Reading Literature

8

Teacher's Edition

Contents

Significant Features of Reading Literature

The first series that really teaches literature and reading in one program!

Many literature programs offer selections without teaching the skills students need to appreciate them. And many reading programs teach skills without providing a meaningful context for using those skills. *Reading Literature* is the only series to give you both! It's a literature program that helps students gain the skills they need to read and enjoy literature, and it's a reading program that provides students with meaningful literature selections for applying those skills.

Photograph by Brent Jones

ISBN: 0-86609-228-5
Reading Literature, Green Level, Teacher's Edition

Faces

SARA TEASDALE

Have you ever wondered about the lives of people you see on the street? Read to find out what this speaker finds in the faces of strangers.

People that I meet and pass
In the city's broken roar,
Faces that I lose so soon
And never found before,

Do you know how much you tell
In the meeting of our eyes,
How ashamed I am, and sad
To have pierced your poor disguise?

Secrets rushing without sound
Crying from your hiding places—
Let me go, I cannot bear
The sorrow of the passing faces.

—People in the restless street,
Can it be, oh, can it be
In the meeting of our eyes
That you know as much of me?

Office Girls, 1936, RAPHAEL SOYER. Oil 26 × 24"

382 POETRY

Outstanding literature selections

Reading Literature brings to your students the best of the world's great literary heritage. The series provides an appealing, highly-readable acquaintance with classical as well as contemporary writers (see pages T4–T5).

Developing Comprehension Skills

1. Tell the main events of each fable in order.
2. Explain the moral "One swallow does not make a summer" in your own words.
3. In "The Fox and the Crow," the fox said to the crow, "You have a voice, madam. What you need are wits." What did the fox mean? Why did he say this?
4. How else could the fox have gotten the cheese from the crow? Can you think of another solution?
5. The man in "The Spendthrift and the Swallow" and the crow in "The Fox and the Crow" each made a similar mistake. What was it?

Reading Literature: Fables

1. **Interpreting Character.** When the spendthrift saw the dead swallow, he became angry. He blamed the swallow for his being cold. What does this tell you about the spendthrift?
2. **Understanding Personification.** What human quality, or characteristic, does each animal in "The Fox and the Crow" stand for? Give reasons for your answers.
3. **Appreciating the Fable.** People who tell fables often use animals as their main characters rather than people. Why is it easier to accept the moral of a fable when the characters are animals?

Developing Vocabulary Skills

Understanding Expressions. Following are some words and expressions that make use of the word *crow.* Match the appropriate meaning in column B with the word or expression in column A. Use your dictionary if you need help.

A	B
1. crow's-nest	a. a lookout
2. crowbar	b. the lines around a person's eyes
3. to crow about something	c. to boast, brag
4. crow's-feet	d. in a straight line
5. as the crow flies	e. a tool used for prying

24 FABLES

Developing Writing Skills

1. **Presenting an Opinion.** The proverb "Flattery is the best persuasion" appears as the moral of "The Fox and the Crow." However, there is another proverb about flattery: "Flattery will get you nowhere." Which proverb do you believe is true? Can both proverbs be true? Write one or more paragraphs explaining and defending your opinion.
2. **Understanding Purpose.** The fable of "The Spendthrift and the Swallow" has the purpose of teaching a lesson. Rewrite the fable with a different purpose in mind. Choose one of these purposes or think of another. Change the moral to fit your new purpose.
   a. To sell Northerners airplane tickets to the warm South
   b. To encourage people to open savings accounts
   c. To encourage people to feed birds
   d. To pass a law against spendthrifts

Fox Hunt, 1893, WINSLOW HOMER. Pennsylvania Academy of the Fine Arts, Philadelphia.

Spendthrift, Fox and Crow 25

Solid skills program

Reading Literature provides the most complete presentation of skill development found in any series. Each concept is introduced, then developed, extended, and reinforced several times at each level. With each new selection, students are better able to understand and appreciate what they read (see pages T6–T8).

Strong writing component

No other series offers such a strong writing component. The writing strand serves two important functions: it enhances reading comprehension and it develops essential writing skills (see page T9).

Brings the world's great literature directly to all your students

Reading Literature offers the kinds of selections that develop a genuine appreciation of fine literature. A balance of traditional writers is included, as well as contemporary favorites. Centering around traditional values, the selections express concerns and insights that have meaning for students—now and throughout their lives.

Reading Literature gives students selections they can read.

Students will be able to read the literature with ease and understanding. Chosen for their appeal and readability, the selections can be appreciated on many levels, allowing all students to experience the rewards of fine literature.

Women

ALICE WALKER

"Women" tells about the black women of the past who worked for a better future for their children. How does the speaker feel toward these women?

They were women then
My mama's generation
Husky of voice—Stout of
Step
With fists as well as
Hands
How they battered down
Doors
And ironed
Starched white
Shirts
How they led
Armies
Headragged Generals
Across mined
Fields
Booby-trapped

of Fort Scott, Kansas, 1949.
RDON PARKS

The Learned Son

LEO TOLSTOY

A son once returned from the city to his father, who lived in the country.

"We're mowing today," said the father. "Take a rake and help me."

The son did not want to work, so he said, "I am a scholar and have forgotten all those peasant words. What is a rake?"

As he walked across the yard, he stepped on a
way, and it s
He suddenly
was. Clutchi
fool left a ra

Haystack in Winter, 1891, CLAUDE MONET (Fr. 1840–1926).
Oil on canvas, 25¾ × 36⅜", 1970.253, Gift of the Misses Aimée and Rosamond Lamb in memory of Mr. and Mrs. Horatio A. Lamb, 1970. Courtesy, Museum of Fine Arts, Bosto

When I Was One-and-Twenty

A. E. HOUSMAN

Like the two preceding poems, this poem uses a few unfamiliar words. For example, it refers to units of English money—pounds, guineas, and crowns. Read to find out if its ideas are also unfamiliar.

When I was one-and-twenty
  I heard a wise man say,
"Give crowns and pounds and guineas
  But not your heart away;
Give pearls away and rubies
  But keep your fancy free."
But I was one-and-twenty,
  No use to talk to me.

When I was one-and-twenty
  I heard him say again,
"The heart out of the bosom
  Was never given in vain;
'Tis paid with sighs a plenty
  And sold for endless rue."
And I am two-and-twenty,
  And oh, 'tis true, 'tis true.

Giant Magnolias, 1885–95, MARTIN JOHNSON HEADE. Courtesy of R.W. Norton Art Gallery, Shreveport, Louisiana.

Students benefit from reading literature in its original form.

The series includes a rich variety of timeless selections in their original form. Selections are not rewritten, so that students can appreciate the literature as it was meant to be read.

CHAPTER 7

Nonfiction

Humorous Sketches

Humor delights because of its unexpectedness. Humor often surprises the reader with its contrasts or its exaggerations. Humor may have a serious point, too, about human weaknesses. However, the serious point is usually buried under more than a few laughs. Here are two **humorous sketches** that are examples of humorous essays at their best.

Golconde, 1953, RENÉ MAGRITTE. Private Collection.

The series develops an understanding of major literary types.

The genre organization, coupled with insightful teaching pages, develops in students an in-depth understanding of one literary type at a time. Every level includes study of the short story, poetry, nonfiction, and drama. Other topics covered at one or more grade levels include fables, folklore, legends, myths, the long short story, and specific periods in American and English literature.

Beautiful fine art adds another dimension to literature.

You and your students will be excited and visually stimulated by the beauty of the fine art reproductions throughout the texts. Each illustration enriches understanding by reflecting the theme and the mood of the selection it accompanies.

Teaches the skills students need to read and enjoy literature

Reading Literature selections are carefully coordinated with teaching material that presents the concepts and skills students must develop to understand, appreciate, and evaluate what they read.

Because concepts and skills are reviewed throughout each text, development is progressive and cumulative. Each concept or skill is introduced, then developed, extended, and reinforced several times at each level. With each new selection, students are better able to understand and appreciate what they read.

Introductory pages preview the literary type and teach reading skills.

Each chapter begins with pages that teach the concepts and skills students need to approach the selections.

Reading Literature: Short Stories

What Is a Short Story?

A **short story** is a story short enough to be read from beginning to end at one time. A short story is fiction. It comes from the imagination of a single writer. A short story usually focuses on a single important event in the life of one character.

The History of the Short Story

The short story is a very old form of literature. Stories were told by storytellers long before they were written. Short, fictional stories were written down in Egypt as early as 3000 B.C. The Bible contains many short stories called **parables**.

Two outstanding collections of short stories were written around the year 1350. (This was about one hundred years before Malory wrote *Le Morte d'Arthur.*) An Italian writer, Giovanni Boccaccio, wrote a collection of tales called *The Decameron*.

A few years later, an English writer, Geoffrey Chaucer, wrote *The Canterbury Tales*. In this book, each member of a group of travelers tells a story.

In the 1800's, great writers all over the world became interested in the short story. They each developed slightly different ways of writing short stories.

American poet and writer Edgar Allan Poe studied the short story thoroughly. In his writings, he explained how he thought a short story should be written. He said that the goal of a short story should be to communicate a single idea. Every sentence and every word should be chosen carefully. If it was written correctly, Poe thought, the short story could communicate the writer's entire message before the reader became tired of reading. Poe's ideas strongly influenced later writers.

134 SHORT STORIES

The Elements of the Short Story

The three main elements in a short story are the same as in a legend. They are characters, setting, and plot.

Plot. Many short stories follow the same general plan. It is a logical way of telling a story. Here is that plan.

Introduction: This comes at the beginning of the story. You meet the characters, learn about the setting, and see the beginning of a conflict, or struggle.
Rising Action: The struggle grows more intense.
Climax: This is the most exciting part in the story. It is the turning point.
Falling Action: After the climax, events follow their logical course to the end.
Resolution: All loose ends are tied up. The story ends.

Point of View. If the story is told by a character in the story, it is written from the **first-person point of view**. Then the writer uses words such as *I* and *we*. If a narrator who is not a character in the story is telling what happened, the story is written from the **third-person point of view**. Sometimes this narrator tells only what one person could know. That is the **limited** third-person point of view. Sometimes this narrator knows everything that happens. That is the **omniscient** third-person point of view.

How To Read a Short Story

1. Read carefully. Since these stories are so short, each word is important. You may miss something if you skip words.
2. Decide who is telling the story. Is it a narrator outside the story? Is it one of the characters in the story?
3. Keep track of the order of events.
4. Try to understand why one event leads to the next.

Reading Literature 135

Reading Literature. These pages focus students' attention on the literary form of the chapter. The text clearly defines the genre, outlines a brief history, describes the distinguishing characteristics, and provides guidelines for reading that particular type.

Comprehension. Because comprehension is critical to appreciating any piece of literature, each of these lessons concentrates on skills such as finding the main idea, making inferences, and separating fact from opinion.

Comprehension Skills: Author's Purpose

Understanding the Author's Purpose

When preparing to write, writers decide what they want the piece of writing to do. Their purpose, or reason for writing, could be one or more of the following: 1) to entertain, 2) to express feelings, 3) to experiment with a new way of writing, 4) to teach, 5) to inform, 6) to persuade, 7) to make people laugh, 8) to inspire, 9) to shock, 10) to make people think seriously about a certain social problem.

Usually, a writer knows the purpose before he or she begins a piece of writing. Purpose affects many choices the writer makes, including the choices of topic, form, characters, setting, and plot.

To understand the author's purpose, study your own reaction to the piece. Were you entertained? Were you taught something? Did you gain a better understanding of other people's problems?

Not every writer achieves his or her purpose. Sometimes writers intend their work to be funny, but readers don't laugh. Sometimes a piece is meant to teach, but all it does is bore readers. Only the reader can tell if the writer has succeeded.

Evaluating the Author's Choice of Words

Suppose a story or play is set in the Middle Ages. The way the characters speak should suggest the time in which they live. As a reader, you would expect the characters to sound different from yourself. The writer might have the characters use old-fashioned words such as *thee, prithee,* and *verily.*

Suppose a second story is set in modern t... cer is reporting to the nation. Would you expe... "Don't worry. No problem"? That would n... officer. This is how the general in *Invasion fron*...

uation arising from reported presence of certain individuals of unidentified nature is now under complete control." That sentence sounds believably stiff, formal, and official.

A writer chooses a character's words carefully. The words must fit the character and make him or her sound like a real person. You, as a reader, can judge when a writer has chosen the character's words well.

Exercises: Understanding the Author's Purpose and Choice of Words

A. Identify the purpose of each of these selections.

1. Mel works with scientists called marine archaeologists. They study the wrecks of old ships and all of the things that are brought up from the deep water.
   a. to inform you
   b. to persuade you
   c. to shock you
2. Small bird, forgive me.
   I'll hear the end of your song
   in some other world.
   a. to make you laugh
   b. to express feelings
   c. to teach

B. For each character below, choose the fitting line of dialog.

1. King Arthur:
   a. Thanks, Wiz. It's great to have you here at Camelot.
   b. Blessings upon thee, oh Great Wizard. I welcome thee to Cam-

Vocabulary. To help students develop the language and vocabulary skills they'll need for increased comprehension, each of these lessons focuses on a single word attack skill, such as using context clues, using word parts, or using the dictionary. Skills presented here are developed and extended throughout the chapter.

Vocabulary Skills: Context Clues

Using Context Clues

What do you do when you are reading and you come to a word you can't understand? Do you skip it and go on with your reading, hoping that the word was not important? Sometimes, that's not a bad idea. Usually, however, a better idea is to figure out what the word means by using context clues.

Often you have to guess at the meaning of a new word. Then you test out your meaning in the sentence where you found the word. Here is an example. In these lines from *A Connecticut Yankee in King Arthur's Court,* the new word is underlined:

> **Connecticut Yankee:** The next time I saw Camelot, I knew at once that something was amiss. As I approached the gates of the castle, Clarence ran out to meet me and, by the worried look on his face, I knew that there was trouble.

What could *amiss* mean? To figure it out, first ask yourself what part of speech the new word could be. *Amiss* is probably an adjective because it describes the word *something.* Next, look at other clues. Clarence looked worried. The Yankee knew there was trouble. From all these clues, you can guess that something was wrong. *Amiss* probably means *wrong.*

Test your meaning in the given sentence. Replace *amiss* with *wrong:* "I knew at once that something was wrong." As you read on, you will know more surely whether your guess is correct.

This way of finding the meaning of a new word from context is called *inferring the meaning.* **Inference** is using what the writer has told you to figure out what the writer has not told you.

Here is another example of inferring meaning. This selection is from *Invasion from Mars.* Martians have killed forty people. The radio announcer is trying to keep the audience informed.

> **Announcer:** Ladies and gentlemen, I have just been informed that we have finally established communication with an eyewitness of the tragedy. Professor Pierson . . . will give you his explanation of the calamity.

What does calamity mean? First, decide what part of speech it is. If you reread the sentence, you will see that calamity must be a noun, because the phrase "of the" needs a noun to complete it.

Now look for other clues. Professor Pierson saw a tragedy. You can guess that the thing he will explain will be that tragedy, or disaster. Calamity must mean disaster.

Exercise: Using Context Clues

Use context clues to find the meaning of each underlined word. Choose from the meanings following each selection.

1. **Connecticut Yankee:** Well, sir, there never was a man more dumbfounded than I was. I just couldn't get used to the idea. That's why when I woke again I thought the whole thing a dream, and, when I saw that page boy standing before me, I was more amazed than ever.
   a. Dumbfounded means "stupid."
   b. Dumbfounded means "found by accident."
   c. Dumbfounded means "surprised."
2. **Sound:** Clamor of crowd in the background
   a. Clamor means "silence."
   b. Clamor means "noise."
   c. Clamor means "sight."
3. **Announcer two:** Ladies and gentlemen, I have a grave announcement to make. Incredible as it may seem, those strange beings who landed in the Jersey farmlands tonight are the vanguard of an invading army from the planet Mars.
   a. Vanguard means "part of the army ahead of the main army."
   b. Vanguard means "a kind of vehicle."
   c. Vanguard means "a kind of guard."

Follow-up study questions reinforce literary concepts and reading skills.

Study questions following each selection lead students to a better understanding of content and an appreciation of technique and style. The questions further develop skills in comprehension, reading literature, and vocabulary.

Developing Comprehension Skills

1. In your own words describe the purpose of the Time Distorter.
2. What did Bigelow do to prepare for his trip backwards in time?
3. Why did Bigelow want to prevent Lincoln's assassination?
4. What made Bigelow seem dangerous to the president's bodyguard?
5. Suppose you had been able to speak to Bigelow before he tried to warn the President. What advice would you have given him?

Reading Literature: Short Stories

1. **Recognizing Science Fiction.** Name several elements in the story that make it science fiction. When do you think this story was written? Give evidence from the story to support your opinion.
2. **Understanding Characterization.** The character Bigelow is more than just a good scientist and an admirer of Lincoln. He appears to be extreme and unreasonable. Review the beginning of the story. Find two details about Bigelow that indicate he may be abnormal in his admiration of Lincoln. Why do you think the author developed the character this way?
3. **Diagraming the Plot.** Draw a plot diagram to illustrate the five parts of the story. Include one detail of the introduction, two details of the rising action, a clear statement of the climax, one detail of the falling action, and an explanation of the resolution.
4. **Understanding Irony.** "The Assassin" contains **irony.** That is, the events turn out in a way opposite to what you expected. What did Bigelow expect to happen if he did not achieve his goal immediately? What really happens? What idea does the ending express about machines controlling history?

Developing Vocabulary Skills

Reviewing Ways To Find Word Meaning. You have learned many ways to determine the meaning of an unfamiliar word. Sometimes it is helpful to look at **word parts**—the prefix, suffix, and base word. Other times there may be **context clues** to the meaning. Still other times you need to check a **dictionary** for the meaning of a word.

Read the following sentences about the story "The Assassin." Try to use word parts or context clues to find the meaning of each underlined word. Write the word and its meaning on your paper. Also write which method you used to determine the meaning: *Word Parts* or *Context Clues.* If there are no clues to the meaning, write *Dictionary.*

1. Bigelow had developed a workable time-travel theory, or scientific idea.
2. President Lincoln was known to many people as an emancipator.
3. Bigelow refastened the cover of the Time Distorter after he had pressed the button.
4. The Time Distorter provided Bigelow with an infinity of chances. If he failed, he could return to his own time and make the jump again, over and over, as many times as he needed.
5. Bigelow wanted to prevent the weak and ineffectual Andrew Johnson from becoming the next president.

Additional study questions develop related skills.

In addition to reinforcing comprehension, reading literature, and vocabulary, the study questions develop several related skills. These questions are included to help students respond to the literature and to develop skills they will use across the curriculum.

Writing. Questions in Developing Writing Skills help students develop the analytic and creative writing skills they need to respond to literature.

Critical Thinking. These exercises ask students to apply critical thinking skills to selection content. Students learn to distinguish between fact and opinion, make generalizations, recognize slanted writing, and evaluate and organize information.

4. He requested Mr. Neimand to leave. Mr. Neimand accepted the <u>dismissal</u> politely.
5. When Graham opened the bedroom door, <u>anxiety</u> overtook him. But he forced his face and voice to express a calmness until he had retrieved the gun from his son.

Developing Writing Skills

1. **Writing an Argument.** It is easy to state a personal opinion. However, it is often difficult to support an opinion. Select one of the following opinions about scientists presented in this story:

    Mr. Neimand thinks that scientists should be held responsible for the effect of their work on the world.

    Dr. Graham does not feel that scientists should worry about future uses or effects of their work.

    Write an organized argument to defend your opinion.

    Pre-Writing. Prepare reasons to use in writing your argument. List all the points you can think of to support your opinion. Draw ideas from the story and from current news. Take notes on facts that support each statement you list.

    Number the statements in your list by order of importance. Start with the least important and build to the most important point.

    Writing. Develop an organized argument. Start with a sentence stating your opinion on the subject of scientists' responsibilities. Present your reasons in order of importance. Use key words or phrases to introduce each reason.

    Two types of key words help make an argument clear. Some key words help state the reasons or facts. These include: *because, so, since, if, therefore,* and *as a result.*

    Other key words help to put the reasons or facts in order of importance. These include: *the first reason, second, more important, most important,* and *finally.*

    Revising. Read your argument to a group. Ask the group members to evaluate your argument. Then change any part of your argument that they do not find convincing.

2. **Creating a Setting.** You have read eleven stories in this chapter. Each story has a setting that fits the action. In some stories, such as "The Third Wish," the setting is very detailed and a part of the action. In other stories, the setting is only a background and is not described in detail. This is true in the story "Raymond's Run."

    Create your own setting for a story. Then write a paragraph describing the setting. Identify the time period—the past, present, or future. Tell about the place. Include details that appeal to several of the five senses. Try to make your setting express a mood.

Developing Skills in Critical Thinking

Classifying Science Fiction. Science fiction is a special type of story. Read the introduction on page 305. Then write your own definition of science fiction. As part of your definition, include a list of elements, or characteristics, common to science fiction stories. You may use details from the stories in your textbook as examples. You also may use details from other science fiction works.

318 SHORT STORIES

character. Include a physical description. Also tell how the character behaves. Tell what the character thinks of himself or herself. Explain the character's attitudes toward others.

Developing Skills in Study and Research

Refining a Research Topic. You may want to learn more about running, or track and field events, after you have read "Raymond's Run." One resource to check for information is an encyclopedia. Another is *The Readers' Guide to Periodical Literature.*

Track and Field is a broad, or general, topic. Therefore, each library resource will list many subheadings about it. Each resource will also suggest other closely related topics, called cross references, to research. You could not possibly research the entire topic of track and field. For a broad topic such as this one, you will need to limit your research to a specific area.

Using either an encyclopedia index or *The Readers' Guide,* look up the subject Track and Field. Read through the list of articles. Also check the articles listed under the cross reference topics suggested. Use the information you find to answer the following questions.

1. Suppose as an assignment your teacher asked you to write a report about running. What specific topics within the general subject of track and field might you select? List five possible report ideas.
2. Choose one of the report topics you suggested. Select at least three articles that you think would provide information about the topic. Write down the article titles. For encyclopedia articles, list the encyclopedia, the volume number, and page numbers. For periodical articles, list the magazine title, volume number, date, and page numbers.

Developing Skills in Speaking and Listening

Reading Orally. One of the elements of this story that makes it so successful is the language the writer uses. Squeaky sounds like a real person. Choose a section of the story that you particularly like. Limit yourself to one or two paragraphs. Practice reading the selection the way you think Squeaky would have said it. Read through the selection enough times that you are comfortable with it. Practice a reading speed that seems like normal conversation. Do not rush through the selection.

When you are ready, read the selection aloud to a group. Try to make eye contact with people in your audience. It will help make them feel that you are Squeaky talking to them. Be sure to speak loudly and clearly. Try to make your voice fit Squeaky's personality.

Raymond's Run 289

Study and Research. A study and research skill, such as taking notes or study-type reading, relates directly to the preceding selection.

Speaking and Listening. For these assignments, students may, among other activities, deliver a speech, introduce a guest speaker, interpret poems, or tell a story. Each activity is based on the selection students have just read.

Chapter reviews provide even more reinforcement.

At the end of each chapter, a two-page review helps students pull together and apply what they have learned.

Handbook for Reading and Writing summarizes skills taught.

In the back of the text is a comprehensive resource for independent reference and review. Included are Literary Terms, Summary of Comprehension Skills, Summary of Vocabulary Skills, Guidelines for the Process of Writing, Guidelines for Study and Research, and Summary of Skills in Critical Thinking. Each section includes detailed explanations, examples, and page references.

Study and Research

The Card Catalog

The card catalog lists all the books in the library. The cards are arranged in alphabetical order according to the words on the top line of the card.

Each book has three cards: an author card, a title card, and a subject card. Each card contains the same information, but in a different order. The author card lists the author's name on the first line. The title card lists the title of the book on the first line. The subject card lists the subject or topic of the book on the first line. On the top left corner of each card; you will find the call number.

Your library may also have a catalog for audio-visual materials such as records or films. It is probably organized like the card catalog for books.

Author Card
292 **Gates, Doris**
G259 The warrior goddess Athena. Illustrated by Don Bolognese. New York: Viking Press, ©1972.

Title Card
292 **The warrior goddess Athena.**
G259 **Gates, Doris**
The warrior goddess Athena. Illustrated by Don Bolognese. New York: Viking Press, ©1972.

Subject Card
292 **Mythology**
G259 **Gates, Doris**
The warrior goddess Athena. Illustrated by Don Bolognese. New York: Viking Press, ©1972.

3. Preparing to Study

Preparations in Class

Before beginning an assignment, be sure you know what you are asked for. The first step to studying is listening carefully to directions.

1. Concentrate on only the directions about to be given.
2. Note how many steps there are.
3. Relate a key word to each step, such as *Read, Answer,* or *Write.*
4. If you do not understand a step, ask questions.
5. Repeat the directions to yourself and write them down.

An assignment notebook will help you keep track of what you must do. For each assignment, write the following:

1. The subject
2. The assignment and any details
3. The date the assignment is given
4. The date the assignment is due

Subject	Assignment	Date given	Date due

Guidelines for Study and Research 627

Coordinates literature and reading with writing skill development

Research has shown that writing actually improves students' understanding of what they've read. Therefore, in addition to the writing study questions after selections, each level includes a special chapter devoted to teaching writing.

How Writers Write lets students in on the secret of good writing.

A separate chapter highlights the techniques and processes writers use. By reporting the words and experiences of professional writers, this chapter encourages students to see that writing is a skill that they, too, can acquire.

CHAPTER 4

How Writers Write

Using the Process of Writing

"It's impossible to write a good story by carrying a rabbit's foot in your pocket," says writer Isaac Bashevis Singer. Writers work to create good writing. They follow certain stages called the **process of writing**.

pre-writing—a time of planning
writing
revising—a time of rewriting or reworking

Gregory in the Pool, (Paper Pool 4: A, B, D, G), 1978, DAVID HOCKNEY. Printed and published by Tyler Graphics, Ltd., © Copyright David Hockney/Tyler Graphics Ltd.

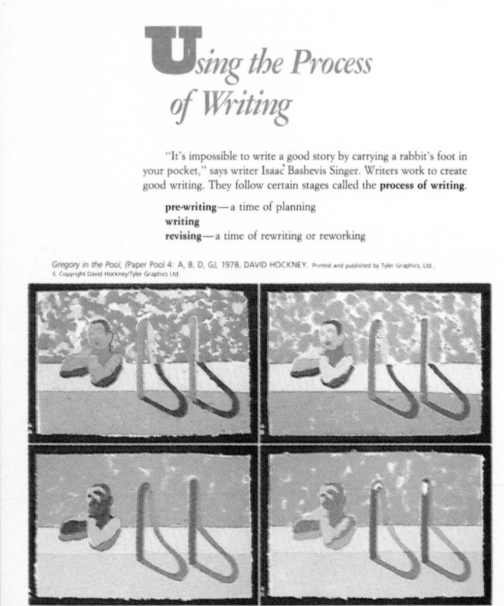

Understanding the Process of Writing

enjoy looking at a statue without knowing exactly how the artist cut and chiseled the stone. You can admire its smoothness and shape, without being an expert.

Imagine, however, that you tried to carve a statue. You would face

Using the Sounds of Language

Words are the writer's tools. The good writer chooses words for both their meaning and their sound. In this section, you will learn about the following ways that writers use the sounds of language:

alliteration rhyme onomatopoeia
rhythm assonance

1979, ROMARE BEARDEN. Private Collection. Courtesy of Sheldon Ross Gallery, Birmingham, Michigan

Special section teaches the process of writing.

One section of the chapter explains and illustrates the three stages in the process of writing: pre-writing, writing, and revising.

Students learn to apply techniques writers use.

Special sections of the chapter teach *Using the Sounds of Language* and *Using Figures of Speech*. Students learn how writers use techniques such as rhythm, simile, and metaphor to make their writing more interesting.

Other McDougal, Littell Programs

McDougal, Littell Literature Revised Edition

These anthologies for Grades 7-12 combine abundant, high-quality selections with comprehensive skills development. You can choose the selections you want to teach without omitting important skills.

Building English Skills

Building English Skills is the only complete, developmental composition and grammar program for grades 1–12. Skills are developed sequentially from one grade to the next, with each level reinforcing and extending the skills learned earlier.

Basic Skills in English

Basic Skills in English for grades 7–12 is the only English series for students reading *below* grade level . . . with content that is *on* grade level.

Guidelines for Managing the Program

Managing the Program

Reading Literature combines literary selections with a carefully structured developmental program of concepts and skills. Students will gain the most from the text if the chapters are presented in order.

It is not realistic, however, to expect that every student will read every selection and work every exercise. In fact, this approach is not necessarily desirable. The text provides ample exercises for teaching, reteaching, review, and enrichment of a wide range of objectives. The teacher should determine which objectives are most important for a particular group of students and then choose selections and activities that develop those objectives.

This Teacher's Edition is designed to help the teacher determine which selections and exercises will be most useful in attaining the objectives he or she has chosen. It also provides direction in the use of supplementary materials for *Reading Literature*.

Understanding the Skills Strand

The seven skills strands in *Reading Literature* are the following:

Reading Literature	Study and Research
Comprehension	Critical Thinking
Vocabulary	Speaking and Listening
Writing	

Lessons developing concepts from each of the first three strands appear at the beginning of each genre chapter; writing, the fourth strand, is the subject of an entire chapter (Chapter 3). Study questions in each of these four strands appear at the end of every selection. In addition, at least one study question in each of the other strands appears in every chapter.

Each set of study questions for Developing Comprehension Skills includes at least one question on each of three thinking and reading levels: Literal, Interpretive, and Critical. (With reference to Bloom's Taxonomy, Literal Reading corresponds roughly to memory and translation; Interpretive Reading to interpretation, application, and analysis; and Critical Reading to synthesis and evaluation.)

Scheduling Your Time

Every teacher using *Reading Literature* should become familiar with the organization of the student text, the format of the Teacher's Edition (pages T12 and T13), and the educational philosophy of the program (pages T14 and T15). To get a broad view of the types of techniques and activities recommended for the program, the teacher should skim the teaching suggestions for individual selections (see pages T12 and T13) and these sections of the T.E.:

Teaching Special Populations (pages T16 and T17)
Suggestions for Enrichment (pages T18 and T19)
Guidelines for Evaluating Composition (pages T24 through T27)

It is also recommended that the teacher use the Reading Experiences Inventory in the *Diagnostic and Mastery Tests* to become acquainted with the students' background and abilities.

Next, considering the curriculum requirements of the school and the abilities of the students, the teacher should determine the major objectives to be developed during the year. The teacher should then examine the chapter and selection lists of objectives to identify the selections and study questions to be developed most thoroughly.

Some selections and study questions may be assigned for independent work, with little class time devoted to them. Others may be developed at length, depending on the needs of the class. If it becomes necessary, because of scheduling limits or other reasons, to omit selections or to take them out of order, the teacher should make sure that no essential skills or concepts are slighted. The lists of objectives in the Teacher's Edition, the indexes of skills at the back of the student text, and the boldface subheads on the study questions will all be useful in assigning priorities and class time.

Significant Features of the Teacher's Edition

The Teacher's Edition includes a complete student text, reduced to a readable 83% of the original size, for convenient reference. Objectives and teaching suggestions for each selection appear next to the reduced pages of that selection. In addition, check tests and notes concerning the fine art are provided where they, too, will be most useful, immediately beneath the material to which they refer.

CHAPTER **4**

The Front Parlor, 1913, WILLIAM McGREGOR PAXTON.
The St. Louis Art Museum. Cora E. Ludwig Bequest, by exchange, and Edward Mallinckrodt, Sr., by exchange.

Chapter Objectives

The following is a list of the major skills developed in study questions throughout this chapter:

Skills in Reading Literature

- To appreciate the short story as a literary form
- To identify the elements of the short story: setting, character, plot
- To understand and interpret characters
- To recognize point of view
- To recognize internal and external conflict
- To recognize examples of irony and personification
- To recognize tone in a short story

Comprehension Skills

- To recall events in the order they occurred (Literal Reading)
- To recognize direct and indirect quotations (Literal Reading)

Objectives. Next to the title page of each chapter is a list of major objectives, in all seven strands, developed in the chapter. More detailed objectives begin the teaching suggestions for each selection.

Appointment in Baghdad

TRADITIONAL STORY
Retold by Edith Wharton

This is a traditional story retold by Edith Wharton, an American writer. Notice how she creates an atmosphere, or mood, of suspense in the story. Watch for the surprise ending that adds to this mood.

Bijar Rug, Late 19th Century. Collection of Joseph W. Fell.

One morning the Sultan was resting in his palace in Damascus. Suddenly the door flew open, and in rushed a young man, out of breath and wild with excitement. The Sultan sat up alarmed, for the young man was his most skillful assistant.

"I must have your best horse!" the youth cried out. "There is little time! I must fly at once to Baghdad!"

The Sultan asked why the young man was in such a rush.

"Because," came the hurried reply, "just now, as I was walking in the palace garden, I saw Death standing there. When Death saw me, he raised his arms in a frightening motion. Oh, it was horrible! I must escape at once!"

The Sultan quickly arranged for the youth to have his fastest horse. No sooner had the young man thundered out through the palace gate, than the Sultan

Appointment in Baghdad 157

About the Art

Turkish Bijar rugs are hand made. There are approximately 180,000 hand tied knots to every square meter. Tightly woven, they form a very deep and thick pile. In addition to their fine quality, these rugs are noted for their jewel-like colors and intricate ornamental designs.

Check Test

1. In what city was the Sultan's palace located? (Damascus)

2. Where did the young man see Death for the first time? (in the palace garden)

3. Where will Death see the young man again? (in Baghdad)

Objectives

- To identify the elements of a short story, including setting, main character, and conflict
- To appreciate personification
- To recognize the use of irony
- To apply literal, interpretive, and critical reading skills to a selection
- To distinguish between direct and indirect quotations

Preparing the Students

Essential Vocabulary. The words presented here are essential to the understanding of the selection.

Write *sultan, Damascus,* and *Baghdad* on the board. Point out that Damascus is the capital of Syria, and Baghdad is the capital of Iraq. If possible, have students locate these places on a map. Explain that a *sultan* is a ruler.

If students need additional help with the vocabulary of this selection, encourage them to use context clues to determine word meaning. As needed, direct them to the **Glossary** at the back of the text or to a classroom dictionary.

Motivation. Point out that this short story is retold by the author. Remind the students that they have read fables that were retold, in Chapter 1.

Have the students read the introductory paragraph on page 157. Discuss what atmosphere, or mood, means.

Presenting the Selection

1. Have the students read "Appointment in Baghdad."

2. Make sure that everyone has read the selection by administering the **Check Test** at the bottom of page 157 in the T.E.

3. Remind the students that the introduction to the story asked them to watch for the surprise ending. Call on several students to explain the surprise ending. Make sure the students understand that the young man has not escaped Death by fleeing to Baghdad.

4. Develop the study questions as suggested in **Using the Study Questions**, beginning on page 158.

Reinforcing the Lesson

To reteach, reinforce, or extend the skills in this lesson, see the following:

Skills Practice Book, Red Level—pages 89 and 90

157

Preparing the Students. Ideas for introducing essential vocabulary and for motivating students.

Presenting the Selection. Step-by-step suggestions for leading the students through the selection. These suggestions emphasize important content and concepts.

Reinforcing the Selection. A listing of the pages of the Skills Practice Book to be used after the lesson.

Special Populations. Specific recommendations for helping such students as those who speak English as a second language, speakers of nonstandard English, and students with learning disabilities or handicaps.

Encouraging Independent Reading. Questions or activities to stimulate students to read on their own.

Art Notes. Beneath each reproduction of fine art is a brief discussion of the artist or the work of art.

Check Tests. Questions for testing literal comprehension after the first reading.

Additional Resource. A listing of the diagnostic and mastery tests for the chapter.

. . . keta . . . Then another, moving slowly from the other direction: cla . . . keta . . . cla . . . keta. . . .

Keplik shouted toward the trains, "Thank you, Mister Motorman! Tomorrow, I am going to start a great new masterpiece! The Second Avenue el from Fourteenth Street to Delancey Street! Thank you for slowing up your trains!"

First one motorman, then the other, blew his train whistle as the trains moved on, into the night beyond. "Ah, how I am *gebentsht*," said Keplik to himself. "In America there are kind people everywhere. All my life, the el train has shaken my hands. But tonight, it has shaken my heart."

Keplik worked for the rest of the night on a little project. The next morning, Keplik hung this sign made from matches outside his window, where every passing el train motorman could see it:

Developing Comprehension Skills

Literal Reading	1. In the first six paragraphs of the story, the author tells much about Mr. Keplik. How does he tell the reader that Mr. Keplik feels that he has been blessed? What little stories are given to show how Mr. Keplik reacts to problems?
Literal Reading	2. Why does Mr. Keplik start to make models out of matchsticks?
Interpretive Reading	3. On page 205, why does Mr. Keplik call to the el train and say, "I'll never make an el train out of matches"?
Interpretive Reading	4. At the end of the story, Mr. Keplik says that the el train has shaken his heart. What does he mean by that? How does he feel?

Keplik, the Match Man 207

Using the Study Questions

It is recommended that students always read and answer the questions in **Developing Comprehension Skills** in class discussion. Whenever possible, they also should read the other categories together and discuss the answers.

Developing Comprehension Skills

Question 1. Encourage students to find proof of their answers in the selection.

Question 2. Refer students to page 202, paragraph 6.

Question 3. Have the students reread paragraphs 5 through 8 on page 205 before they answer the question.

Question 4. Point out to the students that *shaken* is used as figurative language in this expression.

Question 5. After students answer this question, ask them to try to think of similarities between their own homes and Mr. Keplik's. (Possible similarities: noise of trains or traffic, stairs.)

Challenge Question. What characteristics does Keplik have that enabled him to finish such a complicated piece of work? (Interpretive Reading)

Reading Literature: Short Stories

Question 1. After students have identified the problems, ask them to tell whether these conflicts were external or internal.

Question 2. Read and discuss. Make sure the students understand how much the project meant to the old man.

Question 3. You may wish to give the students some background information on Lithuania and the many immigrants who came to the United States from that country.

Question 4. Before students answer the question, you may wish to have them read aloud the paragraphs expressing the moods.

Challenge Question 1. Is this story written from the omniscient or limited third-person point of view?

Challenge Question 2. Read this sentence about the bridge: "But the bridge seemed to enjoy waiting for the next train to shake it apart again." How is this sentence an example of personification?

Answers to Study Questions

Developing Comprehension Skills

1. The author tells us that Keplik loves his work. Keplik says that he is *gebentsht*, meaning "blessed." Stories include his reaction when the elevated train goes by, his calm response to an upset customer, his decision to cure his emptiness with a hobby.

2. Keplik takes up the hobby because his hands seem empty and useless without work. (He quit work because he was getting too old to climb the stairs.) He uses matchsticks because he has them in the house.

3. Keplik is annoyed that the el train keeps going by and disturbing his matchstick creations.

4. When he says that his heart has been shaken, Keplik means that he can feel in his heart the kindness of the motormen who gave him the hour he needed to finish his project.

5. The setting is realistic. It is easy to picture Keplik working on watches—a job in the real world—and matchstick creations, and stopping his work for the el trains.

Challenge. Keplik is a very patient person. He doesn't mind spending a lot

(continued on page 208)

207

Using the Study Questions. Guidance in the most effective use of the study questions. For each question in Developing Writing Skills, for example, techniques in pre-writing, writing, and revising are suggested.

Answers to the Questions. Answers, and suggested answers to questions requiring independent thinking.

Challenge Questions. One or two higher-level thinking questions for each selection, provided for optional assignments or further discussion.

Supplementary Materials

Skills Practice Book

The *Skills Practice Book* reinforces the concepts and skills developed in the student text. Each page is an independent lesson, related to an introductory lesson or to a study question. Because successful completion of the skills page does not depend on the selection it follows, these pages are excellent for use in reteaching. The Teacher's Edition of the *Skills Practice Book* contains an answer key to the exercises.

Diagnostic and Mastery Tests

The *Diagnostic and Mastery Tests* include the following:

A reading experiences inventory to be administered at the beginning of the year to familiarize the teacher with the students' reading habits

A diagnostic test for each chapter, to help in identification of serious weaknesses

A mastery test for each chapter

An end-of-year mastery test

The Teacher's Edition of the test booklet includes an answer key to the exercises.

Integrating Reading, Writing, and Thinking

In the recent past, reading has been taught apart from literature, often as a sequence of unconnected subskills. Writing, too, has been relatively isolated, taught more in conjunction with grammar than with reading. The study of thinking skills has not been a major concern within the study of language arts.

Today, much research in the language arts finds this fragmented approach inadequate in developing students' abilities to process language meaningfully. In its place, researchers and educators are calling for an integration of the various areas of language arts. With these developments in mind, the writers and editors of the *Reading Literature* series have organized the selections, teaching material, and study questions so as to integrate language arts and related skills with the study of literature.

Research

In his article "Relating Reading and Other Language Arts: A Need for Reasoned Decisions" (in *Teaching Reading with the Other Language Arts*, 1983), Mark W. Aulls reported the following:

> At least five principles of instruction follow from psycholinguistic processing models of reading and language.
>
> 1. Language, whether oral or written, is a highly interdependent system which should not be fractionated into atomistic units for all aspects of instructions. . . .
>
> 4. Knowledge and awareness of relationships between language and print are not sufficient to produce or comprehend efficiently written text. It is also necessary for children to learn strategies for predicting, organizing, reflecting upon, and monitoring what is read, written, or spoken.
>
> 5. . . . As students grow older, they are increasingly more capable of consciously self-regulating their language knowledge and deliberately using it to judge, manipulate, or coordinate its structures and meanings during reading, writing, speaking, and listening.

Aulls concluded that

> Growth in understanding the potential interrelationships among reading, speaking, listening, and writing depends upon the opportunity for the learner to participate in each process and play different roles (author, reader, listener) when the processes are combined for different purposes. Hence, artificially dichotomizing reading and other language arts into separate subjects totally ignores the transfer learning benefits derived by interfacing similar tasks such as learning about the function of topical relationships when reading text, writing text, or planning a speech.

Researchers in the writing process have long been asserting the connections between writing and reading, and between writing and thinking. Margaret Hunsberger, writing in the *Journal of Reading*, has summarized widely-accepted beliefs as follows:

> A concept that reading researchers and teachers have always known but have sometimes forgotten is that reading is one aspect of language. It must be viewed as being within our total language experience, not as somehow distinct from language. There is a particularly strong link between reading and writing, as the receptive and expressive parts of literacy.
>
> For teachers it is important to remember that reading and writing facilitate each other. That is, learning and practicing writing helps develop reading ability and vice versa. Reading and writing need to be learned in concert. Graves's work with children's writing shows the valuable contribution writing can make to children's language development and that writing in school can be transformed from a school exercise to a thought-out expression of something the child wishes to say . . .
>
> If reading gives us ideas and provides food for thought, then writing facilitates the development of that thought: indeed it makes possible a kind of thinking that cannot be achieved otherwise. A closely reasoned philosophic or scientific argument must be developed through writing. The original idea may be entirely in the mind, but its full development can evolve only as the thinking is done through writing.
>
> Children will sometimes say that they don't know how their stories are going to end because they haven't written them yet. For adults, working at the most intense level of abstract thought, the same is often true. Clearly, planning the writing is important, but in addition the writing evokes, shapes, and sharpens ideas. This, in turn, facilitates reading more widely and critically, which extends thinking further, and so on in ever expanding circles. Teachers do their students a great injustice if they ignore the teaching of writing in conjunction with reading.

. . . learning and practicing writing helps develop reading ability and vice versa.
(Hunsberger)

The influence of one's reading on one's writing and thinking has been examined, as reported by Dennis Adams, in his article "Does What You Read Influence How You Write?" (in *The Leaflet*, the Journal of the New England Association of Teachers of English, Spring 1983). Adams described a comparison of writing by children using two different reading series.

> . . . students who used the reading series with the most elaborate linguistic structures tended to write more complex stories. Students seemed to internalize specific linguistic features of their reading textbook. Those with the least elaborate text wrote with the least elaborate structures—those with the more elaborate text wrote with more elaborate structures.

Adams's article also pointed out a relationship between reading, writing, grammar, and the mechanics of writing:

> Stotsky, in her review of the literature, finds from several studies that additional reading is at least as good as grammar in improving the grammatical structure of writing. In fact, students who did additional reading made as much or more improvement in grammar, usage, and other writing concerns, than those who studied formal grammar. . . . It seems that writing programs are not nearly as effective if they exist in a reading vacuum.

. . . writing programs are not nearly as effective if they exist in a reading vacuum.
(Adams)

Clearly, the benefits of integrating reading, writing, thinking, and related skills are varied and valuable.

Applications in *Reading Literature*

The basis of *Reading Literature* is the belief that classic literature endures for two reasons: it expresses concerns that are as real and vital today as when they were first recorded, and it expresses those concerns in a style that excites the imagination of generation after generation of readers. Such literature condenses for young readers a whole approach to thinking that reflects the development of civilization, and, in particular, the American culture. At the same time, of course, a systematic study of this literature introduces students to the elements and conventions of various genres of writing.

In itself, this body of knowledge deserves attention in the curriculum. As the center of a balanced study of the language arts, it provides content that proves to students the value of attaining the skills being developed.

The two-pronged organization of *Reading Literature* takes advantage of the numerous benefits of combining literature with the development of language arts skills. The chapter organization, by genres, makes possible an understanding and an appreciation of the literature. The skills organization, by strands, builds upon the interrelationships among skills.

For an example, consider the study questions for "Summer of the Beautiful White Horse" by William Saroyan (pages 211 to 217).

In Developing Comprehension Skills, there are questions on the literal (1), interpretive (2, 3, 4), and critical (5) reading levels. Besides aiding in comprehension of the story, these questions develop thinking skills of varying difficulty.

Questions 2 and 3 in Reading Literature: Short Stories develop the student's understanding of setting and character, and lay the groundwork for the two writing assignments, which concern these topics.

The awareness of the multiple meanings of words developed in the Comprehension, Vocabulary, and Writing questions is reinforced and enriched by the exercise in defining terms assigned in Developing Skills in Critical Thinking.

Bibliography

Adams, Dennis. "Does What You Read Influence How You Write?" in *The Leaflet* (Journal of the New England Association of Teachers of English), Volume 82, Number 2, subtitled "Integrating Reading, Writing, and Thinking": pages 2–5.

Aulls, Mark W. "Relating Reading and Other Language Arts: A Need for Reasoned Decisions" in *Teaching Reading with the Other Language Arts*, edited by Ulrick H. Hardt. Newark, Delaware: International Reading Association, 1983.

Hunsberger, Margaret. "Commentary," in *Journal of Reading*, Volume 25, Number 7: pages 629–633.

Teaching Special Populations

Many students have special language needs. They include students with learning disabilities (LD), those learning English as their second language (ESL), and others who speak a nonstandard dialect of English (NSD). A teacher who recognizes the special needs of these students can anticipate and avoid difficulties they are likely to encounter in the classroom.

Following are some general strategies for modifying lessons and assignments to help LD, ESL, and NSD students overcome some of their difficulties. In addition, specific suggestions for teaching individual selections and skills appear in the teaching suggestions for those selections. (There, strategies with no limiting label are useful for all three groups.)

Learning Disabled Students

LD students typically have average or above average potential, but have specific difficulties hindering the processing of information and acquisition of skills. Specific areas of dysfunction include auditory memory and discrimination, visual memory and discrimination, fine and gross motor coordination, and written and oral expression.

It is important for the teacher to realize that these learning difficulties are caused by some physical impairment and beyond the students' control. Learning disabilities may be the result of brain damage, central nervous system dysfunction, mild cerebral palsy, or other physical impairment.

Whenever possible, the teacher should work with counselors and special education teachers to determine the specific nature of a student's disability. This will allow the teacher to devise strategies for circumventing the disability, in addition to the general strategies presented here.

General Strategies. There are several strategies the teacher can use to counter learning disabilities.

1. Seat the students at the front of the room where there are few distractions.
2. Present essential information, including assignments, both orally and in writing. Supply visual aids for reinforcement.
3. Whenever possible, supply visual aids to reinforce material from the text.
4. Repeat important ideas frequently, and begin each lesson with a summary of material covered the previous day.
5. Demonstrate the correct way to complete an assignment. Work a sample on the board. Break down the assignment into steps.
6. Avoid making long-term assignments. Assign reading and exercises on a step-by-step basis.
7. Simplify assignments. When possible, allow students to select a few of several questions. For writing assignments, allow students to work with partners or to put first drafts on tape.

English as a Second Language

The problems of students whose first language is not English fall into two categories: difficulty with the language and unfamiliarity with cultural references.

General Strategies: Language Differences. To help students overcome the difficulties posed by an unfamiliar language, these strategies are helpful:

1. Whenever possible, have selections read aloud while the ESL student follows the reading in the text. Provide tapes so that the student can listen to any selection more than once.
2. Read aloud any study questions before assigning them, allowing time for explanations, examples, and the answering of questions.
3. Define any abstract concept, such as *opinion*, as concretely as possible, and review such concepts frequently. Give as many specific examples as possible.
4. Shorten assignments. Allow extra time for these students to acquire concepts.
5. Build into the activities as many visual and concrete experiences as possible. Illustrate and demonstrate meanings.
6. Suggest that students work in a group or with a partner.
7. Precede every writing activity with a similar oral activity.
8. Encourage ESL students to keep personal journals in English, without concern for grammar, spelling, and pronunciation.
9. Recruit advanced students to help the ESL students.

General Strategies: Cultural Differences. Unfamiliarity with cultural references may make it difficult, for example, to determine sender from proper names alone or to understand references to national holidays, sports, or famous people. To help students overcome such difficulties, the following strategies are useful:

1. Encourage class discussion to clarify cultural references.

2. Encourage discussion of differences and similarities between the ESL student's native language and English.

3. Encourage ESL students to write about their native folklore, customs, songs, and stories.

4. Encourage ESL students to read material, on an appropriate level, about specifically American people, places, and events.

Speakers of Nonstandard Dialects

Everyone speaks some sort of dialect. Sometimes, however, the dialect common to a particular group departs so much from the most widely used dialects that it is termed "nonstandard."

Teachers must be aware that nonstandard dialects are legitimate language variations. These dialects follow regular phonological and semantic rules. Speakers of nonstandard dialects are not necessarily careless speakers of English, nor should the variant features of these dialects be considered "errors." However, speakers of these dialects should be led to recognize that they cannot participate fully in mainstream American society without understanding and using its language, standard English.

General Strategies. The following strategies are helpful:

1. Encourage students to learn the patterns and usages of standard English for use in contexts where it is appropriate: for example, in classroom discussions and presentations.

2. Encourage students to use the dialect that sounds natural to both speaker and listener in informal, casual settings, such as at sports or social events.

3. Have the NSD students keep journals of observations and experiences in whatever dialect is natural and comfortable. Read the journals periodically and, without "correcting" variations from standard English, comment in writing about the possible use of the material in class-oriented compositions.

4. Establish group workshops of four or five students, and have them collaborate in revising written work. This may educate all of the students about the various dialects spoken in class.

5. Note any areas of grammatical variation that appear consistently in the NSD students' work. Speakers of so-called Black English, for example, may have trouble with verb usage. Speakers of Hawaiian dialect may encounter difficulties with articles and pronouns.

Provide extra coaching to help students master the unfamiliar aspects of standard dialect.

Suggestions for Enrichment

Readers Theater

Readers Theater is an oral interpretation of a text rewritten in script form. There are few, if any, props, and the audience imagines the settings and actions through active listening.

Readers Theater develops fluency in oral reading and provides for meaningful listening. Because it eases students into script-writing by allowing them to use text models, it promotes student writing. This enrichment activity creates a shared literary experience in which students of various reading abilities can participate with enjoyment.

The easiest pieces to script are short stories that include several characters and much dialogue. In *Reading Literature, Green Level,* the legends are excellent for introducing Readers Theater to the students. "The Six Horsemen" and "Lazy Peter and His Three-Cornered Hat" would make good choices. All the short stories lend themselves to scripting.

However, any piece of text can be scripted. In the nonfiction chapter, episodes from any of the autobiographies, biographies, or the vignette can easily be used as the basis of Readers Theater productions. In addition, of course, the selections in the drama chapter could be presented either with props and scenery, in the traditional way, or in the Readers Theater style.

Here are the steps for using Readers Theater:

1. Choose the story. If the story is short, all of it may be scripted. If it is long, it may need editing.
2. Decide on the number of readers needed. Usually two or more narrators are required, as well as characters.
3. Script the text, putting as much plot development into characters' speeches as possible. Information that must be presented in narration should be split among the narrators. The scripting can be done as a group activity or by individual students.
4. Assign parts for reading. Here it is important for the teacher to be aware of the relative difficulty of each part and to assign students appropriately.
5. Provide each reader with a complete script, which each narrator and character will hold during the production. The pages should be stapled and placed in a folder. Students may highlight their individual parts with a pastel marker or by underlining.
6. Have the readers practice individually and then as a group. (See also page 503 of the student text.)
7. Decide on staging and any props. A prop should be used only if it adds to the clarity of the story. The readers may stand or sit on stools or chairs. Swivel stools, or chairs turned sideways, allow characters to face away from the audience when they are not "on stage." Placing the narrators at the two ends of the stage or classroom performing area lends visual balance to the setting of the production.
8. Have a dress rehearsal; make any staging changes that may be needed.
9. Present the performance.

Dictation

Dictation is the reading of well written, interesting, and complete passages for students to transcribe. Besides developing the power of concentrated listening, it gives practice in spelling, capitalization, punctuation, grammar, handwriting, and proofreading in a meaningful context. In addition, it helps students become actively familiar with the language of literature. Its structured and focused practice on specific skills is thought to be particularly beneficial for ESL, LD, and other students with special needs. The practice of dictation is recommended for use with any of the prose chapters of *Reading Literature.*

Here are the steps for using dictation:

1. The teacher selects a short passage, preferably without dialogue, and marks it off in syntactic groups appropriate for the students' span of attention. Beginning with three or four sentences is recommended; this allows for the development of a smooth procedure and gradually longer passages.
2. Students should clear their desks. They should be reminded to leave adequate margins and to skip every other line, leaving space for corrections.
3. The teacher reads the passage three times.

The first reading is to give the sense of the passage; the students only listen. The teacher may stop then to write difficult words on the board.

The second reading should be slower, with pauses between phrases as the students write. In order to lengthen the students' span of attention, there should be no repetitions during this reading. Depending on the focus of the lesson, punctuation may be given orally.

The third reading should again be at normal speed; students check for missing or incorrect words and errors in spelling, punctuation, capitalization, and word order.

4. Next, the students proofread their writing against the text and make corrections. The teacher then proofreads the paper. He or she grades each paper only on the errors the student has failed to correct. The student is responsible for finding and correcting those mistakes. Grading on only missed errors encourages careful proofreading by the student; requiring the student to reread his or her own work brings home the need for legible handwriting.

Fine Arts

The study of literature should be integrated with the other fine arts in two ways:

1. Students should be exposed to paintings, sculpture, and other works of visual art, and to works of the great composers and contemporary musicians, which reflect the selections in their reading.
2. Students should be allowed to express their responses to the selections in artistic or musical forms.

The student text of *Reading Literature* is rich in reproductions of fine art that reflect the topics and themes of the selections. In addition, where relevant, the text mentions works of art and music that relate to the selections. It is important to remind the students frequently to examine, compare, and contrast the illustrations throughout the text.

This Teacher's Edition provides short notes about each of the reproductions. These notes could be used as the basis for a steady broadening of the students' understanding and appreciation of art. They could be supplemented by visits to art museums and galleries by individual students or by class groups.

Students should also be encouraged to listen to recordings of music that relate to the reading selections. If possible, make some class time available for this activity. The music department in your school or system may be able to provide recordings and suggest appropriate selections.

In their responses to the literature, students should be encouraged to produce original art or music that reflects their personal understanding or vision of the topics discussed. Great literature should engage and inspire the whole person; provide opportunities for students to apply all their senses and talents in this study.

Bibliography

Stotsky, Sandra. "Dictation: Building Listening, Writing, and Reading Skills Together," in *The Leaflet,* Volume 82 Number 2: pages 6–12.

The T-numbered pages continue following the annotated student text pages.

See pages T21 through T48 at the back of this Teacher's Edition for these features:

management materials
contents of *Reading Literature*, 7–12
an overview of skills taught in *Reading Literature*, 7–12

Reading Literature

Purple Level
Yellow Level
Blue Level
Orange Level
GREEN LEVEL
Red Level

About the Cover Art

Primary shapes—circles, rectangles, and squares—dominate the paintings of Kenneth Noland (born 1924). His paintings, like the one on the cover, often create the illusion that the colors and shapes are moving. This style of painting has been called minimal art. It has little concern for external reality, that is, it does not depict recognizable objects from daily life or traditional subjects such as people or landscapes.

About the Art

The Unicorn in Captivity is the last tapestry from a magnificent series of seven called *The Hunt of the Unicorn.* The tapestries were woven in the fifteenth century in western Europe. The series begins with the *Start of the Hunt* and ends with this one showing the unicorn corraled after the hunt.

The tapestries were probably intended as a wedding gift, perhaps for the couple whose initials are embroidered into the tapestry itself. Large tapestries such as this one added color to the interior of castles or cathedrals, and they helped retain whatever warmth was afforded by the fireplace. The unicorn, a mythological animal, was a symbol of purity and courtly love, an elaborate chivalric system of courtship and romance. Notice in this tapestry how the simple form of the unicorn contrasts with the richly detailed pattern of the flowers.

Reading Literature

Green Level

The McDougal, Littell English Program

Jacqueline L. Chaparro
Curriculum Coordinator, English Language Arts
San Diego County Office of Education,
San Diego, California

Mary Ann Trost
Specialist in Educational Materials
for the Middle Grades, Cleveland Heights, Ohio

McDougal, Littell & Company
Evanston, Illinois
New York Dallas Sacramento

Special-Populations Consultants

Grace Holt, Project Facilitator, Bilingual Education, Elk Grove Unified School District, Sacramento, California

M. Gene Millard, Educational Consultant, Palm Harbor, Florida

Eleanor Thonis, Ph.D., District Psychologist, Wheatland Elementary School District, Wheatland, California

Virginia Woods, Secondary Resource Teacher (Specific Learning Disabilities), Dripping Springs, Texas

Consultants

James Dedes, Teacher, Holmes Junior High School, Mount Prospect, Illinois

Richard H. Gray, Chairman, English Department, Enfield High School, Enfield, Connecticut

Patricia West Jeffries, High school teacher and freelance writer on basic skills for the Memphis (Tennessee) City Schools.

Aramenta Kirkpatrick, Teacher, Warrensville Heights Junior High School, Cleveland, Ohio

Neeta Lewis, Teacher, Richardson Junior High School, Richardson, Texas

Sandra J. Nash, Teacher, Salt Rock Junior High School, Huntington, West Virginia

Jeane S. Travis, Teacher, Griffin Middle School, Smyrna, Georgia

Virginia Vargas, Teacher, Berta Cabaza Middle School, San Benito, Texas

H. Vance White, Department Chair, English, Walker Junior High School, La Palma, California

Frontispiece: *The Unicorn Tapestries VII: Unicorn in Captivity,* about 1500.
Metropolitan Museum of Art, gift of John D. Rockefeller, Jr., the Cloisters Collection, 1937.

Acknowledgments

Ricardo E. Alegría: For "Lazy Peter and the Three-Cornered Hat" by Ricardo E. Alegría, from *The Three Wishes,* a Collection of Puerto Rican Folktales. Isaac Asimov: For "The Disappearing Man" by Isaac Asimov, as it appeared in *Boy's Life,* June 1978. Brandt & Brandt Literary Agents, Inc.: For "Western Wagons," "Abraham
(continued on page 605)

ISBN: 0-86609-229-3

87 88 89 90 / 15 14 13 12 11 10 9 8 7 6 5 4 3

Contents

CHAPTER 1 *Legends*

CHAPTER 4 *Short Stories* 133

CHAPTER 6 *Nonfiction* 351

Letters

Speeches

Vignette

Handbook for Reading and Writing 531

Dear Educator,

Reading Literature brings to your students the greatest literature of all time. In this age of computers and VCR's, precious little of the world's great literary heritage filters through to our new generation. I don't believe you want your students to go through life without being acquainted with the tales of King Arthur. I don't believe you want your students to be unacquainted with the stories and poems of Geoffrey Chaucer, Pearl Buck, Emily Dickinson, and Henry Wadsworth Longfellow. This kind of reading can provide your students with a quickened sense of life's drama and a new sense of life's possibilities. The time is now. The opportunity is here.

Your students will be reading literature in its original form. Selections are not adapted. We have searched through the world's great literature to find selections that will stretch the students' minds, sharpen their senses, and enrich their lives.

Throughout, *Reading Literature* integrates reading and writing. Writing is presented as a process. A thorough foundation for writing is presented in a complete chapter, "How Writers Write" (see Chapter 3). The universal themes and ideas revealed by great literature make easy the task of teacher and text in guiding students to discover topics for their own writing.

I hope you will be as proud to offer *Reading Literature* to your students as we are to present it to you. I hope, too, that *Reading Literature* will assist you in helping the students to read happily, to think critically, and, above all, to meet the wondrous challenge that is life. Great writers of our time, and of earlier times, can help students in this process of growth. No other writers can do it as well.

Joseph F. Littell
Editor-in-Chief
McDougal, Littell & Company

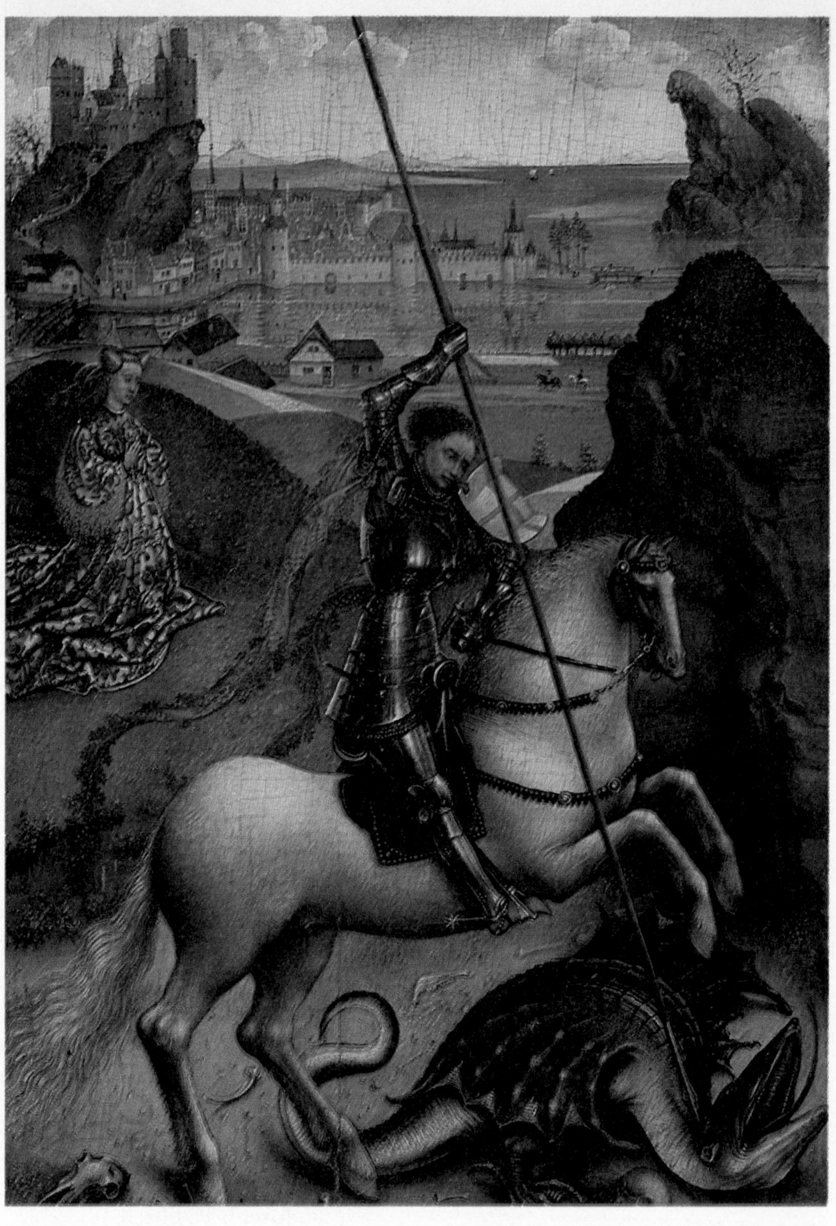

About the Art

Although he did not sign any of his paintings, Rogier van der Weyden (about 1399-1464) is well known. He is considered the finest painter in the Netherlands during the fifteenth century. Born in Flanders, van der Weyden moved to Brussels, where he became the official City Painter, a position of wealth and respect he held for the rest of his life. Van der Weyden's individual portraits, especially his emotionally charged religious scenes, have strongly influenced artists.

A richly colored and detailed painting, *St. George and the Dragon* presents a popular subject for painters: the legendary rescue of the king's daughter by St. George. The overall presentation may seem very calm for such a dramatic event, but this composure is perhaps appropriate to highlight the assured victory of good over evil. Except for the dragon writhing under St. George's spear, all is relatively calm. St. George effortlessly combats the dragon while the king's daughter, the near victim of the dragon, kneels in prayer. In the background, life seems to go on as usual, as if nothing out of the ordinary were taking place outside the city gates.

CHAPTER 1

St. George and the Dragon, about 1432, ROGIER van der WEYDEN.
National Gallery of Art, Washington, D.C., Ailsa Mellon Bruce Fund, 1966.

Chapter Objectives

The following is a list of the major skills developed throughout this chapter:

Skills in Reading Literature

- To appreciate the legend as a form of literature
- To identify the characteristics of a legend, such as the blending of fact and fiction
- To examine such elements of legend as characters, setting and plot

Comprehension Skills

- To identify main ideas and details in a paragraph (Literal Reading)
- To recall events in the order they occurred (Literal Reading)
- To make inferences about characters' motives (Interpretive Reading)
- To evaluate the believability of events (Critical Reading)

Vocabulary Skills

- To use definition and restatement context clues to discover meanings of words
- To use synonyms and antonyms as context clues
- To infer the meanings of words from context

Writing Skills

- To write a comparison of two characters (Analytical Writing)
- To write an explanation of an opinion (Analytical Writing)
- To write an original conversation (Creative Writing)
- To write a legend from a new point of view (Creative Writing)

Study and Research Skills

- To understand how to use the Dewey Decimal System and card catalog
- To become familiar with library resources

Critical Thinking Skills

- To classify legends
- To separate fact and fiction
- To recognize slanted writing

Speaking and Listening Skills

- To read a selection orally, expressing mood
- To recognize and compare rhythms in prose writing
- To tell a legend to a group

Reading Literature

The lesson in **Reading Literature** on pages 2 and 3 gives the students important background to help them enjoy and appreciate legends. First, the text explains what a legend is. Then it presents a brief history of this form of literature and describes some of its major characteristics. Last, it presents the students with specific suggestions to aid them in reading legends.

Preparing the Students

Write the titles of the following legends on the chalkboard: "The Legend of Robin Hood," "The Legend of King Arthur," and "The Legend of Davy Crockett." Ask the students if they recognize any of these titles. Have any students who are familiar with the stories tell something about them. Ask if anyone knows of any other legends. Tell the class that they will learn more about legends in this chapter and will have a chance to read many legends from different countries and times.

It is recommended that you administer the **Chapter 1 Diagnostic Test** at this time. The results of this pretest will serve as a guide for measuring student needs and progress in achieving chapter objectives.

If you have not yet had the students fill out and turn in the **Reading Experiences Inventory** in the test booklet, this would be a good time to do so. The **Inventory** will give you a better understanding of the student's personal reading habits and strengths.

Presenting the Lesson

1. Have one student read aloud **What Is a Legend?** on page 2. Discuss what a legend is. Make sure the students realize that legends are part fact and part fiction. You may need to review the meaning of the word *fictional.* Have one student explain what *oral tradition* means.

2. Have one student read **The History of the Legend.** Then discuss the information there. Stress that legends are based on fact. They are, therefore, different from tall tales or fairy tales that have no relation to reality. Ask if anyone is familiar with the legends of St. George (the saint who killed a dragon to save a princess's life), Robin Hood (the noble outlaw who robbed from the rich to help the poor), and Pocahontas (the Indian princess who saved the life of John Smith, an early colonist).

To demonstrate how a story can change with each retelling, you may want to play

Reading Literature: Legends

What Is a Legend?

A **legend** is a story about heroes and heroines and extraordinary events of the past. Some parts of legends are true and some parts are fictional. Legends are part of the **oral tradition.** That is, they have been passed on orally from parents and storytellers to children for many years.

The History of the Legend

People need heroes and heroines. When they find someone who is brave, strong, kind, and intelligent, they spread the good news. That is how legends begin.

Most legends are based on fact. However, when a true story is repeated many times, it changes. One teller may exaggerate a bit. The next teller adds a new event. Someone else remembers an old tale he or she once heard and includes that story, too. Soon, the true story is buried under exaggerations and additions. The new story that is created is a legend—a mix of fact and fiction.

Legends can be about characters as different as St. George, Robin Hood, and Pocahontas. Each group of people has its own favorite legends. Their heroes and heroines have qualities that the group admires, such as honesty or loyalty. There are some qualities that all of these characters have. They defend their beliefs bravely, they lead others, and they never give up.

For hundreds of years, people preserved legends by repeating them to each new generation. When printing was invented, people wrote the stories down. That is how we have them today.

From official records, we know that some of the characters in these legends, such as William Tell, were real people. However, we don't know if any of these adventures ever happened.

The Elements of a Legend

Legends are stories. The three major elements of any story are **characters, setting,** and **plot.**

Characters. The characters are the people or animals who take part in the story. Usually, in a legend, one of the characters is a brave, good person. He or she may have powers greater than the normal person. This hero or heroine is often joined by followers. Opposing them, there is usually a powerful, evil character.

Setting. The setting tells when and where the story takes place. It is often described early in the legend. However, details all through the story help you picture the setting.

Plot. The plot is the series of events that takes place in the story. The plot includes a struggle, or **conflict,** that the hero or heroine must face. In a legend, he or she must show courage or cleverness to win over evil forces.

Some events in legends are unbelievable. For example, one hero is carried down a mountain on an eagle's back. Uncommon happenings are common in legends.

Narrator. The narrator is the person telling the story. Most legends are told by a narrator who does not take part in the plot. This narrator knows everything—even what characters think.

How To Read a Legend

When you read a legend, remember these guidelines:

1. Identify the setting. Does the legend take place in the time of knights and castles? Is it set in a forest or a jungle?
2. Accept impossible happenings. The imaginations of many storytellers are at work in legends. Enjoy their creativity.
3. Decide what the legend tells you about what makes a person heroic. Do the people who created the legend value courage, loyalty, patience, intelligence, or some other quality?

the game called "Telephone." To play the game, one person whispers a message to another person who then passes the message along to a third person. After the message has been passed to several people, compare the final message to the original statement. Usually, you will find that significant changes will have been made.

3. Direct the students to read **The Elements of a Legend** on page 3. Discuss the major elements of character, setting, and plot. Have one student describe the two kinds of characters that usually appear in legends. Make sure that everyone knows what conflict is and what the narrator does.

4. Call on volunteers to read **How To Read a Legend**. Discuss the three guidelines that are presented.

Reinforcing the Lesson

To reteach, reinforce, or extend the concepts in this lesson, see the following:

Skills Practice Book, Green Level—pages 1 and 2

Additional Resources

Diagnostic and Mastery Tests, Green Level—Reading Experiences Inventory, pages 1 and 2; Chapter 1 Diagnostic Test, pages 3 and 4

Comprehension Skills

The lesson in **Comprehension Skills** on pages 4 and 5 stresses the concept of main idea and explains the difference between important and less important details. Recognition of main idea and details will be emphasized throughout this chapter, and it will be reviewed frequently in other chapters.

Preparing the Students

Read this paragraph to the class. Then ask them to tell you, in one sentence, the most important idea it is saying.

> When you use power tools, it is important to follow the rules. You should always wear goggles to protect your eyes from flying particles. Keep your attention on your work at all times. Make sure that everyone around you stays a safe distance away.

The students should recognize that the most important idea is that people using power tools should follow certain rules. Explain that the most important idea is also called the main idea. Tell the students that they will learn more about the main idea of paragraphs in the next section.

Presenting the Lesson

1. Have the class read **Understanding Main Idea and Details** on page 4. Discuss what a main idea is and how it is different from a topic. Make sure that everyone realizes which sentence is the topic sentence in the paragraph about Hamelin. Stress that every sentence in a paragraph must be related to the main idea.

2. Read to the class the first paragraph and excerpt (page 4 only) in **Important and Less Important Details.** Ask the students to identify the main idea of the sample paragraph. List the details from the paragraph on the board, and ask the class to identify the more important details from the list. Then have the rest of that section, page 5, read aloud, and discuss it. Emphasize that, while all the details are related to the main idea, some are necessary while others are not.

3. Have the students read **Exercise A** silently. You may wish to explain that this is a paragraph from a traditional native American legend that they will read later in the chapter. Discuss the main idea together.

Have the students complete **Exercise B** independently. Discuss the answers. Have the students explain why they felt some details were more important than others.

Comprehension Skills: Main Idea

Understanding Main Idea and Details

Every paragraph has a main idea. The **main idea** is the most important idea in the paragraph. Do not confuse the main idea with the topic of the paragraph. The topic is simply what the paragraph is about. The main idea is what the writer is telling you about the topic.

Read this sample paragraph.

> Hamelin, a little German town, was overrun by rats. They were so fierce and numerous that they attacked the cats and drove the dogs away. All kinds of traps were laid, but the rats just flipped them about. They were everywhere.

The main idea of a paragraph is often stated in a topic sentence. In the paragraph above, the topic sentence is underlined. Read the paragraph again. See how the underlined sentence states the most important idea. Notice, also, that the other sentences give details about how Hamelin was overrun by rats. All the detail sentences tell more about the main idea.

Every sentence in a paragraph must be related to the main idea. To introduce a new idea, writers begin a new paragraph.

Important and Less Important Details

Some details are more important to the main idea than other details. Here is an example.

> One evening in autumn, Blondel came to an unusually large castle in the middle of a wild forest. It had a grim look, dark and desolate. Two equally grim guards stood in front of the drawbridge.

You learn a lot of details in this short paragraph. The most important idea, or main idea, is that Blondel found an unusually large castle in a forest. One important detail is the grim look of the place. Another important detail is that it was guarded.

Some other details are not important to the story. For example, it does not matter much that Blondel came to the castle on one evening in autumn. It is not important to know that the forest was wild or where the guards were standing. These details make the story fun to read, but they are not absolutely necessary for an understanding of the story.

Exercises: Understanding Main Idea and Details

A. What is the main idea of this paragraph?

Their raid was not a success. The Pahani were watchful. The young warriors got nowhere near the Pahani horse herd. Not only did they capture no ponies, but they even lost their own mounts, because, while they were trying to creep up to their enemies' herd, the Pahani found their horses. The two young men had a hard time getting away on foot because their enemies were searching for them everywhere.

B. Read the following paragraph. Then match the items below.

Like autumn leaves in a storm, this promise was carried through the Hausa towns. It came to the ears of a certain young prince who was, himself, the son of a chief. Fadebi, he was called, and he was well known for his brave deeds.

1. This sentence states the main idea.
2. This sentence states an important detail.
3. This sentence tells a less important detail.

a. "The promise was carried like autumn leaves in a storm."
b. "The promise came to the ears of a certain young prince."
c. "Fadebi was well known for his brave deeds."

Reinforcing the Lesson

To reteach, reinforce, or extend the concepts in this lesson, see the following:

Skills Practice Book, Green Level—pages 3 and 4

Special Populations

LD. These students may frequently confuse the main idea with the topic. In most cases, this distinction is of relatively small importance and should not be stressed with these students. They may need much reinforcement in identifying the main idea of a paragraph.

Since many LD students tend to have a literal approach, you may need to stress the fact that not every paragraph states its main idea in a single, topic sentence. Remind them that they must read and think about the whole paragraph and decide what the main idea is, before looking for it in a single sentence.

Answers to Exercises

A. The raid by the two young men was not a success.

B. Matching items and sentences:

1. b.
2. c.
3. a.

Vocabulary Skills

The lesson in **Vocabulary Skills** teaches students how to use a definition or restatement clue and a synonym in context to understand a new word. Study questions throughout the chapter develop and provide drill in this skill, applying it to words in the chapter selections.

Preparing the Students

Ask the students if they have ever come across a word they did not understand in their reading. Find out how they handled the problem. Tell them that in this text they will learn several different ways to unlock the meaning of these unknown words. They will begin in Chapter 1 by learning how to recognize and use context clues.

If you like, have the students begin a vocabulary notebook, or a vocabulary section of their class notebook, in which they will record all the techniques for discovering word meanings as they learn them.

Presenting the Vocabulary Lesson

1. Have the students read the first paragraph of **Using Context Clues.** Ask what is meant by *context.* Have the rest of the section read aloud, stopping to make sure students can identify the clues in the sample sentences.

After they have read the section, ask students to explain in their own words what a definition or restatement clue is. List on the chalkboard the key words that signal a definition or restatement clue. Have the students copy this information in their notebooks. For additional reinforcement, ask students for original sentences that use definition or restatement clues using each of the key words. The sentences can define simple words such as *umbrella, blizzard,* or *train.*

2. Have **Synonyms** read aloud. Make sure everyone understands that in a synonym clue, the synonym simply replaces the unfamiliar word in the next place where that word could have appeared. This differs from a restatement clue, where the unfamiliar word is immediately followed by its meaning and the meaning is brought in specifically to explain the unfamiliar word, not to develop the story.

3. Make sure the students understand the directions for **Exercises A** and **B**. Assign the exercises to be completed independently. Discuss the answers.

Vocabulary Skills: Context Clues

Using Context Clues

As you read, you often come upon new and unfamiliar words. Writers know that you may not understand every word. They leave clues in the context to help you. The **context** means the sentences and paragraphs in which a word appears. In this chapter, you will learn about different context clues, including definition or restatement clues, and synonyms.

Definition and Restatement Clues. Sometimes a writer gives you the meaning of a new word. The **definition clue** may appear in the same sentence as the new word or in the following sentence.

> The man held a pipe. A pipe is a tube of wood or metal used as a musical instrument.

Other times a writer repeats the new word in a slightly different way. This is a **restatement clue.**

> The children trooped, or marched, behind the piper.

Certain key words and key punctuation tell you to look for definition and restatement clues. Here are some of these keys:

is	*that is*	*in other words*	parentheses	
or	*who is*	*which is*	commas	dashes

Find the definition or restatement clue that explains the underlined word in each sentence below. Identify any key words or punctuation.

1. A gale, which is a strong wind, blew the ships off course.
2. King John served sumptuous, that is, magnificent, meals.
3. He calls himself a patriot—a person who loves his country.

4. Blondel was a minstrel, a poet who was also a singer.
5. He looked into the abyss (a very deep hole in the earth).

Synonyms. A **synonym** is a word that means almost the same thing as another word. For example, a synonym for *azure* is *blue*. Writers often use a new word and then, as soon as they can, use a synonym for it. In this way, you understand the new word. This sentence uses a synonym to explain *lariat*. From the synonym in the sentence, you know that a lariat is a rope.

> Black Crow took his rawhide *lariat,* made a loop in it, put the *rope* around Spotted Eagle's chest under his armpits, and lowered him down.

Exercises: **Using Context Clues**

A. For each underlined word, find the definition or restatement.

1. Gessler was a tyrant. A tyrant is a cruel ruler.
2. Tell took hold of the rudder, which is a movable piece of wood used for steering a boat.
3. All that you possess will be forfeited, that is, lost, to me.
4. The piper was pied. In other words, his clothes had patches of two different colors.

B. For each sentence, identify the word that has been restated, the key words or punctuation that helped you find the restatement clue, and the meaning of the restated word.

1. A deeper meaning was concealed—hidden—in the song.
2. The mayor summoned, or called together, his councilors.
3. Spotted Eagle lived on the ledge with the eagle fledglings (young birds).
4. Black Crow wore a sash, a type of scarf, around his waist.
5. The Abbot of Canterbury, the head of the English church, lived as well as the king.

Reinforcing the Lesson

To reteach, reinforce, or extend the skills in this lesson, see the following:

Skills Practice Book, Green Level—pages 5 and 6

Special Populations

LD. Make a ditto or wall chart with information from this lesson, showing the key words and punctuation for definition and restatement clues. Encourage students when doing the exercises to refer to the chart in order to review the words to look for in determining the type of context clues.

Answers to Exercises

A. Definitions

1. cruel ruler
2. movable piece of wood used for steering a boat
3. lost
4. patches of different colors

B. Word, key, and meaning

1. concealed, dashes, hidden
2. summoned, commas, called together
3. fledglings, parentheses, young birds
4. sash, commas, type of scarf
5. Abbot of Canterbury, commas, head of English church

Objectives

- To recognize and appreciate legend as a form of literature
- To recognize character traits
- To apply literal, interpretive, and critical reading skills to a selection
- To determine the main idea of a paragraph
- To use definition and restatement context clues to determine word meaning
- To analyze the structure of a story
- To understand the library's system of categorizing books

Preparing the Students

Essential Vocabulary. It is suggested that students complete **Developing Vocabulary Skills** at this time. Have the students use the context clues in the sentences on page 13 to determine the meanings of the underlined words.

If the students need additional help with the vocabulary of this selection, encourage them to use context clues to determine word meaning. As needed, direct them to the **Glossary** or to a classroom dictionary.

Motivation. Briefly discuss the Crusades. (The Crusades were a series of expeditions by European Christians to recapture the places where Jesus had lived from the Muslims, people of the Islamic faith, who had conquered the Holy Land. There were eight different crusades during the eleventh, twelfth and thirteenth centuries. Richard the Lion-Hearted of England met Saladin, the Muslim leader, in battles during the Third Crusade. Richard never captured Jerusalem, but he was successful in making a pact with Saladin allowing Christians to visit their sacred shrines in peace.)

Have the students read the introductory paragraph at the top of page 8 and state in their own words what they should try to find out as they read this legend.

Presenting the Selection

1. Have the students read "Richard the Lion-Hearted: Saved by a Song" on pages 8 to 11.

2. After students have finished reading, use a map to point out the Holy Land, the area Richard passed through on his way home, and the countries where he was held prisoner.

3. Remind students of the introduction. Ask several students for their answers to the questions posed there.

4. Make sure that everyone has read

Richard the Lion-Hearted: Saved by a Song

Even heroes need saving sometimes. In this story, a hero is saved through something more powerful than weapons or treasure. As you read, look for that powerful quality.

TRADITIONAL TALE

Retold by Louis Untermeyer

Richard the First lived in the twelfth century. He is considered one of the greatest English kings, although he spent comparatively little time in England. Wars in Europe as well as the Crusades in the Holy Land kept him abroad during most of his reign. He was in the forefront of every battle he fought. When he wielded his huge battle-axe, none could withstand him. So fearless was he that he was known not merely as King Richard the Mighty but as Richard the Lion-Hearted. Enemies fled when he charged upon them shouting his battle cry, "God be with us!"

Richard had gone on the Third Crusade against the Saracens, hoping to drive them out of Jerusalem so that Christians could visit the holy places in safety. He had been aided by two other European kings, but he quarreled with his allies and grew to respect his enemies more than his friends. Saladin, king of Saracens, returned his respect and welcomed Richard as his guest. After mutual acts of courtesy and expressions of good will, a three-year truce was proposed.

"We of the East believe greatly in the number three," said Saladin. "It is a powerful number. Man is a threefold creature made of body, soul, and spirit, and the enemies of man are three: the world, the flesh, and the devil. Do you not believe so, you of the North?"

"It is so," replied Richard. "The Greeks taught us that man's life depends on the three fates—the three daughters of the night who spin the thread of life—that nature is divided into three kingdoms—animal, vegetable, and mineral—and that there are three prime colors: red, yellow, and blue."

"That being true," said Saladin, "let us make our truce really binding. Let it be

Stories of the Emperors: Soliman Against the Christians, 15th Century. Paris Biblioteque de l'Arsenale. Courtesy of Art Resource, New York.

for three years, three months, three days, and three hours. And let us take an oath that nothing shall break such a truce."

The two leaders swore to keep the peace for that length of time and, if they were still friends, for the rest of their lives. Then Richard withdrew his troops from the Holy Land. He set sail for England by way of Cyprus, but a gale blew his ships off their course and drove them to Italy. Worse weather occurred when he resumed the journey. Storms overwhelmed the fleet with waves like battering-rams, and knife-sharp winds tore the sails. After a grueling week, the boats lost contact with each other. King Richard's ship was thrown against a rocky coast and destroyed. His men were drowned, and he himself barely managed to survive.

After wandering for weeks, he found himself in the land of one of his worst enemies, Duke Leopold of Austria. He was recognized at once and captured. The Duke of Austria shut him up in a dungeon and then asked a huge ransom for his release. When Henry, Emperor of Germany, heard of this, he compelled Leopold to give up his prize. Instead of freeing Richard, Henry imprisoned him in one of his own castles and demanded a still more staggering ransom. So that no one would know where the King of

the legend by administering the **Check Test**, at the bottom of page 11 of this T.E.

5. Develop the study questions as suggested in **Using the Study Questions,** beginning on page 12. That section also provides a challenge question for further discussion, if needed. (For answers to questions, see T.E. pages 12 to 14.)

Reinforcing the Lesson

To reteach, reinforce, or extend the skills in this lesson, see the following:

Skills Practice Book, Green Level—pages 7 through 10

Special Populations

LD. The exercise under **Developing Vocabulary Skills** on page 13 may need to be simplified for the LD student. Present the following chart for the student to fill in:

	Word	Clue	Meaning
1.			
2.			
3.			

LD, ESL. In general, LD students will have difficulty completing exercises in **Developing Writing Skills** as individual assignments due to lack of ability to generalize and make inferences, and because they have limited imaginations. ESL students face language difficulties and differences in background experiences. Both groups will have greater success when students are paired with partners, assigned to small groups, or given opportunities for pre-writing group discussions.

About the Art

Stories of the Emperors: Soliman Against the Christians depicts a historical event but might seem more like propaganda than history. The Christian artist shows the Christian army, to the left, in orderly formation and seemingly confident of the outcome of the battle. Soliman and the Turks, identifiable by their exotic armor, turban-like helmets, and curved scimitars, are shown in disarray and retreat to the right. Soliman the Magnificent was Sultan of the Ottoman Empire from 1520 to 1566. A great warrier, he led his armies against the Christians in a bold military campaign. He was also a man of culture who surrounded himself with statesmen, poets, architects, and lawyers.

Encouraging Independent Reading

Students may enjoy reading *Ivanhoe* by Sir Walter Scott or seeing the movie made from the novel. Another novel about this time of history is *Richard I, King of England* by Martha Rufheart.

England was hidden and attempt to rescue him, he was moved at various times from one secret stronghold to another.

Meanwhile, things were going badly in England, where Richard's absence had caused much confusion. There were rumors that the demand for ransom was a deception to get money for the German emperor and that Richard was really dead. His brother John robbed the treasury and plotted to seize the throne; the country was in a state of turmoil and anxiety. No one thought of clarifying the situation by finding out whether Richard was alive or dead. No one except Blondel de Nesle.

Blondel was a minstrel, a poet who was also a singer. He had been a boon companion to Richard in his youth. Richard and Blondel had spent many hours together making up tunes, matching rhymes, and composing songs on any subject that came to mind. It was Blondel who asked for permission to look for the king.

"But how do you expect to conduct so wild a hunt?" inquired Richard's minister. He was the person who had been appointed by Richard to take care of his court duties while he was away. "Where will you start?"

"I cannot tell you how until I begin," answered Blondel. "But I can tell you where. The demands for the ransom have come from Germany, so Germany is the most likely place to start."

"How many men will you require?" asked the minister.

"None," said Blondel. "I will go alone."

"You will, I hope, be well armed. What weapons will you need?"

"One weapon only," said Blondel, "if you can call it that. I will take along my little hand harp. It will be all I need."

For three months Blondel wandered up and down Germany. He played his harp and sang his songs in taverns, inns, courtyards, and castles. He was always welcome, for people in every land delight to hear songs of war and wooing, of gallant deeds and lovely ladies, especially when they are sung as beautifully as Blondel sang them. He was offered large sums of money to remain in many a palace; he heard much gossip and was told many things in confidence. But never a word did he hear about King Richard.

One evening in autumn he came to an unusually large castle in the middle of a wild forest. It had a grim look, dark and desolate. Two equally grim guards stood in front of the drawbridge.

"Keep back," one of them said. "We make short work of spies."

"I am no spy," said Blondel. "I am a minstrel. I go from place to place to entertain lords and ladies. I am sure those inside would like to hear me."

"There is no one inside who cares for merrymaking," said the other guard. "Your eyes must be poor if you think this is a place for entertainment. It is not so much a castle as a prison."

"Indeed?" said Blondel. "I would not have suspected it."

"Yes," said the first guard, a note of pride coming into his voice. "It is one of the strongest prisons in Europe and one of the least known. And the curious part is this: it houses only one prisoner."

"And who might that be?" Blondel asked eagerly. "Who has an entire prison to himself?"

"That we can't tell you," replied the second guard. "In fact, we ourselves don't know. All we know is that he must be someone very important, someone who has to be watched very carefully."

"Well," said Blondel. "That is very interesting. But, after all, it has nothing to do with me. If I cannot get a welcome here I will try elsewhere. Before I go, perhaps you would like to hear a song."

"Go ahead," said the first guard. "A song never hurt anyone."

"Nor helped them, either," added the second. "But go ahead."

Blondel tuned his harp and began:

My lady sits within her bower;
She sings "alas" right dolefully:
She lingers hour after hour.
For her true lord. But where is he?

Blondel paused. It was a song that he and King Richard had made up and sung together years ago. It had a new meaning for them now.

Then another voice was added to his, completing the second stanza:

O tell my lady that the fates
Have kept her lord away from men;
But patiently her lover waits
The day he can come home again.

The guards were startled to hear the second voice. They did not guess the meaning concealed in the song. Nevertheless, they were angry with themselves for having let the minstrel linger.

"That's enough!" shouted the guards. "On your way!"

Blondel went, but he had found what he had been seeking. Also, the captured king knew that Blondel had discovered where he had been hidden. He did not have to wait long to be freed.

Three months later his release was accomplished and he was brought back to England. More powerful than ever, King Richard restored his country to peace.

A Twelfth-Century Signet Ring of Richard I, 1189–99.
The British Museum, London.

About the Art

The signet ring was often decorated with a personal initial or family crest. In addition to symbolizing royalty, the signet provided a practical way to authenticate, identify, and seal both personal and official documents. An impression of the seal could be made by pressing the ring into soft wax. The signet ring might be thought of as a predecessor to today's notary seal.

Check Test

1. Who was the king of the Saracens? (Saladin)

2. How many guards were at the drawbridge of the castle in the forest? (two)

3. What did Blondel do to find out if Richard was in the castle? (He sang a song.)

4. How long did it take for King Richard to be released after Blondel found him? (three months)

Using the Study Questions

It is recommended that students always read and answer the questions in **Developing Comprehension Skills** in class discussion. Whenever possible, they should also read the questions in the other categories together and discuss the answers.

Developing Comprehension Skills

Question 1. Make sure that students understand the meaning of *truce*. Discuss briefly what both Richard and Saladin say about the number three.

Question 2. Since Richard reached Henry's prison in a complicated way, students may need to reread this part of the legend for the answer. Encourage students to find proof of their answers in the selection.

Question 3. Explain that students will not be able to find a direct statement to answer this question. They must infer the relationship using clues in the story.

Question 4. Ask what kind of rescue party the enemy was probably expecting. Why would it be easy for a minstrel to learn secret information and slip by unnoticed?

Question 5. Have the students skim the legend looking for major events. List the major events on the board. Have them decide whether each event was possible.

Challenge Question. Why didn't Blondel let the guards know he had found Richard? (Interpretive Reading)

Reading Literature: Legends

Question 1. To be sure the students know what types of actions or attitudes they should look for, discuss how a person might show self-confidence, loyalty, and cheerfulness.

Question 2. Read and discuss.

Question 3. Ask the students to think about who was actually helped by the song and who was hurt by it.

Question 4. Be sure that all students know which paragraph to read before directing them to answer the question.

Developing Vocabulary Skills

Read the directions to the exercise aloud. Review with students the meaning of definition or restatement clues. If you wish, have students reread the explanation on pages 6 and 7 in the introduction. You may want to complete the first question together with the students. Have

Developing Comprehension Skills

Literal Reading	1. What led Richard and Saladin to make a truce? How long was the truce to last?
Literal Reading	2. How did Richard come to be in Henry's prison?
Interpretive Reading	3. How do you know that the relationship between Richard and his brother John was not good?
Interpretive Reading	4. Why was Blondel the best person to find Richard?
Critical Reading	5. Do you think any of the events in this story could really have happened? Which ones? Give reasons for your answer.

Reading Literature: Legends

1. **Recognizing Character Traits.** Heroes and heroines of legends are noted for their personal qualities, or **traits.** These traits are admired by the group that created the legends. Pick one of the three traits below and tell how Blondel showed that trait.

   a. self-confidence b. loyalty c. cheerfulness

2. **Understanding Setting.** The actions in a story may take place in several different settings. The storyteller or writer may describe one setting more clearly than other settings in the story.

   "Richard the Lion-Hearted" takes place in several settings: in the Holy Land, at sea, in Austria, in prisons in Germany, in England, in taverns and castles in Germany, and at one particular prison in Germany. Only one of these settings is described clearly. Which is it? Can you think of a reason why the writer described that one setting?

3. **Recognizing Irony.** Often a writer lets the reader know more than a character knows. The character thinks one thing is true, but the reader knows the opposite is true. When what appears to be true is not true at all, the writer is using **irony.**

   For example, on page 11, Blondel asks the guards if he may sing. Not knowing his real purpose, the guards agree:

   > "Go ahead," said the first guard. "A song never hurt anyone."
   >
   > "Nor helped them, either," added the second.

   Explain how both guards are wrong.

Answers to Study Questions

Developing Comprehension Skills

1. Richard quarreled with his allies and grew to respect his enemy. Richard was welcomed as a guest by Saladin and their friendship led to the truce. It was to last three years, three months, three days, and three hours.

2. After his ship wrecked, Richard was captured by Duke Leopold of Austria and held for ransom. Henry, emperor of Germany, forced Leopold to give up his prisoner. Then Henry held him for ransom.

3. In Richard's absence, John was plotting to steal the throne and had already robbed the treasury.

4. Because he was a minstrel, Blondel was welcome almost everywhere he went and was frequently taken into people's confidence and heard much gossip. All of this could help to lead him to Richard without arousing suspicion. In addition, his close friendship with Richard gave him more knowledge of the king than others would have.

5. Answers may vary. Some possible events include the following:

Richard making a truce with Saladin

Richard being captured and held for ransom (These events would not be unusual for a king.)

4. **Determining the Main Idea.** Reread paragraph 5 in column 2 on page 10. What is the main idea of the paragraph? State the main idea in your own words. Then list one of the details in the paragraph that explains the main idea.

Developing Vocabulary Skills

Using Context Clues in Sentences. The underlined words in the following sentences were drawn from the story. The meaning of each word can be figured out by a definition or restatement clue. For each underlined word below, write the following on your paper:

a. Whether each sentence contains a definition or restatement clue
b. The key words or key punctuation that helped you find the meaning of the word
c. The meaning of the underlined word

1. The fighting between the two countries ended after mutual acts of courtesy. In other words, the leaders of the countries acted courteously toward each other.
2. Wars in Europe kept King Richard away during most of his reign—his time in power.
3. The Greeks believed that man's life depended on fate. Fate is what happens to a person beyond the person's control.
4. The Duke of Austria shut Richard up in a dungeon and then asked for a huge ransom, the price asked for his release.
5. When Henry heard of this he compelled, or forced, Leopold to give up his prize.
6. There were rumors that the demand for ransom was a deception (trick) to get money for the German Emperor.
7. The guards were angry with themselves for having let the minstrel linger, or stay around.
8. More powerful than ever, King Richard restored, that is, brought back, peace to his country.

Developing Writing Skills

Analytical Writing

1. **Relating the Parts of a Story.** After the first six paragraphs, the legend does not mention Saladin. Can you explain why Saladin was in

Blondel looking for Richard (A good friend would do this.)

Richard being released and returning to England

Challenge. Blondel was alone, and he knew he could not rescue the king by himself. As long as Henry did not know that the king had been found, he would not move him again. That would make it easier to free the king later.

Reading Literature: Legends

1. Possible examples of Blondel's character traits:

a. Self-confidence—He never doubted that he could rescue Richard alone and unarmed.

b. Loyalty—He was willing to devote all his time to searching for Richard.

c. Cheerfulness—He was well-liked everywhere he went, and his happy nature even softened the grim guards outside the castle where Richard was being held.

2. The one particular castle in Germany is described more clearly than any other setting. This setting is where the most important action of the story occurs—Bondel finds Richard.

(continued on page 14)

them complete the assignment independently. Discuss the answers together.

Developing Writing Skills

Read and discuss the three assignments. Then have each student choose and complete one of the three.

Note that there are no answers to **Developing Writing Skills** in the box labeled **Answers to Study Questions.** The writing assignments are to be graded on an individual basis. See pages T24 to T27 of this Teacher's Edition for suggestions and a form for evaluating student writing.

Question 1. This question asks students to decide why certain details were included in the legend. It helps the students appreciate that decisions about what to include were made by the writer deliberately, not accidentally.

Pre-Writing. Review the reasons for Richard's trip to the Holy Land and the cordial relationship between Richard and Saladin. Have the students think about the questions in the text and make notes on their answers. Have the students use their notes to decide why it was essential to the rest of the story to tell about Saladin and Richard in the Holy Land. Emphasize that there may be many reasons, not just one right answer.

Writing. Allow sufficient time for the students to write their first drafts.

Revising. When students have completed their first drafts, ask them to read their drafts to partners. The partners should be able to explain the writers' reasons why the legend mentions Saladin and Richard in the Holy Land. Allow sufficient time for any necessary revisions.

Question 2. It may help some students to work with partners and exchange ideas about what arguments might work.

Pre-Writing. Have the students brainstorm to think of any possible arguments Henry could have used on Leopold. Encourage them to list all ideas, no matter how unlikely. Then direct each student to choose the one idea he or she has the most to say about. To help set the tone of the conversation, have students decide whether Henry and Leopold are friends or enemies. If they wish, students may write a conversation using an informal, modern way of speaking.

Writing. Remind students that readers need to know who is speaking throughout the conversation. You might suggest that they indicate the speaker as a playwright does, that is, by putting the name followed by a colon in front of the speaker's words. Have them read the conversations aloud as they write in order to test whether they make sense and sound natural.

Revising. Allow time for students to read their conversations to the class, ask for responses, and improve the final product.

Question 3. In this question, the students have an opportunity to write part of a story. It will give inexperienced writers a gradual introduction to creating stories.

Pre-Writing. Have students imagine their relationships to the king, whether they are servants, relatives, fellow knights, or in another position. Have them decide what capabilities they would have had because of their occupations or relationships with the king and court. Suggest that students take notes about the character they are pretending to be and list possible ways in which that character could find the king. Then have students choose the way they like best.

Writing. Allow students enough time to write the paragraph. Remind them to write in the first-person, using "I" and "me."

Revising. Have students share their new endings with each other in small groups. While reading their stories, students may find things they wish to revise. If so, allow sufficient time for the revisions.

It is suggested that you briefly examine the **Handbook** section of the text with the class, pointing out the **Process of Writing** section. Suggest that the section will be useful for students as they work on their writing assignments.

Developing Skills in Study and Research

Together with the students, read **Finding Information in the Library**. Emphasize that the Dewey Decimal System and the Library of Congress System are two ways of making it easy to locate books in a library. Knowing these two systems, the students can find books in any library in the country.

If possible, answer the two questions with the class in a visit to the school or local library. At this time, you may want to show the students where books in the major categories are shelved.

Have the students turn to page 560 in the **Handbook** to examine the chart on the **Dewey Decimal System**. Urge them to use the chart when trying to locate books.

the story at all? What do we learn about Richard from his friendship with the Saracen leader? How does Richard's trip to the Holy Land set the stage for the rest of the legend? Write at least a paragraph that tells why the story mentions Saladin and Richard's activities in the Holy Land.

Creative Writing

2. **Writing a Conversation.** The story says that Henry forced Leopold to hand over Richard. Create a short conversation that shows how Henry might have persuaded Leopold to give up Richard.

Creative Writing

3. **Suggesting Another Ending.** If you had been a friend of King Richard, how would you have tried to find him? Write at least one paragraph explaining your solution to the problem. Use information from the story to make your plans. If you prefer, write a new version of the story, putting yourself in Blondel's place.

Developing Skills in Study and Research

Finding Information in the Library. This legend about Richard the Lion-Hearted may be based on fact. How could you find out what parts of the story are true? The way to begin is to learn what information your school or local library can give you.

All books in the library are separated into two large groups, fiction and nonfiction. The fiction books are shelved alphabetically, according to the author's last name. The nonfiction books can be separated into smaller groups, according to their topics.

One system for grouping books is the **Dewey Decimal System**. In this system, every nonfiction book is assigned to one of ten categories. Each category has a range of a hundred numbers between 0 and 999. When a book is assigned to a category, it is given a number within that range. For example, the category that includes history has the numbers from 900 to 999. Any history book will have a 900 number. Nonfiction books are shelved, then, in numerical order.

Another system, the **Library of Congress System**, assigns numbers in a different way.

Use information posted in your library to answer the questions below. If necessary, ask the librarian for help.

1. Which system does your library use to number nonfiction books?
2. What are the major categories used in the system?

(continued from page 13)

3. The song hurt the guards and Henry because it provided Blondel with the information he was looking for. The singing helped both Blondel and Richard by allowing them to communicate with each other without the guards' knowledge.

4. The main idea is that Blondel wandered through Germany looking for Richard. Responses may vary; any of the sentences offer acceptable details.

Developing Vocabulary Skills

1. mutual—*In other words;* shared by both

2. reign—dash; time in power

3. fate—*is;* what happens to a person beyond the person's control

4. ransom—comma; the price asked for a person's release

5. compelled—*or;* forced

6. deception—parenthesis; trick

7. linger—*or;* stay around

8. restored—*that is;* brought back

Developing Skills in Study and Research

The answers will vary depending on the library used.

King John and the Abbot:
The Three Questions

King John was noted for his greed, his jealousy, and his cruelty. However, this legend says that he had at least a few good qualities. As you read the legend, look for those good qualities.

TRADITIONAL TALE
Retold by Louis Untermeyer

Upon the death of Richard the Lion-Hearted, his younger brother John became king. King John lived not only richly and royally but, even for a king, extravagantly. He had many castles, and each of them outshone the other with lordly towers, marble floors, bronze doors, and tapestries that made the walls sing with color. He dressed his servants in cloth of gold; he presented his guests with garments of heavy silk, jewelled rings, and coats of precious furs. He served the most sumptuous meals on plates of pure silver. No one in the kingdom lived as well as its king—no one except the Abbot of Canterbury, the head of the English church.

For a while King John permitted the abbot to rival him in luxury. Finally, he could control his jealousy no longer. He summoned the abbot.

"Father Abbot," he began quietly, "I hear that you have a hundred knights to wait on you every day. I hear that you furnish them with velvet coats and gold chains. In short, I hear that you keep a far better household than I do. This, you know, is treason."

"Your Majesty," replied the abbot, "I would be the last man in your kingdom to have even the smallest thought of disloyalty. As to treason—I spend only what is my own. It is true that I entertain my guests in fair style; but that does credit to the abbey and, in a broad sense, to England."

"Yes, yes, I knew you would say something of the sort," said King John, beginning to lose his temper. "Surely you know that all property in England belongs to the crown. But I didn't bring you here to argue with you. I brought you here to tell you that you are guilty of treason, that you deserve to be executed, and that all your possessions should be given to me."

Objectives

- To recognize and appreciate the legend as a form of literature
- To recognize the elements of setting, and conflict in a legend
- To apply literal, interpretive, and critical reading skills to a selection
- To make a time line
- To use synonym context clues to find word meanings
- To write a comparison of characters
- To understand and use the card catalog in a library
- To read a legend aloud

Preparing the Students

Essential Vocabulary. The words presented here are essential to the understanding of the selection.

Write the following sentences on the chalkboard, have them read aloud, and ask the students to use context clues to determine the meanings of the underlined words.

abbot	forfeit
extravagant	treason

1. The abbot was in charge of the monastery where the young monks lived.
2. The king expected extravagant, or overly expensive, gifts.
3. Because you have not paid the taxes on your farm for five years, you must forfeit all of your property to the government.
4. You have betrayed your own country. You are guilty of treason.

If you like, discuss and assign **Developing Vocabulary Skills** (pages 19 and 20) before introducing the selection.

If students need additional help with the vocabulary of this selection, encourage them to use context clues to determine word meaning. As needed, direct them to the **Glossary** or to a classroom dictionary.

Motivation. Review with students what King John did in the last story. Then have the students read the introduction to "King John and the Abbot" on page 15. Ask students to restate what they should look for as they read the selection.

Presenting the Selection

1. Have students read "King John and the Abbot" (page 15 to 18).

2. Remind students that the introduction asked readers to look for King John's good qualities. Ask several students for their answers.

3. Make sure that everyone has read the selection by administering the **Check Test**, at the bottom of page 18 of this T.E.

4. Develop the study questions as suggested in **Using the Study Questions**, beginning on page 18. That section also provides challenge questions for further discussion, as needed. (For answers to questions, see T.E. pages 18 to 20.)

Reinforcing the Lesson

To reteach, reinforce, or extend the skills in this lesson, see the following:

Skills Practice Book, Green Level—pages 11 through 14

Special Populations

ESL. When discussing **Reading Literature: Legends, 4,** check to make sure students are familiar with the children's stories cited as further examples of the importance of the number three. Elicit other stories the students may be familiar with that use three as an important number. ESL students may have folk tales or children's stories from their native country to share with the class (possibilities might be "Les Trois Mousquetaires," "Los Tres Gatitos," "El Zapatero y las Duendes," or "Los Tres Puercos").

LD. Students who have difficulty making the time line for **Comprehension, 2,** could be given the following reinforcement activities: Give students a list of events that have been mixed up and ask the students to put them in the correct order, or give the list with a few events missing. Ask the students to fit the missing events into the correct spot on the time-line.

A general suggestion for students having difficulty with the writing exercises is to present questions for the student to answer, gradually asking for more complex forms of answers. Initially, require yes/no or single answers to questions. (For example: Fill in the rest of this sentence: "Dressed like the abbot, the shepherd carried ________ and ________.") The student can be asked to find answers and copy key phrases or sentences. Then have the student dictate answers to questions to a partner. Finally, have the student develop short, very simple sentences and combined sentences.

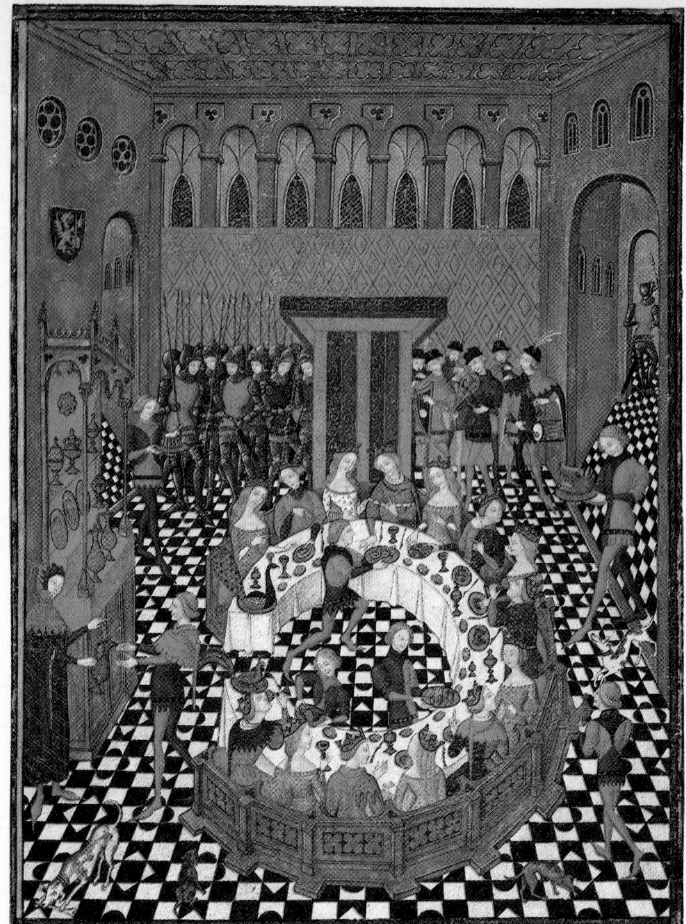

Royal Banquet Scene (detail) 19th Century, SPANISH FORGER. The Norton Simon Foundation.

"Your Majesty," cried the abbot. "I cannot believe—"

"Keep your belief for your sermons," angrily interrupted the king. "However," he resumed, calming himself, "as everyone knows, I am a merciful monarch. I will spare your life as well as your property if you can convince me of your wisdom by answering three questions."

"I shall try, your Majesty," said the abbot. "What are the three questions?"

"First," said King John, "as I sit here with this crown of gold on my head, you must tell me to the day how long I shall

About the Art

The *Royal Banquet Scene,* a nineteenth century painting, is done in the style of medieval art. The artist, the "Spanish Forger," pretends not to understand the use of perspective—the hallway to the right becomes a steep ramp, the banquet table looks as if it could slide off the surface of the picture. He also pretends to be obsessed with the problem. Notice his insistent use of tiled floor, a device that painters have always used to emphasize perspective. Actually, the way the patterned floor advances and recedes serves to tie the various elements of the picture together.

live. Second, you must tell me how long it will take me to ride around the entire world. Third, you must tell me what I am thinking."

"But—" began the abbot.

"No more buts," snapped the king. "I will give you seven days to decide on your answers. If you are not here with the right answers exactly one week from today, your life and lands and all the things you possess will be forfeit to me."

Sadly the abbot rode away. He went to Oxford, hoping a scholar at one of the great colleges there could supply the answers. When none could help, he rode to Cambridge; but the learned men there were no wiser. Shaking his head—a head that would, alas, soon be severed from his shoulders—he turned toward home. He had wasted four days; there were only three days left.

As he neared his abbey, he met a shepherd. "Welcome back, master," said the shepherd. "What news do you bring from court and King John?"

"Bad news," replied the abbot. "Bad news indeed. I have only three days to live unless I answer three questions."

"Surely that should not be hard for you," said the shepherd. "What are the questions?"

When the doleful abbot told him what they were, the shepherd grinned. "Cheer up, master. Do not despair. Sometimes a fool may teach a wise man something. Let me, the fool, go to London. Lend me some of your servants, a few of your knights, your horse, and your gown. Begging your pardon, but it has often been said that my features resemble yours and, with a hood over my head, it would be hard to tell the difference between us. Let me do what I suggest—perhaps this fool can fool the king."

"But the questions?" said the abbot. "What will you do when you stand in front of King John?"

"I think I know a way to satisfy him—and save you, too," said the shepherd.

The next day the shepherd, accompanied by a splendid retinue, rode into London. Dressed like the abbot, he carried the gold staff and other symbols of the abbot's churchly office.

"Welcome, Sir Abbot," said King John. "You are prompt; you are even two days ahead of time. That is good. However, prompt as you are, I trust you haven't forgotten our bargain. You must answer my three questions in order to save your life and your property. Are you ready?"

"I am ready, your Majesty," said the disguised shepherd.

"First, as I sit here with this crown of gold on my head, tell me to the day how long I shall live."

"That's easy, your Majesty," replied the shepherd. "You will live until you die, not one day longer and not one hour less."

The king laughed. "A very clever answer. Your wit has saved you this time.

Encouraging Independent Reading

Ask the students what they know about Robin Hood. Explain that the legend of Robin Hood takes place during the reigns of both kings — Richard and John. Have students do some independent reading about Robin Hood. Ask them to notice how either Richard the Lion-Hearted or King John is portrayed in the Robin Hood legend.

Using the Study Questions

It is recommended that students always read and answer the questions in **Developing Comprehension Skills** in class discussion. Whenever possible, they should also read the questions in other categories together and discuss the answers.

Developing Comprehension Skills

Question 1. Briefly discuss some of the causes of jealousy. Then have students answer the question.

Question 2. Discuss how a time line helps a reader remember the order of events in a story. Then have one or more students record the events for King John on a time line on the chalkboard as the class decides what events should be included.

Question 3. Students must offer opinions here, but they should base their answers on details in the story.

Question 4. Read and discuss.

Question 5. Discuss with students how the ideas in a paragraph are all linked to the main idea, although some give less important information than others. Then have a student read the paragraph aloud and have the students answer the question independently. Finally, discuss the answer and help everyone come to an agreement.

Challenge Question. What is ironic about an abbot living like a king? (Critical Reading)

Reading Literature: Legends

Question 1. After the students have answered the text question, point out that having great power is not one of the qualities that makes the shepherd a hero. In terms of position, the shepherd is the least important man in the story, but he is still the hero.

Question 2. Have students find and read aloud any description of King John's castle. Then read and discuss the question.

Question 3. Review the definition of *conflict* with the class. Have them give several different examples of conflict from sources other than this legend. Then discuss the answer to the question.

Question 4. Have students look over or think about the events in this legend. Ask them to see if anything was done or said three times. Also have them find any other mention of the number three.

Now for the second question. How long will it take me to ride around the world?"

"That, your Majesty, is even easier. If at sunrise you get up and ride with the sun and continue to ride with it until it rises again the next morning, you will have ridden around the entire world in exactly twenty-four hours."

King John laughed still more heartily. "I didn't think it could be done so easily," he said. "You are as wise as you are witty. Now for the last and hardest question. Tell me what I am thinking."

This time it was the shepherd who laughed. "That's the easiest of all," he said. "You are thinking I am the Abbot of Canterbury, but I am only a poor foolish shepherd dressed in his robes. And I have come here to ask pardon for him."

For a moment the king frowned. Then he chuckled. Then he roared with laughter until he had to hold his sides.

"You rogue!" he cried. "I ought to have you hanged! Instead I will make you Lord Abbot of Canterbury, in place of the one who is hiding there."

"Thank you, your Majesty," said the shepherd, snatching off the abbot's cap and bowing deeply. "But that's impossible. I can neither read nor write."

"In that case," smiled the king, "I will see that you get a reward, four pieces of silver every week. The joke was worth it. And when you get home, you can tell the abbot that, thanks to your cleverness, he has a pardon from King John. Tell him I wish him to live long—but not quite so well."

Developing Comprehension Skills

Literal Reading — 1. Why was King John jealous of one of his subjects?

Literal Reading — 2. A **time line** is a way of showing the events of a story in a short form. To make a time line, begin by drawing a straight line. Then draw a dot on the line for each important event in the story.

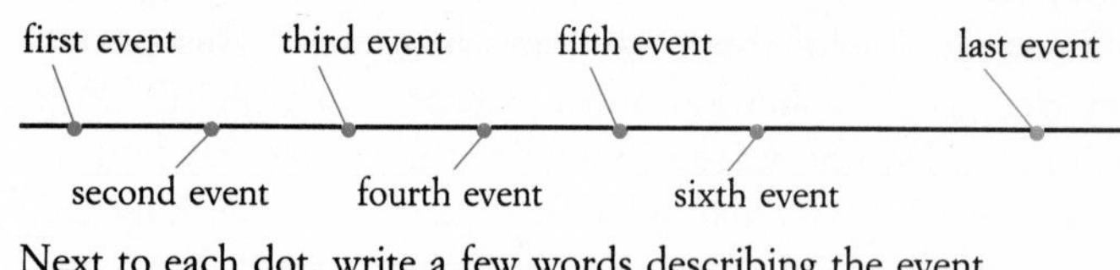

Next to each dot, write a few words describing the event.

Check Test

1. What crime did King John accuse the abbot of committing? (treason)

2. How many questions did King John ask the abbot? (three)

3. What was the shepherd's reward? (four pieces of silver a week)

Answers to Study Questions

Developing Comprehension Skills

1. King John was jealous of the abbot because the abbot lived as well as the king did.

2. Sentences may vary, but should include most of these events:

The abbot goes to Oxford to look for the answers.

The abbot goes to Cambridge to look for the answers.

The abbot meets the shepherd and tells him his story.

The shepherd fools the king and answers the riddles.

Complete the time line for "The King and the Abbot."

(1) King John becomes jealous of the abbot.

(2) King John sentences the abbot to die unless he can answer three riddles.

Interpretive Reading — 3. What changes do you think the abbot will make in his lifestyle?

Critical Reading — 4. Create a new law you think King John might make for his country after this experience.

Interpretive Reading — 5. Reread paragraph 4, column 2 on page 17. ("The next day the shepherd. . . .") State its main idea in one sentence. Then identify one important detail. Last, identify one less important detail.

Reading Literature: Legends

1. **Examining a Character.** Who is the hero in this legend? What are some of the qualities that make him a hero?

2. **Examining Setting.** Why is the setting of King John's castle important to this story?

3. **Identifying Conflict.** What is the conflict, or struggle, in this story? How is it settled?

4. **Recognizing the Use of Three's.** In "Richard the Lion-Hearted," Richard and Saladin discussed the importance of the number three. Many stories make use of this number. You have probably noticed this in children's stories, such as "Cinderella," "The Three Bears," "The Three Billy Goats Gruff," and many others.

   In "King John and the Abbot," events and other things come in groups of three. Identify two groups of three in the tale.

Developing Vocabulary Skills

Using Synonyms as Context Clues. Sometimes a writer will give a clue to the meaning of an unfamiliar word by repeating, or explaining, an idea with a word or phrase that means the same thing. Words that have almost the same meaning are called **synonyms**.

The shepherd is awarded four pieces of silver every week.

3. The abbot's lifestyle will be less grand.

4. Answers may vary. One possibility: No one in the kingdom may have more money or live in a grander style than the king.

5. Main idea: The shepherd went to London.

Important Detail: He was dressed like the abbot.

Less Important Details: He was accompanied by a splendid retinue. He carried the gold staff and other symbols of the abbot's office.

Challenge. The abbot is an official of the church. You would expect that someone in that position would not be concerned about worldly riches, but this abbot loves wealth and luxury.

Reading Literature: Legends

1. The shepherd; wisdom, wit, courage

2. The luxurious setting of the palace makes it clear that King John thinks luxuries are very important. As King, he would want to have the most extravagant possessions.

(continued on page 20)

Challenge Question. What was the positive characteristic of King John that was partially responsible for saving the abbot's life? Why is this characteristic considered positive? That is, what is good about it?

Developing Vocabulary Skills

Have the students read the first paragraph of the exercise and give some examples of pairs of synonyms. Then have them read the directions at the top of page 20. Make sure they understand what is required. Assign the exercise to be completed independently. Discuss the answers with the class.

Developing Writing Skills

Read and discuss the two assignments. Then have each student choose and complete one of the two.

Question 1. This question builds on the analytical skills the students practiced in **Reading Literature, 1**. This time, students not only analyze one character, but also compare him with a character in another legend.

Pre-Writing. Briefly review the events and characters in the legend "Richard the Lion-Hearted: Saved by a Song." Have students list on the board any important details they remember about Blondel, including his occupation, his abilities, and his character traits. Ask students to list in another column similar information about the shepherd.

Have each student study the lists and choose a similarity and a difference to discuss. Suggest that the students review both stories, looking specifically for details that give information about those topics and noting them on paper. Finally, have each student write a topic sentence that states the main idea of the paragraph he or she intends to write.

Writing. Suggest that students use connecting words that show comparison or contrast. For example, to show comparison, they could connect ideas using *in the same way* or *just as*. To show contrast, they could use *on the other hand* or *however*.

Revising. Have students exchange paragraphs with partners. Have the partners comment on whether the likenesses and differences are clear. Allow time for revisions.

Question 2. After students have written their arguments, you may want to have them read them to the class and have the students decide whether the arguments would have persuaded King John to spare their lives.

Pre-Writing. Have students decide whether they will appeal to the king's sense of fairness, his friendship with the abbot, his mercy, his greed, his desire for power, or some other quality. Then they should list possible statements or arguments that will appeal specifically to the chosen quality.

Writing. Remind students to write an argument that leads the listener or reader logically to the conclusion that the king should forgive the abbot. Allow sufficient time for students to write their first drafts.

Revising. Ask students to reread their arguments and decide which of their reasons are more important than the others. Have them rearrange the reasons, if necessary, to progress from the least important to the most important reason. Allow time for making a clean copy and proofreading.

Developing Skills in Study and Research

Reading **Finding Information in the Library** (pages 20 and 21) with the class. If possible, show the class examples of cards from the card catalog. Make sure the students know what they are to look for; you may wish to have them work with partners or teams. Have them complete the exercise independently.

In addition to the assigned topics, you may want to have the students record the titles, authors, and numbers of books on other selected subjects, for example, some topic in science or social studies.

Developing Skills in Speaking and Listening

Have a student read **Reading a Story Aloud**. Discuss what a good speaker should remember as he or she tells or reads a story.

Have students choose a page of the legend to read aloud and ask them to prepare their readings outside of class. Set a time in class for the students to read the selections to each other. Working in small groups will save time and allow everyone to participate.

Each of the following sentences or groups of sentences uses words drawn from the story "King John and the Abbot." The meaning of the underlined word may be unfamiliar to you. Read over the sentence or group of sentences carefully. Find a synonym for each underlined word. On your paper, write the word and its synonym.

1. King John accused the abbot of treason, but the abbot declared he had no thought of disloyalty to his country.
2. The abbot hoped some scholars at Oxford could supply the answers, but none could help. He then rode to Cambridge, but the learned men there were no wiser.
3. "However," he resumed, "as everyone knows, I am a merciful monarch. As your king, I will spare your life as well as your property."
4. The next day the shepherd was accompanied by a splendid retinue. The attendants rode to London with him.
5. "Welcome, Sir Abbot," said King John. "you are prompt. However, on time as you are, I trust you haven't forgotten our bargain."

Developing Writing Skills

Analytical Writing

1. **Comparing Characters.** How is the hero of this story different from the hero of "Richard the Lion-Hearted"? How are the two characters alike?

Creative Writing

2. **Writing a Defense.** Imagine that the abbot could not find the answers to the riddles, and no one volunteered to help him. Write a speech that the abbot could make to King John to save his life.

Developing Skills in Study and Research

Finding Information in the Library. In the library, nonfiction books are assigned numbers according to the Dewey Decimal system, the Library of Congress system, or some other system. After each book has been assigned a number, the number is stamped on the outside of the book. The books are shelved in numerical order.

At the same time, the librarians record the name and number of every book on cards that are placed in the **card catalog**. The author and the topic of the book are also recorded on the cards. Three cards are made for each book.

(continued from page 19)

3. The conflict is between King John and the abbot. The king objects to the abbot's lifestyle and wishes to have him executed; the abbot wants to stay alive and to continue to live well.

The king gives the abbot three questions or riddles to answer. The abbot finds the shepherd, who answers them for the abbot and saves his life.

4. Three questions: three days left to solve the riddles; the shepherd was the third source from which the abbot sought answers to the questions.

Challenge. King John had a sense of humor and was able to appreciate the shepherd's wit. A sense of humor is a characteristic that makes life more enjoyable. Without humor, life would often seem drab and dull.

Developing Vocabulary Skills

1. treason—disloyalty
2. scholars—learned men
3. monarch—king
4. retinue—attendants
5. prompt—on time

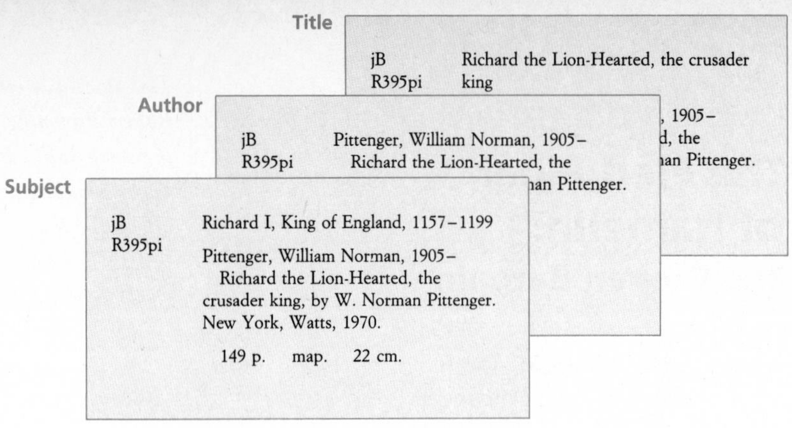

title card—the title of the book appears on the first line
author card—the author's name appears on the first line
subject card—the subject of the book appears on the first line

If you want to find a book, you first look it up in the card catalog to find its number. You can look for the **title card**, the **author card**, or the **subject card**. Each one of these cards will tell the number of the book. Then you look on the shelves for the book with that number.

Investigate your school or local library. Find out if it has any books about King Richard the Lion-Hearted (Richard I) or King John (John I). Look up each ruler in the card catalog. Then find on the shelves at least one of the books listed in the catalog. On your paper, write the name, author, and number of the book you found. Tell whether you used a subject card, a title card, or an author card in your search.

Your local library may have this information on a computer.

Developing Skills in Speaking and Listening

Reading a Story Aloud. Legends were originally passed along by storytellers. Even though they have now been written down, they are still good entertainment when they are spoken rather than read silently.

Choose approximately one page of this legend. Prepare to read it to a group. If the part you choose includes the words of one or more characters, try to have your voice show that a character is speaking. The narrator's statements should sound different from each character, and each character should have a special sound.

When you are ready, present your selection to a group.

Objectives

- To recognize and appreciate the legend as a form of literature
- To identify the climax of a story
- To apply literal, interpretive, and critical reading skills to a selection
- To write a description of an imaginary setting
- To separate fact and fiction
- To present a reading, expressing mood

Preparing the Students

Essential Vocabulary. The words presented here are essential to the understanding of the selection.

Write the following sentences on the chalkboard. Have the students determine the meaning of each underlined word by the way it is used in the sentence.

pied lame

1. The piper's clothes were pied, that is, they had patches of different colors.
2. Because of his lame foot, the boy had trouble walking.

If the students need additional help with the vocabulary of this selection, encourage them to use context clues to determine word meaning. As needed, direct them to the **Glossary** or to a classroom dictionary.

Motivation. Have students read the introduction on page 22. Ask them to restate what they are to identify and judge as they read the story.

Presenting the Selection

1. Have the students read "The Pied Piper of Hamelin" on pages 22 to 25.

2. After students have finished reading, have them turn to the painting on pages 24 and 25. Ask them which part of the story is pictured there. Have them compare the piper in the painting with the description in the legend.

3. Remind the students that the introduction on page 22 asked them if the mayor made the right decision. Ask for responses to the question.

4. Make sure that everyone has read the selection by administering the **Check Test**, at the bottom of page 25 in this T.E.

5. Develop the study questions as suggested in **Using the Study Questions** on pages 26 to 28. That section also provides a challenge question for further discussions, if needed. (For answers to questions, see T.E. pages 26 to 28.)

This story was made famous by Robert Browning in his poem of the same name. In the story, the mayor makes a fast decision that affects the lives of many other people. Did the mayor make the right decision?

The Pied Piper of Hamelin:
The Broken Bargain

TRADITIONAL TALE
Retold by Louis Untermeyer

Not many people know that this story was hundreds of years old when the nineteenth century poet Robert Browning rewrote it. Here is the original.

Hamelin, a little German town in the duchy of Brunswick, was overrun by rats. They were so fierce and so numerous that they attacked the cats and drove the dogs out of the city. All kinds of traps were laid, but the rats just flipped them about. The creatures swarmed through the streets, broke into the houses, filled the attics, invaded the kitchens, sprang on the tables, and raced through the bedrooms. They were everywhere.

In poetry, Robert Browning describes them this way:

Rats!
They fought the dogs, and killed the cats,
  And bit the babies in the cradles,
And ate the cheeses out of the vats,
And licked the soup from the cook's
  own ladles,
Split open the kegs of salted sprats,
Made nests inside men's Sunday hats,
And even spoiled the women's chats,
  By drowning their speaking
  With shrieking and squeaking
In fifty different sharps and flats!

The townspeople complained bitterly. "What kind of a mayor have we got," they said, "who allows such a thing to happen! He sits in his elegant office, gazes out of the window, and does nothing about it!"

The mayor summoned his councilors, but they were no help. Day after day they met, but nothing they thought up had the slightest effect on the plague of rats. It grew worse every hour.

One summer morning—sometime around the year 1300—a tall, odd-looking stranger entered Hamelin and came straight to the town hall. Browning saw him this way.

His queer long coat from heel to head
Was half of yellow and half of red;
And he himself was tall and thin,
With sharp blue eyes, each like a pin,
And light loose hair, yet swarthy skin.
No tuft on cheek nor beard on chin,
But lips where smiles went out and in—
There was no guessing his kith and kin.
And nobody could enough admire
The tall man and his quaint attire.

The stranger entered the councilors' room, advanced to the council table, and spoke directly to the mayor.

"I hear," he said, "you are troubled with rats. I can help you, for I happen to be a rat-catcher. By means of a certain power—call it music or call it magic—I can rid your town of the pests that are such a plague to you. People call me the Pied Piper."

The mayor looked up at the man and noticed that at the end of the stranger's red and yellow scarf there hung a small pipe, and the stranger's fingers kept twitching as though they wanted to be playing on it.

"Yes," continued the strange figure, "I have freed many cities of rats, as well as gnats and bats. I will do the same for you—" he paused for a moment and coughed gently, "only you will have to pay me a thousand guilders."

"A thousand guilders?" echoed the mayor. "Make it fifty thousand! If you can really clear Hamelin of rats, it will be well worth it."

The piper stepped into the street and played a shrill tune on his pipe. As he played, rats came tumbling out of the houses. It was as if an army were on the run, murmuring and muttering. The muttering grew to a grumbling, the grumbling to a mighty rumbling, and still the rats kept coming. Great rats, small rats, lean rats, tall rats, young rats, old rats, big rats, bold rats, rats of every size and color. They followed the piper wherever he went. Still playing, he led them to the river Weser. Into the river went the rats, and every single rat was drowned.

The piper returned to the city hall and asked politely for his thousand guilders. The mayor looked blank.

"You must be joking," said the mayor. "Surely you wouldn't expect anyone to pay such a huge sum of money for getting rid of a few rats. Besides, the river did most of the work for you. A thousand guilders? Don't be silly. Come, take fifty."

The piper's face grew dark. "I don't drive bargains," he said. "I want the full payment agreed upon. If not, you will be sorry that you didn't keep your promise. See, I still have my pipe. And if you force me, I can play a different tune."

"What!" exclaimed the mayor angrily. "You dare to threaten me! The mayor of Hamelin is not to be insulted by a fool in crazy clothes! Do your worst! Blow on your pipe until you burst!"

The piper did not say another word. Instead, he left the council room and

Reinforcing the Lesson

To reteach, reinforce, or extend the skills in this lesson, see the following:

Skills Practice Book, Green Level—pages 15 through 18

Special Populations

LD. For help in completing the question under **Developing Vocabulary Skills** on page 26, draw the following clue chart on the chalkboard and have the students copy it and fill it out. Stress that if a sentence uses key words or punctuation, the clue is a definition or restatement clue; synonym clues do not use key words or punctuation.

Word		
Restatement or Definition?		
Key Words or Punctuation?		
Synonym?		
Meaning?		

ESL. These students should complete the exercise for **Developing Skills in Speaking and Listening,** on page 28, by reading the passage with a partner. Portions of the text can also be taped for listening by ESL students. Students should read along, gaining practice in intonation, phrasing, and pronunciation while learning to express the mood of the story by raising and lowering their voices, and speeding up or slowing down the dialog. Allow students to present their reading to a very small group. ESL students may need extra time to prepare the material for the presentation.

stepped out into the street. Putting his lips to the pipe, he blew again. This time the sound was anything but shrill. It was sweet and low, a dreamy tune, full of delightful turns and twists, gentle and at the same time fun, promising all manner of marvelous things. As he played, there came a sound of little hands clapping and feet pattering, of small voices chattering, like chicks in a barnyard when corn and grain are scattering. Out of the houses came boys and girls, flocking to the piper, tripping and skipping, following after the magic music with shouting and laughter.

People looked on in amazement. The mayor cried "Stop!" But the children paid no attention to anything or anyone except the piper. Singing and dancing, they followed him out of town.

This time the piper did not guide them toward the river but toward the hills. When they came to the Köppelberg, a side of this mountain opened as though it were a door and all the children—one hundred and thirty of them—trooped inside. Then the hill closed up again. Not one of these boys and girls was ever seen again.

It would never have been known what the piper's music promised, what was inside the hill, had it not been for one lame boy. He never tired of saying how dull it was in Hamelin without his playmates nor of telling what he remembered.

Pied Piper, 1909, MAXFIELD PARRISH. Courtesy of the Palace Hotel, San Francisco.

About the Art

Maxfield Parrish (1870-1966) was an illustrator of books and magazines who also designed posters and painted murals. The *Pied Piper* is a mural in the Palace Hotel Bar in San Francisco. It shows twenty-seven children being led off into the mountains by a tall, thin man dressed in strange attire and blowing on a pipe. Like much of Parrish's work, the Pied Piper mural evokes a world of magic and fantasy. The costumes and setting are vaguely medieval, suggesting the "once-upon-a-time" setting of all legends and fairy tales.

"Because of my lame foot," he said, "I was a little behind the others. We were all happy as on a holiday. We were all looking forward to the place the piper—I mean the piper's music—told us about. It was a land where all things were beautiful and all people were good. A dozen rivers flowed there, each with a different sweet flavor. The flowers were larger and lovelier than anywhere else on earth. The sparrows were not dull brown, as they are here, but brighter than peacocks. Dogs ran faster than deer and never barked. Bees had lost their sting. Horses were born with eagles' wings. No one was ever sad or sick, and anyone who came to the place with anything wrong—like a lame foot—was instantly cured. Just as I was about to catch up with the other children, the door in the side of the mountain closed, the music stopped, and I was left on the Köppelberg, alone."

All of this happened (or was believed to have happened) centuries ago. But still, they say, no one is allowed to play the pipe in Hamelin. Besides, they say that in Transylvania (now a part of Romania) there lives a strange group of people who wear outlandish garments of red and yellow, and have names something like those of the families that once lived in Hamelin. Not one of them, they say, ever breaks a promise.

Check Test

1. What country was the town of Hamelin in? (Germany)

2. How much did the piper charge for driving the rats out of Hamelin? (one thousand guilders)

3. Who was left outside the door in the mountain? (the lame boy)

4. What does the strange group who lives in Translyvania never do? (break a promise)

Using the Study Questions

It is recommended that students always read and answer the questions in **Developing Comprehension Skills** in class discussion. Whenever possible, they should also read the questions in the other categories together and discuss the answers.

Developing Comprehension Skills

Question 1. Read and discuss. Students may have some different theories on how the Piper's magic worked.

Question 2. Have the students relate the mayor's situation to ones they can identify with more easily. For example, ask them to talk about a problem or illness they have had to deal with. Focus on the idea that once the problem was gone it didn't seem nearly as bad as it had when they were in the middle of it.

Question 3. There will be a variety of answers. Emphasize that students should support their opinions with logical reasons.

Question 4. Read and discuss.

Challenge Question. There is a common expression that in most situations in life we have to "pay the piper." What do you think is meant by that statement? How does it relate to this selection? (Interpretive Reading)

Reading Literature: Legends

Question 1. Have students skim the story to find other descriptive passages. Have a few of them read aloud and point out how the descriptive details express particular moods, such as fear or excitement.

Question 2. If students have difficulty answering this question, discuss what the piper did that was wrong. Discuss how the mayor worked at his job. Have students decide what traits each showed through their actions.

Question 3. Make sure the students understand the meaning of *climax*. Stress the phrase *turning point*, explaining that everything before this point leads to the climax, and everything following it is a result of the climax. These hints should be enough to lead the students to recognize the argument between the mayor and the piper as the climax.

Developing Vocabulary Skills

Review with students the meanings of *definition or restatement clues* and *synonyms*. If necessary, refer to pages 6 and 7 to review the concepts. Then read to the

Developing Comprehension Skills

Literal Reading — 1. How did the piper get the rats to leave?

Interpretive Reading — 2. Why do you think the mayor decided not to pay the piper?

Critical Reading — 3. Was the piper right to do what he did after the mayor's decision? Why or why not?

Literal Reading — 4. What good quality did the people of Hamelin learn to respect?

Reading Literature: Legends

1. **Recognizing Descriptions.** The setting of this story is described with many details. Both paragraph 2 on page 22 and the first section quoted from Browning's poem tell what the town was like when the rats were there. There are several other clear, detailed descriptions in this legend. Find three of them. Tell what is being described (the main idea). Then list several details that help the reader picture what is happening.

2. **Examining Characters.** In legends, the heroes and villains can be identified fairly easily. For example, the hero of this tale is the piper, while the villain is the mayor. However, heroes can have bad traits, and villains can have good ones. What bad trait do you find in the piper? Does the story suggest a good trait in the mayor? Explain.

3. **Identifying the Climax.** In every story, there is one point that is the turning point. Here the conflict, or struggle, reaches its peak. In "The Pied Piper," the conflict between the mayor and the piper reaches its peak quickly. What scene is the climax, the turning point of the story?

Developing Vocabulary Skill

Using Context Clues in Sentences. Read the following sentences about "The Pied Piper of Hamelin." Figure out the meaning of each underlined word from the context. Write **definition or restatement clue** or **synonym** to tell which clue you used to find the meaning of the word. Then write the meaning of the word.

1. Hamelin is a little German town in the duchy of Brunswick. A duchy is the land ruled by a prince or a duke.
2. The rats were so numerous that they attacked the cats. There were so many that they even drove the dogs out of the city.

26 LEGENDS

Answers to Study Questions

Developing Comprehension Skills

1. The piper played his pipe.

2. Once the problem was gone it didn't seem as bad as it had while the rats still ran through the town. It didn't seem like the piper had done enough to earn all that money.

3. Answers may vary. Possible answers are the following:

Yes, he had been promised something and was not given it, so he had the right to take something in its place; or, No, although a promise was broken, taking all of the children in the town was too terrible a punishment.

4. They learned to value honesty.

Challenge. The saying is based on this legend, and it means that we must pay for the good things that happen to us. We must remember that very few things we get are entirely free. We don't always pay with money. There are other ways the piper gets paid, too.

Reading Literature: Legends

1. There are several possible answers. Some examples are the following:

a. the piper—page 23, column 1
b. the rats following the piper—

3. The strange figure informed the mayor that he would have to give him a thousand guilders. He wanted the coins in exchange for freeing the town of rats.

4. When the piper asked politely for his thousand guilders, the mayor looked blank, without understanding.

5. The boy was behind the others because of his lame foot. In other words, he was unable to walk as well as the other children.

6. They say that in Transylvania there lives a strange group who wear outlandish garments of red and yellow. The same strange clothes were worn by the pied piper.

Developing Writing Skills

Analytical Writing

1. **Explaining Your Opinion.** In the first two legends that you read, the things that happened were all possible. We could call those stories **realistic**. That is, they could really have happened. In this legend, several things that happened were impossible. We would call this story **fantastic**. That is, there was fantasy in the story.

   Do you prefer one kind of story? If so, do you prefer realistic or fantastic stories? Or do you enjoy both kinds of stories? Write at least one paragraph telling your opinion and explaining your reasons.

Creative Writing

2. **Putting Yourself into the Story.** Imagine that you are one of the townspeople of Hamelin. Describe what life is like with all the rats. If you wish, write your answer as a letter to a friend in another town.

Developing Skills in Critical Thinking

Separating Fact and Fiction. It is clear that most of this story was made up. However, some parts of it might have happened, and then a storyteller added the rest to make it interesting. Think about each event listed below. Tell which events might have happened. Tell which events could not have happened.

1. Rats overran a town.
2. The mayor and the council searched for a solution to the rat problem.
3. A stranger said he could help.
4. The stranger asked for a thousand guilders as pay.

page 23, column 2

c. the children following the piper—page 24, column 1

d. the land the piper promised—page 25, column 1

2. The piper is cruel to the people of Hamelin when he takes their children. The mayor is concerned about his town. He tries to do his job and get rid of the rats.

3. The climax comes when the piper returns to ask for his money and the mayor refuses to pay the agreed upon price.

Developing Vocabulary Skills

1. duchy—definition or restatement clue; a land ruled by a prince or duke

2. numerous—synonym; so many

3. guilders—synonym; coins

4. blank—definition or restatement clue; without understanding

5. lame—definition or restatement clue; unable to walk as well as others

6. outlandish—synonym; strange

(continued on page 28)

class the exercise directions on page 26. Have the students complete the assignment independently. Discuss the answers with the class.

Developing Writing Skills

Read and discuss the two assignments. Then have each student choose and complete one of the two.

Question 1. Many students may never have thought about whether they prefer realistic or fantastic writing. They may be surprised to find out, in pre-writing or post-writing discussion, that some people feel strongly one way or the other.

Pre-Writing. Discuss the difference between realism and fantasy. Have several students give their opinions about the two kinds of stories. Encourage them to give examples of other stories they like or dislike, and to identify elements of those stories that are fantastic or realistic. Then have each person make up his or her own mind on the question and state that opinion in a topic sentence.

Writing. Remind students to support their opinions with reasons that will make sense to the reader.

Revising. Students who have not given this question much thought before may have trouble making up their minds, and may change their opinions several times as they write. Allow them time to revise their paragraphs more than once.

Before students turn in their paragraphs for evaluation, have them revise and proofread them using the guidelines in the **Checklist for the Process of Writing** on pages 556 and 557.

Question 2. Students can use their creative abilities to answer this question while they remain firmly based in the facts of the story. This activity may suit students who have trouble writing original stories.

Pre-Writing. Ask students to think of words to describe the sights, sounds, and smells of life in Hamelin before the piper did his magic. List student suggestions on the board.

Writing. Have students write a description using some of the words on the board. Remind them that, if they wish, they may write it in friendly letter form. (The purpose of suggesting that students write their descriptions in a letter is to enable them to express their thoughts from the first-person point of view. The emphasis should be on content, not form, at this time.)

Revising. Have students read their descriptions aloud in small groups. Have listeners point out at least three details in each description. If listeners are unable to find three details, have the writer add descriptive details.

Developing Skills in Critical Thinking

The exercise on page 27 is best done in class discussion. Read the directions to the class. Call on students to read the statements and to evaluate whether or not each describes a possible event. Require reasons for each evaluation, perhaps relating the statement to the students' personal experiences. If there are disagreements, discuss the different opinions until the students come to an agreement.

Developing Skills in Speaking and Listening

Discuss with students the art of oral interpretation. To communicate moods, they can vary their speed, their volume, their tone, and their pitch. Encourage them to read almost as if they were acting out a part in a play.

Have the exercise on page 28 read aloud. As time allows, have students locate the passages referred to and have a few students read, without preparation, to show the moods listed. Point out the good qualities in any of these readers' voices, and make constructive suggestions about pacing, pauses, and pitch, as well as clear pronunciation.

Ask the students to prepare their readings outside of class, and set a time for presenting the readings. At that time, you may choose to have the students meet in small groups so that everyone has a turn.

See page T28 of this Teacher's Edition for suggestions for evaluating the speakers.

5. The mayor promised to pay what the man asked.
6. The stranger charmed the rats with music on his pipe.
7. The mayor refused to pay.
8. The stranger threatened the mayor.
9. The stranger charmed the children of the town with pipe music.
10. The children went inside a mountain.

Developing Skills in Speaking and Listening

Expressing Mood. The **mood**, or the feeling you get from reading a story, changes several times in "The Pied Piper of Hamelin." For example, at the beginning of the story, when the rats are described, the mood is one of anxiety and disgust. Then there is a mood of excitement when the rats are being led into the river and, again, when the children are being led away. There is a mood of sadness and longing in the lame boy's explanation of what he saw and heard. Choose one of these passages. Prepare to read it to a group. Let your voice express the mood of the passage. Also, practice speaking clearly so that your listeners will understand every word. Then present your reading to a group.

(continued from page 27)

Developing Skills in Critical Thinking

Events that might have happened: 1, 2, 3, 4, 5, 7, 8

Events that could not have happened: 6, 9, 10

William Tell:
The Archer and the Apple

TRADITIONAL TALE
Retold by Louis Untermeyer

William Tell, the hero of the Swiss people, was willing to die for a belief. What is this belief? What does this legend tell us about what is important to the people of Switzerland? As you read, look for the answers.

William Tell died in the fourteenth century, but he continues to live, not only in legend but in literature. The German poet Schiller wrote a stirring drama about this national hero of Switzerland, and the Italian composer Rossini glorified him in a popular opera.

William Tell was Switzerland's greatest champion in its war of independence against Austria. Albert of Austria had determined to deprive Switzerland of its long-held freedom and to bring it under his autocratic rule. To do this he had appointed Gessler, a real tyrant, to act as governor and subdue the people. A group of Swiss patriots met near the Lake of Lucerne to discuss what might be done. Their leaders were three mountain-men, Arnold von Melchtal, Walter Fürst, and Walter's son-in-law, William Tell.

"Gessler has sworn that he will break the country into pieces," said Arnold von Melchtal. "He has spies in every canton, and he will punish anyone who dares to utter the word 'liberty.' "

"I have heard that he is planning something worse," said Walter Fürst. "I hear that he's going to set his cap on top of a pole, and anyone who fails to salute it will be thrown into jail or banished from the country."

"Our people are too proud to bend the knee to a tyrant," said William Tell. "I, for one, would not bow to Gessler himself, let alone his cap."

A week later Tell was walking with his seven-year-old son through the town of Altdorf.[1] There, in the center of the village square, was a tall pole, and on top perched an Austrian cap. A dozen soldiers loafed in front of an inn facing the village square. Tell walked by without bending his head or even glancing at the

1. **Altdorf**, a Swiss town in the Alps at the foot of Lake Lucerne, is still in existence.

Objectives

- To appreciate the legend as a form of literature
- To recognize the significance of the themes of legends
- To apply literal, interpretive, and critical reading skills to a selection
- To identify and use antonyms as context clues to find word meanings
- To rewrite a legend
- To become familiar with library resources
- To recognize slanted writing

Preparing the Students

Essential Vocabulary. The words presented here are essential to the understanding of the selection.

Write the following words and their definitions on the board. Read them with the students. Then erase the words and ask students to recall them. Rewrite the words, erase the definitions, and ask students to recall the definitions.

contempt—scorn

archer—one who shoots with bow and arrow

tyrant—a ruler who is cruel and harsh

patriot—a person who loves his or her country

If the students need additional help with the vocabulary of this selection, encourage them to use context clues to determine word meaning. As needed, direct them to the **Glossary** or to a classroom dictionary.

Motivation. Use a wall map or a map shown on an overhead projector to point out the location of Switzerland and Austria. Discuss briefly Switzerland's status as a free and independent country, and its neutrality in all recent wars. Have students read the introduction on page 29.

Presenting the Selection

1. Have the students read "William Tell: The Archer and the Apple," pages 29 to 31.

2. Remind students that the introduction asked them to look for the belief for which William Tell is ready to die. Discuss the responses.

3. Make sure everyone has read the selection by administering the **Check Test** at the bottom of T.E. page 31.

4. Develop the study questions as suggested in **Using the Study Questions**, on pages 32 to 34. That section also provides a challenge question for further discussion, if needed. (For answers to questions, see T.E. pages 32 to 34.)

Reinforcing the Lesson

To reteach, reinforce, or extend the skills in this lesson, see the following:

Skills Practice Book, Green Level—page 19

Special Populations

Exercise 2 under **Developing Writing Skills** on page 33 is a good activity for most special-populations students. Have the students work in a small group or with a partner. Have part of the group dictate the story, part write it as an experience chart using easy-to-understand words, and part of the group illustrate the story.

It will be necessary for special-populations students to work the **Developing Skills in Critical Thinking** exercise on page 34 as a group exercise, as suggested in **Using the Study Questions** (see page 34).

Encouraging Independent Reading

Play in class a recording of the overture to the opera *William Tell*, by Gioacchino Rossini. (Some students will recognize it as the Lone Ranger theme.) Explain that many legendary heroes have been portrayed in musical compositions. Then play another of these compositions, such as an excerpt from *Till Eulenspiegel's Merry Pranks* by Richard Strauss, and encourage the students to read about the hero of that composition.

pole. The soldiers pounced upon him. Collaring the boy too, they dragged father and son to Gessler.

Gessler, dark and hateful, sat staring coldly at William Tell.

"They tell me you call yourself a patriot," he said. "They also tell me that you are quite an archer. Well, I give you a chance to prove your skill. I could have you imprisoned, but I am a kind man. I will give you a chance."

"I do not need your 'kindness,' " said Tell.

"We shall see about that," said Gessler. "You," he said, turning to one of his soldiers, "bring me an apple. Take that boy a hundred steps from here and place the apple on his head. Now you," he said, turning back to Tell, "shoot that apple off your son's head. If you do it, both of you shall go free. If you fail, both of you shall die."

The crowd that had followed from the village square gasped with horror; even the soldiers shuddered. But Tell did not flinch. He looked at Gessler with contempt. He took two arrows from his quiver, hid one inside his shirt, and silently fitted the other to his crossbow. The shaft sped to its mark—the tense silence was broken as the apple split in half and fell to the ground. The Swiss shouted for joy, while the Austrian soldiers tried not to show their admiration.

"Very pretty," said Gessler sarcastically. "But I saw you take two arrows. Evidently you weren't so sure of your first shot. You kept the second in case you should miss. Am I right?"

"You are wrong," said Tell. "The second arrow was for you had I as much as scratched my son."

"Enough!" cried Gessler. "You have spoken your own doom. Put him in chains," he told the soldiers. "Carry him across the lake to the castle at Küssnacht. Let him lie in the darkest dungeon, far from the light of the sun, and let him be a prey to the rats and reptiles that lodge there. I will go with you to see it done."

Tell was bound and thrown into a boat. Hardly had the vessel left the shore when the sky was covered with black clouds. A great storm sprang up bringing huge gusts of rain and driving the boat wildly in the darkness. The rowers were helpless.

"If you take off my chains," said Tell, "I will guide the boat for you. I know the lake, and I am used to this weather."

Gessler nodded, the chains were removed, and Tell took hold of the rudder. He steered straight toward the shore, heading for a slippery shelf of rock. Picking up his crossbow where it lay in the bottom of the boat, Tell leaped swiftly out. Then, as Gessler stood up in the tossing boat, he fitted the second arrow and shot the tyrant dead.

William Tell's example gave heart to other patriots. Crowds rose to challenge the rule of the Austrian oppressors. The land was cleared of tyranny, and the Swiss were—and have remained—a free people ever since. The rock where Tell leaped is now honored with a chapel, and a statue in the village square of Altdorf stands where the fearless archer shot the apple from his son's head.

Check Test

1. What country had sent Gessler to govern Switzerland? (Austria)

2. What did Tell refuse to salute? (Gessler's cap)

3. How was Gessler killed? (Tell shot him with an arrow.)

Using the Study Questions

It is recommended that students always read and answer the questions in **Developing Comprehension Skills** in class discussion. Whenever possible, they should also read the questions in the other categories together and discuss the answers.

Developing Comprehension Skills

Questions 1 and 2. Have the students find proof of their answers in the selection.

Question 3. Briefly discuss the kind of character a tyrant might have liked. Then have students point out how Tell differed from Gessler's ideal.

Question 4. Students' opinions may vary a great deal on this question. Make sure that they are able to give reasons.

Challenge Question. There are two sides to every disagreement. Do you think the Austrian government would consider William Tell a hero? How do you think the rulers would describe his actions? (Critical Reading)

Reading Literature: Legends

Question 1. Review Gessler's actions and words. Point out these times when Gessler's soldiers react to events: when Gessler orders Tell to shoot the apple from his son's head and when Tell successfully shoots the apple.

Question 2. Have students discuss the elements of legends before attempting to answer this question. You may wish to refer to the information in the introduction to this chapter, pages 2 and 3.

Developing Vocabulary Skills

Have the students read the directions for the exercise on page 32 and discuss the example. Have the students give some of their own examples of antonyms. Then have them complete the exercise independently. Discuss the answers together.

Developing Writing Skills

Read and discuss the two assignments. Then have each student choose and complete one of the two.

Question 1. This question strengthens students' abilities to make connections, not only between events in one story, but also between events in different stories. It reminds them that there are standards that can be applied to all legends.

Pre-Writing. Have students list the major actions of the rulers in all four legends.

Developing Comprehension Skills

Literal Reading — 1. What did William Tell have to shoot from his son's head? Why did he have to do it?

Literal Reading — 2. Put these four events in the right order:

a. Tell jumped out of the boat.
b. Gessler was made governor.
c. Gessler declared a new rule about his cap.
d. Tell proved he was a good archer.

Interpretive Reading — 3. Why do you think Gessler hated William Tell?

Critical Reading — 4. Do you believe William Tell was right in shooting Gessler? Why or why not?

Reading Literature: Legends

1. **Examining a Character.** In this legend, it is easier than in most stories to pick out the hero and the villain. Reread the paragraphs that discuss Gessler. Look for information about what he does, what he says, and what others say or think about him. What qualities do you find in him? Do his own men like him? Refer to sentences or paragraphs in the story that support your answer.

2. **Recognizing the Value of a Legend.** Imagine that someone proved that William Tell never shot an apple off his son's head. However, the person also proved that everything else in the story was true. How would this affect the value of the legend? Would the legend no longer be worth telling? Or would the point of the story stay the same? Before you answer, be sure you understand the purpose of a legend. That is, be able to answer these questions: Why do people tell legends? Must they believe that every event in a legend is true? Must they believe that the qualities of the hero or heroine are worthwhile?

Developing Vocabulary Skills

Recognizing Antonyms as Context Clues. You can sometimes figure out the meaning of an unfamiliar word by looking for a word that is opposite in meaning. These words are called **antonyms.** An antonym may be found in the same sentence or in a nearby sentence. It is usually in the same position as the unfamiliar word. Read this example:

Answers to Study Questions

Developing Comprehension Skills

1. an apple; Gessler, the governor, ordered Tell to do it.

2. The order of events is as follows: b, c, d, a.

3. Gessler hated William Tell because Tell was courageous, independent, and proud, too proud to salute the cap of a man he did not respect.

4. Answers will vary. A possible answer is that Tell was right in shooting Gessler because Gessler was an enemy of his country and as such deserved death. Another possible answer is that Tell should not have killed Gessler since Gessler was unarmed and not expecting an attack.

Challenge. The Austrian government would probably say that William Tell was a traitor and criminal who had disobeyed the law and murdered the governor. His acts would be called crimes.

Reading Literature: Legends

1. Answers will vary. Possible qualities and sentences that show those qualities:

a. oppressive—page 29, paragraphs three and four
b. sarcastic—page 30, paragraphs three and seven

This lion cub is not vicious. He is gentle.

The opposite of *vicious* is *gentle.*

Read these sentences about legends you have read. Find the antonym of each underlined word. Write the word and its antonym.

1. Richard quarreled with his allies, but grew to respect his enemies.
2. The country was in a state of turmoil. During Richard's absence there was no peace.
3. The abbot was doleful as he rode away. He was not happy about his chances of answering the three questions.
4. When the shepherd heard the bad news, he grinned, "Do not despair, master. Be hopeful."
5. The shepherd knew the king would never recognize a poor, simple shepherd when he wore elegant clothes.
6. A dozen soldiers were loafing in front of the inn. Instead of working, they simply watched the people walk by.
7. The crowd was tense as the apple was placed on the boy's head, but Tell remained calm.
8. The land was cleared of tyranny, and the people have kept their freedom ever since.

Developing Writing Skills

Analytical Writing

1. **Understanding Legends.** All four legends that you have read had something to say about rulers. Only one ruler, Richard the Lion-Hearted, was pictured in a favorable way. Consider what these legends reveal about the people who told them. What do people expect of their rulers? What are some of the evils or failings that people criticize in their rulers? Write at least one paragraph to answer these questions.

Creative Writing

2. **Rewriting a Legend.** Rewrite this story so that you can tell it to a first grader. Replace words that are too hard with easier words that mean almost the same thing. If you think that the story needs an explanation of what a tyrant is, add the explanation. If you feel the ending is too violent for a child, bring the story to an end after Tell successfully shoots the apple from his son's head.

c. revengeful and cruel—page 30, last paragraph

d. untrusting—page 30, last sentence

Gessler's own men probably didn't like him. They shuddered when Gessler ordered Tell to shoot the apple from his son's head. They admired Tell's shooting.

2. It wouldn't matter that William Tell didn't really shoot the apple from his son's head. The point of the story, that people should fight to keep their freedom, would stay the same. The legend would still tell of the value the Swiss people place on independence.

People tell legends to pass on their values. It is not important that every event be true. The qualities of the hero and heroine are still worthwhile.

Developing Vocabulary Skills

1. allies—enemies
2. turmoil—peace
3. doleful—happy
4. despair—hopeful
5. elegant—poor and simple
6. loafing—working
7. tense—calm
8. tyranny—freedom

(continued on page 34)

Have students decide which of those actions were approved of by the people who wrote the legends. Have them decide which actions were disapproved of. Ask students to look over their lists and make a general statement about what people want from their rulers. Have them use that general statement as a topic sentence for their paragraphs.

Writing. Remind students to support their main idea with proofs and details from the legends. Have them make sure they have included proof from more than one legend.

Revising. Have students exchange papers with partners. Have the partner read the paragraph and on another paper, write the main idea and the details that support the main idea. Then have each writer compare the reader's main idea and details to what he or she was trying to say. If the student feels that more work is necessary, allow sufficient time for revision.

Question 2. This question focuses students' attention on the importance of style and vocabulary in accomplishing the author's purpose and in reaching a specific audience.

Pre-Writing. Have students suggest reasons for the types of changes suggested in the question. Ask whether students can think of any other changes that might be needed to make this legend understandable and appealing to a first grader, and list those additional changes on the chalkboard. Ask students to list the major events in the legend. Remind them of the value the legend places on freedom and of the need to retain this theme in their retelling.

Writing. Encourage students to imagine they are speaking directly to a first grader as they write their versions of the legend. Remind students to cover the main points and convey the main idea of the tale. Encourage them to keep the retelling short.

Revising. If possible, have students read their legends to a class or small group of first or second grade children. Discuss beforehand what clues they should watch for to determine the children's interest in the story, such as silence or the asking of relevant questions, appropriate facial expressions, and requests for more of the story. Ask them to be aware of the children's reaction and to report whether the younger children understood and enjoyed the story.

Developing Skills in Study and Research

Review with students the information they have already learned about their school or local library, especially where certain information is located. Read the exercise on page 34 to the students. Have them complete the assignment for homework. If possible, have teams of students look for the information in different libraries. Perhaps one student could find the play or a recording of the opera and bring it in to class.

Developing Skills in Critical Thinking

You may want to complete this exercise with the students. Read and discuss the directions on page 34. Have students skim the story, starting on page 29. Have them look for the positive or negative words and list them on the board. The words can be nouns (*tyrant*), verbs (*leaped*), adjectives (*hateful*), or adverbs (*sarcastically*). Then have the students compare the lists and answer the exercise questions.

Developing Skills in Study and Research

Becoming Familiar with Your Library. As the first paragraph of this story noted, William Tell has been made the hero of both a play and an opera. If you wanted to read the play or hear the opera, would your school or local library be of any help? In the Dewey Decimal system, plays are usually grouped with other literature, in the 800's. However, the play mentioned in the story was written in German. The play might be grouped with books in other languages, in the 400's. Records are shelved apart from books, and often they have a separate card catalog.

Investigate your library. Use the card catalog to find the following information:

1. Does the library have any writing by Johann Christoph Friedrich von Schiller?
2. Is that writing grouped under literature or languages?
3. Are records listed in the same card catalog as books? If not, where are they listed? How is the information organized?
4. Does the library have a record of the opera named *William Tell* by Gioacchino Rossini?
5. Does the library have any other recordings of works by Rossini? What are their titles?

Developing Skills in Critical Thinking

Recognizing Slanted Writing. Make two lists of words used in "William Tell." On one list, write all the words used to describe Gessler. On the other, write all the words used to describe Tell. Which list has almost all words with **positive,** or good, feelings? Which has almost all words with **negative,** or bad, feelings? What does this choice of words tell you about the writer's opinion of each of the characters?

(continued from page 33)

Developing Skills in Critical Thinking

Answers will vary. Possible words:

Gessler—tyrant, dark, hateful, coldly, sarcastically

Tell—hero, champion, proud, patriot, fearless

The choice of words shows that the writer thought Gessler was a cruel leader and that Tell was very brave.

Spotted Eagle and Black Crow

TRADITIONAL AMERICAN INDIAN LEGEND
Retold by Jenny Leading Cloud

The first four legends were from European peoples. This one is from American Indians. As you read, ask yourself: What qualities are admired by both groups? What other qualities of heroes are shown in this legend?

This is a story of two warriors, of jealousy, and of eagles. This legend is supposed to have been a favorite of the great *Mahpiya Luta*—Chief Red Cloud of the Oglalas.

Many lifetimes ago, there lived two brave warriors. One was named *Wanblee Gleska*—Spotted Eagle. The other's name was *Kangi Sapa*—Black Crow. They were friends but, as it happened, they both loved the same girl, *Zintkala Luta Win*—Red Bird. She was beautiful, a fine tanner and quill-worker, and she liked Spotted Eagle best, which made Black Crow very jealous.

Black Crow went to his friend and said, "Let us, you and I, go on a war party against the Pahani. Let us get ourselves some fine horses and earn eagle feathers." Spotted Eagle thought this a good idea. The two young men purified themselves in a sweat bath. They got out their war medicine and their war shields. They painted their faces. They did all that warriors should do before a raid. Then they went against the Pahani.

Their raid was not a success. The Pahani were watchful. The young warriors got nowhere near the Pahani horse herd. Not only did they capture no ponies, but they even lost their own mounts, because, while they were trying to creep up to their enemies' herd, the Pahani found their horses. The two young men had a hard time getting away on foot because their enemies were searching for them everywhere. At one time, they had to hide themselves in a lake, under the water, breathing through long, hollow reeds which were sticking up above the surface. They were so clever at hiding themselves that the Pahani finally gave up searching.

Objectives

- To recognize and appreciate the legend as a form of literature
- To identify the conflict in a story
- To apply literal, interpretive, and critical reading skills to a selection
- To infer the meaning of a word from context in the sentence
- To rewrite a legend, changing the point of view
- To recognize the rhythm of a legend by reading passages aloud

Preparing the Students

Essential Vocabulary. The words presented here are essential to the understanding of the selection.

Have the students use the context clues in the following sentences to determine the meanings of the underlined words.

lariat enmity sash

1. He made a loop in the end of his lariat and used it to lasso the new calf as it tried to escape.
2. The enmity between the two countries grew until they finally went to war.
3. The governor wore a red sash, or ribbon, around his waist at the ceremony.

Motivation. Have the students read the introduction on page 35. Ask students what they know about native Americans and their heroes. Briefly talk about some of the qualities they might expect Indians to admire. Suggest that as they read they should test their expectations against what they find in the story.

Presenting the Selection

1. Have the students read "Spotted Eagle and Black Crow," on pages 35 to 39, reminding them to pay attention to the qualities that are shown to be important in a hero.

2. Make sure everyone has read the selection by administering the **Check Test** at the bottom of page 39 of this T.E. Questions 1 and 2 pertain to pages 35 to 37, column 2, paragraph 1, ending with the sentence "Let the eagles help me, let me succeed." Questions 3 and 4 pertain to page 37, column 2, to the end.

3. Remind students of the question posed in the introduction. Ask several students for their answers.

4. Develop the study questions as suggested in **Using the Study Questions**, on pages 40 through 42. That section also provides challenge questions for further discussion, as needed. (For answers to questions, see T.E. pages 40 to 42.)

Reinforcing the Lesson

To reteach, reinforce, or extend the skills in this lesson, see the following:

Skills Practice Book, Green Level—pages 20 through 22

Special Populations

There may be some students of native American ancestry in the class. Provide opportunities for them, and others who are interested, to tell the class about Indian customs and traditions or lifestyles. Also consider having a student find out information on how Indians live today.

LD. Developing Comprehension Skills, 2, on page 40 asks the students to do a task that is difficult for many special-populations students. Direct the students' attention to page 37, paragraph 1, for clues to the answer.

For assistance in completing **Reading Literature: Legends, 2**, on page 40, discuss examples of conflict from the students' experience or from stories they have read in the past.

Encouraging Independent Reading

Challenge students to do research on any of the following topics, or one of their choice, related to native American art, customs, or beliefs, and to create a poster to explain or illustrate what they learned:

1. Masks
2. Headdresses
3. Shields
4. Blankets
5. Kachinas
6. Totems and totem poles

Brulé Sioux Shield with Feather Decoration.
Museum of the American Indian, Heye Foundation.

The young men had to travel home on foot. It was a long way. Their moccasins were tattered, their feet bleeding. At last they came to a high cliff. "Let us go up there," said Black Crow, "and see whether our enemies are following us." They climbed up. They could see no one following them; but on a ledge far below them, halfway down the cliff, they spied a nest with two young eagles in it. "Let us at least get those eagles," Black Crow proposed. There was no way one could climb down the sheer rock wall, but Black Crow took his rawhide lariat, made a loop in it, put the rope around Spotted Eagle's chest under his armpits, and lowered him down. When his friend was on the ledge with the nest, Black Crow said to himself, "I will leave him there to die. I will come home alone, and then Red Bird will marry me." And he threw his end of the rawhide thong down and left without looking back and without listening to Spotted Eagle.

Spotted Eagle cried in vain. He got no answer, only silence. At last it dawned on him that his companion had betrayed him, that he had been left to die. The lariat was much too short for him to lower himself to the ground; there was an abyss of two hundred feet yawning beneath him. He was left with the two young eagles screeching at him, angered that this strange, two-legged creature had invaded their home.

Black Crow came back to his village. "Spotted Eagle died a warrior's death,"

About the Art

The Sioux Indians made shields of buffalo hide on which they incised images or scenes, such as scenes of warfare, which were thought to impart strength or bravery to the warriors carrying them into battle. The shield reproduced here shows a mounted Sioux warrior in a war bonnet pointing a gun at a Pawnee. It is elaborately decorated with hanging cloth and feathers and may have been used as a dance ornament.

he told the people. "The Pahani killed him." There was loud wailing throughout the village because everybody had liked Spotted Eagle. Red Bird grieved more than the others. She slashed her arms with a sharp knife and cut her hair to make plain her sorrow to all. But in the end she became Black Crow's wife, because life must go on.

But Spotted Eagle did not die on his lonely ledge. The eagles got used to him. The old eagles brought plenty of food—rabbits, prairie dogs, or sage hens—and Spotted Eagle shared this raw meat with the two chicks. Maybe it was the eagle medicine in his bundle, which he carried on his chest, that made the eagles accept him. Still, he had a very hard time on that ledge. It was so narrow that, when he wanted to rest, he had to tie himself with the rawhide thong to a little rock sticking out of the cliff, for fear of falling off the ledge in his sleep. In this way he spent a few very uncomfortable weeks; after all, he was a human being and not a bird to whom such a crack in the rock face is home.

At last the young eagles were big enough to practice flying. "What will become of me now?" thought the young warrior. "Once these fledglings have flown the nest for good, the old birds won't be bringing any more food up here." Then he had an inspiration. "Perhaps I will die. Very likely I will die. But I will try it. I will not just sit here and give up." He took his little pipe out of the medicine bundle and lifted it to the sky and prayed, "*Wakan Tanka, onshimala ye.* Great Spirit, pity me. You have created man and his cousin, the eagle. You have given me the eagle's name. I have decided to try to let the eagles carry me to the ground. Let the eagles help me. Let me succeed."

He smoked and felt a surge of confidence. He grabbed hold of the legs of the two young eagles. "Brothers," he told them, "you have accepted me as one of your own. Now we will live together or die together. *Hokahay.*" And he jumped off the ledge. He expected to be shattered on the ground below, but with a mighty flapping of wings the two young eagles broke his fall and all landed safely. Spotted Eagle said a prayer of thanks to the Ones Above. He thanked the eagles, telling them that one day he would be back with gifts and have a giveaway in their honor.

Spotted Eagle returned to his village. The excitement was great. He had been dead and had come back to life. Everybody asked him how it happened that he was not dead, but he would not tell them. "I escaped," he said, "and that is all." He saw his love married to his treacherous friend, but he bore it in silence. He was not one to bring enmity to his people, to set one family against the other. Besides, what happened could not be changed. Thus he accepted his fate.

A year or so later, a great war party of Pahani attacked his village. The enemy outnumbered them tenfold. There was no chance of victory for Spotted Eagle's band. All the warriors could do was to fight a slow rear-guard action, which would give the women, children, and old folks a chance to escape across the river. Guarding their people this way, the few warriors at hand fought bravely, charging the enemy again and again, making them halt and regroup. Each time, the warriors retreated a little, taking up a new position on a hill, or across a gully. In this way they could save their families.

Showing the greatest courage, exposing their bodies freely, were Spotted Eagle and Black Crow. In the end they alone faced the enemy. Then, suddenly, Black Crow's horse was hit by several arrows in succession and collapsed under him. "Brother, forgive me for what I have done," he cried to Spotted Eagle. "Let me jump up on your horse behind you."

Spotted Eagle answered, "You are a Fox. Pin yourself and fight. Then, if you survive, I will forgive you; and if you die, I will forgive you also."

What Spotted Eagle meant was this: Black Crow was a member of the Fox Warrior Society. The braves who belong to it sing this song:

I am a Fox.
If there is anything daring,
If there is anything dangerous to do,
That is a task for me to perform.
Let it be done by me.

Foxes wear a long, trailing sash, decorated with quillwork, which reaches all the way to the ground even when the warrior is on horseback. In the midst of battle, a Fox will sometimes defy death by pinning his sash to the earth with a special wooden pin, or with a knife or arrow. This means: I will stay here, rooted to this spot, facing my foes, until someone comes to release the pin, or until the enemies flee, or until I die

Black Crow pinned his sash to the ground. There was no one to release him, and the enemy did not flee. Black Crow sang his death song. He was hit by lances and arrows and died a warrior's death. Many Pahani died with him.

Spotted Eagle had been the only one to see this. He finally joined his people, safe across the river. The Pahani had lost all taste to follow them there. "Your husband died well," Spotted Eagle told Red Bird. After some time had passed, Spotted Eagle married Red Bird. And much, much later he told his parents, and no one else, how Black Crow had betrayed him. "I forgive him now," he said, "because once he was my friend, and because he died like a warrior should, fighting for his people, and also because Red Bird and I are happy now."

After a long winter, when spring came again, Spotted Eagle told his wife, "I must go away for a few days to fulfill a promise. I must go alone." He rode off by himself to that cliff. Again he stood at its foot, below the ledge where the eagles' nest had been. He pointed his sacred pipe to the four directions, down to Grandmother Earth and up to the Grandfather, letting the smoke ascend to the sky, calling out: "*Wanblee, misunkala.* Little eagle brothers, hear me."

High above him in the clouds appeared two black dots, circling. These were the eagles who had saved his life. They came at his call, their huge wings spread majestically, uttering a shrill cry of joy and recognition. Swooping down, they alighted at his feet. He stroked them with a feather fan, and thanked them many times, and fed them choice morsels of buffalo meat, and fastened small medicine bundles around their legs as a sign of friendship, and spread sacred tobacco offerings around the foot of the cliff. Thus he made a pact of friendship and brotherhood between *Wanblee Oyate*—the Eagle Nation—and his own people. After he had done all this, the stately birds soared up again into the sky, circling motionless, carried by the wind, disappearing into the clouds. Spotted Eagle turned his horse's head homeward, going happily back to Red Bird.

Dakota Sioux Shield, about 1870.
The Denver Art Museum.

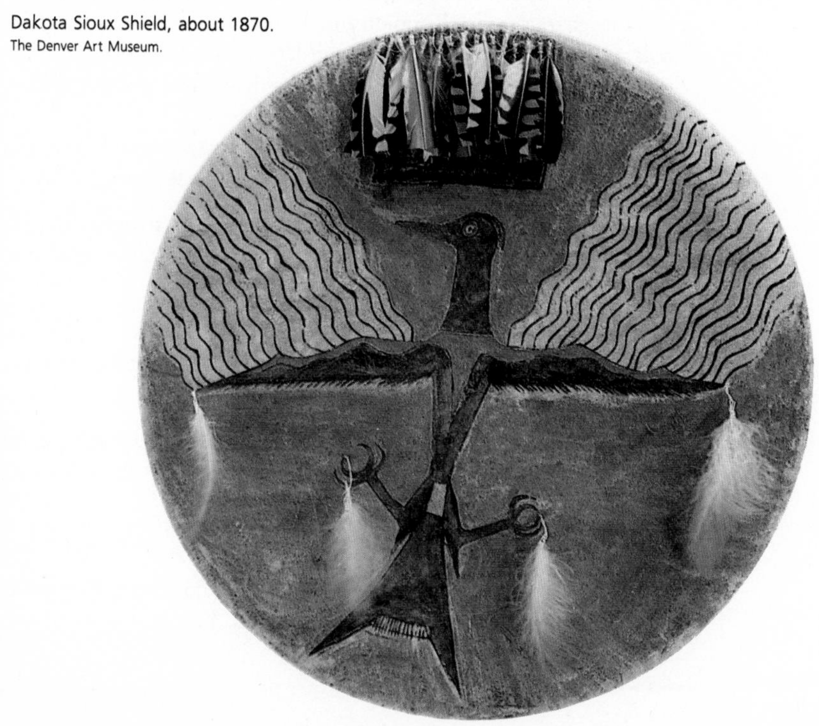

About the Art

The Sioux Indians often decorated their shields with visions revealed to them in dreams. These visions, considered powerful magic, were thought to provide as much protection as the tough skin of the shield itself. Feathers were used as decoration and also as a symbol of the wearer's achievements, much like contemporary medals of valor. The shield shown here has on it the image of a bird with outstretched wings and claws, suggesting a bird of prey swooping down for the kill, an appropriate theme for a battle shield.

Check Test

1. What was the name of the woman loved by both warriors? (Red Bird)

2. What did Spotted Eagle eat to stay alive on the ledge? (raw meat—rabbits, prairie dogs, sage hens)

3. How did Black Crow die? (in battle, hit by lances and arrows)

4. What did Spotted Eagle feed the eagles as a gift of thanks? (buffalo meat)

Using the Study Questions

It is recommended that students always read and answer the questions in **Developing Comprehension Skills** in class discussion. Whenever possible, they should also read the questions in the other categories together and discuss the answers.

Developing Comprehension Skills

Question 1. Have one student volunteer to write the time line on the board as students list events. Stress the fact that only major events should be included.

Question 2. Point out to students that they are being asked to make inferences here. This question is not answered directly in the story, only indirectly.

Question 3. Instruct students to find each event in the story to answer this question.

Question 4. Read and discuss.

Challenge Question. Do you think Spotted Eagle should have let Black Crow climb onto his horse? Should he have forgiven Black Crow before he died? Give reasons for your answer. (Critical Reading)

Reading Literature: Legends

Question 1. Point out that in real life it is rare that someone is all good or all bad. Have two students write lists on the board for each warrior.

Question 2. Discuss the meaning of conflict. Have students explain how this conflict lasts through most of the story.

Question 3. Discuss the meaning of climax. Explain that the climax is often the point at which an important decision is made. Then have students answer the question.

Question 4. Read and discuss the question. Remind students that many legends include impossible events.

Challenge Question. Why do you think this story is told so simply, using easy words, short sentences, and few details?

Developing Vocabulary Skills

Have the students read the directions for this exercise. Be sure that students know what is meant by the word *infer*. Complete the exercise with the class. For each word ask students to explain what helped them to figure out the meaning of the word.

Developing Comprehension Skills

Literal Reading — 1. Make a time line showing the major events in this story.

Interpretive Reading — 2. State two ways in which you can tell that Red Bird preferred Spotted Eagle.

Literal Reading — 3. Find a reason given in the story for each of these events.

a. Black Crow abandoned Spotted Eagle on the eagles' ledge.
b. Red Bird married Black Crow.
c. Spotted Eagle told only his parents of Black Crow's actions.
d. Black Crow pinned his sash to the ground and fought till he died.

Critical Reading — 4. Do you think that the events in this story could have really happened? Give reasons for your answer.

Reading Literature: Legends

1. **Examining Characters.** Unlike the narrator of "William Tell," the narrator of "Spotted Eagle and Black Crow" does not tell the reader that one character is a champion and the other is a villain. Instead, she tells what each young man does and lets the reader judge these actions. She even shows that Black Crow had some good qualities, despite his weaknesses.

   For each warrior, list those actions that suggest good qualities. Then list actions that suggest bad qualities or weaknesses.

2. **Identifying the Conflict.** What is the conflict, or struggle, in this story? Keep in mind that the conflict must be part of the story almost from beginning to end.

3. **Identifying the Climax.** What is the turning point in the conflict? In what scene does Black Crow face the result of his betrayal of his friend? How does he face this?

4. **Recognizing Elements of Legends.** Name some events in this story that are impossible.

Developing Vocabulary Skills

Choosing the Correct Meaning. A writer does not always give obvious clues to the meaning of an unfamiliar word. You may not find any

Answers to Study Questions

Developing Comprehension Skills

1. Events that should be included:
Black Crow and Spotted Eagle raid the Pahani.
Black Crow leaves Spotted Eagle on a cliff to die.
Black Crow announces Spotted Eagle's death to the tribe and marries Red Bird.
Spotted Eagle is saved by the eagles.
Spotted Eagle returns to his village.
Pahani attack the village.
Black Crow dies a warrior's death.
Spotted Eagle marries Red Bird.
Spotted Eagle goes back to thank and honor the eagles.

2. Red Bird grieved more than the others when she heard of Spotted Eagle's death. She married Black Crow only because "life must go on."

3. Reasons given in the story:

a. Black Crow decided that if Spotted Eagle were dead, Red Bird would marry him.

b. She believed that life must go on.

c. At first, Spotted Eagle didn't want to bring enmity to his people and besides, what had happened

key words or key punctuation to help you find a context clue. Then you must try to understand the important idea of the sentence or paragraph in which the word is found. From that, you may figure out the meaning of the word. In other words, you can **infer** the meaning of the word.

Read these sentences drawn from the story of "Spotted Eagle and Black Crow." For each underlined word, choose the meaning that best fits the sentence. Write the letter of your answer on your paper.

1. There was no way one could climb down the sheer rock wall.
   a. very steep c. shiny
   b. beautiful d. flat
2. Spotted Eagle cried in vain. He got no answer, only silence.
   a. too softly c. unkindly
   b. too loudly d. without success
3. At last it dawned on him that his companion had betrayed him, that he had been left to die.
   a. felt sorry for him c. forgave him
   b. misled him d. become angry with him
4. Red Bird grieved over the news of Spotted Eagle's death. She slashed her arms with a sharp knife and cut her hair to make plain her sorrow to all.
   a. was saddened c. showed no feeling
   b. smiled shyly d. lost interest
5. Over their shoulders, the Fox Indians wear a long, trailing sash, decorated with quillwork.
   a. soft-leathered shoes c. headband
   b. a long strip of cloth d. a piece of armor

Developing Writing Skills

Analytical Writing

1. **Understanding the Legend.** In this legend, both Spotted Eagle and Black Crow show courage. However, the legend suggests that courage is not enough to make a good warrior into a hero. What are some of the differences between Spotted Eagle and Black Crow? What qualities does Spotted Eagle show that make him a better person? Your answer should be at least one paragraph long.

Developing Writing Skills

Read and discuss the two assignments. Then have each student choose and complete one of the two.

Question 1. This question is an extension of the character analysis begun in **Reading Literature, 1.**

Pre-Writing. Have students refer to their answers to **Reading Literature, 1.** Looking at a list of the two characters' strengths and weaknesses will help students decide why Spotted Eagle is considered to be the hero even though Black Crow also shows courage.

Writing. Allow sufficient time for students to complete their first drafts.

Revising. Have students revise their own paragraphs. Refer them to the **Checklist for the Process of Writing** on pages 556 and 557.

Question 2. This question strengthens students' familiarity with the concept of point of view. By experimenting with writing from various points of view, they will learn how to identify another writer's point of view.

Pre-Writing. Have students reread the parts of the legend in which the eagles appear. Have them list details about sights, sounds, and feelings the eagles might know about. Point out that the eagles have a very limited knowledge of Spotted Eagle's adventures.

Writing. Remind students to use the pronouns "I," "me," "we," or "us." Have them make sure that they don't include details that the eagles could not have known, but on the other hand, make it clear that they are not limited to describing only what is described in the legend.

Revising. Have students read their stories aloud in small groups. Encourage students to comment, especially if they enjoyed another writer's wording or choice of detail.

could not be changed. He accepted his fate. After Black Crow died, Spotted Eagle forgave him. He didn't want people to know of Black Crow's betrayal.

d. He was a Fox, and members of the Fox Warrior Society defied death in this way.

4. Answers may vary. Some events could happen and some could not. It seems unlikely that a man could live several weeks on a narrow ledge or that two eagles could safely fly a man to the ground. All the other events probably could have happened.

Challenge. Answers may vary. Possible answers are the following: Spotted Eagle did the right thing. He gave Black Crow another chance to prove he was a true friend.

Spotted Eagle should have helped Black Crow. Even though Black Crow made a terrible mistake, Spotted Eagle would have shown goodness and strength if he had forgiven him.

Reading Literature: Legends

1. Black Crow's good qualities:
- fought bravely against the Pahani
- faced death courageously

Black Crow's bad qualities:
- left his friend to die
- lied about his friend's death
- married his friend's girl friend

Spotted Eagle's good qualities:
- didn't give up even when it looked like he should
- did not complain about Black Crow's actions
- fought bravely against the Pahani
- praised his enemy in his death
- kept his promise to the eagles

Spotted Eagle's bad qualities:
- did not try to save Black Crow from the Pahani

(continued on page 42)

Developing Skills in Speaking and Listening

Students may be more accustomed to talking about rhythm when discussing poetry. At first, it may be hard for them to hear the rhthym in these selections. Emphasize that rhythm is easier to identify when the selection is read aloud. Remind the students that they need to listen very carefully in order to hear the rhythm.

Read the passages aloud to the class. As you read, have them listen for the way the legend's sentences are put together. Do they have many clauses or series of phrases or are the sentences simple? Is the rhythm fast or slow? Is it tense or peaceful? Explain that the rhythm helps to create the mood or feeling you get when you read the legend. Discuss the students' perceptions of the rhythm after each passage is read and again after all have been read.

Creative Writing

2. **Changing the Point of View.** The term **point of view** refers to the narrator of a story. All of the legends have been told from the point of view of someone outside of the story. If this legend had been told by Spotted Eagle, we would say it was told from his point of view.

Rewrite the story from the point of view of one of the eagles who befriended Spotted Eagle. Imagine that you are one of the baby eagles. Tell what you see happening, the way an eagle might understand the events. In your version, tell about only the things that the eagles saw and heard.

Developing Skills in Speaking and Listening

Comparing Rhythms. Each legend you have read has a slightly different rhythm. **Rhythm** is the pattern of accented and unaccented syllables. The length of sentences is part of the rhythm. The way in which phrases go together is part of the rhythm. The length of individual words, the number of commas, and the amount of repetition are part of the rhythm. The rhythm can be fast or slow, regular or irregular, smooth or jerky, exciting or matter-of-fact or dull. Even when you read silently, you can tell differences in rhythm. When you read aloud, those differences should be much more noticeable.

Do this exercise in a small group. Each of you should take turns reading the passages listed below. Then discuss what you heard. What adjectives could you use to describe the rhythm of each passage?

1. "Richard the Lion-Hearted," page 9; three paragraphs beginning with "After wandering for weeks" through "to look for the king."
2. "The Pied Piper of Hamelin," page 22; two paragraphs beginning with "Hamelin, a little German town," through "and does nothing about it."
3. "Spotted Eagle and Black Crow," page 37; two paragraphs beginning with "Spotted Eagle returned to his village," through "they could save their families."

(continued from page 41)

2. The conflict is between Spotted Eagle and Black Crow because both men love Red Bird.

3. The climax is the scene when both braves face the Pahani and Black Crow asks Spotted Eagle to save his life and Spotted Eagle tells him to stand and fight. Black Crow accepts Spotted Eagle's decision and faces his death bravely.

4. Possible answers:

A man living on a ledge for several weeks

Two eagles carrying a man to the ground from a high cliff

The final meeting Spotted Eagle has with the eagles

Challenge. The simplicity helps readers or listeners concentrate on the events that take place. The legend may also have been told simply so that even little children could hear it and understand its meaning.

Developing Vocabulary Skills

1. a
2. d
3. b
4. a.
5. b.

Developing Skills in Speaking and Listening

Descriptions of the rhythms will vary. Here are some possible answers:

1. The long, complicated sentences, with many words between pauses, tend to produce a slow, solid rhythm.

2. The many short phrases produce a fast and exciting rhythm.

3. The phrases are all of approximately the same length, producing an even, slow, and dignified rhythm.

The Six Horsemen

TRADITIONAL WEST AFRICAN LEGEND
Retold by Frances Carpenter

This story has not one but six heroes. What quality enables them to succeed? What does the importance of that quality tell us about the people from whom we get this legend?

"The chief's daughter is gone!" they heard. "Nassa has been kidnaped by Ballo, the Robber."

The news spread through the Hausa towns of Northern Nigeria. People shook their heads with dismay. All knew this Ballo, the chief of a neighboring tribe. They called him "The Robber" because he often carried off a camel or a horse from right under their eyes.

Now he had taken Nassa, the fair daughter of the chief himself. Everyone loved this girl. She was known to be the kindest and the most beautiful of all the girls in that countryside. It is no wonder that this Ballo should wish her for his wife. The marvel was that he could have stolen her out of her bed without waking the guards. But that he had done.

The chief, father of Nassa, was beside himself with sadness. "I offer my daughter as bride to any good young man of our tribe who shall bring her home safe and sound. Half of my riches shall be their wedding gift."

Like autumn leaves in a storm, this promise was carried through the Hausa towns. It came to the ears of a certain young prince who was, himself, the son of a chief. Fadebi, he was called, and he was well known for his brave deeds.

"I will bring back the chief's daughter," Fadebi declared. He had seen Nassa. He admired her. Indeed, he was already in love with her. He saddled his fastest mare, and he galloped away toward the strong fortress where she was.

Fadebi had not ridden far before he met another traveler. After the custom on the highroad, the two reined in their steeds to give each other greeting.

"Allah give thee peace!" they said. When Fadebi was asked where he was going, he replied bravely: "I go to find Nassa, daughter of our chief. She is shut up in the fortress of Ballo, the Robber."

Objectives

- To recognize and appreciate the legend as a form of literature
- To recognize magic and riddles as elements of legends
- To apply literal, interpretive, and critical reading skills to a selection
- To appreciate the importance of setting
- To identify context clues to word meaning
- To rewrite a legend as a realistic narrative
- To locate reference materials in a library

Preparing the Students

Essential Vocabulary. It is suggested that students complete the exercise for **Developing Vocabulary Skills** on page 49 at this point in order to introduce them to unfamiliar vocabulary in this selection. The words presented there are essential to the understanding of the selection. Students should be asked to look up in the dictionary those words not defined by context clues.

If the students need additional help with the vocabulary of this selection, encourage them to use context clues to determine word meaning. As needed, direct them to the **Glossary** or to a classroom dictionary.

Motivation. Have students read the introduction to "The Six Horsemen" on page 43. Have them restate in their own words what they should look for as they read this legend. Point out that this legend is from West Africa and encourage the students to look for ways in which the setting affects the legend.

Presenting the Selection

1. Have the students read "The Six Horsemen" on pages 43 to 47. You may wish to assign the reading in two parts: page 43 through the first paragraph on page 45, and page 45 to the end. The first three questions of the **Check Test** correspond with the first half of the story. The second two are answered in the second half.

2. Make sure everyone has read the selection by administering the **Check Test** at the bottom of page 47 of this T.E.

3. Remind students of the questions in the introduction. Ask several students for their answers. You might choose to postpone the following discussion until the students have read and discussed **Reading Literature: Legends, 3.**

4. Develop the study questions as suggested in **Using the Study Questions**, on pages 48 to 50. That section also provides a challenge question for further discussion, if needed. (For answers to questions, see T.E. pages 48 to 50.)

Reinforcing the Lesson

To reteach, reinforce, or extend the skills in this lesson, see the following:

Skills Practice Book, Green Level—pages 23 through 28

Special Populations

This legend may have a strong appeal for students of African ancestry. They may want to research the lifestyle and customs of a particular African tribe.

LD. If the writing exercises on pages 49 and 50 are beyond some students' capability, you may want to modify the assignment in any of the following ways:

1. Assign a student tutor or partner to complete the exercise as a team.
2. Assign alternate activities such as designing a poster that illustrates a character or setting from the story.
3. Have a student dictate on tape a story about a rescue attempt that he or she has seen on TV or in a movie.

For the exercise **Using the Card Catalog To Find Reference Materials**, on page 50, students may need to be assigned partners.

Encouraging Independent Reading

Many other stories tell of a group of characters with special powers or qualities who work together. Ask the students to read these three stories and compare them to "The Six Horsemen": *The Five Chinese Brothers* by Claire H. Bishop, *The Fool of the World and the Flying Ship* by Arthur Ransome, *The Bremen Town Musicians* by the Brothers Grimm.

Challenge students to find a fairy tale with the same type of characters such as "The Six Travelers" in *Fifty Famous Fairy Tales* (published by Whitman Publishing Co., 1965).

Invite students to read, and then retell to the class, another African tale.

The other horseman shuddered. Everyone feared Ballo, the Robber in that part of Africa. His fortress of mud bricks was strong. His soldiers were just as cruel as he was himself.

"You should not go alone," he cried. "You should have a companion to help you. I'll give you my help." He, too, was young, and he, too, liked adventure.

"Two are always better than one," Fadebi agreed. "Come along if you wish." Then the two horsemen rode on together.

It was not long before they met a third traveler. When that one heard the story of their bold errand, he also wanted to join them.

"If two are better than one, then three are better than two, I suppose." Fadebi gave his consent. He did likewise to three other young horsemen whom they met on the highroad.

They were now a company of six. Their horses' hoofs made a clatter as they galloped over the land. With Fadebi in the lead, they swam their horses across the river that divided their country from that of Ballo, the Robber.

In the town on the other side of this river, they found shelter for the night in a small inn. The young woman who served their evening meal gave them news of fair Nassa.

"I know the girl well," she said. "Each morning I go into Ballo's fortress to dress the hair of his wives. Nassa is the prettiest of them all, but she also is the saddest. My heart aches when I see her tears. If I could, I would set her free."

Thus, Fadebi found out that even the people of Ballo's own tribe hated his fearful cruelty.

"My father is rich, girl," Fadebi said to the hairdresser. "You shall have a bolt of fine cloth, if you will do a service for me. Another bolt will come with it, if no one finds out that I come from Nassa's land." The girl nodded consent, and Fadebi continued.

"Tell Nassa I come from her father. I will bring her out of her prison, but she must help me find the way in."

Next morning, while the girl from the inn went to the fortress, Fadebi called his five companions around him. "You have offered your help," he said. "Pray tell me what each one of you can do best. If we succeed and I marry the chief's daughter, you shall have your rewards."

"I have great wisdom," said the first horseman. "There is no question on earth that I cannot answer."

"I can see into the future," the second horseman declared. "I know what is to happen before the time comes."

"I can dig a long tunnel in the wink of an eye." The third one was speaking now. The fourth then cried out, "I can build a large boat before anyone knows I have begun it."

"As for me," said the fifth horseman, "I have a strong JuJu. With my magic I can change myself into any form I wish."

You can know by these words that the six horsemen lived in the fairy-tale times of long ago.

At that very moment, in the fortress of Ballo, the Robber, the hairdresser was combing Nassa's long black hair. She was whispering Fadebi's message into the girl's listening ear.

"A handsome young man is this Fadebi who has come here from your father," she was saying. "He promises to get you out of this prison, if you will tell him how he may make his way into the fort."

Nassa was quiet until the hairdresser had finished combing her hair. Then, without speaking a word, she put into the girl's hands three little bundles.

The hairdresser hastened to hide them under her brushes.

"Will Fadebi know how to use them?" she asked. The chief's daughter nodded her head.

Fadebi, too, was puzzled when he opened the three bundles. In one there was a fig leaf. A strange leaf it was, like none the young man ever had seen. In the second bundle there was a bone, with bits of meat still upon it. And in the third, there was only a bunch of green grass.

"What am I to do with this fig leaf, this bone, and these blades of grass?" He turned to his companion who had said he could answer all questions.

"It is quite simple," the wise young fellow nodded his head. "The leaf is from the tree that reaches to Nassa's window.

Carved Ivory Equestrian Figure from the Oyo Area.
Private Collection. Courtesy of the Pace Gallery, New York City.

About the Art

From a Western cultural viewpoint, African art may seem primitive, but it is really very sophisticated. It is closely tied to and expressive of the political, social, and religious structures of the community. Works of art are not just decorative objects. They represent abstract ideas or concepts. The African artist intentionally chooses not to depict his subjects realistically. Instead, he simplifies and distorts them in order to make them more powerful, to convey some social or religious truth, or to express an idea about man's relationship to nature.

The Oyos, a great tribal nation in the seventeenth and eighteenth centuries, produced beautiful carvings of wood and ivory. This equestrian figure is a carved ivory sculpture of a man riding a horse. The artist has made the man much larger than the horse, suggesting, for one thing, man's dominance over animals.

The bone is for the watchdog at the foot of the tree, so that he shall not bark. And when the Robber's horse, who is tied there, is about to whinny a warning to his master, this green grass will stop his cry."

This young man truly had wisdom. For that night, when the moon rose, Fadebi climbed over the garden wall. It was easy to find the tree with the strange leaf. Before the watchdog could bark, the bone was in his mouth. Then, before the Robber's horse could make even one whinny, it was munching the grass.

Without trouble, Fadebi went up the tree and in through the open window where Nassa was waiting. With sweet words he told her of her father's promise that she should marry that young man who would bring her home safe and sound. He spoke of how he would love her and how happy they would be. They talked and they talked as they waited for a dark cloud to cover the moon, so that they could get away without being seen.

Although they spoke softly, the watchful chief, Ballo, heard them as he walked in the garden. At once he called for the guards.

"A strange man is with Nassa! I have heard his voice. He must not escape. Beat the drums! Call all the people! I have work for them to do."

When all the town was wakened, Ballo, the Robber gave his commands. "A thief is in my fortress. You shall see it for yourselves. Lift off its roof. Take first one tile, then another, so that he may not leap through. Then take down its walls, one mud brick at a time. The stranger cannot run away with so many of us in wait for him."

The people began the work. In the crowd, looking on, were the young hero's five companions.

"Our friend is in trouble," whispered the One-who-knew-what-was-going-to-happen-before-the-time. "Ballo means to kill him. I see it all clearly. We must find some way to get Fadebi and Nassa out of the fort."

Then the One-who-could-dig-a-long-tunnel-in-the-wink-of-an-eye began to work on the opposite side of the fortress. In the ground at the back, out of sight of the crowd, he dug and he dug. Before anyone knew it, Fadebi and Nassa had crept out through his tunnel. Their horses were waiting. With Nassa riding behind him on his swift mare, Fadebi led the way out of the Robber's town.

Meanwhile, the roof of the fortress had been taken off, tile after tile. Its walls were coming down, one brick at a time, but no stranger was there. Gone, too, was Ballo's pretty prisoner, Nassa. Ballo flew into a rage, "My horse! Bring me my horse!"

Ballo was soon in the saddle. With soldiers riding behind him, he was galloping across the land after Fadebi and Nassa.

The river slowed up the six fleeing young horsemen. They heard clearly the hoofbeats of their pursuers. They feared they would never be able to swim across the river in time.

Then it was the turn of the One-who-could-build-a-large-boat-in-a-jiffy. Before Ballo could come up with them, the six horsemen and the chief's daughter were safe in a huge vessel out in the stream. It was so big that their horses, too, were aboard.

Ballo leapt from his steed and threw himself into the river. With flashing arms and legs he swam like a big fish, trying to catch up with the boat. He might have succeeded if Fadebi's fifth companion had not remembered his JuJu. By its strong magic, he turned himself into a giant eagle. White as a cloud was this eagle, larger than an elephant! So strong was the great bird that it could lift the boat high up into the air. Its passengers were well out of Ballo's reaching hands.

When they were set safely down on the other side of the river, the man's JuJu worked once more. It changed the giant eagle into a huge crocodile, with rows of teeth as big as an elephant's tusk. With one bite, that crocodile made an end of Ballo, the Robber. Never again would he trouble the chief's gentle daughter.

Her father rejoiced to have Nassa again at home, safe and sound. He gladly kept his promise to the young man who had saved her.

The wedding feast was splendid. The five horsemen who had helped Fadebi were the most honored guests. Each one of them went home with five handsome horses as his reward.

Check Test

1. What name did the Hausa people give Ballo? (The Robber)

2. Why did Fadebi decide to rescue Nassa? (He was in love with her.)

3. What did Fadebi promise to give the hairdresser to reward her for her helping him? (two bolts of cloth)

4. What three things did the chief's daughter send to Fadebi? (a leaf, a bone, and grass)

5. How did Fadebi and Nassa get out of the fortress? (They crept through a tunnel.)

Using the Study Questions

It is recommended that students always read and answer the questions in **Developing Comprehension Skills** in class discussion. Whenever possible, they should also read the questions in other categories together and discuss the answers.

Developing Comprehension Skills

Question 1. Read and then discuss the question together.

Question 2. If necessary, refer students to pages 45 to 47. Have individual students list each horseman and his contribution on the board.

Question 3. Ask students to explain the difference between main idea and details. You may want to refer to pages 4 and 5 to review these concepts. Then have a student read the paragraph aloud and answer the question.

Question 4. After the students have answered the questions, point out that, with her bundles, Nassa was testing Fadebi. Have the students explain why she made her message tricky, and how she would have reacted to Fadebi if he had not understood the bundles.

Question 5. Students may refer to the list on the board from question 2, above, to help answer this question.

Challenge Question. Eagles played a part in two legends you have read, "Spotted Eagle and Black Crow" and "The Six Horsemen." What qualities does the eagle make you think of? (Interpretive Reading)

Reading Literature: Legends

Question 1. In discussing attitudes of an entire group, students may tend to generalize more than the information in the stories warrants. Help them to avoid using stereotypes and to qualify their statements to keep them accurate.

Question 2. Students may be able to identify additional stories that hinge on riddles, or to relate the concept of riddles to mystery novels.

Question 3. Ask students how the six horsemen accomplished their goal. Then read and discuss this question. It is possible that students may find not one, but several traits that appear in other legends too.

Question 4. Ask students to define both conflict and climax. Then discuss this question. If necessary, point out that the fifth companion's action as an eagle ended the danger and was, therefore, the turn-

Developing Comprehension Skills

Literal Reading

1. Which of these words names the chief's daughter? What or whom does each of the others name?

   a. Ballo b. Hausa c. Nassa d. JuJu

Literal Reading

2. How does each of the six horsemen contribute to the success of the adventure? Who else aids in Nassa's escape?

Interpretive Reading

3. Reread paragraph 3 on page 46. Below are listed three ideas from that paragraph. Decide which is the main idea, which is an important detail, and which is a less important detail that was included just to make the paragraph more interesting.
   a. Fadebi used sweet words.
   b. Fadebi got into Nassa's room and explained his mission.
   c. Fadebi and Nassa waited for a dark cloud to cover the moon.

Interpretive Reading

4. When the hairdresser tells Nassa that Fadebi needs her advice on how to get into the fortress, Nassa gives her three little bundles. What does Nassa's action tell about her? What does she expect from Fadebi?

Critical Reading

5. Which events and characters in this legend are realistic, or believeable? Which ones are fantastic? Give reasons for your opinions.

Reading Literature: Legends

1. **Recognizing Elements of Legend: Magic.** The Pied Piper carried enchantment in his pipe. Spotted Eagle carried eagle medicine in his bundle. One of the six horsemen has a strong JuJu. How do these types of magic show similarities among the groups who made up these legends? What differences do the types of magic point out?
2. **Recognizing Elements of Legend: Riddles.** The three bundles that Nassa sends to Fadebi must be interpreted. They are like riddles he must answer to save her. What other legend involved riddles? What might be proved by an ability to answer riddles?
3. **Comparing Character Traits.** Like "Spotted Eagle and Black Crow," this legend says that courage is not enough to make a person a hero. What character trait shared by the six horsemen enabled them to defeat Ballo? Was this character trait important in any of the other legends you have read?

Answers to Study Questions

Developing Comprehension Skills

1. a. Nassa—the chief's daughter
b. Hausa—an African tribe
c. Ballo—the Robber who stole Nassa
d. JuJu—magic power

2. The six horsemen gave the following:

One answers the question of the meaning of the bundles Nassa sent to Fadebi.

One sees into the future and warns that Ballo wants to kill Fadebi.

One builds a tunnel to help Fadebi and Nassa escape.

One builds a boat to help them escape.

One turns himself into an eagle and then a crocodile.

The sixth horseman is Fadebi, who assembles the rescue party and goes into the fortress for Nassa.

The hairdresser also aids in Nassa's escape.

3. a. less important detail
b. main idea
c. important detail

4. She is clever and does what she can to help herself. She expects Fadebi to be

4. **Identifying Conflict and Climax.** What is the conflict in this story? Which scene is the climax, or turning point?

5. **Recognizing the Purpose.** Why do you think storytellers told this legend? Why did someone eventually write it down? Was the purpose mainly to teach about Hausa beliefs? Was it to tell a good story? Was it to show how good triumphs and evil is destroyed? Or was there a combination of reasons? Explain your opinion.

Developing Vocabulary Skills

Identifying Context Clues. You cannot always figure out the meaning of an unfamiliar word by looking for context clues, synonyms, or antonyms. You must refer to the dictionary or glossary to find the meaning of the word. Read this example of a sentence that contains no clue to the meaning of the underlined word.

Monica is a very loquacious person.

You cannot figure out from the context of the sentence that *loquacious* means "fond of talking."

Read each of these sentences using words drawn from the story. Try to figure out the meaning of the underlined word by using context clues. If there are clues, write the meaning of the word. If there are no clues, write *No clues—use dictionary.*

1. People shook their heads in dismay—sadness—at the news of Nassa's kidnapping.
2. Fadebi saddled his fastest mare and galloped toward the fortress.
3. Fadebi had ridden far on his steed and stopped to give the horse a drink of water and some rest.
4. The travelers reined, or guided, their horses in greeting each other.
5. Fadebi gave his consent—that is, he approved—and the third traveler joined them.
6. The hoofbeats of their pursuers could be heard easily.

Developing Writing Skills

Analytical Writing

1. **Understanding Setting.** What does this legend tell about life in the Hausa towns at the time of the story? Describe what you have learned about how people lived. For example, what were some of the jobs

ing point. His action as a crocodile simply confirmed the victory of Fadebi's team.

Question 5. Have students speculate about what it takes to make a story worth passing on.

Developing Vocabulary Skills

Briefly review with the students the different types of context clues: definition or restatement, synonym, antonym, and inference. Read to the class the directions for **Identifying Context Clues,** on page 49. Have the students complete the exercise independently. Discuss the answers together.

Developing Writing Skills

Read and discuss the two assignments. Then have each student choose and complete one of the two.

Question 1. This question emphasizes that even small details can tell a great deal about the people who created legends. It may show students that literature can be appreciated on different levels and for different purposes.

Pre-Writing. Suggest that students reread the story, this time looking for the answers to the questions in the text about Hausa life. Have them make notes on the answers to those questions as well as on any other details that could give a more complete look at the Hausa culture. Ask each student to group all the details that lead to a single conclusion about Hausa customs or attitudes. If they like, they could concentrate on stating and proving one conclusion they have come to, or they could briefly explain several conclusions.

Writing. Remind students to use the notes they made as they write and to stay on one topic long enough to make clear

just as clever and to understand what the bundles mean. She hopes these clues will help Fadebi know how to rescue her.

5. Possible answers include the following. Reasons will vary. Ballo seems realistic and the act of kidnapping a young girl seems possible. Fadebi setting out to save her seems realistic. The actions of the wise horseman and the horseman who could see what was going to happen before the time are possible. Building a tunnel and a boat so quickly and turning into an eagle are fantastic events.

Challenge. Answers may vary. A possible answer is that the eagle suggests strength and independence.

Reading Literature: Legends

1. All the groups thought that magic had to be in some object or power outside of people's normal make-up. One group felt that music could cause magic; the second group's magic required the help of living creatures, the eagles; the third group thought that magic could be a gift given only to special people. For each culture, the magic accomplished particular kinds of tasks that were important in that culture.

2. In "King John and the Abbot," King John asks the abbot three riddles. The ability to answer riddles proves wisdom or cleverness, and gives the person a special power.

3. Cooperation was the most important trait shared by the six horsemen. No other legend in the chapter showed several heroes working together, depending on and trusting one another.

4. The conflict is between Ballo and Fadebi over Nassa's kidnapping. The climax comes when the fifth horseman turns himself into a giant eagle that lifts the boat out of the air to save Nassa and the others.

5. Answers will vary somewhat. The purpose was a combination of reasons. People pass on legends that are entertaining, but for a legend to survive it should

(continued on page 50)

the conclusion they have drawn and the thinking behind it.

Revising. Have students exchange papers with partners. Ask the partners to read the paragraphs and check to see whether they agree with the writers' conclusions. If they do not, they should let the writers know what their objections are and give the writers an opportunity to explain in further detail or to revise their arguments.

Question 2. In legends, there is a fine line between reality and fantasy. This question forces students to examine this legend and identify the fantastic elements.

Pre-Writing. Refer students to the answer to **Developing Comprehension Skills, 5**, for a list of the fantastic or unbelievable events in the story. Explain that these events must be rewritten so that readers will believe that the rescue really could have taken place. Make it clear that the students can simply retell the rest of the legend in their own words.

Writing. Allow sufficient time for students to write their first drafts.

Revising. Have students refer to the **Checklist for the Process of Writing** on pages 556 and 557 for help in revising and proofreading their stories.

Developing Skills in Study and Research

Read **Using the Card Catalog To Find Reference Materials** with the class. If possible, make available a specialized dictionary, an unabridged dictionary, and an atlas. Show them to the students and demonstrate how to locate information in each.

Assign the card catalog search for homework. Discuss the students' findings.

they held? How were they ruled? What objects were valuable to them? What feelings did they respect?

Creative Writing

2. **Rewriting a Legend More Realistically.** Most legends are based on actual events. However, as the legend is told and retold, other happenings are added to the actual events. These new happenings may be fantastic, that is, not possible in the real world. Suppose that "The Six Horsemen" started as an account of an actual rescue. Write a short version of the story the way you think it could have really happened. Replace the magical events with realistic adventures. Make your version about six to twelve paragraphs long.

Developing Skills in Study and Research

Using the Card Catalog To Find Reference Materials. In this story, the term *JuJu* may be unfamiliar to you. Because it is not used frequently in English, some dictionaries might not list it. If you wanted to know more about what it means, you might need to find it in an **unabridged dictionary** or a **specialized dictionary**.

Perhaps you want to know where each of the legends in this chapter came from. You would want to look at an **atlas**. An atlas would include an index of countries, listed in alphabetical order. The index would tell which of the maps in the atlas show each country.

To find the reference materials you want, you would begin with the card catalog. Start with the headings *Dictionaries* and *Atlases*. Under those classifications, there may be cards listing all the dictionaries and atlases in the library. There may be cards referring you to other headings, such as *Foreign Language Dictionaries*.

Make a list of the dictionaries and atlases your school or local library has. If you can find an entry for *JuJu* in any of the dictionaries, write down the name of the dictionary, its call number, and the information it gives about the term. In an atlas, find a map that shows western Africa. List five countries of western Africa.

(continued from page 49)

have something else, too. It should serve a purpose—to tell about a people's beliefs or to teach values.

Developing Vocabulary Skills

1. dismay—sadness
2. fortress—no clue, use dictionary
3. steed—horse
4. reined—guided
5. consent—approval
6. pursuers—no clue, use dictionary

Developing Skills in Study and Research

Information about JuJu will vary according to the dictionary used. Possible countries in western Africa—Algeria, Mali, Senegal, Niger, Nigeria, Guinea, Ghana, Gambia, Morocco, Ivory Coast, Liberia, Sierra Leona, and Upper Volta.

The number three is used again and again in legends. Watch how important it is in this story.

Lazy Peter and His Three-Cornered Hat

TRADITIONAL PUERTO RICAN LEGEND

Retold by Ricardo E. Alegría and translated by Elizabeth Culbert

This is the story of Lazy Peter, a shameless rascal of a fellow, who went from village to village making mischief.

One day Lazy Peter learned that a fair was being held in a certain village. He knew that a large crowd of country people would be there selling horses, cows, and other farm animals and that a large amount of money would change hands. Peter, as usual, needed money, but it was not his custom to work for it. So he set out for the village, wearing a red three-cornered hat.

The first thing he did was to stop at a stand and leave a big bag of money with the owner, asking him to keep it safely until he returned for it. Peter told the man that when he returned for the bag of money, one corner of his hat would be turned down, and that was how the owner of the stand would know him. The man promised to do this, and Peter thanked him. Then he went to the drugstore in the village and gave the druggist another bag of money, asking him to keep it until he returned with one corner of his hat turned up. The druggist agreed, and Peter left. He went to the church and asked the priest to keep another bag of money and to return it to him only when he came

Objectives

- To recognize and appreciate the legend as a form of literature
- To compare characters from different legends
- To identify the theme of a story
- To apply literal, interpretive, and critical reading skills to a selection
- To write an opinion supported by examples
- To classify legends
- To tell a legend to a group

Preparing the Students

Essential Vocabulary. It is suggested that students complete the exercise for **Developing Vocabulary Skills** at this time. This will introduce them to unfamiliar vocabulary they will encounter while reading this selection.

If the students need additional help with the vocabulary of the selection, encourage them to use context clues. As needed, direct them to the **Glossary** or to a classroom dictionary.

Motivation. Have students read the introduction to this selection. Ask them to recall what Richard the Lion-Hearted and Saladin said about the number three. Ask them to give examples of other uses of the number three in some of the other legends they have read.

Presenting the Selection

1. Have students read "Lazy Peter and His Three-Cornered Hat," pages 51 to 55.

2. Make sure that students have read the story by administering the **Check Test** at the bottom of page 55 in this T.E.

3. Develop the study questions as suggested in **Using the Study Questions** on pages 55 to 57. That section also provides challenge questions for further discussion, as needed. (For answers to questions, see T.E. pages 55 to 57.)

Reinforcing the Lesson

To reteach, reinforce, or extend the skills in this lesson, see the following:

Skills Practice Book, Green Level—pages 29 and 30

Special Populations

LD. The exercise **Classifying** on page 57 is good practice for the special-populations students in organizing likenesses and differences they've seen in the legends.

ESL. To supplement the exercise **Telling a Legend**, on page 57, ESL students might want to share a favorite folk legend from their native country. The student might dictate the legend to another student, who writes the story to give to the class, or the ESL student may teach the legend to a small group to be acted out before the class.

back with one corner of his hat twisted to the side. The priest said fine, that he would do this.

Having disposed of three bags of money, Peter went to the edge of the village where the farmers were buying and selling horses and cattle. He stood and watched for a while until he decided that one of the farmers must be very rich indeed, for he had sold all of his horses and cows. Moreover, the man seemed to be a miser who was never satisfied but wanted, always, more and more money. This was Peter's man! He stopped beside him. It was raining, and, instead of keeping his hat on to protect his head, he took it off and wrapped it carefully in his cape, as though it were very valuable. It puzzled the farmer to see Peter stand there with the rain falling on his head and his hat wrapped in his cape.

After a while he asked, "Why do you take better care of your hat than of your head?"

Peter saw that the farmer had swallowed the bait. Smiling to himself, he said that the hat was the most valuable thing in all the world and that was why he took care to protect it from the rain. The farmer's curiosity increased at this reply, and he asked Peter what was so valuable about a red three-cornered hat. Peter told him that the hat worked for him. Thanks to it, he never had to work for a living because, whenever he put the hat on with one of the corners turned over, people just handed him any money he asked for.

The farmer was amazed and very interested in what Peter said. As money-getting was his greatest ambition, he told Peter that he couldn't believe a word of it until he saw the hat work with his own eyes. Peter assured him that he could do this, for he, Peter, was hungry, and, since he had no money with which to buy food, the hat was about to start working.

With this, Peter took out his three-cornered hat, turned one corner down, put it on his head, and told the farmer to come along and watch the hat work. Peter took the farmer to the stand. The minute the owner looked up, he handed over the bag of money Peter had left with him. The farmer stood with his mouth open in astonishment. He didn't know what to make of it, but of one thing he was sure—he had to have that hat!

Peter smiled and asked if he was satisfied, and the farmer said yes, he was. Then he asked Peter if he would sell the hat. This was just what Lazy Peter wanted, but he said no, that he was not interested in selling the hat because, with it, he never had to work and he always had money. The farmer said he thought that was unsound reasoning because thieves could easily steal a hat. Wouldn't it be safer to invest in a farm with cattle? So they talked, and Peter pretended to be impressed with the farmer's arguments. Finally he said yes, that he saw the point.

If the farmer would make him a good offer, he would sell the hat. The farmer, who had made up his mind to have the hat at any price, offered a thousand pesos. Peter laughed aloud and said he could make as much as that by just putting his hat on two or three times.

As they continued haggling over the price, the farmer grew more and more determined to have that hat until, finally, he offered all he had realized from the sale of his horses and cows—ten thousand pesos in gold. Peter still pretended not to be interested, but he chuckled to himself, thinking of the trick he was about to play on the farmer. All right, he said, it was a deal. Then the farmer grew cautious and told Peter that, before he handed over the ten thousand pesos, he would like to see the hat work again. Peter said that was fair enough. He put on the hat with one of the corners turned up and went with the farmer to the drugstore. The moment the druggist saw the turned-up corner, he handed over the money Peter had left with him. At this the farmer was convinced and very eager to set the hat to work for himself. He took out a bag containing ten thousand pesos in gold and was about to hand it to Peter, when he had a change of heart and thought better of it. He asked Peter please to excuse him, but he had to see the hat work just once more before he could part with his gold. Peter said that that was fair enough, but now he would have to ask the farmer to give him the fine horse he was riding as well as the ten thousand pesos in gold. The farmer's interest in the hat revived, and he said it was a bargain!

Lazy Peter put on his hat again and doubled over one of the corners. He told the farmer that, since he still seemed to have doubts, this time he could watch the hat work in the church. The farmer was delighted with this, his doubts were stilled, and he fairly beamed thinking of all the money he was going to make once that hat was his.

They entered the church. The priest was hearing confession, but when he saw Peter with his hat, he said, "Wait here, my son." He went to the sacristy and returned the bag of money Peter had left with him. Peter thanked the priest, then knelt and asked for a blessing before he left. The farmer had seen everything and was fully convinced of the hat's magic powers. As soon as they left the church, he gave Peter the ten thousand pesos in gold and told him to take the horse, also. Peter tied the bag of pesos to the saddle, gave the hat to the farmer, begging him to take good care of it, spurred his horse, and galloped out of town.

As soon as he was alone, the farmer burst out laughing at the thought of the trick he had played on Lazy Peter. A hat such as this was priceless! He couldn't wait to try it. He put it on with one corner turned up and entered the butcher shop. The butcher looked at the hat, which was

very handsome indeed, but said nothing. The farmer turned around, then walked up and down until the butcher asked him what he wanted. The farmer said he was waiting for the bag of money. The butcher laughed aloud and asked if he were crazy. The farmer thought that there must be something wrong with the way he had folded the hat. He took it off and doubled another corner down. But this had no effect on the butcher. So he decided to try it out some other place. He went to the Mayor of the town.

The Mayor, to be sure, looked at the hat but did nothing. The farmer grew desperate and decided to go to the druggist who had given Peter a bag of money. He entered and stood with the hat on. The druggist looked at him but did nothing.

The farmer became very nervous. He began to suspect that there was something very wrong. He shouted at the druggist, "Stop looking at me and hand over the bag of money!"

The druggist said he owed him nothing, and what bag of money was he talking about anyway? As the farmer continued to shout about a bag of money and a magic hat, the druggist called the police. When they arrived, he told them that the farmer had gone out of his mind and kept demanding a bag of money. The police questioned the farmer, and he told them about the magic hat he had bought from Lazy Peter. When he heard the story, the druggist explained that Peter had left a bag of money, asking that it be returned when he appeared with a corner of his hat turned up. The owner of the stand and the priest told the same story.

I am telling you, the farmer was so angry that he tore the hat to shreds and walked home.

Developing Comprehension Skills

1. (Literal Reading) In this story, there are at least three sets of three. Tell, in order, three sets of events that come in threes.
2. (Literal Reading) Why did the farmer think the hat was worth a great deal of money?
3. (Interpretive Reading) Peter took advantage of one of the farmer's qualities. What was that quality? How did Peter use it against the farmer?
4. (Critical Reading) Would you call this story realistic? That is, do you think it could really happen? Why or why not?

Reading Literature: Legends

1. **Comparing Characters.** Lazy Peter, Blondel, and the shepherd in "King John and the Abbot" were all very clever. Did they use their cleverness in the same way? Which ones do you admire? Why?

Check Test

1. What color was Peter's hat? (red)

2. What did Peter give to the owner of the stand? (a bag of money)

3. What, besides ten thousand pesos in gold, did the farmer agree to give Peter for the hat? (his horse)

4. What did the farmer do with the hat at the end of the story? (tore it to shreds)

Answers to Study Questions

Developing Comprehension Skills

1. Three sets of three:

Peter gives a bag of money to three different people.

Peter takes the farmer to collect the money from the owner of the stand, a druggist, and a priest.

The farmer tries to collect money from the butcher, the mayor, and the druggist.

2. The farmer thought the hat would supply its owner with money whenever he wanted it.

(continued on page 56)

Using the Study Questions

It is recommended that students always read and answer the questions in **Developing Comprehension Skills** in class discussion.

Developing Comprehension Skills

Questions 1 and 2. Read and discuss.

Question 3. Have the students refer to the story to point out how Peter discovered this trait in the farmer.

Question 4. Have students explain what is meant by realistic by giving examples of both realistic and fantastic events in some of the other legends they have read. Then discuss this question.

Challenge Question. Usually you feel sorry for the victim of a trick. Do you feel sorry for the farmer? Why or why not? (Critical Reading)

Reading Literature: Legends

Question 1. There may be a variety of opinions in answer to this question. Have students give specific examples of how each character used his cleverness and reasons why the student considers each example admirable or undesirable.

Question 2. After students have read this question, emphasize that the theme is a general statement; it must not apply only to the story from which it is taken. Then have them answer the question.

Question 3. Discuss with students how the conflict in this story is different from the conflict in "The Six Horsemen." They might get a better feel for the differences in tension and mood, also, if you ask them to choose the actors to play Fadebi and Lazy Peter (and possibly the Robber and the farmer) in imaginary movies about the legends. Ask, also, for suggestions for background music for the two movies.

Question 4. Allow for differences of opinion concerning the answer to the first question. To help students decide how the story would change if the farmer had shouted at the Mayor, have students reread pages 54 and 55. Ask them what the druggist knew that the Mayor didn't know.

Challenge Question. What makes the legend "Lazy Peter and His Three-Cornered Hat" different from all the other legends you have read in this chapter? Examine the characters. How are they different from some of the others you have met in these stories?

Developing Vocabulary Skills

Throughout this chapter, students have learned how to use various types of context clues. The exercise on page 56 reviews most of these types of clues. Have the students read the directions to **Recognizing Context Clues, Synonyms, and Antonyms** and complete the exercise independently in class. Discuss the answers.

Developing Writing Skills

Read and discuss the two assignments. Then have each student choose and complete one of the two.

Question 1. This question reminds students that not every hero will be totally admirable.

Pre-Writing. Review the events of the legend of Lazy Peter. List the major events on the board. Ask students to consider Peter's part in the events. Then have each student decide whether Peter is a person he or she would want to imitate. Have the student list two or three reasons supporting that decision.

Writing. Suggest that students write their paragraphs as if they were trying to persuade someone to agree with them. Remind them to use examples from the story to support their opinions.

Revising. Have students share their opinions in small groups. If a student wishes to rewrite the paragraph, allow time for revisions.

Question 2. This question reinforces the concept of point of view. Remind the students that the retelling is not simply an outsider's viewpoint. It is the point of view of someone who will have strong reactions to the events.

Pre-Writing. Review the events that involve the farmer. Make sure students avoid listing events the farmer had no part in, such as Peter's leaving the money bags

2. **Identifying Theme.** The **theme** of a story is a general statement that it makes about life. For example, the theme of "William Tell" might be worded this way: "Liberty is more important than life itself." The theme of "The Six Horsemen" might be, "Cooperation will bring success." How would you state the theme of "Lazy Peter"?

3. **Identifying Conflict.** In "Lazy Peter," the conflict is not a physical one, as in "The Six Horsemen." What is the conflict in this story? How is it settled?

4. **Examining the Use of Three's.** What would happen to the story if Lazy Peter had left a fourth bag of gold with another person? Would that make the story even more interesting, or would it simply make the story longer? What would happen if the farmer had started shouting at the Mayor instead of going on to the druggist? Would that simply shorten the story, or would it lose a connection between the parts of the story? Explain your answer.

Developing Vocabulary Skills

Recognizing Context Clues, Synonyms, and Antonyms. Read each of the following sentences or groups of sentences. On your paper, write this information about each underlined word:

a. Whether you found a *definition or restatement clue*, a *synonym*, or an *antonym* to help you figure out the meaning of the word
b. Any key words or punctuation that helped you find the clue
c. The meaning of the word

1. Lazy Peter disposed of, or got rid of, three bags of money.
2. The farmer seems to be a miser who is never satisfied but always wants more and more money.
3. Seeing the bag of money was such a surprise, the farmer stood with his mouth open in astonishment.
4. Peter saw that the farmer had swallowed his bait. In other words, he had fallen for Peter's trick.
5. The farmer offered a thousand pesos, Spanish coins, for the hat.
6. The farmer said Peter used unsound thinking because thieves could easily steal a hat. Wouldn't it be more reasonable, he said, to invest in a farm with cattle?

(continued from page 55)

3. He took advantage of the farmer's greed. When Peter saw how much the farmer loved money, he knew the farmer's greed would overshadow his common sense.

4. There is nothing in the story that is pure fantasy. It is all possible.

Challenge. It is difficult to feel sorry for the farmer. He was greedy and also was willing to cheat Peter.

Reading Literature: Legends

1. The three used their cleverness for different purposes. Blondel used his cleverness to save the king, the shepherd used it to help the abbot, and Peter used it to make money. Answers will vary as to which characters are admirable. Most students will approve of Blondel and the shepherd. As for Peter, however, many will say that he was just as greedy as the farmer and does not deserve admiration.

2. Possible theme: It does not pay to be greedy.

3. The conflict in "Lazy Peter" is between Peter and the farmer over whether Peter can trick the farmer into buying the hat.

4. The better readers will recognize that using the number three allows for a pattern to be set up. Most students will probably say that leaving a fourth bag would just make the story longer.

If the farmer had shouted at the mayor, the police and others might never have discovered that Lazy Peter had left money with the druggist. The trick would never have been revealed.

Challenge. This legend does not have a hero. There is no one who is very good or very brave. The farmer is not really evil, simply greedy. Peter is the main character, but he is not a hero because his actions are not courageous or noble.

7. When the druggist handed Peter the bag of money, the farmer was convinced of the hat's power. He was sure the hat would work for himself, too.
8. The priest had left the bag of money in the sacristy—the place where sacred items of the church were kept.

Developing Writing Skills

Analytical Writing

1. **Stating Your Opinion.** Is Lazy Peter a good model or a bad model? Give your opinion and explain your reasons. Use examples from the story to support your statements.

Creative Writing

2. **Changing the Point of View.** Imagine that you are the farmer. Tell the story of "Lazy Peter and His Three-Cornered Hat" from the farmer's point of view.

Developing Skills in Critical Thinking

Classifying. There are many different ways in which to classify, or group, the legends in this chapter. For example, you could group those stories that are about kings and those that are about tricksters. The same story might be classified in more than one group. For example, "King John and the Abbot" was about both a king and a trickster.

Think of three different classifications in which to group these legends. Then decide which stories fit in each of your classifications.

Developing Skills in Speaking and Listening

Telling A Legend. Prepare to tell the story of "Lazy Peter and His Three-Cornered Hat" to a group of younger students. First, read the story several times until you know the order in which things happen. If you like, take notes that will help you remember the events. Then, practice telling the story to yourself. Use your own words. Make up speeches that Lazy Peter and the other characters might say to each other. Try to make their voices sound different from each other and different from the narrator. If you can find or make a three-cornered hat, practice showing how Peter used it throughout the tale.

Finally, tell the story to a group. Remember to look into your listeners' eyes. If your listeners start to laugh at the story, remember to pause until they can hear your next words. Make sure you sound interested in what you are saying.

with the stand owner, the druggist, and the priest. When the students have listed the events the farmer knows about, have them list his possible reactions to each event, so they can include his feelings.

Writing. Allow sufficient time for students to write their first drafts. Remind students to use their notes as they write. Encourage them to include details that will make the story come alive.

Revising. Have students revise and proofread their own papers and make a clean final copy. Refer them to pages 556 and 557 for suggestions. Display the finished papers on a classroom bulletin board.

Developing Skills in Critical Thinking

Have a student read aloud the exercise on page 57. Ask students to brainstorm possible classifications. If necessary, start them off with one or two titles from the answer box. As each classification is suggested, have the title written on the board while students name the stories that would belong in that group. After four or five ways of classifying have been listed, challenge the students each to come up with three new groups and to list the stories in each group, using all seven stories at least once each.

Developing Skills in Speaking and Listening

Have students read **Telling a Legend.** Make sure the instructions are clear.

Remind students that legends started as oral tradition and were always told by professional storytellers. Make sure they understand that they are to tell the story, not read it from the book or notes.

If possible, arrange for the students to tell their stories to younger students (not necessarily in the primary grades).

Developing Vocabulary Skills

1. disposed—definition or restatement; *or*; got rid of
2. miser—definition or restatement; *who is*; someone who is never satisfied
3. astonishment—synonym; surprise
4. swallowed the bait—definition or restatement; *in other words*; fallen for a trick
5. pesos—definition or restatement; commas; Spanish coins
6. unsound—antonym; not reasonable
7. convinced—synonym; sure
8. sacristy—restatement; dash; the place where sacred items of the church were kept

Developing Skills in Critical Thinking

The following are possible groups:

Legends about kings—"Richard the Lion-Hearted," "King John and the Abbot," and "William Tell"
Legends using the number three—"Richard the Lion-Hearted," "King John and the Abbot," "The Six Horsemen," and "Lazy Peter and His Three-Cornered Hat"
Legends using magic—"The Pied Piper," "Spotted Eagle and Black Crow," "The Six Horsemen"
Legends involving women—"Spotted Eagle and Black Crow," "The Six Horsemen"

Using the Review

This review should be completed before the administration of the **Chapter 1 Mastery Test.** Students will have an opportunity to recall important concepts from this chapter and apply them. Teacher observation during the review can reveal which students still have not mastered the skills.

Using Your Skills in Reading Legends

Have the students read the directions and the paragraph. Allow a few minutes for them to write their answers independently. Then call on individuals to identify Roland's qualities and details in the description that suggest these qualities.

Watch for students who need further practice in recognizing or appreciating these elements.

Using Your Comprehension Skills

With the class, read the directions. Have the students read the excerpt independently. Tell them to write the main idea. Remind them that the main idea may or may not be found in a topic sentence. Have them select and write important details, also. Then discuss the answers. Again, watch for any students who need additional practice.

Using Your Vocabulary Skills

Have the students read the directions and restate them in their own words. Make sure that students understand that they must not only identify the meaning for each underlined word, but also identify the type of context clue used to find the meaning.

Have the students complete this exercise independently. Then discuss the answers and sentences with the class, noting any students who need more practice with this skill.

Using Your Writing Skills

Have the students read the directions. Point out that they should complete only one of the two assignments. Either exercise will show understanding of the elements of a legend. The first exercise is more analytic; the second is more creative. This allows each student to choose the type of writing he or she prefers.

Give the students time to complete the writing in class or assign it for homework. Remind students to use all the information and skills they have learned in this chapter.

CHAPTER 1 

Chapter 1 Review

Using Your Skills in Reading Legends

The following paragraph is from a legend about Roland, a knight. Tell in your own words what you learn about him in this paragraph. What do you find out about him from the description of his armor?

> Some of Roland's ancestors were the noblest heroes the world had ever seen. The blood of heroes flowed in the lad's veins. Of all the knights and warriors in Charlemagne's kingdom, Roland was the bravest and most skillful. When he reached manhood, he was given suitable armor for the knight of a king. His helmet was made of steel and inlaid with pearls, and engraved on it were battle scenes. His shield was made of copper and gold.

Using Your Comprehension Skills

The following is from a legend you will read in Chapter 2 of this book. Read the paragraph. Then state the main idea of the paragraph. Also, identify an important detail that makes the main idea clear.

> Arthur immediately mounted his horse and led his men out of the castle. They fiercely attacked the enemy camp. Arthur was always at the front of the battle, doing marvelous deeds of arms. In the thick of fighting his horse was killed beneath him. King Lot came upon Arthur just then. To save himself, Arthur drew his magic sword. It was so bright that it blinded Lot and his men. They turned and ran, leaving Arthur the victor.

Using Your Vocabulary Skills

The following sentences are from "The Legend of King Arthur," which you will read in Chapter 2. Use context clues to determine the meaning of each underlined word. Tell the meaning in your own words. Then tell which kind of context clue you used: definition or restatement, synonym, antonym, or inference.

Answers to Questions

Using Your Skills in Reading Legends

The materials used in Roland's armor were very valuable, proving that the king (or whoever gave him the armor) considered him valuable, too, and wanted to honor him.

Using Your Comprehension Skills

The main idea is how Arthur won the battle.

Students may choose any of the following main ideas:

Arthur led his men into the battle.

The men attacked the enemy camp fiercely.

Arthur was always at the front of the battle.

King Lot came upon Arthur after his horse was killed under him.

Arthur's sword blinded Lot and his men.

Using Your Vocabulary Skills

1. stayed by himself; definition or restatement clue

2. inn; synonym

1. For many months, Lancelot isolated himself in the forests. He avoided all human contact.
2. When Arthur returned to his lodgings, he found the inn empty and locked.
3. Then Arthur's foster father revealed the secret of Arthur's birth. He told the boy that Merlin had arranged for Sir Ector to raise him, but his real father was King Uther Pendragon.
4. Arthur rode back quickly and, without stopping to read the inscription, yanked the sword from the stone.
5. When Joseph arrived in England, he brought with him the cup Jesus had used at the Last Supper. The cup was called the Holy Grail.

Using Your Writing Skills

Choose one of the writing assignments below.

1. Choose one of the legends you have read in this chapter. Identify which of the following can be found in the legend: (a) a powerful hero or heroine; (b) a powerful evil character; (c) some unbelievable event or events.
2. Create your own hero or heroine. Decide on one admirable quality for which your character will be known. Write a one-paragraph description of this character. Be sure to describe both the character's physical appearance and his or her admirable quality.

Using Your Study and Research Skills

The following questions can be answered through the information available in a library. Read each question; then look at the card-catalog headings listed below. For each question, identify the headings that would be useful in locating answers.

1. Who are the other members of the family of Richard the Lion-Hearted and King John I?
2. Did the German town of Hamelin ever really exist?
3. How do the Swiss honor their national hero, William Tell?

a. William	b. Richard I (the Lion-Hearted)	c. Hamelin
d. towns	e. Tell, William	f. Germany

Collect and evaluate these papers according to the guidelines on pages T26 through T27 of this T.E. It is strongly recommended that you discuss and explain your evaluation with the student, and that you provide an opportunity for the students to revise and resubmit their writing.

Using Your Skills in Study and Research

Have a student read the exercise aloud. Either have the students answer the questions independently before discussion, or complete the exercise as a group activity. Make sure the students recognize why only a few of the headings are useful for answering each question.

Reinforcing the Lesson

To reteach, reinforce, or extend the skills in this lesson, see the following:

Skills Practice Book, Green Level—pages 31 and 32

Additional Resource

Diagnostic and Mastery Tests, Green Level—Chapter 1 Mastery Test, pages 5 through 8

3. uncovered, made known, told; inference or synonym

4. something written; inference

5. the cup Jesus had used at the Last Supper; definition or restatement

Using Your Skills in Study and Research

1. b

2. c, f

3. e

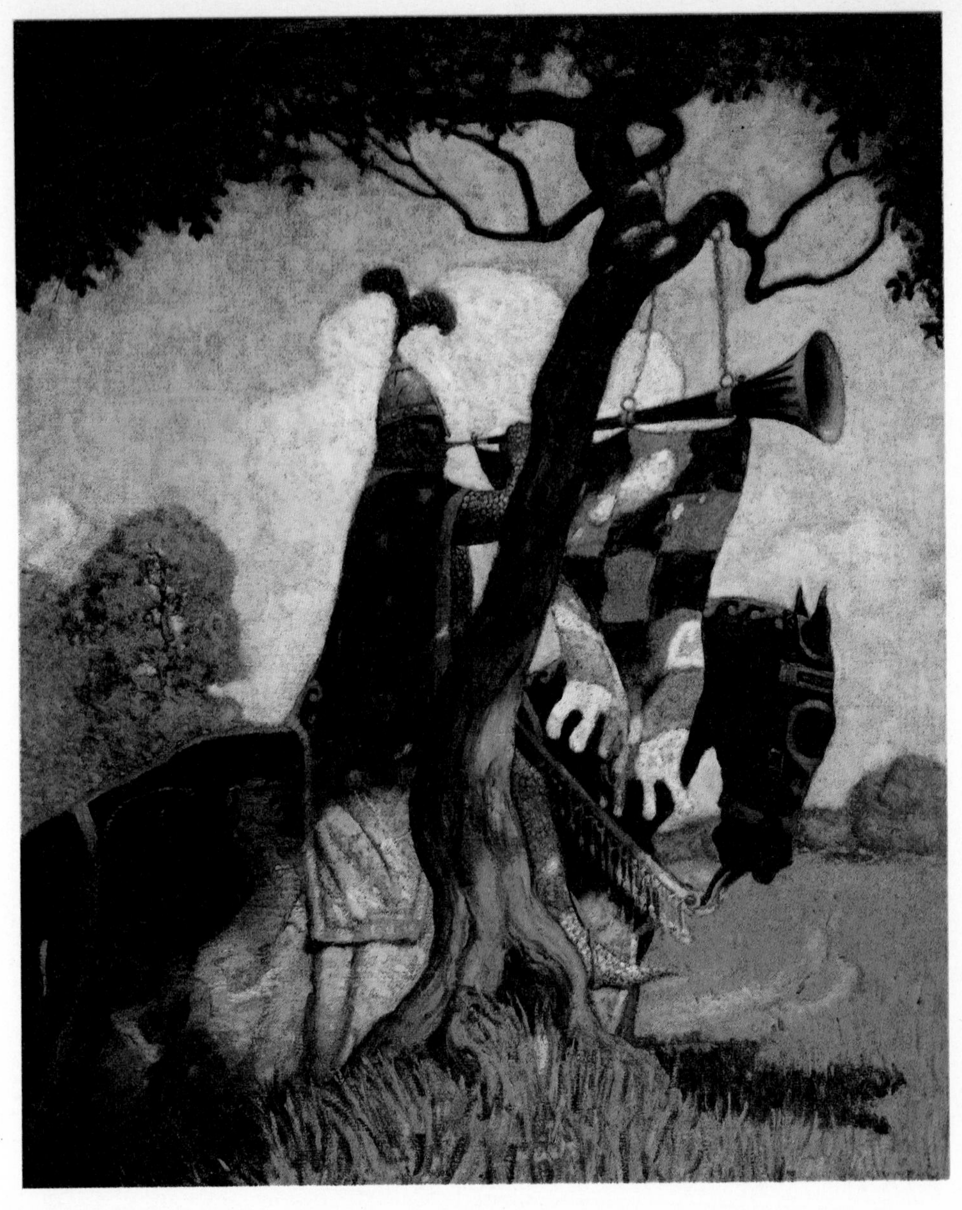

About The Art

N.C. Wyeth (1882–1945), considered one of the greatest American illustrators of children's books, made pictures for such classics as *Treasure Island, Robin Hood,* and *Robinson Crusoe.* Although his illustrations were eventually reduced to page size, Wyeth painted the originals in oils on a large canvas. *He Blew Three Deadly Notes* is an oil painting that was an illustration for *The Boy's King Arthur.* The legend of King Arthur and his knights provided a rich source of inspiration for Wyeth, who loved stories of romance, of triumph and defeat, and of the deeds of heroes.

CHAPTER 2

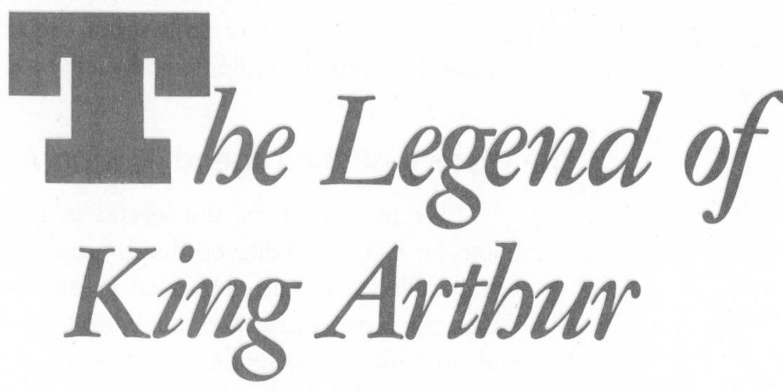

The Legend of King Arthur

He Blew Three Deadly Notes, 1917, N.C. WYETH.
Brandywine River Museum, Chadds Ford, Pennsylvania.

Chapter Objectives

The following is a list of the major skills developed in study questions throughout this chapter:

Skills in Reading Literature

- To recognize and appreciate the Arthurian legend as a form of literature
- To examine and understand characters in a legend
- To identify characteristics of legend such as the use of magic and the episodic nature of the plot

Comprehension Skills

- To recall events in the order in which they occurred (Literal Reading)
- To make inferences from one's reading (Interpretive Reading)
- To draw conclusions from one's reading (Interpretive Reading)
- To make evaluations concerning characters and events (Critical Reading)

Vocabulary Skills

- To recognize base words and affixes
- To use prefixes and suffixes to determine word meaning
- To recognize word parts from Greek and Latin, and to use them in determining word meaning

Writing Skills

- To write a character analysis (Analytical Writing)
- To write an explanation of an opinion, giving reasons (Analytical Writing)
- To write a new ending for a legend (Creative Writing)

Study and Research Skills

- To use and evaluate encyclopedias
- To find and use other reference sources

Critical Thinking Skills

- To make comparisons

Speaking and Listening Skills

- To interpret a character's words orally
- To interpret the mood of a legend orally

Reading Literature

The lesson in **Reading Literature** on pages 62 and 63 introduces the students to the legend of King Arthur. It presents a short history of the story and takes a close look at the elements of *character, setting,* and *plot* as they apply to this particular legend. Last, it provides students with specific suggestions for reading and understanding the legend of King Arthur.

Preparing the Students

In an encyclopedia or other reference book, locate a picture of a knight, a castle, or some other related subject. As you show it to the class, find out how much they know about this period in history. Ask where and when knights lived, what a knight's responsibility was, and whether any student can name any knights from history or legend. Tell the students that in this chapter they will read the best-known and best-loved legend of knighthood. The stories in this book were taken from Malory, *Le Morte d'Arthur,* and rewritten especially for this book.

It is recommended that you administer the **Chapter 2 Diagnostic Test** at this time. The results of this informal pretest will serve as a guide for measuring student needs and progress in achieving chapter objectives.

Presenting the Lesson

1. Have one student read **What is the Legend of King Arthur?** aloud. Review the subject of the legend and the countries where it has been most popular. If possible, point out on a world map or map of Europe the island on which lie the countries of Scotland, Wales, and England, and explain that these three countries, along with Northern Ireland, make up Britain.

2. Call on students to read aloud the first three paragraphs of **The History of the Legend of King Arthur**. Refer to the map to make sure students see the geographic origin and spread of the legend. Have the students read the rest of this section silently. Then, in discussion, emphasize the following major points: 1) history tells us that there probably was a real Arthur; 2) his story was first written down around 600 A.D.; 3) details in the legend have been added by storytellers and writers; 4) many accounts of Arthur's legend have been made popular in Britain, France, and the United States.

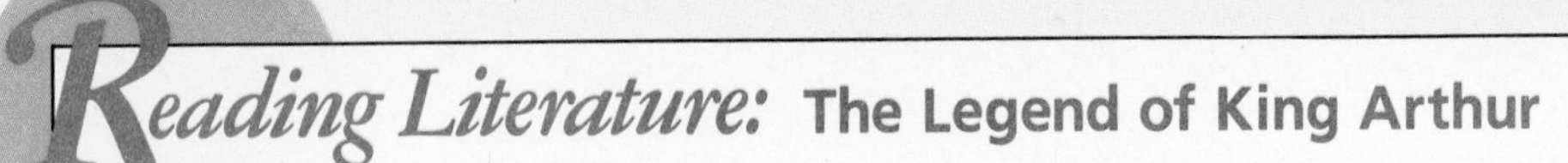

Reading Literature: The Legend of King Arthur

What Is the Legend of King Arthur?

The legend of King Arthur is one of the best loved legends of Britain, France, and the United States. It is also called the Arthurian legend. This legend tells about the noble Arthur, King of Britain, his court of knights, and their bold adventures.

The History of the Legend of King Arthur

Like most legends, the legend of King Arthur is probably based on fact. It is believed that the real Arthur was a leader of a group called the Celts. He lived in Britain in the sixth century. When the Saxons from Germany began to invade Britain, Arthur and his followers defended their land. Arthur was defeated and was killed in battle, but his courage was not forgotten.

Some of his followers fled south to Wales and some to Brittany in France. There they told everyone about Arthur. They began to create a legend that was more exciting than the facts.

Arthur's bravery was first mentioned in print in a Welsh poem as early as 600 A.D. By the twelfth century, Arthur was a national hero in Britain. Some people even believed that King Arthur, as he was soon called, would someday return.

The legend of Arthur also had become popular in France. The French wrote stories and poems about King Arthur, adding details to his legend. For example, during the age of knighthood, some writers decided that Arthur must have been a knight. A French writer invented the Round Table, King Arthur's table where all seats were of equal importance. His knights, the storytellers said, were known for their bravery, honesty, and courtesy.

In 1470, Sir Thomas Malory of England combined many French and British poems and stories about Arthur in a work called *Le Morte d'Arthur*. In the nineteenth century, Alfred, Lord Tennyson of England wrote a book-length poem, *Idylls of the King,* based on this legend. In our own century, T. H. White wrote a book about Arthur, *The Once and Future King,* and an American musical play, *Camelot*, retold the legend for modern audiences.

The Elements of the Legend of King Arthur

Characters. In the legend of King Arthur, you will meet many people. Besides the noble Arthur and his wife Guinevere, there are his knights Lancelot, Galahad, and many others. These characters are not always presented realistically. They are often symbols of qualities such as loyalty, purity, or greed.

Setting. This legend is set in Britain about 500 A.D. It pictures Arthur and his friends as knights. In reality, the age of knighthood would come hundreds of years later. To enjoy the story, ignore that fact and imagine the action taking place in castles among knights in armor and ladies in flowing gowns.

Plot. Many stories were combined over hundreds of years to make this legend. The version you will read, based on Malory's *Le Morte d'Arthur,* is a combination of shorter stories. Each story has its own plot, or series of events. When you read the whole legend, you read all these plots one after the other.

How To Read the Legend of King Arthur

1. Notice all the ways in which King Arthur shows his goodness and courage. By studying Arthur, you can understand why this legend has survived for so long.
2. Read each name carefully the first time it appears. The names may be hard to remember. Especially important and possibly confusing are Merlin, Morgan Le Fay, and Mordred.
3. Appreciate the way this legend takes you out of this ordinary world and into a land of magic and beauty.

3. Have individual students read the separate paragraphs about each element under **The Elements of the Legend of King Arthur**. Stress that students will find fact and fantasy mixed in this legend. For example, note that, although Arthur is a character based on fact, many other characters are just symbols, and that the whole legend is set in a romantic time very dissimilar from the actual era when Arthur lived.

4. Have the class read **How To Read the Legend of King Arthur**. Discuss the hints together. You might want to suggest that as they read the legend, students write a note about each character when he or she is introduced.

Reinforcing the Lesson

To reteach, reinforce, or extend the concepts in this lesson, see the following:

Skills Practice Book, Green Level—pages 33 and 34

Additional Resource

Diagnostic and Mastery Tests, Green Level—Chapter 2 Diagnostic Test, pages 9 and 10

Special Populations

LD. Students might be familiar with other presentations of the tales of King Arthur and the Knights of the Round Table such as the Disney production of *The Sword and the Stone*. Encourage the class to contribute any background information they might have about England and the customs and lifestyles of the people during the time the legend was supposed to have been created.

To help students understand the setting of the legend, bring in pictures of castles, knights, kings, and ladies of the court. As they complete the parts of the selection, encourage students to make posters or illustrations depicting some of the scenes that take place in this legend. Students might look for illustrations done by other artists in the encyclopedia, history books, or children's storybooks. Several students might want to make a three-dimensional model of a castle as an outside-of-class group project.

Comprehension Skills

On pages 64 and 65, the lesson in **Comprehension Skills** introduces the skills of making inferences and drawing conclusions. These skills will be emphasized throughout this chapter and will be reviewed frequently in other chapters.

Preparing the Students

Describe this situation to the class: A man is getting ready to go outside. First he pulls on heavy, tall boots. Then he puts on a wool sweater and a down jacket. Last he wraps a scarf around his neck and puts on a ski cap. Ask the students what kind of weather he is preparing for and what clues gave them the answer. Point out that when they read they can use clues like these to understand things that are not specifically stated. In this section, they will learn how to spot and use the clues the writers give them.

Presenting the Lesson

1. Have the students read silently **Getting All the Meaning from the Words**. Ask them to identify some of the habits of good readers. (They look for relationships, make inferences, and draw conclusions.) Then have students read the first two paragraphs of **Making Inferences** and explain what is meant by this phrase.

Call on students to read aloud the paragraphs concerning characters, setting, and mood.

Discuss the types of questions that a reader can ask to help himself or herself make inferences.

2. Have the class read and discuss **Drawing Conclusions**. Point out that inferences may be based on a very small amount of information or a slight hint, while conclusions should be drawn from a substantial body of evidence.

Give the students practice in drawing conclusions using the following model or similar models:

Beth will swim only when the water temperature is above 70 degrees.

Beth tested the water temperature today.

Beth is swimming today.

Conclusion: The water temperature is above 70 degrees.

3. Complete the exercise with the class. Discuss why some of the inferences are sensible while others are not.

Comprehension Skills: Inferences and Conclusions

Getting All the Meaning from the Words

Reading is an activity. It does not just happen. You make it happen. Good readers throw themselves into their reading. They are always thinking and looking for relationships. As they read, they make inferences and draw conclusions.

Making Inferences

An **inference** is information that the reader draws from the evidence by reasoning. That is, he or she uses what the writer states as clues. By thinking about these clues, the reader can discover ideas or facts that the writer did not state.

When people write, they count on readers to catch the hints they drop. They try not to make their writing so detailed that it becomes boring. Writers expect you to recognize and use the clues in their writing. Only when you make logical guesses based on evidence in the story can you understand what happens and why.

What evidence should you look for? Keeping these questions in mind as you read will help you make sensible inferences.

1. **Characters:** How is the character described? Does the character grow and develop during the story? What is the mood of the character? How does he or she treat other people? What do other characters say about this character? Does the writer give any clues about what has happened to the character in the past? Are there clues that suggest the character's hopes for the future? Do these clues explain the character's actions?
2. **Setting:** What is the setting? How does the setting affect what happens in the story? Why does the author mention details about the setting at particular points in the story?

3. **Mood:** Can you find words or phrases that give you a certain feeling? Which events or situations are described strongly enough to make you feel certain emotions?

Drawing Conclusions

Think of how detectives work. They collect all the evidence, put all the clues together, and come up with a conclusion. A **conclusion** is the final decision in a chain of thinking or reasoning. When you read, you are often asked to draw conclusions. Here is a model for you to follow.

You know these facts:

1. Only the true king can pull the magic sword from the stone.
2. Many people try to pull the sword out, but they fail.
3. Arthur pulls the sword from the stone easily.

You draw this conclusion: Arthur is the true king.

Exercise: Getting All the Meaning from the Words

Read the following paragraphs from "The Legend of King Arthur." They tell what happens when Sir Kay sends Arthur to get a sword for him. Then decide which inferences are sensible.

> Arthur yanked the magic sword from the stone. Then he hurried back to Sir Kay with the borrowed sword.
>
> As soon as he saw the sword, Sir Kay knew where it had come from. He grabbed it, ran to his father, and said, "Sir! Look! I have the sword from the stone, so I must be the rightful King of England!"

1. Sir Kay is the rightful King of England.
2. Sir Kay is not very honest.
3. Sir Kay is not very old.
4. Arthur tries to please Sir Kay.
5. Arthur is handsome.
6. Arthur has no time to lose.

Reinforcing the Lesson

To reteach, reinforce, or extend the skills in this lesson, see the following:

Skills Practice Book, Green Level—pages 35 and 36

Special Populations

LD. Many LD students lack the ability to make inferences, generalize, or draw conclusions. They might need help in determining what would be a "logical guess" when asked to make inferences. Take time to develop the introductory information in this lesson thoroughly with these students. In specific reading situations, relate making inferences to "solving a puzzle." Ask the students to state the puzzle (for example, to find out if a statement is true or false); then have them apply and answer the questions listed on this page.

Stressing logic, order and sequence of events, and cause-and-effect relationships can provide the student with some concrete tools to help understand these areas.

Answers to Exercise

The sensible inferences are 2, 3, 4, and 6.

Vocabulary Skills

The lesson in **Vocabulary Skills** on pages 66 and 67 teaches the students to recognize and understand words built with base words and affixes, and words that use Greek and Latin word parts. Study questions throughout the chapter develop these skills by having students apply them to words in the chapter selections.

Preparing the Students

Write these words on the board in two columns.

write	rewrite
appoint	disappoint
kind	kindness
help	helpless

Ask the students how each word in the first column was changed to make the word in the second column. Make sure they realize that letters were added at the beginning or the end of each word. Point out how these additions changed the meaning of the first column words. Tell the class that in the next lesson they will learn more about word parts and how they affect meaning.

Presenting the Lesson

1. Have the students read silently the first paragraph and the examples in **Using Word Parts** on page 66. Ask them to define each of the terms printed in bold face. Then have individuals read the second paragraph and the box. Write on the board each of the prefixes and suffixes in the box. Ask for additional examples of words that use each of the word parts, and have a student record them on the board. If necessary, suggest any of the following examples: reconsider; mismatch; inattentive; immodest; irrational; illegible; discourage; roundness; thoughtless; meaningful; officious.

2. Have individual students read aloud **Word Parts from Greek and Latin**, including the examples in the box. Ask for other examples of words that use these word parts and record any responses on the board. (Suggestions include *monolog, binary, triplets, decathlon, multi-purpose, omnipotent,* and *geology.*) You may want to look up any suggested words in the dictionary to be sure everyone knows the correct meanings.

3. Have the students complete **Exercise A** independently. Discuss the answers.

Vocabulary Skills: Word Parts

Using Word Parts

Words in our language are formed in many ways. Some words are formed by adding a beginning or an ending to a **base word**. A word part added to the beginning of a base word is called a **prefix**. A word part added to the end of a word is called a **suffix**.

Prefix	+	**Base Word**	=	**New Word**
re	+	use	=	reuse

Base Word	+	**Suffix**	=	**New Word**
care	+	ful	=	careful

Adding a prefix or a suffix to a base word makes a new word with a different meaning. Read the following lists of prefixes and suffixes. What is the meaning of each new word?

Prefixes	**New Words**
re– means "again."	retake
mis– means "wrong" or "wrongly."	miscount
in–, im–, ir–, and **il–** mean "not."	inactive, immortal, irresistible, illegal
dis– means "the opposite of."	displease
Suffixes	**New Words**
–ness means "the quality of" or "state of being."	goodness
–less means "without."	hopeless
–ful, –ous mean "full of" or "having."	wonderful, dangerous

Word Parts from Greek and Latin

Many English words are based on Greek and Latin words. Greek and Latin words are shortened and used as prefixes and suffixes. Here are some Greek and Latin word parts that you may find in your reading. Knowing their meanings will help you understand the meaning of the English words that they are part of.

Meaning	Greek	Latin	Examples
one	mono–	uni–	monotone, unicycle
two	di–	bi–, duo–	dioxide, bicycle, duet
three	tri–	tri–	triangle
ten	deca–	deci–	decade, decimal
many	poly–	multi–	polygon, multitude
half	hemi–	semi–, hemi–	semiannual, hemisphere
all	pan–	omni–	panorama, omnipresent
science of	–ology		biology

Exercises: Using Word Parts

A. In each sentence, find a word with a prefix or suffix from page 66. Identify each word part and tell what the word means.

1. One seat at the Round Table was called the "Seat Perilous."
2. Merlin could vanish and reappear by magic.
3. The punishment for being disloyal was death.
4. The knights tried to avoid needless fighting.

B. Use the chart of Greek and Roman forms. Answer these questions.

1. How many colors are there in a *tricolored* flag?
2. If *lateral* means "sided," what does *multilateral* mean?
3. If *cornu* is the Roman word for "horn," how many horns does a unicorn have?
4. If *bios* is Greek for "life," what does *biology* mean?

Complete **Exercise B** with the students. Ask them if they can think of any other words that use the Greek and Latin word parts mentioned here.

Reinforcing the Lesson

To reteach, reinforce, or extend the skills in this lesson, see the following:

Skills Practice Book, Green Level—pages 37 and 38

Special Populations

LD. You may wish to reproduce the chart on page 66 on a poster or worksheet to be used by the students as they come across unfamiliar words in their reading.

ESL. ESL students whose native languages are related to Greek or Latin may be able to give further examples from their native languages of words using word parts in the chart on page 67.

Answers to Exercises

A. Identifying word parts and meanings:

1. perilous—peril + ous; full of peril
2. reappear—re + appear; appear again
3. disloyal—dis + loyal; not loyal
4. needless—need + less; without need

B. Understanding Greek and Roman forms:

1. three colors
2. many sided
3. one horn
4. the science of life

Objectives

- To appreciate the Arthurian legend as a form of literature
- To recognize separate episodes that form a legend
- To apply literal, interpretive, and critical reading skills to a selection
- To make inferences about a character
- To recognize word parts drawn from Greek and Latin
- To write a first-person account of events
- To become familiar with the encyclopedia

Preparing the Students

Essential Vocabulary. The words presented here are essential to the understanding of the selection.

Write the following sentences on the chalkboard. Have the students use the context clues in the sentences to determine the meanings of the underlined words.

anvil siege sheath barge

1. The blacksmith laid the white-hot iron rod on the smooth surface of the anvil and hammered it into shape.
2. The town withstood the siege for three days, but at last they could hold back the enemy no longer.
3. As the fighter pulled his knife from its protective sheath, the blade shone in the sun.
4. The barge would be more useful to them than a regular boat because its flat bottom would not scrape the bed of the shallow river.

If the students need additional help with the vocabulary of this selection, encourage them to use context clues to determine word meaning. As needed, direct them to the **Glossary** or to a classroom dictionary.

Motivation. Have the students read the introductory paragraph at the top of page 68 and state in their own words what they should be looking for as they read this selection.

Note to the teacher. You may wish to acquaint the students with some of these pronunciations:

Uther (o͞o′ thər)
Pendragon (pən′ drag′ ən)
Igraine (ī′ grān)
Merlin (mʉr′ lən)
Ector (ek′ tər)
Arthur (är′ thər)
Leodegrance (lē ō′ də gräns)
Guinevere (gwin′ ə vir′)
Camelot (kam′ ə lät)

In this part of the legend, you will learn how the young Arthur gained the throne and began his court. Which men did Arthur trust? Why? Why did other men trust Arthur? As you read, look for clues to these answers.

The Legend of King Arthur: Part One

A retelling of Le Morte d'Arthur by Sir Thomas Malory

Centuries ago, when Uther Pendragon reigned as King of England, he and his wife Igraine had a son named Arthur. Uther's close aide, the magician Merlin, foresaw that Arthur would need special training. Therefore, he talked the King into keeping the birth of his son secret. At Merlin's urging, Uther sent his baby son away. Safe from the dangers and distractions of court life, Arthur could learn the ways of knighthood.

Merlin took Arthur to Sir Ector and his wife to raise, along with their own son Kay. Together the boys trained to become knights.

While Arthur was still a young boy, King Uther Pendragon became seriously ill. Merlin asked him, "Do you wish Arthur to become king after your death?"

The King replied, "Yes, the throne is his by right of birth."

Shortly after that, Uther died. His enemies began to take over his lands and there was much unrest. When Merlin saw this, he went to the Archbishop of Canterbury. He suggested that a call be issued to all the lords of the kingdom. He asked that the lords gather on Christmas Eve in a church in London. There they could search for a sign that would show who should be the next King of England.

When they assembled, everyone was amazed. In the churchyard they found a large block of marble. In the marble was a steel anvil with a sword driven into it. Gold letters on the sword read: "Whoever pulls this sword out of the stone and anvil is the King of England by right of birth."

Immediately, several knights tried to pull the sword out of the stone. No matter how hard they tried, no man could even budge it. The sword in the stone was left in the churchyard, a challenge to all.

On New Year's Day, there was to be a tournament of jousts and matches in the

fields outside London. Each man would test his strength and skill against each of the others. Sir Ector brought Sir Kay, recently knighted, and Arthur to witness this great event. On New Year's Eve, the three arrived in London and found an inn at which to stay. The next day they rode out to the site of the tournament.

When they arrived at the field, Sir Kay realized he had forgotten his sword. He asked Arthur to ride back to their lodgings in town and get it for him.

Arthur found the inn empty and locked. Upset, he remembered the sword and anvil he had seen as he had ridden past the church. He rode back quickly and, without stopping to read the inscription, yanked the sword from the stone. Then he hurried back to Sir Kay with the borrowed sword.

Presenting the Selection

1. Because this is a fairly long selection, it is advisable to assign the beginning section and the two subheadings, "Excalibur" and "Arthur and Guinevere," as three separate reading assignments. Remind the students that, as they read, they should look for clues that will help them answer the questions asked in the introduction. You may wish to ask the appropriate questions of the **Check Test** after each section (see step 3, below).

The version of the legend provided here is a modern-language adaptation of the major episodes of Sir Thomas Malory's *Morte d'Arthur.* Wherever possible, especially in the characters' speeches, Malory's words have been retained. However, in order to condense the events and avoid unnecessarily confusing vocabulary, the editors paraphrased the language of the original.

2. Students may understand the events in the beginning section (pages 68 to 71) better if they know that at that time the Archbishop of Canterbury was a powerful leader, not only in the Church but also in the government. It was not unusual for political leaders to seek his support.

3. Make sure that everyone has read the selection by administering the **Check Test** at the bottom of page 74 of this T.E. This may be done as each reading assignment is completed or after students have completed all of Part 1. (Questions 1, 2, and 3 deal with the beginning section; questions 4 and 5 deal with "Excalibur"; and the last two questions refer to "Arthur and Guinevere.")

4. Develop the study questions as suggested in **Using the Study Questions** on pages 75 to 77 of this T.E. That section also provides challenge questions for further discussion, as needed. (For answers to questions, see T.E. pages 75 to 77.)

Reinforcing the Lesson

To reteach, reinforce, or extend the skills in this lesson, see the following:

Skills Practice Book, Green Level—pages 39 through 44

Special Populations

ESL. It may be necessary to give some historical background to the students; their understanding of the time and the customs could be very limited. You might want to describe tournaments between the knights, to explain why some of the characters are called Sir or Lady, or how a man could become a knight; and to list some of the jobs people from this time in history might have had.

LD, ESL. Assign partners for the special-populations student to work with on library assignments such as those suggested under **Developing Skills in Study and Research** on page 77. Understanding and finding information in encyclopedias can be particularly difficult for the ESL students, especially those students who have difficulty with spelling and alphabetical order of words.

The suggestions found under the **Developing Skills in Study and Research** sections could become a special unit of study all by itself for many of the special-populations students to complete with the help of the LD or ESL instructor. The material presented provides the students with valuable tools with which they can help themselves solve problems they may encounter in understanding some of the materials they read.

Encouraging Independent Reading

1. Ask your more capable students to locate a copy of *Idylls of the King* by Alfred, Lord Tennyson or *The Once and Future King* by T.H. White. Challenge them to find the parts that parallel this version of the legend. Have them make a chart showing specific ways in which the versions differ.

2. Many students will be interested in doing independent reading on the topics of knights, castles, wizards, ladies, and mythical beasts such as dragons and unicorns that often appear in legends about knights. Encourage them to report on their reading by setting up a bulletin board labeled "Days of Knighthood—Facts and Fantasies." Allow students to post 3 x 5 cards on which they have reported a historical fact (such as the weight of a suit of armor or the value of some medieval crown) or described an imaginary beast or feat of magic believed in by the people of the Middle Ages. On each card, the writer should list the source of his or her information.

The following are books students might find in their school or local library:

Tales of King Arthur and His Knights by Howard Pyle

Knight of the Cart by Constance Hieatt

As soon as he saw the sword, Sir Kay knew where it had come from. He grabbed it, ran to his father, and said, "Sir! Look! I have the sword from the stone, so I must be the rightful King of England!"

Sir Ector took his son and Arthur to the church. There he demanded that Sir Kay tell the truth. Unwilling to lie in a holy place, Sir Kay admitted that Arthur had brought the sword to him. Sir Ector questioned Arthur, and then pondered things over in his mind. At last he told Arthur, "Now I know you must be the rightful King of England."

Arthur asked, "But, sir, how can this possibly be?"

First, Sir Ector explained the magic of the sword in the stone. Only the man fit to be the next King of England would have the power to draw that sword out of the stone. Then Arthur's foster father revealed the secret of Arthur's birth. He told the boy that Merlin had arranged for Sir Ector to raise him, but his real father was King Uther Pendragon.

Arthur declared, "You, Sir, and your wife have raised me from my birth. I owe you love and honor for all you have done for me."

Sir Ector replied, "Arthur, I ask only one thing of you when you become King of England. Make Sir Kay the keeper of all your lands."

Arthur was mightily surprised at this news of his birthright and at the thought that he should be king. Yet something inside him told him what to do and say. Without hesitation he answered, "Sir, your wish is granted. Sir Kay shall retain his office as long as he and I shall live."

Sir Ector took Arthur to the Archbishop. He pointed out the magic sword in Arthur's hands and explained how Arthur had drawn it from the stone. As the word spread, onlookers hurried from the tournament fields to the church. The crowds watched Arthur put the sword back into the stone. Several knights and barons tried to pull the sword out again. Over and over they tried, but no one could do so. Finally, Arthur stepped up to the stone once more. Effortlessly, he slid the sword out and raised it before all the people.

Many knights were angry that a mere boy could accomplish this feat. They convinced the Archbishop that many more knights deserved a chance to draw the sword. Several times over the next few months, nobles and knights gathered so that all might have an opportunity to pull the sword from the stone. Still, none could do so except Arthur.

Finally, the people cried, "We will wait no longer. We want Arthur for our king. We will fight anyone who opposes him."

Then the knights accepted Arthur despite his youth. He was immediately declared a knight. Shortly after that, Sir Arthur was officially crowned King of England.

As soon as he took office, the young king promised to right the wrongs that had been committed since his father's death. The people's hearts were filled with joy. Once again peace and justice would rule the land.

Excalibur

After he was made king, Arthur decided to give a great feast. He sent messengers out with gifts for all the kings of the neighboring counties. He dressed in his finest clothes and waited for their arrival.

However, when his messengers returned they brought back his gifts. They told him that the neighboring kings had refused the presents. They had called Arthur a boy of low birth. They did not recognize his right to rule as king. In fact, they were on their way to take Arthur's lands away from him.

Alarmed, Arthur gathered an army of men to help him. He and his five hundred followers gathered supplies and went into a strong castle.

When the rivals came, Arthur and his men withstood a siege that lasted for fifteen days. Then Merlin made his way into the camp of Arthur's enemies. The leaders recognized Merlin and asked him, "Why has a young boy like Arthur been made king?"

Merlin told them how Sir Ector had raised Arthur, but that Arthur's father actually was King Uther Pendragon and the throne was his by right of birth. He convinced some of the leaders of Arthur's claim to the throne. Others, however, laughed at Merlin.

"Even if your story is true," they said, "the boy Arthur hasn't proved himself. He must show by victories that he deserves to be our king."

Merlin warned them, "It would be good for you to accept him and end this resistance. Even if there were ten times as many of you as there are now, you would never defeat Arthur."

"Should we be afraid of this dream-reader?" King Lot, one of the leaders, mocked Merlin.

At that, Merlin vanished. He reappeared before King Arthur, inside his fortress.

"Begin the attack," Merlin told Arthur. "They won't listen to reason. But be careful. The fighting will be fierce. Do not use the sword you have acquired by magic until you have no choice. Then do your best with it."

Arthur immediately mounted his horse and led his men out of the castle. They fiercely attacked the enemy camp. Arthur was always at the front of the battle, doing marvelous deeds of arms. In the thick of the fighting, his horse was killed beneath him. King Lot came upon Arthur just then. To save himself, Arthur drew his magic sword. It was so bright that it blinded Lot and his men. They turned and ran, leaving Arthur the victor.

Now that he had established himself as a leader, Arthur relaxed by going out hunting. In the forest, he came across a knight who insisted on fighting him. They were both strong and skillful swordsmen. For a long time the fight was even, each man giving and taking wounds. Then the two swords smashed together, and King Arthur's magic sword broke in two. The strange knight was about to kill Arthur. Suddenly Merlin arrived. He quickly put an enchantment on the knight, who fell to the ground in a deep sleep.

"What have you done, Merlin?" Arthur cried. "Have you killed this good knight by your crafts? He was the bravest and strongest knight I have ever come across! I would have wanted him to fight under me."

"Don't worry," Merlin assured him. "He's in better health now than you are. He will wake soon. In the future he will do you much good service."

For three days King Arthur rested from the fight. Then he became worried because he had no sword.

"Come with me," Merlin said. "I will take you to one."

Merlin led Arthur to a wide lake. At the center of the lake was an arm reaching up out of the water. Its hand held up a sword encased in a sheath.

"Look," said Merlin. "That is the sword I spoke of. And here comes the Lady of the Lake. Speak courteously to her, and she will give you a sword."

"Fair Lady," Arthur asked the Lady of the Lake, "what sword is this which an arm holds above the water? I wish to have that sword because I no longer have my own."

"The sword is mine," said the Lady. "You may have it, if you will give me a gift when I ask for it."

Arthur agreed. The Lady pointed out a barge that Arthur could use. He rowed across the lake. When he reached the arm, he grasped the sword by the handle. The arm slowly went back under the water.

When Arthur returned to the shore, Merlin told him, "Your sword is called

Excalibur. Keep it close to you as long as you live."

As they rode back to court, Merlin asked Arthur, "Which do you like better, the sword or the sheath?"

Arthur answered, "The sword, of course."

"The sheath is far more valuable than the sword," said Merlin. "While you wear it, you will lose no blood, even if you are badly wounded. Always keep it nearby."

From that day on, Arthur felt more capable of fighting against his enemies. He began to have a large following who recognized him as a good and strong leader.

Arthur and Guinevere

Once Arthur began to get his kingdom in order, he decided it was time to marry. He consulted with Merlin.

"Have you seen anyone fit to be the Queen?" Merlin asked.

"Yes," said Arthur. "The most beautiful woman I have ever seen is Guinevere, the daughter of King Leodegrance. She is the woman I wish to marry."

Merlin wasn't happy about Arthur's choice. With his gift of foresight, he knew that Guinevere would love another as well as Arthur. Merlin advised Arthur, "She is not the woman I would have chosen for you. I could find you a woman who would make you even happier."

Arthur answered, "No. I want only Guinevere for my wife. Go and settle matters for me with her father."

King Leodegrance had been an ally of Arthur's father. For his wedding present, Uther Pendragon had sent Leodegrance an enormous round table. The table was so large that one hundred and fifty knights could sit around it.

King Leodegrance was very happy that Arthur wanted to marry his daughter. He told Merlin, "Arthur does not need any more lands. I will give him the finest gift I can offer him. I will give him the Round Table that his father gave to me long ago."

With the Round Table went one hundred knights who would help Arthur to make decisions and protect his lands. Still, there were fifty empty seats to be filled.

Merlin, Guinevere, and the Knights of the Round Table set off for Arthur's castle at Camelot. When Arthur saw Guinevere, she looked even more beautiful than he had remembered her. He was delighted with the gift of the Round Table and the hundred knights. These were men of maturity and experience whom he could count on.

Arthur set a high standard for his knights. He declared that the knights of the Round Table could not fight each other and could not start battles just to gain power or riches. Instead, they were to protect people in need, including the poor. They were to guard the kingdom against dangers from lawbreakers within the country and enemies outside the borders. They must always show courage and courtesy.

In order that the empty seats of the Round Table would be filled, a custom was established. The feast of Pentecost came in early summer, the seventh Sunday after Easter. Every year at this time more knights would be added to the Round Table, as they proved themselves worthy of this great honor. When a new knight sat in one of the seats, the seat was magically labeled with his name in letters of gold. One seat, called "Seat Perilous," was left empty. If anyone unworthy sat there, he would be destroyed.

When Guinevere became Arthur's queen, she was overwhelmed by the splendor of Arthur's kingdom. She quickly established herself in his court, and his knights became devoted to her. Her love for Arthur, and Arthur's love for her, grew steadily.

In the meantime, Merlin also fell in love. The lake in which Arthur had found his sword, Excalibur, also held a great rock. Underneath the great rock was a palace. The Lady of the Lake lived there. One day she cast her spell and persuaded Merlin to come and live with her. That was the last time anyone ever saw Merlin the magician.

Check Test

1. Who was Arthur's real father? (Uther Pendragon, the King of England)

2. What was the name of Arthur's magician friend? (Merlin)

3. How did Arthur become King of England? (He pulled a sword from a stone.)

4. What happened to Arthur's first magic sword? (It broke in half.)

5. Who gave Arthur his second sword, Excalibur? (the Lady of the Lake)

6. What gift did Leodegrance, Guinevere's father, give Arthur as a wedding present? (the Round Table)

7. With whom did Merlin fall in love? (the Lady of the Lake)

Answers to Study Questions

Developing Comprehension Skills

1. b, e, a, c, d

2. People thought Arthur was too young to be king. They also thought he was a boy of low birth.

Arthur proved his right by establishing himself as a leader in battle and by restoring justice. He was also the only one able to remove the sword from the stone.

Developing Comprehension Skills

Literal Reading

1. Arrange the following events from the legend in the correct order.
   a. Arthur visited the Lady of the Lake and got a sword.
   b. Merlin suggested that Arthur be raised by Sir Ector.
   c. Arthur married Guinevere and received the gift of the Round Table.
   d. Merlin disappeared and was not heard from again.
   e. Arthur pulled the sword from the stone.

Literal Reading

2. At first, Arthur was not accepted easily as king. Name two objections against him. Then tell at least two ways Arthur proved his right to be king.

Interpretive Reading

3. After Arthur drew the sword from the stone, Sir Ector told him his real father was Uther Pendragon and that Arthur was the rightful King of England. Arthur immediately declared, "I owe you love and honor for all you have done for me," and he promised to make his foster brother the keeper of his lands. What can you infer about Arthur's character from these statements? That is, what do these statements tell you about the kind of person Arthur was?

Critical Reading

4. Did Arthur put too much trust in Merlin? In your answer, identify several important instances in which Arthur did exactly as Merlin advised. Also, identify other instances in which Arthur acted without Merlin's help or approval. Do you think Merlin's disappearance will be good or bad for Arthur? Explain your answer.

Reading Literature: The Legend of King Arthur

1. **Understanding Setting.** The term **setting** refers to the place and the time in which a story is set. When a story is set in a time different from our own, the characters often think differently from modern people. Use clues in this story to decide what the characters might think about these modern statements. Explain your answers.
   a. Magic is just tricks.
   b. In a good government, people elect their leaders.
   c. A woman should decide for herself whether to marry.

2. **Studying Plot.** In the introduction to Chapter 2, you learned that the legend of King Arthur was a combination of many shorter tales. In this part of the legend there are at least five separate **episodes,** or

These proofs backed up Merlin's statement that he was King Uther's son.

3. Possible answers: Arthur was loving, loyal, generous, and honorable.

4. Students' conclusions about whether Arthur put too much trust in Merlin will vary, but all answers should include occasions when Arthur trusted Merlin as well as times when he did not rely on him. Arthur trusted Merlin when he began his battle, and when he asked the Lady of the Lake for the sword. He did not heed Merlin's advice in choosing a wife. Merlin's disappearance may make Arthur stand on his own; however, he will not have Merlin's protection.

Challenge. Answers may vary but all answers should include reasons. One possible answer: Since Arthur believed in magic, he probably decided that following Merlin's advice was the wisest course of action. He followed Merlin's advice because he was strong, not weak.

Reading Literature: The Legend of King Arthur

1. Answers may vary but should include reasons.

a. The characters would probably disagree with the statement. Sev-

(continued on page 76)

Using the Study Questions

It is recommended that students always read and answer the questions in **Developing Comprehension Skills** in class discussion. Whenever possible, they should also read the questions in other categories together and discuss the answers.

Developing Comprehension Skills

Question 1. Have a volunteer list the events in the proper order on the board.

Question 2. Read and discuss.

Question 3. Review the meaning of *infer.* If necessary, have students refer to the section on making inferences on pages 64 and 65. Ask them to consider other possible reactions to news such as the information Sir Ector gave Arthur, and to compare the possibilities with Arthur's reaction. For example, they should recognize that a less responsible boy might have decided that, as King, he no longer owed Sir Ector anything.

Question 4. Have each student list the occasions when Arthur followed Merlin's advice and the occasions when he did not. Help them make their own predictions about the effect Merlin's disappearance will have on Arthur. Encourage them to compare their predictions with what actually happens as they continue to read the legend.

Challenge Question. Arthur was willing to follow Merlin's directions in most cases. Does that show a weakness of character or does it show a mature willingness to take good advice? Give reasons for your answer. (Critical Reading)

Reading Literature: The Legend of King Arthur

Question 1. Briefly review various aspects of the setting of this legend that demonstrate its difference from modern times, such as the importance of knighthood, the dominance of kings, and the belief in magic. Then have the students predict how specific characters might react to the statements.

Question 2. Read and discuss. There may be some disagreement on an exact point at which any episode begins or ends, but it should not be difficult to agree on a few major events that identify episodes. List on the board the short tales on which the students agree before you ask the class to explain how the episodes are related to each other.

Question 3. Have the students give examples of how Arthur treats other people and of his sense of honor. Also have them examine his actions and decisions, such as his choice of a wife, his dependence on Merlin's advice, and his fight with the knight in the forest.

Question 4. Ask students to identify places in the story where magic changed the course of events.

Challenge Question. Notice the words and word order used in this legend. Would you say it is a formal or informal way of writing? Why is this style an appropriate way to present this legend?

Developing Vocabulary Skills

1. Have the students read the directions to this exercise. Have the lists of Greek and Latin words and word parts, and their meanings, read aloud.

2. Have the students complete the exercise, without the help of a dictionary. As they give the meaning for each underlined word, have them tell which word part is used.

Developing Writing Skills

Read and discuss the two assignments. Then have each student choose and complete one of the two.

Question 1. Emphasize that the assignment is not simply to describe Merlin's physical appearance, but to decide whether or not he acts like a real person.

Pre-Writing. Encourage students to read the portions of the legend that refer to Merlin and to take notes on what he did, what he said, and how he looked. Students should use the notes to help them decide whether or not Merlin acts like a real person. Remind them that their goal is to present evidence that will make the reader agree with their decision.

Writing. Allow sufficient time for the students to write their first draft. Remind them to prove their point of view with evidence from the legend.

Revising. Let students who chose this question meet in small groups to discuss and compare their conclusions as well as the evidence they chose to include. Then allow time for revising the drafts, in case some writers find that they must explain their reasons more clearly. Make sure, however, that students do not assume that there is one right answer, or that the papers should match.

series of events. Identify as many of the five short tales as possible. How are these short tales related to each other?

3. **Examining Character.** The hero or heroine of a legend must be better than the average person in some ways. Name some of the ways in which Arthur is special. Are there other ways in which he is like other men? Describe them.

4. **Appreciating the Legend.** Magic is an important element in "The Legend of King Arthur." It sets off Arthur's world from ours and makes everything that happens unusual. Point out several places where magic affects the story.

Developing Vocabulary Skills

Using Word Parts from Greek and Latin. Examine the chart below. Note the meaning of each Greek and Latin word and word part listed. Then read the sentences below the chart. The underlined word in each sentence is based on one or more of the words or word parts on the chart. Use the information on the chart and the context clues in each sentence to figure out the meaning of each underlined word.

mono–, uni–	one	hemi–	half	scientia	knowledge
di–	two	omni–	all	archein	to rule
multi–	many				

1. Arthur wanted to unite all of England under his rule.
2. His enemies led a multitude against Arthur's men.
3. Since the author knows everything that happened, we can tell the story uses an omniscient point of view.
4. The government of England has been a monarchy for about 1200 years.
5. Arthur was faced with a dilemma. Should he listen to Merlin or should he listen to his heart?

Developing Writing Skills

Analytical Writing

1. **Examining a Character.** Does Merlin act like a real person? What is special about his abilities? What kinds of unusual feats can he accomplish? Write at least one paragraph describing Merlin.

(continued from page 75)

eral events in the story involve magic, and the characters are willing to accept magic as a real force.

b. The characters would not agree because they believed that being born in the ruling family, or marrying into it, gave a man or woman the right to rule.

c. The characters would not agree because they felt that a woman should do whatever was planned for her by her parents; she did not have a choice.

2. Possible episodes:
Arthur's life until he removes the sword from the stone
Arthur's beginning as king, until he defeats his enemies
Arthur's fight with the knight who broke his sword, and the gift of Excalibur
Arthur's marriage to Guinevere
The beginning of the Knights of the Round Table
Merlin's disappearance
Each episode follows in time order.

3. Possible heroic qualities: Arthur had a high moral code and was dedicated to

Creative Writing

2. **Describing Actions.** Imagine that you were one of the people at the tournament on the day that young Arthur drew the sword from the stone. Write an eyewitness account of what happened for your hometown paper. Remember to use only the information that a traveler to the tournament would know.

Developing Skills in Study and Research

Using the Encyclopedia. A general encyclopedia is a collection of articles on a wide variety of topics. The articles are arranged alphabetically by title and often fill several separate books, or **volumes.** The encyclopedia **index** lists all the titles of the articles and tells the volume and page where you will find each article. Sometimes one article may discuss several related topics. The title of the article may name only one of the topics. The other related topics are also listed in the index as separate entries. There you will find the title of the article or articles that discuss the topic.

You can often get an idea of how important a topic is by seeing how much space an encyclopedia gives to that topic. In your school or local library, choose one set of encyclopedias. Look up each of the following names and terms in that encyclopedia. Find out which names and terms are given separate articles, and how long each article is. Find out which names and terms are discussed only in articles under other titles. Use the index to save yourself from looking up entries that do not exist.

Arthur or King Arthur	Guinevere
Round Table	Merlin
Arthurian Legend	Uther Pendragon
Lady of the Lake	Sir Ector
Knighthood	Camelot

Question 2. This assignment calls for a journalistic style of writing, such as might be used in newspapers, TV, and radio. Encourage the students to have fun with it, making up details as needed.

Pre-Writing. Discuss the ways in which reporters present their stories. Some newspaper reports are dry and factual, while others take a more sensational approach. Provide students with a few front page news stories from different types of papers to familiarize themselves with the styles. If a newspaper is unavailable, remind students of the way TV and radio newscasters report their stories. Have each student choose one of those styles for this assignment.

Ask students to give one or two examples of the kind of information an eyewitness would and would not know. For example, an eyewitness would not know why Arthur tried to take the sword, and a traveler might not know the significance of Arthur's feat. Have the writers reread the account of the tournament, list the events, and decide which would be known to bystanders.

Writing. Remind the students to stick to the style they chose in pre-writing. They may choose to write in the concise, no-nonsense style of a serious newspaper reporter or they may write in a broader, flashier way similar to the style of some tabloids or local news stations.

Revising. Have the students share their accounts in small groups. Ask them to decide which details were most effective in getting across a clear understanding of what happened.

Developing Skills in Study and Research

Call on students to read aloud the directions for this assignment. If possible, bring to class an encyclopedia index and a few volumes to show to the students before they begin the assignment. Make sure students are familiar with the format and purpose of encyclopedias. Give special attention to the index.

Have students complete the exercise outside of class. If you like, have them investigate the available texts in teams of two or three.

Discuss the students' findings in class.

his country. He was kind and courageous. He ignored personal danger.

Possible weaknesses: Like other men, Arthur sometimes allowed his emotions (such as love) to overrule his judgment. Also, Arthur's power was limited.

4. Only Arthur could pull the sword from the stone. Arthur used his magic sword and blinded his enemies. Merlin cast a spell on the knight. Arthur received Excalibur from the Lady of the Lake.

Challenge. This legend is written in a formal style. This is appropriate for a legend that tells about courageous heroes who should be honored and admired.

Developing Vocabulary Skills

1. unite—to make one
2. multitude—many people
3. omniscient—all-knowing
4. monarchy—rule by one person
5. dilemma—choice between two things

Developing Skills in Study and Research

Answers will vary according to the encyclopedias used.

Objectives

- To appreciate the Arthurian legend as a form of literature
- To recognize the use of a character to represent one quality
- To identify mood
- To apply literal, interpretive, and critical reading skills to a selection
- To make inferences about characters
- To recall events in the order in which they occurred
- To use prefixes and suffixes in determining word meaning
- To write a comparison of characters
- To compare the content of two or more encyclopedias
- To interpret a character's speech orally

Preparing the Students

Essential Vocabulary. The words presented here are essential to the understanding of the selection. Introduce the vocabulary listed below. Write the sentences on the board, have them read aloud, and ask students to use context clues to determine the meanings of underlined words.

potion	treachery	vessel
severity	cloister	hermitage

1. As the wizard drank his magic potion, I watched to see if its spell would work.
2. When the doctor saw the severity of Gail's injury, he rushed her to the hospital.
3. Your treachery disappoints me because I trusted you. I never imagined you would turn against me.
4. Because she was raised in a cloister by nuns, the girl had no idea what the outside world was like.
5. Lady Anne always drank her wine from a jeweled vessel which was a copy of a drinking glass used by King Henry VIII.
6. The holy man had lived alone in his hermitage on the mountain for 35 years.

Motivation. Have the students read the introduction to "The Legend of King Arthur: Part Two" on page 78. Ask them what types of qualities they would expect King Arthur's knights to have. Have them refer to Part One for help with their answers. Then remind them to compare their answers with what the legend actually tells them as they read.

Note to the teacher. You may wish to acquaint the students with some of these pronunciations:

Lancelot (län′ sə lät′)
Morgan La Fay (môr′ gən lə fā′)

The Legend of King Arthur: Part Two

A retelling of Le Morte d'Arthur by Sir Thomas Malory

Lancelot, Tristram, and Galahad are three of the bravest and noblest of King Arthur's knights. Each is faced with a different challenge. As you read, look for the qualities that enable each man to meet his challenge.

These are the stories of three of the most respected of King Arthur's knights.

Sir Lancelot

One of the finest and bravest knights of King Arthur's court was a young man named Lancelot. He became Arthur's closest friend. Earlier in his life, he had met Guinevere at her father's castle and had fallen in love with her. Now that she was King Arthur's wife, he kept his love for her in his heart and tried to avoid her in the court.

Lancelot fought valiantly in battles. No one could win over him. One night he was attacked by four knights. He killed two and the other two fled in terror.

Later, he discovered Sir Kay in the midst of a battle. He fought off the three attackers easily. Then he exchanged horses and armor with Sir Kay, so that Sir Kay could ride home in safety.

Lancelot was often pursued by the ladies of the court. Since none of them seemed to him as beautiful as Guinevere, he had no time for them. Once, Arthur's sister, Morgan Le Fay, found Lancelot asleep in a forest. She cast a spell on him and had him transported to her castle. When he woke up, four women were standing over him. They told him they knew his heart belonged to Guinevere, but he must choose one of them for his wife or face death in prison.

After thinking it over, Lancelot declared, "I choose to die rather than to have one of you as my wife. As for Guinevere, she is faithful to her husband."

Very discouraged and knowing they were defeated, the four women let Lancelot go on his way. When his friends at the court heard this story, they respected him even more.

By this time, Guinevere had learned of Lancelot's love for her. She had no desire to leave King Arthur or to offend him. Still, she enjoyed the fact that the finest knight in all the court would love no woman but her. She became jealous if she heard any rumor that Lancelot had paid attention to anyone else.

Once she believed that Lancelot had fallen in love with the lady Elaine, daughter of King Pelleas. Furious with Lancelot, Guinevere insulted him, calling him a traitor. "Leave the court immediately!" she demanded. "And never again come into my sight!"

Filled with sorrow, Lancelot went mad and fled to the countryside. Guinevere soon regretted her angry words. She sent messengers to find him, but he could not be found anywhere.

For many months, Lancelot isolated himself in the forests and lived like an animal. He survived by eating fruits and berries. He avoided all human contact. When he at last went into a town, he could not remember who he was. The people of the town, feeling sorry for the crazy man, gave him enough food to survive.

Finally, Elaine happened to see this crazy person, and she recognized Lancelot. As he slept, her knights carried him to a tower.

In the tower was hidden the most precious object in all England. Hundreds of years before, Joseph of Arimathea had come to England. This was the man who had given his tomb to the Apostles for the burial of Jesus. When Joseph arrived in England to spread the Gospel, he brought with him the cup Jesus had used at the Last Supper. This cup was called the Holy Grail. Joseph left the Grail in the keeping of a good family.

After a time the people of England fell into evil habits. They were no longer worthy to see the Holy Grail. From then on, the Grail was hidden in the tower of the good family with whom it had been left. It was that tower to which Elaine had Lancelot taken.

As Lancelot lay near the Grail, he was cured of his madness. When he awoke, he remembered who he was. He recognized Elaine and her father Pelleas. He became ashamed of his madness and what he had done while he was out of his mind.

Elaine wanted him to marry her, but Lancelot would not listen. As soon as he heard that Guinevere wanted him back in court, he returned to Camelot.

Sir Tristram

Another of King Arthur's knights was named Tristram. His name meant "sorrowful birth." He got his name from his mother shortly before she died. Tristram's mother had heard that her husband, King Melodius, had unjustly been thrown into prison. She set off to help him and died from exposure to the cold on a winter's night. The next day, King Melodius was freed. He returned home to find that his son had been born and his wife had died.

Elaine (ē lān')
Pelleas (pel' ē əs)
Arimathea (ar' ə mə thē' ə)
Melodius (mə lō' dē əs)
Tristram (tris' trəm)
Marhaus (mär' hous)
Anguish (aŋ' gwish)
Isoud (ē sōd')
Hoel (hō ël')
Galahad (gal' ə had')
Pentecost (pen' tə kôst')
Gawaine (gä' wān)

Presenting the Selection

1. Have the students read Part Two of "The Legend of King Arthur." Because this is a fairly long selection it may be more manageable if read in three parts. Assign each subheading, "Sir Lancelot," "Sir Tristram," and "Sir Galahad," as a separate assignment. (There are two **Check Test** questions for each assignment.)

2. Before assigning each section, remind the students that the introduction asked them to look for the challenges that called for special qualities in each of the knights. Encourage students to look for both the challenges and the special qualities.

3. Make sure everyone has read Part Two of the legend by administering the **Check Test** in the box at the bottom of page 83. This may be done in parts, as each reading assignment is completed, or as a whole upon completing Part Two.

4. Develop the study questions as suggested in **Using the Study Questions**, on pages 84 to 86. That section also provides challenge questions to be used for the more capable students. (For answers to the questions, see T.E. pages 84 to 86.)

Reinforcing the Lesson

To reteach, reinforce, or extend the skills in this lesson, see the following:

Skills Practice Book, Green Level—pages 45 to 50

Special Populations

ESL. Additional background history would help these students to understand some of the events in the story. Some students may not know the history of Jesus and the Last Supper, or they may not understand the value of the cup called the Holy Grail to the people of that time.

For the page 85 exercise on **Developing Vocabulary Skills**, students might need help finding the words built from base words. Present a copy of the chart on page 66 and ask the student to identify every word that contains a word part listed on the page.

The exercise under **Developing Skills in Speaking and Listening** may be difficult for ESL students or students with difficulty reading, especially if these students are asked to read aloud before the entire class. Encourage the student to practice with a partner or in a small group. Insecurity due to difficulty with syntax, vocabulary, pronunciation, verb tense or organization of ideas can hamper participation in public speaking. When the student participates in oral recitations, do not make an issue of incorrect pronunciation or different patterns of intonation. Alternative activities the instructor might use include allowing the student to tape record the reading; or allowing two or more students to read as a group or to alternate sentences; or having the student read along with a tape-recorded version of the dialog.

Making eye contact while speaking is considered impolite by some cultures. The instructor should explain that in the American culture it is important to look at the audience when speaking.

Encouraging Independent Reading

Many nonfiction books have been written about the days of chivalry and knighthood. Have the students research this historical period and develop scenery or costumes from that period of time, either in drawings or in three-dimensional form, for example, dioramas using shoe boxes. If possible, schedule time for a fashion show, and allow students to put together costumes based on historical reports of the clothing of the day.

Seven years later, King Melodius married again. His new wife became jealous of Tristram and decided to poison him. By mistake, one of her own sons drank the potion and died.

When Melodius heard about this, he condemned his wife to be burned at the stake as a traitor. Tristram begged for her life to be spared. He could not accept the severity of this punishment. The King agreed, but sent his son off for his own safety to learn the ways of knighthood.

Tristram left for France. There he learned to play beautiful music on the harp. He also learned to fight bravely, and he became a knight.

When Tristram returned home to Cornwall, he threw himself into battle. When he was fighting with the Irish Sir Marhaus, Tristram thrust his sword into his opponent's skull. Tristram's sword was chipped, and the chip stayed in Marhaus's skull. Sir Marhaus went home to Ireland to die.

Tristram had been wounded seriously in this fight. He boarded a ship, intending to go in search of a doctor who could heal him. Strong winds drove the ship to Ireland. There he was given hospitality by King Anguish. Tristram fell in love with Anguish's daughter, Isoud.

One day a servant noticed Tristram's broken sword. It matched the piece that had killed Isoud's uncle, Sir Marhaus. Tristram was asked to leave King Anguish's house immediately. Before he left, he pledged his love for Isoud. She promised to keep her love for him, too.

On his return home, Tristram talked constantly of his fair maiden Isoud. His uncle, King Mark, jealous of Tristram, decided to marry Isoud himself.

To overcome his grief at the marriage of Mark and Isoud, Tristram plunged into his duties as a knight. Once he saved a knight from being killed by two enemies and discovered that it was King Arthur he had rescued.

In gratitude, Arthur awarded Tristram a seat at his Round Table. There the knight became well known and loved. The knights and ladies of Camelot appreciated his gift for music.

Tristram's uncle, hearing of his latest honor, traveled to Camelot with two knights. He planned to surprise and kill Tristram. However, when he told his plan to the knights, they rejected it in horror. Instead, they went to King Arthur and told him of Mark's treachery. Arthur quickly had Mark arrested.

Brought before King Arthur, Mark confessed his crime. Arthur forgave him this time. However, he warned Mark that if he tried again to harm Tristram, he would be severely punished. Mark agreed to leave Tristram alone. Then he returned to Cornwall.

Trying to forget Isoud, Tristram went to Brittany in search of adventure. There he fought bravely for King Hoel. In gratitude, the king offered to Tristram marriage with his daughter, another Isoud. She was known as Isoud of the White Hands.

By now, Tristram realized that he was never to win his first love. He liked Isoud of the White Hands well enough, and he decided to marry her. They lived happily for a while, until Tristram was badly wounded in another battle. Despite the loving care of his wife, Tristram grew weaker and weaker.

Tristram remembered how badly wounded he had been when he had landed in Ireland. He remembered how Isoud, his first love, had nursed him to health. He asked his wife to send for her. Perhaps, he reasoned, she might bring him back to health again.

At first, Isoud of the White Hands agreed. She sent messengers to Cornwall to ask Isoud to come and help. If Isoud agreed to come, the ship was to return bearing white sails. If Isoud refused, the ship was supposed to use black sails.

After the ship with the messengers left, Tristram's wife began to worry. What was to stop her husband from falling in love once more with the first Isoud?

When she saw the ship return with white sails, Isoud of the White Hands made up her mind. She went to her husband where he lay ill. She told him that

the ship had returned with black sails. Tristram turned away sorrowfully.

"Alas, my beloved," Tristram sighed, "we shall never see each other again." Then he died.

When the ship landed, Isoud heard the terrible news. She was led to Tristram's bedroom. There she, too, died of grief.

The bodies of Tristram and Isoud were returned to Cornwall. King Mark sadly buried them in his own chapel.

Sir Galahad

Throughout the years, the seat at the Round Table called "Seat Perilous" had remained empty. Finally, a man came to court who was worthy to sit there.

A young man named Galahad, the son of Elaine, King Pelleas's daughter, had been raised by the nuns in a quiet cloister. He had been taught wisdom, understanding, and purity of heart. Now that Galahad had become a young adult, he had been sent out to learn the ways of knighthood.

It was the feast of Pentecost, and the knights were waiting for one of the seats at the Round Table to be filled.

A squire came into the court and told the knights that he had seen a great red stone with a sword stuck in it floating on the river. Immediately, they all rushed out to the river see if they could capture the sword. When they got there, not one man could do so. Disappointed, they returned to the court.

Later, when they were again seated at the Round Table, an old man led a young man into the room. In the young man's hand was the sword from the red rock in the river. Amazed, they watched the old man lead this young man to the Table. He led the youth to the "Seat Perilous," but now the words read, "This is the seat of Sir Galahad, the high prince." King Arthur remembered how he, too, had pulled a sword from a stone. From that moment on, Sir Galahad was treated with the greatest honor and respect.

At this same season, a vision appeared to the knights as they sat at the Round Table. There was a bright light and a clap of thunder. Then the Holy Grail, covered so that no one could see it, appeared at one end of the hall. It passed before all the knights and disappeared. After a moment Sir Galahad stood up.

"I make a holy vow," he declared. "I am starting now on a search for the Holy Grail. I will not return until I have succeeded in finding it."

All the knights knew that only a man of pure heart could see this holy vessel. In spite of this, each one of them wanted to be the first person to see it.

Every Knight of the Round Table took up the challenge to search for the Holy Grail. King Arthur's heart was filled with sadness. He knew his Round Table would never be the same. Many knights would never return from this quest.

Galahad rode off unarmed. He had no

shield to protect himself. While he was riding, he saw a white abbey. When he stopped there, a white knight told him, "Here is a shield which only you, sir, are fit to wear. Take it and ride in safety."

As Galahad rode on, he discovered the Castle of Maidens. He wounded and chased away seven knights who were barring his entrance to it. Once inside, Galahad set free hundreds of people who had been imprisoned there by the seven wicked knights he had just fought.

As he traveled on, Galahad stopped at a hermitage to share a meal with an old man who lived there. A woman came to the door and asked for him by name. "Galahad, come with me. I will show you the greatest vision you have ever seen."

She led Galahad to a ship. He, with two of his friends, Sir Bors and Sir Percival, sailed to a castle in the city of Sarras.

When they arrived, Galahad was met by the vision of Joseph of Arimathea. Joseph told Galahad that he would take him to see the Holy Grail. Galahad entered the holy place in fear and trembling. He knew that he would not survive once he had seen the vision. He also knew it would be the greatest vision he had ever seen. When he saw the Holy Grail, he fell on his knees in a state of rapture and happiness. Galahad felt his life had now been fulfilled.

He came out, briefly, to say farewell to his friends. Then his friends saw Galahad's soul carried up into the heavens. With him went the Holy Grail.

After this remarkable experience, Sir Bors entered a holy hermitage. Sir Percival returned to King Arthur's court to recount the amazing story.

Now that the search for the Holy Grail had ended, the remaining knights returned to the Round Table. King Arthur was overjoyed at their return.

Check Test

1. Whom did Lancelot love? (Guinevere)

2. What did Morgan Le Fay do to Lancelot? (She cast a spell on him.)

3. Why did Arthur have King Mark, Tristram's uncle, arrested? (because of Mark's plan to kill Tristram)

4. What did it mean if the ship sent to bring Isoud to Tristram returned bearing black sails? (that Isoud had not come)

5. How did Sir Galahad earn a seat at the Round Table? (He pulled a sword from a red stone in the river.)

6. What did all of Arthur's knights set out to find? (the Holy Grail)

Using the Study Questions

It is recommended that students always read and answer the questions in **Developing Comprehension Skills** in class discussion. Whenever possible, they should also read the questions in the other categories together and discuss the answers.

Developing Comprehension Skills

Question 1. If necessary, have students find the passage in the legend that explains the Holy Grail. Have a student read this aloud. You might explain that the great majority of people in England and Europe all practiced the same religion at this time.

Question 2. Discuss again with students what is meant by inferences. Make sure they understand that a reasonable inference is based on common sense. They should be able to use their own understanding of human nature to identify reasons for or against each lettered statement.

Question 3. Discuss what is needed for one to draw a logical conclusion. If necessary, have students reread the information on page 65 on drawing conclusions. Remind them that in this case, King Anguish is the one drawing the conclusion. Ask them if Anguish's evidence was sufficient.

Question 4. Explain to students that the answer is not stated directly. They must infer the answer from the text.

Question 5. As proof for their answers, challenge students to provide examples of the reactions of ordinary people in similar situations.

Challenge Question. Do you think Sir Galahad could have been a real person? Could the character have been based on a real person? Or was the character entirely made up? Give reasons for your answer. (Critical Reading)

Reading Literature: The Legend of King Arthur

Question 1. Make it clear that each of the three knights displays many different traits but that one particular quality of each is stressed more than others. If students suggest different answers, have the class examine each section to determine the number and importance of the instances showing each trait. Discuss the possibilities to try to come to a consensus.

Question 2. Students should be familiar with how to make a time line. Point out that only important events should be included in a time line.

Question 3. Ask the students how they felt after they read this episode. Have them identify events or even words that helped create those feelings.

Challenge Question. In both "Sir Lancelot" and "Sir Tristram" the men are in love with women, but the love is not returned or fulfilled. This is often referred to as *unrequited* love. It is seen in many works of literature. Why do you suppose this is such a common topic in literature?

Developing Vocabulary Skills

Read the directions for this exercise to the students. Ask for volunteers to explain the meaning of *base word, prefix,* and *suffix*. Briefly review with them the prefixes and suffixes on page 66. Have them complete the exercise independently. Check the answers together.

Developing Writing Skills

Read and discuss the three assignments. Then have each student choose and complete one of the three.

Question 1. Point out that this question asks students to give equal attention to King Arthur and Sir Galahad.

Pre-Writing. Discuss each of the characters. Have students list on the board notes about what each character does and how he or she acts. In the group discussion, identify some likenesses and differences. Then ask the students to decide for themselves how they will compare the two characters and to write their topic sentences, telling what the paragraph will be about.

Developing Comprehension Skills

Literal Reading

1. Explain what the Holy Grail was and how it came to be in England.

Interpretive Reading

2. Tristram's uncle, Sir Mark, wanted to marry Isoud after he found out that Tristram loved her. What inferences can you draw from this?
   a. Sir Mark was brave and gallant.
   b. Sir Mark was jealous of Tristram.
   c. Sir Mark loved Isoud and didn't want to hurt Tristram.
   d. Sir Mark cared only about himself.

Literal Reading

3. Why did King Anguish order Tristram to leave his house? What evidence upset him? What conclusion did he draw?

Interpretive Reading

4. Sir Galahad was the only man who saw the vision of the Holy Grail. What can you guess about his character that made this possible?

Critical Reading

5. Lancelot's character was shown in two extremes, as very gallant and brave in defending Sir Kay and as outraged and crazy after his fight with Guinevere. Do you think an ordinary person would act as he did in those two incidents? Give reasons for your answer.

Reading Literature: The Legend of King Arthur

1. **Examining Characters.** Lancelot, Tristram, and Galahad were three of the greatest Knights of the Round Table. Each one **represents,** or stands for, a particular quality that was admired by people who heard this legend. What quality does each of the three knights stand for? Give a reason for your answer.

2. **Making a Time Line.** As you learned in Chapter 1, a time line is a list, in order, of the main events in a story. Each event is represented by a dot printed on a straight line. (See page 18, question 2.) Choose one of the three episodes in Part 2. Make a time line for that episode.

3. **Recognizing Mood.** Each story gives its readers a certain **mood**, or feeling. For example, in the story of Sir Galahad there is a feeling of suspense and anticipation. Each event—from Galahad's appearance at court with the magic sword to his disappearance in the sky with the Grail—carries the story steadily forward. What do you think is the mood of the story of "Tristram and Isoud"? What feeling or feelings do you get reading it?

Answers to Study Questions

Developing Comprehension Skills

1. According to legend, the Holy Grail was the cup Jesus had used at the Last Supper. It was brought to England by Joseph of Arimathea, who had come to spread the Gospel.

2. b, d

3. Tristram's broken sword matched the piece that had killed Sir Marhaus. King Anguish, therefore, concluded that Tristram had killed Sir Marhaus. Because of this, he ordered Tristram from his house.

4. It was known that only a man "of pure heart" would be allowed to see anything so holy as the Grail. Therefore, Galahad must have been a good and virtuous man, better than all the other knights.

5. It is not unusual for people to react differently from one situation to another, but Lancelot's reactions are more extreme than those of the average person. His reaction to the argument with Guinevere is particularly exaggerated.

Challenge. Answers will vary. Some students may feel that there are enough realistic traits in Galahad to suggest that the character was based on a real person. Others may consider Galahad completely unrealistic, and believe that he was invented simply to teach a lesson.

Reading Literature: The Legend of King Arthur

1. Answers may vary, but the following are the most likely. Lancelot stands for honor; he kept his love for Guinevere a secret but decided not to marry anyone else. Tristram stands for goodness and kindness in spite of ill treatment and sorrow. He forgave his enemies. Galahad stands for purity of heart. Only he was able to see the Holy Grail.

Developing Vocabulary Skills

Using Prefixes and Suffixes To Determine Word Meaning. Each of the following sentences from "The Legend of King Arthur" includes a word built from a base word and one of the prefixes and suffixes discussed on page 66. Identify the word, separate it into its base word and prefix or suffix, and tell what it means.

1. The Holy Grail passed before all the knights and then disappeared.
2. Furious with Lancelot, Guinevere insulted him, calling him a traitor.
3. Tristram saved a knight from being killed by two enemies and discovered that it was King Arthur he had rescued.
4. Arthur slid the sword from the stone with an effortless pull.
5. Arthur was always at the front of the battle, doing marvelous deeds of arms.
6. The sorrowful Tristram died when he thought Isoud would not come to him.
7. Lancelot told the women that Guinevere was faithful to her husband.
8. The knights dismounted and fought with swords.

Developing Writing Skills

Analytical Writing

1. **Comparing Characters.** Compare Sir Galahad with King Arthur. Think about what each one does. Also think about what sort of person each one is. How are they alike? How are they different? Write at least one paragraph comparing the two characters.

Creative Writing

2. **Creating Other Solutions.** When Lancelot faced the trickery of Morgan Le Fay and the other women, he made a daring statement and they spared his life. How else could he have outwitted them? Write an original solution to his problem. Keep Lancelot's character true to the legend: He would never harm the women or forget his love for Guinevere.

Creative Writing

3. **Writing a New Ending.** Is there any way that the story of Tristram and Isoud could have a happy ending? Write a new ending for the story. Keep the characters the same but change enough of the happenings to make a different ending.

Writing. Remind students to use the notes on the board. Suggest that they compare the two characters in a logical order. They could describe one character first and then the other, or they could compare them trait by trait.

Revising. Have students exchange papers with a partner. The partner should point out any sentences he or she doesn't understand. The partner should also be able to tell at least one important way in which Arthur and Galahad are alike or different.

Question 2. Make sure the students see that Lancelot himself must solve his problem: they may not introduce a new character, such as King Arthur or Merlin, to get Lancelot out of his difficulty.

Pre-Writing. Review on page 78 the part of the story this question deals with. Have students meet in small groups of three or four to brainstorm possible new solutions to the problem.

Writing. Allow sufficient time for students to write their first drafts. Remind them to keep Lancelot's character the same as it was in the legend.

Revising. Have students share their finished stories orally or in a classroom display. You may wish to have the group decide which version blends in with the rest of the legend best.

Question 3. This question asks students to change the ending of the story of Tristram and Isoud. Some students may welcome this assignment since the story was so sad.

Pre-Writing. Ask students to skim the story of Tristram to find turning points where the story could be changed. They may find it helpful to refer to the time lines they developed for **Reading Literature, 2,** above. Suggest that students plan the new story in their minds or in rough

2. The time line for Lancelot's story may include the following events:

a. Lancelot falls in love with Guinevere.
b. Lancelot saves Sir Kay.
c. Morgan Le Fay casts a spell on Lancelot; he says he'd rather die than marry anyone but Guinevere.
d. Guinevere becomes jealous and orders Lancelot to leave the court.
e. Lancelot flees and goes mad.
f. Elaine takes Lancelot to a tower where the Holy Grail is kept.
g. Lancelot is cured of madness and returns to Camelot.

The time line for Tristram's story may include the following:

a. Tristram's mother dies; Melodius remarries.
b. Tristram's stepmother tries to kill him, fails, and is forgiven by Tristram.
c. Tristram goes to France and becomes a knight.
d. Tristram returns to Cornwall, fights Sir Marhaus, and is wounded.
e. He travels to Ireland for a cure and falls in love with Isoud.
f. King Anguish banishes Tristram from Ireland.
g. Tristram's uncle marries Isoud.
h. Tristram saves King Arthur in a fight and becomes a member of the Round Table.
i. King Mark plots to kill Tristram and is sent back to Cornwall.
j. Tristram goes to Brittany and marries Isoud of the White Hands.
k. Tristram is wounded in battle and requests Isoud to come.
l. Isoud of the White Hands lies to Tristram and he dies of grief.

The time line for Galahad's story may include the following:

(continued on page 86)

notes. Some might prefer writing out a more complete, informal outline.

Writing. Remind students to be sure that events follow each other logically. Have them make the connection between events clear.

Revising. Have students share their stories in small groups. Encourage members of the group to tell the writer when events are not logically connected. Allow time for revisions and for the students to write clean copies. See also the T.E. suggestions for revision of Question 2, above.

Developing Skills in Study and Research

Read the exercise on page 86 to the students and discuss it with them to make sure they understand what is required.

Students should be familiar with encyclopedias from the **Study and Research** assignment following the first part of "The Legend of King Arthur." Point out to students that the purpose of the exercise on page 86 is to compare two encyclopedias and then make a judgment about which one is more useful to them.

Developing Skills in Speaking and Listening

Talk with students about how language changes with time. This can be done by presenting examples of dated slang, for example, *twenty-three skidoo, the cat's meow, groovy.* Another technique would be to have students listen to recordings of parts of Shakespeare's plays or the words of writers from other eras to hear how the style of language has changed.

Then have the students read and discuss this assignment. Set a time for students to read to the class, and have them prepare independently.

Developing Skills in Study and Research

Comparing Encyclopedias. Most school and local libraries have at least two different sets of encyclopedias. One reason for this is that each encyclopedia includes slightly different amounts of information. One encyclopedia may provide more information on one topic, while a second encyclopedia may tell more about a different topic.

Look up each of these topics in at least two different encyclopedias. Compare the amount and the kinds of information given by the different encyclopedias. Which encyclopedia has more lines of writing about the topics? Which one has more pictures, charts, or maps? Which one looks easier to read and understand? If you were going to buy one of the sets, which one would you choose?

Arthur *or* King Arthur
Knights *or* Knighthood
Legends
Britain, Great Britain, *or* United Kingdom

Developing Skills in Speaking and Listening

Interpreting a Character's Speech. In "The Legend of King Arthur," the characters use a language that is a bit more formal than our everyday language. This helps to make the characters sound like the knights and ladies they were. Choose one of the characters whose exact words are given in one of the passages. Prepare to read that character's words to the class. Make sure you speak clearly, so that everyone can hear each word. However, try to make the words sound natural, as if the character would normally speak that way.

(continued from page 85)

a. Galahad is raised in a cloister.
b. Galahad takes the sword from the red stone and gains Seat Perilous at the Round Table.
c. The Knights of the Round Table share a vision of the Holy Grail and decide to search for it.
d. Galahad is given a special shield.
e. Galahad saves the Castle of Maidens.
f. Galahad, Bors, and Percival sail to Sarras where Galahad meets a vision of Joseph of Arimathea.
g. Galahad sees the Holy Grail and his soul is carried up to heaven.

3. The mood is one of sadness. Things seem to keep going wrong for Tristram. There seems to be nothing he can do about it; it is his fate.

Challenge. The fact that the characters are unhappy in love makes for a more interesting story. Every story needs some sort of conflict, and the unrequited love often provides that conflict.

Developing Vocabulary Skills

1. disappeared; dis-, appeared; did not appear
2. furious; fury, -ous; full of fury
3. discovered; dis-, covered; uncovered
4. effortless; effort, -less; without effort
5. marvelous; marvel, -ous; full of marvels
6. sorrowful; sorrow, -full; full of sorrow
7. faithful; faith, -ful; having faith
8. dismounted; dis-, mounted; got off

Developing Skills in Study and Research

Answers will vary according to encyclopedias used.

The Legend of King Arthur: Part Three

A retelling of Le Morte d'Arthur by Sir Thomas Malory

King Arthur loves his queen, Guinevere. He also values highly the trust and friendship of his knights. What happens when he must choose between wife and friends? Is there any easy solution?

Spring was at hand, so Queen Guinevere decided to go "a-Maying." She and ten of her knights went out, unarmed, to pick the lovely flowers from the fields.

Sir Meliagrance, who had fallen in love with the Queen, seized this opportunity to strike. He rode out into the field to capture the Queen. When he declared his love and asked her to come with him, she responded angrily. She told him she would rather cut her throat than go with him. However, when his men began attacking her unarmed knights, she agreed to go with him if her knights could go, too.

When they arrived at Meliagrance's castle, Queen Guinevere waited for her chance. Then she sent a secret message to Sir Lancelot telling him of her plight. Lancelot set out immediately. While he was still at a distance, Meliagrance's men shot his horse from under him. Lancelot walked a long way, hampered by his heavy armor. Then he borrowed a woodsman's cart to ride the rest of the way.

When he finally arrived at the castle, Lancelot shouted to Meliagrance that the "knight of the cart" had come to fight. Meliagrance, knowing he couldn't win against Lancelot, begged and obtained mercy from the Queen. Lancelot, greatly disappointed that he couldn't fight with Meliagrance, rode away with Guinevere and delivered her safely home.

The Breakup of the Round Table

Two of King Arthur's nephews, Sir Mordred and Sir Agravaine, hated Queen Guinevere. They knew their words would be much more powerful than their swords. Therefore, they began to plant vicious rumors about the love Queen Guinevere felt for Sir Lancelot.

Together, they set a trap for Lancelot. They arranged for King Arthur to stay out hunting one night. Then they hid outside Guinevere's chamber. As they had hoped,

Objectives

- To appreciate the Arthurian Legend as a form of literature
- To make inferences about character motivation
- To draw conclusions concerning the author's purpose
- To recognize themes of a legend
- To apply literal, interpretive, and critical reading skills to a selection
- To form words with affixes
- To present an opinion in writing, providing reasons for it
- To become familiar with specialized reference books
- To interpret the mood of a selection orally

Preparing the Students

Essential Vocabulary. The words presented here are essential to the understanding of the selection.

Introduce the vocabulary listed below. Write the sentences on the board, have them read aloud, and ask students to use context clues to determine the meanings of the underlined words.

chaos banishment woe
penance councilors

1. There was total chaos during the fire drill, with people crowding out doors, tripping down steps, shouting, and running in different directions.
2. His penance for breaking the window was mowing and raking the lawn for one month.
3. Punished by banishment, the knight was never allowed to return to his homeland.
4. The king called his council together to get the advice of his councilors.
5. Helen was filled with unbearable woe when she learned of the death of her parents.

Motivation. Have the introductory paragraph on page 87 read aloud. Ask students to explain why it is sometimes necessary to choose between friends. If they can, have them present examples of this situation. Ask them what could possibly make it necessary for a king to choose between his wife and his friends.

Note to the teacher. You may wish to acquaint the students with some of these pronunciations:

Gawaine (gä' wān)
Meliagrance (mə lé ə grans')
Mordred (môr' drid)
Agravaine (aǵ rə vān')
Lucan (lo͞o' kən)
Bedivere (bed' ə vir')

Presenting the Selection

1. "The Legend of King Arthur: Part Three" is a long selection. It is advisable to assign it in several segments. There are five episodes in Part Three. You may want to handle each episode as a separate assignment, group the first three and the last two, or have the introductory episode read aloud in class and the following episodes assigned in two's. If you like, you can administer the **Check Test** in parts, as described in Step 3, below.

2. Remind students of the questions raised in the introduction. Have several students give their answers.

3. Make sure everyone has read the selection by administering the **Check Test** at the bottom of page 94 of this T.E. This may be done at the conclusion of Part Three or upon completion of each reading assignment. Question 1 pertains to the introductory section, questions 2 through 4 to "The Breakup of the Round Table," question 5 to "Sir Mordred," questions 6 and 7 to "The End of the Round Table," and question 8 to "Lancelot and Guinevere."

4. Develop the study questions as suggested in **Using the Study Questions**, on pages 94 through 97.

Reinforcing the Lesson

To reteach, reinforce, or extend the skills in this lesson, see the following:

Skills Practice Book, Green Level—pages 51 to 56

Encouraging Independent Reading

Students who enjoy the elements of magic, fantasy, and adventure that pervade these legends may enjoy reading the *Lord of the Ring* series by J.R.R. Tolkien. Mythological creatures, quests, dangers, and valor are all present in this modern "legend."

Special Populations

ESL. For the exercise in **Developing Skills in Speaking and Listening** on interpreting mood, portions of the story could be taped for listening by ESL students. Students should read along, gaining practice in intonation, phrasing, and pronunciation, while learning to express the mood of the story by raising and

Lancelot came to talk with the queen. As soon as he entered her room, they pounded on the door.

"Come out, traitor," they cried.

Lancelot had no choice. He had to open the door to try to escape. When he did so, the fight began.

Lancelot wounded Mordred. He killed Agravaine and the other knights. Finally, he escaped. Mordred rushed to tell King Arthur about Lancelot's disloyalty and his killing of the knights.

King Arthur's heart was broken. He could no longer trust his queen or his good friend Lancelot. They must both be punished.

One of Arthur's nephews, Sir Gawaine, was a good friend of Lancelot. He argued in Lancelot's defense. "Lancelot has defended the queen several times," Gawaine pointed out. "Perhaps she called him to her chamber to reward him. And perhaps she feared the rumors that would start if he were seen visiting her. That may be why she called him at night, when she thought no one was about.

"Lancelot is your best friend, your finest knight. You must believe that he and your queen wish you no harm."

Still, Mordred argued strongly against Gawaine. "They have loved each other for a long time. Everyone knows it!"

At last, Mordred convinced Arthur that Guinevere was guilty. Sorrowfully, the king sentenced Guinevere to be burned at the stake for treason.

Just as the wood piled about Guinevere was to be set afire, Lancelot rushed in with his forces and saved the queen. He rode off with her to his castle, Joyous Gard. In the chaos of the fight and the escape, Lancelot unknowingly killed two brothers of his friend Sir Gawaine.

When Gawaine heard that news, his friendship turned to vengeful hatred.

Hearing all that had taken place, King Arthur arrived with his men to lay siege on Lancelot's castle. For fifteen weeks Lancelot kept his men inside, refusing to fight Arthur.

At last Arthur stood before Lancelot's castle and called to him, "Come forth, if you dare, and fight me!"

"I cannot fight my king, the man who made me a knight," Lancelot replied.

"I am no longer your king! I am your enemy! You have killed my men and stolen my queen."

"I never wanted to hurt your men. They forced me to, in order to save myself. And how could I let your innocent queen die because of me? I had fought to defend her often enough before. I am heartily willing to return her to you. She is here only for her safety. She is true to you. Take her back, I beg you, and end this needless war."

Arthur weakened. He wanted to believe his old friend. Yet, Sir Gawaine remembered his dead brothers.

"Liar! Traitor! Killer!" Gawaine yelled. "I will forever make war against you!"

"I repent of your brothers' deaths," Lancelot said. "I will do whatever penance you ask."

Gawaine would not listen. Angrily he reminded Arthur of all the evidence against Lancelot and Guinevere. He pointed out the damage they had caused to the Round Table. Arthur once again resolved to fight Lancelot, and he broke off discussions with him. Sadly, Lancelot told his men that they could leave the castle to fight. He ordered them, however, not to harm his friends Arthur and Gawaine.

For the next several days, the fighting was hard and bloody. Several times Lancelot came upon Arthur and Gawaine. Each time he held back from killing either man. When he saw his own men attacking his old friends, he stepped in to save Arthur and Gawaine.

Hundreds of knights were killed on both sides. The number of deaths became

lowering their voices, and by speeding up or slowing down the dialog. Allow students to read along with a partner or to mimic the vocal expressions of a partner during practice readings.

so great that the Pope decided to intervene. He issued a decree that Arthur must take back Queen Guinevere and that peace must once again exist between King Arthur and Sir Lancelot.

Lancelot sent word to King Arthur that he would personally deliver the queen back to the court. The queen's ladies and knights arrived riding in a procession, all dressed in the finest green velvet. Behind them rode Lancelot and Guinevere, dressed in robes of white. They dismounted and knelt before the king. All who stood by wept.

Lancelot addressed the king in his finest words. He repeated what he had said before the battle. He blamed all the trouble on lies and swore unending loyalty to Arthur. Once more he asked that their friendship begin anew.

Gawaine, at Arthur's side, answered first. "The king may do as he pleases," Gawaine said bitterly, "but I will never forgive you."

"I am taking back Guinevere as my queen only because the Pope has commanded me to do so," Arthur stated wearily. "As for you, I will not fight you. But you must leave Camelot at once, forever."

Lancelot, hearing these words, turned and rode away. He bent his head in the deepest sorrow he had ever known.

Feeling he had lost everything, Lancelot called his knights together. He told them about his banishment from King Arthur's court. They cried, "We will remain with you forever. Wherever you go, we go."

Lancelot felt comforted. Together, he and his knights sailed for France. When they arrived, they were well accepted. Their reputation for helping the poor and downtrodden had preceded them.

Sir Mordred

Even though Lancelot had declared his sorrow at killing Gawaine's brothers, Gawaine was not satisfied with Lancelot's banishment. He continued to stir up King Arthur to take revenge. Despite the Pope's order, Arthur decided to take up the fight with Lancelot once again.

Before leaving for France, King Arthur gave his nephew Mordred complete charge of his kingdom and power to rule over his affairs.

Lancelot, hearing of Arthur's and Gawaine's arrival in France, sent a message to them, begging for peace. They would not hear of it, and the siege began again.

Both sides were equally matched. Hundreds were again killed in battle. Lancelot seriously wounded Gawaine. The battle raged on for months.

In the midst of the fighting, King Arthur received word that Sir Mordred had taken over all his lands in England. Mordred had ordered his men to write from abroad proclaiming that King Arthur had been killed. He had persuaded the Archbishop to crown him king. Now he was planning to make Guinevere his queen.

Guinevere had reluctantly agreed to Mordred's demands, but she first made a special request. She asked to travel to London to buy a new wardrobe. Mordred agreed. Once in the city, Guinevere locked herself up in the Tower of London to protect herself from Mordred.

King Arthur and his men left the siege in France and quickly returned to England. Mordred and his men attacked them as they left their ships. Sir Gawaine, not fully recovered from the wound Lancelot had given him in France, was again wounded seriously. Arthur found him lying half-dead. The king mourned, "Are you going to leave me too? You and Lancelot were my best knights. Will I lose you both? In you two I most had my joy. Losing you, I will lose all joy in life."

Sir Gawaine, realizing death was near, at last regretted his actions.

"I see now," he said, "that my willfulness has caused this disaster. If I had forgiven Lancelot, you and he would have come to terms. Then he would have been at your side, and this war with Mordred would never have begun. And now you will miss Lancelot."

Then Gawaine asked for ink and paper. He wrote a letter to Lancelot, asking his forgiveness for the pain he had caused. He begged Lancelot to come to Arthur's aid. Then he took his last breath.

The End of the Round Table

On the next morning, Arthur's army took the field against Mordred's. Many were slain, but at the end Mordred fled. Arthur took several days to have the dead buried and to let the wounded recover. Then he set a date to meet Mordred again.

The night before the battle, Arthur had a strange dream. In the dream Gawaine appeared to him.

"I advise you," Gawaine said, "in no way should you go to battle tomorrow. If you fight tomorrow, you will cause your own death and the death of many others. Postpone the battle for a month. By then Lancelot will arrive and slay Mordred."

Then Gawaine vanished.

Arthur told his councilors about his dream. He asked them to make a treaty with Mordred. In order to postpone the battle, he would agree to any conditions.

The councilors arranged the treaty. All that was left was for Arthur and Mordred to meet to complete the arrangements. Each was to bring fourteen men.

Before going to the meeting, Arthur warned his men, "I don't trust my nephew. This may be a trap. If any sword is drawn, strike immediately." Mordred gave his men the same message.

While they were negotiating, a snake crawled onto a knight's foot and bit him. Without thinking, the knight pulled his sword and struck at the snake. With that movement, fighting broke out at once.

The battle raged all day. Hundreds of men were killed. At the end, King Arthur had only two knights left, Sir Lucan and Sir Bedivere. Sir Mordred stood alone.

"Look, Sir Lucan," Arthur cried, "there is the man who has caused all this woe. Give me my spear."

"Sir," Lucan argued, "remember your dream. Leave him alone. We can finish this tomorrow."

Arthur ignored the warning. He shouted to Mordred, "Even if this is the end of me, I will not leave this life without killing such a traitor as you are, Mordred."

With that, Arthur grabbed his spear and ran at Mordred. The spear passed into Mordred and through his body. Mordred knew he was dying. Despite the spear, he pushed himself closer to Arthur and brought his sword down on Arthur's helmet. The blow was so strong that it cut through the helmet and into Arthur's head. Then Mordred fell dead.

Sir Lucan and Sir Bedivere carried Arthur to a chapel near the lake to recover. Arthur said to Bedivere, "Take my sword, Excalibur, and throw it into the water. Then tell me what you see."

Twice Sir Bedivere pretended to do so, each time returning and saying nothing had happened. Arthur said to him, "Would you betray me at the very end? Do as I say!"

Bedivere finally threw the sword into the water. As soon as he did so, an arm and a hand reached out of the water, grabbed the sword, shook it three times, and vanished with the sword underneath the water.

Arthur was greatly relieved when he heard the report. "Now," he said, "take me to the waterside."

When Sir Bedivere carried him there, they found a small barge on the lake. In the boat were Arthur's sister, Morgan Le Fay, and two other women. The women took Arthur into the boat and rowed him across the lake.

Sir Bedivere cried, "My lord Arthur, what will become of me? You are leaving me alone among my enemies!"

"Comfort yourself," Arthur replied. "Do as well as you can by yourself, for in

me there is nothing left to trust. I am going to the valley of Avalon. If you never hear of me again, pray for my soul."

The next morning Sir Bedivere discovered a chapel with a freshly-dug grave outside it. The hermit who lived at the chapel said that during the night several women had brought to him the body of a warrior to be buried.

Bedivere knew that the warrior must have been King Arthur. He decided to stay in this chapel and spend the rest of his life in prayer and fasting.

Lancelot and Guinevere

The news finally reached Lancelot that Sir Mordred had been crowned King of England and would not allow Arthur to return. He also heard that Guinevere had locked herself up in the Tower of London for safety.

Quickly, Lancelot gathered his men and returned to England. In the meantime, Guinevere, learning that Arthur had been killed, fled to the peace and quiet of a convent in Almesbury.

Arriving in England, Lancelot learned about King Arthur's death. He set out to search for Guinevere. He finally found her in the cloister where she was living.

When Guinevere saw Lancelot, she cried, "Lancelot, because of us, a good king and thousands of knights have been killed. We must never see each other again. I will stay here and live a life of prayer. You must leave at once."

Using the Study Questions

It is recommended that students always read and answer the questions in **Developing Comprehension Skills** in class discussion. Whenever possible, they should also read the questions in the other categories together and discuss the answers.

Developing Comprehension Skills

Question 1. After the students read the question, allow a few minutes for them to review the story. Then have the class work together to select and list the major events of the story. Frequently ask the students to identify the cause and effect relationships linking the events; this will both improve comprehension and help order the time line events. See also the Challenge Question below.

Question 2. Before having the students answer this question, discuss the concept of cause and effect. Explain that every action has a cause. Give students some examples. Provide the cause and let them provide the effect.

Example:

Cause: It rained for three days in a row.

Effect:

Then provide the effect and let students provide the cause.

Example:

Effect: She missed school for a week.

Cause:

Question 3. If necessary, review main ideas and details, pages 4 and 5.

Question 4. Encourage each student to present a personal opinion to answer the second half of the question.

Question 5. Ask students to explain what is meant by inference and then discuss the question.

Lancelot left, greatly saddened, knowing that he, too, must find peace. As he rode along, he heard a bell ringing from a chapel. There he found Sir Bedivere and vowed to spend the rest of his life at the chapel with his friend and the hermit who had buried Arthur.

Six years went by. One day Lancelot received a sad message. Guinevere had died, leaving a note for Lancelot. She asked that he bury her beside her husband, King Arthur. Lancelot obeyed her request and brought her body back to the chapel.

There, he and the others buried Guinevere in a grave next to that of Arthur. Losing all interest in life, Lancelot grieved for the death of his king and his queen. He sorrowed for his part in the destruction of their kingdom.

And there, in six weeks, Lancelot died. His body was carried to his castle, Joyous Gard, as he had requested. At last he would rest in peace.

Developing Comprehension Skills

Literal Reading

1. Make a time line showing the end of King Arthur's reign. Begin with Mordred's setting the trap for Lancelot and Guinevere. Show all the important events. Be sure to include each point at which Arthur makes a major decision.

Literal Reading

2. Find a reason stated in the story for each of these actions:
   a. Gawaine's friendship for Lancelot turned to hate.
   b. King Arthur stopped fighting Lancelot in France and returned to England.
   c. Guinevere locked herself up in the Tower of London.
   d. Bedivere threw Excalibur into the lake.

Interpretive Reading

3. Reread paragraph 2 on page 90. The main idea of the paragraph is that Lancelot brought Guinevere back to Camelot. Identify two or three important details in this paragraph. Then identify two less important details.

Critical Reading

4. When Sir Gawaine lay dying, he realized that Arthur needed Lancelot's friendship and help. He also saw that Arthur and Lancelot would have made up their quarrel long before if only he, Gawaine, had not stood between them. How did Sir Gawaine try to correct this situation before he died? Do you feel he was doing the right thing? Tell why or why not.

Check Test

1. What means of travel did Lancelot use to rescue Guinevere from Sir Meliagrance's castle? (horse, foot, and cart)

2. Who set the trap for Lancelot and Guinevere? (Mordred and Agravaine)

3. Why did Sir Gawaine begin to hate Lancelot? (Lancelot killed two of his brothers.)

4. Why did Arthur take Guinevere back? (The Pope ordered him to take her back.)

5. Where did Guinevere go after Mordred said he was going to marry her? (the Tower of London)

6. What warned Arthur of disaster if he were to fight Mordred? (Gawaine appeared to him in a dream.)

7. How did Arthur leave Sir Bedivere? (He was carried off on a barge with his sister, Morgan Le Fay, and two other women.)

8. Where was Guinevere when she died? (in a convent)

Answers to Study Questions

Developing Comprehension Skills

1. The time line may include these events (*indicates major decision):

a. Mordred and Agravaine arrange for Arthur to be out hunting.
b. Lancelot comes to talk with Guinevere, is accused of treason, and must fight his way out.
*c. Arthur decides that Lancelot and Guinevere have betrayed him and sentences Guinevere to be burned at the stake.

Interpretive Reading

5. After Arthur's death, both Lancelot and Guinevere chose to live the rest of their lives in prayer and fasting. Which of the following inferences can be reasonably drawn from that fact?
   a. Lancelot and Guinevere were searching for peace.
   b. They were tired of the glory of King Arthur's court.
   c. They wanted to repent for their part in causing Arthur's death.
   d. They were hiding from enemies.

Reading Literature: The Legend of King Arthur

1. **Recognizing Contrasts.** Part 3 begins with the story sometimes called "The Knight of the Cart" and ends with the death of Guinevere and Lancelot. What are some of the contrasts that you see between the two episodes? Are the characters the same, or have they changed? How has the setting changed? Is the mood of the story (the feeling it gives you) the same in the two episodes? What other differences do you find?
2. **Recognizing the Author's Purpose.** Review your answer for the question above. Then suggest an answer for this question: Why did the author begin this section with the story of the knight of the cart?
3. **Understanding Reasons for Actions.** The story states that Mordred and Agravaine hated Queen Guinevere and plotted against her and Lancelot. It does not state reasons for their hate. Consider what happened both before and after they hatched their plot. Can you infer any reasons for Mordred's eagerness to make Lancelot look bad? Can you think of any possible reasons for Agravaine's attitude?
4. **Examining Characters.** In Part 2, the characters of Lancelot, Tristram, and Galahad were not drawn very fully. Each character could stand for a single human quality. In Part 3, however, the characters are drawn more fully. Arthur, Lancelot, Gawaine, and Mordred all have good qualities and bad qualities. Choose one of these four characters. Describe both the good and bad qualities of this character. Tell whether you think the character is believable—that is, whether you learn enough about him to believe he could be a real person you might know.
5. **Recognizing Themes.** A **theme** is a general statement that the writer makes about life. For example, in Part 1 the writer pictured Sir Ector

Challenge Question. The plot becomes extremely complicated after Arthur no longer trusts Guinevere and Lancelot. How else might Arthur have reacted? How would the plot have been changed in that case? (Critical Reading)

Reading Literature: The Legend of King Arthur

Question 1. Have students cite examples from both episodes to prove what changes have taken place. Have them note how the characters act and what they say. Help them to find specific words and phrases in each episode that help develop the mood.

Question 2. If students do not come up with the idea of contrast on their own, ask whether they would choose to paint a picture of a white rabbit on snow or a black bird in shadows. Have them provide reasons for avoiding such combinations, and point out that a good writer, too, tries to avoid monotony and to highlight changes.

Question 3. Encourage students to think creatively about the clues suggested in the question.

Question 4. Encourage students to see that even heroes have weaknesses and villains usually have some good points.

Question 5. Have students quote examples from the selection to show how Arthur dealt with his friends and how he felt about friendship. Help the students to state themes about friendship in general terms that can apply to everyone, not just the characters in this story.

Developing Vocabulary Skills

Be sure students understand the directions to the exercise. If necessary, review the discussion of base words, suffixes, and prefixes on page 66. Have each

d. Lancelot rescues Guinevere, killing Sir Gawaine's brothers in the fight.
*e. Lancelot's efforts to satisfy Arthur fail, and Arthur's and Lancelot's armies fight.
f. The Pope declares Arthur must take back Guinevere and make peace with Lancelot.
*g. Lancelot is banished; he goes to Britanny.
*h. Arthur leaves England to fight Lancelot again.
i. Mordred takes over Arthur's lands, is crowned King, and demands Guinevere for his queen.
*j. Guinevere goes to London and locks herself in the Tower of London; Arthur brings his army back to fight Mordred.
k. Gawaine is fatally wounded and writes to Lancelot for forgiveness and for help for Arthur.
*l. As he plans for battle Arthur receives a warning from Gawaine in a dream; his councilors arrange a treaty.
m. During negotiations, a knight strikes a snake and the battle begins again.
*n. Despite the warning in his dream, Arthur kills Mordred and is himself fatally wounded.
o. Arthur has Bedivere throw Excalibur into the water.
*p. Arthur is taken across the lake to Avalon in a barge; he is never seen again.

2. Reasons for actions are:
a. Lancelot killed two brothers of Gawaine.
b. Arthur received word that Mordred had taken over his lands and planned to make Guinevere his queen.

(continued on page 96)

student complete the exercise independently and discuss the answers.

Developing Writing Skills

Read and discuss the two assignments. Then have each student choose and complete one of the two.

Question 1. The question asks students to present an opinion supported by details from the story. A wide variety of opinions is possible.

Pre-Writing. Ask students who they feel was responsible for the ruin of Arthur's court and why that person was to blame. List the names on the board. Discuss at which points in the story it would have been possible to change the course of events. Encourage a variety of opinions. Make sure that students recognize that not everyone will accept an opinion not supported by evidence or good reasons. Have each student write a topic sentence telling his or her opinion about who or what destroyed the kingdom. Ask each student to list three reasons for that opinion. Remind them that they don't have to blame just one person.

Writing. Have students support their opinions with reasons and details from the story.

Revising. Have students exchange papers with a partner. If the partner cannot restate the topic sentence or explain the writer's reasoning, have the writer revise his or her paragraph.

Question 2. Let the students know how much detail you would like to see in this answer, from a one- or two-paragraph summary to a story that uses description and direct quotations.

Pre-Writing. Have the students form small groups and brainstorm to come up with possible solutions to Guinevere's problem. Have one student serve as secretary.

as wise, honest, and concerned about both his son and his foster son. In this way, the writer made the statement that a good knight could also be a good and loving father.

In Part 3, the writer is very concerned about the idea of friendship and the demands that friendships make on a person. Review what Arthur does in his struggle to keep both of his friends, Lancelot and Gawaine. Reread Arthur's statements to his friends, particularly to the dying Gawaine. What are some of the statements about friendship that you find in this legend?

Developing Vocabulary Skills

Forming Words with Prefixes and Suffixes. In each sentence below, a word is missing. The base word is given in parentheses, but one of the prefixes or suffixes from page 66 must be added to the base word. Read the rest of the sentence. Choose the correct **affix** (prefix or suffix) that will change the base word into a word that makes sense in the sentence. On your paper, write the complete sentence, filling in the new word.

1. Guinevere caused problems when she acted in a ___(thought)___ manner.
2. The damage to the Round Table could never be repaired; in other words, it was ___(reparable)___.
3. When Arthur became king, the identity of his father was ___(known)___.
4. For several weeks, Lancelot raved in delirium. Elaine found him while he was ___(wit)___.
5. It was ___(legal)___ for a knight to visit the Queen alone.
6. Despite his ___(sorrow)___ life, Tristram brought music and many pleasant moments to the people of the court.
7. Galahad was noted for his ___(truthful)___ and other virtues.
8. Merlin accomplished by magic many tasks that were otherwise ___(possible)___.

Developing Writing Skills

Analytical Writing

1. **Presenting Your Opinion.** Who was responsible for the ruin of King Arthur's court? Was it one person? Was it a combination of people? Was there any one point at which a different decision by Lancelot or

(continued from page 95)

c. Guinevere wanted to avoid marrying Mordred.

d. Arthur was dying and ordered Bedivere to throw the sword in the lake.

3. Some important details are that Lancelot sent word to Arthur that he would personally deliver the queen back to the court, Lancelot and Guinevere arrived behind the queen's ladies and knights, and they knelt before the king. Some less important details are that the ladies and knights were dressed in green velvet, Lancelot and Guinevere dressed in white, and all who stood by, wept.

4. Sir Gawaine wrote to Lancelot asking forgiveness for the pain he had caused and asking Lancelot to help Arthur. Answers to the second part of the question will vary, but most students will agree that Gawaine was probably correct in doing this, hoping to make amends.

5. a, c

Challenge. Answers may vary. Arthur may have chosen to believe in Lancelot and Guinevere. If he had, it is possible that the Round Table would not have been destroyed.

Reading Literature: The Legend of King Arthur

1. Between the first and last episodes, much has changed. In the beginning, Guinevere and Lancelot act almost like children—Guinevere goes "a-Maying" and Lancelot is disappointed when he doesn't get to fight Sir Meliagrance. They are still friends with Arthur. The kingdom is at peace. The mood of the story is adventurous and cheerful.

By the end, Guinevere and Lancelot have grown older and wiser. They live with guilt because they have caused many deaths and Arthur, whom they have hurt,

Gawaine or Arthur could have saved the kingdom? State your opinion and give reasons.

Creative Writing

2. **Writing a New Legend.** In the story of the knight of the cart, Guinevere saves her unarmed knights but must wait for Lancelot to free all of them from Sir Meliagrance. Write a new ending to this episode. Have Guinevere outwit Meliagrance and free herself and her knights. However, do not use any modern inventions in your new legend. All of the characters and the setting should remain the same as they are described in the original legend.

Developing Skills in Study and Research

Finding Other Reference Sources. A general encyclopedia has articles on topics in many fields—history, science, literature, art, and so on. There are also encyclopedias in special fields, such as history, science, literature, and art. A school library or public library will have numerous specialized encyclopedias and other reference books as well as general encyclopedias.

Examine the reference section of your school or local library. Make a list of any reference books in which you can find information about either the book entitled *Le Morte d'Arthur* or its author, Sir Thomas Malory. Write down both the title and the author(s) or editor(s) of each reference book on your list.

Developing Skills in Speaking and Listening

Interpreting Mood. Do this activity with a partner. One member of the team should prepare to tell the story of the knight of the cart, while the other should prepare "The End of the Round Table."

First, review your answers to the first question in Reading Literature: The Legend of King Arthur. Decide what the mood is in the story of the knight of the cart and in "The End of the Round Table." Decide for each story whether you want your listeners to laugh or to cry. Then prepare your story. You may read the text. If you prefer, you may tell the story in your own words, adding details to make the effect you want.

Then tell your stories, one after another, to a group. Ask the group to let you know if the mood of each story was clear and different from the other.

Writing. He or she should record the ideas and read them back to the group frequently. Encourage all students to participate to make sure their group has a good legend. You might ask each group to write a new legend, or have the groups separate so that each member can write independently. Remind students to keep the characters and setting the same.

Revising. Have the groups (or students) share their legends with each other orally and choose the legend that has the most creative solution.

Developing Skills in Study and Research

Read and discuss the exercise. Review with the students how they can discover if information about *Le Morte D'Arthur* or Sir Thomas Malory is contained in a particular set of reference books (by using the index). Discuss sources likely to have such information, including biographical dictionaries and literary reference works.

Assign the work for independent completion or to be done by teams. Later, discuss the students' findings.

Developing Skills in Speaking and Listening

Read and discuss the exercise on **Interpreting Mood** on page 97.

Assign a partner to each student. Have the partners decide which one will read each episode. After students have rehearsed their presentations, separate the class into groups of four to six to share their presentations. Encourage students to put expression in their voices and think about what they are reading.

If time is a problem, have each pair read only part of the episode. Be sure to reserve time to discuss the effectiveness of each pair of presentations.

is dead. The kingdom is destroyed. The mood is sad and regretful.

Students may point out additional contrasts.

2. The section begins with "The Knight of the Cart" to show the contrast between the cooperation and happiness of Camelot in the beginning and the sorrow of the ruined kingdom at the end.

3. Mordred and Agravaine were Arthur's nephews. They wanted to overthrow Arthur and didn't want Guinevere or Lancelot to interfere. Guinevere would have supported Arthur, and Lancelot would have fought for him if they had not been branded as traitors. Since Mordred later wanted to marry Guinevere, it is possible he had wanted her for himself all along.

4. Some good and bad qualities of each character are as follows. Opinions about their believability will vary.

Arthur—brave, generous, responsible, sensitive, loving; hasty, unforgiving, overly dependent on the advice of others

Lancelot—a good friend, brave, patient, gallant, loyal, loving; unable to control his emotions, unable to see how his actions would affect others

Gawaine—a good friend and loyal brother, persuasive, courageous; revengeful, unyielding, insensitive to the problems of others

Mordred—brave in battle, able to win other men to his side; cunning, spiteful, untrustworthy

5. Possible answers:
Friendship is of utmost importance.
Friends never betray each other.
Friends should trust each other.
True friendship will survive hurts and disappointments.

Developing Vocabulary Skills

1. thoughtless
2. irreparable
3. unknown
4. witless
5. illegal
6. sorrowful
7. truthfulness
8. impossible

Using the Review

This review should be completed before the administration of the **Chapter 2 Mastery Test**. Students will have an opportunity to recall important concepts from this chapter and apply them to new contexts. Teacher observation during the review can reveal which students still have not mastered the skills.

Using Your Skills in Reading the Legend of King Arthur

Have the students read the exercise and answer the question independently. Discuss the answers together. Note which students seem slow to write or to participate in the discussion, or collect papers after the review lesson to see who needs further help in this or other areas of study.

Using Your Comprehension Skills

Read the directions to the exercise to the students. If you are working the Review orally, let the students read the excerpt to themselves to avoid having a good reader give away too many clues by his or her oral interpretation of the passage. Discuss the questions, and then have the excerpt read aloud.

If you wish the students to answer in writing, make it clear that the second question is simply a clarification of the first, not a separate question. Allow sufficient time for them to read the excerpt and answer the questions. Discuss the answers, and then have the excerpt read aloud.

See the suggestion above for evaluation.

Using Your Vocabulary Skills

Read the directions to the exercise to the students. If you like, briefly review the chart on page 67 with the class. Then let the students work independently to read the paragraph, locate the five words, and figure out their meanings.

Discuss the answers. Note which students still have difficulty identifying or using context clues.

Using Your Writing Skills

Call on students to read aloud the two assignments; make sure they understand that they are to choose only one. Answer any questions students may have about the assignments. If you are asking the students to complete their writing in class, let them know how much time they have and that they may turn in a marked-up

CHAPTER 2 Review

Using Your Skills in Reading the Legend of King Arthur

Read this paragraph from another story about King Arthur's knights. Explain what is magical and unreal in the events.

> Once, a rich gentleman asked Arthur's knights for help.
>
> "Not long ago," the gentleman said, "I was in a joust. During the contest I was twice defeated by a certain knight. He attacked my son and wounded him. Now my son cannot be healed until I have defeated the knight in combat. Yet how can I find him? I don't even know his name. I only know that, when he wants to, he can become invisible."

Using Your Comprehension Skills

The following paragraph is from a short story you will read in Chapter 4. Read it carefully. From the information given by the speaker, what do you think his attitude is toward his family? Is he ashamed or proud of his background? How can you tell?

> We were poor. We had no money. Our whole tribe was poverty-striken. Every branch of the Garoghlanian family was living in the most amazing and comical poverty in the world. Nobody could understand where we ever got money enough to keep food in our bellies, not even the old men of the family. Most important of all, though, we were famous for our honesty. We had been famous for our honesty for something like eleven centuries, even when we had been the wealthiest family in what we liked to think was the world.

Using Your Vocabulary Skills

In the following paragraph, there are five words that use Greek or Latin word parts listed on page 67. Read the paragraph and locate those five words. Review the information on the chart on page 67. Then use

Answers to Questions

Using Your Skills in Reading the Legend of King Arthur

These are the magical events in the passage: the health of the gentleman's son depends on the gentleman defeating a knight in combat; the knight can become invisible when he wants to.

Using Your Comprehension Skills

The speaker is proud of his family. He doesn't seem to care that the family was poor, because he says the family was living in "amazing and comical poverty." He says that the most important thing about the family was that "we were famous for our honesty."

Using Your Vocabulary Skills

The words and meanings are as follows:

a. multi-talented—with many talents or abilities
b. monopoly—a power given to one person only
c. omnipotent—having all powers
d. decade—a period of time involving the number ten (Most stu-

that information and the context clues in the paragraph to figure out a possible meaning for each word.

It was common knowledge around King Arthur's court that Merlin, the multi-talented magician, was a very special person. He was thought to have a monopoly on magic. He alone knew how to cast spells. His powers were so great that he seemed almost omnipotent. King Arthur knew that, even if he searched for a decade, he would never find another person like Merlin. Merlin was unique.

Using Your Writing Skills

Choose one of the writing assignments below.

1. Choose an instance when magic is used in "The Legend of King Arthur." Explain why the magical event appears believable. To support your explanation, list the details used to make the scene seem possible. Think about the ways the character or characters involved react to the event. List any way you believe their reactions make the magic seem realistic.
2. Write another adventure for some of the characters in this legend. Use the adventure to show off certain personality traits that you have seen in the characters. For example, you might "test" the goodness of a knight by having him tempted by a rich or beautiful enemy of the king. In your adventure, make the characters agree with what they were like in the legend. Continue the same relationships among the characters.

Using Your Skills in Study and Research

In addition to providing written information, an encyclopedia provides maps, photographs, charts, and other illustrations. Imagine that you have been asked to examine an encyclopedia. Your assignment is to locate drawings of King Arthur and the knights and ladies of this legend. Describe the steps you would follow. Under what headings or guide words would you look? How would you determine which pictures would best illustrate the characters in this story?

first draft. Remind them to skip lines to leave space for corrections. If you are asking them to do the writing outside of class, you may require clean copies.

Using Your Skills in Study and Research

Read the directions for this exercise to the students. Make sure they understand that there are three parts to the assignment: to describe the steps in using an encyclopedia; to list several headings under which information about the appearance of medieval knights and ladies might be found; and to state some standards for choosing appropriate pictures to illustrate the legend the students have read in this chapter.

Depending on the abilities of your students, you may prefer to work this exercise as a group activity.

Reinforcing the Lesson

To reteach, reinforce, or extend the skills in this lesson, see the following:

Skills Practice Book, Green Level—pages 57 and 58

Additional Resource

Diagnostic and Mastery Tests, Green Level—Chapter 2 Mastery Test, pages 11 through 14

dents will recognize the term as meaning *ten years,* but the context clues and word parts chart do not provide that information.)

e. unique—one of a kind

Using Your Skills in Study and Research

Students should suggest looking in the index of the encyclopedia to search for likely entry headings. They should find out whether headings they have thought of independently appear in the encyclopedia. They should also mention looking up the articles listed in the index and using the information and cross-references in the articles to find other possible headings. They might suggest such headings as "King Arthur," "Knighthood," "Middle Ages," "clothing styles," and "armor."

To determine which pictures might illustrate this story, students could suggest the possibilities of referring to the pictures in the text and comparing pictures and captions in different articles or different encyclopedias.

About the Art

At the start of his career, Henri Matisse (1869-1954) was a leader of the Fauve movement. The Fauvists were noted for their use of bright, bold colors with which they achieved striking emotional effects. At the end of his life, when he was too old and ill to paint at an easel, Matisse made paper cut-outs which he pasted on backgrounds of contrasting color. He said, "There is no break between my painting and my cut-outs. Only, with something more of the abstract and the absolute, I have arrived at a distillation of form. . . . Of this or that object which I used to present in all its complexity in space, I now keep only the sign."

Mimosa is one of Matisse's late works. The forms are abstract flowers but the earlier Fauvist fascination with bold color contrasts remains.

CHAPTER 3

How Writers Write

Mimosa, 1945–51, HENRI MATISSE.
Ikeda Museum of 20th Century Art, Japan.

Chapter Objectives

Using the Process of Writing

- To understand that writing is a thinking process
- To recognize the three stages in the process of writing: pre-writing, writing, and revising

Using the Sounds of Language

- To identify the use of alliteration, rhyme, rhythm, and onomatopoeia in prose and poetry
- To be aware of the effects of these sounds of language in writing

Using Figures of Speech

- To identify the use of simile, metaphor, personification, and hyperbole in prose and poetry
- To understand the effects of figures of speech in writing

Preparing the Students

If the students do not have class notebooks, they will need notebook paper for recording some important information about writing as you guide them through this chapter.

Ask for a show of hands from students who have ever had difficulty completing a writing assignment, such as a short story or an essay.

Tell the students that the chapter they are about to read contains detailed information about writing that will help them learn how to select ideas, organize them, and state them more clearly.

If you are presenting Chapter 3 early in the year and if the students have not yet completed any of the writing questions in the previous chapters, have them read only the section of this chapter entitled **Using the Process of Writing** (pages 102 through 110) at this time. The sections on **Using the Sounds of Language** and **Using Figures of Speech** should be read later, when the students have experience in using the process of writing.

It is recommended that you administer the **Chapter 3 Diagnostic Test** at this time. The results of this pretest will serve as a guide for measuring students' needs and progress in achieving the chapter objectives.

Additional Resource

Diagnostic and Mastery Tests, Green Level—Chapter 3 Diagnostic Test, pages 15 and 16

Using the Process of Writing

Objectives

- To understand the five steps in the pre-writing process
- To recognize useful techniques for writing a first draft
- To understand the steps in the revising process
- To understand how and when to prepare a final copy

Presenting the Lesson

Ask the students to think of something they now do very well that took a lot of practice to become good at. Have them share their skill with the class. (Students will probably share abilities in such areas as sports, academics, and music.) Then ask the students to try to think back to the first time they performed that particular activity. Ask them if they performed skillfully that first time or whether their performance showed a need for practice. (Most will indicate that their performance lacked skillfulness.) Stress the fact that becoming very good at something takes considerable practice.

Ask the students to suggest things other than practice that helped them to improve in the areas they do well in. Help them to recognize that certain people may have given them advice or actually shown them how something should be done (for example, a parent showing a child how to hold a baseball bat correctly). They may have even observed and learned to imitate certain techniques that professionals use.

Read and discuss the introductory paragraph on page 102. Then have volunteers read aloud the section entitled **Understanding the Process of Writing** on page 103.

Point out that, just as we enjoy a concert or baseball game or any other event more when we realize the hard work that went into making it a good quality performance, we can also better appreciate the selections we read once we have learned about the techniques that successful writers use to write good quality literature.

Using the Process of Writing

Writers do not possess a magical power that enables them to write masterpieces on the first attempt. Writers work hard and long to produce good writing. Usually they follow a set of steps called the **process of writing.** The three main stages are:

pre-writing—a planning stage
writing
revising—a rewriting or reworking stage

Morning Light, 1916, OSCAR BLUEMNER. Hirshhorn Museum and Sculpture Garden, Smithsonian Institution, Washington, D.C.

About the Art

Trained as an architect, the painter Oscar Bluemner (1867-1938) composed his paintings in a logical, ordered, geometric manner, breaking his subjects into planes. His work resembles a multiple exposure photograph. The repeated views, each one a little different, convey the sense of a process or progression, in this painting the progression of the rising sun.

Bluemner was interested in color and light. *Morning Light* explores the effects of light and color as the sun rises over a row of houses. The mountains in the background are bathed in a pink glow. The houses and the street are in brilliant white and cool blue-green shadows.

Understanding the Process of Writing

Have you ever seen professional musicians play a piano or a guitar or a saxophone? They make it look easy. In fact, it looks so simple that you may think you could do as well with a little practice.

If you really do learn to play an instrument, you will find out how difficult it is. You will begin to appreciate how well the musician plays.

If you study an instrument such as the piano for a while, you will become a better listener. Instead of simply listening to the entire sound of a piano piece, you will listen for certain techniques. You can decide whether the pianist performs well or poorly. You would probably be happier listening to a good performance than would someone who had never studied piano.

Reading someone else's writing is similar to hearing someone play an instrument. When you know what to listen for at a concert, you can better appreciate the quality of the performance. When you know what to look for as you read, you can enjoy the writing more fully.

In this chapter, you will learn how writers produce their writing. You will learn about techniques they use to make their writing clear and vivid. You will get a chance to try some of these techniques yourself. As a writer, you will become a more appreciative reader.

Pre-Writing

The first stage of the writing process is called **pre-writing.** During the pre-writing stage, writers prepare to write. They think and plan before they put one word down on paper. These are the pre-writing steps writers follow:

1. Choose and limit a topic. Think of possible topics. Do you know a great deal about one topic? Would you like to learn more

Understanding the Process of Writing

Pre-Writing

Ask the students why builders need a plan to follow in constructing a building. Have them tell you what the effects would be if no detailed plan were made before a building was erected.

Point out that writers also need to make a plan before they begin to write. Without one, a writer's work would be disorganized and confusing, just like a building that has been constructed without first planning the design.

Have the students read the paragraph under **Pre-Writing** (page 103) silently as you list the five pre-writing steps on the board (pages 103 through 105). Then have them copy the steps into their notes, leaving ample space between headings for the important details about each one to be filled in later.

1. Choose and Limit a Topic. Ask a student to read aloud the first three paragraphs of this section (pages 103 and 104). Then have the students suggest topics that interest them and list these on the board.

Have another student read aloud the remainder of this step. To help students understand the sequence of steps they should follow, select and circle any one of the topics on the board and have them suggest ideas about it. List that information on the board as well. Then have the students look over the list and decide which ideas are related and could be combined into a single piece of writing. Circle the items that the students group together and cross out the ones that they exclude.

For reinforcement, ask the students to suggest the important details of this section in logical order. Write these on the board under the **Pre-Writing** heading. Their answers should be similar to the following ideas and presented in the order given here:

a. list all the topics that interest you
b. choose the topic that you most want to write about
c. list anything you can say about the topic
d. decide which ideas are related and circle them

Then have the students copy the list into their notes.

2. Decide on Your Purpose. Point out to the students that deciding why you are writing a selection helps you to narrow down the ideas that should be included, thereby simplifying the task. Have the students read the paragraph for step 2 silently. Then ask them to state the four purposes for writing that the paragraph mentions. List these on the board.

3. Decide on Your Audience. Have the students read this step (pages 104 and 105) silently. Then have them state in their own words why it is important to decide who will be reading their writing. Their answers should reflect the fact that this step will help them choose the appropriate level of language and details to include. List all correct responses on the board to reinforce understanding of this step in the pre-writing process. Then have the students copy the list into their notes.

4. Gather Supporting Information. Have the students read the first paragraph on page 105 silently. Then have them state the three ways a writer can gather information. As each item is stated, list it on the board. Their answers should be similar to the following ideas and presented in the order given here:

a. list the things you already know about the topic
b. compose questions that need to be answered before you can write
c. use every possible resource to help you find the answers

Have the students copy the list into their notes.

Now direct the students to read the remainder of this step silently. Have them find a similarity and a difference between the methods the two authors used for gathering the information they needed (similarity: both obtained information from people who were knowledgeable about the topic; difference: Bonham consulted reference materials, such as books and journals, but Brink didn't). Ask the students why Bonham needed to do library research and Brink didn't. Help them to understand that a writer's topic determines the kind of reference sources that need to be consulted.

5. Organize Your Ideas. Have a student read aloud the first two paragraphs of this section (pages 105 and 106). Then ask another student to state what should be done after the unnecessary details have been eliminated (answer: choose an order for presenting the ideas).

Have the students read the remainder of this step silently. Then call on students to state in their own words the various

about another? List all the topics that interest you. Then go over this list of ideas again. Choose the one that you most want to write about.

Professional writers search for ideas for topics too. Jean Craighead George describes where she gets her ideas.

> Ideas for my stories come from memories of my childhood, from events that happen to the people I love, live, and work with—and from reading. I mean all reading—ads, books, magazines, newspapers, scientific journals, trashy stuff, classics, my children's homework, postcards, even legal papers. Ideas do not come out of thin air.

Now think about the topic you have chosen. Make another list. This time include anything you can say about the topic. Decide which of these ideas belong in your story, poem, or other writing. Then limit your topic. Which of these ideas can be covered adequately in the space available?

As you choose and limit your topic, keep in mind two related considerations: your purpose and your audience.

2. Decide on your purpose. What do you want to accomplish with your writing? Do you want to entertain your readers? Do you want to teach them facts they didn't know before? Do you want to persuade them to think a certain way? Do you want to share a feeling? The way you treat your topic depends on your purpose.

3. Decide on your audience. In any library, you can probably find a variety of books about a popular topic such as race car driving. You may find a story about a trip to the race track in the pre-school room. In the children's room there may be a book describing important races that have been run. The adult room may have a biography of a famous driver. Each book on this topic is aimed at a different audience.

For each audience, you write differently. If you are writing for pre-schoolers, you use simple words and tell about events five-year-olds can understand. For school-age children, you might write about fast-paced action. You might use slang words. Writing for adults, you would probably use a more formal style.

Once she has chosen her topic, author Mary Lewis thinks about her audience carefully.

> When a story idea seems to be a good one, I next must think of exactly what age group I am going to write it for. The age group must be more definite than just for children. I write the story for children of one special age and then try to make the story interesting also to children who are a few years younger or older.

4. Gather supporting information. The next pre-writing step is to gather information about your chosen topic. Make a list of things you already know about the topic. Then list questions you need to answer before you can write. Use every possible resource to help you find the answers.

Author Frank Bonham gives this advice to writers beginning their research: "Take notes—notes on anything you might possibly need later. Never trust your memory." He varies his research.

> For a book I wrote about dolphins, I read all I could find about these delightful animals in books and scientific journals. I visited them at Marineland. Then I talked to marine biologists. I talked, finally, to tuna fishermen who find the tuna by spotting schools of dolphins feeding on the fish.

Carol Ryrie Brink wrote *Caddie Woodlawn,* a book based on her grandmother's childhood adventures. Looking at her information, she began to see how each piece was related to the other.

> My grandmother had told me many stories of her childhood. I had to sort them out in my mind and decide which things were most important, where natural climaxes should come, and how one story could be woven into another so that they made a unified whole.

5. Organize your ideas. Read over the list of details you have gathered. Some will be useful for your writing. Others will not fit

methods writers use for organizing their information.

Now have the students suggest the main ideas of this step and list these on the board. Their answers should include the following:

a. choose an order for your ideas
b. go back and continue your research if your information is incomplete
c. choose a method of organization that works well for you

Have the students copy this list into their notes.

Reinforcing the Lesson

To reteach, reinforce, or extend the skills in this lesson, see the following:

Skills Practice Book, Green Level—pages 59 and 60

Special Populations

Many special-populations students have difficulty with the process of writing because of limited fine-motor ability, trouble with organizing ideas, unfamiliarity with language usage, and limited expressive-language abilities due to perceptual problems or limited vocabulary. To compensate for some of these difficulties, you may wish to pair students with partners to whom they can dictate their thoughts; or you may wish to conduct the lesson as a small group activity or allow students to prepare their stories or exercises by tape recording their ideas.

To help special-populations students with pre-writing, you might encourage them to choose partners with whom they can do research to gather supporting information. You or the partner may need to outline specific questions to be researched to guide the special-populations student in finding information about the topic. This student would also benefit from individualized help in applying the suggestions under step 5, **Organize Your Ideas**.

in. Cross out any details that are not related to what you want to say. Your research may have uncovered interesting new information on a different topic. You may decide to change your topic.

Once you have settled on a topic, it is time to organize your information. In what order will you present your ideas or appropriate facts? Choose an order. Stories are usually arranged in time order. Details of descriptions often are arranged according to the order in which they are noticed. Writing meant to convince or persuade lists reasons in the order of importance.

As you begin to picture the direction your writing will take, you may discover areas where your information is incomplete. If so, go back and continue your research.

Most writers organize their material in some type of outline. Matt Christopher, writer of sports books, tells how he goes about writing his outline.

> Working with sheets of paper containing the scenes of my proposed book, I begin my outline, writing chapter after chapter, usually about half a page in length.

Mary Lewis finds that her outline depends on the type of writing she is doing.

> For a short picture book I do not find I need a detailed outline, just a list of notations of what is going to happen. But for a longer and more complicated story, I need a long and detailed outline.

Other writers organize their writing in special ways that make sense to them. Marguerite Henry, writer of exciting books about horses, has her own method of organizing:

> Conventional outlines are not for me. I construct a kind of skeleton skyscraper which foretells the story as visibly as steel girders and beams give promise of the building to come. This framework tells me more, in one glance, than all the I, II, III's and a, b, c's of a normal outline.

You, the writer, can choose any type of organizing or outlining that makes sense to you.

Writing the First Draft

You have done your research. You have organized your ideas. Now begin to write. Write quickly. Concentrate on getting your ideas down. Try to follow your outline as much as possible. As you write, skip lines to leave room for later corrections and changes.

Writers know that facing a blank sheet of paper can be frightening. Nevertheless, anyone who writes has to overcome that fear and plunge in, as these writers advise:

> Get your ideas into words and put the words down on paper. Don't worry about how you scribble them down or about anything else. —Louis Slobodkin

> Get it down. Take chances. It may be bad, but it's the only way you can do anything really good.
> —William Faulkner

Pura Belpré, storyteller and author, describes the way she begins to write:

> I write my first draft by hand and always in pencil. I do it just as soon as I finish doing the research, and I am careful that I have covered everything that is needed for the story. Drafting quickly is important so that the freshness of the material is not lost.

Writers write the first draft quickly, knowing that they will come back to it later when they begin to revise.

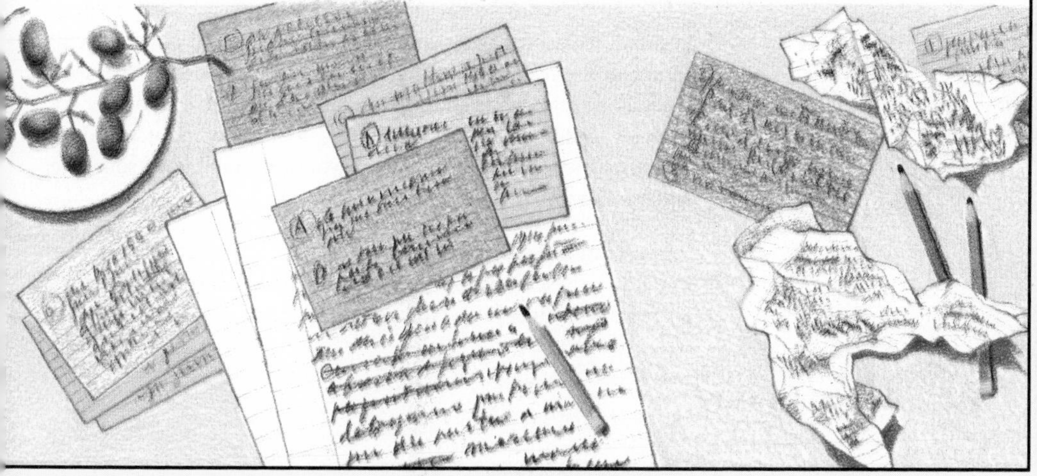

Writing the First Draft

Have the students write the heading "Writing the First Draft" in their notes. Direct them to read this section (page 107) silently and raise their hands as soon as they determine the most important idea about writing a first draft. As soon as the majority of students have their hands up, call on a student to give the answer (getting your ideas down quickly). Have the students write the answer in their notes.

Ask students to share what they think are common mistakes that beginning writers make when writing the first draft (possible answers: they spend time on such things as correcting sentence structure, grammar, and punctuation instead of just getting their ideas down; they don't leave enough space between the lines for later corrections and changes).

Reinforcing the Lesson

To reteach, reinforce, or extend the skills in this lesson, see the following:

Skills Practice Book, Green Level—page 61

Special Populations

LD. Stress the concept of "write and write quickly." Often students become lost making corrections of their work and rapidly lose their story line. Allowing the student to dictate thoughts initially could help, as would allowing the student to use a word processor, if the student is familiar with such equipment and if the equipment is available.

Revising

Have the students write the heading "Revising" in their notes. Then ask a student to read aloud the first portion of this section (page 108) through the four questions. Point out that making corrections is necessary and advisable in order to improve the clarity of your writing.

Direct the students to the page of revised manuscript on page 109. Ask them to explain how the author added, omitted, or changed words and to point out an example of each of these kinds of changes. Write each example on the board. For reinforcement, have the students refer to the examples on the board to help them state in their own words how changes in the wording of the first draft can be made. List all appropriate responses on the board. Then have the students copy the list and the examples into their notes.

Have a volunteer read aloud the remainder of this section up to the section entitled **Proofreading** on page 110. To reinforce the importance of revising, ask the students to suggest some arguments they could use to convince someone that revising is not a punishment for having written incorrectly the first time; it is a natural and logical next step in the writing process (possible answers: even the most experienced and successful writers revise; sometimes we find that the words we chose don't quite say what we want them to say).

At this time, explain to the students that a writer often asks other people for help during the revising stage. Emphasize that feedback from others can help us realize the weaknesses as well as the strong points of our work. If your students will be working with others later during revising, you might want to define *self-evaluation, peer evaluation,* and *teacher evaluation* for the students. (See the suggested evaluation form and explanation on T.E. pages T24 through T27.)

Proofreading. Have the students write the subtitle "Proofreading" in the **Revising** section of their notes. Then have them suggest what kinds of commonly made errors in writing have not yet been discussed (possible answers: grammar, spelling, punctuation, and capitalization). Now have a volunteer read aloud the section about proofreading in the text (page 110). Ask another student to state the main idea of this section (answer: correct any errors in grammar, spelling, punctuation, and capitalization) and write it on the board. Have the students copy it into their notes.

Revising

Just because you wrote it doesn't mean it's good.
—Frank Bonham

When you revise, you have another chance to get your ideas and words written just right. To begin revising, read over what you have written with these questions in mind:

1. Will readers think my writing is interesting? Will my writing hold their attention?
2. Did I stick to my topic? Did I include any unnecessary words or sentences? Do I need to add any important details?
3. Is my organization logical? Will the readers be able to follow my ideas as I've connected them?
4. Did I use complete sentences? Did I choose the best words to express my meaning?

On your first draft, mark any changes or corrections. Draw lines through words you have decided to omit. Note the words and sentences you want to add. Don't be surprised if your paper becomes so marked up that you have trouble reading it. If that happens, copy the page.

Beginning writers are not the only ones who have to revise. All writers think of revising as the natural and logical next step in the writing process.

Each writer has favorite techniques for revising.

> Sometimes words seem stubborn and don't say what we have in mind. So we try again and sometimes again and again. Having someone else read what we have written often helps. So does leaving it alone for a while and then coming back to give it another try. Both of these help us find a "fresh" look. Reading it aloud, or sometimes just telling it as though you were talking to someone, helps in rewriting. —Glenn O. Blough

> In rewriting, I add details here and there, rearrange sentences for more directness, and where a sentence is long, shorten it or turn it into two sentences. —Holling C. Holling

By the end of that winter it was clear to everyone that Barry was the best rescue dog the monks had ever had. In a snow storm Barry was the first to find people buried under the snow. He was the fastest at digging them free. He worked hardest at warming them up. Sometimes, after the other dogs gave up, Barry went on licking a frozen face until finally there was movement, a moan, an opening eye. Then the great dog grew wild with joy.

Years passed. Werner grew tall and thin. He put aside his school books and gave all of his time to the dogs. He worked with Brother Luigi every day feeding the dogs, playing with them, training the pups. He was completely happy.

In 1806 Barry was six years old, and Werner was eighteen. It was the most terrible winter ever to strike the mountains. Rescue trips were made every day. Half of the dogs in the monastery died that winter, trying to save the travelers' lives. Almost half of the monks died in icy traps as they went about their rescues.

One night in March Werner and Barry were walking slowly up the trail toward home. Werner's face was stiff with cold and even Barry seemed tired. It had been a terrible winter for both of them.

Author Lynn Hall shows how she corrected a page of her manuscript while writing the story *Barry, the Bravest St. Bernard.*

Direct the students to turn back to page 109 and look in the revised manuscript for corrections that were made in grammar, spelling, capitalization, and punctuation. Have them explain how the changes were made, pointing out an example of each kind. Write each example on the board. Then have the students add these to their notes.

To reinforce the fact that corrections in form should not be made until all corrections have been made in the area of content, ask the students to explain why they think these kinds of errors should not be corrected until the wording has been revised (possible answer: it would be a waste of time to make such changes before sentences have been reworded and reorganized).

Preparing the Final Copy. Have the students read this section (page 110) silently. Then ask them to tell you the three most important ideas that should be remembered about preparing the final copy (answers: make it neat and easy to read; make all the necessary changes and corrections; check it again for any mistakes that were missed) and list these on the board. Then have the students copy the list into their notes.

Reinforcing the Lesson

To reteach, reinforce, or extend the skills in this lesson, see the following:

Skills Practice Book, Green Level—pages 62 and 63

Special Populations

Emphasize that revising is a necessary and expected part of writing, that making changes or correcting mistakes does not mean that the writing the student has done during the pre-writing and writing stage is of poor quality. Some students may need additional support for this portion of the writing process. They may get such support from classmates if they are working in small, congenial groups in which members help each other with the revising and proofreading; or they can get support from partners to whom they can dictate their ideas or changes.

Practicing the Process of Writing

Ask a student to read this section (page 110) aloud. Then have the students turn to the **Guidelines for the Process of Writing** on pages 552 through 555. Allow time for them to read through the pages silently to see if there are any other details they would like to add to their notes that would help them in their writing.

Now have the students turn to the **Checklist for the Process of Writing** on pages 556 and 557. Tell them that this is a quick, easy-to-use reference tool to guide them through their writing.

> I read and write my drafts with a critical ear. I test every sentence for meaning and for sound. I keep testing the book as I type. I'm a noisy writer. I mumble as I work because I have to find out how a sentence sounds when read aloud.
>
> —Ann Petry

> One thing is certain: you have to be able to look at your own writing objectively and critically, as a stranger would.
>
> —H. A. and Margaret Rey

"Revise!" urges writer Frank Bonham. "Only the sculptor has the disadvantage of being stuck forever with what he has chipped out."

Proofreading. You have revised your writing so it says what you want it to say. Now make sure that careless mistakes don't prevent readers from understanding you. Reread your marked-up draft. This time look for errors in grammar, spelling, punctuation, and capitalization. Mark any corrections.

Preparing the Final Copy. Your final copy should be neat and easy to read. When you write it or type it for the last time, remember to make all necessary changes and corrections.

Finally, proofread your writing again to check yourself.

Practicing the Process of Writing

Use the ideas in this chapter when you write. Also, refer to the Process of Writing section in the Handbook for Reading and Writing. It contains guidelines for the process of writing, for revising, and for proofreading.

As you read, think as a writer would think. Do as Carol Ryrie Brink suggests:

> If you have enjoyed a passage in a book, ask yourself why. Was it because the words were well chosen or because it expressed a feeling that you had often had yourself? Could you write such a passage? You could try.

Using the Sounds of Language

Every word has both a sound and a meaning. Writers use sound and meaning to appeal to readers' senses as well as their reason. In this chapter, you will see how writers use the sounds of language in five ways:

alliteration	rhyme	onomatopoeia
assonance	rhythm	

The Blue Guitar, 1982, DAVID HOCKNEY. Courtesy of the Pantechnicon, London.

About the Art

The Blue Guitar by British artist David Hockney (born 1937) is a series of Polaroid photographs which together form a disjointed still life of flowers, fruit, and guitar. By piecing together photos showing various and sometimes overlapping views of the same object, Hockney achieves, in a somewhat farcical and therefore humorous way, a cubist effect by breaking up the picture plane. The title seems to be an allusion to Picasso, the founder of Cubism, who did a famous painting of a man playing a blue guitar. However, this allusion is humorous, too, since, as we can see, Hockney's guitar isn't blue at all.

Using the Sounds of Language

Objectives

- To identify the use of alliteration, assonance, rhyme, rhythm, and onomatopoeia in prose and poetry
- To be aware of the effects of the sounds of language in writing

Presenting the Lesson

In preparation for this lesson, copy the following sentences onto the board. Do not write the word in parentheses.

1. The night was so cold that even his two heavy wool blankets did not keep him warm. (touch)
2. The aroma of chocolate chip cookies filled the air as Mother did her weekly baking. (smell)
3. John laughed loudly even though he had heard the joke so many times before. (hearing)
4. The white sails glistened in the afternoon sun as the boats approached the harbor. (sight)
5. Thoughts of delicious foods filled his head as the shipwrecked sailor ate yet another meal of fruits and berries. (taste)
6. The clanging bells signaled the approach of the train. (hearing)

Before the students turn to the first page of this section on the sounds of language, call on volunteers to name the five senses. List these on the board. Now direct the students to read from the board the six sentences that you prepared earlier. Call on students to read aloud the sentences that strongly appeal to the sense of hearing. As a review, you may wish to name the other senses, one at a time, and ask students to read aloud the sentence that appeals to that particular sense.

Now have the students follow along as you read the introductory paragraph on page 111. Have them pronounce each of the five writing techniques after you. Then ask them which one of their senses all of these techniques will appeal to.

Alliteration

Before you begin this lesson, copy the poetry samples by Hoberman and Longfellow (pages 112 and 113) onto the board or on an overhead transparency for use during the lesson.

Present an example of alliteration orally to the students (the silver rocket streaked across the star-strewn sky) and ask them what is similar about the sounds of some of these words. Then ask a student to read aloud the definition and example of alliteration in the box on page 112.

Alliteration in Prose. Now direct the class's attention to the section entitled **Alliteration in Prose** (page 112). Define prose as the everyday language people use in speaking and writing. Ask a volunteer to read this section aloud. After the samples of prose are read, have the students explain how alliteration is used in each one. Next, ask them which example repeats a consonant sound someplace other than just at the beginning of words.

Alliteration in Poetry. Have the students read this section, down to the bottom of page 112, silently. Then ask a volunteer to come to the board or overhead projector and underline the examples of alliteration in the poem by Hoberman that you prepared earlier. Have another student explain how the use of alliteration creates a humorous mood.

Have the students read the remainder of this section (top of page 113) silently. Then ask students to underline the examples of alliteration in Longfellow's poem.

Encourage the students to think of their own examples of alliteration to share with the class. Write each appropriate response on the board. Then have the students write the definition of alliteration in their notes along with one of the examples on the board or one of their own.

Reinforcing the Lesson

To reteach, reinforce, or extend the skills in this lesson, see the following:

Skills Practice Book, Green Level—page 64

Alliteration

> **Alliteration** is the repetition of consonant sounds.
>
> Example: rough and ready
>
> Usually, the repeated consonant sound appears at the beginning of the words.

Alliteration in Prose. You probably already use alliteration without knowing it. It is fun to use. We find alliteration in phrases such as "tried and true" and "making a mountain out of a mole-hill." We use it in comparisons such as "hungry as a horse" and "green as grass." And our tongue twisters are usually built with alliteration: "She sells seashells by the seashore."

When writers want to be sure the readers will pay attention to certain words, they often use alliteration. Here are some examples. Notice how sometimes the writers repeat the consonant sound in places other than the beginning of words.

> The silver rocket lay in the light of the moon. And beyond the rocket stood the yellow lights of his home, a block away, burning warmly. —Ray Bradbury, "The Rocket"

> Again the stream slowed into long, lazy stretches sparkling in the sun. —Edwin Way Teale, *Journey into Summer*

Alliteration in Poetry. Sometimes poets use alliteration for a humorous effect, as in the following example.

GAZELLE

O gaze on the graceful gazelle as it grazes
It grazes on green growing leaves and on grasses
On grasses it grazes, go gaze as it passes
It passes so gracefully, gently, O gaze!

—Mary Ann Hoberman

Alliteration is a favorite way of using sound in poetry. Read this example from Longfellow. Look for the many repeated consonant sounds.

The tide rises, the tide falls,
The twilight darkens, the curlew calls;
Along the sea-sands damp and brown
The traveler hastens toward the town,
And the tide rises, the tide falls.
—Henry Wadsworth Longfellow,
"The Tide Rises, the Tide Falls"

Exercises: **Using Alliteration**

A. Each of these selections uses alliteration. Identify the consonant sounds that are repeated at the beginnings of words.

1. The fair breeze blew, the white foam flew,
The furrow followed free;
We were the first that ever burst
Into that silent sea.
—Samuel Taylor Coleridge, "The Rime of the Ancient Mariner"
2. There once was a witch of Willowby Wood,
and a weird wild witch was she.
—Rowena Bennett, "The Witch of Willowby Wood"
3. He sprang through the sleeping camp and in swift silence dashed through the woods.
—Jack London, *The Call of the Wild*
4. They climbed higher on the hill, cutting the briers and brushes and tree branches and stacking them neatly into piles.
—Jesse Stuart, "The Clearing"
5. All that day Hugh sat at the clearing's edge, still as a stone.
—Jane Yolen, "The Hundredth Dove"

B. Write three sentences using alliteration. Try to repeat the consonant sound at least three times at the beginning of words.

Special Populations

Provide additional examples of alliteration for the students to hear. Draw phrases from the students' texts in other subjects; from newspaper and magazine headlines and articles; and from dialog in class, on TV programs, or movies or plays that the students may be familiar with. Use the phrases on work sheets or individual cards, and ask the students to identify the phrases that are alliterative.

Using the Exercises

Read and discuss the directions for each exercise before assigning the questions for independent work.

Exercise A. You may wish to discuss the selections with the class first and then have the students write their answers on paper.

Exercise B. After the students complete this exercise, have them share their sentences with the class.

Answers to Exercises

A. Consonant sounds:

1. The fair breeze blew, the white foam flew,
The furrow followed free;
We were the first that ever burst
Into that silent sea.

2. There once was a witch of Willowby Wood, and a weird wild witch was she.

3. He sprang through the sleeping camp and in swift silence dashed through the woods.

4. They climbed higher on the hill, cutting the briers and brushes and tree branches and stacking them neatly into piles.

5. All that day Hugh sat at the clearing's edge, still as a stone.

B. Answers will vary.

Assonance

It is suggested that you supply yourself with two colors of chalk or overhead markers for this lesson (one piece of each color is sufficient). Also, before the lesson, copy the poetry samples by Tennyson and Coleridge (pages 114 and 115) onto the board or an overhead transparency for use during the lesson.

Ask the students if they enjoy listening to their favorite songs over and over. (Most students will indicate that they do.)

Tell them that hearing certain vowel sounds over and over in a piece of prose or poetry is also enjoyable because the repetition creates a music-like effect. Have a student read the definition and example of assonance in the box on page 114.

Assonance in Prose. Ask a student to read this section (page 114) aloud. Discuss the examples of assonance in the prose samples. For review, you may wish to have the students identify the use of alliteration (Buck brooded; roamed relentlessly; task, slash, snap).

Assonance in Poetry. Ask a student to read this section aloud, to the bottom of page 114. Then have a volunteer come to the board or overhead transparency that you prepared earlier and underline all the examples of assonance in one color. Have another student underline all the examples of alliteration in the other color. Ask the students what other type of repetition is used besides the repetition of beginning letters (answer: repetition of words), and have them find examples of it. Next, discuss the mood. (Students will probably identify the mood as sad.) Point out how the use of alliteration, assonance, and word repetition helps to create that mood.

Ask a student to read aloud the remainder of this section at the top of page 115 and to point out the repeated words in the poem by Coleridge. Then follow the same procedure for underlining the examples of assonance and alliteration that was used for the Tennyson poem. Next, have the students share the feelings they get as they read the poem (possible answers: loneliness, fear). Discuss the use of assonance, alliteration, and word repetition in creating the mood of this poem.

Encourage the students to think of their own examples of assonance to share with the class. Write each correct response on the board. Then have the students write the definition of assonance in their notes along with one of the examples from the book or one of their own.

Assonance

Assonance is the repetition of vowel sounds within words.

Example: Rain, rain, go away!

Assonance in Prose. The repetition of vowel sounds helps writers produce a musical quality in their writing. Your ears simply enjoy hearing certain sounds over and over. In addition, assonance creates different moods, depending on which sounds are repeated.

In the following selections, assonance emphasizes the meanings the writer wants his or her words to express. The *oo* sound in the first sample emphasizes the sadness that the character felt. On the other hand, the sharp, rough, short *a* sound in the second sample suggests a more active mood.

> All day Buck brooded by the pool or roamed restlessly above the camp.
>
> It was no task for him to learn to fight with cut and slash and the quick wolf snap.
>
> —Jack London, *The Call of the Wild*

Assonance in Poetry. Poets use assonance in poetry for the same reasons that other writers use it in prose. It creates moods and it emphasizes the music-like qualities of our language.

In this sample, notice how the poet has combined assonance with alliteration.

> Our echoes roll from soul to soul,
>   And grow for ever and for ever.
> Blow, bugles, blow, set the wild echoes flying,
> And answer, echoes, answer, dying, dying, dying.
>
> —Alfred, Lord Tennyson, "The Splendor Falls"

This poem repeats both sounds and words to create its mood.

Alone, alone, all, all alone,
Alone on a wide wide sea!
—Samuel Taylor Coleridge, "The Rime of the Ancient Mariner"

Exercises: **Using Assonance**

A. Find the assonance in each selection. Identify the vowel sounds that are repeated.

1. Break, break, break
On thy cold grey stones, O Sea!
—Alfred, Lord Tennyson, "Break, Break, Break"

2. I saw . . . the soft and nearly imperceptible waving of the sable draperies . . . —Edgar Allan Poe, "The Pit and the Pendulum"

3. who knows if the moon's
a balloon, coming out of a keen city
in the sky—filled with pretty people?
—e.e. cummings, "who knows if the moon's"

4. O beautiful for spacious skies,
For amber waves of grain.
—Katharine Lee Bates, "America, the Beautiful"

5. The first second of flight was only a flurry of awkward wings. Then Itchi-ban surged away, the air thick about it, its body beating against the dark, the feel of life on a leash, spinning, cartwheeling to dive, crashing into the river.
—Eve Bunting, "Magic and the Night River"

B. Write three sentences using assonance. Each sentence should use the same vowel sound at least twice. Assonance can sound comical or beautiful, depending on how you use it. Make sure that the effect of the assonance fits with the meaning of the sentence.

Reinforcing the Lesson

To reteach, reinforce, or extend the skills in this lesson, see the following:

Skills Practice Book, Green Level—page 65

Special Populations

Provide additional examples of assonance for the students to hear. Give exercises asking the students to sort a series of phrases that show assonance; the instructor might adapt the exercise that was suggested for practice with alliteration (see T.E. page 112) for use with assonance. For variation, have the students sort the phrases into three groups: those using alliteration, those using assonance, and those using neither technique.

Using the Exercises

Read and discuss the directions for each exercise before assigning the questions for independent work.

Exercise A. You may wish to discuss these selections with the class first, and then have the students write their answers on paper.

Exercise B. After the students complete this exercise, have them share their sentences with the class.

Answers to Exercises

A. Vowel sounds:

1. Break, break, break
On thy cold grey stones, O Sea!

—long a, long o

2. I saw . . . the soft and nearly imperceptible waving of the sable draperies.

—ô (au, aw), short i, long a

3. who knows if the moon's a balloon, coming out of a keen city in the sky—filled with pretty people?

—oo, long e, short i

4. O beautiful for spacious skies,
For amber waves of grain.

—or, long a

5. The first second of flight was only a flurry of awkward wings. The Ichi-ban surged away, the air thick about it, its body beating against the dark, the feel of life on a leash, spinning, cartwheeling to dive, crashing into the river.

—ir, short i, long ē, long i, ar

B. Answers will vary. Note the requirements stated in the question.

Rhyme

Have a student read aloud the definition and example of rhyme in the box on page 116. Then write a word on the board—for example, sun, book, or day— and give the students one minute to list as many words as they can think of that rhyme with the word. Have a few students read their lists to the class. You might like to challenge your students further by asking them to make up two rhyming lines of verse using two or more words in their list and to share their verses with the class.

Rhyme in Prose. Call on a volunteer to read this section (page 116) aloud. Discuss the mood of the selection and the effect that the rhyming words have on that mood. Ask the students what other techniques, besides rhyme, the author uses to emphasize that the play is ending (repetition of words). Have the students identify the words that are repeated. Point out how this repetition draws attention to the rhyme.

Rhyme in Poetry. Have students read this section (pages 116 and 117) aloud up to the end of Robert Frost's poem. After each poem is read, have students identify the lines that rhyme.

Direct the students to read and study the section about rhyme schemes as you copy the poem by Tennyson (page 114) onto the board. Call on a student to come to the board and label the lines with letters of the alphabet to show its rhyme scheme.

Now have the students write the definition and an example of rhyme in their notes.

Reinforcing the Lesson

To reteach, reinforce, or extend the skills in this lesson, see the following:

Skills Practice Book, Green Level—page 66

Rhyme

Rhyme is the repetition of sounds at the ends of words.

Example: Jack and Jill
Went up the hill.

In poems, rhymes are usually found at the ends of lines.

Rhyme in Prose. Prose does not usually use rhyme. Sometimes, though, it is used for special effect. For example, the near-rhyme of *poem* and *home* in this final speech of a play stresses the fact that the play is ending.

> That's why, when I look at her now through this window, I remember that time and that poem, and she really seems to say, Whoever you are, wherever you come from, Welcome All. Welcome Home. —Arthur Miller, *Grandpa and the Statue*

Rhyme in Poetry. Poems rhyme in different patterns. Sometimes the lines that rhyme come one after another.

Dreaming of honeycombs to share
With her small cubs, a mother bear
Sleeps in a snug and snowy lair.
—Harry Behn, "Waiting"

Sometimes every other line rhymes, as in the following poem.

All day the snow fell on that Eastern town
With its soft, pelting, little, endless sigh
Of infinite flakes that brought the tall sky down
Till I could put my hands in the white sky.
—Stephen Vincent Benét, *John Brown's Body*

This poem has a third pattern of rhyme. Can you find it?

Whose woods these are I think I know.
His house is in the village though;
He will not see me stopping here
To watch his woods fill up with snow.
—Robert Frost, "Stopping by Woods on a Snowy Evening"

The pattern of rhyme in a poem is called a **rhyme scheme**. We use a special code to represent the rhyme scheme. The ending sound in each line of a poem is assigned a different letter of the alphabet. If one ending sound is repeated at the end of another line, the same letter is used to label both lines. Here is an example:

I never saw a moor, *a*
I never saw the sea; *b*
Yet I know how heather looks, *c*
And what a wave must be. *b*
—Emily Dickinson, "I Never Saw a Moor"

Notice that the second and fourth lines rhyme. Therefore, they are both labeled with the same letter.

Here are the rhyme schemes for the other examples:

WAITING	JOHN BROWN'S BODY	STOPPING BY WOODS
a	*a*	*a*
a	*b*	*a*
a	*a*	*b*
	b	*a*

Exercises: **Using Rhyme**

A. Turn to pages 112 and 113. Show the rhyme scheme for each of the poems you find there.

B. Make a list of rhyming words for each of the words below. Then, using any rhyme scheme, write a two- or a four-line poem. Use your list of rhyming words.

moon tree skate ball race money

Special Populations

LD. To ease these students into using letters to indicate rhyme schemes, have them copy one or more sample poems from the text and circle the rhyming words with colored pencils, using a different color for each rhyming ending. Have students see the rhyme patterns by pointing out the repetition of different colors throughout the poem. Then ask the student to go back over the poem, assigning letters to the lines with a letter for each color. Some students may be confused when they find no rhyming word for every line. With the use of color, the student should be able to see the rhyming pairs more easily and can assign letters to show the rhyme scheme efficiently, giving the nonrhyming words the next letters in sequence.

Using the Exercises

Read and discuss the directions for each exercise before assigning the questions for independent work.

Exercise A. You may wish to do this exercise as a class activity.

Exercise B. You might like to demonstrate to the students how they can discover rhyming words by substituting the beginning sound of the given word with each letter of the alphabet. As the students are working, provide individual help for those students who are having difficulty. Create a bulletin board display so students can share their work with each other.

Answers to Exercises

A. a b b c; a a b b a; a b c b

B. Answers will vary.

Rhythm

Before introducing this lesson, copy Carl Sandburg's "Early Moon" (page 118) and Robert Frost's "The Pasture" (page 119) onto the board or an overhead transparency for use during the lesson.

Read aloud the definition and example of rhythm in the box on page 118. Define stressed syllables as those word parts that are said with greater intensity. Write examples on the board, such as:

Th̆e wéathĕr wăs sŏ pléasănt wĕ dĕcídĕd tŏ háve ă pícnĭc.

Clap the syllables for the students, giving heavier claps for the stressed syllables. Then have them clap the syllables of other examples along with you.

Rhythm in Prose. Have a student read aloud the paragraph below the definition box (page 118). Read the example to the students, having them pay close attention to the relationship between the changes in the intensity of your voice and the accent marks above the words. Ask a student to read the next paragraph aloud. Then read the example to the students so they can hear how the rhythm of the writing quickly speeds up and affects the mood. Now direct the students' attention to Carl Sandburg's "Early Moon" on the chalkboard or transparency that you prepared earlier. Have them help you add the marks for the accented and unaccented syllables.

Rhythm in Poetry. Ask a volunteer to read aloud the introductory paragraph and poem on page 119. Now direct the students' attention to Robert Frost's "The Pasture," on the board or on a transparency that you have prepared earlier. Tap the rhythm and have students help you add the marks for the accented and unaccented syllables, one line at a time. Then ask a student to identify the line where the rhythm changes (answer: the last line). Finally, read the poem aloud and tap the rhythm together.

Have the students write the definition and an example of rhythm in their notes.

Reinforcing the Lesson

To reteach, reinforce, or extend the skills in this lesson, see the following:

Skills Practice Book, Green Level—page 67

Rhythm

Rhythm is the pattern of accented and unaccented syllables in a sentence or a line of poetry. The pattern is shown by marking each syllable with these symbols:

/ for accented, or stressed syllables

◡ for unaccented, or light syllables

Example: Jack be nimble, Jack be quick.
Jack jump over the candlestick.

Rhythm in Prose. Language has a natural rhythm. Occasionally, the rhythm of some prose is so strong that we can easily hear the rhythm pattern, as in the following example. The accent marks above each word tell you which syllables to stress.

> The wind was howling up from the sea, beating the waves against the wharves.
>
> —Esther Forbes, *Johnny Tremain*

Writers use the rhythm of language to express mood. In the following example, the writer uses the rhythm of his words to stress their meaning. The result is growing excitement.

> They had drums among the Indians, the Chinese, the Egyptians, thousands of years ago. And the words of their poetry move along like drum-beats, keeping time, now fast, now slow, drumming easy and slow at the opening of a war dance, drumming faster and faster, wild and furious, till it is so swift only the best-trained warriors can stand the speed of the dance that is drummed.
>
> —Carl Sandburg, *Early Moon*

The rhythm of the writing speeds up with the drum beats.

Rhythm in Poetry. Rhythm in poetry catches and holds your attention. In addition, it works with the meaning of the words to express the poet's thought. The first stanza of this poem has a gentle, easy rhythm. Can you find where the rhythm changes slightly to emphasize the words?

I'm going out to clean the pasture spring;
I'll only stop to rake the leaves away
(And wait to watch the water clear, I may):
I shan't be gone long.—You come too.
—Robert Frost, "The Pasture"

Exercises: Using Rhythm

A. Read these two prose selections from the same story. Compare their rhythms. Describe the mood that the words and the rhythm express.

Somehow the people who made tennis shoes knew what boys needed and wanted. They put marshmallows and coiled springs in the soles and they wove the rest out of grasses bleached and fired in the wilderness. Somewhere deep in the soft loam of the shoes the thin hard sinews of the buck deer were hidden. The people who made the shoes must have watched a lot of winds blow the trees and a lot of rivers going down to the lakes. Whatever it was, it was in the shoes, and it was summer.

"Bang! I deliver your packages, pick up packages, bring you coffee, burn your trash, run to the post office, telegraph office, library! You'll see twelve of me in and out, in and out, every minute."
—Ray Bradbury, "The Sound of Summer Running"

B. Copy these lines. Mark the stressed and unstressed syllables.

Honey, pepper, leaf-green limes,
Pagan fruit whose names are rhymes,
Mangoes, bread-fruit, ginger-roots,
Grenadillas, bamboo-shoots.
—Agnes Maxwell-Hall, "Jamaica Market"

Special Populations

Ask students to clap their hands or tap their desks softly as you read examples of various rhythm. Try to find varied examples, showing rhythm that is gentle and relaxing and rhythm that is rapid and exciting.

Using the Exercises

Read and discuss the directions for each exercise before assigning the questions for independent work.

Exercise A. You may wish to do this exercise as a class activity. Copy the first two lines of the two prose selections onto the board as the students read the passages silently. Read each sample aloud to the students and have them help you mark the accented and unaccented syllables. Then have the students read the samples aloud with you to help them feel the rhythm and recognize the mood of each one. Have the students describe the mood that the words and rhythm of each selection create.

Exercise B. Have the students copy the poem. You may wish to read it to them and have them listen and mark the accented and unaccented syllables they hear.

Answers to Exercises

A. Possible answers: The mood of the first selection is humorous and carefree. The mood of the second selection is tense and hurried.

B. Hóneў, péppĕr, léaf-grĕen límes,
Págăn frúit whŏse námes ăre rhýmes,
Mángŏes, bréad-frŭit, gíngĕr-rŏots,
Grénădíllăs, bámbŏo-shŏots.

Onomatopoeia

Have a student read aloud the definition and examples of onomatopoeia in the box on page 120. Ask the students to name actions or objects that could make the sound each example word suggests.

Onomatopoeia in Prose. Have the students read this section (page 120) silently. Then have them invent new words of their own that describe sounds. If time permits, you may wish to have them illustrate an object making its sound and label it boldly for a bulletin board display.

Onomatopoeia in Poetry. Have the students read this section (page 120) silently. Then suggest a situation (a picnic, a birthday party), and direct the students to try to imagine themselves in that particular situation. Encourage them to think of words that imitate sounds they might hear. As each word is given, list it on the board and have the student tell what would make that sound. You might like to challenge your students further by having them write their own two-line verses using any of the sound words on the board.

Have the students write the definition and an example of onomatopoeia in their notes.

Reinforcing the Lesson

To reteach, reinforce, or extend the skills in this lesson, see the following:

Skills Practice Book, Green Level—page 68

Special Populations

Ask students to find examples of onomatopoeia in comic strips or from songs they hear on the radio.

ESL students may be able to think of examples of words from their native language that sound like what they mean.

Using the Exercises

Read and discuss the directions for each exercise before assigning the questions for independent work.

Exercise A. Ask the students what technique other than onomatopoeia is used in each sentence (first sentence—alliteration: steeples, telling, it, time, to, about; second sentence—alliteration: tube, flutes, tweet-tweet; assonance: tuba, oomphs, flutes).

Exercise B. Ask students to share their sentences with the class.

Onomatopoeia

> **Onomatopoeia** is the use of words that imitate sounds.
>
> Examples: bang, thump, whizz

Onomatopoeia in Prose. When writers need a word to tell about a sound, they often invent a new word, for example:

> The pounding of the cannon increased; there was the rat-tat-tatting of machine guns, and from somewhere came the menacing pocketa-pocketa-pocketa of the new flame throwers.
>
> —James Thurber, "The Secret Life of Walter Mitty"

Onomatopoeia in Poetry. In the example below, the poet imitates sounds you might hear at a July Fourth fireworks display.

> A white sky bomb fizzed on a black line.
> A rocket hissed its red signature into the west.
> —Carl Sandburg, "Fourth of July Night"

Exercises: Using Onomatopoeia

A. Find the onomatopoeia in the following sentences.

1. The bells in the steeples cling-clanged, telling people it was time to be up and about.
   —Esther Forbes, *Johnny Tremain*
2. The tuba oomphs, the flutes tweet-tweet;
   —William Cole, "Here Comes the Band"

B. Write three sentences using words that sound like their meanings. Your words might imitate the sounds of animals, weather, tools, musical instruments, or anything else that makes a sound.

Answers to Exercises

A. 1. cling-clanged
2. oomphs, tweet-tweet

B. Answers will vary.

Using Figures of Speech

Figures of speech are a special way of using language. Writers and speakers use figurative language and figures of speech often because they make language colorful and lively. In this part of the chapter, you will read and study these figures of speech:

simile	personification
metaphor	hyperbole

The Starry Night, 1889, VINCENT van GOGH. Oil on canvas, 29″ × 36¼″. Collection, The Museum of Modern Art, New York. Acquired through the Lillie P. Bliss Bequest.

Using Figures of Speech

Objectives

- To identify the use of simile, metaphor, personification, and hyperbole in prose and poetry
- To recognize the effects of figures of speech in writing

Presenting the Lesson

Read aloud the introductory paragraph on page 121. Then explain that the term *figure of speech* describes an expression that uses words to create a picture in our minds.

Special Populations

You may want to make a handout that lists and defines the four types of figures of speech presented. As each figure of speech is introduced, give the students lists of phrases or put the phrases on cards to be distributed to the group. Ask the students to sort the phrases according to category.

About the Art

Vincent Van Gogh (1853-1890) loved brilliant color, through which he tried to make his paintings express the secrets of nature. His subjects were birth, life, death, and rebirth. In *The Starry Night* we see his vision of the universe set down in bold and energetic brushstrokes.

The painting is both a private and public landscape. The little village in the valley rests peacefully under the protection of the church spire, as the stars and planets in the heavens swirl and explode in a way that is violent but also, somehow, benign. The bright yellow stars are set off against the blue and violet of the night sky. The huge tree in the foreground, deep green and brown, seems to stand as a sentinel against the threatening darkness.

Simile

In preparation for this lesson, copy the poems by Zolotow and Cavafy (pages 122 and 123) onto the board or an overhead transparency for use during the lesson.

Have a student read aloud the definition and examples of simile in the box on page 122. Ask students to identify the objects that are being compared in each example and to explain how the two things are alike.

Similes in Prose. Read aloud the first two paragraphs on page 122. Then present examples of clichés (like giving candy to a baby; as white as snow) and have students explain the comparisons. Encourage the students to think of some original similes to share with the class and write these on the board. Now read the remainder of this section. After each sample is read, have students tell you what two things are being compared and how they are alike.

Similes in Poetry. Call on students to read this section (pages 122 and 123) aloud. After each poem is read, ask students to identify the objects being compared and explain what they have in common. As a review, call on students to come to the board or the overhead projector and underline the examples of alliteration in poems that you prepared earlier.

Have the students write the definition of simile in their notes along with one of the examples from the board or one of their own.

Reinforcing the Lesson

To reteach, reinforce, or extend the skills in this lesson, see the following:

Skills Practice Book, Green Level—page 69

Simile

> A **simile** is a comparison that uses *like* or *as*. It points out how two unlike things are alike in some way.
>
> Examples: The star is like a diamond in the sky.
> The dancer was as graceful as a cat.

Similes in Prose. By using similes, writers help you see your familiar world in a new way. A good simile should make you say, "That's exactly what it's like! I never thought of it that way before."

Writers, therefore, try to invent similes that are fresh and original. Overused similes can become **clichés**. You have heard them so often that you do not really listen to them anymore.

The following samples use similes. Look for the two things that are compared in each one.

A pale smile, like a gleam of cold sun on a winter's evening, passed over the old man's face.

—J.R.R. Tolkien, *The Return of the King*

The mothers stayed back in the kitchen, washing and drying, putting things away, recrossing their traceless footsteps like the lifetime journeys of bees.

—James Agee, *A Death in the Family*

Similes in Poetry. This poem compares trees to pencil strokes. At the same time, it puts a clear image into our minds.

Scene
Little trees like pencil strokes
black and still
etched forever in my mind
on that snowy hill.

—Charlotte Zolotow

The next poem takes objects we can see—candles—and compares them to things we cannot see.

The days of our future stand before us
Like a row of little lighted candles—
Golden, warm, and lively little candles.
—C.P. Cavafy, "Candles", translated by Rae Dalven

Exercises: **Using Simile**

A. For each example, tell what two things are being compared. Also tell what they have in common.

1. I wandered lonely as a cloud
   That floats on high o'er vales and hills.
   —William Wordsworth, "I Wandered Lonely as a Cloud"
2. The fence had lost many of its pickets and stood propped against the tangle like a large comb with teeth missing.
   —Elizabeth Enright, "Nancy"
3. The fuel was in the rocket and the men ran away from it on the ground like ants running lickety from a metal god—
   —Ray Bradbury, "R Is for Rocket"
4. Black snake! Black snake!
   Curling on the ground,
   Rolled like a rubber tire,
   Ribbed and round.
   —Patricia Hubbell, "The Black Snake"

B. Write three original similes. If you are having trouble getting started, you may want to use these beginnings.

1. The engine sounded as quiet as ________.
2. The wind was like ________.
3. The cake we made in cooking class tasted like ________.
4. The water in the pool looked like ________.

Using the Exercises

Read and discuss the directions for each exercise before assigning the questions for independent work.

Exercise A. You may wish to do this exercise orally with the class.

Exercise B. Have students share their similes with the class.

Answers to Exercises

A. Comparing things:

1. The author is comparing himself to a cloud. Their needs are similar: both are alone.

2. A fence is being compared to a large comb. They look alike: both are missing many of their parts.

3. The men are being compared to ants. They look alike: they both run off in all directions.

4. A black snake is being compared to a rubber tire. They look alike: both are rolled into a round shape and have grooves.

B. Answers will vary.

Metaphor

Read aloud the definition and examples of metaphor in the box on page 124. Have a student explain the difference between simile and metaphor. Then discuss what the two things in each of the examples have in common.

Metaphor in Prose. Direct the students to read this section (page 124) silently. Help them to recognize the difference between the way these examples and those in the box at the top of the page are stated: the examples at the top of the page use the words is and was between the objects compared, but the other examples do not. Next, have the students explain how the two things in each comparison are alike. As a review, you may wish to have them find and identify the use of alliteration in the last sample (long lances and sunlight; foliage and far).

Metaphor in Poetry. Call on a volunteer to read this section (pages 124 and 125) aloud. Ask the students if the metaphor in the poem is directly stated (no, it is not) and what clues are given to help the reader see what two things are being compared (the title, "The dinosaurs are not all dead," and "iron head"). Have the students explain how the steam shovel is like a dinosaur.

Encourage the students to think of metaphors of their own to share with the class. List these on the board. Then have the students write the definition and an example of metaphor in their notes.

Reinforcing the Lesson

To reteach, reinforce, or extend the skills in this lesson, see the following:

Skills Practice Book, Green Level—page 70

Special Populations

LD. Stress to the students that the difference between metaphor and simile is the use of the words *like* or *as*, and that a metaphor states that one thing is another thing. Metaphors are sometimes difficult for students to find. Provide as many examples as you can locate for the students to discuss.

Metaphor

A **metaphor** is a comparison that states that one thing is another, unlike thing. It shows how the two things have something in common.

Examples: Your mind is a complex computer.
The spider's web was strung with diamonds.

In the first example, your mind is compared to a computer. In the second example, drops of water on a spider's web are compared to diamonds.

Metaphors in Prose. Read the sample below. Try to picture the street scene in this comparison.

> The air was filled with snowstorms of torn paper; strangers hugged each other in the streets. The war was over.
> —Alice Dalgliesh, *The Silver Pencil*

Metaphors are stated in a variety of ways. They don't always say clearly that one thing *is* another. It is up to the reader to figure out what two things are being compared and how they are alike. What two things are compared in each example below?

> Now and then Tom and Huck came upon snug nooks carpeted with grass and jeweled with flowers.
>
> . . . long lances of sunlight pierced down through the dense foliage far and near. . . .
> —Mark Twain, *The Adventures of Tom Sawyer*

Grass is compared to a carpet. Flowers are compared to jewels. Shafts of sunlight are compared to lances.

Metaphors in Poetry. Read the following part of a poem called "Steam Shovel." To what is the steam shovel compared?

The dinosaurs are not all dead.
I saw one raise its iron head
To watch me walking down the road
Beyond our house today.
Its jaws were dripping with a load
Of earth and grass that it had cropped.
It must have heard me where I stopped,
Snorted white steam my way,
And stretched its long neck out to see,
And chewed, and grinned quite amiably.
—Charles Malam, "Steam Shovel"

In this poem, the steam shovel is like a huge dinosaur.

Exercises: **Using Metaphor**

A. Find the metaphors in the following selections. What two things are compared? How are they alike?

1. The bones of the sea
are on the shore,
shells
curled into the sand.
—Lilian Moore, "Shells"

2. The tundra was an ocean of grass.
—Jean Craighead George, "Amaroq, the Wolf"

3. All the world's a stage,
And all the men and women merely players.
—William Shakespeare, *As You Like It*

4. Fingers of fear squeezed his stomach.
—Carl Henry Rathjen, "The Runaway Rig"

B. Write three sentences containing original metaphors. These questions may start you thinking. Use these ideas or your own.

1. To what can you compare your school when the bell rings?
2. To what can you compare snow?
3. To what can you compare a rocket?

Using the Exercises

Read and discuss the directions for each exercise before assigning the questions for independent work.

Exercise A. You may wish to do this exercise orally with the class.

Exercise B. Have volunteers share their sentences with the class.

Answers to Exercises

A. Comparisons:

1. Shells are being compared to bones. Both are hard substances that give animals their shape.

2. The tundra is being compared to an ocean. Both are flat and far-reaching.

3. The world is being compared to a stage. Both are occupied for a period of time by people with a role or a special purpose for being there.

4. Fear is being compared to fingers. The fear has a physical effect on the character, just as fingers squeezing would.

B. Answers will vary.

Personification

In preparation for this lesson, copy Carl Sandburg's "Chicago" (page 126) onto the board or an overhead transparency for use during the lesson.

Ask a student to read aloud the definition and examples of personification in the box on page 126. Discuss the use of personification in these examples.

Personification in Prose. Have the class read this section silently. As you discuss each of the last two excerpts, call on students to tell what is being compared to humans and in what way it is like humans. Then have them describe the mood of these excerpts and show how the use of personification emphasizes the contrast between the pleasantness of the first scene and the unpleasantness of the second.

Personification in Poetry. Have the students read this section silently, down to the bottom of page 126. Then have them explain how Chicago is personified.

Now, direct the class's attention to the poem "Chicago" on the board or on a transparency that you prepared earlier. As you read the poem aloud, have students help you mark the accented and unaccented syllables. Then discuss the differences in mood and image between this poem and Forbes's *Johnny Tremain* prose excerpt (page 126), and show how the words, rhythm, and personification contribute to these differences. Help the students to recognize that Chicago is portrayed as productive, active, and somewhat unruly while Boston is depicted as quiet and slow-paced.

Have the students read the remainder of this section silently. Then have them tell what is being compared to humans in each poem and how these things are like people.

Now have the students write the definition and an example of personification in their notes.

Reinforcing the Lesson

To reteach, reinforce, or extend the skills in this lesson, see the following:

Skills Practice Book, Green Level—page 71

Personification

Personification is the giving of human qualities to an object, an animal, or an idea.

Examples: The train whistle screamed.
The hail tap-danced on the roof.

Personification in Prose. Personification, like other figures of speech, puts a picture in the reader's mind.

In this sample, a whole city takes on the qualities of one person. The reader can picture the way that person wakes up.

> Boston slowly opened its eyes, stretched, and woke.
> —Esther Forbes, *Johnny Tremain*

Personification also helps the writer express a mood.

> In the distance a beautiful island covered with palm trees and flowers beckoned invitingly from the sparkling water.
> —Norton Juster, *The Phantom Tollbooth*

> The ice talked, grinding its teeth, sending out every now and then a singing crack.
> —Norah Burke, "Polar Night"

Personification in Poetry. In this poem, another city is personified. Read how Carl Sandburg describes Chicago. See how he uses the meaning and rhythm of his words as well as personification to communicate an image and a mood.

> Hog Butcher for the World,
> Toolmaker, Stacker of Wheat,
> Player with Railroads and the Nation's Freight Handler;
> Stormy, husky, brawling,
> City of the Big Shoulders.
> —Carl Sandburg, "Chicago"

Each of these examples of poetry gives human qualities to different things. How is each shown to be like people?

Snowy Benches
Do parks get lonely
in winter, perhaps,
when benches have only
snow on their laps?
—Aileen Fisher

The telephone poles
have been holding their
arms out a long time now.
—Donald Justice, "Crossing Kansas by Train"

Exercises: Using Personification

A. In each example, tell what is being compared to humans. Tell why it is like humans.

1. On all sides, green-clad mountains gazed down upon us.
—Edwin Way Teale, *Journey into Summer*
2. Ten thousand daffodils saw I at a glance,
Tossing their heads in sprightly dance.
—William Wordsworth, "Daffodils"
3. The wind stood up, and gave a shout;
He whistled on his fingers, and
Kicked the withered leaves about,
And thumped the branches with his hands.
—James Stephens, "The Wind"

B. Use personification to describe each thing listed below. Consider how the object looks and what it does. Then think about similar ways people look and act. If possible, let your personification express a mood.

1. a mailbox
2. an apple tree bearing fruit
3. a radio

Using the Exercises

Read and discuss the directions for each exercise before assigning the questions for independent work.

Exercise A. You may wish to do the exercise orally with the class.

Exercise B. Encourage the students to make an illustration for each description. You may wish to use their completed work to create a bulletin board display.

Answers to Exercises

A. Comparisons:

1. The mountains are like people looking down on what is below them.

2. The movement of the daffodils reminds the speaker of people tossing their heads.

3. The wind is noisy; it whistles, kicks, and thumps branches as if it had hands.

B. Answers will vary.

Hyperbole

Have a student read aloud the definition and example of hyperbole in the box on page 128. Use other examples to help the students understand that, in exaggeration, facts are slanted so strongly that there is little or no truth left in them (the skyscraper was so tall that it touched the sky; John is always so late that, even if we arrive two months late, he still won't be there).

Hyperbole in Prose. Call on students to read this section (page 128) aloud. After each excerpt is read, ask a student to explain what is humorous about it. To emphasize the strong effect that hyperbole has on the mood of a selection, you may wish to have the students restate each excerpt, preserving the main idea but eliminating the exaggeration. Have them compare the mood of their restatements with the mood of the excerpts.

Hyperbole in Poetry. Direct the students to read Silverstein's "Strange Wind" (page 128) silently. Then have a student identify its use of hyperbole. Discuss the effect that hyperbole has on the mood of the poem.

Now have the students read the remainder of this section. Discuss its use of hyperbole. Then have the students describe how Millay must have felt when she wrote it. Help them to recognize how hyperbole intensifies the mood of the poem.

Encourage the students to think of their own examples of hyperbole to share with the class. Write each appropriate response on the board. Then have the students write the definition of hyperbole in their notes along with one of the examples on the board or one of their own.

Reinforcing the Lesson

To reteach, reinforce, or extend the skills in this lesson, see the following:

Skills Practice Book, Green Level—page 72

Special Populations

For extra practice in understanding hyperbole, ask students to bring in comic strips for the class to find examples of highly exaggerated statements or behavior.

Hyperbole

Hyperbole is exaggeration that puts an image into the reader's mind. A hyperbole is often funny.

Example: It was so hot, you could fry an egg on the sidewalk.

Hyperbole in Prose. In hyperbole, the exaggerated pictures fit in well with the fun-loving mood of tall tales and folk humor. The following examples of hyperbole are from American tall tales.

> There is a family in this town that is so lazy it takes two of them to sneeze. One throws his head back. And another goes AH-CHOO!
>
> There is a man nearby whose feet are so large that, when it rains, he lies down and uses them as umbrellas.

Writers also use hyperbole to describe exciting moments, as in the following example.

> The swing accelerated ever more wildly: soon it would take off entirely, depart from its hinges, fly through the air, burn a hole through the sky!
>
> —Elizabeth Enright, "Nancy"

Hyperbole in Poetry. Hyperbole gives this poem a carefree and humorous mood.

> What a strange wind it was today,
> Cool and clear from a sky so grey
> And my hat stayed on but my head blew away—
> What a strange wind it was today.
>
> —Shel Silverstein, "Strange Wind"

The writer of this poem chose hyperbole to express her strong emotions.

I will be the gladdest thing
Under the sun!
I will touch a hundred flowers
And not pick one.
—Edna St. Vincent Millay, "Afternoon on a Hill"

Exercises: Using Hyperbole

A. Identify which of the following selections use hyperbole.

1. And I will love thee still, my dear,
Till all the seas go dry.
—Robert Burns, "A Red, Red Rose"
2. It was hot. Only the black ants didn't feel it, and they would be happy in a furnace.
—"Arap Sang and the Cranes," retold by Humphrey Harman
3. Mr. Johansen was a gentle, white-haired, elderly man; he walked slowly with a slight stoop and had a kindly, sad face with large, dark eyes. —Joan Aiken, "The Serial Garden"
4. I heard all things in the heaven and in the earth. I heard many things in hell. —Edgar Allan Poe, "The Tell-Tale Heart"
5. There is a man who is so forgetful that one night he put his cat to bed and put himself outside. He did not discover his mistake until a dog chased him and he found he could not climb a tree.

B. Write an original hyperbole. If you wish, you may begin with one of these phrases.

1. My bedroom is so messy that ________.
2. Our car is so small that ________.
3. The speaker talked so long that ________.

Using the Exercises

Read and discuss the directions for each exercise before assigning the questions for independent work.

Exercise A. After the students have identified the selections with hyperbole, discuss what is being exaggerated in each one.

Exercise B. Encourage the students to illustrate at least one of their exaggerations. You may wish to display their work on a bulletin board.

Answers to Exercises

A. Identifying hyperbole: 1, 2, 4, 5

B. Answers will vary.

Review

Understanding the Process of Writing

Read and discuss the directions for **Understanding the Process of Writing** on page 130. Then assign the exercise for independent work. When the students have finished, call on volunteers to tell the answers. Make sure students can cite evidence from the statements to support their answers.

Understanding Sounds of Language

Read the directions for **Understanding Sounds of Language** with the class. Have the students copy the two samples onto their papers, leaving a line of space between every two lines of writing, as you list the following step-by-step directions on the board:

1. Underline the examples of alliteration and assonance in both samples.
2. Using letters of the alphabet, write the rhyme scheme of the poem.
3. Mark the stressed (′) and unstressed (˘) syllables in both samples.
4. Make a list of the words that imitate sounds.

Direct the students to follow the directions on the board and complete the exercise independently. When they have finished, discuss their answers.

Understanding Figures of Speech

Have a student read the directions aloud. Then have the students complete the exercise on their own. Remind them to identify the comparisons and tell how the two things being compared are alike. When the students have finished, discuss their answers.

CHAPTER 3 Review

Understanding the Process of Writing

Read the following statements by writers. Each one tells about one stage of the writing process—pre-writing, writing or revising. About which stage is each one speaking?

1. I read the manuscript aloud to myself and discover awkward words or phrases that had escaped me when I read them silently. In the final draft I have been known to spend several hours working over one page, or sometimes one paragraph, in order to get it as close to what I am trying to create as possible.
   —Robert M. McClung
2. Many writers find it useful to keep a notebook. In my own, I keep ideas for plots, characters observed from real life, scenes, scraps of speeches, even single phrases that flash into the mind.
   —Geoffrey Trease
3. I do not worry about length or the order in which the material is written down. Neither do I worry about incomplete sentences, spelling, or grammar. . . . This first draft is like an artist's quick sketch of a landscape or a figure.
   —Ann Petry

Understanding Sounds of Language

Read each of the following samples. Look for examples of these sounds of language. Identify each example you find. If you can, tell how the use of sound helps the reader to understand the example.

alliteration   rhythm
assonance   onomatopoeia
rhyme

Reinforcing the Lesson

To reteach, reinforce, or extend the skills in this lesson, see the following:

Skills Practice Book, Green Level—pages 73 and 74.

Additional Resource

Diagnostic and Mastery Tests, Green Level—Chapter 3 Mastery Test, pages 17 and 18

Answers to Study Questions

Understanding the Process of Writing

1. revising
2. pre-writing
3. writing

Understanding Sounds of Language

Alliteration in poetry sample: SUSHES, some, still, so, loudness, laughs, lovely; whiteness, whitely, whirs, white.

Alliteration in prose sample: light, leaves, like, little, laps, lawn, crab, crawling, cars; roof, roots, regarding; street, seaweed, sat, silent, substantial; was, water, were, would, wearing.

Assonance in poetry sample: SUSHES, hushes; flitter-twitters; laughs, laughs; whiteness, whitely, white.

Assonance in prose sample: afternoon, through, roof, roots; street, leaves, green, seaweed, eat, regarding, people; parked, cars, regarding.

Rhyme in poetry sample: SUSHES, hushes; flitter-twitter; me, be; shirts, hurts.

Rhythm in poetry sample:

CYNTHIA IN THE SNOW

Ĭt SÚSHĚS.

CYNTHIA IN THE SNOW

It SUSHES.
It hushes
The loudness of the road.
It flitter-twitters,
And laughs away from me.
It laughs a lovely whiteness,
And whitely whirs away
To be
Some otherwhere,
Still white as milk or shirts.
So beautiful it hurts.

—Gwendolyn Brooks

It was a beautiful afternoon. The street was very high with elms. The light that came through their roof of leaves was green and trembling like light through water. Fiona became a little crab crawling among the roots of seaweed. The parked cars were fishes which would eat her up, danger was everywhere. . . .

The houses sat back from their green laps of lawn, silent and substantial, regarding her like people wearing glasses.

—Elizabeth Enright, "Nancy"

Understanding Figures of Speech

Reread each sample above. Look for the following figures of speech:

simile	personification
metaphor	hyperbole

Identify each figure of speech you find. If you find a comparison, identify the two things being compared and tell how they are alike.

Ĭt húshĕs
Thĕ lóudnĕss ŏf thĕ róad.
Ĭt flĭttĕr-twĭttĕrs.
Ănd laúghs ăwáy frŏm mĕ.
Ĭt laúghs ă lóvelў whíteněss,
Ănd whítelў whírs ăwáy
Tŏ bé
Sŏme óthĕrwhére,
Stĭll whíte ăs mílk ŏr shírts.
Sŏ beaútĭfŭl ĭt hurts.

Rhythm in prose sample: Ĭt wăs ă bĕautĭfŭl ăftĕrnoón. Thĕ streét wăs vĕrў hígh wíth elms. Thĕ líght thăt căme thrŏugh thĕir róof ŏf leáves wăs gréen ănd trĕmblĭng lĭke líght thrŏugh wátĕr. Fíónă bĕcáme ă líttle crab cráwlĭng ămŏng thĕ róots ŏf séawĕed. Thĕ parked cárs wĕre físhĕs whĭch wŏuld éat hĕr úp, dángĕr wăs évĕrywhĕre. . . .

Thĕ hoúsĕs săt báck frŏm thĕir gréen láps ŏf láwn, sílĕnt ănd sŭbstántĭăl, rĕgárdĭng hĕr lĭke péople wéarĭng glássĕs.

Onomatopoeia in poetry sample: SUSHES, hushes, flitter-twitters, whirs.

Understanding Figures of Speech

Simile. Poem: The whiteness of the road is compared to that of milk and shirts. Prose: The light coming through the roof of leaves is green and trembling like light that goes through water. The houses seem to sit back and observe like people who wear glasses.

Metaphor. Prose: Fiona's movements are compared to a crawling crab. The parked cars are compared to dangerous fish surrounding her. The leaves of the trees are compared to a roof.

Personification. Poem: The road sushes and hushes, flitter-twitters, and laughs. Prose: The light trembles. The houses sit back and watch.

Hyperbole. The road is so beautiful, it hurts to look at it.

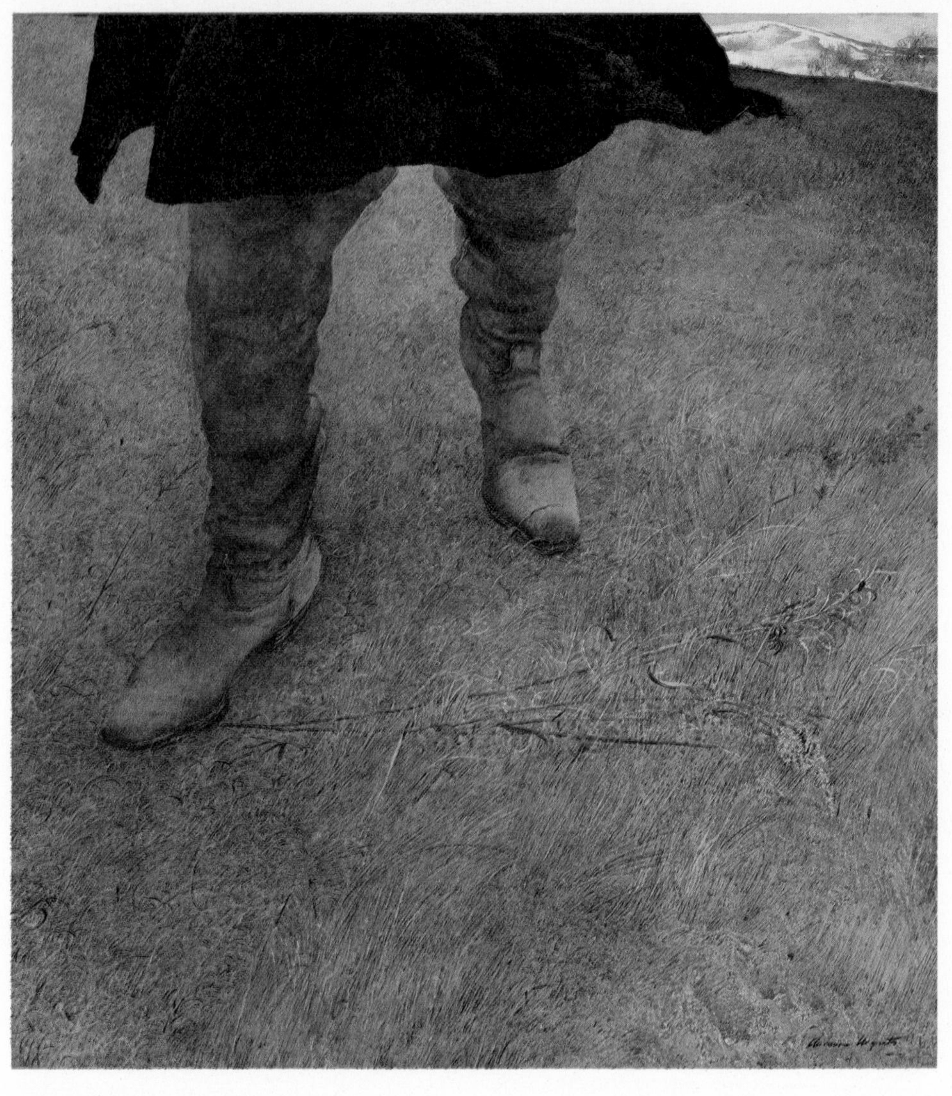

About the Art

Andrew Wyeth (born 1917) is well known for his realistic paintings of the countryside in Maine and Pennsylvania. Although the viewer is provided with a clear objective focus in his work, there always seems to exist beyond what can be seen the sense of an intimate and mysterious relationship between man and nature.

Wyeth heightens this relationship in *The Trodden Weed* by concentrating on one small area of ground. With his characteristic complete and patient attention to detail, he depicts the individual blades of grass with the same care as he gives to the pair of boots. At the same time, he has cut off the figure, and restricted our view of the countryside. Both the person's identity and the exact physical locale are withheld. Only the view into the distance in the upper right provides a clue that we are on a hillside, and allows us to adjust our tilted perspective.

Andrew Wyeth is the son of the artist N.C. Wyeth, one of whose illustrations appears on page 60.

CHAPTER 4

Short Stories

The Trodden Weed, 1951, ANDREW WYETH.
Private Collection.

Chapter Objectives

The following is a list of the major skills developed in study questions throughout this chapter:

Skills in Reading Literature

- To recognize and appreciate the short story as a form of literature
- To identify the characteristics of the short story, with special emphasis on plot, conflict, and characters
- To recognize the theme of a short story

Comprehension Skills

- To recall events in the order they occurred (Literal Reading)
- To understand cause and effect relationships (Interpretive Reading)
- To evaluate the believability of characters (Critical Reading)

Vocabulary Skills

- To recognize and use words with multiple meanings
- To recognize and use different levels of language
- To recognize the meanings of slang words and colloquialisms
- To complete analogies

Writing Skills

- To write an analysis of the effect of point of view (Analytical Writing)
- To write an evaluation of a character (Analytical Writing)
- To write a diary using events from a story (Creative Writing)
- To write an original short story (Creative Writing)

Study and Research Skills

- To compare reference sources
- To conduct a poll
- To identify the organization of an encyclopedia article
- To use the card catalog

Critical Thinking Skills

- To make generalizations from specific details
- To recognize the need to define terms
- To recognize deductive reasoning

Speaking and Listening Skills

- To act out an interview
- To read a dialog to express a mood

Reading Literature

Reading Literature: Short Stories contains information that will help the students understand and appreciate the short stories they will read in this chapter. After defining a short story, the text presents a brief history of the short story. Next it describes the element of plot in greater depth than the previous chapters have and explains the concept of point of view. Last it provides students with suggestions to aid them in reading short stories.

Preparing the Students

Ask the students if they have ever read any short stories before. They may have read them in other classes or in magazines or books from the library. Briefly discuss the short stories they remember. Tell the students that in this chapter they will learn more about short stories and will read a variety of short stories from many different times and places.

It is recommended that you administer the **Chapter 4 Diagnostic Test** at this time. The results of this pretest will serve as a guide for measuring student needs and progress in achieving chapter objectives.

Presenting the Lesson

1. Have the students read **What Is a Short Story?** Emphasize that each short story was created by one specific person. Also stress that since it is short, this type of story usually focuses on only one important event in the life of one character.

2. Have the class read **The History of the Short Story**. Explain that although stories have been told for thousands of years, the popularity of the short story written by one specific person is fairly recent. It is only since the 1800's that the short story has been a serious and respected way of writing. Stress the importance of each word of a short story in communicating the writer's message.

3. Have the students read **The Elements of the Short Story**. Discuss the element of plot in depth. Make sure the students know what happens in the introduction, rising action, climax, falling action, and resolution.

4. Discuss point of view. Have students restate sentences in the first-person as sentences in the third-person. For example, you might say, "I closed the window." The student would respond, "She [or he] closed the window." When discussing lim-

Reading Literature: Short Stories

What Is a Short Story?

A **short story** is a story short enough to be read from beginning to end at one time. A short story is fiction. It comes from the imagination of a single writer. A short story usually focuses on a single important event in the life of one character.

The History of the Short Story

The short story is a very old form of literature. Stories were told by storytellers long before they were written. Short, fictional stories were written down in Egypt as early as 3000 B.C. The Bible contains many short stories called **parables**.

Two outstanding collections of short stories were written around the year 1350. (This was about one hundred years before Malory wrote *Le Morte d'Arthur*.) An Italian writer, Giovanni Boccaccio, wrote a collection of tales called *The Decameron*.

A few years later, an English writer, Geoffrey Chaucer, wrote *The Canterbury Tales*. In this book, each member of a group of travelers tells a story.

In the 1800's, great writers all over the world became interested in the short story. They each developed slightly different ways of writing short stories.

American poet and writer Edgar Allan Poe studied the short story thoroughly. In his writings, he explained how he thought a short story should be written. He said that the goal of a short story should be to communicate a single idea. Every sentence and every word should be chosen carefully. If it was written correctly, Poe thought, the short story could communicate the writer's entire message before the reader became tired of reading. Poe's ideas strongly influenced later writers.

The Elements of the Short Story

The three main elements in a short story are the same as in a legend. They are characters, setting, and plot.

Plot. Many short stories follow the same general plan. It is a logical way of telling a story. Here is that plan.

Introduction: This comes at the beginning of the story. You meet the characters, learn about the setting, and see the beginning of a conflict, or struggle.
Rising Action: The struggle grows more intense.
Climax: This is the most exciting part in the story. It is the turning point.
Falling Action: After the climax, events follow their logical course to the end.
Resolution: All loose ends are tied up. The story ends.

Point of View. If the story is told by a character in the story, it is written from the **first-person point of view**. Then the writer uses words such as *I* and *we*. If a narrator who is not a character in the story is telling what happened, the story is written from the **third-person point of view**. Sometimes this narrator tells only what one person could know. That is the **limited** third-person point of view. Sometimes this narrator knows everything that happens. That is the **omniscient** third-person point of view.

How To Read a Short Story

1. Read carefully. Since these stories are so short, each word is important. You may miss something if you skip words.
2. Decide who is telling the story. Is it a narrator outside the story? Is it one of the characters in the story?
3. Keep track of the order of events.
4. Try to understand why one event leads to the next.

ited and omniscient third-person point of view, examine the word parts that are combined in the word *omniscient*. *Omni* is a Latin prefix meaning "all." *Sciens* is a form of a Latin verb meaning "to know." Therefore *omniscient* means "all-knowing."

5. Have individual students read **How To Read a Short Story** orally. Discuss the suggestions for reading and understanding the short story.

Reinforcing the Lesson

To reteach, reinforce, or extend the concepts in this lesson, see the following:

Skills Practice Book, Green Level—pages 75 and 76

Additional Resource

Diagnostic and Mastery Tests, Green Level—Chapter 4 Diagnostic Test, pages 19 and 20

Comprehension Skills

In this lesson, students will learn the necessity of finding relationships in order to understand what they read. The two specific relationships that will be discussed are time order and cause and effect relationships. Exercises will give the students practice in identifying and understanding each type of relationship.

Preparing the Students

Remind the students that the plot of a story is composed of a series of events. To understand any story, a reader has to see how each of the events is connected to the rest. Explain that in this section the students will learn about two important ways in which events in stories are connected to each other and will learn how to spot those relationships.

Presenting the Lesson

1. Have the students read **Finding Relationships Among Events** down to **Cause and Effect**. List the words that signal time order. Explain that these signal words are not used every time there is a time order relationship. Often the reader must simply assume that the events that are described first happened first.

2. Have the students read **Cause and Effect**. Make sure that they understand that this relationship refers to what happened and to the forces that made it happen. Emphasize how this relationship differs from time order relationship. List the words that signal a cause and effect relationship and again explain that writers do not always use these words. Stress that it is up to the reader to figure out what is the cause and what is the effect.

3. Have the students complete Exercises A and B independently. Discuss the answers together.

Reinforcing the Lesson

To reteach, reinforce, or extend the skills in this lesson, see the following:

Skills Practice Book, Green Level—pages 77 and 78

Special Populations

The lesson beginning on page 136 is one of considerable importance for special-populations students. Many students, especially LD students, have difficulty with

Comprehension Skills: Relationships

Finding Relationships Among Events

As you read, it is important to see how one event is connected to another. If you do not see the connections, the story will not make sense. Sometimes the writer tells how one event is related to others. Sometimes he or she gives clues, and you must figure out what the relationship is. Two important relationships to watch for are **time order** and **cause and effect**.

Time Order. Writers know that the order of events in their stories should be clear. Often, they leave clues to help you. Certain words are signals that tell you that time order is being explained. A few of these signal words are *after*, *before*, *finally*, *then*, *now*, *soon*, *next*, and *at last*.

Read the following paragraph. What event comes first? What comes last? The underlined words give you clues about time order.

> There was a meeting, about eleven in the morning, at the Town Hall. After that, everyone had a picnic on the green. Then the procession formed to escort the old soldiers out to the Burying Ground, where they put flags on the graves.

Cause and Effect. Sometimes the events in a story just occur in a certain order. Other times an early event is the reason for a later event. Then the early event is a **cause**, a reason why something happens. The later event is an **effect**, what happens as a result of the cause. Here is an example.

> I can't run because my running shoes are worn out.

Cause	**Effect**
My running shoes are worn out.	Therefore, I can't run.

Notice the underlined word in the sample sentence. *Because* is a key word to look for when you want to identify the reasons for something happening in a story. Some other key words are *so*, *for this reason*, *since*, *therefore*, and *that is why*.

A writer will not always provide signal words. However, you may still find a cause-and-effect relationship. For example, the sample sentence could have been stated in any one of these ways:

I can't run. My running shoes are worn out.
I need new running shoes. My old shoes are worn out.
My running shoes are worn out, and I can't run.

As you can see, you cannot only look for key words. You must think about each event and how it goes with other events.

Exercises: Understanding Time Order and Cause and Effect

A. Read this sentence from one of the stories in this chapter. Does it show a time-order relationship or cause and effect?

The old man hadn't heard this because he was so deaf.

B. Read this selection. Then answer the questions below.

Esmeralda stared at the coin she held in her hand. It was a shilling. She had never had any money before and was quite puzzled to know what she should buy with it. Almost without realizing what she was doing, she began to wander along the stalls, looking at different things offered for sale. Then she came to the toy counter.

1. What did Esmeralda do first? second? third?
2. The writer used two key words to show time order. Name one.
3. Why was Esmeralda puzzled?
   a. She stared at the coin in her hand.
   b. She had never had any money before.
   c. She began to wander along the stalls.
4. How was Esmeralda going to decide what to buy?

exercises asking them to find relationships or understand cause and effect events. Whenever possible, give extra attention to this skill, and provide additional examples to give the students practice understanding these concepts.

Answers to Exercises

A. cause and effect

B. Answers concerning paragraph:

1. First, Esmeralda stared at the coin. Second, she wandered along the stalls, looking at things for sale. Third, she came to the toy counter.
2. before, Then
3. b
4. She was going to see what was for sale and choose among the things.

Vocabulary Skills

In this vocabulary lesson on multiple meanings, students learn to use context clues to choose among the meanings of words with multiple meanings. They also learn that the meaning of a word may depend on the level of language in which it is used.

Exercises give students an opportunity to practice using context clues and levels of language to understand words with multiple meanings.

Preparing the Students

Ask the students to choose the meaning of the word *run* from this list of definitions: 1) to move on foot at a pace faster than a walk; 2) to make a short, quick trip; 3) to unravel along a line; 4) to continue; 5) a small, fast-moving stream; 6) an unbroken series of events; 7) an outdoor enclosed space for an animal. After they have made a guess, tell them that these are all definitions for *run*. Explain that in some dictionaries there are more than sixty definitions for that one word. Tell the students that there are many words like *run* that have more than one meaning. In this section, students will learn how to choose the meaning the writer intended.

Presenting the Lesson

1. Have the students read **Using Words with Multiple Meanings**. Ask individual students for original sentences using any of the meanings of *bit* and have the rest of the class choose the meaning that was used in each sentence. Review the meaning of *context*. Have students answer the questions about which definition of *bit* is used in the sentences in the text.

2. Have one student read **Levels of Language** aloud. Ask for examples of current slang words and their meanings.

3. Have the students complete Exercises A and B independently or as a group exercise. Discuss the answers together.

Reinforcing the Lesson

To reteach, reinforce, or extend the skills in this lesson, see the following:

Skills Practice Book, Green Level—pages 79 and 80

Vocabulary Skills: Multiple Meanings

Using Words with Multiple Meanings.

Can potatoes see with their eyes? If you're bright, do I need sunglasses to look at you? The underlined words in these sentences have more than one meaning. Many words in our language have multiple meanings. Often this fact makes it difficult for us to understand what a speaker or writer is saying.

For example, here are seven dictionary definitions for *bit*.

1. *n.*, a metal mouthpiece on a bridle
2. *n.*, the part of the key that turns the lock
3. *n.*, the cutting part of a tool
4. *n.*, a tiny piece
5. *n.*, a short time
6. *adj.*, very small: as, *he has a bit part*
7. *n.*, in computers, the smallest unit of information

The dictionary can tell you all the meanings of a word. However, in order to know exactly which definition is meant, you need to read the word in **context**—in a sentence or a paragraph.

Which definition of *bit* is meant in each sentence below?

1. The wild horse hated the feel of the bit in its mouth.
2. I'll be happy if I get even a bit part in the play.
3. In computer class, we learned that a bit is zero or one.

Levels of Language

Often the meaning of a word depends on the level of language in which it is used. The two major levels of our language are standard and nonstandard English. **Standard English** is accepted anywhere. **Formal standard English** is used in most writing. **Informal standard English** is used in everyday conversations.

Nonstandard English, unlike standard English, is not accepted everywhere. Baby talk, for example, is a kind of nonstandard English. Another kind of nonstandard English is **slang**. Slang includes new words or words with new meanings that are not used by everyone. For example, in standard English, you might say that an accident left your bike a total wreck. In slang, you might say that you totalled your bike. Some dictionaries label nonstandard words or meanings as slang.

Exercises: Using Multiple Meanings

A. Choose the correct definition for each underlined word.

1. Let us decide by lot which of us shall go into town.
   That movie was filmed on the back lot.
   a. lot—an object used to decide a matter by chance; the person who draws it from a container of like objects wins
   b. lot—in movies, a studio and its surrounding area
2. Be sure to lock the door with the bolt.
   How many bolts of cloth will it take to make the drapes?
   a. bolt—a roll of cloth or paper
   b. bolt—a sliding bar used to lock a door or gate
3. She had never met her cousins who lived in a distant city.
   The young woman's glance fell upon the prisoner with a distant, swift disinterest.
   a. distant—cool in manner, reserved
   b. distant—widely separated, far away

B. Choose one of the numbered definitions to answer each question.

tip (1) in baseball, to hit the ball a glancing blow
(2) **tip off** to give secret information to
(3) **tip one's hand** [slang] to reveal a secret

1. Which definition gives a meaning that is special for one sport?
2. Which definition gives a slang meaning?
3. Which definition gives a meaning used mostly in conversation?

Special Populations

ESL. The lesson on **Levels of Language** may need to be previewed or reinforced by the ESL specialist working with the ESL student. Understanding of the concepts presented will be related to the student's fluency and understanding of what constitutes "standard English." Many students may have difficulty distinguishing among formal standard English, informal standard English, and some examples of nonstandard English that include popular slang words. The student might need additional assistance from you, the ESL specialist, or a student tutor to complete the reading exercises pertaining to this lesson.

Answers to Exercise

A. Definitions:
1. a, b
2. b, a
3. b, a

B. Definitions of *tip*:
1. (1)
2. (3)
3. (2)

Great Classic Stories

Call on a student to read page 140 to the class. Point out that a model is someone or something that is copied, and ask in what ways modern writers might copy from these classic stories. If necessary, have the students reread the paragraph and notice the emphasis on setting, characters, and events, and the importance of making these imaginary things seem real. Suggest that, as the students read the selections in this part of the text, they watch for the variety of ways in which a writer leads readers to believe in what he or she has written.

Great Classic Stories

The first meaning of *classic* listed in the dictionary is "being a model of its kind." These stories by famous writers of the past are truly models for today's writers. They suggest how a short story can make a certain setting or character or event real for the reader. Even though they range in age from about eighty years to over five hundred years old, they still touch our feelings and lead us to think.

Eskimo Finger Masks, 1880, Private Collection. Photograph by Peter Furst.

About the Art

The art of nomadic peoples, such as the Eskimos of the Northwest, is small and scaled down so that it can be carried with the tribe as it moves in search of food. The finger masks shown here were made to be worn on the hand—two fingers are inserted into the holes at the base—and were probably used in religious ceremonies. They are based on the human face, but the features have been simplified and their significance is symbolic. Traditionally, one of the masks is male and one female.

The folklore of the Eskimos is an oral tradition that has been passed on to succeeding generations in stories and dances. The masks probably represented characters in those stories. They are very similar in appearance to the traditional smiling and frowning comedy and tragedy masks of Western culture.

How the Three Young Men Found Death

GEOFFREY CHAUCER

This story is set in the Middle Ages, when the disease called the Black Death killed one out of every four people throughout Europe. Read to find out what happened when three young men tried to stop Death.

In Flanders there was once a company of young men who devoted themselves to folly of all kinds: rioting, gambling, and drinking. They danced and played dice both day and night and drank more than they should.

One day, as three of these young men sat in a tavern, they heard the clanging bell of a funeral procession. One of them called out to a waiter, "Go and ask what corpse is passing by here."

"Why, sir," said the boy, "there is no need to ask. Only a short time ago someone told me. The dead man was a friend of yours. Last night as he sat drinking on his bench, suddenly the thief that men call Death came by and, with his spear, cut his heart in two and then went away without another word. He has taken thousands with his plague, and I would suggest that you be careful to avoid his presence."

The innkeeper then said, "The boy is telling the truth; for Death has taken many—men, women, and children—in the village this year. It seems as if he has made his home here."

"Is there such danger in meeting him?" one young man asked. "Why, then I shall look for him in every street. Let the three of us make a pact. Let us hold up our hands and swear to be brothers and to find and kill this traitor who has killed so many others!"

So together these three made their pact: to live and die for each other as brothers. And they started off to find Death, shouting that Death was as good as dead, if only they could find him.

When they had gone less than half a mile, they came upon an old man, who gave them a friendly greeting.

The proudest of the three young men spoke for all three. He said to the man, "You scoundrel, why are you all covered except for your face? How have you lived to be so old?"

Objectives

- To recognize and appreciate the short story as a form of literature
- To identify character traits
- To recognize foreshadowing
- To make a plot diagram
- To apply literal, interpretive, and critical reading skills to a selection
- To arrange events in the order they occurred
- To recognize multiple meanings of words
- To write a story using personification
- To make generalizations from specific details

Preparing the Students

Essential Vocabulary. The words presented here are essential to the understanding of the selection.

Have the students use the context clues in the following sentences to determine the meanings of the underlined words.

scoundrel betray apothecary

1. That scoundrel is known for lying, stealing, and cheating.
2. I will never betray you. I will be your faithful friend.
3. The apothecary made the medicine and poured it into a little bottle.

If the students need additional help with the vocabulary of this selection, encourage them to use context clues to determine word meaning. As needed, direct them to the **Glossary** or to a classroom dictionary.

Ask the students to tell you the qualities a true friend would have. List these on the board. Then suggest that as they read this next story, they should compare the actions of the three major characters with the list.

Motivation. Have the students read the introductory paragraph at the top of page 141 and state in their own words what they should try to find out as they read this short story. Point out that the author of this story, Geoffrey Chaucer, lived during the fourteenth century. This is the oldest story in this text.

Presenting the Selection

1. Have the students read "How the Three Young Men Found Death" on pages 141 to 144 independently. The English language has changed so much since this story was written that the original version is difficult to read; this is a modern English translation.

2. Make sure that everyone has read the assignment by administering the **Check Test** at the bottom of T.E. page 144.

3. Remind the students that the introduction to the story asked them to find out what happened when the three young men tried to stop Death. Have the students discuss the answer to this question.

4. Develop the study questions as suggested in **Using the Study Questions** beginning on page 145. That section also provides challenge questions for further discussion, as needed. (For answers to questions, see T.E. pages 145 to 147.)

Reinforcing the Lesson

To reteach, reinforce, or extend the skills in this lesson, see the following:

Skills Practice Book, Green Level—pages 81 through 84

Special Populations

When assigning the selections throughout this section, encourage the students to list words with which they are unfamiliar in their class notebooks. Have them copy key phrases along with the words in order to help them stay aware of context clues. After each word (and phrase), the student should write a definition, either from context clues or a dictionary.

Encouraging Independent Reading

Some students may be interested in learning more about the Black Death, or bubonic plague. Encourage them to research the subject in an encyclopedia to find out what kind of sickness it was, how many people it killed, when the major outbreaks occurred, and any other information they think is interesting. Have them give short oral reports about the plague to the class.

The Hunt of the Unicorn II: The Unicorn Dips His Horn into the Stream To Rid It of Poison (detail).
The Metropolitan Museum of Art, Gift of John D. Rockefeller, Jr., the Cloisters Collection, 1937.

The old man answered, "Even if I were to walk as far as India, I would not be able to find, in any town or village, a man who would be willing to exchange his youth for my age. And, therefore, I shall keep my age for as long as I live. So I walk around the earth in my shroud like a restless slave and hope for death. But you show no manners in speaking unkindly to an old man. You should treat an old man who has done you no harm as kindly as you would want to be treated in your old age—if you live so long. Now I must go."

"Oh, no, old dog," said the youth. "You shall not leave so easily. You just spoke now of the traitor Death, who has

About the Art

According to legend, the unicorn was able to purify a stream by dipping its horn into the waters. This is the story behind the detail of the tapestry reproduced here. It is the second tapestry of *The Hunt of the Unicorn* series (see **About The Art** on the frontispiece, the page opposite the title page of this book). In the detail, several gentlemen are shown with their attendants and dogs. They have just sighted the unicorn kneeling beside the stream below them. Note the detail of their facial expressions, the gestures of their hands, and also the color and texture of their clothing.

been killing all our friends in this area. I think that you are his spy, and I demand that you tell me where he is. Surely you are one of his helpers."

"Now, sirs," the old man said, "if you are so eager to find Death, turn up this crooked path. I left him under a tree in that grove, and there he will stay. Death will not hide from your boasting. Do you see that oak? You will find him there."

So together the three young men ran until they came to the tree. But there was no one there; instead they found eight bushels of coins—round and shiny gold pieces. The sight of such wealth drove all thoughts of Death from their minds, and they sat down by their treasure.

"Brothers," said one, "listen closely to what I say. Fortune has given us this treasure, and we shall spend it as easily as we found it. Once this gold is carried away from this place, to my house or to yours (for we know that all this gold is ours), then all will be well.

"But, after all, we cannot do it by daylight. Then people would say that we were thieves and hang us for our treasure. It must be carried away by night as carefully and secretly as we can. Therefore, let us draw lots to see which of us shall go into town to bring back food and drink. And two of us shall keep guard over the treasure. Then, when it is night, we shall carry it to wherever we agree is the best place."

The lot fell on the youngest of the three, and he went off toward the town. As soon as he was gone, one said to the other, "You know that you are my sworn brother, and now I will tell you your reward. Our friend has gone into town, but here is the gold (and plenty of it!) to be divided among the three of us. But if I can help it, it shall only be divided between us two. Isn't this a great favor to do a friend?"

The other answered, "I don't know how that can be. What will we do? What will we say to him?"

"Will you keep it a secret?" asked the first man. "If so, I will tell you in a few words how we will bring it about."

"I promise, by my honor," said the other, "that I will not betray you."

"Now," said the first, "there are two of us, and two are stronger than one. When he comes back, watch when he sits down and right away stand up as though you want to wrestle with him; and while you struggle with him, as in sport, I will run him through the side. Then, with your dagger, you do the same. And then, my dear friend, all this gold will be divided only between you and me; and we can both have everything we want and gamble as much as we like." And so these two agreed to kill the third.

On his way into town, the youngest thought of nothing but the bright and shiny gold coins. He thought, "If only I could have all that gold for myself; then there would be no man in all the world so happy as I."

At last he thought that he would buy poison with which to kill his two partners. When he got into town, he went straight to the apothecary and asked for poison to kill some rats.

The apothecary answered, "I will give you something that no being can withstand. Once you have given it, the creature will be dead before you have walked a mile—it is so strong and violent."

The young man took the box of poison; and on the next street he met a man from whom he bought three large bottles. He poured the poison into two and kept the third clean for his own drink. When he had filled the three bottles with wine, he returned to the grove where his friends waited for him.

Just as they had planned, the other two killed him as soon as he returned. And when they had done this, one said, "Let us sit down and drink and celebrate. We will bury him later." So he took one of the bottles with the poisoned wine and drank it down. Then he gave the other to his friend.

And soon, like their friend, the two found Death.

Vanitas, 1603, JACQUES de GHEYN the ELDER.
The Metropolitan Museum of Art; Curtis Marquand, Victor Wilbour Memorial, Charles B. and Alfred N. Punnett Endowment Funds 1974.

About the Art

Jacques de Gheyn the Elder (1565-1629) was a prominent Dutch painter. Originally an engraver who made pictures in black and white, he began to do oil paintings in 1603. He received many commissions from wealthy patrons, among them the Queen of France. *Vanitas*, painted in 1603, makes use of symbolic objects. The skull reminds us that beauty, like life, is only temporary, and vanity, the pride in and desire to possess temporary things like beauty, is useless and foolish. The bubble is a symbol, too. It suggests that our lives are short and can end suddenly at any time.

Check Test

1. How was Death killing thousands of people? (with the plague)

2. Where did the old man tell the young men they could find Death? (under a tree in a grove)

3. How did the youngest man kill his friends? (He poisoned them.)

Developing Comprehension Skills

Literal Reading — 1. Why do the three young men go to look for Death?

Interpretive Reading — 2. How do you think the old man knew exactly where Death was? Why do you think so?

Critical Reading — 3. These three young men put their desire for gold above their loyalty to each other. Can you think of any situation in which you would be justified in turning against a friend?

Literal Reading — 4. Rearrange the events listed below in terms of time order. Identify which happen first, second, and so on.

a. The youngest is killed by the other two young men.
b. The three young men find the coins.
c. All three young men find Death.
d. A corpse is carried past the tavern.
e. The three young men meet the old man.
f. The two young men drink the poisoned wine.
g. The youngest man goes to town for food and drink.
h. The three young men swear to be brothers.

Interpretive Reading — 5. In looking at this story as a whole, what do you think the author is telling you about life? In other words, what is the theme of this story? Can you identify another theme? What might it be?

Reading Literature: Short Stories

1. **Identifying Character Traits.** Reread the conversation of the three young men with the old man. Only one young man spoke, but the others did not object, so they must have agreed with their friend. What does this conversation tell you about the qualities, or traits, of the three young men? Find two other parts of the story that make you sure that your opinion of them was right.

2. **Making Inferences.** Often a writer will drop a hint about, or foreshadow, an event that happens later in the story. What is there in the old man's speech that contains a clue to the outcome of the story?

3. **Making a Plot Diagram.** Review the events listed in Developing Comprehension Skills, 4, above. Find the place for each event in the plot diagram below. More than one event may belong in each category. The correct position of two events has already been marked on the

Using the Study Questions

It is recommended that students always read and answer the questions in **Developing Comprehension Skills** in class discussion. Whenever possible, they should also read the questions in the other categories together and discuss the answers.

Developing Comprehension Skills

Question 1. Read and discuss. Encourage students to find proof of their answers in the text.

Question 2. Point out to the students the friendly, gentle way the old man acts and the wisdom in what he says. Ask how the old man shows his understanding of human nature.

Question 3. Have students think about times when friends have let them down and times when they have lost friends. Direct students to relate general situations, not persons' names or the details of their own experiences.

Question 4. You may wish to have the students identify just the first three events in class discussion, list these on the board, and then have them complete the exercise independently. If you use this procedure, be sure to discuss the answers together. Have the students retain these lists for use in **Reading Literature, 1** and **3.**

Question 5. Ask students to define *theme* in their own words (possible answer: a main idea of a selection). Explain that many themes can be found in this story. One major theme involves the relationship between life and death.

Challenge Question. Is death presented as an evil force or is it pictured as neither good nor bad? To answer this question, pay more attention to what Death does than to what people say about Death. (Interpretive Reading)

Reading Literature: Short Stories

Question 1. Have the students reread the last paragraph on page 141 through paragraph 2 on page 143. Then ask them whether they would have liked these men and why or why not. To help students find the appropriate parts of the story that support their opinions, have them look over the lists of major events they prepared in **Developing Comprehension Skills,** 4.

Question 2. Refer the students to the same conversation as was read in **Reading Literature,** 1.

Question 3. Draw a plot diagram on the board. Explain that this diagram may be used for many stories the students

Answers to Study Questions

Developing Comprehension Skills

1. The young men want to kill Death.

2. Possible answer: The old man had lived long enough to know that money usually causes trouble between people, especially cruel and unfeeling people like the young men. He knew that the money under the tree would bring either trouble or death. He knew the coins were there, since he left them there himself.

3. Answers will vary. Possible answer: You might be justified in turning against a friend if your friend decided to do something he knew was wrong.

4. Order of events: d, h, e, b, g, a, f, c

5. Answers will vary. Possible answers: No one can escape death. Death is part of life. Money causes nothing but trouble.

Challenge. Death is not evil. It takes people because that is what it has to do. The young men are the cause of their own deaths. Death is the result of their deeds.

Reading Literature: Short Stories

1. The young men are proud, disloyal, and cruel. They show their pride when

(continued on page 146)

read, and provide the following explanation of its shape: After the introduction, all events lead up to a climax. That is why the climax is placed at the highest point in the diagram. After the climax, events decrease in excitement, so they are placed on the diagram on a downward slanting line. The resolution is flat because there is no tension or suspense left in the story by that point.

Then have the students complete the diagram.

Question 4. Have students locate the parts of the story where Death is referred to as if it were a person. Explain that the humor in this story is subtle. It pokes fun at proud and stupid people.

Challenge Question. You were probably not sad when the young men died. How did the writer make sure that you would not care about these men?

Developing Vocabulary Skills

Read the directions for **Recognizing Multiple Meanings of a Word** together with the class. Complete the first pair of sentences with the students to make sure they know what they are to do. Have them complete the exercise independently and discuss the answers.

Developing Writing Skills

Read and discuss the two assignments. Then have each student choose and complete one of the two.

Question 1. Note that this question asks students to explain how the story would have been different if written from a first-person point of view. It does not ask students to rewrite it themselves.

Pre-Writing. Have students discuss which events were known by only one or two of the young men. Draw two columns on the board. In one column, list the events that would have been left out if the narrator were the young man who went to town. In another column, list the events that would have been left out if the narrator had been one of the men who plotted to stab him. Have students examine the differences between the lists. Remind them that the text question asks for an explanation of those differences.

Writing. Allow sufficient time for the students to write their first drafts. Remind them to use the notes on the board.

Revising. Have students exchange papers with a partner. Partners should read the paragraphs and identify the ways the writers feel the first-person account would have differed from the story as Chaucer

diagram. The letters *b* and *d* refer to the letters identifying the items in the Comprehension exercise on page 145.

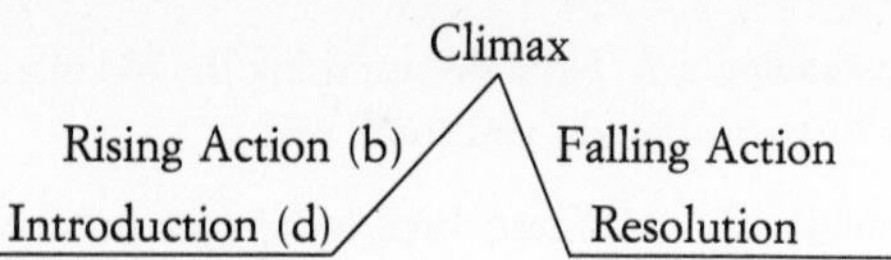

4. **Examining the Effect of Personification.** Death is a person in this story. How does this add to the interest of the story? How does it provide humor? Find at least three sentences in which there is a double meaning caused by thinking of Death as a person. Do you think these lines are humorous?

Developing Vocabulary Skills

Recognizing Multiple Meanings of a Word. Read the following pairs of sentences. In each pair, both sentences use a word drawn from the story. However, each sentence uses a different meaning of the word. Choose the correct meaning of the underlined word in each sentence from the definitions given.

1. Death came by and took away thousands with his <u>plague</u>.
2. Mosquitoes were annoying all day, but at dusk they became a <u>plague</u>.

   a. a very dangerous disease that spreads rapidly and often causes death
   b. a thing or person that torments or troubles

3. The sailors tied a secure <u>shroud</u> to the mast of the ship.
4. The old man had walked around the earth in his <u>shroud</u> like a restless slave.

   a. a rope stretched from a ship's side to the top mast.
   b. a wrap or garment used for burial

5. Not a <u>spear</u> of grass was found in the garden.
6. Death took his <u>spear</u> and cut the man's heart in two.

   a. a weapon used for thrusting or throwing
   b. a sprout or shoot of a plant

(continued from page 145)
they think they can kill Death. They show they are not true friends when they all decide to kill each other. They show their cruelty when they carry out their plans and stab and poison each other.

2. The first hint is the old man's comment about the young men in their old age—"if you live so long." When the young men question him, he says that Death is waiting under a tree and that Death will not hide from them.

3. Events on the plot diagram:
Introduction—d
Rising Action—h, e, b, g
Climax—a
Falling Action—f
Resolution—c

4. Since Death is a person, the reader pictures it and it becomes more real. It is humorous that anyone would think Death could be killed.

Sentences that show double meaning can be found in these parts of the story: the boy tells the men that Death has taken their friend, they vow to kill Death, the old man says that Death is waiting under a tree, and all three men eventually find Death. The following are possible answers:

7. The young man thought of nothing but the bright gold coins.
8. Alexis is very bright in math but not in science.
   a. clever
   b. radiating or reflecting light
9. Jon's favorite area of science is astronomy.
10. Many people in the area of the village had died suddenly.
    a. a field of study
    b. a particular geographical region

Developing Writing Skills

Analytical Writing

1. **Appreciating Point of View.** "How the Three Young Men Found Death" was written from the point of view of the all-knowing, or omniscient, author. Imagine that, instead, one of the young men had told the story to a passerby who found him dying of poison. Then the story would have been written from the first-person point of view. What parts of this story would the young man not know? What would he have left out? Would he have added anything? Write one or more paragraphs explaining how the story would have been different if it had been told from the first-person point of view.

Creative Writing

2. **Using Personification.** Write a story of no more than twelve paragraphs about three young people of today who go searching for one of these: Peace, Happiness, Excitement, or Wisdom. Personify the quality you choose. If you like, your heroes or heroines can meet and talk with the personified quality.

Developing Skills in Critical Thinking

Making Generalizations from Specific Details. List details given in this selection that show the character of the three young men. From this list, write three generalizations about the men. A **generalization** is a statement about a group that supposedly is true of all the members of the group. Your generalizations should be as accurate as possible.

Then make one generalization that is inaccurate and unfair to the men. Rewrite your generalizations in any order. Then exchange papers with a partner. The partners must identify the unfair generalizations.

wrote it. Allow time for students to improve the clarity and accuracy of their work.

Question 2. As students use personification in completing this writing assignment, they will see for themselves the effects it can create.

Pre-Writing. Group the students in small groups to brainstorm about the quality they can personify in their stories. If you wish, you can have the members of the group cooperate to write a story. Have the students make notes about the characters in their stories, the qualities they are seeking, and the setting. Have the students list the events in the order they will happen so that they will have an outline to work from.

Writing. Remind students to work from their outlines. However, tell them that they can alter the outline if they get a better idea. Allow sufficient time for the students to write their first drafts.

Revising. Have individual students or groups share their stories with the class or in small groups. Ask for criticisms, both positive and negative, from the listeners. Allow time for revisions to be made.

Developing Skills in Critical Thinking

Read the directions for **Making Generalizations from Specific Details** on page 147 with the students. On the board, list students' suggestions of details that show the characters of the young men. Ask the students to write and rewrite their generalizations according to the exercise directions. Then have them exchange papers with partners and identify the unfair generalizations. Discuss their generalizations together.

"Death has taken many—men, women, and children—in the village this year. It seems as if he has made his home here."

"And they started off to find Death, shouting that Death was as good as dead, if only they could find him."

"And soon, like their friend, the two found Death."

Some students may see the humor while others will not. The humor lies in the impossibility of killing Death and the play on words.

Challenge. The writer included only negative details about the men. He showed the men to be mean and greedy. They plot against each other and kill each other for money. When they die, the reader feels that they got what they deserved.

Developing Vocabulary Skills

1. a **2.** b **3.** a **4.** b **5.** b **6.** a **7.** b **8.** a **9.** a **10.** b

Developing Skills in Critical Thinking

Some possible generalizations are the following:

All three young men loved riches more than they loved their friends.

All three men liked to gamble, dance, and drink more than they should.

Some unfair generalizations are the following:

These men never did one good thing their whole lives.

All three men are lazy.

Objectives

- To recognize and appreciate the short story as a form of literature
- To identify internal conflict
- To identify the tone of a short story
- To apply literal, interpretive, and critical reading skills to a selection
- To choose the correct dictionary meaning for a word using context clues
- To analyze the role of a minor character
- To compare reference sources

Preparing the Students

Essential Vocabulary. The words presented here are essential to the understanding of the selection.

Write the following words and their definitions on the board. Have individual students read the words and their meanings aloud. Explain to the students that they will encounter these words in the following short story.

galleys—large ships propelled by oars and sails

hideous—ugly

sermonizing—speaking as though delivering a sermon

wavered—swung back and forth

gendarmes (zhän′ därm)—name for French police officers

recollection—memory

monseigneur (mōn sē nyôr′)—a French title of honor given to a person of high rank

monsieur (mə syur′)—a French title equivalent to Mister, used alone or prefixed to the name of a Frenchman

Mme, abbreviation for madame (me däm′)— French title equivalent to Mrs. for a married woman

Mdlle, abbreviation for mademoiselle (mad′ ə mä zel′)—an unmarried French girl or woman and used as a title equivalent to Miss

If the students need additional help with the vocabulary of this selection, encourage them to use context clues to determine word meaning.

Motivation. Discuss the meaning of *temptation*. Then ask the students to try to think back to the times they found it difficult to choose between right and wrong and ask them what prompted them to make the decisions they did. Tell them that in this story, they will read about a man who is faced with a temptation and the consequences of his decision.

Have the students read the introductory paragraph at the top of page 148 and state in their own words what they should

The Bishop's Candlesticks

VICTOR HUGO

In this short story, which is part of a novel, the two major characters act in ways that may surprise you. Try to find and understand the reasons each man had for acting as he did.

Les Miserables tells the story of Jean Valjean, a French peasant who stole a loaf of bread for his sister's starving children. He was sentenced to the galleys for five years. Because he repeatedly tried to escape, Jean's time in prison was increased until he had served nineteen years.

At last he was set free; and four days later something happened that changed his whole life.

The scene is the small house the bishop chose to live in rather than in the bishop's palace, which he had turned over for use as a hospital. The time is 1815.

As the bishop entered the dining-room, Mme. Magloire, the old servant, had just finished setting the table for supper. She was talking with some warmth to Mdlle. Baptistine, the bishop's sister, about the need for a lock for the front door. It seems that while she had been out making provision for supper, she had heard talk about a suspicious vagabond who was lurking somewhere in the town. It was said that some unpleasant adventures might befall those who came home late that night, and that everyone ought to bolt his door most carefully.

"We are not safe at all," said Mme. Magloire, "for nothing could be more horrible than a door that opens by a latch on the outside. And monseigneur has the habit of always saying, 'Come in,' even at midnight."

At this moment there was a violent knock on the door.

"Come in," said the bishop.

The door opened.

A man entered. He was a man of middle height, strong and hardy; he might have been forty-six or forty-seven years old. A slouched leather cap half hid his face, tanned by the sun and wind. He wore a coarse yellow shirt, open at the neck; shabby blue trousers, white on one knee and with holes in the other; an old ragged gray blouse patched on one side with a piece of green cloth sewed with twine. Upon his back was a well-filled knapsack, strongly buckled and quite new. In his hand he carried an enormous knotted stick; his stockingless feet were in hobnailed shoes; his hair was shorn but bristly, for it seemingly had not been cut for some time.

He came in, took one step, and paused, leaving the door open behind him. There was a rough, hard, tired, and fierce look in his eyes, as seen by the firelight. He was hideous.

Mme. Magloire had not even the strength to scream. She stood trembling, with her mouth open.

Mdlle. Baptistine turned, saw the man enter, and started out half alarmed; then slowly turned back again toward the fire. She looked at her brother, and her face resumed its usual calmness and serenity.

The bishop looked upon the man with a tranquil eye.

As he was opening his mouth to speak, doubtless to ask the stranger what he wanted, the man, leaning with both hands upon his club, glanced from one to another in turn, and, without waiting for the bishop to speak, said in a loud voice:

"See here! My name is Jean Valjean. I am a convict; I have been nineteen years in the galleys. Four days ago I was set free; today I have walked twelve miles. When I reached this place this evening, I went to an inn, and they sent me away. I went to another inn; they said: 'Get out!' I went to the prison and the turnkey would not let me in. In the square I laid down upon a stone; a good woman showed me your house and said: 'Knock there!' I have knocked. What is this place? Is it an inn? I have money; my savings, 109 francs and 15 sous, which I have earned in the galleys by my work for nineteen years. I will pay. I am very tired—and I am so hungry. Can I stay?"

"Mme. Magloire," said the bishop, "put on another plate."

The man stepped foward. "Stop," he exclaimed, as if he had not been understood. "I am a galley slave—a convict—I am just from the galleys." He drew from his pocket a large sheet of yellow paper, which he unfolded. "This is my passport, yellow, as you see. That is enough to have me thrown out wherever I go. It says, 'This man is very dangerous.' There you have it. Everybody has thrust me out. Will you receive me? Can you give me something to eat? Have you a stable where I can sleep?"

"Mme. Magloire," said the bishop, "put some sheets on the bed in the alcove." Then he turned to the man. "Monsieur, sit down and warm yourself. We are going to take supper presently, and your bed will be made ready."

try to find out as they read this short story. Explain that this story is taken from a long novel, but it contains all the elements of a short story.

Presenting the Selection

1. Read aloud and discuss the explanation of the story on page 148. Be sure the students understand the situation before they begin to read.

2. Have the students read "The Bishop's Candlesticks" silently. Since it is a long selection, you may want to assign it in two parts. The first part would then end on page 152, after the fourth full paragraph ("he fell on the bed, dressed as he was, into a sound sleep.")

3. Make sure that everyone has read the short story by administering the **Check Test**, at the bottom of T.E. page 154. If the story was read in two parts, administer Questions 1 and 2 after the first part and Questions 3 and 4 after the second part.

4. Remind students that the introduction to the story asked them to try to find and understand the reasons each man had for acting as he did. Ask several students for their answers to the question.

5. Develop the study questions as suggested in **Using the Study Questions** beginning on page 154. That section also provides challenge questions for further discussion, as needed. (For answers to questions, see T.E. pages 155 to 157).

Reinforcing the Lesson

To reteach, reinforce, or extend the skills in this lesson, see the following:

Skills Practice Book, Green Level—pages 85 through 87

Special Populations

LD. In this story and others of any length, encourage the students to list the characters and their actions in the story.

The first writing exercise on page 157, **Understanding a Minor Character**, talks about the author's purpose for introducing a character. Students may need help seeing the relationship of Mme. Magloire's dialog telling her fears to the introduction of Jean Valjean. To help them focus on the role that Mme. Magloire has in increasing the feeling of suspense or apprehension, ask the students to list some of the fear-producing statements or descriptions used on the first two pages of the story.

Encouraging Independent Reading

After reading "The Bishop's Candlesticks," some students may be interested in reading the entire story of Jean Valjean in the novel, *Les Misérables*. They may wish to find out if Valjean leads an honest life after the bishop pledges Valjean's soul to God. They may also wish to learn about the events that led up to Valjean's arrest and subsequent years in prison. Encourage the students to write a report on the important events in Valjean's life and the effects these have on his character. Remind them to refer to the **Checklist for the Process of Writing** on pages 556 and 557.

At last the man understood; his face, the expression of which till then had been gloomy and hard, now expressed stupefaction, doubt and joy, and became absolutely wonderful. He began to stutter like a madman.

"What? You will keep me? You won't drive me away—a convict? You call me 'monsieur' and don't say, 'Get out, dog!' as everybody else does. I shall have a supper! a bed like other people, with mattress and sheets—a bed! It is nineteen years since I have slept on a bed. I will pay well. I beg your pardon, Mr. Innkeeper, what is your name? You are an innkeeper, aren't you?"

"I am a priest who lives here."

"A priest," said the man. "How stupid I am. I didn't notice your cap."

While speaking, he deposited his knapsack and stick in the corner, replaced his passport in his pocket, and sat down.

Mme. brought in a plate and set it on the table.

"Mme. Magloire," said the bishop, "put this plate as near the fire as you can." Then turning toward his guest, he added: "The night wind is raw in the Alps; you must be cold, monsieur."

Every time he said the word "monsieur" with his gently solemn and heartily hospitable voice, the man's face lighted up. "Monsieur" to a convict is a glass of water to a man dying of thirst at sea.

"The lamp," said the bishop, "gives a very poor light."

Mme. Magloire understood him and, going to his bedchamber, took from the mantel the two silver candlesticks, lighted the candles and placed them on the supper table.

"Monsieur, you are good; you don't despise me. You take me into your house, you light your candles for me, and I haven't hid from you where I come from."

The bishop touched his hand gently and said, "You need not tell me who you are. This is not my house; it is the house of Christ. It does not ask any comer whether he has a name, but whether he has an affliction. You are suffering; you are hungry and thirsty. Be welcome. Whatever is here is yours. What need have I to know your name? Besides, before you told me, I knew it."

The man opened his eyes in astonishment. "You knew my name?"

"Yes," answered the bishop, "Your name is my brother."

Meantime Mme. Magloire had served up supper. It consisted of soup, a little pork, a scrap of mutton, a few figs, a green cheese, and a large loaf of rye bread. She had added, without asking, a bottle of fine old wine.

"To supper!" said the bishop briskly. When they were seated, he asked the blessing and then served the soup. Suddenly he said: "It seems to me something is lacking on the table."

Mme. Magloire understood the remark; without a word she went out and, a moment afterward, returned with the three extra silver plates that they always had on the table when there were guests.

The man ate with the voracity of a starving man, paying no attention to anyone. Meanwhile, the bishop chatted pleasantly of Pontarlier, to which place Jean Valjean said he must be on his way by daybreak. He told of the many paper-mills, tanneries, and iron foundries there, saying that, during the revolution when his family was ruined, he himself had worked there. Without giving the stranger any advice, he let him know where there was a place that he could stay and where he was sure to find work. Never once did he bring into the conversation any sermonizing.

Immediately after the dessert, the bishop said, "You must be in great need of sleep." Bidding goodnight to his sister, he took one of the silver candlesticks from the table, handed the other to his guest, and said to him:

"Monsieur, I will show you to your room."

To reach the alcove where Jean Valjean was to sleep, they had to pass through the bishop's sleeping-chamber. As they went through this room, Mme. Magloire was just putting up the silver in the cupboard at the head of the bed. The bishop left his guest in the alcove before a clean, white bed. The man set down the candlestick upon a small table.

"A good night's rest to you," said the bishop. "Tomorrow morning before you go, you shall have a cup of warm milk from our cows."

"Thank you, monsieur," said the man. A moment afterward, so completely exhausted was he that, after blowing out the candle, he fell on the bed, dressed as he was, into a sound sleep.

As the cathedral clock struck two, Jean Valjean awoke.

He had slept only four hours, but he could not get to sleep again. Many thoughts came to him, but there was one that continually presented itself and that drove away all others. He had noticed the six silver plates and the large ladle that Mme. Magloire placed in the cupboard at the head of the bishop's bed. They were solid and old silver. With that big ladle, they would bring at least 200 francs; double what he had got for nineteen years' labor.

His mind wavered a whole hour, in fluctuation and in struggle. The clock struck three. He opened his eyes, got up hastily in bed, and put his feet on the floor. All at once, he stooped down and took off his shoes. Then he rose to his feet, hesitated for a moment longer, and listened. He placed his belongings near the window and, with stealthy steps, moved toward the door of the bishop's room. On reaching it he found that it was unlatched. He pushed it a little, then more boldly. This time a rusty hinge sent out into the darkness a harsh creak. For a moment he thought he was lost. But minutes passed, and he ventured to look into the room. The bishop had not stirred.

A deep calm filled the chamber. As Jean Valjean paused before the bed, suddenly the dark clouds parted, and a ray of moonlight, crossing the window, lighted up the bishop's face. The effect was startling. The expression of content, hope, and happiness on his countenance became radiant, and he appeared as if in a halo.

Jean Valjean, standing in the shadow, erect, motionless, was terrified. He had never seen anything comparable to it. He did not remove his eyes from the old man. One would have said he was hesitating between two realms—that of the doomed and that of the saved.

In a few moments, he raised his left hand slowly to his forehead and took off his cap. He stood for some time looking at the sleeping bishop. Then, suddenly he put on his cap, passed quickly to the cupboard, turned the key, opened it, took the basket of silver, passed quickly to the window in the alcove, stepped out, ran across the garden, leaped over the wall like a tiger, and fled.

The next day at sunrise, as the bishop was walking in the garden, Mme. Magloire came running, quite beside herself, to tell him that the silver was stolen, the man was gone! The bishop was silent for a moment, then, raising his serious eyes, he said mildly:

"Mme. Magloire, I have for a long time wrongfully withheld this silver. It belonged to the poor. Who was this man? A poor man evidently."

A short time later, the bishop and his sister were having breakfast when there was a knock at the door.

"Come in," said the bishop.

The door opened. A strange, fierce group appeared on the threshold. Three men were holding a fourth by the collar. The three were gendarmes; the fourth, Jean Valjean. One of them stepped forward and addressed the bishop.

"Monsiegneur," said he.

The bishop rose and approached as quickly as his great age permitted. "Ah, there you are," he said, looking toward Jean Valjean. "I am glad to see you. But I gave you the candlesticks also, which are silver like the rest and would bring 200 francs. Why did you not take them along with your plates?"

Jean Valjean opened his eyes and looked at the bishop with an expression that no human tongue could describe.

"Monseigneur," said the gendarme, "then what this man said was true? We met him. He was going like a man who was running away, and we arrested him in order to see. He had this silver."

"And he told you," interrupted the bishop, with a smile, "that it had been given him by a good old priest with whom he had passed the night. I see it all. And you brought him back here? It is all a mistake."

"If that is so," said the gendarme, "we can let him go."

"Certainly," replied the bishop.

The gendarmes released Jean Valjean, who shrank back.

"You can go. Do you not understand?" said one of them.

"My friend," said the bishop, "before you go away, here are your candlesticks. Take them." He went to the mantelpiece, took the two candlesticks, and brought them to Jean Valjean, who was trembling in every limb. He received the two candlesticks mechanically.

"Now," said the bishop, "go in peace." To the gendarmes he said, "Messieurs, you can retire." The gendarmes withdrew.

Using the Study Questions

It is recommended that students always read and answer the questions in **Developing Comprehension Skills** in class discussion. Whenever possible, they should also read the questions in the other categories together and discuss the answers.

Developing Comprehension Skills

Question 1. Have students find proof of their answers in the text.

Question 2. Review the crime Valjean was punished for and the reasons he had been forced to serve for nineteen years. Also have the students consider the way people had treated him since he was released from jail.

Question 3. Ask a student to read aloud the bishop's final speech on page 154. Have students discuss the way the bishop acts throughout the story.

Question 4. Explain that although the story gives no definite answer to this question, students can make guesses based on the characters and the situations involved.

Challenge Question. Do you think that Jean Valjean should have been punished for stealing the silver? (Critical Reading)

Reading Literature: Short Stories

Question 1. Read and discuss.

Question 2. Have students suggest the two courses of action. Write them in two columns on the board. Then have students suggest the advantages and disadvantages and list these in the appropriate columns.

Question 3. Have students consider the descriptions of each character, as well as what they say and do.

Jean Valjean felt like a man who is about to faint.

The bishop approached him and said in a low voice, "Forget not, never forget that you have promised me to use this silver to become an honest man."

Jean Valjean, who had no recollection of this promise, stood confused. The bishop had laid much stress upon these words as he uttered them. He continued solemnly:

"Jean Valjean, my brother, you belong no longer to evil, but to good. It is your soul that I am buying for you. I withdraw it from dark thoughts and from the spirit of perdition, and I give it to God."

Developing Comprehension Skills

Literal Reading	1. Why was Jean Valjean directed to knock on the bishop's door?
Interpretive Reading	2. Describe Jean Valjean's life for the past nineteen years. What things had happened to him that would make it possible for him to consider taking the silver?
Critical Reading	3. What does the bishop say his reasons are for giving the silver to Jean Valjean? Do you think these are his real reasons? Explain your answer.

Check Test

1. Why did the townspeople turn the stranger away? (He was a convict.)

2. What word or title of respect did the bishop repeatedly use when he spoke to Jean Valjean? (monsieur)

3. What did Valjean steal? (the bishop's silver)

4. How did the bishop save Valjean from going to jail? (He told the gendarmes that he gave Valjean the silver.)

Answers to Study Questions

Developing Comprehension Skills

1. The woman knew that the bishop would give the man a place to sleep for the night.

2. For nineteen years, Jean Valjean had been a convict working on a galley. Since his crime had been so small and he had served so much time for it, he probably thought he deserved the silver. He may also have remembered the poor treatment he had been given by other people, and may have been afraid he could not get the job.

3. The bishop says that Valjean promised to use the silver to become an honest man. Valjean never said he would do this. However, the bishop hoped that by giving Valjean the silver he would save him from hatred and despair and give the man's soul to God.

4. Answers will vary. Some possible answers are the following:

Valjean will become an honest man. He didn't really want to steal the silver. He took over an hour to talk himself into stealing it. ("His mind wavered ... in struggle.") Now that he has money, he won't have to steal.

Critical Reading

4. Do you think Jean Valjean will use the silver to become an honest man, able to support himself? Why or why not? Quote any passages you can find from the story to support your answer.

Reading Literature: Short Stories

1. **Identifying the Plot Line.** On your paper, fill in the missing parts of this plot diagram for "The Bishop's Candlesticks."
   a. Introduction: Jean Valjean comes to the Bishop's house and is fed and housed.
   b. Rising Action: Jean Valjean wakes in the night and runs off with the bishop's silver, but is brought back by three gendarmes.
   c. Climax:
   d. Falling Action: the gendarmes leave him with the bishop.
   e. Resolution:

2. **Identifying Internal Conflict.** When he woke at 2:00 A.M., Jean Valjean's "mind wavered a whole hour, in fluctuation and in struggle." Describe the two opposing courses of action that Valjean was considering. For each course, list both advantages and disadvantages for him. Then tell why you think he chose the one he did.

3. **Identifying Tone.** The **tone** of a story is the author's attitude toward the theme, plot, and characters. The approach may be a serious one, a somber one, or a light and happy one. For example, the tone of "How the Three Young Men Found Death" was somewhat amused. The narrator seemed to think the young men were foolish and not worth feeling sorry for. How would you describe the tone of "The Bishop's Candlesticks"? Is the author making fun of the characters, or is he concerned about them? What parts of the story make you think as you do?

4. **Understanding Character.** In the third paragraph from the end of the selection, the bishop tells Jean Valjean, "Forget not, never forget that you have promised me to use this silver to become an honest man." Valjean cannot remember the promise. Did he make it? Is the bishop imagining things? Consider the bishop's other actions and statements, particularly his reaction to Mme. Magloire's news that the silver was stolen and his final statement. Then tell what reasons you think he might have had for telling Valjean about his "promise."

Question 4. Explain to students that people sometimes give promises without stating the promises directly. For example, people who join a club are promising to follow the rules of the club even though they might not say so. Ask them how Valjean could have given a promise without saying the words.

Ask students to figure out what the bishop wanted Valjean to do with his life.

Challenge Question. Reread the first three paragraphs on page 151. Then interpret the following metaphor. "Monsieur" to a convict is a glass of water to a man dying of thirst at sea.

Developing Vocabulary Skills

Read the directions for **Identifying Multiple Meanings in a Dictionary Entry** on page 156 with the class. Be sure that the students understand the directions. Then have them complete the exercise independently. Discuss the answers together.

Developing Writing Skills

Read and discusss the two assignments. Then have each student choose and complete one of the two.

Question 1. As they write an answer to this question, students will see how each detail in a short story works toward accomplishing the author's purpose.

Pre-Writing. Have the students skim pages 148 and 149 to find details about Mme. Magloire. On the board, list these details about her, including what she talks about and what she does. Then discuss with the class how Mme. Magloire's character and actions affect the mood of the story. Briefly review the text question and

Valjean will not be able to be honest. People have been cruel to him ("When I reached this place ... let me in.") and will continue to be since he is a convict, and he will have trouble getting a job. He will be forced into crime because he can't make an honest living.

Challenge. Answers will vary. Possible answers are the following: Valjean should not have been punished. He had been treated unfairly for nineteen years and deserved a chance to start his life over again.

Valjean should have been punished. He stole, and stealing is a crime. Anyone who breaks the law should be punished, or the laws will become worthless.

Reading Literature: Short Stories

1. Climax: The bishop tells the gendarmes that he gave the silver to Valjean.

Resolution: The bishop tells Valjean not to forget that he has promised to be an honest man. The bishop says that he has saved Valjean's soul.

2. One course of action: Valjean could steal the silver. An advantage would be that he could sell the silver and have enough money to make a new start. A disadvantage would be that he would have committed another crime and would be a wanted man. Equally important, he would have betrayed a person who was kind to him, and he obviously regretted doing that.

Other course of action: Valjean could resist the temptation to steal the silver. An advantage would be that he could respect himself for being honest and trustworthy, but a disadvantage would be that he would still be poor.

Valjean probably chose to steal because he was angry at the injustice done to him

(continued on page 156)

point out the two basic questions that must be answered: Why is Mme. Magloire in the story? How does she fill that role?

Writing. Suggest that students begin their paragraphs with topic sentences. Allow sufficient time for the students to write their first drafts.

Revising. Have students refer to the **Checklist for the Process of Writing** on pages 556 and 557 to revise and proofread their paragraphs before they hand them in.

Question 2. You may want to complete the list of details with the class and then have them write their paragraphs independently.

Pre-Writing. Have students skim the story, looking for details that describe Valjean. List these on the board and discuss how each detail adds to the mood.

Writing. Allow sufficient time for the students to write their first drafts. Remind them to use the notes on the board. Encourage the students to use the details to create a mood in their descriptions.

Revising. Have students exchange papers with a partner. You may want to pair up strong writers with weaker writers. Have the partners identify the mood the writers created in their descriptions. Allow time for papers to be revised and recopied.

Developing Skills in Study and Research

Read aloud the directions for **Comparing Reference Sources** on page 157. Have the students read silently the biography of Victor Hugo on page 586. Discuss the information given there. Then assign the remainder of the exercise for homework or schedule a visit to the school library. Discuss students' findings with them.

Developing Vocabulary Skills

Identifying Multiple Meanings in a Dictionary Entry. Several words in "The Bishop's Candlesticks" have more than one dictionary meaning. Each of the following pairs of sentences uses one of those words with two of its meanings. Below the pair of sentences is part of the dictionary entry for the underlined word. For each, choose the definition that best fits the context of the sentence. On your paper, write the letter of your choice.

1. There was a rough, tired, and fierce look in the man's eyes.
2. Miss David asked for a rough outline of the project.
   a. having a coarse or uneven surface: *rough road*
   b. shaggy and tangled: *a dog with a rough coat*
   c. harsh; rude; ungentle: *a rough manner*
   d. not completed; hastily done as a first try: *a rough idea*
   e. in golf, any part of the course bordering the fairway

3. The convict was looking for a stable in which he could sleep.
4. The concrete poles supporting the tent were quite stable.
   a. a building for lodging and feeding of horses
   b. not likely to fall or give way
   c. able or likely to continue or last: *a stable government*
   d. in chemistry, resisting molecular or chemical change: *a stable compound*

5. In the town square, Jean Valjean lay down upon a stone.
6. "Find the square of four," asked Mr. Jenkins.
   a. a rectangle having all four sides of equal length
   b. an open area bounded by streets in a city or town, used as a park
   c. in math, the product of a number multiplied by itself.

7. While speaking, the man had deposited his knapsack and stick in the corner.
8. The miners found rich deposits of iron.
   a. to put, place, or set down
   b. to insert (a coin) in a coin-operated device
   c. to place money for safekeeping in a bank account
   d. a natural accumulation of oil or ore
   e. money placed in a bank account

156 SHORT STORIES

(continued from page 155)

and he was worried that he would never be able to get a job and support himself.

3. The tone is sympathetic. The author seems to care about these characters. The bishop welcomes Valjean into his home and trusts him. Valjean hesitates a long time before taking the bishop's silver.

4. Valjean never made the promise in words, but when he allowed the bishop to save him, he became indebted to the bishop. The bishop didn't really care about the silver. In fact, he thought that he should give it to the poor anyway. He decided that he should use the silver to give Valjean's soul to God.

Challenge. Valjean needed the bishop's kindness and courtesy to feel alive.

Developing Vocabulary Skills

1. c **4.** b **7.** a **9.** c
2. d **5.** b **8.** d **10.** a
3. a **6.** c

9. Mrs. Barnes hurried to the sale to bid for the old chair.
10. The bishop bid goodnight to his sister and took one of the silver candlesticks from the table.

    a. to say as a greeting, or wish: *to bid the visitors farewell*
    b. in cards, to enter a bid of a given suit: *to bid hearts*
    c. to make an offer to purchase at a price
    d. an invitation

Developing Writing Skills

Analytical Writing

1. **Understanding a Minor Character.** Look at the beginning of the selection and list the details that are given about Mme. Magloire. What is her role in the Bishop's household? What does she talk about? What are her fears?

   Why did Victor Hugo write about Mme. Magloire in the beginning of this selection? What was the author's purpose? How does the description of Madame Magloire achieve this purpose? Write at least one paragraph discussing her role in setting the mood of the story.

Creative Writing

2. **Creating a Mood.** In this story, Victor Hugo and the translator chose words deliberately. They carefully created the mood of fear and suspense that hovers about the character of Jean Valjean. List at least ten of the words and phrases used to describe Valjean that establish this mood. Then use several of those words and phrases in a single paragraph describing Valjean.

Developing Skills in Study and Research

Comparing Reference Sources. Read the short biography of Victor Hugo in the Handbook for Reading and Writing in this book. What does it tell you about this author? Also, look up Victor Hugo in at least two other reference books:

a dictionary	an almanac
an encyclopedia	your choice of any other reference books

Find the answers to these questions: Do both of the books you looked into list Victor Hugo? Which tells the most about him? Which tells the least? Which entry is the most interesting to you?

Objectives

- To recognize and appreciate the short story as a form of literature
- To understand the function of the introduction
- To recognize irony
- To apply literal, interpretive, and critical reading skills to a selection
- To relate cause and effect
- To use parts of speech in determining word meanings
- To recognize slang words and colloquialisms
- To write a comparison of characters
- To make inferences

Preparing the Students

Essential Vocabulary. The words presented here are essential to the understanding of the selection.

Have the students use the context clues in the following sentences to determine the meanings of the underlined words.

influx	counterfeiting
forestalled	petition

1. After the doors of the hall were opened, the <u>influx</u> of ticketholders was so great that in minutes all the seats were filled.
2. The squirrels <u>forestalled</u> winter starvation by gathering nuts in the fall.
3. The man was arrested for <u>counterfeiting</u>, or making fake copies of, twenty dollar bills.
4. The governor refused the <u>petition</u> that asked him to pardon the convicted killer.

If the students need additional help with the vocabulary of this selection, encourage them to use context clues to determine word meaning. As needed, direct them to the **Glossary** or to a classroom dictionary.

Motivation. Have the students read the introductory paragraph at the top of page 158 and state in their own words what they should try to find out as they read this short story. Discuss with the students how they would have handled the situation described in the introduction.

Presenting the Selection

1. Have the students read "Hearts and Hands" on pages 158 to 160 silently.

2. Make sure that everyone has read the assignment by administering the **Check Test**, at the bottom of T.E. page 160.

Hearts and Hands

O. HENRY

Have you ever walked down a street and met someone you once knew? How do you explain what has happened to yourself in the meantime? Read the story to see how two people handled this situation.

At Denver there was an influx of passengers into the coaches on the eastbound express. In one coach there sat a very pretty young woman dressed in elegant taste and surrounded by all the luxurious comforts of an experienced traveler. Among the newcomers were two young men, one of handsome presence with a bold, frank countenance and manner; the other a ruffled, glum-faced person, heavily built and roughly dressed. The two were handcuffed together.

As they passed down the aisle of the coach, the only vacant seat offered was a reversed one facing the attractive young woman. Here, the linked couple seated themselves. The young woman's glance fell upon them with a distant, swift disinterest; then with a lovely smile brightening her face and a tender pink tingeing her rounded cheeks, she held out a little gray-gloved hand. When she spoke, her voice, full, sweet, and deliberate, proclaimed that its owner was accustomed to speak and be heard.

"Well, Mr. Easton, if you will make me speak first, I suppose I must. Don't you ever recognize old friends when you meet them in the West?"

The younger man roused himself sharply at the sound of her voice. He seemed to struggle with a slight embarrassment which he threw off instantly, and then clasped her fingers with his left hand.

"It's Miss Fairchild," he said, with a smile. "I'll ask you to excuse the other hand; it's otherwise engaged just at present."

He slightly raised his right hand, bound at the wrist by the shining "bracelet" to the left one of his companion. The glad look in the girl's eyes slowly changed to a bewildered horror. The glow faded from her cheeks. Her lips parted in a vague, relaxing distress. Easton, with a little

laugh as if amused, was about to speak again when the other forestalled him. The glum-faced man had been watching the girl's expression with veiled glances from his keen, shrewd eyes.

"You'll excuse me for speaking, miss, but I see you're acquainted with the marshal here. If you'll ask him to speak a word for me when we get to the pen, he'll do it, and it'll make things easier for me there. He's taking me to Leavenworth prison. It's seven years they give for counterfeiting."

"Oh!" said the girl, with a deep breath and returning color. "So that is what you are doing out here? A marshal!"

"My dear Miss Fairchild," said Easton, calmly, "I had to do something. Money has a way of taking wings unto itself, and you know it takes money to keep step with our crowd in Washington. I saw this opening in the West, and—well, a marshalship isn't quite as high a position as that of ambassador, but—"

"The ambassador," said the girl, warmly, "doesn't call any more. He

3. Remind students of the introduction. Ask them how the two characters reacted to the chance meeting.

4. Develop the study questions as suggested in **Using the Study Questions** beginning on page 161. That section also provides a challenge question for further discussion, if needed. (For answers to questions, see T.E. pages 161 to 164.)

Reinforcing the Lesson

To reteach, reinforce, or extend the skills in this lesson, see the following:

Skills Practice Book, Green Level—pages 88 through 90

Special Populations

LD. The irony of the switch of characters in the story may be so subtle that it is lost to some students. Make sure students have the correct answer for the first question under **Developing Comprehension Skills** before going on to other questions.

Students may need further help in determining second meanings for statements listed under **Recognizing Irony** on page 162. First, make sure the students understand the meaning that might be implied from Miss Fairchild's point of view. Then ask the students to reread the phrases (or the paragraph including each of the phrases) and see if they can see the meaning of the sentences, knowing that Mr. Easton is actually the criminal. This exercise can be coupled with the one on page 164, **Making Inferences**, to establish a better understanding of what actually was happening in the story.

Encouraging Independent Reading

Tell the students that O. Henry wrote a number of stories that, like "Hearts and Hands," have surprise endings. If this intrigues them, refer them to one of the many existent O. Henry anthologies, such as *O. Henry Stories*, with an introduction by Henry Golden.

needn't ever have done so. You ought to know that. And so now you are one of these dashing Western heroes, and you ride and shoot and go into all kinds of dangers. That's different from the Washington life. You have been missed."

The girl's eyes, fascinated, went back, widening a little, to rest upon the glittering handcuffs.

"Don't you worry about them, miss," said the other man. "All marshals handcuff themselves to their prisoners to keep them from getting away. Mr. Easton knows his business."

"Will we see you again soon in Washington?" asked the girl.

"Not soon, I think," said Easton. "My butterfly days are over, I fear."

"I love the West," said the girl, irrelevantly. Her eyes were shining softly. She looked away out the car window. She began to speak truly and simply, without the gloss of style and manner: "Mamma and I spent the summer in Denver. She went home a week ago because Father was slightly ill. I could live and be happy in the West. I think the air here agrees with me. Money isn't everything. But people always misunderstand things and remain stupid—"

"Say, Mr. Marshal," growled the glum-faced man. "This isn't quite fair. I'm needin' a drink, and haven't had a smoke all day. Haven't you talked long enough? Take me in the smoker now, won't you? I'm half dead for a pipe."

The bound travelers rose to their feet, Easton with the same slow smile on his face.

"I can't deny a petition for tobacco," he said, lightly. "It's the one friend of the unfortunate. Good-bye, Miss Fairchild. Duty calls, you know." He held out his hand for a farewell.

"It's too bad you are not going East," she said, reclothing herself with manner and style. "But you must go on to Leavenworth, I suppose?"

"Yes," said Easton, "I must go on to Leavenworth."

The two men sidled down the aisle into the smoker.

The two passengers in a seat nearby had heard most of the conversation. Said one of them: "That marshal's a good sort of chap. Some of these Western fellows are all right."

"Pretty young to hold an office like that, isn't he?" asked the other.

"Young!" exclaimed the first speaker, "why—Oh! didn't you catch on? Say—did you ever know an officer to handcuff a prisoner to his right hand?"

Check Test

1. Where was the young man going? (to Leavenworth Prison)

2. What was Easton's crime? (counterfeiting)

3. How did the nearby passenger know that Easton was not the marshal? (His right hand was in the handcuff.)

Answers to Study Questions

Developing Comprehension Skills

1. Mr. Easton was the prisoner, and the glum-faced man was the marshal. A marshal never handcuffs a prisoner to his right hand and Mr. Easton's right hand was cuffed. That's why he couldn't shake Miss Fairchild's hand. Some readers will realize that Easton is not the marshal earlier in the story, but everyone should realize it after the final paragraph.

2. They had known each other in Washington ("it takes money to keep step with our crowd in Washington"). They had known each other a long time ago

Developing Comprehension Skills

Literal Reading 1. Which man was the prisoner and which the marshal? How do you know? When, in reading the story, did you know?

Literal Reading 2. Where, when, and how well had Miss Fairchild and Mr. Easton known each other before this meeting? Give statements from the story to support your answer.

Interpretive Reading 3. Why does Miss Fairchild say, "I could live and be happy in the West"? What is she trying to tell Easton?

Interpretive Reading 4. What does the author mean when he says Miss Fairchild "reclothed herself with manner and style"? When had she removed manner and style and for what reason?

Critical Reading 5. Do you think the marshal showed good manners and sensitivity by doing what he did? Which person did he help more, Miss Fairchild or Easton? Do you think he showed the proper regard for his office?

Reading Literature: Short Stories

1. **Identifying Time Order.** List these events in the proper time order. Number them from one to five.

    Miss Fairchild and Mr. Easton meet and speak on the train.
    Mr. Easton is arrested and convicted for counterfeiting.
    Miss Fairchild and Mr. Easton part forever.
    Mr. Easton goes West to seek his fortune.
    The marshal pretends to be the prisoner.

    At which of these events does this story begin?

2. **Understanding the Introduction.** In a short story, the reader should be made to feel at home in the story as soon as possible. In the first paragraph of this story, what do you learn about these topics:

    a. who the characters are
    b. what kind of person each character is
    c. where the action will take place

3. **Understanding Cause and Effect.** The marshal acts quickly when he decides to pretend he is the prisoner. What occurrence on the train caused him to make this decision? What are some of the effects of the decision?

("Don't you ever recognize old friends ..."). They had known each other well enough to know each others' friends ("The ambassador doesn't call any more. He needn't ever have done so. You ought to know that.")

3. Miss Fairchild is trying to tell Mr. Easton that she would be willing to stay in the West to be with him.

4. Miss Fairchild's manner became formal again. She had removed manner and style when she spoke about how much she wanted to stay in the West. She did this to impress upon Mr. Easton how much she wanted to be with him again.

5. The marshal showed kindness and sensitivity by pretending to be the prisoner. He kept Mr. Easton from being embarrassed because of his situation. To a lesser degree, he was also kind to Miss Fairchild in letting her think her friend was doing well and saving her from the disgrace of being friendly with a criminal. Opinions about whether he showed the proper regard for his office will vary.

Challenge. The marshal probably knew that Miss Fairchild was expecting to renew her relationship with Mr. Easton. He stopped the conversation so that neither one would get too involved and get hurt.

(continued on page 162)

Using the Study Questions

It is recommended that students always read and answer the questions in **Developing Comprehension Skills** in class discussion. Whenever possible, they should also read the questions in the other categories together and discuss the answers.

Developing Comprehension Skills

Question 1. Read and discuss.

Question 2. Explain that students will need to infer the answer to this question based on evidence in the story.

Question 3. Have students discuss the probable relationship between Mr. Easton and Miss Fairchild considering their reactions to each other.

Question 4. Ask students how people usually act when talking to acquaintances rather than close friends. Ask students to find the references in the story to Miss Fairchild's changes in behavior.

Question 5. Explain that this question asks students to form a personal opinion.

Challenge Question. Why did the marshal stop the conversation and ask to go to the smoker car? (Interpretive Reading)

Reading Literature: Short Stories

Question 1. Ask a student to identify the event that happened first and write it on the board. Then have the students complete the exercise independently. Be sure to discuss the order of events together.

Question 2. Have a student read the introduction aloud. Then list the three topics on the board, leaving ample space between each one. Ask students to identify the details from the paragraph that describe the topics.

Question 3. Refer students to the bottom of page 158, paragraph 6, through page 159, paragraph 3.

Question 4. Have the students reread the passages that contain the given quotations. Have them consider what they thought the sentence meant the first time they read it, and then have them identify the second meaning they know now.

Developing Vocabulary Skills

Question 1. In preparation for this lesson, list the parts of speech and their abbreviations on the board.

Read and discuss the directions to **Using Parts of Speech To Determine Meanings** on page 162. Be sure that students have located the four words in the text before assigning the exercise. Remind them to refer to the parts of speech on the board. Then have students complete the exercise independently and discuss the answers together.

Question 2. Define *slang words* for the students (language peculiar to a particular group) and give a few examples (such as *hogwash, wing it, put the lid on*). Discuss the meaning of each example. Then ask a student to read aloud the directions on page 163. Have the students complete the exercise independently and discuss the answers together.

Question 3. Ask a student to read the directions aloud. Then have students complete the exercise independently and discuss the answers together.

Developing Writing Skills

Read and discuss the two assignments. Then have each student choose and complete one of the two.

Question 1. To answer this question, students will need to recall the traits of a character in "The Bishop's Candlesticks." Their comparison requires the skill of analysis as well as evaluation.

Pre-Writing. Have students skim "The Bishop's Candlesticks" to refresh their memories about the major events in the story. Then ask for suggestions about the character traits of each of the criminals in the two stories. List students' suggestions on the board. Have students compare the descriptions of the two characters and write a topic sentence stating their opinions of either one or both of the characters.

Writing. Encourage students to look for differences as well as similarities between the characters. Have them explain at least three ways that the characters were alike or different. Remind them to include their opinions about both characters. Allow sufficient time for the students to write their first drafts.

Revising. Have students exchange papers with partners. Have the partner look for three ways in which the characters were alike or different. Allow time for corrections and revisions to be made.

Question 2. Have the students approach this question realistically, emphasizing events that are believable.

Pre-Writing. Have students get together in small groups and brainstorm about possible alternate endings. Have them answer the questions on page 164 in their groups.

Writing. Have each student write a new outcome to the story independently. Allow sufficient time for the students to

4. **Recognizing Irony.** This story uses a special form of irony. Dramatic irony occurs when the truth is known to everyone in the story except the principal character. The facts of this story are known to everyone except Miss Fairchild. She must talk and act on the wrong assumption until the end. She takes at face value everything that is said by Easton or the sheriff. What is the second meaning that can be understood in the following quotations from their conversations?
   a. Easton: "I found this opening in the West."
   b. Easton: "It takes money to keep step with our crowd in Washington."
   c. Marshal: "Mr. Easton knows his business."
   d. Easton: "My butterfly days are over, I fear."
   e. Miss Fairchild: "But people always misunderstand things and remain stupid—"
   f. Marshal: "This isn't quite fair."
   g. Easton: "I must go on to Leavenworth."

Developing Vocabulary Skills

1. **Using Parts of Speech To Determine Meanings.** Many words in the English language can be used as more than one part of speech. For example, the word *design* is used as a noun in the first sentence below and as a verb in the second.

   That wallpaper has a bold design.
   Ms. Forbes will design a new building.

   Several words in "Hearts and Hands" may be used as more than one part of speech. Find the words *express, coach, taste,* and *comforts* in the first paragraph of the story. Decide from the context of the sentence how each word is used. Then read the dictionary entry below for each word. On your paper, write the part of speech of the word in that sentence. Then write the dictionary definition that best fits the context of the sentence.

   a. **express** *v.* **1.** put into words. **2.** show by look, voice, or action. **3.** to press or squeeze out. *-adj.* **4.** clear and definite. **5.** especially direct or fast. *-n.* **6.** a train or bus that carries passengers, packages, money. **7.** a quick means of sending, *by express.*

(continued from page 161)

Reading Literature: Short Stories

1. The following is the proper order of events:

Mr. Easton goes West to seek his fortune.
Mr. Easton is arrested and convicted for counterfeiting.
Miss Fairchild and Mr. Easton meet and speak on the train.
The marshal pretends to be the prisoner.
Miss Fairchild and Mr. Easton part forever.

2. The details in the introduction include the following:

a. The characters are a wealthy young woman, a handsome young man, and a roughly-dressed older man.

b. The young woman is used to luxuries and travel. The young man looks brave and honest. The older man is heavily-built, uncheerful, and roughly-dressed.

c. The action will take place aboard an eastbound train.

3. The marshal pretends to be the prisoner when he notices how distressed the young woman becomes when she sees the handcuffs. Some effects of the decision: The conversation between Easton and Miss Fairchild is then pleasant instead of painful. Miss Fairchild tries to

b. **coach** *n.* **1.** a large old-fashioned, horse-drawn carriage. **2.** a passenger car of a railroad train. **3.** a class of airline travel. **4.** a person who trains or teaches athletes. **5.** a private tutor. *-v.* **6.** to give instruction or advice. **7.** to study with or be instructed by a coach.

c. **taste** *v.* **1.** to try or test the flavor of something. **2.** to eat or drink a little bit of. **3.** to experience; have: *to taste freedom.* **4.** to have a particular flavor; *this tastes of garlic.* *-n.* **5.** sensation, flavor, or quality of something: *the taste of lemons.* **6.** a liking for something: *taste for art.* **7.** the sense of what is fitting or beautiful.

d. **comfort** *v.* to soothe or console; cheer; *comfort him in his loss.* **2.** to make physically comfortable. *-n.* **3.** a person or thing that gives consolation: *The child was a great comfort to her.* **4.** a cause of satisfaction: *It was a comfort to see him.* **5.** freedom from hardships: *He enjoys his comforts.*

2. **Recognizing the Meaning of Slang Words.** Many slang words are used about and by criminals. Identify the meaning of each word listed below. Tell whether you used context clues, the dictionary, or both to find the meaning.

   a. bracelet (page 158, column 2, paragraph 5)
   b. pen (page 159, column 1, paragraph 2)

3. **Recognizing the Meaning of Colloquialisms.** A phrase used mostly in everyday conversation is called a **colloquialism**. Find these colloquialisms in the story. Use context clues to determine their meanings. On your paper, tell what each phrase means.

   a. to keep step (page 159, column 2, paragraph 2)
   b. I'm half dead (page 160, column 2, paragraph 1)
   c. speak a word for me (page 159, column 1, paragraph 2)

Developing Writing Skills

Analytical Writing

1. **Comparing Characters.** In both "The Bishop's Candlesticks" and "Hearts and Hands," one of the major characters is a lawbreaker. Jean Valjean and Mr. Easton are very different characters, however. Write a paragraph or more comparing Valjean and Easton. How do you feel toward each of them?

write their first drafts. Remind them to use realistic reactions and details.

Revising. Assign students to new groups and have them read their stories aloud. Have them share their feelings about whether they like the O. Henry story with its surprise ending better than their realistic stories. You may wish to have the students make clean copies of their stories for a bulletin board display entitled "Imagine That!"

Developing Skills in Critical Thinking

Have students read **Making Inferences** on page 164. Make sure they understand the directions and then give them enough time to reread the story, looking for clues. Tell them to take notes as they read. Discuss the clues they found.

renew her close friendship with Mr. Easton and even expresses her desire to remain out West with him.

4. Students should identify the following second meanings:

a. I saw a chance to make money illegally in the West.

b. I felt pressure to have enough money to keep up with our crowd of friends.

c. Mr. Easton knows the crime he has committed; or, Mr. Easton knows that I know my business.

d. I'll be in prison for quite a while.

e. I hope you understand what I am saying.

f. It isn't fair to mislead Miss Fairchild this way.

g. I must go to prison.

Developing Vocabulary Skills

1. Parts of speech and meanings are:
- **a.** noun; 6. a train or bus that carries passengers, packages, money.
- **b.** noun; 2. a passenger car of a railroad train.
- **c.** noun; 7. the sense of what is fitting or beautiful.
- **d.** noun; 5. freedom from hardships.

2. Slang words mean:
- **a.** bracelet—handcuffs, context clues
- **b.** pen—penitentiary, context clues or dictionary

3. Colloquialisms mean:
- **a.** to keep step—to keep up with
- **b.** I'm half dead—I really need
- **c.** Speak a word for me—Help me by saying something good about me.

(continued on page 164)

Creative Writing

2. **Changing the Outcome of a Story.** Imagine that the marshal in "Hearts and Hands" had not pretended to be the prisoner. Then write a short story of what might have happened in this encounter on the train. Before you write, consider these questions:
   a. What elements in the O. Henry story will be missing in yours?
   b. How will the characters change in different circumstances? For instance, does Miss Fairchild get angry, or does Mr. Easton show remorse?

Developing Skills in Critical Thinking

Making Inferences. Now that you know the story of "Hearts and Hands," reread it for clues that might have told you the truth, that Mr. Easton was the prisoner and the burly man was the marshal. Identify at least two clues.

(continued from page 163)

Developing Skills in Critical Thinking

The following are clues that might be used:

Page 158, column 2—The younger man roused himself sharply at the sound of her voice. He seemed to struggle with a slight embarrassment which he threw off instantly.

Page 159, column 1—The marshal interrupted Easton when he saw Miss Fairchild's reaction to the handcuffs. A prisoner probably wouldn't have done this.

Page 160, column 1—Easton says, "My butterfly days are over," meaning that he will not be free for a long time.

The Bet

ANTON CHEKHOV

Think of how you have changed in the last five years. Then imagine spending three times as long, alone. What might those years do to you? In this story, does the lawyer expect what happens to him?

It was a dark autumn night. The old banker was pacing from corner to corner in his room, recalling to his mind the party he had given in the autumn fifteen years before.

There had been many clever people at that party. There was much good talk. They talked, among other things, of capital punishment. The guests for the most part disapproved of it. They found it old-fashioned and evil as a form of punishment. They thought it had no place in a country that called itself civilized. Some of them thought that capital punishment should be replaced right away with life in prison.

"I don't agree with you," said the host. "In my opinion, capital punishment is really kinder than life in prison. Execution kills instantly; prison kills by degrees. Now, which is better? To kill you in a few seconds, or to draw the life out of you for years and years?"

"One's as bad as the other," said one of the guests. "Their purpose is the same, to take away life. The government is not God. It has no right to take a human life. It should not take away what it cannot give back."

Among the company was a young lawyer, a man about twenty-five. "Both are evil," he stated, "but if offered the chance between them, I would definitely take prison. It's better to live somehow than not to live at all."

"Nonsense!"

"It is so!"

"No!"

"Yes!"

The banker, who was then younger and more nervous, suddenly lost his temper. He banged his fist on the table. Turning to the young lawyer, he cried out:

"It's a lie! I bet you two million you couldn't stay in a prison cell, even for five years."

"Do you mean that?" asked the young lawyer.

The banker nodded eagerly, his face an angry red.

Objectives

- To recognize and appreciate the short story as a form of literature
- To recognize character development
- To understand internal and external conflict
- To identify the mood of a short story
- To apply literal, interpretive, and critical reading skills to a selection
- To recognize cause and effect relationships
- To complete and explain analogies
- To examine the use of the flashback as a literary technique

Preparing the Students

Essential Vocabulary. The words presented here are essential to the understanding of the selection.

Have the students use the context clues in the following sentences to determine the meanings of the underlined words.

capital punishment　　despise
haphazardly

1. The killer was sentenced to capital punishment, or death.
2. Phil didn't seem to follow any plan for getting the job done. He just worked haphazardly.
3. I despise radishes and I hate green peppers too.

If the students need additional help with the vocabulary of this selection, encourage them to use context clues to determine word meaning. As needed, direct them to the **Glossary** or to a classroom dictionary.

Motivation. Have the students read the introductory paragraph at the top of page 165 and state in their own words what they should try to find out as they read this short story.

Presenting the Selection

1. Have the students read "The Bet" on pages 165 to 169 independently.

2. Make sure that everyone has read the assignment by administering the **Check Test,** at the bottom of T.E. page 169.

3. Remind students that the introduction asked them to find out if the lawyer expects what happens to him. Have them answer the question.

4. Develop the study questions as suggested in **Using the Study Questions** beginning on page 170. That section also provides challenge questions for further discussion, as needed. (For answers to questions, see T.E. pages 170 to 173.)

Reinforcing the Lesson

To reteach, reinforce, or extend the skills in this lesson, see the following:

Skills Practice Book, Green Level—pages 91 through 93

Special Populations

LD, ESL. The exercise **Completing Analogies** on page 172 gives a good sequential follow through for the student to gain a better understanding of the relationships of analogies. ESL students, in particular, may need individual assistance completing the exercise.

Encouraging Independent Reading

Since "The Bet" is a story of a person who is isolated from the outside world for several years and shows the effects that the experience has on the person's character, you may wish to recommend a book with a similar plot, such as *Anne Frank: The Diary of a Young Girl* or *Island of the Blue Dolphins* by Scott O'Dell.

"Then I accept your bet," the lawyer said simply. "But I'll stay not five years but fifteen."

"Fifteen! Fifteen!" cried the banker. He was now wild, as though he had already won the bet. "Done, then. The people here are our witnesses. I stake two million rubles. You stake fifteen years of your freedom."

So this foolish, senseless bet came to pass. At the time, the banker had too many millions to count. He was beside himself with joy. All through dinner he kept talking about the bet. He said to the lawyer jokingly, "Come to your senses, young man. It's not too late yet. Two million is nothing to me, but you stand to lose three or four of the best years of your life. I say three or four, not fifteen. You'll never stick it out longer than that, I can tell you. And they'll just be wasted years. Not the smallest coin do I give you if you leave earlier than fifteen years. Why, just think of it! My jail will have no bars, no locks. You'll be able to walk out of it any time you want to. That thought will be like poison to you. So you will walk out, I know that. Sooner or later, you will!"

Now the banker, pacing from corner to corner, recalled all this and asked himself, "Why did I make this bet? What's the good? The lawyer loses fifteen years of his life, and I throw away two million. That bet was a mistake. On my part, it was the foolishness of a well fed man. On the lawyer's part, it was pure greed for gold."

He remembered, further, what happened after the evening party. It was decided that the lawyer's "prison" would be in the garden wing of the banker's house. For fifteen years the lawyer was not to go through its door. He was not to see living people or to hear a human voice. He was not to receive letters or newspapers. Musical instruments, however, were to be permitted. He could also read books and write letters. Some other things, he could order. He had only to pass his order note through a special window. A guard would bring anything allowed.

Thus, the smallest details of the bet were discussed and settled. At twelve noon on November 14, 1870, the prison term began. It was to last until twelve noon on November 14, 1885. The lawyer must make no attempt to break the rules agreed upon. Any attempt to escape, even for two minutes, would free the banker from having to pay the two million.

The lawyer's first year, as far as it was possible to judge from his short notes, was one of suffering. He grew lonely and bored. From his wing, day and night, came the sound of the piano. Short, easy novels were his only reading—love stories, crime, and comedy.

In the second year, the piano was heard no more. The lawyer asked only for classics. By the fifth year, music was heard again. Guards who peeked into his room said that he yawned often and talked angrily to himself. Books he did not read

now. Sometimes at night, he would sit down to write. He would write for a long time and then tear it all up in the morning. More than once, he was heard to weep.

In the second half of the sixth year, the prisoner began zealously to study languages, philosophy, and history. He fell on these subjects with hunger. The banker hardly had time to get books enough for him. In four years' time, about 600 volumes were brought at his request. Later on, after the tenth year, the lawyer sat before his table and read only the New Testament. Then he went on to the history of religions.

During the last two years, the prisoner read a huge amount, quite haphazardly. He would ask for books on science. Then it would be Shakespeare. Notes used to come from him, asking at the same time for books on chemistry, religion, and medicine, as well as for a novel. He read as though he were swimming in a sea among broken pieces of wreckage. In his desire to save his life, he was eagerly grasping at one thing after another.

The banker recalled all this and thought, "Tomorrow at noon he receives his freedom. Under the agreement, I shall have to pay him two million. But if I pay, it's all over with me. I shall be ruined forever."

Fifteen years before, he had had too much money to count. Now, he did not know which he had more of, money or debts. He had gambled on the stock market—and lost. He had made business deals that turned sour. The fearless, proud man of business had become an ordinary person, trembling with worry about money.

"That cursed bet!" murmured the old man. "Why didn't the lawyer die? He's only forty years old. He will take all my money. He will marry and enjoy life. To him, I will look like an envious beggar, and he will say, 'Look, let me help you.

After all, I owe my happiness to your money.' Oh, such shame!

"Ruin and shame," the banker went on. "No—it's too much. Too much for anyone. I must escape ruin and shame, even if he has to die—even if he has to die!"

The clock struck three. The banker stood, listening. In the house everyone was asleep, and he could hear only the frozen trees whining outside the windows. He put on his overcoat and went out of the house. The garden was dark and cold. It was raining. A damp wind argued with the noisy trees. Nearing the garden wing, he called the guard twice. There was no answer. "Good," the banker thought. Evidently the guard had taken shelter from the bad weather. The man was probably sleeping in the kitchen or greenhouse.

"If I have the courage to kill this man," thought the old banker, "the guard will get the blame."

In the darkness he groped for the door. It opened without a sound. In the prisoner's room, a candle was burning dimly. The prisoner sat by the table. Only his back, the hair on his head, and his hands were visible. Open books lay everywhere—on the table, on the two chairs, on the carpet.

Five minutes passed, and the prisoner never once stirred. "Probably asleep," thought the old banker. He stepped forward. Before him, at the table, sat a man unlike an ordinary human being. It was a skeleton, with tight skin, long curly hair like a woman's, and a shaggy beard. The face was yellow. The cheeks were sunken. The hands were so long and skinny that they were painful to look upon. His hair was already silvering with gray, and no one who looked at the thin, aging face would have believed that he was only forty years old. On the table before his bent head, lay a sheet of paper covered with tiny handwriting.

"Poor devil," thought the banker. "He's asleep and probably seeing millions in his dreams. I only have to throw this

half-dead thing on the bed. Then I'll smother him in a moment with the pillow. But first, let's read what he has written."

His eyes dropped to the paper:

> Tomorrow, at noon, I am to have my freedom. I shall have the right to mix with people. But before I leave this room, I want to say a few words to you. My conscience is clear, and I stand before God, who sees me. I declare to you that I despise all that your books call the blessings of the world.
>
> For fifteen years I have studied earthly life. In your books I hunted deer and sang songs. In your books I climbed Mt. Blanc. I saw from there how the sun rose in the morning. In your books I worked miracles, burned cities to the ground, preached new religions, conquered whole countries—
>
> Your books gave me wisdom. I know that I am cleverer than you all. You are mad and gone the wrong way. You worship things, not ideas. You take falsehood for truth and ugliness for beauty. So do I marvel at you, you have traded heaven for earth. I do not want to understand you.
>
> To show that I despise all that you live by, I give up the two million I once so desired. Can your money buy wisdom? No. I shall come out of here five minutes before noon tomorrow. I shall thus break our agreement.

When he had read this, the banker kissed the head of the strange man. He began to weep. He went out of the wing. Never, not even after his terrible losses in the stock market, had he felt such hatred for himself. Back in his own room, he lay down on the bed. Tears of guilt kept him a long time from sleeping.

The banker slept late the next morning. About noon the poor guard came running to him. The prisoner had escaped! He had walked out into the garden! He had gone to the gate and disappeared!

The banker instantly went with his servants to the wing. Yes, the prisoner was gone. To avoid rumors, he picked up the note on the table. He made two neat folds. And on his return, he locked it in his safe.

Check Test

1. How long did the lawyer bet he could stay alone in a room? (fifteen years)

2. Why did the banker want to kill the lawyer? (The banker would be ruined if the lawyer won the bet.)

3. How did the banker win the bet? (The lawyer left before the end of the fifteen years.)

Using the Study Questions

It is recommended that students always read and answer the questions in **Developing Comprehension Skills** in class discussion. Whenever possible, they should also read the questions in the other categories together and discuss the answers.

Developing Comprehension Skills

Question 1. Encourage students to find evidence for their answers from the text.

Question 2. Have students prepare their lists independently. Then ask students for suggestions for a class list to be written on the board. Have students compare their lists with the class list.

Question 3. Before discussing the question, have students reread the letter on page 169.

Question 4. Explain to students that this question is not answered directly in the text. To answer, they must formulate personal opinions, but their opinions should be based on events in the story.

Question 5. Have the students reread page 166, column 1, in which the banker jokes with the lawyer about the bet. Then have them answer the question.

Challenge Question 1. Do you think that the lawyer wasted the years of his imprisonment, or did he make better use of those years than most people do? (Critical Reading)

Challenge Question 2. Why did the lawyer insist on extending his term of imprisonment from five to fifteen years when the bet was made? (Interpretive Reading)

Developing Comprehension Skills

Literal Reading

1. What is being discussed at the party? What are the young lawyer's thoughts on this topic? What are the banker's thoughts on the topic?

Literal Reading

2. Rearrange the events listed below in terms of time order. Identify which happened first, second, and so on.
   a. The banker reads the letter written by the lawyer.
   b. The banker and lawyer make the bet at the party.
   c. The banker decides to kill the lawyer.
   d. The banker is pacing from corner to corner in his room, worried about the consequences of his bet.
   e. The guard finds the prisoner has escaped.
   f. The prisoner reads books on many different subjects.
   g. The banker places the letter in the safe.
   h. The banker loses his temper and challenges anyone to a bet.

Interpretive Reading

3. According to the letter found on the lawyer's desk, why was he going to break the bet? What does this suggest about the reason he took the bet in the first place?

Critical Reading

4. Because the lawyer left the room before the noon deadline, the banker won the bet. Remembering that the original argument was about capital punishment as opposed to life imprisonment, who do you think won the argument?

Interpretive Reading

5. Did the lawyer walk out before the deadline for the reason the banker said he would?

Reading Literature: Short Stories

1. **Understanding Cause and Effect.** As you know, a **cause** is a reason why something happens. An **effect** is what happens as a result of the cause. Read each passage below and identify at least one cause and one effect discussed in each.

   a. "Why did I make this bet? What's the good? The lawyer loses fifteen years of his life, and I throw away two million. That bet was a mistake. On my part, it was the foolishness of a well fed man. On the lawyer's part, it was pure greed for gold."

Answers to Study Questions

Developing Comprehension Skills

1. Capital punishment is being discussed at the party. The young lawyer believes that it is better to live in prison than not at all. The banker thinks capital punishment is kinder than life imprisonment.

2. The following is the correct order of events: h, b, f, d, c, a, e, g.

3. The lawyer was going to break the bet because through his studies he became wiser than the rest of society that had gone the "wrong way." He no longer respected or wanted to be like the rest of society. He probably took the bet in the first place to make money, and he no longer wants even that.

4. Opinions may vary. Some students may feel that the banker won the argument because it was more cruel to make the lawyer live alone all those years than to kill him. Others may think that the lawyer became a better person and so imprisonment was proven to be kinder than death.

5. The banker had thought that the lawyer would not be able to resist the urge to be free,since he would not be locked in. The lawyer actually did resist that urge but left before the deadline because he didn't want the money anymore.

Challenge 1. Opinions will vary, but all opinions should be supported by logical reasons. Some students may feel it was worthless for the lawyer to live those years alone when he could have been learning about life by living it with other people. Others may feel that the lawyer learned more about life than most people ever know, by reading the thoughts of thousands of writers.

Challenge 2. The lawyer wanted to prove that a man can withstand the torment of a long prison term.

b. "Tomorrow at noon he receives his freedom. Under the agreement, I shall have to pay him two million. But if I pay, it's all over with me. I shall be ruined forever."

2. **Recognizing Character Development.** The banker changes from a confident, arrogant man, to an insecure, troubled person. Scattered through the story are passages that show him as he was at the time of the party and as he was fifteen years later. These passages show how he has changed. Here is an example:

Young Banker	Old Banker
At the time, the banker had too many millions to count. (page 167, column 2, paragraph 5)	"He will take all my money. He will marry and enjoy life. To him I will look like an envious beggar." (page 167, column 2, paragraph 4)

Can you find at least two more descriptions of the young banker and two more of the old banker? Then find at least three descriptions of the lawyer at the beginning of the bet and three of him at the end of the bet.

3. **Understanding Conflict.** Both external and internal conflicts are presented in this story. The external conflict involves the disagreement between the lawyer and the banker. What is the internal conflict the lawyer has to cope with during the fifteen years? What is the internal conflict the banker has to cope with on the night before the fifteen years ends?

4. **Making a Plot Diagram.** Review the events listed in Developing Comprehension Skills, 2, on page 170. Choose the most important of these events, and add others to fill in the plot diagram below.

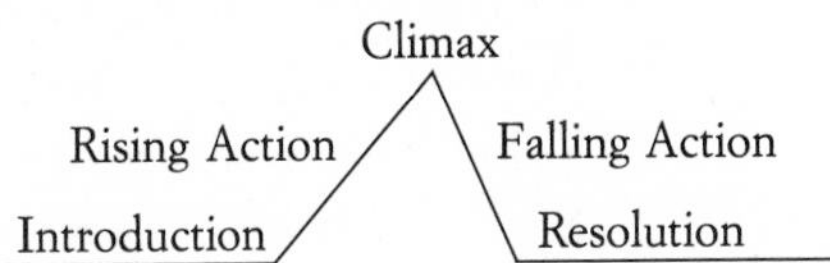

5. **Identifying Mood.** How would you describe the mood of this story—the feelings you get as you read it? Reread the first paragraph. Can you point out words that set that mood?

Reading Literature: Short Stories

Question 1. You may want to complete this exercise with the students. Have individual students read the two passages aloud. After each passage is read, ask for suggestions of causes and effects and list them on the board. Discuss why one event causes the other.

Question 2. Have students skim the story, looking for descriptions of the lawyer and banker and how they changed over the years. After students have completed the question independently, compare answers.

Question 3. Ask a student to define *internal.* The definition should be similar to the following: Existing within the mind. Then have them answer the question.

Question 4. Draw a plot diagram on the board as students discuss their answers. Then have them suggest the important events that belong in each category as you fill in the diagram.

Question 5. Read the first paragraph aloud to the students, emphasizing the words and phrases that best communicate the mood.

Challenge Question. Is the story written from the third-person limited or third-person omniscient point of view? Explain your answer.

Developing Vocabulary Skills

Read to the class the explanation in **Completing Analogies** on page 172, up to the paragraph of directions preceding the eight numbered items.

If you feel your students need to practice analogies using opposites, write these analogies on the board.

Reading Literature: Short Stories

1. Possible answers:

a. Cause 1: the bet
Effect 1: Lawyer loses fifteen years of his life.
Banker loses two million rubles.
Cause 2: foolishness
Effect 2: the bet
Cause 3: greed
Effect 3: the bet

b. Cause 1: Lawyer fulfills the agreement.
Effect 1: Banker pays money.
Cause 2: Banker pays money.
Effect 2: Banker is ruined.

2. Possible answers:

Young Banker: "Two million is nothing to me,..." Old Banker: "But if I pay, it's all over with me. I shall be ruined forever."

Young Banker: "He was now wild, as though he had already won the bet." Old Banker: "Why did I make this bet?"

Young Lawyer: "It's better to live somehow than not to live at all." Old Lawyer: "I despise all that you live by."

Young Lawyer: "...I accept your bet." Old Lawyer: "I give up the two million I once so desired."

Young Lawyer: "He grew lonely and bored." Old Lawyer: "Your books gave me wisdom."

3. The lawyer has to deal with the internal conflict of whether to remain in his prison. The banker has to decide whether to kill the lawyer or not.

4. Parts of the plot diagram are:

Introduction: The banker recalls the discussion of capital punishment and how he and the lawyer made a bet.

Rising Action: The banker remembers how the lawyer went through several stages during his imprisonment.

The banker decides to kill the lawyer.

(continued on page 172)

Young is to old as little is to ____ .

new child big baby

Hot is to cold as black is to ____ .

dark white freezing gray

Then write the following analogies on the board to practice analogies using synonyms.

Sad is to unhappy as happy is to ____ .

joyful crying laughing good

Lamb is to sheep as bunny is to ____ .

ram rabbit jump wool

Discuss the sample analogies. Make sure that students understand that other analogies may require them to make different connections.

Now ask a student to read aloud the exercise directions. Have students complete the exercise independently. (Discussion of answers is called for in the exercise for **Developing Skills in Critical Thinking**.)

Developing Writing Skills

Read and discuss the two assignments. Then have each student choose and complete one of the two.

Question 1. Before asking students to complete this assignment, make sure they can identify the places in the story where the flashback is used.

Pre-Writing. Have students list on the chalkboard, in order, the various times when the story takes place and what takes place at those times. Have them circle the events that take place in the past. Note the ones that take place in the present. Briefly discuss the questions in the text.

Writing. Allow sufficient time for the students to write their first drafts. Remind them to answer all three questions in the text.

Revising. Have students revise and proofread their own papers using the **Checklist for the Process of Writing** on pages 556 and 557.

Question 2. This question builds on the understanding of the changes that came over the lawyer's character discussed in **Reading Literature, 2.**

Pre-Writing. Have the students pinpoint where the story begins to describe the lawyer's activities during those fifteen years (page 166, paragraph 7). As they reread each paragraph through paragraph 4 on page 167, have them identify and make a list of the different phases that the lawyer went through during his years of isolation. Ask them to think of possible

Developing Vocabulary Skills

Completing Analogies. In an analogy there are two pairs of related words. Each pair is related in the same way. Here are two examples:

a. Lion is to cat as wolf is to dog.

b. Tall is to short as pretty is to ugly.

In the first example, the relationship between *lion* and *cat* is that the lion is a wild animal and the cat is a tame animal in the same family. In the same way, the *wolf* and *dog* are wild and tame members of the same family.

In the second example, the words in each pair are opposites.

In an analogy question, you are given the first pair of words and must complete the second pair. To work the question, you must first figure out the relationship between the first two words. Then you must find the missing word that will form the same relationship with the third word given. Here is an example:

Really is to actually as seemingly is to ____.

usually apparently carefully terribly

The first two words are synonyms. Therefore, the missing word must be a synonym for *seemingly*. If you remember the meaning of *seemingly*, you will choose the answer *apparently*.

The following analogies use words you have read in the stories in Chapters 1, 2, and the first part of Chapter 4. Choose the word that will complete each analogy. If necessary, refer to the Glossary of this book or to a dictionary for meanings of words.

1. Principal is to teachers as abbot is to ____.
   knights robbers monks councilors
2. Joy is to sadness as order is to ____.
   chaos cloister contempt
3. Teach is to school as preach is to ____.
   house court market cathedral
4. Car is to road as ____ is to water.
   train barge horse eagle
5. Raise is to lower as welcome is to ____.
   rouse pace shudder banish

(continued from page 171)

Climax: The banker finds and reads the lawyer's letter, and leaves him alive.

Falling Action: The guard finds the prisoner gone.

Resolution: The banker places the letter in the safe.

5. The mood is tense, sad, and regretful. Some words that suggest this are "dark autumn night" and " pacing from corner to corner."

Challenge. The story is written from the third-person omniscient point of view. The narrator can see everyone's situation, knows their thoughts, and can move backward and forward in time. The narrator is all-knowing.

Developing Vocabulary Skills

1. monks **5.** banish
2. chaos **6.** fortress
3. cathedral **7.** garments
4. barge **8.** abyss

Developing Skills in Critical Thinking

1. Abbots supervise monks just as principals supervise teachers.

6. Room is to chamber as castle is to ______.
   cliff fortress passport disposition
7. Pillow is to pillowcase as person is to ______.
   hassle garments jousts grove
8. Up is to down as peak is to ______.
   abyss apothecary blubber feat

Developing Writing Skills

Analytical Writing

1. **Examining Literary Techniques.** This story uses the technique of a **flashback**, a passage that tells what happened at a time before the story began. Without the flashback, the story would have begun at the party and moved forward, year by year, to the night before the bet was to end.

   Write one, two, or three paragraphs discussing the use of the flashback in "The Bet." How does it affect the introduction? How does it keep the story short? How does it focus attention on the conflict between the two men?

Creative Writing

2. **Writing a Diary.** "The Bet" gives a short description of the activities of the lawyer during his fifteen-year confinement. There is a slow change in his behavior and reading habits. Find the part in the story that describes this and reread it carefully.

   Write a diary that tells about the changes in the lawyer. Write the diary from the first-person point of view. Imagine that you are the lawyer, speaking to no one but yourself for fifteen years. Use the following time divisions to indicate the changes in your thinking and personality. For each time division, write one or two paragraphs.

   a. first year
   b. second year
   c. fifth year
   d. tenth year
   e. last two years

Developing Skills in Critical Thinking

Understanding Analogies. Refer to Developing Vocabulary Skills, on pages 172 and 173. Explain the reason for each of your choices.

reasons why one type of behavior logically followed the next. You may want students to work with partners to explore the emotions of a person in this situation. Have students list nouns, verbs, adjectives, and adverbs that they could use in their diaries.

Writing. Remind students to use the notes they made in pre-writing. This question may be completed most efficiently as a homework or long-term assignment.

Revising. Give students an opportunity to share their diaries either orally or on a bulletin board.

Developing Skills in Critical Thinking

Discuss the analogies with the students. Have dictionaries available for student reference when they encounter new words.

2. The words are opposites.
3. A cathedral is a place where preaching is done as teaching is done in a school.
4. A barge is a type of transportation on water just as cars are a type of transportation on roads.
5. The words are opposites.
6. The words are similar in meaning.
7. Garments cover a person just as a pillowcase covers a pillow.
8. The words are opposites.

Objectives

- To recognize and appreciate the short story as a form of literature
- To recognize point of view in a story
- To recognize special uses of language
- To apply literal, interpretive, and critical reading skills to a selection
- To list events in the order they occurred
- To choose the correct meaning from a dictionary entry
- To compare literature to life
- To conduct a poll

Preparing the Students

Essential Vocabulary. The words presented here are essential to the understanding of the selection.

Have the students use the context clues in the following sentences to determine the meanings of the underlined words.

famine meanest marveled

1. The country was suffering through a famine. The crops had failed, the cattle had died, and there was nothing left to eat.
2. He lived in the meanest house in the village. It was small, cold, dark, and in bad repair.
3. The people wondered how Keesh stayed alive and they also marveled at his great luck in hunting.

If the students need additional help with the vocabulary of this selection, encourage them to use context clues to determine word meaning. As needed, direct them to the **Glossary** or to a classroom dictionary.

Motivation. Ask the students to try to think back to a time they defended what they believed in in the face of strong opposition. Then ask them to share how they felt in such a situation. Tell the class that the young boy in the next story stands up for what he feels is right in spite of the consequences.

Have the students read the introductory paragraph at the top of page 174 and state in their own words what they should try to find out as they read this short story.

Presenting the Selection

1. Prior to presenting this lesson to the students you should be thoroughly familiar with "The Story of Keesh." It is important to recognize and, in discussions, help the students to see that the boy's harsh method of killing animals is an act of desperation to avoid starvation. At this

The Story of Keesh

JACK LONDON

In the Arctic only strong people or those with strong friends and family can survive. Usually, a thirteen-year-old is not considered to be a strong person. Find out how young Keesh proves his strength.

The winter darkness, when the north gales make their long sweep across the ice pack and the air is filled with flying white and no man may venture forth, is the chosen time for the telling of how Keesh, from the poorest igloo in the village, rose to power.

Keesh lived long ago on the rim of the polar sea. He was a bright boy, healthy and strong, who had seen thirteen years. His father had been a very brave man who had met his death in a time of famine, when he sought to save the lives of his people by taking that of a great polar bear. In his eagerness, he had come to close grapples with the bear, and his bones had been crushed. But the bear had had much meat on him, so the people were saved.

Keesh was his only son and lived alone with his mother. But people are forgetful, and the deed of his father was forgotten. Keesh being but a boy, and his mother only a woman, they, too, were swiftly forgotten. Soon they were reduced to living in the meanest of all the igloos.

At a council one night in the big igloo of Klosh-Kwan, who was chief, Keesh showed the blood that ran in his veins and the manhood that stiffened his back. With the dignity of an elder, he rose to his feet and waited for silence amid the babble of voices.

"It is true that meat is apportioned me and mine," he said. "But it is ofttimes old and tough, this meat, and, moreover, it has an unusual quantity of bones."

The hunters, both the grizzled and gray and the lusty and young, were aghast—a child that talked like a grown man and said harsh things to their very faces!

Steadily and with seriousness, Keesh went on. "Because I know my father, Bok, was a great hunter, I speak these words. It is said that Bok brought home more meat than any of the best hunters, that with his own hands he attended to the division of it, that with his own eyes he saw to it that the least old woman and the last old man received fair share."

"Na! Na!" the men cried. "Put the child out!" "Send him off to bed!"

He waited calmly till the uproar died down.

"My mother has no one save me; wherefore I speak. As I say, though Bok be dead because he hunted overkeenly, it is just that I, who am his son, and that Ikeega, who is my mother and was his wife, should have meat in plenty so long as there is meat in plenty in the tribe. I, Keesh, the son of Bok, have spoken."

He sat down.

"That a boy should speak in council!" old Ugh-Gluk was mumbling.

"Shall the babes in arms tell us men the things we shall do?" Massuk demanded in a loud voice. "Am I a man that I should be made a mock by every child that cries for meat?"

Their anger boiled to white heat. They ordered him to bed, threatened that he should have no meat at all, and promised him sore beatings. Keesh's eyes began to flash and his blood to pound darkly under his skin. In the midst of the abuse, he sprang to his feet.

"Hear me, ye men!" he cried. "Take this now for my last word. Bok, my father, was a great hunter. I, too, his son, shall go and hunt the meat that I eat. And be it known now, that the division of that which I kill shall be fair. And no widow nor weak one shall cry in the night because there is no meat, when the strong men are groaning in great pain because they have eaten overmuch. And in the days to come there shall be shame upon the strong men who have eaten overmuch. I, Keesh, have said it!"

Jeers and scornful laughter followed him out of the igloo, but his jaw was set and he went his way, looking neither to right nor to left.

The next day he went forth along the shore line where the ice and the land met together. Those who saw him go noted that he carried his bow, with a goodly supply of bone-barbed arrows, and that across his shoulders was his father's big hunting spear. And there was laughter, and much talk, at the event. It was an unprecedented occurrence. Never did boys of his tender age go forth to hunt, much less to hunt alone. Also, there were shaking of heads and prophetic mutterings. The other women looked pityingly at Ikeega, and her face was grave and sad.

"He will be back ere long," they said cheeringly.

"Let him go; it will teach him a lesson," the hunters said. "He will come back shortly, and he will be meek and soft of speech in the days to follow."

But a day passed, and a second, and on the third a wild gale blew, and there was no Keesh. Ikeega tore her hair and put soot of the seal oil on her face in token of her grief; and the women assailed the men with bitter words in that they had mis-

time, it might be helpful to discuss with the students the difference between killing animals needlessly and killing as a means of survival.

2. Have the students read "The Story of Keesh" on pages 174 to 180 independently. Since this is a long selection, you may want to assign it for homework.

3. Administer the **Check Test** at the bottom of T.E. page 180.

4. Remind students of the introduction. Have several students explain how Keesh proves his strength.

5. Develop the study questions as suggested in **Using the Study Questions** beginning on page 181. That section also provides challenge questions for further discussion, as needed. (For answers to questions, see T.E. pages 181 to 184.)

Reinforcing the Lesson

To reteach, reinforce, or extend the skills in this lesson, see the following:

Skills Practice Book, Green Level—pages 94 through 98

Special Populations

LD, ESL. "The Story of Keesh" is one that may need to be divided into smaller readings for some students. ESL students may also have difficulty with some of the nonstandard use of English or dialect throughout the story. Check frequently for comprehension, interpreting phrases into more familiar English when necessary. Point out some of the unfamiliar phrases to the class to complete Comprehension question 4, **Recognizing Special Uses of Language**, on page 181.

For the following exercises on page 183 under **Developing Writing Skills**, you may wish to assign alternate activities for students with limited writing abilities.

Assignment 1: Illustrate a comic strip or a poster depicting a heroic action a thirteen-year-old might take.

Assignment 2: Write a letter to Keesh, asking him several questions about his life that might show a difference from our lives.

ESL. You might wish to adapt the exercise under **Developing Skills in Speaking and Listening** on page 184 to provide an opportunity for ESL students to interview a family member or be interviewed by another member of the class. See what likenesses and differences the class can find in some of the customs or backgrounds each of us have. This could be turned into a class study of our own families and our heritage.

Encouraging Independent Reading

Students who wish to read more about Eskimos and their lives may enjoy *Julie of the Wolves*, by Jean Craighead George. In this imaginitive novel, George not only presents an insider's view of Eskimo life, but she also addresses the problems that Eskimos, particularly Eskimo women, face in modern society.

Polar Bear and Cub in Ice, 1959, NIVIAKSIAK.

treated the boy and sent him to his death; and the men made no answer, preparing to go in search of the body when the storm abated.

Early the next morning, however, Keesh strode into the village. He came not shamefacedly. Across his shoulders he bore a burden of fresh-killed meat. There was importance in his step and arrogance in his speech.

"Go, ye men, with the dogs and sledges, and take my trail for the better part of a day's travel," he said. "There is much meat on the ice—a she-bear and two half-grown cubs."

Ikeega was overcome with joy, but he received her demonstrations in manlike fashion, saying, "Come, Ikeega, let us eat. And after that I shall sleep, for I am weary."

He passed into their igloo and ate profoundly, and, after that, he slept for twenty running hours.

There was much doubt at first, much doubt and discussion. The killing of a polar bear is very dangerous, but thrice dangerous is it, and three times thrice, to kill a mother bear with her cubs. The men could not bring themselves to believe that the boy Keesh, single-handed, had accomplished so great a marvel.

But the women spoke of the fresh-killed meat he had brought on his back, and this was an overwhelming argument

About the Art

Niviaksiak (1918-1959), an Eskimo artist, was also a hunter who was particularly fascinated with bears. Bears appear again and again in his work. In this print, notice how the great sweeping curve of color frames the powerful head and paw of the mother and seems to protect the cub. There is a story that while hunting with a friend, Niviaksiak came upon a polar bear that, surprisingly, did not try to attack the men. Niviaksiak prepared to shoot. Before he could, he fell to the ground dead. His friend ran for help. When he returned with a group of hunters, they found Niviaksiak's body frozen but untouched and the bear gone. It was said that the Bear Spirit was angry because the artist had tried to capture the essence or being of the bear in his art, and the Bear Spirit punished him for this with sudden death.

against the men's unbelief. Finally, the men departed, grumbling greatly that in all probability, if the thing were so, he had neglected to cut up the carcasses.

Now, in the north it is very necessary that this should be done as soon as the kill is made. If not, the meat freezes so solidly as to turn the edge of the sharpest knife, and a three-hundred-pound bear, frozen stiff, is no easy thing to put upon a sled and haul over the rough ice. However, arriving at the spot, they found not only the kill, which they had doubted, but that Keesh had quartered the beasts in true hunter fashion and removed the entrails.

Thus began the mystery of Keesh, a mystery that deepened and deepened with the passing of the days. His very next trip he killed a young bear, nearly full grown, and, on the trip following, a large male bear and his mate. He was ordinarily gone from three to four days, though it was nothing unusual for him to stay away a week at a time on the ice field. Always he declined company on these expeditions, and the people marveled.

"How does he do it?" they demanded of one another. "Never does he take a dog with him, and dogs are of such great help."

"Why dost thou hunt only bear?" Klosh-Kwan once ventured to ask him.

Keesh made fitting answer. "It is well known that there is more meat on the bear," he said.

However, there was also talk of witchcraft in the village. "He hunts with evil spirits," some of the people contended, "wherefore his hunting is rewarded. How else can it be, save that he hunts with evil spirits?"

"Mayhap they be not evil, but good, these spirits," others said. "It is known that his father was a mighty hunter. May not his father hunt with him so that he may attain excellence and patience and understanding? Who knows?"

Nonetheless, his success continued, and the less skillful hunters were often kept busy hauling in his meat. In the division of it, Keesh was just. As his father had done before him, he saw to it that the least old woman and the last old man received a fair portion, keeping no more for himself than his needs required. Because of this and of his merit as a hunter, he was looked upon with respect and even awe; and there was even talk of making him chief after old Klosh-Kwan. Because of the things he had done, they looked for him to appear in the council, but he never came, and they were ashamed to ask.

"I am minded to build me an igloo," he said one day to Klosh-Kwan and a number of the hunters. "It shall be a large igloo, wherein Ikeega and I can dwell in comfort."

"Aye," they nodded gravely.

"But I have no time. My business is hunting, and it takes all my time. So it is but just that the men and women of the village, who eat my meat, should build me my igloo."

The igloo was built accordingly, on a generous scale that exceeded even the dwelling of Klosh-Kwan. Keesh and his mother moved into it, and it was the first prosperity she had enjoyed since the death of Bok. Nor was material prosperity alone hers, for, because of her wonderful son and the position he had given her, she came to be looked upon as the first woman in all the village; and the women were given to visiting her, to asking her advice, and to quoting her wisdom when arguments arose among themselves or with the men.

But it was the mystery of Keesh's marvelous hunting that took chief place in all their minds. And one day Ugh-Gluk taxed him with witchcraft to his face.

"It is charged," Ugh-Gluk said ominously, "that thou dealest with evil spirits, wherefore thy hunting is rewarded."

"Is not the meat good?" Keesh made answer. "Has one in the village yet to fall sick from the eating of it? How dost thou know that witchcraft be concerned? Or dost thou guess, in the dark, merely because of the envy that consumes thee?"

Ugh-Gluk withdrew, discomfited, the women laughing at him as he walked away. However, in the council one night after long deliberation, it was determined to put spies on Keesh's track when he went forth to hunt, so that his methods might be learned. So on his next trip Bim and Bawn, two young men, the craftiest of hunters, followed after him, taking care not to be seen. After five days they came back, their eyes bulging and their tongues a-tremble, to tell what they had seen. The council was hastily called in Klosh-Kwan's dwelling, and Bim took up the tale.

"Brothers! As was commanded, we journeyed on the trail of Keesh, and cunningly we journeyed, so that he might not know. And midway of the first day, he picked up with a great he-bear. It was a very great bear."

"None greater," Bawn corroborated and went on himself. "Yet was the bear not inclined to fight, for he turned away and made off slowly over the ice. This we saw from the rocks of the shore, and the bear came toward us, and after him came Keesh, very much unafraid. And he shouted harsh words after the bear, and waved his arms about, and made much noise. Then did the bear grow angry, and rise up on his hind legs, and growl. But Keesh walked right up to the bear."

"Aye," Bim continued the story. "Right up to the bear Keesh walked. And the bear took after him, and Keesh ran away. But as he ran he dropped a little round ball on the ice, and the bear stopped and smelled of it, and then swallowed it up. And Keesh continued to run away and drop little round balls, and the bear continued to swallow them up."

Exclamations and cries of doubt were being made, and Ugh-Gluk expressed open unbelief.

"With our own eyes we saw it," Bim affirmed.

Bawn repeated, "Aye, with our own eyes. And this continued until the bear stood suddenly upright, and cried aloud in pain, and thrashed his forepaws madly about. And Keesh continued to make off over the ice to a safe distance. But the bear gave him no notice, being occupied with the misfortune the little round balls had wrought within him."

"Aye, within him," Bim interrupted. "For he did claw at himself, and leap about over the ice like a playful puppy—save from the way he growled and squealed it was plain it was not play but pain. Never did I see such a sight!"

"Nay, never was such a sight seen," Bawn took up the strain. "Furthermore, it was such a large bear."

"Witchcraft," Ugh-Gluk suggested.

"I know not," Bawn replied. "I tell only of what my eyes beheld. And after a while the bear grew weak and tired, for he was very heavy and he had jumped about with exceeding violence, and he went off along the shore ice, shaking his head slowly from side to side and sitting down ever and again to squeal and cry. And Keesh followed after the bear, and we followed after Keesh, and for that day and three days more we followed. The bear grew weak and never ceased crying from his pain."

"It was a charm!" Ugh-Gluk exclaimed. "Surely it was a charm!"

"It may well be."

Bim relieved Bawn. "The bear wandered, now this way and now that, doubling back and forth and crossing his trail in circles, so that at the end he was near where Keesh had first come upon him. By this time the bear was quite sick and could crawl no farther, so Keesh came up close and speared him to death."

"And what then?" Kosh-Kwan demanded.

"Then we left Keesh skinning the bear and came running that the news of the killing might be told."

In the afternoon of that day, the women hauled in the meat of the bear while the men sat in council assembled. When Keesh arrived, a messenger was sent to him, bidding him come to the council.

Keesh sent reply, saying that he was hungry and tired; also that his igloo was large and comfortable and could hold many men.

Curiosity was so strong on the men that the whole council, Klosh-Kwan to the fore, rose up and went to the igloo of Keesh. He was eating, but he received them with respect and seated them according to their rank. Ikeega was proud and embarrassed by turns, but Keesh was quite composed.

Klosh-Kwan recited the information brought by Bim and Bawn, and at its close he said in a stern voice: "So explanation is wanted, O Keesh, of thy manner of hunting. Is there witchcraft in it?"

Keesh looked up and smiled. "Nay, O Klosh-Kwan. It is not for a boy to know aught of witches, and of witches I know nothing. I have but devised a means whereby I may kill the ice bear with ease, that is all. It be headcraft, not witchcraft."

"And may any man?"

"Any man."

There was a long silence. The men looked in one another's faces, and Keesh went on eating.

"And—and—and wilt thou tell us, O Keesh?" Klosh-Kwan finally asked in a tremulous voice.

"Yea, I will tell thee." Keesh finished sucking a marrowbone and rose to his feet. "It is quite simple. Behold!"

He picked up a thin strip of whalebone and showed it to them. The ends were sharp as needle points. The strip he coiled carefully, till it disappeared in his hand. Then, as he suddenly released it, it sprang straight again. He picked up a piece of blubber.

"So," he said, "one takes a small chunk of blubber, thus, and thus makes it hollow. Then into the hollow goes the whale bone, so, tightly coiled, and another piece of blubber is fitted over the whalebone. After that it is put outside where it freezes into a little round ball. The bear swallows the little round ball, the blubber melts, the whalebone with its sharp ends stands out straight, the bear gets sick, and, when the bear is very sick, why, you kill him with a spear. It is quite simple."

Ugh-Gluk said, "Oh!" and Klosh-Kwan said, "Ah!" and each said something after his own manner, and all understood.

This is the story of Keesh, who lived long ago on the rim of the polar sea. Because he exercised headcraft and not witchcraft, he rose from the meanest igloo to be head man of his village, and, through all the years that he lived, it is related, his tribe was prosperous. Neither widow nor weak one cried aloud in the night because there was no meat.

Eskimo Ivory Bag Fastener. Department of Anthropology, Smithsonian Institution, Washington, D.C.

About the Art

Superb sculptors and carvers, the Eskimos have created beautiful works of art from bone, ivory, and driftwood. While many of the works have symbolic or religious significance, the Eskimos engraved many items for everyday, household use, such as the ivory bag fastener shown here. Eskimo women keep their sewing equipment in cloth pouches with embroidered flaps that are rolled around the pouch and secured with an ivory fastener. The bag fastener reproduced here, carved in the image of a smiling face flanked on either side by seals, is an exquisite example of Eskimo craftsmanship.

Check Test

1. How did Keesh's father die? (He was killed by a bear.)

2. How did the villagers explain Keesh's good luck in hunting? (They thought he was using witchcraft.)

3. What did Keesh use as bait for the bears? (a coiled whalebone wrapped in blubber)

Developing Comprehension Skills

Literal Reading 1. Why did Keesh complain to the council?

Literal Reading 2. Why did Keesh's talk to the council make its members so angry?

Literal Reading 3. When Keesh hunted, he followed a definite method. Tell, in order, the steps he used to kill a bear.

Interpretive Reading 4. What did Keesh mean when he said that he exercised headcraft, not witchcraft?

Creative Writing 5. Keesh is a very mature thirteen-year-old boy. Do you think that he is a realistic character? Considering what you know of teenagers, do you believe a thirteen-year-old could do what he did? Explain your answer.

Reading Literature: Short Stories

1. **Appreciating the Setting.** This story could be set only above the Arctic Circle in the lands of the Eskimos. It tells about the people in one Alaskan village and shows some of the customs of these people. What are some of the customs or activities that are different from your own? Would you have as much difficulty persuading your town council that a particular need of yours should be met?

2. **Recognizing Point of View.** Who is the narrator of this story? Is it one of the characters in the story or someone outside the story who knew and told everything that happened? Or is it someone outside the story who knew and told something, but not everything, about what was going on? We call these points of view the first-person, the third-person omniscient, and the third-person limited. Which did you choose? Select several passages from the story to support your answer.

3. **Outlining the Plot.** In the order of their happening, list the events in this story. List only the most important events, because a great many things happen in this story. Then tell which event is the climax of the story. You can identify the climax because everything that happens after it explains how the characters in the story react to their new knowledge.

4. **Recognizing Special Uses of Language.** In "The Story of Keesh," the author was writing about a culture quite different from ours. He

Using the Study Questions

It is recommended that students always read and answer the questions in **Developing Comprehension Skills** in class discussion. Whenever possible, they should also read the questions in the other categories together and discuss the answers.

Developing Comprehension Skills

Questions 1 and 2. Read and discuss.

Question 3. If necessary, have the students reread Keesh's explanation on page 180, paragraphs 7 and 8.

Question 4. Explain to students that they must infer the answer. It is not stated directly in the story.

Question 5. Students should express their personal opinions in answering this question and support their answers with solid reasoning.

Challenge Question 1. Why do you think Keesh kept secret his method of killing the bear? (Critical Reading)

Challenge Question 2. Sometimes our imaginations can run wild when we cannot figure out what someone is doing or why. We arrive at conclusions that are often based on inaccurate or incomplete observations. How was this true with the villagers? (Interpretive Reading)

Reading Literature: Short Stories

Question 1. Have students skim the story to find village customs. As each one is identified, list it on the board.

Question 2. Point out how the story includes only what could be known by a person observing the action. Private feelings are not known except when they are obvious to an observer. Have students find instances when no one knew what would happen next, for example, when Keesh was lost in a storm.

Question 3. Draw a plot diagram on the board as the students skim the story and make their lists of the most important events. Then have them help you fill in the events of the story in their proper places on the diagram.

Question 4. Have the students skim the story, point out the locations of the sentences they find by page and paragraph numbers, read the sentences aloud, and then rephrase them.

Challenge Question. Do you like the formal, old-fashioned way of writing in this story? Explain your reasons why or why not.

Answers to Study Questions

Developing Comprehension Skills

1. Keesh complained that he and his mother were given meat that was old, tough, and bony, and that not everyone was getting a fair share.

2. The council members did not like having a child speak harshly to them.

3. Keesh took a small chunk of blubber and hollowed it out. Next he put a coiled whalebone in the blubber and then put more blubber over it. He put the ball outside to freeze. The bear swallowed the ball. When the blubber melted, the whalebone uncoiled, making the bear sick. Keesh then killed the bear with his spear.

4. Keesh thought of a smart way to solve his problem, rather than using magic.

5. Opinions will vary depending on the individual students' experiences. Nothing was definitely beyond the capabilities of a thirteen-year-old, but some students might not think a boy of that age would feel confident to try to hunt by himself in such a hostile environment.

Challenge 1. Answers may vary. Keesh may have kept his method secret because he wanted the village council to come to him to ask for help, since he had freely

(continued on page 182)

Developing Vocabulary Skills

Read the directions for **Choosing the Correct Meaning from a Dictionary Entry** on page 182 with the students. Make dictionaries available to the class before asking them to complete this exercise independently. You may want to have students with very weak dictionary skills complete this exercise with a more skilled partner. Discuss the answers together.

Developing Writing Skills

Read and discuss the four assignments. Then have each student choose and complete one of the four.

Question 1. This question requires creative thinking and strengthens student understanding of the relationship between literature and life.

Pre-Writing. Have the students brainstorm about possible ways a thirteen-year-old could win recognition and respect. List any suggestions on the board. Then have each student choose one of the ideas and write a topic sentence for his or her paragraph.

Writing. Allow sufficient time for the students to write their first drafts.

Revising. Have students revise and proofread their own paragraphs using the **Checklist for the Process of Writing** on pages 556 and 557.

Question 2. Students should review all three stories before choosing which story to analyze.

Pre-Writing. On the board, have students list the major events of each of the three stories. Ask for suggestions about the events that are hard to believe. Then have each student choose one of the stories to write about.

Writing. Make sure that students include at least two or three unbelievable events in their paragraphs. Allow time for

wanted the reader to keep that in mind throughout the story. One way to show the difference was by having the characters speak in an unusual way. Therefore, the writer had the characters use old forms of common words, as in "He will be back ere long" instead of "he will be back before long." In addition, the characters—and even the narrator—use very formal sentence patterns and unusual word choices. For example, Keesh says, "My mother has no one save me; wherefore I speak" instead of "Since my mother has no one else to help her, I have to say something to you."

Choose five other sentences from the story that use old-fashioned forms or unusual sentence patterns and words. Restate each sentence as you would say it naturally.

Developing Vocabulary Skills

Choosing the Correct Meaning from a Dictionary Entry. Sometimes it is not easy to choose the correct definition of a word in the dictionary. The meanings of the word may be only slightly different. There may be many to choose from. Often there is a sample sentence after the definition. This sentence will help you choose the correct meaning.

Read these sentences drawn from the story. Find each underlined word in the dictionary. Choose the best meaning. Examine how the word is used in each sentence. On your paper, write the word, its part of speech, and the dictionary definition you chose.

1. With the dignity of an elder, he rose to his feet and waited in silence.
2. The men prepared to go in search of the body when the storm abated.
3. The igloo was built on a generous scale that exceeded even the dwelling of Klosh-Kwan.
4. One day Ugh-Gluk taxed him with witchcraft to his face.
5. He received the men of the council with respect and seated them according to their rank.
6. Ikeega was proud and embarrassed by turns, but Keesh was quite composed.

(continued from page 181)

offered his ideas before and they had refused to consider them. He may have felt that, since he discovered the method, only he should get to use it.

Challenge 2. The villagers didn't know how Keesh was hunting so successfully, so they imagined that he was using witchcraft. They thought this might be true because he used methods they knew nothing about.

Reading Literature: Short Stories

1. Some customs include the following: having the council of men, dividing the meat among all villagers, hunting for food, living in igloos. A young person of today would probably still have as much difficulty as Keesh in persuading the town council to listen to him or her.

2. The narrator is third-person limited. The reader knows only what can be observed. Some possible passages that show this are: page 175, column 2—"Those who saw him go noted that he carried his bow,..." and page 175, column 2—"Ikeega tore her hair...and the women assailed the men with bitter words in that they had mistreated the boy and sent him to his death." This happened before Keesh returned home safely.

3. The major events are the following:

a. Keesh complains to the council. (Introduction)
b. The council refuses to listen to him. (Introduction)
c. Keesh goes hunting. (Rising Action)
d. Keesh becomes a great hunter and is fair to everyone. (Rising Action)
e. Keesh is suspected of using witchcraft. (Rising Action)
f. Hunters follow Keesh on his hunting trip. (Rising Action)
g. Keesh explains his hunting method to the council. (Climax)

Developing Writing Skills

Analytical Writing

1. **Comparing Literature to Your Life.** After Keesh proved himself a worthy hunter and a fair provider of meat, he received rewards from the villagers. Can you think of ways a thirteen-year-old could achieve similar honor in our culture? Write at least a paragraph describing how a thirteen-year-old boy or girl could win recognition and respect from the community.

Analytical Writing

2. **Comparing Plots to Reality.** While reading a well-written story, a reader believes that the events could really happen, even though he or she knows they did not. Afterwards, the reader often sees ways that the story does not match reality. Think about the last three stories: "Hearts and Hands," "The Bet," and "Keesh." Choose one and write a paragraph that points out hard-to-believe events in that story.

Creative Writing

3. **Preparing for an Interview.** In an interview, one person questions another to obtain information. The questions are usually prepared in advance and should be worded so that the person interviewed gives in-depth answers.

   Imagine that you will interview Keesh after the village finds out his unique way of killing bears. Write six questions that you could ask him. The questions may be on his personal background, his hunting method, how he worked out his method, or his plans for the future.

Creative Writing

4. **Changing Point of View.** Rewrite the story of Keesh as he might have told it to his son, many years later. Remember that the point of view will change. You will write the story as though you had lived it yourself. What character traits of Keesh would show as he tells this story to his son? Your story should be at least six paragraphs long.

Developing Skills in Study and Research

Conducting a Poll. A poll is a collection of opinions on a subject. The poll can be of a selected group or a random group. A selected group would be one certain type, for example, all eighth-grade students in your school or all people over thirty years of age. A random group would be without a definite pattern, for example, people at the supermarket or people on the street.

students to write their paragraphs independently.

Revising. Have students exchange paragraphs with partners. Have them identify the events that the writer found difficult to believe. Have the readers decide whether they agree or disagree with the writers' choice of events. If, after discussing the events they chose, the writers wish to revise their paragraphs, allow time for revisions to be made.

Question 3. Note that the questions that students prepare in answering this question will be used in **Developing Skills in Speaking and Listening** on page 184.

Pre-Writing. Ask students if they have ever seen an interview on television, heard one on the radio, or been interviewed themselves. Underscore that the key to a good interview is the questions that are asked. Encourage students to think of questions that require more than a yes or no response.

Writing. Allow sufficient time for students to write at least six good questions.

Revising. Have students work with partners. Have them ask their partners the questions they wrote and have the partners give the answers Keesh would have given. If, after hearing the answers, the writers wish to revise their questions, allow time for revisions to be made.

Question 4. Emphasize to students that this retelling should include personal details that were missing from the original story.

Pre-Writing. Have students list the major events of the story. Have them imagine how Keesh's adventures sounded and looked. Then ask them to imagine how Keesh felt about the false accusations of witchcraft. Before they begin to write, have students think about the character traits they wish to bring out in their retelling.

h. The council understands and accepts Keesh's hunting method. (Falling Action)
i. Keesh becomes a respected man, the head of the village. (Resolution)

4. Answers may vary. Possible answers include the following:

a. "...who had seen thirteen years" means "who was thirteen years old."
b. "...the deed of his father was forgotten" means "what his father had done was forgotten."
c. "But it is ofttimes old and tough" means "It is often old and tough."
d. "Shall the babes in arms" means "Shall the young children..."
e. "...they have eaten overmuch" means "they have eaten too much."

Challenge. Opinions will vary but should be supported by logical reasons.

Developing Vocabulary Skills

Answers may vary, depending on the dictionary used.

1. dignity; noun; nobility
2. abated; verb; lessened
3. generous; adjective; large
4. taxed; verb; accused
5. rank; noun; social division or class
6. composed; adjective; calm

Writing. Remind students to write in the first-person. Also remind them of the audience Keesh is writing for. This last consideration may affect which details or emotions are included.

Revising. Allow class time for students to share their stories. After a few accounts have been read, have students make comparisons between stories as to which events were described, which events seemed most realistic, and which characters seemed most alive.

Developing Skills in Study and Research

Read the directions for **Conducting a Poll** on pages 183 and 184 with the students. Have the students complete the assignment of conducting the poll for homework. Some students may benefit from working in small groups to prepare the four different types of graphs.

Developing Skills in Speaking and Listening

Read aloud the directions to the exercise on page 184. Allow time in class for students to prepare and present their interviews as directed in **Presenting an Interview** on page 184. Alert the students who will be in the role of the interviewer to listen closely to their partner's responses, which may contain information they should follow up on with further questioning or clarification.

Conduct a random poll of five people outside this class. The poll will be about voting age. Ask each person: "Are you in favor of lowering the voting age to sixteen?" The answer must be one of the following:

a. Yes, I am.
b. No, I am not.
c. Only under certain conditions.
d. I don't know.

After everyone in the class has obtained five responses, pool the results. Add all the responses in each of the four categories. Then work together to show the combined results using all of the following reporting methods:

a. raw numbers
b. percentages
c. a bar graph
d. a circle graph

Examples:

a. 100 total: 40 in favor, 40 opposed, 15 conditional, 5 undecided
b. 40% in favor, 40% opposed, 15% conditional, 5% undecided

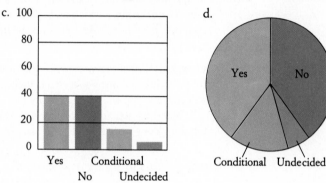

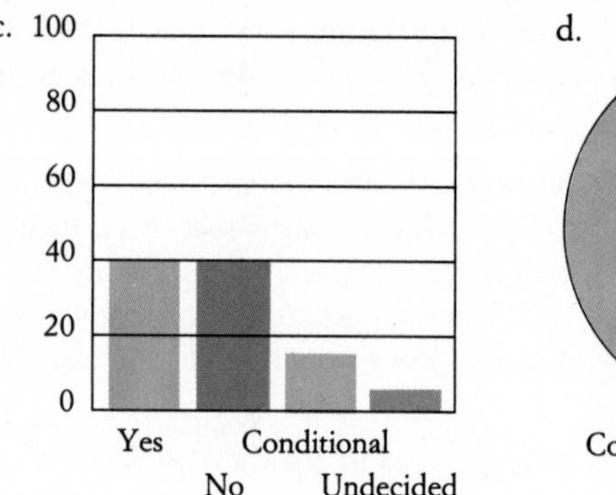

Developing Skills in Speaking and Listening

Presenting an Interview. With a partner, act out a news interview. (Use any questions you wrote for the third activity in Developing Writing Skills, page 183.) When one partner asks his or her prepared questions, the other partner takes the part of Keesh.

Great Modern Stories

These stories were all written in the middle of the twentieth century. In most of them, the plot covers a longer time span than it does in the classic stories you read. Also, there are more minor characters. However, like the older stories, each of these focuses attention on one particular problem faced by the characters. Each one helps us see a certain part of life more clearly.

The Great Wave Off Kanagawa, 1831–33. KATSUSHIKA HOKUSAI.
The Metropolitan Museum of Art; Bequest of Mrs. H.O. Havemeyer, 1929. The H.O. Havemeyer Collection.

Great Modern Stories

Ask students to turn to page 185, look at the painting reproduced there, and tell what they see at first. Most students will see only the tremendous wave in their first glance. They will need a few moments of closer examination to note the fishing boats and the men crouching in their places.

Then have a student read the text on page 185 aloud. Ask the students to relate the painting to what the text says about a short story. As needed, lead them to realize that in both, one particular problem or part of life gets special attention.

About the Art

The Japanese woodblock printmaker Katsushika Hokusai (1760-1849) produced a series of prints entitled *Thirty-six Views of Mt. Fuji. The Great Wave Off Kanagawa* is a print from this series, showing Japan's highest mountain peak as seen from the sea. Hokusai's design is bold and simple. His sensitive use of line and color gives the sense of the water's movement, the powerful rush of water as it crests and curls and breaks in waves on the boats below. In this print, man is shown dwarfed by the powerful forces of nature, tiny in contrast to the immensity of the sea and sky. However, Hokusai introduces into this print a sense of humor and sympathy with the plight of man.

See also pages 200 and 203 for two other views of Mt. Fuji. Hokusai did this series of prints for the Japanese equivalent of postcards, advertising the most popular tourist attraction, Mount Fuji.

Reading Literature

This lesson provides more detail on major elements of short stories that could not be discussed fully on pages 134 and 135, **Reading Literature: Short Stories**. It discusses characters, and points out different ways characters can be grouped. It summarizes briefly the definitions of external and internal conflict. It also develops more fully the concepts of *theme* and *mood*.

Preparing the Students

Remind the students that, in the lesson entitled **Reading Literature: Short Stories**, they learned about plot and point of view in a short story. Remind them, also, that the study questions for the selections in the first part of this chapter have not been limited to those two elements of stories. Point out that this lesson will take up several other major elements of short stories.

Presenting the Lesson

1. Have the students read **More About the Elements of a Short Story** on page 186. Then ask them to identify the element with which conflict is closely related (plot).

2. Have students read silently the two paragraphs concerning **Characters.** Then ask them to distinguish between major and minor characters, and between static and dynamic characters. Discuss the examples provided in the text, and ask students for other examples, either from their reading or from television shows or movies.

3. Have students read **Conflict** silently. Ask them to define external and internal conflict in their own words, with their own examples.

4. Call on students to read aloud each of the sections on page 187, **Theme** and **Mood**. Pause after each section to discuss the meaning of the term and the fact that each of these terms may be used with several different ideas, even when discussing one selection.

Reinforcing the Lesson

To reteach, reinforce, or extend the concepts in this lesson, see the following:

Skills Practice Book, Green Level—pages 99 through 101

Reading Literature: More About Short Stories

More About the Elements of a Short Story

You know that the most important elements of a short story are its characters, setting, and plot. On these pages you will learn more about characters and about the element of the plot called **conflict**. You will also learn about the theme and the mood of a short story.

Characters. Characters can be either major or minor. A **major character** is a main character. The story is really about the major characters. In a short story, there is often only one major character. A **minor character** is less important to the story. His or her actions matter only if they are connected in some way to the main character. In "Hearts and Hands," for example, the young woman, the sheriff, and the prisoner are the major characters. The other two passengers are included in the story only to bring out the truth about the major characters.

Characters are either static or dynamic. **Static characters** stay the same throughout the whole story. **Dynamic characters**, on the other hand, change and grow during the story. This difference can be seen in a comparison of "Hearts and Hands" with "The Bet." In "Hearts and Hands," the reader finds out the truth about the characters; they do not change. In "The Bet," the characters also find out some truths; they do change.

Conflict. The plot of a short story describes the struggle between opposing forces, called the **conflict**. Every story needs conflict. There are two kinds.

External conflict is a struggle between a character and another character or the forces of nature. External conflict can even include the character's battle with supernatural forces. Examples of external conflict include the struggles of the three young men with each other and with Death, in the tale "How the Three Young Men Found Death."

Internal conflict refers to the clash of different feelings and thoughts inside a character. The struggle within Jean Valjean in "The Bishop's Candlesticks" is an example.

Learning About Theme and Mood

Theme. In each piece of writing, a writer focuses on one thing he or she has learned about life. That main idea that the writer shares with the reader is called the **theme**.

To determine the theme, review the story. Decide what the writer is telling you about the characters. Then, decide how the things you learned from them can be applied to your own life. Last, state this idea so that it can be applied to everyone.

It is possible that different readers will find somewhat different themes in the same story. This is because each of us brings different experiences to the story. For example, in "The Story of Keesh," a reader might find any of these themes:

Age doesn't necessarily make a person wise.
In order to survive, a person must use his or her wits.
Determination and bravery will bring success.

Mood. The **mood** of a piece of writing is the feeling you get as you read it. You may feel worried, joyful, or fearful. Writers know the kind of mood they want you to feel. To create that mood, they choose their words carefully. They choose words both for their meanings and for the feelings the words give you.

Note how the beginning of this story reminds you of a fairy tale. The mood is funny in one way and scary at the same time.

> There was once a little girl called Esmeralda who lived with her wicked stepmother. Her father was dead. The stepmother, who was called Mrs. Mitching, was very rich and lived in a large but hideous house in a suburb.

Objectives

- To recognize and appreciate the short story as a form of literature
- To understand character descriptions
- To identify the theme of a short story
- To apply literal, interpretive, and critical reading skills to a selection
- To identify homographs
- To develop a character for a short story
- To identify the organization of an encyclopedia article

Preparing the Students

Essential Vocabulary. The words presented here are essential to the understanding of the selection.

Write the following words and their definitions on the board. Call on students to read aloud the words and their meanings. Explain that students will encounter these words in the next story.

chaise—a light, open carriage drawn by one horse

lament—to express sorrow

recruit—to sign up new members

barracks—structures resembling sheds or barns that provide temporary housing for soldiers

proceed—to go forward or onward

Ask students to copy the words in alphabetical order. Then erase the definitions, and have students recall them.

If the students need additional help encourage them to use context clues to determine word meaning. As needed, direct them to the **Glossary** or to a classroom dictionary.

Motivation. Make sure all the students are aware that the American Revolution made possible the creation of the United States, and that the Fourth of July commemorates the birth of the country.

Tell the students that although this story is set in the year 1848, it was written by a modern author. Have the students read the introduction on page 188 and state in their own words what they are to find out as they read this short story.

Presenting the Selection

1. Have the students read "The Old Soldier" on pages 188 to 195. Since this is a long selection, you may want to divide it into two assignments, ending the first assignment after page 191, column 2, "but they had always seen the old long gun, laid on the pegs over the fireplace, and the old belt hung with it."

The Old Soldier

DOROTHY CANFIELD

The title of this story gives attention to one character. Is he the most important character? As you read, decide whether the story is mainly about the old soldier or about someone else.

No matter how I set this story down, you will take it, I fear, as a fable. But it is not. It is as literally true as a local news item in your this-morning's newspaper. It happened up the state aways from our town, "over the mountain," as we call that middle upland valley of Vermont.

For a long time, after the Revolution, the citizens of the little town of Sunmore had made a great day out of the Fourth of July. They seemed to hear, more clearly than some other towns, the very sound of the old Liberty Bell in Philadelphia as it rang out in joy over the signing of the Declaration of Independence. They had not at all forgotten what the Fourth meant. As the years went by, a set form grew up for the day's celebration. At dawn, the big boys fired off again and again the old cannon that stood on the village common. There was a meeting, about eleven in the morning, at the Town Hall, where people made speeches and sang patriotic songs. After that, a picnic lunch was eaten out on the green. If it rained, the lunch was eaten inside the Town Hall. Then, rain or shine, the procession formed to escort the old soldiers out to the Burying Ground, a mile from town, where they put flags on the graves of their comrades among the Sunmore men who, like them, had been soldiers in the Revolution.

The boys looked forward to this celebrating from one year to the next chiefly, of course, because to share in the firing of the cannon marked a long step forward in growing up. The cannon was generally said to have been in the Battle of Bennington in 1777. Ordinary people said yes, of course it was. But more careful folks said this was not sure. As the years went by after that battle, twenty, forty, fifty; and finally by the time of this story, in 1848, seventy years, fewer and fewer people could remember it. Also, of course, there were fewer and fewer old Sunmore men who had been Revolutionary soldiers.

Until they were past eighty, they had walked in the procession like everybody else. After that, Dr. White, who of course took care of them all when they were sick, said their joints were too stiff. He took them out in his own chaise, behind his slow, ancient roan horse. Dick was rather stiff in his joints too, and was glad to walk with ceremonial slowness.

Dr. White knew more about medicine than anyone else in town. This was to be expected because nobody else knew anything at all about it. But on the subject—local history—of which many people knew a great deal, he was also the local specialist. On the shelves of his library, mixed up with his medical books, stood more histories of Vermont than the rest of Sunmore people had, all put together. When anyone wanted to find out something about what had happened in the past, Dr. White was asked. He always knew the answer.

When May and June came in, people began to plan for the Fourth of July celebration. But there were no old soldiers left. For four or five years there had been only two. Both of them were very old, of course, for the year 1848 was seventy-one years after the Battle of Bennington. One had been ninety, and the other eighty-six. Now both were gone. The older one had died in the winter, and the family of the other one had moved away out west into York State and taken the old man with them.

It was too bad. Everybody was saying that the celebration wouldn't be much without an old soldier in it, to connect the town with the Revolution. Without one, how would people remember what the Fourth of July was really about? The ancients had always sat on the platform of the Town Hall, while the singing and speech-making went on, their long firearms across their knees, their soldier's leather belts strapped on over their Sunday coats. Of course what uniforms they had had, had gone all to pieces, if they'd ever had any, which was unlikely, buckskin being the wear in those early days. They had ridden in Dr. White's chaise, just behind the fife and drum corps and the little girls in white dresses carrying the bouquets, ahead of the marching men and women, four abreast in the road. When the procession reached the cemetery, the little girls handed the flowers to the big boys, and they passed them out to the hobbling old soldiers, who laid them on the graves of their comrades in the Revolution. The smaller boys had the honor of planting fresh American flags on the graves, waving above the flowers.

One of the boys in town, one of the Bostwick family, heard his folks lamenting that the celebration would not seem right with no old soldiers at all. He was the third child; Andrew was his name. He was about ten years old when this happened. He went to the nearby district school and read in the fourth reader, but

2. Make sure that everyone has read the short story by administering the **Check Test**, at the bottom of T.E. page 195. If the story was read in two parts, administer questions 1 and 2 after the first reading assignment and questions 3 and 4 after the second assignment.

3. Remind students of the introduction and the question posed there. Ask several students whether the story is mainly about someone other than the old soldier, and if so, who is it about. Have them cite evidence from the story to support their answers.

4. Develop the study questions as suggested in **Using the Study Questions** beginning on page 196. That section also provides challenge questions to be used for further discussion, as needed. (For answers to questions, see T.E. pages 196 to 198.)

Reinforcing the Lesson

To reteach, reinforce, or extend the skills in this lesson, see the following:

Skills Practice Book, Green Level—pages 102 and 103

Encouraging Independent Reading

1. Suggest that students do some reading on the Hessian soldiers who fought with the British in the Revolutionary War. How did the alliance develop between Britain and Germany? When did the Hessians begin to fight in America? Encourage students to share their findings with the class.

2. Have the students form teams to investigate the history of their town or city. Take some class time to discuss possible sources of information—City Hall, the local library, the local newspaper archives—and set a deadline for each team to bring in facts on a given topic, such as the reason for the name of the town, the date of founding, the first hospital, and so on.

long before he knew his alphabet, he knew about the Battle of Bennington and the Revolutionary War.

He was just getting to be old enough to help fire off the cannon, and to hand the flowers to the old soldiers in the cemetery. And now they were all gone.

One day in June, when he was sent out to look for a cow which, the night before, hadn't come back to the barn from the mountain pasture, he met a schoolmate up there, Will Hunter. Will's mother had sent him out to pick wild strawberries on that sloping clearing. After the two boys met, the cow and the strawberries were forgotten. They sat down on a ledge to have a talk. Before long, Andrew said something about the Fourth of July celebration with no old soldier left, not a single one.

The other boy said, "There's an old fellow lives with the Hawleys, 'way up Haw-

A Beautiful World, 1948, GRANDMA MOSES.

About the Art

Anna Mary Robertson Moses (1860-1961), known as "Grandma Moses," was always involved in artistic activity, but her daily obligations made a serious art career impossible until her later years. In her seventies, Anna Moses taught herself to paint the rural scenes of New England. Her acute sense of color, pattern, and spatial depth make her one of America's foremost folk artists.

ley Hollow from our house. He's their great-grandfather, I think. Maybe he was a soldier in the Revolution. He's old enough. They say he's ninety. More."

Andrew's ten-year-old mind was already firmly lodged behind the tight narrow wall of the idea of the Town. "They don't live in Sunmore," he said. "We have to have a Sunmore old soldier for our Fourth."

"Yes, they do too, live in Sunmore," said the other boy. "They don't trade at the Summore stores, because from that end of the Hollow where their house is, it's easier to go out the far end to Canbury. But they vote in our Town Meeting."[1]

The two boys looked at each other. Thinking no more of the missing cow and the wild strawberries, they set out for the Hollow.

So there was to be a Revolutionary soldier after all for the Fourth of July celebration! Everybody was talking about the old man, eighty-nine years, or maybe ninety, maybe more, back up on the far side of Westward Mountain, who had been remembered just in time.

When the two boys told their fathers about him, two of the Selectmen of the town had gone over the mountain to see him. They said his back was bent with rheumatism, he was almost stone deaf, and he hobbled along with two canes to steady him. But he still had his old rifle, and even his cracked leather soldier's belt, just as the others had. And they reported that when, shouting loudly in his ear, they had asked him if he had fought in the Revolutionary War, he had nodded his head. Then they asked had it been in the Battle of Bennington? When he finally heard what they were asking, he nodded his head and told them, "Yes, yes, sir, it certainly was."

They said the Hawleys up there, for all he was so old, thought a great deal of him. It was his great-grandson's family he was with—young people they were, had been married only five or six years. When the last of his grandchildren had died, these young people had left their little cottage in Canbury and gone up to take care of him. An arrangement often made, in our country—he was to leave them his house and farm and they were to provide for his old age. They had never heard, naturally, what he had been doing seventy years ago—neither of them was over twenty-five—but they had always seen the old long gun, laid on the pegs over the fireplace, and the old belt hung with it.

On the morning of the Fourth, Andrew's father got up early, took the boys, and drove his farm wagon all the way around the mountain and up into the Hollow to bring the old man back. It was ten o'clock when they came back into Sunmore Street. A crowd was waiting in

1. **Town Meeting.** In New England, this is an annual meeting of citizens 18 years and older. They vote on issues affecting the town. The town is an area larger than a village, much like the Midwest township.

front of the Town Hall. They began to clap their hands and cheer when Mr. Boswick helped lift the bent old man out of the wagon and led him into the Hall. Andrew and Will, the Young Guard of Honor, carried his ancient gun in and put it across his knees. He had his rusty belt strapped on over his coat.

When they took his gun to carry, he gave them such a pleasant smile of thanks that they understood why his great-grandchildren thought so much of him. He was a very nice-looking old man, everybody thought, clean and neat, with quiet, gentle eyes; and although he hadn't a tooth left, his mouth still looked as though he liked jokes.

The people came into the Town Hall, took their seats, and began fanning themselves. It was a hot day, as the Fourth often is. The speaker was there, a lawyer from Canbury. The chorus of local singers stood below the platform, facing the audience. Their leader rapped his stick. They stood at attention. But they did not begin to sing. For at this point Dr. White, who always sat on the platform with the Selectmen and the speaker, called out to Andrew, "Here! Let me look at that gun! Pass it over to me."

Andrew was surprised. He put his hand on the gun and, leaning down to the old man's ear, said as loudly as he could, "Dr. White wants to see your gun."

He shouted with all his might but he could not make himself heard. The old soldier was almost stone deaf. But he was willing to do anything that was wanted. His cheerful old face was bright. He felt the friendliness that was all around him. He smiled, nodded, and passed his gun to Andrew.

The doctor took one sharp look at it and motioned to the singers in the chorus. "Wait a minute!" he told them.

Then he put on his glasses and looked very carefully at a certain place near the trigger. Everybody kept still, wondering what was in his mind.

When he looked up, his face was all astonishment. He spoke so loudly that everybody in the whole Town Hall could hear him. "This is a Hessian[2] gun! The old man must have been one of the Hessians who fought against the Americans."

There was such a silence in the Town Hall you could hear a wasp buzzing at one of the windows.

He was a Hessian! He had fought on the other side. People's mouths dropped open, they were so taken back.

The old man hadn't heard any of this because he was so deaf. He sat quietly there, between the two little boys, his gentle old eyes looking around at the people in the hall.

For a minute nobody said a word. Nobody could think of what to say. Or what to do.

2. **Hessians,** well-trained soldiers from Hesse-Kassel, Germany, were hired by the British to fight the colonists during the Revolutionary War.

Then Andrew ran out to the front of the platform and began to talk very fast. "Listen," he said. "That was a hundred years ago. Well, more than seventy years, anyhow. No matter how mad you are at somebody, you don't keep it up forever. He's lived close to us all that time, and farmed it like anybody, and had his family, and paid his taxes. He's old, so old—it would be mean of us to—"

Andrew had never even spoken a piece in school. He had forgotten where he was. When he realized what he was doing, he stopped talking and hung down his head. He went back and put one hand on the old man's shoulder. The wrinkled face lifted to smile at him. Andrew smiled back. But his lips were trembling.

People began to rustle and move their feet. But when Dr. White stood up as if to say something, they became still again, to listen.

He said, "I remember now, when I first came to Sunmore to practice medicine and first began to be interested in Vermont history, I did hear some very old people talk about a young Hessian soldier who had been wounded in the Battle of Bennington, and was picked up unconscious, in the woods, the day after. One of the old history books in my Vermont collection says that he was carried to a farmhouse and taken care of there. By the time he was well enough to get around, many months afterwards, there were no more soldiers or armies around. He was only nineteen by that time, and he had come to love the way of life he saw around him. He wanted to be an American and live here.

"That history book didn't say anything more about him. But I heard something else from old Mr. Hale." The doctor looked down into the audience at a middle-aged man in the second row. "He was your grandfather, Jim Hale. He was sort of connected, in-laws somehow, with the Bennington family that took in the Hessian boy. He told me they always liked him, the young soldier, I mean. When he learned enough English, he told them his story. He had always had it hard in the Old Country, he said. He was an orphan, very poor, seventeen years old, when a recruiting gang picked him up off the street and carried him off to the barracks in Brunswick. He never liked soldiering, he said. He never understood what the fighting was about. He never knew any English till he learned it from the Vermont family who cared for him."

The doctor still held the old rifle in his hands. He turned around now and laid it back on the old man's knees. Then he said to the audience, "I rather think Andrew Bostwick was right. Seventy years is too long to go on being mad. I think our celebration would better go on. Maybe the Reverend Hardwick might have something to say to us about this."

The minister stood up, stooped in his black clergyman's clothes. He stood silent a long time. Then he said, "May war pass and peace be with us. Amen."

He sat down. The Moderator of the Town stood up. He was a burly, powerful, middle-aged man, with a serious, responsible face. He said, soberly, "I think this is something we ought to take a vote on. Don't you think so, Mr. Hardwick?"

The minister nodded. "Yes. It is something for each one of us to decide. But before we vote, I think we ought to sit quiet for a moment. And think."

The Moderator reached for the clergyman's cane, and with it struck a gavel-like blow on the table. In his Moderator's voice, he said, "The question before this House, is whether we can live in peace when war has long gone by."

They all sat still.

The deaf ears of the old soldier had, of course, not heard any of this. It looked all right to him. He was very much bent with rheumatism. His hands lay thin and knotted on the arms of his chair. His clean old

Colonel Glover's Fishermen Leaving Marblehead for Cambridge, 1775, about 1920, J.O.J. FROST.
New York Historical Association, Cooperstown.

About the Art

Like Grandma Moses, who began painting later in life and had no formal training (see **About The Art** on page 190), John Orne Johnson Frost (1858-1928) began painting when he was in his late sixties. Corresponding to Grandma Moses's work, his paintings are in a naive, or unsophisticated, style. Most of his art depicts scenes from early American history, usually events that occurred in his native state of Massachusetts.

In this painting, a Revolutionary War scene, notice how the soldiers appear rigid and flat, almost as if they had been cut out and pasted on the canvas rather than painted. Observe the men's strength and sense of purpose as they march in rhythm and how this contrasts with the free brushwork of the sky.

face was calm. In the silence, he looked from one person to another in the audience. He smiled a little. After a moment, he turned his white head to look back at his little-boy guard of honor. There they were, one on each side of his chair. He nodded and leaned back as if to say, "It's all right, if you are there."

The water came into Andrew's eyes.

The people in the rows of chairs on the floor were all looking up at the old soldier and the little boys.

A man stood up and said, "Mr. Moderator, I move that our celebration proceed."

Several voices said, "I second the motion."

Then the vote was taken. Everybody voted "aye."

That afternoon, after the usual speaking and singing had been done, and the picnic lunch eaten out on the Common, the procession formed as usual, to march out to the cemetery.

The old soldier looked very tired by this time, but still cheerful. He came out of the Town Hall on Dr. White's arm, and was helped up into the chaise. The Young Guard of Honor held their flags high, so that they stirred in the breeze. The little girls in white dresses were pushed by their mothers into line, two by two. They carried the flowers——lilies, roses, carnation pinks.

The men and women formed, four by four. The doctor slapped the reins over the old horse's back. The leader of the band lifted his hand and said, commandingly, "A–a–ll ready!"

The marchers held their flags straight, ready to go.

"Forward, march!" cried the bandmaster.

The fifes sang out, "Whee-dee-deedle-dee" in thin high voices.

In a deep roar, the drums said, "Boom! boom! boom!"

And away they all went.

Check Test

1. For what celebration did Sunmore want an old soldier? (the Fourth of July celebration)

2. On what subject was Dr. White an expert? (local history)

3. Why did Dr. White stop the celebration? (He saw that the old soldier was carrying a Hessian gun.)

4. What did the townspeople decide to do about the celebration? (to continue the celebration)

Using the Study Questions

It is recommended that students always read and answer the questions in **Developing Comprehension Skills** in class discussion.

Developing Comprehension Skills

Question 1. Read and discuss.

Question 2. After the students answer this question, ask them how they think Andrew felt about the honors he was given. Have them support their answers with evidence from the story.

Question 3. Explain that this question asks personal opinions. Point out, however, that their opinions should be based on information in the story.

Question 4. Read and discuss.

Challenge Question. Firing the cannon "marked a long step in growing up" in Sunmore. Can you think of any modern day ceremonies that mark the passage from childhood into adulthood? (Critical Reading)

Reading Literature: Short Stories

Question 1. Have students identify the setting of the story, both the place and time.

Question 2. Have one student read the paragraph. Review the definition of *metaphor*. Have students discuss their answers to this question.

Question 3. Have students discuss why it was so important that the old soldier be from Sunmore.

Question 4. Ask students to think about their reactions to the old soldier. Point out that if they like him, it is probably because the author wants them to like him. Have students skim the story and find descriptions of the old soldier.

Question 5. If necessary, refer students to page 193, column 1.

Question 6. As a review, ask a student to define *external conflict*. Discuss what would make an external conflict political in nature. Then have the students answer.

Challenge Question. Why was it important to the story that the old soldier be deaf? How would the story have changed if he could have heard?

Developing Vocabulary Skills

Read the directions for **Identifying Homographs** on page 197 to the students. Have them complete the exercise

Developing Comprehension Skills

Literal Reading — 1. Why did the townspeople of Sunmore need an old soldier for the Fourth of July celebration? How would the ceremonies have been different without an old soldier?

Literal Reading — 2. Of what importance was the celebration to the boys of Sunmore? Why was Andrew so interested in this year's celebration?

Critical Reading — 3. Would you have voted to continue or not to continue with the ceremony? Explain your answer.

Interpretive Reading — 4. Why was the idea of the soldier being Hessian such a surprise to the townsfolk? Why had they never thought of this possibility?

Reading Literature: Short Stories

1. **Appreciating the Setting.** Why is the small-town setting important for an understanding of this story? How is the date important?

2. **Understanding Metaphor.** Examine this passage from the story.

   > Andrew's ten-year-old mind was already firmly lodged behind the tight narrow wall of the idea of the Town. "They don't live in Sunmore," he said. "We have to have a Sunmore old soldier for our Fourth."

   How is "the idea of the Town" like a wall? What is it holding in? What is it keeping out?

3. **Identifying Unstated Cause and Effect.** Reread the passage in question 2, above. It states that Andrew thought of the town as a wall. Then it reports that Andrew insisted on the old soldier being from Sunmore. What is the relationship between these two facts?

4. **Understanding Character Descriptions.** Sometimes the author wants the reader to feel a certain way about a character. What feeling does the author want the reader to develop about the old soldier? Find several passages from the story that support your answer.

5. **Identifying Theme.** In the first paragraph, the author assures the reader that the story is not a fable. She insists that the story is as true as a newspaper notice. However, one way the story is like a fable is that its theme is stated as the moral of a fable often is. Find the theme as stated in Andrew's words.

Answers to Study Questions

Developing Comprehension Skills

1. In the ceremony, the old soldiers put flowers on the graves of their comrades. Without an old soldier, there would be no guest of honor and no link with the past.

2. The older boys were allowed to fire off the cannon. This marked a big step in growing up. Andrew was supposed to help fire the cannon this year and was to be a member of the guard of honor for the old soldier.

3. Opinions will vary. Most students will probably say that since the battle was so long ago, and since the old soldier hadn't really wanted to fight in the first place, the ceremony should have continued.

4. The townsfolk might have thought that all the Hessian soldiers had gone home. Other answers are possible, as long as they are logical.

Challenge. Answers will vary. Graduation is one ceremony that marks a passage. Many religions have such ceremonies. The cultural backgrounds of your students may include more examples of rites of passage.

6. **Identifying Conflict.** What is the external political conflict that almost started because of the Hessian soldier? How is it avoided?

Developing Vocabulary Skills

Identifying Homographs. In the dictionary you may find two or three entry words that look the same. For example, there are three words that are spelled *r-o-w*. Read these dictionary entries:

row[1] (rō), a line or rank
row[2] (rō), to move by oars
row[3] (rou), a noisy quarrel

Words like *row* are called **homographs**. They are spelled the same, but their meanings are completely different. These words often have the same pronunciation, but sometimes, as in *row,* they do not. The dictionary enters and defines each homograph separately.

The following sentences are drawn from stories you have read. Each underlined word is a homograph. Find each homograph in a dictionary. On your paper, write the definition that fits the context of the sentence.

1. The young woman had a lovely smile, and her rounded cheeks were a tender pink.
2. "The other hand is engaged at present," he told Miss Fairchild.
3. He would write for a long time and then tear it all up.
4. They were reduced to living in a mean igloo.
5. Several voices said, "I second the motion."

Developing Writing Skills

Analytical Writing

1. **Identifying the Narrator.** "The Old Soldier" is told by a specific character. The author asks you to imagine the character from the first sentence, where the narrator refers to himself or herself twice:

   > No matter how I set this story down, you will take it, I fear, as a fable.

   Throughout the story, the narrator uses conversational phrases and offers personal opinions.

   What image did you develop of the narrator as you read the story? What sort of person do you think he or she is? Write a paragraph

Reading Literature: Short Stories

1. In a small town, people are not used to dealing with many different kinds of people. They are cut off from many influences. It might have been harder for a small-town person to accept the old Hessian soldier. The date is important because it had been so many years since the Revolution that many people were not angry about it anymore.

2. The idea of the town was like a wall because it limited Andrew's thinking. He was so used to the way things had been done before that he couldn't imagine new ways.

3. Since people from the town should follow tradition, and traditionally the town celebrated on its own, then the old soldier should be one of the town's citizens.

4. The author wants the reader to like the old soldier. The following passages describe the old soldier in a positive way:

Page 191, column 2—"They said the Hawleys up there, for all he was so old, thought a great deal of him."
Page 192, column 2, paragraph 1
Page 193, column 2, paragraph 2
Page 194, last paragraph, through page 195, first paragraph

(continued on page 198)

independently and discuss the answers together. For reinforcement, you may wish to have the students suggest sentences of their own that fit the other definitions of each underlined word.

Developing Writing Skills

Read and discuss the two assignments. Then have each student choose and complete one of the two.

Question 1. To answer this question, students must reread the story carefully, this time noticing the style of the narrator.

Pre-Writing. Have the students try to describe the overall feeling they have about the narrator. Ask for suggestions of adjectives that could be used to describe him or her. List a few of these on the board. Urge students to identify lines in the story that made them feel as they do and list these next to their corresponding adjectives. Have students write topic sentences.

Writing. Remind students to support their opinions about the narrator with examples from the story. Tell them that they may use the examples on the board but they should include other lines from the story to support their conclusions. Allow sufficient time for the students to write their first drafts.

Revising. Have students exchange papers in small groups. Have the group decide whether each writer included enough references to the story to justify his or her conclusion.

Question 2. The characters developed in this question will be used later when students write an original short story.

Pre-Writing. Explain to students that this character will appear in a short story they will write soon. Encourage them to choose a character they will want to write about. Have students list words and phrases that describe the character, following the list of suggestions in the text.

Writing. Remind students to use specific words to describe their characters.

Revising. Have the students put this description aside for a few days. Then ask them to reread it and decide whether they still want to write about that character. If they have changed their minds, allow time for them to write new descriptions.

Developing Skills in Study and Research

Have students read **Using the Encyclopedia** on page 198. Make sure they understand what the assignment is asking for. Have your class visit the school library, or make several encyclopedias available for use in class.

explaining what you think the narrator is like. Include references to lines of the story that led you to your conclusions.

Creative Writing

2. **Developing a Character.** Begin to assemble the parts of a short story. Think of a character. You can base your character on someone you know but change the name and at least one character trait, or quality. Describe this character in as much detail as you can. Tell about things such as these:

how the person dresses
the color of the person's hair
his or her size
his or her personality traits

Give examples of how this person does things.

Developing Skills in Study and Research

Using the Encyclopedia. Sometimes a great deal of information is presented about a subject or topic in the encyclopedia. So much information is presented that it is necessary to divide or outline the subject. Boldface headings or titles are used to introduce the different sections within a single article.

In your school or local library, select an encyclopedia. Find the volume that has the article on the "American Revolution" or the "Revolutionary War." On your paper, list the boldface headings or titles that are used to organize the information in the article. Then describe the type of organization used. Was it chronological? Were certain periods discussed separately? Were the periods broken down further by topics or themes? Were the same topics or themes discussed for each time period?

(continued from page 197)

Page 195, column 2—"The old soldier looked very tired by this time, but still cheerful."

The students may find other passages to support their answers.

5. "No matter how mad you are at somebody, you don't keep it up forever."

6. If Andrew and Dr. White hadn't spoken up in defense of the old soldier, the townspeople would probably have openly expressed their differences of opinion, creating much discontent in the community.

Challenge. If the soldier had been able to hear, he probably would have been upset that people weren't sure they wanted him in their celebration. He might have gotten angry and then people might have become angry with him, and the ceremony would probably have not taken place. But because he was kind and gentle, people were able to see that it was time to forgive their enemies.

Developing Vocabulary Skills

Wording will vary according to the dictionary used.

1. tender—soft quality or delicate tone
2. present—existing or happening now
3. tear—to pull apart into pieces
4. mean—low in quality
5. second—to indicate one's approval or support of (a motion) before discussing a vote on it

The Big Wave

PEARL S. BUCK

In this story of a Japanese fishing village, the destructive forces of nature win a major victory. Read the story to see how the good in people helps them deal with the situation.

Kino lived on a farm that lay on the side of a mountain in Japan. The mountain rose so steeply out of the ocean that there was only a strip of sandy shore at its foot. Upon this strip was a small fishing village where Kino's father sold his vegetables and rice and bought fish.

Kino often looked down upon the thatched roofs of the village. The village houses faced one another, and those which stood beside the sea did not have windows toward it. Since Kino enjoyed looking at the waves, he often wondered why the village people did not, but he never knew until he came to know Jiya, whose father was a fisherman. Jiya's house did not have a window toward the sea either.

"Why not?" Kino asked him. "The sea is beautiful."

"The sea is our enemy," Jiya replied.

"How can you say that?" Kino asked. "Your father catches fish from the sea and sells them, and that is how you live."

Jiya shook his head. "The sea is our enemy," he repeated.

It was hard to believe this. On hot sunny days Kino and Jiya threw off their clothes and swam far out toward a small island that they considered their own. Actually, it belonged to an old gentleman whom they had never seen except at a distance.

Kino longed to sleep on the island some night, but Jiya was never willing. Even when they spent only the afternoon there, he looked often out over the sea.

"What are you looking for?" Kino asked one day.

"Only to see that the ocean is not angry," Jiya replied.

But certainly the ocean was not angry now. The sun sparkled deep into the clear water, and the boys swam over the silvery surface of rippling waves. Beneath them, the water was miles deep. When Kino dived, he went down, down, down, until he struck icy-still water.

Objectives

- To recognize and appreciate the short story as a form of literature
- To identify the internal conflict of a character in a short story
- To appreciate description
- To understand the function of the introduction, or exposition, of a short story
- To apply literal, interpretive, and critical reading skills to a selection
- To recognize different pronunciations of a word
- To develop a setting for a short story
- To read a dialog expressing a mood

Preparing the Students

Essential Vocabulary. The words presented here are essential to the understanding of the selection.

Have the students use the context clues in the following sentences to determine the meanings of the underlined words.

zenith   terraces

1. When the sun is at its highest point in the sky, we say it is at its zenith.
2. To farm on mountainsides, farmers make terraces, flat-topped areas of earth with sloping sides.

If the students need additional help with the vocabulary of this selection, encourage them to use context clues to determine word meaning. As needed, direct them to the **Glossary** or to a classroom dictionary.

Motivation. Explain to students that the next story takes place in a setting quite different from the small town in New England where the last story took place. It is set in a fishing village in Japan. If a wall map is available, ask a volunteer to point out the location of Japan.

Tell the class that the writer, Pearl Buck, knew a lot about life in China and Japan and wrote many books about that part of the world. As they read this story, they will see some similarities and differences between the way of life of the Japanese and that of their own. Have the students read the introductory paragraph at the top of page 199 and state in their own words what they should try to find out as they read this short story.

Presenting the Selection

1. Have the students read "The Big Wave" in two parts. The first part ends at the bottom of column 2 on page 203.

2. Make sure that everyone has read the short story by administering the **Check**

Test, at the bottom of T.E. page 207. The first two questions refer to the first part of the story, and the second two questions refer to the second part.

3. Ask several students to explain how the good in the people of the village helped them get through the difficult situation.

4. Develop the study questions as suggested in **Using the Study Questions** beginning on page 208. That section also provides challenge questions to be used for further discussion, as needed. (For answers to questions, see T.E. pages 208 to 210.)

Reinforcing the Lesson

To reteach, reinforce, or extend the skills in this lesson, see the following:

Skills Practice Book, Green Level—pages 104 through 106

Special Populations

LD. The exercise **Recognizing Exposition** on page 209 may be altered slightly for some students by asking them to choose from the following statements the facts found in the first five paragraphs:

Setting:

- The farm is on the side of a mountain.
- The mountain rises steeply out of the ocean.
- The village has the mountains to protect it from the sea. (incorrect)
- The fishing village is located on a thin strip of sandy shore.
- Village windows do not face the sea.
- The farm was on the shore by the sea. (incorrect)
- The waves come from the sea.

Characters:

- Kino is a boy living on a farm.
- Kino's father sells vegetables, rice; buys fish.
- Lama is a girl living on the island. (incorrect)
- Jiya is a boy living in the village.
- Jiya's father catches and sells fish.
- Jiya's mother grows vegetables. (incorrect)

ESL. ESL students may need individual help completing the vocabulary exercise, **Recognizing Different Pronunciations of a Word**, on page 209. Give the students other examples of the italicized or underlined words used in a sentence, stressing the correct pronunciation. The students may not be familiar with the usage of some of these words.

The Coast of Tago, 1823–29, KATSUSHIKA HOKUSAI. The Metropolitan Museum of Art, Rogers Fund, 1922.

Today when he felt the coldness grasp his body, he understood why Jiya was afraid, and he darted upward again to the sun. On the beach he threw himself down and was happy again. But Jiya looked often at the sun. When he saw it sinking toward the west, he called to Kino: "Come quickly. We must swim home."

After supper that evening, Kino turned to his father. "Why is Jiya afraid of the ocean?" he asked.

"The ocean is very big," Kino's father replied. "We do not understand the ocean."

"I am glad we live on the mountain," Kino went on. "There is nothing to be afraid of on our farm."

"But one can be afraid of the land too," his father replied. "Do you remember the volcano we visited last autumn?"

Kino did remember. They had gone to visit a great volcano twenty miles away. Kino had looked down into the yawning mouth of the volcano, and he had not liked it. Great curls of yellow smoke were rolling about it, and a white stream of melted rock was crawling slowly from one corner.

200 SHORT STORIES

About the Art

The Coast of Tago, a print by the master *Ukiyo-e* printmaker Katsushika Hokusai (1760-1849), shows fishermen in boats on the sea and farmers working the fields along the coastline. In the background, rising above and dominating the scene, is Japan's most famous landmark, Mt. Fuji. (See also **About the Art** on pages 185 and 203.)

The art of Japanese woodblock printmaking known as *Ukiyo-e,* which means "pictures of the floating world," depicted the fleeting pleasures of everyday life. It portrayed popular actors, professional wrestlers, and beautiful women of the day, as well as common scenes and famous sights. Before this, Japanese art followed the tradition of Chinese painting, which took as its subject religious and philosophical themes.

"Must we always be afraid of something?" Kino asked.

His father looked back at him. "No," he replied. "I did not mean that. It is true that on any day, an ocean may rise into storm and a volcano may burst into flame. We must accept this fact, but without fear. We must say, 'Some day I shall die, and does it matter whether it is by ocean or volcano, or whether I grow old and weak?' "

"I don't want to think about such things," Kino said.

"It is right for you not to think about them," his father said. "Enjoy life and do not fear death. That is the way of a good Japanese."

There was much in life to enjoy. In the winter Kino went to a school in the fishing village, and he and Jiya shared a seat. In the summer Kino worked on the farm, helping his father. Even his little sister, Setsu, and the mother helped when the rice seedlings had to be planted and when the grain was ripe and had to be threshed.

Sometimes if it were not seedtime or harvest, Kino went fishing with Jiya and Jiya's father. "I wish my father were a fisherman," he would say. "It is stupid to plow and plant and cut the sheaves, when I could just come out like this and reap fish from the sea."

Jiya shook his head. "But when the storms come, you would wish yourself back upon the earth," he said.

On days when the sky was bright and the winds mild, the ocean lay so calm and blue that it was hard to believe that it could be cruel and angry. But when the deep water moved and stirred, ah, then Kino began to be glad that his father was a farmer and not a fisherman!

Yet it was the earth that brought the big wave. Deep under the deepest part of the ocean, fires raged in the heart of the earth. At last the fires grew so strong that they forced their way through the mouth of the volcano. That day Kino saw the sky overcast halfway to the zenith. "Look, Father!" he cried. "The volcano is burning again!"

His father gazed anxiously at the sky. "It looks very angry," he said. "I shall not sleep tonight."

All night Kino's father kept watch. When it was dark, the sky was lit with red and the earth trembled under the farmhouse. Down at the fishing village, lights in the little houses showed that other fathers watched too.

When morning came, the sky was red and, even here upon the farm, cinders fell from the volcano.

In the house the mother took down everything from the walls that could fall or be broken. Her few good dishes she packed into straw in a basket and set them outside.

"Shall we have an earthquake, Father?" Kino asked as they ate breakfast. "After the volcano burns?"

Encouraging Independent Reading

Ask for volunteers to do some research projects on life in Japan. You may wish to present the following categories and divide these up according to the number of volunteers you have:

- Education
- Recreation
- Dress
- Family Life
- Industry
- Religious Beliefs and Practices
- Government

Encourage the students to consult a variety of reference sources other than just an encyclopedia to obtain the information they need (e.g., magazine articles; a Japanese relative, friend, or acquaintance; someone they know who has visited Japan; travel books and brochures). Suggest to the students that they might enjoy making illustrations to accompany their reports. If time permits, have students give oral presentations of their findings to the class. You may wish to make a display of the students' projects.

"I cannot tell, my son," his father replied. "Earth and sea are struggling together against the fires inside the earth."

No fishing boats set sail that hot summer morning. The sea lay dead and calm, but when Kino looked at it he felt afraid.

No one stirred from home that day. Kino's father sat at the door, watching the sky and the oily sea, and Kino stayed near him. He did not know what Jiya was doing, but he imagined that Jiya, too, stayed by his father.

Early in the afternoon, the sky began to grow black. The air was as hot as though a forest fire were burning. The glow of the volcano glared over the mountaintop, blood-red against the black. All at once a deep-toned bell tolled over the hills.

"What is that bell?" Kino asked.

"It is a bell in the temple inside the walls of Old Gentleman's Castle," his father replied. "Old Gentleman is calling people to come up out of the village and find shelter within his walls."

"Will they come?" Kino asked.

"Not all of them," his father replied. "Parents will try to make the children go, but the children will not want to leave their parents. Mothers will not want to leave fathers, and the fathers will stay by their boats. But some will want to be sure of life."

"I wish Jiya would come up to our farm," Kino said. "Do you think he will see me if I stand on the edge of the terrace and wave my sash?"

"Try it," his father said.

Kino took off the strip of white cloth which he wore instead of a belt, and he waved it high above his head. Jiya, far down the hill, saw the two figures and the waving strip of white. For Jiya was already on his way up the mountain toward Old Gentleman's Castle. He was crying as he climbed and trying not to cry. He had not wanted to leave, but his father said, "If the ocean yields to the fires, you must live after us."

"I don't want to live alone," Jiya said.

"It is your duty to obey me, as a good Japanese son," his father told him.

So Jiya had run out of the house, crying. Now when he saw Kino, he decided that he would go there instead of to the castle, and he began to hurry up the hill to the farm.

Kino's father put out his hand to help Jiya climb over the stone wall of the terrace, and Kino was just about to shout out his welcome, when suddenly a hurricane wind broke out of the ocean. Kino and Jiya clung together and wrapped their arms about the father's waist.

"Look, what is that?" Kino screamed.

The purple rim of the ocean seemed to lift and rise against the clouds. Under the deep waters of the ocean, the earth had yielded at last to the fire. It groaned and split open, and the cold water fell into the middle of the boiling rocks. Steam burst out and lifted the ocean high into the sky in a big wave.

The Red Fuji, 1831–33, KATSUSHIKA HOKUSAI. The Metropolitan Museum of Art, Rogers Fund, 1914.

The wave rushed toward the shore, green and solid, frothing into white at its edges.

"I must tell my father!" Jiya screamed. But before Jiya could scream again, the wave reached the village and covered it fathoms deep in swirling wild water. Upon the beach where the village had stood, not a house remained.

Jiya gave a wild cry, and Kino felt him slip to the ground. Jiya was unconscious. What he had seen was too much for him. His family and his home were gone.

Kino's father gathered Jiya into his arms and carried him into the house. "It is better that he is unconscious," he said gently. "Let him remain so until his own will wakes him. I will sit by him."

"What shall we say to Jiya when he wakes?" Kino asked his father.

"We will not talk," his father replied. "We will give him warm food and let him rest. We will help him to feel he has a home still."

"Here?" Kino asked.

"Yes," his father replied.

About the Art

The Red Fuji, a woodblock print by the master printmaker Katsushika Hokusai (1760-1849), shows the mountain at sunset bathed in red light. Hokusai did a series of thirty-six prints of this mountain from different viewpoints and in different seasons. (See also **About the Art** pages 185 and 200.) Since a separate block had to be carved for each color, the printmaker usually limited himself to only a few colors. In this print, the simplicity of the color scheme is echoed in the simplicity of the design. Only a few lines are needed to depict the mountain, the forest at the base of the mountain, and the sky above.

"I don't think Jiya can ever be happy again," Kino said sorrowfully.

"Yes, he will be happy some day," his father said. "Life is always stronger than death. Soon now he will open his eyes, and we must be there, you to be his brother and I to be his father. Call your mother, too, and little Setsu."

So they went back into the house. Jiya's eyes were still closed, but he was sobbing in his sleep. Kino ran to fetch his mother and Setsu, and they all gathered about the bed, kneeling on the floor.

In a few minutes, Jiya's eyelids fluttered and then he opened his eyes. He did not know where he was. He looked from one face to the other as though they were strangers.

None of them said anything for a long time. They continued to kneel about him, waiting. But Setsu could not keep quiet. She clapped her hands and cried, "Jiya has come back!"

The sound of her voice made him fully awake. "My father—my mother," he whispered.

Kino's mother took his hand. "I will be your mother now, dear Jiya," she said.

"I will be your father," Kino's father said.

"I am your brother now, Jiya," Kino faltered.

"Jiya will live with us!" Setsu said joyfully.

Then Jiya understood. He got up from the bed and walked to the door. He looked down the hillside to the beach where the fishing village had stood.

Kino's heart ached for his friend–brother. Kino's mother was wiping her eyes, and even little Setsu looked sad. She stood beside Jiya and took his hand and stroked it. "Jiya, I will give you my pet duck," she said.

But Jiya could not speak. He kept on looking at the ocean.

"We ought all to eat something," Kino's mother said. "I have a fine chicken for dinner."

"I'm hungry," Setsu cried.

"Come, my son," Kino's father said to Jiya. Jiya was not hungry, but, when Kino begged him, he took up his chopsticks and ate some of the meat and rice. His mind was still unable to think, but his body was young and strong and glad of the food.

When they had all finished, Kino said, "Shall we go up the hillside, Jiya?"

But Jiya shook his head. "I want to go to sleep again," he said.

Each day Jiya was still tired. He did not want to think or to remember. He only wanted to sleep. One day when the work was over and Jiya still had not waked, Kino and his father sat together on the threshold. "Father, are we not very unfortunate people to live here?" he asked.

"Why do you think so?" his father asked in reply.

"Because the volcano is behind our house and the ocean is in front and, when they make the earthquake and the big wave, we are helpless. Often many of us are lost."

"To live in the midst of danger is to know how good life is," his father replied.

"But if we are lost in the danger?" Kino asked anxiously.

"To live in the presence of death makes us brave and strong," Kino's father replied.

"What is death?" Kino asked.

"Death is the great gateway," Kino's father said. His face was not at all sad.

"The gateway—where?" Kino asked again.

Kino's father smiled. "Can you remember when you were born?"

Kino shook his head. "I was too small."

Kino's father laughed. "I remember very well when you were born," he said. "And oh, how hard you thought it was to be born! You cried, and you screamed."

"Didn't I want to be born?" Kino asked.

"No," his father told him, smiling. "You wanted to stay where you were, in the warm dark house of the unborn. But the time came to be born, and the gate of life opened."

"Did I know it was the gate of life?" Kino asked.

"You did not know anything about it, and so you were afraid," his father replied. "But see how foolish you were! Here we were waiting for you, your parents, already loving you and eager to welcome you. And you have been very happy, haven't you?"

"Until the big wave came," Kino replied. "Now I am afraid again because of the death that the big wave brought."

"You are only afraid because you don't know anything about death," his father replied. "Some day you will wonder why you were afraid, as today you wonder why you feared to be born."

While they were talking, the dusk had deepened, and now, coming up the mountainside, they saw a flickering light. "I wonder who comes?" Kino exclaimed.

In a few minutes they saw that their visitor was Old Gentleman coming from the castle. "Is this the house of Uchiyama, the farmer?" Old Gentleman asked.

At this, Kino's father stood up, and so did Kino. "Please, Honored Sir," Kino's father said. "What can I do for you?"

Old Gentleman came forward. "Do you have a lad here by the name of Jiya?"

"He lies sleeping inside my house," Kino's father said.

"It is my habit when the big wave comes to care for those who are orphaned," said Old Gentleman. "Three times the wave has come, and three times I have searched out the orphans and widows, and I have fed them and sheltered them. I have heard of this boy Jiya and I wish to do even more for him. I will make him my own son."

"But Jiya is ours!" Kino cried.

"Hush," his father replied. "We must think of Jiya's good. We are only poor people." Then he said to Old Gentleman, "Sir, it is very kind of you to propose this for Jiya. I had planned to take him for my own son, now that he has lost his parents, but I am only a poor farmer and I cannot pretend that my house is as good as yours. Tomorrow when he wakes, I will tell him of your kind offer. He shall decide."

"Very well," Old Gentleman said. "But let him come and tell me himself, so that I will know how he feels."

As soon as Kino woke the next morning, he remembered Jiya and the choice he had to make. After breakfast Kino went to the field to weed the cabbages, but his father stayed home to talk to Jiya.

For a long time Kino stayed in the field, working alone. Then, when the sun was nearing zenith, he heard his father calling. He got up at once and walked between the terraces until he reached the doorway. There his father stood with Jiya.

"I have told Jiya that he must not decide until he has seen all that Old Gentleman can give him for a home," Kino's father said. "Jiya, you know how our house is—these four rooms and the kitchen, this little farm upon which we have to work so hard for our food. We have only what our hands can earn."

Then he returned to Kino again. "You are to go with Jiya, and when you see the castle you must persuade him to stay there, for his own sake."

So the two boys went down the mountainside to the castle. The gate was open, and the garden was most beautiful. A gardener was sweeping the green moss, but he left his work to lead them to the house. There they took off their shoes and followed the gardener through a great door. Inside this, they met a manservant who dismissed the gardener and said to the boys, "Follow me."

So they followed him through a wide passageway. On both sides of the passageway, panels slid back to show beautiful rooms, and in each room were a vase of flowers, an exquisite scroll, a few pieces of dark polished furniture. Neither Jiya nor Kino had ever seen such a house.

Then far in the distance, they saw Old Gentleman sitting beside a small table. The table was set in front of the open sliding panels that looked into the garden, and Old Gentleman was writing.

When the two boys came near, he looked at Jiya. "Well," he said. "Will you be my son?"

Jiya turned very red. He had not expected to have the question put to him so directly.

Old Gentleman saw he found it hard to speak. "Say yes or no," he told Jiya.

"No," Jiya said. "I thank you, but I have a home—on the farm," he added.

Check Test

1. What did Kino's family do for a living? (They farmed.)

2. Why did the Old Gentleman have the bell rung? (to call people to come up to his house)

3. What did the Old Gentleman want to do for Jiya? (make him his son)

4. With whom did Jiya finally decide to live? (Kino's family)

For a moment Kino was filled with pure joy. Then he remembered the small farmhouse, the four little rooms and the old kitchen. "Jiya," he said solemnly, "remember how poor we are."

Old Gentleman was smiling a half-sad little smile. "They are certainly very poor," he said to Jiya. "And here, you know, you would have everything."

Jiya looked about him. Then he shook his head again.

Old Gentleman took up his brush[1] again. "Very well," he said. "I will do without a son."

The manservant motioned to them and they followed, and soon they were out in the garden.

"How foolish you are," the manservant said to Jiya. "You would have everything here."

"Not everything," Jiya replied.

They went out of the gate and across the hillside and back to the farmhouse. Setsu came running to meet them, the sleeves of her bright kimono flying and her feet clattering in wooden sandals.

"Jiya has come back home!" she cried.

And Jiya, seeing her happy little face, opened his arms and gave her a great hug. For the first time, he felt comfort creep into his heart.

1. **Brush.** The written Japanese language consists of pictographs, or characters that have evolved from pictures. The writer uses a brush to draw them.

Their noonday meal was ready, and Kino's father came in from the field. When he had washed, they all sat down to eat. "How happy you have made us," he told Jiya.

"Happy indeed," Kino's mother said.

"Now I have my brother," Kino said.

Jiya smiled. Happiness began to live in him again. The good food warmed him, and his body welcomed it. Around him, the love of the people who received him glowed like a warm and welcoming fire upon the hearth.

The Suido Bridge and Suruga Plain from "One Hundred Famous Views of Edo," 1857, ANDO HIROSHIGE.
Cooper Hewitt Museum, Smithsonian Institution, Washington, D.C.

About the Art

The Japanese woodblock printmaker Ando Hiroshige (1797-1858) began his career in the *Ukiyo-e* tradition, producing prints of the popular actors and beautiful women of his day. (See **About the Art** on page 200.) Later he turned to landscapes. The print shown here is a view of the bridge and city of Edo, modern-day Tokyo, with Mt. Fuji in the background. Like another famous printmaker, Hiroshige's rival, Katsushika Hokusai (see also pages 185, 200, and 203), Hiroshige depicted his landscapes from a distance and from an unusual point of view. However, Hiroshige's works are thought to be gentler and more poetic.

Here, the fish in the foreground is actually a banner blowing in the wind. Beneath and beyond, we can see the people, a bridge, towers of the city, and other flying fish.

Using the Study Questions

It is recommended that students always read and answer the questions in **Developing Comprehension Skills** in class discussion.

Developing Comprehension Skills

Question 1. Read and discuss.

Question 2. For reinforcement, you may wish to have the students reread items *c* and *d* and state some other effects of those events.

Question 3. Refer students to the discussion between Kino and his father on page 205, column 1, paragraph 5, through column 2, paragraph 3. You may want to have a student read this section aloud.

Question 4. Have students discuss what wealth could have given Kino and what life would be like with Kino's family.

Question 5. Emphasize that the answer to this question is a personal opinion. Remind students to use information from the story to help them form their opinions.

Challenge Question. Two short stories, "How the Three Young Men Found Death" and "The Big Wave," deal with the subject of death. Do the stories treat the subject in the same way or differently? Explain. (Literal Reading)

Reading Literature: Short Stories

Question 1. Explain that there is a clear winner in the conflict between the people and the sea. However, there is no real winner in the internal conflict that Jiya struggles with. For reinforcement, discuss the internal conflict that Kino has (his struggle to understand death).

Question 2. You may want to work out part of this question with the students.

Developing Comprehension Skills

Literal Reading

1. At first Kino and Jiya have different ideas about the sea. How does Jiya feel about the sea? How does Kino feel about the sea?

Literal Reading

2. List the following events from the story in the order in which they happened. Some are related only by time. Others are connected by cause-and-effect relationships. Identify at least two events that are related by cause and effect, and explain which is the cause and which is the effect.

   a. Jiya's father and mother died.
   b. Kino and Jiya went swimming.
   c. The Old Gentleman talked with Kino's father.
   d. A tremendous wave washed over the fishing village.
   e. The Old Gentleman talked with Jiya.

Interpretive Reading

3. Kino's father uses a comparison, a metaphor, to explain his idea of death. What is the comparison? What is he saying about death?

Interpretive Reading

4. What did the Old Gentleman have to offer Jiya? What did Kino's family have to offer Jiya? Why did Jiya choose Kino's family as opposed to the Old Gentleman's castle?

Creative Writing

5. Do you agree with Jiya's choice? Why or why not?

Reading Literature: Short Stories

1. **Identifying the Conflict.** The external conflict in this story is the characters' struggle against a force in nature. This force in nature is the sea. Who wins the conflict?

   Kino and Jiya both must face internal conflict. Explain the internal conflict for Jiya after his parents die. How does he resolve it?

2. **Appreciating Description.** In the following paragraphs from the story, the author paints a clear word-picture of the sea and the volcano. She wants the readers' senses to come alive. She uses concrete, vivid words to create these descriptive word pictures.

   Read the two descriptions. Then write the words and phrases that help you see the ocean and the volcano.

   > Certainly the ocean was not angry now. The sun sparkled deep into the clear water, and the boys swam over the silvery surface of

Answers to Study Questions

Developing Comprehension Skills

1. Jiya considers the sea his enemy. Kino thinks the sea is beautiful.

2. The following is the correct order of events: b, d, a, c, e.

Cause: d, Effect: a
Cause: a, Effect: c
Indirectly, *d* is also the cause of *c* and e, and *c* is the cause of e.

3. Kino's father says that death is like a great gateway. People don't know what is beyond the gate, so they fear it. Kino's father is telling Kino not to fear death, that it is a new beginning.

4. The Old Gentleman could give Jiya wealth and power. Kino's family, although they were poor, could offer Jiya love, friendship, and family life. Jiya chose Kino's family because he knew that with them he would be loved and wanted.

5. Opinions may vary. Some students may decide that Jiya made the right decision, since he needed someone to love him and care about him. Other students may feel that Jiya should have gone to live with the Old Gentleman, since he could have stayed friends with Kino even though he had lived with the Old Gentleman, and he could have enjoyed his wealth too.

Challenge. Death is treated more sympathetically in "The Big Wave" than it is in "How the Three Young Men Found Death." In the Chaucer story, Death is shown to be cruel, a thing to be feared. In the Buck story, Death is shown as a natural event that may lead to further good when it is experienced.

Reading Literature: Short Stories

1. The sea wins the external conflict. The people who lived in the sea's path lost their struggle against it.

Jiya's first internal conflict is whether he can ever be happy again without his

rippling waves. Beneath them, the water was miles deep. When Kino dived, he went down, down, until he struck icy-still water.

Kino did remember. They had gone to visit a great volcano twenty miles away. Kino had looked down into the yawning mouth of the volcano, and he had not liked it. Great curls of yellow smoke were rolling about it, and a white stream of melted rock was crawling slowly from one corner.

Find at least three other examples of descriptive phrases. These do not necessarily have to describe the sea or the volcano.

3. **Recognizing Mood.** How would you describe the mood of this story? Is it fearful and pessimistic or carefree and optimistic? Is the mood some combination of these and other feelings? Do the examples you chose for question 2 make the mood clear?

4. **Recognizing Exposition.** The introduction, or **exposition**, in a short story introduces the characters and the setting. This must be done in the opening paragraphs of the story. The exposition also gives clues or signals that tell the reader what to look for in the coming pages. These clues or signals may be what the characters say, what the narrator says, and even the title of the story.

   List the facts that are told in the first five paragraphs of "The Big Wave," the exposition portion of this story. How does this introduction prepare the reader for what happens in the story?

Developing Vocabulary Skills

Recognizing Different Pronunciations of a Word. Sometimes a word can be pronounced two different ways, but it is not a homograph. There is only one dictionary entry for the word. The accent may change from one syllable to another, depending on its part of speech. Read these sentences.

Owen's *present* was a ten-speed bike. (pres′ent)
The drama class will *present* a play tonight. (pre sent′)

In the first sentence, *present* is accented on the first syllable and is used as a noun. In the second, *present* is accented on the second syllable and is used as a verb. The dictionary gives both pronunciations for the word. It also indicates which definitions use each of the pronunciations.

Have individual students read the passage. Ask students to identify descriptive words and phrases from the paragraphs and list them on the board. Have students find other descriptive phrases from the story independently. Discuss their findings.

Question 3. Before this question is read, discuss the difference between *optimistic* and *pessimistic.* Now direct the students to read the question with you. Then have them think about the feeling they get when they consider both the events and the characters in the story. Also have them look over the examples they chose when answering **Reading Literature, 2.** As the mood of the story is discussed, have students cite those examples or others from the story to support their answers.

Question 4. Be sure that students realize that *exposition* is another word for *introduction.* Explain that *exposition* is more precise because *to expose* means "to reveal," and the first part of a short story reveals information about the characters, the setting, and the conflict.

Call on students to list facts from the first five paragraphs on the board. Then have them suggest ways in which these early facts are developed later in the story.

Challenge Question. State one or more of the themes of this short story.

Developing Vocabulary Skills

Have a student read aloud **Recognizing Different Pronunciations of a Word** on pages 209 and 210. Repeat the two pronunciations for the word *present,* giving marked emphasis to the accented syllables. After you are sure the students understand the directions, have them complete the exercise independently. Discuss the answers with the students.

parents. This conflict is made more clear in Jiya's second conflict, whether to live with Kino's family or the Old Gentleman. Both conflicts are resolved when Jiya decides to live with Kino and his family.

2. The descriptive words and phrases in the first passage are the following: *angry, the sun sparkled deep into the clear water, silvery surface of the rippling waves, miles deep, icy-still water.*

In the second passage, the following phrases are descriptive: *yawning mouth, great curls of yellow smoke were rolling about it, white stream of melted rock, crawling slowly.*

Other descriptive phrases can be found in the following sentences and in many others. Students need not write the entire sentence; just the descriptive phrase is enough.

a. "When it was dark, the sky was lit with red and the earth trembled under the farmhouse."
b. "When morning came, the sky was red and, even here upon the farm, cinders fell from the volcano."
c. "The sea lay dead and calm."
d. "The air was as hot as though a forest fire were burning. The glow of the volcano glared over the mountaintop, blood-red against the black."

3. Answers may vary somewhat. The mood of the story is sad but not pessimistic. it is hopeful and comforting.

4. Some facts revealed in the first five paragraphs are the following:

a. Kino lives on a farm on a mountain near the ocean.
b. The windows in the fishing village below do not face the ocean.
c. Kino thinks the sea is beautiful.

(continued on page 210)

Developing Writing Skills

Read and discuss the two assignments. Then have each student choose and complete one of the two.

Question 1. Many students need practice in recognizing and explaining irony. The irony in this situation is clear.

Pre-Writing. Have the students think about the value many people place on money. Then ask them to compare that with Jiya's attitude. Have each student write a topic sentence.

Writing. Allow sufficient time for the students to write their first drafts.

Revising. Have students revise and proofread their paragraphs using the **Checklist for the Process of Writing** on pages 556 and 557.

Question 2. The setting that students describe in this question will be used in an original short story they will write later.

Pre-Writing. Remind students that setting refers to both place and time. The setting should be as specific as possible. Explain that a vague concept such as "the country" is not specific enough. Encourage students to picture their settings in their minds. Have them prepare a list of nouns, adjectives, and phrases that will describe the settings. Remind them that the character they described after the last selection must fit logically into the setting.

Writing. Have students use the notes they made in pre-writing. Allow sufficient time for the students to write their first drafts.

Revising. Have students reread their descriptions of the characters that will appear in their stories. They may want to change some aspect of either their characters or their settings to make them fit together. Allow time for revisions to be made.

Developing Skills in Speaking and Listening

Read aloud the directions on page 210 for **Reading a Dialog**. Have students identify and turn to the passages referred to in the exercise.

Page 199 (Kino and Jiya talk about the sea.)
Page 205 (The father explains death to Kino.)
Pages 206 and 207 (The Old Gentleman, Jiya, and Kino discuss Jiya's future.)

Have the students choose partners, or assign them. Allow ten to fifteen minutes of preparation time. Then call on volunteers to read to the class, or reassign partners and have each student read to his or her new partner.

Read each of the sentences concerning stories you have read. Then find each underlined word in your dictionary. On your paper write the following:

a. the underlined word separated into syllables with the correct accent marked
b. the part of speech of the word as it is used in the sentence
c. the meaning of the word as it is used in the sentence

1. The man said in a loud voice, "See here! I am a <u>convict</u>; I have been nineteen years in the galleys."
2. When she spoke her voice was full, sweet, and <u>deliberate</u>.
3. He said with a smile, "Will you please <u>excuse</u> the other hand?"
4. Then, rain or shine, the procession would <u>escort</u> the old soldiers out to the Burying Ground.
5. During the lawyer's fifteen years in prison, they did <u>permit</u> him to have musical instruments.

Developing Writing Skills

Analytical Writing

1. **Recognizing Irony.** The term **irony** is used to describe a situation in which what is expected does not happen. Write a paragraph explaining what is ironic about Jiya's decision to live with Kino's family rather than with the Old Gentleman.

Creative Writing

2. **Developing a Setting.** Continue preparing for the short story you started in connection with "The Old Soldier." Then, you wrote about a character. Now, describe the setting in which you imagined this character. Tell about the time and place in which he or she lives. Use specific words and phrases.

Developing Skills in Speaking and Listening

Reading a Dialog. There are several places in "The Big Wave" where two or more people are speaking. Find each of the passages described below. Decide what the mood of each dialog is. Then work with one or two partners. Prepare to read one of these dialogs. Try to express the mood of the story in your voice.

Kino and Jiya talk about the sea.
The father explains about death to Kino.
The Old Gentleman, Jiya, and Kino discuss Jiya's future.

(continued from page 209)

d. Jiya, the son of a fisherman, says that the sea is their enemy.

Those five paragraphs make the reader feel uneasy about the sea. The reader wonders why Jiya feels so strongly about the sea. The reader may also begin to wonder whether the sea really is the characters' enemy and what disaster might be in store for them.

Challenge. Possible answers include the following:

Love is more important than money.
Knowing you must die someday makes life more precious.
Living with danger makes a person strong.

Developing Vocabulary Skills

Wording of definitions may vary according to the dictionary used.

1. con′ vict; noun; a person found guilty of a crime

2. de lib′ er ate; adjective; carefully thought out or formed

3. ex cuse′; verb; to pardon

4. es cort′; verb; to go with or accompany

5. per mit′; verb; to allow

The Summer of the Beautiful White Horse

WILLIAM SAROYAN

William Saroyan wrote about growing up in the San Joaquin Valley area of California. Note his use of the first-person point of view. How does this help to make the account of this magical summer enjoyable?

One day back there in the good old days when I was nine and the world was full of every imaginable kind of magnificence and life was still a delightful and mysterious dream, my cousin Mourad (Mo͞o'räd), who was considered crazy by everybody who knew him except me, came to my house at four in the morning and woke me up by tapping on the window of my room.

"Aram," he said.

I jumped out of bed and looked out the window.

I couldn't believe what I saw.

It wasn't morning yet but it was summer, and with daybreak not many minutes around the corner of the world it was light enough for me to know I wasn't dreaming.

My cousin Mourad was sitting on a beautiful white horse.

I stuck my head out of the window and rubbed my eyes.

"Yes," he said in Armenian. "It's a horse. You're not dreaming. Make it quick if you want to ride."

I knew my cousin Mourad enjoyed being alive more than anybody else who had ever fallen into the world by mistake, but this was more than even I could believe.

In the first place, my earliest memories had been memories of horses and my first longings had been longings to ride.

This was the wonderful part.

In the second place, we were poor.

This was the part that wouldn't permit me to believe what I saw.

We were poor. We had no money. Our whole tribe was poverty-stricken. Every branch of the Garoghlanian (Gar'ə glän'yən) family was living in the most amazing and comical poverty in the world. Nobody could understand where we ever got money enough to keep us with food in our bellies, not even the old

Objectives

- To recognize and appreciate the short story as a form of literature
- To recognize the tone of a short story
- To appreciate the setting of a short story
- To appreciate the technique of repetition as an element of style
- To apply literal, interpretive, and critical reading skills to a selection
- To evaluate an opinion
- To choose the best meaning for a word from a dictionary entry
- To write an evaluation of a character
- To describe a conflict
- To recognize the need to define terms

Preparing the Students

Essential Vocabulary. The words presented here are essential to the understanding of the selection.

Write the following words and definitions on the board. Have individual students read the words and their meanings. Explain that the students will encounter these words in the following story.

poverty—the condition of being poor

descendant—a person descended from others, offspring

capricious—irregular; apt to change suddenly

vagrant—wandering from place to place

surrey—a vehicle with two seats pulled by a horse

Give students a few minutes to study the definitions. Then erase the meanings and ask students to recall them. If the students need additional help with the vocabulary of this selection, encourage them to use context clues to determine meaning. As needed, direct them to the **Glossary** or to a dictionary.

Motivation. Ask the students to try to remember a summer when everything seemed to go right, a summer they wish they could live over again. Explain that this story tells about such a summer. Have the students read the introductory paragraph at the top of page 211 and state in their own words what they should try to find out as they read this short story.

Presenting the Selection

1. Have the students read "The Summer of the Beautiful White Horse" on pages 211 through 217. You may want to have some students read part of the story aloud to appreciate its conversational style (for instance, page 214, paragraph 3 through page 215, paragraph 8).

2. Make sure that everyone has read the short story by administering the **Check Test**, at the bottom of T.E. page 217.

3. Remind students about the question posed in the introduction. Have several students explain why the first-person point of view makes the story enjoyable.

4. Develop the study questions as suggested in **Using the Study Questions** beginning on page 218. That section also provides challenge questions to be used for further discussion, as needed. (For answers to questions, see T.E. pages 218 to 221.)

Reinforcing the Lesson

To reteach, reinforce, or extend the skills in this lesson, see the following:

Skills Practice Book, Green Level—pages 107 and 108

Special Populations

The exercise on page 219, **Reading Literature: Short Stories**, requests students to find examples of the techniques used to avoid monotony. This may be too broad in scope for some special-populations students. To simplify the task slightly, ask students to find examples of the techniques, but point out general areas (page numbers or paragraphs, depending upon the student's reading ability) in which they should look.

LD. A lead-in to the second writing assignment on page 220 could be for the student to describe a conflict from his or her own experience, one in which he or she was involved or in which a friend or family member was involved. This provides an intermediate step, that of recalling an incident. This could precede the step (as stated in question 2) that asks the student to create an incident, a conflict, for a character.

ESL, NSD. The exercise **Recognizing the Need To Define Terms** on pages 220 and 221 is very good for special-populations students, especially those needing to improve their language skills. To supplement the exercise, the instructor might also take the list created by the class and write a series of possible meanings for the words. Ask the students to choose the most appropriate meanings and to create sentences using the rest of the meanings.

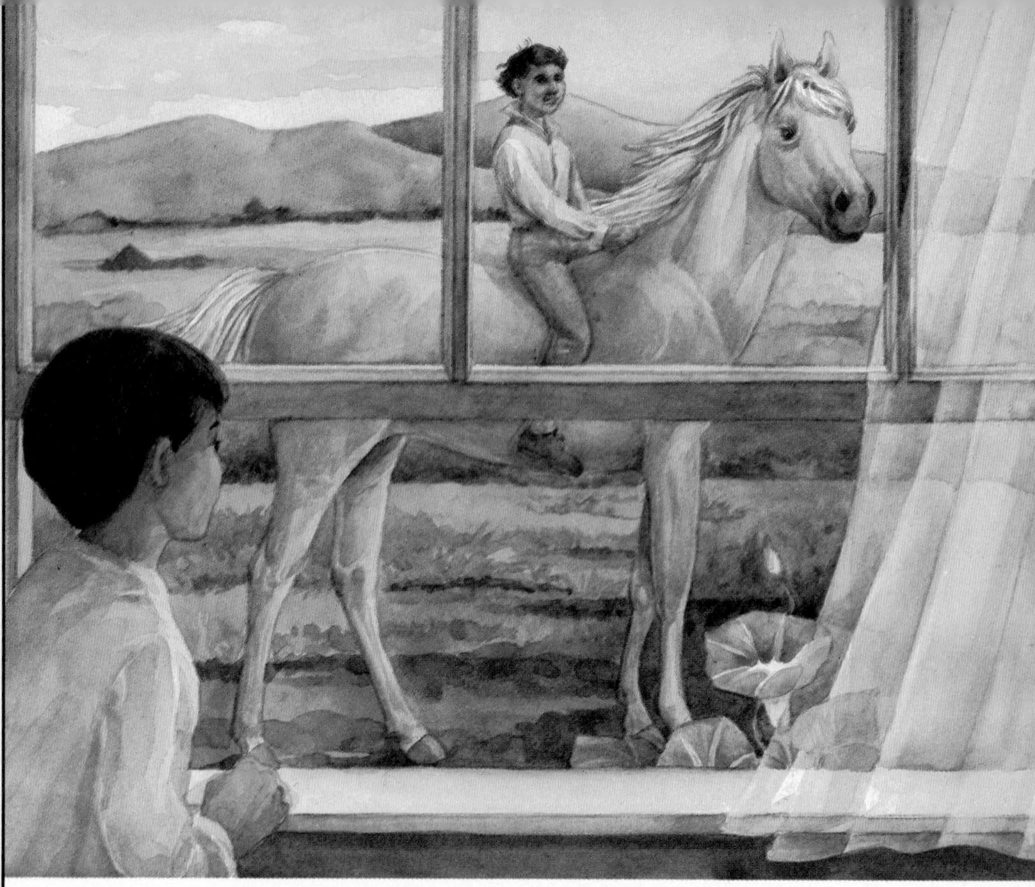

men of the family. Most important of all, though, we were famous for our honesty. We had been famous for our honesty for something like eleven centuries, even when we had been the wealthiest family in what we liked to think was the world. We were proud first, honest next, and after that we believed in right and wrong. None of us would take advantage of anybody in the world, let alone steal.

Consequently, even though I could see the horse, so magnificent; even though I could smell it, so lovely; even though I could hear it breathing, so exciting; I couldn't believe the horse had anything to do with my cousin Mourad or with me or with any of the other members of our family, asleep or awake, because I knew my cousin Mourad couldn't have bought the horse, and, if he couldn't have bought it he must have stolen it, and I refused to believe he had stolen it.

No member of the Garoghlanian family could be a thief.

I stared first at my cousin and then at the horse. There was a pious stillness and humor in each of them, which on the one hand delighted me and on the other frightened me.

"Mourad," I said, "where did you steal this horse?"

"Leap out of the window," he said, "if you want to ride."

It was true, then. He had stolen the horse. There was no question about it. He had come to invite me to ride or not, as I chose.

Well, it seemed to me stealing a horse for a ride was not the same thing as stealing something else, such as money. For all I knew, maybe it wasn't stealing at all. If you were crazy about horses the way my cousin Mourad and I were, it wasn't stealing. It wouldn't become stealing until we offered to sell the horse, which of course I knew we would never do.

"Let me put on some clothes," I said.

"All right," he said, "but hurry."

I leaped into my clothes.

I jumped down to the yard from the window and leaped up onto the horse behind my cousin Mourad.

That year we lived at the edge of town, on Walnut Avenue. Behind our house was the country: vineyards, orchards, irrigation ditches, and country roads. In less than three minutes we were on Olive Avenue, and then the horse began to trot. The air was new and lovely to breathe. The feel of the horse running was wonderful. My cousin Mourad, who was considered one of the craziest members of our family, began to sing. I mean, he began to roar.

Every family has a crazy streak in it somewhere, and my cousin Mourad was considered the natural descendant of the crazy streak in our tribe. Before him was our uncle Khosrove (Käsh′rôv), an enormous man with a powerful head of black hair and the largest mustache in the San Joaquin Valley, a man so furious in temper, so irritable, so impatient that he stopped anyone from talking by roaring, "It is no harm; pay no attention to it."

That was all, no matter what anybody happened to be talking about. Once it was his own son Arak running eight blocks to the barber shop, where his father was having his mustache trimmed, to tell him their house was on fire. This man Khosrove sat up in the chair and roared, "It is no harm; pay no attention to it." The barber said, "But the boy says your house is on fire." So Khosrove roared, "Enough, it is no harm, I say."

My cousin Mourad was considered the natural descendant of this man, although Mourad's father was Zorab (Zo͞o′räb), who was practical and nothing else. That's how it was in our tribe. A man could be the father of his son's flesh, but that did not mean that he was also the

Encouraging Independent Reading

Students who enjoyed "The Summer of the Beautiful White Horse" may also enjoy reading the following books about horses:

- *The Horse Comes First* by Mary Calhoun
- *Runaway Stallion* by Walt Morey
- *All Creatures Great and Small* by James Herriot
- *Black Stallion* by Walter Farley
- *National Velvet* by Enid Bagnold

father of his spirit. The distribution of the various kinds of spirit of our tribe had been from the beginning capricious and vagrant.

We rode and my cousin Mourad sang. For all anybody knew we were still in the old country where, at least according to some of our neighbors, we belonged. We let the horse run as long as it felt like running.

At last my cousin Mourad said, "Get down. I want to ride alone."

"Will you let me ride alone?" I said.

"That is up to the horse," my cousin said. "Get down."

"The horse will let me ride," I said.

"We shall see," he said. "Don't forget that I have a way with a horse."

"Well," I said, "any way you have with a horse, I have also."

"For the sake of your safety," he said, "let us hope so. Get down."

"All right," I said, "but remember you've got to let me try to ride alone."

I got down and my cousin Mourad kicked his heels into the horse and shouted, *Vazire,* run. The horse stood on its hind legs, snorted, and burst into a fury of speed that was the loveliest thing I had ever seen. My cousin Mourad raced the horse across a field of dry grass to an irrigation ditch, crossed the ditch on the horse, and five minutes later returned, dripping wet.

The sun was coming up.

"Now it's my turn to ride," I said.

My cousin Mourad got off the horse.

"Ride," he said.

I leaped to the back of the horse and for a moment knew the worst fear imaginable. The horse did not move.

"Kick into his muscles," my cousin Mourad said. "What are you waiting for? We've got to take him back before everybody in the world is up and about."

I kicked into the muscles of the horse. Once again it reared and snorted. Then it began to run. I didn't know what to do. Instead of running across the field to the irrigation ditch, the horse ran down the road to the vineyard of Dikran Halabian (Dik′rən Hä läb′yän) where it began to leap over vines. The horse leaped over seven vines before I fell. Then it continued running.

My cousin Mourad came running down the road.

"I'm not worried about you," he shouted. "We've got to get that horse. You go this way and I'll go this way. If you come upon him, be kindly. I'll be near."

I continued down the road and my cousin Mourad went across the field toward the irrigation ditch.

It took him half an hour to find the horse and bring him back.

"All right," he said, "jump on. The whole world is awake now."

"What will we do?" I said.

"Well," he said, "we'll either take him back or hide him until tomorrow."

He didn't sound worried and I knew he'd hide him and not take him back. Not for a while, at any rate.

"Where will we hide him?" I said.

"I know a place," he said.

"How long ago did you steal this horse?" I said.

It suddenly dawned on me that he had been taking these early morning rides for some time and had come for me this morning only because he knew how much I longed to ride.

"Who said anything about stealing a horse?" he said.

"Anyhow," I said, "how long ago did you begin riding every morning?"

"Not until this morning," he said.

"Are you telling the truth?" I said.

"Of course not," he said, "but if we are found out, that's what you're to say. I don't want both of us to be liars. All you know is that we started riding only this morning."

"All right," I said.

He walked the horse quietly to the barn of a deserted vineyard, which at one time had been the pride of a farmer named Fetvajian (Fet vä' jən). There were some oats and dry alfalfa in the barn.

We began walking home.

"It wasn't easy," he said, "to get the horse to behave so nicely. At first it wanted to run wild, but, as I've told you, I have a way with a horse. I can get it to want to do anything I want it to do. Horses understand me."

"How do you do it?" I said.

"I have an understanding with a horse," he said.

"Yes, but what sort of an understanding?" I said.

"A simple and honest one," he said.

"Well," I said, "I wish I knew how to reach an understanding like that with a horse."

"You're still a small boy," he said. "When you get to be thirteen you'll know how to do it."

I went home and ate a hearty breakfast.

That afternoon my uncle Khosrove came to our house for coffee. He sat in the parlor, sipping and remembering the old country. Then another visitor arrived, a farmer named John Byro, an Assyrian who, out of loneliness, had learned to speak Armenian. My mother brought the lonely visitor coffee, and he sipped and then at last, sighing sadly, he said, "My white horse which was stolen last month is still gone. I cannot understand it."

My uncle Khosrove became very irritated and shouted, "It's no harm. What is the loss of a horse? Haven't we all lost the homeland? What is this crying over a horse?"

"That may be all right for you, a city dweller, to say," John Byro said, "but what of my surrey? What good is a surrey without a horse?"

"Pay no attention to it," my uncle Khosrove roared.

"I walked ten miles to get here," John Byro said.

"You have legs," my uncle Khosrove shouted.

"My left leg pains me," the farmer said.

"Pay no attention to it," my uncle Khosrove roared.

"That horse cost me sixty dollars," the farmer said.

"I spit on money," my uncle said.

He got up and stalked out of the house, slamming the screen door.

My mother explained.

"He has a gentle heart," she said. "It is simply that he is homesick and such a large man."

The farmer went away, and I ran over to my cousin Mourad's house.

He was sitting under a peach tree, trying to repair the hurt wing of a young robin which could not fly. He was talking to the bird.

"What is it?" he said.

"The farmer, John Byro," I said. "He visited our house. He wants his horse. You've had it a month. I want you to promise not to take it back until I learn to ride."

"It will take you a year to learn to ride," my cousin Mourad said.

"We could keep the horse a year," I said.

My cousin Mourad leaped to his feet.

"What?" he roared. "Are you inviting a member of the Garoghlanian family to steal? The horse must go back to its true owner."

"When?" I said.

"In six months at the latest," he said.

He threw the bird into the air. The bird tried hard, almost fell twice, but at last flew away, high and straight.

Early every morning for two weeks my cousin Mourad and I took the horse out of the barn of the deserted vineyard where we were hiding it and rode it, and every morning the horse, when it was my turn to ride alone, leaped over grape vines and small trees and threw me and ran away. Nevertheless, I hoped in time to learn to ride the way my cousin Mourad rode.

One morning on the way to Fetvajian's deserted vineyard, we ran into the farmer John Byro who was on his way to town.

"Let me do the talking," my cousin Mourad said. "I have a way with farmers."

"Good morning, John Byro," my cousin Mourad said to the farmer.

The farmer studied the horse eagerly.

"Good morning, sons of my friends," he said. "What is the name of your horse?"

"*My Heart,*" my cousin Mourad said in Armenian.

"A lovely name," John Byro said, "for a lovely horse. I could swear it is the horse that was stolen from me many weeks ago. May I look into its mouth?"

"Of course," Mourad said.

The farmer looked into the mouth of the horse.

"Tooth for tooth," he said. "I would swear it is my horse if I didn't know your parents. The fame of your family for honesty is well known to me. Yet the horse is the twin of my horse. A suspicious man would believe his eyes instead of his heart. Good day, my young friends."

"Good day, John Byro," my cousin Mourad said.

Early the following morning we took the horse to John Byro's vineyard and put it in the barn. The dogs followed us around without making a sound.

"The dogs," I whispered to my cousin Mourad. "I thought they would bark."

"They would at somebody else," he said. "I have a way with dogs."

My cousin Mourad put his arms around the horse, pressed his nose into the horse's nose, patted it, and then we went away.

That afternoon John Byro came to our house in his surrey and showed my mother the horse that had been stolen and returned.

"I do not know what to think," he said. "The horse is stronger than ever. Better-tempered, too. I thank God."

My uncle Khosrove, who was in the parlor, became irritated and shouted, "Quiet man, quiet. Your horse has been returned. Pay no attention to it."

Check Test

1. From whom did Mourad steal the horse? (from John Byro, a neighbor)

2. Where did the boys hide the horse? (in the barn of a deserted vineyard)

3. How much had John Byro paid for the horse? (sixty dollars)

4. Why did John Byro look in the horse's mouth? (to see if the horse's teeth matched the teeth of the horse he lost)

Using the Study Questions

It is recommended that students always read and answer the questions in **Developing Comprehension Skills** in class discussion. Whenever possible, they should also read the questions in other categories together and discuss the answers.

Developing Comprehension Skills

Question 1. To emphasize the tradition of honesty in the Garoghlanian family, ask a student to read aloud the first paragraph on page 212.

Question 2. Remind students that this group of people had just come to America from another country. Ask them why Aram's family was especially important to him.

Question 3. Have students consider how the boys and their family would have felt if someone had caught them stealing. Remind the students that John Byro was a friend of the family.

Question 4. Read and discuss.

Question 5. This question asks students to evaluate a character's statement concerning stealing. It should be thoroughly discussed with the students. As you discuss students' answers, be sure to have them consider the problems the horse's loss caused John Byro.

Challenge Question. What did Mourad mean when he said he had a way with animals? (Interpretive Reading)

Reading Literature: Short Stories

Question 1. Discuss students' descriptions of the tone. Have several students read passages aloud to show the tone of the story.

Developing Comprehension Skills

Literal Reading
1. Why was Aram so surprised to see his cousin with a horse?

Interpretive Reading
2. Why do you think the speaker presented so much information on his Armenian "tribe"? List some of the characteristics of his "tribe."

Interpretive Reading
3. When he met Mourad and Aram on the road in the early morning, John Byro inspected the white horse. Why did he not take the horse from Mourad and Aram? Do you think he knew that it was his horse? Explain your answer.

Interpretive Reading
4. Byro mentions two positive things that happened to the horse during its absence. What are these positive things? Why do you think the horse had made these changes in attitude?

Critical Reading
5. Comment on this statement from the story: "Well, it seemed to me stealing a horse for a ride was not the same thing as stealing something else, such as money." Do you agree or disagree with this statement? Explain your answer.

Reading Literature: Short Stories

1. **Recognizing Tone.** The attitude that an author shows toward his or her work is called **tone**. The author must choose words very carefully to let the reader recognize the tone. In "The Summer of the Beautiful White Horse," the boys keep a horse without permission, knowing they should not. Is the author's tone critical of the boys? Is it preachy? Would you describe the tone as forgiving or amused, or would you describe it with some other term? How does Saroyan's use of the first-person point of view affect the tone?

   Pick out two or three passages that support your comments on the tone of the story.

2. **Appreciating Setting.** Is the setting important in "The Summer of the Beautiful White Horse"? Could the setting have been in present-day New York City or some other large urban area? Explain your answer.

3. **Understanding Characters.** What type of person was Uncle Khosrove? What do you think Uncle Khosrove meant when he said, "It's no harm, pay no attention to it"? Do you believe there are real people like Uncle Khosrove? Explain your answer.

Answers to Study Questions

Developing Comprehension Skills

1. Aram was surprised to see his cousin with a horse because Aram had always longed for a horse. In addition, his cousin was too poor to have been able to buy the horse, which meant that he must have stolen it. This seemed impossible to Aram because their family was well known for its honesty.

2. The speaker presented so much information on his Armenian "tribe" to impress upon the reader that since Aram's family had recently come to America, they depended on each other and stayed together even more than most families. Aram's family was important to him, and through his family the reader learns about Aram. Some characteristics of his "tribe" are honesty, pride, and a belief in right and wrong. They were also very poor.

3. John Byro probably knew it was his horse. He didn't take it because he didn't want to embarrass the boys. Since honesty was important to their family, he knew that accusing the boys of stealing would have hurt them and their family.

4. The horse was stronger than ever and better tempered. Mourad's patience, kindness, and training are the probable reasons for the changes in the horse.

5. Opinions may vary. Following are some possible answers:

If someone steals a horse, but is definitely going to give it back, it is not quite as bad as stealing something and never returning it. It is more like borrowing it. (It should be pointed out that this line of thinking can get people into a lot of trouble. How can anyone know what someone else intends to do in that situation?)

When you steal anything, whether it is a horse or money, you are hurting someone else. It makes no difference what you steal. Stealing is wrong.

4. **Recognizing Sounds of Language.** Throughout this story, the author uses various kinds of repetition. This repetition helps Saroyan to express his ideas clearly and to create interesting patterns of sound.

There is repetition of ideas.

> We were poor. We had no money. Our whole tribe was poverty-stricken.

There is repetition of phrases.

> I have a way with a horse.
> I have a way with farmers.
> I have a way with dogs.

There is repetition of sentence patterns.

> Consequently, even though I could see the horse, so magnificent; even though I could smell it, so lovely; even though I could hear it breathing, so exciting; I couldn't believe the horse had anything to do with my cousin Mourad or with me.

Saroyan avoids monotony by letting some patterns grow more complex gradually. For example, "We were poor" grows into "Our whole tribe was poverty-stricken." Another way he avoids monotony is by making a sudden change in sentence length. An example of this occurs at the end of the sentence above, beginning with "Consequently." Only part of the sentence is shown above; the complete sentence is eighty-eight words long. The sentence following it is only ten words long. In other places, several very short sentences are followed by a very long one.

Find at least one other example of each of these techniques:

a. Repetition of ideas
b. Repetition of phrases
c. Repetition of sentence patterns
d. Sudden change in sentence length

Developing Vocabulary Skills

Choosing the Best Meaning. Each of the following sentences was drawn from "The Bet" or "The Summer of the Beautiful White Horse." Most of the underlined words have more than one meaning. Find the entry in the dictionary for each underlined word. Test each listed meaning in the context of the sentence. Find the meaning that best fits the sentence. Write that meaning on your paper.

Question 2. Remind students of what Mourad stole and what the boys did with the horse.

Question 3. Have students reread the sections of the story that tell about Uncle Khosrove (page 215, column 2, paragraph 8 through page 216, column 1, paragraph 9).

Question 4. To answer this question, students will have to go over the story carefully. They may need to complete the assignment at home. Note that the different effects often overlap; the same phrase may be an example of two or more techniques.

Challenge Question. In the beginning of the story, the writer mentions dreaming a few times. The rest of the story has a dreamlike quality—nothing frightening happens, no one gets angry at the boys, the horse is returned easily. Why do you think the writer made this story seem like a dream?

Developing Vocabulary Skills

Be sure the students understand the directions for **Choosing the Best Meaning** on page 219. Explain that, in 1, 2, 3, and 5, they will need to look up the base word rather than the form of the word that is used in the sentence.

Developing Writing Skills

Read and discuss the two assignments. Then have each student choose and complete one of the two.

Question 1. You may want to have students complete this assignment after they define the term *crazy* as suggested in the teaching notes below for **Recognizing the Need To Define Terms** on pages 220 and 221.

Challenge. Mourad thought that animals liked him and would do whatever he wanted them to do.

Reading Literature: Short Stories

1. The tone is amused and accepting. The author is not judging whether the actions were right or wrong. He is simply telling what happened. Because it is written in the first-person, the reader feels the closeness and the caring between characters, adding to the forgiving tone.

Some possible passages that show the tone are the following:

"It was true, then. He had stolen the horse. There was no question about it. He had come to invite me to ride or not, as I chose."

"Are you telling the truth?" I said.

"Of course not," he said, "but if we are found out, that's what you're to say. I don't want both of us to be liars. All you know is that we started out riding only this morning."

"All right," I said.

2. The rural setting is important to this story since Mourad had stolen a horse. It would be difficult to steal a horse in an urban setting. He would have great difficulty hiding the horse in a city or riding it without being noticed.

3. Uncle Khosrove is rough on the outside but gentle on the inside. He has been through many hard times and has found that not paying attention to problems is sometimes the only way to survive. When he says, "It's no harm, pay no attention to it," he means not to take problems too seriously.

Opinions will vary as to whether there are real people like Uncle Khosrove, depending on students' experiences.

4. Some examples of the techniques used in this story are the following:

a. Page 215, column 2, paragraph 8, beginning "My white horse which

(continued on page 220)

1. The old banker was pacing from corner to corner in his room.
2. Execution kills instantly; prison kills by degrees.
3. In the second year the piano was heard no more. The lawyer asked only for classics.
4. I must escape ruin and shame.
5. In the darkness he groped for the door.
6. The feel of the horse running was wonderful.
7. A man could be the father of his son's flesh, but that did not mean that he was also the father of his spirit.
8. Don't forget that I have a way with horses.

Developing Writing Skills

Analytical Writing

1. **Evaluating a Character.** In this story, Aram mentions several times that his cousin Mourad was considered crazy by everyone. Was he crazy? Make a list of the things you learned about Mourad. You can begin with the following:

   He woke Aram up before daybreak.
   He was riding a white horse.

   Add ten or more items to this list. When you have listed about a dozen specific things that Mourad did, make a judgment on what kind of person Mourad is. Write a paragraph explaining your opinion of whether Mourad was crazy or not.

Creative Writing

2. **Describing a Conflict.** You have written about a character and you have imagined a setting for that character. Now describe a conflict for that character in that setting. For example, the character may have to move away from the setting or possibly the setting changes. Write a few paragraphs describing this conflict and giving details about how the character feels about it.

Developing Skills in Critical Thinking

Recognizing the Need To Define Terms. Frequently, we use terms whose definitions we think we know. However, not everyone may agree on those definitions. In the story of "The Summer of the Beautiful White Horse," for example, Aram thinks he understands what honesty and

Pre-Writing. Many students will benefit from working in small groups of three or four. Have each group prepare a list of ten or more things that Mourad did. Then ask each student to summarize in a single sentence what kind of a person he or she thinks Mourad was.

Writing. Have each student write his or her own paragraph about Mourad. Remind students to include their opinions about whether Mourad was crazy or not. Urge students to use examples from the story to prove their points.

Revising. Have students assemble again in the same groups they worked with in pre-writing. Have them read their paragraphs to each other. Ask the listeners to identify the evidence the writer gives for his or her point of view. If the evidence doesn't support the opinion adequately, have the writer revise the paragraph.

Question 2. Students may have partially worked out the conflict as they pictured the character and the setting in previous writing assignments.

Pre-Writing. Remind students that a conflict may be either external or internal. If their conflicts are external, have students identify and describe the opposing person or force. If the conflict is internal, have them describe the character's feelings. Have students make notes about how the character becomes involved in the conflict.

Writing. Allow sufficient time for the students to write their first drafts. Remind them to use their notes.

Revising. Have the students work with partners. You may want to pair a stronger writer with a weaker writer. Have them read each other's paragraphs. Ask each student to comment on whether the conflict is clear and logical. If the reader cannot understand the conflict, have the writer revise it to make the conflict more obvious.

(continued from page 219)

was stolen last month," through page 216, column 1, paragraph 6, "I spit on money," my uncle said.

b. Page 211, paragraph 5 through paragraph 8, "...it was light enough for me to know I wasn't dreaming..."

   "Yes, it's a horse. You're not dreaming."

c. Page 211, column 2, paragraph 3: "In the first place, my earliest memories had been memories of horses and my first longings had been longings to ride."

d. Page 211, paragraphs 1 and 2: "One day back there in the good old days ...on the window of my room.

   "Aram," he said.

Challenge. The writer remembers this summer as a happy time in his life. It happened so long ago that he remembers only the good things about it. That could be the reason why he wrote it as if it were a dream.

Developing Vocabulary Skills

1. pace—to walk back and forth

2. degree—amount or extent; *by degrees* means little by little

3. classic—a very fine old book or other work of art

4. ruin—destruction, very great damage

5. grope—to feel about with the hands

6. feel—perception by touching or feeling

7. spirit—the essential force in a person, the will

8. way—the ability to handle or deal with something or someone

stealing are. Then Mourad brings a horse to his window, and suddenly Aram is no longer sure what *stealing* means. The term *crazy,* too, is used to describe Mourad. Aram's meaning for *crazy,* however, is probably different from another person's meaning.

For one day, carefully listen to conversations, commercials, and other announcements. Listen particularly for words that seem familiar, but whose meanings you cannot easily explain. List at least three such words, and keep a record of how you heard each word used. Then, in class or in a small group, discuss the words you and the other group members listed. Without using a dictionary, try to agree on meanings that fit the situations in which you heard the words.

Spring Tryout, 1944, THOMAS HART BENTON. Charles H. MacNider Museum, Mason City, Iowa.

Developing Skills in Critical Thinking

After students have read **Recognizing the Need To Define Terms** on pages 220 and 221, discuss how Aram would have defined stealing before and after his cousin stole the horse. Also have them discuss the different ways *crazy* can be defined. Then assign the observation for homework and allow time to discuss students' findings with them.

About the Art

Thomas Hart Benton (1889-1975) was called a "regionalist painter" because he depicted the small town and rural life of the American Midwest. He wished to create an authentic American art using subjects from America's own everyday experience. *Spring Tryout* lightheartedly captures a moment when, certainly with chores to be done, two boys have been carried away by the exhilarating feeling of confidence and playfulness accompanying the emergence of spring.

Objectives

- To recognize and appreciate the short story as a form of literature
- To compare types of stories
- To recognize the theme of a short story
- To apply literal, interpretive, and critical reading skills to a selection
- To evaluate the believability of a character
- To plan the plot of an original story
- To use the card catalog to find information

Preparing the Students

Essential Vocabulary. The words presented here are essential to the understanding of the selection.

Have the students use the context clues in the following sentences to determine the meanings of the underlined words.

hideous forlorn moping
melancholy impertinence

1. The monster, with its green skin, bulging eyes, and huge teeth, was hideous.
2. I love melancholy movies. They make me cry.
3. The puppy looked so forlorn, sitting alone in the rain, that Sara took him home with her.
4. It would be an impertinence to slap the President on the back and say, "How are you doing, Bud?" if you don't know him very well.
5. The child was moping around the house after her father left on his trip, but she became cheerful again when he returned.

If the students need additional help with the vocabulary of this selection, encourage them to use context clues to determine word meaning. As needed, direct them to the **Glossary** or to a classroom dictionary.

Motivation. Have the students read the introductory paragraph at the top of page 222 and state in their own words what they should try to find out as they read this short story.

Presenting the Selection

1. Have the students read "The Rocking Donkey" on pages 222 to 227. Explain that this story uses several terms that are common in England, where the story was written, but are practically unknown here. Some unfamiliar terms have been defined in footnotes at the bottom of the pages on which they appear.

The Rocking Donkey

JOAN AIKEN

In this story you will find a wicked stepmother, an innocent child, and magic. Does it sound like a fairy tale? As you read it, try to decide whether "The Rocking Donkey" is a fairy tale or not.

There was once a little girl called Esmeralda who lived with her wicked stepmother. Her father was dead. The stepmother, who was called Mrs. Mitching, was very rich, and lived in a large but hideous house in a suburb with a dusty, laurelly garden, and a lot of ornamental iron fencing.

Mrs. Mitching was fond of opening things, and getting things up. The things she opened were mostly hospitals, or public libraries, or new bypasses, or civic centers. The things she got up were sales of work,[1] and bazaars, and flag days. She was, in fact, a public figure and was very little at home. When she was, she spent her time receiving callers in her fringy, ornamented drawing room.

"How is your little girl?" they would sometimes ask. "Is she still at home, or has she gone to boarding school?"

"Oh, she's at home," Mrs. Mitching would reply, "but she has her own playroom, you know, so that we needn't disturb one another. I don't believe in grownups bothering children all the time, do you?"

Mrs. Mitching could not afford school for Esmeralda, as she needed all her wealth for opening and getting up. She always took Esmeralda along to the openings in a white muslin dress, painfully starched at the neck and wrists, because people liked to see a child on the platform. But for the rest of the time, Esmeralda had to manage in her old brown dress, much too short now, and a torn pair of gym shoes. She had her meals in the kitchen, and they were horrible—bread and margarine, boiled fish, and prunes.

However, the most melancholy part of Esmeralda's life was that she had nothing to do. The playroom which Mrs. Mitching spoke of was a large, dark basement

1. **Sale of work** is a sale of handmade goods, such as needlework and crafts.

room, shadowed by the laurels which overhung the area. There was nothing in it at all, not even a chair. No one ever came into it; and it would have been thick with dust had not Esmeralda, who was a tidy creature, once a week borrowed a broom from the housemaid's cupboard and swept it. She had no toys. Once Mr. Snye, the man who came to cut the laurels, had given her a length of garden twine. She used this as a skipping rope, to keep herself warm. She became a very good skipper, and could polka, double-through, swing the rope, and other fancy variations. If she felt inclined to do plain skipping, she could go on almost all day without a fault.

There were no books to read in the house. She was not encouraged to go into Mrs. Mitching's rooms or outside because of her shabby clothes, though she sometimes took a stroll at dusk.

One day Mrs. Mitching was to open a jumble sale.[2] She was being driven to it by the mayor in his Rolls-Royce; so she told Hooper, the housemaid, to bring Esmeralda by bus, dressed in her white muslin, and meet her at the hall. Then she went off to keep an appointment.

"Drat," said Hooper. "Now what am I do to? Your muslin's still at the laundry from last week."

"I'll have to go as I am," said Esmeralda, who quite liked openings. At least, they made a change from wandering about in the basement.

"I don't know what Madam'll say," said Hooper doubtfully, "but I should catch it if I didn't take you, sure enough." So they went as they were, Esmeralda in her old brown dress and shoes.

When Mrs. Mitching saw them, she gave a cry of dismay.

"I can't let you be seen like that! You must go home at once," and she hurriedly left them before anyone should connect her with the shabby child.

Hooper had set her heart on a violet satin pincushion she had noticed on one of the stalls, so she pushed Esmeralda into a corner and said, "You wait there. I shan't be a moment. It won't matter; no one will know who you are."

Esmeralda stood looking quietly about her. An elderly gentleman, Lord Mauling, making his way to the platform, noticed what seemed to him a forlorn-looking little creature. Stopping by her, he took a coin from his pocket and said, "Here, my dear. Buy yourself a pretty toy."

Esmeralda gave him a startled look as he went on his way. Then she stared at the coin she held in her hand. It was a shilling. She had never had any money before and was quite puzzled to know what she should buy with it. Almost without realizing what she was doing, she began to wander along the stalls, looking at the differ-

2. **Jumble sale** is the British name for rummage sale, a sale of assorted new or used items, usually to raise money for charitable causes.

2. Make sure that everyone has read the short story by administering the **Check Test**, at the bottom of T.E. page 227.

3. Develop the study questions as suggested in **Using the Study Questions** beginning on page 228. The question posed in the introduction is answered there. That section also provides challenge questions for further discussion, as needed. (For answers to questions, see T.E. pages 228 to 230.)

Reinforcing the Lesson

To reteach, reinforce, or extend the skills in this lesson, see the following:

Skills Practice Book, Green Level—pages 109 and 110

Special Populations

LD, ESL. The exercise **Doing Background Reading** would be most successfully done with a partner or as a small group activity. Assign topics pertinent to the story such as old English toys or family life in England (or another country). Have the groups find information and related topics in the following sources: encyclopedias, children's story books, card catalogs.

Students with more limited reading ability could concentrate on finding shorter articles from encyclopedias or magazines; other group members could find information from short stories, novels, or biographies. Have the groups present a summary of information from their topic.

Encouraging Independent Reading

Plenty of sources are available for students who might want to read more of Joan Aiken's work; she is a prolific author. Other writings by Aiken include:

Black Hearts in Battersea
The Cuckoo Tree
Not What You Expected
The Stolen Lake
The Wolves of Willoughby Chase

ent things offered for sale. There were books, clothes, bottles of scent, flowers—all the things she saw seemed beautiful, but she could not imagine buying any of them. Then she came to the toy counter. Toys! She had never had one. The only time she ever touched a toy was sometimes when Mrs. Mitching opened a children's ward at a hospital, and Esmeralda would present a ceremonial teddy bear to a little patient. She gazed at dolls, puzzles, engines, without noticing that most of them were shabby and secondhand. Then at the end of the counter, she saw what she wanted. There was no hesitation in her mind; she knew at once.

It was a rocking donkey—gray, battered, weather-beaten, with draggling ears and tangled tail. On the side of his rockers his name was painted—"Prince." It hardly seemed the name for someone so ancient and worn. The price ticket pinned to his tail said one shilling.

"I'd like the donkey, please," said Esmeralda timidly to the lady at the stall, holding out her coin. The lady glanced from the coin to the ticket and said, "Good gracious. Can this really be going for only a shilling? Surely they mean ten? Mr. Prothero," she called to a gentleman farther down the room, but he was busy and did not hear.

"Oh, well," she said to Esmeralda. "You take it. You won't often get a bargain like that, I can tell you." She took the coin and put the donkey on the floor.

"How will you get him home?" she asked.

"I don't know," said Esmeralda. She was lucky though. As she stood hesitating with her hand on Prince's bridle, someone familiar stopped beside her. It was Mr. Snye, the man who cut the hedges.

"You bought that donkey?" he said. "Well, I'm blest. That'll be a bit of fun for you, I reckon. Like me to take it home for you in the van? I've got it outside—been bringing some flowers along for the platform."

"Oh thank you," Esmeralda said. So he shouldered Prince, nodded to her, and said, "I'll be home before you are, like as not. I'll just leave him in the shrubbery for you."

Esmeralda went to find Hooper, who had bought her pincushion, and they caught their bus home.

As soon as dusk fell and no one was about, she slipped up the back steps and half dragged, half carried Prince from his hiding place down through the basement passage to her playroom. She put him in the middle of the floor and sat down beside him.

It was a strange moment. For as long as she could remember, she had had no company at all, nothing to play with. Now here, all of a sudden, was a friend. She felt sure of that. She put an arm over his cold, smooth neck. He rocked down and gently touched the top of her head with his nose.

"Prince," she said quietly and almost wondered if he would reply, but he was silent. She combed out his tangled mane and tail. Then she sat with him until the room was quite dark, and it was time to put herself to bed.

As she went to her tiny room upstairs, it occurred to her that he might be cold, alone in that dark basement. She took one of the two blankets off her bed, slipped down again in her nightdress, and tucked it over him. Back in bed, she tried to settle but could not. It was a chilly night, and one blanket was not enough to keep her warm. Also, she could not help wondering if Prince felt lonely and perhaps homesick for wherever he had come from? So presently she was tiptoeing back to the playroom with the other blanket. She made a sort of nest for the two of them and slept all night on the floor, curled up between his front rockers. If she wanted company, all she had to do was reach up, and pull on a rein to bring down his cold, friendly nose against her cheek.

She was never lonely again. She never rode on Prince—she felt that would be almost an impertinence with someone who was so much a friend and who, moreover, looked so weary and battered. But she would set him off rocking while she skipped, so that they seemed to be keeping each other company; and she talked to him all the time, while he nodded intelligently in reply. Every night she crept

down with her two blankets and slept curled up between his feet.

One day, Mrs. Mitching decided to give a whist drive[3] in her house for the wives of chimney sweeps. It occurred to her that the basement playroom would be just the right size for the purpose. She went along to inspect and found Esmeralda having her weekly cleanout with brush and dustpan.

"That's right, that's right," she said absently, glancing about. "But what is this? A rocking horse?" Esmeralda stood mute.

"Do you not think you are a little old for such toys? Yes, yes, I think it had better be given away to some poor child. It is the duty of children who live in rich houses, such as you, Esmeralda, to give away your old toys to the little slum children who have nothing. It can be taken away when the van for the Bombed Families[4] calls here tomorrow morning. But you must certainly clean it up a little first. You should be quite ashamed to pass on such a shabby old toy without doing your best to improve its appearance. After all, you know, it may gladden some poor little life in Stepney or Bethnal Green. So give it a good scrub this evening. Now what was I doing? Ah, yes, seventeen feet by sixteen, ten tables—let me see—"

Esmeralda passed the rest of the day in a sort of numbness. After tea, she took some sugar soap and a scrubbing brush from the housemaid's cupboard and started to scrub Prince.

"Well," she thought, "perhaps I didn't deserve to be so happy. I never thought of scrubbing him. Perhaps someone else will take better care of him. But oh, what shall I do, what shall I do?"

She scrubbed and scrubbed and, as the shabby gray peeled away, a silvery gleam began to show along Prince's back and sides. His mane and tail shone like floss. By the time she had finished, it was quite dark. A long ray of moonlight striking across the floor caught his head and, for a moment, dazzled her eyes.

For the last time she went up, fetched her blankets, and settled herself beside him. Just before she fell asleep, it seemed to her that his nose came down and lightly touched her wet cheek.

Next day Esmeralda hid herself. She did not want to see Prince taken away. Mrs. Mitching superintended this.

"Good gracious," she said, when she saw him shining in the sun. "That is far too valuable to be taken to Stepney. I shall give it to the museum." So the Bombed Families van dropped Prince off at the museum before going on to Stepney.

All day Esmeralda avoided the basement playroom. She felt that she could

3. **Whist Drive** is a fund-raising activity involving the card game of whist, a game that is similar to bridge.

4. **Bombed Families** were families left homeless as a result of the bombing raids over England during World War II.

not bear to look at the empty patch in the middle of the floor.

In the evening, Hooper felt sorry for her, she seemed so restless and moping, and took her out for a stroll. They went to the museum, where Hooper liked to look at the models of fashions through the ages. While she was studying crinolines and bustles, Esmeralda wandered off. Soon, around a corner, she came on Prince, railed off from the public with a red cord, and with a notice beside him that read, "Donated by the Honorable Mrs. Mitching, November 19—"

Esmeralda stretched out her hand, but she could not quite touch him over the cord.

"Now, miss," said an attendant. "No touching the exhibits, please." So she looked and looked at him until Hooper said it was time to go home.

Every day after that she went to the museum to look at Prince. Hooper said to Cook, "That child doesn't look well." Mrs. Mitching was away from home a good deal, organizing the grand opening of a new welfare center and clinic, so she did not notice Esmeralda's paleness or her constant visits to the museum.

One night something woke Esmeralda. A long finger of moonlight lay lightly across her closed eyes. She got up quietly and put on her old brown dress and thin shoes. It was easy to steal out of that large house without anyone hearing. Once outside, she slipped along the empty streets like a shadow. When she reached the museum, she went at once, as if someone had called her, to a little door at one side. Somebody had left it unlocked, and she opened it softly and went into the thick dark.

The museum was a familiar place by now. She went confidently forward along a passage and presently came out into the main hall. It did not take her long to find Prince, for there he was, shining like silver in the moonlight. She walked forward, stepped over the rope, and put her hand on his neck.

"Esmeralda," he said. His voice was like a faint, silvery wind.

"You never spoke to me before."

"How could I? I was choked with gray paint."

"Oh," she cried, "I'm so terribly lonely without you. What shall I do?"

"You never rode on me," he said.

"I didn't like to. You were so old and tired, it would have seemed like taking a liberty."

"Ride on me now."

Timidly she put her foot into the stirrup and swung herself onto his back.

"Settle yourself in the saddle and hold tight. Are you all right?"

"Yes," she said.

Like a feather in the wind, they went rocking up the ray of moonlight and passed through the high window as if it had been a mist. Neither of them was ever seen again.

Check Test

1. Why didn't Mrs. Mitching let Esmeralda go outside to play? (She didn't want anyone to see Esmeralda's shabby clothes.)

2. How much did the rocking donkey cost? (one shilling)

3. Where did Mrs. Mitching take the donkey? (to the museum)

4. What did the rocking donkey do when Esmeralda put her hand on him the last night in the museum? (He spoke to her.)

Using the Study Questions

Developing Comprehension Skills

Question 1. Have the students read and discuss the question.

Question 2. If necessary, have the students reread the passage that describes Esmeralda's relationship with Prince (page 224, paragraph 2, through page 226, paragraph 1).

Question 3. Explain that Esmeralda's reaction included both her feelings and her actions.

Question 4. Point out that this question asks students to formulate opinions based on information in the story.

Question 5. Point out that this question calls for a statement of personal preference or opinion. There is no single correct answer.

Challenge Question. Did you like Esmeralda? Explain your reasons. (Critical Reading)

Reading Literature: Short Stories

Question 1. You may want to complete this question with the class. Divide the class into small groups, assign one method to each group, and have the students skim the story, looking for examples of that method of describing Mrs. Mitching. Appoint one member of each group as the group leader and direct these individuals to record the page number and paragraph number of each example given by the other members of the group. Ask each group leader to report his or her group's findings to the class, citing the location of each example for quick reference by the other groups.

Question 2. Draw two columns on the board, one labeled "Like a Fairy Tale" and

Developing Comprehension Skills

Literal Reading — 1. How did Mrs. Mitching treat Esmeralda? To Esmeralda, what was the worst part of her treatment?

Literal Reading — 2. Describe a typical day and night for Esmeralda and Prince. How was this different from Esmeralda's life before Prince came?

Interpretive Reading — 3. Mrs. Mitching said that the rocking donkey should be cleaned up before being given away to the slum children. What was Esmeralda's reaction? Was this typical of Esmeralda?

Critical Reading — 4. Do you think Mrs. Mitching knew how badly she treated Esmeralda? Have you ever met someone like Mrs. Mitching? Can you believe in this type of character? Why or why not?

Critical Reading — 5. Do you think the ending was happy? Why or why not?

Reading Literature: Short Stories

1. **Finding Character Traits.** As we have seen, the reader can determine the personality of a character by considering the following:
   a. what the character says
   b. what others say about the character
   c. what the narrator says about the character
   d. what the character does

   Describe the personality of Mrs. Mitching. List ways the author tells about her personality. For each method, select an example.

2. **Comparing Types of Stories.** Certain features or elements appear over and over in fairy stories. The tales usually begin with "Once upon a time . . ." or "Long, long ago . . ." Both good and bad characters usually appear in the same story. Good characters are totally good and bad characters are totally bad. One incident often occurs three times in a fairy tale. Fairies have magical powers. They can take the shape of humans or animals. Most fairy tales end happily, with ". . . and they lived happily ever after."

   Identify at least three ways in which "The Rocking Donkey" is like a fairy tale. Also, identify any ways you can think of in which it is different. Then tell your opinion of whether or not it is a fairy tale.

3. **Identifying Elements of a Plot.** Make a plot diagram for this story.

Answers to Study Questions

Developing Comprehension Skills

1. Mrs. Mitching treated Esmeralda very badly. She ignored her, used her, and gave her no new clothes or toys. The worst thing for Esmeralda was that she had nothing to do.

2. Esmeralda never rode on Prince. She set him rocking while she skipped rope, and she talked to him constantly. At night, Esmeralda brought Prince a blanket and slept at his feet. Before Prince came, Esmeralda had been very lonely. She had no toys, and her only fun was skipping rope and sometimes taking a walk at dusk.

3. Esmeralda obeyed her stepmother. She felt numb, and began to think that she hadn't deserved the donkey. This was a typical reaction for Esmeralda.

4. Mrs. Mitching may not have realized how badly she was treating Esmeralda because she was too busy with her own business. Opinions concerning Mrs. Mitching's believability may vary, but all opinions should be supported by logical reasons and examples drawn from the story or from experience.

5. Opinions will vary. Possible answers:

The ending was happy because Esmeralda got away from her cruel stepmother.

The ending was unhappy because Esmeralda never came back.

Challenge. Opinions will vary. Some students may have liked Esmeralda because she was sweet, generous, and kind. Others may not have liked her because she didn't stand up for herself.

Reading Literature: Short Stories

1. Answers may vary. Mrs. Mitching is a selfish, thoughtless person. She is described in the following ways:

4. **Recognizing Theme.** A writer can say something about real life even in a story that is not realistic. Can you identify the theme of "The Rocking Donkey," what the author wanted to say about life?

Developing Vocabulary Skills

Reviewing Context Clues. Read each of the following groups of sentences from the stories you have read. Use context clues to figure out the meaning of each underlined word. Look for definitions, restatements, synonyms, and antonyms. You may have to infer the meaning from the other words in the sentence. Write the meaning of each word from the clues given.

1. Mdlle. Baptistine looked at her brother, and her face resumed its usual calmness and serenity.
2. One would have said he was hesitating between two realms—that of the doomed and that of the saved.
3. We were poor. We had no money. We were poverty-stricken.
4. Uncle Khosgrove was a man so furious in temper, so irritable, so impatient, that he stopped anyone from talking by roaring.
5. Esmeralda had horrible meals in the kitchen. However, the most melancholy part of Esmeralda's life was that she had nothing to do.
6. Esmeralda, who was a tidy creature, would borrow a broom from the housemaid's cupboard and sweep the room.
7. It was a shilling. She had never had any money before and was quite puzzled to know what she should buy with it.
8. It was a gray rocking horse—battered, weather-beaten, with dragging ears and tangled tail.

Developing Writing Skills

Analytical Writing

1. **Discussing Point of View.** Try to imagine "The Rocking Donkey" being told in the first-person point of view. How would the story have changed if Esmeralda had told it? How would it have changed if Mrs. Mitching had given her view? Could the yardman have told the story in the way it is written? Write at least a paragraph about the point of view in this story. Point out some of the effects of the third-person, omniscient point of view on the story and on the reader.

the other labeled "Not Like a Fairy Tale." As each feature is suggested, write it in the appropriate column.

Question 3. Discuss the major events of the story with the students. List them on the board. Then draw a plot diagram on the board. Ask students where each of the major events belongs on the plot diagram and have them fill it in.

Question 4. Read and discuss the question.

Developing Vocabulary Skills

Read the directions for **Reviewing Context Clues** with the students. Have them complete the exercise independently and discuss the answers together.

Developing Writing Skills

Read and discuss the three assignments. Then have each student choose and complete one of the three.

Question 1. This is the students' final preparation for writing their own short stories.

Pre-Writing. Review the major developments in each of the five parts of the plot. Refer to the box on page 135, or review the parts as you write a class plot outline. Describe a character and a setting. Ask for suggestions from the students about the events that could happen. Have the students choose the events they want in the story. List them on the board in order, perhaps on a plot diagram.

Writing. Have students write their own individual plot outlines. Remind them that the outlines need not be written in formal outline form.

Revising. Have students exchange their outlines with partners. Have the partners discuss their outlines with each other. Readers should point out anything that is

a. what the character says: "Do you not think you are a little old for such toys? Yes, yes, I think it had better be given away to some poor child."
b. what others say: "...I should catch it if I didn't take you, sure enough."
c. what the narrator says: "Mrs. Mitching could not afford school for Esmeralda, as she needed all her wealth for opening and getting up."
d. what the character does: gives away Esmeralda's plaything.

Other examples are possible.

2. Possible answers: Like a fairy tale, the story begins "There was once..." In the story, the good people are totally good, the wicked stepmother is totally bad, magic powers are used to rescue Esmeralda, and good wins out over evil. This story is different from a fairy tale because one person wrote it using carefully-chosen words. Also, unlike fairy tales, it is set in modern times.

Opinions about whether it is a fairy tale or not may vary. Some may think that because it is like a fairy tale in many ways, it is a fairy tale itself. Others may decide that a fairy tale cannot be written by one person in words that can't be changed with retelling. The modern setting, too, may make some students decide it is not a fairy tale.

3. The plot diagram should include:
Introduction: Introduction of characters and setting
Rising Action: Esmeralda buys the rocking donkey.
Mrs. Mitching takes the donkey away from Esmeralda.
Esmeralda visits the donkey at the museum.

(continued on page 230)

illogical or difficult to follow or understand, so the writers can revise.

Question 2. This question builds on the analysis begun in **Developing Comprehension Skills, 5.**

Pre-Writing. Have each student think independently about how he or she would change the story's ending. Have them skim the last page of the story and list specific events that would not occur in their stories. Then have them decide on a series of different events that would make the story more to their liking. Have them arrange those events in the order they would happen.

Writing. Remind students to follow their plan, unless they think of better ideas as they write. Explain that, if they change their plan, they had better be sure the new events follow logically.

Revising. Direct the students to read over their writing and make any changes that would improve it. Allow time in class for students to share their new endings.

Question 3. Emphasize that this question is not asking students to rewrite the story from a different point of view, but simply to analyze why the third-person omniscient point of view works so well.

Pre-Writing. Have students discuss the answers to the questions in the text concerning the ways the story would have been different if it had been told in the first-person. Have them identify the events and reactions that would have been missing from first-person accounts. Ask what effect each change would have on the plot or the mood of the story. After discussing several of these possible changes and effects, ask the students to list two or three statements about the story that depend on the point of view not changing.

Writing. Remind students not only to name an effect, but also to give an example of it. Allow sufficient time for students to write their first drafts.

Revising. Have students revise and proofread their own paragraphs using the **Checklist for the Process of Writing** on pages 556 and 557.

Developing Skills in Study and Research

Have students read **Doing Background Reading** on page 230. Discuss why an encyclopedia may not always be the best source for information. Arrange a visit to the library and have students complete the assignment, or assign it for homework. Discuss students' findings together.

Creative Writing

2. **Planning Your Own Story.** In writing activities for the first three stories of this section, you have had an opportunity to create a character and a setting, and to describe a conflict facing the character. To do this activity, you may use that character, setting, and conflict, or you may invent new ones.

   Develop a plot outline for a story about your character. The outline should be between five and ten sentences long. Write at least one sentence for each of the parts in the plot diagram below.

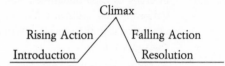

Creative Writing

3. **Writing a New Ending.** The ending of this story may have seemed too sudden to you. You may have felt that the rest of the story seemed possible, but the ending brought in impossible events. Perhaps you felt that the ending was too sad or left too many loose ends. Can you think of an ending more satisfying to you? Decide at what point you would begin to change the story. Then write your own ending, beginning at that point.

Developing Skills in Study and Research

Doing Background Reading. The story of "The Rocking Donkey" is by an English author. She used many terms common in England, but not necessarily in America. For example, the phrases "sales of work," "jumble sale," and "whist drive" probably were unfamiliar to you. To understand the story a bit better, you might want to know something about customs in England. An encyclopedia article is very limited; it might not tell you much about how the average person lives. To learn more about life in England, you might want to do some background reading, that is, reading of fiction and nonfiction books on the topic.

Use the card catalog of your school or local library. Find the titles of at least three books that might give you information about the lives of typical people in England or another country of your choice. Begin by looking up the name of the country and go on to the other categories listed there. To select the three books, read the short descriptions that are given on the cards. You could include biographies, novels, or books about events in the country of your choice since World War II.

(continued from page 229)

One night Esmeralda goes to the museum to see the donkey.

Climax: The donkey speaks to Esmeralda.

Falling Action: She gets on his back, and they ride away.

Resolution: Neither one is ever seen again.

4. Answers may vary. Some possible themes are the following: Children should be treated kindly. Good people will eventually be rewarded. People who do good deeds in public may not always be as good in private.

Developing Vocabulary Skills

Answers will vary. Possible answers:

1. serenity—calmness
2. doomed—people who can't be saved
3. poverty-stricken—poor
4. irritable—easily annoyed
5. melancholy—unhappy
6. tidy—neat
7. shilling—a coin
8. battered—beaten up

The Disappearing Man

In detective stories the reader should be aware of evidence or small clues that help in solving the crime. Can you find the clues in this story? Can you predict the outcome?

ISAAC ASIMOV

I'm not often on the spot when Dad's on one of his cases, but I couldn't help it this time.

I was coming home from the library that afternoon, when a man dashed by me and ran full speed into an alley between two buildings. It was rather late, and I figured the best thing to do was to keep on moving toward home. Dad says a nosy fourteen-year-old isn't likely to make it to fifteen.

But in less than a minute, two police officers came running. I didn't wait for them to ask. "He went in there," I said.

One of them rushed in, came out, and shouted, "There's a door open. He went inside. Go 'round to the front."

They must have given the alarm, because in a few minutes three police cars drove up, there were plainclothes officers on the scene, and the building was surrounded.

I knew I shouldn't be hanging around. Innocent bystanders get in the way of the police. Just the same, I was there when it started and, from what I heard the police saying, I knew they were after this man, Stockton. He was a loner who'd pulled off some pretty spectacular jewel robberies over the last few months. I knew about it because Dad is a detective on the force, and he was on the case.

"Slippery fellow," he said, "but when you work alone, there's no one to double-cross you."

I said, "Doesn't he have to work with someone, Dad? He's got to have a fence—someone to peddle the jewels."

"If he has," said Dad, "we haven't located him. And why don't you get on with your homework?" (He always says that when he thinks I'm getting too interested in his cases.)

Well, they had him now. Some jeweler must have pushed the alarm button.

The alley he ran into was closed on all sides but the street, and he hadn't come out. There was a door there that was

Objectives

- To recognize and appreciate the short story as a form of literature
- To appreciate timing in a detective story
- To analyze relationships between characters
- To apply literal, interpretive, and critical reading skills to a selection
- To predict outcomes
- To recognize standard and nonstandard English
- To write an original short story
- To recognize and use deductive reasoning

Preparing the Students

Essential Vocabulary. The words presented here are essential to the understanding of the selection.

Have the students use the context clues in the following sentences to determine the meanings of the underlined words.

loner evacuate stimulated

1. The robber lived alone and worked alone. He was a real <u>loner</u>.
2. When they were ordered to <u>evacuate</u> the building, everyone left immediately.
3. The quarterback's surge of energy <u>stimulated</u> the fans too. They began to stamp and yell.

If the students need additional help with the vocabulary of this selection, encourage them to use context clues to determine word meaning. As needed, direct them to the **Glossary** or to a classroom dictionary.

Motivation. Explain to students that the next story is a detective story. People usually like detective stories because they give readers a chance to figure out a crime at the same time as the detective. Have the students read the introductory paragraph at the top of page 231 and state in their own words what they should be looking for as they read this short story.

Presenting the Selection

1. Have the students read "The Disappearing Man" on pages 231 to 234.

2. Make sure that everyone has read the assignment by administering the **Check Test**, at the bottom of T.E. page 234.

3. Ask if any students were able to predict the outcome of the story before it was revealed. Have them tell what clues they used.

4. Develop the study questions as suggested in **Using the Study Questions**

beginning on page 235. That section also provides challenge questions for further discussion, as needed. (For answers to questions, see T.E. pages 235 to 237.)

Reinforcing the Lesson

To reteach, reinforce, or extend the skills in this lesson, see the following:

Skills Practice Book, Green Level—pages 111 through 114

Special Populations

Direct the class's attention to the introduction on page 231 suggesting that readers keep track of any clues they spot. Have the students make a list as they read.

ESL. ESL students may need individualized assistance with the exercises under **Developing Vocabulary Skills** on pages 235 and 236. It is important that students understand the discussion accompanying the exercise.

LD. When discussing **Recognizing Deductive Reasoning** on page 237, remember that you are requiring students to deal with some relatively complex abstractions that are difficult for many LD students.

open, and he must have gone in. The police had the possible exits guarded. They even had a couple of officers on the roof.

I was just beginning to wonder if Dad would be involved, when another car came up, and he got out. First thing, he saw me and stopped dead. "Larry! What are you doing here?"

"I was on the spot, Dad. Stockton ran past me into the alley."

"Well, get out of here. There's liable to be shooting."

I backed away, but I didn't back off all the way. Once my father went into the building, I got into his car. The driver knew me, and he said, "You better go home, Larry. I'm going to have to help with the search, so I can't stay here to keep an eye on you."

"Sure, you go on," I said. "I'll be leaving in a minute." But I didn't. I wanted to do some thinking first.

Nobody leaves doors open in New York City. If that door into the alley was open, Stockton must have opened it. That meant he had to have a key; there wasn't time to pick the lock. That must mean he worked out of that building.

I looked at the building. It was an old one, four stories high. It had small businesses in it, and you could still see the painted signs in the windows in the fading light.

On the second-floor window, it said, "Klein and Levy, Tailors." Above that was a theatrical costumer, and on the top floor was a jeweler's. That jeweler's made sense out of it.

If Stockton had a key to the building, he probably worked with that jeweler. Dad would figure all that out.

I waited for the sound of shots, pretty scared Dad might get hurt. But nothing happened. Maybe Stockton would see he was cornered and just give in. I hoped so. At least they didn't have to evacuate the building. Late on Saturday, I supposed, it would be deserted.

After a while, I got tired of waiting. I chose a moment when no police officers were looking and moved quickly to the building entrance. Dad would be hopping mad when he saw me, but I was curious. I figured they had Stockton, and I wanted to see him.

They didn't have him.

There was a fat man in a vest in the lobby. He looked scared, and I guess he was the watchman. He kept saying, "I didn't see anybody."

Police officers were coming down the stairs and out of the old elevator, all shaking their heads.

My father was pretty angry. He said, "No one has anything?"

A police sergeant said, "Donovan said no one got out on the roof. All the doors and windows are covered."

"If he didn't get out," said my father in a low voice that carried, "then he's in the building."

"We can't find him," said the sergeant. "He's nowhere inside."

My father said, "It isn't a big building——"

"We had the watchman's keys. We've looked everywhere."

"Then how do we know he went into the building in the first place? Who saw him go in?"

There was a silence. A lot of police officers were milling about the lobby now, but no one said anything. So I spoke up. "I did, Dad."

Dad whirled and looked at me and made a funny sound in the back of his throat that meant I was in for it for still being there. "You said you saw him run into the alley," he said. "That's not the same thing."

"He didn't come out, Dad. There was no place else for him to go."

"But you didn't actually see him go in, did you?"

"He couldn't go up the side of the buildings. There wouldn't have been time for him to reach the roof——"

Dowagiac, 1983, ED PASCHKE. Private collection. Courtesy of Phyllis Kind Gallery, Chicago. Photograph by William H. Bengtson,

About the Art

The recent work of Chicago-born painter Ed Paschke (born 1941) suggests the strange lighting and image effects of television. The central image of *Dowagiac* is a human face that seems to emerge from the glowing bands and stripes of color. The pattern of the painting and its vibrant, electrical colors are reminiscent of a television on the blink. The eerie light also evokes an X-ray image.

Paschke often makes up words for his titles, words that echo the strangeness of his paintings. However, this title, possibly of native American origin, is the name of a real town in southwest Michigan.

But Dad wasn't listening. "Did anyone actually see him go in?"

Of course no one said anything, and I could see my father was going to call the whole thing off, and then, when he got me home, I was going to get the talking-to of my life.

The thought of that talking-to must have stimulated my brain, I guess. I looked about the lobby desperately and said, "But, Dad, he did go into the building, and he didn't disappear. There he is right now. That man there." I pointed, and then I dropped down and rolled out of the way.

There wasn't any shooting. The man I pointed to was close to the door—he must have been edging toward it—and now he made a dash for it. He almost made it, but a police officer who had been knocked down grabbed his leg and then everyone piled on him. Later they had the jeweler, too.

I went home after Stockton was caught, and, when my father got home much later, he did have some things to say about my risking my life. But he also said, "You got onto that theatrical costume bit very nicely, Larry."

I said, "Well, I was sure he went into the building and was familiar with it. He could get into the costumer's if he had to, and they would be bound to have police uniforms. I figured that, if he could dump his jacket and pants and get into a uniform quickly, he could just walk out of the building."

Dad said, "You're right. Even after he got outside, he could pretend he was dealing with the crowd and then just walk away."

Mom said, "But how did you know which police officer it was, Larry? Don't tell me you know everyone by sight."

"I didn't have to, Mom," I said. "I figured if he got a police uniform at the costumer's, he had to work fast and grab any one he saw. And they wouldn't have much of an assortment of sizes anyway. So I just looked around for a police officer whose uniform didn't fit, and, when I saw one with trouser legs stopping above his ankles, I knew he was Stockton."

Check Test

1. What crime was Stockton suspected of committing? (jewel robbery)

2. In what city does the story take place? (New York City)

3. How did Stockton try to escape? (by dressing in a police uniform)

4. How did Larry know that the thief wasn't a real police officer? (His pants were too short.)

Answers to Study Questions

Developing Comprehension Skills

1. Larry is coming home from the library when he sees the man dash by. Larry stays because he is interested in the case.

2. Larry knew the man had run into the building and hadn't come out. He thought that the man must have had a key to the building, since no one leaves a door unlocked in New York. Therefore, the man must have worked in the building and known about the costumer there. Since the police hadn't found him when they searched the building, Larry decided that the thief must have pretended to be a police officer after changing into a police officer's uniform that he got at the costume shop.

3. Possible reasons: Maybe the police officers weren't as interested in this case. Maybe they didn't know that this thief always worked alone and had escaped capture for many months, so they weren't looking for such a clever escape plan. Possibly Larry was trying harder because he was afraid his father would be angry with him later.

4. Opinions will vary. Opinions should be supported by logical reasons. Possible answers include the following:

Developing Comprehension Skills

Literal Reading 1. Why is Larry right there on the spot for this particular case? Why does he stay at the scene although he knows his father will be angry?

Literal Reading 2. What are the clues that lead Larry to Stockton?

Interpretive Reading 3. Why do you think the police officers did not note the same clues as Larry did?

Critical Reading 4. Do you think Stockton could have been caught without Larry's help?

Reading Literature: Short Stories

1. **Appreciating Timing in a Detective Story.** After reading the end of "The Disappearing Man," you realize that the speaker noticed several seemingly unimportant things that he put together to solve the mystery. List them. Could all of the clues have been presented in the first paragraph? Would it have been a different story if they had? Would it have made a better story if it had been written that way? Why or why not?

2. **Analyzing the Plot.** Make a plot diagram for this story.

3. **Analyzing Relationships Between Characters.** Larry and his father obviously had a close relationship. Find at least three references Larry makes about his father that show the understanding between them.

Developing Vocabulary Skills

1. **Recognizing Standard and Nonstandard English.** Standard English is English that is understood by all speakers of English. It is acceptable at all times and in all places. It is the kind of English that is used in writing, speeches, and conversations with most people. All of the stories in this chapter are written in standard English.

   A second level of language, nonstandard English, is not acceptable at all times and places. One kind of nonstandard English that is sometimes acceptable is **slang.** If it is not overused, slang is acceptable in conversation, especially with close friends. Slang words and slang meanings for accepted words may be used by a small group of people or by many people for a short time. If the group stops using the word,

Using the Study Questions

It is recommended that students always read and answer the questions in **Developing Comprehension Skills** in class discussion.

Developing Comprehension Skills

Question 1. Read and discuss.

Question 2. Have each student prepare a list. Together, list student suggestions on the board. Then have students compare their lists with the class list.

Question 3. Remind students of Larry's special interest and motivation.

Question 4. Explain that this question asks students to formulate an opinion based on information in the story.

Challenge Question. Larry was a successful detective because he was curious and observant. In what other professions would these qualities be useful? (Interpretive Reading)

Reading Literature: Short Stories

Question 1. As you discuss this question, have the students suggest the clues and list them on the board.

Question 2. Draw a plot diagram on the board. Ask students to suggest events that belong at the various points.

Qustion 3. Have students skim the story and look for the way Larry and his father treat each other and think about each other.

Challenge Question. Do you think that this story is written the way a fourteen-year-old would write it? Give one or two reasons why you feel this way.

The police wouldn't have caught Stockton without Larry. He is the only one who put the clues together quickly enough to capture the thief before he could escape.

The police eventually would have caught Stockton, since they knew that he would come back to the jewelry store in this building. They would have been ready for him the next time.

Challenge. Answers will vary. Some possible answers include the following: A scientist needs to be curious and observant. So do a mechanic, a police officer, a reporter, a salesperson, a lawyer, and many others.

Reading Literature: Short Stories

1. The following clues helped Larry:
   a. Larry saw the man enter the building.
   b. The man got in so quickly that he must have had a key. That meant that he worked there.
   c. There was a jeweler and a theatrical costumer in the building.
   d. No one had come out.
   e. The police had searched the building thoroughly.
   f. Everyone in the building was together in that one room.
   g. No one would suspect a police officer of being the thief.
   h. If the thief had taken a police officer's uniform from the costumer, he wouldn't have had time to find one that fit perfectly.

It wouldn't have made sense to put all the clues in the first paragraph. The story was fun to read and easy to understand because the clues were presented one at a time, as Larry noticed them.

2. The plot diagram should include:
   Introduction: Larry sees the man run into the building.
   Rising Action: The police arrive on the scene and search the building.

(continued on page 236)

Developing Vocabulary Skills

Question 1. Have individual students read **Recognizing Standard and Nonstandard English** aloud. Discuss the difference between these two levels of language. Ask students for examples of current slang words or expressions and their meanings. Have students complete the exercise independently. Remind them that they are looking for phrases as well as words. Discuss the answers together.

Question 2. Have students look over each of the stories in this chapter, including the classic stories at the beginning of the chapter, before answering this question. Have them cite examples of the level of language that each story uses.

Developing Writing Skills

Read and discuss the three assignments. Then have each student choose and complete one of the three.

Question 1. This question asks students to condense the story into a few succinct sentences. Students must understand the story well to state it so briefly.

Pre-Writing. Write the questions that should be answered in five columns on the board. Have students suggest the answers that belong in each column. To appreciate the style of a radio broadcast, you may want to have the students listen to a newscast and then discuss the way the news is presented on it. Students should notice that news reports usually avoid slang words and phrases. They are normally presented in formal standard English, with occasional departures into informal standard English.

Writing. Remind students to avoid slang words and phrases. Allow sufficient time for the students to write their first drafts.

Revising. Have students read their radio news reports to partners. Have the partner note whether the writer forgot an important detail or neglected to answer one of the questions. Allow time for students to add the missing details or answers.

Question 2. Through analysis questions such as this one, students learn not only to identify point of view, but also to appreciate the effects of point of view on a story.

Pre-Writing. Have students describe the mood and tone of each of the stories. Then have them compare the two stories. Point out the detachment of the third-person point of view. Point out the involvement in the story that is created by the first-person point of view, stressing the insight it gives us into the characters' personal thoughts and feelings.

it dies. Sometimes the word is accepted generally, and everyone begins to use it. At that point, the word is not considered slang anymore. It becomes part of standard English. Because slang is constantly changing, slang words are not always in the dictionary.

In the sentences below, identify the slang words or phrases. Use either the dictionary or context clues in the sentence to determine the meaning of the slang.

a. When you go to that theater, look at your seat carefully before you sit down. Some of the seats are so grungy you wouldn't want to touch them!

b. Stand up for yourself! Don't be a pushover!

c. In the shoot-out at the end of the western, the outlaw got the drop on the sheriff.

d. I can't buy your excuse for being late.

e. Ginny pretends to be friendly, but I've got her number. I wouldn't trust her with any of my secrets!

2. **Recognizing Formal and Informal Standard English.** The story of "The Disappearing Man" was written in the first-person point of view. Larry is speaking as though he were having a conversation with someone. He uses **informal standard English.** Compare the language in "The Disappearing Man" to that in "The Big Wave." Notice how casual Larry's language sounds when compared to the **formal standard English** of "The Big Wave."

Find another story in this chapter that is written in informal standard English. Find another written in formal standard English.

Developing Writing Skills

Analytical Writing

1. **Writing a Brief News Report.** Imagine that a radio news program reported the arrest of Stockton. Like a newspaper article, a radio news report must answer the five W questions:

Who? Where? When? What happened? Why?

Write a one-paragraph news report in which you answer all five questions. Use the information Larry gave in "The Disappearing Man." Make sure your sentences can be understood by someone hearing them read on the radio.

(continued from page 235)

Larry notices a number of important clues.

Climax: Larry points out the thief in a policeman's uniform.

Falling Action: The criminal is caught.

Resolution: Larry explains how he solved the mystery.

3. Answers may vary. Possible references:

a. Larry's father tells him to go home so he won't get hurt.

b. Larry is afraid that his father might get hurt.

c. Larry's father compliments Larry on his good detective work.

d. Larry's father talks the case over with him at home.

Challenge. The story is written in an informal way that is close to the way a fourteen-year-old would speak.

Developing Vocabulary Skills

1. The following slang words and phrases should be identified and defined:

a. grungy—dirty

b. pushover—a person who is easily taken advantage of

c. shoot-out—gunfight; got the drop on—surprised *or* had an advantage over

Analytical Writing

2. **Comparing Points of View.** "The Rocking Donkey" was written in the third-person point of view, while "The Disappearing Man" was written in the first-person point of view. Can you find some differences in the kinds of stories they are and the effects their authors wanted to have on readers? How do the different points of view help to make these differences clear?

Creative Writing

3. **Writing Your Own Story.** You may have already written a plot diagram for the writing exercise following "The Rocking Donkey" (page 230, Developing Writing Skills, 2). Using that plot diagram, write your own story It must be about one main character and must include all five parts of a plot. Your story should be at least ten paragraphs long.

Developing Skills in Critical Thinking

Recognizing Deductive Reasoning. The kind of thinking Larry used in "The Disappearing Man" is called **deductive reasoning.** In deductive reasoning, you begin with a general statement that is always or almost always true, such as "All three-sided figures are triangles." Then you compare a specific case with the general rule and make a decision, for example, "That sign has three sides. Therefore, that sign is a triangle."

Larry began with the general statement, "All doors in New York are locked." He decided, therefore, that the door in the surrounded building was locked. Next, he realized that "To open a locked door, you need a key." Stockton opened the locked door, so Larry deduced that he had a key.

Here are three other general statements that Larry must have thought of as he unlocked the mystery. Read the general statement and figure out the specific statement that Larry deduced from it, using the rest of the information he had.

a. No one can carry materials (such as disguises) past police officers without being seen.

b. A person being chased doesn't have time to explore a new hiding place.

c. The police officers would have noticed anyone not in their group.

Discuss, also, what information is known or not known to the narrator, and therefore to the reader. Ask students to consider how the detective story would have changed had the speaker been an all-knowing third person. Have each student decide whether to write about mood, tone, plot, or some combination of these elements. Tell each writer to write a topic sentence about that element or elements. Then have the students review the text question to see what else needs to be covered in their answers.

Writing. Allow sufficient time for the students to write their first drafts.

Revising. Encourage students to revise and proofread their own paragraphs before handing them in. Refer them to the **Checklist for the Process of Writing** on pages 556 and 557.

Question 3. This is the culmination of several writing assignments aimed at preparing students to write their own original short stories.

Pre-Writing. Have students refer to their plot diagrams prepared after the last selection. They may want to use the same characters and settings that they prepared on pages 198 and 210, or to revise all three elements in note stage before beginning writing.

Writing. Remind students to include all five parts of the plot. Have them try to make the characters come alive through the use of details and descriptive language. Remind them to describe each setting where the action takes place.

Revising. Display students' revised and proofread stories on a classroom bulletin board. You may want to make the stories available during a class reading time. Stories can be signed out, as books are signed out of a library.

Developing Skills in Critical Thinking

To be sure that students understand the concept of deductive thinking, you may want to discuss the explanation and complete the exercise with them. Have a student read **Recognizing Deductive Reasoning** on page 237 aloud. Make sure that everyone realizes that deductive thinking begins with a general rule that is then applied to a specific case. Complete the exercise together.

d. buy—accept, believe
e. I've got her number.—I understand what she's really doing.

2. Stories written in formal standard English are the following:
"How the Three Young Men Found Death"
"The Bishop's Candlesticks"
"Hearts and Hands"
"The Bet"
"The Story of Keesh"
"The Rocking Donkey"
Stories written in informal standard English are the following:
"The Old Soldier"
"The Summer of the Beautiful White Horse"

Developing Skills in Critical Thinking

a. The thief must have found a disguise and put it on in the building.
b. The thief must have been familiar with the building.
c. The thief must have been in the group of officers.

Using the Review

This review should be completed before the administration of the **Chapter 4 Mastery Test**. Students will have an opportunity to recall important concepts from this chapter and apply them to new contexts. Teacher observation during the review can reveal which students still have not mastered the skills.

Using Your Skills in Reading Short Stories

Read the directions to the exercise aloud. Have the students read the excerpt silently and write the answers to the questions. Discuss the answers together. Collect papers after the review lesson to see who needs further help in this or other areas of study.

Using Your Comprehension Skills

Read the directions to the exercise to the students. Ask students for definitions of the terms *cause* and *effect*. Then read the poems aloud, and explain that *primal* means "early" or "prehistoric." Allow the students time to identify a cause and its effect. Discuss the answers.

See the suggestions above for evaluation.

Using Your Vocabulary Skills

Have the students read the directions to the exercise to themselves. Then call on volunteers to explain what they are to do in the exercise. Have the students complete the exercise independently in writing. Then discuss the answers.

Using Your Writing Skills

Call on students to read aloud the two assignments. Point out that they should complete only one of them. Either exercise will show understanding of the elements of a short story. The first exercise is more analytic; the second is more creative. This allows each student to choose the type of writing he or she prefers.

Answer any questions students may have about the assignments. If you are asking the students to complete their writing in class, let them know how much time they have and that they may turn in a marked-up first draft. Remind them to skip lines to leave space for corrections. If you are asking them to do the writing outside of class, you may require clean copies.

Collect and evaluate these papers according to the guidelines on pages T24

CHAPTER 4 Review

Using Your Skills in Reading Short Stories

The following paragraph is the introduction of the short story "Charles" by Shirley Jackson. Read it carefully. Then answer these questions: From what point of view is the story being told? Who is the narrator? What have you learned about Laurie?

> The day my son Laurie started kindergarten, he rejected corduroy overalls with bibs and began wearing blue jeans with a belt. I watched him go off the first morning with the older girl next door, seeing clearly that an era of my life was ended, my sweet-voiced nursery-school tot replaced by a long-trousered, swaggering character who forgot to stop at the corner and wave good-bye to me.

Using Your Comprehension Skills

Read the following poem from Chapter 5, "The Termite," by Ogden Nash. It contains at least two examples of cause and effect. Identify at least one effect and its cause. Then identify any clue words that helped you, and explain how they helped.

> Some primal termite knocked on wood
> And tasted it, and found it good,
> And that is why your cousin May
> Fell through the parlor floor today.

Using Your Vocabulary Skills

The following sentences are from poems you will read in Chapter 5. Each underlined word has more than one meaning and may be used as more than one part of speech. The possible parts of speech of the underlined word are listed after the sentence. If you were looking up the word in the dictionary, for which part of speech would you look?

Answers to Questions

Using Your Skills in Reading Short Stories

The story is told from the first-person point of view.

The narrator is Laurie's mother.

The introduction gives the following information about Laurie:

- He started kindergarten.
- He rejected his babyish clothes and started wearing blue jeans.
- He became a "swaggering character" who forgot to wave good-bye to his mother.

Using Your Comprehension Skills

The fact that a termite tasted wood had the effect of making termites like to eat wood.

The fact that termites like to eat wood caused the parlor floor to give way under cousin May. The clue words are "And that is why."

Using Your Vocabulary Skills

1. verb
2. verb
3. verb
4. verb
5. verb

1. I have nothing I treasure more. noun, verb, adjective
2. The Barn Owl blunders on her way. noun, verb, adjective
3. Every day that dawns, you must say to yourself, "I was born today!" noun, verb, adjective
4. He clasps the crag with crooked hands. noun, verb
5. You gull up there, dive down! noun, verb, adverb, preposition

Using Your Writing Skills

Choose one of the writing assignments below.

1. Choose, from any story in this chapter, the character whom you could picture the best. In one to three paragraphs, explain why you chose this character. Did the author describe him or her at length? Did the character's words or actions tell a great deal about him or her? Did you feel strongly about the character, either for or against? Use details from the story to support your statements.
2. You have learned that in the introduction to a short story, the writer usually describes the setting. Imagine that you are going to write a mystery story set in your own home or school. Write the introduction to your short story, concentrating only on the setting. Be as specific as possible. Provide details that describe the setting exactly. Use words that appeal to the senses.

Using Your Skills in Critical Thinking

You have learned that a generalization is a general statement about many specific things or events. You have also learned that some generalizations are not true. Of what use, then, are generalizations? Explain at least one way in which generalizations are helpful to us in our thinking or in explanations. Also, describe one way in which the use of generalizations might be harmful. (You may wish to review the use of generalizations in deductive reasoning. See Developing Skills in Critical Thinking on page 237.)

through T27 of this T.E. It is strongly recommended that you discuss and explain your evaluation with the student, and that you provide an opportunity for the students to revise and resubmit their writing.

Using Your Skills in Critical Thinking

This exercise asks students to evaluate the usefulness of generalizations, applying what they have learned in this chapter in a new way. It is recommended that the exercise be done as a class activity, rather than graded on an individual basis.

Read the directions to the students. Allow them time to review page 237, if they like, and to think about their answers. Then ask for suggestions concerning the helpfulness and harmfulness of generalizations. List several on the chalkboard and discuss them.

Reinforcing the Lesson

To reteach, reinforce, or extend the skills in this lesson, see the following:

Skills Practice Book, Green Level—pages 115 and 116

Additional Resource

Diagnostic and Mastery Tests, Green Level—Chapter 4 Mastery Test, pages 21 through 24

Using Your Skills in Critical Thinking

Possible good uses of generalizations include: Generalizations make it easy for us to discuss whole groups of things or people. They can summarize steps in thinking. They can help us to see major differences between groups.

Possible harms in using generalizations include: An inaccurate generalization may distort the truth about a whole group. A carelessly-used generalization may be used on a person or thing that does not belong in a particular group. Sometimes generalizations blind people to real differences among group members.

About the Art

Joan Miró (1893-1983) was a Spanish artist whose work exhibits childlike as well as dreamlike qualities. His *Equinox*, for instance, might be seen as an adolescent or primitive charting of this phenomenon. An equinox occurs two times during the year, at the beginning of spring and at the beginning of fall. At this time, the sun crosses the equator, and day and night all over the earth are of equal length. In this painting, Miró uses simple forms and bright colors to suggest the earth and the heavens. The composition of black lines may suggest, too, some primeval stone structure such as Stonehenge in England, thought to have been built for rituals relating to the sun's movement. On the other hand the painting may simply be an expression of stylistic freedom and unrestricted play that is so much a part of a young person's painting.

CHAPTER 5

Equinox, 1968, JOAN MIRÓ. Etching and aquatint, 41 1/16" × 29". Collection, Museum of Modern Art, New York City. Gift of Studebaker Worthington, Inc.

Chapter Objectives

Skills in Reading Literature

- To appreciate poetry as a form of literature
- To identify such characteristics of poetry as rhythm and rhyme
- To recognize and appreciate the use of sounds and images in poetry
- To identify the mood, theme, and tone of poetry

Comprehension Skills

- To restate poetry in everyday language (Literal Reading)
- To make inferences and predict outcomes in poetry (Interpretive Reading)
- To interpret figurative language (Interpretive Reading)
- To evaluate the effectiveness of the images in a poem (Critical Reading)

Vocabulary Skills

- To use context clues such as examples, comparisons, contrasts, and inferences to determine word meanings
- To complete analogies
- To use a thesaurus

Writing Skills

- To write an opinion (Analytical Writing)
- To write an analysis comparing two or more poems (Analytical Writing)
- To write a poem with rhyme (Creative Writing)
- To write a haiku (Creative Writing)

Study and Research Skills

- To use the encyclopedia and the thesaurus
- To become familiar with such library resources as the record and tape collection, biographies and autobiographies, and the atlas

Critical Thinking Skills

- To identify slanted language in poetry
- To classify poems using specific criteria
- To recognize faulty generalizations
- To evaluate the historical accuracy of a poem
- To define terms

Speaking and Listening Skills

- To interpret a poem orally
- To listen to and evaluate oral presentations of poetry
- To interpret a poem with a group

Reading Literature

Information in **Reading Literature: Poetry** will help students enjoy and appreciate the poetry they will read in this chapter. After presenting a definition and a short history of poetry, the text discusses the following elements of poetry: rhythm (including regular rhythm and free verse), rhyme, sounds in a poem, and figurative language. Much of the material about the elements of poetry was introduced in Chapter 3. In this chapter, however, these elements are related specifically to poetry. Students are then given suggestions which will help them get the most out of the poetry they will read.

Preparing the Students

Tell the students that they will learn about a special kind of literature in this chapter. They will learn about poetry. Explain that not only will they take a close look at how poets have written their works, but they will also experiment with creating their own poetry.

It is recommended that you administer the **Chapter 5 Diagnostic Test** at this time. The results of this pretest will serve as a guide for measuring student needs and progress in achieving chapter objectives.

Presenting the Lesson

1. Have one student read **What Is Poetry?**. Ask how poetry differs from the literature they have read so far in the text. Point out poetry's emphasis on sounds, pictures, and feelings.

2. Have the class read **The History of Poetry** silently. After they have finished, review the ways poetry has been used (songs, chants, epics, plays). Make sure the students understand that poetry is always changing.

3. Have the students read **The Elements of Poetry** independently. Ask one student to define rhythm. Ask two other students to explain regular rhythm and free verse. Rhyme is a familiar concept. Students should be reminded, however, that rhymes at the ends of lines are referred to as end rhymes. Review the meanings of alliteration, onomatopoeia, figurative language, simile, metaphor, personification, and hyperbole. If necessary, have the class refer to the appropriate pages in Chapter 3.

4. Have individual students read **How To Read a Poem** aloud. Stress the impor-

Reading Literature: Poetry

What Is Poetry?

Poetry is a special way of using words. It appeals to your senses and your imagination. Poets choose words with particular meanings and sounds and combine them so as to create vivid pictures and feelings. Poets help you see your world in a new way.

The History of Poetry

Poetry is the oldest form of literature. In poetry, people of long ago were able to tell about and relive exciting experiences in their imagination. They could use the rhythm of words to make their poems music-like and easy to remember. Early songs, chants, prayers, and stories were all poems.

The ancient Greeks and Romans appreciated the beauty and power of carefully arranged words. Therefore, they wrote their plays in poetry. For thousands of years, stories about heroes and brave adventures, called **epics**, were told in poem form. In more recent times, William Shakespeare, perhaps the greatest English playwright, wrote his plays as poetry.

Poets pay attention to what is happening in the world. In their work, they show their feelings about current events and ideas. Because of this, styles in poetry change with the times. In some periods, poets have tried to be logical and controlled. At other times, they have been imaginative and free-thinking.

The Elements of Poetry

Rhythm. The pattern of stressed and unstressed beats in a poem is called **rhythm**. There are two types of rhythm: 1) regular, steady rhythm; and 2) free verse.

In words of more than one syllable, certain syllables are stressed. Others are not stressed. In a poem with **regular rhythm,** words are arranged to make a regular pattern of stressed and unstressed beats. An example is "One, two, buckle my shoe."

In **free verse**, words are arranged more freely. The pattern of beats is not regular. Every line of a free verse poem may have a different pattern of stressed and unstressed beats.

Bring me all of your
Heart melodies
That I may wrap them.

Rhyme. Words that **rhyme** end with the same sound. When rhyming words appear at the ends of lines, the rhyme is called **end rhyme**.

Sounds in a Poem. To a poet, the sounds of words are just as important as their meanings. Poets choose words for special effects, including those you learned about in Chapter 3, such as alliteration, onomatopoeia, and rhyme.

Figurative Language. As you learned in Chapter 3, **figurative language** is a way of speaking or writing that makes you look at familiar things in a new way. Types of figurative language in poetry include similes, metaphors, personification, and hyperbole.

How To Read a Poem

1. Read each poem aloud. Hearing the sounds of a poem makes the meaning clearer and adds to your enjoyment.
2. Decide who is speaking in the poem. Is the poet speaking? Is the poet imagining the words another person might say?
3. Take time to imagine the things or feelings the poet describes.
4. Give each poem a chance. You will like some poems more than others. Everyone does. But remember that each of these poems has something to give you, if you want to take it.

tance of the sounds in poetry. Urge the students to approach poetry with an open mind.

Reinforcing the Lesson

To reteach, reinforce, or extend the concepts in this lesson, see the following:

Skills Practice Book, Green Level—pages 117 and 118

Additional Resource

Diagnostic and Mastery Tests, Green Level—Chapter 5 Diagnostic Test, pages 25 and 26

Comprehension Skills

In **Comprehension Skills: Inferences and Outcomes,** students will review the skills of making inferences and drawing conclusions, this time specifically relating these skills to poetry. They will also see how the skill of predicting outcomes can help them understand poetry.

Preparing the Students

Tell the students that many of the skills that helped them read other forms of literature will help them understand poetry too. Remind them how, in Chapter 2, they learned to make inferences and draw conclusions. In this section, they will see how those same skills can aid them in enjoying poetry. In addition, they will learn another skill, predicting outcomes, that can be used when they read other forms of literature as well as poetry.

Presenting the Lesson

1. Have one student read the first two paragraphs under **Making Inferences in Poetry**. Have another student read the lines of poetry. You may want to read down to **Predicting Outcomes in Poetry** yourself, allowing time enough after each question for students to locate the answers in the poem. Point out that although the poem does give the reader much information, its purpose is not simply to report facts. If it were, the information could have been given in a much simpler way. The purpose of this poem is to create a clear picture of a single moment.

2. Have students read **Predicting Outcomes in Poetry.** Ask one student to tell how a reader can predict outcomes. Ask how a reader would benefit by predicting outcomes.

3. As a class, complete the exercises and discuss the answers.

Reinforcing the Lesson

To reteach, reinforce, or extend the skills in this lesson, see the following:

Skills Practice Book, Green Level—pages 119 and 120

Special Populations

LD. Be sure to check comprehension frequently. Pause periodically while read-

Comprehension Skills: Inferences and Outcomes

Making Inferences in Poetry

Most poets use as few words as possible. To understand poetry, you need to work with the clues that are given. In other words, you have to become skilled at making inferences.

Read these beginning lines from a poem about a close basketball game and its final tense seconds.

With two 60's stuck on the scoreboard
And two seconds hanging on the clock,
The solemn boy in the center of eyes,
Squeezed by silence,
Seeks out the line with his feet,
Soothes his hands along his uniform,

It's amazing how much you can learn from this short section of the poem. By building on the evidence in those six lines, you can answer all the following questions.

1. What's the score of the game? (The clues can be found in Line 1). *60–60*
2. How many seconds are left? (Line 2) *two seconds*
3. What are the fans doing? (Line 3) *watching the boy*
4. What is the atmosphere in the gym? (Line 4) *tense. The boy feels the silence pressing in on him from all sides.*
5. What is the boy about to do? (Line 5) *make a foul shot*
6. How does the boy feel? How do you know? (Line 6) *He's so nervous that his palms are damp. He has to wipe them off.*

After you have collected enough evidence and made logical inferences, you may use what you know to **draw a conclusion**. To do this, you study your evidence and decide what it means when taken as a whole.

Predicting Outcomes in Poetry

Some poems describe a situation and then invite you to figure out what might happen next. If you read carefully, you will usually find clues to help you. Combined with your common sense and knowledge from past experiences, they will point you in the right direction so that you can predict a logical outcome.

Even if you are reading a poem that tells a complete story, it's a good idea to think about what might happen next. When you do, you will discover that you have started reading more carefully just to find out if your guess is right or wrong.

Exercises: Understanding Inferences, Drawing Conclusions, and Predicting Outcomes

A. Which line of the following poem tells you that the eagle is perched on a high mountain?

He clasps the crag with crooked hands;
Close to the sun in lonely lands,
Ringed with the azure world, he stands.

B. Which conclusion can you draw about Abe Lincoln from this stanza of a poem about him? Remember that conclusions are based on more than one piece of evidence.

He liked telling stories,
He liked telling jokes.
"Abe's quite a character,"
Said quite a lot of folks.

a. Abe liked to tell jokes.
b. Abe was interesting and fun to be with.

C. Which sentence below tells what the eagle may do next?

He watches from his mountain walls,
And like a thunderbolt he falls.

a. He will attack a small animal below.
b. He will crash into the rocks below.

ing the selections to ask students: "What could happen next?" This will help build skills in predicting outcomes.

Answers to Exercises

A. He clasps the crag with crooked hands

B. b

C. a

Vocabulary Skills

In **Vocabulary Skills: Context Clues,** students will learn how to use context clues to discover the meaning of unknown words. The kinds of context clues they will work on are example clues, comparison clues, contrast clues, and words in a series. They will learn how to identify each type of clue and recognize key words and phrases. An exercise gives them practice in using these skills.

Preparing the Students

Tell the students that they should not feel helpless when they come upon an unfamiliar word. Many clues right in the poem or story can help them discover the meaning of the word. In this section, they will learn about four different types of context clues that they can use in their reading.

Presenting the Lesson

1. Have the students read **Using Context Clues** down to **Comparison Clues**. List the key words and phrases for example clues on the chalkboard. Ask the students for sentences using each of the key words and phrases.

2. Follow the same procedure for **Comparison Clues** and **Contrast Clues**.

3. Have one student read **Words in a Series.** Read the students the following sentence and have them guess what a condor is.

The wildlife book devoted one chapter to hawks, eagles, condors, and vultures.

4. Have the class complete the exercise independently. Discuss the answers together.

Reinforcing the Lesson

To reteach, reinforce, or extend the skills in this lesson, see the following:

Skills Practice Book, Green Level—pages 121 and 122

Special Populations

LD, ESL, NSD. Create a reference chart listing all the key words from pages 246 and 247 for the students to use throughout the year.

Vocabulary Skills: Context Clues

Using Context Clues

Do you take a dictionary along with you when you go to the movies? Do you keep a dictionary on your lap when you watch TV at home? You would never think of it. Yet, even without using a dictionary, you can probably define new words you have heard at the movies or on TV. You know that you can usually guess at the meaning of a new word if you pay attention to clues in the story.

Learning the meanings of new words that you read can be just as easy. All you need to do is know which clues to look for. Here are a few kinds of context clues that can help you.

Example Clues. Writers often explain unfamiliar words by examples. Some key words and phrases to look for in example clues are *for example*, *one kind*, *for instance*, *like*, *especially*, *and other*, and *such as*.

Jeff is fascinated by dangerous sea creatures, such as the stingray and the great white shark.

From this example clue, you can guess that a *stingray* is a dangerous sea creature. The key phrase is *such as*.

Comparison Clues. When writers want to relate similar ideas, they use comparison clues. Often you will find the meaning of an unfamiliar word in one of the related ideas. Some key words and phrases to look for are *in addition*, *also*, *too*, *moreover*, *besides*, *another*, *other*, *both*, *the same*, *and all*.

Lisa was ecstatic at winning first prize. Moreover, her parents and friends also felt joyful.

From this clue, you can guess that *ecstatic* means "joyful."

Contrast Clues. Contrast clues tell you that the writer is talking about opposite meanings. You can sometimes understand a new word after you know its opposite. Some key words and phrases are *although*, *but*, *however*, *on the other hand*, *as opposed to*, *unlike*, *different from*, *in contrast*, and *not the same.*

> The grasshopper's frivolous attitude was very different from the practical, matter-of-fact attitude of the ant.

From this clue, you can guess that *frivolous* means "silly" or "not serious." The key phrase is *different from*.

Words in a Series. Writers sometimes use a series of words to explain a new word. They know that you may understand other words in the series. They hope that you will be able to transfer your knowledge of the known words to the unknown word.

> The salesperson opened the cabinet. He showed his customer the necklaces, bracelets, brooches, and rings.

You can see that a *brooch* must be a type of jewelry because all the other items in the series are jewelry.

Exercise: Using Context Clues

Use context clues to figure out the meaning of each underlined word. Be prepared to tell why you believe that you are right. Also, identify the key words that helped you find the meaning.

1. Casey doffed his cap when the crowd cheered, unlike Jones who aways kept his cap on.
2. We studied moles and other small mammals that live underground.
3. You're not half as spry as I am. For instance, I can climb up the trees more quickly and gracefully than you can.
4. In addition to the tumult out on the playing field, there was also noisy confusion in the locker room.
5. Although he felt skittish inside, outwardly he acted calm.

Answers to Exercise

1. doffed—took off; unlike
2. moles—small mammals; and other
3. spry—quick and graceful; for instance
4. tumult—noisy confusion; also
5. skittish—nervous; although

Poems About Individual Growth

Call on a student to read page 248 to the class. Remind the students that they have learned in other chapters that there is not necessarily just one theme to a selection; rather, several themes may be found in a single poem or other piece of writing. Stress the idea that identifying theme does not need to be a search for a single right answer but rather an examination of what a poem is saying to each individual.

Ask the students to look at the picture on page 248 and suggest their ideas of what the theme of this picture might be.

Poems About Individual Growth

As you know, the **theme** of a piece of writing is the main idea that the writer wants to share with you. It is the meaning of the piece of writing. Every poem has a theme.

In this section, every poem is about individual growth. As you read, try to answer this question: Does this poem set goals for me?

Portrait of Mademoiselle Violette Heymann, 1909, ODILON REDON.
The Cleveland Museum of Art, Cleveland, Ohio, Honmun B. Hurlbut Collection.

About the Art

The French painter Odilon Redon (1840-1916) was a member of an art and literary movement called "Symbolism." Like the Symbolists with whom he was associated, Redon was not interested in mere representation in art but rather wanted to convey a poetic feeling or idea, to open up a window on the unseen world of thought and imagination. Redon allowed his subconscious free play, giving shape in his paintings to dreams and fantasies. The rich, sensual quality of his colors and the softness of his forms give his work a dreamlike quality. The young woman portrayed here seems lost in thought. She is surrounded by flowers, but whether these flowers are real or exist only in her or the artist's imagination, as part of a daydream, is not clear.

The Dream Keeper

LANGSTON HUGHES

Have you ever given up a dream because someone told you it wasn't practical? Read to find out what Langston Hughes would like to do with that dream.

Bring me all of your dreams,
You dreamers,
Bring me all of your
Heart melodies
That I may wrap them
In a blue cloud-cloth
Away from the too-rough fingers
Of the world.

Developing Comprehension Skills

Interpretive Reading	1. Why does the poet think our dreams need special care?
Literal Reading	2. To whom is the poem addressed?
Interpretive Reading	3. What does the poet offer to do? What do you think he means?
Interpretive Reading	4. What do you think a heart melody is?

Check Test

1. What is the dream keeper telling us to do? (He wants us to bring him our dreams.)

2. What will the speaker do with our dreams? (He will wrap them in a blue cloud-cloth and keep them away from the world.)

Answers to Study Questions

Developing Comprehension Skills

1. Dreams are fragile and easily destroyed.

2. The poem is addressed to anyone who has a dream.

3. He offers to wrap dreams in a blue cloud-cloth to keep them safe. He means that he will help dreamers protect their dreams. He knows that dreams are important and have to be cared for or they die.

4. A heart melody could be the ideas a person thinks about to help him or her feel happy.

(continued on page 250)

Objectives

- To recognize and appreciate poetry as a form of literature
- To identify the sounds of language in a poem
- To recognize the effect of personification
- To identify the theme of a poem
- To apply literal, interpretive, and critical reading skills to a selection

Preparing the Students

Motivation. Encourage the students to think about, and if they wish, to share their dreams or hopes for the future. Now have the students read the introductory paragraph at the top of page 249 and state in their own words what they should try to find out as they read this poem.

Presenting the Selection

1. Read "The Dream Keeper" aloud to the students. Have them read the poem silently once more, and then ask for one or two volunteers to read it aloud.

2. Make sure that everyone has understood the literal meaning of the poem by administering the **Check Test**, at the bottom of this page.

3. Develop the study questions as suggested in **Using the Study Questions** beginning on page 249. The question posed by the introduction is answered there.

Using the Study Questions

It is recommended that students always read and answer the questions in **Developing Comprehension Skills** in class discussion. Whenever possible, they should also read the questions in **Reading Literature** together and discuss the answers.

Developing Comprehension Skills

Question 1. Make sure that students understand that the term *dreams* refers to our hopes for the future. Discuss what can happen to dreams when other people think they are foolish or impossible. Explain that this answer is not stated directly in the poem.

Question 2. Read and discuss the question.

Question 3. Remind students that they must look below the surface meaning of the speaker's words to find the real meaning.

Question 4. Read and discuss the question.

Reading Literature: Poetry

Question 1. Review with the students the meaning of personification. If necessary, have the students reread pages 126 and 127 in Chapter 3.

Question 2. Before students begin to look for examples of repetition of letters in other parts of words, explain that they should look for repetition of consonant sounds, not only letters.

Questions 3 and 4. Read and discuss the questions.

Reading Literature: Poetry

1. **Understanding Figures of Speech.** In lines 7 and 8 the poet uses a figure of speech, **personification**:

   the too-rough fingers
   Of the world

   What can a person's "too-rough" fingers do to a delicate object? In what way can the whole world be compared to a single person handling a dream?

2. **Identifying Sounds of Language.** This poem does not use rhymes or a regular rhythm to give a pattern to the poem. Instead, it uses repetition of letters at the beginning of words (alliteration), repetition of letters in other parts of words, and repetition of whole words. Find an example of each of these uses of language.

3. **Recognizing Special Terms.** This poem uses several terms that were made up just for the poem. We can understand these terms because each of them combines words we already know. The way in which the poet combined the words, however, gives them a fresh meaning. For example, the term "heart melodies" combines two ideas: things that are close to you personally, and songs that may bring beauty or happiness. What two ideas are combined in each of these terms: "cloud-cloth" and "dream keeper"? What do you think each term means? Could the poet have used different words and still expressed the same meaning and the same feeling?

4. **Identifying Theme.** In "The Dream Keeper," the poet is saying something about dreams. What general statement do you get from the poem? Do you think the poet is right?

(continued from page 249)

Reading Literature: Poetry

1. Rough fingers can break a delicate object. The experiences a person has in the world can make him or her think the dream will never come true. One person can break an object just as the world can destroy a dream.

2. Possible examples:

Alliteration—cloud-cloth

Repetition of sounds in other parts of words—rough fingers

Repetition of words—dreams, dreamers, bring me all

3. *Cloud-cloth* reminds the reader of a soft, white cloth made of clouds. *Dream keeper* is a person who can put dreams in a safe place. These words are probably the only words that could have expressed the exact meaning and feeling the poet meant to express.

4. Answers will vary. Possible themes: Dreams need to be protected because they are easily broken. Dreams are precious. Agreement or disagreement should be supported by logical reasons.

The Duel

EMILY DICKINSON

Little David, the Bible says, killed the giant Goliath with just a small stone thrown by David's slingshot. As you read, find the answer to this question: Is the speaker in this poem as successful as David?

I took my power in my hand
And went against the world;
'Twas not so much as David had,
But I was twice as bold.

I aimed my pebble, but myself
Was all the one that fell.
Was it Goliath was too large,
Or only I too small?

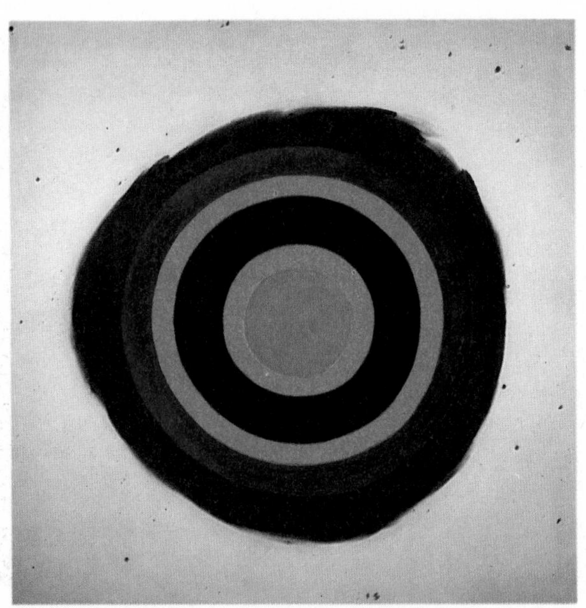

Song, 1958, KENNETH NOLAND. Whitney Museum of American Art, New York City. Gift of the Friends of the Whitney Museum of American Art.

Objectives

- To recognize and appreciate poetry as a form of literature
- To recognize allusions
- To identify rhythms of poems
- To apply literal, interpretive, and critical reading skills to a selection

Preparing the Students

Motivation. You may want to ask volunteers to tell what they know about the story of David and Goliath. Then have the students read the introductory paragraph at the top of page 251 and state in their own words what they should try to find out as they read this poem.

Presenting the Selection

1. Have the students read "The Duel" silently.

2. Make sure that everyone has read the poem by administering the **Check Test**, at the bottom of this page.

3. Have volunteers read the poem aloud. Have them emphasize its meaning and avoid reading it in a sing-song manner.

4. Develop the study questions as suggested in **Using the Study Questions** on page 252. That section answers the question posed in the introduction and also provides a challenge question for further discussion, if needed.

Encouraging Independent Reading

Ask a student, or group of students, to look up the story of David and Goliath and report to the class.

Using the Study Questions

It is recommended that students always read and answer the questions in **Developing Comprehension Skills** in class discussion. Whenever possible, they should

About the Art

Kenneth Noland (born 1924) reveals in his paintings his interest in how colors react to each other. See **About the Cover Art**. The combinations often create the illusion of movement. In *Song*, the red concentric circles framing the black ring might be seen to pulsate around the center circle. On the other hand, the inner black ring might be seen to move while the red ones remain stable. In addition, the entire composition itself might be floating in the white space and just the scattered black particles might be moving about. This visual play is a central feature in all of Noland's work.

Check Test

1. With whom does the speaker compare herself? (David)

2. With whom does the speaker compare the world? (Goliath)

3. Name one possible reason why the speaker fell. (Goliath was too large. The speaker was too small.)

also read the questions in **Reading Literature** together and discuss the answers.

Developing Comprehension Skills

Question 1. Read and discuss the question.

Question 2. Explain to students that the pebble stands for something else. The poet is using figurative language. Have them reread the poem to see what the speaker is really trying to do.

Question 3. Read and discuss the question. Ask a student to find and read aloud the words that tell who won.

Challenge Question. The speaker seems to think that the way to approach the world is to fight it. That is what duelers do. Do you agree with this approach? (Critical Reading)

Reading Literature: Poetry

Question 1. Since this poem refers to a Biblical story, it is fair to assume that it has a religious meaning. Point out that this meaning is one that the poet believes and is not necessarily one that everyone must agree with.

Question 2. Write the poem on the board. Read it with the class, marking the accented and unaccented syllables as you read. Then have the class read it aloud again. The regular rhythm should become obvious.

Question 3. Read and discuss the question.

Question 4. Have students first consider whether the suggestions in the text explain the theme adequately or if they leave out important ideas from the poem. Suggest that students think about the mood of the poem to understand its theme.

Developing Comprehension Skills

Literal Reading — 1. This poem uses personification. The speaker pictures a duel between herself and another person, but what does the poem say her opponent really was?

Interpretive Reading — 2. What does the speaker mean by these lines?

I aimed my pebble, but myself
Was all the one that fell.

What do you think the "pebble" might be? What is the speaker trying to do with it?

Interpretive Reading — 3. Which side won the duel? How do you know?

Reading Literature: Poetry

1. **Recognizing Allusions.** Frequently, writers refer, or **allude**, to other writings. These references are called **allusions**. When you know something about the work to which the writer alludes, you often understand more of what the writer means to say.

   Throughout "The Duel," the poet alludes to the Biblical story of David and Goliath. David was a prayerful person, who usually gave credit for his successes to God. How does that information affect the meaning of this poem?

2. **Identifying Rhythms.** Read "The Dream Keeper" and "The Duel" aloud. "The Dream Keeper" has an irregular rhythm. The accented syllables are not in any particular pattern, and the length of the lines varies. Does "The Duel" have a regular or an irregular rhythm?

3. **Identifying Mood.** As you learned in Chapter 4, the **mood** of a piece of writing is the feeling you get when reading it. Which of the following words best describes the mood of this poem? Be prepared to explain your choice.

   angry puzzled proud

4. **Understanding Theme.** Does this poem tell us not to fight against problems we see in the world? Is it telling us to give up without trying? What do you think it is suggesting?

Answers to Study Questions

Developing Comprehension Skills

1. Her opponent was the world.

2. The speaker fought against the world and failed. The "pebble" might stand for the speaker's talents or abilities. She is trying to use her abilities to defeat forces that are against her.

3. The world won the duel. We know that by the phrase "myself was all the one that fell."

Challenge. Opinions may vary. Possible answers: It is more effective to work together with forces you feel you are against, and change them gradually.

Sometimes it is necessary to fight against the world, or else you will become just like the people or forces you feel you are against.

Reading Literature: Poetry

1. The speaker, unlike David, relied only upon herself. She thinks that maybe if she had a faith in a power greater than herself, as David had, she would have succeeded.

2. "The duel" has a regular rhythm.

Ĭ tóok mȳ pówĕr ín mȳ hánd
Ănd wént ăgáinst thĕ wórld;
'Twăs nót sō múch ăs Dávīd hád,
Bŭt Í wăs twíce ăs bóld.

3. Puzzled. The speaker can't pinpoint the reason why she failed when she had expected to win, just as David did.

4. Themes will vary. Possible answers: Don't expect to win every battle. Sometimes we need help to win our fights.

What's the best thing we could inherit from our parents? Read to find out what this poet thinks.

The Courage That My Mother Had

EDNA ST. VINCENT MILLAY

The courage that my mother had
Went with her, and is with her still:
Rock from New England quarried;
Now granite in a granite hill.

The golden brooch my mother wore
She left behind for me to wear;
I have no thing I treasure more:
Yet, it is something I could spare.

Oh, if instead she'd left to me
The thing she took into the grave!—
That courage like a rock, which she
Has no more need of, and I have.

Check Test

1. What did the speaker's mother leave for her to wear? (a golden brooch)
2. What does the speaker need? (her mother's courage)

Objectives

- To recognize and appreciate poetry as a form of literature
- To recognize the form and organization of a poem
- To identify irony in a poem
- To apply literal, interpretive, and critical reading skills to a selection

Preparing the Students

Essential Vocabulary. The words presented here are essential to the understanding of the selection.

Have the students use the context clues in the following sentences to determine the meanings of the underlined words.

brooch quarry granite

1. The brooch pinned to her blouse had a diamond at its center.
2. Workers quarried the stone from this mountain. They blasted it and dug it out.
3. Since granite is such a hard and durable rock, it is often used in gravestones.

If the students need additional help with the vocabulary of this selection, encourage them to use context clues to determine word meaning. As needed, direct them to the **Glossary** or to a classroom dictionary.

Motivation. Have the students suggest some of the things that people inherit from their parents. Then have them read the introductory paragraph at the top of page 253 and state in their own words what they should try to find out as they read this poem.

Presenting the Selection

1. Read "The Courage That My Mother Had" aloud to the class. In this way, you can be sure that they are not distracted by the line endings, but can concentrate on the meaning.
2. Ask volunteers to read the poem aloud, with expression.
3. Administer the **Check Test** on this page.
4. Develop the study questions as suggested in **Using the Study Questions** on page 254. That section also answers the question posed in the introduction and provides a challenge question.

Special Populations

LD, ESL. For help with question 2, **Identifying Irony** on page 254, give students other examples from their experience of instances of irony (for instance, members of a baseball team who recognize their poor performance but rarely take the time to practice; a person who complains to his or her doctor about not feeling well yet doesn't follow the doctor's advice) and call on students to suggest what is ironic about each one.

For question 3, **Determining Theme** on page 254, write a somewhat broad list of general statements on the board and have individual students choose and explain the ones that reveal what this poem may be suggesting about life. This list could include the following statements:

Some people don't appreciate their parents until their parents are gone.
Sometimes we aim too high.
People are soon forgotten after they are gone.

Using the Study Questions

It is recommended that students always read and answer the questions in **Developing Comprehension Skills** in class discussion. Whenever possible, they should also read the questions in **Reading Literature** together and discuss the answers.

Developing Comprehension Skills

Question 1. Read and discuss the question.

Question 2. Have students find and read the lines in which her mother's courage is compared to rock (lines 3 and 4, stanza 1; line 3, stanza 3).

Question 3. Read and discuss the question.

Question 4. Refer students to the last line of the poem.

Challenge Question. How does the speaker feel about her mother? Give evidence from the poem for your answer. (Interpretive Reading)

Reading Literature: Poetry

Question 1. Have students write a sentence for each stanza, to express its main idea. Discuss their answers together.

Question 2. Refer students to the last stanza for the answer to this question.

Question 3. Point out that there may be more than one theme in this poem. Encourage students to suggest themes freely, since there is no one correct answer. List their suggestions on the board.

Developing Comprehension Skills

1. (Literal Reading) The mother in this poem has died and left a golden brooch, or pin, for her daughter. What does the speaker wish she had instead of the pin?
2. (Interpretive Reading) To what does the speaker compare her mother's courage?
3. (Literal Reading) Do you know from the poem where the mother's birthplace was? Which words tell you?
4. (Interpretive Reading) Why does the speaker regret that the mother took her courage "into the grave"?

Reading Literature: Poetry

1. **Recognizing Organization.** Prose writing is written in sentences, and the sentences are grouped in paragraphs. Each paragraph has a main idea. In poetry, the ideas may or may not be expressed in sentences. They are written in **lines**. The lines are grouped in **stanzas**—sets of two or more lines separated from other stanzas by a line of space. Often, there is a main idea in each stanza.

   How many stanzas are there in this poem? Are the lines in each stanza all about one main idea? If so, what is the main idea of each of the stanzas?

2. **Identifying Irony.** The term **irony** usually refers to a situation in which one thing seems to be true but actually the opposite is true. It can also refer to a situation in which one action seems right or needed, but it doesn't happen. This poem uses irony in the second sense. What is ironic in the situation that the speaker describes?

3. **Determining Theme.** A reader might say that this poem is talking about one woman's death and one daughter's feelings about her mother's death. However, most readers would feel that the poet is suggesting something more general. Think about the irony in this poem. Think about what you have received from your parents, grandparents, and other ancestors. Then decide on a general statement about life that this poem may be making.

Answers to Study Questions

Developing Comprehension Skills

1. She wants her mother's courage.

2. Her courage was like a rock.

3. The mother's birthplace was New England. The words that tell this to us are "Rock from New England quarried."

4. The speaker needs that courage now.

Challenge. We know that the speaker respected her mother, since she admires her courage. We also know that she must have loved her mother, since she treasures the brooch she gave her.

Reading Literature: Poetry

1. There are three stanzas in this poem. The lines in each stanza are all about one main idea. Stanza 1: My mother's courage went with her. Stanza 2: She left me a brooch, which I love but could do without. Stanza 3: I wish I had her courage.

2. Her mother had courage, but doesn't need it anymore. The speaker needs courage, but doesn't have it.

3. Possible answers: The strengths in people's characters are more valuable than gold or money. People are more important than things or money. No one can give someone else courage.

All But Blind

WALTER de la MARE

Some animals, the poet points out, see very poorly. They are blinded by bright daylight. As you read, look for a comparison that the poet makes between these animals and another creature.

All but blind
  In his chambered hole
Gropes for worms
  The four-clawed Mole.

All but blind
  In the evening sky,
The hooded Bat
  Twirls softly by.

All but blind
  In the burning day
The Barn-Owl blunders
  On her way.

And blind as are
  These three to me,
So, blind to Someone
  I must be.

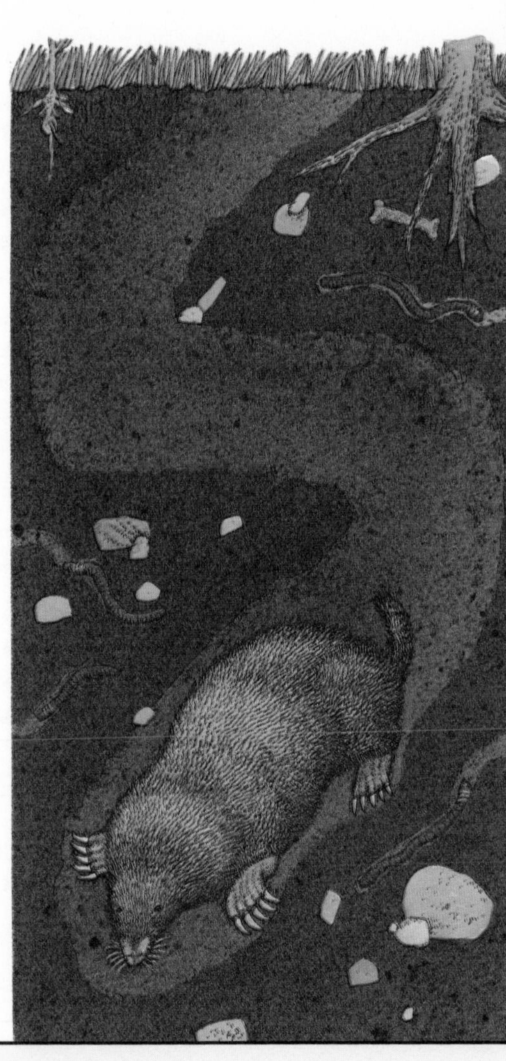

Check Test

1. List the animals mentioned in the poem. (mole, bat, barn-owl)

2. How does the speaker describe himself? (He says he must be blind, too.)

Objectives

- To recognize and appreciate poetry as a form of literature
- To identify the rhythm pattern of a poem
- To apply literal, interpretive, and critical reading skills to a selection
- To use context clues to determine the meanings of words
- To write a short poem
- To compare the information available in the card catalog and the encyclopedia
- To orally interpret the mood of a poem

Preparing the Students

Essential Vocabulary. The words presented here are essential to the understanding of the selection.

Have the students use the context clues in the following sentences to determine the meanings of the underlined words.

chambered gropes blunders

1. A chamber is a room. Something that is chambered has rooms.
2. I groped along the wall in the dark room, feeling for the light switch.
3. During the day, the owl blunders, that is, she moves in a clumsy way and bumps into things.

Motivation. Have the students read the introductory paragraph at the top of page 255 and state in their own words what they should try to find out as they read this poem.

Presenting the Selection

1. Have the students read "All But Blind" silently.

2. Make sure that everyone has read the poem by administering the **Check Test** at the bottom of this page.

3. Choose four students to each read one of the four stanzas aloud.

4. Help students see that the creature mentioned in the introduction is the speaker, who is comparing his limitations to the blindness of the animals.

5. Develop the study questions as suggested in **Using the Study Questions** beginning on page 256. That section also provides a challenge question.

Reinforcing the Lesson

To reteach, reinforce, or extend the skills in this lesson, see the following:

Skills Practice Book, Green Level—pages 123 and 124

Special Populations

ESL. Simplify the wording of the question under **Developing Skills in Speaking and Listening** on page 258 by asking students to answer the following:

1. In what ways does someone show he or she cares about another person?
2. If someone were creating a dance about dreams, how would that person move?

Talk about mood presented by some favorite popular songs. Bring in some examples to play for the class.

Have the students examine the illustration on page 259 and tell how it makes them feel. Talk about its colors and how they help to create the mood. Encourage the students to talk about their favorite colors. Discuss commonly used colors for such things as rooms, clothing, and cars and ask students to explain how each of the colors makes them feel.

Remember, too, that some students may have trouble seeing color and would, therefore, not be able to distinguish the subtle color differences in *Ocean Park #114*. If these students would like to discuss the problem of color deficiency with the class, encourage them to do so.

Using the Study Questions

It is recommended that students always read and answer the questions in **Developing Comprehension Skills** in class discussion. Whenever possible, they should also read the questions in the other categories together and discuss the answers.

Developing Comprehension Skills

Question 1. Explain that the poet has reversed the usual order of the subject and

Developing Comprehension Skills

Literal Reading
1. In the first stanza, the poet does not use the normal order of words in a sentence. Explain in your own words what he is saying.

Literal Reading
2. The poem lists three examples of "all but blind" animals. Does their poor vision hurt these animals? Does it prevent them from doing what they need to do in order to survive?

Interpretive Reading
3. In the last stanza, the person who is speaking compares himself to the three animals. In what way does he think he is like them? Who might the "Someone" be?

Reading Literature: Poetry

1. **Looking at Rhyme.** In each stanza of this poem, the second and the fourth lines rhyme. How does this affect the word order, especially in the first stanza?
2. **Recognizing Repetition of Words and Phrases.** The poet uses the word "blind" five times and the phrase "all but blind" three times. How does this repetition establish a pattern in the poem?
3. **Identifying Rhythm.** The **rhythm pattern** of a poem can be shown in writing. To do this, copy the poem, leaving extra space between lines. Then draw this mark, /, over each accented syllable and this mark, ◡, over each unaccented syllable. Here is the first stanza of "All But Blind" with the rhythm marked:

   /   ◡   /
   All but blind
   ◡   ◡   /   ◡   /
   In his chambered hole
   /   ◡   /
   Gropes for worms
   ◡   /   /   /
   The four-clawed Mole.

   Figure out the rhythm pattern for the other three stanzas of the poem. One of the stanzas will be slightly different from this basic pattern. Which stanza has a different pattern? Can you think of any reason the poet would want it to sound different?
4. **Identifying Theme.** A poet expresses his or her personal beliefs in poetry. Not everyone will agree with what the poet says. What general statement about life is the writer of "All But Blind" making? Can you explain why some people will not agree with this statement?

Answers to Study Questions

Developing Comprehension Skills

1. Not seeing well, the four-clawed mole gropes for worms in his hole with many rooms.

2. The three animals have found ways to survive even though they can't see well. They all are able to feed and find shelter for themselves.

3. The speaker compares himself to the animals because he feels that there are many things that he can't understand. There may even be things that he doesn't know exist. Like the animals, he can survive, but only in a very limited way. The "Someone" is probably God.

Challenge. The speaker has the power to see that his understanding is limited. The animals do not know that they are limited. They don't have the power to think about and evaluate themselves as people do.

Reading Literature: Poetry

1. To rhyme the second and fourth lines in the first stanza, the poet changes the usual order of subject and predicate. The normal word order is changed slightly in the fourth stanza, too ("So, blind to Someone I must be").

2. The poem begins and ends with sentences about blindness and the first line of every stanza begins with either "All but blind" or "And blind as are," emphasizing the importance of blindness.

3. The rhythm pattern is as follows:

Áll bŭt blínd
  Ĭn thĕ évenĭngský,
Thĕ hoódĕd Bát
  Twĭrls sóftlў bý.

Áll bŭt blínd
  Ĭn thĕ búrnĭng dáy

Developing Vocabulary Skills

Using Context Clues. Read the following sentences. Each underlined word was taken from one of the first four poems of this chapter. You can determine the meaning of each word by using one of these types of clues: example, comparison, or contrast. Write the meaning of the word. Also, identify the type of clue that helped you find the meaning.

1. The duels between the knights were more serious than the hand-to-hand fights they had practiced as young squires.
2. Hard rocks like granite are made up of coarse grains and crystals.
3. The ancient Egyptians quarried huge blocks of limestone with copper chisels, unlike the later method of cutting stone with iron tools.
4. Emily blundered her way through the math test. However, she made no mistakes on the science quiz.
5. Marta wore several pieces of jewelry, including two bracelets, a necklace, and a brooch.
6. The mole's chambered hole had, for example, a room to eat in and a separate room to sleep in.

Developing Writing Skills

Analytical Writing

1. **Explaining Your Opinion.** Which of the four poems that you have read in this chapter do you like best? Do you like it for its sounds, for the pictures it brings to mind, for its ideas, or for some other reason? Tell your choice and explain your reason or reasons. Remember that every reader may make a different choice, or may base the choice on different reasons.

Creative Writing

2. **Writing a Poem.** Three of the four poems you have read are organized in four-line stanzas. In two of the three poems, the second and fourth lines rhyme. The fourth poem was written in free verse, with no regular rhythm or rhyme. Choose one of these two forms, a four-line stanza with rhyme or a poem in free verse.

   Next, think about a good topic for a short poem. Your poem may have a serious theme, like the four poems in this section. It may have a lighter theme, if you prefer. Try to think of a topic you might discuss with your friends in conversation. Then turn it into a poem. Make your poem no longer than twelve lines long.

predicate, putting the subject, "The four-clawed Mole," last. You may wish to have students practice reversing sentences such as the following:

Across the prairie galloped the buffalo.

On a high tree branch waits the vulture.

Question 2. Have students explain how these animals manage without the ability to see during the day.

Question 3. After students have discussed how the speaker compares himself to the animals, note the capital *S* in "Someone." Explain that references to God are usually capitalized.

Challenge Question. The speaker imagines that he must seem blind to "Someone" with greater powers than he. How does the power to think make him different from the animals? (Critical Reading)

Reading Literature: Poetry

Question 1. Remind students of the unusual word order discussed in **Developing Comprehension Skills, 1.**

Question 2. Have students point out where the repetition occurs.

Question 3. After students have written the poem and its rhythm pattern on paper, write the poem on the board. Have three students indicate the rhythm pattern above the words. Have the class compare the pattern on the board with the ones on their papers.

Question 4. Read and discuss the question.

Developing Vocabulary Skills

Have a student read the directions for **Using Context Clues** on page 257. Make sure that students understand the directions and can recognize example, compar-

The Barn-Owl blunders
  On her way.

And blind as are
  These three to me,
So, blind to Someone
  I must be.

The last stanza has a slightly different pattern in the first and second lines. Its meaning is different from the other stanzas' meanings. They tell about animals, and the last stanza tells about a person.

4. Possible themes: There is much that people can't understand. People shouldn't feel too proud, because they aren't as smart as they think they are. There is a Person much greater and more powerful than we are. Answers to the second part of the question will vary. (Possible answer: People who don't believe in God may feel that man is the highest and most knowledgeable form of life.)

Developing Vocabulary Skills

1. duels—fights, comparison
2. granite—hard rocks, example
3. quarried—dug out, contrast
4. blundered—made mistakes, contrast
5. brooch—a certain kind of jewelry, example
6. chambered—having rooms, example

Developing Skills in Study and Research

1. Langston Hughes: *The Big Sea, I Wonder As I Wander, The Panther and the Lash*

Emily Dickinson: No books published during her lifetime.

(continued on page 258)

ison, and contrast clues. You may wish to have them reread pages 246 and 247 and use these pages as a reference tool. Have them complete the exercise independently.

Developing Writing Skills

Read and discuss the two assignments. Then have each student choose and complete one of the two.

Question 1. Emphasize that students must explain the reasons why they chose certain poems as their favorites.

Pre-Writing. Have students read all four poems again. Have each student pick his or her favorite poems. Then have the students list the things they like about their chosen poems. Have them notice if most of the reasons they like the poem can be grouped under *Sounds, Images,* or *Ideas.* Have them write their topic sentences for their paragraphs.

Writing. Urge students to include at least two or three reasons why they chose the poems they did. Allow sufficient time for the students to write their first drafts.

Revising. Have students exchange papers. Have partners list the reasons why the writers liked their chosen poems. If the reasons are unclear, allow time for revisions.

Question 2. Students will use their understanding of regular rhythm, free verse, and rhyme in writing a poem.

Pre-Writing. Have students reread "The Dream Keeper" (free verse) and "The Courage That My Mother Had" and "All But Blind" (regular rhythm, rhyming second and fourth lines). Have them point out the poems that have rhyming lines and the poem that was written in free verse. Ask each student to make a list of possible topics—things he or she thinks about or talks about. Have students think about what they can say about each topic and then choose the one for which they have the most to say. Have them decide whether they will write a poem with regular rhythm and rhyme or free verse.

Writing. Allow sufficient time for the students to write their first drafts.

Revising. Have each student read his or her poem to a partner. Have the partner determine whether the poem was written to have a regular rhythm or in free verse. If the poem is supposed to have regular rhythm, have the partner note any places where the rhythm seems forced or unnatural. Have the partners work together to improve the rhythm of the lines.

Developing Skills in Study and Research

Have the students read the directions for **Discovering the Quickest Way To**

Developing Skills in Study and Research

Discovering the Quickest Way To Find Information. The major purpose of the card catalog is to direct library users to specific books. It is useful in other ways, too. Each card provides some important facts about the book and author listed. Sometimes you can get all the information you need from the card catalog itself, without going on to the books listed. This exercise will help you use the card catalog to its fullest.

First, look up one of these writers in the card catalog of your school or public library: Langston Hughes, Emily Dickinson, Edna St. Vincent Millay, Walter de la Mare. (They are the poets whose poems you have just read.) Use the information in the card catalog to answer the following questions:

1. Did the poet write complete books? List some titles.
2. Which of the poet's books are in this library?
3. Did the poet write anything that is not poetry? Give the title or titles.
4. When was the poet born? When did he or she die?

Next, choose a general encyclopedia in your school or local library. Look up the same poet. In the encyclopedia article for that writer, look for the answers to the four questions above.

Last, compare the information you got from each source. Which facts were you able to learn from both the card catalog and the encyclopedia? Which were in only one source? Which questions were answered more clearly or more completely in the encyclopedia?

Developing Skills in Speaking and Listening

Interpreting the Mood of a Poem. Before reading a poem aloud, you must understand its mood. You should read it over several times, asking yourself questions about the person making the statements in the poem. For example, for Langston Hughes's "The Dream Keeper," you might ask such questions as these:

> What kind of person would care about the dreams of others? What kind of person would want to save those dreams, to wrap them up and protect them? If you were that person, what tone would you use

(continued from page 257)

Edna St. Vincent Millay: *Renascence and Other Poems, A Few Figs from Thistles, Second April, The Harp Weaver and Other Poems, Make Bright the Arrows, Collected Sonnets, Collected Lyrics*

Walter de la Mare: *The Listeners and Other Poems, The Fleeting and Other Poems, Collected Poems, Inward Companion*

2. Answers will vary according to the library used.

3. Hughes: Essay—"The Negro Artist and the Racial Movement." *The Big Sea* (autobiography)

Dickinson: Nothing that was not poetry

Millay: Wrote a libretto for an opera, *The King's Henchman*

de la Mare: Wrote a novel, *Memoirs of a Midget*

4. Hughes: Born February 1, 1902. Died May 22, 1967.

Dickinson: Born December 10, 1830. Died May 15, 1886.

Millay: Born February 22, 1892. Died October 19, 1950.

de la Mare: Born April 25, 1873. Died June 22, 1956.

to speak to dreamers? Would you use any gestures? Is there any place in the poem you should pause in order to make a point?

Prepare to read aloud one of the four poems you have read so far in this chapter. If you choose "The Dream Keeper," use the above questions. If you choose one of the others, think of similar questions for yourself. When you are ready, present the poem to a group. You may read it or, if you prefer, recite it from memory.

Ocean Park #114, 1979, RICHARD DIEBENKORN.
Private Collection, Toronto. Courtesy of M. Knoedler and Co., Inc., New York City.

Find Information on page 258. Schedule a visit to a library or assign the exercise for homework. Discuss the students' findings together.

Developing Skills in Speaking and Listening

Have a student read **Interpreting the Mood of a Poem** on pages 258 and 259 to the class. Have each student choose one poem to read aloud, perhaps the poem he or she selected for **Developing Writing Skills, 1.** Allow time for students to present their poems to small groups.

About the Art

Earlier in his career, Richard Diebenkorn (born 1922), a West Coast artist, depicted recognizable figures and landscapes in his paintings. In recent years, his work has become more abstract. *Ocean Park #114,* one of a series of paintings with the same title, is a seascape, though it has none of the traditional elements of a seascape. There is no recognizable coastline, no breaking waves, no seagulls. And yet, through color and composition, the artist is able to evoke the sea, giving us a sense of open space and light. The painting is a variety of ocean-blue and green color tones, and the canvas is criss-crossed by lines that perhaps suggest the horizon line between sea and sky, or the "line" where the sea meets the shore, or an aerial view. The name of the series, *Ocean Park,* comes from the section of Santa Monica, California, where Diebenkorn has his studio.

Objectives

- To recognize and appreciate poetry as a form of literature
- To understand the shape of a poem
- To recognize onomatopoeia
- To apply literal, interpretive, and critical reading skills to a selection

Preparing the Students

Essential Vocabulary. There is no difficult vocabulary in this selection.

Motivation. Have the students read the introductory paragraph at the top of page 260 and state in their own words what they should try to find out as they read this poem.

Presenting the Selection

1. Read "Magic Words To Feel Better" to the students. Have the students read the poem silently to themselves once more, and then call on a volunteer to read it aloud.

2. Administer the **Check Test** at the bottom of this page.

3. Remind students that the introduction asked them to decide what the speaker wants. Have students give their answers.

4. Develop the study questions as suggested in **Using the Study Questions** on page 261.

Special Populations

ESL. After "Magic Words To Feel Better" on page 260 has been read, define "mind's eye" for the students.

Encouraging Independent Reading

Some students may be interested in finding other poems that create a positive feeling (joy, hope, enthusiasm) in the reader for an oral presentation to the class. Suggest the following poetry collections:

Pictures That Storm Inside My Head, edited by Richard Peck

Alone Amid All This Noise, edited by Ann Reit

Strings: A Gathering of Family Poems, selected by Paul B. Janeczko

An Anthology of Concrete Poetry, edited by Emmett Williams

Remind the students that the tone of their voices should reflect the happy mood of the poem.

As you read this poem, decide what the speaker wants. The title gives you a clue.

Magic Words To Feel Better

NETSILIK ESKIMO

SEA GULL
who flaps his wings
over my head
                    in the blue air,

you GULL up there
dive down
                come here
take me with you
                    in the air!

Wings flash by
my mind's eye
and I'm up there sailing
in the cool air,
                    a–a–a–a–a–ah,
                                        in the air.

Check Test

1. What does the speaker want the gull to do? (to take the speaker into the air)

2. What happens to the speaker at the end of the poem? (He flies into the sky in his imagination.)

Answers to Study Questions

Developing Comprehension Skills

1. In the first and second stanzas, the speaker talks to the gull. In the third stanza, the speaker talks to the reader.

2. The speaker envies the sea gull. He asks the gull to dive down and take him up in the air.

3. In the third stanza, the mood changes from hopeful and waiting to joyful and relaxed. Before the third stanza, the speaker longs to fly, and during the last stanza, the speaker gets his wish.

Multi-Feathered Bird, 1961, KENOJUAK.
Reproduced with the permission of the West Baffin Eskimo Cooperative.
Cape Dorset, N.W.T., Canada.

Developing Comprehension Skills

Literal Reading
1. To whom is the speaker talking in the first stanza? In the second stanza? In the third stanza?

Interpretive Reading
2. How does the speaker feel about the sea gull?

Interpretive Reading
3. During the poem, the speaker changes the mood. Where does the change come? Explain the change.

Interpretive Reading
4. Does the speaker actually fly at the end of this poem? If not, how does the speaker get the feeling of flying?

Reading Literature: Poetry

1. **Understanding the Shape of a Poem.** Sometimes the way a poem is printed adds to its message. How does this poem make the reader see that "in the air" is an important phrase?

2. **Recognizing Onomatopoeia.** The term **onomatopoeia** refers to words that sound like what they are describing, such as the *clop-clop* of horses' hooves. In this poem, the made-up word *a-a-a-a-a-ah* suggests what its stanza is describing. What action or feeling does it bring to your mind? If it were dropped from the stanza, what idea or feeling would the poem lose?

3. **Understanding Theme.** Explain how the title, "Magic Words To Feel Better," is right for this poem.

You may wish to challenge the students further by encouraging them to find musical accompaniments to their poems that will enhance the mood.

Using the Study Questions

It is recommended that students always read and answer the questions in **Developing Comprehension Skills** in class discussion. Whenever possible, they should also read the questions in **Reading Literature** together and discuss the answers.

Developing Comprehension Skills

Questions 1 and 2. Have students give evidence from the poem to support their answers.

Question 3. Have students find the place in the poem where the speaker stops talking to the gull and have them identify the change in feeling this creates.

Question 4. After the students answer this question, have them point out the phrase that refers to the speaker's imagination ("mind's eye").

Reading Literature: Poetry

Question 1. Have students notice that "in the air" is given special treatment in the poem.

Question 2. Have several students describe the action or feeling they experience. Encourage them to include details in their descriptions.

Question 3. Read and discuss the question.

4. The speaker doesn't really fly, but has looked at the gull so long, and wished so hard, that he imagines that he is flying.

Reading Literature: Poetry

1. The poet puts "in the air" on a separate line and places it to the right of the other lines.

2. Answers may vary slightly. The word may make readers picture a gull gliding through the air without using its wings, effortlessly. If it were dropped, the poem would lose that image as well as the feeling of freedom and release.

3. The words of this poem lift the reader from the ground up into the air with the gull. They give a free and happy feeling. In this way, they are almost like magic words that lift readers from sadness to happiness.

About the Art

Printmaking was first introduced to the Eskimos in Cape Dorset in 1958. Superb sculptors and craftsmen by tradition, Eskimo artists used their highly developed carving skills to make stone cut prints. In this process, a design or shape is traced onto the surface of the stone. The artist then carves out the surrounding area so that when the block is inked only the raised surface receives the ink and makes the print. Eskimo artists often depict scenes from nature, especially animals (see *About the Art* on page 176).

The Cape Dorset artist Kenojuak (born 1927) often takes birds as her subjects. *Multi-Feathered Bird* shows a bird in flight. The stylized feathers and wings radiate from the simple shape of the bird's body like the rays of the sun.

Objectives

- To recognize and appreciate poetry as a form of literature
- To understand metaphors
- To apply literal, interpretive, and critical reading skills to a selection

Preparing the Students

Essential Vocabulary. The words presented here are essential to the understanding of the selection.

Write the following words and their definitions on the board. Have students read the words and their meanings. Explain that they will encounter these words in reading this poem.

solitary—alone
pilgrim—traveler
foreign—outside one's own country
stray—wander
staff—strong stick that travelers use to help them walk
lot—fate
comrade—friend

Motivation. Have the students read the introductory paragraph at the top of page 262 and state in their own words what they should try to find out as they read this poem.

Presenting the Selection

1. Have the students read "The Song by the Way" silently. Then have four volunteers each read one stanza aloud.

2. Make sure that everyone has understood the poem by administering the **Check Test** at the bottom of this page.

3. Have students answer the question posed in the introduction.

4. Develop the study questions as suggested in **Using the Study Questions** on page 263. That section also provides challenge questions for further discussion, as needed.

The Song by the Way

Imagine walking alone from town to town. What would you take along? Read to see what this person takes.

FRANCISCO A. de ICAZA

A solitary pilgrim I;
Through foreign lands I stray;
Yet am I not alone—my song
Goes with me all the way.

And if the night around be black,
I make it bright as day;
I sing, and then the song lights up
The darkness of the way.

I do not sigh for weariness
However far I stray;
The heavenly staff of song makes brief
The distance of the way.

Ah, sad indeed that pilgrim's lot
Who goes along all day,
Nor has, for comrade of his march,
A song along the way!

Check Test

1. What keeps the pilgrim from feeling alone? (his song)

2. How does a song help when the night is black? (A song lights up the darkness.)

3. Whom does the pilgrim feel sorry for? (any pilgrim who doesn't have a song)

Answers to Study Questions

Developing Comprehension Skills

1. a solitary pilgrim

2. The pilgrim goes through foreign lands but never feels alone and lonely. Sometimes the night is black, but a song lights it up. The pilgrim travels far but is never weary, because a song is like a staff that makes the distance seem shorter.

3. Answers will vary. *Song* could also refer to memories, dreams, or plans.

Challenge 1. Possible answers: Sailors often sing sea chanties to help them

Shepherd Showing Travellers Their Way, 1857, JEAN FRANCOIS MILLET.
The Corcoran Gallery of Art. William A. Clark collection.

Developing Comprehension Skills

Literal Reading 1. Who is speaking in this poem?

Literal Reading 2. Name one difficulty the speaker faces and the thing that helps him through that difficulty.

Interpretive Reading 3. The word *song* may refer only to a melody. However, can you think of some other things, such as "hopes," that it might stand for?

Reading Literature: Poetry

1. **Recognizing Rhyme and Rhythm.** Is the rhythm in this poem mostly regular or mostly irregular? What is somewhat unusual about the rhyming words in this poem? How do the patterns of rhythm and rhyme help to give the reader the idea of a long, steady hike?

2. **Understanding Metaphors.** This poem uses three different metaphors to show the importance of the speaker's song. In the second stanza, the speaker says the song "lights up the darkness," comparing it to the sun. In the third and fourth stanzas the speaker compares a song to two other things. What are those things? What does the speaker mean by each comparison?

Using the Study Questions

It is recommended that students always read and answer the questions in **Developing Comprehension Skills** in class discussion. Whenever possible, they should also read the questions in **Reading Literature** together and discuss the answers.

Developing Comprehension Skills

Questions 1 and 2. Read and discuss the questions.

Question 3. Have students suggest the ideas that cheer them up when they are feeling down.

Challenge Question 1. Can you think of any other individuals or groups of people who sing to make their jobs easier? (Critical Reading)

Challenge Question 2. Have you ever used a song to help make you feel better or to make a job go quicker? Explain your answer. (Critical Reading)

Reading Literature: Poetry

Question 1. Read the poem aloud, exaggerating the regular rhythm. At the same time, record the rhythm pattern for each stanza on the board. Ask students whether the pattern is regular or irregular. Then have volunteers list the rhyming words for each stanza on the board and ask the class what they notice about all the words. Have students answer the final part of the question in discussion.

Question 2. Remind students that metaphors are not always expressed obviously. Readers need to make inferences about comparisons. Have individual students read the metaphors aloud. Discuss their meanings with the students.

perform their tasks. Marching soldiers sometimes sing. Hikers sing marching songs, too.

Challenge 2. Answers will vary depending on students' experiences.

Reading Literature: Poetry

1. The rhythm is mostly regular. All the rhyming words rhyme with each other (they all rhyme with *way*). The steady patterns of rhythm and rhyme are like the regular strides of a walker who has a long way to go.

2. The song is compared to a staff in the third stanza and a comrade in the fourth stanza. The pilgrim depends on his song, just as a walker leans on his or her staff. A song is like a comrade because it keeps the traveler company and is always there when he needs it.

About the Art

The Barbizon School was the name given to a group of French painters who painted directly from nature. They sought to advance landscape painting in its own right rather than as a backdrop to mythological or religious subjects. Jean Francois Millet (1814-1875), a principal member of this group, was less interested in the countryside than in the peasants who inhabited it. Millet did not believe that painting should depict prominent people only. Instead, he painted men and women at work in the fields, or as in this picture, a shepherd and his flock. He painted them without sentimentality, showing their simplicity and quiet dignity.

Objectives

- To recognize and appreciate poetry as a form of literature
- To understand the effect of repetition
- To apply literal, interpretive, and critical reading skills to a selection
- To make inferences in poetry
- To infer word meaning from context
- To classify poems according to moods
- To understand how to use the encyclopedia and card catalog
- To understand how reading techniques affect the listener

Preparing the Students

Essential Vocabulary. The words presented here are essential to the understanding of the selection.

Have the students use the context clues in the following sentences to determine the meanings of the underlined words.

essence resolve

1. The essence of any thing is the quality that sets it apart from anything else. The essence is the most important part.
2. I made a resolve, or a firm decision, to save my money.

Motivation. Have the students read the introductory paragraph at the top of page 264 and state in their own words what they should try to find out as they read this poem.

Presenting the Selection

1. Read "I Was Born Today" aloud to the students. Have the students read the poem silently, and then ask for volunteers to read stanzas of the poem aloud.

2. Administer the **Check Test** at the bottom of this page.

3. Remind the students that the introduction to the poem asked them to find out what the poet has to say about starting over. Have them answer the questions.

4. Develop the study questions as suggested in **Using the Study Questions** beginning on page 265. That section also provides a challenge question for further discussion, if needed.

Reinforcing the Lesson

To reteach, reinforce, or extend the skills in this lesson, see the following:

Skills Practice Book, Green Level—pages 125 through 127

I Was Born Today

AMADO NERVO

When things don't work out, wouldn't it be good sometimes to start all over? Find out what this poet has to say about starting over.

Every day that dawns, you must say
to yourself,
"I was born today!
The world is new to me.
This light that I behold
Strikes my unclouded eyes for the
first time;
The rain that scatters its crystal drops
Is my baptism!

"Then let us live a pure life,
A shining life!
Already, yesterday is lost. Was it bad?
Was it beautiful?
. . . Let it be forgotten.
And of that yesterday let there remain
only the essence,
The precious gold of what I loved
and suffered
As I walked along the road . . .

"Today, every moment shall bring
feelings of well being and cheer.
And the reason for my existence,

Take-Off, 1983, JOANNE CULVER.

About the Art

Joanne Culver (born 1947) has an MFA degree in Electronic Visualization. She is interested in liberating images from electronic screens and in creating the appearance of movement without actually producing movement. *Take-Off* is a computer generated work. Culver produced the image on a mini-computer, having written the software herself. It might be viewed as a landscape in which the upper, blue portion is the sky, and the lower half, dominated by earth tones, is the land. In addition, the series of lines and the "drops of rain" create an afterimage, similar to that left by a rocket taking off.

Check Test

1. What should you say to yourself each day? (I was born today!)

2. What does the speaker say is the reason for existence? (to spread happiness all over the world)

My most urgent resolve,
Will be to spread happiness all over the world,
To pour the wine of goodness into the
eager mouths around me . . .

"My only peace will be the peace of others;
Their dreams, my dreams;
Their joy, my joy;
My crystal tear,
The tear that trembles on the eyelash of another;
My heartbeat,
The beat of every heart that throbs
Throughout worlds without end!"

Every day that dawns, you must say to yourself,
"I was born today!"

Developing Comprehension Skills

Literal Reading 1. What does the speaker tell you to do each day? What does he suggest you do about the past?

Literal Reading 2. What does the speaker believe should be the attitude of every person toward other people?

Critical Reading 3. The mood of this poem is very cheerful and optimistic. The poem asks the reader to "spread happiness" and to see each day as a new beginning. Would it be easy to put the ideas of this poem into practice? Give a reason for your opinion.

Reading Literature: Poetry

1. **Understanding Rhythm and Repetition.** In "I Was Born Today," the poet does not use rhyme or regular rhythm. Instead, he emphasizes important ideas by repeating them in slightly different words. For

Answers to Study Questions

Developing Comprehension Skills

1. You should treat each day as if it were the first day of your life. Forget the past and let only the essence of your yesterdays affect your life.

2. The speaker believes that all people should feel a union with everyone else in the world. Their goals should be to spread happiness and goodness.

3. Opinions will vary. Most students will say that it is difficult to remain cheerful and good all the time, especially when you are faced with problems.

Challenge. Opinions will vary. Some students may feel that you should remember yesterday, especially if it was beautiful, since the memory could make you happy. Others may agree with the speaker. You should forget yesterday because it is done and you cannot change it or relive it. You can only learn from it and then move on.

Reading Literature: Poetry

1. Similar phrases:
- **a.** a pure life—a shining life
- **b.** the reason for my existence—my most urgent resolve

(continued on page 266)

Using the Study Questions

It is recommended that students always read and answer the questions in **Developing Comprehension Skills** in class discussion. Whenever possible, they should also read the questions in the other categories together and discuss the answers.

Developing Comprehension Skills

Question 1. Read and discuss the question.

Question 2. Refer students to stanzas three and four for the answer to this question.

Question 3. Explain that this question asks students to formulate their own opinions. Emphasize that students should present logical reasons for their opinions.

Challenge Question. The speaker in this poem tells you to forget yesterday, no matter whether it was bad or beautiful. Do you think this is good advice? Tell why you agree or disagree. (Critical Reading)

Reading Literature: Poetry

Question 1. Read and discuss the question.

Question 2. Have students read aloud the lines that answer the questions.

Question 3. Help students see that the harsh process that gold ore goes through doesn't destroy it but makes the product, gold, more valuable. Help students relate that process to the difficulties everyone faces in life.

Question 4. Encourage students to express that theme as they see it. There is no single statement that expresses it best.

Developing Vocabulary Skills

Have the students read **Inferring Word Meaning from Context** on page 266. Students should be familiar with the skill of inference already. Make sure that students understand the directions. Have them complete the exercise independently. Discuss the answers together.

Developing Writing Skills

Read and discuss the two assignments. Then have each student choose and complete one of the two.

Question 1. This assignment involves categorizing poems based on mood. Many students may benefit from working with partners.

Pre-Writing. Direct the students to reread all seven poems that have been studied so far. Then have them list the names of all seven poems on a sheet of paper. Beside each title, have students describe the mood of the poem. When they are finished, ask students to group poems with similar moods together. Have them write topic sentences for paragraphs that explain why those poems were grouped together. If, for example, a student has three groups, he or she should write three topic sentences.

Writing. Have students write a paragraph about each group of poems. Allow sufficient time for the students to write their first drafts.

Revising. Have students exchange papers with partners. Ask the partners to comment to the writers on whether the reasons for the groupings were clear and logical. Allow time for revisions.

Question 2. This question asks the students to write a poem about a personal experience. Point out that the directions for this assignment do not mention rhyme or rhythm.

Pre-Writing. Have the students brainstorm about possible subjects for their poems. You may want to record these on the board. Have each student choose his or her topic. Have students make lists of details they could include in their poems. The details could describe sights, smells, sounds, and emotions.

Writing. Allow sufficient time for the students to write their first drafts.

Revising. Have students share their poems in small groups. Ask listeners to restate the experience described in the poem in everyday language. If the listeners have difficulty in restating the poem, have the writer revise it, this time including more clues about what is happening.

Developing Skills in Study and Research

Have students read the directions to **Using Sources** on page 267 and 268 silently. Have them write the answers to the questions. Then schedule a visit to the library, so students can verify their answers. Students may find that their answers are too general. Encourage them to make their answers specific enough to be of real use. Discuss students' findings at a later class.

Developing Skills in Speaking and Listening

Remind the students of the qualities of good public speaking: speaking the words

example, in the first stanza, after stating "I was born today," he says "The world is new to me." Then he gives two examples of how it is new: he is seeing the light for the first time, and the rain is his baptism. For each of the phrases below, find another phrase that states almost the same idea:

a. a pure life
b. the reason for my existence
c. to spread happiness

2. **Making Inferences in Poetry.** Not every day is peaceful and joyful. Is there any indication in the poem that the speaker knows this? What lines in the poem suggest that the speaker has known unhappiness? Does the speaker realize that everyone is going to have bad days? What makes you think so?

3. **Recognizing Metaphors.** Gold ore is a combination of small particles of gold with large amounts of other, mostly worthless materials. The process of separating the gold from the other materials is called *refining*. In order to refine gold, the ore is crushed, heated, and treated with chemicals that pull the ore apart. In the second stanza of "I Was Born Today," find the metaphor that uses gold. What is being compared to gold? How is life like the process of refining gold?

4. **Understanding Theme.** What is the theme of this poem?

Developing Vocabulary Skills

Inferring Word Meaning from Context. Frequently you can figure out the meaning of a word from the sentence in which it appears, even though there are no specific context clues. This is called **inferring** the meaning. For example, read this sentence:

> Joan's reason for being late seemed *plausible*, so the teacher excused her.

From the meaning of the sentence as a whole, you can guess that *plausible* means "believable" or "apparently acceptable."

The following sentences about the poems in this section use terms that may be new to you. Use the information in the sentence to find the meaning of each underlined word or phrase. On your paper, copy the underlined word or phrase and write the definition you have inferred from the sentence context.

(continued from page 265)

c. to spread happiness—to pour the wine of goodness into the eager mouths around me

2. Lines that suggest the speaker has known unhappiness:

And of that yesterday let there remain only the essence,
The precious gold of what I loved and suffered
As I walked along the road.

The speaker knows that others will have bad days as inferred in the following lines:

My crystal tear,
The tear that trembles on the eyelash of another.

3. Gold is compared to the essence of yesterday, what the speaker has loved and suffered. Life is like refining gold because the problems you face in life are like the crushing and heating that gold has to go through. The knowledge you gain as you overcome those problems is as precious as gold.

4. Possible theme: Every day you get a new chance to start your life over.

Developing Vocabulary Skills

1. myopic—almost unable to see *(Myopia* is the inability to see distant things

1. The mole's eyes are so myopic that the poet calls the animal "all but blind."
2. In "The Dream Keeper," the poet coined the terms *cloud-cloth* and *heart-melodies*.
3. The living speaker had need of the courage that was superfluous to her dead mother.
4. A song cheered the traveler during his peregrinations.
5. The poem "Magic Words To Feel Better" evokes the feeling of flying or floating in the air.
6. In "I Was Born Today," the speaker expresses a desire for empathy with others when he says, "My only peace will be the peace of others; Their dreams, my dreams; Their joy, my joy."

Developing Writing Skills

Analytical Writing

1. **Comparing Moods.** Some of the selections in Poems About Individual Growth had a somewhat discouraged mood. Others had a very positive, enthusiastic mood. A few had a mood somewhere between these two feelings. Which poems would you place in each group? Explain your choices in a paragraph or more.

Creative Writing

2. **Describing an Experience in a Poem.** "Magic Words" tells about a very simple experience. The speaker sees the soaring gull and feels like flying with it. In imagination, the speaker sails in the cool air.

   Think of some simple, natural thing that has cheered you up or made you feel excited. Write a poem about it. Speak to the animal or object in some part of the poem. End by telling how you feel.

Developing Skills in Study and Research

Using Sources. One of the poems in the group you have just read was by an Eskimo poet. Two of them were by poets from South America. Suppose you wanted to find out more about poems from other lands. How would you search for information or more poems? Choose either Eskimo poetry or poetry from South America, and answer both questions below.

1. How would you use the encyclopedia to find out more about the kind of poetry you chose? Tell at least two topics you might look up to

clearly and loudly enough to be heard, using expression in your voice that reflects the mood, and having eye contact with your listeners. Point out to the students that they should not pause or stop at the end of a line of poetry unless a punctuation mark indicates it.

Then read to the class **Listening to Poetry** on page 268, and group the students in small groups of three to five.

You may wish to complete this exercise in two sessions. In the first session, students should choose the poems they want to use and should prepare them. In the second session, students should present their poems and answer the evaluative questions on page 268.

Select one person to be recordkeeper and spokesperson for each large group. Have these students report to the class on their groups' responses to the questions.

clearly. This exact meaning is not obvious from the context.)

2. coined—invented
3. superfluous—not needed
4. peregrinations—travels
5. evokes—creates
6. empathy—a feeling that someone else's experiences are your own experiences

Developing Skills in Study and Research

1. Information about Eskimo or South American poetry could be listed under *Eskimo, South America, Poetry, Literature,* or the names of the poets whose poems appear in this chapter. The information in these articles would be general, but the articles might mention other subjects that students could consult for more specific information.

2. The card catalog might list *Poetry—Eskimo* or *Poetry—South American.* Students may also find related information under the names of the groups of people or countries involved. Under each heading you would expect to find the title of the book, the author, a brief summary, and the copyright date.

begin your search for information. Describe the sort of information you think you might find in these articles.

2. How would you use the card catalog to find out more about the kind of poetry you chose? List at least two different headings you might look up to find references to useful books. Tell what sort of material you might find listed under each heading.

Developing Skills in Speaking and Listening

Listening to Poetry. You have learned that in a poem every word is important. Therefore, when you listen to a poem, it is important to listen very carefully. This activity will help you think about and improve your listening habits.

Work in groups of three to five. Each group should choose one of the poems in this section, Poems About Individual Growth. One person in the group should prepare to read the entire poem; the other members should each choose and prepare one stanza.

Two or more groups should join to listen to each other's presentations. First, each poem should be read by the students who prepared one stanza each. Then have the entire group discuss these questions:

1. Does the speed at which poetry is read change with the reader?
2. What effect does a change in reading speed have on the listener?
3. Are there any skills that may help a listener adjust to different reading speeds?
4. Does hearing someone read a poem make it easier to understand the poem than just reading it silently? Why or why not?

Second, those students who prepared entire poems should present their poems. Then the entire group should discuss these questions:

5. Is it easier to listen to a poem of four or more stanzas when it is read by one person or when it is read by several persons? Are there some advantages to each way? What are those advantages?
6. Is it easier to listen to a short poem, of three stanzas or fewer, read by one person or by more than one person? What are the advantages and disadvantages of each way?
7. What should a listener do to develop listening skills for any of these situations?

Poems About Animals

Very often a poet invents a character as well as a poem. The poem sounds as if the character were talking, not the poet. The person speaking in any poem is called the **speaker**. When you read a poem, it is important for you to decide who the speaker is. It may be the poet. It may be an invented human character. It may even be an animal character!

Endangered Species: Bald Eagle, 1983, ANDY WARHOL.
Courtesy of Ronald Feldman Fine Arts, New York City, Photograph by D. James Dee.

Poems About Animals

Have the students read page 269 silently and then explain the term *speaker.* Then have them suggest what tone of voice they might expect the eagle in the painting to use if it were the speaker of a poem.

About the Art

Andy Warhol (born 1927) became famous in the 1960's for his paintings of Campbell's Soup cans and for multiple-image paintings from photographs of celebrities, such as Marilyn Monroe. He began his career as a commercial artist. He produced window displays, illustrated cookbooks, and designed greeting cards. Much of his notable work uses images found in the commercial media—magazines, newspapers, comic strips, advertising, billboards, and television.

Endangered Species: Bald Eagle is one painting from a series concerned with conservation. The viewer's attention is fixed on the blown-up detail of the eagle's head. The image heightened by color focuses our attention solely upon the beauty and majesty of this American treasure that is faced with possible extinction.

Reading Literature

This lesson builds on the lesson on pages 242 and 243, **Reading Literature: Poetry.** It focuses the students' attention on the shapes of poems, their rhyme schemes, and the distinction between narrative and lyric poems. The lesson ends with a discussion of mood as it is created by poets.

Preparing the Students

Ask the students for their personal preferences among the poems they have read so far. Have each student who names a favorite suggest a reason for choosing that poem. There should be enough variety of choices and reasons for you to point out that theme, sound, and imagery are only part of poetry. Explain that the next lesson will discuss certain features of poetry in greater detail.

Presenting the Lesson

1. Have the students read silently **More About the Elements of Poetry** and the first paragraph in **The Shapes of Poems**. Ask them to describe what stanzas are. Then have them read the next two paragraphs and explain what concrete poems and haikus are.

2. Call on a student to read aloud **Rhyme Scheme** on pages 270 and 271. Make sure the students understand the example. If time allows, have the students turn back to pages 253, 255, or 262, and analyze the rhyme scheme of the poem on each page.

3. Have students read **Narrative and Lyric Poems**. Ask them to define the two types of poems in their own words.

4. Call on students to read aloud the section on **Mood**. Make sure students understand the difference between *denotation* and *connotation.* Ask for examples of words with strong or little connotation in any of the poems they have read so far in this chapter. Ask, also, for one or more examples of informal language, or of formal language, in those poems. (Any student who has memorized other poems could be encouraged to cite examples from memory, where applicable.)

Reinforcing the Lesson

To reteach, reinforce, or extend the concepts in this lesson, see the following:

Skills Practice Book, Green Level—pages 128 and 129

Reading Literature: More About Poetry

More About the Elements of Poetry

You have already learned that a poem uses sounds and figures of speech to express its meaning. The information on these pages will help you see how a poet can make use of these elements.

The Shapes of Poems

Poems are organized according to **lines** rather than sentences. The lines are grouped in **stanzas** rather than paragraphs. The length of lines and of stanzas can vary, even within one poem.

Concrete Poems. Poets are very inventive. They think of every possible way to use words to get across their ideas. Sometimes they arrange their words to form a shape. That shape tells more about the subject of their poem. A poem whose shape reminds you of the subject of the poem is called a **concrete poem.** For example, a poem about a kite might be shaped like a kite.

Haiku. In this section, you will read two haikus. A *haiku* is a poem with seventeen syllables. Usually it has three lines, five syllables in the first line, seven in the second line, and five in the last line. Usually, a haiku is about one thing. It describes the thing so clearly that you can picture it in your mind. The haiku gives one, sensory image.

Rhyme Scheme

In poems with rhyme, the rhyming words usually form a pattern. This pattern is called **rhyme scheme.** It is possible to keep track of, or chart, the rhyme scheme of a poem. To do this, you label every line in the poem with a letter of the alphabet. Use the same letter for lines that end with words that rhyme. The rhyme scheme of the following poem has been labeled.

Lincoln was a long man. *a*
He liked the out of doors. *b*
He liked the wind blowing *c*
And the talk in country stores. *b*

Many different rhyme schemes are possible. Besides *a b c b*, some of the most common are these: *a a b b, a b a b, a b b a.*

Narrative and Lyric Poems

A poem can be either a narrative poem or a lyric poem. A **narrative poem** tells a story. Narrative poems are usually quite long. The epic poems of long ago that told of courageous adventures were narratives. So are a few of the poems you will read in the next section.

In a **lyric poem**, the poet expresses his or her personal emotions. A lyric poem seems almost like a song. It does not tell a story. Many examples of lyric poems are in this chapter.

Mood

The **mood** of a poem is the feeling the poem gives you. The mood is not created by accident. It is the result of the poet's efforts to choose the right words. The perfect word does two things: it communicates the meaning the poet has in mind; it stirs up in the reader the emotions and ideas the poet has in mind. That is why poets take into account both the **denotation** and the **connotation** of a word. The denotation of a word is its dictionary meaning. Its connotation consists of the thoughts and emotions it brings to your mind.

Poets can create a mood by the level of language they use. Informal language can give a casual, friendly, down-to-earth feeling. Formal language can make you feel serious and respectful.

Special Populations

LD, ESL. For suggestions in helping the students understand rhyme scheme, refer to the suggestions on page 117, in Chapter 3, concerning use of colored markers to set off rhyming words.

Objectives

- To recognize and appreciate poetry as a form of literature
- To understand the rhythm of a poem
- To apply literal, interpretive, and critical reading skills to a selection

Preparing the Students

Essential Vocabulary. Explain that a *jamcloset* is pictured on page 272.

Motivation. If some students have cats, have them share some interesting habits that their cats have. Allow other students to share behavior they have observed in cats. Then tell the class to turn to pages 272 and 273, examine the picture there, and, based on what they know about cats, explain what a real cat would probably do next in the same kind of situation.

Have the students read the introductory paragraph at the top of page 272 and state in their own words what they should try to find out as they read this poem.

Presenting the Selection

1. Have the students read "Poem" silently.

2. Make sure that everyone has read the poem by administering the **Check Test** at the bottom of this page.

3. Read the poem aloud to the class slowly, to emphasize the care with which the cat moves.

4. Develop the study questions as suggested in **Using the Study Questions** on page 273. A question there reminds students of the question posed in the introduction.

Poem

WILLIAM CARLOS WILLIAMS

Imagine a cat walking on a narrow, cluttered shelf. As you read this poem, can you find ways in which the poem suggests the care with which the cat moves?

As the cat
climbed over
the top of

the jamcloset
first the right
forefoot

carefully
then the hind
stepped down

into the pit of
the empty
flowerpot.

Check Test

1. What did the cat climb over? (the jamcloset)

2. Where were the cat's feet at the end of the poem? (in the pit of the empty flowerpot)

Answers to Study Questions

Developing Comprehension Skills

1. The cat's right forefoot went first, followed by the hind foot.

Developing Comprehension Skills

Literal Reading

1. What part of the cat moves first into the flowerpot? What part follows after?

Critical Reading

2. Reading this poem is much like watching a film. It simply describes what happens. Why do you think anyone would write about something so simple?

Reading Literature: Poetry

1. **Understanding Rhythm.** This poem has no rhyming words and no regular rhythm. Two techniques the poet uses, however, give the poem a cat-like rhythm: short lines and repeated phrases.
   a. Read the poem aloud, pausing very briefly at the end of every line. What does the shortness of the lines tell about the way the cat is moving?
   b. Find the first verb, *climbed.* It is followed by a phrase that tells where, *over the top,* and one that gives an added detail, *of the jamcloset.* Where is this pattern repeated?
2. **Identifying Mood.** Does this poem show any particular feeling about the cat? What mood did you feel as you read the poem?

Using the Study Questions

It is recommended that students always read and answer the questions in **Developing Comprehension Skills** in class discussion. Whenever possible, they should also read the questions in **Reading Literature** together and discuss the answers.

Developing Comprehension Skills

Question 1. Read and discuss the question.

Question 2. Explain that this question asks students to formulate an opinion.

Reading Literature: Poetry

Question 1. Call on a volunteer to read the poem aloud before discussing the first part of this question.

Question 2. Read and discuss the question.

2. Answers may vary. Possible answer: The poet enjoyed observing the cat's movements and wanted to recreate them in words.

Reading Literature: Poetry

1. Rhythm:
- **a.** The cat is using short movements.
- **b.** The word *stepped* is followed by *down into the pit* and *of the empty flowerpot.*

2. The cat is shown to be cautious and careful. This creates a mood of tension and suspense.

Objectives

- To recognize and appreciate poetry as a form of literature
- To understand patterns of rhyme
- To find examples of alliteration in a poem
- To understand simile and metaphor
- To apply literal, interpretive, and critical reading skills to a selection

Preparing the Students

Essential Vocabulary. The words presented here are essential to the understanding of the selection.

Have the students use the context clues in the following sentences to determine the meanings of the underlined words.

technique baton condenses

1. Technique is skill in doing something.
2. The conductor pointed her baton at the violin section, telling them when to play.
3. Cats seem to condense. They seem to make themselves smaller at times.

Motivation. Have the students read the introductory paragraph at the top of page 274 and state in their own words what they should try to find out as they read this poem.

Ask a student to look up the word *catalog* in a dictionary and read the definition aloud to the class. Remind them to look for the relationship between the meaning of the word and the meaning of the poem as they read the poem.

Presenting the Selection

1. Have the students read "Catalog" silently.

2. Make sure that everyone has read the poem by administering the **Check Test** at the bottom of this page.

3. Have volunteers read stanzas aloud. Remind students not to pause at the end of lines unless they see punctuation.

4. Remind students of the question posed in the introduction. Ask several students to identify the double meaning.

5. Develop the study questions as suggested in **Using the Study Questions** on page 275. That section also provides a challenge question for further discussion.

Special Populations

ESL. ESL students may need to work with a partner to complete question 1, **Understanding Patterns of Rhyme,** on page 275.

The title of this poem is a pun. Look up the meaning of the word catalog. Then read the poem and find the double meaning in its title.

Catalog

ROSALIE MOORE

Cats sleep fat and walk thin.
Cats, when they sleep, slump;
When they wake, stretch and begin
Over, pulling their ribs in.
Cats walk thin.

Cats wait in a lump,
Jump in a streak.
Cats, when they jump, are sleek
As a grape slipping its skin—
They have technique
Oh, cats don't creak.
They sneak.

Cats sleep fat.
They spread out comfort underneath
them
Like a good mat,
As if they picked the place
And then sat;
You walk around one
As if he were the City Hall
After that.

If male,
A cat is apt to sing on a major scale;
This concert is for everybody, this
Is wholesale.
For a baton, he wields a tail.

(He is also found,
When happy, to resound
With an enclosed and private sound.)

A cat condenses.
He pulls in his tail to go under bridges,
And himself to go under fences.
Cats fit
In any size box or kit,
And if a large pumpkin grew under one,
He could arch over it.

When everyone else is just ready to go
out,
The cat is just ready to come in.
He's not where he's been.
Cats sleep fat and walk thin.

Check Test

1. Name one thing a cat does when it sleeps. (Possible answers: slumps, spreads out comfort underneath it like a good mat)

2. What do cats do when they go under fences? (They pull in their tails.)

3. What do cats want to do when everyone else is ready to go out? (come in)

Answers to Study Questions

Developing Comprehension Skills

1. Cats become fat and thin, they wait in a lump and jump in a streak, they condense, and they arch their backs. It moves its tail like a baton and pulls it in when going under fences.

2. A cat "sings on a major scale" and will sometimes "resound with an enclosed and private sound."

3. A cat who has chosen its resting place is compared to the City Hall because it won't move. It expects everyone else to go around it.

Developing Comprehension Skills

Literal Reading 1. What are some of the changes in a cat's shape that this poem describes? In what different ways does the cat move its tail?

Literal Reading 2. Besides describing the appearance of a cat, this poem describes two of its sounds. Name them.

Interpretive Reading 3. Why is a cat who has chosen its resting place compared to the City Hall?

Interpretive Reading 4. Does the speaker seem to admire cats or dislike them? Explain your answer.

Reading Literature: Poetry

1. **Understanding Patterns of Rhyme.** Each stanza of this poem uses a different rhyme scheme. Which stanza matches each of the rhyme schemes shown below? Why do you suppose the poet did not stick to one pattern of stanza length and rhyme?

(a)	(b)	(c)	(d)	(e)	(f)	(g)
a	*a*	*a*	*a*	*a*	*a*	*a*
b	*b*	*b*	*a*	*b*	*b*	*a*
a	*a*	*a*	*a*	*b*	*b*	*b*
c	*a*	*c*		*c*	*b*	*a*
a	*a*	*c*		*b*		*a*
d		*d*		*b*		
e		*c*		*b*		
a						

2. **Finding Alliteration.** There are several examples of alliteration in this poem. In a few stanzas, one particular sound appears repeatedly, both at the beginning of words and in other positions. The use of this single sound helps to hold the stanza together.

   Find at least two examples of alliteration—that is, the use of the same sound at the beginning of several words found close together. Also, identify one sound that is used several times in the same stanza, not only at the beginnings of words.

3. **Understanding Simile and Metaphor.** Find similes in stanzas 2 and 3 and a metaphor in stanza 4. In each comparison, identify the two things being compared to each other. In what way are the two things alike? How does each comparison add to the feelings you are getting about cats?

Using the Study Questions

It is recommended that students always read and answer the questions in **Developing Comprehension Skills** in class discussion. Whenever possible, they should also read the questions in **Reading Literature** together and discuss the answers.

Developing Comprehension Skills

Questions 1 and 2. Have the students skim the poem to find and read aloud the words and phrases that answer the questions.

Question 3. Remind students of the meaning of *simile* and *metaphor* and ask which of these figures of speech this is. Ask students what some of the physical characteristics of City Hall are.

Question 4. Have students think about the connotations of the words the poet chose. Have them decide whether they are positive or negative.

Challenge Question. Does this poem give a realistic picture of a cat? Choose details that support your opinion. (Critical Reading)

Reading Literature: Poetry

Question 1. Write the poem on the board or on a transparency and work out the rhyme scheme together with the students.

Question 2. Together with the students, examine each stanza of the poem. First, look for repeated consonant sounds. Then, look for other repeated sounds. Have students examine the stanza for rhyming sounds, as well.

Question 3. Read and discuss the question.

---

4. The speaker seems to admire cats. The speaker uses words with positive connotations such as *sleek* and *technique.* The speaker seems to admire the independence, skill, and pride of cats.

Challenge. Most students will agree that this is a realistic picture of a cat. Any detail from the poem can be used to support the opinion.

Reading Literature: Poetry

1. **(a)** stanza 3; **(b)** stanza 1; **(c)** stanza 6; **(d)** stanza 5; **(e)** stanza 2; **(f)** stanza 7; **(g)** stanza 4.

The poet makes the rhymes and the rhyme pattern match the meaning of each stanza.

2. Alliteration—stanza 1: when they sleep, slump; stanza 2: sleek as a grape slipping its skin; stanza 3: picked the place; stanza 4: male, major; stanza 6: a cat condenses

Sound used several times—stanza 1: *n*; stanza 2: *k, m*; stanza 3: *d, t*; stanza 4: *l*; stanzas 5, 6, and 7: *n*.

3. Stanza 2—"Cats are sleek as a grape slipping its skin." The cat is compared to a grape. They both can move easily and quickly.

Stanza 3—"They spread out comfort underneath them like a good mat." Comfort is compared to a mat. Cats always find a way to get comfortable.

"You walk around one as if he were the City Hall." Cats who are settled down are like City Hall because they refuse to move. Cats expect people to respect them.

Stanza 4—"For a baton, he wields a tail." The cat's tail is compared to a baton. The cat swings the tail back and forth enthusiastically and confidently like a conductor directing an orchestra.

Each comparison adds to the reader's feeling of respect for cats.

Objectives

- To recognize and appreciate poetry as a form of literature
- To understand similes
- To apply literal, interpretive, and critical reading skills to a selection

Preparing the Students

Essential Vocabulary. There is no difficult vocabulary in this selection.

Motivation. Have the students read the introductory paragraph at the top of page 276 and state in their own words what they should try to find out as they read this poem.

Presenting the Selection

1. Have the students read "Sea Lions" silently.

2. Make sure that everyone has read the poem by administering the **Check Test,** at the bottom of this page.

3. Ask one or two volunteers to read the poem aloud.

4. Remind students of the question posed in the introduction. Ask several students for their answers.

5. Develop the study questions as suggested in **Using the Study Questions** on page 277. That section also provides a challenge question for further discussion, if needed.

Special Populations

ESL, LD. This poem is a good one to read to the class or put onto a tape recording to give students the opportunity to hear it read smoothly. Many students might find this poem difficult to read at first, having the habit of reading the words in phrases, stopping at the ends of the lines. After the students have heard the poem read through once, ask them to read it aloud to themselves, watching for the punctuation marks to cue them to pause in their reading.

Did you ever wonder how zoo animals like being in zoos? Read to find out how this poet might answer that question.

Sea Lions

VALERIE WORTH

The satin sea lions
Nudge each other
Toward the edge
Of the pool until
They fall like
Soft boulders
Into the water,
Sink down, slide
In swift circles,
Twist together
And apart, rise again
Snorting, climb
Up slapping
Their flippers on
The wet cement.
Someone said
That in all the zoo
Only the sea lions
Seem happy.

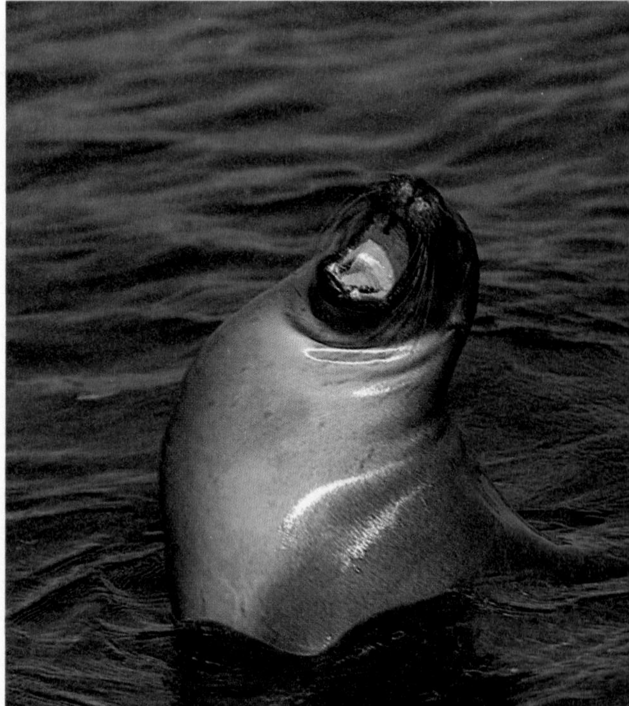

Sea Lion. Photo Researchers, Inc., New York City.

Check Test

1. What do the sea lions do under water? (They slide in circles and twist together and apart.)

2. What do the sea lions do when they reach the surface? (They snort and climb up, slapping their flippers on the cement.)

Developing Comprehension Skills

Interpretive Reading 1. Think of the sea lions you have seen in a zoo or on television. Why do you think the speaker calls them "satin"?

Literal Reading 2. Identify the line that tells these two facts about the animals: they are heavy, and they are flexible.

Interpretive Reading 3. Reread the last four lines of the poem. What has the rest of the poem said to support the statement in these lines?

Reading Literature: Poetry

1. **Understanding Sounds in a Poem.** In this poem, alliteration helps to suggest the movements of the sea lions. What sound do you hear at the beginning of words throughout the poem? Is it a hard sound or a soft sound? How does it relate to the sea lions' actions?

2. **Understanding Similes.** A simile says that two unlike things are alike in some way. Frequently, a good simile suggests several ways in which the two things are alike. For example, consider the simile in lines 5 to 7:

   They fall like
   Soft boulders
   Into the water.

   Comparing seals to boulders stresses the weight of the seals. It also stresses their size. It even suggests their color. In what way does it describe their movements?

Using the Study Questions

It is recommended that students always read and answer the questions in **Developing Comprehension Skills** in class discussion. Whenever possible, they should also read the questions in **Reading Literature** together and discuss the answers.

Developing Comprehension Skills

Question 1. Make sure that students can describe satin cloth before they try to answer this question.

Question 2. Explain that students should be able to find both facts in a single line.

Question 3. Have a student read the last four lines aloud. Ask individuals to suggest proofs for the statement from the poem and list them on the board.

Challenge Question. Do you agree that "in all the zoo only the sea lions seem happy"? If you disagree, tell what other animals seem happy. If you agree, explain why. (Critical Reading)

Reading Literature: Poetry

Question 1. Read and discuss the question.

Question 2. Make sure students can see how the lines suggest the weight, size, and color of the sea lions before asking them to answer the question.

Answers to Study Questions

Developing Comprehension Skills

1. Sea lions' wet fur looks as smooth and soft as satin.

2. Line 6—soft boulders

3. The sea lions play with each other by pushing each other into the water; they swim in circles as if they enjoy swimming; they seem to do tricks in the water, twisting around each other; and they enthusiastically snort and slap their flippers on the cement.

Challenge. If students disagree with the statement, they should suggest other animals that seem happy and describe the ways they show their contentment. If they agree, students should give reasons.

Reading Literature: Poetry

1. You hear the soft sound of *s* throughout the poem. It makes readers think of the smoothness, grace, and speed of the sea lions.

2. The movements of the sea lions are not forced or stiff. They are easy and natural.

Objectives

- To recognize and appreciate poetry as a form of literature
- To understand a concrete poem
- To apply literal, interpretive, and critical reading skills to a selection

Preparing the Students

Essential Vocabulary. Explain that mercury, a shiny silver element in liquid form, is often called *quicksilver.*

Encourage students to use context clues, a classroom dictionary, or the **Glossary** to find out the meanings of any words they do not understand.

Motivation. Have the students read the introductory paragraph at the top of page 278 and state in their own words what they should try to find out as they read this poem.

Presenting the Selection

1. Make sure students notice the unusual shape of this poem. Then have them read "Seal" silently.

2. Administer the **Check Test** at the bottom of this page.

3. Develop the study questions as suggested in **Using the Study Questions** on page 279. That section also provides a challenge question for further discussion, if needed.

The sea lions in Valerie Worth's poem moved softly and smoothly. Read William Jay Smith's poem. Pay special attention to the words that describe the seal's actions.

Seal

WILLIAM JAY SMITH

See how he dives
From the rocks with a zoom!
See how he darts
Through his watery room
Past crabs and eels
And green seaweed,
Past fluffs of sandy
Minnow feed!
See how he swims
With a swerve and a twist,
A flip of the flipper,
A flick of the wrist!
Quicksilver-quick,
Softer than spray,
Down he plunges
And sweeps away;
Before you can think,
Before you can utter
Words like "Dill pickle"
Or "Apple butter,"
Back up he swims
Past stingray and shark,
Out with a zoom,
A whoop, a bark;
Before you can say
Whatever you wish,
He plops at your side
With a mouthful of fish!

Check Test

1. Name two things the seal swims by. (Possible answers: crabs, eels, seaweed, minnow feed, stingray, sharks)

2. Name two sounds the seal makes. (whoop and bark)

Answers to Study Questions

Developing Comprehension Skills

1. dives, zoom, darts; The seal is moving rapidly.

Developing Comprehension Skills

Literal Reading 1. Read over the first eight lines and list all the words you can find that show movement. Is the seal moving rapidly or slowly?

Interpretive Reading 2. Do you think the seal in this poem is swimming in a zoo pond or in the sea? Use phrases from the poem to support your answer.

Interpretive Reading 3. Is the mood of "Seal" serious or light-hearted? Which words or phrases helped you decide?

Reading Literature: Poetry

1. **Understanding Concrete Poems.** A **concrete poem** uses shape to remind a reader of its subject. "Seal" is a concrete poem because the way it is printed on the page reminds the reader of something about the seal. Explain what you think it is.

2. **Understanding Rhyme.** What is the rhyme scheme of the first four lines of "Seal"? Is this rhyme scheme repeated anywhere else in the poem? If so, where?

   The poem is written as one long stanza. It could have had a more complicated rhyme scheme, as in the longer stanzas of "Catalog." Why do you think the poet kept to the rhyme scheme that you identified?

3. **Identifying Rhythm.** As you learned earlier in this chapter, the rhythm pattern of a poem can be shown in writing. Write the first eight lines of this poem, leaving space after every line. Then mark each stressed syllable with this accent, /, and each unstressed syllable with this accent, ˘. (If you like, review Reading Literature 3, for "All But Blind," page 256.) You will find that the number and position of unstressed syllables vary. How many stressed syllables are there in every line?

Using the Study Questions

It is recommended that students always read and answer the questions in **Developing Comprehension Skills** in class discussion. Whenever possible, they should also read the questions in **Reading Literature** together and discuss the answers.

Developing Comprehension Skills

Question 1. List students' answers on the board as they find them.

Question 2. Ask several students for evidence from the poem that proves their answers.

Question 3. Read and discuss the question.

Challenge Question. Why do you think that this poet and the writer of "Sea Lions" like these animals so much? What is attractive about seals? (Interpretive Reading)

Reading Literature: Poetry

Question 1. Encourage the students to point out hints in the poems that help us understand why this shape was used.

Question 2. Ask individual students to chart the rhyme scheme of four successive lines and record the rhyme schemes on the board.

Question 3. You may want to answer this question with the class, writing the lines either on the board or an overhead transparency.

2. The seal is swimming in the sea. He swims "past crabs and eels and green seaweed" and "past stingray and shark." These things couldn't be found in a pond.

3. The mood is light-hearted. Some of the phrases are "with a zoom;" "a flip of the flipper, a flick of the wrist;" "out with a zoom, a whoop, a bark;" and "he plops at your side with a mouthful of fish."

Challenge. Answers may vary. Students may say that seals are attractive because they are energetic and enthusiastic. They seem so happy that they make you happy when you watch them.

Reading Literature: Poetry

1. The shape of the poem reminds you of the way the seal swims through the waves in the sea.

2. Rhyme scheme: a b c b. The rhyme scheme is repeated six more times consecutively to the end of the poem. The poet might have used this regular rhyme scheme to imitate the regularity of the seal's swimming movements.

3. There are two stressed syllables for every line in this poem.

Seé hŏw hĕ díves
Frŏm thĕ rócks wĭth ă zoóm!
Seé hŏw hĕ dárts
Thrŏugh hĭs wátĕrў roóm
Păst crábs ănd eéls
Ănd greén sĕaweéd,
Păst flúffs ŏf sándў
Mínnŏw feéd!

There are two accented syllables in each line.

Objectives

- To recognize and appreciate the haiku as a form of poetry
- To identify sensory images in a poem
- To apply literal, interpretive, and critical reading skills to a selection

Preparing the Students

Essential Vocabulary. There is no difficult vocabulary in this selection.

Motivation. Have the students read the introductory paragraph at the top of page 280 and state in their own words what they should try to find out as they read this poem.

Presenting the Selection

1. Have the students read "Woodpecker" silently.
2. Administer the **Check Test** at the bottom of this page.
3. Ask the students to take a minute to visualize the poem. Then ask volunteers to read it aloud once or twice.
4. Develop the study questions as suggested in **Using the Study Questions** below. That section also provides a challenge question for further discussion, if needed.

Reinforcing the Lesson

To reteach, reinforce, or extend the skills in this lesson, see the following:

Skills Practice Book, Green Level—page 130

Using the Study Questions

Developing Comprehension Skills

Question 1. Read and discuss the question.

Question 2. Have students identify the three words that do these three things: describe a quality of the woodpecker, tell how long the bird has been working, and tell what it has been doing.

Reading Literature: Poetry

Question. Have one student read the poem aloud again before having the students answer the question.

Challenge Question. Find an example of alliteration in this poem.

Woodpecker

ISSA

This haiku distributes its seventeen syllables over four lines. It pictures one moment of a long day. However, can you tell what has been happening throughout the day?

Stubborn woodpecker
   Still hammering
   At twilight
At that single spot.

Developing Comprehension Skills

Literal Reading

1. In your own words, tell what the poet describes in "Woodpecker."

Interpretive Reading

2. This poem has only ten words. Three of them give clues about the woodpecker's actions during the day and the speaker's attitude toward the woodpecker. Identify the three words, and tell what you can infer from them.

Reading Literature: Poetry

Identifying Sensory Images. Usually, a haiku has three lines. Although this poem has four lines, its use of seventeen syllables shows that it is a haiku. It is also like other haiku in its presentation of a single sensory image. That is, it describes one experience so clearly that the reader imagines that he or she can see or hear or feel the thing described. To what sense does this haiku appeal? When you read it, do you imagine seeing, hearing, or feeling something?

Check Test

1. What has the woodpecker been doing all day? (hammering at a single spot)
2. What time of day is it now? (twilight)

Answers to Study Questions

Developing Comprehension Skills

1. The poet describes a woodpecker who has been hammering at a single spot in a tree all day and is still hammering at twilight.

2. *Stubborn, still,* and *hammering* describe the bird's actions throughout the day and the speaker's attitude toward the woodpecker. Using these words, you can infer that the woodpecker is persistent and untiring and that its actions irritate the speaker.

Reading Literature: Poetry

This haiku appeals to the sense of hearing.

Challenge: The letter *s* is repeated four times at the beginning of the following words: stubborn, still, single, and spot.

As you read this haiku, decide which parts of it might be shown in a picture.

Fall

SALLY ANDRESEN

The geese flying south
In a row long and V-shaped
Pulling in winter.

The Twelve Months (detail), 1823–31, KATSUSHIKA HOKUSAI. Freer Gallery of Art, Smithsonian Institution, Washington, D.C.

About the Art

Katsushika Hokusai (1760-1849), best known for his woodblock prints of Mt. Fuji, Japan's highest mountain (see **About the Art,** pages 185, 200, and 203), was a keen and sensitive observer of nature. *The Twelve Months,* a detail of which is reproduced here, presents images from nature for the twelve months of the year. Here we see three birds in flight against a backdrop of fall colors. Suggested is the seasonal migration of the geese as they make their way to a warmer climate for the winter.

Check Test

1. Where are the geese flying? (south)

2. In what type of formation are they flying? (a long, V-shaped line)

Objectives

- To recognize and appreciate the haiku as a form of poetry
- To compare the forms of two poems
- To compare the tones of two poems
- To apply literal, interpretive, and critical reading skills to a selection
- To use the context clues of example, comparison, contrast, and series
- To write a haiku

Preparing the Students

Essential Vocabulary. There is no difficult vocabulary in this selection.

Motivation. Have the students read the introductory paragraph at the top of page 281 and state in their own words what they should try to find out as they read this poem.

Presenting the Selection

1. Have the students read "Fall" silently. Have them try to visualize the poem.

2. Make sure that everyone has read the poem by administering the **Check Test** at the bottom of this page.

3. Ask students to describe the image that comes to mind as we read this poem and to point out the parts of the poem that suggest the image.

4. Develop the study questions as suggested in **Using the Study Questions** beginning on page 282. That section also provides a challenge question for further discussion, if needed.

Reinforcing the Lesson

To reteach, reinforce, or extend the skills in this lesson, see the following:

Skills Practice Book, Green Level—pages 131 and 132

Special Populations

LD. To help the students organize answers to the first writing assignment, **Comparing Images,** on page 283, set up a comparison chart to be filled in, such as the one on the next page:

	POEM 1	POEM 2
a. What do the animals look like?		
b. How do the animals move?		
c. Tell about the animal's personality.		
d. How does the writer feel about the animal?		

Add any other questions to the chart that you feel might help the students make a better comparison between the two poems.

Using the Study Questions

It is recommended that students always read and answer the questions in **Developing Comprehension Skills** in class discussion. Whenever possible, they should also read the questions in the other categories together and discuss the answers.

Developing Comprehension Skills

Questions 1 and 2. Read and discuss the questions.

Challenge Question. When you see geese flying south, you know that winter is coming. What else can you see in the fall that indicates that winter is on its way? (Critical Reading)

Reading Literature: Poetry

Question 1. Students can compare the two poems easily by turning to the previous page in the text. Have them count the number of syllables in each line and add them. Then ask students to comment on the presence or absence of rhyme.

Question 2. Read and discuss the question.

Developing Vocabulary Skills

Have students read the directions to the exercise and explain in their own words what they are to do. If you wish, work the first two sentences with them. Have them complete the exercise independently. Discuss the answers.

Developing Writing Skills

Read and discuss the two assignments. Then have each student choose and complete one of the two.

Developing Comprehension Skills

Literal Reading — 1. To which of your senses does this poem appeal?

Interpretive Reading — 2. In order to understand this poem, you must know something about geese. What fact about geese explains why the poet says this flock is "Pulling in winter"?

Reading Literature: Poetry

1. **Examining Form.** How does the form of this haiku differ from the form of "Woodpecker"? Compare both the number of lines and the number of syllables per line.

   Basing your answer on these two haiku, would you say that rhyme is an important element in haiku poetry?

2. **Comparing Tone.** As you learned in Chapter 4, the **tone** of a piece of writing is the attitude the writer takes toward the subject. Both "Woodpecker" and "Fall" are about birds. Do the speakers in each poem take the same attitude toward birds? Give a reason from the haiku for your answer.

Developing Vocabulary Skills

Using Context Clues. In Chapter 1 you learned that an unfamiliar word can be figured out by finding a definition or restatement clue or a synonym. In this chapter you learned four other context clues: **example**, **comparison**, **contrast**, and **series**. Read the following sentences or groups of sentences. Each underlined word was used in one of the poems you have read. Figure out the meaning of the word by using context clues. Write the meaning of the word and the type of context clue you used to find the meaning.

1. In contrast to her day at the office, where she is constantly dealing with people, Mrs. Jordan enjoys a solitary evening at home.
2. Mr. Dexter often has lunch with his comrades at the university. He and his companions share their ideas and thoughts.
3. Jessica resolved not to quit the swim team, and she also decided to join the drama club.
4. The owner of this store buys his materials at wholesale prices. In other words, he buys them in large quantities at lower prices.

Answers to Study Questions

Developing Comprehension Skills

1. This poem appeals to the sense of sight.

2. The geese fly south to escape from winter. Their flight signals the beginning of fall and the preparation for winter. They fly in a V-shaped formation.

Challenge. Other warnings of winter are shorter days and longer nights, the changing of the leaves' colors, fall flowers, the beginning of school, the beginning of the football season, cooler weather, the harvest season, and the activities of animals.

Reading Literature: Poetry

1. "Woodpecker" has four lines; "Fall" has three lines. The first lines in both poems have five syllables. The second line in "Fall" has seven syllables. The second line in "Woodpecker" has four syllables and its third line has three syllables. The last lines in both poems have five syllables.

Rhyme must not be important in haikus since neither poem uses it.

2. The speakers seem to have different attitudes toward birds. In "Woodpecker,"

5. Large boulders, or rocks, slid from the steep mountain and blocked the highway.
6. The artist painted shades of blue, such as azure, in the background.
7. The snake-like eel is really a fresh- or salt-water fish.
8. Some people prefer the reserved techniques of a cat to the outgoing manners and style of dogs.

Developing Writing Skills

Analytical Writing

1. **Comparing Images.** You have just read two poems about cats, two about seals, and two about birds. Choose one of these pairs of poems. Compare the word pictures of the animals in the two poems. Did the animal move differently in each poem? Did it have a different personality? Did it affect the speaker in a different way?

   Imagine that you were a pet shop owner selling these animals. If you were to use one of the poems in an ad, which of the two poems would you expect to draw more customers?

   Write at least one paragraph comparing the poems.

Creative Writing

2. **Writing a Haiku.** These two statements are true for every haiku: It presents a single sensory image, and it uses seventeen syllables. Think of experiences you have had. Try to remember something you saw clearly and vividly. You may remember a particular sound or touch or taste. Choose one of those sensations for the topic of your poem. Then list as many words and phrases as you can to describe it. Be as specific as possible.

   When you have listed all the words and phrases you can think of, choose the ones that describe the sensation best. Then write a haiku, using those words and phrases in your poem if you can. Remember that the number of syllables must be exactly seventeen. Make sure that the sensory image is clear.

the tone is a little irritated, although the speaker also seems to admire the persistence of the bird. The tone in "Fall" is more respectful. The speaker seems to be awed by the power of the birds.

Developing Vocabulary Skills

1. solitary—alone, contrast
2. comrades—companions, synonym
3. resolved—decided, comparison
4. wholesale—lower, definition or restatement
5. boulders—rocks, restatement
6. azure—blue, example
7. eel—fish, definition
8. techniques—manners and style, comparison

Question 1. Students may choose to write about the poems they enjoyed the most or they may wish to write about the poems in which they see the most differences.

Pre-Writing. Have the students reread all the poems about animals. You may want to have them work in small groups with individuals reading the poems aloud. Then have each student choose the pair of poems he or she wishes to write about. Encourage them to draw charts comparing the way the poems presented the animals according to movements, personalities, effects on the speaker, attractiveness of the animals, and any other quality they can think of.

Writing. Allow sufficient time for the students to write their first drafts.

Revising. Have students revise and proofread their own paragraphs using the guidelines given in the **Checklist for the Process of Writing** on pages 556 and 557.

Question 2. Students may benefit from reading additional examples of haikus. If possible, make available a few anthologies that feature haikus for student reference.

Pre-Writing. Have students brainstorm about possible topics for their haikus. List possibilities on the board. Urge students to choose a topic with which they have personal experience, not just a sight or sound they have seen in pictures or heard on the radio or TV. Have them list sensory details that describe the experience.

Writing. Remind students that their goal is to create a clear image for the reader and to include at least two or three sensory details.

Revising. Have students share their haikus in small groups. Have one student record the topics of the haikus for each group. After everyone has read his or her haiku to the group, ask volunteers to read their haikus to the class. Have the recorder report on the topics in each group. Help students appreciate the variety of topics and the variety of treatments.

Objectives

- To recognize and appreciate poetry as a form of literature
- To identify the speaker in a poem
- To recognize personification
- To apply literal, interpretive, and critical reading skills to a selection

Preparing the Students

Essential Vocabulary. There is no difficult vocabulary in this selection.

Motivation. Have the students read the introductory paragraph at the top of page 284 and state in their own words what they should try to find out as they read this poem.

Presenting the Selection

1. Read "Bee! I'm Expecting You!" aloud to the students. Emphasize the conversational tone of the poem. Have one or two students read it aloud.

2. Administer the **Check Test** at the bottom of this page to see if the students understand the literal meaning of the poem.

3. Develop the study questions as suggested in **Using the Study Questions** on page 285. The question posed in the introduction is answered there. That section also provides a challenge question for further discussion, if needed.

Special Populations

ESL. It will aid in comprehension to paraphrase the poem slightly, filling in the words that the writer left out. Suggested additions are the following: "(I) Was saying Yesterday;" "(They) are settled, and at work;" "(As for the) Birds, (they're) mostly back."

Bee! I'm Expecting You!

EMILY DICKINSON

The following poem takes the form of a letter between two rather unusual friends. Read to find out who they are.

Bee! I'm expecting you!
Was saying Yesterday
To Somebody you know
That you were due—

The Frogs got Home Last Week—
Are settled, and at work—
Birds, mostly back—
The Clover warm and thick—

You'll get my Letter by
The seventeenth; Reply
Or better, be with me—
Yours, Fly.

About the Art

There is little biographical information about the Japanese artist Sosen. He was a floral and figure painter, often confused with a well-known, eighteenth-century artist of the same name.

In his painting, which is a detail from a scroll, the insects, flowers, and leaves are drawn precisely and meticulously, with great technical skill and careful attention to detail. Yet the artist also invests his work with poetic beauty. The simple design of the branches, which flows freely and rhythmically across the paper, is graceful and lyrical.

Check Test

1. Who are some of the fly's friends? (the bee, the frogs, and the birds)

2. Why is the fly expecting the bee? (It's the right time of year. The bee is due to come back now.)

Developing Comprehension Skills

Literal Reading 1. Who is the speaker in this poem?

Literal Reading 2. Who is being addressed and what does the speaker want him or her to do?

Literal Reading 3. What season is celebrated in this poem?

Reading Literature: Poetry

1. **Identifying Rhyme.** In this poem, Emily Dickinson's rhyme scheme is not simple. Identify all the words that rhyme, either at the ends of lines or within one line.

2. **Recognizing Personification.** This poem personifies several animals and insects. Name them and the ways in which they are said to be like humans.

Flowers of Four Seasons (detail), 17th Century. SOSEN. The Philadelphia Museum of Art, Gift of Mrs. John C. Atwood.

Using the Study Questions

It is recommended that students always read and answer the questions in **Developing Comprehension Skills** in class discussion. Whenever possible, they should also read the questions in **Reading Literature** together and discuss the answers.

Developing Comprehension Skills

Questions 1 and 2. Read and discuss the questions.

Question 3. Explain to the students that they will not find the answer to this question stated directly in the poem. They must infer the answer using hints in the poem. Have them list the details that told them the season. (The bee is due back and bees come back in the springtime; frogs are active in the spring after a winter of inactivity; birds return from the South in spring; clover begins to bloom then, too).

Reading Literature: Poetry

Question 1. Write the poem on the board or on an overhead transparency. Identify the rhyming words along with the students.

Question 2. Be sure that students name all the ways each animal and insect is like humans, not just one way.

Challenge Question. Why do you think the poet capitalized certain words even though they were not proper nouns or the first words in sentences?

Answers to Study Questions

Developing Comprehension Skills

1. The fly is the speaker.

2. The bee is being addressed. The speaker wants him or her to come back and join the others.

3. Spring is celebrated.

Reading Literature: Poetry

1. Stanza 1 rhyming words: *you, due* in lines 1 and 4; *saying, yesterday* in line 2; *to, you* in line 3; *you, due* in line 4.

Stanza 2: no obvious rhyming words. However, some students may recognize the near rhyme—*week, thick.*

Stanza 3: *my, by, Reply, Fly* in lines 1, 2, and 4; *be, me* in line 3.

2. The bee can read and has friends who are expecting its return. The fly can write a letter and speak. The frogs arrived home and are settled in and back to work just like humans after a vacation.

Challenge. The poet probably capitalized certain words to show their importance. As you read the poem, you emphasize those words because they are capitalized.

Objectives

- To recognize and appreciate poetry as a form of literature
- To apply literal, interpretive, and critical reading skills to a selection
- To understand figurative language

Preparing the Students

Essential Vocabulary. The words presented here are essential to the understanding of the selection.

Have the students use the context clues in the following sentences to determine the meanings of the underlined words.

clasp crag azure

1. When they meet, people often clasp hands in a friendly handshake.
2. Even the best of mountain climbers couldn't reach the top of that steep crag.
3. The artist tried many different blues before he found one that matched the azure of the sky.

Motivation. Have the students read the introductory paragraph at the top of page 286 and state in their own words what they should try to find out as they read this poem.

Presenting the Selection

1. Have the students examine the picture on page 287 before they read "The Eagle" silently. This examination will help them understand the mood of the poem. Ask a volunteer to read the poem aloud.

2. Administer the **Check Test** at the bottom of this page to see if the students understand the literal meaning of the poem.

3. Develop the study questions as suggested in **Using the Study Questions.** The suggestion made in the introduction is discussed there. That section also provides a challenge question for further discussion, if needed.

Encouraging Independent Reading

Some students may want to find other poems in which animals are personified. Tell these students to copy the poems and illustrate them for a bulletin board display. Emphasize that their illustrations should bring out the personification in the poem, as well as its mood. Explain that very humorous illustrations could be made to accompany poems of a lighthearted na-

As you read this poem, discover all the images that tell of the dignity and power of the eagle.

The Eagle

ALFRED, LORD TENNYSON

He clasps the crag with crooked hands;
Close to the sun in lonely lands,
Ringed with the azure world, he stands.

The wrinkled sea beneath him crawls;
He watches from his mountain walls,
And like a thunderbolt he falls.

Developing Comprehension Skills

Literal Reading — 1. At least three phrases tell you where the eagle of the poem is. Identify these phrases.

Literal Reading — 2. Explain this simile:

And like a thunderbolt he falls.

Interpretive Reading — 3. Reread line 5. Can you suggest a cause-and-effect connection between that and line 6?

Critical Reading — 4. The poet uses many images in this poem to help us see the eagle as he does. Which one do you like best? Explain why.

286 POETRY

Check Test

1. Does the eagle live among people or does it live alone? (alone)

2. What is beneath the eagle? (the sea)

3. To what is the eagle compared? (a thunderbolt)

Answers to Study Questions

Developing Comprehension Skills

1. "He clasps the crag"; "close to the sun in lonely lands"; "the wrinkled sea beneath him"; "ringed with the azure world"; "from his mountain walls"

2. A thunderbolt is a streak of lightning. The eagle falls so swiftly that it seems as fast as lightning. Like lightning, it is full of power.

3. The eagle probably saw some prey so he flew after it.

4. Answers will vary. Each student should explain why he or she chose a particular image. Possible images: the eagle on a high, rocky crag; the blue sky all around him; the sea so far away that its waves look like wrinkles; the eagle falling swiftly and powerfully.

Wallowa Lake, 1927–28, STEVE HARLEY. Abbey Aldrich Rockefeller Folk Art Center, Williamsburg, Virginia.

Reading Literature: Poetry

1. **Identifying Rhyme and Rhythm.** Copy the first stanza of this poem, leaving a line of space after each line. Mark the stressed and unstressed syllables with these marks: ˊ, ˘. Then write the rhyme scheme, using as many letters of the alphabet as you need.
2. **Recognizing Alliteration.** Which letter is used repeatedly at the beginning of words in stanza 1? How does it stress the harshness of the setting?

   Can you find examples of alliteration using other letters, also?
3. **Understanding Personification.** Some of the words used to describe the eagle make it seem almost human. What are some of the words? How does this personification make the eagle more interesting?

ture. The following books include poems about animals and may be helpful to the students:

A Light in the Attic and *Where the Sidewalk Ends* by Shel Silverstein
Early Moon and *The Sandburg Treasury—Prose and Poetry for Young People* by Carl Sandburg
Poems by Rachel Field
Selected Poems by Marianne Moore

Using the Study Questions

Developing Comprehension Skills

Question 1. Read and discuss the question.

Question 2. Be sure that students know why this phrase is a simile.

Question 3. Explain to students that they must infer the answer to this question. It is not stated directly.

Question 4. Include in this discussion a reminder about the directions in the introduction. As students discuss favorite images, have them point out the ones that show the eagle's dignity and power.

Challenge Question. Name another animal that seems as dignified and powerful as the eagle. (Critical Reading)

Reading Literature: Poetry

Question 1. Have students complete this question independently. Then have them compare their answers to the rhythm pattern and rhyme scheme you write on the board.

Question 2. Read and discuss the question.

Question 3. Have students look for details about the eagle's appearance or actions.

Challenge. Answers will vary. Possible answers: a lion, a horse, a tiger, a wolf.

Reading Literature: Poetry

1. Rhythm pattern:

Hĕ cláps thĕ crág wĭth cróokĕd hánds;
Clóse tŏ thĕ sún ĭn lónelў lánds,
Rínged wĭth thĕ ázŭre wórld, hĕ stánds.

Rhyme scheme: a a a

2. The repeated letter is *c.* Since it is a hard *c,* it has a harsh, rough sound that reinforces the harshness of the setting.

Other examples of alliteration: lonely lands, world...watches...walls

3. Phrases: *clasps, crooked hands, he stands, he watches*

The personification makes the eagle easy to picture and gives him a personality.

About the Art

Wallowa Lake, a painting by the folk artist Steve Harley, shows an eagle in flight reflected in a lake surrounded by tall, snow-capped mountains. In the foreground, deer browse on grasses and shrubs. Like the work of many other self-taught artists, Harley's painting is a panoramic view filled with careful detail. Such work often has a narrative quality to it; that is, it attempts to describe or tell a story. Compare this painting with Grandma Moses' *A Beautiful World* on page 190 or the painting on pages 194 to 195 by another untrained artist, J.O.J. Frost.

Objectives

- To recognize and appreciate poetry as a form of literature
- To understand the characters in a poem
- To apply literal, interpretive, and critical reading skills to a selection

Preparing the Students

Essential Vocabulary. The words presented here are essential to the understanding of the selection.

Write the following words and definitions on the board. Have the students read them before reading the poem.

prig—a smug and narrow-minded person

former—the first of two things mentioned

latter—the second of two things mentioned

spry—active, lively

If the students need additional help with the vocabulary of this selection, encourage them to use context clues to determine word meaning. As needed, direct them to the **Glossary** or to a classroom dictionary.

Motivation. Have the students read the introductory paragraph at the top of page 288 and state in their own words what they should try to find out as they read this poem. Be sure that students know what a fable is and what a moral is.

Presenting the Selection

1. Have the students read "The Mountain and the Squirrel" silently.

2. Make sure that everyone has read the poem by administering the **Check Test** at the bottom of this page.

3. Have three volunteers read the poem aloud, taking the parts of the narrator, the mountain, and the squirrel.

4. Develop the study questions as suggested in **Using the Study Questions** on page 289. The question posed in the introduction is answered there. That section also provides a challenge question for further discussion, if needed.

The Mountain and the Squirrel

This poem is very much like some of the fables you have read. Look for a moral stated in two words.

RALPH WALDO EMERSON

The mountain and the squirrel
Had a quarrel,
And the former called the latter "Little prig;"
Bun replied,
"You are doubtless very big;
But all sorts of things and weather
Must be taken in together
To make up a year,
And a sphere.
And I think it no disgrace
To occupy my place.
If I'm not so large as you,
You are not so small as I,
And not half so spry.
I'll not deny you make
A very pretty squirrel track.
Talents differ; all is well and wisely put;
If I cannot carry forests on my back,
Neither can you crack a nut!"

Check Test

1. What did the mountain call the squirrel? (little prig)

2. What can the mountain do that the squirrel can't do? (carry forests on his back)

3. What can the squirrel do that the mountain can't do? (crack a nut)

Ielerang or Javan Squirrel, 1850. Hand-colored lithograph from a drawing by Edward Lear. Field Museum of Natural History.

Developing Comprehension Skills

Literal Reading — 1. You will find three speakers in this poem. Identify each.

Literal Reading — 2. Read the first four lines carefully. Who is Bun?

Interpretive Reading — 3. Which of these words would you use to describe the squirrel?
a. shy b. self-confident c. bold d. overbearing

Literal Reading — 4. Identify the words of the poem that state its moral. Then explain the moral in your own words.

Reading Literature: Poetry

1. **Identifying Rhyme.** The rhyme scheme in this poem is unusual. Use letters of the alphabet to label the first eleven lines of the poem. Does every line rhyme with another line?

2. **Understanding Characters.** The squirrel tells the mountain:

   I'll not deny you make
   A very pretty squirrel track.

   Is the squirrel trying to insult the mountain or to compliment it? How do you think the mountain would react to the comment? Does the comment tell you anything about the squirrel's view of the world?

Using the Study Questions

It is recommended that students always read and answer the questions in **Developing Comprehension Skills** in class discussion. Whenever possible, they should also read the questions in **Reading Literature** together and discuss the answers.

Developing Comprehension Skills

Question 1. Read and discuss the question.

Question 2. Remind students of the meanings of *former* and *latter*.

Question 3. Have students tell why they chose their descriptions. Point out that the squirrel knows his own value. He is not afraid to express his opinion to something much bigger than he is, although that opinion may not be welcomed.

Question 4. Ask students first to define a moral. Then have students read the line aloud that contains the moral.

Challenge Question. This poem says that the mountain and the squirrel had a quarrel during which the mountain called the squirrel a name. What could a mountain and a squirrel possibly quarrel about? (Critical Reading)

Reading Literature: Poetry

Question 1. Write the last words of each line on the board. Have students label them, starting with the letter *a*.

Question 2. Read and discuss the question.

About the Art

Edward Lear (1812-1888), the youngest of twenty-one children, perhaps best known as a writer of nonsense verse, earned his living from the age of fifteen by drawing, first for the Zoological Society of London and later for the British Museum. Eventually he became one of England's finest illustrators of birds and animals, and gave a series of drawing lessons to Queen Victoria.

The drawing reproduced here shows Lear's keen powers of observation and his sensitivity to line and color. The precise detail and realistic pose give a sense of vitality to the animal, and it seems almost alive. The exacting work of drawing animals affected Lear's eyesight, and in 1835 he turned from illustration to landscape painting.

Answers to Study Questions

Developing Comprehension Skills

1. The speakers are the narrator, mountain, and squirrel.

2. Bun is the squirrel.

3. Correct choices are *b* or *c*.

4. Moral: Talents differ. This means that everyone has different abilities, but no one's abilities are more important than anyone else's. All are needed. Everything is as it should be.

Challenge. Answers will vary. Any creative or logical answer is acceptable.

Reading Literature: Poetry

1. a b c d c e e f f g g
Lines 1, 2, and 4 don't rhyme with any other lines. Lines 1 and 2 end in near rhymes; some students may show the rhyme scheme as follows:
a a b c b d d e e f f

2. The squirrel is probably trying to compliment the mountain. The mountain is probably insulted that the squirrel is mentioning one of his least important characteristics. The squirrel's comment tells us that he thinks only useful things are valuable.

Objectives

- To recognize and appreciate poetry as a form of literature
- To make inferences
- To apply literal, interpretive, and critical reading skills to a selection
- To recognize context clues
- To write a response to a poem from a different point of view
- To identify slanted language

Preparing the Students

Essential Vocabulary. The following word is essential to the understanding of the selection.

Have the students use the context clues in the following sentence to determine the meaning of the underlined word.

condescend

Since all her friends were busy, Anna <u>condescended</u> to play with her little sister.

If the students need additional help with the vocabulary of this selection, encourage them to use context clues to determine word meaning. As needed, direct them to the **Glossary** or to a classroom dictionary.

Motivation. Make sure that everyone has read the title of the poem. Then have the students read the introductory paragraph at the top of page 290 and state in their own words what they should try to find out as they read this poem.

Presenting the Selection

1. Have the students read "The Dog (As Seen by the Cat)" silently.

2. Make sure that everyone has understood the poem by administering the **Check Test** at the bottom of this page.

3. Ask volunteers to read the poem with the expression that the cat would have used.

4. Develop the study questions as suggested in **Using the Study Questions** beginning on page 291. The challenge that the introduction gave is answered here. That section also provides a challenge question for further discussion, if needed.

Reinforcing the Lesson

To reteach, reinforce, or extend the skills in this lesson, see the following:

Skills Practice Book, Green Level—page 133

The Dog
(As Seen by the Cat)

OLIVER HERFORD

We usually think of dogs and cats as not getting along well with each other. Read this poem to get an insider's view of the relationship!

The dog is black or white or brown,
And sometimes spotted like a clown.
He loves to make a foolish noise,
And Human Company enjoys.

The Human People pat his head
And teach him to pretend he's dead,
And beg, and fetch, and carry, too;
Things that no well-bred Cat will do.

At Human jokes, however stale,
He jumps about and wags his tail,
And Human People clap their hands
And think he really understands.

They say "Good Dog" to him. To us
They say "Poor Kit" and make no fuss.
Why Dogs are "good" and Cats are "poor"
I fail to understand, I'm sure.

To Someone very Good and Just,
Who has proved worthy of her trust,
A Cat will sometimes condescend—
The Dog is Everybody's friend!

Check Test

1. According to the poem, which animal acts foolish? (the dog)

2. How does the dog respond to human jokes? (He jumps about and wags his tail.)

3. With whom will a cat be friends? (someone very good and just who has proved worthy of her trust)

Answers to Study Questions

Developing Comprehension Skills

1. The cat is the speaker.

2. Some of the phrases are the following: "He loves to make a foolish noise"; "And beg, and fetch, and carry, too; Things that no well-bred Cat will do"; "He jumps about and wags his tail"; "The Dog is Everybody's friend."

3. Answers may vary. Possible answers: People who aren't very bright and need something to boss around would

Developing Comprehension Skills

Literal Reading 1. Who is the speaker in this poem?

Interpretive Reading 2. The dog is compared to a clown. What other phrases show that the cat looks down on him?

Interpretive Reading 3. If you believe this speaker, what kind of people would want cats for pets? What kind would like dogs?

Interpretive Reading 4. In what tone of voice should the last two lines be read?

Reading Literature: Poetry

1. **Understanding Rhyme.** Write the rhyme scheme of the first stanza of this poem. Do all the stanzas use the same pattern?
2. **Making Inferences.** This cat states its opinion of dogs quite clearly. The cat also suggests its opinion of humans. What is that opinion? What lines in the poem support your answer?

Developing Vocabulary Skills

Recognizing Context Clues. The following paragraph is about eagles. This is an example of a paragraph you may read in a textbook or a book about eagles. Read the paragraph and answer the four questions that follow.

> Eagles can be identified by three distinguishing habits. They are diurnal birds, as opposed to nocturnal fliers. That is, eagles fly and hunt for food by day, rather than by night as do the owls. An eagle is a raptorial bird, one who preys upon other birds and animals, seizing them in its talons and sometimes in its bill. Eagles are believed to mate for life, not a common occurrence among birds.

1. What phrase in the second sentence tells you that the sentence is a contrast statement?
2. The third sentence gives a clue to the meanings of the words *diurnal* and *nocturnal* found in the second sentence. What type of clue is it? What does each of the words mean?
3. In the fourth sentence what type of clue gives the meaning of a *raptorial* bird? What does the term mean?

Using the Study Questions

It is recommended that students always read and answer the questions in **Developing Comprehension Skills** in class discussion. Whenever possible, they should also read the questions in the other categories together and discuss the answers.

Developing Comprehension Skills

Questions 1 and 2. Read and discuss the questions.

Question 3. Have students reread any lines in the poem that deal with humans. Students must infer this answer.

Question 4. Have the students decide whether the cat admires the dog for being "Everybody's friend." That understanding will help them decide how the lines should be read.

Challenge Question. Do you think the cat is jealous of the dog? Do you think that she would like all the attention that he gets from humans? Support your answer with details from the poem. (Interpretive Reading)

Reading Literature: Poetry

Question 1. After students see that the first two lines rhyme and the second two lines rhyme, have them check for the same pattern in all stanzas.

Question 2. Make sure students refer to specific lines, not just the general impression the poem gives.

Developing Vocabulary Skills

Have students read the directions for the exercise and the paragraph silently. Have them complete the exercise independently and discuss the answers together.

like dogs for pets. People who are good, just, trustworthy, and don't demand that their pets do everything they say would want cats for pets.

4. The lines should be read in a disapproving or sarcastic voice.

Challenge. The cat doesn't seem to be jealous of the dog. She thinks he is foolish and she doesn't have a high opinion of humans either. She doesn't wish for the friendship of humans. Instead, she condescends to be friendly to humans she thinks are worthy.

Reading Literature: Poetry

1. a a b b
All stanzas use the same pattern.

2. The cat doesn't respect humans very much. Humans ask the dog to do "things that no well-bred Cat will do" (stanza 2, line 4); "they tell stale jokes" (stanza 3, line 1); "they think a dog understands when he doesn't" (stanza 3, line 4). They have poor judgment since they call the dog "good" and the cat "poor" (stanza 4, lines 1 and 2).

Developing Vocabulary Skills

1. as opposed to

2. Definition or restatement clue; *diurnal* means flying and hunting for food by day; *nocturnal* means flying and hunting for food by night.

3. Definition or restatement clue; *raptorial* means preying upon other birds and animals.

4. *Talons* are the claws of a bird of prey.

(continued on page 292)

Developing Writing Skills

Read and discuss the two assignments. Then have each student choose and complete one of the two.

Question 1. Explain that different people may decide on different qualities. Not everyone will agree; there is no single right answer.

Pre-Writing. Have students reread "The Eagle" on page 286. Have each student decide on the quality that he or she feels was emphasized the most. Then have students look over the poem, finding the words and phrases that support their opinions.

Writing. Allow sufficient time for the students to write their first drafts.

Revising. Have students revise and proofread their paragraphs using the **Checklist for the Process of Writing** on pages 556 and 557.

Question 2. Make sure students understand that they should choose only one of the suggested responses.

Pre-Writing. Have the students read the directions for their chosen responses carefully. Directions change for each one. For example, parts **a** and **c** suggest that students may write in either prose or poetry. Have students reread the poems they chose to respond to. Then have them list possible responses to those poems.

Writing. Remind students to write in the first-person.

Revising. Have students who answered the same question read their poetry or prose to each other. Have listeners comment on at least one aspect of the writing that they enjoyed. Students might comment on the naturalness of conversation, the attention to detail, the logic of any arguments, or the cleverness of approach.

Developing Skills in Critical Thinking

Have a student read the explanation aloud. Then have each student independently list words and phrases that show the cat's slanted language. After each student completes his or her own list, have the students give suggestions for a class list to be written on the board.

4. The word *talons* is in the fourth sentence. Use the context of the sentence to infer what the word might mean. What is the exact meaning found in the dictionary?

Developing Writing Skills

Analytical Writing

1. **Analyzing a Poem.** What quality of eagles is most important in "The Eagle"? Write at least one paragraph explaining your opinion. Point out words or phrases from the poem that support your answer.

Creative Writing

2. **Taking a Different Point of View.** Write one of these responses to poems you have read about animals.
   a. Imagine that you are the bee to whom the fly is writing in "Bee! I'm Expecting You!" Explain why you are late. Write in poetry, using four-line stanzas, or in prose.
   b. Imagine that you are the mountain in "The Mountain and the Squirrel." Add some lines to the poem, giving the mountain's point of view. You might comment on what a mountain is good for, or what a mountain can do that a squirrel cannot do.
   c. Imagine that you are a dog. Write an answer to the cat speaker in "The Dog (As Seen by the Cat)." Use examples of what cats and dogs do, and how they behave with humans, to make your points. Write in either prose or poetry.

Developing Skills in Critical Thinking

Identifying Slanted Language. Frequently a writer appears to be stating facts when he or she is actually expressing an opinion. The writer does not directly state that he or she likes or dislikes the thing being described. Instead, the writer uses words that make the thing look good or bad. For example, instead of saying that a person is *quiet*, the writer says the person is *dull.*

Reread "The Dog (As Seen by the Cat)." The cat looks down on the dog but never says so directly. The cat's slanted language, however, shows its opinion. Find four examples of language that is used to make the dog look inferior.

(continued from page 291)

Developing Skills in Critical Thinking

Possible answers:

1. The cat compares the dog's spots to a clown's costume: "sometimes spotted like a clown."

2. The cat calls the dog's bark "a foolish noise."

3. The dog does things "no well-bred Cat will do."

4. The dog "jumps about and wags his tail" at human jokes, no matter how bad the jokes are.

5. The dog doesn't choose his friends carefully enough. He is willing to be "Everybody's friend."

The Panther

OGDEN NASH

Perhaps you know the difference between leopards and panthers. See if you agree with Ogden Nash.

The panther is like a leopard,
Except it hasn't been peppered.
Should you behold a panther crouch,
Prepare to say Ouch.
Better yet, if called by a panther,
Don't anther.

Developing Comprehension Skills

Literal Reading
1. Explain line 2 in your own words. Then explain line 6.

Interpretive Reading
2. Is the poem serious or humorous? Refer to specific words and phrases in the poem that support your answer.

Reading Literature: Poetry

1. **Understanding the Poet's Choice of Words.** If a panther were to spring at you, you would probably not cry, "Ouch!" Why does the poet use this word instead of a more serious cry for help?

2. **Understanding Figurative Language.** The first line of the poem uses the word *like* to compare the two animals. Is this a simile? Explain your reasons.

Objectives

- To recognize and appreciate humorous poetry
- To apply literal, interpretive, and critical reading skills to a selection

Preparing the Students

Essential Vocabulary. Explain that *behold* means "see."

Motivation. Ask the students to think about what they know about the similarities and differences between panthers and leopards. Then have the students read the introductory paragraph at the top of page 293 and state in their own words what they should try to find out as they read this poem.

Presenting the Selection

1. Have the students read "The Panther" silently.

2. Administer the **Check Test.**

3. Ask a volunteer to read the poem aloud.

4. Develop the study questions as suggested in **Using the Study Questions.**

Reinforcing the Lesson

To reteach, reinforce, or extend the skills in this lesson, see the following:

Skills Practice Book, Green Level—page 134

Using the Study Questions

Developing Comprehension Skills

Question 1. Emphasize the lighthearted humor of the poem.

Question 2. Have students think about both the subject matter and the vocabulary.

Reading Literature: Poetry

Question 1. Have students think about the mood of the poem and how other cries would not have fit together with that mood. Have them suggest other cries for help that would have had a less humorous effect.

Question 2. Read and discuss the question.

Challenge Question. Chart the rhyme scheme of this poem.

Check Test

1. How does a panther differ from a leopard? (He isn't peppered.)

2. What should you do if you are called by a panther? (Don't answer.)

Answers to Study Questions

Developing Comprehension Skills

1. A panther has no spots. The poet wanted a rhyme for *panther,* so he wrote the word *answer* as *anther.*

2. The poem is humorous. It is written informally, using words such as "Ouch" and "Don't anther." The contrast of Nash's lighthearted approach to a dangerous situation creates a humorous mood in the reader.

Reading Literature: Poetry

1. "Ouch" adds to the humorous mood.

2. It is not a simile. The two animals are very similar. Similes compare unlike things.

Challenge. a a b b c c

Objectives

- To recognize and appreciate poetry as a form of literature
- To apply literal, interpretive, and critical reading skills to a selection

Preparing the Students

Essential Vocabulary. Explain that *primal* means "first."

Motivation. Call on a volunteer to explain what instinct is. If necessary, have a student read aloud the dictionary definition of the word.

Have the students read the introductory paragraph at the top of page 294 and state in their own words what they should try to find out as they read this poem.

Presenting the Selection

1. Have the students read "The Termite" silently.

2. Make sure the students have read the poem by administering the **Check Test** at the bottom of this page.

3. Have the students read the poem in unison.

4. Develop the study questions as suggested in **Using the Study Questions** below. That section also provides a challenge question for further discussion, if needed.

Using the Study Questions

It is recommended that students always read and answer the questions in **Developing Comprehension Skills** in class discussion. Whenever possible, they should also read the questions in **Reading Literature** together and discuss the answers.

Developing Comprehension Skills

Question 1. Have students identify the cause and effect relationship between events.

Question 2. Have students think about their feelings about the termite. Do they like it or dislike it?

Reading Literature: Poetry

Question 1. Read and discuss the question.

Question 2. Have students think about how the termite is described and the vocabulary used.

Do you know what instinct is? This poem gives an example of the results of termite instinct.

The Termite

OGDEN NASH

Some primal termite knocked on wood
And tasted it, and found it good,
And that is why your Cousin May
Fell through the parlor floor today.

Developing Comprehension Skills

Literal Reading — 1. Explain in your own words why May fell through the floor.

Interpretive Reading — 2. Have you ever heard a superstitious person use the phrase "knock on wood"? That person may think that knocking on wood is a way to keep away bad luck. Why did the poet use that phrase in the poem? How does it affect your feelings toward the termite?

Reading Literature: Poetry

1. **Recognizing the Sounds of Language.** Rhyme and the repetition of the *t* sound and the *d* sound give shape to this poem. Write the rhyme scheme. Then list all the words that use the *t* sound or the *d* sound and underline the letters that make the sound. Can you explain why those two sounds work well in this poem?

2. **Understanding Mood.** This poem discusses termites and a dangerous home accident. You might expect these topics to be discussed seriously. Is the poem serious? In what ways does it set its mood?

Check Test

1. What did the primal termite do? (knocked on wood)

2. Who fell through the parlor floor? (Cousin May)

Answers to Study Questions

Developing Comprehension Skills

1. May fell through the floor because termites had eaten it.

2. The phrase "knocked on wood" makes you think that the termite is almost human. It just had a natural taste for wood, so it shouldn't be blamed for its actions.

Reading Literature: Poetry

1. a a b b; *t* sound: termite, tasted, it, that, today, knocked

These sounds remind the reader of the sound a termite might make when eating.

2. The mood is lighthearted. The termite is presented as an insect that is simply following its nature, not meaning any harm. The words the poet uses are short and simple.

The Hippopotamus

OGDEN NASH

There is an old saying that beauty is in the eye of the beholder. In this poem, find out whose eye sees beauty in a hippo.

Behold the hippopotamus!
We laugh at how he looks to us,
And yet in moments dank and grim
I wonder how we look to him.
Peace, peace, thou hippopotamus!
We really look all right to us,
As you no doubt delight the eye
Of other hippopotami.

Hippopotamus from the Egyptian tomb of Senbi, about 17th century B.C.
The Metropolitan Museum of Art, Gift of Edward S. Harkness, 1917.

Developing Comprehension Skills

Literal Reading — 1. The speaker addresses two audiences. Who are they and at what line does the change take place?

Interpretive Reading — 2. What does the speaker think hippos may feel about people? What line or lines make you think this?

Reading Literature: Poetry

Understanding Patterns of Rhythm. Certain rhythm patterns are used frequently in poems because they sound much like natural speech. One of these is iambic rhythm. **Iambic** rhythm alternates an unstressed beat and a stressed beat, shown this way: ∪ / ∪ / ∪ /. Is this poem mostly iambic or mostly some other pattern?

Objectives

- To recognize and appreciate poetry as a form of literature
- To identify iambic rhythm
- To apply literal, interpretive, and critical reading skills to a selection

Preparing the Students

Essential Vocabulary. Explain that *dank* means "unpleasantly damp" and *hippopotami* is the plural for *hippopotamus*.

Motivation. Have the students read the introductory paragraph at the top of page 295 and state in their own words what they are to find out as they read.

Presenting the Selection

1. In preparation, copy "The Hippopotamus" onto the board or onto an overhead transparency for later use.

2. Read "The Hippopotamus" aloud to the students. Have volunteers reread it.

3. Administer the **Check Test**.

4. Discuss the introduction.

5. Develop the study questions as suggested in **Using the Study Questions**.

Using the Study Questions

Developing Comprehension Skills

Question 1. Ask how the poet made the audience change clear.

Question 2. This answer isn't stated directly. Students must infer the answer.

Reading Literature: Poetry

Direct attention to the poem on the board or on the overhead transparency. Have them help you mark the rhythm.

About the Art

The ancient Egyptians believed in life after death in a material as well as a spiritual sense. They buried food, clothing, and furniture with the dead person for use in the afterlife. They also decorated the tomb with wall paintings and sculpture depicting activities enjoyed in life so the person might enjoy them again in the next world. The Egyptians hunted duck, crocodile, and the dangerous hippopotamus from boats using long spears. This clay sculpture of a hippopotamus, decorated with lotus flowers, was found in the tomb of the Egyptian Senbi.

Check Test

1. Why do we laugh at the hippopotamus? (He is funny-looking.)

2. Who thinks that hippos are beautiful? (other hippopotami)

Answers to Study Questions

Developing Comprehension Skills

1. The speaker addresses the reader in Lines 1 through 4 but then addresses the hippopotamus from Line 5 until the end.

2. The speaker thinks hippos may find us funny-looking. The lines that make us think this are the following: Line 4—"I wonder how we look to him"; Line 6—"We really look all right to us."

Reading Literature: Poetry

The poem is mostly iambic rhythm.

Objectives

- To recognize and appreciate poetry as a form of literature
- To apply literal, interpretive, and critical reading skills to a selection

Preparing the Students

Essential Vocabulary. The words presented here are essential to the understanding of the selection.

varies   revolting   moulting

1. This restaurant's special dinner varies from day to day. On Monday, it is spaghetti and on Tuesday, it is steak.
2. Leo liked the painting, but Gertrude said it was revolting.
3. When a bird is moulting, it sheds its old feathers.

Motivation. Have the students read the introductory paragraph at the top of page 296 and state in their own words what they should try to find out as they read this poem.

Presenting the Selection

1. Have the students read "The Canary" silently.
2. Make sure the students have read the poem by administering the **Check Test** at the bottom of this page.
3. Have one or two volunteers read the poem aloud.
4. Develop the study questions as suggested in **Using the Study Questions.**

Using the Study Questions

Developing Comprehension Skills

Question 1. Read and discuss the question.

Question 2. Ask students how people usually react to a sound that never changes.

Reading Literature: Poetry

Question 1. As a review, point out the iambic pattern in a few lines from "The Hippopotamus." Be sure to show how the lines usually begin with an unaccented syllable and end with an accented syllable. Then have students compare that pattern with the rhythm pattern of "The Canary." You may want to write the poem on the board and have students mark the rhythm.

Question 2. Allow students adequate time for the completion of their poems.

The Canary

Most people think a canary is a pretty little bird that cheers us all with its song. Does this poet agree?

OGDEN NASH

The song of canaries
Never varies,
And when they're moulting
They're pretty revolting.

Developing Comprehension Skills

Literal Reading 1. What does the poet find "revolting" about canaries?

Interpretive Reading 2. Do you think the poet likes the canaries' song? Give your reasons.

Reading Literature: Poetry

1. **Recognizing Rhythm.** Copy this poem, leaving space between the lines. Mark the stressed syllables. Is this poem mostly iambic or mostly another pattern? (If necessary, review page 295.)

2. **Understanding Mood.** The mood of this poem is critical and negative toward canaries. Write your own version of this poem, following these directions and keeping the same mood:
   a. Change the first line to read "A canary's song."
   b. Change the second line so that it rhymes with "song."
   c. Replace the last two lines with another statement critical of canaries. The ending words in the last two lines should rhyme.

Check Test

1. What about the canary is always the same? (its song)
2. How does it look when it's moulting? (revolting)

Answers to Study Questions

Developing Comprehension Skills

1. He feels it's revolting to see them lose their feathers.
2. Since the poet says the song never varies, it seems that he is tired of it.

Reading Literature: Poetry

1. The rhythm pattern is irregular:

Thĕ sóng ŏf cănárĭes
Névĕr várĭes,
Ănd whén thĕy're móultĭng
Thĕy're préttў rĕvóltĭng.

The rhythm pattern is mostly a pattern other than iambic.

2. Answers will vary. The rhyme pattern should be a a b b. The mood should be negative and critical of canaries.

This professor was an excellent scientist. Does he seem to be an excellent person?

The Purist

OGDEN NASH

I give you now Professor Twist,
A conscientious scientist.
Trustees exclaimed, "He never bungles!"
And sent him off to distant jungles.
Camped on a tropic riverside,
One day he missed his loving bride.
She had, the guide informed him later,
Been eaten by an alligator.
Professor Twist could not but smile.
"You mean," he said, "a crocodile."

Developing Comprehension Skills

Literal Reading — 1. List at least two phrases or words that describe the Professor.

Interpretive Reading — 2. In line 9, why did Professor Twist smile?

Interpretive Reading — 3. We can presume the professor has two loves. What were they and which was first in importance for him?

Reading Literature: Poetry

1. **Understanding Elements of Poetry.** Compare this poem to others by Ogden Nash, considering the following:

   a. rhyme scheme b. mood

2. **Understanding Theme.** Most of the other poems by Ogden Nash in this book are humorous, with no particular message. It is possible, however, to find a rather serious message in this funny poem. Can you state that message, or theme, in your own words?

Check Test

1. Where did the trustees send Professor Twist? (to distant jungles)

2. What happened to his bride? (She was eaten by a crocodile.)

Answers to Study Questions

Developing Comprehension Skills

1. The professor is "conscientious," and he "never bungles."

2. He was amused that the guide used the wrong word to name the animal that ate his wife. It was a crocodile, not an alligator.

3. The professor loves the correct use of words and also loves his bride. He seems to love words more than his bride.

Reading Literature: Poetry

1. Possible comments:

a. All of the Odgen Nash poems in the section have the same rhyme scheme—a a b b c c, etc.

(continued on page 298)

Objectives

- To recognize and appreciate poetry as a form of literature
- To understand the theme of a poem
- To apply literal, interpretive, and critical reading skills to a selection
- To complete analogies
- To imitate a poet's writing style
- To become familiar with various library resources
- To read a humorous poem effectively

Preparing the Students

Essential Vocabulary. The words presented here are essential to the understanding of the selection. Write the words and their definitions on the board. Have individual students read them aloud.

purist—one who practices strict correctness, especially in the use of words

conscientious—careful and thorough

bungle—make a mistake

Motivation. Have the students read the introductory paragraph at the top of page 297 and state in their own words what they should try to find out as they read this poem.

Presenting the Selection

1. Have the students read "The Purist" silently.

2. Make sure that everyone has read the poem by administering the **Check Test** at the bottom of this page.

3. Remind the students of the question posed in the introduction. Have them answer the question.

4. Develop the study questions as suggested in **Using the Study Questions** beginning on page 298. That section also provides a challenge question for further discussion, if needed.

Reinforcing the Lesson

To reteach, reinforce, or extend the skills in this lesson, see the following:

Skills Practice Book, Green Level—page 135

Special Populations

ESL. For the first activity under **Developing Skills in Speaking and Listening** on page 299, ESL students might be able to use samples of humorous poetry or songs from their native countries to interpret for the class.

Encouraging Independent Reading

Suggest to the students that, for their own enjoyment, they read other poems by Ogden Nash, such as *Parents Keep Out—Elderly Poems for Youngerly Readers,* by Ogden Nash. To stimulate their interest in his poetry further, you may wish to find a few more of Ogden Nash's more humorous poems to read aloud to the class.

Using the Study Questions

It is recommended that students always read and answer the questions in **Developing Comprehension Skills** in class discussion. Whenever possible, they should also read the questions in the other categories together and discuss the answers.

Developing Comprehension Skills

Question 1. Read and discuss the question.

Question 2. Remind students of the meaning of the word *purist.* If necessary, point out that the professor was reacting to the misuse of the word instead of the bad news.

Question 3. Have students think about the professor's reaction to the news that his bride was eaten. Ask how he would have reacted if she had been his first love.

Reading Literature: Poetry

Question 1. Direct the students to reread Nash's poems on pages 293 through 296 and to determine the rhyme scheme and mood of each one.

Question 2. Have students examine the way the professor treats people and what he considers important in life. Have them decide what the poet's opinion of the professor is.

Developing Vocabulary Skills

Have students read the directions for the exercise. Make sure they understand them and then have them complete the exercise independently. Encourage them to use the **Glossary** or a classroom dictionary to check on meanings they are unsure of. Discuss the answers together.

Developing Vocabulary Skills

Completing Analogies. As you learned in the vocabulary exercise for "The Bet" in Chapter 4 (page 172), an analogy consists of two pairs of related words that are related in the same way. Here is an example:

Herd is to cow as flock is to bird.

The first term in each pair, herd and flock, is the group name for the animal named in the second term, cow and bird. Other relationships include synonyms and antonyms.

Each incomplete analogy below uses words from the prose and poetry selections you have already read in this book. For each, choose the word that will complete the relationship. Be able to explain why you chose that word.

1. Weary is to tired as eager is to ____.
   zealous valiant tranquil severe
2. Quack is to whinny as duck is to ____.
   bear turkey horse dog
3. Venture is to hesitate as superintend is to ____.
   obey direct agree tell
4. Cow is to hay as ____ is to wood.
   panther termite hippopotamus canary
5. Friend is to loyal as enemy is to ____.
   slow prophetic vengeful enthusiastic
6. Reed is to grass as stingray is to ____.
   seal fish glass danger
7. Surrey is to horse as car is to ____.
   road driver tires engine
8. Tremulous is to firm as monotony is to ____.
   treason variation rascal vagabond

Developing Writing Skills

Analytical Writing

1. **Examining Humor in Poems.** All four poems by Ogden Nash in this text were funny. Can you explain, in one or more paragraphs, how his

Developing Writing Skills

Read and discuss the two assignments. Then have each student choose and complete one of the two.

Question 1. Encourage students to choose just one of the ways of examining the rhyme, rhythm, or surprising words of the poetry. To try to examine all aspects in one or two paragraphs would mean that the examination would be incomplete and superficial.

Pre-Writing. Have students reread the poems. Then have each student decide which aspect to examine—rhyme, rhythm, or surprising words. Ask each student to

(continued from page 297)

b. The mood of all the poems is light and humorous.

2. Possible theme: You can become so wrapped up in your job that you forget to care about people.

Developing Vocabulary Skills

1. zealous; both pairs are synonyms

2. horse; the first two terms are animal sounds and the second two are the animals that make those sounds

3. obey; both pairs are antonyms

rhymes helped create the humor? If you prefer, you can write about his rhythms or about his use of words that surprise the reader.

Creative Writing

2. **Imitating a Poet.** The poetry of Ogden Nash is easy to imitate, especially with the regular rhythms used in "The Termite," "The Purist," and "The Hippopotamus." Think of some subjects you could use to make people laugh: joggers, TV watchers, video-game players, sports fans. Write a poem of at least four lines, using some of Ogden Nash's rhythm and rhyme patterns and his surprising mix of words.

Developing Skills in Study and Research

Becoming Familiar with Other Library Resources. A library contains more than books. In your school or local library, find the record and tape collection. Also, locate the section of the card catalog in which these resources are listed. Notice that some records are of music and some are of non-musical presentations, such as poetry readings.

Find out if your library has any records or tapes of any of the poems in this chapter. List the title of the record or tape, and the name of the person who did the reading.

Your library may have no records or tapes of poems in this book. However, it may have recordings of other poems by the poets you have read. If so, list those records and tapes.

Ogden Nash wrote funny poems to be read to the music of *Carnival of the Animals* by the French composer Emile Saint-Saens. Does your library have a recording of the music along with the poems? If so, list both the conductor and the narrator.

Developing Skills in Speaking and Listening

1. **Reading Humorous Poems.** Is there one Ogden Nash poem you liked best? Perhaps you have found another poem by the same author in another source. Prepare to read or recite your favorite Nash poem to your class. Remember that these funny poems are very short. Give your audience time to get the humor by using pauses or gestures.

2. **Changing the Interpretation of a Poem.** If you located "Carnival of the Animals" in the Study and Research activity above, you might want to listen to and copy some of the verses you like. Recite them with the record. Then prepare and recite your own interpretations, using different expressions.

4. termite; the first term in each pair is the name of an animal and the second term is the food it eats

5. vengeful; the second term in each pair is a characteristic of the first term

6. fish; the first term in each pair is an example of the second term

7. engine; the second term in each pair is one part of the first term

8. variation; both pairs are antonyms

make notes on that aspect for each poem, and to write a topic sentence that explains what the writer intends to show in the paragraph.

Writing. Allow sufficient time for the students to write their first drafts.

Revising. Have students work with partners. Have them read their partners' paragraphs and check to make sure that their topic sentences tell the main idea, and that there are examples from each of the four poems.

Question 2. Encourage students who have not written a poem yet to try this question.

Pre-Writing. Have students brainstorm about possible subjects for a light, short poem. Encourage them to choose subjects with which they are familiar or ones that are so silly that they will be funny to the reader. Have them make notes on what their subject looks like or does.

Writing. Have students keep the first line of an Odgen Nash poem with the rhythm pattern marked on it in front of them as they write. This will help them maintain the regular iambic rhythm pattern. Also remind them to make sure their rhyme scheme is the same.

Revising. Have students share their poems in small groups. You may wish to create a poetry corner in your classroom and display their completed works there.

Developing Skills in Study and Research

Have the students read the explanation and directions. If possible, arrange a visit to a library so students can complete the exercise during class time. If this is not possible, visit the library yourself and bring back records or tapes of poetry readings. Explain how you located the various materials in the library.

Developing Skills in Speaking and Listening

1. Make available a number of poems by Ogden Nash. You may want to encourage students to recite more than one poem if the poems they choose are extremely short. Remind the students to express the mood of the poem in their voices and to observe the punctuation marks.

2. If the class has a recording of Nash's poems along with the "Carnival of the Animals," allow time for individuals or small groups to work on a presentation. Students may recite the poems along with the record or alone.

Poems About Sports

Call on a student to read the first paragraph of page 300. For a few minutes, allow the students to discuss favorite sports and favorite moments in sports. Then have another student read the rest of the page. Have the students tell in their own words the main idea of this page.

Poems About Sports

Most of us enjoy taking part in sports. We like the feelings that the activity and excitement give us. We also enjoy watching sports. The power and grace of an athlete are a pleasure to watch.

The poems in this section try to put into words what we feel or see in sports. As you read these poems, notice how the figures of speech make the sports action come alive.

Sandlot Game, 1964, RALPH FASANELLA. Private Collection.

About the Art

Ralph Fasanella (born 1914) chooses his subjects from the New York City urban environment in which he grew up. The son of Italian immigrants who settled in Greenwich Village, he learned to know the city while working in his father's ice-hauling business. He took up painting in middle age.

Sandlot reflects Fasanella's love of baseball and of the activity—the sights and sounds—of the urban environment. The canvas is filled with color and colorful details of the sandlot play as well as of the city setting. Fasanella's lack of formal training in perspective can be seen in the flatly formed figures and in the slightly tilted playing field. His work also reveals, though, his active sense of humor. Notice the name on the hotdog vendor's cart.

The Base Stealer

ROBERT FRANCIS

As you read this poem, decide who is speaking. Is it the base stealer? Or is it someone watching the base stealer?

Poised between going on and back, pulled
Both ways taut like a tightrope-walker,
Fingertips pointing to opposites,
Now bouncing tiptoe like a dropped ball
Or a kid skipping rope, come on, come on,
Running a scattering of steps sidewise,
How he teeters, skitters, tingles, teases,
Taunts them, hovers like an ecstatic bird,
He's only flirting, crowd him, crowd him,
Delicate, delicate, delicate, delicate—now!

Check Test

1. What type of performer is the base stealer compared to? (a tightrope-walker)
2. What word indicates that the base stealer has made his move? (Now)

Objectives

- To recognize and appreciate poetry as a form of literature
- To understand the rhythm of free verse
- To make inferences and predict outcomes in poetry
- To understand similes
- To apply literal, interpretive, and critical reading skills to a selection

Preparing the Students

Essential Vocabulary. The words presented here are essential to the understanding of the selection.

Have the students use the context clues in the following sentences to determine the meanings of the underlined words.

poised taunt ecstatic hover

1. The tightrope walker stood poised for a moment to be sure she had her balance before she began another trick.
2. Never taunt my dog by holding his bone just out of his reach.
3. My sister was ecstatic when the letter she had been eagerly waiting for finally arrived.
4. The spaceship did not move ahead or land. It just hovered over the open field.

Motivation. Have the students read the introductory paragraph at the top of page 301 and state in their own words what they should try to find out as they read this poem.

Presenting the Selection

1. Have the students read "The Base Stealer" silently. Tell them to pay particular attention to the movements described in the poem.
2. Make sure that everyone has read the poem by administering the **Check Test** at the bottom of this page.
3. Develop the study questions as suggested in **Using the Study Questions** on page 302. A question there reminds students of the question posed in the introduction.

Special Populations

LD, ESL. This would be a good poem to tape record or read through to the class. Students might need help with correct phrasing of the poem.

To add the excitement of actually being at a ballpark, point out the words that need to be read louder or more rapidly, reading as if you were an announcer at a game, shouting the phrases to the rest of the fans.

ESL. ESL students may be unfamiliar with the game of baseball and unable to visualize the action taking place. Ask students to act out the poem, or try to show a videotape of part of a baseball game to point out the actions to the ESL student.

Using the Study Questions

It is recommended that students always read and answer the questions in **Developing Comprehension Skills** in class discussion. Whenever possible, they should also read the questions in **Reading Literature** together and discuss the answers.

Developing Comprehension Skills

Question 1. Have students cite evidence from the poem that explains who the speaker is.

Question 2. As a review, discuss the meaning of simile. Make sure students know that it is a comparison using "like" or "as."

Question 3. Explain that this question asks students to formulate their own opinions. There is no single right answer.

Reading Literature: Poetry

Question 1. Have the students read aloud the lines that support their decisions.

Question 2. Have students find proof for their answers in the poem.

Question 3. Have a student read the last two lines aloud. Have him or her emphasize the beat. Discuss with students how this rhythm is similar to the movements of a base stealer.

Developing Comprehension Skills

Literal Reading
1. Who is the speaker in this poem, the base stealer or someone watching him? What makes you think as you do?

Literal Reading
2. Find four similes in this poem. To what four different things is the base stealer compared?

Critical Reading
3. Which of the four similes do you think pictures the action best? Why did you choose that one?

Reading Literature: Poetry

1. **Making Inferences in Poetry.** Do you think that the base stealer is experienced at stealing bases? Find two lines that you feel support your decision.

2. **Predicting Outcomes in Poetry.** Is it possible to make an accurate prediction about whether or not the base stealer succeeds? Why or why not?

3. **Understanding Rhythm.** This poem has been written in free verse, which means it has a free, or irregular, arrangement of stressed and unstressed beats. Copy the following lines and put an accent mark, ′, over the syllables that are stressed. Notice how the rhythm of each line makes you feel the movement of the base stealer.

   How he teeters, skitters, tingles, teases,
   Delicate, delicate, delicate, delicate—now!

Answers to Study Questions

Developing Comprehension Skills

1. The speaker of the poem is someone other than the base stealer. The speaker says "he" when referring to the base stealer.

2. The base stealer is compared to a tightrope-walker, a dropped ball, a kid skipping rope, and an ecstatic bird.

3. Answers will vary. Students should give logical reasons for their choices.

Reading Literature: Poetry

1. The students will probably feel that the base stealer seems to be in control of the situation. He seems to be experienced as evidenced in the following lines:

"Taunts them, hovers like an ecstatic bird" (Line 8)

"He's only flirting" (Line 9)

2. Answers may vary. Some students may say that he succeeds because he waits until the right moment and he is an experienced runner. Others, especially those who play baseball, may insist that the outcome cannot be predicted from the information given.

3. Accents:

How he teéters, skítters, tíngles, teáses,
Délicate, délicate, délicate, délicate—nów!

The Double-Play

ROBERT WALLACE

In this poem, things happen fast—too fast for the speaker to repeat a name, even when that person is involved in two actions. If you are unsure what or who is acting, go back to the last thing or person named.

The Wide Swing, about 1975,
HARVEY DINNERSTEIN.
Capricorn Galleries, Bethesda, Maryland.

In his sea lit
distance, the pitcher winding
like a clock about to chime comes down with

the ball, hit
sharply, under the artificial
banks of arc lights, bounds like a vanishing string

over the green
to the shortstop magically
scoops to his right whirling above his invisible

About the Art

Harvey Dinnerstein (born 1928) is a representational artist who paints scenes from contemporary life, such as the baseball scene shown here. *The Wide Swing* isolates our interest on one of the most dramatic moments in baseball: the batter following through and watching the results of his swing. It looks like the batter here did hit the ball, and we might be left in suspense had not Dinnerstein placed Hall-of-Famer Joe DiMaggio at the plate. DiMaggio, one of the best hitters in baseball history, played for the New York Yankees between 1936 and 1951. His lifetime batting average was a high .325.

Objectives

- To recognize and appreciate poetry as a form of literature
- To understand figurative language
- To recognize the form of a poem
- To apply literal, interpretive, and critical reading skills to a selection

Preparing the Students

Essential Vocabulary. The words presented here are essential to the understanding of the selection.

Have the students use the context clues in the following sentences to determine the meanings of the underlined words.

pirouette deception

1. At this point in the ballet, the dancers pirouette, or turn around on the tips of their toes.
2. The magician practices fooling people. In fact, he is a master of deception.

If the students need additional help with the vocabulary of this selection, encourage them to use context clues to determine word meaning. As needed, direct them to the **Glossary** or to a classroom dictionary.

Motivation. Have the students read the introductory paragraph at the top of page 303 and state in their own words the directions that are given to help them understand the poem.

Presenting the Selection

1. Before students begin to read silently, read the first nine lines with them. Show them how they can understand confusing passages better if they repeat the last thing or person named and make it the subject of the next part of the sentence. (Examples: "the pitcher ... comes down with the ball;" "the ball ... bounds like a vanishing string.")

Have the students read the entire poem silently.

2. Administer the **Check Test** at the bottom of T.E. page 304.

3. Develop the study questions as suggested in **Using the Study Questions** beginning on page 304. That section also provides a challenge question.

Reinforcing the Lesson

To reteach, reinforce, or extend the skills in this lesson, see the following:

Skills Practice Book, Green Level—page 136

shadows
in the dust redirects
its flight to the running poised second baseman

pirouettes
leaping, above the slide, to throw
from midair, across the colored tightened interval,

to the leaning-
out first baseman ends the dance
drawing it disappearing into his long brown glove

stretches. What
is too swift for deception
is final, lost, among the loosened figures

jogging off the field
(the pitcher walks), casual
in the space where the poem has happened.

Developing Comprehension Skills

Literal Reading	1. In your own words, describe the course of this double play.
Literal Reading	2. In the sixth stanza, the speaker says the first baseman "ends the dance." Find another word or phrase that compares the action to a dance or the players to dancers.
Interpretive Reading	3. Find the words listed below in the poem. What comparison do they suggest? In what ways is the comparison accurate?

artificial	vanishing	magically
invisible	disappearing	deception

Special Populations

LD. To increase students' ability to visualize the action, you might want to sketch a baseball diamond on the board and have a student plot the flight of the ball in the poem.

ESL. See the suggestions for **Special Populations** on T.E. page 301.

Reading Literature: Poetry, 3 on page 305 is necessary to the understanding of this poem for many special-populations students. Ask for help from other members of the class to demonstrate or illustrate the actions and descriptions made.

Using the Study Questions

It is recommended that students always read and answer the questions in **Developing Comprehension Skills** in class discussion. Whenever possible, they should also read the questions in **Reading Literature** together and discuss the answers.

Developing Comprehension Skills

Question 1. Point out how each stanza follows the flight of the ball from one player to the next. Have several students describe the action.

Question 2. Have students picture a dancer and then find words in the poem that describe a dancer's movements.

Question 3. Have students think of a type of entertainment that is often associated with those words.

Reading Literature: Poetry

Question 1. Have students find the clues and read them aloud.

Question 2. Read the first and second stanzas. Compare their irregular rhythm to the regular rhythm of the last stanza. You may want to write the last stanza on the board and mark its accented and unaccented syllables.

Question 3. Read and discuss the question.

Question 4. Have students find and read aloud the exact words that emphasize the ordinariness of the inning.

Challenge Question. Describe the mood of the poem.

Check Test

1. To whom does the shortstop throw the ball? (to the second baseman)

2. Why do the players leave the field after the double play? (It must have been the second and the third outs. The inning is over.)

Answers to Study Questions

Developing Comprehension Skills

1. The pitcher throws the ball. The ball is hit. The shortstop catches the ball and throws it to the second baseman, who touches second base and makes the first out. He whirls, avoiding the runner's slide, and throws the ball to the first baseman, who makes the second out.

2. The poised second baseman pirouettes and leaps.

3. All the words are associated with magic or magicians. The double play is like magic because the ball changes hands so quickly that the eye can't follow it, just as a magician moves faster than the eye can follow.

Reading Literature: Poetry

1. **Making Inferences in Poetry.** Was this game played at night or during the day? What clues in the poem give you the answer?

2. **Understanding Rhythm.** This poem may be difficult to read because throughout most of the poem the rhythm is irregular. Why do you suppose the poet used this irregular rhythm?

   Reread the poem, listening for a break between the irregular rhythm and a regular rhythm at the very end. What is the effect of this change in rhythm?

3. **Recognizing Figurative Language.** Reading this poem is almost like watching a slow-motion instant replay. It draws your attention to little details that you do not ordinarily notice. Yet it does so in only a few words that suggest setting, action, and mood all at once. In your own words, explain each of these phrases:

   a. the pitcher winding
   like a clock about to chime
   b. the ball . . .
   bounds like a vanishing string
   c. the shortstop . . .
   whirling above his invisible
   shadows
   in the dust
   d. the running poised second baseman
   e. the leaning-
   out first baseman . . .
   drawing it disappearing into his long brown glove
   f. the loosened figures
   jogging off the field

4. **Recognizing Form.** This poem separates sharply into two parts: the action of the double play and the closing comments. There is a change in rhythm and a change in language, too. The first seven stanzas are full of details squeezed together, comparisons, and precise words. The last stanza, however, uses very ordinary language in a normal speaking tone. What detail about the players' actions does this stanza mention that makes the end of this inning like the end of a typical, ordinary inning?

Reading Literature: Poetry

1. The game was played at night. The phrases that give us the answer are the following: "under the artificial banks of arc lights" and "whirling above his invisible shadows."

2. The irregular rhythm matches the irregular movements of the players.

The irregular rhythm conveys the swiftness and hurried quality of the action. The regular rhythm at the end of the poem makes the reader feel that everything is back to normal. The change emphasizes that the action is done.

3. Possible answers:

a. The pitcher winds up, ready to pitch.
b. The ball streaks through the air.
c. The shortstop turns and leaps to catch the ball.
d. The second baseman is running and ready to catch the ball from the shortstop.
e. The first baseman leans toward second base and catches the ball in his glove.
f. The players, now relaxed and loose, jog off the field.

4. The players jog and the pitcher walks off the field casually.

Challenge. Answers may vary. The mood is one of tension and excitement.

Objectives

- To recognize and appreciate poetry as a form of literature
- To recognize the rhythmical quality of poetry
- To recognize hyperbole
- To examine levels of language
- To apply literal, interpretive, and critical reading skills to a selection

Preparing the Students

Essential Vocabulary. The words presented here are essential to the understanding of the selection.

Have the students use the context clues in the following sentences to determine the meanings of the underlined words.

patrons	doff	haughty
pallor	defiance	vengeance

1. The fans of a baseball team are sometimes called its patrons.
2. After a long winter spent indoors, Rina's face had a pallor instead of a tan.
3. Ballplayers often take off their caps when the fans cheer. When they doff their caps like that, they are thanking the fans.
4. It was clearly an act of defiance when the young child firmly refused to obey his mother.
5. Chuck was sure that he was the best player on the team. His haughty attitude annoyed the other players.
6. Since the man did not believe in vengeance, he refused to try to get even with the hoodlums who destroyed his car.

If the students need additional help with the vocabulary of this selection, encourage them to use context clues to determine word meaning. As needed, direct them to the **Glossary** or to a classroom dictionary.

Motivation. Have the students read the introductory paragraph at the top of page 306 and state in their own words what they should try to find out as they read this poem.

Presenting the Selection

1. Explain that this poem tells a story. Have the students read "Casey at the Bat" silently. Then have volunteers read one or two stanzas each. Since this poem has such a strong, regular rhythm, allow students to emphasize the rhythm as they read.

2. Make sure that everyone has understood the literal meaning of the poem by

Casey at the Bat

This is one of the best known poems about sports that has ever been written. As you read, consider what it is that has made this poem so popular.

ERNEST LAWRENCE THAYER

It looked extremely rocky for the Mudville nine that day;
The score stood two to four, with but an inning left to play.
So, when Cooney died at second, and Burrows did the same,
A pallor wreathed the features of the patrons of the game.

A straggling few got up to go, leaving there the rest,
With that hope which springs eternal within the human breast.
For they thought: "If only Casey could get a whack at that,"
They'd put even money now, with Casey at the bat.

But Flynn preceded Casey, and likewise so did Blake,
And the former was a pudd'n, and the latter was a fake.
So on that stricken multitude a deathlike silence sat;
For there seemed but little chance of Casey's getting to the bat.

But Flynn let drive a "single," to the wonderment of all.
And the much-despised Blakey "tore the cover off the ball."
And when the dust had lifted, and they saw what had occurred,
There was Blakey safe at second, and Flynn a-huggin' third.

Then from the gladdened multitude went up a joyous yell—
It rumbled in the mountaintops, it rattled in the dell;
It struck upon the hillside and rebounded on the flat;
For Casey, mighty Casey, was advancing to the bat.

The Autograph, 1980, OSCAR de MEJO, 20″ × 16″ from the book, *My America,* Harry N. Abrams, Inc., New York.

There was ease in Casey's manner as he stepped into his place,
There was pride in Casey's bearing and a smile on Casey's face;
And when responding to the cheers he lightly doffed his hat,
No stranger in the crowd could doubt 'twas Casey at the bat.

Ten thousand eyes were on him as he rubbed his hands with dirt,
Five thousand tongues applauded when he wiped them on his shirt;
Then when the writhing pitcher ground the ball into his hip,
Defiance glanced in Casey's eye, a sneer curled Casey's lip.

And now the leather-covered sphere came hurtling through the air,
And Casey stood a-watching it in haughty grandeur there.
Close by the sturdy batsman the ball unheeded sped;
"That ain't my style," said Casey. "Strike one," the umpire said.

administering the **Check Test,** at the bottom of T.E. page 308.

3. Ask the students what they think has made this poem so popular.

4. Develop the study questions as suggested in **Using the Study Questions** beginning on page 309. That section also provides challenge questions for further discussion, as needed. (For answers to questions, see T.E. page 309.)

Encouraging Independent Reading

Students who are interested in baseball may be encouraged to read biographies about famous persons, past or present, in professional baseball. Tell them to prepare to share with the class the accomplishments of the sports figures they choose and any events that contributed to their success.

About the Art

Originally commissioned by *Sports Illustrated* magazine, *The Autograph* by Oscar de Mejo (born 1911) is of a baseball player from an early era of the game, as indicated by the out-of-style uniform. The artist encircled the figure with outstretched hands and pencils of exaggerated proportions, emphasizing the urgency of the fans' requests for autographs. The homespun cartoon-like quality of the drawing also lends the composition a folk art effect, evoking the past era when baseball players, real ones such as Babe Ruth, or fictitious ones such as Casey, became folk heroes.

From the benches, filled with people, there went up a muffled roar,
Like the beating of the storm waves on the stern and distant shore.
"Kill him! Kill the umpire!" shouted someone on the stand;
And it's likely they'd have killed him had not Casey raised his hand.

With a smile of honest charity great Casey's visage shone;
He stilled the rising tumult, he made the game go on;
He signaled to the pitcher, and once more the spheroid flew;
But Casey still ignored it, and the umpire said, "Strike two."

"Fraud!" cried the maddened thousands, and the echo answered "Fraud!"
But one scornful look from Casey and the audience was awed;
They saw his face grow stern and cold, they saw his muscles strain,
And they knew that Casey wouldn't let the ball go by again.

The sneer is gone from Casey's lips, his teeth are clenched in hate,
He pounds with cruel vengeance his bat upon the plate;
And now the pitcher holds the ball, and now he lets it go,
And now the air is shattered by the force of Casey's blow.

Oh, somewhere in this favored land the sun is shining bright,
The band is playing somewhere, and somewhere hearts are light;
And somewhere men are laughing, and somewhere children shout,
But there is no joy in Mudville: Mighty Casey has struck out.

Check Test

1. What was the score at the beginning of the poem? (four to two)

2. What did the crowd do when Casey came up to bat? (It cheered wildly.)

3. How did Casey make the last out? (He struck out.)

Answers to Study Questions

Developing Comprehension Skills

1. The fans were almost hopeless of winning the game. "A pallor wreathed (their) features" is a figurative way of saying that the fans looked and felt sick, thinking about how their team would lose the game.

2. The fans became hopeful that Casey would get a chance at bat when "Flynn let drive a single to the wonderment of all and the much-despised Blakey 'tore the cover off the ball.'"

3. Casey was so confident that he could hit anything that he felt he could afford to wait for the perfect ball to hit. He probably wanted to hit a home run.

4. The reader is expecting to hear that Casey hit the ball. When the poem shifts away from the ball game, the reader becomes curious and uneasy. In addition, the line says that "somewhere" the sun is shining, making the reader fear that that is happening somewhere else, not in Mudville.

Challenge. Casey is proud and haughty. He feels that he can save the team from defeat single-handedly. He even seems to feel that he is in charge of the whole game. He quiets the crowd and signals to the pitcher to throw the ball. He makes a big show of being determined to hit the last ball.

Developing Comprehension Skills

Literal Reading 1. How do you think the "patrons" or fans felt at the beginning of the poem? What is meant by, "A pallor wreathed (their) features"?

Literal Reading 2. What caused the feelings of the crowd to change? Find the lines that are the first indication that their feelings have changed.

Interpretive Reading 3. Why do you think Casey let the first two strikes go by?

Interpretive Reading 4. The poem doesn't reveal what happened until the last two words. However, we begin to get the feeling that something went wrong in the line, "Oh, somewhere in this favored land the sun is shining bright." Explain why this line gives the reader that feeling.

Reading Literature: Poetry

1. **Identifying Rhythm and Rhyme Patterns.** Does this poem have a mostly regular rhythm or a mostly irregular rhythm?

   What is the rhyme scheme of the poem? Does every stanza follow the same pattern?

2. **Recognizing Hyperbole.** As you know, **hyperbole** is an extreme exaggeration that often brings to mind an absurd image. This poem has numerous examples of hyperbole, such as in stanzas 3 and 5:

   So on that stricken multitude a deathlike silence sat

   Then from the gladdened multitude went up a joyous yell—
   It rumbled in the mountaintops, it rattled in the dell;
   It struck upon the hillside and rebounded on the flat;
   For Casey, mighty Casey, was advancing to the bat.

   Find other examples of hyperbole in "Casey at the Bat."

3. **Examining Levels of Language.** One characteristic that makes this poem funny is its very serious tone, in contrast to its not very serious subject. In addition, it mixes slang terms, like "whack," and terms with special sports meanings, like "huggin' third," with rather formal terms, such as "stricken multitude." Make two lists. On the first, write at least five terms or phrases used in "Casey at the Bat" that are more formal than you would normally use in conversation. On the second, write at least five terms or phrases from the poem that are either slang or sports jargon.

Using the Study Questions

It is recommended that students always read and answer the questions in **Developing Comprehension Skills** in class discussion. Whenever possible, they should also read the questions in **Reading Literature** together and discuss the answers.

Developing Comprehension Skills

Questions 1 and 2. Read and discuss the questions.

Question 3. Remind students of Casey's reputation and self-confidence before asking them to answer this question.

Question 4. Point out that since the poem switches away from the action of the game at this crucial time, that fact alone should alert the reader that something has gone wrong.

Challenge Question. Describe Casey's personality, basing your answer on details from the poem. (Interpretive Reading)

Reading Literature: Poetry

Question 1. Read and discuss the question.

Question 2. Have students look for exaggerations in descriptions of actions or feelings.

Question 3. After students have made individual lists, have them suggest items for a class list to be written on the board.

Challenge Question. Why do you think Thayer changed his writing to present tense form in stanza 12?

Reading Literature: Poetry

1. This poem has a mostly regular rhythm. Every stanza follows the same rhyme pattern: a a b b.

2. Possible answers:

From the benches, filled with people, there went up a muffled roar (stanza 9)
Like the beating of the storm waves on the stern and distant shore (stanza 9)
And it's likely they'd have killed him had not Casey raised his hand (stanza 9)
And now the air is shattered by the force of Casey's blow (stanza 12)

3. Possible answers:

Formal language: *a pallor wreathed the features of the patrons of the game; hope which springs eternal within the human breast; gladdened multitude; it struck upon the hillside and rebounded on the flat; leather-covered sphere; the ball unheeded sped; great Casey's visage shone; the spheroid flew.*

Slang or sports jargon: *Cooney died at second; the former was a pudd'n, and the latter was a fake; single; tore the cover off the ball; a-huggin' third; "That ain't my style;" "Kill the umpire;" struck out.*

Challenge. Possible answer: Thayer may have wanted to create a feeling in the reader of being right there at the game during its most exciting part.

Objectives

- To recognize and appreciate poetry as a form of literature
- To understand concrete poetry
- To understand figurative language
- To recognize and understand personification
- To apply literal, interpretive, and critical reading skills to a selection
- To use context clues and word parts to define unknown words
- To write an evaluation of a poem
- To interpret a humorous poem

Preparing the Students

Essential Vocabulary. The words presented here are essential to the understanding of the selection.

Write the following words and their definitions on the board. Have individual students read them aloud.

solemn—serious

hesitate—to pause briefly because of uncertainty

exasperate—to make angry or irritated

Motivation. Have the students read the introductory paragraph at the top of page 310 and state in their own words what they should try to find out as they read this poem.

Presenting the Selection

1. Read "Foul Shot" aloud to the students. This initial reading will help them understand what is happening in the poem. Then have them read the poem silently.

2. To see if students understand the literal meaning of this poem, administer the **Check Test** at the bottom of this page.

3. Remind students of the question posed in the introductory paragraph. Have a student read the lines from the poem that answer the question. Call on another student to state the meaning of those two lines in his or her own words.

4. Develop the study questions as suggested in **Using the Study Questions** beginning on page 311. That section also provides a challenge question.

Reinforcing the Lesson

To reteach, reinforce, or extend the skills in this lesson, see the following:

Skills Practice Book, Green Level—page 137

Foul Shot

The following poem is not about just any foul shot. Read the first few lines carefully to find out what made this shot special.

EDWIN A. HOEY

With two 60's stuck on the scoreboard
And two seconds hanging on the clock,
The solemn boy in the center of eyes,
Squeezed by silence,
Seeks out the line with his feet,
Soothes his hands along his uniform,
Gently drums the ball against the floor,
Then measures the waiting net,
Raises the ball on his right hand,
Balances it with his left,
Calms it with fingertips,
Breathes,
Crouches,
Waits,
And then through a stretching of
stillness,
Nudges it upward.

The ball
Slides up and out,
Lands,
Leans,
Wobbles,
Wavers,
Hesitates,
Exasperates,
Plays it coy
Until every face begs with
unsounding screams—

And then
And then
And then,

Right before ROAR-UP,
Dives down and through.

Check Test

1. Why is the boy so nervous? (He has to make an important foul shot.)

2. What does the crowd do when the ball drops through the hoop? (It roars.)

Answers to Study Questions

Developing Comprehension Skills

1. Main ideas:

Stanza 1: The nervous boy is getting ready to make an important foul shot.

Stanza 2: The ball wavers on the rim.

Stanza 3: The suspense builds.

Stanza 4: The ball drops through the net.

2. The boy is the center of attention for all the fans and the other players. He is also in the center of the court.

Developing Comprehension Skills

Literal Reading 1. There are four stanzas in this poem. The third stanza has only six words in it. What is the main idea of each stanza?

Interpretive Reading 2. Give two meanings for this line: "The solemn boy in the center of eyes."

Reading Literature: Poetry

1. **Understanding Personification.** In this poem, the poet uses personification when he describes the ball. Find four words or phrases that suggest that the ball is a person.
2. **Understanding Concrete Poetry.** Many times the way the words are arranged in a poem helps to make the meaning of the poem clear. In two parts of "Foul Shot," there is only one word on each line. What effect does this have on the way you read the poem? What effect does it have on the feeling you get from the poem?
3. **Understanding Figurative Language.** This poem presents both the sights and sounds of a basketball game. Each phrase below mentions sound or the absence of sound. Explain both the sound and the feeling that the phrase expresses.
   a. Squeezed by silence (stanza 1, line 4)
   b. through a stretching of stillness (stanza 1, line 15)
   c. every face begs with unsounding screams (stanza 2, line 10)
   d. Right before ROAR-UP (stanza 4, line 1)

Developing Vocabulary Skills

Using Context Clues and Word Parts. Read the following sentences based on the poems you have just read. The meaning of each underlined word can be figured out by using context clues or word parts. Choose the correct answer. Then write the meaning of the word.

1. The base stealer teases, <u>taunts</u>, flirts as he skitters back and forth.
   a. restatement clue b. comparison clue c. words in a series
2. The shortstop scoops up the ball, and <u>redirects</u> its flight to the running second baseman.
   a. word parts b. example clue c. definition clue

Reading Literature: Poetry

1. The boy "calms" the ball. The ball "leans," "wavers," "hesitates," "exasperates," "plays it coy," and "dives down."

2. Having one word to a line makes the reader pause between words. It adds to the suspense of the moment.

3. The sounds and the feelings the phrases express:

a. no sound at all; the feeling is tension

b. silence; the feeling is expectant; the crowd is waiting for something to happen

c. There is still silence, but the reader begins to think about the shrill sound of screams; the feeling is excitement

d. the powerful sound of an excited crowd; the feeling is a combination of relief and happiness

Challenge. Answers will vary.

Developing Vocabulary Skills

1. c **4.** b
2. a **5.** a
3. c

Special Populations

ESL. The action will need to be explained to students unfamiliar with the game of basketball.

LD, ESL. Alternative activities that could accompany or replace the exercise **Interpreting a Humorous Poem** could be:

Have students act out the poem as a small group.
Illustrate the poem.
Add sound effects as if reading the poem on the radio.

Using the Study Questions

It is recommended that students always read and answer the questions in **Developing Comprehension Skills** in class discussion. Whenever possible, they should also read the questions in the other categories together and discuss the answers.

Developing Comprehension Skills

Question 1. Read and discuss the question.

Question 2. Have students think about two ways in which the boy is in the center.

Reading Literature: Poetry

Question 1. Read and discuss the question.

Question 2. Have one student read the poem pausing at the ends of lines, and have another student read the lines without pausing. Ask students to decide which method of reading reminded them more of a real foul shot. Ask how they would naturally read the poem since the words are spread out.

Question 3. Ask several students for their answers to each part of the question.

Challenge Question. Which of the figures of speech or sensory details in this poem are most realistic? Name at least three details and explain why you chose them.

Developing Vocabulary Skills

Have students read the directions to the exercise. Then have them complete it independently. Discuss the answers together.

Developing Writing Skills

Read and discuss the two assignments. Then have each student choose and complete one of the two.

Question 1. Emphasize that each student may choose a different poem. There is no "best" poem.

Pre-Writing. Have students think about the four poems. They may want to reread all four. After each student chooses the poem that helps him or her experience the moment best, ask the student to write a list of figures of speech, sounds of language, or sensory images found in that poem.

Writing. Have students use the list of figures, sounds, or images. Allow sufficient time for the students to write their first drafts.

Revising. Have students reread their drafts. Have them decide whether they have included enough references to the poem of their choice.

Question 2. Make sure that the students know that they can write either prose or poetry.

Pre-Writing. Suggest that students think of a moment of tension or beauty in any sport. Then have them list verbs, nouns, and adjectives that they could use to describe the moment. Have students read and follow the directions in the text.

Writing. Allow sufficient time for the students to write their first drafts.

Revising. Have students exchange papers with a partner. Have partners point out any details that are unclear. Allow time for revisions. Post poems or paragraphs on a writing bulletin board.

Developing Skills in Speaking and Listening

Have students read the directions. You may want to divide the poem into parts so that several students can read a few stanzas. Remind students to emphasize the exaggerations in the poem.

3. The pitcher ground the ball into his hip and sent the leather-covered sphere hurtling through the air.
   a. words in a series b. contrast clue c. synonym
4. The sneer is gone from Casey's lips, his teeth are clenched in hate; he pounds with cruel vengeance his bat upon the plate.
   a. word parts b. inference clue c. contrast clue
5. The player leans, wobbles, wavers, and hesitates as he throws the ball.
   a. words in a series b. comparison clue c. example clue

Developing Writing Skills

Analytical Writing

1. **Evaluating a Poem.** Consider the four poems about sports that you have just read. Which one do you think did the best job of helping you experience the moment? Do not choose a poem just because you like the sport. Write a paragraph or more explaining why you chose the poem. Tell which figures of speech or sounds of language or sensory images meant the most to you.

Creative Writing

2. **Using Specific Vocabulary.** "The Base Stealer," "The Double Play," and "Foul Shot" are all trying to do the same thing. They try to recreate the feeling of a specific moment in sports. You can do the same thing. First, think of the most exciting moment you have experienced in playing or watching a sport. Quickly list words and phases that describe the actions involved in the situation. Write every word that comes to mind as you relive the moment. Be as specific as possible. Also list any words that describe your feelings about the moment.

   Then, review your list. Choose the five best words or phrases. If you like, combine several separate words to form five strong phrases. Then use your five best phrases in a description of the moment. Write no more than ten lines or sentences in either poetry or prose.

Developing Skills in Speaking and Listening

Interpreting a Humorous Poem. "Casey at the Bat" provides an excellent opportunity for a dramatic reading. Practice reading this poem aloud. Your goal is to help your listeners experience the drama and emotion of that day. Sometimes silence in the right place adds to the drama. Look for places where pauses might be appropriate.

The Women's 400 Meters

LILLIAN MORRISON

This poem describes the racers as they prepare for and begin their run. Listen for the rhythm.

Skittish,
they flex knees, drum heels and
shiver at the starting line

waiting the gun
to pour them over the stretch
like a breaking wave.

Bang! they're off
careening down the lanes,
each chased by her own bright tiger.

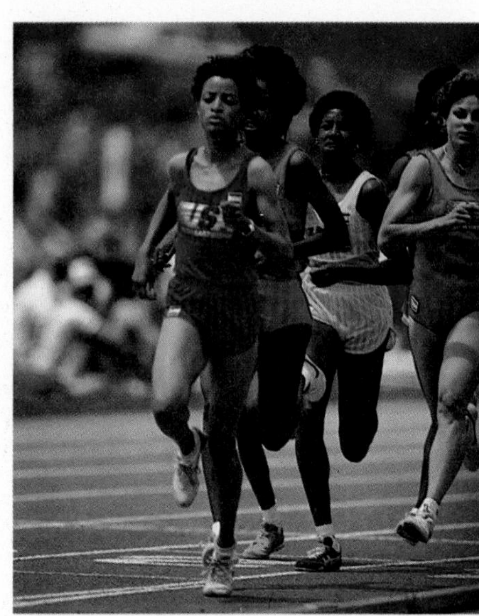

The Image Bank. Photograph by John Kelly.

Developing Comprehension Skills

Literal Reading — 1. What does "careening down the lanes" mean?

Interpretive Reading — 2. Explain the simile in lines 5 and 6. How are the runners like a wave?

Interpretive Reading — 3. Is the poet concerned with who will win this race? If not, what is she concerned with? Give a reason for your answer.

Reading Literature: Poetry

Appreciating Rhythm. Copy lines 5 and 9 on your paper, leaving space above each line. Mark each stressed beat with an accent, ʹ. How many stressed beats do you find in line 5? How many are in line 9? How does the rhythm help to express the meaning of the line?

Objectives

- To appreciate the rhythm of a poem
- To apply literal, interpretive, and critical reading skills to a selection

Preparing the Students

Essential Vocabulary. Tell the students that *skittish* means "nervous" and *careen* means "move out of control."

Motivation. Have the students read the introductory paragraph at the top of page 313 and state in their own words what they are to find out as they read.

Presenting the Selection

1. Have the students read "The Women's 400 Meters" silently and aloud.
2. Administer the **Check Test.**
3. Develop the study questions as suggested in **Using the Study Questions.**

Using the Study Questions

Developing Comprehension Skills

Question 1. Discuss the meaning of *careen.*

Question 2. Suggest that students picture the race from above.

Question 3. Explain that students must infer the answer to this question.

Reading Literature: Poetry

Question. You may want to complete this question with the students.

Challenge Question. There are no tigers actually chasing the women in the race. What might these tigers stand for?

Check Test

1. Name one action of the runners before the race begins. (Possible answers: They flex knees, drum heels, shiver.)
2. What sound are they waiting for? (the sound of the starting gun)

Answers to Study Questions

Developing Comprehension Skills

1. "Careening down the lanes" means running so fast they are almost out of control down the lanes on the track.

2. The runners are spread out in a curve, like a wave breaking on the shore.

3. The poet does not care who wins the race. She only cares about the feelings and movements of the runners. There is no mention of a winner, but there are several references to the runners' feelings and motivations.

Reading Literature: Poetry

Line 5:

tŏ póur thĕm óvĕr thĕ strétch

There are three stressed beats in Line 5.

Line 9:

éach chásed bў hĕr ówn bríght tígĕr

There are five stressed beats in line 9.

The greater number of stressed beats in Line 5 as compared to the previous lines suggests that the race is about to begin and that the runners will be spread out across the track shortly. The even greater number of stressed beats in line 9 indicates that the race is well under way.

Challenge. The tigers may symbolize each woman's ambition to win.

Objectives

- To recognize and appreciate poetry as a form of literature
- To appreciate rhyme in a poem
- To recognize onomatopoeia
- To apply literal, interpretive, and critical reading skills to a selection

Preparing the Students

Essential Vocabulary. The words presented here are essential to the understanding of the selection.

Have the students use the context clues in the following sentences to determine the meanings of the underlined words.

wary skirt

1. It's a good idea to be wary of strange dogs. Don't be afraid; just be cautious.
2. The child skirted the edge of the puddle, coming close but not stepping into it.

Motivation. Have the students read the introductory paragraph at the top of page 314 and state in their own words what they should try to find out as they read this poem.

Presenting the Selection

1. In preparation for this lesson, you may wish to copy "Skating" from page 314 onto the board or an overhead transparency for later use.

2. Have the students read "Skating" silently. Read it aloud to the students, emphasizing the grace of the poem created by the rhythm and word choice.

3. To see if the students understand the literal meaning of the poem, administer the **Check Test** at the bottom of this page.

4. Remind students of the directions in the introduction. Ask several students for their opinions about how the poem imitates the graceful movements of a good skater.

5. Develop the study questions as suggested in **Using the Study Questions** on page 315. That section also provides a challenge question for further discussion, if needed.

Skating

HERBERT ASQUITH

Have you ever watched an ice skater? Have you skated yourself? As you read this poem, watch for the ways the poem imitates the graceful movements of a good skater.

When I try to skate,
My feet are so wary
They grit and they grate;
And then I watch Mary
Easily gliding;
Skimming and curving,
Out and in,
With a turn of her head,
And a lift of her chin,
And a gleam of her eye,
And a twirl and a spin;
Sailing under
The breathless hush
Of the willows, and back
To the frozen rush
Out to the island
And round the edge,
Skirting the rim
Of the crackling sedge,
Swerving close
To the poplar root,
And round the lake
On a single foot,
With a three, and an eight,
And a loop and a ring;
Where Mary glides,
The lake will sing!
Out in the mist
I hear her now
Under the frost
Of the willow bow
Easily sailing,
Light and fleet,
With the song of the lake
Beneath her feet.

Check Test

1. Is Mary skating on a lake or on an indoor rink? (on a lake)

2. Who skates better—Mary or the speaker? (Mary)

Developing Comprehension Skills

Literal Reading — 1. Is the speaker an experienced ice skater? Which lines in the poem give you the answer to that question?

Literal Reading — 2. Name three or more proofs that Mary is a good skater.

Interpretive Reading — 3. The speaker says that "Where Mary slides, The lake will sing." Is the lake making a sound? Is there any other kind of "song" to which this line could refer? Explain your opinion.

Reading Literature: Poetry

1. **Appreciating Rhyme.** Using letters of the alphabet, show the rhyme scheme of the first four lines of the poem. Then identify the rhyme in the next eleven lines the same way. Continue to use the same letter of the alphabet for the same rhyming sound.

   Examine the patterns of rhyme that you have found. Are the lines in this one long stanza grouped mostly in threes or in fours? Do you find a rhyme scheme repeating itself? Where is the rhyme different? Can you think of a reason why the poet used a different pattern of rhyme on certain lines?

2. **Recognizing Onomatopoeia.** This poem contrasts two kinds of skaters. It suggests the differences between them in the sounds of the words describing them.

   Find an example of alliteration in the first three lines. These lines describe the speaker's skating ability. What effect does the alliteration have on the description? Do the repeated sounds suggest any sound that the speaker's skates might make? If so, is the sound smooth or rough?

   Read over the rest of the poem. If possible, read it aloud. Note the number of times you hear each of these sounds, either at the beginning of a word or in any other position: *s, sh, z, l, r, w, th* as in *thick*. What effect do these sounds have on the description? What sorts of sounds do they suggest Mary's skates make?

Using the Study Questions

It is recommended that students always read and answer the questions in **Developing Comprehension Skills** in class discussion. Whenever possible, they should also read the questions in **Reading Literature** together and discuss the answers.

Developing Comprehension Skills

Question 1. Refer students to the beginning of the poem for the answer.

Question 2. Call on individual students to read aloud the phrases that describe Mary's skating ability.

Question 3. Read and discuss the question.

Reading Literature: Poetry

Question 1. Have the students complete the first half of this question independently. It may help some students to show the rhyme scheme of the entire poem, not just the first fifteen lines. Complete the second half of the answer with the students.

Question 2. As a review, discuss the meaning of *onomatopoeia* with the students. If necessary, refer them to page 120. Read and discuss the exercise. To help the students find all the *s, sh, z, l, r, w,* and *th* sounds, direct their attention to the poem on the board or transparency that you prepared earlier. Have them help you find and underline the letters that make each of these sounds.

Challenge Question. Is the rhythm of this poem mostly regular or irregular? How does this rhythm fit together with the subject of the poem?

Answers to Study Questions

Developing Comprehension Skills

1. The speaker is not an experienced skater. The lines that give the answer are the following: When I try to skate,/My feet are so wary/They grit and they grate

2. The poem describes Mary as "easily gliding;" "Skimming and curving;" "sailing;" "round the lake on a single foot, with a three, and an eight, and a loop and a ring;" "easily sailing." Other answers are possible.

3. Possible answer: Mary's skates against the ice may make a sound, but *song* probably also refers to the beauty Mary creates when she skates on the lake.

Reading Literature: Poetry

1. a b a b ; c d e f e g e h i j i

The lines are grouped mostly by fours.

The second and fourth lines rhyme in groups of four lines.

Line 5 doesn't fit with this pattern.

Lines 10 and 11 make a pattern of 6 lines with Lines 6, 7, 8, 9.

Possible reason why the poet used a different pattern of rhyme on certain lines: Those lines introduce the reader to Mary, so they are set apart.

2. Alliteration: grit, grate. The hard *g* is a rough sound, suggesting the speaker's poor skating.

S sound: 16 times; sh: 2 times; z: 5 times; l: 24 times; r: 28 times; w: 10 times; th: 6 times.

These are all smooth, soft sounds. They suggest the speed, grace, and skill with which Mary skates.

Challenge. The rhythm is mostly regular. Mary probably skates with a regular rhythm, too.

Objectives

- To recognize and appreciate poetry as a form of literature
- To make inferences in poetry
- To apply literal, interpretive, and critical reading skills to a selection

Preparing the Students

Essential Vocabulary. The words presented here are essential to the understanding of the selection.

Write the following words and their definitions on the board. Have students read them aloud.

1. ascend—go up
2. descent—the act of coming down
3. horizon—1. the line where the sky seems to meet the earth; 2. the range of a person's abilities or interests

Motivation. Have the students read the introductory paragraph at the top of page 316 and state in their own words what they should try to find out as they read this poem.

Presenting the Selection

1. Have the students read "Pole Vault" silently.

2. Make sure that everyone has read the poem by administering the **Check Test** at the bottom of this page.

3. Develop the study questions as suggested in **Using the Study Questions** below.

Using the Study Questions

It is recommended that students always read and answer the questions in class discussion.

Developing Comprehension Skills

Question 1. Read and discuss the question.

Question 2. Discuss how the pole vaulter must have felt when he failed to clear the crossbar.

Question 3. Ask students to think of other things they try to do and often fail at.

Reading Literature: Poetry

Question. Have students point out the words that imply the answer.

Pole Vault

SHIRO MURANO

In a competition, an athlete concentrates on the track, mat, or other space in which he or she must perform. That space becomes the athlete's whole world. What is the horizon in the pole vaulter's small world?

He is running like a wasp,
Hanging on a long pole.
As a matter of course he floats in the sky,
Chasing the ascending horizon.
Now he has crossed the limit,
And pushed away his support.
For him there is nothing but a descent.
Oh, he falls helplessly.
Now on that runner, awkwardly fallen
on the ground,
Once more
The horizon comes down,
Beating hard on his shoulders.

Developing Comprehension Skills

Literal Reading 1. Restate line 7 in your own words.

Interpretive Reading 2. At the beginning of the poem, the pole vaulter is aiming for his "horizon," the crossbar. Is he successful? Which lines led you to your answer?

Critical Reading 3. Do you think this poem is only about the physical effort of the pole vaulter? Is there any way that a person's efforts in other parts of life could be like a pole vault contest?

Reading Literature: Poetry

Drawing Inferences in Poetry. Reread the last four lines of the poem. What do these lines tell you about this athlete? Has he failed to clear the crossbar on other jumps, too?

Check Test

1. What is the runner running toward? (the bar)

2. What does the runner do after he crosses his limit? (He pushes away his support and falls.)

Answers to Study Questions

Developing Comprehension Skills

1. Answers will vary slightly. Possible answer: The runner can do nothing but fall.

2. The pole vaulter is not successful. This is indicated in the following lines: The horizon comes down, / Beating hard on his shoulders.

3. This poem is not only about the physical effort of the pole vaulter. There are many tasks we must practice to perform correctly. We fail many times before we finally succeed. As we learn how to do one thing, we constantly raise our goals, just as the crossbar is always being raised.

Reading Literature: Poetry

The words *once more* imply that this is not the first time the vaulter has failed.

Sky Diving

RICHMOND LATTIMORE

Not many of us will ever sky dive, except in our imagination. As you read "Sky Diving," try to see and feel what the divers are experiencing.

They step from the high plane and begin
to tumble
down. Below is the painted ground, above
is bare sky. They do not fumble
with the catch, but only fall; drop sheer;
begin to move

in the breakless void; stretch and turn, freed
from pressure; stand in weightless air
and softly walk across their own speed;
gather and group, these dropping
bundles, where

the neighbor in the sky stands, reach touch
and clasp hands, separate and swim
back to station (did swimmer ever
shear such
thin water?) falling still. Now at last
pull the slim

cord. Parasols bloom in the air, slow
the swift sky fall. Collapsed tents cover
the ground. They rise up, plain people now.
Their little sky-time is over.

Freelance Photographers, New York.

Objectives

- To recognize and appreciate poetry as a form of literature
- To recognize the mood of a poem
- To apply literal, interpretive, and critical reading skills to a selection
- To choose the correct meaning of a word from context
- To write a sports poem
- To locate biographies and autobiographies in the library
- To classify poems

Preparing the Students

Essential Vocabulary. The words presented here are essential to the understanding of the selection.

Have the students use the context clues in the following sentences to determine the meanings of the underlined words.

sheer void shear parasols

1. The rock dropped sheer, straight down, into the water below.
2. A void is an empty space.
3. The swimmers sheared, cut through, the water.
4. Women used to carry parasols, little umbrellas that protected their faces from the sun.

Motivation. Have the students read the introductory paragraph at the top of page 317 and state in their own words what they should try to find out as they read this poem.

Presenting the Selection

1. Have the students study the photograph on page 317. Read "Sky Diving" aloud to the class and encourage them to put themselves into the sky diving experience in their imaginations. Then have them read "Sky Diving" silently.

2. To see if the students understand the literal meaning of the poem, administer the **Check Test** at the bottom of this page.

3. Develop the study questions as suggested in **Using the Study Questions** beginning on page 318. That section also provides a challenge question for further discussion, if needed.

Reinforcing the Lesson

To reteach, reinforce, or extend the skills in this lesson, see the following:

Skills Practice Book, Green Level—pages 138 and 139

Check Test

1. Name three things the sky divers do in the air as they fall. (Possible answers: stretch, turn, stand, walk, gather, group, clasp hands, separate, pull the cord)

2. What happens when the divers pull the slim cord? (Their parachutes open.)

Special Populations

LD. For the critical thinking exercise **Classifying Poems** on page 320, the student might need help selecting categories into which the poems can be sorted. Some you might want to suggest are these: humorous/serious; long/short; rhymed/unrhymed; baseball/basketball/track; team activities/individual activities.

Encouraging Independent Reading

Students who are interested in sports may be encouraged to read more on the subject. Recommend the following prose and poetry titles:

The Sidewalk Racer and Other Poems of Sports and Motion by Lillian Morrison
An Anthology of Concrete Poetry, edited by Emmett Williams
Hans Brinker by Mary Mapes Dodge
Four Stars from the World of Sports by Clare Gault and Frank Gault

Using the Study Questions

It is recommended that students always read and answer the questions in **Developing Comprehension Skills** in class discussion. Whenever possible, they should also read the questions in the other categories together and discuss the answers.

Developing Comprehension Skills

Question 1. Have students think about where the sky divers are and the meaning of the word *void.*

Question 2. Ask a student to find and read aloud the phrases that tell what the divers do during the brief time of their fall.

Challenge Question. Why do you think people participate in dangerous hobbies such as sky diving? Would you like to try it someday? (Critical Reading)

Reading Literature: Poetry

Question 1. Have students concentrate on the mood the poem creates, not only on the feelings they themselves have toward sky diving.

Questions 2 and 3. Read and discuss the questions.

Developing Comprehension Skills

Literal Reading 1. What is meant by "the breakless void"?

Interpretive Reading 2. How can you tell that these skydivers are experienced and have planned exactly what they will do as they fall?

Reading Literature: Poetry

1. **Recognizing Mood.** Which of these words would you use in describing the mood of this poem?

   excitement wonder danger surprise fear delight

2. **Recognizing Rhyme and Rhythm.** Examine the way this poem looks, paying special attention to the ends of the lines. Does it look as if it has a strong, regular pattern of rhyme? Then reread the first two stanzas. Do you hear the rhymes clearly? Or do the rhymes blend in with the other words so that you hardly notice them? Reread the first two stanzas once more, listening for the rhythm. Is there a strong, steady rhythm, or an irregular rhythm?

   How do the patterns of rhyme and rhythm in this poem stress the meaning? How do they express the mood?

3. **Understanding Figurative Language.** Two metaphors are used to describe the parachutes. What are they? Why does the poet need two different metaphors? Are the parachutes in one metaphor different from the parachutes in the other?

Developing Vocabulary Skills

Choosing the Right Meaning for the Context. Read the following pairs of sentences. One sentence from each pair was drawn from the poems. Choose the correct meaning for the underlined word in each sentence.

1. Bob stretched his bubble gum until it broke.
2. The runners waited for the signal to pour them over the stretch.

   a. extend one's body or limbs; *stretch one's legs.*
   b. draw out to great length or size.
   c. a straight section of a race course or track.
   d. slang, a term of imprisonment; *served a two-year stretch.*

Answers to Study Questions

Developing Comprehension Skills

1. "The breakless void" is empty space with nothing to stop the fall.

2. They meet each other in the air and then return to their "stations." Such a maneuver must have been planned.

Challenge. Answers will vary. Possible reasons why people sky dive: People sky dive because they enjoy excitement and danger. They enjoy the sensation of flying. Opinions about whether students would like to sky dive will vary.

Reading Literature: Poetry

1. delight; wonder; possibly excitement

2. The poem looks as if it should rhyme, but the rhyme is lost when the poem is read. There is an irregular rhythm.

The poet may want to show that the sky divers are free when they are in the air. They are not bound to ordinary life, and the poet is not bound to typical rhyme and rhythm patterns.

3. Parachutes are compared to parasols when they are in the air and collapsed tents when they are on the ground. The

3. When I try to skate, my feet are so wary that they grit and grate.
4. His constant gum chewing grates on my nerves.
   e. a framework of iron to hold a fire.
   f. to have an annoying or unpleasant effect.
   g. to scrape or rub with rough or noisy friction; *to grate one's teeth.*
   h. to wear down or grind off in small pieces; *to grate cheese.*
5. The sky divers do not fumble with the catch, but only fall and drop sheer.
6. After the game, all of players dropped to their seats in sheer exhaustion.
   i. very thin; almost transparent; *a sheer blouse.*
   j. unmixed, complete; *There was sheer emptiness.*
   k. straight up and down; steep.
   l. swerve; turn aside; turn from a course.
7. This contract made ten years ago is now void.
8. The sky divers began to move in the breakless void.
   m. empty; vacant.
   n. something experienced as a loss; *When his friend moved, there was a void in his life.*
   o. an empty space.
   p. without force; not binding in law.
9. Don traced his descent from a family who came to America in the early years of our country.
10. For the pole vaulter there is nothing but a descent.
    q. coming or going down from a higher to lower place.
    r. a downward slope.
    s. deriving from a family line.
    t. a sudden attack.

Developing Writing Skills

Analytical Writing

1. **Analyzing Action Words in Sports Poems.** People who write about sports and athletes need to develop a good vocabulary in order to help other people share their excitement and enthusiasm. Choose any three poems in this section. List all the verbs you can find in these

poet used two different metaphors because the parachutes look different, depending on where they are.

Developing Vocabulary Skills

1. b. **6.** j.
2. c. **7.** p.
3. g. **8.** o.
4. f. **9.** s.
5. k. **10.** q.

Developing Skills in Critical Thinking

Answers will vary according to categories chosen. It should be clear why certain poems fit into certain categories.

Developing Vocabulary Skills

Have students read the directions for the exercise. Make sure they understand the directions. Encourage them to read all the choices before choosing the correct meaning. Have students complete the exercise independently. Discuss the answers together.

Developing Writing Skills

Read and discuss the two assignments. Then have each student choose and complete one of the two.

Question 1. The first challenge question for "The Women's 400 Meters" prepared students for this question.

Pre-Writing. As a review, discuss the difference between active and passive verbs. Students should be familiar with the difference between present and past tense. Have students draw a chart labeled *Active, Passive, Present Tense,* and *Past Tense.* Then examine the poems carefully and list the verbs that belong in each category. Have each student examine the words listed and develop a generalization about the verbs used, which he or she will explain in this writing assignment.

Writing. Allow sufficient time for the students to write their lists and their first drafts.

Revising. Have students share what they have learned about sports poetry by taking turns reading their paragraphs aloud in small groups.

Question 2. Have students refer to the notes they wrote in **Developing Writing Skills, 1,** to answer this question.

Pre-Writing. Encourage students to choose a sport in which they have experience. Explain that it is impossible to write well unless you know your subject. Have students read and follow the directions in the text concerning lists of descriptive words. Encourage them to make up a list that includes not only verbs but some nouns and adjectives as well.

Writing. Allow sufficient time for the students to write their poems.

Revising. Assemble a notebook of original sports poems. Have each student contribute at least one poem that has been read and approved by two classmates.

Developing Skills in Study and Research

Have a student read the directions to the exercise aloud. Either schedule a visit to the library or assign the exercise for homework. Discuss the students' findings together.

Developing Skills in Critical Thinking

Have a student read the explanation of the exercise aloud. Students may use the categories mentioned or may invent their own. Have students complete the exercise independently and discuss the answers together.

three. Put the verbs into categories, such as active or passive, present tense or past tense. Study your lists and then write a paragraph or more in which you explain what you have discovered about writing sports poetry.

Creative Writing

2. **Writing a Sports Poem.** You have been reading poems about athletes, their skill and their grace, their courage and determination.

   Choose one sport you know something about, either through participation or by seeing it as a spectator. Make a list of at least ten words that you think best describe the sport. Include some words that show your attitude toward the sport, also.

   Using these words as a starting place, try to write a poem in which you share just one feeling or idea about the subject you chose. Be sure you describe one event, and be sure you have included someone's feelings or attitude. The speaker may be either a participant or a spectator.

Developing Skills in Study and Research

Finding Biographies and Autobiographies. Find out how the biographies and autobiographies are grouped in your local or school library. On your paper, list the number or numbers assigned to biographies and autobiographies in the classification system used by your library. Then use the card catalog to locate a biography or autobiography of an author whose work you have read. Write on your paper the title, author, and the Dewey Decimal or other number assigned to the book.

Developing Skills in Critical Thinking

Classifying Poems. In this text, the poems have been grouped, or classified, according to themes or topics, including Individual Growth, Animals, Sports, and American History. The same poems could have been grouped according to other ideas, such as short poems and long poems, rhymed and unrhymed poems, humorous and serious poems. Choose your own system of classifying the poems you have read in this section, Poems About Sports, or in the first three sections of poetry. List the titles of your categories and, under each category title, the titles of the poems that fit in the category. Use two to four categories. Be sure to find a category for each poem in the group of poems you chose.

Poems About American History

The poems in this section are about people and events that happened in the past. Notice how the poets picture these people and events as clearly as if they were happening now. Notice, too, that each poet leaves us with a feeling about the person or event in the poem. Would you like to meet these people? Would you like to share in their adventures?

Three Flags, 1958, JASPER JOHNS. Encaustic on canvas, 30⅞" × 45½" × 5". Collection of Whitney Museum of American Art. 50th Anniversary gift of the Gilman Foundation, Inc., The Lauder Foundation, A. Alfred Taubman, (and purchase) Acq. #80.32.

Poems About American History

Call on a student to read aloud the text on page 321. Challenge the students to explain the decision to use that particular piece of art with this text.

Special Populations

ESL, LD. It is important throughout this section of the chapter to be aware of possible limitations in understanding of or knowledge of historical events. Check comprehension frequently, providing supplementary reading or explanations of events as needed.

About the Art

Jasper Johns (born 1930) is probably best known for his series of paintings of the American flag laid out perfectly flat, like a tablecloth. They are in encaustic, a technique that uses paint mixed with hot wax that is then heated and applied to the canvas more like soft butter than paint. The result is a thick layer of paint with a sensuous surface texture. Some art critics believe that, by depicting the flag simply as a pattern on a cloth, Johns has transformed the flag into simply a visual image, and one denied of its usual symbolic and patriotic meaning. By producing this image in triplicate and in three dimensions, however, the symbolic and emotional content may seem heightened.

Objectives

- To recognize and appreciate poetry as a form of literature
- To apply literal, interpretive, and critical reading skills to a selection
- To understand unstated cause and effect relationships

Preparing the Students

Essential Vocabulary. The words presented here are essential to the understanding of the selection.

Have the students use the context clues in the following sentences to determine the meanings of the underlined words.

plunder inviolate perish hover

1. The pirates became rich by plundering, or robbing, the ships loaded with gold.
2. The plastic wrap was still intact on the medicine bottle. It was inviolate.
3. All humans need food and water, or they will perish.
4. Helicopters are useful for observing traffic because they can hover over highways and watch what is happening.

Motivation. Have the students read the introductory paragraph at the top of page 322 and state in their own words what they should try to find out as they read this poem.

Presenting the Selection

1. Have the students read "Like Ghosts of Eagles" silently. Before you ask volunteers to read it aloud, write the following names on the board and pronounce them: Susquehanna, Shenandoah, and Tombigbee. Ask a few students to repeat the pronunciations.

2. Make sure that everyone has read the poem by administering the **Check Test**.

3. Develop the study questions as suggested in **Using the Study Questions** on page 323. A question there reminds the students of the question posed in the introduction. That section also provides a challenge question for further discussion, if needed.

Special Populations

ESL. Ask ESL students to bring in any poems from their culture depicting historic events that shaped the future of the people or customs of their native countries.

Like Ghosts of Eagles

The title of the poem is really a simile with the first word missing. Think carefully and decide who or what are "like ghosts of eagles."

ROBERT FRANCIS

The Indians have mostly gone
but not before they named the rivers
the rivers flow on
and the names of the rivers flow with them
    Susquehanna   Shenandoah

The rivers are now polluted plundered
but not the names of the rivers
cool and inviolate as ever
pure as on the morning of creation
    Tennessee   Tombigbee

If the rivers themselves should ever perish
I think the names will somehow somewhere hover
like ghosts of eagles
those mighty whisperers
    Missouri   Mississippi.

Check Test

1. Who named the rivers? (the Indians)

2. What has happened to the rivers? (They have been polluted and plundered.)

3. What does the speaker think will live on after the rivers have perished? (their names)

Answers to Study Questions

Developing Comprehension Skills

1. Answers will vary slightly.

Stanza 1: Indians who named the rivers in the past are gone but the rivers flow on.

Stanza 2: The rivers are now polluted but the names are still pure.

Stanza 3: If, in the future, the rivers die, the names will live on.

2. The rivers are now polluted and plundered. People have polluted the rivers by throwing chemicals and waste in them. They have plundered them by killing their plants and animals. Answers to the

The Oxbow, 1836, THOMAS COLE. The Metropolitan Museum of Art. Gift of Mrs. Russell Sage, 1908.

Developing Comprehension Skills

Literal Reading — 1. This poem consists of three stanzas. Tell the main idea of each stanza in your own words. Be sure to mention the time about which each stanza speaks.

Interpretive Reading — 2. What changes in the rivers does the poet tell about? What has caused some of the changes? What might cause the final change?

Interpretive Reading — 3. The title is a simile. What does the poem compare to ghosts of eagles? What do the two things have in common?

Critical Reading — 4. Does the speaker in the poem have an opinion about the changes in the rivers? If so, what is the speaker's opinion? What is yours?

Reading Literature: Poetry

Looking for Cause and Effect. Does the speaker say there is any connection between the Indians going and the rivers being polluted? Did one event cause the other? Or is it possible that both events were caused by something else not mentioned in the poem?

Using the Study Questions

It is recommended that students always read and answer the questions in **Developing Comprehension Skills** in class discussion. Whenever possible, they should also read the questions in **Reading Literature** together and discuss the answers.

Developing Comprehension Skills

Question 1. Have the students reread each stanza before suggesting its main idea.

Question 2. The answer to the second part of this question is not stated. Students should use their knowledge of the past of the country to answer it. Discuss what could occur in the future.

Question 3. Read and discuss the question.

Question 4. Have students think about the mood of the poem, the feeling they get when they read it, to discover the speaker's opinion. Have them formulate their own opinions about the rivers.

Reading Literature: Poetry

Question. Have the class discuss what might have caused the disappearance of the Indians and the pollution of the rivers.

Challenge Question. Look at the names of the rivers. What about these names made them fit into the meaning of this poem?

final part of the question will vary. Possible answer: The final change could come in a nuclear explosion or some other disaster.

3. The names of the rivers are compared to the ghosts of eagles. They are the only things left when something beautiful, proud, and powerful dies.

4. The speaker seems to feel that the changes in the rivers are unfortunate and unnecessary. The speaker makes you feel that something wonderful has been hurt and someday it could be lost forever. Students' opinions will probably be similar to the speaker's opinions.

Reading Literature: Poetry

There is no stated connection between the departure of the Indians and the pollution of the rivers. They both could have been caused by the great number of people who settled all over America. So many people came so quickly that the Indian way of life was destroyed and the rivers were thoughtlessly misused.

Challenge. The names of the rivers contain the sounds of *s, sh,* and long *e.* These soft sounds make the names sound like whispers or the ghosts the speaker is talking about.

About the Art

Thomas Cole (1801-1848) was the most famous member of the Hudson River School, a group of American landscape painters who worked from about 1825 to 1870. They painted nature scenes ranging from the Hudson River and the Catskill Mountains in New York State to the Far West. Cole believed that nature bore the stamp of God's creative power and perfection, and that landscape painting had a fundamental moral purpose and message. *The Oxbow* shows us the beauty of the American wilderness stretching far into the distance.

Objectives

- To recognize and appreciate poetry as a form of literature
- To appreciate sound patterns
- To apply literal, interpretive, and critical reading skills to a selection
- To use a thesaurus
- To compare and contrast poems
- To use the atlas and the dictionary
- To recognize faulty generalizations

Preparing the Students

Essential Vocabulary. The words in this selection are, for the most part, familiar ones. Explain that *gore* means "to stab with a horn or tusk."

Motivation. Have the students read the introductory paragraph at the top of page 324 and state in their own words what they should try to find out as they read this poem.

Presenting the Selection

1. Have the students read "The Flower-Fed Buffaloes" silently.

2. Administer the **Check Test**.

3. Remind students of the introduction. Discuss their findings.

4. Develop the study questions as suggested in **Using the Study Questions** beginning on page 325. That section also provides a challenge question for further discussion.

Reinforcing the Lesson

To reteach, reinforce, or extend the skills in this lesson, see the following:

Skills Practice Book, Green Level—pages 140 through 142

About the Art

William Jacob Hays (1830-1875) is considered the most significant painter of the buffalo. He vied, consciously or not, for this distinction with the famous naturalist John James Audubon, who, it seems, composed his buffalo pictures from taxidermic models. Although Hays lived most of his life in New York City, his paintings also gained him a reputation as an expert on life on the western frontier. Hays gained his direct experience taking several trips along the Missouri River Valley. His first was in 1860, from which he painted many works including the *Herd of Buffalo*.

Keep "Like Ghosts of Eagles" in mind as you read this next poem. Look for ways in which the two poems are alike. Also look for ways in which they are different.

The Flower-Fed Buffaloes

VACHEL LINDSAY

The flower-fed buffaloes of the spring
In the days of long ago,
Ranged where the locomotives sing
And the prairie flowers lie low:—
The tossing, blooming, perfumed grass
Is swept away by the wheat,
Wheels and wheels and wheels spin by
In the spring that still is sweet.
But the flower-fed buffaloes of the spring
Left us, long ago.
They gore no more, they bellow no more,
They trundle around the hills no more:—
With the Blackfeet, lying low,
With the Pawnees, lying low,
Lying low.

Herd of Buffalo (detail), 1862, WILLIAM JACOB HAYS. The Denver Art Museum.

Check Test

1. What machine has replaced the buffalo on the prairie? (the locomotive)

2. What grows on the prairie in place of flowers? (wheat)

Answers to Study Questions

Developing Comprehension Skills

1. Locomotives and wheat have replaced the buffalo, the grass, and the prairie flowers. People and progress made it impossible for them to stay.

2. When people planted wheat, there was no more room for the buffalo to graze. Buffalo need miles of open country to graze upon.

3. These tribes and the buffalo are almost extinct. There are very few of them left.

Reading Literature: Poetry

1. Phrases describing the locomotive are the following:

the locomotives sing;
wheels and wheels and wheels spin by.

Developing Comprehension Skills

Literal Reading

1. The speaker tells us that the buffalo, the grass, and the prairie flowers have gone. Tell in your own words what has taken their place.

Interpretive Reading

2. Can you see any connection between the planting of wheat and the disappearance of buffalo?

Interpretive Reading

3. The Blackfeet and Pawnees are native Americans. Like the buffalo, they are, the speaker says, "lying low." Tell what you think he means.

Reading Literature: Poetry

1. **Looking at Language.** Read again the first eight lines of the poem. Make a list of words the author uses to describe the locomotive and its movement. Do the words have pleasant or unpleasant sounds? Are these words intended to make the reader dislike the locomotive? Or do the words avoid giving the reader any strong feeling? Which line tells us the prairie spring has not completely changed?

2. **Appreciating Sound Patterns.** The poet repeats certain sounds frequently in this poem. List as many examples as you can find of each of these sounds. (The same sound may be spelled different ways.)

   f r l s ou w m o͞o ō ôr

   What effect do these sounds have? Are they soft and flowing or harsh and disruptive?

3. **Identifying Rhyme Patterns.** "The Flower-Fed Buffaloes" makes use of rhyme. Use letters to identify the rhyme scheme.

4. **Recognizing Mood.** How would you describe the mood of this poem? Would you use any of the words listed below or others?

   sad angry happy thoughtful threatening tired

Developing Vocabulary Skills

Using a Thesaurus. You have learned that you can use a dictionary to find the exact meaning. Some dictionaries will also list synonyms for a word. A **thesaurus** is another book to use when you need to find a synonym for a word.

To use a thesaurus, read the directions at the front of the book. Follow the directions to find the information about a word.

Special Populations

LD, ESL. The students may not have the historic and geographic knowledge needed to understand this poem. They may need additional information in order to answer the questions under **Developing Comprehension Skills** on page 325.

The activities explained under **Developing Vocabulary Skills** and **Developing Skills in Study and Research** will be difficult for many special-populations students. Pair the students with others from the class.

Encouraging Independent Reading

Call on volunteers to research one of the Indian tribes mentioned in the poem (Blackfeet, Pawnees) and prepare to point out to the class the tribe's location on a large wall map. They may also wish to share a few interesting facts about the tribe. You may also wish to recommend the following books to the students for their enjoyment:

Sequoyah, Leader of the Cherokees by Alice Marriott
The Last of the Mohicans by James Fenimore Cooper
The Sounds of Flutes and Other Indian Legends by Richard Erdoes

Using the Study Questions

Developing Comprehension Skills

Question 1. Read and discuss the question.

Question 2. Have students think about where the herds of buffalo used to roam and the amount of land needed for wheat fields.

The words have pleasant sounds. They don't give the reader any strong feeling about the locomotive, but are more positive than negative.

You know that the spring has not completely changed because the poem mentions "the spring that still is sweet."

2. Possible answers:

f—flower, fed, buffaloes, perfumed, left, Blackfeet
r—flower, spring, ranged, prairie, perfumed grass, gore, more, trundle, around
l—flower, buffaloes, long, locomotives, lie, low, blooming, wheels, still, left, bellow, trundle, hills, Blackfeet, lying
s—spring, sing, tossing, grass, swept, spin, still, sweet, us
w—flower, swept away, wheat, wheels, sweet, with
m—locomotives, blooming, perfumed, more
o͞o—blooming, perfumed
ō—buffaloes, ago, locomotives, low, bellow, no
ôr—gore, more

These sounds are soft and flowing and help us to imagine the sounds we would hear out on the prairie.

3. a b a b c d e d a b f f b b b

4. The mood is sad and thoughtful. Other answers are possible, but they should not include obviously incorrect answers such as happy.

Challenge. The buffalo (really the American bison) is found only in America. It roamed over the American prairies in vast numbers but is now almost extinct. Like much of nature in America in the past, it was wild and powerful and has been replaced by civilization.

(continued on page 326)

Question 3. Relate this question with the poem just read, "Like Ghosts of Eagles." Point out the many things of the past that are gone now.

Reading Literature: Poetry

Question 1. Have a student read aloud the first eight lines of the poem before answering the question.

Question 2. Students will need to read the poem aloud to listen for the sounds. You may want to answer this question with the students.

Question 3. List the last words of all the lines on the board. Have students write the letters of the rhyme scheme beside the words.

Question 4. Encourage students to describe the mood using different words if they don't see the exact word they are looking for in the suggestions.

Challenge Question. Why is the buffalo a good symbol for the American past?

Developing Vocabulary Skills

Have a student read the explanation of the use of a thesaurus aloud. If possible, have a number of thesauruses available for student use. You may want to complete the exercise with the students to be sure that they all understand how to use the thesaurus.

Developing Writing Skills

Read and discuss the two assignments. Then have each student choose and complete one of the two.

Question 1. Make it clear that students need not compare and contrast the poems in all the ways suggested. You might suggest that they choose no more than three different ways.

Pre-Writing. Have students examine each of the poems. Have them describe the features they considered. When both poems have been examined, have students choose the ways in which they will compare the poems in their paragraphs. Have them write topic sentences for their paragraphs.

Writing. Allow sufficient time for the students to write their first drafts.

Revising. Have students exchange their writing with partners. Have partners comment on whether all the sentences in each paragraph stuck to the topic sentence.

Question 2. Some students may not want to share such a personal statement with their classmates. Explain before stu-

The entry words are grouped according to topic. After each entry word is a list of words that mean the same or almost the same thing. Most importantly, synonyms with different connotations, or feelings, are listed. The right synonym for any sentence will depend on the context of the sentence.

Reread the poem lines that contain the words listed below. Find each word in a thesaurus. Choose a synonym that could replace the word in the poem.

"Foul Shot"

1. soothes, line 6
2. crouches, line 13
3. exasperates, line 24

"Like Ghosts of Eagles"

4. perish, line 11
5. hover, line 12

"The Flower-Fed Buffaloes"

6. perfumed, line 5

Developing Writing Skills

Analytical Writing

1. **Comparing Poems.** Reread both "Like Ghosts of Eagles" and "The Flower-Fed Buffaloes." Make a list of ways in which the poems are alike. Make a separate list of ways they are different. Then write from one to three paragraphs comparing and contrasting the poems.

   Here are some features you might examine:

topic	rhythm	stanza form	theme
mood	rhyme	sound patterns	your reaction

Creative Writing

2. **Writing About Change.** Both "Like Ghosts of Eagles" and "The Flower-Fed Buffaloes" were about change. They expressed some personal ideas and emotions about the subject. Think about changes in your life, both welcome and unwelcome. Then, either in prose or in poetry, describe your ideas or feelings about change. If you write prose, write no more than a paragraph. If you write a poem, it may be rhymed or unrhymed and no more than twelve lines long.

Developing Skills in Study and Research

Using Reference Sources: Maps and Dictionaries. Maps of different states and countries can be found in an **atlas.** Find in your library an atlas that includes a map of the United States as a whole. The atlas should also include maps of individual states or groups of states. The **index** of the atlas should include the names of the rivers listed in the poem "Like

(continued from page 325)

Developing Vocabulary Skills

Answers will vary, depending on the thesaurus used. Possible answers:

1. calms
2. stoops
3. annoys
4. be destroyed
5. stay near
6. sweet-smelling

Developing Skills in Study and Research

The rivers and the states they flow through are the following:

Susquehanna—Pennsylvania and Maryland
Shenandoah—Virginia and West Virginia
Tennessee—Tennessee, Kentucky, Mississippi, and Alabama
Tombigbee—Mississippi and Alabama
Missouri—Missouri, Nebraska, Iowa, South Dakota, and North Dakota

Ghosts of Eagles." Using the index, locate each of those rivers on the maps. If you cannot find an atlas, find the rivers on a wall map, instead. On your paper, list the states through which each of the rivers flows.

There are many other rivers named by the native American Indians, and many states also bear Indian names. How can you find out which names came from the Indians? A dictionary can help you. Most desk dictionaries list not only a word and its meaning, but also the **origin**, or source, of the word. Usually the origin is shown after the pronunciation. If you look up *Susquehanna,* for example, you will find this:

[<Iroquoian tribal or stream name]

After *Shenandoah,* the dictionary may show some uncertainty:

[<AmInd. (? Iroquois)]

Using both the atlas and dictionary, find at least five names of states or rivers (not in the poem) from American Indian languages.

Developing Skills in Critical Thinking

Recognizing Generalizations. Imagine that you are discussing these poems with two other people. One of them says that life in America was better when the Indians were the only inhabitants because there was no pollution. The second person says that life is better now because we have so many modern conveniences.

Each of these statements is a **generalization**. A generalization is a general statement that describes all the items in a certain category. Some generalizations are always true, for example, "all triangles have three corners." Other generalizations are true only in certain cases. A generalization that is not always true is called a **faulty generalization**. An example is this statement: "Bike riders are careless in traffic." It is true that some bike riders do not follow traffic rules. However, there are other cyclists who follow the rules carefully.

Some faulty generalizations can be changed to be more accurate. For example, limiting the terms in the generalization about cyclists would make it true:

Some bike riders are careless in traffic.

Examine the two statements about life in the past and the present. Are they accurate or faulty generalizations? If they are faulty, how could they be changed and limited to be made accurate?

dents begin to write that this assignment will be read by you alone.

Pre-Writing. Have students think of changes that have occurred in their lives. Have them make notes on what has changed and have them describe their feelings. After they have made their notes, have them decide whether they will write prose or poetry.

Writing. Allow sufficient time for the students to write their first drafts.

Revising. Have students revise and proofread their writing using the guidelines on pages 556 and 557 in the **Checklist for the Process of Writing** before handing in their papers to you.

Developing Skills in Study and Research

Have a student read the directions for this exercise aloud. Make several atlases and dictionaries available to the students. You may either work the entire exercise with the students or just do the first river name with them and have them complete the exercise independently. Discuss the answers together.

Developing Skills in Critical Thinking

Call on volunteers to read aloud the explanation and directions for the exercise on page 327. Give the students practice in recognizing and limiting generalizations by writing the following generalizations on the board and having the students tell why they are faulty and how to limit them:

All spring days are windy.

It always rains when I plan a picnic.

Everyone enjoys vacations by the ocean.

Then have students work together to limit the statements in the text.

Mississippi—Louisiana, Mississippi, Arkansas, Tennessee, Kentucky, Missouri, Illinois, Iowa, Wisconsin, and Minnesota

The names of states or rivers from native American languages that students suggest will vary. Possible answers:

Massachusetts
Illinois
Delaware
Chippewa River
Big Sioux River
Potomac River
Chattahoochee River
Cuyahoga River

They are both faulty generalizations. Changes in the two generalizations will vary slightly. Possible answers:

Some aspects of life were better when the Indians were the only inhabitants.

Some aspects of life are better now.

Objectives

- To recognize and appreciate poetry as a form of literature
- To differentiate between narrative poetry and lyric poetry
- To apply literal, interpretive, and critical reading skills to a selection

Preparing the Students

Essential Vocabulary. The words presented here are essential to the understanding of the selection.

Have the students use the context clues in the following sentences to determine the meanings of the underlined words.

proverbs sage dynamo wrench

1. Franklin wrote wise sayings called proverbs.
2. Many people thought his advice was sage, but some thought it was foolish.
3. This dynamo, or generator, produces electrical power for the hospital.
4. By pulling hard, I was able to wrench the bat out of my brother's hands.

If the students need additional help with the vocabulary of this selection, encourage them to use context clues to determine word meaning. As needed, direct them to the **Glossary** or to a classroom dictionary.

Motivation. Have the students read the introductory paragraph at the top of page 328 and state in their own words what they should keep in mind as they read this poem.

Presenting the Selection

1. Have the students read "Benjamin Franklin 1706-1790" silently.

2. Make sure that everyone has read the assignment by administering the **Check Test** at the bottom of this page.

3. Ask five volunteers to read one stanza each aloud.

4. Develop the study questions as suggested in **Using the Study Questions** on page 329. That section also provides a challenge question for further discussion, if needed.

Special Populations

LD, ESL, NSD. The instructor may need to give definitions for some of the more unfamiliar words such as these: *gempmun, almanac, pip, was the rage, dynamos, palate, had a taking eye.*

Benjamin Franklin
1706–1790

Ben Franklin was famous for many things. Two of his talents were writing and inventing. Keep these in mind as you read the poem.

STEPHEN VINCENT BENÉT
and ROSEMARY BENÉT

Ben Franklin munched a loaf of bread while walking down the street
And all the Philadelphia girls tee-heed to see him eat,
A country boy come up to town with eyes as big as saucers
At the ladies in their furbelows, the gempmun on their horses.

Ben Franklin wrote an almanac, a smile upon his lip,
It told you when to plant your corn and how to cure the pip,
But he salted it and seasoned it with proverbs sly and sage,
And people read "Poor Richard" till Poor Richard was the rage.

Ben Franklin made a pretty kite and flew it in the air
To call upon a thunderstorm that happened to be there,
—And all our humming dynamos and our electric light
Go back to what Ben Franklin found, the day he flew his kite.

Ben Franklin was the sort of man that people like to see,
For he was very clever but as human as could be.
He had an eye for pretty girls, a palate for good wine,
And all the court of France were glad to ask him in to dine.

But it didn't make him stuffy and he wasn't spoiled by fame
But stayed Ben Franklin to the end, as Yankee as his name.
"He wrenched their might from tyrants and its lightning from the sky."
And oh, when he saw pretty girls, he had a taking eye!

Check Test

1. What two places are mentioned in the poem? (Philadelphia and France)

2. What did Franklin write? (an almanac)

3. Which word describes Franklin better, stuffy or clever? (clever)

Answers to Study Questions

Developing Comprehension Skills

1. He was eating bread as he walked down the street and was staring at everything.

2. He put in proverbs that were funny and wise.

3. The stanza tells of the discovery of electricity.

4. Ben Franklin at first was young and unaware of the manners of a city. At the end, Franklin was much older and had become very sophisticated. He was still a simple man, though, to the end.

Developing Comprehension Skills

Literal Reading — 1. When Ben Franklin first came to town, what made the girls laugh at him?

Literal Reading — 2. When Franklin wrote his almanac, he wanted large numbers of people to read it. What did he put in it to "spice it up" and make it interesting?

Literal Reading — 3. The third stanza tells about a famous discovery. What was it?

Interpretive Reading — 4. Carefully reread the first and fourth stanzas. How has Ben Franklin changed?

Interpretive Reading — 5. Read the last two lines of the poem. What does each tell you? Explain how the two lines give two different sides of Franklin's personality.

Reading Literature: Poetry

1. **Recognizing Mood.** Would you say the mood of this poem is serious or light? Is it respectful or critical? Find some words and phrases in the poem that support your answer. Your examples should also show whether the level of language is formal or informal.

2. **Identifying Rhythm Patterns.** Choose any stanza of the poem and copy it, leaving space between lines. Mark the accents. You will find that the rhythm is very regular. How many syllables per line are stressed?

3. **Recognizing Narrative Poetry.** A poem that tells a story is called **narrative poetry**. A poem that emphasizes a mood or feeling, or shares one idea with the reader is called **lyric poetry**. Which kind of poem is "Benjamin Franklin"?

Using the Study Questions

It is recommended that students always read and answer the questions in **Developing Comprehension Skills** in class discussion. Whenever possible, they should also read the questions in **Reading Literature** together and discuss the answers.

Developing Comprehension Skills

Question 1. Read and discuss the question.

Question 2. Ask a student to find and read aloud the phrases from stanza 2 that means the same as "spiced it up."

Question 3. This question is not answered directy in the poem. Students must infer the answer.

Question 4. As students read the two stanzas, have them consider the age of Franklin in the first stanza and last stanza.

Question 5. Have several students restate these lines in their own words before you ask them to explain how the lines show the different sides of Franklin's personality.

Challenge Question. Most times, you read about only the extraordinary things that historical figures did. Why do you think it is a good idea to see that they were human, too? (Critical Reading)

Reading Literature: Poetry

Question 1. Make sure that students see that you can describe a person in a light way without being disrespectful.

Question 2. Have several students write the stanzas they chose on the board and mark the accented syllables. Compare the number of accented syllables in each line in several stanzas.

Question 3. Have students explain their answers.

5. The first line says that Franklin dealt with serious problems bravely and the second line reminds readers that he kept his good humor and humanity.

Challenge. When we see famous people's human side, we see that they are not so different from the rest of us. The kinds of things they did might be possible for others to do, too.

Reading Literature: Poetry

1. The poem has a light, but respectful mood. Some words that create the mood are the following: *munched, tee-heed, gempmun, pretty kite, an eye for pretty girls, as Yankee as his name*. The examples show that the level of language is informal.

2. The following rhythm pattern is found in each stanza:

Bĕn Frӑ́nklĭn mŭ́nched ӑ lṓaf ŏf brĕ́ad
  whĭle wӑ́lkĭng dṓwn thĕ strḗet
Ӑnd ӑ́ll thĕ Phĭlӑ́dĕ́lphĭa gĭ́rls tḗe-hḗed tŏ
  sḗe hĭm ḗat,
Ӑ cṓuntrȳ bṓy cōme ŭ́p tŏ tṓwn wĭth ḗyes
  ӑs bĭ́g ӑs sӑ́ucĕrs
Ӑt thĕ lӑ́dĭes ĭ́n thĕir fŭ́rbĕlṓws, thĕ gĕ́mp-
  mŭn ṓn thĕir hṓrsĕs.

There are seven stressed syllables in each line.

3. "Ben Franklin" is a narrative poem.

Objectives

- To recognize and appreciate poetry as a form of literature
- To recognize a narrative poem
- To recognize the tone of a poem
- To apply literal, interpretive, and critical reading skills to a selection
- To use inference to determine word meaning
- To write a paragraph expressing an opinion
- To evaluate historical accuracy of a poem
- To interpret a narrative poem

Preparing the Students

Essential Vocabulary. The words presented here are essential to the understanding of the selection.

Write the following words and their definitions on the board. Have students read them aloud.

aloft—very high up

belfry—a tower where bells are hung

tread—footstep

peril—danger

If the students need additional help with the vocabulary of this selection, encourage them to use context clues to determine word meaning. As needed, direct them to the **Glossary** of the text or to a classroom dictionary.

Motivation. Students will get more out of this poem if they know the background attached to it and the significance of Paul Revere's ride. Tell students the story of his ride and what happened as a result of it before they read the introduction. Have the students read the introductory paragraph at the top of page 330 and state in their own words what they should try to find out as they read this poem.

Presenting the Selection

1. Since this poem is long and uses difficult words, it may be best if you read it aloud to the students. Read a few paragraphs at a time and have students summarize what has happened so far. Have the students read "Paul Revere's Ride" again for homework.

2. Make sure that everyone has understood the poem by administering the **Check Test** at the bottom of T.E. page 334.

3. Remind students of the directions in the introductory paragraph. Ask several

Paul Revere's Ride

HENRY WADSWORTH LONGFELLOW

This long poem narrates the exciting events of the night of April 18, 1775. As you read, watch for words that make real for you the excitement of that long-ago night.

Listen, my children, and you shall hear
Of the midnight ride of Paul Revere,
On the eighteenth of April, in Seventy-five;
Hardly a man is now alive
Who remembers that famous day and year.

He said to his friend, "If the British march
By land or sea from the town tonight,
Hang a lantern aloft in the belfry arch
Of the North Church tower as a signal light,—
One, if by land, and two, if by sea;
And I on the opposite shore will be,
Ready to ride and spread the alarm
Through every Middlesex village and farm,
For the country folk to be up and to arm."

Then he said, "Good-night!" and with muffled oar
Silently rowed to the Charlestown shore.
Just as the moon rose over the bay,
Where swinging wide at her moorings lay
The Somerset, British man-of-war;
A phantom ship, with each mast and spar
Across the moon like a prison bar,
And a huge black hulk, that was magnified
By its own reflection in the tide.

Meanwhile, his friend, through alley and street,
Wanders and watches with eager ears.
Till in the silence around him he hears
The muster of men at the barrack door,
The sound of arms, and the tramp of feet,
And the measured tread of the grenadiers,
Marching down to their boats on the shore.

Then he climbed the tower of the Old North Church,
By the wooden stairs, with stealthy tread,
To the belfry-chamber overhead,
And startled the pigeons from their perch
On the sombre rafters, that round him made
Masses and moving shapes of shade,—
By the trembling ladder, steep and tall,
To the highest window in the wall,
Where he paused to listen and look down
A moment on the roofs of the town,
And the moonlight flowing over all.

Beneath, in the churchyard, lay the dead,
In their night-encampment on the hill,
Wrapped in silence so deep and still
That he could hear, like a sentinel's tread,
The watchful night-wind, as it went
Creeping along from tent to tent.
And seeming to whisper, "All is well!"
A moment only he feels the spell
Of the place and the hour, and the secret dread
Of the lonely belfry and the dead;
For suddenly all his thoughts are bent
On a shadowy something far away,
Where the river widens to meet the bay,—
A line of black that bends and floats
On the rising tide, like a bridge of boats.

students to suggest words and details that made the adventure seem real.

4. Develop the study questions as suggested in **Using the Study Questions** beginning on page 335. That section also provides a challenge question for further discussion, if needed. (For answers to questions, see T.E. page 335.)

Reinforcing the Lesson

To reteach, reinforce, or extend the skills in this lesson, see the following:

Skills Practice Book, Green Level—pages 143 and 144

Special Populations

LD, ESL. Divide this poem into several readings, carefully defining unfamiliar words. List the events on a time line. The instructor might also want to make a map on the chalkboard to show the progress Paul Revere makes as the poem is read. Encourage students to bring in any available paintings of the villages or people from this time in history. Give necessary background information about the struggle between the colonists and the English as our country was developed.

The exercise **Evaluating Historical Accuracy** on page 337 will be difficult for most ESL and LD students because of limited recognition of historical background and the inaccuracies found in the poem. It is suggested that you substitute another assignment for the student, such as finding dates of events that take place during the time of the poem.

ESL. For the exercise under **Developing Skills in Speaking and Listening,** tailor the reading or interpretation of the narrative poem to reinforce correct diction, pronunciation and rhythm. Allow the students time to work with other students to practice phrasing and pronunciation. If necessary, allow the ESL student to tape record the reading or read along with another student.

Encouraging Independent Reading

Let students know that *The World of Paul Revere,* by Esther Forbes, gives an easy-to-follow description of life in Revolutionary America, and a warm, realistic portrayal of the major leaders of the day.

The Paul Revere Event—Four Views (detail), 1968, LARRY RIVERS. Jason McCoy, Inc., New York City.

Meanwhile, impatient to mount and ride,
Booted and spurred, with a heavy stride
On the opposite shore walked Paul Revere.
Now he patted his horse's side,
Now gazed at the landscape far and near,
Then, impetuous, stamped the earth,
And turned and tightened his saddle-girth;
But mostly he watched with eager search
The belfry-tower of the Old North Church,
As it rose above the graves on the hill,

About the Art

Larry Rivers (born 1923) combines carefully drawn detail with elements of abstract art. He uses blurred images, and he often leaves parts of his canvases bare or unfinished as a way of calling attention to the process of painting. In *The Paul Revere Event—Four Views* he views a serious historical subject humorously. The sequence of images and cartoon elements, such as the comic strip "talk balloon" or banner, make the work a kind of comic motion picture. The artist focuses on the story-telling side of art in a delightful visual way.

Lonely and spectral and sombre and still.
And lo! as he looks, on the belfry's height
A glimmer, and then a gleam of light!
He springs to the saddle, the bridle he turns,
But lingers and gazes, till full on his sight
A second lamp in the belfry burns!

A hurry of hoofs in a village street,
A shape in the moonlight, a bulk in the dark,
And beneath, from the pebbles, in passing, a spark
Struck out by a steed flying fearless and fleet:
That was all! And yet, through the gloom and the light,
The fate of a nation was riding that night;
And the spark struck out by that steed in his flight,
Kindled the land into flame with its heat.

He has left the village and mounted the steep,
And beneath him, tranquil and broad and deep,
Is the Mystic,[1] meeting the ocean tides;
And under the alders that skirt its edge,
Now soft on the sand, now loud on the ledge,
Is heard the tramp of his steed as he rides.

It was twelve by the village clock,
When he crossed the bridge into Medford town.
He heard the crowing of the cock,
And the barking of the farmer's dog,
And felt the damp of the river fog
That rises after the sun goes down.

It was one by the village clock,
When he galloped into Lexington.
He saw the gilded weathercock
Swim in the moonlight as he passed,
And the meeting-house windows, blank and bare,

---

1. The Mystic is a river that flows into Boston harbor.

Gaze at him with a spectral glare,
As if they already stood aghast
At the bloody work they would look upon.

It was two by the village clock,
When he came to the bridge in Concord town.
He heard the bleating of the flock,
And the twitter of birds among the trees,
And felt the breath of the morning breeze
Blowing over the meadows brown.
And one was safe and asleep in his bed
Who at the bridge would be first to fall,
Who that day would be lying dead,
Pierced by a British musket-ball.

You know the rest. In the books you have read,
How the British Regulars fired and fled,—
How the farmers gave them ball for ball,
From behind each fence and farm-yard wall,
Chasing the redcoats down the lane,
Then crossing the fields to emerge again
Under the trees at the turn of the road,
And only pausing to fire and load.

So through the night rode Paul Revere;
And so through the night went his cry of alarm
To every Middlesex village and farm,—
A cry of defiance and not of fear,
A voice in the darkness, a knock at the door,
And a word that shall echo forevermore!
For, borne on the night-wind of the Past,
Through all our history, to the last,
In the hour of darkness and peril and need,
The people will waken and listen to hear
The hurrying hoof-beats of that steed,
And the midnight message of Paul Revere.

Check Test

1. Where were the lanterns hung? (in the belfry of the Old North Church tower)

2. What did the two lanterns signal? (The British were moving by sea.)

3. Name the three towns that Revere rode through. (Medford, Lexington, Concord. Note: Middlesex County might be mistaken for a town. It may be accepted as correct.)

Answers to Study Questions

Developing Comprehension Skills

1. If the British troops began to march on land, the friend was to hang one lantern in the Old North Church tower. If they got into boats, he was to hang two lanterns. Paul would be waiting on the opposite shore of the river where he could see the signals.

2. The British moved by sea (stanza 1, lines 6 and 7 on page 331).

3. The future of the United States depended on Paul Revere getting through to warn of the British movements.

4. This poem's purposes are to keep alive the memory of the brave people who began our country and also to tell an exciting story. Most students will feel that it achieves its purposes—many people remember the story of Paul Revere's ride and the courage of the early Americans. People also read the story just for fun.

Challenge. Answers may vary. Possible answer: This fact does not make the poem less effective or enjoyable. Whoever the rider's name was, the ride was exciting and courageous. The poem is still fun to read because of the feelings it gives you and the enjoyable rhythm and rhyme.

Developing Comprehension Skills

Literal Reading — 1. Paul Revere and his friend agreed on signals. Tell in your own words what they were. Where was Paul to watch for the signals?

Literal Reading — 2. How did the British begin their move—by land or by sea?

Interpretive Reading — 3. What is meant by this line in stanza 2, line 6, on page 333: "The fate of a nation was riding that night"?

Critical Reading — 4. What is the purpose of this poem? Is it to teach history or to tell an exciting story? Do you believe it achieves its purpose?

Reading Literature: Poetry

1. **Recognizing Tone.** Compare the tone of the poem with that in "Benjamin Franklin." How does the poet feel about the subject? Does he provide any funny or informal pictures? Is the tone of the poem humorous? The poem about Franklin sketched his entire life and suggested his personality. This poem limits itself to one dangerous night in Revere's long life. Does this difference affect the tone?
2. **Understanding Rhythm.** Choose any four lines in the poem. Copy them, leaving space between lines, and mark the stressed syllables. Count the stressed syllables in each line. Are they close together or far apart? Would you describe the rhythm as slow or fast? How does the rhythm reflect the topic of the poem?
3. **Examining Form.** The length of stanzas and the pattern of rhyme change throughout this poem. Examine stanzas 1, 2, 4, 5, and 6. For each stanza, tell the following:
   a. the number of lines
   b. the rhyme scheme, using letters of the alphabet

Developing Vocabulary Skills

Using Inference To Determine Word Meaning. Sometimes the context clues in a sentence will provide a clear and fairly exact meaning for an unfamiliar word. Other times the clues can only steer you in the right direction—you can tell which meanings cannot fit, at least. Read each of the following excerpts from "Benjamin Franklin" and "Paul Revere's Ride." From the possible meanings below each sentence, choose the meaning for the underlined word that seems most reasonable to you.

Reading Literature: Poetry

1. This poem takes its subject more seriously. There are no humorous or informal pictures in it. Since this poem tells about only one dangerous and important event in Revere's life, the poet reacts only to Revere's bravery. The poem's tone is respectful.

2. The following four lines show the rhythm of the poem:

Óne, if by lánd, and twó, if by séa;
And Í on the ópposite shóre will bé,
Réady to ríde and spréad the alárm
Through évery Míddlesex víllage and fárm

The rhythm is fast, like the hoofbeats of a running horse. The stressed syllables are close together.

3. Length and pattern are:
Stanza 1: lines—5; rhyme scheme—*a a b b a*
Stanza 2: lines—9; rhyme scheme—*a b a b c c d d d*
Stanza 4: lines—7; rhyme scheme—*a b b c a b c*
Stanza 5: lines—11; rhyme scheme—*a b b a c c d d e e d*
Stanza 6: lines—15; rhyme scheme—*a b b a c c d d a a c e e f f*

(continued on page 336)

Using the Study Questions

It is recommended that students always read and answer the questions in **Developing Comprehension Skills** in class discussion. Whenever possible, they should also read the questions in the other categories together and discuss the answers.

Developing Comprehension Skills

Question 1. Refer students to the second stanza for the answer to this question.

Question 2. Have students find proof for their answers in the poem.

Question 3. Read and discuss the question.

Question 4. Explain that the poem could have more than one purpose.

Challenge Question. In reality, Paul Revere never reached some of the people he set out to warn. He was captured by the British, and another rider warned the people in Concord of the British troop movements. Does this historical fact make the poem less effective? Does it make it less enjoyable? Give reasons for your answer. (Note to the teacher: You may want to ask this question after the students complete **Developing Skills in Critical Thinking** on page 337.) (Critical Reading)

Reading Literature: Poetry

Question 1. Direct the students to examine the difference in their own feelings toward the two men. Explain that readers' attitudes are influenced by the tone of the poem.

Question 2. Have the students help you mark the stressed syllables on four lines of the poem at the board. Then have students mark another four lines independently. Compare and discuss students' findings.

Question 3. As the students tell the letters of the rhyme scheme for each stanza, write the letters on the board.

Developing Vocabulary Skills

Have students read the directions for the exercise silently. Be sure they understand what they are to do. Then have them complete the exercise independently. Discuss the answers together.

Developing Writing Skills

Read and discuss the two assignments. Then have each student choose and complete one of the two.

Question 1. Encourage students not to choose the same type of writing assignment every time. If they chose the creative writing last time, urge them to try this analytical writing assignment.

Pre-Writing. Have students look over the poems they have read so far and choose the ones they like best. Have them note how many of the chosen poems are lyric poetry and how many are narratives. Ask students to list the qualities they like best about each type of poem.

Writing. Remind students to use their notes. Since they are writing about both types, for clarity they may want to write two paragraphs.

Revising. Have students revise and proofread their paragraphs using the **Checklist for the Process of Writing** on pages 556 and 557.

Question 2. As a review discuss the meaning of first-person point of view. Stress the use of the pronouns *I* and *me*.

Pre-Writing. First have students choose the approach they want to use from the suggestions in the text. Have them list the events and ideas they want to include. Have them arrange these items in time order.

Writing. Allow sufficient time for the students to write their first drafts.

Revising. Ask volunteers to share their writing with the rest of the students. Have those who did not wish to read their poems aloud post them on a writing bulletin board.

Developing Skills in Critical Thinking

Have a student read the directions aloud. Make sure that students understand that they are not only expected to locate the books but they should also find out the answers to the questions about Paul Revere given in the text. Have them complete the assignment independently. Discuss the answers together.

Developing Skills in Speaking and Listening

Form small groups for this assignment. Have them read the directions in the text. Allow time for them to present their interpretations in class.

1. A country boy come up to town with eyes as big as saucers
   At the ladies in their furbelows, the gempmun on their horses.

   a. saddles b. gentlemen

2. And all our humming dynamos and our electric light
   Go back to what Ben Franklin found, the day he flew his kite.

   a. a person who hums
   b. a machine that makes a humming sound

3. He wrenched their might from tyrants.

   a. took b. used a wrench

4. Just as the moon rose over the bay,
   Where swinging wide at her moorings lay
   The Somerset, British man-of-war.

   a. a tract of open land with poor drainage
   b. something by which a ship is fixed in place, such as a cable.

5. In the silence around him he hears
   The muster of men at the barrack door,
   The sound of arms, and the tramp of feet,
   And the measured tread of the grenadiers.

   a. soldiers b. weapons

6. He could hear, like a sentinel's tread,
   The watchful night-wind, as it went
   Creeping along from tent to tent.

   a. one who keeps watch b. the wind

Developing Writing Skills

Analytical Writing

1. **Expressing Your Opinion.** "Casey at the Bat," "Benjamin Franklin," and "Paul Revere's Ride" are narrative poems, poems that tell stories. Almost every other poem in this chapter is a lyric poem, a poem that shares one idea or feeling. Which type of poetry do you prefer? Or do you enjoy both kinds, for different reasons? Write a paragraph or more explaining how you feel about the two types of poetry. Give reasons for your opinions.

Creative Writing

2. **Using the First-Person Point of View.** Write a short poem of four to twenty lines, rhymed or unrhymed, from the point of view of Paul

(continued from page 335)

Developing Vocabulary Skills

1. b	**3.** a	**5.** a
2. b	**4.** b	**6.** a

Developing Skills in Critical Thinking

Answers will vary, depending on library resources. Paul Revere did try to warn of the British movements, but William Dawes and Samuel Prescott also rode toward Concord that night. Revere was captured by the British, Dawes had to turn back, and only Prescott got through.

Revere's friend. The poem may use any tone you like. It may include ideas and events that are not in "Paul Revere's Ride," perhaps even made-up events. Here are three possible ideas for your poem:

a. A suspense-filled poem about sneaking up to the window of the British officers' meeting room to listen to their plans.
b. A humorous poem about being jealous of Paul for getting a long poem written about him, while your name isn't mentioned.
c. A proud or bragging poem about your part in the adventure.

Developing Skills in Critical Thinking

Evaluating Historical Accuracy. The poem about Paul Revere focuses on one single act performed by one man. In the history of the long War for Independence, it was a small event. Longfellow made it famous by his poem. Did the poet stick to the facts or did he make the event more dramatic than it really was? Did he report some events inaccurately because of the rhyme or rhythm?

How would you find out how accurate his version really is? Using the card catalog and then the indexes of the books listed in the catalog, locate at least three reference books in your library that will give you information about that time in United States history. Remember that you can use biographies as well as more general reference sources.

Developing Skills in Speaking and Listening

Interpreting a Narrative Poem. "Paul Revere's Ride" can be an enjoyable poem to read aloud. Work with a group of your classmates to prepare a reading for the students in another class.

Remember that you can't read a poem well until you understand and feel exactly what the speaker is telling. The group should first take the time to discuss the events in the poem. They should decide which parts should sound loud or soft, slow or fast. Then, work together to decide how the speakers will take turns. Will each person in the group speak one or more stanzas alone or will small groups speak together? Next, the group members should decide who will read what parts. Each member should practice his or her own parts. Last, the group members should practice the poem all together once or twice. Then they can present it to an audience.

Objectives

- To recognize and appreciate poetry as a form of literature
- To identify the speaker in a poem
- To recognize irony
- To understand the mood of a poem
- To apply literal, interpretive, and critical reading skills to a selection

Preparing the Students

Essential Vocabulary. The words presented here are essential to the understanding of the selection.

Have the students use the context clues in the following sentences to determine the meanings of the underlined words.

schooners legions

1. The covered wagons the pioneers took across the prairies reminded some people of schooners, a type of sailing ship. That's why they called them prairie schooners.
2. Pioneers went west in legions, that is, in large numbers.

Motivation. Have the students read the introductory paragraph at the top of page 338 and state in their own words what they should try to find out as they read this poem.

Presenting the Selection

1. Have the students read "Western Wagons" silently.

2. Make sure everyone has read the poem by administering the **Check Test** at the bottom of this page.

3. Have volunteers read the poem aloud. Urge them to imitate the personalities and mood of the optimistic pioneers.

4. Remind students of the questions raised in the introduction. Have several students give their answers.

5. Develop the study questions as suggested in **Using the Study Questions** on page 339. That section also provides a challenge question for further discussion, if needed.

Western Wagons

STEPHEN VINCENT BENÉT
and ROSEMARY BENÉT

This poem captures the spirit of the men and women who settled the American West in the mid-to-late 1800's. Did they consider themselves heroic? As you read, decide whether you would want to join them.

They went with ax and rifle, when the trail was still to blaze,
They went with wife and children, in the prairie-schooner days,
With banjo and with frying pan—Susanna, don't you cry!
For I'm off to California to get right out there or die!

We've broken land and cleared it, but we're tired of where we are.
They say that wild Nebraska is a better place by far.
There's gold in far Wyoming, there's black earth in Ioway,
So pack up kids and blankets, for we're moving out today!

The cowards never started and the weak died on the road,
And all across the continent the endless campfires glowed.
We'd taken land and settled—but a traveler passed by—
And we're going West tomorrow—Lordy, never ask us why!

We're going West tomorrow, where the promises can't fail.
O'er the hills in legions, boys, and crowd the dusty trail!
We shall starve and freeze and suffer. We shall die, and tame the lands.
But we're going West tomorrow, with our fortune in our hands.

Check Test

1. Name three places the settlers were headed for. (Possible answers: California, Wyoming, Nebraska, Iowa)

2. What did the pioneers hope to find in Wyoming? (gold)

Answers to Study Questions

Developing Comprehension Skills

1. The pioneers moved west to mine gold and to farm the black earth.

2. The people in the poem were both brave and foolhardy. They took tremendous risks and faced them bravely, but there didn't seem to be any good reason for them to go west except their desire to do so.

Challenge. Answers will vary. Possible answers:

The people in the picture look determined to make new lives for themselves.

Settlers moved West in great numbers after the Homestead Act of 1862. Denver Public Library.

Developing Comprehension Skills

Literal Reading — 1. According to the poem, why did the pioneers move west? Give two reasons.

Critical Reading — 2. What kind of people were the pioneers as described in the poem? Do you consider them likable? Were they brave or foolhardy or both?

Reading Literature: Poetry

1. **Identifying Speakers.** In the first stanza of the poem, a speaker is telling about the pioneers: "they" went, the speaker says. Who is the speaker in the other three stanzas?
2. **Recognizing Irony.** Read again the last stanza. The speaker says that in the West "promises can't fail." Just two lines further, however, the speaker says that pioneers will die. Why might a pioneer say the promises can't fail even though death is always a possibility?
3. **Understanding Mood.** We know that the kinds of people this poem is about succeeded in settling the West. Does the mood of this poem give you an indication of why they succeeded? Explain.

Using the Study Questions

It is recommended that students always read and answer the questions in **Developing Comprehension Skills** in class discussion. Whenever possible, they should also read the questions in **Reading Literature** together and discuss the answers.

Developing Comprehension Skills

Question 1. Have students find proof of their answers in the poem.

Question 2. Students must formulate their own opinions to answer this question. Make sure they base their opinions on evidence in the poem.

Challenge Question. Examine the people in the photograph on page 339. Do you think the people in the picture would agree with the ideas in the poem? Can you picture them saying the words of this poem? Why or why not? (Interpretive Reading)

Reading Literature: Poetry

Question 1. Help students notice the first person pronouns that are used.

Question 2. Have students first focus on the promises the speaker is referring to. What was promised? What were the pioneers' hopes? Then ask students what type of attitude is required to risk home and security as these pioneers did.

Question 3. Read and discuss the question.

They look like they could face any hardship bravely. They would have agreed with the words of the poem.

The people in the picture look tired. They look sorry that they began the trip. They probably would not agree with the poem.

Reading Literature: Poetry

1. The speaker is one of the pioneers going West.

2. If the pioneers had believed that they probably would not succeed, but would die, they would never have begun the dangerous trip. To take such a chance, you must believe that you are going to succeed. Also, part of the promise of the new land might mean gaining the freedom to take risks. The pioneer might have been willing to pay the price for living his or her life freely.

3. The mood of this poem is optimistic and enthusiastic. The spirit of the pioneers seems to be that nothing is impossible. Their attitude helped them overcome the difficulties that faced them.

Objectives

- To recognize and appreciate poetry as a form of literature
- To recognize metaphors
- To apply literal, interpretive, and critical reading skills to a selection

Preparing the Students

Essential Vocabulary. There is no difficult vocabulary in this selection.

Motivation. You may want to point out that this poem was written by the same poets who wrote "Benjamin Franklin 1706-1790."

Have the students read the introductory paragraph at the top of page 340 and state in their own words what they should try to find out as they read this poem.

Presenting the Selection

1. Have the students read "Abraham Lincoln 1809-1865" silently.

2. Make sure that everyone has read the poem by administering the **Check Test** at the bottom of this page.

3. Ask volunteers to each read one or two stanzas aloud.

4. Develop the study questions as suggested in **Using the Study Questions** on page 341. A question there reminds students of the question posed in the introduction. That section also provides a challenge question for further discussion, if needed.

Reinforcing the Lesson

To reteach, reinforce, or extend the skills in this lesson, see the following:

Skills Practice Book, Green Level—page 145

Encouraging Independent Reading

For students who need challenge, suggest Stephen Vincent Benét's novel-length poem, *John Brown's Body,* or any of its passages that can be separated from the whole.

Abraham Lincoln
1809–1865

Today, the name of Abraham Lincoln is one of the most respected in the history of this country. This poem gives us a view of the man before he became President. Was he always highly respected?

STEPHEN VINCENT BENÉT
and ROSEMARY BENÉT

Lincoln was a long man.
He liked out of doors.
He liked the wind blowing
And the talk in country stores.

He liked telling stories,
He liked telling jokes.
"Abe's quite a character,"
Said quite a lot of folks.

Lots of folks in Springfield
Saw him every day,
Walking down the street
In his gaunt, long way.

Shawl around his shoulders,
Letters in his hat.
"That's Abe Lincoln."
They thought no more than that.

Knew that he was honest,
Guessed that he was odd,
Knew he had a cross wife
Though she was a Todd.

Knew he had three little boys
Who liked to shout and play,
Knew he had a lot of debts
It took him years to pay.

Knew his clothes and knew his house.
"That's his office, here.
Blame good lawyer, on the whole,
Though he's sort of dear.

"Sure, he went to Congress, once.
But he didn't stay.
Can't expect us all to be
Smart as Henry Clay.

"Need a man for troubled times?
Well, I guess we do.
Wonder who we'll ever find?
Yes—I wonder who."

That is how they met and talked,
Knowing and unknowing.
Lincoln was the green pine.
Lincoln kept on growing.

Check Test

1. Where did Lincoln live? (in Springfield)

2. How many children did Lincoln have? (three)

3. What was Lincoln's profession? (He was a lawyer.)

Answers to Study Questions

Developing Comprehension Skills

1. Lincoln's neighbors didn't think he was great. He was just like anyone else, an ordinary person.

2. The people thought Lincoln wasn't smart enough.

Challenge. When people know someone for a long time, they see the person having both successes and failures. They probably think a great person never fails at anything, so the person they know so well can't be great. They might think that a

Abraham Lincoln, 1887,
Artist believed to be ROBERT KRINER. Wood Carving,
Collection of Allan L. Daniel. Courtesy of E. P. Dutton, Inc.

Developing Comprehension Skills

Literal Reading 1. Did the people of Springfield see Abraham Lincoln as a great man? Explain your answer in your own words.

Interpretive Reading 2. Why did the people think Lincoln didn't stay in Congress?

Reading Literature: Poetry

1. **Recognizing Metaphor.** A metaphor compares two unlike things without using "like" or "as." Find a metaphor in this poem and tell what two things or persons are compared. Explain how they are alike.

2. **Predicting Outcomes.** Does this poem lead you to believe that Abe Lincoln will be the "man for troubled times" the people in Springfield say is needed? Support your answer with evidence from the poem.

Using the Study Questions

It is recommended that students always read and answer the questions in **Developing Comprehension Skills** in class discussion. Whenever possible, they should also read the questions in **Reading Literature** together and discuss the answers.

Developing Comprehension Skills

Questions 1 and 2. Read and discuss the questions.

Challenge Question. Why do people often overlook the great qualities of people they have known for a long time? (Critical Reading)

Reading Literature: Poetry

Question 1. Refer students to the last stanza.

Question 2. Have students look for hints that there is greatness in Lincoln even though his neighbors can't see it.

great person must be special in every way. When they see that a person is ordinary in many ways, they overlook his or her greatness.

Reading Literature: Poetry

1. "Lincoln was the green pine" is the metaphor. Lincoln is compared to a green pine, a tree that is growing and getting stronger, just as Lincoln was growing and learning and gaining experience.

2. There were signs that Lincoln will be the "man for troubled times." He was thought to be honest, he paid his debts, he was a good lawyer, and he went to Congress. All the while, Lincoln was growing in skills and experience.

About the Art

National heroes often emerge in times of national crisis. Abraham Lincoln emerged from the Civil War as a national hero and folk figure, and became the subject of much folk art produced in this country. This piece, thought to be the work of the folk artist Robert Kriner, shows Lincoln against the backdrop of the American flag. It is a handsome wood relief carving. The forthright lines and contours of th figure are echoed in the distinct patt the American flag that serves a bolic background.

Objectives

- To recognize and appreciate poetry as a form of literature
- To understand figurative language
- To identify the tone of a poem
- To apply literal, interpretive, and critical reading skills to a selection

Preparing the Students

Essential Vocabulary. There is no difficult vocabulary in this selection.

Motivation. Have the students read the introductory paragraph at the top of page 342 and state in their own words what they should try to find out as they read this poem.

Presenting the Selection

1. Read "Women" aloud to the students and have them follow along in their texts. Then ask one or two volunteers to read the poem aloud again.

2. To see if students understand the literal meaning of the poem, administer the **Check Test** at the bottom of this page.

3. Develop the study questions as suggested in **Using the Study Questions** on page 343. A question there reminds students of the question posed in the introduction. That section also provides a challenge question for further discussion, if needed.

Special Populations

ESL. Students will need help with the phrasing in this poem when they read this selection orally because of the lack of punctuation or cues for the students to pause in the reading.

"Women" tells about the black women of the past who worked for a better future for their children. How does the speaker feel toward these women?

Women

ALICE WALKER

They were women then
My mama's generation
Husky of voice—Stout of
Step
With fists as well as
Hands
How they battered down
Doors
And ironed
Starched white
Shirts
How they led
Armies
Headragged Generals
Across mined
Fields
Booby-trapped
Ditches
To discover books
Desks
A place for us
How they knew what we
Must know
Without knowing a page
Of it
Themselves.

Mrs. Lucy Jefferson of Fort Scott, Kansas, 1949.
Copyright © 1949. GORDON PARKS

About the Art

Early in his career Gordon Parks (born 1912) worked for a time as a photographer for the Federal Security Agency and the Standard Oil Company; for a much longer time, 1948-1972, he worked for *Life* magazine. Throughout his life he has been creatively active as a writer, film producer, and music composer.

Parks was born in Fort Scott, Kansas, where he took this photograph of Mrs. Lucy Jefferson. The titles of Parks's own publications express the nature of his photographic work as revealed in this portrait—*A Poet and His Camera, Whispers of Intimate Things,* and *Born Black.*

Check Test

1. Who were the headragged generals? (the women)

2. What did the women discover for their children? (books and desks—education)

Answers to Study Questions

Developing Comprehension Skills

1. one stanza
2. strength

Developing Comprehension Skills

Literal Reading 1. How many stanzas do you find in this poem?

Interpretive Reading 2. What quality does the speaker imply is part of these women when she describes them in these words: "Husky of voice—Stout of Step, With fists as well as Hands"?

Interpretive Reading 3. Why did the women "batter" down doors? Did they literally break down a door? Think of what we mean when we say someone "broke into" some group or organization.

Critical Reading 4. The women generals led the armies across "mined fields" to discover books and desks. From what you know of the history of minorities in this country, what do you suppose might be represented by the term "mined fields"?

Reading Literature: Poetry

1. **Understanding Metaphor.** Reread the last five lines of the poem. Does the word "page" stand for what can be learned from a book? Or is the speaker referring to something broader? Explain your answer.

2. **Recognizing Rhythm and Rhyme.** Look at the pattern of this poem. Look for rhyme or regular rhythm. What kind of poem is this?

3. **Identifying Tone.** How would you describe the attitude of the poet towards the women about whom she is writing?

Using the Study Questions

It is recommended that students always read and answer the questions in **Developing Comprehension Skills** in class discussion. Whenever possible, they should also read the questions in **Reading Literature** together and discuss the answers.

Developing Comprehension Skills

Question 1. Read and discuss the question.

Question 2. Have students picture a person like that and describe her with an adjective.

Question 3. Explain that this is an example of figurative language. It gets across its meaning in a special way.

Question 4. Have students discuss the barriers that minorities have had to overcome.

Reading Literature: Poetry

Question 1. Read and discuss the question.

Question 2. Write a few lines on the board and have students mark its stressed and unstressed syllables and look for a rhyme scheme. Then have them describe the rhythm and rhyme of the poem.

Question 3. Have students point out both the phrases that describe the women and what the women did.

Challenge Question. Look at the form of this poem. It is written in short lines. Sometimes there is only one word to a line. Why do you think that the poet often put only one word on a line?

---

3. The women did not literally break doors. They worked hard and forced people to change unfair rules. They made sure that their children would not be faced with the same barriers as they had to face.

4. Possible answer: "Mined fields" are the situations where people blocked minorities' chances for success. One of these was the unfairness in education.

Reading Literature: Poetry

1. "Page" may refer to any small part of something. In this poem, it may refer to a small part of education.

2. This poem is written as free verse. There is no regular rhythm or rhyme.

3. She admires the women. She respects them for their strength and their willingness to work for the happiness of their children while ignoring their own needs.

Challenge. With only one word on a line, the poet stresses the importance of that word. This technique causes the reader to pause for a moment and think about the word.

Objectives

- To recognize and appreciate poetry as a form of literature
- To identify internal rhyme
- To understand the mood of a poem
- To apply literal, interpretive, and critical reading skills to a selection
- To use context clues
- To compare poems
- To define terms

Preparing the Students

Essential Vocabulary. The words presented here are essential to the understanding of the selection.

Have the students use the context clues in the following sentences to determine the meanings of the underlined words.

shed	thoroughfare	liberate
strife	alabaster	

1. The clouds shed rain on the mountains last night.
2. The main thoroughfares into the city were blocked by traffic.
3. The liberating army freed the prisoners.
4. Strife can take many forms, from arguments between friends to wars between nations.
5. She imagined an alabaster city, one made entirely of white stone.

If the students need additional help with the vocabulary of this selection, encourage them to use context clues to determine word meaning. As needed, direct them to the **Glossary.**

Motivation. You might want to mention that the poet was inspired to write this poem after looking out over the view from Pike's Peak in Colorado. Have the students read the introductory paragraph at the top of page 344 and state in their own words what they should try to find out as they read this poem.

Presenting the Selection

1. Have the students read "America the Beautiful" silently.

2. Administer the **Check Test.**

3. Have volunteers read one stanza each. Remind the students not to pause at the end... hey see punctua-

...questions as sug-
...ly Questions. A
...tudents of one
...en in the intro-
...provides a chal-
...discussion.

343

America the Beautiful

Since this poem is usually sung, you probably think of it with its melody. This time, treat it as a poem rather than a song. As you read it, try to picture its images.

KATHARINE LEE BATES

O beautiful for spacious skies,
For amber waves of grain,
For purple mountain majesties
Above the fruited plain!
America! America!
God shed His grace on thee
And crown thy good with brotherhood
From sea to shining sea!

O beautiful for pilgrim feet,
Whose stern, impassioned stress
A thoroughfare for freedom beat
Across the wilderness!
America! America!
God mend thine every flaw,
Confirm thy soul in self-control,
Thy liberty in law!

O beautiful for heroes proved
In liberating strife,
Who more than self their country loved,
And mercy more than life!
America! America!
May God thy gold refine
Till all success be nobleness
And every gain divine!

O beautiful for patriot dream
That sees beyond the years
Thine alabaster cities gleam
Undimmed by human tears!
America! America!
God shed His grace on thee
And crown thy good with brotherhood
From sea to shining sea!

Check Test

1. What does the speaker ask God to shed on America? (his grace)

2. What did the heroes love more than they loved themselves? (their country)

Answers to Study Questions

Developing Comprehension Skills

1. The heroes fought liberating wars, wars to free someone or something. Patriots dream about societies in which all people can find happiness.

2. The reasons are the following: the beauty of America, its freedom, its heroes, and its dreams.

3. The poem could also be considered a prayer. The speaker is asking God to help America.

4. The poet wishes for brotherhood, self-control, and nobleness for America.

The Grand Canyon of the Yellowstone, 1893–1901, THOMAS MORAN. National Museum of American Art, Smithsonian Institution, Washington, D.C. Gift of George G. Pratt.

Developing Comprehension Skills

Literal Reading — 1. In the third stanza, what kind of wars did the heroes fight? In the final stanza, what kind of society do the patriots dream about?

Interpretive Reading — 2. This poem answers the question, "Why is America beautiful?" with four different reasons. What are the four qualities of America and Americans that the speaker considers beautiful?

Interpretive Reading — 3. In addition to being a poem and a song, "America the Beautiful" could also be considered something else. Look at the last three lines of each stanza. What else could this piece of writing be called?

Literal Reading — 4. List three qualities the poet wishes for America.

Reading Literature: Poetry

1. **Finding Figurative Language.** Explain what is meant by each of these phrases:

   a. A thoroughfare for freedom

   b. May God thy gold refine
      Till all success be nobleness

Reinforcing the Lesson

To reteach, reinforce, or extend the skills in this lesson, see the following:

Skills Practice Book, Green Level—page 146

Special Populations

ESL. The exercise under **Developing Skills in Critical Thinking** on page 347 explores the many different points of view people can have about a single idea. The exercise could be elaborated upon to include different viewpoints from people of other cultures, young people, older people, different members of a family and so on. Some interesting differences in opinion may be found by the students. Encourage them to share their findings with the rest of the class.

Using the Study Questions

It is recommended that students always read and answer the questions in **Developing Comprehension Skills** in class discussion. Whenever possible, they should also read the questions in the other categories together and discuss the answers.

Developing Comprehension Skills

Question 1. Call on students to read aloud the lines that answer the question and restate those lines in their own words.

Question 2. Students must understand the main idea of each stanza to answer this question.

Question 3. Read and discuss the question.

Question 4. Refer students again to the last three lines of each stanza.

Challenge. Answers will vary. Possible answers: peace, racial equality, an end to pollution, respect for our wilderness areas, a job for everyone who wants one.

Reading Literature: Poetry

1. Possible answers:

a. a way for everyone to gain freedom

b. May all of America's trials make it stronger and more noble.

2. *a b a b c d e d*

3. The second last line in every stanza contains internal rhyme: good, brother-

(continued on page 346)

About the Art

Thomas Moran (1837-1926), an engraver and landscape painter born in Lancashire, England, was a fervent American nationalist after he moved to the United States. Much of his enthusiasm was generated by the accessibility of America's unspoiled natural beauty. His watercolor sketches for his painting *The Grand Canyon of the Yellowstone,* made during his first trip to Yellowstone in 1871, helped to persuade Congress to establish the area as a national park. It was the first wilderness area to be protected in the United States and the world.

The scene reproduced here is of the lower falls of the Grand Canyon, painted after Moran's second trip to Yellowstone in 1892. At the time of the trip he wrote: "It is as glorious as ever and I was completely carried away by its magnificence. I think I can paint a better picture of it than the old one after I have made my sketches."

Challenge Question. If you were to write a poem about America, what wishes for our country would you include? (Critical Reading)

Reading Literature: Poetry

Question 1. Remind students of the meaning of *thoroughfare.* Also remind them of another reference to refining gold in "I Was Born Today" on page 264.

Question 2. Have students work out the rhyme scheme independently. Discuss their answers together.

Question 3. Help students locate the first example of internal rhyme in Stanza 1, Line 7. Have them find the other three lines independently.

Question 4. Explain that there is no single right answer for this question. Make sure students understand that they should find words or phrases in the poem that support their opinions.

Developing Vocabulary Skills

Have a student read the directions for the exercise aloud. Stress that students should try to guess the meanings of each of the words from context before they look them up in the dictionary. Have them complete the exercise independently. Discuss the answers together.

Developing Writing Skills

Read and discuss the two assignments. Then have each student choose and complete one of the two.

Question 1. Emphasize that students should compare the poems by analyzing types of qualities in both. For example, if the student describes the tone in one poem, he or she should also describe the tone in the other poem.

Pre-Writing. Have students reread the six poems mentioned in the text. Have them choose two poems to compare. Have them read each poem slowly, answering the questions in the text for each one. Students should make notes on the answers to these questions. After both poems are analyzed, have students look for the similarities and differences between the two poems.

Writing. Allow sufficient time for the students to write their first drafts.

Revising. Have each student exchange his or her paper with a partner. Ask the partner to read the paper and check to see if the writer compared the same qualities in both poems.

2. **Identifying Rhyme Scheme.** Each stanza contains the same rhyme scheme. Using letters, tell what it is. (In stanza one, consider the words "skies" and "majesties" as rhymes.)
3. **Recognizing Internal Rhyme.** When two words in the same line rhyme, the poet is using **internal rhyme**. Find four examples of internal rhyme in this poem. What pattern do you notice?
4. **Understanding Mood.** What feeling do you get reading this poem? Write a list of the words that give you this feeling.

Developing Vocabulary Skills

Putting Context Clues into Use. Without using a dictionary, determine the meanings of the underlined words in the following excerpts from poems in this section. Use all types of context clues and also word parts. Write your meaning on your paper. Then look up the word in the dictionary. Copy the dictionary definition after yours.

1. The rivers are now polluted plundered
   but not the names of rivers
   cool and inviolate as ever
   pure as on the morning of creation.
2. Lots of folks in Springfield
   Saw him every day,
   Walking down the street
   In his gaunt, long way.
3. God mend thine every flaw,
   Confirm thy soul in self-control,
   Thy liberty in law.
4. A hurry of hoofs in a village street,
   And beneath, from the pebbles, in passing, a spark
   Struck out by a steed flying fearless and fleet.
5. A cry of defiance and not of fear.
6. O beautiful for heroes proved
   In liberating strife,
   Who more than self their country loved,
   And mercy more than life!

(continued from page 345)
hood; soul, self-control; success, nobleness; good, brotherhood

4. Answers will vary. Possible answers: pride in America because of words such as beautiful, majesties, freedom, liberty, patriot; hope for the future because of words such as brotherhood, grace, dream that sees beyond the years

Developing Vocabulary Skills

Students' personal definitions will vary. The following are sample dictionary definitions:

1. inviolate—intact, untouched
2. gaunt—thin and bony
3. confirm—to make firmer or stronger
4. fleet—moving rapidly
5. defiance—open resistance to authority
6. strife—bitter struggle

Developing Skills in Critical Thinking

Students' definitions of the terms will vary.

Developing Writing Skills

Analytical Writing

1. **Comparing Poems.** Six of the poems in this section are concerned with heroes and heroines. However, only "America the Beautiful" uses the term "heroes."

   Choose two of the other poems: "Benjamin Franklin," "Paul Revere's Ride," "Western Wagons," "Abraham Lincoln," or "Women." Then write two or more paragraphs comparing how the poems present their heroes or heroines. Consider questions such as these: Does each poem tell about a short period of the person's life or the whole life? Does it picture one heroic act or an average day? Does it describe specific places and actions or suggest the person's activities in a very general way? Is the tone of each poem admiring, amused, matter-of-fact, or something else? What quality or qualities of the hero or heroine does each poem concentrate on?

Creative Writing

2. **Writing About Heroes and Heroines.** Think about your heroes and heroines. Is there one man or woman whom you feel is great? What makes that person great? Is it courage, intelligence, humor, or some special talent? Or is there a group of people you admire greatly? What do these people have in common that makes them heroic in your eyes? Write from one to three paragraphs of prose or a short poem (eight to forty lines long) about your heroes or heroines.

Developing Skills in Critical Thinking

Defining Terms. In order to communicate clearly with other people, both you and the other people should understand words in the same way. It is important to agree on what the words, or terms, mean. The process of stating what you mean by certain words is called **defining your terms**. Heroism, for example, can mean different things to different people. Perhaps you and others in your class wrote about heroes and heroines for the second writing activity above. If so, each of you probably wrote about different people and different heroic qualities. Choose one of the terms below. Look it up in a dictionary and discuss it with at least three other people, either separately or in one group meeting. Try to form a definition of the term that is acceptable to all of you. Your definition may not disagree with the dictionary meaning. Write a paragraph or more to explain the meaning you have agreed on.

honesty   fairness   beauty   leadership   trust   humor

Question 2. This question allows some flexibility. Students may write about either one person or a group of people, and may write either in prose or in poetry.

Pre-Writing. Have students think about their personal heroes and heroines. Then have them list the qualities that they admire about this person or these people. Have students make notes on details that represent these qualities. Last, ask students to decide whether they wish to write prose or poetry.

Writing. Have students include at least three reasons why this person or these people are great.

Revising. Have students check over their writing. Have them make sure they have described enough qualities to make the reader understand why they consider their subjects to be great.

Developing Skills in Critical Thinking

Read the directions to the exercise aloud to the students. Divide the class into groups of four students each. Direct them to choose one of the terms to define and to discuss what that term means to each of them. Then ask each student to write a paragraph summarizing the group's definition.

The following are the dictionary definitions for the words:

- honesty—integrity, trustworthiness
- fairness—justice
- beauty—a pleasing quality associated with harmony in form, color, sound, or other properties
- leadership—the ability to lead
- trust—firm belief in the reliability of someone or something
- humor—the ability to create or appreciate something that is funny

Using the Review

This review should be completed before the administration of the **Chapter 5 Mastery Test.** Students will have an opportunity to recall important concepts from this chapter and apply them to new contexts. Teacher observation during the review can reveal which students still have not mastered the skills.

Using Your Skills in Reading Poems

Have the students read and complete the exercise independently. Discuss the answers together. Collect papers after the review lesson to see who needs further help in this or other areas of study.

Using Your Comprehension Skills

Read the directions to the exercise to the students. If you wish them to answer the questions in writing, suggest that they number their answers from 1 to 3. (Make sure they recognize that the second and third sentences go together, and that the fourth and fifth sentences go together.)

Allow time for the students to read the excerpt and decide on their answers. Remind students who are writing the answers to number them. Then discuss the inferences and predictions they have made.

See the suggestion above for evaluation.

Using Your Vocabulary Skills

Read the directions to the exercise to the students. Make sure they understand what they are to do. Have the students complete the exercise independently in writing. Then discuss the answers.

Using Your Writing Skills

Call on students to read aloud the two assignments. Point out that they should complete only one of them. Either exercise will show understanding of the elements of a poem. The first exercise is more analytic; the second is more creative. This allows each student to choose the type of writing he or she prefers.

Answer any questions students may have about the assignments. If you are asking the students to complete their writing in class, let them know how much time they have and that they may turn in a marked-up first draft. Remind them to skip lines to leave space for corrections. If you are asking them to do the writing outside of class, you may require clean copies.

Collect and evaluate these papers according to the guidelines on pages T-24 through T-27 of this Teacher's Edition. It

CHAPTER 5 Review

Using Your Skills in Reading Poems

Read the following part of the poem "City," by Langston Hughes. Then follow these directions.

1. Using letters of the alphabet, write the rhyme scheme of the poem.
2. Identify the type of rhythm used in the poem. Is it a regular, steady rhythm or free verse?
3. Identify one metaphor used in the poem. To what is the city being compared? How are the two things alike?

> In the morning the city
> Spreads its wings
> Making a song
> In stone that sings.

Using Your Comprehension Skills

Read these paragraphs from a selection in Chapter 6. Then explain Betty Marie's inner struggle. What decision must she make? Next, predict the outcome of her struggle. What do you think Betty Marie will choose? What evidence in the paragraph did you use to come to your conclusion?

> In high school, Betty Marie's favorite subject was writing. Once she wrote about trying to decide between music and dancing. At fifteen, she was performing at the piano and studying ballet with a great Russian teacher, Mme. Bronislava Nijinska.
>
> Mme. Nijinska was also a choreographer—a person who makes up dances. She gave Betty Marie a leading part in one of her ballets. The performance took place before an enormous audience. As she danced, Betty Marie felt strong and free. Afterward, everyone told her how well she had done.

Answers to the Exercise

Using Your Skills in Reading Poems

1. a b c b
2. a regular, steady rhythm
3. The city is compared to a bird. The noise of the city in the morning, to the speaker, is like the song of a bird

Using Your Comprehension Skills

Betty Marie must make a decision between music—playing the piano—and dancing—ballet.

Using Your Vocabulary Skills

Read the following sentences from selections in Chapter 6. Use context clues to figure out the meaning of each underlined word. Write the meaning in your own words. Then tell which type of context clue you used: example, comparison, contrast, or words in a series.

1. Hjalmar's horse needed an incentive to act up, but all I had to do to my horse was to say "People"; she would dance from one side of the street to the other.
2. There I had my first lessons in the beneficence of nature. But I also had an experience which taught me that nature is not always kind.
3. He had survived against floods, forest and prairie fires, snake-bites, chills, fevers, ague, malaria.
4. The youth found a job on a boat, a square-rigger with tall white sails destined for Hong Kong.

Using Your Writing Skills

Choose one of the writing assignments below. Follow the directions carefully.

1. Select the poem in this chapter that you liked best. Write one clear paragraph reporting your choice. In your paragraph, give three reasons for your choice, in increasing order of importance.
2. Write a poem about a game or a hobby. Use free verse or a regular rhythm and rhyme scheme. Your tone may be serious or humorous. Make your poem no longer than twelve lines. Be sure to include some figurative language in it.

Using Your Skills in Study and Research

Imagine that you have been asked to put together a collection of poems on nature and the seasons. Explain how you would locate in a library some poems you might consider. Explain, also, how you would find poems on these topics in a poetry anthology. Last, tell how you would look for information on the writers of your poems.

is strongly recommended that you discuss and explain your evaluations with the student, and that you provide an opportunity for the students to revise and resubmit their writing.

Using Your Skills in Study and Research

Read the directions to the exercise to the students. Ask them to write on their papers at least two notes (not necessarily in sentence form) to answer each of the three questions. Then discuss the three questions, asking a volunteer to record on the board all the usable suggestions from individuals.

Reinforcing the Lesson

To reteach, reinforce, or extend the skills in this lesson, see the following:

Skills Practice Book, Green Level—pages 147 and 148

Additional Resource

Diagnostic and Mastery Tests, Green Level—Chapter 5 Mastery Test, pages 27 through 30

Students should guess from paragraph 2 that Betty Marie will choose ballet.

Clues include the statement that Betty Marie felt strong and free when performing for an audience and the fact that she received many compliments on her dancing.

Using Your Vocabulary Skills

1. a reason or command, something to cause a certain action; contrast clue

2. kindness; contrast

3. a sickness; words in a series

4. a type of boat; example

Using Your Skills in Study and Research

For finding poems, students should mention using the card catalog and examining books in the poetry sections (in the 800's of the Dewey system).

For examining an anthology, students should suggest looking at the table of contents to discover patterns of organization, and at the index for promising titles or first lines.

For finding information on writers, students might suggest the encyclopedia, a specialized dictionary of poets, or the card catalog once more.

About the Art

Chicago artist Ed Paschke (born 1941) portrays Lincoln as legend—remote, enduring, an object of awe. Even in his lifetime, when he was known as "the rail splitter," Abraham Lincoln had become a national folk figure. After his assassination on Good Friday, the day that commemorates the crucifixion of Christ, he became a hero-martyr.

Artists during Lincoln's lifetime depicted Lincoln as a man—thoughtful, concerned, amused—though slightly larger than life. (See *About the Art* on pages 341, 428, and 439.) Over the past century, the legends about Lincoln have grown, and he has become as much a myth as a man. Glossed in neon-like colors, the painting tends to deify Lincoln and the title of the work echoes this idea. An icon is a religious image, often a picture presented as an object of devotion.

One of Paschke's later paintings, on page 233, shows progress toward depersonalizing his portraits.

CHAPTER 6

Nonfiction

Icon-Ero, 1980, ED PASCHKE.
Courtesy of Phyllis Kind Gallery, New York and Chicago.
Photograph by Eric Pollitzer

Chapter Objectives

Skills in Reading Literature

- To recognize and appreciate nonfiction as a form of literature
- To identify various forms of nonfiction, including autobiographies, biographies, anecdotes, essays, letters, speeches, and vignettes
- To recognize elements of nonfiction, including point of view, organization, purpose, and style
- To identify themes in nonfiction
- To identify humor and irony

Comprehension Skills

- To restate passages (Literal Reading)
- To make inferences about characters (Interpretive Reading)
- To differentiate between denotation and connotation (Interpretive Reading)
- To separate fact and opinion (Critical Reading)

Vocabulary Skills

- To use the dictionary, the Glossary, and the encyclopedia to find information
- To use base words and affixes to unlock the meanings of words
- To choose the best method for finding correct meanings

Writing Skills

- To analyze organization (Analytical Writing)
- To write an autobiographical account (Creative Writing)
- To compare works of nonfiction (Analytical Writing)
- To write a speech (Creative Writing)

Study and Research Skills

- To take notes on written information
- To read a map
- To use the *Readers' Guide*
- To use study-reading skills
- To compare encyclopedias

Critical Thinking Skills

- To understand word connotations
- To analyze slanted writing
- To identify unstated opinions

Speaking and Listening Skills

- To understand and use gestures
- To introduce a guest speaker
- To perform a humorous saying
- To read an essay orally
- To deliver a speech

Reading Literature

Reading Literature: Nonfiction introduces students to nonfiction in its man forms. First, nonfiction is differentiate from fiction. In the following discussion of the history of nonfiction, students learn about the wide variety of nonfictional works. To help students get the most out of nonfiction, the text reviews the element of point of view and relates it to the nonfiction they will read. The text then introduces the two types of organization students will find in these works—chronological order and logical order. Since the element of tone is also important for understanding the writer's attitude toward a subject, tone is also discussed. The lesson ends with guidelines for reading nonfiction, which will help students read the material in this chapter.

Preparing the Students

Tell the students that much of what people read every day is based on fact. Ask the students if they can suggest any types of writing that do not tell a story about fictional characters. If necessary, give them a few examples of factual writing such as newspaper articles or lists of sports records. List their responses on the board. Tell the class that they will learn more about this type of writing, called *nonfiction*, in the next chapter. They will also get a chance to read many different types of nonfiction.

It is recommended that you administer the **Chapter 6 Diagnostic Test** at this time. The results of this pretest will serve as a guide for measuring student needs and progress in achieving chapter objectives.

Presenting the Lesson

1. Have the students read **What Is Nonfiction?**, on page 352. Discuss how nonfiction differs from fiction.

2. Have the students read **The History of Nonfiction** silently. Then discuss the reasons why people through the ages have written nonfiction. Review the categories of nonfiction that are listed and then ask the students if they can think of any nonfiction categories that do not appear on the list.

3. Call on individual students to read aloud **The Elements of Nonfiction**, with each student taking one paragraph. After the paragraph on point of view, ask the students which types of nonfiction are written from the first-person point of view.

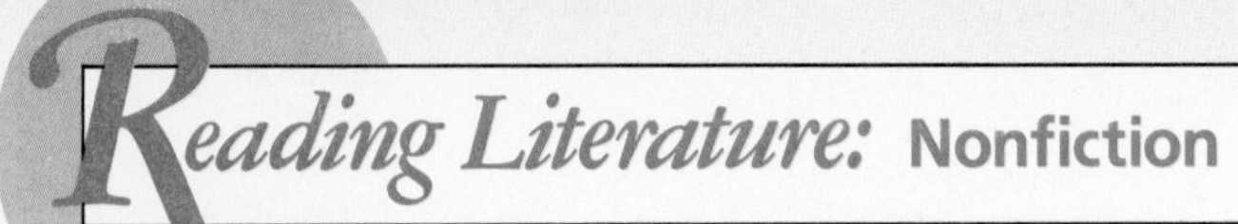

Reading Literature: Nonfiction

What Is Nonfiction?

Nonfiction is writing that tells about real people, places, and happenings. Nonfiction is based on facts. In this important way it is different from fiction, which comes from the writer's imagination.

The History of Nonfiction

Nonfiction has existed as long as people have had news to tell or important facts to remember. Before writing was invented, listeners had to depend on the memory and accuracy of the person reporting the news or facts. The first purpose of writing was to put the facts in a more permanent form.

Nonfiction consists of every kind of writing that people have done that has not come from their imaginations. Whenever people have needed to record, explain, describe, or inform, they have written nonfiction. Here are some categories of nonfiction:

1. Records of the lives, achievements, words, and personalities of famous and not-so-famous people
2. Records of a person's own life and achievements
3. True adventure stories telling of remarkable experiences
4. Records of journeys, including the sights, the events, and the people the traveler met
5. Letters communicating news and private thoughts
6. Memorable speeches first delivered by talented speakers
7. Essays telling personal thoughts and opinions
8. Reports concerning theories and information from research
9. Newspaper and magazine articles recording important events and passing on timely information
10. Special reports and documentaries for television and radio

The Elements of Nonfiction

Point of View. Some works of nonfiction are written from the **first-person point of view**. Autobiographies, letters, speeches, and essays are usually written in this way. Other works are written from the **third-person point of view**. In those cases, writers simply report the facts. They are not part of the action.

Organization. Like short stories and legends, some forms of nonfiction are organized according to **chronological order**. That is, they tell about events in the order in which they happen. These include autobiographies, biographies, anecdotes, and any other forms that tell of people's lives or of events.

Other forms of nonfiction are organized according to **logical order**. In logical order, ideas are arranged so as to explain or prove a statement, or to lead to a certain conclusion. Forms of nonfiction that discuss ideas use logical order. These include essays, letters, and speeches.

Tone. The **tone** of a piece of writing is the way in which the writer lets you know his or her attitude toward a subject. In some cases, the writer may want you to take the subject seriously. The tone could be, for example, admiring or angry. The piece could, on the other hand, be written with a carefree tone that asks you to relax and enjoy it. To understand the meaning of a piece of writing, the reader must be aware of its tone.

How To Read Nonfiction

1. Decide who is speaking. Is the piece written from the first-person or the third-person point of view?
2. Use information in the title. Some titles tell the topic of the piece or its main idea. Others give clues about the tone.
3. Learn what you can about when and where the events take place. The setting affects the events.
4. Make use of your own experience with the topic. What you know will help you understand what you read.

After the paragraph about organization, ask the class what the difference is between chronological order and logical order. Review which types of nonfiction would use each kind of order and why.

In a discussion of tone, ask a student to tell in his or her own words what tone is. Ask why it is important that readers of nonfiction recognize tone.

4. Ask students to read silently **How To Read Nonfiction.** Then ask them to close their books and list the four suggestions for reading nonfiction. Allow them to reread the material on page 353 as needed in order to recall all four suggestions. Stress that the suggestions are useful only when the students apply them to personal reading.

Reinforcing the Lesson

To reteach, reinforce, or extend the concepts in this lesson, see the following:

Skills Practice Book, Green Level—pages 149 and 150

Additional Resource

Diagnostic and Mastery Tests, Green Level—Chapter 6 Diagnostic Test, pages 31 and 32

Special Populations

Incidental learning is sometimes limited for special-populations students. This means that they may not pick up commonly understood information that others in the class have. Limited backgrounds might also affect understanding of some of the material presented. Before assigning each selection in this chapter, check the students' knowledge of historical facts or information vital to the understanding of the stories.

Several selections could benefit from additional background or historical information as they are presented. You may want to ask students to find specific information about some of the famous people written about in this chapter. Students could be encouraged to make use of the card catalog, encyclopedias, biographical dictionaries, or *Readers' Guide* Students could also bring from home or from the library books that give additional information about the people in this chapter.

Comprehension Skills

Comprehension Skills: Connotations, Denotations presents the students with guidelines for distinguishing fact from opinion and for identifying slanted writing. Students are made aware of the power of the connotations as well as the denotations of words. Exercises give the students practice in separating fact from opinion and in recognizing positively and negatively slanted statements.

Preparing the Students

Tell the students to listen to these two statements about one team's performance in basketball playoffs. Ask them to decide how the statements are different.

> Our team was awarded second prize for its excellent playing.
>
> Our disappointing team could do no better than a weak second–place finish.

Point out that the facts are the same in each statement—the team finished in second place. However, the writer showed how he or she felt about the second place finish through his or her choice of words. Tell the students that in this section, they will learn how writers slant their writing.

Presenting the Lesson

1. Tell the students to read silently **Identifying Opinions and Slanted Writing** down to **Slanted Writing**. Ask what an opinion is. Discuss how a reader can check to find out whether a statement is a fact or an opinion.

2. Call on students to read aloud the rest of the section, down to the exercises. Ask if they have ever heard or read any slanted writing. If necessary, point out that sports and weather reports in the newspapers are good sources for slanted treatment of the facts.

Ask the students to identify the positive, negative, and neutral statement among these sentences.

> There is a 70% chance of rain on Saturday.
>
> It looks like the rain is going to spoil another Saturday.
>
> The chances are good that our crops will be saved by a steady rain on Saturday.

3. Have the students complete Exercise A independently and discuss the answers together.

4. Complete Exercise B together with the students.

Comprehension Skills: Connotations, Denotations

Identifying Opinions and Slanted Writing

When people feel strongly about a topic, they often include their opinions in their writing. Sometimes they identify their opinions. Other times, though, they mix their opinions with the facts. As a reader, you must be alert to the ways in which writers try to persuade readers to agree with their opinions.

Fact and Opinion. An opinion is one person's belief. It may or may not be based on facts. Opinions are often stated as if they were facts. For example, "February is the shortest month" is a fact. "February is the worst month" is an opinion.

If a statement is really a fact, it can be proved to be true. You can check it in a source such as an encyclopedia. Sometimes you can observe that it is true by using what you see around you.

Slanted Writing. Sometimes it may seem as if the writer is reporting only the facts. Even facts, however, can be presented so that they favor one side of an issue. A writer who enjoys football, for example, may report only the exciting moments of a particular game. A writer who does not care for the sport may report that the weather that day was cold and wet, that the crowd was unruly, and that several players were injured.

When writing "leans" to one side of an argument, or shows only one view of an event, the writer has used **slanted writing**. Slanted writing is also called **biased writing**.

Connotation and Denotation. The **denotation** of a word is its dictionary meaning. Its **connotation** is the combination of ideas and emotions that the word brings to your mind. Writers can slant their writing by choosing words that have the connotations they want.

Connotations can be positive (good), negative (bad), or neutral (neither good nor bad). Even when words are close in meaning, their connotations can differ widely. The underlined words in the following sentences are similar in denotative meaning. Notice how the picture in your mind changes with each sentence.

1. The crowd left the auditorium. (Neutral)
2. The crowd filed out of the auditorium. (Positive)
3. The crowd escaped from the auditorium. (Negative)

Exercises: Identifying Opinions and Slanted Writing

A. Decide which sentences are facts and which are opinions.

1. I was born on June 27, 1880, in Tuscumbia, Alabama.
2. December goes by too quickly.
3. Abraham Lincoln was our sixteenth president.
4. Training a horse takes care and effort.
5. April just isn't April without robins.

B. Match each sentence with a positive slant to a similar sentence with a negative slant.

Sentences with a Positive Slant

1. The explorers were brave.
2. Abe was so interested that he studied for hours.
3. The general avoided risking the lives of his men needlessly.
4. Maria devoted all her time to her favorite activity, dancing.
5. Helen's teacher was young, lively, and enthusiastic.

Sentences with a Negative Slant

1. The general stubbornly refused to attack.
2. Helen's new teacher was inexperienced.
3. It took Abe hours to understand even the simplest ideas.
4. The explorers took foolish chances.
5. Maria never did anything but dance.

Reinforcing the Lesson

To reteach, reinforce, or extend the skills in this lesson, see the following:

Skills Practice Book, Green Level—pages 151 and 152

Special Populations

ESL. These students may need additional practice assigning good (positive), bad (negative) or neutral labels to English words.

Answers to Exercises

A. Facts: 1, 3, 4. Opinions: 2, 5.

B. Positive sentences, followed by matching negative sentences:

1. 4
2. 3
3. 1
4. 5
5. 2

Vocabulary Skills

In **Vocabulary Skills: Reference Sources** students learn about the reference sources that can help them discover the meanings of unknown words. Students learn the types of information that can be found in a dictionary, a glossary, and an encyclopedia.

One exercise focuses on using the dictionary while the other reviews the information in each source.

Preparing the Students

Review the ways the students have already studied in which readers can find out the meanings of words (using word parts and context clues). Tell the students that, by using reference sources, they can find meanings quickly and accurately. Ask them if they know the names of any reference sources. Tell them that they will learn how to use three reference sources in this section.

Presenting the Lesson

1. Have the students read silently the first paragraph under **Using Reference Sources**. Ask them which reference sources will be discussed in this section.

2. Call on students to read aloud **The Dictionary**. Review the five types of information that can be found in the dictionary. If students have individual dictionaries, choose another word for them to look up, and record the information that they find there. If only one dictionary is available, ask a volunteer to find and report the information.

3. Have the class read silently **The Glossary** and **The Encyclopedia**. Point out that all these reference sources are arranged in alphabetical order. Make sure students recognize that the glossary of a book lists only words from that book that could be unfamiliar to the reader, while the encyclopedia gives more information about the word than just the definition and pronunciation.

4. Have the students complete the exercises independently. Discuss the answers together.

Reinforcing the Lesson

To reteach, reinforce, or extend the skills in this lesson, see the following:

Skills Practice Book, Green Level—pages 153 and 154

Vocabulary Skills: Reference Sources

Using Reference Sources

When you come across an unfamiliar word, you should first try to figure out its meaning from context clues or word parts. If those approaches don't help, turn to a reference source. Three reference sources you should become familiar with are the dictionary, the glossary, and the encyclopedia.

The Dictionary. The **dictionary** lists words in alphabetical order and gives you useful information about them. Each word that is listed is called an **entry word**. For each entry word, the dictionary gives some or all of the following information.

1. **How to divide the word into syllables.** The syllables may be separated by a space or by a centered dot: for est, for•est.
2. **How to pronounce the word.** The pronunciation is usually given in parentheses: (for′ist). The **respelling** identifies the sounds in the word. Each dictionary has a pronunciation key that helps you pronounce each sound correctly. **Accent marks** (′) within a respelling show which syllables to stress.
3. **The part of speech of the word.** The **parts of speech** are abbreviated as follows:

n.	noun	*pro.*	pronoun	*prep.*	preposition
v.	verb	*adv.*	adverb	*conj.*	conjunction
		adj.	adjective	*interj.*	interjection

4. **The origin of the word.** The word may have come into our language in one of a number of different ways. Its **origin**, or source, is printed in brackets such as these: { }.
5. **The definition of the word.** If there is more than one **definition**, each meaning is assigned a number. Often a sample phrase or sentence will show you how to use the word.

The Glossary. A **glossary** of a book lists all the words in that book that may be new or unfamiliar. There is usually a glossary at the back of a nonfiction book. The glossary lists words in alphabetical order and gives pronunciations and definitions.

The Encyclopedia. When you need more information than just the definition or the pronunciation of a word, it sometimes helps to look the word up in an encyclopedia. There may be an article to explain that term, or a cross-reference to an article that does. Like dictionary entries, encyclopedia articles are listed in alphabetical order. Each article is a short factual report.

Exercises: Using Reference Sources

A. Use this dictionary entry to answer the questions below.

en•gaged (in gājd'), *adj.* {Fr. and OFr. engager} **1.** pledged. **2.** pledged in marriage. **3.** occupied; employed; busy. **4.** involved in combat, as troops. **5.** attached to or partly set into (a wall, etc.): as engaged columns. **6.** interlocked; meshed; in gear.

1. How is *engaged* divided into syllables?
2. Is the accent on the first or the second syllable?
3. What part of speech is *engaged*?
4. Which meaning is used in each of these sentences?
   a. Now we are engaged in a great civil war.
   b. His telephone is engaged at this moment.
   c. The couple was engaged for six months before the wedding.

B. Copy these sentences, filling in each blank correctly.

1. A ______ lists words in alphabetical order and gives pronunciations, parts of speech, origins, and meanings.
2. An ______ gives a short report to explain each entry word.
3. A ______ lists and defines the new or unfamiliar words in a particular book in alphabetical order.

Answers to Exercises

A. Dictionary information:

1. The word has two syllables; the break comes after *en*.
2. second syllable
3. adjective
4. Meanings:
a. 4 **b.** 3 **c.** 2

B. Missing words

1. dictionary
2. encyclopedia
3. glossary

Autobiographies

Have the students read page 358. Ask them to define autobiography, and to discuss what advantages an autobiography has over a biography. Point out that the next two selections are autobiographical.

Special Populations

Many selections in this chapter are longer than most of the readings presented in the book thus far. Select assignments carefully for the special-populations students; base your selection on reading level, understanding of vocabulary presented, and ability to process information given within the reading. Material may be adapted in the following ways: allow students extra time to complete the reading; tape-record portions of the story to reinforce correct pronunciation and comprehension skills; omit assignments known to be beyond the capability of the student until individual help can be received from a teacher or a student tutor; ask specialists to provide outside-of-class assistance with the reading; divide reading assignments into small, manageable sections.

Autobiographies

An **autobiography** is the story a person writes about his or her own life. An autobiography may tell a person's whole life story up to that point or only parts of it. It is written from the first-person point of view. An autobiography can give you information you cannot find anywhere else. You learn about the subject's personal feelings and reasons for certain actions. You also get a glimpse of how the person thought and expressed himself or herself.

Rhododendron Bower, 1920, CHARLES C. CURRAN.
Courtesy of Fred and Maureen Radl, Cragsmoor, N.Y.

About the Art

Charles C. Curran (1861-1945) was born in Hartford, Kentucky and, even as a small child, showed a talent for drawing. He attended the Cincinnati School of Design and studied at the Art Students League in New York City. In 1886, at the age of twenty-five, he was an associate member of the National Academy of Art. Two years later he went to Paris to study at the Académie Julien, where he won many awards for his painting. He returned to the United States, and in 1904 he was admitted into the National Academy as a full member.

Curran is best known for his paintings of women and flowers. *Rhododendron Bower* shows both—a young lady posed in profile, surrounded by flowers. A very special light outlines the woman and causes the flowers to glow. The artist has captured an intimate moment so sensitively that you can almost hear the woman's thoughts.

I Get a Colt To Break In

LINCOLN STEFFENS

This selection describes an enjoyable time in Lincoln Steffens's boyhood. It also tells some of his private thoughts and feelings. What are some of these thoughts and feelings? Do you agree with him?

Colonel Carter gave me a colt. I had my pony, and my father meanwhile had bought a pair of black carriage horses and a cow, all of which I had to attend to when we had no "man." My hands were pretty full, and so was the stable. But Colonel Carter seemed to think that he had promised me a horse. He had not; I would have known it if he had. No matter. He thought he had, and maybe he did promise himself to give me one. That was enough. The kind of man that led immigrant trains across the continent and delivered them safe, sound, and together where he promised, would keep his word. One day he drove over from Stockton, leading a two-year-old which he brought to our front door and turned over to me as mine. Such a horse!

She was a cream-colored mare with a black forelock, mane, and tail and a black stripe along the middle of her back. Tall, slender, high-spirited, I thought then—I think now that she was the most beautiful of horses. Colonel Carter had bred and reared her with me and my uses in mind. She was a careful cross of a mustang mare and a thoroughbred stallion, with the stamina of the wild horse and the speed and grace of the racer. And she had a sense of fun. As Colonel Carter got down out of his buggy and went up to her, she snorted, reared, flung her head high in the air, and, coming down beside him, tucked her nose affectionately under his arm.

"I have handled her a lot," he said. "She is as kind as a kitten, but she is as sensitive as a lady. You can spoil her by one mistake. If you ever lose your temper, if you ever abuse her, she will be ruined for ever. And she is unbroken. I might have had her broken to ride for you, but I didn't want to. I want you to do it. I have taught her to lead, as you see; had to, to get her over here. But here she is, an unbroken colt; yours. You take and you

Objectives

- To recognize and appreciate autobiography as a form of literature
- To define autobiography and identify its elements
- To apply literal, interpretive, and critical reading skills to a selection
- To distinguish fact from opinion
- To choose the correct respellings of words in order to identify appropriate meanings
- To write an analysis of the author's purpose for writing a selection
- To take notes
- To recognize and understand the effect of the connotations of words

Preparing the Students

Essential Vocabulary. The words presented here are essential to the understanding of the selection.

Introduce to the students the words listed below. Write the sentences on the board, have them read aloud, and ask the students to use context clues to find the meaning of each underlined word.

conceit	boring	reproachful
literally	conspicuous	

1. Since he talked only about himself and his accomplishments, everyone thought the man was filled with conceit.
2. The treatment of the prisoners was, literally, inhuman. Their food came in a horse's feed bag, and they slept in a barn.
3. The man was boring through the crowd by shoving people aside, one by one.
4. The object was conspicuous because of its enormous size and bright colors.
5. The woman looked reproachful. It was clear that she meant to scold her children as soon as the visitors left.

If the students need additional help with the vocabulary of this selection, encourage them to use context clues to determine word meaning. As needed, direct them to the **Glossary** or to a classroom dictionary.

Motivation. Encourage students to share with the class information about their pets, including any tricks they have taught their pets and the procedures they used. Then have the students read the introductory paragraph on page 359 and ask them to state in their own words what they should try to find out as they read the story.

Presenting the Selection

Have the students read "I Get a Colt To Break In" silently. Since it is a long selection, you may want to assign it in two parts. The first part would end on page 362, after the first full paragraph ("...my sisters had to lead her while I rode.")

1. Make sure that everyone has read the assignment by administering the **Check Test,** at the bottom of T.E. page 366. If the story was read in two parts, administer questions 1, 2, and 3 after the first part and questions 4 and 5 after the second part.

2. Remind the students that the introduction to the story asked them to find out some of Lincoln Steffens's private thoughts and feelings and to decide if they agree with him. Have students respond to those questions.

3. Develop the study questions as suggested in **Using the Study Questions,** beginning on page 366. That section also provides a challenge question for further discussion, if needed. (For answers to questions, see T.E. pages 366 to 369.)

Reinforcing the Lesson

To reteach, reinforce, or extend the skills in this lesson, see the following:

Skills Practice Book, Green Level—pages 155 through 157

Special Populations

Students who have been responsible for a pet or farm children who have taken responsibility for a particular farm animal may want to present a panel discussion to the class on the methods they have used to train and raise animals.

ESL. The first exercise in **Developing Vocabulary Skills, Choosing the Correct Respelling,** may be a confusing activity for ESL students who are concentrating on being able to recognize and pronounce regular spelling of words. To help them with this activity, first present a list of the respelled words and then a list of words to choose from that includes the correct words.

Encouraging Independent Reading

Students may be encouraged to do more extensive reading in the books they located while completing the **Study and**

break her. You're only a boy, but if you break this colt right, you'll be a man—a young man, but a man. And I'll tell you how."

Now, out west, as everybody knows, they break in a horse by riding him in his wild state, lassoing, throwing, and saddling him; then they let him up, frightened and shocked, with a yelling broncho-buster astride of him. The wild beast bucks, the cowboy drives his spurs into him, and off they go, jumping, kicking, rearing, falling, till by the weight of the man, the lash, and the spurs, the horse is broken—in body and spirit. This was not the way I was to break my colt.

"You must break her to ride without her ever knowing it," Colonel Carter said. "You feed and you clean her—you, not the stable man. You lead her out to water and to walk. You put her on a long rope and let her play, calling her to you and gently pulling on the rope. Then you turn her loose in the grass lot and, when she has romped till tired, call her. If she won't come, leave her. When she wants water or

food, she will run to your call, and you will pet and feed and care for her." He went on for half an hour, advising me in great detail how to proceed. I wanted to begin right away. He laughed. He let me lead her around to the stable, water her, and put her in the stable and feed her.

There I saw my pony. My father, sisters, and Colonel Carter saw me stop and look at my pony.

"What'll you do with him?" one of my sisters asked. I was bewildered for a moment. What should I do with the little red horse? I decided at once.

"He's yours," I said to my sisters.

"No," said Colonel Carter, "not yet. You can give your sisters the pony by and by, but you'll need him till you have taught the colt to carry you and a saddle—months; and you must not hurry. You must learn patience, and you will if you give the colt time to learn it, too. Patience and control. You can't control a horse unless you can control yourself."

He went off downtown with my father, and I started away with my colt. I fed, I led, I cleaned her, gently, as if she were made of glass; she was playful and willing, a delight. When Colonel Carter came home with my father for supper, he questioned me.

"You should not have worked her today," he said. "She has come all the way from Stockton and must be tired. Yes, yes, she would not show fatigue; too fine for that, and too young to be wise. You have got to think for her." He went on to draw on my imagination a centaur; the colt as a horse's body—me, a boy, as the head and brains of one united creature. I liked that. I would be that. I and the colt: a centaur.

After Colonel Carter was gone home, I went to work on my new horse. The old one, the pony, I used only for business: to go to fires, to see my friends, run errands, and go hunting. But the game that had all my attention was the breaking in of the colt, the beautiful cream-colored mare, who soon knew me—and my pockets. I carried sugar to reward her when she did right, and she discovered where I carried it; so did the pony, and when I was busy they would push their noses into my pockets, both of which were torn down a good deal of the time. But the colt learned. I taught her to run around a circle, turn and go the other way at a signal. My sisters helped me. I held the long rope and the whip (for signaling), while one of the girls led the colt. One would lead the colt round and round till I snapped the whip; then she would turn, turning the colt, till the colt did it all by herself. The colt was very quick. She shook hands with each of her four feet. She let us run under her, back and forth. She was slow only to carry me. Following Colonel Carter's instructions, I began by laying my arm or a saddle strap over her back. If she trembled, I drew it slowly off. When she could abide it, I tried buckling it, tighter and

Research assignment. If some students have pets, they can actually try some of the suggestions in the book and report to the class on how well they worked.

tighter. I laid over her, too, a blanket, folded at first, then open, and, at last, I slipped up on her myself, sat there a second, and, as she trembled, slid off. My sisters held her for me, and when I could get up and sit there a moment or two, I tied her at a block, and we, my sisters and I, made a procession of mounting and dismounting. She soon got used to this and would let us slide off over her rump, but it was a long, long time before she would carry me.

That we practiced by leading her along a high curb where I could get on as she walked, ride a few steps, and then, as she felt me and crouched, slip off. She never did learn to carry a girl on her back; my sisters had to lead her while I rode.

While we were breaking in the colt, a circus came to town. The ring was across the street from our house. Wonderful! I lived in that circus for a week. I saw the show but once, but I marked the horse-trainers, and in the mornings when they were not too busy I told them about my colt, showed her to them, and asked them how to train her to do circus tricks. With their hints I taught the colt to stand up on her hind legs, kneel, lie down, and balance on a small box. This last was easier than it looked. I put her first on a low, big box and taught her to turn on it; then got a little smaller box upon which she repeated what she did on the big one. By and by we had her so that she would step on a high box so small that her four feet were almost touching, and there also she would turn.

The circus man gave me one hint that was worth all the other tricks put together. "You catch her doing something of herself that looks good," he said, "and then you keep her at it." It was thus that I taught her to bow to people. The first day I rode her out on to the streets was a proud one for me and for the colt, too, apparently. She did not walk, she danced; perhaps she was excited, nervous; anyhow I liked the way she threw up her head, champed at the bit, and went dancing, prancing down the street. Everybody stopped to watch us, and so, when she began to sober down, I picked her up again with heel and rein, saying, "Here's people, Lady," and she would show off to my delight. By constant repetition I had her so trained that she would singlefoot, head down, along a country road till we came to a house or a group of people. Then I'd say, "People, Lady," and up would go her head, and her feet would dance.

But the trick that set the town talking was her bowing to anyone I spoke to. "Lennie Steffens' horse bows to you," people said, and she did. I never told how it was done; by accident. Dogs used to run out at us, and the colt enjoyed it; she kicked at them sometimes with both hind hoofs. I joined her in the game, and being able to look behind more conveniently than she could, I watched the dogs until they were in range, then gave the colt a

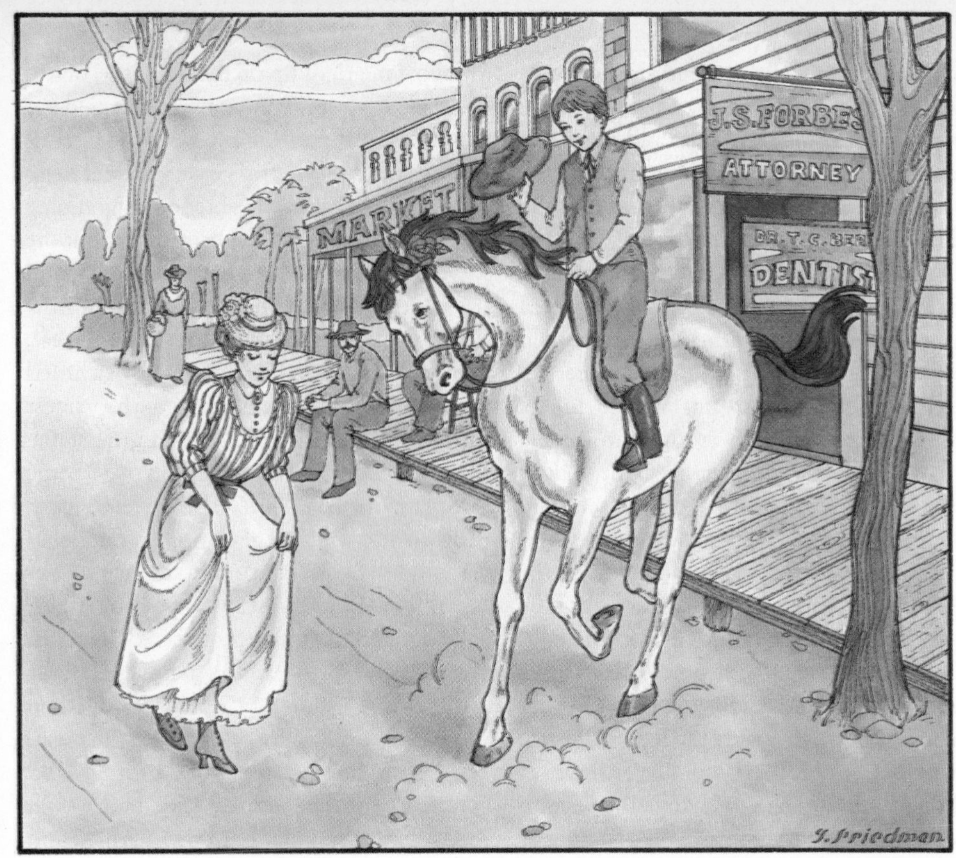

signal to kick. "Kick, gal," I'd say, and tap her ribs with my heel. We used to get dogs together that way; the colt would kick them over and over and leave them yelping in the road. Well, one day when I met a girl I knew, I lifted my hat, probably muttered a "Good day," and I must have touched the colt with my heel. Anyway, she dropped her head and kicked—not much; there was no dog near, so she had responded to my unexpected signal by what looked like a bow. I caught the idea and kept her at it. Whenever I wanted to bow to a girl or anybody else, instead of saying "Good day," I muttered "Kick, gal," spurred her lightly, and—the whole centaur bowed and was covered with glory and conceit.

Yes, conceit. I was full of it, and the colt was quite as bad. One day my chum Hjalmar came into town on his Black Bess, blanketed. A great fistula had been cut out of her shoulder, and she had to be kept warm. I expected to see her weak and dull, but no, the good old mare was champing and dancing, like my colt.

"What is it makes her so?" I asked, and Hjalmar said he didn't know, but he thought she was proud of her blanket. A great idea. I had a gaudy horse blanket. I put it on the colt and I could hardly hold her. We rode down the main street together, both horses and boys so full of vanity that everybody stopped to smile.

We pranced, the black and the yellow, all the way down J Street, up K Street, and agreed that we'd do it again, often. Only, I said, we wouldn't use blankets. If the horses were proud of a blanket, they'd be proud of anything unusually conspicuous. We tried a flower next time. I fixed a big rose on my colt's bridle just under her ear and it was great—she pranced downtown with her head turned, literally, to show off her flower. We had to change the decoration from time to time, put on a ribbon, or a bell, or a feather, but really, it was not necessary for my horse. Old Black Bess needed an incentive to act up, but all I had to do to my horse was to pick up the reins, touch her with my heel, and say, "People"; she would dance from one side of the street to the other, asking to be admired. As she was. As we were.

I would ride down to my father's store, jump off my prancing colt in the middle of the street, and run up into the shop. The colt, free, would stop short, turn, and follow me right up on the sidewalk, unless I bade her wait. If anyone approached her while I was gone, she would snort, rear, and strike. No stranger could get near her. She became a frightened, frightening animal, and yet when I came into sight she would run to me, put her head down, and as I straddled her neck, she would throw up her head and pitch me into my seat, facing backward, of course. I whirled around right, and off we'd go, the vainest boy and the proudest horse in the state.

"Hey, give me a ride, will you?" some boy would ask. "Sure," I'd say, and jump down and watch that boy try to catch and mount my colt. He couldn't. Once a cowboy wanted to try her, and he caught her; he dodged her forefeet, grabbed the reins, and in one spring was on her back. I never did that again. My colt reared, then bucked, and, as the cowboy kept his seat, she shuddered, sank to the ground, and rolled over. He slipped aside and would have risen with her, but I was alarmed and begged him not to. She got up at my touch and followed me so close that she stepped on my heel and hurt me. The cowboy saw the point.

"If I were you, kid," he said, "I'd never let anybody mount that colt. She's too good."

That, I think, was the only mistake I made in the rearing of Colonel Carter's gift-horse. My father differed from me. He discovered another error or sin, and thrashed me for it. My practice was to work hard on a trick, privately, and when it was perfect, let him see it. I would have the horse out in our vacant lot doing it as he came home to supper. One evening, as he approached the house, I was standing, whip in hand, while the colt, quite free, was stepping carefully over the bodies of a lot of girls, all my sisters and all their girl friends. My father did not express the admiration I expected; he was frightened and furious. "Stop that," he called, and he came running around into the lot, took the whip, and lashed me with it. I tried to explain; the girls tried to help me explain.

I had seen in the circus a horse that stepped thus over a row of prostrate clowns. It looked dangerous for the clowns, but the trainer had told me how to do it. You begin with logs, laid out a certain distance apart; the horse walks over them under your lead, and whenever he touches one you scold him. By and by he will learn to step with such care that he never trips. Then you substitute clowns. I had no clowns, but I did get logs, and, with the girls helping, we taught the colt to step over the obstacles even at a trot. Walking, she touched nothing. All ready thus with the logs, I had my sisters lie down in the grass, and again and again the colt stepped over and among them. None was ever touched. My father would not listen to any of this. He just walloped me, and, when he was tired or satisfied and I was in tears, I blubbered a short excuse: "They were only girls." And he whipped me some more.

My father was not given to whipping; he did it very seldom, but he did it hard when he did it at all. My mother was just the opposite. She did not whip me, but she often smacked me, and she had a most annoying habit of thumping me on the head with her thimbled finger. This I resented more than my father's thoroughgoing thrashings, and I can tell why now. I would be playing Napoleon and, as I was reviewing my Old Guard, she would crack my skull with that thimble. No doubt I was in the way; it took a lot of furniture and sisters to represent properly a victorious army; and you might think as my mother did that a thimble is a small weapon. But imagine Napoleon at the height of his power, the ruler of the world on parade, getting a sharp rap on his crown from a woman's thimble. No. My father's way was more appropriate. It was hard. "I'll attend to you in the morning," he would say, and I lay awake wondering which of my crimes he had discovered. I know what it is to be sentenced to be shot at sunrise. Also, it hurt in the morning when he was not angry but very fresh and strong. You see, he walloped me in my own person; he never shamed Napoleon or my knighthood, as my mother did. I learned something from his discipline, something useful.

I learned what tyranny is and the pain of being misunderstood and wronged, or,

Using the Study Questions

It is recommended that students always read and answer the questions in **Developing Comprehension Skills** in class discussion. Whenever possible, they should also read the questions in the other categories together and discuss the answers.

Developing Comprehension Skills

Question 1. Read and discuss. After the students have answered this question, ask them what kind of man Colonel Carter was. They should find evidence in the story to support their answers.

Question 2. It is important that the students can relate the steps that were carried out in teaching the colt this trick. If necessary, have them refer to page 362 of the story.

Question 3. Have students reread page 360, paragraph 2, through page 361, paragraph 1, before answering this question. Explain that although the story does not state the answer directly, students can make reasonable guesses based on the situations described. Then, as students answer the question, have them explain the difference between breaking a horse in body and breaking him in spirit.

Question 4. Lennie's attitude toward girls is hinted at in other instances in the story, as well. After students have answered the text question, have them try to find other passages that help illustrate this attitude in Lennie (e.g., "...my sisters had to lead her while I rode").

Question 5. Make sure students can clearly explain the three methods of training. Then have them defend their choice for the best one.

Challenge Question. Reread the passage on page 365, paragraph 3, that describes Lennie's reaction to his parents' discipline. Describe how he reacts to his mother's discipline and his father's discipline. What does this tell you about his character? (Interpretive Reading)

Reading Literature: Nonfiction

Question 1. After students have identified the point of view, discuss the difference between a biography and an autobiography.

Question 2. Draw two columns on the board. Label one "The Elements of Fiction" and the other "I Get a Colt To Break In." Have the students turn to the introduction for Chapter 4, on page 135, to find the items that belong in column one. Next, have them refer to the selection and check

if you please, understood and set right. They are pretty much the same. He and most parents and teachers do not break in their children as carefully as I broke in my colt. They haven't the time that I had, and they have not some other incentives I had. I saw this that day when I rubbed my sore legs. He had to explain to my indignant mother what had happened. When he had told it his way, I gave my version: how long and cautiously I had been teaching my horse to walk over logs and girls. Having shown how sure I was of myself and the colt, while my mother was boring into his silence with one of her reproachful looks, I said something that hit my father hard.

"I taught the colt that trick, I have taught her all that you see she knows, without whipping her. I have never struck her; not once. Colonel Carter said I mustn't, and I haven't."

And my mother, backing me up, gave him a rap: "There," she said, "I told you so." He walked off, looking like a thimble-rapped Napoleon.

Developing Comprehension Skills

Literal Reading	1. Why did Colonel Carter give Lennie a colt?
Literal Reading	2. How did Lennie teach the colt to balance and turn on a small box?
Interpretive Reading	3. On page 360, paragraph 2, you learned how most horses were broken to ride in the Old West. Compare that way of breaking a horse to the way Colonel Carter told Lennie to break his new colt. What is the difference in the trainers' attitudes? How does the effect on the horse differ?
Interpretive Reading	4. Lennie's father whipped him for having his colt step over his sisters. Lennie defended himself by saying, "They were only girls." On the next page (page 365), Lennie described how it shamed him to get "a sharp rap on his crown from a woman's thimble." From these two examples, what can you tell about Lennie's attitude toward girls and women when he was young?
Critical Reading	5. The author describes three ways of training children or horses. One is his mother's way of training him, one his father's way, and the third one is the way he himself trained his colt. Tell which way you think is

Check Test

1. Who gave Lennie the colt? (Colonel Carter)

2. Had anyone ever ridden her before? (no)

3. What is a centaur? (a creature with a horse's body and a man's head)

4. Where did Lennie learn how to teach Lady most of the tricks she performed? (the circus)

5. Why did the author get whipped by his father? (for having his horse step over his sisters' bodies)

Answers to Study Questions

Developing Comprehension Skills

1. Either the Colonel thought he had promised Lennie a colt or he had promised himself to give Lennie one.

2. Lennie had the colt do it first on a large low box and then on smaller and smaller ones until she was able to balance on a very small high box.

3. Colonel Carter believed in using gentle persuasion in training a horse. He told Lennie to be kind and patient, not to hurt the colt or use punishment but to reward for good behavior. The cowboys in the Old West believed they had to over-the best of these three ways for raising children. Give your reasons for answering the way you do.

Reading Literature: Nonfiction

1. **Identifying Point of View.** Is this story told from the first-person or the third-person point of view? How does the point of view help you know whether the story is from a biography or an autobiography?
2. **Examining Nonfiction Writing.** This selection is presented in the nonfiction chapter, so you know it is based on real happenings. Can you tell from the selection itself that it is nonfiction rather than fiction? Are there similarities? Are there differences? What are they?
3. **Distinguishing Fact and Opinion.** In telling about his parents' ways of disciplining him, Lennie says, "My father's way was more appropriate." Is this a fact or an opinion? How can you tell?
4. **Describing Tone.** In the introduction to this chapter, you read that nonfiction writing can have different tones. The tone can be serious—admiring, for instance, or angry. Or it can be carefree, asking the reader just to relax and enjoy it. How would you describe the tone of this selection? Give examples from the story to support your answer.

Developing Vocabulary Skills

1. **Choosing the Correct Respelling.** You know that the dictionary and glossary show how words are pronounced. The words are respelled with special symbols to stand for certain sounds. The pronunciation key in the dictionary or glossary explains these respelling symbols by using key words. Here is the pronunciation key from the glossary of this text.

at, āte, fär; pen, ēqual; sit, mīne; sō, côrn, j**oi**n, t**o͝o**k, f**o͞o**l, **ou**r; us, t**ur**n; **ch**ill, **sh**op, **th**ick, ***th***ey, si**ng**; **zh** *in* measure; 'l *in* idle; ə *in* alive, cover, family, robot, circus.

Use the key to help you pronounce each respelling in the following list. Then read the following sentences from or about the story. Choose the respelling of the word that would make sense in each

power a horse to train it. They trained their horses by hurting and frightening them. The method that was used in the Old West left the horse broken in both body and spirit. Colonel Carter's method makes the horse gentle, sensitive, and patient.

4. Answers will vary but should include the idea that Lennie was not considerate of females or didn't think that they were very important.

5. The three methods are humiliation as punishment, physical punishment for wrong doing, and patience with rewards for good behavior. Students should give logical reasons for the method they think is best.

Challenge. Answers should indicate that Lennie expresses resentment toward his parents' discipline. This shows pride because he more readily recognizes the faults of others before his own.

Reading Literature: Nonfiction

1. It is written from the first-person point of view, which tells us that the person wrote about his own life. Therefore, it is an autobiography. If it were told

(continued on page 368)

off in column two all the elements found in the nonfiction selection. Explain that not every nonfiction selection has a clear plot, as this one does, but this selection illustrates that that is possible.

Question 3. Briefly discuss the difference between fact and opinion. If necessary, have the students reread the information about fact and opinion on page 354. Then provide students with some examples and ask them to distinguish between the two. You may wish to use the following examples:

1. My father is a good cook.
   My father plays golf on Saturdays.
2. Spring is the best time of the year.
   Spring starts on March 20th and ends on June 20th.
3. Mount Everest is the tallest mountain on earth.
   Mount Everest is the most beautiful mountain on earth.

Question 4. Ask a student to define *tone*. If necessary, have the students turn back to page 353 and reread the explanation about tone given there. As a review, remind them that in Chapter 4 "How the Three Young Men Found Death" had an amusing tone, whereas the tone of "The Bishop's Candlesticks" was sympathetic. Now have students answer the question.

Developing Vocabulary Skills

Question 1. Read the directions for **Choosing the Correct Respelling** on page 367 with the class. Ask a student to read aloud and complete the first sentence in the exercise. Then have the students complete the exercise independently. Discuss the answers together.

Question 2. Read and discuss the information in **Accent Marks and the Schwa Sound** on page 368. After the exercise directions are read, point out that the schwa sound can represent any vowel. Have the students complete the exercise independently and then write their answers on the board for class checking.

Developing Writing Skills

Read and discuss the three assignments. Then have each student choose and complete one of the three.

Question 1. This question asks the students to analyze the author's views on child discipline as well as what he thought of his mother's and father's methods.

Pre-Writing. Draw three columns on the board as the students reread page 365, paragraph 3, to the end of the story. Have them suggest words or phrases that describe Lincoln Steffens's attitude about discipline, and list those on the board in the first column. Then have them suggest words or phrases that describe how he felt about his parents' methods of discipline, and list those in the other two columns, headed "Mother" and "Father."

Writing. Tell students to write a topic sentence that explains what the paragraph will be about. Remind them to include in the paragraph all the information requested in the text questions and to use the notes from the three lists to support their statements.

Revising. Have the students refer to the **Checklist for the Process of Writing** on pages 556 and 557 to revise and proofread their paragraphs before they turn them in.

Question 2. To answer this question, the students will need to analyze the words and actions of Lincoln Steffens to determine what kind of a person he was when he was a boy.

Pre-Writing. Have the students skim the story and point out some of Lincoln Steffens' words and actions. List each description of Lincoln Steffens on the board. Then have the students explain what each description tells us about him.

Writing. Remind students to explain and support their descriptions with evidence from the story. Allow sufficient time for students to complete the assignment.

Revising. Have the students review their answers to make sure that none of their statements about Lincoln Steffens contradict each other and that their proofs from the story are directly related to the statements. Ask them to correct statements and add proofs as needed.

Question 3. Begin development of this assignment by asking the students to list quickly at least three things thay have done that they are proud of.

Pre-Writing. Encourage the students to think of words to share with the class that suggest pride, and list these on the board. Then ask a few volunteers to identify achievements on their lists. Make it clear that the achievements need not be important to others, as long as they are important to the students involved. Give the students several more minutes to add other events to their lists, and then to choose their topics from these possibilities.

Writing. Tell the students to write their stories in a way that lets the reader understand the pride they feel about what they have done. Remind them that, since this is an autobiography, they must write from the first-person point of view. Events must be true and told in chronological order. Allow sufficient time for students to complete the assignment.

sentence. Write both the respelling and the word that the respelling stands for.

(1) sen′ sə tiv	(3) stal′ yən	(5) sen′ tôr
(2) sub′ stə tüt	(4) pā′ shəns	(6) shug′ ər

a. The horse was a cross of a mustang mare and a thoroughbred ______.

b. The horse and I were like one united creature. We were a ______.

c. "She is a very ______ horse and if you lose your temper and abuse her, she will be ruined forever," he warned.

d. "Training the pony will take much ______," said Colonel Carter.

e. Lennie carried ______ to reward Lady when she did right.

f. The circus trainer told him to begin training the horse to step over logs, and then ______ people.

2. **Accent Marks and the Schwa Sound.** Each of the words above has one accent mark. The respellings of some of the words found in the story have more than one accent. Here is an example:

ad′ mə rā′ shən

The heavy, dark accent is called the **primary accent**. That syllable gets the most stress. The lighter accent is called the **secondary accent**. That syllable gets a lighter stress.

Look again at the words in the exercise above. In some of them you see this symbol: ə. This is called the **schwa**. It represents the sound of the vowel heard in the unaccented syllable.

Find these words in the dictionary. Write them in syllables. Mark the primary and secondary accents. Underline any syllables that have a schwa sound.

a. decoration	c. bewilder	e. repetition
b. continent	d. attention	f. convenient

Developing Writing Skills

Analytical Writing

1. **Understanding the Author's Purpose.** This is mostly a story about breaking a colt. However, at the end of the story, Lincoln Steffens also tells his feelings about how to discipline a child. Write a paragraph explaining how he felt about this subject. Include what he thought of his mother's method and his father's method. Why did he tell his parents how he taught his colt to step over the girls?

(continued from page 367)
from a third-person point of view, it would be a biography.

2. One cannot tell from the selection itself that it is nonfiction rather than fiction. The selection is similar to fiction because fiction is often told in the first-person point of view with the events presented in chronological order. There are no special elements in nonfiction that cannot be found in fiction except the fact that the events described in nonfiction really happened. A reader needs information outside the selection itself to know that the events were not made up.

3. It is an opinion—it is how the young boy felt. It cannot be proven to be true.

4. Possible answers: amusement at the writer's own faults and the actions of his parents; understanding; satisfaction.

Developing Vocabulary Skills

1. The respellings and words:
- **a.** stal′ yən; stallion
- **b.** sen′ tôr; centaur
- **c.** sen′ sə tiv; sensitive
- **d.** pā′ shəns; patience
- **e.** shug′ ər; sugar
- **f.** sub′ stə tüt; substitute

2. **Inferring from Indirect Description.** In this selection, the author does not describe himself directly. The reader learns about him from his words and actions. Write a paragraph describing in your own words what Lincoln Steffens was like when he was a boy. Use passages from the story to explain and support your description.

3. **Writing an Autobiography.** Lincoln Steffens was proud of his accomplishment in training his colt. Write a story about something you have done that you are proud of. Your story should be at least two paragraphs long.

Developing Skills in Study and Research

Taking Notes. Do you have a favorite animal? Go to the library. Use the card catalog to find at least one book on how to train one animal. Write notes on what the book says about one important part of training, for instance, how to train the animal to do tricks. Be sure to record the name of your book, the author, and the chapter and page from which you take your notes. You may also take notes on notebook paper. Be sure to include all of the information asked for here.

Developing Skills in Critical Thinking

Understanding Connotation. In the introduction to this chapter, you learned that the connotation of words can be positive (good), negative (bad), or neutral. In the following sentence from the story, the author tells us that he learned about being bossed around. He also tells how bad it feels to be misunderstood. Read the sentence. One part of it is written with a positive slant and the other part with a negative slant. Tell which part of the sentence is positive and which is negative. Then tell what the author means in this sentence:

> I learned what tyranny is and the pain of being misunderstood and wronged, or, if you please, understood and set right; they are pretty much the same.

2. The words should be written as follows:

- **a.** dec´ o ra´ tion
- **b.** con´ ti nent
- **c.** be wil´ der
- **d.** at ten´ tion
- **e.** rep´ e ti´ tion
- **f.** con ve´ nient

Developing Skills in Critical Thinking

The negative part of the statement tells of being "misunderstood and wronged," while the positive part tells of being "understood and set right."

The author means that at the time he was punished he thought he was misunderstood and therefore was being punished unfairly. However, he sees now that he may have been understood more than he realized, and that his punishment may have been fair. Either way, the punishment hurt just as much.

Revising. After the assignment is completed, students may wish to read their autobiographies aloud. You may want to create an autobiography bulletin board and display clean copies of the students' writings. Students may also wish to attach to their papers photographs, medals, or other items that their story tells about.

Developing Skills in Study and Research

Read and discuss the directions for **Taking Notes** on page 369.

Direct students to choose an animal that is usually trained. Point out that it may be easy to find a book on tropical fish but difficult to find any information on how to train them.

Have students describe how they will examine any books they find in order to locate the information they are looking for. Make sure they realize that they should first examine the table of contents and the index to make sure the book contains the information. If it does, they should then record the information that the text exercise specifies.

Discuss how to take notes. Explain to the students that when they are taking notes they do not need to write down every word, only the main points that they need to remember. Have them complete the exercise for homework.

Developing Skills in Critical Thinking

It is advisable to discuss the meaning of connotation before assigning this question. Provide some examples of positive, negative, and neutral connotations, such as:

> My mother is a very thrifty shopper and always buys things on sale.
> My sister is so cheap that she won't buy anything unless it is reduced to half-price.
> The woman is an economical shopper.

Discuss these sentences and ask the students to provide a few examples of their own. Then discuss the assignment.

Objectives

- To define autobiography and identify its elements
- To understand how literature is a reflection of culture
- To recognize such elements of autobiography as personal insights, tone, and a writer's personal style
- To apply literal, interpretive, and critical reading skills to a selection
- To recognize base words and affixes
- To write a description using specific details and descriptive words
- To analyze slanted writing
- To understand and use gestures to convey meaning

Preparing the Students

Essential Vocabulary. The words presented here are essential to the understanding of the selection.

Introduce the words listed below. Write the sentences on the board, have them read aloud, and ask the students to use context clues to find the meanings of the underlined words.

languor	beneficence
instinctively	gamut
irresolute	spontaneous

1. Staying awake all last night has caused a languor in me today. I just can't seem to get going.
2. The little girl instinctively placed the note on the hallway table, as if she knew that would be the first place her mother would look.
3. The jury was irresolute in reaching a verdict. It couldn't come to a decision.
4. The man was long remembered for his beneficence. He had performed many acts of charity during his lifetime.
5. Susan's semester grades ran the gamut from poor to excellent.
6. Their spontaneous parties were always more fun than the ones that were planned.

If the students need additional help with the vocabulary of this selection, encourage them to use context clues to determine word meaning. As needed, direct them to the **Glossary** or to a classroom dictionary.

Motivation. Ask students to imagine what it would be like to be blind and deaf. Have them share their thoughts with the class. Then have the students read the introductory paragraph on page 370 and ask them to state in their own words what they will be looking for as they read.

From

The Story of My Life

HELEN KELLER

Helen Keller's childhood was very different from yours. See how her autobiography can help you understand an experience you have not had yourself.

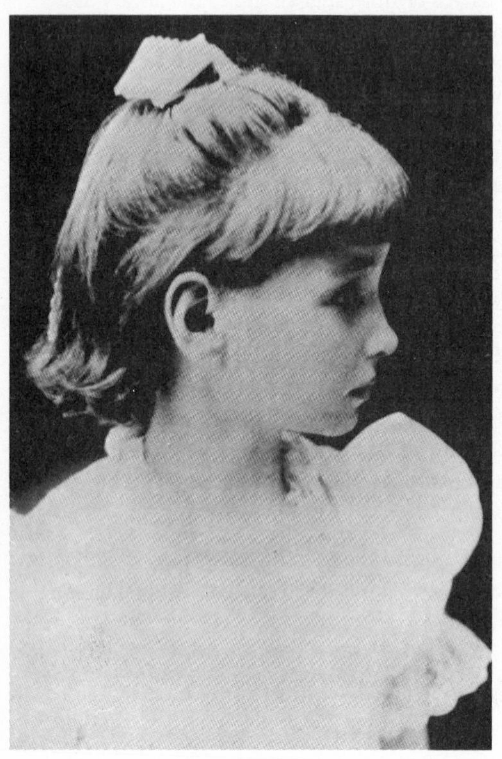

Helen Keller at age seven. Photograph by Ira F. Collins. American Foundation for the Blind.

I was born on June 27, 1880, in Tuscumbia, a little town of northern Alabama. The beginning of my life was simple and much like every other little life. I came, I saw, I conquered, as the first baby in the family always does.

I am told that while I was still in long dresses I showed many signs of an eager, self-asserting disposition. Everything that I saw other people do I insisted upon imitating. At six months, I could pipe out "How d'ye," and one day I attracted everyone's attention by saying "Tea, tea, tea" quite plainly. Even after my illness I remembered one of the words I had learned in these early months. It was the word "water," and I continued to make some sound for that word after all other speech was lost. I ceased making the sound "wah-wah" only when I learned to spell the word.

They tell me I walked the day I was a year old. My mother had just taken me out of the bath-tub and was holding me in her lap, when I was suddenly attracted by the flickering shadows of leaves that danced in the sunlight on the smooth floor. I slipped from my mother's lap and almost ran toward them. The impulse gone, I fell down and cried for her to take me up in her arms.

These happy days did not last long. One brief spring, musical with the song of robin and mocking-bird, one summer rich in fruit and roses, one autumn of gold and crimson sped by and left their gifts at the feet of an eager, delighted child. Then, in the dreary month of February, came the illness that closed my eyes and ears and plunged me into the unconsciousness of a new-born baby. They called it acute congestion of the stomach and brain. The doctor thought I could not live. Early one morning, however, the fever left me, as suddenly and mysteriously as it had come. There was great rejoicing in the family that morning, but no one, not even the doctor, knew that I should never see nor hear again.

Night

I cannot recall what happened during the first months after my illness. I only know that I sat in my mother's lap or clung to her dress as she went about her household duties. My hands felt every object and observed every motion, and in this way I learned to know many things. Soon I felt the need of some communication with others and began to make crude signs. A shake of the head meant "No" and a nod, "Yes;" a pull meant "Come" and a push, "Go." Was it bread that I wanted? Then I would imitate the acts of cutting the slices and buttering them. If I wanted my mother to make ice cream for dinner, I made the sign for working the freezer and shivered, indicating cold. My mother, moreover, succeeded in making me understand a good deal. I always knew when she wished me to bring her something, and I would run upstairs or anywhere else she indicated. Indeed, I owe to her loving wisdom all that was bright and good in my long night.

I understood a great deal of what was going on about me. At five I learned to fold and put away the clean clothes when they were brought in from the laundry, and I knew my own from the rest. I knew by the way my mother and aunt dressed when they were going out, and I always begged to go with them. I was always sent for when there was company, and when the guests took their leave, I waved my hand to them, I think with a vague remembrance of the meaning of the gesture.

I do not remember when I first realized that I was different from other people; but I knew it before my teacher came to me. I had noticed that my mother and my friends did not use signs as I did when they wanted anything done, but talked with their mouths. Sometimes I stood between two persons who were conversing and touched their lips. I could not under-

Presenting the Selection

1. Call on students to read aloud the first section, which ends in the first column on page 371. Then ask a student to state the cause of Helen's loss of sight and hearing.

Have the students read the remainder of "The Story of My Life" silently. Since this is a relatively long selection, it may be easier for students to handle it if it is assigned in parts. Depending on the students' abilities, choose one of the following:

a. Assign the autobiography in two readings.
   The second part would then begin with the section entitled "Nature," on page 376.
b. Assign the autobiography in five short readings, using the headings as natural breaks.

2. Make sure that everyone has read the assignment by administering the **Check Test**, at the bottom of T.E. page 380.

If the story was read in two parts, administer Questions 1, 2, and 3 after the first part and Questions 4 and 5 after the second part. If the story was read in five short readings, administer one question for each part.

3. Refer to the introductory paragraph and ask the students to discuss what it must have been like to grow up deaf and blind. Elicit comments about whether this selection helped them to imagine what it must be like even though they have not had the experience themselves.

4. Develop the study questions as suggested in **Using the Study Questions**, beginning on page 380. That selection also provides challenge questions for further discussion, as needed.

Page 376 shows an example of a card with Braille writing. Your students may be able to see books written in Braille in the public library. Many children's books are available that talk about Braille reading, finger spelling, and signing for the deaf and hard of hearing. This can be related to the discussion for **Reading Literature, 2,** on page 381. **Understanding the Author's Purpose**. Encourage students to use the library or talk to exceptional-education specialists to see if they can find other examples of helpful devices for people who have various disabilities.

Reinforcing the Lesson

To reteach, reinforce, or extend the skills in this lesson, see the following:

Skills Practice Book, Green Level—page 158

Special Populations

If there are any children in the class who have handicaps or know someone with a handicap, have them present to the class a narrative about doing something that was difficult and frightening. Have them be sure to include the feelings they experienced once they were successful.

ESL. For the exercise in **Developing Skills in Speaking and Listening** on page 383, note that some gestures from the ESL students' cultures may be different from those common in America. Ask the students to demonstrate and explain some of the differences in gestures.

LD, ESL. This exercise in speaking and listening on page 383 might be a valuable activity for special-populations students. It would give them a chance to become aware of some forms of nonverbal communication. You might suggest that the students limit observation to one or two people for a period of 15 minutes. This could be done in the cafeteria, waiting for a bus, or sitting in the libary or study hall. Another source of observation would be to have the students turn the sound off while they watch an action-TV show. Have them try to record the communication between characters.

Encouraging Independent Reading

Some students may be interested in finding information about the Braille system of writing. Perhaps two students could work together to prepare an oral presentation using a display chart of the Braille alphabet and short messages in Braille to aid their explanation of how the system works.

stand and was vexed. I moved my lips and gestured frantically without result. This made me so angry at times that I kicked and screamed until I was exhausted.

I think I knew when I was naughty, for I knew that it hurt Ella, my nurse, to kick her, and when my fit of temper was over I had a feeling similar to regret. But I cannot remember any instance in which this feeling prevented me from repeating the naughtiness when I failed to get what I wanted.

Many incidents of those early years are fixed in my memory, isolated, but clear and distinct, making the sense of that silent, aimless, dayless life all the more intense.

One day I happened to spill water on my apron, and I spread it out to dry before the fire which was flickering on the sitting-room hearth. The apron did not dry quickly enough to suit me, so I drew nearer and threw it right over the hot ashes. The fire leaped into life; the flames encircled me so that in a moment my clothes were blazing. I made a terrified noise that brought Viny, my old nurse, to the rescue. Throwing a blanket over me, she almost suffocated me, but she put out the fire. Except for my hands and hair I was not badly burned.

About this time I found out the use of a key. One morning I locked my mother up in the pantry, where she was obliged to remain three hours, as the servants were in a detached part of the house. She kept pounding on the door, while I sat outside on the porch steps and laughed with glee as I felt the jar of the pounding. This most naughty prank of mine convinced my parents that I must be taught as soon as possible.

The Search for Help

Meanwhile the desire to express myself grew. The few signs I used became less and less adequate, and my failures to make myself understood were invariably followed by outbursts of passion. I felt as if invisible hands were holding me, and I made frantic efforts to free myself. I struggled—not that struggling helped matters, but the spirit of resistance was strong within me; I generally broke down in tears and physical exhaustion. If my mother happened to be near, I crept into her arms, too miserable even to remember the cause of the tempest. After awhile, the need of some means of communication became so urgent that these outbursts occurred daily, sometimes hourly.

My parents were deeply grieved and perplexed. We lived a long way from any school for the blind or the deaf, and it seemed unlikely that anyone would come to such an out-of-the-way place as Tuscumbia to teach a child who was both deaf and blind. Indeed, my friends and relatives sometimes doubted whether I could be taught. My mother's only ray of hope came from Dickens's "American Notes." She had read his account of

Laura Bridgman, and she remembered vaguely that Laura was deaf and blind, yet had been educated. But she also remembered with a hopeless pang that Dr. Howe, who had discovered the way to teach the deaf and blind, had been dead many years. His methods had probably died with him; and, if they had not, how was a little girl in a far-off town in Alabama to receive the benefit of them?

When I was about six years old, my father heard of an eminent eye doctor in Baltimore, who had been successful in many cases that had seemed hopeless. My parents at once determined to take me to Baltimore to see if anything could be done for my eyes.

When we arrived in Baltimore, Dr. Chisholm received us kindly, but he could do nothing. He said, however, that I could be educated. He advised my father to consult Dr. Alexander Graham Bell, of Washington, who would be able to give him information about schools and teachers of deaf or blind children. Acting on the doctor's advice, we went immediately to Washington to see Dr. Bell, my father with a sad heart and many misgivings, I wholly unconscious of his anguish, finding pleasure in the excitement of moving from place to place. Child as I was, I at once felt the tenderness and sympathy which endeared Dr. Bell to so many hearts. He held me on his knee while I examined his watch, and he made it strike for me. He understood my signs, and I knew it and loved him at once. But I did not dream that that interview would be the door through which I should pass from darkness into light, from isolation to friendship, companionship, knowledge, love.

Dr. Bell advised my father to write to Mr. Anagnos, director of the Perkins Institution in Boston, the scene of Dr. Howe's great labors for the blind, and ask him if he had a teacher able to begin my education. This my father did at once. In a few weeks there came a kind letter from Mr. Anagnos with the comforting assurance that a teacher had been found. This was in the summer of 1886, but Miss Sullivan did not arrive until the following March.

Miss Sullivan Comes

The most important day I remember in all my life is the one on which my teacher, Anne Mansfield Sullivan, came to me. I am filled with wonder when I consider the immeasurable contrasts between the two lives that it connects. It was the third of March, 1887, three months before I was seven years old.

On the afternoon of that eventful day, I stood on the porch, expectant. I guessed vaguely from my mother's signs and from the hurrying to and fro in the house that something unusual was about to happen, so I went to the door and waited on the steps. The afternoon sun penetrated the mass of honeysuckle that covered the porch and fell on my upturned face. My fingers lingered almost unconsciously on the familiar leaves and blossoms that had just come forth to greet the sweet southern spring. I did not know what the future held of marvel or surprise for me. Anger and bitterness had preyed upon me continually for weeks and a deep languor had followed this passionate struggle.

Have you ever been at sea in a dense fog, when it seemed as if a tangible white darkness shut you in, and the great ship, tense and anxious, groped her way toward the shore with plummet and sounding-line, and you waited with beating heart for something to happen? I was like that ship before my education began, only I was without compass or sounding-line and had no way of knowing how near the harbor was. "Light! give me light!" was the wordless cry of my soul, and the light of love shone on me in that very hour.

I felt approaching footsteps. I stretched out my hand as I supposed to my mother. Someone took it, and I was caught up and held close in the arms of her who had come to reveal all things to me and, more than all things else, to love me.

The morning after my teacher came, she led me into her room and gave me a doll. The little blind children at the Perkins Institution had sent it and Laura Bridgman had dressed it; but I did not know this until afterward. When I had played with it a little while, Miss Sullivan slowly spelled into my hand the word "d-o-l-l." I was at once interested in this finger play and tried to imitate it. When I finally succeeded in making the letters correctly, I was flushed with childish pride and pleasure. Running downstairs to my mother, I held up my hand and made the letters for doll. I did not know that I was spelling a word or even that words existed; I was simply making my fingers go in monkey-like imitation. In the days that followed, I learned to spell in this uncomprehending way a great many words, among them *pin*, *hat*, *cup*, and a few verbs like *sit*, *stand*, and *walk*. But my teacher had been with me several weeks before I understood that everything has a name.

One day, while I was playing with my new doll, Miss Sullivan put my big rag doll into my lap also, spelled "d-o-l-l" and tried to make me understand that "d-o-l-l" applied to both. Earlier in the day we had had a tussle over the words "m-u-g" and "w-a-t-e-r." Miss Sullivan had tried to impress it upon me that "m-u-g" is *mug* and that "w-a-t-e-r" is *water*, but I persisted in confusing the two. In despair she had dropped the subject for the time, only to renew it at the first opportunity. I became impatient at her repeated attempts and, seizing the new doll, I dashed it upon the floor. I was keenly delighted when I felt the fragments of the broken doll at my feet. Neither sorrow or regret followed my passionate outburst. I had not loved the doll. In the still, dark world in which I lived there was no strong sentiment or tenderness. I felt my teacher sweep the fragments to one side of the hearth, and I had a sense of satisfaction that the cause of my discomfort was removed. She brought me my hat, and I knew I was going out into the warm sunshine. This thought, if a wordless sensation may be called a thought, made me hop and skip with pleasure.

We walked down the path to the well-house, attracted by the fragrance of the honeysuckle with which it was covered. Some one was drawing water, and my teacher placed my hand under the spout. As the cool stream gushed over one hand, she spelled into the other the word *water,* first slowly, then rapidly. I stood still, my whole attention fixed upon the motions of the fingers. Suddenly I felt a misty consciousness as of something forgotten—a thrill of returning thought; and somehow the mystery of language was revealed to me. I knew then that "w-a-t-e-r" meant the wonderful cool something that was flowing over my hand. That living word awakened my soul, gave it light, hope, joy, set it free! There were barriers still, it is true, but barriers that could in time be swept away.

I left the well-house eager to learn. Everything had a name, and each name gave birth to a new thought. As we returned to the house, every object which I touched seemed to quiver with life. That was because I saw everything with the strange, new sight that had come to me. On entering the door, I remembered the doll I had broken. I felt my way to the hearth and picked up the pieces. I tried vainly to put them together. Then my eyes filled with tears; for I realized what I had done. For the first time I felt repentance and sorrow.

Helen Keller and Annie Sullivan, 1890.
American Foundation for the Blind.

I learned a great many new words that day. I do not remember what they all were; but I do know that *mother*, *father*, *sister*, *teacher* were among them—words

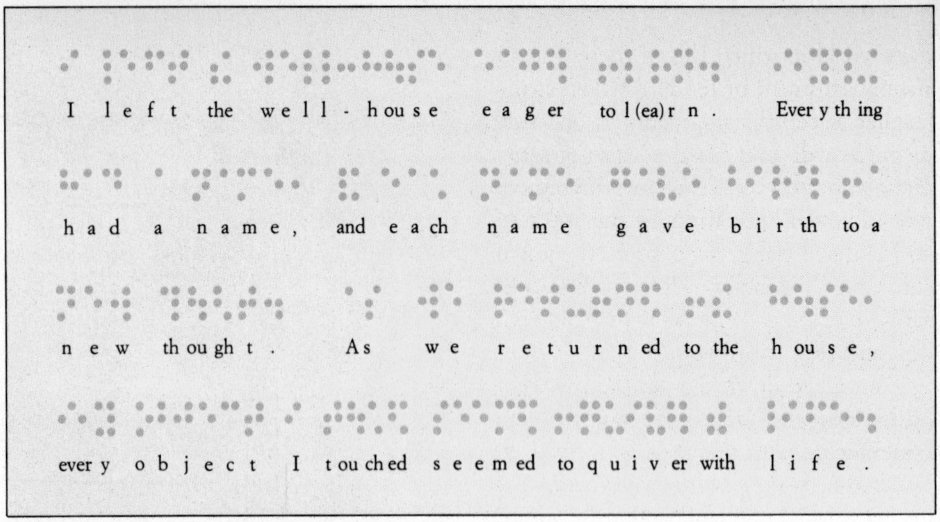

I left the well-house eager to l(ea)rn. Ever y th ing

had a name, and each name gave birth to a

new th ou gh t. As we returned to the house,

ever y object I tou ch ed seem ed to quiver with life.

Above is the Braille writing for the last three sentences in column one on page 375. Helen Keller wrote her autobiography this way. The dots are raised on paper with a special machine much like a typewriter. The writing is read by touch.

that were to make the world blossom for me, "like Aaron's rod, with flowers." It would have been difficult to find a happier child than I was as I lay in my crib at the close of that day and lived over the joys it had brought me, and for the first time longed for a new day to come.

Nature

I recall many incidents of the summer of 1887 that followed my soul's sudden awakening. I did nothing but explore with my hands and learn the name of every object that I touched; and the more I handled things and learned their names and uses, the more joyous and confident grew my sense of kinship with the rest of the world.

When the time of daisies and buttercups came, Miss Sullivan took me by the hand across the fields, where men were preparing the earth for the seed, to the banks of the Tennessee River. There, sitting on the warm grass, I had my first lessons in the beneficence of nature. I learned how the sun and the rain make to grow out of the ground every tree that is pleasant to the sight and good for food; how birds build their nests and live and thrive from land to land; how the squirrel, the deer, the lion, and every other creature finds food and shelter. As my knowledge of things grew, I felt more and more the delight of the world I was in. Long before I learned to do a sum in arithmetic or describe the shape of the earth, Miss

Sullivan had taught me to find beauty in the fragrant woods, in every blade of grass, and in the curves and dimples of my baby sister's hand. She linked my earliest thoughts with nature, and made me feel that "birds and flowers and I were happy peers."

But about this time I had an experience which taught me that nature is not always kind. One day my teacher and I were returning from a long ramble. The morning had been fine, but it was growing warm and sultry when at last we turned our faces homeward. Two or three times we stopped to rest under a tree by the wayside. Our last halt was under a wild cherry tree a short distance from the house. The shade was grateful, and the tree was so easy to climb that with my teacher's assistance I was able to scramble to a seat in the branches. It was so cool up in the tree that Miss Sullivan proposed that we have our luncheon there. I promised to keep still while she went to the house to fetch our lunch.

Suddenly a change passed over the tree. All the sun's warmth left the air. I knew the sky was black, because all the heat, which meant light to me, had died out of the atmosphere. A strange odor came up from the earth. I knew it, it was the odor that always precedes a thunderstorm, and a nameless fear clutched at my heart. I felt absolutely alone, cut off from my friends and the firm earth. The immense, the unknown, enfolded me. I remained still and expectant; a chilling terror crept over me. I longed for my teacher's return; but above all things I wanted to get down from that tree.

There was a moment of sinister silence, then a multitudinous stirring of the leaves. A shiver ran through the tree, and the wind sent forth a blast that would have knocked me off had I not clung to the branch with might and main. The tree swayed and strained. The small twigs snapped and fell about me in showers. A wild impulse to jump seized me, but terror held me fast. I crouched down in the fork of the tree. The branches lashed about me. I felt the intermittent jarring that came now and then, as if something heavy had fallen and the shock had traveled up till it reached the limb I sat on. It worked my suspense up to the highest point, and just as I was thinking the tree and I should fall together, my teacher seized my hand and helped me down. I clung to her, trembling with joy to feel the earth under my feet once more. I had learned a new lesson—that nature "wages open war against her children, and under softest touch hides treacherous claws."

After this experience, it was a long time before I climbed another tree. The mere thought filled me with terror. It was the sweet allurement of the mimosa tree in full bloom that finally overcame my fears. One beautiful spring morning when I was alone in the summer-house reading, I became aware of a wonderful, subtle fragrance in the air. I started up and instinctively stretched out my hands. It seemed as if the spirit of spring had passed through the summer-house. "What is it?" I asked, and the next minute I recognized the odor of the mimosa blossoms. I felt my way to the end of the garden, knowing that the mimosa tree was near the fence, at the turn of the path. Yes, there it was, all quivering in the warm sunshine, its blossom-laden branches almost touching the long grass. Was there ever anything so exquisitely beautiful in the world before! Its delicate blossoms shrank from the slightest earthly touch; it seemed as if a tree of paradise had been transplanted to earth.

I made my way through a shower of petals to the great trunk and for one minute stood irresolute; then, putting my foot in the broad space between the forked branches, I pulled myself up into the tree. I had some difficulty in holding on, for the branches were very large and the bark hurt my hands.

I had a delicious sense that I was doing something unusual and wonderful, so I kept on climbing higher and higher, until I reached a little seat which somebody had built there so long ago that it had grown part of the tree itself. I sat there for a long, long time, feeling like a fairy on a rosy cloud. After that I spent many happy hours in my tree of paradise, thinking fair thoughts and dreaming bright dreams.

Love

I had now the key to all language, and I was eager to learn to use it. Children who hear acquire language without any particular effort; the words that fall from others' lips they catch on the wing, as it were, delightedly, while the little deaf child must trap them by a slow and often painful process. But whatever the process, the result is wonderful. Gradually, from naming an object, we advance step by step until we have traversed the vast distance between our first stammered syllable and the sweep of thought in a line of Shakespeare.

At first, when my teacher told me about a new thing, I asked very few questions. My ideas were vague, and my vocabulary was inadequate; but as my knowledge of things grew and I learned more and more words, my field of inquiry broadened, and I would return again and again to the same subject, eager for further information. Sometimes a new word revived an image that some earlier experience had engraved on my brain.

I remember the morning that I first asked the meaning of the word "love." This was before I knew many words. I had found a few early violets in the garden and brought them to my teacher. She tried to kiss me, but at that time I did not like to have anyone kiss me except my mother. Miss Sullivan put her arm gently round me and spelled into my hand, "I love Helen."

"What is love?" I asked.

She drew me closer to her and said, "It is here," pointing to my heart, whose beats I was conscious of for the first time. Her words puzzled me very much because I did not understand anything unless I touched it.

I smelled the violets in her hand and asked, half in words, half in signs, a question which meant, "Is love the sweetness of flowers?"

"No," said my teacher.

"Is this not love?" I asked, pointing the direction from which the heat came. "Is this not love?"

It seemed to me that there could be nothing more beautiful than the sun, whose warmth makes all things grow. But Miss Sullivan shook her head, and I was greatly puzzled and disappointed. I thought it strange that my teacher could not show me love.

A day or two afterward, I was stringing beads of different sizes in symmetrical groups—two large beads, three small ones, and so on. I had made many mistakes, and Miss Sullivan had pointed them out again and again with gentle patience.

Finally I noticed a very obvious error in the sequence, and for an instant I concentrated my attention on the lesson and tried to think how I should have arranged the beads. Miss Sullivan touched my forehead and spelled with decided emphasis, "Think."

In a flash I knew that the word was the name of the process that was going on in my head. This was my first conscious perception of an abstract idea.

For a long time I was still—I was not thinking of the beads in my lap, but trying to find a meaning for "love" in the light of this new idea. The sun had been under a cloud all day, and there had been brief showers; but suddenly the sun broke forth in all its southern splendor.

Again I asked my teacher, "Is this not love?"

"Love is something like the clouds that were in the sky before the sun came out," she replied. Then in simpler words than these, which at that time I could not have understood, she explained: "You cannot touch the clouds, you know; but you feel the rain and know how glad the flowers and the thirsty earth are to have it after a hot day. You cannot touch love either; but you feel the sweetness that it pours into everything. Without love you would not be happy or want to play."

The beautiful truth burst upon my mind—I felt that there were invisible lines stretched between my spirit and the spirits of others.

From the beginning of my education Miss Sullivan made it a practice to speak to me as she would speak to any hearing child; the only difference was that she spelled the sentences into my hand instead of speaking them. If I did not know the words and idioms necessary to ex-

Using the Study Questions

It is recommended that students always read and answer the questions in **Developing Comprehension Skills** in class discussion. Whenever possible, they should also read the questions in the other categories together and discuss the answers.

Developing Comprehension Skills

Question 1. Students should refer to the selection if necessary.

Question 2. Ask the students to explain the difference between fact and opinion. Then discuss each quotation.

Question 3. If necessary, have students reread page 374, paragraph 4, through page 375, paragraph 2. After students have explained how Helen learned that everything has a name, tell them to use younger children they know as examples in explaining how normal children learn language.

Question 4. Have the students skim the pages and read aloud descriptive passages that are based on visual imagery to support their opinions.

Point out to the students that people who lose their sight, even very early in life as Helen Keller did, may have certain recollections of how things look. This may explain why Helen is able to give descriptions that are visual in nature.

Question 5. Suggest that students compare Helen's tantrums with those of a typical two-year-old. Are the causes similar? Make sure students are aware of Helen's parents' predicament. The fact that they had no way of communicating on any but a very simple level made it difficult for them to understand what was going on in Helen's head.

Challenge Question 1. How do you think Helen's awareness of the world around her would have been different if a teacher hadn't been found for her? (Interpretive Reading)

Challenge Question 2. Name an abstract idea (other than love) and try to remember how you came to understand what it means. How would you explain it to a young child? (Critical Reading)

Reading Literature: Nonfiction

Question 1. Have students skim the story to find passages that answer the question and have those read aloud. Discuss why these bits of information could not be found in any writing other than an autobiography.

Question 2. Ask students how they would react if they met a deaf and blind

Iris and Wild Roses, 1887, JOHN LA FARGE. The Metropolitan Museum of Art, Gift of Priscilla A.B. Henderson, 1950.

press my thoughts she supplied them, even suggesting conversation when I was unable to keep up my end of the dialog.

This process was continued for several years; for the deaf child does not learn in a month, or even in two or three years, the numberless idioms and expressions used in the simplest daily intercourse. The little hearing child learns these from constant repetition and imitation. The conversation he hears in his home stimulates his mind and suggests topics and calls for the spontaneous expression of his own thoughts. This natural exchange of ideas is denied to the deaf child. My teacher, realizing this, determined to supply the kinds of stimulus I lacked. This she did by repeating to me as far as possible, verbatim, what she heard, and by showing me how I could take part in the conversation. But it was a long time before I ventured to take the lead and still longer before I could find something appropriate to say at the right time.

The deaf and the blind find it very difficult to acquire the amenities of conversation. How much more this difficulty must be augmented in the case of those who are both deaf and blind! They cannot distinguish the tone of the voice or, without assistance, go up and down the gamut of tones that give significance to words; nor can they watch the expression of the speaker's face, and a look is often the very soul of what one says.

About the Art

Like the work of the late nineteenth-century French Impressionist painters, the work of John La Farge (1834-1910), an American painter and designer of stained glass, focuses on color and light. There is a translucent quality to the colors in the painting *Iris and Wild Roses* that is reminiscent of stained glass. Although muted, the colors seem to glow. La Farge was best known for his still lifes and flowers, both in his paintings and in glass.

Check Test

1. What naughty trick did Helen perform after she learned the use of a key? (She locked her mother in the pantry.)

2. What was Dr. Alexander Graham Bell's advice to Helen's father? (Find a teacher for Helen.)

3. What was the first word that Helen's teacher made her understand? (water)

4. What happened to Helen once while she sat in the tree? (A sudden storm came and frightened her.)

5. What abstract idea did Helen struggle to understand? (the meaning of love)

Developing Comprehension Skills

Literal Reading

1. How did Helen Keller become deaf and blind?

Critical Reading

2. Here are five quotations from the story. Tell if each one is a fact or an opinion:
   a. I was born on June 27, 1880, in Tuscumbia.
   b. I owe to her loving wisdom all that was bright and good in my long night.
   c. One morning I locked my mother up in the pantry.
   d. Dr. Bell advised my father to write to Mr. Anagnos.
   e. It would have been difficult to find a happier child than I was as I lay in my crib at the close of that eventful day.

Interpretive Reading

3. How did Helen learn that everything has a name? Compare this with how children who are not deaf and blind learn the same thing.

Critical Reading

4. Do you think a blind person can understand how things look? Give examples from the story to support your opinion.

Interpretive Reading

5. Helen describes how she used to have temper tantrums when she was very young. What does she say caused her to act that way? Now imagine that she had never been educated and did not write her autobiography. What do you suppose her parents would think caused her temper tantrums?

Reading Literature: Nonfiction

1. **Understanding Elements of Autobiography.** Autobiographies give you information you cannot get anywhere else. Give one example from the story for each of these categories:
   a. the reasons why Helen acted in a particular way
   b. one of Helen's personal, secret feelings
2. **Understanding the Author's Purpose.** Helen Keller did not have sight or hearing, two senses that most of us take for granted. How does her autobiography help you understand what it is like to be deaf and blind? What are some of the problems shared by deaf and blind people with people who do not have these handicaps? What are some of the additional problems faced by deaf and blind people? Refer to the selection to support your answer.

person today. Would they treat this person normally? Would they stare? Did this autobiography change how they might react?

Question 3. If necessary, before the students answer this question, review the meaning of *tone*. Then help students identify the tone of each selection. Remind them to be prepared to support their answers with examples from the story.

Question 4. Have students identify modern conveniences that were not part of Helen Keller's life a hundred years ago.

Question 5. You may wish to write the list of examples on the board and underline the paired words and phrases.

Challenge Question. What might be a drawback in using literature to find out about a culture distant in time or place?

Developing Vocabulary Skills

As a review, have the students turn back to page 66 and read the information about base words and affixes together. Make sure students recognize that the term *affix* refers to both prefixes and suffixes. Then call on students to read aloud the prefixes, their meanings, and the **New Words** in the box.

Now read the exercise on page 382 and 383 with the class. As the students are completing the exercise independently, copy the numbered words onto the board. Then, as the answers are discussed, have students come to the board and circle the base words of the words containing prefixes. For reinforcement, you may wish to have some students suggest additional words that contain these affixes. Have them write these on the board and state the meanings of these words. Direct them to call on other students to identify the base words.

Answers to Study Questions

Developing Comprehension Skills

1. She had a severe illness as a baby.

2. The five quotations are identified as follows:

a. fact **d.** fact
b. opinion **e.** opinion
c. fact

3. Helen learned that everything has a name through her experience with water. Her teacher had been spelling words into her hand for many weeks. Finally Helen realized what it meant as a stream of water gushed over one hand and her teacher spelled the word *water* into Helen's other hand. Children who are not deaf or blind would learn what water is by seeing it, hearing the word repeatedly, and imitating what they heard.

4. Answers may vary. Examples from the story must be given and should show some of the visual description in the story (e.g., "...feeling like a fairy on a rosy cloud.")

5. She says her inability to communicate caused her tantrums. Her parents might have realized her frustration, or they might have found other reasons for her actions, such as that they had been too permissive in the way they raised her due to her handicaps.

Challenge 1. Answers should include the ideas that Helen would have continued to be frustrated and very dependent upon her parents.

Challenge 2. Answers will vary.

Reading Literature: Nonfiction

1. Answers will vary. Some possible answers:

a. Helen became angry and had a temper tantrum when she could not understand how people communicate by moving their mouths (page 371, paragraph 5). She be-

(continued on page 382)

Developing Writing Skills

Read and discuss the two assignments. Then have each student choose and complete one of the two.

Question 1. In preparing the students for this assignment, give special attention to the task of limiting the topic.

Pre-Writing. Point out that both similarities and differences should be considered when writing a comparison. Have students suggest some similarities and differences between the two selections and list these on the board, similarities in one column and the differences in another.

Have the students choose topics from the information on the board. Remind them that they have the choice of writing about the whole selections, or comparing just the two main characters, the authors' purposes, or the tones of the two selections. Tell them that if they choose to write about the whole selections, they should include all or any of the features in the pre-writing lists.

Next, have the students gather as much information from the stories as they can to support their comparisons. Then have them select and organize their details.

Writing. Allow sufficient time for students to write their first drafts.

Revising. Have students refer to the **Checklist for the Process of Writing** on pages 556 and 557. Allow time for revisions to be made.

Question 2. This question calls on students to describe vivid memories, so the writing must be based on experiences that left strong impressions. Before reading the text question, you might wish to have an informal discussion about experiences of any kind—pleasant, scary, sad—that the students remember in detail.

Pre-Writing. In preparation for this lesson, direct the students to reread the passage about Helen sitting in a tree

3. **Identifying Tone.** You have now read two selections of autobiography. Are the tones of the two selections alike or different? Give examples to support your answer.

4. **Understanding Literature as a Reflection of Culture.** Literature often reflects the culture of the time and place in which it was written. Name at least two things you learned about life a hundred years ago from this story.

5. **Recognizing Personal Style.** Every person who writes frequently will develop a personal style. The language in that person's writing becomes different from everyone else's. Even though the writer might not sign every page of his or her writing, a good reader could tell whether two pages were by the same person.

   One of the marks of Helen Keller's style is the frequent use of paired words or phrases. Here are some examples:

   > Then, in the dreary month of February, came the illness that <u>closed</u> my <u>eyes</u> and <u>ears</u> and <u>plunged</u> me into the unconsciousness of a new-born baby.
   >
   > They called it acute congestion of the <u>stomach</u> and <u>brain</u>.
   >
   > Early one morning, the fever left me as <u>suddenly</u> and <u>mysteriously</u> as it had come.
   >
   > My hands <u>felt every object</u> and <u>observed every motion</u>.
   >
   > My parents were deeply <u>grieved</u> and <u>perplexed</u>.

   Identify at least five other sentences in which you find paired words or phrases.

Developing Vocabulary Skills

Recognizing Base Words and Affixes. Several words found in the story of Helen Keller contain some of the affixes you learned in Chapter 2 on page 66. Other words contain the same letters as an affix, but the letters are part of the base word. They cannot be separated from the base word. For example, in the word *rewrite*, *re* is a prefix. However, in *read*, *re* is part of the base word.

Each of the following words contains the letters of an affix. If the letters are an affix added to a base word, write the meaning of the

(continued from page 381)

gan to make crude signs out of the need to communicate with others (page 371, paragraph 5).

b. Helen was delighted when she felt the pieces of the broken doll (page 374, paragraph 5).

She compared herself to a ship lost in the fog before she began her education (page 374, paragraph 2).

She felt like a fairy on a rosy cloud as she sat in the mimosa tree (page 378, paragraph 3).

2. Helen shares the thoughts and feelings she experienced being deaf and blind. Problems shared by deaf and blind people and people without handicaps include such difficulties as illness and protecting oneself when faced with danger (fire, natural disasters, and the like). Additional troubles faced by deaf and blind people are such problems as having difficulty carrying on conversations because of an inability to distinguish the tone of the voice or see facial expressions (page 380, paragraph 3). Any other answers supported or suggested by passages in the selection should be accepted.

3. Students should recognize that Helen Keller is more serious in tone and less carefree than Lincoln Steffens is. However, they might also point out that certain attributes, such as determination and patience, are found in both of them.

4. Answers will vary. Examples may include the following: fewer educational facilities, outdoor water pumps, less advanced medical knowledge, and scarcity of telephones.

5. These are possible answers:

a. I *fell down* and *cried* for her to take me up in her arms. (page 371, paragraph 1)

b. Indeed, I owe to her loving wisdom all that was *bright* and *good* in my long night. (page 371, paragraph 3).

word. Use the affix as a clue to meaning. If the letters are part of the base word, write the dictionary or glossary definition.

1. disposition
2. image
3. unconciousness
4. discomfort
5. immeasurable
6. invisible
7. renew
8. impatient

Developing Writing Skills

Analytical Writing

1. **Comparing Two Autobiographies.** *The Story of My Life* and "I Get a Colt To Break In" are both selections of autobiography. Write a paragraph comparing the two. What are some things they have in common? What are some differences? You may write about the whole selection, or you may choose to compare just the two main characters, the authors' purposes, or the tone of the two selections.

Creative Writing

2. **Writing a Description.** Helen Keller describes vividly how she felt sitting in a tree during a thunderstorm. Write a description of something that made you feel frightened or helpless. Use specific details and descriptive words to tell your readers what it was like. Appeal to as many senses as you can, including sight, sound, touch, and smell.

Developing Skills in Critical Thinking

Analyzing Slanted Writing. Helen Keller used words and phrases with a positive connotation to describe herself as a child. Find two examples of descriptions that are slanted to make little Helen seem good or cute. Rewrite the sentences with a neutral connotation (neither good nor bad). Do you think Helen Keller was unfair to write about herself with a positive slant? If some writing is slanted, does that mean it is not true?

Developing Skills in Speaking and Listening

Understanding and Using Gestures. At the beginning of her autobiography, Helen Keller describes several ways she communicated before she knew any language. People who can see and hear often use "body language," too. Observe yourself and your friends and family for a few days. Take notes on ways you notice people communicating without language. Then show the class some of the things you noticed. See if your classmates can tell what you mean by your motions.

during a thunderstorm (page 377, paragraphs 3 and 4). Have them point out sentences that appeal to the senses of smell and touch.

Writing. Remind students that their use of detail and descriptive words should appeal to as many senses as possible.

Revising. After the assignment is completed, students may wish to read their descriptions aloud to the class. Have them proofread and make clean copies of their work. You may wish to assemble their papers in a classroom notebook.

Developing Skills in Critical Thinking

As needed, review the terms *denotation* and *connotation* (see page 354 and 355). Ask a student to state the meaning of *connotation* (possible answer: the feelings, ideas, and thoughts a word brings to the reader's mind) and the difference between a positive connotation and negative connotation. Encourage students to think of examples to share with the class.

Ask a student to read **Analyzing Slanted Writing** on page 383. Have the students skim the story to find examples of slanted writing. Direct them to specify the location of their examples by page number and paragraph number. After each description is read aloud, have the students rephrase it. Discuss the last two questions in the text exercise.

Developing Skills in Speaking and Listening

Read and briefly discuss the exercise on page 383. Have students provide some examples of facial gestures and body movements that are used for communication before you have them complete the assignment. Urge them to look for less obvious body language signals.

c. Many incidents of those early years are fixed in my memory, isolated, but *clear* and *distinct*, making the sense of that silent, aimless, dayless life all the more intense. (page 372, paragraph 3)
d. I generally broke down in *tears* and *physical exhaustion*. (page 372, paragraph 6).
e. After that I spent many happy hours in my tree of paradise, *thinking fair thoughts* and *dreaming bright dreams*. (page 378, paragraph 3)

Challenge. Literature is always an interpretation and may not be strictly factual.

Developing Vocabulary Skills

1. one's general nature or mood
2. a likeness
3. not in the state of being conscious
4. opposite of comfort
5. not able to be measured
6. not visible
7. to make new again
8. not patient

Developing Skills in Critical Thinking

Answers will vary. Possible examples of words and phrases with a positive connotation:

a. "like every other little life"
b. "eager, self-asserting child"
c. "I could pipe out"
d. "eager, delighted child"
e. "laughed with glee"
f. "I was keenly delighted"

Students should recognize that Helen Keller may have written about herself in a positive way because that is the way she remembered those events. If some writing is slanted, it does not mean that it is not true. Helen may have communicated the facts fairly accurately even though she chose words to create certain ideas and feelings in the reader.

Biographies

Ask the students to read page 384 and to identify the differences it lists between biographies and autobiographies. (If necessary, have students review page 358.) Point out that the subject's own words are a valuable resource in biography, just as in autobiography.

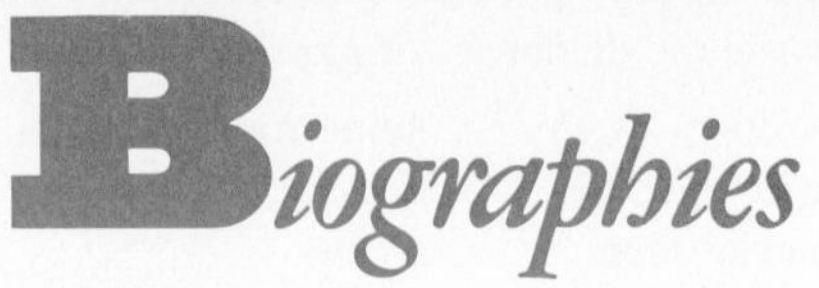

Biographies

A **biography** is a true story of a real person's life. Unlike the autobiography, it is written by another person, usually from the third-person point of view.

Biographers research their subjects thoroughly. They read everything written about them or by them. Then, in writing about a subject, the biographer tells both the good qualities of that person and some of the less admirable ones. Wherever possible, the writer uses the subject's own words.

The Firebird, 1945, MARC CHAGALL. Sketch for the stage curtain of Igor Stravinsky's ballet. Private collection. Photography by Musée National d'Art Moderne, Centre Georges Pompidov, Paris.

About the Art

Marc Chagall (1887-1985) was born in Russia, the son of a poor Jewish fish merchant. Much of his work draws its inspiration from his Russian-Jewish heritage. His paintings of clowns, flying lovers, fantastic animals, and fiddlers on rooftops are full of childlike wonder and delight. In 1945, he designed the backdrops and costumes for a New York production of the Russian composer Igor Stravinsky's ballet *The Firebird,* based on an old Russian folktale. Chagall's sketch for the curtain for *The Firebird* is painted in rich, beautiful colors. Its central image of a woman and bird in flight, seemingly merging into one, suggests the wonderful world of fairy tales.

The Firebird ballet was created by Balanchine for Maria Tallchief. See "Maria Tallchief," beginning on page 404.

Peculiarsome Abe

CARL SANDBURG

In this selection from a biography of Abraham Lincoln, you will learn about Abe's boyhood. As you read, see if you can tell why its title is "Peculiarsome Abe."

The farm boys in their evenings at Jones's store in Gentryville talked about how Abe Lincoln was always reading, digging into books, stretching out flat on his stomach in front of the fireplace, studying till midnight and past midnight, picking a piece of charcoal to write on the fire shovel, shaving off what he wrote, and then writing more—till midnight and past midnight. The next thing Abe would be reading books between the plow handles, it seemed to them. Once, trying to speak a last word, Dennis Hanks said, "There's suthin' perculiarsome about Abe."

He wanted to learn, to know, to live, to reach out; he wanted to satisfy hungers and thirsts he couldn't tell about, this big boy of the backwoods. Some of what he wanted so much, so deep down, seemed to be in the books.

This was one thing meant by Dennis when he said there was "suthin' peculiarsome" about Abe. It seemed that Abe made the books tell him more than they told other people. All the other farm boys had gone to school and read "The Kentucky Preceptor," but Abe picked out questions from it, such as "Who has the most right to complain, the Indian or the Negro?" Abe would talk about it, up one way and down the other, while they were in the cornfield pulling fodder for the winter. When Abe got hold of a storybook and read about a boat that came near a magnetic rock, and how the magnets in the rock pulled all the nails out of the boat so it went to pieces and the people in the boat found themselves floundering in water, Abe thought it was funny and told it to other people. After Abe read poetry, especially Bobby Burns's poems, Abe began writing rhymes himself. When Abe sat with a girl, with their bare feet in the creek water, and she spoke of the moon rising, he explained to her it was the earth moving and not the moon—the moon only seemed to rise.

Objectives

- To recognize and appreciate biography as a form of literature
- To define and identify the elements of biography
- To analyze the author's viewpoint
- To apply literal, interpretive, and critical reading skills to a selection
- To write a short biography based on a personal interview
- To scan for specific information

Preparing the Students

Essential Vocabulary. The words presented here are essential to the understanding of the selection.

Introduce the words listed below. Write the sentences on the board, have them read aloud, and ask the students to use context clues to find the meaning of the underlined words.

peculiar suspicion drollery
fodder floundering

1. Since the new boy was different from everyone else, his neighbors thought he was peculiar.
2. The farmer went into the barn to give the cows some fodder at feeding time.
3. Although they weren't sure, the children had a suspicion that a quiz was coming soon.
4. The floundering child was rescued when her frantic movements caught the attention of the lifeguard.
5. The man was well-known for his drollery. People would listen for hours as he told one humorous story after another.

If the students need additional help with the vocabulary of this selection, encourage them to use context clues to determine word meaning. As needed, direct them to the **Glossary** or to a classroom dictionary.

Motivation. Ask students if they know anything about Abraham Lincoln. Point out that much information they have may be based on legends and folk tales. Have them read the introductory paragraph on page 385 and state in their own words what they should be looking for as they read. Ask them to decide how this biography differs from some of the folklore that they already know about Lincoln.

Presenting the Selection

1. Read aloud the explanation about biographies on page 384. Then have the students read "Peculiarsome Abe" silently.

(The original material has been abridged for length.)

2. Make sure that everyone has read the selection by administering the **Check Test** at the bottom of T.E. page 388.

3. Remind the students that the introduction to the story asked them to find out why the title of this selection is "Peculiarsome Abe." Have them answer the question.

4. Develop the study questions as suggested in **Using the Study Questions** beginning on page 389. That section also provides a challenge question for further discussion if needed.

Reinforcing the Lesson

To reteach, reinforce, or extend the skills in this lesson, see the following:

Skills Practice Book, Green Level— pages 159 and 160

Special Populations

LD. Scanning exercises can be difficult for LD students. The exercise on page 391, **Scanning for Specific Information**, could be modified slightly by grouping the students into small groups to complete the assignment; choosing books available within the classroom and giving students specific pages (or paragraphs) to scan, depending upon their abilities to find information; or doing the activity together as a class.

Another aid would be to list on the board or a copy master the separate questions to be answered, step by step.

Encouraging Independent Reading

Expand upon the topics assigned in the **Study and Research** section. Some students may read one of the biographies they found and report on their reading by giving answers to the following questions:

1. What is the title of the book?

2. Who is the author?

3. Is the story limited to a specific time and place in Abraham Lincoln's life?

4. Tell something interesting you found.

5. Why did you like or dislike the book?

Perhaps several different biographies reported upon orally could lead to a class discussion about which seemed to be the most useful, the most factual, or the most slanted version. If possible, written reports should be displayed in the classroom.

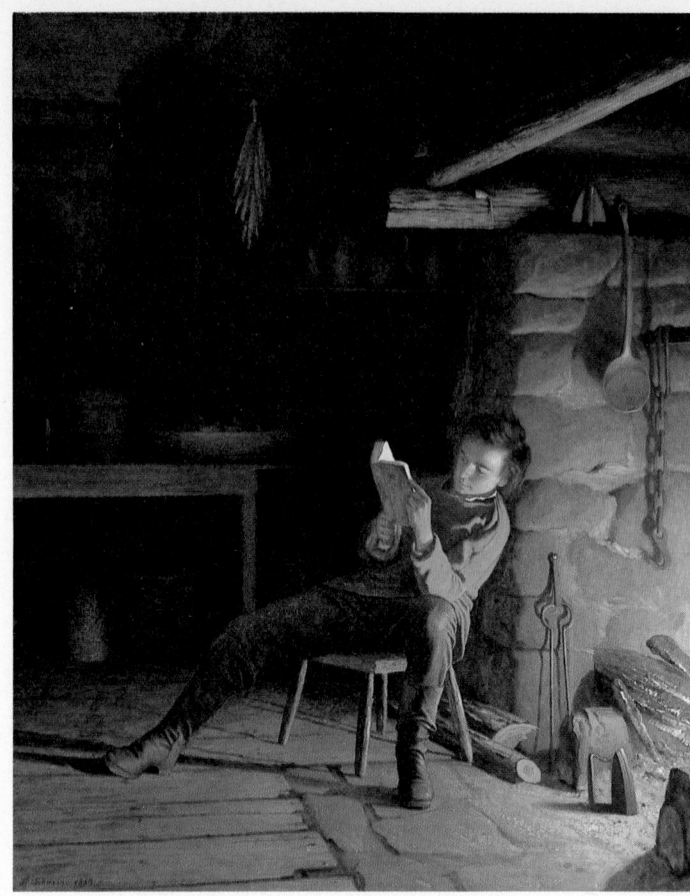

Boyhood of Lincoln, 1868, EASTMAN JOHNSON. Oil on canvas. The University of Michigan Museum of Art; bequest of Henry C. Lewis.

He liked to explain to other people what he was getting from books; explaining an idea to some one else made it clearer to him. The habit was growing on him of reading out loud; words became more real if picked from the silent page of the book and pronounced on the tongue; new balances and values of words stood out if spoken aloud. When writing letters for his father or the neighbors, he read the words out loud as they got written. Before writing a letter, he asked questions such as: "What do you want to say in the letter? How do you want to say it? Are you sure that's the best way to say it? Do you think we can fix up a better way to say it?"

About the Art

Eastman Johnson's (1824-1906) painting of Abraham Lincoln as a boy presents one of the best-loved elements of the Lincoln legend—his self-education through long hours of study by firelight. Born in Lowell, Massachusetts, Johnson studied art in Europe, first in Germany and them in Holland where he was influenced by the work of the seventeenth century Dutch painters, particularly Rembrandt. Rembrandt is famous for his use of dramatic light and shadow effects, and Johnson learned some of this from the master. In this painting, the glow of the fire highlights young Lincoln's face and the pages of his opened book, casting long shadows on the cabin floor. The intensity of the light and the surrounding darkness of the room give the painting a sense of concentration and solemnity.

As he studied his books, his lower lip stuck out, Josiah Crawford noticed it was a habit and joked Abe about the "stuck-out lip." This habit too stayed with him.

What he got in the schools didn't satisfy him. He went to three different schools in Indiana, two in Kentucky—altogether about four months of school. He learned his A,B,C's, how to spell, read, write. And he had been with the other barefoot boys in butternut jeans learning "manners" under the school teacher, Andrew Crawford, who had them open a door, walk in, and say, "Howdy do?" Yet what he tasted of books in school was only a beginning, only made him hungry and thirsty, shook him with a wanting and a wanting of more and more of what was hidden between the covers of books.

He kept on saying, "The things I want to know are in books; my best friend is the man who'll git me a book I ain't read." He said that to Pitcher, the lawyer over at Rockport, nearly twenty miles away, one fall afternoon, when he walked from Pigeon Creek to Rockport and borrowed a book from Pitcher. Then when fodder-pulling time came a few days later, he shucked corn from early daylight till sundown along with his father and Dennis Hanks and John Hanks, but after supper he read the book till midnight, and at noon he hardly knew the taste of his corn-bread because he had the book in front of him. It was a hundred little things like these which made Dennis Hanks say there was "suthin' peculiarsome" about Abe.

Besides reading the family Bible and figuring his way all through the old arithmetic they had at home, he got hold of "Aesop's Fables," "Pilgrim's Progress," "Robinson Crusoe," and Weems's "The Life of Francis Marion." The book of fables, written or collected thousands of years ago by the Greek slave known as Aesop, sank deep in his mind. As he read through the book a second and third time, he had a feeling there were fables all around him, that everything he touched and handled, everything he saw and learned had a fable wrapped in it somewhere.

The style of the Bible, of Aesop's fables, the hearts and minds back of those books, were much in his thoughts. His favorite pages in them he read over and over. Behind such proverbs as, "Muzzle not the ox that treadeth out the corn," and "He that ruleth his own spirit is greater than he that taketh a city," there were the music of simple wisdom and the mysteries of common everyday life that touched deep spots in him.

Book talk was a comfort against the same thing over again, day after day, so many mornings the same kind of water from the same spring, the same fried pork and corn-meal to eat, the same drizzles of rain, spring plowing, summer weeds, fall fodder-pulling, each coming every year, with the same tired feeling at the end of the day, so many days alone in the woods or the fields or else the same people to talk with, people from whom he had learned all they could teach him. Yet there ran through his head the stories and sayings of other people, the stories and sayings of books, the learning his eyes had caught from books; they were a comfort; they were good to have because they were good by themselves; and they were still better to have because they broke the chill of the lonesome feeling.

Already, Abe knew more than his father; he was writing letters for the neighbors; they hunted out the Lincoln farm to get young Abe to find his bottle of ink with blackberry brier root and copperas in it, and his pen made from a turkey buzzard feather, and write letters. Abe had a suspicion sometimes his father was a little proud to have a boy that could write letters, and tell about things in books, and outrun and outwrestle and rough-and-tumble any boy or man in Spencer County. Yes, he would be different from his father; he was already so; it couldn't be helped.

In growing up from boyhood to young manhood, he had survived against lonesome, gnawing monotony and against floods, forest and prairie fires, snakebites, horse-kicks, ague, chills, fever, malaria, "milk-sick."

A comic outline against the sky he was, hiking along the roads of Spencer and other counties in southern Indiana in those years when he read all the books within a fifty-mile circuit of his home. Stretching up on the long legs that ran from his moccasins to the body frame with its long, gangling arms, covered with linsey-woolsey, then the lean neck that carried the head with its surmounting coonskin cap or straw hat—it was, again, a comic outline—yet with a portent in its shadow. His laughing "Howdy," his yarns and drollery, opened the doors of men's hearts.

Check Test

1. What did Dennis Hanks say about Abe? ("There's suthin' peculiarsome about Abe.")

2. What did Abe spend much of his time doing? (reading)

3. What did Abe do for his father and neighbors that they were unable to do for themselves? (He wrote letters for them.)

Developing Comprehension Skills

1. How much time did Abe Lincoln spend in school? Was this because he did not like school? How do you know?
2. Why did Abe like to read?
3. Explain why "Peculiarsome Abe" is a good title for this biography.
4. The story says that Abe was bored with "the same people to talk with, people from whom he had learned all they could teach him." The phrase "all they could teach him" is a generalization. Do you think it was true in all cases? If not, can you limit the statement in some way to make it true?

Reading Literature: Nonfiction

1. **Identifying Biography.** Name one way you can tell that this is a biography and not an autobiography.
2. **Analyzing the Author's Viewpoint.** Most modern biographies tell both the good qualities of the person they are describing and some of the bad ones. Does this biography show both sides? Explain your answer.
3. **Understanding Elements of Biography.** Find at least one small detail about Abe that helps the reader see him as a real person.
4. **Understanding the Setting.** What is the importance of the setting of Abe's early life? How would his youth have been different in another setting?
5. **Recognizing Persuasive Writing.** A biography tells us something about what life was like at the time and place the main character lived. It can also help persuade a reader to have a certain opinion about the person and the times. Does this biography give you a certain opinion about Abe Lincoln? Explain your answer.

Developing Vocabulary Skills

Identifying Dictionary Terms. Review the information about the dictionary on page 356 and the study questions for Developing Vocabulary Skills on pages 367 and 368. Then match each of the following dictionary

Answers to the Study Questions

Developing Comprehension Skills

1. Abe Lincoln spent only four months in school because he had too much work to do to spend time in school. Two proofs that he would have liked more schooling are the following: he tried five different schools; he spent all his free time reading.

2. The things Abe wanted to know were in books. By reading, Abe could get away from his everyday life. He could learn things no one else nearby could teach him.

3. Abe's reading habits and thirst for knowledge were unusual.

4. The generalization was probably not true in all cases. Limitations to the statement may vary. Any of the following phrases could be added to the statement: "that could be useful to him"; "that could lead him to new truths"; "that could excite his imagination."

Reading Literature: Nonfiction

1. This story is told from the third-person point of view.

(continued on page 390)

Using the Study Questions

It is recommended that students always read and answer the questions in **Developing Comprehension Skills** in class discussion. Whenever possible, they should also read the questions in the other categories together and discuss the answers.

Developing Comprehension Skills

Question 1. Have the students find proof of their answers in the selection.

Question 2. Ask students why they read or like to read. Have them compare their reasons with Abe's.

Question 3. Have a student look up the definition of *peculiar* in the dictionary and read it aloud. Then have students answer this question. Point out that even though he was different, Abe seemed to be well-liked. Have them find evidence of this in the story.

Question 4. Discuss the meaning of *generalization*. Point out that generalizations can be either true or false. Give an example of a false generalization, then a true one. Examples:

All dictionaries contain illustrations. (false generalization)
All dictionaries contain words. (true generalization)

After the students answer this question, ask them to explain what point the author is trying to get across.

Reading Literature: Nonfiction

Question 1. Read and discuss. If necessary, have a student reread aloud the information about autobiographies and biographies on pages 358 and 384.

Question 2. Before students answer this question, discuss the meaning of the terms *good qualities* and *bad qualities*.

Question 3. Students may find it easy to answer this question once they realize they are looking for things that they themselves or people they know might do too.

Question 4. Remind the students that the term *setting* refers to the time and the place in which the events of the story occur. Have them describe the setting of this story. Ask them to point out some modern conveniences and entertainments that didn't exist then.

After students answer the first question, have them describe a different setting and how it might have affected Lincoln's youth.

Question 5. Have students decide whether they would have liked or disliked Abe. Have them find reasons for their answers in the selection.

Challenge Question. The author of a biography usually gives his own point of view about the subject. Describe how you would go about finding out whether the author's point of view is accurate.

Developing Vocabulary Skills

Read and discuss the exercise directions. Have the students reread the information on pages 356, 367, and 368 independently. Then have them complete the exercise in class in writing as a measure of how well they reviewed. Be sure to discuss the answers together in class.

Developing Writing Skills

Read and discuss the two assignments and then have students choose and complete one of the two.

Question 1. This question builds on the details used in answering Questions 3, 4, and 5 in **Reading Literature**. In addition, it calls for use of comparison and contrast skills.

Pre-Writing. Have students list details from the selection that tell them about daily life in Lincoln's time. Then have them suggest some similarities between life in Lincoln's time and our own time and list those on the board in one column. Have them suggest some differences and list those in another column.

Writing. Students may use the suggestions discussed in class in their writing, but encourage them to look for other similarities and differences on their own. Allow sufficient time for them to complete the assignment independently.

Revising. Have students share their work with others who answered the same question to see if their details are accurate. Allow time for revisions.

Question 2. This question gives students an opportunity to select details to include in a biography about a twentieth century subject. Interviewing skills are stressed.

Pre-Writing. Have the students think of someone they want to interview and make a list of questions they want to ask that person. Then make sure the students understand how to take notes. Tell them that they should jot down just the important words that will help them remember how the question was answered. You may wish to have a list of questions prepared beforehand and role play an interview. You may play the role of the interviewer and a student may play the role of the interviewee. Following the interview, you could share your notes with the class.

terms in column A with the definitions in column B. Write the letter on your paper.

A	B
1. entry words	a. A list of sample words that show the symbols used in identifying sounds in words
2. respelling	b. The heavy mark that indicates which syllable has the strongest stress
3. pronunciation key	c. The symbol that represents the vowel sound heard in an unaccented syllable
4. syllable	d. Entry words that are spelled the same but have two different meanings, and may be pronounced differently
5. primary accent	e. More than one definition
6. secondary accent	f. The lighter mark on a syllable that has a lighter stress
7. schwa sound	g. All the words entered in alphabetical order in a dictionary or glossary
8. homographs	h. The pronunciation of a word shown in parentheses immediately after an entry word
9. multiple meanings	i. A part of a word that consists of one vowel sound alone or with one or more consonant sounds

Developing Writing Skills

Analytical Writing

1. **Learning About Human Experience Through Literature.** Nonfiction writing can play a valuable role by reflecting the culture, or way of life, of a certain time and place. Write a paragraph telling what you learned from reading this selection about life in Indiana in Abe Lincoln's time. What things were different from our times? What were the same?

Creative Writing

2. **Writing Biography.** This biography tells the reader what life was like when Abe was growing up. It describes the kinds of things people did and how they lived. Try writing a short biography of someone you know, someone your age or a little older. The person you choose must be someone you can interview.

(continued from page 389)

2. This biography points out mostly good qualities about Abe: he was thoughtful, hard-working, intelligent, and friendly. However, it admits he was different looking, also, and often uninterested in those around him. Students should recognize that this is a basically positive description of Lincoln.

3. Possible answers: He had the habit of reading out loud. He liked to sit by a creek with his bare feet in the water. He told humorous stories.

4. Abe lived a simple life in the country. Since he had little entertainment, books were important to him. In another setting, he might have had more distractions to prevent him from reading.

5. Answers will vary, but students' answers will probably reflect the positive tone of this selection.

Challenge. Possible answers. Examine the author's reference sources. Refer to other biographies. Read the subject's journals, letters, or other autobiographical writings.

Developing Vocabulary Skills

1. g **4.** i **7.** c
2. h **5.** b **8.** d
3. a **6.** f **9.** e

Before you interview your subject, prepare questions you wish to ask him or her. Include questions about such facts as the subject's birth date, schools he or she has attended, and jobs or hobbies he or she has had. Also include questions about feelings and opinions, such as favorite songs or sports or classes, or most important memories. Write out the questions so that you won't forget them as you talk with your subject.

During the interview, take notes on the subject's answers. Write down the main ideas, not every word.

After the interview, use your questions and the subject's answers to write about that person's life. Be sure to include details of daily life as in Carl Sandburg's biography of Lincoln. Write so that someone reading your biography a hundred years from now could learn something about life in the twentieth century. Your biography should be at least eight paragraphs long.

Developing Skills in Study and Research

Scanning for Specific Information. Many biographies have been written about Abe Lincoln besides Carl Sandburg's. Go to the library and find at least three of them. On your paper, write the author and title of each biography you have chosen. Then look inside the books. Skim the table of contents and index. Examine the bibliography, if there is one, to see how many books the author referred to in writing the book. Read a few sample pages of each book to see if the writing is slanted. Does the author quote from reference sources to let you know where he or she got the information? Or does the writer just tell the story? Does the writer tell about the character's personal thoughts without telling how he or she found out that the character thought that way? Does the writer include personal opinions? If a writer does not identify sources for information, but does give personal opinions, you have a clue that the writing is slanted.

After you have examined the table of contents, index, and bibliography, and have read to discover slanted writing, put the three books in order. The first book on your list should be the one that you think would have the most accurate information about Abe. The last book on the list should be the one you consider the least accurate. Write a few brief notes about each book to explain your ranking.

Set a date by which time all the writers will have interviewed their subjects. If you wish, review their notes to make sure they have sufficient information. Have students arrange the events in their notes in time order.

Writing. Allow sufficient time for the students to write their biographies. Suggest they follow the time order indicated in their notes. Remind them to include details that will help reveal the culture and the setting of the person they interview.

Revising. Allow as many students as possible to share their biographies orally with the class. After each biography is read, have the class discuss what someone who read that biography a hundred years from now could learn about our culture. Allow time for any revisions that should be made.

Developing Skills in Study and Research

Have the directions for the exercise read aloud. Remind students to use the card catalog to help them locate the material they want. If necessary, review with them how to do so. You may wish to refer students to page 561 in the **Handbook** for a review of the card catalog. Also, it would be helpful to obtain a one-volume biography of Abraham Lincoln and discuss the information given in the table of contents, index, and bibliography. Remind the students that they are to scan, that is, read quickly looking for specific information. Then, before they complete this assignment, have them explain in detail how they will distinguish between a book that is slanted and one that is probably accurate. You may want to assign this exercise to groups of three or four students, having each student examine a book and report his or her findings to the group. The group should then decide on the most and least accurate book of the group.

Objectives

- To recognize and appreciate biography as a form of literature
- To recognize the importance of literature in recording and interpreting human experience
- To compare the effects of two different approaches used in the writing of biographies
- To apply literal, interpretive, and critical reading skills to a selection
- To select the most appropriate method for determining the meaning of an unfamiliar word in context
- To write a personal anecdote illustrating courage
- To interpret various features of a map
- To make a formal introduction of a speaker

Preparing the Students

Essential Vocabulary. The words presented here are essential to the understanding of the selection.

Introduce the words listed below. Write the sentences on the board, have them read aloud, and ask the students to use context clues to find the meanings of the underlined words.

expedition	undaunted
grueling	ordained
convalescence	mutilated

1. Carrying all their food and supplies on their backs, the group set out on an expedition that would include many adventures.
2. The trip across the desert was so grueling that most of the men hoped they'd never have to do it again.
3. After she injured her back it took six months of convalescence before Mary could work again.
4. Ignoring his own danger, the undaunted man rushed into the burning house to save his family.
5. It seemed that the shipwrecked explorer was ordained to a life of loneliness after repeated attempts to locate him had failed.
6. After the dog chewed on the slippers, they were too mutilated to be worn ever again.

If the students need additional help with the vocabulary of this selection, encourage them to use context clues to determine word meaning. As needed direct them to the **Glossary** or to a classroom dictionary.

Motivation. Display a large map of the world and point out the location of the North Pole, the Arctic Circle, and various

Matthew A. Henson

LANGSTON HUGHES

To reach the North Pole, Robert Peary and Matt Henson faced bitter cold, starvation, and other dangers. Look for clues that suggest why Matt Henson was willing to take such great risks.

The North Pole was discovered on April 6, 1909, by Rear Admiral Robert E. Peary of the United States Navy. With Admiral Peary at the North Pole was Matthew Henson. In fact, Henson was the trail breaker for Peary's expedition and, as such, went ahead first to the Pole, reaching it some forty-five minutes before the Admiral himself. So Henson was actually the very *first* person to stand at the top of the world.

At the Pole, the latitude is 90 degrees North and from there all directions are South. In Admiral Peary's Log Book his arrival at the North Pole is recorded thus: "Arrived here today, 27 marches from Cape Columbia, I have with me five men, Matthew Henson, colored, Ootah, Eginwah, Seegloo, and Ookeah, Eskimos; five sledges and thirty-eight dogs. The expedition under my command has succeeded in reaching the POLE . . . for the honor and prestige of the United States of America." To Henson then, his only English speaking companion, Peary is reported to have said, "This scene my eyes will never see again. Plant the Stars and Stripes over there, Matt—at the North Pole."

Portrait of Matthew Henson. The Bettmann Archive, Inc. New York City.

Born on a farm in Charles County, Maryland, the year after the close of the War Between the States, Matthew Alexander Henson had a harsh childhood. When he was two years old, his mother died and his father married again. Matt was only eight when his father died, too. His stepmother was not kind to him. She made him work very hard, would not allow him to go to school, and often whipped him severely. When he was eleven years old, in the middle of the winter, Matt decided to run away. While everyone else was asleep in the house, in the dark of night he started out on foot, heading toward Washington. There, a kind woman who ran a small lunch room took him in, fed him, and gave him a job as her dishwasher at a dollar and a half a week. For a number of years he was happy, until the urge came over him to travel further. Matt had heard that in Baltimore there were docks and great ships that sailed away into all the waters of the world. Young Henson wanted to be a sailor.

Life at Sea

Matt was lucky. After walking from Washington to Baltimore, it was not long before the thirteen-year-old youth found a job on a boat, a square-rigger with tall white sails destined for Hong Kong, a port halfway around the world. Matt was signed on as a cabin boy. Added to this good fortune was the fact that the *Katie Hines* was in command of a kind-hearted captain who took an interest in the brave youngster who could hardly read or write. The captain decided to teach him to read and write before the ship got back to Baltimore. In those days it was a voyage of many months to China. Every day the captain gave Matt a private class in his cabin. In this way, Matt acquired the groundwork of a good education on a windjammer rocking and rolling through the troughs of the sea.

For five years Matt Henson sailed on the *Katie Hines*, learning seamanship, learning from books, learning from people of all nationalities, and growing into a man. One entire winter the ship was locked in by ice at the Russian harbor of Murmansk. Matt learned to speak Russian, hunt wolves, and drive sleighs. Later he saw the pagodas of Japan, the gypsies of Spain, the palm trees of the West Indies, and the great rivers of Africa. Matt picked up a smattering of many languages, and some he learned well. He acquired a knowledge and understanding of strange peoples and strange ways, and he learned to take foreign customs in his stride and to mingle in a friendly way with everybody. This ability to get along with strangers and live with folks whose language he did not speak stood him in good stead later in life, for it was his destiny to become an explorer.

The good captain of the *Katie Hines*, who introduced the world to Matt, died when Matt was seventeen. His ship had

other places mentioned in the selection, such as Greenland, England, and China. Have the map available for students as they read. Tell the students that the story they are about to read is about Matt Henson, the first person to reach the North Pole. Then have them read the introductory paragraph on page 392 and ask them to state in their own words what they should look for as they read the story.

Presenting the Selection

1. Have the students read "Matthew A. Henson" silently. Since this is a relatively long selection, it may be easier for students to handle if it is assigned in two segments. Begin the second assignment on page 395 with the section subtitled "Second Trip to the Arctic."

This selection has been abridged because of space limitations.

2. Make sure that everyone has read the assignment by administering the **Check Test** on T.E. page 400. If the selection was assigned in two parts, the **Check Test** may be split, questions 1 and 2 asked after the first part and questions 3 and 4 after the second part.

3. Remind students that the introduction asked them why Matt took the risks he did. Discuss what some of those risks were. Ask for several opinions about why Matt took risks. Then discuss what might motivate the students themselves to take risks.

4. Develop the study questions as suggested in **Using the Study Questions** beginning on T.E. page 400. That section also provides challenge questions for further discussion if needed.

Reinforcing the Lesson

To reteach, reinforce, or extend the skills in this lesson, see the following:

Skills Practice Book, Green Level—pages 161 and 162

Special Populations

This selection may have special appeal to black students. Ask those who are interested to find information on blacks who conquered new frontiers or achieved recognition in their particular field. Have each student make a brief presentation to the class, or develop a poster or bulletin board display about the chosen individual's accomplishments.

ESL. The past four selections have told the stories of several Americans and their achievements. Ask ESL students to contribute stories of people famous in their native countries.

Encouraging Independent Reading

Members of minorities have contributed much to American society. Suggest that students try to locate biographies of members of American minorities who are remembered for their special achievements. Have students present reports to the class that describe the contributions of those individuals.

just left Jamaica heading through the Caribbean for Baltimore. With the Captain in his cabin when he died was the boy he had guided toward manhood, young Matthew Henson. The master of the ship was buried at sea.

Matt did not sail on the *Katie Hines* again. He shipped instead on a fishing boat, but quit when it reached Newfoundland. In Boston and other cities along the coast as far as New York, young Henson worked at various jobs ashore—nightwatchman, ditch digger, coachman.

Matt Works for Robert Peary

When he was nineteen, Matt Henson went back to Washington again. There, two years later, working as a stockroom clerk in a men's furnishing store, he met young Robert Peary, a civil engineer for the Navy, who came in to the store to buy a sun helmet for use in the tropics. Peary offered Matt Henson a job as his personal attendant on a surveying trip to Nicaragua for the government. Henson did not like the idea of being anyone's man-servant, but he felt intuitively that the job might lead to something better. Having adventure in his blood, he accepted it. In no time at all, Peary recognized in the youth qualities of value far beyond those of a personal servant, so he promoted him to his surveying crew as a field helper. For twenty-three years thereafter, Henson was associated with Peary in his work and his trips.

Peary was not a rich man so he could not always personally afford to pay Henson for his services. But on their return from Central America, a job was secured for Henson on government pay as a messenger in Peary's office at the Navy Yard in Philadelphia. About a year later, Peary told young Henson about a proposed expedition to Greenland. He intended to explore the northern icecaps, and he said he desired very much to take Matt along. But since the trip had very meager backing, there was no money to pay for Henson's services. Matt Henson volunteered to go without pay. In this he was joined by a number of other adventurers.

First Trip to the Arctic

In 1888 the party set out for Baffin Bay.[1] In spite of the fact that Peary suffered a broken leg shortly after his arrival in Greenland, he and the whole party elected to allow their ship to depart, leaving them isolated for a year at the foot of a glacier they hoped to cross.

Matt built a house for Peary, his wife, and the rest of the party and aided in the construction of sledges for their inland trips. From the Eskimos, he learned how to handle a team of eight to sixteen dogs to pull sledges across the ice. Matt's light

1. **Baffin Bay**. A body of water on the southwestern coast of Greenland. It separates Canada's Baffin Islands from Greenland. It is the farthest north a ship can go and tie up to land.

tan skin at first caused the Eskimos to think him one of them. In short order, he had established friendly relations with the native peoples and soon began to learn their language. That winter they taught him a great many things useful to know in the frozen North, especially how to hunt, trap, and fish for food.

Since Henson put his newly acquired knowledge at the disposal of the entire party of explorers, he became a most valuable man to Peary's expedition. Lieutenant Peary realized his value and respected Henson accordingly. Matt, in turn, sympathized deeply with Peary's aims and marvelled at his determination. Soon between the two men there sprang up a relationship of mutual admiration and dependence. When the party set out in the face of stinging sleet through sub-zero weather to conduct its explorations, Matt was considered one of the most important men in the group. By then, on the part of others, his race had been entirely forgotten. Here in the frozen North, no one thought of color lines. In the primitive Arctic, a man was a man—and that was that.

When the expedition returned to New York in 1892, Peary told Matt Henson, "We are going back to the Arctic again—but next time, all the way to the North Pole." At the turn of the century, no one knew what lay at either the North Pole or the South Pole. At the earth's axis would there be snow-covered land, or only drifting ice floes impossible of crossing? Nobody could tell. And how could a man reach the North Pole? By land or by sea? No one knew. In those days there were no radios to keep up communications with the rest of the world. There were no airplanes to survey terrain from the air, or to drop food if explorers were stranded, or to effect a quick rescue if they were isolated. To make an attempt to reach the North Pole was considered by most people to be a foolhardy adventure indeed, but Henson and Peary both wanted to attempt it.

Second Trip to the Arctic

In 1895 a party of eleven men and two women again headed for Greenland, with Peary intending to go further North this time. After a year of Arctic hardships and frustrations, all but two of the men returned to the United States. Only Matt Henson and one other, Hugh Lee, stuck by Peary, electing to remain another year, sticking out a second winter that they might go forward in the spring. Peary's first attempt that year to reach the Pole had been unsuccessful, and their supplies were buried in a frozen drift of snow and ice. In April, the party made another attempt in the face of icy winds that bore down from the North under the cold but continuous glare of a twenty-four-hour sun on blindingly white snow. In their three dog-sledges, the men often lost contact in the swirling blizzards through which they travelled. It was slow and dangerous going over ice that might split and isolate one dog team from another.

At one time Lee was lost. Peary and Henson made camp trusting he would catch up to them, but he did not. To keep warm while waiting and hoping, the two men slept huddled in furs as close together as they could, that their body heat might keep each other from freezing. After three days, Henson went in search of the third man and, luckily, found him. Lee was almost frozen on the top of his dog sledge, though still alive. Henson rescued him and treated him for frostbite and extreme exposure.

When their food supply got so low the men could not share any of it with the dogs, they would each day kill a dog and feed that one to the other animals. Finally, the men were reduced to eating dogs themselves. After a month, however, the three pioneers had covered six hundred miles. They were too exhausted by then and their supplies too low to hope to go any further and expect to make the long trek back to civilization alive. Besides, scurvy, the dreaded disease caused by malnutrition, set in. They had failed.

Nevertheless they brought back to New York from the Greenland coast two large meteorites of scientific interest, leaving behind one of many tons that was too large to be loaded aboard their small ship. In 1897 they secured a larger ship and stronger tackle, sailed again to Greenland, and this time brought back to New York the largest meteorite in the world. This gained Peary wide newspaper publicity as well as a profitable lecture tour. Matt, meanwhile, was employed by the American Museum of Natural History as an assistant in the mounting of Arctic animals and arranging true-to-nature panoramas of the beasts and backgrounds of the far North.

Later Trips to the Arctic

In England, Peary's lectures and interviews were so successful that a publisher presented him with a ship, the *Windward*, especially equipped for Arctic travel. On his return to America, he immediately began to plan another Polar search, this time working out details most carefully in advance, selecting a full complement of assistants to cover each lap, and preparing to spend at least four years on the expedition. He alerted Matt to be ready to accompany him.

Off again in 1898, Peary and Henson steamed past the Statue of Liberty, but ice prevented the *Windward* from penetrating as far north as Peary had hoped. They got only to Cape d'Urville on Ellesmere Island. From there, Peary decided to go by sledge overland to Fort Conger, deserted fifteen years before by another exploring party that had left behind a large stock of supplies. This trip to Conger was one of two hundred and fifty miles

Icebergs, 1861, FREDERICK CHURCH. The Dallas Museum of Fine Arts, anonymous gift. Photograph by David Wharton.

through deep snowdrifts over mountains of ice, but Matt and Peary, with a group of Eskimos, got there. On arrival, Peary's feet were frozen so badly that some of his toes snapped off as his shoes were removed. For three months at Conger, Matt cared for Peary, treating his frozen feet and trying to prevent gangrene from setting in. When they could travel again, they returned to Cape d'Urville where all of Peary's remaining toes, except one on either foot, had to be amputated. This great misfortune left him a partial cripple for life. Convalescence did not keep him from remaining for two years more in Greenland, but again he failed on this trip to reach the Pole. At Etah, Matt and Peary passed many months alone, except for the Eskimos, and they were the first to define for map makers the northern rim of Greenland. When they returned to New York in 1902, they had added to the geographical knowledge of the world by this major exploration.

Over a period of many years, from youth to middle-age, the still determined Robert Peary made a total of eight unsuccessful attempts to reach the Pole, and, on

About the Art

Supported by his father, a wealthy Hartford, Connecticut, insurance man, Frederick Edwin Church (1826-1900) received the finest art education offered in America at that time. He studied with, and later became the protégé of, Thomas Cole, a foremost American painter. (See **About the Art** on page 323.)

Church began to travel to find more dramatic subjects than the traditional picturesque scenes he had been painting. His *Heart of the Andes* (1859), painted after his trip to South America, sold for $10,000, the highest price paid till then for a work by a living American artist.

In 1861, he traveled to Nova Scotia to paint icebergs. Often hampered by fog, freezing weather, and sea-sickness, Church made many quick sketches during the trip but completed very few paintings of them afterwards. The sketches made bold use of color and were completely different than the paintings. One of the completed works, *The Icebergs* was lost. An engraving of it was made, though, a copy of which is reproduced here.

all but one, Matt Henson accompanied him. Henson became an expert in his knowledge of the Arctic and its winds and weather. In the frozen North, far away from the centers of civilization, he developed into a sort of Jack-of-all-trades since there was nothing Matt would not do to be of value to himself or his party. He learned to harpoon walrus; to hunt reindeer, bear, and musk-oxen; to skin and stuff animals; to cook over a hole in the ice; and to build igloos as an ice shelter against zero gales. He could not only build a boat but navigate it. He could interpret for the white men and the Eskimos. He was so good at manipulating heavily loaded dog sledges, even in blizzards of 50 degrees below, that Peary once said of Henson, "He is a better dog driver and can handle a sledge better than any man living except some of the best Eskimo hunters themselves." With the Eskimos no one could form closer friendships or achieve cooperation more quickly than could Henson. He not only learned to speak their language but to understand their jokes, eat their food, and wear their clothes. He adopted an orphan Eskimo boy, Kudlooktoo. And once when Henson slipped on an ice floe and went into the freezing water, it was an Eskimo who saved his life.

On the expedition begun in 1905, they went by ship as far as Cape Sheridan, then by sledge and on foot across the ice of the Polar Sea. That year Peary and Matt Henson reached a new farthest North, 87°6", only 175 miles from the Pole. Here again they were stymied by all the conditions that make travel in the Land of the Midnight Sun excessively difficult—the breaking ice floes, the towering cliffs of frozen snow, the swirling blizzards and the terrors of complete isolation. With supplies gone, dogs emaciated and the Eskimos exhausted, for days they faced death on floating ice fields as they tried to make their way back to their base camp. Again defeated, Matt and Peary reached New York on Christmas Eve, 1906.

Success at Last

In 1907, Henson got married, but marriage did not keep Matt at home. The call came again to seek, with the undaunted Peary, a foothold at the top of the world. Two more determined men than Peary and Henson have never been known in the annals of exploration. One disappointment after another plus the ridicule of the press of the world at his continual failures only made Peary more firm in his ambition to reach 90 degrees North, where no person had ever stood before. On each expedition his accompanying members changed, but Matt Henson remained with him. Henson was forty-two years old when again he left the United States on July 8, 1908, once more heading for familiar Cape Sheridan. This time President Theodore Roosevelt came aboard their ship in New York Harbor to see the expedition off and to cheer its departure.

Leaving the ship at Cape Sheridan, the party travelled overland ninety-three miles across the snow to Cape Columbia where a base was established. From here, it was four hundred uncharted miles across seas of ice to the Pole. The temperature was so cold that often the men's beards were frozen stiff from the moisture from their breath. Eighteen years of determination lay behind Peary when on February 28, 1909 he began another attempt to reach the Pole.

The party got off to a good start. But in March a great lead of water that they could not cross—an Arctic river between the ice—stopped their progress and made it appear they might never get further. Fortunately, after a week of waiting, the weather went even further below zero. Then the water froze, permitting lightly loaded sledges to cross and re-cross, conveying supplies to the other side. When they were a hundred and thirty miles from the Pole, the last of the supporting parties turned back. Now Peary and Henson were left alone with four Eskimos, five sledges, and a group of huskies for their final dash northward, destined, if successful, to make history. Matt was to blaze the trail, Peary to follow.

A grueling trail it was, over a white wilderness of snow and ice, but they pushed forward. "Day and night were the same," wrote Henson later in his autobiography, *A Negro at the North Pole*. "My thoughts were on the going and the getting forward and on nothing else. The wind was from the southeast and seemed to push us on and the sun was at our backs, a ball of livid fire rolling its way above the horizon in never ending day." But on this last lap, he continued, "As we looked at each other we realized . . . the time had come for us to demonstrate that we were the men who, it had been ordained, should unlock the door which held the mystery of the Arctic."

By April 5 they were thirty-five miles from the Pole. Peary with his mutilated feet was then fifty-three years old, and Matt was not young either. Could it be that at last their dream of so many years would come true? Henson and Peary could not sleep from the excitement of it. A part of Matt's job as trailblazer was to build an igloo of ice at each stopping point so that when Peary got there they could rest until time to start again. On the day when Henson, forging ahead, finally arrived at a point where North no longer existed, he knew he had reached the Pole. With Ootah's assistance, there he began to build an igloo. Forty-five minutes later, with Eskimos and a team of dogs, Peary arrived. To Matt Henson, Peary gave the honor of planting the American flag at the North Pole while he stood in salute. It was April 6, 1909.

Eleven years later Admiral Peary died, but Matt Henson lived to be eighty-eight

Using the Study Questions

It is recommended that students always read and answer the questions in **Developing Comprehension Skills** in class discussion. Whenever possible, they should also read the questions in the other categories together and discuss the answers.

Developing Comprehension Skills

Question 1. Read and discuss.

Question 2. Remind students that they are looking for details that bring out the human qualities in Matt, not the traits that make him seem a larger-than-life explorer.

Question 3. Encourage students to focus on Matt's entire youth, not just the negative things that happened to him early in life. Discuss the major events of Matt's youth up to the point when Robert Peary gave Matt a job as his personal manservant. List those events on the board. Then discuss the question.

Question 4. Point out the differences between the late 1800's and now in terms of laws, institutions, and individual expectations for children's behavior.

Question 5. Read and discuss. Emphasize that there is no single correct answer and that opinions should be supported by reasons.

Challenge Question. Matt Henson was a black man who grew up just after slavery was ended in the United States. How did racial prejudice affect his life? (Interpretive Reading)

Reading Literature: Nonfiction

Question 1. Discuss the meaning of "recording human experience." Point out that the phrase can include a wide range of topics from one individual's private life to worldwide events. Have students decide what major event was described in this biography. After students suggest other possible ways to learn about this topic, ask them to explain the strong and weak points of each source.

Question 2. Emphasize that this question asks about the boyhoods only of the two men.

Question 3. Ask students to decide which person they feel they know better. Stress that the question asks them to evaluate which type of biography helps them know about the subject better. Explain that there is no single correct answer, but that answers should be supported by reasons. Ask them to keep these ideas in mind as they discuss the question.

years old. He passed away in New York City in 1955. In tribute to his long series of explorations, Matt Henson received a Congressional Medal, a gold medal from the Chicago Geographical Society, and a loving cup from the Bronx Chamber of Commerce. A building has been named after him at Dillard University. On the occasion of the forty-fifth Anniversary of the Discovery of the North Pole, President Eisenhower honored Matt Henson at the White House.

Matthew Henson stands before the American flag at the North Pole, 1909.

The Bettmann Archive, Inc. New York City.

Check Test

1. Why did Matt run away from home? (His stepmother was cruel to him.)

2. How did Matt learn to read and write? (The captain of the *Katie Hines* taught him.)

3. Name two problems that stopped Peary and Henson on their first seven attempts to reach the North Pole. (Possible answers: blizzards, icy winds, snow drifts, low food supplies, illness and frostbite, breaking ice floes, uncharted rivers)

4. When the expedition team finally reached the North Pole, who planted the American flag there? (Matt Henson)

Answers to Study Questions

Developing Comprehension Skills

1. The captain of the *Katie Hines* taught him when he served as a cabin boy on a long trip to China.

2. Possible answers: Matt ran away from home when he was young. He had close friendships with people. He did not like the idea of being anyone's manservant. He learned languages quickly. He became one of the best dog drivers. He adopted an Eskimo boy.

3. Matt's early life was harsh, so he learned to accept hardships and depend on himself, two necessary qualities in an

Developing Comprehension Skills

Literal Reading 1. How did Matt happen to learn to read and write aboard a ship?

Literal Reading 2. A good biography should make its subject seem real. Name two or three small details in this biography that made Matt seem real to you.

Interpretive Reading 3. Do you think that the way Matt grew up helped him become an explorer as an adult? Give a reason for your answer.

Critical Reading 4. What would happen if a child living today tried to do what Matt did when he was a boy?

Critical Reading 5. Do you think life was better for a child growing up in the 1860's and '70's or in the 1980's? Give some reasons for your answer.

Reading Literature: Nonfiction

1. **Learning About Human Experience Through Literature.** Nonfiction writing is an important way of recording human experience. In this biography, you learned about the life of Matt Henson. What other important experience did you learn about? In what other ways might you learn about the same topic? Do you think reading a biography is as good a way to learn as these other ways, or better, or worse? Give a reason for your answer.

2. **Comparing Two Characters.** Compare what you have learned about Matt Henson and about Abe Lincoln when they were boys. How were they different? How were they similar? Give at least two answers for each question.

3. **Comparing Biographies.** The biography of Matt Henson covers most of his life. That of Abe Lincoln covers only part of his boyhood. How does this difference affect the two biographies? Does it affect how well you get to know the subject (main character)? How does it affect the author's choice of events? Which approach do you think works better in helping you know about the subject of the biography? Or do you feel that the approaches are equally good? Give a reason for your answer.

4. **Comparing Autobiography and Biography.** Consider the two autobiographies and two biographies you have read. An autobiography can tell you some things that a biography cannot tell as accurately and completely. A biography can tell other things that an autobiography

Question 4. Discuss the differences between autobiography and biography. Discuss the strengths of each type of writing. Then ask the students to use details in the four selections they have read as examples to prove these strengths.

Question 5. Discuss the concept that opinions frequently are based on fact and therefore are reasonably correct.

Challenge Question. Find as many examples as you can in this selection of the author stating his opinion. If an opinion is based on fact, include evidence from the story to support your answer.

Developing Vocabulary Skills

Have the first paragraph and list of methods on page 402 read aloud. Depending on your students' ability, you may wish to discuss the three methods of figuring out the meaning of an unfamiliar word. Ask students for examples of words that have affixes, write them on the board, and ask them to explain how the affix affects the meaning of the word. Discuss what is meant by context clues. Have the students suggest original example sentences that contain context clues.

Students not needing this thorough review may be referred to the **Vocabulary Skills** section in the **Handbook for Reading and Writing** at the back of the student text.

Remind the students that a dictionary should be consulted when an exact definition is needed or if the context in which the word appears does not provide adequate information for determining the meaning of an unfamiliar word.

Read the exercise directions to the students and have them complete the exercise independently. Check the answers together.

---

explorer. Also, he traveled a lot as a boy and probably liked the adventures of visiting new places as an explorer would.

4. A child today probably would not succeed in doing what Matt did due to the laws concerning child labor, legal custody of children, and enrollment in school.

5. Answers will vary. Possible answers: Life was better for children in the 1860's because they had more freedom to get jobs and earn their own money. Life is better in the 1980's because children are protected by laws. They are taken care of until they are older.

Challenge. Possible answers: Peary first gave Matt the job of man-servant, a position commonly held by black people during those times . Henson did not gain the widespread publicity that Peary did for his accomplishments. Peary was the one who spoke before groups and who received the gifts and praise.

Reading Literature: Nonfiction

1. This biography describes the discovery of the North Pole. Some other sources for learning about this topic are history books, encyclopedias, and autobiographical accounts. Answers to the last question will vary. Possible answers: Biography is a good way to learn since it tells about how events affect people. Biography includes interesting events and important details. Encyclopedia articles and history books are factual, but they don't often tell about people's feelings. Autobiographical accounts, such as journals, sometimes tell about details that are not important.

Biography is not always the best way to learn, since it is often slanted. It sometimes uses facts in a limited way.

2. Possible answers: Similarities—They both had a strong desire to learn about different people, places, and things. They both obtained an education outside of

(continued on page 402)

Developing Writing Skills

Read and discuss the two assignments. Then have each student choose and complete one of the two.

Question 1. This question asks the students to draw conclusions based on information in Henson's biography.

Pre-Writing. Have the students find passages in the story that suggest Henson's personality traits and read them aloud. Discuss what each passage reveals about his character. You may want to list some descriptive words on the board.

Writing. Remind the students to include details from the story concerning Matt Henson's actions and activities that will support their description of him. If they wish, they can use the descriptive words from the list on the board. Allow sufficient time for students to complete the assignment independently.

Revising. Have each student reread his or her own paragraph, making sure that each character trait is supported by details from the selection.

Question 2. Some students may feel that this question asks them to brag and may be reluctant to answer it. Emphasize that by answering this question, they will see that courage is found in many forms.

Pre-Writing. Point out that there are many types of courage and that the incident they write about does not have to be dangerous. Have students suggest situations that commonly cause feelings of fear or anxiety in people. Possible suggestions might include these: riding in an airplane for the first time, making a speech in front of a large group of people, going to the hospital for an operation. List students' ideas on the board. Then have each student select one of those ideas or one of his or her own, make a list of the important details that should be included, and organize them into the correct time order.

cannot tell as accurately and completely. Find evidence in the four selections to prove each of these statements.

5. **Evaluating an Opinion.** Read this sentence from the biography: "A kind woman who ran a small lunchroom took him in, fed him, and gave him a job as her dishwasher." Calling the woman "kind" is an opinion. From the information in the rest of the sentence, do you think the opinion is based on facts? Give a reason for your answer.

Developing Vocabulary Skills

Reviewing Ways To Find Correct Meanings. You have learned these methods for figuring out the meaning of an unfamiliar word:

a. Word Parts. Knowing the meaning of affixes and how they change the meaning of a base word.

b. Context Clues. Considering the sentence or paragraph in which a specific word appears. Frequently, context clues give the information you need to understand the use of the word.

c. Dictionary and Glossary. Finding the exact meaning of a word in a dictionary or glossary.

Read these sentences about events in Matthew Henson's life. Decide which method you want to use for figuring out the meaning of each underlined word. On your paper, write the meaning of the word. Also write which of the methods you used to find the meaning.

1. Later he saw the pagodas of Japan, the gypsies of Spain, and the palm trees of the West Indies.
2. The men were too exhausted to go any further. Besides, scurvy, the dreaded disease caused by malnutrition, set in.
3. It was not long before young Henson found a job on a boat, a square-rigger with tall white sails destined for Hong Kong.
4. Peary's first attempt to reach the pole had been unsuccessful.
5. The men faced the cold but continuous glare of a twenty-four-hour sun on blindingly white snow.
6. With supplies gone, dogs emaciated, and the Eskimos exhausted, they faced death on floating ice fields.
7. Peary's toes, except one on either foot, had to be amputated.

(continued from page 401)

school. They were both well-liked by people. Differences—Much of what Abe Lincoln learned came from books, but Matt Henson learned from personal experience. Lincoln spent his childhood at home, but Henson spent his out in the world.

3. Most likely answer: The biography of Abe Lincoln, which covers only a portion of his boyhood, helps the reader get to know the subject better than the biography of Matt Henson, which concentrates on the important events in the subject's life. The writer who tells about just part of the subject's life can include interesting details. Answers about whether one approach is better than the other will vary. The evaluation depends on what the reader wants to know.

4. An autobiography gives information about the subject's personal feelings:

> I learned what tyranny is and the pain of being misunderstood and wronged, or, if you please, understood and set right. They are pretty much the same. ("I Get a Colt to Break In,"—page 365, last paragraph)

> I left the well-house eager to learn. As we returned to the house, every object which I touched seemed to quiver with life. That was because I saw everything with the strange, new sight that had come to me. ("The Story of My Life,"—page 375, paragraph 3)

A biography can give an outsider's view of the subject. It can give the subject its proper place in history. Examples:

> The farm boys in their evenings at Jones's store in Gentryville talked about how Abe Lincoln was always reading, digging into books,.... ("Peculiarsome Abe"—page 385, paragraph 1)

> In fact, Henson was the trail breaker for Peary's expedition and, as such, went ahead first to the Pole, reaching it some forty-five minutes before the Admiral himself. So Henson was actually the very *first* person to stand at the top of the world. ("Matthew A. Henson,"—page 392, paragraph 1)

8. Matt worked in the American Museum of Natural History arranging true-to-nature panoramas. These pictures depicted the beasts and backgrounds of the far North.

Developing Writing Skills

Analytical Writing

1. **Analyzing a Character.** After reading this biography, what kind of a person do you think Matt Henson was? Write a paragraph describing Matt's character and personality. Use details from the story to support what you write.

Creative Writing

2. **Writing About Courage.** Think about a time when you had to show courage. You may have been frightened when you learned to swim. Perhaps large dogs or other animals upset you. You may have been lost in a strange place. How did you face your problem? Write one or more paragraphs explaining how you showed courage.

Developing Skills in Study and Research

1. **Reading a Map.** Find and examine a map that shows the area of the North Pole. Look at the **legend**, the box that explains the symbols used on the map. How does the map show land and water? Is the North Pole on land or is it a sea covered by ice? Now look at the distance scale in the legend. Using your finger or a ruler, estimate how far the North Pole is from Ellesmere Island, one of Henson's stops.

2. **Using Two Reference Materials.** Locate magnetic north on a map of the North Pole. Is magnetic north the same as the North Pole? Now look up *magnetic north* in an encyclopedia, dictionary, or atlas. On your paper, write what the term means. Also write how and where you found the meaning.

Developing Skills in Speaking and Listening

Introducing a Guest Speaker. Imagine that you are the chairperson of an explorer's club in 1909. Your club has invited Matt Henson to speak and receive an award. You are given the job of presenting the award and telling Matt why the club thinks he deserves it. Write your speech and practice it. Then present it before a group. Be sure to speak loudly enough for everyone to hear. Give your audience the feeling that you really admire Matt and want him to know it.

Writing. Remind students to explain how they showed courage in the situation they are describing. Have them include details about their feelings during the incident. Remind them that descriptive details will make their accounts come alive for the reader.

Revising. Have the students reread their stories to be sure each explanation is clearly written and contains no irrelevant sentences. Allow time for revisions to be made. Following this activity, you may wish to create an "Acts of Courage" bulletin board display so students can share their stories with each other.

Developing Skills in Study and Research

Question 1. For this exercise, display a large world map or project such a map with an overhead projector. Discuss what is meant by *legend* and the kind of information that it contains. Then have students read and answer the text questions.

Question 2. Have this exercise read aloud. Complete the first part of this question with the class. Then have the students complete the second part independently. Discuss the students' answers and reference sources.

Developing Skills in Speaking and Listening

Read and discuss the exercise. Stress that this speech should be slanted to give a favorable view of Matt Henson.

Assign members to a group, so that students will know the members of their audiences. Then set a date for each speaker, and ask students to prepare outside of class.

For suggestions for teacher or student evaluation of speakers, see pages T28 and T29 of this T.E.

5. The opinion is based on fact, since kindness is being "generous, good, or helpful." The woman's actions prove that she is kind.

Challenge. Possible answers:

a. Matt was lucky.—an opinion
He found a job on a boat sailing for Hong Kong.—fact

b. Matt was a valuable man to Peary's expedition.—opinion
Matt could hunt, trap, and fish for food.—facts

c. Two more determined men than Peary and Henson have never been known in the annals of exploration.—opinion
These men made numerous unsuccessful attempts at reaching the Pole and put up with ridicule.—facts

Developing Vocabulary Skills

1. a temple in the form of a tower, found in Japan or China; c
2. the dreaded disease caused by malnutrition; b
3. a boat; b
4. not successful; a
5. uninterrupted; a or b
6. made very thin; c
7. cut off, surgically; c
8. pictures; b

Developing Skills in Study and Research

1. Ellesmere Island is approximately 400 miles from the North Pole.

2. Magnetic north—the direction in which a magnetic compass points. The magnetic North Pole is some distance from the geographic North Pole and moves a little every year.

Objectives

- To recognize and appreciate biography as a form of literature
- To analyze the organization of a biography
- To describe the tone of a piece of writing
- To apply literal, interpretive, and critical reading skills to a selection
- To identify faulty generalizations
- To understand the effects of connotation
- To use glossaries in other textbooks to determine the meaning of unfamiliar words
- To state and defend in writing a personal opinion
- To use the *Readers' Guide to Periodical Literature*
- To identify unstated opinion

Preparing the Students

Essential Vocabulary. The words presented here are essential to the understanding of the selection.

Introduce the words listed below. Write the sentences on the board, have them read aloud, and ask the students to use context clues to find the meanings of the underlined words.

horrified	enormous
pianist	elaborate

1. The children were horrified when the vicious dog broke loose from his leash and dashed straight towards them.
2. The famous pianist sat down at the piano to begin her concert.
3. The skeleton of the dinosaur was so enormous that it made the people who stood near it look very small.
4. The costumes were elaborate, but the hairstyles were very plain.

If the students need additional help with the vocabulary of this selection, encourage them to use context clues to determine word meaning. As needed, direct them to the **Glossary** or to a classroom dictionary.

Motivation. Ask students if they or someone they know has ever had to make a difficult choice that might affect the rest of their lives. Allow them to share those experiences with the class. Then have the students read the introductory paragraph on page 404, and ask them to state in their own words what they should try to find out as they read the selection.

Maria Tallchief

TOBI TOBIAS

Like most people, Maria Tallchief had to make some important decisions during her life. As you read her biography, look for the moments when she had to make choices. Can you predict her decisions?

In the Osage language, *Ki He Kah Stah* means "the tall chiefs." One of America's greatest ballerinas comes from the native American family with this name. Elizabeth Marie Tallchief was born on January 24, 1925, in Fairfax, Oklahoma, a small town on the Osage reservation in southwestern United States. Her father was a full-blooded Osage; his father had been chief of the tribe. Her mother came from Scottish and Irish people.

Betty Marie's father was an easygoing man. He did not have to work at a regular job because oil had been discovered on the Osage reservation. The tribal council sold this oil and each member of the Osage shared in the profits. Mr. Tallchief loved the outdoors and a relaxed, comfortable life. Gerald, Betty Marie's older brother, was like him.

Mrs. Tallchief was different. She was strict and full of energy. She had great plans for Betty Marie and for her other daughter, Marjorie, who was two years younger. She wanted them to study music and dancing, and she expected them to work hard at everything they did.

Betty Marie was only three when she started taking piano lessons, but she learned music quickly and easily. Mrs. Tallchief dreamed that one day her daughter would play in concerts all over the world.

By the next year, Betty Marie was dancing too. She had ballet lessons with a teacher who came to Fairfax once a week. This teacher did not realize that ballet dancing should be taught slowly and carefully. She showed Betty Marie how to jump and leap and spin like a circus acrobat. She put her in toe shoes and taught her to dance on the tips of her toes. She had Betty Marie on stage when she was only five years old.

When Marjorie began taking lessons and performing with her sister, Mrs. Tallchief decided that the family should move to Los Angeles, where the girls could find better music and dancing teachers. Mr. Tallchief liked the idea. In California's sunshine, he said, he could play golf all year long.

At first Betty Marie felt strange and lonely in her new home. She was glad to settle down to the things she knew best—school, music, and dancing. The sisters went to a fine teacher, Ernest Belcher, for ballet lessons. The first time the eight-year-old Betty Marie danced for Mr. Belcher, he was horrified. "If you really want to dance," he said, "you will have to start all over again, from the beginning. No toe shoes, no fancy tricks, no performing. I'm surprised that your back and feet haven't been ruined by all this nonsense."

Betty Marie felt very disappointed but she was used to doing as she was told. She always tried to please her mother and her teachers. She wasn't afraid of any amount of hard work, either, and she loved to dance. So she began again, this time in the right way, with the simplest exercises and steps.

Mrs. Tallchief still wanted her daughter to become a concert pianist. She felt that dancing was wonderful, as long as it didn't keep Betty Marie away from her music. Betty Marie tried to be perfect in both. Every day she practiced the piano for several hours and went to a two-hour ballet class. She did well in her schoolwork too and even found time to have fun with her friends. At home her mother taught her to cook and sew. But she had no time for dreaming, no time for just doing nothing.

To celebrate her twelfth birthday, Betty Marie gave a concert. For the first half she played the piano, and for the second half she danced. That concert, she said, showed how she felt inside. She was split in half between the two things she loved most. One day she would have to choose between them. In high school, Betty Marie's favorite subject was writing. Once she wrote about trying to decide between music and dancing. At fifteen, she was both performing at the piano and studying ballet with a great Russian teacher, Mme. Bronislava Nijinska.

Mme. Nijinska was also a choreographer—a person who makes up dances. She gave Betty Marie a leading part in one of her ballets. The performance took place before an enormous audience. As she danced, Betty Marie felt strong and free. Afterward, everyone told her how well she had done. Now she realized that, more than anything else, she wanted to be a dancer.

Betty Marie grew to be tall and slim, with a lovely, strong body. Her face was beautiful. She had olive skin, mysterious dark eyes, high cheekbones, a wide, well-shaped mouth, and a cloud of dark hair. She was a quiet, serious girl and, even more than most dancers, a hard worker.

When she was seventeen, Betty Marie finished high school and went to New

Presenting the Selection

1. Have the students read "Maria Tallchief" silently. Although this selection is not too long, it may be helpful for some students if it is assigned in two parts. Begin the second assignment with the first full paragraph on page 407. This selection was revised and updated by the author for this anthology.

2. Make sure that everyone has read the assignment by administering the **Check Test** at the bottom of page 409. If the selection has been assigned in two parts, questions 1 through 3 can be asked in after first part, questions 4 and 5 after the second part.

3. Remind students that the introduction asked them to notice important decisions Maria made. Ask several students what they noticed. They may come up with answers such as the decision to dance with a particular company, the decisions to marry and to divorce, to have a child, and to quit dancing. Briefly discuss the students' opinions about these decisions.

4. Develop the study questions as suggested in **Using the Study Questions**, beginning page 410. Challenge questions are provided for further discussion as needed.

Reinforcing the Lesson

To reteach, reinforce, or extend the skills in this lesson, see the following:

Skills Practice Book, Green Level—pages 163 through 165

Special Populations

If you have students of native American ancestry, ask them to do research and locate information on individual native Americans who have made special contributions to American life. Have them give a brief oral report that includes the following:

1. the name of the individual
2. his or her tribe
3. his or her contribution
4. where they found their information

Encouraging Independent Reading

Students may be encouraged to read the articles they have located in the *Readers' Guide* for the **Developing Skills in**

Study and Research exercise. They could also read about other dancers or other aspects of dance. Ask them to write a one-paragraph summary of the article to hand in. Remind them to include the source from which they got their information.

York City, hoping to find a job in a ballet company. Sergei Denham, the director of the famous Ballet Russe de Monte Carlo, had seen and liked her dancing when she was a student in California. Now he said he would try her out in his company.

Betty Marie went on tour with the Ballet Russe. The company traveled from city to city, giving performances. Betty Marie danced so well that people began to notice her. Soon she had some solo parts.

Ballet life was often hard, though, and Betty Marie was sometimes unhappy. She kept to herself at first, and many people in the company thought she was unfriendly. Some of them were jealous because she was doing so well. She missed her family and wrote long letters home.

When Mr. Denham asked her to stay on in the company, he said that she must have a beautiful stage name. So Betty Marie became Maria. She refused to

The Entrance of the Masked Dancers, 1879, EDGAR DEGAS. Sterling and Francine Clark Art Institute, Williamstown, Massachusetts.

About the Art

Unlike the Impressionists, who were his contemporaries and several of whom were his friends, Edgar Degas (1834-1917), was interested in theatrical rather than natural effects. He liked to paint race horses and ballet dancers.

In *The Entrance of the Masked Dancers,* Degas primarily uses pastels, a soft chalky medium, because the quality of these colors best suggests stage colors and lights. The world of the theater gave Degas the chance to examine the effects of light and movement that were as fresh and varied as the theater and dance productions he loved so well.

change Tallchief, though. She was proud of her native American family name.

Then George Balanchine, a well-known choreographer, joined the Ballet Russe. Maria caught his eye at once. Her dancing was fast and brilliant. She could jump up and cross her long legs together four times in the air. She could turn in the air and land on the points of her strong toes. Her balance was sure. Her leaps were sharp and high. Her turns were quick and powerful.

Day after day, Mr. Balanchine worked with Maria. He was a gentle, patient teacher, but he often asked her to perform steps that seemed impossible. She tried over and over again, until she could do what he wanted. Soon she was dancing better than ever before.

When Maria was twenty-one, she and Mr. Balanchine married. The next year she and her husband went to France to work with the Paris Opéra Ballet. Maria was the first American to dance with this company in more than a hundred years. The French people loved her. When she came out to bow, they greeted her with applause and bouquets of flowers.

Then Mr. Balanchine went back to work at his own studio in New York, the School of American Ballet. He formed a company called Ballet Society with the dancers he had trained there. In time this group would grow into the New York City Ballet and become one of the best companies in the world. Maria joined this company as its leading dancer when she was twenty-two.

In the years that followed, George Balanchine made great changes in ballet. He took old ballets and old steps and made them new and different. He tried out new ways of moving and new ways of making dances. Many people called him a genius.

Mr. Balanchine created marvelous ballets for Maria. In one of them, *Firebird*, she danced the part of a beautiful, wild bird with magic powers. Mr. Balanchine gave her very difficult steps that made the audience gasp with wonder and surprise. Maria flashed across the stage, she flew, she whirled, she slashed through space like a flaming arrow. *Firebird* proved that Maria was truly a ballerina. She was not just a fine dancer but one of the best in the world.

Maria was a very musical dancer. Her years of study at the piano had taught her to love and understand music, and this helped her to work well with Mr. Balanchine. Some of his greatest ballets had no story, no elaborate scenery or costumes. They were just movements to music. Maria's dancing in ballets like *Serenade*, *Concerto Barocco*, *The Four Temperaments*, and *Symphony in C* helped to make the New York City Ballet famous.

Still, Maria's life was almost all hard work. Every morning she took a long ballet class. In the afternoon she rehearsed with the company, went to costume fittings, saw reporters and photographers, and practiced by herself. When evening came, she did her warm-up exercises, put on her stage make-up and costume, and went out on the stage to perform. She had little time to rest and no time for anything outside of ballet. Like most dancers, though, Maria loved her work.

Maria won many honors for her dancing. One came from her hometown. Thousands of people gathered in Fairfax for the celebration. Among them were the leaders of the Osage, the governors of Oklahoma, and Maria's mother and father. There were speeches, songs, dancing, and feasting. The Osage wore native dress and performed a special ceremony that made Maria a princess of the Osage tribe.

Maria's ballet career was a success, but her marriage to Mr. Balanchine had become very unhappy. She wanted to have children, but her husband could not agree. He thought a ballerina should give her whole life to dancing. After several years their marriage ended. Then, when she was thirty-one, Maria married Henry D. Paschen, Jr., an engineer who worked in Chicago. Three years later she became the mother of a little girl whom she named Elise Maria.

In her years with the New York City Ballet, Maria often went on tour with the company. She traveled with other companies, too, as a guest ballerina. She danced in most of the big cities of the United States and Europe. Working with these other groups, Maria performed parts that have made ballerinas famous throughout history. She danced in ballets that the New York City company never presented. She also met new partners who were excellent dancers and who knew exactly how to make a ballerina look her best.

Soon Maria began to see that the New York City Ballet was not the right place for her any more. She felt that a ballerina should have roles that make her look like a star. She wanted to have partners who were stars too. In the New York City Ballet, Mr. Balanchine's choreography was the most important thing. No matter how good they were, the dancers took second place.

Finally Maria decided to join American Ballet Theatre. She toured with this company as its prima, or first, ballerina, for several years and appeared with other companies as well. By the time she was thirty-five, Maria was called America's greatest ballerina. But she was facing a hard question. What should she do next? What would be best for her, as a dancer and as a person?

She could go back to the New York City Ballet. But she felt she did not belong there any more. She could go on dancing with other companies, but these groups were almost always on tour. Maria was tired of traveling all the time. She was tired of dancing the same parts over and over again. Maria Tallchief was one of the

Maria Tallchief and Erik Bruhn, dancing the *Flower Festival at Benzano* Ballet. Photograph by Jack Mitchell.

finest dancers in the history of ballet. Yet the ballet world did not seem to have a place for her.

She had a third choice, though, and now she turned to it. She had once said, "Marriage and dancing are both very important but it is better to take them one at a time." In 1966, when she was forty-one, Maria made her decision. She "hung up her toe shoes," as people in ballet say, and went home to her family in Chicago.

Although Maria left the stage, she did not leave the dance world. She began teaching young people and, in 1980, formed her own dance company, the Chicago City Ballet. Her sister, Marjorie, who also had a fine career as a ballerina, now heads the company's school. Maria has many duties as an artistic director but she likes to think of herself simply as a teacher, passing on what she has learned to a new generation of dancers.

Check Test

1. What two things did Betty Marie work on when she was young? (dancing and the piano)

2. What was Betty Marie's stage name? (Maria) Why wouldn't she change her last name? (She was proud of her native American family name.)

3. Which ballet performance proved that Maria was one of the best ballerinas in the world? (*Firebird*)

4. What important decision did Maria make in 1966 that changed her life? (She left dancing and went home to her family in Chicago.)

Using the Study Questions

It is recommended that students always read and answer the questions in **Developing Comprehension Skills** in class discussion. Whenever possible, they should also read the questions in the other categories together and discuss the answers.

Developing Comprehension Skills

Question 1. Read and discuss.

Question 2. Have students read aloud portions from the biography that answer this question.

Question 3. Emphasize that students must find evidence for their answers.

Question 4. This question is phrased broadly enough to allow students to use other evidence, in addition to this selection, in their answers. However, the points illustrated in Tallchief's experience must be considered as strong arguments against Balanchine's position.

Challenge Question. Maria Tallchief is famous and successful. In what ways did her mother contribute to her career? (Interpretive Reading)

Reading Literature: Nonfiction

Question 1. Have the students review the selection, and list on the board the examples of cause and effect as they discover them.

Question 2. Have students describe their own attitudes toward Maria. Have them find passages in the selection that helped to create their attitudes, that is, descriptions of Maria's character or events in her life that she had to deal with.

Question 3. After the students have read the question, have them list on the

Developing Comprehension Skills

Literal Reading

1. Maria started playing piano and dancing while very young. Who was responsible for her starting out so young?

Interpretive Reading

2. Young Maria was very good at both piano and ballet. As she grew up, she had to make a choice between them. Tell how you know that at first she did not know which she would pick. What caused her to choose ballet?

Critical Reading

3. Find an idea about Maria that the author repeats over and over again in this biography. Do you think that the idea reflects the facts? Give a reason for your answer.

Critical Reading

4. Mr. Balanchine did not want Maria to have children. He thought children would distract her from dancing. Later, Maria had a child. She continued to dance for seven more years, and after that she became a ballet teacher. What do you think of Mr. Balanchine's objections? How did Maria's actions conflict with his ideas? Do you think that taking on the responsibility for a child means that a man or woman cannot perform well in his or her career? Give reasons for your answer.

Reading Literature: Nonfiction

1. **Analyzing Organization.** Most biographies are organized in one of two ways. They are either related in simple, chronological (time) order, or told in terms of cause and effect. "Maria Tallchief" is mainly organized in chronological order, but there are also some examples of cause and effect. Find one of these and tell how the cause and effect relationship affects the author's choice of events and the order in which they are told.

2. **Describing the Tone.** The **tone** of a piece of writing lets you know how the author feels about his or her subject. Some words to describe tone include *serious*, *admiring*, *angry*, *sad*, *carefree*, *amused*. How would you describe the tone of "Maria Tallchief"? Refer to the selection to explain your answer.

3. **Identifying Faulty Generalizations.** As you remember, a generalization is faulty if it can be disproven in even one case. Words like *all*, *always*, and *every* are clues that you may have a faulty generalization.

Answers to Study Questions

Developing Comprehension Skills

1. Her mother was responsible for her starting out so young.

2. Betty Marie worked hard on both skills. After a concert where she danced and played the piano, she said the concert showed how divided she felt inside. She decided to choose ballet when she did well in the leading part in one of Mme. Nijinska's ballets.

3. One of the possible answers: Maria is a hard worker. This is evidenced by the following examples from the selection:

"She wasn't afraid of any amount of hard work. . . ." (page 405, paragraph 3)

"She was a quiet, serious girl and, even more than most dancers, a hard worker." (page 405, paragraph 7)

"She tried over and over again, until she could do what he wanted." (page 407, paragraph 3)

Most students will agree that an idea that is illustrated several times is probably true.

4. Answers will vary. Some students may feel that having children shouldn't keep a person from performing a job well. Other students may feel that some jobs could suffer if a person didn't give the job a lot of time. They might feel that Mr. Balanchine was right in some cases. Opinions should be supported with reasons.

Challenge. Maria's mother had Maria begin dance and music lessons early. She continued to encourage her daughter in these fields. Although Maria's hard work and talent led to her success, her mother clearly influenced Maria's life.

Reading Literature: Nonfiction

1. Examples of cause and effect:

a. Betty Marie danced very well in Mme. Nijinska's ballet. (Cause)

Words like *most* and *almost* usually indicate the generalization is not faulty. Read the following sentences from the story. Decide whether each one is or is not a faulty generalization. Think about whether each statement includes too much to be true. For each sentence, explain why you decided as you did.

a. Maria's life was almost all hard work.
b. Like most dancers, Maria loved her work.
c. Like most women, she wanted to have children.
d. These groups were almost always on tour.

4. **Understanding the Effect of Connotations.** The following sentences from "Maria Tallchief" include words with positive connotations. Identify each word that suggests a strong, favorable feeling. If the author had used only neutral words, would the sentences be more accurate or less accurate? Would they be more or less interesting?

a. She slashed through space like a flaming arrow.
b. They greeted her with applause.
c. Mr. Balanchine created marvelous ballets for Maria.

5. **Identifying Elements of Biography.** Three thousand years ago, biographers told only about a person's great deeds and heroic qualities. Today, biographers tell both the great and the small, the good and the bad, the successful and difficult times of a person's life. If Maria's biography were written by a 3000-year-old-biographer, what parts of this biography do you think would be left out?

Developing Vocabulary Skills

Using Glossaries in Other Textbooks. Most of the textbooks you use in your classes contain a glossary. The glossary in the back of this book contains words that are used in the selection. Your math, social studies, geography, and science books also have glossaries. The glossary of each text contains vocabulary words on that subject. Several words that are used in the selections in this book might also be found in one of your other textbooks. Decide in which of your textbooks you might find each word listed. Then look the word up in that textbook's glossary. If you cannot find the word in the glossary of any other textbook, look it up in the glossary of this text. Write the meaning of each word and tell where you found it.

chalkboard the words that tend to make a generalization faulty. Ask them for others. Some possibilities might be *none, never,* or *no.* Have the students provide examples of both faulty and accurate generalizations. Then have them complete the question together.

Question 4. Review the meaning of *connotation.* Have students complete this question together. Ask students to rewrite each sentence using neutral words. For example, the first sentence could be rewritten, "She danced."

Question Question 5. Explain that certain details prove that the subject of the biography was not perfect. These details don't mean the person was bad, but just human. List those details on the board as they are suggested.

Challenge Question 1. "Peculiarsome Abe" and "Maria Tallchief" are both biographies. How are the selections alike and how are they different?
Challenge Question 2. Compare and contrast the characters of Maria Tallchief and Matthew Henson.

Developing Vocabulary Skills

Have students read the directions for this exercise. Discuss how a glossary differs from a dictionary and how a glossary for a particular book will be unique to that book. Before assigning this drill, read aloud the list of words. Working with the first four words, provide suggestions for what types of books to use.

Then have the students complete the exercise independently. Be sure to discuss the answers together in class.

For extra challenge, ask students to write a paragraph using as many of these words as possible, while still making sense.

Betty Marie realized she wanted to be a dancer. (Effect)
The events that follow show the step-by-step process she undertakes to be the best dancer she can possibly be.

b. Maria felt that a ballerina should look like a star and dance with other stars. (Cause)
She quit the New York City Ballet and joined the American Ballet Theatre. (Effect)

This relationship affects how the author explains Maria's later choice not to return to the New York City Ballet.

2. Possible answers: admiring, serious. Examples from the selection:

"She was a quiet, serious girl and, even more than most dancers, a hard worker." (page 405, paragraph 7)
"Her dancing was fast and brilliant." (page 407, paragraph 1)
"She was not just a fine dancer but one of the best in the world." (page 407, paragraph 6)

3. The answers are as follows:

a. not faulty—It can be proven that she worked in morning, afternoon, and evening.
b. not faulty—It is logical to conclude that most dancers love their work, since they give so much time and hard work to it.
c. Two possible answers:
not faulty—Since the statement doesn't include all women, it could be true.
faulty—Since the group being described ("most women") is so large, and there is no way of verifying the statement, it could be false.
d. not faulty—This statement uses the word *almost.*

4. Words with positive connotations are the following:

(continued on page 412)

1. monarch
2. immigrant
3. sphere
4. meteorite
5. primitive
6. granite
7. continent
8. terrain
9. autocratic
10. magnify
11. allies
12. dynamo
13. irrigate
14. symmetrical

Developing Writing Skills

Analytical Writing

1. **Comparing Writing Styles.** The author of "Maria Tallchief" wanted to give the reader a certain impression of her subject. To do this, she used much descriptive language, emotional appeal, and repetition of certain ideas. Write a paragraph or two comparing this approach with the way the biography of Matt Henson was written. Which style of writing made you feel more as if you knew the person? If possible, quote passages from the selections to make your opinions clear.

Analytical Writing

2. **Presenting Your Opinion.** Abe Lincoln and Matt Henson were both historical figures. Maria Tallchief achieved fame in a cultural field. Is it important to write about achievements in cultural fields? Write at least one paragraph stating your opinion about this question and giving reasons for your opinion.

Developing Skills in Study and Research

Using the Readers' Guide. Many newspaper and magazine articles have been written about Maria Tallchief. The names of these articles and the periodicals (newspaper or magazine) in which they were published are listed in the *Readers' Guide to Periodical Literature*. A new volume of the *Guide* is printed almost every month. This keeps the *Guide* up-to-date. At the end of the year, all the listings for the year are joined in one large volume.

In each volume of the *Readers' Guide*, each article is listed under the subject of the article. The subjects are in alphabetical order. The same article may be listed under several subjects. At the beginning of each volume is an explanation of the abbreviations used in the entries, for example, for the titles of the magazines.

Find a recent volume of the *Readers' Guide* in your school or public library. Look under the subject "ballet" or "dance." See if you can find any entries for articles about Maria or Marjorie Tallchief or George Balanchine. Choose one. If there is none, choose any article about ballet.

Developing Writing Skills

Read and discuss the two assignments. Then have the students choose and complete one of the two.

Question 1. This question expands upon the concepts explained in **Reading Literature**, 1, 2, and 4.

Pre-Writing. Have students think about the way each biography was written. Which one used an emotional appeal? Which one looked at its subject in a factual way? How did each biography create its approach? How were facts organized and described? Have students find passages in each biography that are typical of the writer's approach—emotional or factual.

Suggest that each student choose one aspect of the writing on which to concentrate. That aspect should in some way explain the student's feeling of closeness to the subject of the biography.

Writing. Have students use their notes to write their paragraphs comparing the styles of the selections.

Remind them to include typical passages from the selections. The topic sentence should tell in what way the two selections will be compared.

Revising. Allow students to share their work with others who answered the same question. Have them decide whether the writers have proven the statements in their topic sentences with appropriate passages from the selections. Allow time for papers to be revised and recopied.

Question 2. This question asks students to focus on the appropriateness of selecting certain subjects for biographies. Emphasize that students are not being asked which field, history, or culture is more important. They should simply judge whether cultural figures are appropriate subjects.

(continued from page 411)

a. slashed; flaming arrow
b. greeted; applause
c. marvelous

If the author had used only neutral words, the sentences might have been more accurate, but not necessarily. They definitely would have been less interesting.

5. Possible answers:

Betty Marie was sometimes unhappy (page 406, paragraph 3).

Maria had little time to rest and no time for anything outside of ballet (page 408, paragraph 1).

Maria's ballet career was a success, but her marriage had become an unhappy one (page 408, paragraph 3).

Challenge 1. Possible answers:

Similarities—Both stories have an admiring tone. Both selections reflect the culture of a certain time and place.

Differences—The biography of Abe Lincoln covers only a portion of the subject's life, whereas the biography of Maria Tallchief covers most of the subject's life.

"Peculiarsome Abe" is told in terms of cause and effect and "Maria Tallchief" is mainly organized in chronological order.

Challenge 2. Possible answers:

Similarities—Both of these achieved something that was important to them through hard work and dedication. Both were proud of their heritage.

Differences—Matt had a friendly, open personality while Maria was quiet and reserved. Maria decided to devote her time to her family. Matt didn't give up his explorations to be with his family.

Developing Vocabulary Skills

Many of these words have multiple meanings. Definitions will vary.

On your paper, write the volume of the *Readers' Guide* in which you found the entry. Compare the abbreviations used in the entry with the code to abbreviations at the front of the volume. Then write the following information:

a. the name of the article
b. the name of the periodical the article is in
c. the month or volume number of that issue of the magazine
d. the pages the article appears on

You do not need to find the article itself.

Developing Skills in Critical Thinking

Identifying Unstated Opinions. An author can express an opinion by stating it directly. For example, the author could write, "Vince is a good fielder, but he doesn't hit well under pressure." An author can also express an opinion without stating it directly.

There are two ways the author can express an unstated opinion. First, he or she can simply leave out information. For example, instead of saying that Vince is a weak hitter in tight situations, his biographer may report only his fielding averages and not mention his batting average or, especially, his runs batted in. Second, the writer may include some information on the topic and imply things that are not said. For example, Vince's biographer might report, "The manager surprised everyone by leaving Vince in the lineup going into the tenth inning."

When the writer presents opinions indirectly, the reader may not think about these opinions. Still, he or she may accept the opinions without thinking.

Read the following opinions. Which one is implied, that is, meant but not stated, in "Maria Tallchief"? Find passages in the selection that support the unstated opinion. Which opinions are not supported?

1. Maria made a bad choice when she decided to have a baby.
2. Maria's mother was important in encouraging her career, but her father was not.
3. Maria and her sister did not get along well because they were jealous of each other.

Pre-Writing. Discuss what is meant by the term *cultural fields.* Have students suggest other areas besides dance that would be included. If necessary, remind them of music, painting, sculpture, photography, writing, and other fields. Have students decide whether it is important to write about cultural achievers. Have them list reasons to support their opinions.

Writing. Have students state their opinions in topic sentences. Remind them that they need to give reasons for their opinions. Allow sufficient time for students to complete the assignment independently.

Revising. Have students revise and proofread their paragraphs using the **Checklist for the Process of Writing** on pages 556 and 557.

Developing Skills in Study and Research

Read this assignment aloud. Then, together, examine a volume of the *Readers' Guide.* Have students choose a topic, for example, modern art. Have them look it up and find two or three articles listed in the *Guide.* Have a volunteer copy the information given in the *Guide* exactly as it is printed. Then have the students explain what the entry means. Make sure they are aware of how to find the meanings for the abbreviations in the book.

Assign the exercise to be completed independently, or perhaps by partners. Discuss the students' findings.

Developing Skills in Critical Thinking

Have students read and discuss the directions for this exercise. Then discuss the three statements and complete the exercise with the students. Have students read aloud passages from the selection that support the opinions.

1. a ruler, as a king, queen, or emperor; a large black and orange butterfly

2. relating to those who come into a different land to make a new home

3. the place or range of action or being; a round body whose surface is, at all points, equally distant from the center

4. a small chunk of metal or stone remaining from a meteor that has fallen upon the earth

5. like that of earliest times. (This word also has many specialized definitions in various fields such as mathematics, painting, biology, and geology.)

6. rock used for buildings and monuments

7. any of the large land areas of the earth; adj. restrained or moderate

8. ground or area of land; the character of land

9. having complete power over others; forcing others

10. to make, look, or seem larger than is really so; to increase the size or volume of an image or sound

11. countries joined together by agreement or united for a special purpose; friends

12. a machine for changing mechanical energy into electricity; a very energetic or forceful person

13. to water by means of canals, ditches, or pipes; to wash out with water or medicinal fluid

14. balanced; alike in arrangement

Developing Skills in Critical Thinking

1 and 3 are not stated or implied.

2 is implied. Passages that support it include paragraphs 2, 3, and 6 on page 404.

Humorous Sayings, Writings, and Anecdotes

Call on a student to read aloud the text on page 414. Ask students to define the term *anecdote*.

Then ask students to examine the illustration on page 414. Point out the headline in the newspaper Lincoln is holding, and the title and date of the drawing. Have the students explain what the artist was trying to communicate when he drew Lincoln in this distorted way.

Special Populations

LD, ESL. This section will be popular with many of the ESL and LD students because the reading material is short and generally entertaining. Much of this reading could be substituted for other work that might be beyond the student's capability. Some of the humor may be subtle enough to be missed by a few students. Check for understanding of the irony seen in some of the readings.

Humorous Sayings, Writings, and Anecdotes

Abraham Lincoln must have been a witty man. We know this because so many of his sayings have been remembered for so long. Some of his sayings stand alone. Others can be better appreciated when they are part of a short account of some happening in Lincoln's life. Such an account is called an **anecdote**. The sayings, writings, and anecdotes in this section give a good picture of Lincoln's personality.

Long Abraham Lincoln a Little Longer,
F. BELLEW. Reprinted from *Harper's Weekly,* November 26, 1864. Culver Pictures, Inc., New York City.

About the Art

The artist, Frank Bellew (1828-1894), was the son of a political cartoonist. Because he followed in his father's footsteps, he earned the nickname "Chip," from the phrase "chip off the old block."

The cartoon *Long Abraham Lincoln a Little Longer* is a visual pun. The caricature exaggerates Lincoln's great height, making him "a little longer" and as skinny as one of the rails he was known to have split. He is shown holding his second inaugural address, indicating that he has just been reelected. In other words, he was going to be around as President "a little longer."

Abraham Lincoln Is My Name

ABRAHAM LINCOLN

When Abe wrote this poem, he was about the same age as he was in the biography you read. See what you learn about his personality by reading his poem.

Abraham Lincoln is my nam
And with my pen I wrote the same
I wrote in both hast and speed
and left it here for fools to read

Abraham Lincoln his hand and pen
he will be good but god knows When

Developing Comprehension Skills

Literal Reading — 1. What did Abe write with his pen?

Interpretive Reading — 2. How can you tell this poem was written by a young person?

Critical Reading — 3. What makes this poem funny? Explain your answer.

Reading Literature: Nonfiction

Combining Information from Two Sources. Think about what you learned in the biography of Abraham Lincoln about his schooling. Then proofread this poem, written when Abe was a teenager. Several words are misspelled and some capitalization is incorrect. Why did Abe make these mistakes? Was he just careless or did he have better reasons? Would it be acceptable if you wrote that way?

Check Test

1. How did Lincoln write his name? (Accept either: in haste and speed, with his pen)

2. Who did he think would read his name? (fools)

Answers to Study Questions

Developing Comprehension Skills

1. He wrote his name.

2. errors in spelling, capitalization, and grammar

3. Lincoln pokes fun at himself. He looks at himself and his words good-naturedly. The poem is funny because the reader feels that he or she has been let in on a joke.

Reading Literature: Nonfiction

Possible answers: Lincoln may have been just careless, but, more likely, the mistakes could be due to his lack of formal education.

Errors like these would be acceptable only if they were done on purpose, for special effect. A writer might use errors in a humorous piece. If the errors were not useful, they would not be acceptable.

Objectives

- To compare and contrast the prupose of different types of nonfiction
- To analyze an individual's character through that person's writings
- To apply literal, interpretive, and critical reading skills to a selection

Preparing the Students

Essential Vocabulary. There are no difficult words in this selection.

Motivation. Have the students read the introductory paragraph on page 415 and state in their own words what they should try to find out as they read the selection.

Presenting the Selection

1. Have the students read "Abraham Lincoln Is My Name" silently.

2. Administer the **Check Test**.

3. Remind the students that the introduction to the selection asked them to find out something about Abe Lincoln's personality. Have a volunteer read the selection aloud, and then have students answer the introductory question.

4. Develop the study questions as suggested in **Using the Study Questions.**

Using the Study Questions

It is recommended that students always read and answer the questions in **Developing Comprehension Skills** in class discussion. Whenever possible, they should also read the questions in **Reading Literature** together and discuss the answers.

Developing Comprehension Skills

Question 1. Read and discuss.

Question 2. After the students answer the question, have them point out the errors in spelling, capitalization, and grammar. Write these on the board and discuss why each is incorrect.

Question 3. Emphasize that students should not be looking for one word or phrase that is funny. They should try to identify what in the poem makes the reader smile.

Reading Literature: Nonfiction

Have students discuss Lincoln's education as described in "Peculiarsome Abe."

Then have them answer the questions.

Objectives

- To recognize and appreciate anecdotes as a form of literature
- To analyze an individual's character through his writings
- To recognize sentence patterns and how they affect the tone of a selection
- To apply literal, interpretive, and critical reading skills to a selection

Preparing the Students

Essential Vocabulary. The words presented here are essential to the understanding of the selection.

Introduce the words listed below. Write the sentences on the board, have them read aloud, and ask the students to use context clues to find the meaning of the underlined words.

distress legal morally sprightly

1. The boaters sent a distress signal over the radio to alert the Coast Guard that they were in trouble.
2. The lawyer carefully explained the law so the man would know his legal rights.
3. The children wanted to do what was morally right, so they took the lost wallet to the police station.
4. The dancer gave a sprightly performance. In other words, the performance was full of life and energy.

If the students need additional help with the vocabulary of this selection, encourage them to use context clues to determine word meaning. As needed, direct them to the **Glossary** or to a classroom dictionary.

Motivation. Have the students read the introductory paragraph on page 416. Ask them to state in their own words what they should try to find out as they read the selection. Make sure students understand why the man would need a lawyer.

Presenting the Selection

1. Have the students read "Lawyer Lincoln Turns Down a Case" silently.

2. Make sure that everyone has read the assignment by administering the **Check Test** at the bottom of this page.

3. Have a volunteer read the selection aloud using the same voice tones Lincoln might have used.

4. Develop the study questions as suggested in **Using the Study Questions** below. That section also provides challenge questions for further discussion.

Lawyer Lincoln Turns Down a Case

ABRAHAM LINCOLN

Lincoln wrote this note when he was a lawyer. A man had died, leaving a widow, six children, and a debt of $600. A second man asked Lincoln to help him collect the debt. What advice did Lincoln give?

Yes, we can doubtless gain your case for you; we can set a whole neighborhood at loggerheads; we can distress a widowed mother and her six fatherless children, and thereby get for you six hundred dollars to which you seem to have a legal claim, but which rightfully belongs, it appears to me, as much to the woman and her children as it does to you. You must remember, however, that some things legally right are not morally right. We shall not take your case, but we will give you a little advice for which we will charge you nothing. You seem to be a sprightly, energetic man. We would advise you to try your hand at making six hundred dollars in some other way.

Abraham Lincoln. Library of Congress.

Check Test

1. What was the debt of the man who had died? ($600)

2. What advice did Lincoln give to the man who wanted to collect the debt? (to try his hand at making six hundred dollars in some other way)

Developing Comprehension Skills

Literal Reading 1. What did the man want to hire Lincoln to do?

Literal Reading 2. Why didn't Lincoln want to take the case?

Critical Reading 3. How can something be legally right but not morally right?

Reading Literature: Nonfiction

1. **Learning About a Character.** This note gives a reader insight into Abe's personality. What quality or qualities do you become aware of?

2. **Recognizing Sentence Patterns.** This paragraph is made up of five sentences. The first sentence is as long as the other four combined. This sentence is also complex; that is, it is really made up of several smaller sentences. Why do you think Lincoln joined these sentences in one sentence? Try to imagine Lincoln reading this sentence to the man. What tone of voice do you think he would use?

   The second sentence is short and direct. Following such a long first sentence, what is the effect of a short sentence here? What tone of voice do you imagine Lincoln using for this sentence?

Using the Study Questions

It is recommended that students always read and answer the questions in **Developing Comprehension Skills** in class discussion. Whenever possible, they should also read the questions in **Reading Literature** together and discuss the answers.

Developing Comprehension Skills

Question 1. Read and discuss the question.

Question 2. Have students find proof for their answers in the selection.

Question 3. Students may need to be given some examples here to help them understand the difference between legality and morality. For example, in a war, killing is legally right, but there may be situations where killing is morally wrong. Have students suggest other situations in which an action that is legally right is not morally right.

Challenge Question 1. Do you think Lincoln was right to turn down the case? Explain. (Critical Reading)

Challenge Question 2. How do you suppose the man who got the letter felt about himself or about Lincoln? (Interpretive Reading)

Reading Literature: Nonfiction

Question 1. Focus students' attention on Lincoln's attitudes toward money and needy people.

Question 2. Help students to recognize and restate what Lincoln is trying to say in the first sentence and then the second. After students have discussed this question, have a volunteer read the selection aloud again, paying special attention to tone.

Answers to Study Questions

Developing Comprehension Skills

1. He wanted Lincoln to force the widow to pay him the $600 her dead husband owed him.

2. He didn't want to take the case because he didn't want to cause the widow any further distress and he thought the woman had more need for the money than the man.

3. Answers will vary. The law doesn't cover every possible situation. Sometimes a higher law, a moral law, must be used to bring about justice.

Challenge 1. Answers will vary. Students will probably agree with Lincoln's decision. The widow needed the money badly.

Challenge 2. Answers will vary. The man might have felt angry with Lincoln and might have felt he was treated unfairly. On the other hand, he may have felt ashamed that he had tried to get the money from the widow and grateful that Lincoln made him rethink his position.

Reading Literature: Nonfiction

1. his honesty, morality, lack of greediness, and sympathy for people in trouble

2. By writing such a long sentence, Lincoln emphasizes all the problems that would be created by collecting this debt. He might sound disapproving, as if he were teaching a lesson the man should already know. The second sentence, since it differs in length from the first sentence, emphasizes the contrast between what the man wants Lincoln to do and what Lincoln thinks should be done. The tone of the voice would be decisive and firm.

Objectives

- To recognize and appreciate an anecdote as a form of literature
- To analyze an individual's character through that person's writings
- To analyze the organization of a nonfiction selection and how it affects the tone
- To apply literal, interpretive, and critical reading skills to a selection

Preparing the Students

Motivation. Tell the students that, in the selection they are about to read, Lincoln explains the things that he feels are more valuable than money. Have students predict what he might include. Have the students read the introductory paragraph on page 418 and tell in their own words what they should look for as they read the selection.

Presenting the Selection

1. Have the students read "Lawyer Lincoln Answers an Inquiry" silently.

2. Make sure that everyone has read the assignment by administering the **Check Test** at the bottom of this page.

3. Have a volunteer read the selection aloud.

4. Develop the study questions as suggested in **Using the Study Questions** below.

Using the Study Questions

It is recommended that students always read and answer the questions in **Developing Comprehension Skills** in class discussion. Whenever possible, they should also read the questions in **Reading Literature** together and discuss the answers.

Developing Comprehension Skills

Question 1. Read and discuss the question.

Question 2. Encourage students to discuss the worth of their own lives and the lives of those they love. Why is life considered so priceless? What makes it so valuable?

Question 3. Ask students whether the questioner ever received a straight answer. Did Lincoln want to answer the question? Have students explain why they agree or disagree with Lincoln's treatment of the question.

Lawyer Lincoln Answers an Inquiry

ABRAHAM LINCOLN

Someone asked Lincoln how a neighbor of his stood in terms of money and possessions. Lincoln's answer tells you something about what he thought of the question.

First of all, he has a wife and a baby; together they ought to be worth $500,000 to any man. Secondly, he has an office in which there is a table worth $1.50, and three chairs, worth, say $1.00. Last of all, there is in one corner a large rathole, which will bear looking into.

Respectfully,
A. Lincoln

Developing Comprehension Skills

Literal Reading 1. Was Lincoln's neighbor rich? Give a reason for your answer.

Interpretive Reading 2. Money was worth more a hundred years ago. If we suppose that a penny in Lincoln's time bought what a dime will buy now, then Lincoln placed the value of the man's wife and baby at about five million dollars in today's money. What did he mean by saying the wife and baby were worth that much money?

Critical Reading 3. What did Lincoln think of the question about the financial standing of his neighbor? Do you agree with him?

Check Test

1. What did Lincoln say the wife and baby were worth? ($500,000)

2. What were the table and chairs worth? (table—$1.50; chairs—$1.00)

3. What did Lincoln say was in one corner? (a large rathole)

Answers to Study Questions

Developing Comprehension Skills

1. Possible answers: No, he was not rich; he owned only a table and three chairs. Yes, he was rich in things that matter more than money, such as a family and love.

2. He meant that they were priceless, that they were more than anyone could imagine.

3. Lincoln was serious about placing the man's wife and child above his material possessions in value. But he really avoided answering the question. In his good-natured way, he told the questioner that people's financial standing is their own private business. Opinions of agreement or disagreement will vary.

Reading Literature: Nonfiction

1. **Analyzing the Organization.** In answering the question about his neighbor's finances, Lincoln lists three possessions. The first is priceless, the second is worth a moderate amount of money, and the third is worthless—in fact, ridiculous. Why did Lincoln name those three items in this order? How does the order help make Lincoln's point? How does it make the writing funny?
2. **Learning about Lincoln Through His Writing.** What can you learn about Lincoln from this note that you might not learn from someone else writing about Lincoln?

Appliqué Quilt commemorating the Century of Progress Exhibition of 1933. America Hurrah, New York City.

Reading Literature: Nonfiction

Question 1. Have students identify the three possessions. Ask them which possession Lincoln thought was most important and which was least important.

Question 2. Focus students' attention on Lincoln's use of words—his organization, his style, his humorous approach.

Reading Literature: Nonfiction

1. Lincoln lists the items in the order of importance. The most important things are the ones money can't buy. After these, he lists material items, showing how little they really are worth. He lists the last item, the rathole, both to be funny and to make sure the reader isn't offended.

2. This note tells the reader that Lincoln organized his ideas clearly and didn't waste words in his writing. He enjoyed making use of the multiple meanings of words. When he said the rathole "will bear looking into," he could have meant "should be examined" as well as the literal meaning of looking into a rathole.

About the Art

An appliqué quilt is made by filling two layers of cloth with a soft material and stitching it together in lines or patterns. The overall pattern on the quilt is then created by stitching layers of various materials to the existing fabric ground.

This quilt presents an interesting symmetrical design. The portrait of Lincoln balances that of Washington's. The original colonial flag is paired with the updated one for 1933. The technique as well as the historical subject matter of this appliqué quilt demonstrates the hard work and pioneer spirit of the American people. In addition, the symmetry in the overall design suggests a balance and agreeable harmony celebrated in America.

Objectives

- To appreciate the anecdote as a form of literature
- To understand how irony affects the tone of a selection
- To apply literal, interpretive, and critical reading skills to a selection

Preparing the Students

Essential Vocabulary. Have the students use the context clue to find the meaning of the underlined word.

One of the most important attributes, or qualities, of a good parent is patience.

Preparing the Students

Motivation. Ask the students to describe what a politician is. Then have them read the introductory paragraph on page 420 and ask them to state in their own words what they should try to find out as they read the selection. Have students predict Lincoln's opinion of politicians.

Presenting the Selection

1. Have the students read "On Political Skill" silently.
2. Administer the **Check Test**.
3. Have the selection read aloud.
4. Develop the study questions as suggested in **Using the Study Questions.**

Using the Study Questions

Developing Comprehension Skills

Question 1. Ask students for more examples of cause and effect, such as:

Cause: It rained on Saturday.
Effect: The picnic was called off.

Have students suggest examples of causes that people work for, such as the nuclear freeze movement or the women's movement. Help them see how politicians use those causes.

Question 2. Read and discuss the question.

Reading Literature: Nonfiction

Question 1. Focus students' attention on the double meaning of *cause.* Ask students to find the use of reptition for humorous effect in this selection.

Question 2. Make sure students understand the meaning of *irony.*

This short quote tells you what Lincoln thought of politicians. Was he praising or criticizing them?

On Political Skill

ABRAHAM LINCOLN

Abraham Lincoln, asked what he thought was the best attribute for a politician, said he thought it "would be the ability to raise a cause which would produce an effect and then fight the effect."

Developing Comprehension Skills

Literal Reading

1. The quote deals with cause and effect. Here is an example of the kind of cause and effect Lincoln had in mind.

   Cause: A person holds a lighted match next to a pile of newspapers
   Effect: The newspapers burn up.

   In your own words, say what Lincoln meant by this quote.

Interpretive Reading

2. What did Lincoln think of politicians?

Reading Literature: Nonfiction

1. **Appreciating Humor.** One thing which makes this quote humorous is the way it is worded. What is funny about the wording?

2. **Understanding Irony.** As you may remember, **irony** results when something happens that contradicts what was expected to happen. Often irony is humorous. After reading this quote, do you think it was ironic that Lincoln later went into politics himself? Explain your answer.

Check Test

1. What question did someone ask Lincoln? (to name the best attribute for a politician)

2. What would a politician with this attribute do after producing an effect? (fight the effect)

Answers to Study Questions

Developing Comprehension Skills

1. He meant that a politician often causes the trouble he works hard to fight against.

2. Answers will vary. Possible answers: He thought they were dishonest. He thought they were trouble makers. He thought they were unnecessary.

Reading Literature: Nonfiction.

1. The quote is funny because it is hard to follow, partly because of the long, complicated sentence and partly because of the two meanings of the word *cause.* The repetition of the word *effect* adds to the confusion and the humor.

2. It is ironic that, although it seems that Lincoln dislikes politicians, he eventually became one.

On Fooling the People

ABRAHAM LINCOLN

Lincoln made this statement shortly before he was elected President. People all over the world have repeated it.

You can fool all of the people some of the time, and some of the people all of the time, but you cannot fool all the people all of the time.

Developing Comprehension Skills

Interpretive Reading 1. From reading this statement, do you think Lincoln thought it was a good idea to try to fool people? Give a reason for your answer.

Interpretive Reading 2. What can you learn from this statement about Lincoln's attitude toward people?

Reading Literature: Nonfiction

1. **Understanding the Effect of Literary Style.** One reason this quote has been repeated through the years is its message. Another reason is the way it was written, or its **style**. Identify how Lincoln used repetition of words and balance of ideas. Do you suppose these techniques have contributed to the popularity of this saying? Explain your answer.

2. **Applying Lincoln's Ideas.** According to this saying, Lincoln thought it was wrong for leaders to try to fool people. Do you think his ideas still apply today? Are there any modern leaders who should be reminded of this warning?

Check Test

1. Whom does Lincoln say you can fool some of the time? (all the people)

2. Whom does Lincoln say you can fool all of the time? (some of the people)

Answers to Study Questions

Developing Comprehension Skills

1. No, Lincoln didn't think so. He says you will eventually get caught.

2. In most cases Lincoln respects people and thinks they should be dealt with honestly.

Reading Literature: Nonfiction

1. Lincoln repeats the words *fool, people,* and *time* in similar but slightly different phrases. In the first two phrases, he balances "all" and "some." He concludes by balancing two "all" phrases. The repetition and balance give the reader a satisfied, solid feeling.

2. Answers may vary. Generally, students should feel that it still applies today.

Objectives

- To recognize and appreciate the anecdote as a form of literature
- To analyze an individual's character through that person's writings
- To understand the effect of literary style
- To apply Lincoln's ideas to modern society
- To apply literal, interpretive, and critical reading skills to a selection

Preparing the Students

Essential Vocabulary. There are no difficult words in this selection.

Motivation. Ask students what it means to fool people. Have them share their experiences fooling someone else or being fooled themselves. Then have them read the introductory paragraph and then tell what they should find out as they read the selection.

Presenting the Selection

1. Have the students read "On Fooling the People" silently.

2. Administer the **Check Test**.

3. Ask students if they had ever heard this statement before. Did they know Lincoln was the first to say it?

4. Develop the study questions as suggested in **Using the Study Questions.**

Using the Study Questions

Developing Comprehension Skills

Question 1. Read and discuss the question.

Question 2. Ask students for reasons for their answers.

Reading Literature: Nonfiction

Question 1. Make sure that students understand what is meant by *style*. If necessary, refer to past selections in which elements of style were discussed, such as, "Lawyer Lincoln Turns Down a Case" and "On Political Skill."

Question 2. There is often a great deal of publicity focused on dishonest politicians. If students cannot think of examples themselves, provide them with some from the news, if possible.

If students do not suggest applying Lincoln's words to advertising and, possibly, the entertainment industry, you may wish to bring out these issues.

Objectives

- To recognize and appreciate the anecdote as a form of literature
- To analyze an individual's character through that person's writings
- To recognize and appreciate contrast in producing a humorous effect
- To recognize the style of a selection
- To apply literal, interpretive, and critical reading skills to a selection

Preparing the Students

Motivation. Ask the students if any of them have read or heard of *Uncle Tom's Cabin,* a novel written by Harriet Beecher Stowe. If not, tell them that the book focuses attention on the evils of slavery.

Then have the students read the introductory paragraph on page 422 and ask them to state what they should try to find out as they read the selection.

Presenting the Selection

1. Have one student read "On Meeting Harriet Beecher Stowe" aloud.

2. Administer the **Check Test.**

3. Have a volunteer read the selection aloud again, this time using the tone of voice Lincoln might have used.

4. Remind the students that the introduction to the selection asked them to find out what President Lincoln thought of Stowe. Have them answer the question.

5. Develop the study questions as suggested in **Using the Study Questions.**

Using the Study Questions

Developing Comprehension Skills

Question 1. Remind students that many words have multiple meanings. Ask students to define *great* in another way besides "wonderful," and list the different meanings on the chalkboard. Then have students decide whether *great* has positive connotations when it is used in each of these senses.

Question 2. Students should realize that wars are usually fought for many reasons, not just one reason. Have students decide whether Lincoln would have known that.

Reading Literature: Nonfiction

Questions 1 and 2. Read and discuss the questions.

On Meeting Harriet Beecher Stowe

ABRAHAM LINCOLN

Harriet Beecher Stowe wrote a novel about slavery, Uncle Tom's Cabin. After reading this book, many Northerners wanted to fight to abolish (get rid of) slavery. What did President Lincoln think of Mrs. Stowe?

So you're the little woman who
wrote the book that made this great war!

Developing Comprehension Skills

Literal Reading

1. What did President Lincoln mean when he said "this great war"? Did he mean the war was wonderful?

Critical Reading

2. Do you think Lincoln really felt that Mrs. Stowe made the war? Give a reason for your answer.

Reading Literature: Nonfiction

1. **Appreciating Contrast.** Humor is often developed by making contrasts. For example, the comedians Laurel and Hardy made good use of the contrast between Hardy's round shape and Laurel's thin shape. What contrast does Lincoln make in this quote? In your opinion, does this make the quote humorous?

2. **Recognizing Style.** Compare this quote to Lincoln's other short sayings in this section. Consider such techniques as sentence patterns, balance of ideas, repetition of words, and development from unimportant to important details (or the opposite). Does the style of this saying have anything in common with the other sayings?

   Imagine that Lincoln had said only "So this whole war is your fault!" Would his words have been remembered?

Check Test

1. How did Lincoln describe Harriet Beecher Stowe? (a little woman)

2. What did Stowe's book cause to happen? (a great war; the Civil War)

Answers to Study Questions

Developing Comprehension Skills

1. Lincoln meant that it was a big war, not a wonderful one.

2. No, Lincoln didn't think she caused the war directly. He meant that her book against slavery made a great number of people take a stand against slavery.

Reading Literature: Nonfiction

1. Lincoln made a contrast between a little woman and a great war. Opinions about the humor in the quote will vary.

2. The style of this quote is similar to that of other Lincoln quotes. Proofs will vary. Possible proofs include Lincoln's grouping of ideas or phrases in three's and his sharp contrast.

If Lincoln had not used this style, his words would not have been remembered as well as they are.

What Must God Think?

ABRAHAM LINCOLN

Lincoln wrote this during the Civil War, also called the War Between the States. Does it apply only to that war? Or is it true of every war?

We, on our side, are praying to Him to give us victory, because we believe we are right; but those on the other side pray to Him, look for victory, believing they are right. What must He think of us?

Developing Comprehension Skills

Literal Reading
1. What are both sides praying for?

Interpretive Reading
2. If Lincoln answered his own question ("What must He think of us?"), what do you think he would say? Give a reason for your answer, based on this paragraph.

Reading Literature: Nonfiction

1. **Understanding Irony.** This paragraph can be read seriously. However, suppose you read it as ironic humor. What does it tell you about Lincoln's personality? Does it tell anything about his opinion of human nature?

Objectives

- To recognize and appreciate the anecdote as a form of literature
- To understand ironic humor
- To appreciate how a theme can apply to similar situations in any time period
- To apply literal, interpretive, and critical reading skills to a selection
- To be aware of possible confusion caused by certain words
- To write a humorous personal anecdote
- To use library resources in research
- To present an oral interpretation of an anecdote

Preparing the Students

Motivation. Make sure that all of the students know that the American Civil War, or War Between the States, was fought from 1861 to 1865 and was waged for a number of reasons, particularly because of differences of opinion concerning states' rights and slavery. Then have the students read the introductory paragraph on page 423 and ask them to state in their own words what they should decide as they read the selection.

Presenting the Selection

1. Have the students read "What Must God Think?" silently.

2. Administer the **Check Test.**

3. Have a volunteer read the selection aloud in a tone of voice that reflects Lincoln's attitude about human nature.

4. Remind the students that the introduction to the selection asked them to decide if what Lincoln wrote applies just to the Civil War or to all wars. Have them discuss this question. Ask, also, what other kinds of things the Civil War might have in common with other wars.

Check Test

1. During the war, what are we praying to God to give us? (victory)

2. Why do we pray to God to help us win a war? (We believe we are right.)

Answers to Study Questions

Developing Comprehension Skills

1. Both are praying for victory.

2. God must think humans are proud, stubborn, and confused because both sides think they deserve to win. (Accept any thoughtful answer with this idea.)

Reading Literature: Nonfiction

1. Lincoln seems to understand human nature, but he also becomes impatient with its failings.

2. This saying can apply to any war or conflict. When you are involved in a conflict, Lincoln's words can help you remember that the other person feels he or she is right too.

Challenge. Answers will vary, but students should include the idea that these sayings are a clever way of putting into words something that a lot of people believe.

Developing Vocabulary Skills

a. advice—(5)
b. advise—(3)
c. effect—(1)
d. affect—(6)
e. except—(4)
f. accept—(2)

1. effect, noun
2. affect, verb
3. advise, verb
4. advice, noun
5. except, preposition
6. accept, verb
7. except, preposition
8. advise, verb

5. Develop the study questions as suggested in **Using the Study Questions.** That section also provides a challenge question for further discussion.

Reinforcing the Lesson

To reteach, reinforce, or extend the skills in this lesson, see the following:

Skills and Practice Book, Green Level
—pages 166 and 167

Special Populations

LD, ESL. These students may have difficulty translating the respelling of the words for the exercise **Recognizing Confusing Words** on page 424. Students will need assistance to complete this exercise.

Encouraging Independent Reading

John F. Kennedy, like Lincoln, was known for his witty and humorous sayings. Challenge students to find quotations from Kennedy that show his feelings about human nature, war, or politics. Have students report their findings to the class.

Using the Study Questions

It is recommended that students always read and answer the questions in **Developing Comprehension Skills** in class discussion.

Developing Comprehension Skills

Question 1. Read and discuss.

Question 2. Students should realize that Lincoln is giving an opinion about war in this comment. He is subtlely stating a disapproval of it.

Reading Literature: Nonfiction

Question 1. Have two volunteers read the selection aloud. The first should read it in a serious tone of voice. The second should try to read it with a wry, humorous tone. You may want to read it aloud yourself with a humorous tone.

Question 2. Stress the idea that great literature contains ideas that are meaningful to people in a wide variety of places and times. Point out that it is because of this characteristic of literature that anecdotes and sayings can be classified as literature, despite their brevity. Students should recognize that these anecdotes have appeal and meaning not only to people who are informed about and interested in the Civil War, but also to people facing similar situations today.

Challenge Question. Why have sayings and writings such as these lasted for a century?

Developing Vocabulary Skills

Have students read the directions and complete the exercise independently. As the exercise is discussed in class, make sure students know how to distinguish between each pair of words and how to use each word correctly. Then have them suggest sample sentences of their own, using words from the given word list. They should spell the word they used, and the class should determine if they used the given word correctly.

Developing Writing Skills

Read and discuss the two assignments. Then have the students choose and complete one of the two.

Question 1. You may want to have groups of students work together on the pre-writing section of the assignment.

2. **Appreciating Theme.** Some things are written or said to apply only to a specific time and place. Other writings and sayings can apply to similar situations at any time. In which category would you place this saying by Lincoln? How does this help make Lincoln's words worth remembering?

Developing Vocabulary Skills

Recognizing Confusing Words. Some of the words in the selections you have read are often confused with other words. They look very much alike and may have similar meanings. Read the following list of words. Match each word with its respelling. Then read the sentences below. Choose the correct word to fill in each blank. Write the part of speech of each word as it is used in the sentence. You may use a dictionary if you need to.

a. advice	(1) ə fekt′
b. advise	(2) ək sept′
c. effect	(3) əd vīz′
d. affect	(4) ek sept′
e. except	(5) əd vīs′
f. accept	(6) a fekt′

1. Abraham Lincoln thought that a good politician should be able to raise a cause which would produce an _____.
2. Exercise can _____ the way we feel.
3. Dr. Chisholm did _____ my father to consult Dr. Alexander Graham Bell.
4. Acting on the doctor's _____, we immediately took a train to Washington.
5. At that time I did not like to have anyone kiss me _____ my own mother.
6. Having adventure in his blood, Henson did _____ Peary's offer for the job.
7. Peary once said of Henson, "He is a better dog driver than any man living _____ for some of the best Eskimo hunters themselves."
8. We would _____ you to try your hand at making six hundred dollars in some other way.

Developing Writing Skills

Analytical Writing

1. **Identifying Humor.** Choose a saying that you think is funny. Write a paragraph telling why you think your choice is humorous.

Creative Writing

2. **Writing Humor.** In the humorous sayings and writings you have read, Lincoln used several means of making his statements funny. Sometimes he made a funny contrast. Sometimes irony made the writing funny. At other times there was a build-up of details. Using these or other techniques, write a humorous paragraph about some event in the news or in your own life.

Developing Skills in Study and Research

Using Library Skills. Other people besides Abe Lincoln have made humorous statements. Go to your library to find some books containing humorous quotations. First, you will need to find out how collections of quotations are listed. Make use of the card catalog. If necessary, ask the librarian for help. Once you have found several books of humorous quotations and sayings, write down their titles and authors. Explain briefly how you found the books.

Now read at least one short passage from one of the books you found. Be ready to explain whether you thought it was humorous, and to tell why or why not.

Developing Skills in Speaking and Listening

Performing a Humorous Saying. Most of these sayings and writings have a serious side as well as a humorous side. They were said for a reason. Choose one of the sayings and memorize it. Practice saying it so that your audience will understand the serious part of it but will also see the humor. As you practice, consider these questions: What should the **pitch** of your voice be? Should the whole saying be said at the same level, or should your voice go up and down with the meaning? What **pace**, or speed, should you use? Can you make **eye contact** with your audience? Is there **feeling** in your voice?

Working together may help students remember funny sayings.

Pre-Writing. Make it clear to students that they need not limit their choices to Lincoln's sayings. Briefly review some of the techniques Lincoln used for humorous effect—such as complicated sentences, balanced sentences with words repeated, contrast, irony, exaggeration—and list them on the chalkboard.

Give students time to remind each other of funny sayings they have heard. Group members should discuss several of those sayings, identifying which of the techniques listed on the board, or others, make each saying funny.

Then, working independently, each student should select a single saying to write about, and should note all the reasons he or she can think of for its humorous effect. Last, the student should number the reasons in decreasing order of importance. Leave the techniques on the board for the students to refer to while they are working.

Writing. Have students begin their papers by writing the saying first, separate from the paragraph. Then they should start the paragraph with a topic sentence that gives an opinion about the saying or about the causes for its humor. The causes should then be listed and explained. Allow sufficient time for students to complete the assignment independently.

Revising. Have the students exchange papers with partners. Have the partners check to make sure they understand what the saying was and why the writer felt it was funny. Allow time for revisions.

Question 2. Writing humor is extremely difficult for some students. This question should be assigned only to students who want to try it.

Pre-Writing. Have each student make his or her own list of possible topics. Ask students to think about what they can say about each. Have them decide which techniques might work with their topics.

Writing. As students write, they may find that the topic is not workable after all. Encourage students to return to the pre-writing stage if they are stuck. Remind them to use the techniques for humorous writing that they learned in the past few selections, as well as other techniques they already know.

Revising. Have volunteers read their stories to the class. You may wish to assemble clean copies into a "book" called *A Funny Thing Happened.*

Developing Skills in Study and Research

Call on students to read aloud the directions for this assignment. Remind them of the various skills they have acquired in using the library and explain that they need to be able to find information independently.

When students bring back the information they have found, have them compare the methods they used for locating the material they wanted. As they discuss their methods, have them decide which ones were the most efficient.

Developing Skills in Speaking and Listening

Have students read aloud the directions for this assignment. Discuss with the whole class the questions and techniques listed in the assignment. Students who have found quotes or sayings that they particularly like while they were completing their research assignment might be allowed to substitute those for the Lincoln excerpts.

Since these sayings are so short, you may be able to schedule all the students to present their choices to the class as a whole. Set a date for presentations and have students practice outside of class.

When the presentations are made, the listeners could give instant ratings on the effectiveness of the speaker's pitch, variation, pacing, and eye contact.

Objectives

- To appreciate the anecdote as a form of literature
- To recognize the use and purposes of humor in nonfiction
- To apply literal, interpretive, and critical reading skills to a selection

Preparing the Students

Motivation. Remind the students that an anecdote is a short account of some happening in a person's life, and that frequently anecdotes are humorous. Ask the students what they learned about Lincoln's personality by reading his sayings. Then have the students read the introductory paragraph on page 426 and ask them to state in their own words what they should try to find out as they read this anecdote.

Presenting the Selection

1. Have the students read "Horse Trade" silently.

2. Administer the **Check Test.**

3. Have a volunteer read the selection aloud.

4. Remind the students that the introduction to the selection asked them to find out something about Abraham Lincoln. Have them answer the question.

5. Develop the study questions as suggested in **Using the Study Questions.**

Using the Study Questions

Developing Comprehension Skills

Question 1. Read and discuss the question.

Question 2. Students may not agree with Lincoln's opinion. Discuss with them Lincoln's reasoning.

Challenge Question: Why do you think Lincoln stared in silence at the old horse so long? (Interpretive Reading)

Reading Literature: Nonfiction

Point out that this anecdote sounds like a joke, and may not have really happened. However, people were willing to believe it happened to Lincoln. Can students identify characteristics in previous sayings and writings known to be Lincoln's that would make people connect this joke with Lincoln?

Horse Trade

BEATRICE SCHENK de REGNIERS

Before there were cars, horses provided the fastest transportation. A horse trade was an important event. What can you learn about Abraham Lincoln from this anecdote?

Lincoln and the judge were joking about who could make the better horse trade. At last they agreed to meet in the morning to swap horses. Lincoln would not see the judge's horse beforehand. And the judge would not see Lincoln's horse.

The next morning a crowd gathered. Who would get the better of the trade?

The judge came first, dragging behind him the oldest, sorriest, boniest nag that ever managed to stand on four feet.

While the crowd was still laughing, Lincoln came along, carrying a carpenter's wooden saw horse. For a full minute Lincoln stared at the judge's horse without saying a word.

"Judge," said Lincoln at last, "this is the first time I ever got the worst of it in a horse trade."

Developing Comprehension Skills

Literal Reading — 1. Lincoln brought a horse to the horse trade. Was it the kind of horse that everyone expected?

Interpretive Reading — 2. Why did Lincoln decide that he had gotten the worst of the trade?

Reading Literature: Nonfiction

Inferring Character Traits. Lincoln's sense of humor comes through in his bringing a saw horse to the trade. He is playing a joke on the judge. After it is all over with, at whom else is he laughing? What does this tell you about his personality?

Check Test

1. What kind of horse did Lincoln bring to the trade? (a sawhorse)

2. Whom did Lincoln think got the worst of the trade? (himself)

Answers to Study Questions

Developing Comprehension Skills

1. No, people expected a live horse. Lincoln brought a wooden sawhorse.

2. The judge's old nag was of no use, while Lincoln's sawhorse was useful.

Challenge. Lincoln might have been trying to decide who got the better of the deal. He might have been thinking about what to say. He might have been setting up the crowd to appreciate his punch line.

Reading Literature: Nonfiction

He is laughing at himself, which shows that he is not too proud to see humor in his own actions.

Here is a funny story about Abraham Lincoln. Can you explain what is funny about it?

No Trouble

BEATRICE SCHENK de REGNIERS

Lawyer Lincoln, so they say, was walking along a dusty road. Along came a farmer driving his wagon to town.

Lincoln. Would you be good enough to take my overcoat to town for me?
Farmer. Glad to. But how will you get it back again?
Lincoln. No trouble at all. I'm going to stay right inside it!

Developing Comprehension Skills

Literal Reading — 1. What was "no trouble"?

Interpretive Reading — 2. What was Lincoln really asking the farmer?

Reading Literature: Nonfiction

1. **Understanding Tone.** What is the tone of this anecdote; that is, what is the attitude of the author?

2. **Applying Your Knowledge.** From your knowledge of Abraham Lincoln, do you think this occurrence really happened, or that he made up this story, or that someone else invented it about him? Give a reason for your answer.

Check Test

1. What did Lincoln ask the farmer to take to town? (his overcoat)

2. What did the farmer ask Lincoln? (how Lincoln would get his coat back again)

Answers to Study Questions

Developing Comprehension Skills

1. Getting the coat back was "no trouble."

2. Lincoln was asking for a ride to town.

Reading Literature: Nonfiction

1. Possible answers: The tone is humorous, good-natured, and light. There is also admiration and appreciation of Lincoln's wit.

2. Answers may vary. The story is consistent with Lincoln's personality, so it is possible that this event really happened.

Objectives

- To define and identify the characteristics of an anecdote
- To recognize and appreciate humor in nonfiction
- To apply one's knowledge of an author to determining the origin of a written account
- To apply literal, interpretive, and critical reading skills to a selection

Preparing the Students

Motivation. Tell the students to examine the appearance of this next anecdote. Have them notice the names in boldface print and the placement of the sentences. Explain that the form means that the selection is a conversation.

Then have the students read the introductory paragraph on page 427. Ask them to state in their own words what they should try to find out as they read the selection.

Presenting the Selection

1. Have the students read "No Trouble" silently.

2. Make sure that everyone has read the assignment by administering the **Check Test** at the bottom of this page.

3. Have volunteers read the parts of Lincoln and the farmer aloud.

4. Remind the students of the question in the introduction. Have them answer it.

5. Develop the study questions as suggested in **Using the Study Questions.**

Using the Study Questions

It is recommended that students always read and answer the questions in **Developing Comprehension Skills** in class discussion. Whenever possible, they should also read the questions in **Reading Literature** together and discuss the answers.

Developing Comprehension Skills

Question 1. Read and discuss.

Question 2. Once students have answered this question, ask them why Lincoln would choose to ask for a ride in this way.

Reading Literature: Nonfiction

Question 1. Read and discuss.

Question 2. Encourage students to refer to specific selections they have read to help prove their opinions.

Objectives

- To identify the anecdote as a form of literature
- To compare types of literature
- To understand the role of setting
- To apply literal, interpretive, and critical reading skills to a selection

Preparing the Students

Motivation. Ask students to examine the illustration of the statue of Abraham Lincoln on page 428. Have them point out the physical characteristics the sculptor was emphasizing in his representation of Lincoln. Then have the students read the introductory paragraph at the top of the same page and ask them to state in their own words what they should think about as they read the selection.

Presenting the Selection

1. Have the students read "The Longest Leg" silently.

2. Make sure that everyone has read the assignment by administering the **Check Test** at the bottom of this page.

3. Have a volunteer read the selection aloud.

4. Remind the students of the questions posed in the introduction to the selection. Ask several students for their answers.

5. Develop the study questions as suggested in **Using the Study Questions** on page 429. That section also provides a challenge question for further discussion, as needed.

The Longest Leg

BEATRICE SCHENK de REGNIERS

As you read this anecdote, consider two questions: Do you think this event really happened? Do you think Mr. Lincoln was being rude?

One day a man came to Abraham Lincoln's law office. He saw Lincoln sitting with one leg stretched across the desk.

"Why Mr. Lincoln," said the man, "that's the longest leg I've ever seen!"

"Here's another just like it," said Lincoln. And he put his other leg across the desk.

Abraham Lincoln, 1938–39, WILLIAM NORRIS.
Wood carving from a single log. Abbey Aldrich Rockefeller Folk Art Center, Williamsburg, Virginia.

About the Art

William Norris (1861-1946) is said to have carved this wood sculpture of Abraham Lincoln from a single log, using a pocket knife for the details. The single log recalls that, as a young man, Lincoln worked for a time as a rail splitter, fencing in the Illinois farmland. The young Lincoln was noted for the strength and skill with which he could wield an ax. Norris seems to have exaggerated Lincoln's height and his thinness; the head seems tiny in comparison to the body. The left hand holds the lapel of the simple coat in the pose of a country lawyer or orator. (See also page 414.)

Check Test

1. What was stretched across Lincoln's desk? (his leg)

2. What was the man's comment about what he saw? ("That's the longest leg I've ever seen.")

Developing Comprehension Skills

Interpretive Reading 1. Why do you think the man commented on Abe's leg?

Critical Reading 2. In Lincoln's time, as today, putting your leg on your desk would be considered impolite or undignified. What does this story show about Lincoln's attitude toward rules of polite behavior? Give a reason for your answer.

Reading Literature: Nonfiction

1. **Comparing Types of Literature.** The sayings of a famous person are usually brief quotes by that person about specific topics. Anecdotes are humorous stories about the person. In what ways is this anecdote like the legends or short stories you have read? What elements do they have in common?
2. **Understanding the Role of Setting.** What is the setting of this anecdote? Would it matter if the event took place somewhere other than in Lincoln's own office?
3. **Analyzing the Tone.** Judging from his words, what do you think was the attitude of the man coming to Lincoln's office? Was he shocked? Was he kidding or criticizing? What was the tone of Lincoln's response? Was he being rude? Give reasons for your answers.

Using the Study Questions

It is recommended that students always read and answer the questions in **Developing Comprehension Skills** in class discussion. Whenever possible, they should also read the questions in **Reading Literature** together and discuss the answers.

Developing Comprehension Skills

Question 1. If any students object to the idea that the visitor had the motive of criticism, point out that the visitor would probably have considered it rude to criticize Lincoln face to face in an open fashion.

Question 2. After students have answered this question, ask them what part Lincoln's background might have played in his attitude toward manners.

Challenge Question. Suppose you went to a lawyer's office and the lawyer kept his legs up on the desk throughout your visit. What would you think of the lawyer's personality? (Critical Reading)

Reading Literature: Nonfiction

Question 1. Briefly review the elements of legends and short stories. List them on the board before students answer this question.

Question 2. To answer this question, have students decide whether they act more relaxed in their own homes than they do at friends' homes.

Question 3. Have students reread the anecdote. Stress that there is no single right answer to this question, but that students must be able to give reasons for their answers.

Answers to Study Questions

Developing Comprehension Skills

1. He commented because it was so long. It may also have been a hint that Lincoln should take his leg off his desk.

2. It shows that he didn't think that rules of polite behavior were important at all times. Lincoln made sure the visitor knew his attitude by putting his other leg up, too.

Challenge. Answers may vary. Possible answers:

a. The lawyer was relaxed and comfortable, treating me as a close friend.

b. The lawyer was rude and sloppy, treating me without respect.

Reading Literature: Nonfiction

1. All three types feature characters in a setting. They all have plots and themes, and the way they are presented creates a mood.

2. Yes, Lincoln would feel freer to do as he pleased in his own office. In another person's office, such an act might be insulting.

3. Answers will vary. Accept any interpretation that is supported by logical reasoning.

Objectives

- To recognize the anecdote as a form of literature
- To recognize how literature reflects its time
- To apply literal, interpretive, and critical reading skills to a selection

Preparing the Students

Motivation. Have students read the introductory paragraph on page 430 and ask them to state in their own words what they should try to find out as they read.

Presenting the Selection

1. Have the students read "A Lincoln Riddle" silently.

2. Administer the **Check Test**.

3. Ask volunteers to read the parts of Lincoln and the man aloud. Have another student read the final paragraph.

4. Remind the students that the introduction to the selection directed them to find out something else about Lincoln. Ask them what they learned about him.

5. Develop the study questions as suggested in **Using the Study Questions**.

Encouraging Independent Reading

Building on the theme of riddles, suggest students do any of the following:

1. Make a collection of riddles.

2. From a book on quotations, find a quote that they feel Abraham Lincoln might have liked.

3. Collect riddles some of the students have written and provide them in a notebook for the rest of the class to read.

A Lincoln Riddle

BEATRICE SCHENK de REGNIERS

Now you will read two riddles. We are not sure if Lincoln made them up, but he did use them. As you read this first riddle, see what it tells you about Mr. Lincoln.

Lincoln. If you call a sheep's tail a leg, how many legs will a sheep have?

Man. Five legs, of course.

Lincoln. Wrong. A sheep has four legs. Even if you call a tail a leg, it is still a tail.

Lincoln used this riddle to help him win an argument. Lincoln was trying to explain that just *saying* a thing is true does not make it true.

Developing Comprehension Skills

Interpretive Reading

1. What kind of argument do you suppose Lincoln was having when he used this riddle? Give a reason for your answer.

Critical Reading

2. Why would Lincoln or anyone else like to use humor in an argument?

Reading Literature: Nonfiction

Recognizing How Literature Reflects Its Time. The example Lincoln used in this riddle, sheep, is a reflection of his environment. In modern times, we might use a different example. What does the example used tell you about his environment?

Using the Study Questions

Developing Comprehension Skills

Question 1. If students have difficulty with this question, have them reread the paragraph that follows the riddle.

Question 2. Ask students what happens when two people are arguing and becoming angry, and then one of them suddenly says something funny.

Reading Literature: Nonfiction

After students answer this question, ask them what kinds of examples might be used in modern times.

Check Test

1. How many legs did the man say a sheep might have? (five)

2. Why did Lincoln use this riddle? (to help him win an argument)

Answers to Study Questions

Developing Comprehension Skills

1. Answers should include the idea that it was an argument in which his opponent was claiming that something was true without proof.

2. Arguments can turn mean and spiteful. Humor can sometimes prevent people from losing their tempers.

Reading Literature: Nonfiction

The environment was agricultural, and so many people were familiar with farm animals.

Another Riddle

Read the first part of this riddle. Then stop and see if you can answer it yourself before you read the answer.

BEATRICE SCHENK de REGNIERS

Lincoln may have heard this riddle when he was a boy in Indiana. He used it when he was President to show that the right answer in arithmetic can sometimes be the wrong answer when you are dealing with pigeons or people:

Lincoln. If there be three pigeons on the fence, and you fire and kill one, how many will there be left?

Answer. Two?

Lincoln. No. There will be none left. For the other two birds, frightened by the shot, would have flown away.

Developing Comprehension Skills

Literal Reading

1. The answer to the question in this riddle seems simple: three pigeons take away one pigeon leaves two pigeons. The simple answer is not correct, however, because an important fact has been left out of the question. What fact was left out?

Critical Reading

2. Why do you think Lincoln used a riddle about pigeons and not about people?

Reading Literature: Nonfiction

Comparing Types of Literature. Sometimes an anecdote can be like a fable. It can teach a lesson and have a moral. "Another Riddle" is an example of this kind of anecdote. Identify the moral of this riddle.

Objectives

- To recognize the anecdote as a form of literature
- To compare types of literature
- To apply literal, interpretive, and critical reading skills to a selection

Preparing the Students

Motivation. Have the students read the introductory paragraph on page 431. Ask them to state in their own words what they are to do.

Presenting the Selection

1. Have the students read "Another Riddle" silently.

2. Make sure that everyone has read the assignment by administering the **Check Test** at the bottom of this page.

3. Ask a student to read the first paragraph aloud. Then ask volunteers to read the parts of Lincoln and the person who answers the riddle.

4. Develop the study questions as suggested in **Using the Study Questions** below.

Using the Study Questions

It is recommended that students always read and answer the questions in **Developing Comprehension Skills** in class discussion. Whenever possible, they should also read the questions in **Reading Literature** together and discuss the answers.

Developing Comprehension Skills

Questions 1 and 2. Read and discuss the questions.

Reading Literature: Nonfiction

Briefly review what a fable is: a short story that teaches a lesson. Make sure students understand that the moral of a story is the lesson it teaches, the point it is making. Then have them identify the moral of this riddle.

Check Test

1. What is the expected answer to the riddle? (two)

2. What was Lincoln's answer to the riddle? (none)

Answers to Study Questions

Developing Comprehension Skills

1. The missing fact is the reaction of the other two pigeons to the shot.

2. By using pigeons instead of people, Lincoln made sure that the moral could apply to anyone, not just the people he mentioned in the story.

Reading Literature: Nonfiction

Possible answers: Things can be more complex than they seem. Don't draw conclusions without all the facts. Also, you can't ignore emotions when you try to solve a problem.

Objectives

- To appreciate the anecdote as a form of literature
- To recognize the use and purposes of humor in nonfiction
- To recognize the organization of an anecdote
- To apply literal, interpretive, and critical reading skills to a selection

Preparing the Students

Motivation. Have the students read the introductory paragraph on page 432 and ask them to state in their own words what they should try to find out as they read this selection.

Presenting the Selection

1. Have the students read "Lincoln Tells a Story About the King, the Farmer, and the Donkey" silently.

2. Make sure that everyone has read the assignment by administering the **Check Test** at the bottom of this page.

3. Have volunteers read the selection aloud.

4. Remind the students that the introduction to the selection asked them to find out how Lincoln used his sense of humor to solve a problem. Have them answer the question.

5. Develop the study questions as suggested in **Using the Study Questions** on page 433. That section also provides a challenge question for further discussion, as needed.

Lincoln Tells a Story About the King, the Farmer, and the Donkey

Abraham Lincoln was a humorous man. Yet he had a serious job, and there was a war going on. See how he used his sense of humor to help solve a real problem.

BEATRICE SCHENK de REGNIERS

One day President Lincoln found twenty men in his office waiting to see him. They all wanted jobs in the government. And they all had letters and other papers with them saying what smart men they were—what good work they could do.

These men didn't seem to understand that the President did not have time to give to the many, many people who came to him for jobs. There was a civil war going on. How could the President turn these job-hunters away without hurting their feelings? Maybe he could do it with a story.

"Gentlemen," said President Lincoln, "let me tell you a story I read long ago."

There was once a King who wanted to go hunting. He called the man who was Chief Weatherman and Court Minister.

"Tell me," said the King, "will it rain today?"

"No, your Majesty," said the Chief Weatherman and Court Minister. "The weather is clear. It won't rain. Good hunting to you!"

The King set out with his hunting party. On the way they met a farmer riding on a donkey. "Don't try to go hunting today, Your Majesty," said the farmer. "It is going to rain."

The King laughed and rode on. Surely the Court Minister knew better than a simple farmer!

But just as the King reached the forest, it began to rain. Oh, how it poured! The King and everyone with him were soaked to the skin.

When the King got home, he fired the Court Minister. Then he sent for the farmer.

"From now on," said the King, "you will have the job of Chief Weatherman and Court Minister. Now tell me, how did you know it would rain?"

"I didn't," said the farmer. "It's my donkey who knows when it is going to rain. He puts his ears forward when wet weather is coming; he puts them back when it's going to be dry. So you see, Your Majesty, I cannot take the job."

The King sent the farmer away and sent for the donkey. And the King gave the donkey the job of Chief Weatherman and Court Minister.

"And that," said Lincoln, "is when the King made a great mistake."

"Why do you say that?" asked one of the job-hunters.

"Why, ever since that time," said Lincoln, "every donkey wants a job with the government."

The men couldn't help laughing. And then Lincoln told them, "Gentlemen, leave your letters and papers with me, and when the war is over, you will hear from me."

Abraham Lincoln, 1861, ALEXANDER GARDNER.
National Portrait Gallery, Smithsonian Institution, Washington D.C.

Developing Comprehension Skills

Literal Reading — 1. Why did President Lincoln tell this fable?

Literal Reading — 2. Why did the King come to the conclusion that he should fire his Chief Weatherman and hire the farmer?

Critical Reading — 3. Do you think that President Lincoln achieved his purpose for telling this story? Give a reason for your answer.

Reading Literature: Nonfiction

Finding the Organization. This anecdote contains two stories. How are they connected? In other words, how is the anecdote organized?

Using the Study Questions

It is recommended that students always read and answer the questions in **Developing Comprehension Skills** in class discussion. Whenever possible, they should also read the questions in **Reading Literature** together and discuss the answers.

Developing Comprehension Skills

Question 1. If necessary, have students reread the beginning of the anecdote to find the answer.

Questions 2 and 3. Have students find evidence for their answers in the selection.

Reading Literature: Nonfiction

Make sure every student can see where the story Lincoln told begins and ends.

Challenge Question. Lincoln compared the job-hunters to donkeys. Why was this more effective than comparing them to other animals, such as the farmer's dog or his chickens?

Check Test

1. Why did the twenty men come to see President Lincoln? (They wanted jobs in the government.)

2. How did the donkey tell the farmer it was going to rain? (by moving his ears forward)

Answers to Study Questions

Developing Comprehension Skills

1. Lincoln told the story to turn away job-seekers without hurting their feelings.

2. His Chief Weatherman had given the King the wrong prediction and the farmer had been right.

3. Lincoln did achieve his purpose. The selection states, "The men couldn't help laughing." They saw that they were the donkeys in the story and knew they would not be getting jobs from Lincoln for a long time.

Reading Literature: Nonfiction

The writer explains why Lincoln told the story first, leading logically into the story. After the story, the writer describes the men's reaction and Lincoln's parting words to them.

Challenge. The word *donkey* has connotations of ignorance and stubbornness. These connotations would communicate Lincoln's meaning more clearly than any connotations attached to any other animals.

Objectives

- To appreciate the anecdote as a form of nonfiction literature
- To learn about history from nonfiction
- To apply literal, interpretive, and critical reading skills to a selection

Preparing the Students

Motivation. Have the students read the introductory paragraph on page 434 and ask them to state in their own words what they should try to find out as they read this selection.

Presenting the Selection

1. Have the students read "A Pass to Richmond" silently.

2. Make sure that everyone has read the assignment by administering the **Check Test** at the bottom of this page.

3. If possible and necessary, point out on a wall map the positions of Washington, D.C., and Richmond, Virginia. Have a volunteer read the selection aloud.

4. Remind the students that the introduction to the selection asked them to find out how Lincoln's humor helped him deal with this problem. Have them answer the question.

5. Develop the study questions as suggested in **Using the Study Questions** on page 435.

Special Populations

LD. Some students may read several of the humorous pieces about Lincoln and not see the subtle twists of logic in them. Ask students to retell the stories in their own words to check for comprehension.

A Pass to Richmond

BEATRICE SCHENK de REGNIERS

During the Civil War, the North needed to take Richmond, Virginia. General McClellan was in charge of this mission but was not doing anything. How did Lincoln's humor help him deal with this problem?

President Lincoln had been trying for a long time to get General McClellan to march south with his army and take the city of Richmond, Virginia.

One day, while Lincoln was worrying about this problem, a businessman came to see him. The man asked for a pass so that he could go to—of all places—Richmond, Virginia.

"A pass to Richmond?" said Lincoln with a sigh. "My dear sir, it would do you no good. I have given McClellan passes for two hundred and fifty thousand men . . . and not one of them has got there yet!"

President Lincoln meeting General George B. McClellan at Antietam, Maryland, 1862. Culver Pictures, New York.

Check Test

1. What did President Lincoln want General McClellan to do? (to march south and take the city of Richmond)

2. Why did the businessman come to see Lincoln? (He wanted a pass to go to Richmond.)

Answers to Study Questions

Developing Comprehension Skills

1. Lincoln's orders for the 250,000 soldiers in McClellan's army to go to Rich-

Developing Comprehension Skills

Literal Reading

1. In what sense had Lincoln given 250,000 men passes? Who were the men? Why hadn't they gotten to Richmond yet?

Interpretive Reading

2. Nowadays, you would not need a pass from the President to travel to another city. In the anecdote, why did the businessman need a pass to travel to Richmond?

Reading Literature: Nonfiction

1. **Learning about History from Literature.** Literature often tells much about the times and places in which it was written. Tell three things about the Civil War that you can learn from this anecdote.

2. **Evaluating Background Information.** Is it possible that Lincoln felt more deeply about the situation than this anecdote shows? Was he using humor because this was a light matter or to relieve a serious, tense problem? What else would you need to know in order to answer these questions?

Anecdotes 435

Using the Study Questions

It is recommended that students always read and answer the questions in **Developing Comprehension Skills** in class discussion. Whenever possible, they should also read the questions in **Reading Literature** together and discuss the answers.

Developing Comprehension Skills

Question 1. Read and discuss the question.

Question 2. If necessary, remind the students that the country was at war.

Reading Literature: Nonfiction

Question 1. List answers on the board as students suggest them.

Question 2. Ask students what happens when they are tense or afraid and someone says something that makes them laugh. Then have them try to relate their own reactions to this question.

mond were the passes. McClellan hadn't led the army there yet.

2. In a war, the government needed to be careful about people traveling near or through enemy lines. A pass would identify the man as a private citizen, not a soldier, the man might need to prove he was not a Confederate spy.

Reading Literature: Nonfiction

1. Possible answers: McClellan was general of the Northern army. The North needed to take control of Richmond, Virginia. McClellan had 250,000 soldiers. Lincoln didn't have complete control of the decisions of his generals. Northern businessmen still had dealings with southern people. During the war, people needed passes to travel.

2. Students should recognize that Lincoln felt that taking Richmond was a serious matter. To know Lincoln's feelings more exactly and certainly, we would need more information about the importance of Richmond and Lincoln's relationship with McClellan.

Objectives

- To identify characteristics of an anecdote
- To understand the tone of a selection
- To recognize irony
- To apply literal, interpretive, and critical reading skills to a selection

Preparing the Students

Motivation. Discuss the meaning of the term *sarcasm*. Have students give examples. Tell them that Lincoln uses sarcasm in this selection. Have the students read the introduction on page 436 and tell what they should think about as they read this selection.

Presenting the Selection

1. Have the students read "Borrow the Army" silently.

2. Administer the **Check Test**.

3. Have a volunteer read the selection aloud.

4. Remind the students that the introduction to the selection asked them to find out how they would react to Lincoln's statement if they were General McClellan. Have several students answer the question.

5. Develop the study questions as suggested in **Using the Study Questions**.

Using the Study Questions

It is recommended that students always read and answer the questions in **Developing Comprehension Skills** in class discussion. Whenever possible, they should also read the questions in **Reading Literature** together and discuss the answers.

Developing Comprehension Skills

Question 1. If necessary, have students reread the previous selection.

Question 2. Point out to students how visualizing something that seems ridiculous makes it funny, for example, borrowing anything as huge as an army.

Reading Literature: Nonfiction

Question 1. Help students to recognize that Lincoln's request may have been asked on two levels: On a surface level, it was humorous, but on a deeper level, it was serious.

Question 2. Discuss with the students both irony and sarcasm. Ask students what Lincoln really means in this anecdote.

Borrow the Army

BEATRICE SCHENK de REGNIERS

President Lincoln makes another joke about General McClellan's slowness. If you were General McClellan, how would you react to this statement?

"If General McClellan is not using the army," said Lincoln, "I would like to borrow it for a while."

Developing Comprehension Skills

Literal Reading

1. From reading the previous selection, tell what Lincoln meant by McClellan "not using the army."

Interpretive Reading

2. Why is it funny for Lincoln to ask to borrow the army? Whose army was it? Could Lincoln borrow it?

Reading Literature: Nonfiction

1. **Understanding the Tone.** What tone of voice do you think Lincoln used when he said these lines?
2. **Understanding Irony.** The term **irony** can mean saying something opposite to what you really mean. In this meaning, *irony* and *sarcasm* are almost synonyms. Is this anecdote an example of irony? Explain your answer.

Check Test

What did Lincoln want to borrow from General McClellan? (the army)

Answers to Study Questions

Developing Comprehension Skills

1. The army was not moving or fighting.

2. The army was actually Lincoln's army. It seems silly to ask to borrow something that belongs to you, and the image of "borrowing" 250,000 men is funny.

Reading Literature: Nonfiction

1. A sarcastic tone would have been used.

2. Yes, Lincoln knew he did not need to "borrow" the army. It was at his command. What Lincoln was really trying to do was to tell McClellan to start using it.

Lincoln Gives a Book Review

In contrast to the anecdotes about McClellan, here President Lincoln is trying to avoid hurting someone's feelings. See how he manages it.

BEATRICE SCHENK de REGNIERS

A well-known man read aloud to President Lincoln some chapters from a book he was writing.

"Tell me, Mr. Lincoln," said the man, "what do you think of my book?"

Lincoln didn't think much of it. But he didn't want to hurt the author's feelings, so he said:

"Well, for those who like that sort of thing, I think it is just about the sort of thing they would like."

Developing Comprehension Skills

Literal Reading 1. Write the last sentence of the story in your own words.

Critical Reading 2. Do you think the man suspected that Lincoln didn't like his book? Give a reason for your answer.

Reading Literature: Nonfiction

Identifying Humor. Find a sentence in the anecdote that is funny partly because of the way it is worded. How does the wording make it funny?

Check Test

1. What did the man ask Lincoln? (what he thought of his book)

2. Did Lincoln like the book he reviewed? (no)

Answers to Study Questions

Developing Comprehension Skills

1. Answers vary. Possibility: "If you usually like that kind of writing, you'll like this book."

2. Yes, the man might have suspected that Lincoln didn't like the book because Lincoln said, "for those who like that sort of thing," implying that he was not one of those people.

Reading Literature: Nonfiction

The last sentence is funny. The repetition of *like* and *sort of thing* helps make it funny. Another thing that makes it funny is the circular, confusing reasoning that, nevertheless, still makes sense.

Objectives

- To identify characteristics of an anecdote
- To appreciate the humor in a selection
- To apply literal, interpretive, and critical reading skills to a selection

Preparing the Students

Motivation. Have the students read the introductory paragraph on page 437 and ask them to state in their own words what they should try to find out as they read this selection.

Presenting the Selection

1. Have the students read "Lincoln Gives a Book Review" silently.

2. Make sure that everyone has read the assignment by administering the **Check Test** at the bottom of this page.

3. Have a volunteer read the selection aloud.

4. Remind the students that the introduction to the selection asked them to find out how Lincoln avoided hurting someone's feelings. Have them explain his technique.

5. Develop the study questions as suggested in **Using the Study Questions** below.

Using the Study Questions

It is recommended that students always read and answer the questions in **Developing Comprehension Skills** in class discussion. Whenever possible, they should also read the questions in **Reading Literature** together and discuss the answers.

Developing Comprehension Skills

Question 1. Warn students that this sentence will be hard to restate since it says very little. Lincoln kept it vague on purpose.

Question 2. Ask students to imagine themselves in the author's place.

Reading Literature: Nonfiction

Students have discussed different methods of creating humor. They should recognize the repetition of phrases that helps to make the statement funny.

Here is another story Mr. Lincoln told. As you read it, try to decide why he liked it.

A Bad Example

BEATRICE SCHENK de REGNIERS

President Lincoln told the story of a governor who visited the state prison.

The governor talked to the prisoners and asked what types of crimes they had committed. Each prisoner said he had never done anything wrong. To hear them talk, you would have thought they were all innocent, good men.

At last the governor came to one prisoner who said, "I am a thief and I deserve to be in jail."

"Then I must pardon you," said the governor, "and get you out of this place. You seem to be the only criminal in this prison, and I don't want you here setting a bad example to all these good men I have been talking to."

Developing Comprehension Skills

Literal Reading

1. What did most of the prisoners tell the governor?

Interpretive Reading

2. Was the last prisoner really "the only criminal in this prison"? Explain your answer.

Reading Literature: Nonfiction

1. **Recognizing Sarcasm or Irony.** The governor told the last prisoner that he would pardon him. Was the reason he gave true, or was he speaking sarcastically (ironically)? What did he mean?

2. **Making Inferences.** From what you now know about Abraham Lincoln, why do you think he liked this story?

Objectives

- To identify the characteristics of an anecdote
- To appreciate humor in nonfiction
- To apply literal, interpretive, and critical reading skills to a selection
- To make inferences based on background information

Preparing the Students

Motivation. Have the students read the introductory paragraph on page 438 and ask them to state in their own words what they are to do.

Presenting the Selection

1. Have the students read "A Bad Example" silently.

2. Administer the **Check Test**.

3. Have a volunteer read the selection aloud.

4. Develop the study questions as suggested in **Using the Study Questions**.

Reinforcing the Lesson

To reteach, reinforce, or extend the concepts in this lesson, see the following:

Skills Practice Book, Green Level—page 168

Using the Study Questions

It is recommended that students always read and answer the questions in **Developing Comprehension Skills** in class discussion.

Developing Comprehension Skills

Question 1. Read and discuss the question.

Question 2. Make sure students understand that the governor knew that all the other criminals were lying.

Reading Literature: Nonfiction

Question 1. If necessary, review what was discussed about irony and sarcasm in "Borrow the Army."

Question 2. Encourage students to mention specific examples from the selections that they have read that help show why Lincoln liked this story. Point out, too, how this story stresses Lincoln's admiration for honesty, a trait not brought out as strongly in the other anecdotes.

Check Test

1. Who visited the state prison? (the governor)

2. What did the last prisoner tell the governor about himself? (that he was a thief and deserved to be in jail)

Answers to Study Questions

Developing Comprehension Skills

1. They said that they were innocent.

2. No, but he was the only one who was honest with the governor.

Reading Literature: Nonfiction

1. The governor was speaking sarcastically. He meant that he really knew that the others were criminals.

2. Lincoln liked using humor to make a point, and he admired honesty.

Lincoln's Favorite Joke

We know that Lincoln could make jokes about other people. He could also laugh at himself. Can you find several reasons why this joke would appeal to him?

BEATRICE SCHENK de REGNIERS

Here is the joke about himself that Lincoln liked best of all. He said it was the best story about himself he had ever read in the papers:

Two Quaker women were talking about who would win the war—President Lincoln for the United States, or Jefferson Davis, who was President of the Confederate States.

First Quaker Woman. I think Jefferson Davis will win.

Second Quaker Woman. Why does thee think so?

First Quaker Woman. Because he is a praying man.

Second Quaker Woman. Abraham Lincoln is a praying man, too.

First Quaker Woman. Yes, but the Lord will think Abraham is joking.

Abraham Lincoln, 1980, L.G. WRIGHT. Collection of Kirby Rodriguez.

Objectives

- To appreciate the anecdote as a form of literature
- To understand an author's purpose for writing a selection
- To apply literal, interpretive, and critical reading skills to a selection
- To locate information in the dictionary and encyclopedia
- To write a riddle
- To recognize the need to use different types of reading for different purposes

Preparing the Students

Motivation. Briefly discuss what a Quaker is so the students will better understand the comments of the two women. Explain that during the Civil War and all subsequent wars, the Quakers, being pacifists, refused to fight at all. Explain too, that they are deeply religious and believe that prayer and meditation can bring a person close to God.

Have the students read the introductory paragraph on page 439. Ask them to state in their own words what they should try to find out as they read this selection.

Presenting the Selection

1. Have the students read the selection silently.

2. Make sure that everyone has read the assignment by administering the **Check Test** at the bottom of this page.

3. Ask a student to read the first two paragraphs aloud. Then have two other students read the parts of the Quaker women.

4. Remind the students that the introduction to the selection asked them to find several reasons why this joke would appeal to Lincoln. Have them answer the question.

5. Develop the study questions as suggested in **Using the Study Questions** beginning on page 440. That section also provides a challenge question for further discussion, as needed.

Reinforcing the Lesson

To reteach, reinforce, or extend the concepts in this lesson, see the following:

Skills Practice Book, Green Level—pages 169 and 170

Check Test

1. Why did the first Quaker woman think Jefferson Davis would win the war? (because he was a praying man)

2. Was Abraham Lincoln a praying man? (yes)

About the Art

Although usually serious, Abraham Lincoln was known for his sense of humor and his appreciation of a good joke. L.G. Wright has captured here in one picture these two sides of Lincoln's character. Wright portrays the President as a serious and purposeful man. His eyes gaze out from beneath heavy eyebrows, and his face is lined. But about his mouth there is the suggestion of a smile, and when we look again at his eyes they seem to have an expression of amusement, a slightly mischievous look.

Special Populations

LD. Many special-populations students will have difficulty with scanning and skimming exercises. It is difficult for them to glance quickly through reading material to sort out the facts they are looking for from the general information presented in the reading. Slower reading rates also affect their success with skimming and scanning for information. The SQ3R method of study is much more successful for many special-populations students. You might want to limit the scanning to words in a list or a single paragraph. The exercise will need to be broken down into very simple steps for the students to be able to complete it successfully.

Encouraging Independent Reading

A wealth of fiction and nonfiction writing on the topic of the Civil War exists. Ask the students provocative questions that will lead them to read more widely. Here are some sample questions:

1. Was the issue of slavery the major cause of the War? If not, what was?

2. Who was the youngest soldier to fight in the War?

3. Which leader in the Union army was best-liked by his men? Why? Who was most liked in the Confederate army? Why?

4. What was the role of women in the war effort for either side? How many women served as spies?

5. What was the role of blacks in the Union army? in the Confederate army?

6. Did native Americans play a role in the outcome of the War? in what way?

Remind students that photography provided a record of this war that does not exist for earlier conflicts. Urge them to investigate the work of such early professional photographers as Matthew Brady, and to find and examine collections of photos from that era. The *American Heritage* magazine contains excellent photographs, some of which pertain to the Civil War. You may wish to recommend this magazine to your students.

Using the Study Questions

It is recommended that students always read and answer the questions in **Developing Comprehension Skills** in class discussion. Whenever possible, they should also read the questions in the other categories together and discuss the answers.

Developing Comprehension Skills

Literal Reading — 1. Where did Lincoln read this joke?

Interpretive Reading — 2. Why would the Lord "think Abraham is joking"?

Reading Literature: Nonfiction

1. **Making Inferences.** What quality of Abraham Lincoln is brought out in this anecdote that you didn't know from the other anecdotes?

2. **Understanding the Author's Purpose.** What do you think was the author's purpose in writing this joke? Was he criticizing President Lincoln, or predicting victory for the South, or commenting on something else? Why do you think President Lincoln liked the joke?

Developing Vocabulary Skills

Locating Information in the Encyclopedia. You have learned to use the dictionary to find the meaning of unfamiliar words in the stories you have read. There are also dictionary entries for the names of famous people or groups of people, places and events. For example, you can find Helen Keller and the Osage Indians entered in most dictionaries. However, the dictionary will give only a brief explanation of these entries. The **encyclopedia** will provide much more information. Words like *meteorite* also need more space for an explanation than a dictionary can provide.

The following words and names appear in the nonfiction selections you have read. Locate each item in the dictionary or glossary. Write the definition. Then locate each item in the encyclopedia. Write two facts about each topic that were not given in the dictionary or glossary.

1. gangrene
2. North Pole
3. Civil War
4. Jamaica
5. Dr. Alexander Graham Bell
6. Robert E. Peary

Developing Writing Skills

Analytical Writing — 1. **Examining Anecdotes.** Not every anecdote about President Lincoln was true. We cannot tell which ones were entirely accurate. However, every anecdote was based on some quality of Lincoln that the people of his time appreciated and talked about. From the anecdotes in this section, what do you think were some of the qualities the people of his

Answers to Study Questions

Developing Comprehension Skills

1. Lincoln read the joke in the papers.

2. The Lord would think so because Lincoln jokes so often.

Challenge. Answers will vary. All answers should include the reasons why the students feel as they do.

Reading Literature: Nonfiction

1. Lincoln was a praying man.

2. Answers may vary. The writer may have been teasing Lincoln about his habit of using humor even in serious situations. Lincoln may have enjoyed the story because it emphasized things he valued—prayer, humor, and the concept that no one is perfect or necessarily better than others—even enemies.

Developing Vocabulary Skills

Dictionary definitions and information from the encyclopedia will vary.

Developing Skills in Study and Research

1. 1826

2. the summer of 1861

3. 1885

time saw in President Lincoln? Write a paragraph explaining your conclusions.

Analytical Writing

2. **Understanding the Use of Humor.** How did President Lincoln's sense of humor help him solve or cope with the problems of being President at a critical time? Write a paragraph or more describing Lincoln's use of humor. Refer to specific sayings or anecdotes to illustrate your statements.

Creative Writing

3. **Writing a Riddle.** Choose one of Abraham Lincoln's riddles on pages 430 and 431. Using this riddle as a pattern, write a riddle of your own. You should use a modern example, but your riddle should have the same meaning as Lincoln's.

Developing Skills in Study and Research

Scanning, Skimming, and Study-Type Reading. A good reader does not always read at the same rate. That is because not all reading is done for the same purpose. Your reason for reading influences how carefully and thoroughly you read. When you are reading for fun, you may concentrate less than when you are reading for information. When you are reading for different kinds of information, you can use different types of reading.

In **scanning,** you look for specific information. For example, you may be searching the sports pages of a newspaper for the mention of your school's team. You may be looking through a chapter of your science book for an explanation of Vitamin C. In both of these cases, nothing else on those pages is of interest to you. You are looking for only one word or phrase. When you scan, you are not reading for understanding. You can go through the pages much more quickly than when you do other kinds of reading.

In **skimming,** you look over the information on the page quickly to see what sort of material is there. You do not read every word, but you find out what topics are discussed. You look at the boldface heads, or heads in dark type. You get a general idea of whether there is anything on the page of interest to you. If there are any difficult words or passages, you skip over them. You are not trying to learn everything that is on the page. Skimming is not as fast as scanning, but it is still fast.

In **study-type reading** you go more slowly than in skimming and scanning. Now you are reading for understanding. You first read over any-

Possible facts: McClellan was the Democratic candidate for President in 1864, but lost to Lincoln. As major general, he cleared western Virginia of Confederate forces. Lincoln relieved him of command as supreme general in March, 1862.

Boldface headings and main ideas will vary depending on the encyclopedia used.

Developing Comprehension Skills

Question 1. Read and discuss.

Question 2. In answering this question, students should consider what they have learned about Lincoln in this chapter.

Challenge Question. Basing your answer on what you have learned about Lincoln in this text, do you think you would have liked him? Give reasons why you feel that way. (Critical Reading)

Reading Literature: Nonfiction

Question 1. Have students consider what they knew about Lincoln's personality before and then find evidence from the selection that describes him in a new way.

Question 2. Students should realize that Lincoln's personality is the focus of this joke. The author's intention was not to comment on how the South would do in the war.

Developing Vocabulary Skills

Make sure a dictionary and appropriate encyclopedias are available for this exercise. Have a student read the directions aloud. Ask a student to look up Helen Keller in the dictionary and read the explanation aloud. Then have the student locate Helen Keller in the eycyclopedia and tell the class two facts that are given there. Use the same procedure for sharing the information given about the Osage Indians in both reference books.

Have the students complete the exercise independently. Be sure to discuss the answers together in class.

Developing Writing Skills

Read and discuss the three assignments. Then have the students choose and complete one of the three.

Question 1. This question asks the students to write a character analysis of Lincoln using evidence from several anecdotes.

Pre-Writing. Have students look over the anecdotes they have read and list the qualities that each one stresses. Have them note a few qualities that are emphasized several times.

Writing. Have students begin with a topic sentence that states some qualities that people saw in Lincoln. Have them explain why they included those particular qualities. Encourage them to use evidence from the selections.

Revising. Have students look over their writing to make sure they gave reasons for their choices of qualities. Allow time for corrections and improvements to be made.

Question 2. This question asks students to organize, in written form, their ideas about a subject that has been discussed throughout this section. It helps students take ideas that have been discussed orally and combine them logically and briefly in writing.

Pre-Writing. Have students locate the selections that refer to Lincoln's problems during the Civil War. To make the organization of this writing assignment easier for the students, write the titles of those selections on the board and the problem that each describes. Suggest the students choose one incident or one recurring problem as an illustration of Lincoln's technique. Remind them, however, that their general statements about Lincoln's use of humor should apply to any and all of the problems on the list.

Writing. Remind students that the topic of their writing is general: How did Lincoln's sense of humor help him as President? They must provide some general answers, supported by specific sayings or anecdotes. Allow sufficient time for students to complete the assignment independently.

Revising. Have students exchange papers. Have the partners look for topic sentences and evidence from the selection to support ideas. Allow time for corrections and improvements to be made.

Question 3. Creating a riddle with a pattern similar to Lincoln's will help students see how ideas can apply to many times and cultures.

Pre-Writing. Discuss the pattern of the riddles on pages 430 and 431. Then have the students suggest a few modern examples that come to mind that could be used to create a riddle with the same meaning as Lincoln's.

Writing. Allow sufficient time for students to complete the assignment.

Revising. Allow as many students as possible to share their riddles with the class.

Developing Skills in Study and Research

Call on students to read aloud the explanation on page 441, stopping after the first (partial) paragraph on page 442. After each paragraph, pause to discuss each type of reading thoroughly. Make sure that students are aware of the different purposes for each rate. Remind them that purpose determines rate.

Stress that students will need to master different reading rates in order to be efficient readers as they continue in school. Explain that a good, efficient reader and a fast reader are not the same thing. A good reader will be able to scan or skim effectively when necessary or to read carefully when it is appropriate.

Once all three rates and the technique for each have been thoroughly discussed, read the directions on page 441 to the students. Have them complete the exercise independently. Be sure to discuss the results together in class.

thing in boldface type to get an idea of what the important ideas on the page are. You also find out how the material is organized. Then you read the material carefully. You stop to look up words in the glossary or dictionary when you need to. You read slowly enough to understand the main ideas in each paragraph.

Look up General George Brinton McClellan in an encyclopedia. First scan the article to find the following information:

1. The date of his birth
2. The date he took command of the Union Army in the East, also called the Army of the Potomac
3. The date of his death

Next, skim the article. On your paper, note three facts about General McClellan that you think are interesting.

Last, do a study-type reading of the article. Determine how the article is organized. On your paper, copy any boldface heads. Also, write the main idea of each paragraph of the article. If several important ideas are in one paragraph, restate them in your own words.

Essays

Most of us like to read about famous and important people. However, we also like to read about people and things closer to our own lives. The selections in this section challenge us to take a closer look at the things around us every day.

Woman with Plants, 1929, GRANT WOOD. Collection of the Cedar Rapids Museum of Art, Iowa.

Essays

Ask students to read page 443 and to examine the painting reproduced there. Have them explain what the upcoming selections and the painting have in common. Bring out the idea that writing and the arts are valuable, not only when they present remarkable people and occurences, but also when they record the average, normal happenings of life.

About the Art

Born on a farm in Iowa, Grant Wood (1892-1942) painted scenes of rural America that evoke the sturdy moral character of the Midwestern farmer. His landscapes show a rural paradise of rolling hills and green meadows. The figures in his paintings are simple, devout, hard-working people, the farmers who till the soil and share in what Wood called "the pagentry of growing things." *Woman with Plants,* a portrait of Wood's mother, shows the relationship between the people and the land, the farmer's special intimacy with the soil and the fruits of labor.

Reading Literature

All of the nonfiction selections in the preceding sections of the chapter reported the happenings in the lives of the writers or their subjects and were organized according to chronological order. This lesson stresses the difference between that type of writing and writing that reports ideas and is organized according to logical order. The lesson explains this difference and defines three types of writing that discuss ideas and opinions: essays, letters, and speeches.

Preparing the Students

Remind the students that the introduction to essays on page 443 warned them that the following selections would have a different purpose from that of the first three groups of nonfiction selections, that is, to examine everyday things. Point out that this different purpose may require some techniques in writing that are different from those of biographical writing. Explain that the text on pages 444 and 445 will discuss some of these differences.

Presenting the Lesson

1. Call on students to read aloud **Two Types of Nonfiction** on page 444. Ask them to describe in their own words the differences between the two types of writing. They should understand that in the first type the emphasis is on actions, while in the second type the emphasis is on thoughts and opinions.

2. Have students read silently the sections on **Essays, Letters,** and **Speeches.** Pause after each section to discuss the characteristics and purposes of each of these types of writing, and the differences among them. Ask students to identify other essays, letters, and speeches with which they are familiar, for example, editorials in the newspaper, friendly letters, and political speeches.

Reinforcing the Lesson

To reteach, reinforce, or extend the concepts in this lesson, see the following:

Skills Practice Book, Green Level—pages 171 and 172

Special Populations

LD, ESL. Remind students that essays, speeches, and letters contain thoughts

Reading Literature: Types of Nonfiction

Two Types of Nonfiction

You have learned that nonfiction includes all writing that is based on facts rather than imagination. In general, there are two types of nonfiction.

In the first type of nonfiction, the writer reports facts about people, places, and events. Autobiographies, biographies, short sayings and writings, and anecdotes are all examples of the first kind of nonfiction. The last selection in this chapter, a vignette, also reports facts. These forms of nonfiction report things that were done or said.

The next three groups of selections belong to the second kind of nonfiction. In this writing, the author discusses ideas and opinions. Essays, letters, and speeches are some of the forms this writing can take. We read them purposely to find out what the writer thinks and feels about the topic.

In both types of nonfiction, the writers use both fact and opinion. In the first type, the writer is most concerned with giving information about people and events. However, in order to make this information clear, he or she often includes opinions.

In the second type, the writers tell what they believe and why. They base their opinions on facts and may use facts to support their statements. Frequently, they try to persuade their readers to agree with them.

Essays

The **essay** is a type of nonfiction writing in which writers state personal opinions and explain their reasons for those opinions. In a good essay, the opinions and reasons are organized. The writer's line of thought is clear and reasonable.

Almost any topic can be the subject of an essay. Some writers speak of common happenings. They give their reactions to these events and their thoughts about everyday life. The selections in this chapter are of this kind. Other writers use the essay form to discuss more serious topics, such as justice, peace, and truth. The writer's attitude, or tone, can range from serious thought to light humor.

Letters

The **letter** is one of the oldest and most popular forms of nonfiction writing. You have probably written letters yourself. Letters are written for many reasons, such as to describe the events of a trip, to tell news of daily life, and to make business arrangements. A writer can also write a letter to explain what he or she has done or what he or she thinks, and to give reasons.

The letters you will read, by Abraham Lincoln, are of this second type. They explain Lincoln's opinions on certain topics and his reasons for his opinions.

Speeches

A **speech** is a form of nonfiction written to be read aloud. The speeches that people remember are the ones that were both written well and presented well by skilled speakers.

Speech writers must have a special talent. They must be able to predict how certain phrases or sentences will be understood by a crowd of people. They must write speeches more boldly than other nonfiction forms, such as essays and letters. A speech should capture the listener's—or reader's—interest quickly. It should hold the attention of the audience. It should sound both important and sincere. Above all, the ideas in a speech must be well organized. A listener or reader should be able to understand the thinking of the speaker immediately and remember the ideas later.

A speech does not need to be long in order to develop its ideas clearly. Some of the best speeches are very short. The speeches by Abraham Lincoln in this chapter will prove that.

and opinions held by the writers and may not be opinions with which many people agree. These may also express examples of slanted writing that may need to be pointed out to the students. Some LD students may take much of what they read literally. Try to find examples for the class showing writing that is to be taken literally and writing that is to be taken figuratively.

For ESL students, the understanding of some of the opinions expressed will be based upon their experience with the content. To be able to make sense of the point of view, you may need to provide a context, particularly for the speeches.

Objectives

- To recognize and appreciate an essay as a form of literature
- To identify mood
- To analyze the organization of a good essay
- To apply literal, interpretive, and critical reading skills to a selection

Preparing the Students

Essential Vocabulary. The words presented here are essential to the understanding of the selection.

Ask the students to use context clues in the sentences below to find the meaning of the underlined words.

comparatively	underrate
strut	deliberately

1. The fireworks display at this year's Fourth of July celebration was not as exciting as last year's, but the music was comparatively good.
2. The trainer taught her horse to strut. Now it walks with the pride and high-stepping foot movements of a show horse.
3. Don't underrate your opponents. They may be better than you think they are.
4. The poet read his poems aloud deliberately, in an unhurried way.

If the students need additional help with the vocabulary of this selection, encourage them to use context clues to determine word meaning. As needed, direct them to the **Glossary** or to a classroom dictionary.

Motivation. Ask students how they can tell when spring is approaching. Encourage them to think of things that appeal to the senses in answering this question.

Have the students read the introductory paragraph on page 446 and ask them to state in their own words what they should try to determine as they read this essay.

Presenting the Selection

1. Have the students read "April and Robins" silently.

2. Make sure that everyone has read the assignment by administering the **Check Test** at the bottom of this page.

3. Have volunteers read the selection aloud.

4. Remind the students that the introduction asked them to see if they could tell why the author wrote it. Have them answer the question.

April and Robins

HAL BORLAND

This essay is about just what the title states: the beginning of April and robins. As you read it, see if you can tell why the author wrote it.

April 2

People who can't tell a bald eagle from a vulture know what a robin looks like, and they know that, when robins strut the lawn, April must be here. April just isn't April, in this part of the world, without robins. Spring couldn't come without them.

The robin long ago became a kind of national bird without a shred of legal backing. It didn't need legal proclamations, for the robin is one of the best known and widely distributed birds in all these United States. Perhaps most important of all, it is a cosmopolitan bird, equally at home in a city park, on a suburban lawn and in the open country. Unlike most other thrushes, it prefers to nest near a house. Being a comparatively large bird, big as a blue jay, and a conspicuous bird with its black head and cinnamon-red breast, the robin simply can't be overlooked. Besides, robins love to strut. And to sing, preferably from a street-side tree.

The robin's song is often underrated, probably because the robin is so common and so vocal. But the robin, after all, is a thrush, and the thrushes are accomplished songsters. The robin sings long, loudly and rather deliberately. Its notes are clear and rich in tone. And no two robins sing exactly the same way; they vary their songs, put the phrases together differently. An individual robin may sing as many as ten different songs, varying with the time of day.

Robins are already singing in many places. Their chorus will increase day by day. After all, it is April, even to a robin.

Check Test

1. What bird do most people recognize easily? (robin)

2. How many different songs can a robin sing? (ten)

Answers to Study Questions

Developing Comprehension Skills

1. The two things are that they look alike and that they come in April.

2. Identification of statements:

a. opinion c. opinion
b. fact d. fact

Developing Comprehension Skills

Literal Reading

1. What two things does the author say almost everyone knows about robins? Look at the first paragraph of the essay to find out.

Critical Reading

2. Read each statement below and decide whether it is a fact or an opinion. Give a reason for your decision.
   a. April just isn't April . . . without robins.
   b. But the robin, after all, is a thrush.
   c. The robin simply can't be overlooked.
   d. An individual robin may sing as many as ten different songs.

Reading Literature: Nonfiction

1. **Analyzing Organization.** A good essay is well organized. Reread each paragraph in this essay. Then in your own words identify the main idea of each paragraph. What is the connection between each main idea and the next?
2. **Identifying Mood.** The mood of a piece of literature is the feeling it gives you when you read it. How would you describe the mood of "April and Robins"?

Reasons will vary, but students should show a clear understanding of the difference between fact and opinion.

Reading Literature: Nonfiction

1. The main ideas are the following:

Paragraph 1—April and robins go together.

Paragraph 2—The robin is a kind of national bird because it is well known, widely distributed, and easy to notice.

Paragraph 3— The robin's song is pleasing and varied.

Paragraph 4—It is April and robins are singing. The first paragraph says that April isn't April without robins. The second paragraph explains why people feel that the robin represents April all over the United States. The second paragraph ends with the fact that robins love to sing. The third paragraph tells more about the robin's song. The last paragraph says that robins are singing now; this connects the last paragraph to the others. The last paragraph also mentions that it is April, connecting it to the first paragraph.

2. Answers may vary. The mood is light and happy. The happy mood comes from the casual style—"People who can't tell a bald eagle from a vulture know what a robin looks like . . . ."

5. Develop the study questions as suggested in **Using the Study Questions** on page 447.

Special Populations

ESL. ESL students may be able to tell the class about springtime in a different country. Have them explain how it is similar to or different from spring in Borland's essay.

Using the Study Questions

It is recommended that students always read and answer the questions in **Developing Comprehension Skills** in class discussion. Whenever possible, they should also read the questions in **Reading Literature** together and discuss the answers.

Developing Comprehension Skills

Question 1. After students have answered this question, ask them if the opening statement is true about the part of the country in which they live.

Question 2. Have students explain the difference between fact and opinion. Then have them discuss each statement. Be sure they can tell why a statement is fact or opinion.

Reading Literature: Nonfiction

Question 1. Ask for a definition of the main idea of a paragraph. If the students have difficulty with this, explain that the main idea of a paragraph is the over-all idea that the paragraph is about. Then have the students read and answer the question. Stress the importance of logical order in explaining or proving how two paragraphs are related.

Question 2. Once students have specified the mood of this selection, have them cite phrases from the essay that caused them to come to their decision.

Objectives

- To recognize an essay as a form of literature
- To appreciate the use of metaphor
- To identify onomatopoeia and alliteration
- To identify word connotations
- To apply literal, interpretive, and critical reading skills to a selection

Preparing the Students

Essential Vocabulary. The words presented here are essential to the understanding of the selection. Ask the students to use context clues in the following sentences to find the meaning of the underlined words.

insistent teeming ultimate

1. The customer was so insistent about returning the dress, the salesperson finally agreed to give her a refund.
2. Unlimited fishing was allowed because the lake was teeming with fish.
3. The skating team had won many city and statewide competitions, but their ultimate achievement was their first-place award at the national level.

If the students need additional help with the vocabulary of this selection, encourage them to use context clues to determine word meaning. As needed, direct them to the **Glossary** or to a classroom dictionary.

Motivation. Discuss thoroughly the meaning of *prelude.* Explain that the word is usually used in reference to a musical introduction to a play, concert, opera, or piece of music.

Have the students read the introductory paragraph on page 448 and state in their own words what they should find out as they read this selection.

A prelude comes before the main event. What is the main event that follows this prelude?

The Prelude

HAL BORLAND

June 6

Early Spring or late, cool May or warm, by June the days are alive with sound. It comes so gradually, increasing day by day from the cold silence of March, that we are scarcely aware of it. We must force our ears to listen. But there it is, in suburb and countryside, even in a city park, the buzz of the bumblebee, the low chirping of the lesser cricket at the grassroot, the scratch and rattle of the brash-winged grasshopper, the harsh rustle of the beetle in flight on stiff, inadequate wings. The insect sounds.

This is the lesser chorus, and it goes with daisies in the meadows and wild roses along the pasture margins. Not one of the sounds is really insistent, even when one listens closely; but in sum they are the voice of early June, untold millions of little hummings and buzzings and rustlings that set the long daylight hours to vibrating.

There is no true silence now, for the world is alive and teeming. What we hear is the urgency of life, the insistence of the unimportant which by its very numbers becomes of ultimate importance. Only the pollen of the trees and the spores of ferns and fungi outnumber the insect eggs, and all those eggs are hatching. Hatched, they must announce and praise life, mate, lay more eggs, perpetuate life. Later will come the high-pitched shrill of the cicada, the clamor of the katydid. But they await hot noontimes and warm evenings. They are the Summer itself. Now we hear the tune-up and the prelude. This, when we listen closely, is the voice of Summer still approaching.

Presenting the Selection

1. Read "The Prelude" aloud to the class. Stress the use of alliteration and onomatopoeia.

2. Make sure that everyone has listened to the selection by administering the **Check Test** at the bottom of this page.

3. Have volunteers read parts of the selection aloud.

4. Remind the students that the introduction to the selection asked them to try to find out what main event follows this prelude. Have them answer the question.

5. Develop the study questions as suggested in **Using the Study Questions** on

Check Test

1. What time of year is this essay about? (spring)

2. Name one sound you hear in early June. (buzz of bumblebee, chirping of cricket, rattle of grasshopper, rustle of beetle)

Developing Comprehension Skills

Literal Reading — 1. What kind of sounds is the author talking about in this essay?

Literal Reading — 2. A prelude is often a part of a piece of music. It is like an introduction. In this essay, the author calls certain sounds of nature a prelude. What are they a prelude to?

Interpretive Reading — 3. Do you think the author likes the coming of summer? Give a reason for your answer.

Critical Reading — 4. Which of these two essays, "April and Robins" and "The Prelude," did you enjoy more? Give a reason for your answer.

Reading Literature: Nonfiction

1. **Recognizing Metaphor.** This essay is organized around a metaphor. A **metaphor** is a type of comparison that is not openly stated. In "The Prelude," the author compares the sounds and seasons to something that he does not openly state. What is it? Use these words from the essay as clues to your answer: *chorus, voice, hummings, high-pitched, tune-up, prelude.*

2. **Finding Onomatopoeia and Alliteration.** The use of words that sound like what they mean is onomotopoeia. For example, "whoosh" is onomatopoetic. Alliteration is the repetition of a single sound usually at the beginning of words. For example, "Peter Piper picked a peck of pickled peppers" is alliterative. In "The Prelude," the author uses both of those techniques. Find at least two examples of each technique. How do these techniques make the meaning of the essay clearer?

3. **Identifying Connotations.** Below are phrases from the essay. For each phrase, state whether the connotation is positive, negative, or neutral.

   a. alive with sound
   b. the harsh rustle of the beetle
   c. the cold silence of March
   d. the voice of early June
   e. high-pitched shrill
   f. stiff, inadequate wings

page 449. That section also provides a challenge question for further discussion, as needed.

Using the Study Questions

It is recommended that students always read and answer the questions in **Developing Comprehension Skills** in class discussion. Whenever possible, they should also read the questions in **Reading Literature** together and discuss the answers.

Developing Comprehension Skills

Questions 1 and 2. Read and discuss the questions.

Question 3. If necessary, ask students whether people usually choose to observe things they enjoy or things they don't like.

Question 4. Make sure students know there is no single right answer. Students should support opinions with reasons.

Challenge Question. The writer tells us that "we must force ourselves to listen" to the sounds of early June. Why do you think he feels we should try to hear these noises? How could it benefit us? (Critical Reading)

Reading Literature: Nonfiction

Question 1. Read and discuss the question.

Question 2. Discuss both onomatopoeia and alliteration. Ask students to provide examples of each. Then have them complete the question.

Question 3. Students should have a clear grasp of connotation at this point. Have them complete the exercise independently and then discuss their answers together in class.

Answers to Study Questions

Developing Comprehension Skills

1. The author is talking about insect noises.

2. The sounds are a prelude to summer.

3. The writer seems to have listened closely to the sounds of the coming of summer. He probably likes the sounds since he pays so much attention to them.

4. Answers will vary. Students should give reasons to explain their answers.

Challenge. Answers will vary. Possible reasons: The writer thinks we will enjoy the season more if we pay attention even to little things like insect noises. He believes humans should stay in touch with nature.

Reading Literature: Nonfiction

1. The author compares the sounds to a symphony or a musical performance.

2. The following are possible answers:
onomatopoeia—buzz, rattle, rustle
alliteration—buzz of the bumblebee, ferns and fungi, clamor of the katydid

These techniques help us to "hear" the sounds of nature the author is describing.

3. Connotations are as follows:
a. positive
b. negative
c. negative
d. neutral
e. negative
f. negative

Objectives

- To recognize and appreciate an essay as a form of literature
- To identify personification
- To apply literal, interpretive, and critical reading skills to a selection
- To use word parts drawn from Greek and Latin in determining word meanings
- To write an original essay
- To present an essay orally with clarity and with expression that reflects the mood

Preparing the Students

Essential Vocabulary. The words presented here are essential to the understanding of the selection.

Ask the students to use context clues in the sentences below to find the meaning of the underlined words.

innate sticklers

1. Some people believe that humans are born with certain characteristics. Others disagree. They say these characteristics are not innate.
2. The office manager expected everyone to come exactly on time. She was a stickler for promptness.

If the students need additional help with the vocabulary of this selection, encourage them to use context clues to determine word meaning. As needed, direct them to the **Glossary** or to a classroom dictionary.

Motivation. Ask the students how they feel about December. Then have them read the introductory paragraph on page 450 and ask them to state in their own words what they are to find out as they read this next essay. Have them compare their own feelings with Mr. Borland's as they read.

Shortest Month

HAL BORLAND

So far, we have read Mr. Borland's comments on spring and summer. Now we can find out how he feels about a winter month.

December 4

December is the shortest month of the year. No argument will be accepted, if it is to the contrary; and those who point to February are merely making gestures. True, December does have thirty-one days, such as they are. But can you really call days those hurried little spans that come zipping past, once Thanksgiving is behind and Christmas lies just ahead? Certainly not. Why, if you even pause to check them off on the calendar, you have no time for anything else! The Thanksgiving turkey vanishes, and you turn around, and there is the Christmas tree waiting to be decorated. New Year's Day is here, and January. December is gone again.

There is no mistake about it, except for those who are innate sticklers. In round figures, December has only 288 hours of daylight; and that counts in even those dreary times when the sun sulks behind a mass of clouds all day. Even March, of evil reputation, can muster that many hours of daylight in twenty-four days. And June, magnificent June, does as well by us in only nineteen days.

What is a December day, anyway? Nine hours of daylight, with a few minutes left over at each end to turn the lights on and off. And fifteen hours of darkness. With a moon, to be sure, and a great many stars. But darkness, just the same. You eat breakfast by lamplight, hurry to work in half-light, and get home in darkness. You have four weekends in which to watch the sun scurry across the southern quadrant of the sky.

December? By sundown tonight we will have had just a little over thirty-seven hours of December daylight. Enough said?

Presenting the Selection

1. Have the students read "Shortest Month" silently.

2. Make sure that everyone has read the assignment by administering the **Check Test** at the bottom of this page.

3. Have volunteers read the selection aloud.

4. Remind the students that the introduction to the selection asked them to see if they could find out how Mr. Borland feels about a certain winter month. Have them answer the question.

5. Develop the study questions as suggested in **Using the Study Questions** (beginning on page 451).

Check Test

1. What, according to the author, is the shortest month? (December)

2. Name one of the reasons that the author considers that month as short. (It has so few hours of sunlight. It's a busy month because of the holidays.)

Arctic Owl and Winter Moon, 1960, CHARLES BURCHFIELD.
Private collection. Courtesy of Kennedy Galleries, New York

Developing Comprehension Skills

Literal Reading

1. What does December have less of than do March and June?

Interpretive Reading

2. The first sentence of this essay is the topic sentence. December isn't really the shortest month, though. Change the underlined word below to another word or words so that the sentence tells what the author really means.

   "December <u>is</u> the shortest month of the year."

Critical Reading

3. What is the author's opinion of December? Do you agree with him? Why or why not?

About the Art

Charles Burchfield (1893-1967) reveled in the beauty and poetry of nature. He found that trees and flowers, wind, snow, and rain, dramatized his personal feelings, whether of exaltation or gloom. His depictions of nature expressed his moods and feelings about life, reflected in the seasons of the year and the different time of day or night.

Rather than deadening his senses, winter inspired Burchfield to paint. He transformed the winter scene in *Arctic Owl and Winter Moon* into an animated and supernatural landscape, illuminated by the light of the moon, haunted by the afterimage of the owl. Vibrant and elongated forms pervade the black and white scene. Just one small bird at the bottom of the evergeen tree appears to maintain its color and composure.

Reinforcing the Lesson

To reteach, reinforce, or extend the skills in this lesson, see the following:

Skills Practice Book, Green Level—page 173

Encouraging Independent Reading

Recommend to students who enjoyed the Borland essays any of Hal Borland's other writings on nature, such as these: *Hal Borland's Book of Days* and *The Golden Circle: A Book of Months.*

In addition, the following collections of essays on nature by Edwin Way Teale are highly recommended: *North with the Spring, Journey into Summer,* and *Wandering Through Winter.*

Annie Dillard's *Pilgrim at Tinker Creek* is another widely praised personal reaction to the small, regular events in nature.

Using the Study Questions

It is recommended that students always read and answer the questions in **Developing Comprehension Skills** in class discussion.

Developing Comprehension Skills

Question 1. Make sure the students distinguish between the number of days and the number of daylight hours.

Question 2. Point out that the way the author has worded this first sentence tells the reader that the piece is personal writing, expressing one writer's opinion.

Question 3. Have students reread the essay, looking for specific examples of expressions of the author's opinion.

Reading Literature: Nonfiction

Question 1. Encourage students to refer to the essay to identify the arguments.

Question 2. Students should realize that a number of elements combine to result in tone. The details included, the connotations of words, and the stated opinions of the author all combine to create tone.

Question 3. Ask students to suggest reasons for the writer's use of personification. Help them see that this technique helps the reader understand more quickly a writer's attitude toward the things he or she is discussing, by recognizing the people of whom those things remind the writer.

Developing Vocabulary Skills

Question 1. Briefly review the three given techniques to find the meaning of an unfamiliar word. You may want to have the students turn to the vocabulary skills section of the **Handbook** (particularly pages 548 and 549) and read the information given there. Then have the students complete the exercise independently and discuss the answers together in class.

Question 2. Have the students read the directions for the exercise. Then have them turn to page 67 and review the Greek and Latin prefixes presented there. Tell students that they may need to use a dictionary to check the spelling of the new words. Have them complete the exercise independently. Check the answers together.

Developing Writing Skills

Read and discuss the two assignments. Then have the students choose and complete one of the two.

Question 1. If you prefer, you could ask your students to write about only one of the essays, discussing the features suggested in the text question.

Pre-Writing. All three essays express opinions about a time of year. Discuss the opinion expressed in each essay. Point out that certain essays use figures of speech and sounds of language more than others. Make a list on the board of the techniques the author uses. Have the students reexamine each essay to find examples of as many of those techniques as they can and take notes on what they find. Make sure students consider these facts before they choose which essay to compare with "Shortest Month." Then have them select one of the other two essays.

Make it clear that this composition should not simply be a list of examples. Provide a few statements regarding techniques for the students to model their writing on, such as the following: "The use of personification in *Shortest Month* helps the writer share his feelings with his readers"; "In *The Prelude,* alliteration almost makes you hear the noises of spring." Have each student write two or three possible statements about each essay he or she has chosen. The students may then select and arrange details to develop these statements.

Writing. Remind the students to discuss both the author's opinions and techniques in both essays, and to use the examples they found to explain and support their statements.

Revising. Ask students to reread the text question and make sure their writing

Reading Literature: Nonfiction

1. **Identifying Organization.** The author presents two arguments to show that December is the shortest month. What are those arguments? Do they use facts or opinions or both?
2. **Understanding Tone.** What is the tone of this essay? Would you call it serious, light, humorous, sad, or some other term?
3. **Recognizing Personification.** A writer using **personification** gives human qualities to non-human things. An example is "the lines of pine trees marched to the cliff's edge." Find at least three examples of personification in "Shortest Month."

Developing Vocabulary Skills

1. **Reviewing Context Clues.** The underlined word in each sentence below is from one of the essays by Hal Borland. The meaning of each underlined word can be figured out by using one of these context clues. On your paper, write each underlined word, its meaning, and the clue you used to figure out the meaning.

   (1) Main idea
   (2) Comparisons which relate ideas
   (3) Examples that explain an idea or word

   a. The robin is a <u>cosmopolitan</u> bird. For instance, it is at home in a city park, on a suburban lawn, and in the open country.
   b. Thrushes are skilled singers. Like all thrushes, the robin is an <u>accomplished</u> songster.
   c. Being a large bird, and a <u>conspicuous</u> bird with its black head and cinnamon-red breast, the robin simply can't be overlooked.

2. **Reviewing Word Parts.** In chapter two, you learned the meaning of several Greek and Latin prefixes. Another Latin prefix used in many English words is *quadra,* or *quadri,* meaning "four." For example, in one of the essays this phrase appears: "across the southern quadrant of the sky." A *quadrant* is one-fourth or one quarter of a circle.

   Read the following sentences. Choose the correct prefix to fill in the blank before each root word. Choose from among *quadri* and the other Latin and Greek prefixes listed on page 67. If you are unsure, check your answers in a dictionary.

Answers to Study Questions

Developing Comprehension Skills

1. December has less daylight.
2. seems like
3. The author does not like December. He describes some parts of December as "dreary times when the sun sulks behind a mass of clouds all day." He says a December day is "nine hours of daylight, with a few minutes left over at each end to turn the lights on and off."

Students' opinions and reasons will vary.

Reading Literature: Nonfiction

1. First, the writer says December seems to go fast because of the holidays, and secondly, it has few hours of daylight. The first is mostly opinion; the second is based on fact.

2. Answers will vary. The tone is light and somewhat humorous. The tone might also be considered disapproving.

3. Examples of personification are the following: "the sun sulks," "March, of evil reputation," "watch the sun scurry," "Christmas tree waiting to be decorated."

a. A __lingual person speaks three languages, and a __lingual speaks four.
b. A __cycle has one wheel and a __cycle has four wheels.
c. A celebration marking the end of two hundred years is a __centennial, and one marking the end of four hundred years is a __centennial.
d. A __syllable word has many syllables, and a __syllable word has four.
e. A __gon is a figure with many sides, and a __agon has ten sides.

Developing Writing Skills

Analytical Writing

1. **Comparing Literary Works.** All three of these essays are related to seasons. Compare "Shortest Month" with either of the other essays. Discuss the author's opinions about the different seasons. Also discuss the author's use of figures of speech, such as personification, and the sounds of language, such as alliteration. Refer to examples from the essays to explain or to support your statements.

Creative Writing

2. **Writing an Essay.** Write a two- or three-paragraph essay that expresses your feelings about a certain time of year. Start by organizing your essay on scratch paper. First, choose one time of year. Then think of two or three reasons for liking or disliking it. Put your reasons in order of importance, beginning either with the most important or with the least important. Think about how to connect your ideas. When you have your ideas well organized, write your essay.

Developing Skills in Speaking and Listening

Reading an Essay Orally. Prepare to read one of these essays by Hal Borland aloud. First make sure you understand the difficult words in the essay. Practice reading the phrases using onomotopoeia and alliteration. Try to read with expression, so that the mood of the essay is clear.

When you are ready to read the essay aloud, join four or five classmates. Members of the group should take turns reading their choices. After everyone has had a turn, discuss the differences between reading these essays silently and hearing them read aloud. Consider such questions as these: In what way is reading silently better? In what way is hearing the essay better? Which way did you understand the meaning better? Why do you think that is so?

Developing Vocabulary Skills

1. Answers:
   - **a.** cosmopolitan, at home in many places, 3
   - **b.** accomplished, skilled, 2
   - **c.** conspicuous, hard to overlook, 1
2. Correct prefixes:
   - **a.** tri-; quadri-
   - **b.** uni-; quadri-
   - **c.** bi-; quadri-
   - **d.** multi-; quadri-
   - **e.** poly-; deca-

has discussed each topic listed there. Also, they should look for statements that tell what the effect of any technique is. Allow time for corrections and improvements to be made.

Question 2. Encourage students to make these essays truly personal.

Pre-Writing. To stimulate creative, individual responses, provide one of the following activities:

a. Show a short film concerning a season, preferably one without narration, just music background.
b. Display several posters showing nature in different seasons.
c. Pass around the class several photographs (perhaps from the library picture file) presenting mood-setting views of nature in different seasons.

Particularly if your school is in an urban setting, include pictures of city scenes indicating seasons, such as flowerboxes or trees surrounded by sidewalk.

Allow several minutes of unguided discussion, encouraging students to react honestly to the photography.

Then have each student work independently for several minutes, following the directions in the text. Remind them that their reasons for liking or disliking a season are personal, and the ranking depends on personal preferences.

Writing. Allow sufficient time for students to complete the assignment.

Revising. Have students reread their papers to check for logical order and clear expression of ideas. Have them use the **Checklist for the Process of Writing** on pages 556 and 557 to revise and proofread their papers.

Developing Skills in Speaking and Listening

Have students read the directions for the exercise. Have each student practice reading one of the essays. Allow class time for students to read their chosen essays in groups of four or five. If possible, have a short class discussion afterwards, so that all the students will benefit from the insights of each group.

Letters

Call on a student to read page 454 to the class. Ask the students to discuss whether they are in the habit of writing letters, and have them suggest reasons why some people write more letters than others. Remind them of the many form letters they have seen, and point out that, as President, Abraham Lincoln must have written hundreds, perhaps thousands, of letters to lawmakers and citizens. Stress the fact that despite the volume of writing he did, he managed to put a bit of himself into each thing that he wrote.

Encouraging Independent Reading

If possible, obtain on extended loan one or more collections of letters by famous people. Then enlist the help of the students in setting up a trivia contest that involves the letters as follows.

1. Divide the class into two teams (or have two classes compete against each other). Set up time limits for steps 2 and 3, at most a week per step for each team.

2. Tell each team to form two groups: question writers and fact checkers. The question writers are to skim the letters for interesting bits of information. (Perhaps each writer could read one letter.) Each writer may write several questions, but must include with each the answer and the page of the anthology on which the answer appears. The questions should follow models such as these:

Who got an idea for a famous novel when he took some children on a picnic?

What famous novel grew out of a story made up during a picnic?

Which President asked his daughter to send him regular reports of her schooling?

Who reported her school progress to a President?

The fact checkers verify all the questions, choose the top twenty (or some other agreed-upon number), and write the selected questions on a copy master or poster for the opposing team's reference. They turn over the answers and lists of proofs to the teacher or some other appointed referee.

3. The teams exchange questions. Each team gets an equal period of time to find the answers.

4. The teacher or referee checks the answers and identifies the champion trivia team.

Letters

Abraham Lincoln is most famous for his actions as President. However, he was not only a leader of his country. He had a family and felt deeply for his friends and acquaintances.

You will read two letters by Abraham Lincoln. One is a personal letter to his brother. The other is a letter he wrote as President. Although this letter is official, Lincoln's human sympathy and kindness shine through his formal words.

Army Boots, 1865, WINSLOW HOMER. Hirshhorn Museum and Sculpture Garden, Smithsonian Institution, Washington, D.C.

About the Art

The American painter Winslow Homer (1836-1910), known for his paintings of the sea, began his career as an illustrator. In 1862 he was hired by the magazine *Harper's Weekly* to cover the Civil War, which he recorded in drawings and paintings. *Army Boots* shows two young boys who are probably freed slaves attached to a Union regiment. Apparently too young to be soldiers, one of their jobs would probably have been to shine the officers' boots, a pair of which we see in the foreground along with an open tin of shoe polish. The two boys, a deck of cards spread out before them, seem to have put aside their task for the moment and are shown relaxing. The life of a regiment consisted not only of long marches and skirmishes with the enemy, but also of such quiet moments in camp as shown here.

Abraham Lincoln:
A Letter to His Step-Brother

Here is a personal letter from Lincoln to his step-brother. Read it carefully to understand Lincoln's reasoning. Do you think it was easy for him to write what he did?

Dec. 24, 1848

Dear Johnston:

Your request for eighty dollars, I do not think it best to comply with now. At the various times when I have helped you a little, you have said to me, "We can get along very well now," but in a very short time I find you in the same difficulty again. Now this can only happen by some defect in your conduct. What that defect is, I think I know. You are not *lazy,* and still you are an *idler.* I doubt whether since I saw you, you have done a good whole day's work, in any one day. You do not very much dislike to work, and still you do not work much, merely because it does not seem to you that you could get much for it.

This habit of uselessly wasting time, is the whole difficulty; it is vastly important to you, and still more so to your children, that you should break this habit. It is more important to them, because they have longer to live, and can keep out of an idle habit before they are in it, easier than they can get out after they are in.

You are now in need of some ready money; and what I propose is, that you shall go to work, "tooth and nail," for somebody who will give you money for it.

Objectives

- To recognize a well-written letter as a form of literature
- To recognize the role of literature in reflecting a culture
- To apply literal, interpretive, and critical reading skills to a selection

Preparing the Students

Essential Vocabulary. The words presented here are essential to the understanding of the selection.

Introduce the words listed below. Write the sentences on the board, have them read aloud, and ask the students to use context clues to find the meaning of the underlined words.

comply deed indebtedness

1. Unless you comply with our rules, you cannot remain a member of the club.
2. The older brother thought he would own the farm someday, and was surprised when his father chose to deed it to his younger brother.
3. The company's indebtedness was so great that it took several years to pay back the money it owed.

If the students need additional help with the vocabulary of this selection, encourage them to use context clues to determine word meaning. As needed, direct them to the **Glossary** or to a classroom dictionary.

Motivation. Explain that, in Lincoln's time, personal letters were the main method of communication. People were more used to writing long letters to friends and family than people are now.

Have the students read the introductory paragraph on page 455 and ask them to state in their own words what they should think about as they read this letter.

Presenting the Selection

1. Read "Abraham Lincoln: A Letter to His Step-Brother" to the students. Stop after each paragraph to make sure students understand the most important ideas.

2. Check comprehension by administering the **Check Test** on page 456.

3. Remind the students that the introduction to the selection asked them to decide if they think it was easy for Lincoln to write what he did in his letter. Ask several students to answer the question.

4. Develop the study questions as suggested in **Using the Study Questions** on page 457. That section also provides a challenge question for further discussion.

Let father and your boys take charge of your things at home—prepare for a crop, and make the crop, and you go to work for the best money wages, or in discharge of any debt you owe, that you can get. And to secure you a fair reward for your labor, I now promise you that for every dollar you will, between this and the first of May, get for your own labor either in money or in your own indebtedness, I will then give you one other dollar.

By this, if you hire yourself at ten dollars a month, from me you will get ten more, making twenty dollars a month for your work. In this, I do not mean you shall go off to St. Louis, or the lead mines, or the gold mines, in California, but I mean for you to go at it for the best wages you can get close to home—in Coles County.

Now if you will do this, you will soon be out of debt, and what is better, you will have a habit that will keep you from getting in debt again. But if I should now clear you out, next year you will be just as deep in as ever. You say you would almost give your place in Heaven for $70 or $80. Then you value your place in Heaven very cheaply, for I am sure you can with the offer I make you get the seventy or eighty dollars for four or five months' work. You say if I furnish you the money you will deed me the land, and if you don't pay the money back, you will deliver possession—

Nonsense! If you can't now live *with* the land, how will you then live without it? You have always been kind to me, and I do not now mean to be unkind to you. On the contrary, if you will but follow my advice, you will find it worth more than eight times eighty dollars to you.

Affectionately,
Your brother,
A. Lincoln

Check Test

1. What did Lincoln's stepbrother ask Lincoln to give him? ($80)

2. Who did Lincoln think should run the farm while his stepbrother was working? (His father and Johnston's sons)

3. What did Lincoln offer to do to encourage his brother to work? (pay him a dollar for every dollar he earned)

Developing Comprehension Skills

Literal Reading — 1. Write the first sentence of the letter in your own words. It might help you to know that "comply" means to agree with or go along with.

Literal Reading — 2. Why did Lincoln refuse to lend his brother the money?

Interpretive Reading — 3. Do you think Abraham Lincoln had a fairly close relationship with his step-brother? Give reasons for your answer.

Critical Reading — 4. Do you believe Lincoln was right to answer as he did? Why or why not?

Reading Literature: Nonfiction

1. **Learning about History through Literature.** This letter reflects the society of the times. For instance, we learn that $80 was worth a lot and took a long time to earn. What else did you learn from this letter about what life was like a century ago?

2. **Recognizing Tone.** What is Lincoln's attitude toward his step-brother's request? What is his attitude toward his own proposal?

Using the Study Questions

It is recommended that students always read and answer the questions in **Developing Comprehension Skills** in class discussion. Whenever possible, they should also read the questions in the other categories together and discuss the answers.

Developing Comprehension Skills

Question 1. Read and discuss the question.

Question 2. Students should find evidence for their answers in the selection.

Question 3. Suggest that students reread the letter, looking for passages that indicate closeness.

Question 4. Students must be able to give solid reasons for their opinions.

Challenge Question. What is the difference between a lazy person and an idler, according to Lincoln? (Interpretive Reading)

Reading Literature: Nonfiction

Question 1. Students may again need to refer to the letter to find specific examples of what life was like at that time.

Question 2. Students must analyze the tone carefully. Lincoln is critical of his brother's actions but he is not negative.

Answers to Study Questions

Developing Comprehension Skills

1. Possible answer: I don't think I should give you the eighty dollars you want right now.

2. Lincoln was afraid that his brother would keep his bad habits and go into debt again. He felt it was better for his brother to be offered a reason to work.

3. Answers will vary, but it seems to be a reasonably close relationship. Possible proofs: Lincoln took the time to write a lengthy letter giving his stepbrother advice that he thought could help him. Lincoln stated in his letter that his stepbrother had always been kind to him. Lincoln promised his stepbrother that he would give him one dollar for every dollar he earned.

4. Answers will vary. Possible answers: Lincoln was right. It was the only way his stepbrother would learn to help himself.

Lincoln was wrong. Since he had the money to give, he should have helped his stepbrother in need and should have trusted him to change his habits.

Challenge. Possible answer: A person who doesn't like to work is lazy. A person who simply doesn't work is an idler.

Reading Literature: Nonfiction

1. Farming was common; people lived in extended families; a worker could earn about ten dollars per month; lead mines and gold mines were places where people thought they could earn a lot of money fast.

2. Lincoln is disappointed in his brother and regretful that he has to refuse Johnston's request, but he is positive and hopeful about his suggestion to Johnston.

Objectives

- To recognize and appreciate well-written letters as a form of literature
- To recognize the role of literature in reflecting a culture
- To analyze connotations of words
- To recognize alliteration as an element of personal style
- To apply literal, interpretive, and critical reading skills to a selection
- To identify the correct respelling, part of speech, and meaning of a word to fit its context
- To write a comparison of two letters
- To analyze the organization of a selection

Preparing the Students

Essential Vocabulary. The words presented here are essential to the understanding of the selection.

Have students use context clues in the following sentences to find the meaning of the underlined words.

fruitless	assuage	consolation
beguile	tendering	
refrain	bereavement	

1. Arguing with Ann was fruitless; she did what she wanted to do anyway.
2. Kim could not beguile her friends into believing that she was as happy as she pretended to be.
3. Since his grades dropped, John's parents said he had to refrain from watching television in the evenings until he finished his homework.
4. Even though he didn't mean to damage his brother's trophy, nothing could assuage Howard's feelings of guilt.
5. The tendering of money to a police officer in payment for special favors is against the law.
6. Since they felt they had lost a good friend, the neighbors shared in the widow's feeling of bereavement.
7. Friends' attempts at consolation didn't work. The grieving mother could not be comforted.

If the students need additional help with the vocabulary of this selection, encourage them to use context clues to determine word meaning. As needed, direct them to the **Glossary** or to a classroom dictionary.

Motivation. Have students examine the photograph on page 459. Looking at this detailed photo might make the war seem more real to the students. Explain that the Civil War took a terrible toll of American lives, both North and South.

Abraham Lincoln:
A Letter to Mrs. Bixby

This letter was written sixteen years after the last one, after Lincoln had become President. It is an official letter, so its style is formal. How did Lincoln feel about Mrs. Bixby's sons?

Executive Mansion
Washington, Nov. 21, 1864

To Mrs. Bixby, Boston, Mass.

Dear Madam,

I have been shown in the files of the War Department a statement of the Adjutant General of Massachusetts that you are the mother of five sons who have died gloriously on the field of battle. I feel how weak and fruitless must be any word of mine which should attempt to beguile you from the grief of a loss so overwhelming. But I cannot refrain from tendering you the consolation that may be found in the thanks of the republic they died to save. I pray that our Heavenly Father may assuage the anguish of your bereavement, and leave you only the cherished memory of the loved and lost, and the solemn pride that must be yours to have laid so costly a sacrifice upon the altar of freedom.

Yours very sincerely and respectfully,
A. Lincoln

Check Test

1. How many of Mrs. Bixby's sons were reported killed? (five)

2. How did Lincoln find that Mrs. Bixby had lost her sons? (War Department files)

Answers to Study Questions

Developing Comprehension Skills

1. Answers should be similar to the following: I hope the thanks that I am expressing on behalf of the people of this country will in some way comfort you.

2. Lincoln was very sad that the sons had died. However, he felt the deaths had not been in vain. Because of them, the republic had been preserved.

3. Answers will vary. Possible answer: The letter probably consoled the mother by letting her know that someone was aware of her sorrow. It also served the purpose of assuring her that her sons'

Union supply base at Cumberland, used during McClellan's Peninsular Campaign in 1862. Library of Congress.

Developing Comprehension Skills

Literal Reading

1. Because this letter was written over a century ago, the language is a little hard to understand. Take some time to "translate" it into modern English. Write the third sentence in your own words. The phrase "beguile you from" means "lead you away from."

Interpretive Reading

2. What was Mr. Lincoln's feeling about these deaths?

Critical Reading

3. Do you think this letter served its purpose? If you were Mrs. Bixby, how might you react to it? Give reasons for your answers.

deaths had not been worthless. Their deaths had saved the republic and helped preserve freedom. Instead of simply feeling grief, the mother could also feel pride.

Challenge. Answers will vary. Possible answers: family, country, beliefs.

Reading Literature: Nonfiction

1. Possible answers: solemn, sad, respectful.

This letter conveys an attitude of gratefulness and respect. The letter to Lincoln's step-brother is more factual, logical, and persuasive.

2. Some possible answers include: gloriously, cherished, solemn, pride, altar of freedom, thanks of the republic.

It helps Lincoln to show the positive outcome of the sons' deaths.

3. It tells you that a terrible number of lives were lost, and that both soldiers and the people at home were deeply committed to their cause.

4. loved and lost; so costly a sacrifice

Challenge. Answers will vary. Point out the lack of permanence in a phone call and also the lack of formality. The letter to

(continued on page 460)

Have students read the introductory paragraph on page 458. Then ask them to state in their own words what they should try to find out as they read this letter.

Presenting the Selection

1. Have the students read "Abraham Lincoln: A Letter to Mrs. Bixby" silently.

2. Make sure that everyone has read the assignment by administering the **Check Test** at the bottom of this page.

3. Have a volunteer read the letter aloud in the tone of voice that reflects how he or she thinks Mr. Lincoln felt as he wrote it. The question posed in the introduction to the selection will be answered directly in connection with **Developing Comprehension Skills, 2.**

4. Develop the study questions as suggested in **Using the Study Questions** beginning on page 459. That section also provides challenge questions for further discussion, as needed.

Reinforcing the Lesson

To reteach, reinforce, or extend the skills in this lesson, see the following:

Skills Practice Book, Green Level— pages 174, 175, and 176

Special Populations

ESL. For the exercise **Identifying the Correct Respelling and Part of Speech** on page 460, you might choose to omit the work concerning respellings and, instead, ask the students to list all of the meanings given for each of the words underlined. Then, have them choose the correct meaning from the list and tell why they feel it is correct.

Using the Study Questions

It is recommended that students always read and answer the questions in **Developing Comprehension Skills** in class discussion. Whenever possible, they should also read the questions in the other categories together and discuss the answers.

Developing Comprehension Skills

Question 1. Have several students read their translations aloud.

Question 2. Read and discuss the question.

Question 3. Students may point out that very little could lessen the grief of losing five sons, but they should recognize that this letter would have accomplished what was possible to do.

Challenge Question. Lincoln thought Mrs. Bixby's sons died for a good cause. Is there something you think would be worth dying for? Explain your answer. (Critical Reading)

Reading Literature: Nonfiction

Question 1. Remind students that *tone* refers to the writer's attitude toward the subject. Have students consider the purpose of each letter in determining the tone of each.

Question 2. List students' suggestions on the board. Have several students describe the feelings that the words with positive connotations reminded them of. Example: "died gloriously"—courage, honor

Question 3. Read and discuss the question.

Question 4. As a review, discuss the meaning of alliteration. Then complete discussion of this question.

Challenge Question. Today, business that once would have been done by letter is done on the telephone. Referring to either one of Lincoln's letters, compare the letter with an imaginary phone call saying the same things. What differences would there be? Which forms of communication do you think suit each subject better?

Developing Vocabulary Skills

Have the students read the directions and complete the exercise. As each answer is discussed, ask for the second pronunciation of the word. Students must be careful to distinguish between the two pronunciations and meanings.

Developing Writing Skills

Read and discuss the two assignments. Then have the students choose and complete one of the two.

Question 1. To answer this question, the student must place himself or herself in Lincoln's situation. Students must imagine Lincoln's feelings.

Pre-Writing. Have students reread each letter and make a list of reasons why it might have been difficult to write it. Then have them analyze each list to determine which reasons would make the task harder. Each student should have a slightly different list and a slightly different order.

Reading Literature: Nonfiction

1. **Comparing the Tone.** What is the tone of this letter? How is it different from Lincoln's letter to his step-brother?
2. **Analyzing Connotation.** Identify in this letter two examples of words with positive connotation. How does this connotation help President Lincoln make his point?
3. **Learning about History through Literature.** What does this letter tell you about the Civil War?
4. **Recognizing Alliteration.** One way that Lincoln made this difficult message easier to accept was by using a stately rhythm in the sentences. Another way was by using alliteration to connect phrases. In the last sentence, identify at least one instance of alliteration.

Developing Vocabulary Skills

Identifying the Correct Respelling and Part of Speech. Read the following sentences drawn from the nonfiction selections you have read. Each of the underlined words can be pronounced two different ways. Each word also has more than one part of speech. Decide how each word is used in the sentence. Then look up the word in the dictionary. On your paper, write the following for each word:

a. The correct respelling
b. The part of speech
c. The correct meaning

1. If you <u>abuse</u> the horse, she will be ruined for ever.
2. My father's way of discipline was more <u>appropriate</u>.
3. I am filled with wonder when I consider the <u>contrasts</u> between the two lives which that day connects.
4. I returned again and again to the <u>subject</u>, eager for more information.
5. I did nothing but explore with my hands and learn the name of every <u>object</u> that I touched.
6. Lincoln was asked what would be the best <u>attribute</u> for a politician.
7. He said the attribute "would be the ability to raise a cause which would <u>produce</u> an effect and then fight the effect."

(continued from page 459)
Lincoln's step-brother might have been handled adequately in a phone conversation, but the letter to the mother was probably done best in its present form. It was formal and solemn and could be read again and again.

Developing Vocabulary Skills

Respellings and definitions will vary depending on the dictionary used, but should be clearly similar to the following. Any shift in accent position indicates an error. Parts of speech are as follows.

1. (ə byo͞oz′); verb; use wrongly
2. (ə prō′ prē it); adjective; suitable, proper
3. (kän′ trasts); noun; differences
4. (sub′ jikt); noun; something thought about, discussed, or studied
5. (äb′ jikt); noun; something that can be seen or touched
6. (á trə byo͞ot); noun; a characteristic belonging to a person
7. (prə do͞os′); verb; bring forward, show
8. (kän′ dukt); noun; way of acting
9. (dē′ fekt); noun; fault
10. (ik skyo͞os′); noun; a reason, real or pretended, that is given

8. Lincoln refused his step-brother eighty dollars because of a defect in the step-brother's conduct.
9. The defect was that his step-brother didn't do a day's work in a day.
10. I blubbered a short excuse: "They were only girls."

Developing Writing Skills

Analytical Writing

1. **Comparing the Two Letters.** Both of these letters must have been difficult for Abraham Lincoln to write, although for different reasons. Write a paragraph telling which you think was harder to write. First, you will have to tell what was hard about writing each one. Then, give reasons to support your opinion.

Creative Writing

2. **Writing a Personal Letter.** Write a letter to an imaginary person. In your letter, deal with a serious topic and serious feelings. It should be a personal letter, not a formal one. The letter should be at least three paragraphs long. There should be a clear development of your ideas.

Developing Skills in Critical Thinking

Analyzing Organization. Lincoln's letter to his step-brother starts out by saying that he doesn't think it is a good idea to send the $80. Lincoln then goes on to say why. He has an organized argument. Outline Lincoln's argument step by step. Here is the beginning of your outline. Use as many numbers as you need.

1. I have helped you before, but you soon had money problems again.
2. You are not lazy, but you are an idler.
3. You have a habit of wasting time.

Writing. Remind students to give reasons that support their opinions. Allow sufficient time for students to complete the assignment.

Revising. Have students reread and revise their paragraphs to make sure that their opinions are supported with strong reasoning, and their ideas are presented in a logical order.

Question 2. Explain that this letter will be read only by you. This assurance might make it easier for some students to deal with subjects that are personally important but private.

Pre-Writing. Have students reread Lincoln's letter to his stepbrother to see the clear development of his ideas. See **Analyzing Organization,** below. Emphasize that students can choose any serious topic from something in the news to a personal problem. Give students time to select a topic. Have them make notes on their topic and then have them organize the notes logically.

Writing. Before students begin writing, have them check their ideas to be sure they are well organized. Have students construct a letter that follows the outline of their ideas. However, let them know that as they write, they might find their ideas changing or their emphasis shifting, from the problem, for example, to a solution. Encourage them to revise their writing plan as they go.

Remind them that their letters should be at least three paragraphs long.

Revising. Have students reread their letters to be sure the ideas are connected from one paragraph to the next. Before collecting the papers, allow time for corrections and revisions to be made.

Developing Skills in Critical Thinking

Read and discuss the assignment. Ask students why organization is a necessary element in writing. Have students write their own outlines for Lincoln's letter. Ask for suggestions for a class outline and, on the board, record students' suggestions for each point. Have students compare their outline with the class outline.

Developing Skills in Critical Thinking

Possible completion of outline:

4. It is important for you to break your habit of wasting time.
5. My suggestion to you is to get a paying job.
6. I will give you one dollar for every dollar you earn.
7. This will get you out of debt and keep you from getting into debt again.
8. You can get seventy or eighty dollars for just four or five months' work.
9. You have promised your land to repay the loan, but I know you wouldn't be able to live without the land.
10. What I am suggesting is more valuable to you than eight times eighty dollars.

Speeches

Have the students read page 462 and identify how public opinion of Lincoln's speeches has changed over the years. Suggest that the students try to recall speeches they have heard. Have them determine what qualities they liked or disliked in those speeches. Then, as they read Lincoln's speeches in this section, they can compare and contrast Lincoln's approach to speech-making with the speeches they have heard.

Speeches

During his lifetime, Abraham Lincoln was not considered one of the great speakers of the country. Many audiences preferred long speeches filled with difficult words and complicated ideas. However, those complicated speeches have long been forgotten while Lincoln's short speeches are still remembered.

The Right To Know (detail), 1968, NORMAN ROCKWELL.

About the Art

Norman Rockwell (1894-1978) is popularly known by his widely circulated illustrations and paintings, reproduced for many years in magazines such as *Saturday Evening Post, Ladies' Home Journal,* and the *American Magazine*. With photographic clarity and attention to detail, Rockwell portrayed, often humorously, the everyday life in America. In 1945, he painted a series called *The Four Freedoms*—"Freedom of Expression," "Freedom of Worship," "Freedom from Fear," and "Freedom from Want." These pieces were intended to illustrate the democratic ideals jointly expressed by Winston Churchill and Franklin Delano Roosevelt at the beginning of World War II.

The Right To Know is in this tradition. Rockwell presents a range of American society, in race, sex, age, and occupation. It seems any one observer who might question the look on these faces would be confronted with the reality that America takes its democratic tradition seriously and challenges any threat to its basic freedoms.

Rockwell placed himself, smoking a pipe, in the right of the painting.

Farewell Address:
Delivered at Springfield, Illinois, February 11, 1861

ABRAHAM LINCOLN

When Lincoln was elected President, he had to move from Illinois to Washington, D.C. This is how he said goodbye to his friends and neighbors in his hometown.

My Friends:

No one, not in my situation, can appreciate my feeling of sadness at this parting. To this place, and the kindness of these people, I owe everything. Here I have lived a quarter of a century, and have passed from a young to an old man. Here my children have been born, and one is buried. I now leave, not knowing when or whether ever I may return, with a task before me greater than that which rested upon Washington. Without the assistance of that Divine Being who ever attended him, I cannot succeed. With that assistance, I cannot fail. Trusting in Him who can go with me, and remain with you, and be everywhere for good, let us confidently hope that all will yet be well. To His care commending you, as I hope in your prayers you will commend me, I bid you an affectionate farewell.

Check Test

1. Where had Lincoln lived before he gave this farewell speech? (Springfield, Illinois)

2. How did he feel about leaving? (sad)

3. When did he plan to return? (He didn't know.)

Objectives

- To recognize speeches as a form of nonfiction literature
- To recognize the literary style of a speech and its effect on the listener
- To apply literal, interpretive, and critical reading skills to a selection
- To identify the important details in a speech
- To complete analogies
- To write the first paragraph of a speech

Preparing the Students

Essential Vocabulary. The words presented here are essential to the understanding of the selection.

Ask the students to use context clues in the sentences below to find the meaning of the underlined word.

The parents will <u>commend</u> their child to the care of his grandparents while they are out of town.

If the students need additional help with the vocabulary of this selection, encourage them to use context clues to determine word meaning. As needed, direct them to the **Glossary** or to a classroom dictionary.

Motivation. Ask students how Lincoln might have felt about leaving his hometown when he became President. Then have them read the introductory paragraph on page 463 and ask them what the subject of the speech will be.

Presenting the Selection

1. Have the students read "Farewell Address" silently.

2. Make sure that everyone has read the assignment by administering the **Check Test** at the bottom of this page.

3. Have a volunteer read the selection aloud.

4. Develop the study questions as suggested in **Using the Study Questions** beginning on page 464.

Using the Study Questions

It is recommended that students always read and answer the questions in **Developing Comprehension Skills** in class discussion. Whenever possible, they should also read the questions in the other categories together and discuss the answers. A challenge question has been provided for further discussion, as needed.

Developing Comprehension Skills

Question 1. Read and discuss.

Question 2. Students are translating into a simpler, more modern form of English. Remind them that they may not change Lincoln's intended meaning.

Question 3. Have students refer to the speech to answer this question. Help them to recognize what Lincoln meant by Washington's great task (starting a new country).

Question 4. Read and discuss.

Question 5. Have students compare this speech with ones given by most other politicians. Ask them how they differ. Help them to recognize the simplicity of Lincoln's speech.

Challenge Question. What in Lincoln's background might have helped him become a skilled speaker? (Interpretive Reading)

Reading Literature: Nonfiction

Question 1. Ask students to use their knowledge of Lincoln's personality, in addition to the speech itself, to answer this question.

Question 2. You may want to list these ideas on the board as students suggest them.

Question 3. Have students read each sentence slowly and carefully, looking first for repetition and, on the second careful reading, looking for balance of words and phrases.

Developing Vocabulary Skills

This is the third exercise about analogies in this text. By this time, students should be able to read the directions and complete the analogies independently. Encourage students to use the dictionary when they find a word they can't understand. Discuss the answers together.

Developing Writing Skills

Read and discuss the two assignments. Then have the students choose and complete one of the two.

Developing Comprehension Skills

Literal Reading — 1. To what or whom did Lincoln feel he owed everything?

Literal Reading — 2. Write the last sentence of the speech in your own words. Here is some information to help you: "His" refers to God; "commending" is like "entrusting," or putting in the care of someone trustworthy.

Interpretive Reading — 3. Did Lincoln think that he was becoming President at an important time in history? Give a reason for your answer.

Interpretive Reading — 4. Remember that this speech was written just before the start of the Civil War. What did Lincoln mean by hoping "that all will yet be well"?

Critical Reading — 5. Very often a person elected to public office makes a speech just to get publicity. Do you feel that this was Lincoln's goal? If not, what was the purpose of this speech?

Reading Literature: Nonfiction

1. **Identifying Tone.** Basing your opinion on this speech, how do you think Lincoln felt when he gave it? Do you think he is being honest about his feelings? Give reasons for your answer.

2. **Identifying Important Details.** A good speech should give you ideas to think about after the speaker is finished. What ideas did Lincoln leave for his listeners to think about? Name at least two.

3. **Recognizing Literary Style.** Abraham Lincoln wrote very effective speeches. He used words, phrases, and sentence patterns carefully to achieve the effect he desired. This care in writing produced a "Farewell Address," which has an almost musical and prayerful quality. Lincoln achieved this quality by using several methods, or **techniques**, in writing.

   One method was the repetition of a certain pattern of words within a sentence. The third sentence, where he uses two related verb phrases, "have lived" and "have passed," is an example of this. Another technique was that of balancing related words or phrases, either within one sentence or in sentences close together. Examples are "born" and "buried," and "when or whether."

   Find in the "Farewell Address" an additional example of repetition of sentence patterns and another example of balance.

Answers to Study Questions

Developing Comprehension Skills

1. Lincoln felt he owed everything to the place where he lived and the kindness of the people there.

2. Possible sentence: I pray that God will take care of you and I hope you will pray the same for me as I tell you good-bye.

3. Yes, Lincoln did. He said his task was greater than Washington's.

4. Lincoln meant he hoped that war could be avoided.

5. Answers may vary but publicity does not seem to be the purpose. Lincoln is not expressing his views on the issues or making promises. Instead, he is merely expressing feelings of gratitude and affection to the people he grew up with.

Challenge. Since Lincoln read so much, he became good at using words. By telling jokes and stories, he became accustomed to speaking to crowds and experienced in predicting audience reaction.

Reading Literature: Nonfiction

1. Possible answers: sad; hopeful; concerned; nervous. Students will probably feel that he is being honest because he has shown in other writings that he values

Developing Vocabulary Skills

Completing Analogies. In a word analogy, there are two pairs of related words. Each pair is related in the same way, for example, as synonyms or as antonyms. Complete the following analogies involving words used in this chapter.

1. intermittent is to constant as meager is to ______.
   abundant gaudy isolated small
2. languor is to listlessness as grief is to ______.
   graciousness sadness height laziness
3. hero is to inspire as sentinel is to ______.
   watch confuse immigrant generation
4. solitary is to isolated as passionate is to ______.
   perplexed emotional rambling sinister
5. stimulus is to response as incentive is to ______.
   action incident rebuke gasp
6. rebuke is to sulky as ______ is to radiant.
   gesture ramble speculate praise
7. stymie is to encourage as obstacle is to ______.
   intuitive multitude assist oculist
8. President is to country as ______ is to state.
   general cabinet member governor congressman

Developing Writing Skills

Analytical Writing

1. **Evaluating the Effectiveness of a Speech.** Lincoln's "Farewell Address" is very short. It probably took no more than a minute or two to deliver it. Did this shortness make the speech more effective or less effective? Would the speech have been better if it had been longer? Write a paragraph telling your opinion.

Creative Writing

2. **Writing a Speech.** Think of a topic you feel strongly about. Write the first paragraph of a speech on this topic. The first paragraph should tell what the speech will be about and give some indication of your opinion. It should also set the tone of the speech.

honesty. Also, he wouldn't have had to win support that he probably already had.

2. Possible answers: What it is like to leave home; the possibility of war and of avoiding war; trust in God; the need for prayer

3. Some of the possible answers are the following (The same phrase may appear in either classification.):

Repetition—"this place," "these people;" "I cannot succeed," "I cannot fail;" "Here" (two times); "Without the assistance," "With that assistance"

Balance—"from young ... to old;" "go with me, and remain with you, and be everywhere;" "commending you," "commend me;" "I now leave" and "I may return"

Developing Vocabulary Skills

1. abundant **5.** action
2. sadness **6.** praise
3. watch **7.** assist
4. emotional **8.** governor

Question 1. Emphasize that there is no single correct answer. Any answer that is supported by logical reasons is acceptable.

Pre-Writing. Make four lists on the board. Label them as follows: *Advantages of a Short Speech, Disadvantages of a Short Speech, Advantages of a Long Speech, Disadvantages of a Long Speech.* Ask students for suggestions to fill in each list. Have them consider how well each type of speech would communicate its message. Then, have the students decide whether the "Farewell Address" accomplished its purpose. Have the students look over the board list and decide whether the speech would have been improved if it had it been longer. Have each student write a paragraph stating his or her opinion.

Writing. Tell students that they can use the ideas in the list on the board to explain their opinions. Allow sufficient time for students to complete the assignment.

Revising. Have students reread their paragraphs to be sure they included topic sentences stating their opinions and logical reasons to support their opinions. Have them refer to the **Checklist for the Process of Writing** on pages 556 and 557 for help in revising and proofreading.

Question 2. This question gives students an opportunity to use some of the techniques they have studied in Lincoln's writing. Encourage able students to complete the speech.

Pre-Writing. Have students suggest topics that interest them and list those on the board. Have them make notes on what they want to say about at least three of the topics or additional topics of their own. The let each student select one of those ideas.

Writing. Remind students that their opening paragraphs should tell their opinions about their chosen topics and should also set the tone. Remind students to use strong verbs and simple, direct language.

Revising. Have students read their speeches aloud to partners or to a small group. Have the listeners explain what the speech is about and list two or three ideas that support the opinion expressed in the speech. If the listeners cannot identify the subjects, the opinions, or any supporting details, have the writers revise their speeches for clarity.

Students who need challenge should also be advised to notice the effect of their reading on their audiences. As a speech, this composition should move the audience to some feeling or understanding. If their words didn't capture their listeners' interest, the writers should examine and improve their style.

Objectives

- To recognize and appreciate speeches as a form of nonfiction literature
- To recognize the role of literature in recording and interpreting human experience
- To recognize theme in a selection
- To identify the author's purpose for writing a speech
- To apply literal, interpretive, and critical reading skills to a selection
- To use a pronunciation key to figure out the pronunciation of a word
- To write a comparison of two selections
- To recognize slanted writing
- To deliver a speech effectively

Preparing the Students

Essential Vocabulary. The words presented here are essential to the understanding of the selection.

Introduce the words listed below. Write the sentences on the board, have them read aloud, and ask the students to use context clues to find the meaning of the underlined words.

hallow nobly

1. We cannot hallow this ground, that is, set it aside as holy.
2. The soldiers acted nobly in giving their lives for others.

If the students need additional help with the vocabulary of this selection, encourage them to use context clues to determine word meaning. As needed, direct them to the **Glossary** or to a classroom dictionary.

Motivation. Ask students if they have ever heard of Gettysburg. Ask them what they know about it. If they are unfamiliar with the battle, let them know the following: It raged for four days (July 1 to 5, 1863) and cost the lives of thousands of men. The site was the farthest north that the Confederate army reached. The fact that Lee's army was defeated at Gettysburg gave the U.S. army renewed hope and the will to fight on to victory.

Have the students read the introductory paragraph on page 466. Have them state in their own words what they should try to find out as they read this famous speech.

Presenting the Selection

1. Read "The Gettysburg Address" aloud to the class. Since many of the words and sentence constructions are difficult, it is important that you emphasize the most important ideas.

2. Make sure that everyone has listened to the selection by administering the **Check Test** on this page.

3. Remind the students that the introduction to the selection asked them to find out what Lincoln wanted his listeners to learn from the battle at Gettysburg. Have several students answer the question.

4. Develop the study questions as suggested in **Using the Study Questions** beginning on page 467.

The Gettysburg Address: Delivered at Gettysburg, Pennsylvania, November 19, 1863

ABRAHAM LINCOLN

In 1863, the Civil War was still raging. That fall, President Lincoln spoke at the dedication of a cemetery on the site of the Battle of Gettysburg. What did he want his listeners to learn from that awful battle?

Four score and seven years ago our fathers brought forth upon this continent a new nation, conceived in liberty, and dedicated to the proposition that all men are created equal.

Now we are engaged in a great civil war, testing whether that nation, or any nation so conceived and so dedicated, can long endure. We are met here on a great battlefield of that war. We have come to dedicate a portion of it as a final resting place for those who here gave their lives that that nation might live. It is altogether fitting and proper that we should do this.

But, in a larger sense, we cannot dedicate—we cannot consecrate—we cannot hallow this ground. The brave men, living and dead, who struggled here, have consecrated it far above our poor power to add or detract. The world will little note nor long remember what we say here, but can never forget what they did here. It is for us, the living, rather to be dedicated here to the unfinished work which they have, thus far, so nobly carried on. It is rather for us to be here dedicated to the great task remaining before us—that from these honored dead we take increased devotion to that cause for which they here gave the last full measure of devotion; that we here highly resolve that these dead shall not have died in vain; that this nation shall have a new birth of freedom; and that this Government of the people, by the people, for the people, shall not perish from the earth.

Check Test

1. Was "The Gettysburg Address" written before, during, or after the Civil War? (during)

2. How long after the founding of the country was "The Gettysburg Address" given? (four score and seven years or 87 years)

3. Why was Lincoln speaking at Gettysburg? (to dedicate a battlefield)

Civil War Drum, 9th Regiment Infantry. Chicago Historical Society.

Developing Comprehension Skills

Literal Reading — 1. Some of the words in this speech may not be familiar to you. In the first sentence, for instance, a "score" is twenty; "conceived" means brought into existence; and a "proposition" is a proposal or a statement. Rewrite the first sentence of the speech in your own words.

Literal Reading — 2. Lincoln came to Gettysburg to dedicate a portion of the battlefield to the soldiers who died there. Then he said that could not be done. How did he arrive at this conclusion?

Literal Reading — 3. Lincoln was asking his listeners to do something. In your own words, say what he wanted them to do.

Interpretive Reading — 4. This speech contains many unusual words. Do you think Lincoln purposely chose words not used in everyday conversation? Why would he do such a thing?

Critical Reading — 5. Why do you suppose this speech is included in a literature book? Do you agree it still has meaning for us today? Why or why not?

Reinforcing the Lesson

To reteach, reinforce, or extend skills in this lesson, see the following:

Skills Practice Book, Green Level—pages 177 and 178

Special Populations

ESL. The unfamiliar vocabulary and syntax of "The Gettysburg Address" might make it initially difficult for ESL students to understand. After you have read the speech to the class, it would be helpful to paraphrase the text of the speech for the students. Be sure the students have the necessary historical background for an understanding of the importance of the speech in our country's history.

ESL students may be hesitant to deliver a speech to the class because of insecurity with their command of the English language. Allow students extra time to prepare for a speech. Pair students with native English-speaking students for practice sessions. Avoid commenting on incorrect pronunciation or different patterns of intonation and phrasing.

LD, ESL. The respelling exercise presented on page 468, **Using a Pronunciation Key,** can be altered for many ESL or LD students. Ask them to choose from a list of the same words spelled as they usually are to find the answers to the questions.

Using the Study Questions

It is recommended that students always read and answer the questions in **Developing Comprehension Skills** in class discussion. Whenever possible, they should also read the questions in the other categories together and discuss the answers.

Developing Comprehension Skills

Question 1. Remind students that they must keep the meaning behind Lincoln's words in their translation.

Question 2. Help students to follow the logic of Lincoln's thinking by discussing that portion of the speech, sentence by sentence or even phrase by phrase.

Question 3. Again, students may need to analyze the last half of the speech, phrase by phrase, beginning with "It is for us, the living ...." Have one volunteer point out the portion of the speech that answers the question, then discuss the meaning of the words together.

Question 4. Remind students that Lincoln often used everyday, informal lan-

Answers to Study Questions

Developing Comprehension Skills

1. Answers will vary. Possible answer: Eighty-seven years ago, our ancestors made a new, free country with the idea that all people are equal.

2. Lincoln felt that the soldiers who died there had already consecrated the battlefield.

3. Lincoln wanted the people to dedicate themselves to preserving the United States, that is, to determine to win the War and to make the country better.

(continued on page 468)

About the Art

Drums have been carried into battle and used as a means of sending signals since the early history of man. During the American Civil War, drums were made by local drummers. The top and bottom of the drum were often made of calfskin with hoops placed over it to create the necessary tension. The tension in the finished drum was controlled by leather slides on the sides of the drums. When a company's drum was delivered, the regiment's insignia were painted onto the body.

guage in his other writing. Help students see that Lincoln always chose his words with care. Have a student list on the board some of the unusual words Lincoln used.

Question 5. Have students discuss why any piece of writing is chosen to be included in a literature book. Have students explain their answers to the question about whether the speech still has meaning today.

Reading Literature: Nonfiction

Question 1. Students should easily recognize the seriousness of this speech. Encourage students to describe several feelings the speech gives.

Question 2. Review the meaning of theme in a class discussion. Students should know that a statement of theme must be a broad, inclusive idea that is not limited to any one time period or location. Have students reread Lincoln's speech to determine its themes.

Question 3. Ask the students to try to imagine the people who were listening to Lincoln's speech. What reaction did he want them to have?

Question 4. Students will find it much easier to answer this question if they read Lincoln's words aloud. If they are working out the answers in class, allow a few minutes for every student to read to himself or herself aloud, simultaneously. Then let the students discuss, in groups of twos or threes, their favorite lines, reading those lines to each other. Last, working as a class, they should answer the question.

If the questions are assigned as homework, encourage students to do these question where they can read aloud.

Developing Vocabulary Skills

Have the students read the instructions silently. Point out the pronunciation key

Reading Literature: Nonfiction

1. **Describing the Mood.** How would you describe the mood of this speech? What feelings do you get when reading it?
2. **Recognizing Theme.** Lincoln thought that people would not remember what he said at Gettysburg. If the speech dealt only with the specific dedication of a battlefield, he probably would have been right. However, people are still reading his speech today. What themes did President Lincoln discuss in this speech that make it worth remembering?
3. **Identifying Author's Purpose.** What was the purpose for which President Lincoln was invited to speak? He had another, more general purpose in mind. What was it?
4. **Examining Style.** The third question under Reading Literature: Nonfiction for Lincoln's "Farewell Address" (page 464) pointed out two methods, or techniques, that Lincoln often used in his writing. These were repetition of sentence patterns and balance of related words or phrases. Lincoln used these techniques in his "Gettysburg Address," also. In addition, he varied the length of sentences to produce a stately, but not heavy, rhythm. Find examples of each of these three techniques in this speech.

Developing Vocabulary Skills

Using a Pronunciation Key. The following respellings are of words found in "The Gettysburg Address." Use the pronunciation key in the glossary of this text (page 569) to figure out the pronunciation of each word. Find the word in the speech to see how it is spelled. Write the word on your paper using the standard spelling. Then answer the questions below. Use context clues or a dictionary to find the answers.

a. kont'n ənt	d. en důr'	g. di vō'shən
b. prop'ə zish'ən	e. kon'sə krāt'	h. ri zolv'
c. ded'ə kāt	f. di trakt'	

1. Which two words in the third paragraph mean "to set apart for a particular reason"?
2. Which word means "a proposal or idea"?
3. Which word means "to last or keep on"?

(continued from page 467)

4. Lincoln wanted to show that this was an occasion of extraordinary importance. It deserved to be noted with special words.

5. Answers may vary. Possible answers: This speech is included in a literature book because it deals with values and ideals common to people of every age. People still believe in dedication to a cause, they believe in love of freedom, and they believe that we owe a debt to those who sacrificed their lives for high ideals.

Reading Literature: Nonfiction

1. The mood is serious and sad, yet hopeful. The speech gives the feelings of sorrow, pride, gratitude, determination.

2. Some possible themes are:

People are capable of amazing courage and dedication to a cause.

The living must carry on the work of the dead.

Freedom shall not perish.

3. President Lincoln was invited to speak about the dedication of a cemetery. His more general purpose was to encourage people to rededicate themselves to the highest principles of our country and to win the war.

4. The following are possible answers. Answers in the first two groups are interchangeable.

Repetition of sentence patterns: "of the people, by the people, for the people;" "that nation, or any nation;" "so conceived and so dedicated;" "we cannot dedicate—we cannot consecrate—we cannot hallow"

Balance of related words and phrases: "living and dead;" "fitting and proper;" "add or detract;" "will little note nor long remember"

Varied length of the sentences: Long followed by short—last two sentences of

4. Which word is a synonym for *dedication?*
5. Which word is the opposite of "add"?

Developing Writing Skills

Analytical Writing

1. **Comparing Two Works.** Compare "A Letter to Mrs. Bixby" and "The Gettysburg Address." Are the themes related? Is the difficulty of the vocabulary similar? Are there any similarities in sentence length or sentence patterns? How do the tones compare? Do you get the same feeling from each?

   If you noted differences, can you suggest any reasons for them? Does the author's purpose affect the answers to the questions above?

Analytical Writing

2. **Examining Style.** "The Gettysburg Address" ends in an emotional climax. Write a paragraph analyzing how the mood of the speech builds toward that climax. Consider the techniques discussed in Reading Literature: Nonfiction, 3, on page 464. Also consider Lincoln's use of words with strong connotations.

Creative Writing

3. **Writing an Appeal.** If you could encourage a large group of people to do something important, what would you urge them to do? Choose a project you really believe is important. Then write a speech of three paragraphs (the length of Lincoln's "Gettysburg Address"). Use words with strong connotations to win the support and enthusiasm of your listeners or readers.

Developing Skills in Critical Thinking

Recognizing Slanted Writing. Slanted writing is not necessarily bad. All writers use it. It is the reader's job to be aware of how it is affecting his or her reactions to the writing.

In "The Gettysburg Address," Lincoln was encouraging his listeners to carry the war to victory. How did he do this? He used both a logical development of ideas and emotion-packed words.

To see more clearly how Lincoln constructed his speech, do the following exercise. Fold your paper in half. On the left half, write an outline of Lincoln's argument, using words with neutral connotations. Here is the first point:

1. Our ancestors started a country based on ideas of liberty and equality.

on page 567. Helping the students use the pronunciation key as reference, call on individuals to pronounce each respelling on page 468. After each is pronounced correctly, have students locate and point out the word in the speech identifying its location by the number of the paragraph and line.

Have the students write the standard word spellings on their papers and the answers to the questions independently. Remind them to use the context clues in the speech itself or a dictionary to help them figure out the meaning of the words. Discuss the answers together in class.

Developing Writing Skills

Read and discuss the three assignments. Then have the students choose and complete one of the three.

Question 1. Explain that students already discussed many of the ideas that will be used to answer this question in **Reading Literature: Nonfiction** for both "A Letter to Mrs. Bixby" and "The Gettysburg Address."

Pre-Writing. On the board, list each of the topics raised in the first paragraph of the question. Point out that each topic deserves one or more paragraphs of discussion. Then have the students review the **Reading Literature Comprehension** and study questions for the two selections and identify any questions after each topic. List these study questions after each topic. Suggest that students review their answers to these questions for ideas.

Pre-Writing. On the board, list each of the topics raised in the first paragraph of the question. Point out that each topic deserves one or more paragraphs of discussion. Then have the students review the **Reading Literature Comprehension** and study questions for the two selections and identify any questions after each topic.

paragraph 2; short to medium length to long—last three sentences of paragraph 3

Developing Vocabulary Skills

a. continent	**1.** e, c
b. proposition	**2.** b
c. dedicate	**3.** d
d. endure	**4.** g
e. consecrate	**5.** f
f. detract	
g. devotion	
h. resolve	

Developing Skills in Critical Thinking

Possible outline:

1. Our ancestors started a country based on ideas of liberty and equality.
2. The war that's going on now will determine if our nation will continue to exist.
3. We have come here to set aside this battlefield as a cemetery for the men who died here.
4. We cannot make this ground holy because the men who died here have already made it so.
5. It is our job to carry on the work the dead soldiers started.
6. Therefore we should make sure that our government continues.

Words with strong connotations:

1. brought forth, conceived, dedicated
2. engaged, great civil war, conceived, dedicated, endure
3. dedicate, resting place
4. dedicate, consecrate, hallow, brave, struggled, detract
5. dedicated, nobly, great task, honored dead, devotion, last full measure
6. resolve, in vain, new birth, perish

List these study questions after each topic. Suggest that students review their answers to these questions for ideas to be used in this assignment.

Encourage students to concentrate on one or two topics. Reread the second paragraph of the study question. Remind students to answer the last two questions no matter which topic in paragraph 1 they concentrate on. Have them find quotes from the selections to prove their opinions.

Writing. Allow sufficient time for students to complete the assignment.

Revising. Have students exchange papers. Ask partners to make sure the writers have stated one or two likenesses or differences. Have them check to see if writers have used quotes from both selections and have considered author's purpose. Allow time for revisions.

Question 2. Style has been emphasized through this chapter. Students should be able to recognize several elements of Lincoln's style that appear in the "Gettysburg Address."

Pre-Writing. Have students recall elements of Lincoln's style that build mood which were discussed before, such as repetition of sentence patterns, balance of related words or phrases, and use of words with strong connotations. Write those on the board. Have students find examples of those techniques in "The Gettysburg Address." Have students read the speech and note the concentration of those elements at the end of the speech.

Ask each student to decide how many techniques to discuss, and in which order.

Writing. Allow sufficient time for students to complete the assignment.

Revising. Refer students to the **Checklist for the Process of Writing** for revising and proofreading suggestions.

Question 3. Encourage the creativity that this question asks for.

Pre-Writing. Have students suggest topics that are important to them and list those on the board. Then have them point out the strong connotative words in Lincoln's "Farewell Address" and "The Gettysburg Address" and remind students how strong connotative words help to create a reaction in the listener or reader.

Writing. Have students select one of the topics on the board or one of their own. Remind them that the opening paragraph should tell what the speech will be about, indicate the writer's opinion about the topic, and set the tone of the speech. Encourage them to use some of Lincoln's techniques.

Revising. Have students reread their speeches to be sure they are clear and interesting. Have volunteers prepare to give their speeches aloud to the class.

The last point on the outline should be this: "Therefore we should make sure that our government continues."

On the right half of the paper, across from each outline statement, list words from the speech with strong connotations. These should be words Lincoln used to express the idea in the outline statement.

After you have completed both halves of your paper, discuss how Lincoln blended both ideas and emotions in his speech.

Developing Skills in Speaking and Listening

Delivering a Speech. Choose one of the two speeches by Lincoln and prepare to say it to a group. For your speech to be effective, you must be sure that you understand exactly what Lincoln meant. Ask your teacher for help if you need it. If you understand what you are saying, your listeners will be able to understand you, too.

When you deliver your speech to the group, speak slowly. These are serious speeches and you should not rush through them. Say the words as if you mean them. Make sure you are standing straight and proud, speaking clearly and loudly, and looking at your audience.

Allow them to use their papers in their presentation but stress the importance of frequent eye contact with their audience. Also remind them of the following qualities of good public speaking: tone of voice that reflects the mood, clear articulation, proper pitch, and good posture.

Developing Skills in Critical Thinking

Students may have difficulty in separating the points of Lincoln's argument. It is suggested that you read and complete this assignment as a group project with the whole class. Have one volunteer record the neutral outline on the board and another list the words with strong connotations.

Developing Skills in Speaking and Listening

Read the exercise on page 470 to the class. When assigning this topic, reinforce the idea that a good speech does not sound as if it is being read. Even though it is usually not memorized, a good speech sounds as if it is just being spoken. Tell students to present it the way they think Lincoln might have.

Vignette

A **vignette** is a short piece of nonfiction writing that studies a person closely. A vignette is sometimes called a character sketch. Using a few words, the writer draws a picture of the person as you would draw a pencil sketch.

In the vignette you will read about Abraham Lincoln, the writer does not try to tell you everything about the man. She is interested only in introducing you to Lincoln as he was on that particular day in his life.

Abraham Lincoln, 1865, ALEXANDER GARDNER.
National Portrait Gallery, Smithsonian Institution, Washington D.C.

Vignette

Have a student read page 471 to the class. Point out that this selection is biographical in nature; it could easily have been placed in the first part of the chapter. Ask the students to decide, as they read the selection, why it was placed at the end of the chapter. Before discussing the study questions for "Day of Light and Shadow," remind the students of this question of placement and ask for their opinions.

Point out, also, that the chapter began with a painting of Lincoln (see page 350) and ends with a photograph of Lincoln. Have the students examine the two illustrations and discuss the different feelings they produce in the viewer. Suggest that the painting, like an essay, allows the artist to include his or her opinions while the photograph, like the upcoming vignette, limits itself to what is (or was).

About the Art

Alexander Gardner (1821-1882) originally worked for the famous Civil War photographer Matthew Brady. He broke with Brady in 1863 to form his own photographic corps because Brady wouldn't credit his cameramen or let them keep negatives of the photos they took on their own time. In 1865-1866, Gardner published a two-volume photographic sketchbook of the war containing over one hundred original prints. The book contains some of the finest photographs of the Civil War. The photograph of Abraham Lincoln reproduced here is a sensitive and incisive portrait of the President, his face deeply lined, his eyes cavernous.

After the war, Gardner went west to photograph the construction of the Union Pacific Railroad. Traveling with a survey expedition, he went as far as California. His work from this time is a thrilling photodocumentation of travel across the continent by wagon train and railroad.

Objectives

- To appreciate vignette as a form of nonfiction literature
- To compare and contrast the purpose of different types of nonfiction
- To recognize foreshadowing in a selection
- To apply literal, interpretive, and critical reading skills to a selection
- To determine the meaning of unfamiliar words by using context clues and word parts
- To write a vignette
- To recognize the organization of a specific example of nonfiction writing
- To identify words with strong connotations

Preparing the Students

Essential Vocabulary. The words presented here are essential to the understanding of the selection.

List the following words on the chalkboard, and then read, one by one, the information below. Ask the students to listen for one or more key words that will help them remember the meanings of the word. Write the brief definition or reminder suggested by students on the board, after the word.

earnestly rebel molest

1. earnestly—in a serious, intense, or determined manner
2. rebel—The Civil War, or War between the States, started when several Southern states declared themselves separate from the United States, calling themselves the Confederate States of America. Northerners, however, refused to recognize the Confederacy as a separate nation. Instead, they called the people of those states rebels, people fighting against the established government.
3. molest—to annoy, interfere with, bother, with the intent to trouble or harm

If the students need additional help with the vocabulary of this selection, encourage them to use context clues to determine word meaning. As needed, direct them to the **Glossary** or to a classroom dictionary.

Motivation. Tell students that this selection is about a day in the life of Abraham Lincoln. Then have the students read the introductory paragraph on page 472, and have them state in their own words what they should try to find out as they read this selection.

Day of Light and Shadow

GENEVIEVE FOSTER

The following selection describes Abraham Lincoln's last day. As you read it, try to separate provable facts from the author's interpretation of the facts. Does the author's opinion of Lincoln show through?

April 14, 1865, was a great day for the United States and a happy one for Abraham Lincoln. Almost exactly four years after it had been fired upon, the Stars and Stripes were raised again above Fort Sumter! War was over! The Union had been saved. Slavery had been abolished. All that Lincoln had pledged himself to do had been accomplished.

The care that had weighed so heavily upon him for the last four years seemed to have slipped now from his shoulders. His lined face was almost radiant.

The last day he began, as usual, working at his desk, and then had breakfast at eight. Robert, his oldest son, now twenty-one, was with him. He had a picture of Robert E. Lee to show his father. Lincoln looked at it earnestly. "It is a good face," he said.

After breakfast he had several interviews and letters to write before the Cabinet meeting that was called for eleven o'clock.

"Today," said the President, "General Grant will be with us."

One by one, the cabinet members came in, entering into casual conversation over the day's news and speculating as to where the leaders of the rebel government had now gone.

"I suppose, Mr. President," said the Postmaster General, "you would not be sorry if they escaped from the country."

"Well, I should be for following them up pretty close to make sure of their going," answered Lincoln in a comical tone.

Then a half cloud passed over Lincoln's face, and he told of a strange dream that he had had the previous night. The dream itself was not so strange, he said, as the fact that he had had it several times before—and each time it had preceded some great victory or disaster.

It was a vague feeling of being on a strange phantom ship, sailing, or floating towards some vast, indefinite, unknown shore.

Someone ventured the suggestion that the anxiety in his mind may have led to the dream.

"Perhaps," said Lincoln thoughtfully, "that may be the explanation."

Stanton burst in—carrying a large roll of papers, and the group around the table was complete. General Ulysses S. Grant was then cordially introduced. Grant nodded and told in the fewest possible words the incidents of the surrender at Appomattox.

"And what terms did you give the common soldier?" asked Lincoln.

"I told them to go back to their homes and families, and that they would not be molested if they did nothing more," said Grant.

The President's face lighted with approval. That was right. There must be no hate shown or vindictiveness. Now that the war was over, everything must be done to help the bankrupt people of the South back to prosperity. So the talk turned to post-war plans. Stanton spread out his big roll of paper, showing charts for reconstruction. These were discussed until the meeting broke up at two o'clock.

As they were leaving, Lincoln spoke of going to the theater that evening to see "The American Cousin." Turning to General Grant, he said that he hoped that he and Mrs. Grant would accompany them. But there seemed to be some misunderstanding, because, though it had been advertised in the papers, General Grant said that they were to leave town that evening. Lincoln, himself, was not too eager about it, but since it had been announced, he thought he'd better go.

He made an appointment for the following day, and then went to lunch, from which his next callers saw him return munching an apple.

Then followed a talk with Vice-President Andrew Johnson. The time was growing short. It was past three o'clock. Lincoln could not stay much longer. There were only a few last things for him to do.

Towards late afternoon, he put on his high black hat and went for a drive with Mrs. Lincoln, alone. No, "just ourselves," he had told her when she had suggested guests. It was a fresh spring day, the lilacs were in blossom, the willows along the river were green, the dogwood was opening. Lincoln's face glowed.

"I never felt so happy in my life," he said, drawing a deep breath.

Returning, he walked across the gravel path to the War Department and "was more cheerful and happy," Stanton thought, "than he had ever seen him." Nevertheless, to the guard who walked back to the White House with him in the gathering dusk, he spoke of men who, he believed, would take his life. When they reached the steps it was "Good-bye, Crooks," that he said, for the first time, not "Good night."

Presenting the Selection

1. Have the students read "Day of Light and Shadow" silently. (This selection has been abridged because of space limitations.)

2. Make sure that everyone has read the assignment by administering the **Check Test** at the bottom of this page.

3. Have volunteers read the selection aloud.

4. Ask for students' reactions to this vignette. Was it what they expected? At this point, you may wish to give a brief explanation of how Lincoln died.

5. Remind the students that the introduction to the selection asked them to find out if the author's opinion of Lincoln showed through. Discuss their answers.

6. Develop the study questions as suggested in **Using the Study Questions** beginning on page 475. That section also provides a challenge question for further discussion, as needed.

Reinforcing the Lesson

To reteach, reinforce, or extend skills in this lesson, the following:

Skills Practice Book, Green Level—pages 179 and 180

Encouraging Independent Reading

1. As a culmination for the chapter, students might be encouraged to read full-length biographies of Lincoln.

2. Point out the illustration of lilacs on page 474 and explain that the blossoms have become symbolic of Lincoln because of the Walt Whitman poem "When Lilacs Last in the Dooryard Bloomed" which concerns the death of Lincoln. Suggest that the students find the poem in an anthology and find out what it had to say concerning Lincoln's death.

The strands of happiness and tragedy that made Abraham Lincoln's life were twisting closely now for, in the next moment, seeing two friends from Illinois, the governor and a congressman, he called to them in the cheeriest tone. Laughing and chatting, he led them to his office, and read them one ridiculous story after another. His son Tad came to call him to supper, and he said he'd be right there. But first he wanted them to hear just one more story, the one perhaps in which the author poked fun at the "Goriller Linkin, whuz rane he had hoped wood be a short wun."

Then the author said, "The Confederacy is ded. It's gathered up its feet, sed its last words, and deceest . . . Linkin will serve his term out—our leaders will die off uv chagrin and inability to live long out uv offis. And so, Farewell, vane world!" And Lincoln left them laughing.

After dinner the Speaker of the House came for a few minutes, to say that, if there was to be no special session of Congress during the summer, he would take a trip to the West Coast where the transcontinental railroad was now being built.

The clock ticked on; it was just time to go to the theater when the congressman from Massachusetts was announced. Lincoln arranged to see him in the morning. Taking a small card he wrote a few words on it, and then he signed his name for the last time.

They were now at the door. Outside, the carriage was waiting. A breath of fresh cool air came in as the door was opened, and they walked out onto the portico in the moist spring night. Abraham Lincoln stood for a moment, then stepped into the carriage, its door closed behind him, the horses started, the carriage rolled down the driveway, the sound of the wheels on the gravel grew fainter and then died away and he was gone. Abraham Lincoln was gone.

Only then could the people of Abraham Lincoln's world realize how great he was. He was too tall when he walked beside them.

Check Test

1. Was the Civil War being fought on the day described in this sketch? (no)

2. What kind of meeting did Lincoln attend that day? (a Cabinet meeting)

3. What was Lincoln traveling on in his dream? (a ship)

4. Who went for a drive with Mr. and Mrs. Lincoln that afternoon? (They went alone, together.)

Developing Comprehension Skills

Literal Reading — 1. President Lincoln liked what General Grant told the common soldiers from the South. What did General Grant tell them? Why did Lincoln like that?

Literal Reading — 2. List at least five of Abraham Lincoln's activities on his last day. How do we know what he did?

Interpretive Reading — 3. The author says that only after Lincoln died did people realize how great he was. How does she phrase this statement?

Interpretive Reading — 4. Why do you think Lincoln told the Cabinet about his dream?

Critical Reading — 5. Why is this sketch called "Day of Light and Shadow"? Is it a good title?

Reading Literature: Nonfiction

1. **Recognizing Images.** In art, a **vignette** usually refers to a picture of someone's face. Find at least two words or phrases used to describe Lincoln's face in this written vignette. What do the words you found have in common with each other?

2. **Separating Fact and Opinion.** Tell which of the following statements are facts and which are opinions:

   a. War was over!
   b. "It is a good face."
   c. There must be no hate shown.
   d. Returning, he walked across the gravel path to the War Department.

3. **Recognizing Foreshadowing.** The vignette you read was written in a very lively and creative style. Even though it reports historical facts, the author develops suspense by dropping hints about what is to happen in the future. Such use of hints is called **foreshadowing**. Find the first hint that this day was Lincoln's last. Then locate at least three other instances of foreshadowing in this selection.

4. **Comparing Types of Writing.** Compare this vignette with the biographies you read earlier in the chapter. Can you identify some similarities? What are some differences?

Using the Study Questions

It is recommended that students always read and answer the questions in **Developing Comprehension Skills** in class discussion. Whenever possible, they should also read the questions in the other categories together and discuss the answers.

Developing Comprehension Skills

Question 1. Read and discuss.

Question 2. Students may need to scan the selection to make a complete list.

Question 3. Have the students read the phrase from the selection. Ask them why the author chose to describe Lincoln's greatness in this way.

Question 4. Students must infer what Lincoln is trying to say here. They should realize that his mentioning it shows that it troubles him.

Question 5. Lead students to understand the figurative language and imagery used in developing this sketch. Have them find specific examples of the contrast between happiness and sorrow in the selection and read them aloud.

Reading Literature: Nonfiction

Questions 1 and 2. Read and discuss the question.

Question 3. Make sure students have a clear understanding of foreshadowing.

Question 4. Draw two columns on the board, one labeled *Similarities* and the other labeled *Differences.* Discuss briefly the characteristics of both vignette and biography. As students compare and contrast these two genres, write each response on the board in the appropriate column.

Challenge Question. Why do you think the writer left a larger-than-usual space between the last two paragraphs?

Answers to Study Questions

Developing Comprehension Skills

1. General Grant told them to go home to their families and nothing would happen to them. Lincoln liked it because he wanted no hate or vindictiveness shown. He thought that everything should be done to help the bankrupt people of the South back to prosperity.

2. Lincoln had breakfast and then several interviews, letters to write, a Cabinet meeting, a talk with the Vice-President, lunch, a drive, a talk with a War Department guard, a meeting with the governor and a congressman from Illinois, supper, a note to the congressman from Massachusetts, and a carriage ride to the theater. People Lincoln spoke with remembered his words. Messages he wrote were found after his death.

3. He was too tall when he walked beside them.

4. Answers should show students realize he thought it was a premonition.

5. Lincoln's last day was a combination of happiness and sadness. Opinions about whether it is a good title may vary, but most students will agree it is an appropriate title.

(continued on page 476)

Developing Vocabulary Skills

Have students read the directions for the vocabulary drill. Have them identify which types of text clues the directions alert them to (synonym and antonym clues). If necessary, have students turn to pages 546 to 549 of the **Handbook** and read the information given there. Then have them complete the exercise independently. Discuss the answers together.

Developing Writing Skills

Read and discuss the three assignments. Then have the students choose and complete one of the three.

Question 1. Answering this question will help students appreciate the unity of the selection—the way every detail fits together.

Pre-Writing. Discuss the definition of metaphor. You may wish to have students turn to page 537 and read and discuss the information about metaphor given there. Have students consider what concrete object the writer was comparing Lincoln's life to. Then have students find some examples of happiness and tragedy in the sketch and write those on the board.

Writing. Remind students that they may use the notes on the board. Tell them to be sure to begin with a topic sentence that tells what the paragraph will be about. Remind them to use examples from the selection.

Revising. Have students revise and proofread their writing using the **Checklist for the Process of Writing** on pages 556 and 557.

Question 2. Emphasize that students are expected to present logical reasons to support their opinions.

Pre-Writing. Encourage students to give their reactions to the nonfiction selections in this chapter. Would they like to read other nonfiction selections primarily for enjoyment? Have each student list in order of importance the reasons why he or she reads nonfiction . Direct students to use these lists as outlines of the ideas they will include in their paragraphs.

Writing. Tell students to follow their outlines as much as possible, but remind them that they can change their outlines if they come up with better ideas as they write. Remind students that their first sentences should state their opinions and that they should include arguments to support their opinions.

Revising. Have students reread their paragraphs to be sure they included strong reasons to support their opinions. Allow time for revisions to be made.

Question 3. Before students choose the days they will write about, explain that they will have an opportunity to read their papers aloud. Knowing their audience will influence the students choices of events and details.

Pre-Writing. Have students choose a day they want to write about and think over the events of that day. The day may be either especially significant or merely typical. Have them write notes on what they remember, discard the unimportant details, and organize the ones they will want to include.

Writing. Tell students to follow their outlines and to make it clear how one event leads to the next. Encourage them

Developing Vocabulary Skills

Reviewing Context Clues and Word Parts. Read these sentences (or groups of sentences) from the selection. Try to figure out the meaning of each underlined word by using context clues or word parts. Look especially for words that are similar or opposite in meaning. On your paper, write your own meaning of the word. Then write whether you used context clues or word parts to figure out the meaning.

1. The Union had been saved. Slavery had been abolished.
2. Lincoln's lined face that had grown so drawn and haggard was almost radiant.
3. The dream was like a vague feeling of being on a strange phantom ship, sailing towards some unknown shore.
4. Everything must be done to help the bankrupt people of the South back to prosperity.
5. Stanton spread out his big roll of paper, showing charts for reconstruction.
6. There seemed to be some misunderstanding with the Grants about the evening.

Developing Writing Skills

Analytical Writing

1. **Explaining Metaphor.** Read this sentence from the story: "The strands of happiness and tragedy that made Abraham Lincoln's life were twisting closely now." Write a paragraph telling what this means. Use examples of happiness and tragedy from the sketch.

Analytical Writing

2. **Writing a Well Organized Paragraph.** Some people think that fiction is read for enjoyment, but that nonfiction is read only for information, not enjoyment. What do you think? Write a paragraph explaining your opinion. Your first sentence should state your opinion. Then you should give arguments to support your opinion.

Creative Writing

3. **Writing a Vignette.** Write a vignette about a day in your own life. First think over what happened on the day you choose. Write notes about the events you want to record. You will have to choose what you think is worth including. When you have made your choices, write at least six paragraphs describing your day. Try to show how

(continued from page 475)

Reading Literature: Nonfiction

1. The words used to describe Lincoln's face are: radiant, lighted with approval, and glowed. The words all show happiness.

2. a) fact
b) opinion
c) opinion
d) fact

3. Examples of foreshadowing are: "the last day ...", "the time was growing short ...", "he spoke of men who, he believed, would take his life", "Good-by Crooks", "strands of happiness and tragedy ... twisting closely now", "he signed his name for the last time", and "Abraham Lincoln was gone"

4. Both reveal facts about Lincoln's life and his character, both give the author's opinions, and they are written from the third-person point of view. The vignette recreates an event or moment more in detail and gives you more detailed information about Lincoln's personality.

Challenge. The writer probably wanted to show that time and events came between the time Lincoln left the White House and the point when people realized how great he was.

one event leads to the next. Include enough details to make your vignette interesting.

Developing Skills in Study and Research

Comparing Encyclopedias. Different encyclopedias often provide slightly different information or organize their entries differently. Using at least two different encyclopedias, look up the entries on Abraham Lincoln. Compare the two entries. Are they organized in the same way? Describe their pattern, or patterns, of organization. Does one encyclopedia provide more information than the other? Are they equally easy to understand? Do they both describe Lincoln's death in the same way? Based on this comparison, would you choose one of these encyclopedias over the other the next time you need to look up something?

Developing Skills in Critical Thinking

Identifying Words with Strong Connotations. Even though the vignette, "Day of Light and Shadow," reports the facts, it also includes many opinions. Frequently the reader does not notice the opinions. They are part of the picture the author draws for us. Examine each of the following sentences from the selection. Then find it in the selection in order to understand its context. What is the effect of the underlined word on the meaning of the passage?

1. Lincoln looked at it earnestly. (page 472, paragraph 3)
2. "Perhaps," said Lincoln thoughtfully, "that may be the explanation." (page 473, paragraph 2)
3. Stanton burst in. (page 473, paragraph 3)
4. The President's face lighted with approval. (page 473, paragraph 6)
5. "I never felt so happy in my life," he said, drawing a deep breath. (page 473, column 2, paragraph 5)

to include sensory details to enliven their vignettes. Allow sufficient time for students to complete the assignment.

Revising. Have students reread their vignettes to see if they are clear and interesting. Allow time for revisions to be made. Refer students to the **Checklist for the Process of Writing** in the Handbook on pages 556 and 557. Then have as many students as possible read their papers to the class.

Developing Skills in Study and Research

Have the students read the directions for the exercise. Either schedule a visit to the library or have available in the classroom as many sets of encyclopedias as possible. Allow time for the students to complete the exercise independently. Discuss their findings with them.

Developing Skills in Critical Thinking

Have a student read the directions for the exercise aloud. You may want to complete the exercise with the class. For each sentence, have a student tell where the sentence can be found in the selection. Have the students reread the passage. Then have another student describe the effect of the underlined word. To help students see the difference the word makes, have them read the sentence without the word. For example, the first sentence would be "Lincoln looked at it." Point out how the underlined word gives a better understanding of Lincoln's feelings and doesn't simply state the facts.

Developing Vocabulary Skills

1. abolished—ended; context
2. haggard—tired; context
3. phantom—ghost-like; context
4. prosperity—success: context
5. reconstruction—building again; word parts
6. misunderstanding—confusion; word parts

Developing Skills in Study and Research

Answers will vary according to encyclopedias used.

Developing Skills in Critical Thinking

Answers will vary. Possible answers:

1. The word *earnestly* emphasizes Lincoln's seriousness.

2. The dream weighed heavily on his mind.

3. Stanton may have been late for the meeting.

4. Lincoln visibly showed his approval. He may have looked sad or serious before hearing this news.

5. Lincoln was contented and relieved.

Using the Review

This review should be completed before the administration of the **Chapter 6 Mastery Test.** Students will have an opportunity to recall important concepts from this chapter and apply them to new contexts. Teacher observation during the review can reveal which students still have not mastered the skills.

Using Your Skills in Reading Nonfiction

Read the directions to the exercise aloud. Have the students read the excerpt silently and write the answers to the questions. Discuss the answers together. Collect papers after the review lesson to see who needs further help in this or other areas of study.

Using Your Comprehension Skills

Read the directions to the exercise to the students. Ask students for definitions of the terms of *fact* and *opinion*. Then ask two students to read aloud the parts of Phillips and Pierson, reminding the listeners to concentrate on Pierson's statements. Allow a few minutes for the students to identify and write at least one fact and one opinion of Pierson's. Point out that each fact need not be proved in this excerpt, but the student must suggest a way to prove it.

Discuss the answers, and have a student write on the chalkboard the facts and opinions the students can identify. Have the students decide which way of proving each fact is most practical or efficient.

Using Your Vocabulary Skills

Students must have access to dictionaries to complete this exercise. If not every student has a dictionary, you could pass a copy through the group while the students develop their pre-writing notes for the writing assignment, and correct their work after every student has had a turn.

Have the students read the directions to the exercise to themselves. Then call on volunteers to explain what they are to do in the exercise. Have the students complete the first part of the exercise independently in writing (see above). Then call on students to pronounce the underlined words correctly, and discuss the answers.

Using Your Writing Skills

Call on students to read aloud the two assignments. Point out that they should complete only one of them.

CHAPTER 6 Review

Using Your Skills in Reading Nonfiction

The following is from *A Portrait of Myself*, by Margaret Bourke-White, a famous photographer for *Life* magazine. Read it. Then answer these questions: From what point of view is it written? How would you describe the tone that the writer is using?

> A few months later, in the spring of 1929, I received a telegram from a man I had never met: HAVE JUST SEEN YOUR STEEL PHOTOGRAPH. CAN YOU COME TO NEW YORK AT OUR EXPENSE? signed: HENRY R. LUCE, TIME, THE WEEKLY NEWS MAGAZINE.
>
> When I arrived, Mr. Luce and his associates explained that they were planning to launch a new magazine, which they hoped to illustrate with the most dramatic photographs of industry that had ever been taken. Did I think this was a good idea, he asked?
>
> A good idea? I went back to Cleveland to pick up my belongings. Before I left again for New York, I wrote my mother: "I feel as if the world has been opened up and I hold all the keys."

Using Your Comprehension Skills

The following dialog is from a play you will read in Chapter 7. In it, Professor Pierson states both facts and opinions. Identify which statements are facts and which are opinions. Explain how each fact can be proved to be true.

Phillips. Professor, would you please tell our radio audience what you see as you observe the planet Mars through your telescope?

Pierson. Nothing unusual at the moment, Mr. Phillips. A red disk swimming in a blue sea. Stripes across the disk. The stripes are merely the result of atmospheric conditions peculiar to the planet.

Answers to Questions

Using Your Comprehension Skills

The selection is told from the first-person point of view.

The tone could be described as excited, confident, or enthusiastic.

Using Your Skills in Reading Nonfiction

Fact: Through the telescope, Mars appears to be a red disk in a blue sea, with stripes across it. This could be verified by looking through the telescope.

Opinions: The view of Mars showed nothing unusual. The stripes are merely the result of atmospheric conditions. The chances against living intelligence existing on Mars are a thousand to one.

Using Your Vocabulary Skills

Wordings of definitions will vary, depending on dictionary used.

1. verb; worked, made
2. noun; actions
3. noun; prisoner
4. verb; express

Phillips. Then you're quite convinced that living intelligence does not exist on Mars?

Pierson. I should say the chances against it are a thousand to one.

Using Your Vocabulary Skills

The following are sentences from the plays you will read in Chapter 7. Locate the definition of the underlined words in the dictionary. On your paper, write the part of speech and the definition that fits the context below. Be prepared to pronounce the word correctly.

1. Merlin hath wrought a spell.
2. Stop the proceedings.
3. Her mistress is a captive in a vast and gloomy castle.
4. I wish I could convey the atmosphere of this fantastic scene.

Using Your Writing Skills

Choose one of the writing assignments below.

1. Choose from the selections in this chapter the person you found most admirable or appealing. Explain, in one to three paragraphs, why that person and his or her experiences interested you. Be sure to include specific examples of personal qualities.
2. Choose a famous modern-day person who interests you. Write two introductions about the person. Write the first as if you were the biographer of the person. Write the second as if you were the person. Remember to use the appropriate viewpoint for each introduction.

Using Your Skills in Critical Thinking

You have learned that one category of nonfiction records the lives, achievements, and personalities of people. List all the people about whom you have read in this chapter. What qualities, or personality traits, do some of the people share? What type of person does it take to overcome obstacles and achieve great things? What generalization can you make about this type of person? Be sure to support your generalization with at least five facts from the selections.

Using Your Skills in Critical Thinking

Generalizations may vary, as long as they are logically drawn from facts reported in the selections.

Answer any questions students may have about the assignments. If you are asking the students to complete their writing in class, let them know how much time they have and that they may turn in a marked-up first draft. Remind them to skip lines to leave space for corrections. If you are asking them to do the writing outside of class, you may require clean copies.

Collect and evaluate these papers according to the guidelines on pages T-24 through T-27 of this T.E. It is strongly recommended that you discuss and explain your evaluation with the student, and that you provide an opportunity for the students to revise and resubmit their writing.

Using Your Skills in Critical Thinking

Throughout this chapter, the students have been asked to identify opinions and to evaluate which of them are reasonable, that is, supported by facts. This exercise asks them to form an original opinion, a generalization, based on facts from the chapter. It is recommended that the exercise be done as a class activity, rather than individually.

Read the directions to the students. Allow them time to skim the biographies, autobiographies, and vignettes, as well as their study questions, to remind themselves of the qualities of the different people about whom they have read.

Then have the students discuss the questions in the exercise, as you record the main points of the discussion on the chalkboard. After students have pointed out at least five facts about the subjects of the selections, have them begin to pull together the information in generalizations. Encourage them to list several more facts and develop at least three to five generalizations that summarize what they have learned.

Reinforcing the Lesson

To reteach, reinforce, or extend the skills in this lesson, see the following:

Skills Practice Book, Green Level—pages 181 and 182

Additional Resource

Diagnostic and Mastery Tests, Green Level—Chapter 6 Mastery Test, pages 33 through 36

About the Art

Within an apparently random combination of blocks of color and a series of wandering lines, Richard Hull (born 1955) has created a dramatic staging of a dramatic stage. A number of forms suggesting the human figure—silhouetted, reversed, upside down, and superimposed on others—emerge from, or seem to be enmeshed in, the stage-like construction. The shadowy and ghostly figures inhabiting the stage help to evoke the spirit and imagination of the theater.

CHAPTER **7**

Deep Bait, 1980, RICHARD HULL.
Photograph by William H. Bengtson,
Courtesy of Phyllis Kind Gallery,
New York and Chicago.

Chapter Objectives

The following is a list of the major skills developed in study questions throughout this chapter:

Skills in Reading Literature

- To recognize and appreciate drama as a form of literature
- To examine such elements of drama as dialog, conflict, and theme
- To recognize plot development
- To identify stereotypical characters
- To understand the development of major characters

Comprehension Skills

- To identify time order of events (Literal Reading)
- To consider possible personal reactions to events in a drama (Interpretive Reading)
- To recognize the author's purpose for writing a selection and to evaluate word choice for its effectiveness in achieving that purpose (Critical Reading)

Vocabulary Skills

- To use context clues to determine the meaning of unfamiliar words

Writing Skills

- To write several paragraphs or a play excerpt predicting the outcome of a play (Analytical or Creative Writing)
- To write a comparison of two plays (Analytical Writing)
- To write a description of an imaginary creature (Creative Writing)
- To write an original radio script (Creative Writing)

Critical Thinking Skills

- To evaluate the literary quality of a radio play

Speaking and Listening Skills

- To present a monolog that reflects the mood of a play

Reading Literature

First, **Reading Literature: Drama** explains that the terms *drama* and *play* are almost synonomous. The lesson then sketches in a few of the major periods in the development of drama and introduces some stylistic features that have developed over the years. The lesson ends with guidelines for reading and appreciating a play.

Preparing the Students

Ask the students whether they have watched a television drama or a movie within the last week. Almost all, if not all, will report seeing one or both. Then ask what reasons the students can offer for the popularity of stories that are acted out. List several of the students' answers on the board.

Then point out that many of the answers have been true for thousands of years, for all stories that are acted out, not just those on TV or film. Explain that the next chapter will discuss drama and some of the qualities that make it different from other forms of storytelling.

It is recommended that you administer the **Chapter 7 Diagnostic Test** at this time. The results of this pretest will serve as a guide for measuring student needs and progress in achieving chapter objectives.

Presenting the Lesson

1. Have the students read **What Is Drama?** on page 482. Then call on students to define the terms *drama* and *play* in their own words. Make it clear that the term *drama* can refer to all plays, in general, or to a single play.

2. Call on students to read the four paragraphs of **The History of Drama** aloud. Then have the students close their books and describe morality plays, tragedies, and comedies. Ask them to identify the countries and the centuries in which Thespis and Shakespeare lived.

3. Point out that in the next section **The Elements of Drama**, the first subtitle limits the topic to written drama: **The Form of Written Drama**. Explain to the students that, when a play is produced, the audience doesn't need to know about all of these elements, but the actors and any readers must understand them in order to make sense of the play when it is merely words on paper.

Have the students read **The Form of Written Drama** to themselves. Then ask

Reading Literature: Drama

What is Drama?

Drama is a form of literature in which a story is told through the words and actions of characters. Another word for a drama is a **play**. Plays are meant to be performed by actors and actresses in front of an audience.

The History of Drama

Drama, like other forms of literature, reflects what writers feel is important about life. Drama, therefore, has changed repeatedly in the thousands of years since the first play was acted out. That was long before the first play was written.

The first written plays we have today came from Greece. Around 600 B.C., a Greek poet named Thespis wrote a new kind of song. One person would pretend to be a character. A chorus of singers would have a conversation with him to tell a story.

Hundreds of years later, in countries such as Germany, France, and England, the Christian church made a different kind of play popular. Plays based on stories from the Bible were acted out. Much later, around 1500, people enjoyed **morality plays**. In these, characters had to choose between good and evil.

If you had lived in England in the late 1500's, you would have sensed the great excitement many people felt about drama. The best known playwright of that time was William Shakespeare. His plays told fascinating stories about kings and soldiers, witches and common people. Shakespeare wrote serious plays that ended in disaster called **tragedies** and light-hearted plays called **comedies**.

In recent times, plays have been written specially to be performed on radio and on television. This chapter has examples of plays written for radio.

The Elements of Drama

The Form of Written Drama. The written form of a play reminds you that the story is told through the words of the characters. The written play first gives the name of the character who is speaking. Then it prints the words, or lines, the character says.

Arthur: Good health to you both!
Clarence: Congratulations, Sir Boss.

Plays are divided into short sections called **scenes**. When the time or place changes, there is a new scene. Long plays are divided into **acts**, which are made up of a number of scenes.

Dramatic Conventions. A **convention** is an agreed-upon way of doing something. **Dramatic conventions** are the customary ways of writing and performing drama. Here are examples:

1. **Dialog**: Dialog refers to the conversations between characters in a play. The dialog tells the story.
2. **Aside**: In an aside, a character talks to the audience and acts as if the other characters cannot hear.
3. **Stage directions**: These are instructions to the director, actors, and actresses. They tell how to enter, move, and behave on the stage. They also help readers picture the play in their minds. They are usually printed in parentheses ( ).
4. **Sound effects**: These are sounds to be made as part of the play. In radio plays, they help listeners picture the action.
5. **Fade in**: In a radio play, this direction tells actors to speak softly and then louder, as if someone is coming closer.

How To Read a Play

1. Picture the play being performed by actors and actresses. Pay special attention to the stage directions and sound effects.
2. Cooperate with the writer. Enter the world he or she has made.

them to identify the two speakers in the excerpt they read and to explain the difference between an act and a scene.

Call on six students to read aloud **Dramatic Conventions** on page 483. After each paragraph, stop for a brief discussion to make sure everyone understands each term. You may wish to point out an example of each convention in one of the selections in this chapter and then to have the students turn to the example briefly. Avoid having them read more than a line or so of each example.

4. Have the students read **How To Read a Play** on page 483, silently. Then ask them to restate each of the directions and to suggest answers for this question: how will following each of the directions help them understand and enjoy a play?

Reinforcing the Lesson

To reteach, reinforce, or extend the concepts in this lesson, see the following:

Skills Practice Book, Green Level—pages 183 and 184

Additional Resource

Diagnostic and Mastery Tests, Green Level—Chapter 7 Diagnostic Test, pages 37 and 38

Special Populations

If the class decides to present either of these plays, choose small portions of the dialog for the special-populations students to memorize or read, based on ability. You may want to pair students for practice readings or tape record the dialogs for the special-populations students to practice with. For the ESL student, stress correct dialect, intonation, pronunciation, and phrasing. Allow students extra time to prepare for a reading or to memorize dialog.

Comprehension Skills

The lesson on pages 484 and 485 directs the students' attention to the author's purpose and to one of the tools the author uses to achieve that purpose, choice of words. Students are made aware of the need to read critically in order to see what effect a playwright intends to have on an audience and how effectively the playwright's words produce that effect.

The lesson ends with exercises requiring students to identify the writer's purpose and to evaluate word choices. After each selection in the chapter, study questions remind the students of the importance of reading critically.

Preparing the Students

Ask each student to try to remember the first thing he or she said this morning, the first thing said at school, and the first thing said in this class. Call on a few volunteers to report their statements, and have the student identify the reasons for each of the statements. For example, a student might have asked someone at home for lunch money: that statement expressed a need. The student might have exchanged greetings with a friend: that exchange expressed a feeling of friendship. The student might have answered a teacher's question: that statement was a response to another person.

After the students have become aware of a variety of purposes for their own communication, point out that writers, too, have a variety of purposes for communicating. Explain that this lesson will discuss this fact.

Presenting the Lesson

1. Call on a student to read aloud the first paragraph of **Understanding the Author's Purpose** on page 484. Ask students to identify legends, stories, poems, or nonfiction pieces that may have been written for each of the ten purposes listed. Ask, also, whether they can add other purposes to the list.

Have the next three paragraphs read aloud. If students wish to report on stories, movies, or TV programs that reached or missed their goals, limit the discussion to only a few minutes but let the students know that in this chapter they will have several opportunities for expressing such opinions.

2. Read **Evaluating the Author's Choice of Words** to the class. Point out that a character in a play can be exagger-

Comprehension Skills: Author's Purpose

Understanding the Author's Purpose

When preparing to write, writers decide what they want the piece of writing to do. Their purpose, or reason for writing, could be one or more of the following: 1) to entertain, 2) to express feelings, 3) to experiment with a new way of writing, 4) to teach, 5) to inform, 6) to persuade, 7) to make people laugh, 8) to inspire, 9) to shock, 10) to make people think seriously about a certain social problem.

Usually, a writer knows the purpose before he or she begins a piece of writing. Purpose affects many choices the writer makes, including the choices of topic, form, characters, setting, and plot.

To understand the author's purpose, study your own reaction to the piece. Were you entertained? Were you taught something? Did you gain a better understanding of other people's problems?

Not every writer achieves his or her purpose. Sometimes writers intend their work to be funny, but readers don't laugh. Sometimes a piece is meant to teach, but all it does is bore readers. Only the reader can tell if the writer has succeeded.

Evaluating the Author's Choice of Words

Suppose a story or play is set in the Middle Ages. The way the characters speak should suggest the time in which they live. As a reader, you would expect the characters to sound different from yourself. The writer might have the characters use old-fashioned words such as *thee, prithee,* and *verily.*

Suppose a second story is set in modern times. An army officer is reporting to the nation. Would you expect the officer to say, "Don't worry. No problem"? That would not sound like a real officer. This is how the general in *Invasion from Mars* speaks: "Situation arising from reported presence of certain individuals of unidentified nature is now under complete control." That sentence sounds believably stiff, formal, and official.

A writer chooses a character's words carefully. The words must fit the character and make him or her sound like a real person. You, as a reader, can judge when a writer has chosen the character's words well.

Exercises: Understanding the Author's Purpose and Choice of Words

A. Identify the purpose of each of these selections.

1. Mel works with scientists called marine archaeologists. They study the wrecks of old ships and all of the things that are brought up from the deep water.
   a. to inform you
   b. to persuade you
   c. to shock you
2. Small bird, forgive me.
   I'll hear the end of your song
   in some other world.
   a. to make you laugh
   b. to express feelings
   c. to teach

B. For each character below, choose the fitting line of dialog.

1. King Arthur:
   a. Thanks, Wiz. It's great to have you here at Camelot.
   b. Blessings upon thee, oh Great Wizard. I welcome thee to Camelot as my right-hand man.
2. Radio Announcer:
   a. Ladies and gentlemen, due to circumstances beyond our control, we are unable to continue the broadcast.
   b. We've been cut off! Oh, no! What'll I do?

ated to make a certain situation clear. For example, it is unlikely that anyone would regularly speak like the general quoted in the second paragraph. However, some people speak like that under certain circumstances, and the playwright chose that style to emphasize the situation.

3. Have the students read and complete Exercises A and B on page 485 independently. Discuss the answers.

Reinforcing the Lesson

To reteach, reinforce, or extend the concepts in this lesson, see the following:

Skills Practice Book, Green Level—pages 185 and 186

Answers to Exercises

A. Purposes:
1. a
2. b

B. More appropriate dialog:
1. b
2. a

Vocabulary Skills

In Chapters 1 and 5, the introductory vocabulary lessons and many vocabulary exercises after each selection developed a recognition of various context clues that were signaled by key words or punctuation. In this lesson, attention is given to those words whose meaning can be inferred from the sense of an entire passage. Although this type of clue may be hard to spot, it is the most frequent and most helpful of context clues. **Using Context Clues**, on pages 486 and 487, provides two examples and examines how students can recognize and use inference clues.

Preparing the Students

Remind the students that they have already learned about several types of context clues, such as definition or restatement clues, comparison and contrast clues, and example clues. Explain that this lesson will discuss another, even more common type of context clue that will help them find word meanings without resorting to a dictionary.

Presenting the Lesson

1. Have students read aloud the first five paragraphs, including the excerpt, in **Using Context Clues**. Discuss the process by which the meaning of *amiss* was uncovered.

Point out that it was necessary to read the entire passage in order to find enough clues to determine the meaning. Explain that sometimes a reader must read several paragraphs, perhaps an entire page, to get enough information to pin down the meaning of a certain word. Advise the students not to panic if they cannot figure out a word immediately from context clues; by continuing to read, they may find the meaning. If, after several more paragraphs, they still can't figure out the word and this uncertainty is interfering with their understanding of the rest of the material, they should then stop and use a dictionary.

2. Read and discuss the rest of the lesson through the middle of page 487.

3. Read the directions for the exercise on page 487 and point out that each item is written according to play style. Have students identify which items present dialog and which present stage directions. Allow time for them to read and answer the questions. Discuss their answers.

Vocabulary Skills: Context Clues

Using Context Clues

What do you do when you are reading and you come to a word you can't understand? Do you skip it and go on with your reading, hoping that the word was not important? Sometimes, that's not a bad idea. Usually, however, a better idea is to figure out what the word means by using context clues.

Often you have to guess at the meaning of a new word. Then you test out your meaning in the sentence where you found the word. Here is an example. In these lines from *A Connecticut Yankee in King Arthur's Court,* the new word is underlined:

> **Connecticut Yankee:** The next time I saw Camelot, I knew at once that something was amiss. As I approached the gates of the castle, Clarence ran out to meet me and, by the worried look on his face, I knew that there was trouble.

What could *amiss* mean? To figure it out, first ask yourself what part of speech the new word could be. *Amiss* is probably an adjective because it describes the word *something*. Next, look at other clues. Clarence looked worried. The Yankee knew there was trouble. From all these clues, you can guess that something was wrong. *Amiss* probably means *wrong*.

Test your meaning in the given sentence. Replace *amiss* with *wrong*: "I knew at once that something was wrong." As you read on, you will know more surely whether your guess is correct.

This way of finding the meaning of a new word from context is called *inferring the meaning*. **Inference** is using what the writer has told you to figure out what the writer has not told you.

Here is another example of inferring meaning. This selection is from *Invasion from Mars*. Martians have killed forty people. The radio announcer is trying to keep the audience informed.

Announcer: Ladies and gentlemen, I have just been informed that we have finally established communication with an eyewitness of the tragedy. Professor Pierson . . . will give you his explanation of the calamity.

What does calamity mean? First, decide what part of speech it is. If you reread the sentence, you will see that calamity must be a noun, because the phrase "of the" needs a noun to complete it.

Now look for other clues. Professor Pierson saw a tragedy. You can guess that the thing he will explain will be that tragedy, or disaster. Calamity must mean disaster.

Exercise: Using Context Clues

Use context clues to find the meaning of each underlined word. Choose from the meanings following each selection.

1. **Connecticut Yankee:** Well, sir, there never was a man more dumbfounded than I was. I just couldn't get used to the idea. That's why when I woke again I thought the whole thing a dream, and, when I saw that page boy standing before me, I was more amazed than ever.
   a. Dumbfounded means "stupid."
   b. Dumbfounded means "found by accident."
   c. Dumbfounded means "surprised."
2. **Sound:** Clamor of crowd in the background
   a. Clamor means "silence."
   b. Clamor means "noise."
   c. Clamor means "sight."
3. **Announcer two:** Ladies and gentlemen, I have a grave announcement to make. Incredible as it may seem, those strange beings who landed in the Jersey farmlands tonight are the vanguard of an invading army from the planet Mars.
   a. Vanguard means "part of the army ahead of the main army."
   b. Vanguard means "a kind of vehicle."
   c. Vanguard means "a kind of guard."

Reinforcing the Lesson

To reteach, reinforce, or extend the concepts in this lesson, see the following:

Skills Practice Book, Green Level—pages 187 and 188

Answers to Exercises

1. c
2. b
3. a

Objectives

- To recognize and appreciate drama as a form of literature
- To examine such elements of drama as dialog and conflict
- To identify the theme of a drama
- To recognize stereotypical qualities of a dramatic character
- To apply literal, interpretive, and critical reading skills to a selection
- To use context clues to determine the meaning of unfamiliar words
- To write a comparison
- To recognize the author's purpose for writing a selection
- To participate in a group dramatic reading

Preparing the Students

Essential Vocabulary. The words presented here are essential to the understanding of the selection.

Introduce the words listed below. Write the sentences on the board, have them read aloud, and ask the students to use context clues to find the meaning of the underlined words.

reminiscent	laurels	amiss
page	revolution	
maundering	montage	

1. Her bobby socks, poodle skirt, and pony tail were reminiscent of the way people dressed in the 1950's; they were reminders of the styles that were fashionable during that period of time.
2. A boy who acts as a servant is sometimes called a page.
3. The speaker confused his audience with his maundering, or rambling and illogical, speech.
4. Even though the politician had received many honors, these laurels alone were not enough to make him win the election.
5. The rebels began a revolution, a struggle to overthrow the old government.
6. The artist created a montage by combining bits and pieces from several different photographs.
7. We thought we had carried out the experiment correctly, but the results showed that something had gone amiss.

If the students need additional help with the vocabulary of this selection, encourage them to use context clues to determine word meaning. As needed, direct them to the **Glossary** or to a classroom dictionary.

Motivation. Explain that the play the students are about to read is a radio play based on a novel by Mark Twain. Students

A Connecticut Yankee in King Arthur's Court

In this play, the Connecticut Yankee goes back in time and lands in King Arthur's Camelot. As you read, decide whether he is a good time-traveler. Can he make himself comfortable in his new surroundings?

MARK TWAIN

Adapted from the novel

CHARACTERS

Connecticut Yankee	Alisande de la Carteloise (al'ə sänd də lä kär tel lwaz)
Worker	Women, *two*
Clarence	Men, *two*
King Arthur	
Merlin	

Music. *Pastoral theme, in and under.*[1]

Connecticut Yankee *(Elderly, as for all narrations).* I am an American, born and reared in Hartford, Connecticut. So, I am a Yankee of the Yankees—and practical. When I was little more than a lad, I went over to the great arms factory and learned my real trade; learned all there was to it. Why, I could make anything a body'd want—anything in the world. It didn't make any difference what; and if there wasn't any newfangled way to make a thing quickly, I could invent one—and do it as easy as rolling off a log. I became a head superintendent—had a couple of thousand men under me. Now with all those men, you can see how easy it would be to fall into an argument. Well, one day. . . .

Music. *Reminiscent theme, in and under.*

Sound. *Factory noises softly in background.*

Conn. Yankee *(Younger than before, as for all dialog sequences).* Is that so, now? Well, sir, it just so happens that there *was* a total eclipse of the sun in the sixth century—matter of fact, it was on

1. **In and under**: a musical direction that directs the music to swell and then fade into the background.

the 21st of June, in the year 528 A.D., and began at three minutes after twelve noon.

Worker. Now look here, just because you're the foreman of this plant doesn't mean that you know everything. Ah, the trouble with you thick-headed types is that you're sure you do know everything.

Conn. Yankee. And just who are you calling thick-headed, sir?

Worker. Just you, sir.

Conn. Yankee. Is that right, now? Well, let me tell you something. . . .

Sound. *Angry voices fade off mike.*

Conn. Yankee *(Older voice).* Well, we argued and argued, and pretty soon we were taking off our shirts for a real fight. Everything was going along pretty smoothly, until he hit me a left under the chin that I didn't expect. The next think I knew, I was floating through space. . . .

Music. *Eerie, hypnotic dream theme, in and under.*

Sound. *Birds twittering gayly.*

Clarence *(A young boy).* Faith, sir, be ye awake?

Conn. Yankee *(Yawning).* Wha . . . Hmm? *(Alarmed)* Great green Jehosophat! Who are you?

Clarence. Clarence is my name. I be a page, sir.

Conn. Yankee. A page? A little thing like you a page? Go 'long, you aren't more than a paragraph. Hey, what is this place anyway? Where am I? Bridgeport?

Clarence. Camelot. You're in prison, sir.

Conn. Yankee. Prison! Then what are you doing all dressed up like you were going to a fancy ball?

Clarence. Marry,[2] sir, this is the latest thing for a page.

Conn. Yankee *(Suspiciously).* What's the date? This isn't April first, is it?

Clarence. No, sir. It's the twentieth of June, 528.

Conn. Yankee. Five twenty . . . look here. Is this a circus, maybe, or a lunatic asylum?

Clarence. No, sir, in faith it isn't.

Conn. Yankee. Well, then, either I am out of my mind, or something awful just happened. Now tell me, honest and true, where am I?

Clarence *(Simply).* Marry, sir, 'tis easy. You are in King Arthur's Court!

Music. *Delightful theme, in and under.*

---

2. **Marry**: exclamation of surprise used in Middle Ages.

will notice many places where music and sounds are needed. Have students read the introductory paragraph on page 488 and state in their own words what they should find out as they read the play.

Presenting the Selection

1. Read the cast of characters to the class and make sure the students can pronounce Alisande's name. Then assign the parts for the Connecticut Yankee, Worker, and Clarence, and have pages 488 and 489 read aloud. (You should read all the stage directions yourself). This section involves three scenes (counting the Yankee's introductory speech as a scene) and may be confusing to some students.

At the end of the reading, discuss the passage and make sure the students can identify the three settings (the present, with the Yankee speaking as an old man; the past, in the factory; and the distant past, in Camelot) and the transitions between them. If time allows, have the first two pages reread for fun.

Then assign the rest of the play to be read independently. If you like, assign the play in two segments. The first reading assignment should end after the second speech at the top of the first column on page 494. (Questions 1, 2, and 3 of the **Check Test** refer to the first assignment; questions 4 and 5 refer to the second assignment.)

2. Make sure that everyone has read the assignment by administering the **Check Test** at the bottom of T.E. page 499. If you have assigned the reading in two parts, ask questions 1, 2, and 3 after the first assignment; ask questions 4 and 5 after the second.

3. If time allows, assign parts to the students and have a portion of the play read aloud in class. Begin at the top of page 490, column one, when the Connecticut Yankee learns that he is in King Arthur's Court, through the first assignment (ending after the second speech of the first column on page 494). Note that the students will be participating in a more formal reading of the play for the **Developing Skills in Speaking and Listening** exercise.

4. Remind the students that the introduction to the play asked them to decide if the Connecticut Yankee is a good time-traveler. Ask several students to express their opinions.

5. Develop the study questions as suggested in **Using the Study Questions**, beginning on page 500. That section also provides challenge questions for further discussion, as needed.

Reinforcing the Lesson

To reteach, reinforce, or extend the skills in this lesson, see the following:

Skills Practice Book, Green Level—pages 189 through 194

Special Populations

ESL. Provide some background information about the period in history in which *A Connecticut Yankee in King Arthor's Court* is supposed to take place. Explain to the students that the unusual syntax and vocabulary in this play are based on language used in the Middle Ages, which may sound very different from what we use today. These students will need individual assistance with context clue exercises on page 501 because of their unfamiliarity with the context from which the vocabulary words are coming. Pair ESL students with native-English-speaking students for help in pronouncing and defining unfamiliar words.

Some of the phrases and words that might be discussed as a class exercise include these: *in faith it isn't, prithee, bides, wrought a spell, forsooth, essay this peril, dominions, show homage, verily, eradicated slavery, knight-errantry,* and *serfdom.*

ESL students may be hesitant to participate in a dramatic reading, such as suggested in the exercise for **Developing Skills in Speaking and Listening** on page 503. See the comments under **Special Populations** on T.E. page 483 for suggestions.

Encouraging Independent Reading

You might like to read the class a portion of one of Mark Twain's humorous short stories to stimulate more interest in his works. The stories suggested below can be found in Twain's *The Mysterious Stranger* :

"The Stolen White Elephant"
"Luck"
"The $1,000,000 Bank-Note"

You may also want to suggest that the students read Twain's novel, *A Connecticut Yankee in King Arthur's Court*, or these other well-known books by Mark Twain:

The Adventures of Tom Sawyer
The Prince and the Pauper

Conn. Yankee *(Older voice).* Well, sir, there never was a man more dumbfounded than I was. I just couldn't get used to the idea. That's why, when I awoke again, I thought the whole thing a dream and, when I saw that page boy standing before me, I was more amazed than ever.

Clarence. Sir! Sir! Wake up!

Conn. Yankee. What? You here yet? Go along with the rest of the dream. Scat!

Clarence. Prithee, what dream?

Conn. Yankee. What dream? Why the dream that I am in Arthur's Court, and that I talk to you, who are nothing but a work of the imagination.

Clarence. Indeed! And is it a dream that you're to be burned at the stake tomorrow? Answer me that!

Conn. Yankee *(Astounded).* What?

Clarence. Aye, by the command of the King. Merlin suggested it!

Conn. Yankee *(Nervously).* Now, Clarence, my boy, you're the only friend I've got. You must help me devise some way to escape from this place.

Clarence. Verily, sir, it is impossible. The corridors are filled with guards, and worse than that, Merlin has woven a spell about this dungeon, and there bides not a man in this kingdom who would dare attempt to escape!

Conn. Yankee. Merlin hath wrought a spell. Merlin, forsooth! That cheap old humbug, that maundering old fake. *(Laughs)*

Clarence *(Frightened).* Oh beware! Any moment these walls may crumble upon us if you say such things!

Conn. Yankee. Do you know why I laughed? Because I'm a magician myself. Why, I knew Merlin seven hundred years ago, and he doesn't amount to shucks as a magician, not next to me! Oh, he's all right for parlor magic and such, but he never learned the rudiments of the big stuff. Now listen to me. I want you to do me a favor; you said today is June 20, didn't you? Well, get word to the King that I am a magician myself, and, if he dares to try burning me tomorrow, I will blot out the sun at noon, and it shall never shine again. The fruits of the earth shall rot for lack of light, and the peoples of the earth shall die. Do you understand?

Music. *Mischievous theme, in and under.*

Conn. Yankee *(Older voice).* Well, the King believed that I was a magician, right enough. But that old fake, Merlin, persuaded him that I was a humbug. And so, at twelve the next day, I found myself tied to a stake in the middle of the courtyard. That didn't bother me, though; I knew that in about a minute and a half, I could expect a total eclipse of the sun.

Sound. *Clamor of crowd in background.*

Conn. Yankee *(Older voice).* Sure enough, just as they were about to light the pile of wood at my feet, I saw the skies darken slightly. Majestically, I raised my arm, pointing at the sun. Then everyone noticed the darkness. Poor fools, they thought I was really going through with my threat. Suddenly, the King rose, and shouted. . . .

Arthur *(Slightly off mike).* Stop the proceedings. Do not light the stake!

Merlin *(An old, crackling voice).* But Your Majesty. . . .

Arthur. Be quiet, Merlin. I, Arthur, King of England, command silence. But look you, the skies grow darker. *(Pleading)* Stranger, I am sorry! I beg of you: do not extinguish the sun!

Conn. Yankee. Stay where you are, all. If any man moves—even the King—before I give him leave, I will blast him with thunder and lightning.

Arthur. Be merciful, fair sir, and essay this peril no further, lest disaster follow. Name any terms, reverend sir, even to the halving of my Kingdom; but banish this calamity! Spare the sun!

Conn. Yankee *(Casually).* Give me time to consider.

Arthur. How long, oh, how long? Be merciful; look, it groweth darker, moment by moment. Prithee, how long?

Conn. Yankee. Oh, not long, Maybe an hour. For a lesson, I will let this darkness proceed, and spread night in the world; but, whether or not I will blot out the sun for good shall rest with you. These are the terms: you shall remain King over all your dominions, but you shall appoint me your perpetual minister and executive, so that I'll be The Boss, and give me as payment, one percent of all revenue I raise for the state. Is it satisfactory?

Arthur. Away with his bonds, and set him free! And show him homage, high and low, rich and poor, for he is a great wizard and magician. Now, sir, banish, if you will, this awful night.

Conn. Yankee *(To himself).* Ah, at last the eclipse is total. Now is the time. *(Aloud majestically)* Let the enchantment dissolve and pass harmless away!

Sound. *Tumultuous cheers in backgound.*

Arthur *(Proclaiming).* Blessings upon thee, oh Great Wizard. I, Arthur, welcome thee to Camelot as my right-hand man. And from this day henceforward, shall thy name be called . . . The Boss!

Sound. *Crowd cheers.*

Arthur *(Shouting).* Make way! Make way! Make way for The Boss!

Music. *Fanfare into royal theme, in and under.*

Conn. Yankee *(Older voice).* Well, that—miracle, shall we call it?—fixed things up as right as right could be. Soon news of it traveled throughout the Kingdom, and everybody knew what a wonderful person I was. Of course, I couldn't rest on my laurels. The Kingdom would get suspicious; besides, I was getting restless. I wanted some new glories. And so, I began—inventing things.

Music. *Out.*[3]

3. **Out**: a musical direction to indicate that the music should stop.

Conn. Yankee. Look, Your Majesty. My newest invention.

Arthur. It is a wondrous looking thing, but—but what is it?

Conn. Yankee. It's an artificial candle. It's cheaper to manufacture—I've already started a factory—and it'll give a hundred times the light that oil lamps give.

Arthur *(With awe).* Indeed! And what do you call your new miracle?

Conn. Yankee. I've given it the name . . . electric light bulb!

Music. *Low-pitched chord.*

Arthur. Another invention, Sir Boss?

Conn. Yankee. Yes. A collapsible sunshade—it'll protect you from rain, too. And when not in use, it can double as a walking-stick. I've got a factory producing twenty thousand of them a day. Do you like it?

Arthur *(In wonder).* Verily, I do. And what do you plan to call this wonderful device?

Conn. Yankee. How about—umbrella?

Music. *Higher chord.*

Conn. Yankee. Yes, Your Majesty, a new invention. It's a box that is capable of transfixing images of real things in miniature on paper. I call it a camera.

Music. *Higher chord.*

Conn. Yankee. It's a solution with which to get your skin much cleaner than with ordinary water. I plan to name it . . . soap.

Music. *Higher chord.*

Conn. Yankee. Yes, Your Majesty, I've just invented shoe polish. *(Pause)* That's right, Sire, it's my newest discovery: whipped cream. *(Pause)* Right again, King Arthur. Another invention: this one's the printing press.

Music. *A succession of chords mounting to a climax, then, fanfare.*

Arthur. I have sent for you, Sir Boss, to ask if you would like an adventure.

Conn. Yankee. An . . . an adventure?

Arthur. Yes. You must be tired of staying here in Camelot year after year, just working your humdrum miracles, so I thought—or, rather, Merlin thought—that you might like to go off on an adventure.

Conn. Yankee. Merlin did, did he?

Merlin. Yes, I did, did I.

Conn. Yankee. I'm awfully sorry, Sire, but much as I'd like to—well, I just couldn't. The factories have been going only a few months, and the Sunday schools have been in operation barely a week.

Merlin. You aren't afraid that I might get the upper hand while you're away, are you?

Conn. Yankee *(Not quite convincing).* Of course not. It's just that—well, what adventure could I go on?

Arthur. Ah, that's all settled. This lady that you see on my right has just come to Camelot with a marvelous tale. It seems that her mistress is a captive in a vast and gloomy castle, along with forty-three other young and beautiful girls.

Alisande *(A sweet, innocent voice).* Forty-four, an it please you, Sire.

Arthur. Ah yes; forty-four young ladies. The master of this castle is a giant, with four arms and one eye—in the center of his forehead. Your adventure is simply this: find the Princess and her ladies! Doesn't it sound exciting? I wish that I could go with you, but Guinevere would never hear of it. Oh, you must be thrilled!

Conn. Yankee *(Downheartedly).* Yes, yes, Sire. Thrilled. I can hardly control myself. *(Weakly, limply)* Three cheers for adventure.

Music. *Pastoral theme, in and under.*

Sound. *Horses trotting on a dirt road.*

Conn. Yankee. I still don't understand why you insist upon accompanying me on this fool's errand, young lady.

Alisande. How else then should you find the castle, Sir Boss?

Conn. Yankee. Oh come, come; you don't mean to say that there really *is* such a place. Your name, please?

Alisande. I'm called the Demoiselle Alisande de la Carteloise, an it please you.

Conn. Yankee. Now, Sandy—it's easier to call you that—have you brought any letters, any documents, any proofs that you are trustworthy and truthful?

Alisande. Of a surety, no; and wherefore should I? Have I not a tongue, and cannot I say all that by myself?

Conn. Yankee. But your saying it and someone else's saying it are different.

Alisande. Different? How might that be? I fear me I do not understand.

Conn. Yankee. Not understand? Can't you see the difference between you—why in Heaven's name do you look so innocent and idiotic?

Alisande *(Innocently).* I? In truth I know not, but it were the will of God.

Conn. Yankee. Oh, for the love of Heaven! *(Regaining his calm)* Now as to this castle—where is it?

Alisande. Oh, as to that, it lieth in a far country, many leagues away.

Conn. Yankee. Never mind the distance; whereabout does the castle lie, in what direction?

Alisande. Ah, please you sir, it hath no direction from here, by reason that the road lieth not straight but turneth evermore.

Conn. Yankee. But have you not a map—a good map?

Alisande *(Puzzled).* Is that peradventure[4] the manner of thing which of late the unbelievers have brought from over the great seas, which being boiled in oil, *(Fading)* and an onion and salt added thereto, doth . . .

4. **Peradventure**: Middle Age word for *perhaps.*

Music. *Pleasant theme, in and under.*

Conn. Yankee *(Older voice).* Ah, I knew right then that the poor girl was a liar from the word "Go," and was only stalling for time. And here was I, a respectable Wizard of the Court of King Arthur, off gallivanting around the countryside with a beautiful young demoiselle named Sandy. Why, it was improper! It was indecent! It was scandalous! Especially since I was engaged to a telephone operator from East Hartford, Connecticut, named Kitty Flanagan. *(Sighs)* Ah, it was doubtful that I'd ever see her again, or ever call her on the telephone, with a "Hello, Operator." At first, I did think that there might be some chance of my returning to the nineteenth century—but as time went on, I realized that such would never be the case. And so, after much wandering around the countryside, I finally decided that it was time that Sandy and I were married. Therefore, we returned briefly to Camelot.

Music. *Wedding March, in and under.*

Note. *The next six speeches overlap each other in sequence, in a montage effect.*

Arthur. Good health to you both! Good health and long life!

Clarence. Congratulations, Sir Boss.

1st Woman. Long live Sir Boss and Lady Alisande!

1st Man. The best of luck in the world to you both.

2nd Woman. My heartiest congratulations and best wishes!

2nd Man. Long live the happy bride and groom!

Music. *Wedding March, in and under.*

Conn. Yankee *(Older voice).* Although the first few months of our marriage were happy ones, in my dreams I still wandered thirteen centuries away. I could not get the face of that telephone operator—the one that I had been engaged to in Hartford—out of my mind. Night after night, I would toss upon my pillow, and whisper fitfully in my sleep: *(Whispering)* Hello, Operator! Hello, Operator! Hello, Operator! *(Pause)* In a little more than a year, Sandy presented me with a child, and, with great magnanimity, she saddled that cry of mine, uttered in my sleep, upon our little daughter, believing it to be the name of some lost darling of mine. It touched me to tears, and it nearly knocked me off my feet, too, when she smiled up at my face and said:

Alisande. The name of one who was dear to thee is here preserved, here made holy, and the music of it will abide always in our ears. Now thou'lt kiss me, as knowing the name I have given the child.

Conn. Yankee. Yes, I know, sweetheart—how dear and good it is of you, too! But I want to hear these lips of yours, which are also mine, utter it first. Then its music will be complete.

Alisande *(With deep feeling)*. I have called our baby . . . Hello-Operator!

Music. *Lively theme, in and under.*

Conn. Yankee *(Older voice)*. After a year and a half of traipsing arond the countryside in search of Sandy's mythical Princess, we returned once more to the Court of King Arthur. At first, I was worried about what I could tell His Majesty, but Sandy fixed that up just fine. She had lied me into the mess. Now, she lied me out again.

Music. *Lighthearted theme, in and under.*

Alisande. Yes, Your Majesty, we *did* find the forty-four maidens—*and* the Princess. But what do you think? They had been turned to swine! So we drove them back to the Kingdom from which they originally came, and the Sorcerer Glacklick turned them back into fair damsels.

Arthur. But why couldn't you turn them back into humans yourself, Sir Boss?

Conn. Yankee. Why, er . . . uh. . . .

Alisande *(Aghast)*. Surely you wouldn't have someone as mighty as The Boss associate with swine, Your Majesty?

Music. *Delightful theme, in and under.*

Conn. Yankee *(Older voice)*. Time marched on, and, I am pleased to say, England was altered. I had eradicated slavery, knight-errantry, serfdom, and ignorance. I had established schools everywhere, and even colleges. Baseball was the national pastime—King Arthur was my prize shortstop! A number of pretty good newspapers were in operation, and I even had established a weekly magazine. Only one thing troubled me; that was Merlin. He seemed jealous and was always slinking around in corners, whispering to his friends in low tones, and sneering whenever I passed. No matter, though, I thought; I had more important business on my mind. Then one day . . . .

Music. *Out.*

Alisande *(Breathless)*. Sir! Sir Boss! Come quickly!

Conn. Yankee *(Kindly)*. Easy, darling, easy. What is it?

Alisande. Hello-Operator. She's sick—the doctor says it's mem . . . membraneous croup. I don't know what that is—it's a word he learned in one of your colleges. But I'm frightened!

Conn. Yankee *(Calling out)*. Clarence! Fetch my staff of physicians! And hurry!

Music. *Urgent theme, in and under.*

Conn. Yankee *(Older voice).* The doctors said we must take the child away if we would coax her back to health and strength again. And she must have sea air. Quickly, I had a yacht outfitted, and Sandy, the baby, and I took off for a cruise on the Mediterranean. I left Clarence in charge of things while I was away, and for three months I did not set foot on English soil.

Music. *Calm theme, in and under.*

Conn. Yankee *(Older voice; seriously, urgently).* The next time I saw Camelot, I knew at once that something was amiss. As I approached the gates of the castle, Clarence ran out to greet me and, by the worried expression on his face, I knew that there was trouble.

Clarence *(Breathless).* Sir Boss, at last you have come!

Conn. Yankee. What is it, Clarence? Speak!

Clarence. It was a plot—all of it—all Merlin's idea. As soon as your sails were out of the harbor, he started a revolution.

Conn. Yankee *(Numb with shock).* A—revo . . . lution?

Clarence. He brought back slavery, nobility—everything that you worked for years to remove. The people were only too ready for things to go back to their old state. It was no good for you to try to change them.

Conn. Yankee *(Heartbroken).* My dreams . . . my dreams of a republic . . . all gone, all smashed. What of the King?

Clarence. Dead. It is no use, I say. No use at all!

Conn. Yankee *(Determined).* Come, Clarence. There is work to do.

Clarence. Work? Where?

Conn. Yankee. We must destroy the schools, the factories, the colleges, lest they fall into Merlin's hands. We must destroy them; else, they destroy all of England.

Music. *Dramatic theme, in and under.*

Sound. *Explosions in the background.*

Conn. Yankee *(Bitterly).* Look at them, Clarence. Factories, schools, everything—blown to smithereens. And by my own hand; that's the irony of it.

Clarence. The work of a lifetime gone, in one fell swoop. What took you three-and-thirty years to build, destroyed in three-and-thirty minutes.

Conn. Yankee. It was the only way. I knew it would come to this, I think; yes, I knew it all along. That's why I had the dynamite charges set under all the buildings as soon as they were completed—in preparation for an event such as this. England simply wasn't ready for me, that's all.

Clarence. But it's not right, it's not fair.

Conn. Yankee. There can be no talk of right and fair. Go; see to the destruction of the newspaper office.

Clarence. The newspaper office? That too?

Conn. Yankee. That too. Go. I'll follow you in a moment.

Music. *Tense theme, in and under.*

Conn. Yankee *(To himself)*. Just these last power lines to cut, and then it's finished. There . . . and . . . *(Exerting pressure)* . . . ugh! There! Now everything's done that must be done.

Merlin. Not everything, Sir Boss.

Conn. Yankee *(Surprised)*. Wha . . . ? Who spoke? Merlin!

Merlin *(Maliciously)*. Aye, Merlin. You see, Sir Boss, I win after all. I still have the upper hand here; I shall always have the upper hand here.

Conn. Yankee. Not as long as I am alive.

Merlin. Just so; and that is the one task that remains in the destruction of your Empire. I will not try magic with you; we understand each other too well for that. I shall only use—this dagger!

Conn. Yankee. Wha . . . ? Aggh!

Sound. *Body falling.*

Merlin. There now, Sir Boss! I, Merlin, am once again triumphant.

Alisande *(Fading on)*. Husband, Clarence told me I might find you here . . . What's this? Merlin! Where is Sir Boss? *(Pause)* Stabbed!

Merlin. He's unconscious; aye, in my power at last!

Alisande *(Sobbing)*. Husband!

Merlin. It is now my turn to work an enchantment—an enchantment to send Sir Boss back to wherever he came from. *(Calling aloud)* Thaglitch! Eerandabar! Sophoclus! Sophoclee!

Conn. Yankee *(A weird, echoing quality in his voice)*. Goodbye, Alisande! Goodbye, Alisande! Goodbyyyyyye, Aaaalliiiiisaaaaaande!

Music. *Rapid succession of ascending chords.*

Sound. *Murmur of bewildered factory workers.*

Conn. Yankee *(Coming out of a coma)*. Alisande! Alisande!

Worker *(Bewildered)*. Alisande? Hey, who's Alisande? Come on, Boss, wake up. I didn't mean to hit you so hard, honest!

Conn. Yankee. Clarence . . . Merlin . . . eclipse.

Worker. Yeah, the eclipse, Boss. You were right about that. Now wake up, Boss. *(Pleading)* Please!

Conn. Yankee. Where . . . where am I?

Worker. You're in the factory, Boss. I was afraid you were never going to come around.

Conn. Yankee. Huh? What? You're sure this isn't Camelot?

Worker. It's the factory, the factory. Where did you think you were?

Conn. Yankee. Why in . . . oh, never mind. You'd probably never believe me, even if I told you. Besides, it was all just a dream.

Merlin *(Eerie and distant, speaking through miles and centuries).* It was the only way, Sir Boss. The only way.

Conn. Yankee *(Bewildered).* That voice. How can it be? It was only a dream. *(Pause)* Or . . . was it?

Music. *Full to finish.*

Check Test

1. Where does the Yankee work? (in a factory in Hartford, Connecticut)

2. Who is the narrator of the play? (the Connecticut Yankee)

3. Who is the first person the Yankee meets in Camelot? (a page named Clarence)

4. What does Alisande name their baby? (Hello-Operator)

5. How does the Yankee get back to his own time period? (Merlin stabs him and then casts a spell.)

Answers to Study Questions

Developing Comprehension Skills

1. The Yankee was hit under the chin. He went to the year 528 because that was the year he and the worker were fighting about.

2. In his own time, the Yankee was engaged to a telephone operator. He feels guilty about marrying Lady Alisande when he is engaged to someone else.

3. No, the Yankee is making things that were invented by others in his own time to impress the people in Camelot.

(continued on page 500)

Developing Comprehension Skills

Literal Reading — 1. What caused the Connecticut Yankee to go back to 528 A.D.?

Interpretive Reading — 2. After the Yankee marries Lady Alisande, whom he calls Sandy, he tosses and turns in bed at night, whispering, "Hello, Operator! Hello, Operator!" Why does he do this? What is disturbing him?

Interpretive Reading — 3. In the factory where he worked in Hartford, Connecticut, the Yankee was head superintendent, with many men working under him. He is knowledgeable about his work. When he reaches Camelot, he uses this knowledge to "invent" things. Is he really inventing anything?

Critical Reading — 4. When the Yankee sets off dynamite charges to destroy all he has built in Camelot, he says, "England simply wasn't ready for me." Why was it wrong for the Yankee to bring about so much change?

Critical Reading — 5. To the Connecticut Yankee, the eclipse of the sun was an event that could be explained by natural causes. To the natives of Camelot, it was magic. Knowing this, can you suggest a definition of magic?

Reading Literature: Drama

1. **Appreciating Differences in Dialog.** This play uses two different speaking styles to show differences in characters and in their time periods. Remember that the Yankee moves back in time to Camelot. How does his style of speech differ from that of the characters he encounters there? Give examples from the early part of the play.

   Find two times that the Connecticut Yankee talks like the natives of Camelot. Does he change his speaking style on purpose? Why?

   Find a scene in which Alisande begins to talk like the Connecticut Yankee. Why does her language change?

2. **Understanding Dramatic Technique.** Look back at the stage directions for times when music is used. Notice that different musical themes, such as "delightful" and "mischievous," are used. These themes reflect the words and actions taking place in the play. Below are three types of musical themes used. Explain how they emphasize what has just taken place, or is taking place, in the play. Be sure to explain what is happening in the play.

   a. mischievous theme (See page 490.)
   b. royal theme (See page 491.)
   c. urgent theme (See page 496.)

Using the Study Questions

It is recommended that students always read and answer the questions in **Developing Comprehension Skills** in class discussion. Whenever possible, they should also read the questions in the other categories together and discuss the answers.

Developing Comprehension Skills

Question 1. Have students find proof of their answers in the selection (page 489).

Question 2. Help students to recognize that the Yankee's reaction demonstrates a commitment to the woman he is engaged to from his own time period.

Question 3. Before the students discuss the question, have a volunteer read the dictionary definition of *invent* aloud.

Question 4. Ask the students why the Yankee "invented" the things he did; that is, what did he expect to gain? Students may note that the Yankee enjoyed being important but that he also may have wanted sincerely to give the people the benefit of the successes of his own time.

Then have students answer the question.

Question 5. After they have answered the question, ask students for examples of other things or events that have been considered magic, such as magicians' tricks. Have them test their definition of magic against these examples.

Reading Literature: Drama

Question 1. Have the students find examples of contrasting speaking styles and read them aloud. To help them figure out why the characters change their speaking styles, have the students think about the situation each character is in.

Question 2. Explain to students that the term *theme*, in this case, means a musical theme. Make sure the students

(continued from page 499)

4. He brought about change too fast and gave the people inventions they weren't ready for yet and didn't need.

5. Answers may vary. A possible answer could be: Magic is something that occurs when the natural or man-made causes for an event are not understood.

Reading Literature: Drama

1. The Yankee's speech is full of slang from modern times, while the speech of the other characters is old-fashioned. He tends to be rude and direct, while the others tend to use both more words and more polite words.

Examples from the early part of the play will vary.

Examples of times that the Connecticut Yankee talks like the natives of Camelot include the following:

When he is ridiculing Merlin: "Merlin hath wrought a spell. Merlin, forsooth" (page 490, column 1).

When he wants the people to believe he is breaking the spell of darkness: "Let the enchantment dissolve and pass harmless away" (page 491, columns 1 and 2).

When he persuades Alisande to tell him the name of their baby: "I want to hear these lips of yours, which are also mine, utter it first" (page 496, column 1).

The Yankee changes his speaking style when it is critical that his words are understood by those who hear him.

In the scene where the baby gets sick (page 496, column 2), Alisande begins to talk like the Yankee. Conversing with him day-to-day has influenced her speaking style.

2. The musical themes are used as follows:

3. **Understanding Conflict.** The Yankee experiences both internal and external conflict in this play. How does he resolve his internal conflict over marrying Sandy instead of the telephone operator? In what way does Sandy try to help him with this problem? How is the Yankee's external conflict with Merlin resolved?

4. **Identifying Theme.** Although this play is more humorous than serious, the author still makes some statements about life. He points out that people tend to develop inventions even when there is no particular need for those inventions. He also points out that some of these inventions are so powerful that they are hard to control. What do you think is the author's opinion of our love of inventions? How does the play express his ideas?

5. **Understanding a Character.** In many ways, the Connecticut Yankee is a stereotype of an American. A **stereotype** person is a character whose ideas, actions, and words fit with a widely held idea of what that type of person is like. A stereotype has no individuality. He or she does only what is expected of that certain type of person. A stereotype does not change or grow.

   One stereotype of Americans pictures us as know-it-alls who are often rude and bossy. According to this stereotype, Americans depend on machines instead of people to solve their problems. This stereotype American believes that whatever is new is good, and whatever is old should be ignored or thrown away.

   The Connecticut Yankee often fits that stereotype in what he says or does. Find at least five details about the Yankee that prove this statement.

   Why would the author of this play want the hero to be a stereotype? With the theme of this play in mind, can you think of a reason? What might that reason be?

Developing Vocabulary Skills

Reviewing Context Clues. As you have learned in other lessons throughout this text, you can determine the meaning of an unfamiliar word from context in many ways. Sometimes there are key words that alert you to the meaning. For example, *is* and *in other words* are key words for definition or restatement clues. A comparison can be signaled by *in the same way,* while a contrast may be introduced with *unlike.*

understand that music is intended to enhance the mood of a movie or play. If possible, play background music from a movie you are familiar with. After the students decide what kind of mood a particular piece creates, describe the scene from which it came. Have the students decide whether the song and theme complement each other. Then discuss the study question.

Question 3. Review the meaning of both internal and external conflict. Then before they answer the question, have the students explain the internal and external conflicts the Connecticut Yankee experiences.

Question 4. Help the students to see how useless many of the Yankee's inventions were to the people in Authur's court.

Question 5. Before asking the students to answer this question, discuss the concept of stereotype thoroughly. See if they can provide some examples of other stereotyped characters used in literature or the movies. Some examples might be the dumb blond, the interfering mother-in-law, and the bratty kid brother.

Challenge Question 1. Twain never gives the Yankee a name. He is referred to as the "Connecticut Yankee" or "Sir Boss". Why does Twain do this?

Challenge Question 2. The character of Lady Alisande contrasts sharply with the character of the Connecticut Yankee. What character traits does she possess that are not found in the personality of the Yankee? Find details in the story that support your answer.

Developing Vocabulary Skills

Read and discuss the directions for this exercise, stopping as needed to clarify any questions. Emphasize that it may be nec-

a. The Connecticut Yankee is setting up Clarence and the others to believe he is a magician. The music emphasizes the humor in the situation.

b. The King has just granted the Yankee his position as Sir Boss. The music emphasizes the Yankee's feeling of power.

c. Hello-Operator is sick and Sir Boss is telling Clarence to get the doctors. The music adds to the worried, rushed feeling.

3. The Yankee resolves his internal conflict by deciding that he will never return to his own time and that he might as well get married to Sandy. Sandy tries to help by naming their baby Hello-Operator.

The Yankee's external conflict with Merlin is resolved when Merlin stabs him and uses magic to send him back to where he came from.

4. Possible answer: The author says that inventions sometimes do not benefit the people they are intended to help and, may create more problems than they eliminate. The play expresses this idea when the Yankee has to destroy the schools and factories so they won't fall into Merlin's hands and be used against the people.

5. Students may list these or other details:

The Yankee was pushy to his workers. That's how he ended up in Camelot in the first place. He was rude to the boy who woke him in Camelot.

He brashly pretended to be a magician.

He took the honors for inventing things he didn't really invent.

He was rude to Sandy and to Merlin.

He changed life in Camelot by introducing schools and factories and

(continued on page 502)

essary to read more than the sentence in which a word is used to discover the meaning of the word.

Work out the first two items with the students to make sure they can find the passages and identify the clues.

Assign the rest of the exercise for independent completion. Compare answers in class discussion.

Developing Writing Skills

Read and discuss the two assignments. Then have each student choose and complete one of the two.

Question 1. This question asks students to compare and contrast the Yankee and Merlin, to explain the causes of their conflict, and to make and support a judgment about the characters. For some students, you may prefer to limit the question to only one part.

Pre-Writing. Before the students begin the assignment, mark off three columns on the chalkboard. Label the first "Connecticut Yankee", label the next "Merlin", and label the last "Both". Suggest a specific character similarity or difference and list it on the board. Have the students decide if it describes the Yankee, Merlin, or both, and put check marks in the appropriate columns. Some suggested character traits for this activity: ambitious (both), clever (both), vengeful (Merlin), rude (Yankee). Be sure students realize that they must support their character descriptions with details from the play. Remind them, also, that their answer must answer three parts of the question:

How are the characters alike and different?

Why are they in conflict?

Which is more interesting, and why?

Have the students write down the three questions to help them remember all three parts in their answer.

Other context clues are not marked by key words. To discover meanings from cause and effect statements, for example, or from the main idea of a paragraph, requires careful reading. Sometimes you can infer the meaning of a word from the single statement in which it appears. Other times you must examine the entire paragraph or several paragraphs around the word.

Find the words listed below in the context of *A Connecticut Yankee.* For each word, read as many sentences or paragraphs as you need to determine the meaning. On your paper, write the word and the meaning you determined from the context. Then look up the word in a dictionary. After your meaning, write the dictionary definition that best fits the context.

1. newfangled (See page 488, The Connecticut Yankee's first speech.)
2. eclipse (See page 488, the Yankee's 2nd speech, and pages 490 and 491, the Yankee's speeches.)
3. devise (See page 490, the Yankee's 5th speech.)
4. humbug (See page 490 column 2, the Yankee's first and last speeches.)
5. homage (See page 491 column 2, Arthur's first speech.)
6. banish (See page 491 column 1, Arthur's 3rd speech and column 2, Arthur's first speech.)
7. humdrum (See page 493 column 2, Arthur's 2nd speech.)
8. gallivanting (See page 495, the Yankee's first speech.)
9. mythical (See page 496, the Yankee's 2nd speech.)
10. smithereens (See page 497 column 2, the Yankee's 4th speech.)

Developing Writing Skills

Analytical Writing

1. **Comparing Characters.** How were the Connecticut Yankee and Merlin similar? How were they different? Why were they in conflict with each other? Think about these questions and then write one or more paragraphs comparing the two characters. End by telling which character you found more interesting and why.

Creative Writing

2. **Predicting Outcomes.** Go beyond the ending of this play. Write about the way the Yankee attempts to explain his experiences in

(continued from page 501)

by getting rid of the old ways of doing things.

He made fun of magic, insisting on the importance of science and machines.

Twain uses a stereotype so that every American could see herself or himself as the one learning the lesson the Yankee learns. Another possible reason was to emphasize the contrast between the people of Camelot, who loved magic, and the people of modern America, who love machines.

Challenge 1. Because the Yankee does not have a name, he seems less personal and less developed as a character; it is easier to make him fit the stereotype.

Challenge 2. Possible answers: Lady Alisande is a very caring person. She names her baby Hello-Operator to honor the person that the Yankee is dreaming about and calling out to in his sleep. She is also polite, as can be seen by her reaction when the Yankee calls her idiotic. She accepts his words and merely states that it is the will of God that makes her the way she is. She may not be very smart, or else she is very clever at pretending not to understand questions. Her conversations sometimes don't make sense, especially when she takes the Yankee on his adventure.

Developing Vocabulary Skills

Students' meanings may vary; dictionary definitions may vary, depending upon the dictionary used.

1. newfangled—new; of the newest style

2. eclipse—the total or partial obscuring of one celestial body by another

3. devise—to plan; to work out a plan by thinking

4. humbug—fake; a person who is not what he or she claims to be

Camelot to his fiancée and the factory employees. Describe how the others will react to his story. Will anyone believe him? Write from two to four paragraphs explaining what you think might happen.

If you prefer, express your ideas in play form. Write an additional scene for the play, in which the Yankee talks with his fellow workers and his fiancée.

Developing Skills in Critical Thinking

Recognizing an Author's Purpose. Think back to Chapter 2 in this book, The Legend of King Arthur. What, if any, are the likenesses between Mark Twain's Camelot, set in 528 A.D., and Thomas Malory's, set in the Middle Ages? Twain was most likely familiar with Malory's legend when he wrote this play. Why do you think he made the changes he made? What was he trying to say in his play that was different from what Malory said in his book?

What tone does Mark Twain take toward Arthur and Merlin? Compare that to the tone Malory expressed. How does this difference in tone help Twain express his theme?

Developing Skills in Speaking and Listening

Giving a Dramatic Reading. Work with a group to present a portion of *A Connecticut Yankee in King Arthur's Court.* Each group member should select a role, study that character, and practice reading that character's lines aloud. Remember that two readers may be needed for the Connecticut Yankee—an older voice for the narrator and a younger voice for the dialog. Several group members should prepare music and produce background noises. Perhaps your music teacher can suggest melodies for the various musical themes asked for in the play.

The group should practice reading the selection together at least once. Make sure that every speaker talks loudly enough to be heard. Try to make your dialog sound as much like natural conversation as possible. Also, rehearse at least once, with sound effects if you plan to use them. Finally, present your reading to the other groups in your class.

5. homage—something done to show respect or honor

6. banish—to get rid of; to clear away

7. humdrum—boring; dull

8. gallivanting—traveling, wandering; going about in search of excitement

9. mythical—make-believe; fabricated, invented, or imagined in an arbitrary way

10. smithereens—bits; fragments

Developing Skills in Critical Thinking

Arthur and Merlin live in Camelot in both works. Malory uses a reverent approach to the legend. He pictures King Author as dignified and brave. He pictures Merlin as a good person dedicated to Arthur. Twain uses a humorous approach. King Arthur is weak and his thinking is easily controlled. Merlin only wants power. Using this critical tone, Twain can get across his theme about people in all ages being fooled into wanting new and different things even when they don't need them. Malory uses his admiring tone because he wants to pass on the legend of bravery and goodness.

Writing. Allow sufficent time for students to complete the assignment, working independently. Remind them to include all the parts you have requested.

Revising. Let students who chose to write this question compare answers with each other. If any disagreements arise, those who disagree should explain what they believe is wrong with the logic or proofs of any writer. Allow time for corrections and improvements to be made.

Question 2. Encourage creativity in students' responses to this question, whichever form—narrative or dramatic—their answers take.

Pre-Writing. Have students brainstorm possible extensions to the play. Remind them of the necessity of keeping the Yankee's personality true to the original play. If some students are writing in play form, you may want to allow them to work with partners. Those who choose to write a scene should be reminded to imitate the form of *A Connecticut Yankee in King Arthur's Court.*

Writing. Allow students time to write their first drafts.

Revising. Have each student check his or her writing to make sure the personality of the Yankee has been preserved and that the reactions of his fiancée and the factory workers have been included. Allow time for revisions. Encourage those who wrote a scene to read or perform it for the class.

Developing Skills in Critical Thinking

Students may need to skim or reread the material from Chapter 2 in order to discuss this question. When you discuss the exercise, help them to recognize the differences in the two works and the differences in the authors' purposes.

Developing Skills in Speaking and Listening

Read the directions to the exercise to the class and discuss them. Review how the students can use the resources of the library to find appropriate music to accompany their reading. Either assign the students to groups or have them form groups on their own. Set up a schedule to allow each group to perform and, before their performance, have group members identify the music they plan to use. Before the groups perform, review good audience habits with the class.

Objectives

- To recognize and appreciate drama as a form of literature
- To identify the elements of a radio play
- To analyze a character by the nature of his or her language
- To apply literal, interpretive, and critical reading skills to a selection
- To choose the most appropriate word-attack technique to determine the meaning of a word
- To write a description of an imaginary creature

Preparing the Students

Essential Vocabulary. The words presented here are essential to the understanding of the selection.

Introduce the words listed below. Write the sentences on the board, have them read aloud, and ask the students to use context clues to find the meaning of the underlined words.

velocity luminous density
straddled martial

1. We knew that the object traveled at a very high velocity, since it took only twenty minutes to cross the entire country.
2. The boy straddled the balcony railing, letting his legs dangle loosely on either side.
3. The luminous object lit up the night sky for miles around.
4. Due to the emergency, the city was placed under martial law. The army was in charge of keeping order and enforcing laws.
5. The drivers had to slow down because the density of the fog made it difficult to see the road ahead.

If the students need additional help with the vocabulary of this selection, encourage them to use context clues to determine word meaning. As needed, direct them to the **Glossary** or to a classroom dictionary.

Motivation. Ask students if they have ever had this experience: They are watching the TV or listening to the radio when suddenly the program is interrupted by a special bulletin. Have students describe their feelings when that happens. Then have the students read the introductory paragraph on page 504 and ask them to state in their own words what they should think about as they read the radio play.

Invasion from Mars

H.G. WELLS
From **The War of the Worlds**
Adapted by Howard Koch

This science fiction radio play uses radio news techniques to tell its story. As you read, think about why these techniques make such an impact upon those who are listening.

October 30, 1938: Shortly after 8 P.M., more than a million Americans, just tuning in their radios, heard a "news commentator" report that Martian invaders had landed in New Jersey. The monsters were reported armed with flames and poison gas and were marching toward New York. In a wave of mass hysteria, thousands of citizens fled to the highways. Churches overflowed. Soldiers and nurses volunteered for duty. A few of the terrified listeners tried to commit suicide; many had to be treated for shock.

The following selection is condensed and adapted from that famous radio broadcast. Announcements before, during, and after the show told listeners that the program was a regular Mercury Theatre presentation, starring Orson Welles. Perhaps, as you read, you'll understand the reactions of those who tuned in late—and didn't wait for the commercial.

ACT ONE

Sound. *Theme.*

Announcer. Ladies and gentlemen: the director of the Mercury Theatre on the Air, Orson Welles. . . .

Orson Welles. We know now that in the early years of the twentieth century this world was being watched closely by beings more intelligent than man and yet as mortal. We know now that, as human beings busied themselves about their various concerns, they were scrutinized and studied, perhaps almost as narrowly as a man with a microscope might scrutinize the tiny creatures that swarm and multiply in a drop of water.

Computerized image of Mars with exaggerated colors. NASA

Across an immense ethereal gulf, intellects vast, cool, and unsympathetic regarded this earth with envious eyes and slowly drew their plans against us. . . .

In the thirty-ninth year of the twentieth century, in the year 1938, came the great awakening.

It was near the end of October. Business was better. The war scare was over. On this particular evening thirty-two million people were listening in on radios. . . .

Fade in . . .

Announcer two. We now take you to the Meridian Room in the Hotel Park Plaza in downtown New York, where you will be entertained by the music of Ramon Raquello[1] and his orchestra.

Sound. *Spanish theme song . . . fades.*

Announcer two. Ladies and gentlemen, we interrupt our program of dance music to bring you a special bulletin from the Intercontinental Radio News. At twenty minutes before eight, Central Time, Professor Farrell of the Mount Jennings Observatory, Chicago, Illinois, reported observing several explosions of incandescent gas, occurring at regular intervals on the planet Mars. The gas seems to be moving toward the

1. **Ramon Raquello**: rä mōn′ rä kāl′yō.

Presenting the Selection

1. Read the opening explanation aloud to the class. Then assign parts to the students and read a portion of the play (as much as you have time for) aloud in class. Have the students read the rest of the first act of "Invasion from Mars" outside of class. Explain that, since this is only the first act, the story will not come to a climax here. This act will set up the conflict.

2. Make sure that everyone has read the assignment by administering the **Check Test** at the bottom of T.E. page 516.

3. Remind the students that the introduction to the play asked them to think about why radio news techniques in this play make such an impact upon those who are listening. Have them suggest answers to the question.

4. Develop the study questions as suggested in **Using the Study Questions**, beginning on page 516. That section also provides a challenge question for further discussion, if needed.

Reinforcing the Lesson

To reteach, reinforce, or extend the skills in this lesson, refer to the following:

Skills Practice Book, Green Level—195 and 196

Encouraging Independent Reading

If you can rent a film version or a reading of *The War of the Worlds*, you might wish to share it with the students and have them compare the different versions. Then they might wish to read the original and make their own Radio Theater version.

earth with enormous velocity. Professor Pierson of the observatory at Princeton confirms Farrell's observation, and describes the phenomenon as (quote) like a jet of blue flame shot from a gun (unquote). We now return you to Ramon Raquello, playing the ever-popular "Stardust."

Sound. *Music.*

Announcer two. Ladies and gentlemen, following on the news given in our bulletin a moment ago, the Government Meteorological Bureau has requested the large observatories of the country to keep an astronomical watch on any further disturbances occurring on the planet Mars. Due to the unusual nature of this occurrence, we have arranged an interview with the noted astronomer Professor Richard Pierson, who will give us his views on this event. We now take you to the observatory at Princeton, New Jersey, where Carl Phillips, our commentator, will interview Professor Pierson.

Sound. *Entire interview in echo chamber; faint ticking sound.*

Phillips. Good evening, ladies and gentlemen. This is Carl Phillips, speaking to you from the observatory at Princeton. I am standing in a large semicircular room, pitch black except for an oblong split in the ceiling. Through this opening I can see a sprinkling of stars that cast a kind of frosty glow over the intricate mechanism of the huge telescope. The ticking sound you hear is the vibration of the clockwork. Professor Pierson stands directly above me on a small platform, peering through the giant lens. Professor, may I begin asking you questions?

Pierson. At any time, Mr. Phillips.

Phillips. Professor, would you please tell our radio audience exactly what you see as you observe the planet Mars through your telescope?

Pierson. Nothing unusual at the moment, Mr. Phillips. A red disk swimming in a blue sea. Transverse stripes across the disk. Quite distinct now because Mars happens to be at the point nearest the earth.

Phillips. In your opinion, what do these transverse stripes signify, Professor Pierson?

Pierson. Not canals, I can assure you, Mr. Phillips, although that's the popular conjecture of those who imagine Mars to be inhabited. From a scientific viewpoint the stripes are merely the result of atmospheric conditions peculiar to the planet.

Phillips. Then you're quite convinced that living intelligence as we know it does not exist on Mars? That there is no life on Mars?

Pierson. I should say the chances against it are a thousand to one.

Phillips. And yet how do you account for these gas eruptions occurring on the surface of the planet at such regular intervals?

Pierson. Mr. Phillips, I cannot account for them.

Phillips. By the way, Professor, for the benefit of our listeners, how far is Mars from the earth?

Pierson. Approximately forty million miles.

Phillips. Well, that seems a safe enough distance——Just a moment, ladies and gentlemen. Someone has just handed Professor Pierson a message. While he reads it, let me remind you that we are speaking to you from the observatory in Princeton, New Jersey, where we are interviewing the world-famous astronomer Professor Richard Pierson. . . . One moment, please. I shall read you the wire that Professor Pierson has just received from Dr. Gray of the Natural History Museum, New York. . . . "Seismograph registered shock of almost earthquake intensity occurring within a radius of twenty miles of Princeton. Please investigate. Signed. Lloyd Gray." . . . Professor Pierson, could this occurrence possibly have something to do with the disturbances observed on the planet Mars?

Pierson. Hardly, Mr. Phillips. This is probably a meteorite of unusual size, and its arrival at this particular time is merely a coincidence. However, we shall conduct a search as soon as daylight permits.

Phillips. Thank you, Professor. Ladies and gentlemen, we've just brought you a special interview with Professor Pierson, at Princeton Observatory. This is Carl Phillips speaking. We now return you to our New York studio.

Sound. *Fade in piano playing.*

Announcer two. Ladies and gentlemen, here is a special announcement from Trenton, New Jersey: "It is reported that at 8:50 P.M. a huge, flaming object, believed to be a meteorite, fell on a farm in the neighborhood of Grovers Mill, New Jersey, twenty-two miles from Trenton. The flash in the sky was visible within a radius of several hundred miles, and the noise of the impact was heard as far north as Elizabeth, New Jersey."

We have dispatched a special mobile unit to the scene, and we will have our commentator, Mr. Phillips, give you a word description as soon as he reaches the farm. In the meantime, we give you Bobby Millette and his orchestra, from the Hotel Martinet in Brooklyn.

Sound. *Swing band for twenty seconds . . . then cut.*

Announcer two. We take you now to Grovers Mill, New Jersey.

Sound. *Crowd noises . . . police sirens.*

Phillips. Ladies and gentlemen, this is Carl Phillips again, at the Wilmuth farm, Grovers Mill, New Jersey. Professor Pierson and I made the eleven miles from Princeton in ten minutes. Well, I . . . I hardly know where to begin, to paint for you a word picture of the strange scene before my eyes, like something out of a modern Arabian Nights.[2] I guess that's the—the *thing* directly in front of me, half-buried in a vast pit. Must have hit with terrific force. The ground is covered with splinters of a tree it struck on its way down. What I can see of the object itself doesn't look very much like a meteor, at least not the meteors I've seen. It looks more like a huge cylinder. It has a diameter of about thirty yards, and the metal on the sheath is—well, I've never seen anything like it. The color is sort of yellowish-white. Curious spectators are pressing close to the object, in spite of police efforts to keep them back.

Here's Mr. Wilmuth, owner of the farm. He may have some interesting facts to add . . . Mr. Wilmuth, would you please tell the radio audience as much as you remember of this rather unusual visitor that dropped in your backyard? Step closer, please. Ladies and gentlemen, this is Mr. Wilmuth.

Wilmuth. I was listenin' to the radio.

Phillips. Closer and louder, please.

Wilmuth. Yes, sir—while I was listenin' to the radio and kinda drowsin', that Professor fellow was talkin' about Mars, so I was half dozin' and half dreamin'——

Phillips. Yes, Mr. Wilmuth, and then you saw something?

Wilmuth. Not first off. First off I heard something.

Phillips. And what did you hear?

Wilmuth. A hissin' sound. Like this: sssssss . . . kinda like a fourt' o'July rocket.

Phillips. Then what?

Wilmuth. I seen a kinda greenish streak and then zingo! Somethin' smacked the ground. Knocked me clear out of my chair!

Phillips. Thank you, Mr. Wilmuth. Thank you.

Wilmuth. Want me to tell you some more?

Phillips. No. That's quite all right, that's plenty. . . . Ladies and gentlemen,

2. **Arabian Nights:** a collection of fanciful Oriental folk tales.

you've just heard Mr. Wilmuth, owner of the farm where this thing has fallen. I wish I could convey the atmosphere of this fantastic scene. Hundreds of cars are parked in a field in back of us. Police are trying to rope off the road leading to the farm, but cars are breaking right through. Their headlights throw an enormous spot on the pit where the object's half-buried. Some of the more daring souls are venturing near the edge. Their silhouettes stand out against the brightness of the metal.

Sound. *Faint humming.*

Phillips. One man wants to touch the thing . . . he's having an argument with a policeman. The policeman wins. . . . Now, ladies and gentlemen, there's something I haven't mentioned in all this excitement, but it's becoming more distinct. Perhaps you've caught it already on your radio. Listen: *(long pause)* . . . Do you hear it? It's a curious humming sound that seems to come from inside the object. I'll move the microphone nearer. Here. *(pause)* Now we're not more than twenty-five feet away. Can you hear it now? Oh, Professor Pierson!

Pierson. Yes, Mr. Phillips?

Phillips. Can you tell us the meaning of that noise inside the thing?

Pierson. Perhaps the unequal cooling of its surface.

Phillips. Do you still think it's a meteor, Professor?

Pierson. I don't know what to think. The metal casing is definitely not found on this earth. Friction with the earth's atmosphere usually tears holes in a meteorite. This thing is smooth and, as you can see, of cylindrical shape.

Phillips. Just a minute! Something's happening! Ladies and gentlemen, this is *terrific!* This end of the thing is beginning to flake off! The top is beginning to rotate like a screw! The thing must be hollow!

Voices. She's a-movin'!

Look, the darn thing's opening up!

Keep back there! Keep back, I tell you.

Maybe there's men in it trying to escape!

It's red hot—they'll burn to a cinder!

Keep back there! Keep those idiots back!

Sound. *The clanking of a huge piece of falling metal.*

Voices. She's off! The top's loose!

Look out there! Stand back!

Phillips. Ladies and gentlemen, this is the most terrifying thing I have ever witnessed. . . . Wait a minute! Someone's *crawling out of the top!* Someone or . . . *something!* I can see peering out of that

black hole two luminous disks . . . are they eyes? It might be a face. It might be——

Sound. *Shout of awe from the crowd.*

Phillips. Good heavens, something's wriggling out of the shadow like a gray snake. Now it's another one, and another. They look like tentacles to me. There, I can see the thing's body. It's as large as a bear, and it glistens like wet leather. But that face. It—it's indescribable. I can hardly force myself to keep looking at it. The eyes are black and gleam like a serpent's. The mouth is V-shaped, with saliva dripping from rimless lips that seem to quiver and pulsate. The monster's rising up! The crowd falls back. They've seen enough. This is the most extraordinary experience. I . . . I'm taking a new position as I talk. Hold on, will you please? I'll be back in a minute.

Announcer two. We are bringing you an eyewitness account of what's happening on the Wilmuth farm, Grovers Mill, New Jersey. We now return you to Carl Phillips at Grovers Mill.

Phillips. Ladies and gentlemen. (Am I on?) Ladies and gentlemen, here I am, back of a stone wall that adjoins Mr. Wilmuth's garden. From here I get a sweep of the whole scene. More state police have arrived. They're drawing up a cordon in front of the pit, about thirty of them. No need to push the crowd back now. They're willing to keep their distance. The captain is conferring with someone. We can't quite see who. Oh, yes, it's Professor Pierson. Now the professor moves around one side, studying the object, while the captain and two policemen advance with something in their hands. I can see it now. It's a white handkerchief tied to a pole—a flag of truce. If those creatures know what that means—what anything means! *Wait!* Something's happening! I don't believe it——

Sound. *Hissing, followed by a humming that increases in intensity.*

Phillips. A humped shape is rising out of the pit. I can make out a small beam of light against a mirror. What's that? There's a jet of flame springing from that mirror, and it leaps right at the advancing men. It strikes them head on! Good Lord, they're turning into flame!

Sound. *Screams and unearthly shrieks.*

Phillips. Now the whole field's caught fire——

Sound. *Explosion.*

Phillips. The woods . . . the barns . . . the gas tanks of automobiles . . . it's spreading everywhere. It's coming this way. About twenty yards to my right——

Sound. *Crash of microphone . . . then dead silence. . . .*

Announcer two. Ladies and gentlemen, due to circumstances beyond our control, we are unable to continue the broadcast from Grovers Mill. Evidently there's some difficulty with our field transmission. However, we will return to that point at the earliest opportunity. In the meantime, we have a late bulletin from San Diego, California: "Professor Indelkoffer, speaking at a dinner of the California Astronomical Society, expressed the opinion that the explosions on Mars are undoubtedly nothing more than severe volcanic disturbances on the surface of the planet." We continue now with our piano interlude.

Sound. *Piano . . . then cut.*

Announcer two. Ladies and gentlemen, I have just been handed a message that came in from Grovers Mill by telephone. "At least forty people, including six State Troopers, lie dead in a field east of the village of Grovers Mill, their bodies burned and distorted beyond all possible recognition." The next voice you hear will be that of Brigadier General Montgomery Smith, commander of the State Militia at Trenton, New Jersey.

Smith. I have been requested by the governor of New Jersey to place the counties of Mercer and Middlesex under martial law. No one will be permitted to enter this area except by special pass. Four companies of State Militia will aid in the evacuation of homes within the range of military operations. Thank you.

Announcer. You have just been listening to General Montgomery Smith, commanding the State Militia at Trenton. In the meantime, further details of the catastrophe at Grovers Mill are coming in. The strange creatures, after unleashing their deadly assault, crawled back into their pit and made no attempt to prevent the efforts of firemen to recover the bodies and extinguish the fire.

We have been unable to establish any contact with our mobile unit at Grovers Mill, but we hope to be able to return you there at the earliest possible moment. In the meantime we take you—uh, just one moment please.

Sound. *Whisper, Long Pause.*

Announcer. Ladies and gentlemen, I have just been informed that we have finally established communication with an eyewitness of the tragedy. Professor Pierson has been located at a farmhouse near Grovers Mill where he has established an emergency observation post. As a scientist, he will give you his explanation of the calamity. Professor Pierson.

Pierson. Of the creatures in the rocket cylinder at Grovers Mill, I can give you no authoritative information—either as to their nature, their origin, or their purposes here on earth. Of their destructive instrument I might venture some explanation. For want of a better term, I shall refer to the mysterious weapon as a heat-ray. It's all too evident that these creatures have scientific knowledge far in advance of our own. It is my guess that they are able to generate an intense heat and project it against any object they choose by means of a polished parabolic mirror of unknown composition—much as the mirror of a lighthouse projects a beam of light.

Announcer. Thank you, Professor Pierson. Ladies and gentlemen, here is a bulletin from Trenton. It is a brief statement informing us that the charred body of Carl Phillips has been identified in a Trenton hospital.

Now here's another bulletin from Washington, D.C.: "Ten units of Red Cross emergency workers have been assigned to the headquarters of the State Militia stationed outside Grovers Mill, New Jersey." Here's a bulletin from State Police, Princeton Junction: "The fires at Grovers Mill and vicinity are now under control. Scouts report all quiet in the pit and no sign of life appearing from the mouth of the cylinder." . . . And now, ladies and gentlemen, in view of the gravity of the situation, we are turning over our entire broadcasting facilities to the State Militia at Trenton, at their request. . . . We take you now to the field headquarters of the State Militia near Grovers Mill, New Jersey.

Captain. This is Captain Lansing of the Signal Corps at Grovers Mill. Situation arising from the reported presence of certain individuals of unidentified nature is now under complete control.

The cylindrical object, which lies in a pit directly below our position, is surrounded on all sides by eight battalions of infantry, adequately armed with rifles and machine guns. All cause for alarm, if such cause ever existed, is now entirely unjustified. The things, whatever they are, do not even venture to poke their heads above the pit. I can see their hiding place plainly in the glare of the searchlights here. With all their reported resources, these creatures can scarcely stand up against heavy machine-gun fire. Anyway, it's an interesting outing for the troops. Now wait a minute! I see something on top of the cylinder. No, it's nothing but a shadow. Now the troops are on the edge of the Wilmuth farm. Seven thousand armed men closing in on an old metal tube. Wait, that wasn't a shadow! It's something moving ... solid metal ... kind of a shieldlike affair rising up out of the cylinder. . . . It's going higher and higher. Why, it's standing on legs—actually rearing up on a sort of metal framework. Now it's reaching above the trees and the searchlights are on it! Hold on! *(Long pause.)*

Announcer two. Ladies and gentlemen, I have a grave announcement to make. Incredible as it may seem, those strange beings who landed in the Jersey farmlands tonight are the vanguard of an invading army from the planet Mars. The battle, which took place tonight at Grovers Mill, has ended in one of the most startling defeats ever suffered by an army in modern times—seven thousand men armed with rifles and machine guns pitted against a single fighting machine of the invaders from Mars. One hundred and twenty known survivors. The rest strewn over the battle area from Grovers Mill to Plainsboro, crushed and trampled to death under the metal feet of the monster, or burned to cinders by its heat-ray. The monster is now in control of the middle section of New Jersey and has effectively cut the state through its center. Communication lines are down from Pennsylvania to the Atlantic Ocean. Railroad tracks are torn. Highways to the north, south, and west are clogged with frantic human traffic. By morning the fugitives will have swelled Philadelphia, Camden, and Trenton, it is estimated, to twice their normal population.

At this time, martial law prevails throughout New Jersey and eastern Pennsylvania. Bulletins too numerous to read are piling up in the studio here. Cables received from English, French, and German scientific bodies offer assistance. Astronomers report continued gas outbursts at regular intervals on planet Mars. Majority voice opinion that enemy will be reinforced by additional rocket machines. . . . Attempts made to locate Professor Pierson at Princeton, who has observed Martians at close range. It is feared he was lost in recent battle.

Langham Field, Virginia: "Scouting planes report three Martian machines visible above tree tops, moving north toward Somerville with population fleeing ahead of them. Heat-ray not in use. Although advancing at express-train speed, invaders pick their way carefully. They seem to be making conscious effort to avoid destruction of cities and countryside. However, they stop to uproot power lines, bridges, and railroad tracks. Their apparent objective is to crush resistance, paralyze communication, and disorganize human society." Here is a bulletin from Basking Ridge, New Jersey: "Coon hunters have stumbled on a second cylinder, similar to the first, embedded in the great swamp twenty miles south of Morristown. U.S. Army fieldpieces are proceeding from Newark to blow up second invading unit before cylinder can be opened and the fighting machines rigged. They are taking up positions in the foothills of Watchung[3] Mountains." Another bulletin from Langham Field, Virginia: "Scouting planes report enemy machines, now three in number, increasing speed northward, kicking over houses and trees in their evident haste to form a conjunction with their allies south of Morristown. Machines also sighted by telephone operator east of Middlesex within ten miles of Plainfield." Here's a bulletin from Winston Field, Long Island: "Fleet of army bombers carrying heavy explosive flying north in pursuit of enemy. . . ." Just a moment, please. Ladies and gentlemen, we've run special wires to the artillery line in nearby villages to give you direct reports in the zone of the advancing enemy. First we take you to the battery of the twenty-second field artillery, located in the Watchung Mountains. . . .

Officer. Projection thirty-nine degrees.

Gunner. Thirty-nine degrees.

Officer. Fire!

Sound. *Boom of Heavy Gun . . . Pause.*

Observer. A hit, sir! We got the tripod of one of them. They've stopped. The others are trying to repair it.

---

3. **Watchung** wä chung′

Sound. *Boom of heavy gun . . . pause.*

Observer. Can't see the shell land, sir. They're letting off a smoke.

Officer. What is it?

Observer. A black smoke, sir. Moving this way. Lying close to the ground. It's moving fast.

Officer. Put on gas masks. *(Pause.)* Get ready to fire. Shift to twenty-four meters.

Gunner. Twenty-four meters. *(Coughs.)*

Officer. Projection, twenty-four degrees. *(Coughs.)*

Gunner. Twenty-four degrees. *(Coughs.)*

Officer. Fire!

Sound. *Boom.*

Observer. Still can't see, sir. The smoke's coming nearer.

Officer. Get the range. *(Coughs.)*

Sound *Fade in coughing. Fade in sound of airplane motor.*

Commander. Army bombing plane, V-8-43, off Bayonne,[4] New Jersey. Lieutenant Voght, reporting to Commander Fairfax, Langham Field. . . . Enemy tripod machines now in sight. Reinforced by three machines from the Morristown cylinder. Six altogether. One par-

4. **Bayonne** bā yōn′

tially crippled machine believed hit by shell from army gun in Watchung Mountains. Guns now appear silent. A heavy black fog hanging close to the earth . . . of extreme density, nature unknown. No sign of heat-ray. Enemy now turns east, crossing Passaic[5] River into Jersey marshes. Another straddles the Pulaski Skyway. Evident objective is New York City. The machines are close together now, and we're ready to attack. Planes circling, ready to strike. A thousand yards and we'll be over the first—800 yards . . . 600 . . . 400 . . . 200 . . . There they go! The giant arm raised. . . . Green flash! They're spraying us with flame! Two thousand feet. Engines are giving out. No chance to release bombs. Only one thing left—drop on them, plane and all. Now we're diving on the first one. Now the engine's gone! . . .

Operator one. This is Bayonne, New Jersey, calling Langham Field. . . .

Operator two. This is Langham Field . . . go ahead. . . .

Operator one. Eight army bombers in engagement with enemy tripod machines over Jersey flats. Engines incapacitated by heat-ray. All crashed. One enemy machine destroyed. Enemy now discharging heavy black smoke in direction of——

5. **Passaic** pə sā′ik.

Operator three. This is Newark, New Jersey. . . . Warning! Poisonous black smoke pouring in from Jersey marshes. Reaches South Street. Gas masks useless. Urge population to move into open spaces . . . automobiles use routes 7, 23, 24 . . . avoid congested areas. Smoke now spreading over Raymond Boulevard. . . .

Sound. *Bells ringing over city gradually diminishing.*

Announcer. I'm speaking from the roof of Broadcasting Building, New York City. The bells you hear are ringing to warn the people to evacuate the city as the Martians approach. In last two hours, an estimated three million people have moved out along the roads to the north. Communication with the Jersey Shore closed ten minutes ago. No more defenses. Our army wiped out. . . . This may be the last broadcast. We'll stay here to the end. . . . People are holding service below us . . . in the cathedral.

Sound. *Voices singing hymn.*

Announcer. Now I look down the harbor. All manner of boats, overloaded with fleeing population, pulling out from docks.

Sound. *Boat whistles.*

Announcer. Streets are all jammed. Noise in crowds like New Year's Eve in city. Wait a minute. . . . Enemy now in sight

Check Test

1. What events were reported on in the first few radio announcements? (explosions on Mars)

2. What is Pierson's occupation? (a scientist)

3. What comes out of the space vehicle? (a creature from space)

4. What does Pierson call the creatures' weapon? (a heat ray)

Answers to Study Questions

Developing Comprehension Skills

1. Advanced knowledge is demonstrated by the alien's ability to travel through space, the heat ray weapon, poisonous black smoke, and the tripod machines. Students may find other examples.

2. Possible answers: Lansing says everything is under control when in fact the army has absolutely no control over the situation. He believes, at that point, that the danger is not great.

Examples of irony: In the beginning, Pierson explains that there is no way there could be life on Mars when in reality, life from Mars just landed on Earth. As the Martians begin their first attack, Professor Indelkoffer blames the explosions on Mars on volcanic disturbances. Other examples of irony are also possible.

3. The scientists try to explain the events as normal occurrences on Earth, such as meteorites. They have their own view of the way the world is and the explosions on Mars. The creatures and their cylinders and weapons are not part of that view.

Reading Literature: Drama

1. The following are major events critical to the narrative:

above the Palisades. Five great machines. First one is crossing river. I can see it from here, wading the Hudson like a man wading through a brook. . . . A bulletin's handed me. . . . Martian cylinders are falling all over the country. One outside Buffalo, one in Chicago, St. Louis . . . seem to be timed and spaced. . . . Now the first machine reaches the shore. He stands watching, looking over the city. His steel, cowlish head is even with the skyscrapers. He waits for the others. They rise like a line of new towers on the city's west side. . . . Now they're lifting their metal hands. This is the end now. Smoke comes out . . . black smoke, drifting over the city. People in the streets see it now. They're running toward the East River . . . thousands of them, dropping in like rats. Now the smoke's spreading faster. It's reached Times Square. People trying to run away from it, but it's no use.

They're falling like flies. Now the smoke's crossing Sixth Avenue . . . Fifth Avenue . . . a hundred yards away . . . it's fifty feet . . . it . . . .

Developing Comprehension Skills

Literal Reading

1. Professor Pierson says that it is "all too evident that these creatures have scientific knowledge far in advance of our own." Find at least three examples that support this statement.

Interpretive Reading

2. Why does Captain Lansing of the Signal Corps say, on page 513, that the situation is under complete control? What is ironic about his statement? Identify two other instances of irony, when an expert says one thing and the exact opposite is true.

Critical Reading

3. How do Professor Pierson and the other scientists quoted on the broadcast first explain the peculiar events that are happening all around? Why do they take so long to realize this is something new?

Reading Literature: Drama

1. **Following Time Order.** Events happen very quickly in this act. Sometimes two things happen simultaneously. This makes it difficult to keep track of what happens when. List the events and number them in the order in which they happen, not when they are described by the radio announcers. Events that happen simultaneously can be given the same number.

(1) Explosions on Mars; gas moves toward Earth.

(2) Radio interview with Pierson.

(2) Spaceship lands in Grovers Mill, New Jersey.

(3) Pierson and Phillips arrive at the scene of the craft's landing.

(4) Craft opens up, creature comes out, Martians attack and kill humans.

(5) Counties of Mercer and Middlesex are placed under martial law.

(6) Captain Lansing announces that everything is under control; infantry surround the cylinder at Grovers Mill.

(7) Seven thousand men are killed at Grovers Mill.

(8) People begin to flee their homes; New Jersey and eastern Pennsylvania are under martial law.

(8) Astronomers report regular outbursts on Mars.

(8) Martian machines are moving north, destroying power and communication lines.

(8) A second cylinder is found in a swamp south of Morristown.

(8) More machines are sighted in various areas of New Jersey.

(9) One of the tripod machines is damaged by artillery gunfire.

(10) Martians release black smoke.

(continued on page 518)

Using the Study Questions

It is recommended that students always read and answer the questions in **Developing Comprehension Skills** in class discussion. Whenever possible, they should also read the questions in the other categories together and discuss the answers.

Developing Comprehension Skills

Question 1. Have the students skim the pages to find the information they need to answer the question. Remind them that this statement is based on our scientific knowledge as it was in the 1930's.

Question 2. Read and discuss. Have students read Captain Lansing's words and characterize his attitude toward the danger. If necessary, review the meaning of irony before attempting to discuss this question.

Question 3. When discussing answers to this question, ask students what would happen if something that they were firmly convinced could not happen, began to happen. Point out that there would likely be a period of disbelief or denial.

Reading Literature: Drama

Question 1. Help students to understand how the events should be listed. Remind them that events are usually reported after they happen. This should be taken into account as they organize the events.

Have the students turn back to the beginning of the story and find the first significant event. Write it on the board. Have the students continue through the act, finding significant events and writing them on the list. Proceed in this manner until all the events are listed in the order that they happened, and numbered appropriately.

Your students may disagree with the answer given in this T.E. If they can give convincing reasons for listing other events, those events should be included. However, try to avoid listing every single happening in the narrative.

Question 2. Direct students to reread Wilmuth's lines on page 508 before they answer this question.

Questions 3 and 4. Read and discuss.

Question 5. Ask students what would be needed to perform a brief scene, such as the first view of the creatures as they crawl out of their craft, on stage. Encourage them to recognize all the props, people, and special effects that would be needed on the stage but aren't necessary when the scene is performed on radio.

Challenge Question. Do you think that Wells provides a complimentary view of scientists in this story? Explain your answer.

Developing Vocabulary Skills

Have the directions of the exercise read aloud. Ask students to explain briefly each of the four techniques listed. If necessary, direct them to the **Vocabulary Skills** section of the **Handbook**, particularly pages 546 through 549.

Remind the students to apply what they learned about figuring out the meaning of an unfamiliar word to their other reading assignments. Explain that when they are reading for pleasure or reading a selection that does not require exact knowledge of every word, they should use what they know about context clues. Point out that if they must know the exact meaning of words in their subject areas, then they will probably need to depend more heavily on the dictionary for word meanings.

Assign the exercise for independent completion. Check the answers together. Help students to see that frequently a combination of methods is necessary.

Developing Writing Skills

Read and discuss the two assignments. Then have each student choose and complete one of the two.

Question 1. This question requires careful reading and rereading of the selection. Having students work in groups will help some students stay on track.

Pre-Writing. Point out to the students that many stories and movies take place over long time periods—often years. Discuss some of the techniques used elsewhere to squeeze time. For example, movies often carry the audience forward

2. **Understanding Dialog.** To show differences in the personalities of his characters, the playwright has the characters use different types of language. For example, the radio announcers speak very formally.

   Reread the dialog of the character named Wilmuth. What is his profession? How does Wilmuth's language contrast with the radio announcers' language? What level of language does Wilmuth use? Why does Phillips cut him off?

3. **Understanding Setting.** Because the play was written for radio, it is easy for the action to jump quickly from one place to another. What are some of the locations mentioned in the play? Why do you think the playwright chose to include so many areas of action, rather than concentrate on just one? What do you think he is trying to show?

4. **Using Description.** A radio play does not use sets, lighting, and costumes as a stage play does. Therefore, it must rely on other techniques to make the setting and actions clear for the listener. One technique is a strong use of description. Find two examples in which a long description explains a setting or an incident. Were you able to picture the place or event in your mind? Try to illustrate one setting or incident, for example, a Martian machine walking toward New York or the cylinder at Grovers Mill surrounded by infantry.

5. **Appreciating the Possibilities of Radio.** This play is more effective for radio than it would have been on stage. Why would you suppose that is true? Think about the many scene changes and the types of characters used to move the action along.

   This play follows the format of a radio news show. How does this fact add to the believability of the invasion from Mars?

Developing Vocabulary Skills

Reviewing Word Parts, Dictionary Skills, and Context Clues. Read the following sentences drawn from the plays. Figure out the meaning of each underlined word by one of these methods:

a. Knowing word parts
b. Using the dictionary
c. Using context clues indicated by key words
d. Using inference context clues

Write the meaning of the word and the method you used to find it.

(continued from page 517)
(11) Martians head for New York City.
(11) Martians and armed forces continue to fight.
(11) Poisonous black smoke covers New Jersey.
(12) Bells ring to warn people to evacuate New York.
(12) Population flees by land and sea.
(12) Enemy approaches New York.
(12) Cylinders land in Buffalo, Chicago, and St. Louis.
(13) Black smoke drifts over New York, killing as it goes.

2. Wilmuth is a farmer. His language is less formal, is considerably less articulate, and includes more slang. He sounds countrified. Phillips cuts him off to go to something he feels is more interesting and more informative. Perhaps Phillips feels that the farmer talks too much or too slowly.

3. Princeton, Grovers Mill, Trenton, and New York are some of the locations. Switching from one place to another builds the tension and excitement. The playwright is trying to show how fast things are happening.

4. Answers will vary.

5. It would be difficult to present all the locations and to handle the scenery and the Martians effectively. The news bulletins sound very realistic. When you listen to the descriptions of a scene, you can imagine it more realistically than a play could present it.

Challenge. Answers will vary. Most students will agree that the scientists seem to be impressed with their own knowledge and unwilling to change their minds when faced with the facts.

Developing Vocabulary Skills

Some students will use the dictionary more frequently than necessary. These are the preferred methods for finding meanings of the words.

1. I am standing in a large semicircular room, pitch black except for an oblong split in the ceiling.
2. That face is indescribable. I can hardly force myself to look at it.
3. Evidently, there's some trouble with our field transmission.
4. Those strange beings who landed in the Jersey farmlands tonight are the vanguard of an invading army from the planet Mars.
5. Enemy tripod machines are now in sight.
6. Oh, he's all right for parlor magic and such, but he never learned the rudiments of the big stuff.
7. You shall give me as payment one percent of all revenue I raise.
8. Have you brought any letters, any documents, any proofs that you are trustworthy and truthful?
9. Why, it was improper—indecent! Especially since I was engaged to a telephone operator from East Hartford, Connecticut.
10. I had eradicated slavery, knight-errantry, serfdom, and ignorance.

Developing Writing Skills

Analytical Writing

1. **Examining Illusions.** This first act of *Invasion from Mars* would take well under an hour to produce. The events it reports would take at least five or six times that long to take place. However, as you read or listen to the play, you get the feeling that you are finding out about the events as they happen. How does the play achieve this effect? How does it carry the audience forward in time without letting the audience notice the shift? Review the play to find some of the techniques the playwright uses to squeeze time. Then write one or more paragraphs explaining his methods. Give examples from the play.

Creative Writing

2. **Creating an Alien.** Many science fiction plays, books, and movies are based on the idea of aliens visiting Earth. There have been evil aliens, as in this play and the movie *The Thing*. There have been friendly aliens, as in the movies *Close Encounters of the Third Kind* and *E.T.*

   Invent an evil or a friendly alien visiting Earth. In one or more paragraphs, describe your alien. Tell about its size, shape, color, and type of skin or fur. Does it have only one head? Are its organs for seeing, smelling, hearing, and eating all located on the head, like ours? Does it walk, ooze, or fly? How does it communicate with others?

in time by momentarily displaying the date at the bottom of the screen. Then have the students skim the play, looking particularly at the first few lines of each character's speech to determine what has happened since the previous speech. List on the board any techniques the students find.

Writing. Remind students to use the notes on the board, as well as any personal findings. Tell them to write a topic sentence that explains what the paragraph will be about. Then have them present examples of techniques as they are used in this play. Allow sufficient time for students to complete the assignment.

Revising. Allow students to share their work with partners who answered the same question to see if they found the same techniques. Allow time for additions, corrections, and improvements to be made.

Question 2. This question asks students to create their own aliens. They can let their imagination run wild.

Pre-Writing. Encourage the students to be original when responding to this question. Tell them to think about the creatures they have seen but to try to make their aliens different from any others. Some students might find it helpful to draw a picture of the alien first. Have students make a list of words to describe the aliens.

Writing. Allow sufficient time for students to complete the assignment. Have them work independently. Remind students to describe the alien in some kind of order, for example, from the top down or from the ground up.

Revising. Have the students check their writing to make sure they have included all details specified in the question. Allow time for revisions to be made. Refer students to the **Checklist for the Process of Writing** in the **Handbook** on pages 556 and 557. Then have as many students as possible read their papers to the class. You may want to ask students who like drawing to illustrate their descriptions.

1. shaped like half a circle—word parts
2. not able to be described—word parts
3. the act of sending out signals by means of radio waves—dictionary
4. the part of the army ahead of the main army—dictionary
5. having three feet or legs—word parts
6. the beginnings or part to be learned —inference context clues
7. money taken in—inference context clues
8. written proofs of something— context clues indicated by key words
9. improper—context clues indicated by key words; *or* not decent—word parts
10. get rid of, erase—dictionary

Objectives

- To appreciate drama as a form of literature
- To recognize plot development
- To understand the development of the central character
- To identify the theme of a radio play
- To apply literal, interpretive, and critical reading skills to a selection
- To use context clues to determine the meaning of unfamiliar words
- To write a script for a radio broadcast
- To evaluate the literary quality of a radio play
- To present a monolog that reflects the mood of a play

Preparing the Students

Essential Vocabulary. The words presented here are essential to the understanding of the selection.

Introduce the words listed below. Write the sentences on the board, have individual students read them aloud, and ask the students to use context clues to find the meaning of the underlined words.

desolate systematic humbled

1. The ruined buildings and empty streets gave the city a desolate look.
2. Bob is no longer bragging. His last-place finish in the race has certainly humbled him.
3. He carried out his project systematically, completing one step at a time.

If the students need additional help with the vocabulary of this selection, encourage them to use context clues to determine word meaning. As needed, direct them to the **Glossary** or to a classroom dictionary.

Motivation. Explain that this is the second act of *Invasion from Mars.* Ask students to predict what will happen next. Have the students read the introductory paragraph on page 520 and state in their own words what they should try to find out as they read the play.

Presenting the Selection

1. Have the students read Act Two of *Invasion from Mars* silently or, preferably, taking parts in class. Alternate speakers after every two or three paragraphs.

2. Make sure that everyone has read the assignment by administering the **Check Test** at the bottom of T.E. page 524.

3. Assign parts to the students and read (or reread) part of Act Two aloud in class. Begin on page 521, column 2, and

It's the end of the Earth as we know it. Or is it? What on Earth can possibly defeat the Martian machines?

Invasion from Mars

H.G. WELLS
From **The War of the Worlds**
Adapted by Howard Koch

ACT TWO

Fade in . . .

Pierson. As I set down these notes on paper, I'm obsessed by the thought that I may be the last living man on earth. I have been hiding in this empty house near Grovers Mill—a small island of daylight cut off by black smoke from the rest of the world. All that happened before the arrival of these monstrous creatures now seems part of another life. I look down at my blackened hands, my torn shoes, my tattered clothes, and I try to connect them with a professor who lived at Princeton, and who, on the night of October 20, glimpsed through his telescope an orange splash of light on a distant planet. My wife, my colleagues, my students, my books, my observatory, my—my world . . . where are they? Did they ever exist? Am I Richard Pierson? What day is it? Do days exist without calendars? Does time pass when there are no human hands left to wind the clocks? . . . In writing down my daily life, I tell myself I shall preserve human history between the dark covers of this little book that was meant to record the movements of the stars. . . . But to write I must live, and to live I must eat. I find moldy bread in the kitchen and an orange not too spoiled to swallow. I keep watch at the window. From time to time I catch sight of a Martian above the black smoke.

The smoke still holds the house in its black coil. . . . Suddenly I see a Martian mounted on his machine, spraying the air with a jet of steam, as if to dissipate the smoke. I watch in a corner as his huge metal legs nearly brush against the house. Exhausted by terror, I fall asleep. . . . It's morning. Sun streams in the window . . . the black cloud of gas has lifted. I venture from the house. I make my way to a road. No traffic.

Here and there a wrecked car, baggage overturned, a blackened skeleton. I push on north. For some reason I feel safer trailing these monsters than running away from them. And I keep a careful watch. I must keep alive. I come to a chestnut tree and fill my pockets. Two days I wander in a vague northerly direction through a desolate world. Finally I notice a living creature—a small red squirrel in a beech tree. I stare at him and wonder. He stares back at me. I believe at that moment the animal and I shared the same emotion—the joy of finding another living being. . . . I push on north. I find dead cows and, beyond, the charred ruins of a dairy. The silo remains standing guard over the wasteland like a lighthouse deserted by the sea. Astride the silo perches a weathercock. The arrow points north. . . . *Fade out.*

Fade in . . .

Next day I came to a city vaguely familiar in its contours, yet its buildings are strangely dwarfed and leveled off, as if a giant had sliced off its highest towers. I reached the outskirts. Newark was undemolished but humbled by some whim of the advancing Martians. Presently, with an odd feeling of being watched, I caught sight of something crouching in a doorway. I made a step toward it, and it rose up and became a man—a man, armed with a large knife.

Stranger. Stop! Where did you come from?

Pierson. I come from . . . many places. A long time ago from Princeton.

Stranger. Princeton, huh? That's near Grovers Mill!

Pierson. Yes.

Stranger. Grovers Mill . . . *(laughs as at great joke)*. . . . There's no food here. This is my country—all this end of town down to the river. There's only food for one. . . . Which way are you going?

Pierson. I don't know. I guess I'm looking for—for people.

Stranger. Say, we're in the open here. Let's crawl into this doorway and talk.

Pierson. Have you seen any Martians?

Stranger. They've gone over to New York. At night the sky is alive with their lights. Just as if people were still living there. By daylight you can't see them. Five days ago a couple of them carried something big across the flats from the airport. I believe they're learning how to fly our airplanes.

Pierson. Then it's all over with humanity. Stranger, there's still you and I. Two of us left.

Stranger. They got themselves in solid; they wrecked the greatest country in

have students read to the top of page 524. Remind students to read lines as naturally as possible.

4. Remind the students that the introduction to this portion of the play asked them to find out if the Martians could be defeated. Have them answer the question.

5. Develop the study questions as suggested in **Using the Study Questions,** beginning on page 524. That section also provides challenge questions for further discussion, as needed.

Reinforcing the Lesson

To reteach, reinforce, or extend the skills in this lesson, see the following:

Skills Practice Book, Green Level—pages 197 through 200

Special Populations

For special-populations students who have difficulty with writing, the exercises suggested on page 526 under **Developing Writing Skills** may be simplified or adapted to one of the following suggestions:

Question 2. List the similarities and differences between the two plays, rather than write a paragraph.

Question 3. Dictate your opinion as to whether a radio play would frighten people today to another student or by using a tape recorder.

Question 4. Write a letter to a friend describing some of the things you saw when a spaceship landed.

Ask students to create a poster advertising the play to other classes. They might be interested in including pictures of the spaceship, the monster, or the crowds fleeing in terror.

Encouraging Independent Reading

Challenge the class to locate at least two science fiction works (short stories, novels, plays, or movies) presenting each of these themes: creatures from other planets are our enemies; such creatures are like humans and can be our friends; such creatures are wiser and more powerful than humans and will help humans; we are wiser and more powerful than creatures from other planets and should help them.

You could suggest the following:

The Angry Planet by Hohn Kier Cross
The Little Prince by Antoine de Saint Exupery
Better readers can try *The Martian Chronicles* or *S Is For Space* by Ray Bradbury.

the world. Those green stars, they're probably falling somewhere every night. They've only lost one machine. There isn't anything to do. We're licked.

Pierson. What will they do to us?

Stranger. I've thought it all out. Right now we're caught as we're wanted. The Martian only has to go a few miles to get a crowd on the run. But they won't keep doing that. They'll begin catching us, systematic like—keeping the best and storing us in cages and things. They haven't begun on us yet!

Pierson. Not begun!

Stranger. Not begun. All that's happened so far is because we don't have sense enough to keep quiet . . . bothering them with guns and such stuff and losing our heads and rushing off in crowds. Now instead of our rushing around blind, we've got to fix ourselves up according to the way things are now.

Pierson. But what is there to live for?

Stranger. There won't be any more concerts for a million years or so, and no nice little dinners at restaurants. If it's amusement you're after, I guess the game's up.

Pierson. And what is there left?

Stranger. *Life* . . . that's what! I want to live. And so do you! We're not going to be exterminated. And I don't mean to be caught, either, and tamed and fattened and bred like an ox.

Pierson. What are you going to do?

Stranger. I'm going on . . . right under their feet. I gotta plan. We men as men are finished. We don't know enough. We gotta learn plenty before we get a chance. And we've got to live and keep free while we learn. I've thought it all out, see.

Pierson. Tell me the rest.

Stranger. Well, it isn't all of us that are made for wild beasts. That's why I watched you. All these little office workers that used to live in these houses—they'd be no good. They haven't any stuff to 'em. I've seen hundreds of 'em running wild to catch their commuters' train in the morning, for fear that they'd get fired if they didn't; running back at night, afraid they wouldn't be in time for dinner. Lives insured and a little invested in case of accidents. The Martians will be a godsend for those guys. Nice roomy cages, good food, careful breeding, no worries. After a week or so of chasing about the fields on empty stomachs, they'll come and be glad to be caught.

Pierson. You've thought it all out?

Stranger. You bet I have! And that isn't all. These Martians will make pets of some of them, train 'em to do tricks. Who knows? Get sentimental over the pet boy who grew up and had to be killed. And some, maybe, they'll train to hunt us.

Pierson. No, that's impossible. No human being——

Stranger. Yes, they will. There's people who'll do it gladly.

Pierson. In the meantime, you and I and others like us . . . where are we to live when the Martians own the earth?

Stranger. I've got it all figured out. We'll live underground. I've been thinking about the sewers. Then there's cellars, vaults, underground storerooms, railway tunnels, subways. And we'll get a bunch of strong men together. Get all the books we can—science books. That's where men like you come in, see? We'll raid the museums, we'll even spy on the Martians. We may not have to learn much before—just imagine this: four or five of their own fighting machines suddenly start off—and not a Martian in 'em. But *men*—men who have learned the way how. It may even be in our time. Imagine having one of them lovely things with its heat-ray wide and free! We'd turn it on Martians, we'd turn it on men. We'd bring everybody down to their knees.

Pierson. That's your plan?

Stranger. You and me and a few more of us, we'd own the world.

Pierson. I see.

Stranger. Say, what's the matter? Where are you going?

Using the Study Questions

It is recommended that students always read and answer the questions in **Developing Comprehension Skills** in class discussion. Whenever possible, they should also read the questions in the other categories together and discuss the answers.

Developing Comprehension Skills

Question 1. Read and discuss the question.

Question 2. Students should be able to point out that the panic and tension of Act I is gone and that Act II is one of very little actual activity.

Question 3. Have students reread Pierson's first speech on pages 520 and 521. Encourage the students to describe the details of Pierson's surroundings and to add details that they would expect to see, hear, or otherwise sense if they were in that situation. When they describe their feelings in such a situation, urge students to go beyond such statements as "I'd feel sad," and to describe how they would face life then.

Question 4. Have the students list on the board the descriptions of present life that Pierson includes. Also, ask them to list the signs that are left of the Martian invasion.

Challenge Question. How did some more recent science fiction films, such as *Close Encounters of the Third Kind*, and *E.T., The Extraterrestrial,* portray alien creatures differently than the Martians in this play? What do these different approaches to life in outer space demonstrate about people's attitudes toward space creatures? Why has the presentation of such creatures changed over the years since this play was written? (Interpretive Reading)

Pierson. Not to *your* world. Goodbye, Stranger. . . .

I came at last to the Holland Tunnel. I entered that silent tube, anxious to know the fate of the great city on the other side of the Hudson. Cautiously I came out of the tunnel and made my way up Canal Street.

I wandered up through the thirties and forties;[1] I stood alone on Times Square. I caught sight of a lean dog running down Seventh Avenue with a piece of dark brown meat in his jaws and a pack of starving mongrels at his heels. He made a wide circle around me, as though he feared I might prove a fresh competitor. I walked up Broadway past silent shop windows displaying their wares to empty sidewalks—past the Capitol Theater, silent, dark—past a shooting gallery, where a row of empty guns faced an arrested line of wooden ducks. I hurried on. Suddenly I caught sight of the hood of a Martian machine, standing somewhere in Central Park, gleaming in the late afternoon sun. An insane idea! I climbed a small hill above the pond at Sixtieth Street. From there I could see, standing in a silent row along the Mall, nineteen of those great metal Titans, their cowls empty, their steel arms hanging listlessly by their sides. I looked in vain for the monsters that inhabited those machines.

Suddenly, my eyes were attracted to the immense flock of black birds that hovered below me. They circled to the ground, and there before my eyes, stark and silent, lay the Martians, with the hungry birds pecking and tearing shreds of flesh from their dead bodies. When their bodies were examined in laboratories, it was found that they were killed by the disease bacteria against which their systems were unprepared . . . slain after all man's defenses had failed.

Strange it now seems to sit in my peaceful study at Princeton writing down this last chapter of the record begun at a deserted farm in Grovers Mill. Strange to see from my window the university spires dim and blue through an April haze. Strange to watch children playing in the streets. Strange to see young people strolling on the green, where the new spring grass heals the last black scars of a bruised earth. Strange to watch the sightseers enter the museum where the disassembled parts of a Martian machine are kept on public view. Strange when I recall the time I first saw it, bright and clean-cut, hard and silent, under the dawn of that last unforgettable day.

Sound. *Music*

1. **Thirties and Forties.** These numbers refer to street numbers in New York City.

Reading Literature: Drama

Question 1. Draw a plot diagram on the board for this exercise. Read the study question and review the meaning of plot and its stages. As the answers are given for each part, write them in the diagram.

Question 2. Review the difference between internal and external conflict before having students answer this question. In addition to the major conflict listed in the answers, students may point out the conflict between Pierson and the Stranger, and Pierson's internal conflict over the purpose of life after the destruction.

Question 3. Have students reread the portion of the play mentioned in the

Check Test

1. Where is Pierson at the beginning of Act II? (in an empty house near Grovers Mill)

2. What is the first living earth creature Pierson sees after two days of wandering? (a squirrel)

3. What kills the Martians? (disease bacteria)

Answers to Study Questions

Developing Comprehension Skills

1. Pierson is writing down notes.

Developing Comprehension Skills

Literal Reading 1. This act shifts from focusing on many characters, as in Act I, to concentrating almost totally on one character. Who is that person? How does he "speak" to the audience?

Interpretive Reading 2. How has the story changed to make possible the shift of focus described in question 1? How does this change affect tone and mood?

Interpretive Reading 3. At the beginning of Act II, Pierson is alone. He is thinking and writing of how his life and surroundings have changed. What does he see around him? How would you feel if you were in Pierson's place?

Critical Reading 4. Pierson informs us that the Martians were destroyed by disease bacteria, which their bodies could not fight. Reread the last paragraph, in which he describes life at present. What does Pierson find strange about it? What does the paragraph suggest about how people have recovered from the Martian invasion?

Reading Literature: Drama

1. **Recognizing Plot Development.** Make a plot diagram for this play. Which events belong in each of the five parts: introduction, rising action, climax, falling action, and resolution?
2. **Understanding Conflict.** Was the conflict in *Invasion from Mars* internal or external? Who or what was the source of that conflict? How was it resolved?
3. **Understanding the Central Character.** Professor Pierson is the central character in this play. As the play progresses, he changes. How is Professor Pierson different at the end of the play than he was in the beginning? Think about how he reacted on page 507 to the question about the seismograph reading. Also, think about your answer for question 3 in Developing Comprehension Skills, Act I (page 517).
4. **Examining Form.** Act II of *Invasion from Mars* has a slower, more thoughtful quality that Act I had. Think about this change of pace and the changes in the numbers of characters. Why did the playwright develop this act differently from the other act?
5. **Identifying Theme.** What general statement is this play making about life? What do Pierson's encounters with the squirrel and the Stranger have to do with the theme? Explain your answer.

2. Pierson is almost alone in a world that has nearly been destroyed. The play is no longer describing events in news report fashion—it is basically describing the aftermath of events. It has changed to a tone of sadness because of the destruction and death. The mood is one of loneliness.

3. Black smoke, destruction, and cinders are all around Pierson. He can see no other people. Answers to the second part of the question will vary. Terrified, lonely, isolated, and sad are likely terms.

4. It is strange that life has totally reverted to the normal routine previous to the Martian invasion. The suggestion is that life has been rebuilt and gone on, almost as if the Martians had not invaded.

Challenge. Answers may vary, but recent portrayals of space life have tended to imagine alien creatures as very different from humans, often with unusual powers but generally kind and humane. A possible reason for this attitude may be that there are people who believe that life in outer space is a possibility, and it is more pleasant and optimistic to think that there are creatures like E.T. than like the Martians in *Invasion from Mars*. Another rea-

(continued on page 526)

question, as well as Question 3 in **Developing Comprehension Skills, Act I** (page 517).

Question 4. Students should recognize that Act I is the action and Act II is the reaction. They should realize that the pace and number of characters in each act help to fulfill that purpose.

Question 5. Briefly review *theme* with the students. Have them reread both of Pierson's encounters, first with the squirrel, then with the stranger.

Challenge Question. What type of reaction do you think the playwright intended to create with this play? Explain your answers.

Developing Vocabulary Skills

Before having students complete this exercise, have them explain the different types of context clues, including antonyms, comparison, definitions, example, main ideas, restatement, cause and effect, and words in a series. Then have them read and complete the exercise. If necessary, work one or two items with the class or a small group needing help. Check the answers together.

Developing Writing Skills

Read and discuss the four assignments. Then have each student choose and complete one of the four.

Question 1. This question asks students to synthesize information discussed in separate study questions in the three selections of this chapter.

Pre-Writing. Encourage students to review both the plays and the study question about the plays, concentrating on the questions that discuss staging techniques. Remind them to refer to notes or answers from these questions.

Suggest that the composition be five or more paragraphs long. The first paragraph should state the main idea, the next three (or more) paragraphs should describe three (or more) techniques and provide proofs, and the last paragraph should summarize the main ideas of the composition. Emphasize that students must include examples to prove their answers.

Writing. Allow sufficient time for students to complete the assignment. Remind students to begin with topic sentences and to include details from the play to prove their points.

Revising. Allow students to share their work with partners who answered the same question. Have the partners restate the writers' main ideas and details. If writers decide that they want to make changes, allow time for corrections and revisions to be made.

Question 2. This question asks students to discover common attitudes in the two plays presented in this text.

Pre-Writing. Students should be able to define *theme*. Remind them that they are comparing both what the Yankee and the Martians tried to do, and what Twain and Wells were trying to do. Suggest that they review the two selections and their study questions, particularly those concerning theme or related elements, such as tone.

Writing. Allow students sufficient time to write their first drafts.

Revising. Because this question invites students to discover common elements that have not been discussed before, they will probably need to revise their writing repeatedly as their ideas become clearer. Encourage them to write as many drafts as they need to until they agree with what they have written.

Question 3. In this question, students are expected to voice their opinions.

Pre-Writing. Encourage the students to consider the many new influences that might cause different reactions today. They might list recent inventions and scientific discoveries, people's attitudes toward life and toward the media, and similar developments. List these factors on the board. Then have them list influences that might cause people of today to react just as people of the 1930's did, such as fear of the unknown and the power of panic. Let students consider the two sets of influences and decide which would be more powerful.

Writing. Have students use the lists on the board to support their opinions.

Revising. Have students who expressed the same opinion for this question share their work with each other. Then have them share their work with others who expressed an opposite opinion. Allow time for corrections and improvements to be made.

Question 4. This question asks students to be original as they create their own radio broadcasts.

Pre-Writing. Remind students that this writing is for a radio news broadcast and they must follow the same restrictions that are placed on a radio play. Have them list the events they will report on. Suggest that they decide on the reaction they will take as reporters of the events.

Writing. Allow adequate time for students to write. Remind them to imitate the style of a news reporter.

Revising. If possible, allow students to

Developing Vocabulary Skills

Reviewing Context Clues. The following words are located in the given paragraphs of the play. Read the paragraph in which each word is found. On your paper, write which context clue helped you figure out the meaning of the word. Also, write the meaning of the word.

1. hysteria (page 504, paragraph 1)
   a. antonym b. main idea c. restatement
2. scrutinize (page 504, Orson Welles' first speech.)
   a. words in a series b. synonym c. antonym
3. distinct (page 506, column 2, Mr. Pierson's second speech)
   a. main idea b. antonym c. words in a series
4. gravity (page 513, line 1)
   a. words in a series b. example c. main idea
5. evacuate (page 516, Announcer, first speech)
   a. synonym b. antonym c. words in a series
6. dissipate (page 520, column 2, paragraph 2)
   a. definition b. comparison c. inference

Developing Writing Skills

Analytical Writing

1. **Developing Techniques for Radio Scripts.** The audience of a radio play cannot see the setting or the action of the play. There are, however, ways in which the playwright can make up for this difficulty. In some ways, in fact, the playwright can take advantage of the situation. List three or more ways in which the playwright can overcome the problem of the audience not seeing the action. Prove your point with examples from either of the two plays in this chapter.

Analytical Writing

2. **Comparing Plays.** In *A Connecticut Yankee in King Arthur's Court*, the central character thinks he can conquer Merlin and change King Arthur's world through his inventions. At first he seems successful. In *Invasion from Mars*, the Martians try to overcome Earth. At first, their superior weapons and machines suggest they will be successful. Are the authors of these two plays concerned with similar themes? If so, in what ways are the themes alike? How are they different? Can you find

(continued from page 525)
son may be that with our own scientific advances, particularly in space travel, we feel more in control in space. People seem to be less afraid of creatures from outer space than they once were.

Reading Literature: Drama

1. Plot diagram for this play:
Introduction: Discussion of events on Mars and meeting Professor Pierson.
Rising action: Landing of Martians, Martian attack.
Climax: End of Act I, Martian capture of New York.
Falling action: Professor Pierson leaves Grovers Mill and heads for New York, trailing the Martians.
Resolution: Pierson's discovery of the dead Martians in Central Park. Life returns to normal.

2. The conflict is external. The Martians are the source, and the conflict is resolved by the death of the Martians.

3. In the beginning, Pierson was rigid, sure that his view was the right and only view. By the end he is more open; he is willing to see more possibilities and to admit he doesn't know everything.

other ways in which these plays correspond to each other? Write one or more paragraphs explaining what you have discovered.

Analytical Writing

3. **Presenting Your Opinion.** When this radio play was first presented, people believed that Martians really had invaded Earth. Some reacted out of fright and tried to run away. Think about what would happen if this play were presented over the radio now. Do you think that people would react the way they did in 1938? Why or why not? Be sure to include strong, solid reasons to support your argument.

Creative Writing

4. **Writing a Radio Script.** For the six o'clock radio news, write a three- or four-minute broadcast describing the landing on Earth of life from another planet. If you created an alien for Developing Writing Skills, 2, for Act I (on page 519), you may use that creature in this script. If you like, include an interview with an eye-witness or an authority.

Developing Skills in Critical Thinking

Evaluating a Radio Play. You have read two complete radio plays in this chapter. If you were going to select a third one to include, what qualities would you look for in a radio play? List your requirements. Think about characters, sound effects, and any other characteristics you consider necessary for a good radio play.

Developing Skills in Speaking and Listening

Presenting A Monolog. Sometimes in a play there is only one character in a scene. The character talks to himself—and the audience. Such a speech is called a **monolog**. At the beginning of Act II of *Invasion from Mars*, Professor Pierson has a long monolog. At the end of the act he has another monolog.

A monolog can be tricky to present, especially in a radio play. Because there is only one person talking, there is less variety in voices and action. An audience can become bored quickly. To avoid boring the audience, the speaker must put strong feeling into his or her voice. The speaker's voice must show changes in mood, even if they are slight.

Work in small groups to practice reading either of Pierson's monologs. Discuss qualities of your speech that you can change, such as the speed with which you talk, the pitch of your voice, and its loudness. Then take turns reading the monolog and applying what you discussed.

share their writing orally with the class. A student who included an interview in his or her script should select a partner to participate in the presentation. Following each broadcast report, have class members first suggest what was especially good about it, then what improvements could be made. Allow time for written revisions to be made.

Developing Skills in Critical Thinking

This question should be used as the basis for a class discussion. Have a volunteer list the qualities suggested by students; in the discussion, determine which of the qualities can be ignored. Try to cut down the list to those qualities that everyone in the class agrees on.

Developing Skills in Speaking and Listening

Have students read the directions for this exercise. Discuss thoroughly the meaning of *monolog*. Make sure students realize the difference between a dramatic monolog and a form that may be more familiar to them, the comic monolog. Then have them complete the exercise, working in groups of two to four.

4. Act I is filled with tension and lots of activity. Act II describes the aftermath and is a reaction to the events in Act I. The purpose of Act II calls for a slower pace—it gives the reader/listener time to react as well as to absorb all the horror.

5. Answers may vary. Some possibilities are the following: Life will continue despite enormous difficulties; Life is precious and worth fighting for; living creatures need other living creatures. Both incidents provide examples of the play's respect and love for life.

Challenge. Answers may vary. Possible goals include—fear, skepticism of scientific "knowledge," and hope.

Developing Vocabulary Skills

1. b; emotional, unthinking disorder
2. b; watch closely
3. a; clear
4. c; seriousness
5. a; move out
6. c; break up

Developing Skills in Critical Thinking

Answers will vary. Some requirements might be funny or interesting characters, an exciting plot, and sound effects that are easy to make.

Using the Review

This review should be completed before the administration of the **Chapter 7 Mastery Test**. Students will have an opportunity to recall important concepts from this chapter and apply them to new contexts. Teacher observation during the review can reveal which students still have not mastered the skills.

Using Your Skills in Reading Plays

Read the directions to the class. Because this excerpt is intentionally written in an inappropriate style, there may be some reaction from alert readers. You may wish to assign roles (Arthur, Merlin, and reader of stage directions) and have the excerpt read aloud, so that you can remind the students to focus on the questions of goals, conflict, and stage directions. Let the students know whether they should write out their answers (particularly the stage directions) completely. Allow time for them to answer the questions.

Discuss the answers together. Note which students seem slow to write or to participate in the discussion, or collect papers after the review lesson to see who needs further help in this or other areas of study.

Using Your Comprehension Skills

If you wish the students to answer in writing, allow sufficient time for them to read the directions and answer each question separately. (Tell them to number their answers from 1 to 5.) If you are working the **Review** orally, for discussion, read the directions to the class, stopping after each question.

For evaluation, see the suggestion above.

Using Your Vocabulary Skills

Read the directions to the exercise to the students and allow sufficient time for them to answer the questions in writing. Discuss the answers. Note which students still have difficulty identifying or using context clues.

Using Your Writing Skills

Call on students to read aloud the two assignments; make sure they understand that they are to choose only one. Answer any questions students may have about the assignments. If you are asking the students to complete their writing in class, let them know how much time they have and that they may turn in a marked-up first draft. Remind them to skip lines to

CHAPTER 7 Review

Using Your Skills in Reading Plays

Read the following part of a play. List the characters in the scene, and briefly explain the goal of each character. What conflict do you see in the goals? Also, identify the stage directions.

ARTHUR AND GUINEVERE

(As the curtain opens, Arthur and Merlin are seated at Arthur's Round Table.)

Arthur. Merlin, my kingdom is in order, and all my subjects are happy. This castle's getting a little empty, though. I guess it's about time I got married.

Merlin. Who's the lucky lady?

Arthur (smiling). The most beautiful woman I've ever seen—Lady Guinevere!

Merlin (alarmed). Guinevere! Oh, no! She's not right for you! Let me fix you up with someone you'd be happier with.

Arthur. Arthur. No, I've made my choice. Guinevere is the only woman I'd ever want to marry. Go see if it's okay with her father, and let's get this show on the road! (He waves Merlin out.)

Using Your Comprehension Skills

The scene above contains dialog that is modern and informal. What effect does the level of language have on the mood of the play? What do you suppose might have been the author's purpose in using this language? Can you suggest a reason for writing a play about King Arthur in modern speech?

Which words in the scene above are not in keeping with a formal court scene? How might you change Arthur's words to create a greater air of royalty and authority?

Answers to Questions

Using Your Skills in Reading Plays

The characters and their goals are as follows:

Arthur—to marry Lady Guinevere
Merlin—to introduce Arthur to another woman

The conflict is the difference of opinion about whom Arthur should marry.

Stage directions: (1) first two lines in italic; (2) smiling; (3) alarmed; (4) He waves Merlin out.

Using Your Comprehension Skills

The modern and informal language creates a light, or somewhat carefree mood.

Possible reason why the author used modern speech: He or she may have wanted the characters to seem more real to the reader.

The words that are not in keeping with a formal court scene and what they might be changed to are as follows:

"I guess it's about time I got married."—"I have decided to wed."

"Go see if it's okay with her father, and let's get this show on the road!"—"Ask

Using Your Vocabulary Skills

Each of these sentences is from a selection in this book. In each, there is an underlined word. If you do not know the meaning of the word, which would be the best way to discover it? For each word, write one of the following: word parts, context clues, the dictionary.

1. You shall appoint me your perpetual minister and executive.
2. The farmer said he thought that was unsound reasoning.
3. The bishop looked upon the man with a tranquil eye.
4. The prisoner began zealously to study languages, philosophy, and history. He fell on these subjects with hunger.
5. Keesh strode into the village. There was importance in his step and arrogance in his speech.

Using Your Writing Skills

Choose one of the assignments below.

1. You have learned that, when reading drama, you should cooperate with the playwright and enter his or her created world. Write from one to three paragraphs describing the world created in *A Connecticut Yankee in King Arthur's Court* or *Invasion From Mars*. Tell how the created world is different from your own.
2. Write one scene of an original play version of the King Arthur legend. If you like, you may use informal English. However, before you write, decide on the tone you will use. It might be, for example, admiring or mocking. Decide, also, on the mood you want your readers to get from your scene. Then, as you write, choose your words carefully to match your tone and mood.

Using Your Skills in Critical Thinking

Compare these three types of literature: short stories, nonfiction, and plays. How are the three alike? How are they different? Think of several categories you could use for discussing these three types of literature. On your paper, set up as many columns as you have chosen categories. Then fill in the columns with information about each of the three.

leave space for corrections. If you are asking them to do the writing outside of class, you may require clean copies.

Using Your Skills in Critical Thinking

Have this exercise read aloud. Allow a few minutes for independent thinking and note-taking, while you draw the following chart on the board:

Categories	Short Stories	Non-Fiction	Plays

Then have the students suggest a few categories and write in the suggestions on your chart. Tell the students that they can use any categories listed on the board and any additional categories they like. Allow at least five minutes for the students to complete the exercise independently.

Discuss the answers.

Reinforcing the Lesson

To reteach, reinforce, or extend the skills in this lesson, see the following:

Skills Practice Book, Green Level—pages 201 and 202

Additional Resources

Diagnostic and Mastery Tests, Green Level—Chapter 7 Mastery Test, pages 39 through 42; End-of-Year Test, pages 43 through 46

her father to grant his permission so we can make plans for the ceremony."

Using Your Vocabulary Skills

1. perpetual; dictionary
2. unsound; word parts
3. tranquil; dictionary
4. zealously; context clues
5. arrogance; dictionary

Using Your Skills in Critical Thinking

Possible Categories	Short Stories	Non-Fiction	Plays
Setting	One time and place	Real time and place	One time and place
Characters	Usually have only one major character	Real characters	Usually have only one major character
Events	One set of events	Real happenings	One set of events
Dialog	Often contains characters' actual words	Often contains characters' actual words	Story told through the words of the characters
Length	Short enough to read in one sitting	Varies from one selection to the next	Long plays divided into acts and scenes

Handbook for Reading and Writing

Literary Terms

Alliteration. The repetition of consonant sounds is alliteration. The repeated sounds usually come at the beginnings of several words in a series of words. Alliteration can be used in prose and poetry.

> He clasps the crag with crooked hands;
> Close to the sun in lonely lands.
> ("The Eagle," page 286)

For more about alliteration, see pages 112 and 113.

Assonance. The repetition of vowel sounds within words is called assonance. Assonance can stress a certain mood and give a musical quality to the work. Notice how the repetition of *o*'s in this example stresses the feeling of smallness.

> The immense, the unknown, enfolded me.
> ("The Story of My Life," page 377)

For more about assonance, see pages 114 and 115.

Autobiography. A story that a person writes about his or her own life is an autobiography. It is written from the first-person point of view. An example of an autobiography is "The Story of My Life" by Helen Keller (pages 370 to 380).

For more about autobiography, see page 358.

Biography. A true account of a real person's life is a biography. It includes important events in a person's life and lets the reader know what the person was like. "Matthew A. Henson" (pages 392 to 400) is an example of a biography.

For more on biography, see page 384.

Character. Each person or animal who takes part in the action of a story, poem, or play is a character. Usually a story has one or two most important characters, called *major characters. Minor characters* would include everyone else in the selection. In "The Rocking Donkey" (pages 222 to 227), Esmeralda is a major character. Mr. Snye is a minor character.

For more about characters, see pages 3, 63, and 186.

See also *Character Trait.*

Character Trait. A quality that a character shows by his or her actions, statements, or thoughts is a character trait. For example, in "The Bet" (pages 165 to 169), the banker exhibits the character trait of greed.

Chronological Order. See *Time Order.*

Climax. The turning point of a story is called the climax. It often involves an important event, decision, or discovery. In "The Old Soldier," for example, the climax comes when the doctor discovers that the old soldier was a Hessian (page 192).

For more about climax, see page 135.
See also *Plot.*

Comparison. A writer uses a comparison to show how two different things have something in common. In this example, children are compared to chicks.

> As he played, there came a sound of little hands clapping and feet pattering, of small voices chattering, like chicks in a barnyard when corn and grain are scattering.
> ("The Pied Piper of Hamelin," page 24)

See also *Contrast, Metaphor, Simile.*

Concrete Poem. See *Poetry.*

Conflict. The struggle that a character faces creates the conflict in a story. That struggle may be within one character, between two characters, or between a character and other forces. Conflict is necessary in any story or play.

For more about conflict, see pages 186 and 187.

See also *External Conflict, Internal Conflict,* and *Plot.*

Contrast. Writers often use contrast to show how different two things are. In "Hearts and Hands," contrast is used to tell about two passengers on the train.

> Among the newcomers were two young men, one of handsome presence with a bold, frank countenance and manner; the other a ruffled, glum–faced person, heavily built and roughly dressed. The two were handcuffed together. (page 158)

See also *Comparison.*

Description. In a description, a writer gives details that help the reader imagine a character, setting, or action. Often the details suggest a visual image, as in this example:

> Before him was our uncle Khosrove, an enormous man with a powerful head of black hair and the largest mustache in the San Joaquin Valley.
> ("The Summer of the Beautiful White Horse," page 213)

A description may also provide details of sound, smell, touch, or other senses. Sometimes a description lists actions or attitudes of a character.

See also *Direct Description* and *Indirect Description.*

Dialog. Conversation between characters in a story or play is called dialog. In writing, the exact words are set off by quotation marks.

"Will you keep it a secret?" asked the first man. "If so, I will tell you in a few words how we will bring it about."

"I promise, by my honor," said the other, "that I will not betray you." ("How the Three Young Men Found Death," page 143.)

For more about dialog, see page 483.

Direct Description. When a writer states how a character looks or acts, he or she is using direct description.

> She was a cream-colored mare with a black forelock, mane, and tail and a black stripe along the middle of her back. Tall, slender, high-spirited, I thought then—I think now that she was the most beautiful of horses. ("I Get a Colt To Break In," page 359)

For more about direct description, see page 208.

See also *Description* and *Indirect Description*.

Drama. A story that is meant to be performed before an audience is a drama, or play. A drama is told through the words and actions of its characters. The word *drama* also refers in general to this type of writing. Like other forms of fiction, drama uses characters, setting, plot, dialog, and sometimes a narrator. In addition, a written drama makes use of stage directions and a cast of characters.

A long play is divided into parts called acts. Each act is divided into smaller scenes. In Chapter 7, there are two examples of drama. "A Connecticut Yankee in King Arthur's Court" is a one-act play. "The Invasion of Mars" is a two-act play.

For more about drama, see pages 482 and 483.

See also *Stage Directions*.

Essay. A type of nonfiction in which the writer expresses his or her own opinion is called an essay. An example of an essay is "April and Robins" by Hal Borland (page 446).

For more about the essay, see pages 444 and 445.

See also *Nonfiction*.

External Conflict. A struggle between two characters, or between a character and a force such as nature, is called external conflict. There are three external conflicts in "Spotted Eagle and Black Crow" (pages 35 to 39): the jealousy between the two warriors, Spotted Eagle's struggle to escape from the narrow ledge, and the battle between the Fox and Pahani tribes.

For more about external conflict, see page 186.

See also *Conflict*, *Internal Conflict*, and *Plot*.

Falling Action. Falling action is that part of the plot in which the story draws to a conclusion. It follows the climax. For example, in "The Six Horsemen" the climax occurs when Fadebi rescues Nassa from the fortress. The falling action occurs when Fadebi's five companions use their magic to get them across the river and away from Ballo (pages 46 to 47).

For more on falling action, see page 135. See also *Plot* and *Climax*.

Fiction. A work of fiction is the one that comes from the writer's imagination. Some types of fiction are short stories, legends, and drama. An example of fiction is "The Legend of King Arthur" (pages 68 to 94).

Figurative Language. A way of speaking or writing that looks at familiar things in a fresh, new way is called figurative language. Some particular kinds of figurative language are called figures of speech. Metaphor, simile, personification, and hyperbole are four figures of speech. They are all examples of figurative language.

Metaphor	The trees were soldiers, standing straight and tall.
Simile	The trees stood as tall as skyscrapers.
Personification	The trees pushed the clouds out of their way.
Hyperbole	A year went by as we stood there, waiting for the cat to climb down.

For more about Figurative Language, see pages 121 to 129.

See also *Hyperbole*, *Metaphor*, *Personification*, and *Simile*.

Humor. Writing that is funny has the quality of humor. A particular action in a story can suggest humor. For example, in "Lazy Peter" (pages 51 to 55), Peter's tricks make fun of the greedy farmer. A certain setting, character, or use of words can also suggest humor. "Casey at the Bat" (pages 306 to 308) has examples of all of these kinds of humor.

See also *Hyperbole* and *Irony*.

Hyperbole. An obvious exaggeration is called hyperbole. It gives the reader a humorous image of what the writer is describing.

> And the much-despised Blakey "tore the cover off the ball."
> ("Casey at the Bat," page 306)

For more about hyperbole, see pages 128 and 129.

Imagery. Imagery is any kind of description that makes an object or experience so real that we can imagine it with our senses. Writers use sensory details to help us see, feel, smell, hear, or taste the things they describe.

> In April, the party made another attempt in the face of icy winds that bore down from the North under the cold but continuous glare of a twenty-four-hour sun on blindingly white snow.
> ("Matthew A. Henson," page 395)

For more about imagery, see page 280.

See also *Figurative Language*.

Indirect Description. A writer who states directly how a character looks or acts is using direct description. Any other way in which the writer leads you to understand the character is indirect description. A character's comments may also tell about himself or herself. For example, this speaker's treatment of his colt shows his patience and love for the animal.

> He went off downtown with my father, and I started away with my colt. I fed, I led, I cleaned her, gently, as if she were made of glass; she was playful and willing, a delight. ("I Get a Colt to Break In," page 361)

A reader can also learn about a character through seeing how other characters react to him or her.

> And curiosity was so strong on the men that the whole council, Klosh-Kwan to the fore, rose up and went to the igloo of Keesh. He was eating, but he received them with respect and seated them according to their rank.
> ("The Story of Keesh," page 179)

For more about indirect description, see page 369.

See also *Description, Direct Description.*

Internal Conflict. The struggle within a character's own self is called internal conflict. This struggle usually involves a decision the character must make. In "The Big Wave" (pages 199 to 207), Jiya must decide where he will live.

For more about internal conflict, see page 187.

See also *Conflict, External Conflict, Plot.*

Introduction. The first part of the plot is the introduction. It introduces the reader to the characters and the setting.

> It was a dark autumn night. The old banker was pacing from corner to corner in his room, recalling to his mind the party he had given in the autumn fifteen years before. ("The Bet," page 165)

For more about the introduction, see page 135.

See also *Plot.*

Irony. The contrast between what is expected, or what seems to be true, and what actually happens is called irony. For example, in "How the Three Young Men Found Death," the young men boast that they will kill death. Instead, they kill each other. The story ends with the ironic statement:

> And soon, like their friend, the two found Death. (page 144)

For more on irony, see pages 12 and 162.

Legend. A legend is a story about notable men and women of the past. Legends are often a mixture of fact and fiction. They reflect the values of the people who told the stories. An example of a legend is "Spotted Eagle and Black Crow" (pages 35 to 40).

For more on legends, see pages 2 and 3.

Lyric Poem. See page 271.

Metaphor. A metaphor is a figure of speech that compares two unlike things having something in common. The comparison is made without the use of *like* or *as*, as in a simile. In the following example, Lincoln is compared to a pine tree.

Lincoln was the green pine.
Lincoln kept on growing.
("Abraham Lincoln," page 340)

For more about metaphor, see pages 124 and 125.

See also *Simile*.

Mood. The feeling you get as you are reading a selection is called the mood of that selection. *Sad* and *cheerful* are two possible moods. The mood of "I Was Born Today" (pages 264 to 265), for example, is hopeful.

For more about mood, see pages 187 and 271.

Narrative Poem. See page 271.

Narrator. A narrator is the person who tells the story. There are different types of narrators. The first-person narrator is usually a character in the story, such as the boy in "The Disappearing Man" (pages 231 to 234). The third-person narrator tells the story from outside the story, as in "King John and the Abbot" (pages 15 to 18).

There are two types of third-person narrator. A narrator who knows how all the characters think and feel is *omniscient*, as in "The Big Wave" (pages 199 to 207). The third-person narrator may also be *limited*, telling only what one character thinks and feels, as in "The Rocking Donkey" (pages 222 to 227).

For more about narrator, see pages 3 and 135.

See also *Point of View*.

Nonfiction. Writing that tells about real people, actual places, and true events is called nonfiction. It is based on fact. An example of nonfiction is "Maria Tallchief" (pages 404 to 409).

For more about nonfiction, see pages 352 and 353.

See also *Autobiography*, *Biography*, and *Essay*.

Onomatopoeia. The use of words that sound like what they describe is called onomatopoeia.

Back up he swims
  Past sting-ray and shark,
    Out with a zoom,
      A whoop, a bark;
("Seal," page 278)

For more about onomatopoeia, see page 120.

Personification. A figure of speech that gives human qualities to animals, objects, or ideas is personification.

The Mountain and the squirrel
Had a quarrel,
And the former called the latter "Little
prig;"
("The Mountain and the Squirrel," page 288)

For more about personification, see pages 126 and 127.

Play. See *Drama.*

Plot. The sequence of events in a story is the plot. In most stories, one event follows the next. Usually, each thing that happens is caused by what comes before it. The parts of the plot include the introduction, the rising action, the climax, the falling action, and the resolution.

For more about plot, see pages 63 and 135.

See also *Introduction*, *Rising Action*, *Climax*, *Falling Action*, and *Resolution*.

Poetry. Poetry is a form of writing in which words are arranged in lines rather than sentences. The sounds of the words and the way they are arranged are important. The lines are arranged in groups called stanzas. "The Dream Keeper" (page 249) has one stanza of eight lines. "Paul Revere's Ride" (pages 330 to 334), in contrast, has fourteen stanzas of varying lengths.

Sometimes a poet writes a poem in a special shape. This is called a *concrete poem*. "Seal" (page 278) is an example.

For more about poetry, see pages 242 and 243.

See also *Rhyme*, *Rhyme Scheme*, *Rhythm*, and *Stanza.*

Point of View. A story may be told from several points of view. This term refers to how the narrator tells the story. It may be a first-person point of view or a third-person point of view. "The Summer of the Beautiful White Horse" (pages 211 to 217) is told from a first-person point of view. "Richard the Lion-Hearted" (pages 8 to 11) is told from a third-person point of view.

For more about point of view, see pages 135 and 353.

See also *Narrator.*

Repetition. When a word or a group of words is repeated in a selection, the writer is using repetition. Poets often repeat a word or phrase to give special emphasis to a thought or action. Here, for example, repetition stresses the suspense of a foul shot.

The ball . . .
Plays it coy . . .
And then
            And then
                        And then,
Right before ROAR-UP,
Dives down and through.
("Foul Shot," page 310)

For more on repetition, see page 219.

Resolution. The loose ends in a story are tied up in the resolution. It is the last part of the plot.

> Jiya smiled. Happiness began to live in him again. The good food warmed him, and his body welcomed it. Around him the love of the people who received him glowed like a warm and welcoming fire upon the hearth.
> ("The Big Wave," page 207)

For more about resolution, see page 135.

See also *Plot*.

Rhyme. The repetition of sounds at the ends of words is called rhyme. In poetry, rhyming words usually come at the ends of lines. The rhyming words in this example are *wore* and *more*, and *wear* and *spare*.

> The golden brooch my mother wore
> She left behind for me to wear;
> I have no thing I treasure more:
> Yet, it is something I could spare.
> ("The Courage That My Mother Had," page 253)

For more about rhyme, see pages 116, 117, and 243.

See also *Rhyme Scheme*.

Rhyme Scheme. Rhyme schemes are the different patterns in which rhyme can be used. When a rhyme scheme is written, different letters of the alphabet are used to stand for different rhyming endings. Here is an example of a rhyme scheme:

> Behold the hippopotamus! *a*
> We laugh at how he looks to us, *a*
> And yet in moments dank and grim *b*
> I wonder how we look to him. *b*
> Peace, peace, thou hippopotamus! *a*
> We really look all right to us, *a*
> As you no doubt delight the eye *c*
> Of other hippopotami. *c*
> ("The Hippopatomus," page 295)

For more about rhyme scheme, see pages 117, 270, and 271.

See also *Rhyme*.

Rhythm. The pattern of accented syllables in poetry is called rhythm. The accented or stressed syllables may be marked with /, while the unaccented or light syllables may be marked with ◡.

> ◡ / ◡ / ◡ / ◡ /
> Some primal termite knocked on wood
> ◡ / ◡ / ◡ / ◡ /
> And tasted it, and found it good
> ◡ / ◡ / ◡ / ◡ /
> And that is why your cousin May
> / ◡ ◡ / ◡ / ◡ /
> Fell through the parlor door today.
> ("The Termite," page 294)

For more about rhythm, see pages 118, 119 and 242.

Rising Action. The second part of the plot is the rising action. In this part it becomes clear that the characters face a problem, or conflict. One event follows the other. In "The Disappearing Man" the rising action occurs when Larry witnesses a man dashing into an alley, followed by two police officers (page 231).

For more about rising action, see page 135.

See also *Plot.*

Sequence. A series of events or ideas may be put in an order, called sequence. Often the writer tells a story in chronological sequence, or time order. Sometimes a selection, such as an essay, has ideas arranged in a logical sequence. The writer might begin with an opinion and follow it with reasons to back it up.

For more on sequence, see page 136.

See also *Time Order.*

Setting. The time and place in which the events of the story occur are referred to as the setting. All stories have a setting, but some are described in more detail than others.

> Kino lived on a farm that lay on the side of a mountain in Japan. The mountain rose so steeply out of the ocean that there was only a strip of sandy shore at its foot. Upon this strip was a small fishing village where Kino's father sold his vegetables and rice. ("The Big Wave," page 199)

For more about setting, see pages 3 and 63.

Short Story. A short story is a work of fiction short enough to be read at one sitting. It usually tells about one major character and one set of events. "Hearts and Hands" (pages 158 to 160) is an example of a short story.

For more about the short story, see page 134.

See also *Fiction.*

Simile. A simile is a figure of speech that compares two things that are not alike, but have something in common. The comparison uses the word *like* or *as.*

> Cats sleep fat.
> They spread out comfort underneath them
> Like a good mat.
> ("Catalog," page 274)

For more about simile, see pages 122 and 123.

See also *Metaphor.*

Stage Directions. In drama, stage directions guide the actors in performing the play. These directions may tell the actors how to speak the words or what background sounds or actions are needed. In "A Connecticut Yankee in King Arthur's Court," the following stage directions may be found: *angry voices fade off mike, birds twittering gayly, yawning, alarmed, suspiciously.* (page 489)

For more about stage directions, see page 483.

Stanza. A group of lines in poetry is called a stanza. There is usually a space between two stanzas of a poem. An example of a poem with several stanzas is "Western Wagons" (page 338).

For more about stanza, see page 254.

Theme. The main idea that the writer wants the reader to understand from a selection is the theme of the selection. In "Lazy Peter and His Three-Cornered Hat" (pages 51 to 55), the theme is that one should not be greedy.

For more about theme, see page 187.

Time Order. Events in a story follow a certain order. It is important to understand which event comes first and how it causes the next event. The progression of events is called time order. For example, look at "The Pied Piper of Hamelin" (pages 22 to 25). From the time the Pied Piper entered the town to the time he left with the children, the events follow one another in time order.

For more about time order, see pages 136 and 353.

Tone. The author's attitude toward what is being said is the tone. For example, in "Borrow the Army" (page 436), Lincoln's tone is sarcastic.

For more about tone, see page 353.

Summary of Comprehension Skills

Cause and Effect. Events are often related by cause and effect. The first event causes the second event. The second event, then, is the effect of the first event.

Some clue words tell the reader to look for cause and effect relationships. Among these clue words are: *because*, *since*, *so that*, *in order that*, and *if—then*.

Here is an example of a cause and an effect. The clue phrase is *so that*.

> Mark reread all of his class notes so that he would do well on the test.

For more about understanding cause and effect, see pages 136 and 137.

Chronological Order. See *Sequence*.

Conclusions. See *Inferences*.

Connotation and Denotation. See *Slanted Writing*.

Details. See *Main Idea*.

Fact and Opinion. Writers often combine fact and opinion. Facts are statements that can be proved. Opinions, on the other hand, are statements that cannot be proved. They only express the writer's beliefs.

Sometimes writers list facts that lead you to believe their opinions, as in the example below. The opinion is underlined. Following the opinion are four sentences that state facts.

> Some of the most unusual scenery in the world is in our national parks. The borders of Grand Canyon Park include most of the mile-deep canyon. In Yellowstone Park, visitors can see numerous geysers. Petrified Forest Park holds both ancient trees that have changed to rock and a brightly colored desert. Hawaii Volcanoes Park has two active volcanoes.

For more about separating fact and opinion, see page 354.

Figurative Language. Figurative language is a way of speaking or writing that forces the listener or reader to look at familiar things in a new way. While the words say one thing, their meaning can be very different.

For example, when people tell you to take a statement with a grain of salt, they don't want you to sprinkle salt on words. The expression "with a grain of salt" means you should not take something seriously. To understand this example of figurative language, you had to think about the words and look for a logical meaning.

For more about understanding figurative language, see pages 121 to 129.

Inferences and Conclusions. An inference is a logical guess based on evidence. You are often expected to make inferences as you read. You must infer what the writer hasn't said from what he or she has said. For example, a writer could describe this situation: A girl walks down a school hall past a boy who says "Hello." The girl doesn't answer. From this information, the reader might infer either that the girl did not hear the boy or that she didn't want to speak to him.

A conclusion is based on several inferences. Suppose that the writer added this information to the situation described above: A door slams loudly as the girl walks past, but she doesn't react. Then she stops to talk with another girl and watches the girl's lips closely during the conversation. From all these clues, the reader could draw the conclusion that the first girl was deaf.

For more about making inferences and drawing conclusions, see pages 64, 65, and 244.

Logical Sequence. See *Sequence.*

Main Idea. A paragraph is a group of sentences that work together to tell about one idea. This idea is the main idea. The main idea is often stated in one sentence called the topic sentence. The topic sentence may be at the beginning, middle, or end of a paragraph. Some paragraphs have no topic sentence at all. However, these paragraphs still have main ideas. All the sentences in a paragraph should be related to the main idea.

Read the following paragraph. The topic sentence has been underlined.

> <u>Software for word processing can speed up your writing.</u> If you misspell a word, you can make the correction cleanly. If you are on your fifth sentence and want to add words to the first sentence, you can move everything else to fit in the new words. If you decide to change the order of sentences, you can rearrange your words without retyping them.

The main idea was stated in the topic sentence. The rest of the sentences gave details about the main idea.

For more about identifying the main idea of a paragraph, see pages 4 and 5.

Opinions. See *Fact and Opinion.*

Outcomes. When you make a reasonable guess about what will happen next in a story, you are predicting an outcome.

Some outcomes are easy to predict. For example, when you hear the band at the ball game play "The Star-Spangled Banner," you can predict that the game will start soon. Predicting other outcomes is not so simple. For example, you would not know at the beginning of the ball game, which team will win.

When you predict outcomes, base your guess on clues the writer gives you. To make a logical prediction, you should use what you know about the character, the plot, the setting, and your personal knowledge of what people usually do in certain situations.

For more about predicting outcomes, see page 245.

Paragraphs. See *Main Idea*.

Purpose. Before beginning any writing, an author decides what he or she wants the writing to do. Some purposes, or reasons for writing, are to entertain, to express feelings, to inform, to persuade, and to make people laugh. The topic of the writing and its organization are affected by the purpose of the writing. So are the choice of such elements as character, plot, and setting. A reader should be aware of the writer's purpose in order to understand the writing completely.

For example, the purpose of "The Disappearing Man" is to challenge the reader to solve the mystery with the same clues as the hero has. For that reason, the author tells the reader all the important clues and very few other details. He saves the explanation of the hero's thinking until the very end of the story.

For more about author's purpose, see pages 484 and 485.

Sequence. To understand a selection, it is important to recognize the sequence, or order, in which the information is presented. Three kinds of sequence are natural order, time order, and logical order.

Natural order is often used in descriptions. In natural order, a writer talks about things in the order in which you would notice them. In the play "Invasion from Mars," for example, Phillips describes "the thing" as he sees it.

> The eyes are black and gleam like a serpent's. The mouth is V-shaped, with saliva dripping from rimless lips that seem to quiver and pulsate. (page 510)

Time order, or **chronological order**, is the order in which events happen. This order is usually used in stories to relate events.

Sometimes events are connected only by time order. Usually, however, the first event must take place before the second event may occur. Here is an example:

> The farmer held the chicken's head with one hand and then reached for the eggs with his other hand.

For more about recognizing time order, see pages 136 and 353, and Drawing a Time Line on pages 18 and 19.

Logical order is usually used to relate ideas or reasons. It may be used in stories to explain why a character does something. For example, read the sixth paragraph on page 38 to find Spotted Eagle's reasons for forgiving Black Crow.

Logical order is also used frequently in essays and similar nonfiction writing. It helps the reader understand why the writer believes or feels as he or she does. For example, read the third paragraph of "April and Robins" on page 446 to find out how the author feels about the robin's song.

Slanted Writing. Some writing appears to be telling nothing but facts, but it is actually presenting the writer's opinions. This kind of writing is called slanted writing. A reader must watch for such clues as those described below.

A writer can mix opinions with fact, as in this example:

> The custom of summer vacation from school started at a time when students were needed for farm work. Since students are no longer needed on farms, we no longer need summer vacation.

A writer can select only those facts that support his or her opinions. For example, support his or her opinions. Suppose you were trying to convince someone that your favorite actor or actress was the best. You might mention only the successful movies in which he or she appeared, and ignore those that got bad reviews.

A writer can report facts with words that lead the reader to feel a particular way about the facts. The writer will carefully choose words with the connotations he or she wants. That is, the writer chooses words that suggest certain ideas or feelings. For example, both sentences below report the same fact. One does it in a favorable way; the other strongly suggests disapproval.

> The school has invested in a new, more efficient copying machine.

> The school has thrown away more money on a newfangled copying machine that's supposed to be faster than the one we already have.

To avoid being influenced unwisely, a reader must watch for slanted writing.

For more about slanted writing, see pages 354 and 355.

Time Order. See *Sequence*.

Word Choice. A writer's choice of words depends on many influences. These include the following: the mood of the piece of writing; the author's tone; the author's personal style; and the setting, if the writing is a story. Characters must sound as if they fit in the time and place described. For example, if the story takes place in modern times, a character might use terms based on space travel, such as *liftoff* and *touchdown*.

For more about word choice for characters, see pages 181, 484, and 500. For more about other influences on word choice, see pages 219, 293, 309, 325, and 421.

Summary of Vocabulary Skills

1. Word Parts

To unlock some unfamiliar words, you can separate each word into two or more parts. If you know the meaning of each word part, you can figure out the meaning of the unfamiliar word. The two kinds of word parts are base words and affixes. There are two kinds of affixes: prefixes and suffixes. Many of the word parts found in English words are based on Greek and Latin words.

Base Word. A word to which other word parts are added is called a base word. For example, the base word in *careless* is *care.* The base word in *reappear* is *appear.* Sometimes the spelling of a base word is changed when other word parts are added to it. For example, the *n* in *win* is doubled when the word is changed to *winner.* For further information about spelling changes caused by combining suffixes and base words, see *Spelling Changes* below.

Prefix. A word part added at the beginning of a base word is called a prefix. Each prefix has a certain meaning. Adding a prefix to the beginning of a word changes the meaning of the word.

Prefix	+	Base Word	=	New Word
in-	+	correct	=	incorrect

For a list of frequently used prefixes, see page 66.

Suffix. A word part added at the end of a base word is called a suffix. Adding a suffix to a word changes the meaning of the word.

Base Word	+	Suffix	=	New Word
hope	+	-ful	=	hopeful

For a list of frequently used suffixes, see page 66.

Spelling Changes. Before endings can be added to some words, one of the following spelling changes may be necessary.

1. When a suffix beginning with a vowel is added to a word ending in silent *e*, the *e* is usually dropped.

   write + -er = writer

The *e* is not dropped when a suffix beginning with a consonant is added.

late + -ly = lately

2. When a suffix is added to a word ending in *y* preceded by a consonant, the *y* is usually changed to an *i*.

happy + -ness = happiness

Note that when the *y* is preceded by a vowel, it is not changed.

joy + -ous = joyous

3. Words of one syllable, ending in one consonant preceded by one vowel, double the final consonant before adding *-ing*, *-ed*, or *-er*.

swim + -ing = swimming

Note that when two vowels appear in a one-syllable word, the final consonant is not doubled.

clean + -er = cleaner

Word Parts from Greek and Latin. Many Greek and Latin words are shortened and used as prefixes and suffixes in English words. Knowing the meaning of these Greek and Latin word parts will help you understand the meaning of English words they are a part of. For example, the Greek prefix *tele-* means "far off," and the word part *-gram* means "something written." For these two word parts, we have the word *telegram*.

For more about Greek and Latin word parts, see page 67.

2. Context Clues

Context refers to the sentence or paragraph in which you find a word. Clues about the meaning of a new word are often given in context. Look for the following kinds of context clues.

Antonyms. An antonym, or opposite, may be given in the same sentence as the new word. It may also be given in a nearby sentence. Often the antonym appears in the same position in its sentence as the new word. Like a contrast clue (page 548), an antonym leads you to understand the meaning of a new word by explaining what it is not.

The group's decision on the date of the picnic was equivocal. However, their decision on the menu was clear and firm.

The antonyms both appear after the verb *was*. *Equivocal* means "the opposite of clear and firm."

For more about antonyms, see pages 32 and 33.

Comparison and Contrast Clues. Writers often compare one idea with another. They sometimes use an unfamiliar word in one part of the comparison. In that case, the other part of the comparison may give you a clue to the meaning of the word. Key words to look for in comparison clues are *like*, *as*, *similar to*, and *than*.

Here is an example of a comparison clue:

> Among people in our city, the diversity in languages is even more noticeable than the differences in foods.

The comparison tells you that *diversity* means "difference."

Writers also use contrast clues to give you hints about the meaning of a new word. Writers show that certain things or ideas are opposites. A contrast clue tells you what the new word is not. Look for these key words in contrast clues: *although*, *but*, *however*, *yet*, *on the other hand*, *different from*, and *in contrast*.

> Many of Karen's ideas are irrational, but her idea for a new city park certainly is sensible.

The contrast clue tells you that *irrational* is the opposite of *sensible*.

For more about comparison and contrast clues, see pages 246 and 247.

Definitions. In a definition clue, the writer tells the meaning of the new word. Certain words signal that a definition will follow. Look for these key words: *is*, *who is*, *which is*, *that is*, and *in other words*.

> The plans for the trip were nebulous. That is, they were not clear.

For more about definitions in context, see pages 6 and 7.

Example Clues. In an example clue, a new word is related to a group of familiar words. The new word may be an example of a familiar term. Other times, the familiar terms are examples of the new word.

Key words and phrases tell you to look for examples in a sentence. Some key words are *an example*, *for example*, *one kind*, *for instance*, *some types*, *such as*.

> Ancient musical instruments, such as the psaltery, were displayed at the museum.

For more about definitions in context, see pages 6 and 7.

Inference: Using Clues from Different Parts of the Sentence. Clues to the meaning of an unfamiliar word can be found in different parts of the same sentence. For example, clues to a new word in the subject can sometimes be found in the predicate.

> The serape that the Indian wore was made of a bright red and yellow wool.

From this sentence, you can guess that a *serape* is a brightly colored garment of some type.

Inference: Using Clues from Different Parts of the Paragraph. Sometimes the sentence in which a new word appears has no clues to its meaning. However, it is often possible to find clues to the meaning somewhere else in the same paragraph.

> This was Jan's first game of lacrosse. The other nine players on her team had all played before. She had a difficult time hitting the small rubber ball with the long-handled racket. To everyone's surprise, she was the first player to make a goal.

You can figure out the meaning of *lacrosse* from this information in the paragraph: lacrosse is a game played by two teams of ten players each; it is played with a long-handled racket; the players try to send the ball into a goal.

For more about inferring meanings from context, see pages 40 and 41.

Main Idea Clues. Sometimes you can figure out the meaning of a new word by understanding the main idea of the paragraph or selection in which it appears. In this example, several clues make the meaning of the underlined word clear.

> Mr. Bailey's decisions were irrevocable. No one ever persuaded him to change his scoring on an event. He was also firm about each contestant's behavior.

The main idea of the paragraph shows that *irrevocable* means "unchangeable."

For more about main idea clues to meanings, see page 502.

Prefixes and Suffixes. Your knowledge of affixes, that is, prefixes and suffixes, can lead you to context clues.

> Don't drink that unsafe water. You must boil it first to make it potable.

In this example, you know that the suffix *-able* means "can be." You can guess that *potable* water is water that can be drunk.

Restatement. To help you understand an unfamiliar word, a writer will often restate it. In other words, he or she says the idea again in a different way. Key words and punctuation tell you to look for the meaning. Some keys are the word *or*, dashes, commas, and parentheses.

> Next on the itinerary, or route, was a visit to the aquarium.

For more about restatements in context, see pages 6 and 7.

Words in a Series. A sentence may have a series of words that are similar in meaning or belong to the same group. If one of the words is unfamiliar to you, you can often guess its meaning by relating it to the familiar words. From the following example, you can guess that *tatting* is closely related to sewing and embroidery.

> Monica was very eager to learn sewing, embroidery, and tatting.

For more about words in a series, see page 247.

3. Denotation, Connotation, and Multiple Meanings

Denotation refers to the dictionary meaning of a word. **Connotation** refers to the feelings, ideas, and thoughts the word brings to the reader's mind. In order to understand most directions, explanations, and statements of fact, you need only recognize the denotation of a word. However, in order to understand most literature, and especially poetry, you need to be aware of the connotations of words.

For example, the denotations of the word *clever* are "bright, intelligent or skillful in doing some particular thing." However, its connotations may include trickery, deceitfulness or foul play in getting what one wants or needs. These are the meanings suggested in the following sentence.

> Josh always has a clever way of getting out of his chores.

For more about the difference between connotation and denotation, see pages 354 and 355.

Multiple Meanings. Many words have more than one meaning. To choose the denotation that the writer intended, read the words in context. Read the words and sentences before and after the word. Try out possible meanings in the context of the sentence.

Use the context of this sentence to figure out which meaning of *knot* the writer intended.

> The ship's speed was twenty knots.

There are at least three dictionary meanings for *knot*:

1. a tying or twining together
2. a unit of speed used on ships
3. a joint on the stem of a plant

Try each of the meanings in the sentence. It is clear that the second meaning must be the one the writer meant.

For more about choosing among multiple meanings, see page 138.

4. Levels of Language

Standard English is English that is acceptable anywhere, either in speaking or writing. It follows traditional rules of grammar and uses words that can be found in the dictionary. Most writing is done in standard English.

Standard English may be formal, as in classroom assignments, in speeches, and in most written literature. It may also be informal, as in conversations and in written literature that is trying to sound like natural speech.

Nonstandard English is English used by particular groups of people in particular circumstances. It may not follow the traditional rules of grammar. It may use **slang**. These are words not usually found as main entries in the dictionary or with meanings not listed in the dictionary. Writers use nonstandard English only for special effects. For example, characters who are close friends might speak to each other in nonstandard English.

For more about recognizing the levels of language, see pages 235 and 236.

5. Reference Books: The Dictionary, Glossary, Encyclopedia, and Thesaurus

A **dictionary** is an alphabetical listing of words and their meanings. Sometimes context clues and word parts do not give enough information to allow you to understand unfamiliar words in your reading. Then you should use a dictionary to find the meaning.

If a word has multiple definitions, or meanings, they will all be listed. These denotations will probably be grouped by part of speech. To choose the right meaning for your selection, test each definition in the sentence in which you found the word.

A **glossary** is often found in the back of a nonfiction book. It contains an alphabetical listing of new or unfamiliar words that are used in the book. The definition given for a glossary word is often limited to the way it is used in a particular selection.

An **encyclopedia** is a book or set of books that gives information on a wide variety of topics. The articles about the topics are arranged alphabetically. You will find more detailed information about a word in an encyclopedia than in a dictionary.

Some dictionaries give information about connotations of a word. Another reference book that gives information about connotations is the **thesaurus**. In a thesaurus, a word is listed with other words of similar meanings, usually with some explanation of the differences.

For more about the dictionary, see page 356; the glossary, page 357; the encyclopedia, page 440; and the thesaurus, pages 325 and 326.

See also *The Dictionary*, *The Encyclopedia*, and *The Thesaurus* under Guidelines for Study and Research.

Guidelines for the Process of Writing

Every time you write, there are certain steps you should follow. Each step is essential for good writing. Together, the steps are called the process of writing.

The process has three stages: **pre-writing**, **writing** the first draft, and **revising**.

Stage 1: Pre-Writing

Pre-writing includes all the preparations you make before you begin to write. During the pre-writing stage, writers think, plan, do research, and organize. Below are the five steps of pre-writing.

1. Choose and limit a topic. Make a list of ideas that interest you. Go over the list carefully. Choose the topic that interests you most. Then list the things you could say about the topic. Limit this list to the ideas you can handle well.

For example, one student was asked to write a paragraph comparing any two legends. She skimmed the legends and chose "Richard the Lion Hearted" and "The Pied Piper of Hamelin." Then she listed all her ideas and circled the one she thought was most interesting.

mood	events	characters
setting	details	(use of music)

2. Decide on your purpose. Decide why you are writing. What do you want to say about your topic? Do you want to explain it, describe it, or criticize it? Are you trying to teach your readers or persuade them to do something?

The student writing about legends decided that the most interesting idea was the use of music. She decided to write her paragraph about music in the legends.

3. Decide on your audience. Decide who will read your writing. Then you will be better able to choose your level of language and the details to include. For example, your language in class will be more formal than at a friend's home.

4. Gather supporting information. List everything you know about the topic. It is possible that you will need more information. You may need to use reference sources, such as encyclopedias.

The student writing about legends reread both her selections. She wrote notes on every part that had to do with music.

"RICHARD"

Richard—Shut up in dungeon, hidden
Blondel—Minstrel and singer
Made up tunes and songs together
Outside prison, Blondel sang song they had made up, and Richard sang back.

"PIED PIPER"

"A power—call it music or call it magic"
Piper played on pipe, led rats to river
Led children to hills
Piper's music told of a magic land.

5. Organize your ideas. Reread your list of details and information. Some details will be useful. Others will not. Cross out the ones that don't belong.

Choose a logical order for the details. For example, you may choose time order if you are writing a story. For a description, you may list details in the order you would notice them. Make a plan, or outline, showing the order in which you will present your ideas. Your outline should make sense to you.

Here is the student's outline for her paragraph. She has written out and underlined her main idea. This will help her keep her sentences on the subject.

COMPARISON OF LEGENDS

Main idea—Music was in both "Richard" and "The Pied Piper."
Important details—
Blondel used music to find Richard.
Pied Piper used music to lead rats away.
Also, to lead the children away.

Stage 2: Writing a First Draft

Now you are ready to get your ideas down on paper. At this point, don't concentrate on getting your words perfect. That careful work will come later. For now, keep your purpose and audience in mind. Follow your outline as much as possible. Remember that you can change your outline if you get better ideas as you write. Leave space between the lines for later corrections and changes.

This is how the student in the example wrote the first draft of her comparison.

First Draft

When I read ''Richard the Lion Hearted I enjoyed reading about how music saved king Richard's life, He was shut up in a dungeon so no one could find him, but Blondels song saved him. In ''the Pied Piper Of Hamelin,'' music got rid of the rats. Also it led the children into a hill, from which They never returned. Music was used in both legends although they were very diffrent.

Stage 3: Revising

Revising means making changes in your writing to improve it. Read over your writing. Ask yourself these questions.

1. Is the writing interesting? Will others want to read it?
2. Did I stick to my topic? Are there any unnecessary details? Should any other details be added?
3. Is the organization easy to follow? Do ideas flow together smoothly?
4. Is every group of words a sentence? Is every word the best word?

Mark any corrections and notes on your first draft. Don't be surprised if you make corrections to your corrections. You may need to write several drafts before you are satisfied with your work.

Proofreading. Your writing should be correct as well as clear and interesting. Read it over again. This time, check for any errors in capitalization, punctuation, grammar, and spelling. Correct your errors. Use the symbols in the box at the top of page 555.

Here is a draft that is being revised. Notice how the writer has improved the piece by crossing out unnecessary words, by adding precise words, and by moving ideas around. The writer has also corrected errors in capitalization, punctuation, grammar, and spelling. The writer has used proofreading symbols shown in the box on page 555. First study this draft, then compare it with the final draft on page 555. See how changes that were marked here have been carried out in the final copy.

Revised Draft

¶ Music was important in both "Richard the Lion-Hearted" and "The Pied Piper of Hamelin."

In ~~When I read~~ "Richard the Lion-Hearted," ~~I enjoyed reading~~

had been hidden

~~about how~~ music saved king Richard's life. He ~~was shut up~~

However, found him.

in a dungeon ~~so no one could find him,~~ but Blondel's song

When Blondel sang a song, the king answered him.

~~saved him~~. In "the Pied Piper Øf Hamelin," music got rid

but magic

of the rats. Also it led the children into a hill ~~from~~

~~which~~ They never returned. Music was used in both ~~legends~~

although they were very diffrent.

legends

Proofreading Symbols

Symbol	Meaning	Example
^	insert	diffrent (e inserted)
≡	capitalize	king
/	make lower case	Of
∿	transpose (trade positions)	Also it
⌒	omit letters, words	theye
¶	make new paragraph	¶ Music
⊙	insert a period	both ⊙

Writing the Final Copy. As soon as you feel your writing is both clear and correct, write your final copy. Use your best handwriting or type carefully. Indent paragraphs correctly. Then proofread your work again. Read it aloud. Look for any errors you might have missed.

Notice that in making this final copy, the student found and corrected an error in punctuation. She also improved the wording of one phrase that had not been marked before.

Final Copy

Music was important in both "Richard the Lion-Hearted" and "The Pied Piper of Hamelin." In "Richard the Lion-Hearted," music saved King Richard's life. He had been hidden in a dungeon. However, the minstrel Blondel found him. When Blondel sang a song, the king answered him. In "The Pied Piper of Hamelin," music got rid of the rats, but it also led the children into a magic hill. They never returned. Although the legends were very different, music was used in both.

Checklist for the Process of Writing

Pre-Writing

1. Choose and limit a topic.
2. Decide on your purpose.
3. Decide on your audience.
4. Gather supporting information.
5. Organize your ideas.

Writing Your First Draft

1. Begin writing. Keep your topic, purpose, and audience in mind at all times.
2. As you write, you may add new details.
3. Concentrate on ideas. Do not be concerned with grammar and mechanics at this time.

Revising

1. Read your first draft. Ask yourself these questions:
   a. Do you like what you have written? Is it interesting? Will others want to read it?
   b. Does your writing make sense?
   c. Is your writing organized well? Do the ideas flow smoothly from one paragraph to the next? Are the ideas arranged in a logical order?
   d. Does each paragraph have a topic sentence? Does every sentence stick to the topic? Should any sentence be moved?
   e. Should any details be left out? Should any be added?
   f. Does every sentence express a complete thought? Are your sentences easy to understand?
   g. Is every word the best possible word?
2. Mark any changes on your paper.

Proofreading

Consider these questions as you check your writing for errors in grammar and usage, capitalization, punctuation, and spelling.

Grammar and Usage

a. Is every word group a complete sentence?
b. Does every verb agree with its subject?
c. Have you used the correct form of each pronoun?
d. Is the form of each adjective correct?
e. Is the form of each adverb correct?

Capitalization

a. Is the first word in every sentence capitalized?
b. Are all proper nouns and adjectives capitalized?
c. Are titles capitalized correctly?

Punctuation

a. Does each sentence have the correct end mark?
b. Have you used punctuation marks such as commas, apostrophes, hyphens, colons, semicolons, question marks, quotation marks, and underlining correctly?

Spelling

a. Did you check unfamiliar words in a dictionary?
b. Did you spell plural and possessive forms correctly?

Preparing the Final Copy

1. Make a clean copy of your writing. Make all changes and correct all errors. Then ask yourself these questions:
   a. Is your handwriting neat and easy to read?
   b. Are your margins wide enough?
   c. Is every paragraph indented?
2. Proofread your writing again. Read it aloud. Correct any mistakes neatly.

Guidelines for Study and Research

1. Using Reference Materials

The Dictionary

A **dictionary** is an alphabetical listing of words, called entry words, and their meanings. The **glossary** of a nonfiction book is a dictionary limited to entry words from that book.

How To Find a Word. In order to find a word in the dictionary, look first at the **guide words** on the pages. Two guide words are usually printed at the top of every page. They show the first and last words on the page. Keep looking until you find the guide words between which your word falls.

For example, here are the guide words for two pages of a dictionary. On which page will *radiant* appear?

radial—radium radius—railway

You needed to compare the guide words to the fifth letter in order to find the answer. *Radiant* will appear on the first page, between *radial* and *radium.*

What the Entry Word Tells You. Use the **entry word** itself, printed in boldface (dark) type, to see how the word is spelled. Use the entry word, also, to find out where to break the word into syllables at the end of a line of writing.

How To Find the Pronunciation. Use the **respelling** that follows the entry word to determine the pronunciation of the word. The respelling usually appears within parentheses. It uses letters and symbols to stand for the sounds of the spoken word. To find out what each letter and symbol stands for, you must refer to the **pronunciation key** on that page or the page across from it. (For the meaning of the symbols in the sample respelling, see the pronunciation key in the Glossary.)

entry word respelling part of speech

ra·di·ant (rā′dē ənt) *adj.* **1.** shining brightly. **2.** showing pleasure. **3.** coming from the sun or other source in rays.

meanings

Accent marks in the respelling indicate which syllable to stress when you say the word. If the word has more than two syllables, it may have more than one accent. The heavy accent is called the **primary accent**. The lighter one is called the **secondary accent**.

How To Find the Part of Speech and the Meaning. Immediately following the respelling is an abbreviation that tells the **part of speech** of the word. Then you will find the **definition**, or meaning, of the word. If the word may be used as more than one part of speech, all the definitions for one part of speech are grouped together. After that you will find a second abbreviation and the definitions that fit that second part of speech, and so on.

After some entries, you will find subentries listed in dark, or bold, type. **Subentries** are familiar phrases in which the entry word appears. The special meaning of the phrase is then listed.

For more on the use of the dictionary, see pages 356, 367, and 368.

The Thesaurus

A **thesaurus** is a list of words followed by related words. You use a thesaurus when you need to find a word to express your exact meaning. The related words may be synonyms for the listed word. Some of the related words may be different parts of speech from the entry word. Other related words are antonyms, words with meanings opposite the entry word.

Imagine, for example, that you needed another word for the term *worried.* You would first find the listing for *worried* in the thesaurus. There you would read words such as *anxious* and *troubled.* You could choose one of those words.

Each thesaurus is organized in a different way. Look in the front of the thesaurus for directions. The index at the back of the book may also help you.

For more about using a thesaurus, see page 325.

The Encyclopedia

The **encyclopedia** is a collection of articles on a wide variety of topics. The articles are arranged in alphabetical order, according to their titles. Usually, if an encyclopedia is several volumes long, an index appears in the last volume.

When you are looking for information in an encyclopedia, begin with the index. The index tells which articles have information on each topic. It tells the volume and page where each article appears.

For more information about using the encyclopedia, see pages 77 and 440.

The Nonfiction Book

When you are looking for detailed information on a topic, your best source may be a nonfiction book concerning the topic. To decide whether the book will be useful to you, examine these parts:

The title page. Does the title mention your topic? Is the author or editor someone with knowledge about the topic?

The copyright page. If you need up-to-date information, is the copyright date a recent one?

The table of contents. Is the organization of the book clear? Do the part titles or chapter titles suggest what you can find in each section of the book, so that you can find your topic easily?

The index. Is there an adequate index? Does it list terms or names that you need information about? Does it use italic or boldface type to indicate the pages with maps, graphs, or illustrations?

2. Finding the Right Book

The Library

Books in a library are divided into two groups: fiction and nonfiction.

Fiction books are stories about imaginary happenings. They are arranged alphabetically according to the last name of the author. The author's last name is usually shown on the spine of the book.

Nonfiction books contain factual information. Most libraries arrange these books according to the **Dewey Decimal System**. Every book is assigned a number in one of ten categories. The number is called a **call number**. It is printed on the spine of the book. The books are then arranged on library shelves in numerical order.

THE DEWEY DECIMAL SYSTEM

000–099	General Works	encyclopedias, almanacs, handbooks
100–199	Philosophy	conduct, ethics, psychology
200–299	Religion	the Bible, mythology, theology
300–399	Social Science	law, education, government, folklore, legend
400–499	Language	languages, grammar, dictionaries
500–599	Science	mathematics, chemistry, physics
600–699	Useful Arts	farming, cooking, sewing, radio, nursing, engineering, television, business, gardening, cars
700–799	Fine Arts	music, painting, drawing, acting, games, sports
800–899	Literature	poetry, plays, essays
900–999	History	biography, travel, geography

The Card Catalog

The best way to locate a book in the library is to use the **card catalog**. The cards are arranged alphabetically according to the words in the top line of each card. On the top left corner of the card, you will find the call number. Using the call number, you can then locate the book on the shelves.

There are usually three cards for every book in the library: an author card, a title card, and a subject card. Each of the three cards contains the same information, but in a different order. The **author card** lists the author's name on the top line. The **title card** lists the title on the top line. The **subject card** lists the subject or topic of the book on the top line.

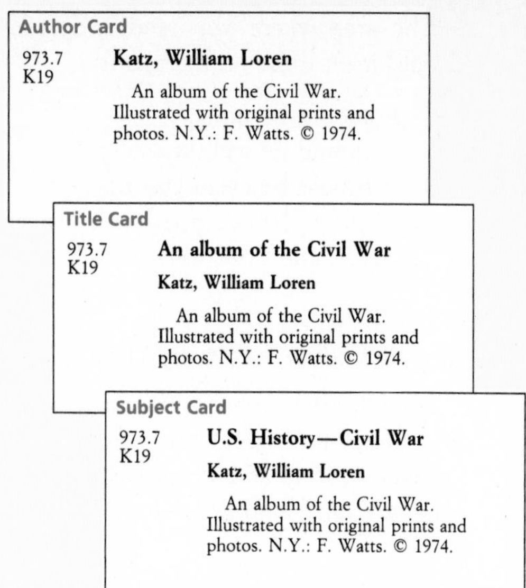

3. Preparing To Study

Preparations in Class

Before you can begin an assignment, you must know what it is you are being asked for. The first step to studying is listening carefully to **directions**.

1. Focus your attention on only the directions about to be given.
2. Note how many steps there are.
3. Relate a key word to each step, such as *Read, Answer,* or *Write.*
4. Ask questions about any step you do not understand.
5. Repeat the completed directions to yourself and then write them down.

Keep an **assignment notebook** for making a record of what you must do. For each assignment, write the following:

1. The subject
2. The assignment and any details
3. The date the assignment is given
4. The date the assignment is due

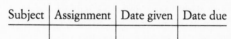

Subject	Assignment	Date given	Date due

Your Study Area

The area where you read and study should meet these requirements:

1. It should be quiet.
2. It should be well lit.
3. It should be clean and neat.
4. It should be equipped with pencils, paper, and a dictionary.

Your Schedule for Study Time

It is important to set aside time to study and complete assignments.

Some reading and writing assignments require a small amount of time. These are called **short-term goals**. To be sure you will do these assignments, set aside a block of time each day to work on your studies.

Assignments that cannot be completed overnight are called **long-term goals**. If you break these assignments into smaller tasks, the job becomes manageable. Decide how long each small task will take. Then develop a plan for completing the tasks, one by one.

To make a **study plan**, write down what you will accomplish each day. On your plan, show the times each day when you will work on the project.

4. Studying

Three Types of Reading

There are three types of reading you can use when you are studying. Each is best for a particular purpose.

Scanning is a type of fast reading. It allows you to locate a specific piece of information quickly. To scan, move your eyes rapidly over the page. Look for key words that will lead you to the facts and ideas you need to answer your question.

Skimming is another type of fast reading. It helps you get an overview of the material you are about to read. To skim, move your eyes quickly over the material. Look for titles, subtitles, and illustrations that will give you clues about the content of the material.

The third type of reading is **study-type reading**. This is slower than scanning and skimming. When you do study-type reading, you are trying to get as much meaning as you can from the words. You are trying to find the order in which the information is arranged, and to make connections between statements. The SQ3R study method is a good description of effective study-type reading.

The SQ3R Study Method

The **SQ3R study method** is a sure way to improve reading and study skills. SQ3R stands for five steps: Survey, Question, Read, Recite, and Review.

Survey. Look over the material to get a general idea of what it is about. Read the titles and subtitles. Look at the illustrations, such as pictures, maps, graphs, or tables. Read the introduction or first few paragraphs. Read the summary.

Question. Read any study questions provided in the book or by your teacher. If there are no study questions, make up some for yourself by turning titles and headings into questions.

Read. Read the material. Identify main ideas. Keep the study questions in mind.

Recite. After reading, recite the answers to the study questions. Write down brief notes to help you remember any other important ideas.

Review. Look back at the study questions and try to answer them without using your notes. You may need to review the material to find the answers. Last, study your notes so that you will be able to remember the information later.

Note-Taking

As you read, you will probably recognize some main ideas and important facts. Write them down in a notebook.

Notes do not have to be written in sentences. They should be in your own words. Write them clearly so that, when you read these notes at a later date, they will still make sense to you.

Taking notes forces you to concentrate on the material. It also helps you understand the material since you are always looking for the most important facts. Besides, notes are useful as a study guide for later review.

Name of encyclopedia | Volume number
World Book Encyclopedia, Volume 15

Title of article | Page numbers
"George Brinton McClellan" pages 266-267

Fact
McClellan became general in chief of all Union armies in 1861. Lincoln removed him in 1862 because of his delay in pursuing the Confederates.

Summary of Skills in Critical Thinking

Analysis. The skill of analysis, or analyzing, is the ability to study something carefully, piece by piece. Many elements go together to make up a story or a poem. When you analyze, you focus on each part individually.

For example, when you analyze a poem, you may want to look at its rhyme scheme, its rhythm, its mood, or another element.

As you study each part separately, you begin to understand the whole selection better. Analyzing also helps you identify the ways in which a particular selection is similar to or different from other writing.

Throughout this text, study questions in Developing Comprehension Skills, Reading Literature, and Developing Writing Skills focus the reader's attention on individual elements in the selections. In addition, questions under Developing Skills in Critical Thinking develop specific skills of analysis on pages 27 and 46.

Evaluation. When you evaluate a piece of writing, you study it carefully and decide on its value. You use certain standards to judge the worth of a selection. Does the writing meet the standards or does it fall short?

Writing can be evaluated in two ways. First, the skill of the writers can be judged. For this type of evaluation you might ask yourself questions such as these: How well has the writer achieved his or her purpose? Has the writer chosen effective ways of presenting ideas? Is the organization logical? Does it help explain the ideas? Are the figures of speech clear?

You can also evaluate what the writers are saying. Is their writing truthful and accurate? How do you know the writers are qualified to write about this subject? Are the writers telling the whole truth or is their view incomplete? Are they biased in any way? What are the qualities of this piece that make it worth reading?

As you evaluate what writers write, stay alert for examples of faulty thinking such as the following:

1. unsupported generalizations
2. hidden confusion of fact and opinion
3. slanted writing

When you write, try to be as skillful and accurate as possible. When you read, demand that other writers do the same.

Some of the many study questions involving evaluation can be found on pages 220, 337, 465, and 530.

Fact and Opinion. Facts can be proved to be true. Opinions are only one person's beliefs. They may or may not be based on facts.

Fact: Water boils at 100 degrees Celsius.
Opinion: This soup is too hot.

As you read, watch out for statements that sound like facts but cannot be proved. The writer's opinions will also influence his or her choice of details, and may result in slanted writing.

Some of the many study questions on identifying fact and opinion in the selections are on pages 402, 413, 475, and 478.

See also *Personal Opinions* and *Slanted Writing*.

Generalizations. Writers sometimes notice that some things occur in a pattern, that is, over and over again. They may make a general statement about what they notice happening. For example, a generalization about spring could be "Many trees grow new leaves in the spring."

Writers can make mistakes in generalizations. Sometimes they don't look at the facts in enough cases. They apply the generalization to more instances than the facts will support. Then the generalizations are too broad. They are not completely true.

For example, this generalization is too broad: *All trees lose their leaves in the fall.* In reality, some trees do not lose their leaves in the fall. In fact, if you can think of one tree that doesn't lose its leaves in fall, the generalization is faulty.

Study questions about generalizations can be found under Developing Skills in Critical Thinking on pages 237 and 327.

Personal Opinions. You are often asked to give your opinion about an issue or question. Your opinion should be based on evidence. You should be able to point out and explain the reasons why you think as you do.

Say, for example, you believe a certain story is realistic. If you want your opinion to be considered valid, you must be ready to back it up with evidence from the story. To explain your opinion, you might find examples of true-to-life situations and conversations in the story. You might point out the ways in which the story is like your own life or the lives of people you know.

Throughout this text, study questions in Developing Comprehension Skills, Reading Literature, and Developing Writing Skills ask the reader to form and present opinions, with supporting reasons. Some of these are on pages 27, 96, 257, and 412.

Slanted Writing. Writers are careful to choose words with the meanings they want. Denotations, or dictionary meanings, are important, of course. However, connotations, or the feelings or ideas the words give you, are equally important. In slanted writing, a writer uses many words with strong connotations. The connotations may lead readers to feel strongly in favor of a point of view. Other words with strong connotations may make a reader feel strongly against a subject.

Be aware of the power of slanted writing as you read. Don't permit the writer to trick you into agreeing with him or her without a good reason.

Read the following three sentences. Although they all deal with the same happening, they are very different. The first sentence is not slanted. The next two sentences are slanted. They use words with strong connotations. Notice how these words affect your reactions.

1. Bill sold his red bike to Todd for fifty dollars.
2. Bill cheated Todd when he sold him his old bike for fifty dollars.
3. Bill practically gave his classic bike to Todd for only fifty dollars.

For more about slanted writing and connotations, see the study questions on pages 292, 383, 411, and 469.

Glossary

The **glossary** is an alphabetical listing of words from the selections, along with their meanings. The glossary gives the following information:

1. **The entry word broken into syllables.**
2. **The pronunciation of each word.** The **respelling** is shown in parentheses. The most common way to pronounce a word is listed first. The Pronunciation Key below shows the symbols for the sounds of letters, and key words that contain those sounds. A key is repeated on every second page.

   A **primary accent** ʹ is placed after the syllable that is stressed the most when the word is spoken. A **secondary accent** ′ is placed after a syllable that has a lighter stress.
3. **The part of speech of the word.** The following abbreviations are used:

   n. noun *v.* verb *adj.* adjective *adv.* adverb
4. **The meaning of the word.** The definitions listed in the glossary apply to selected ways a word is used in these selections.
5. **Related forms.** Words with suffixes such as *-ing, -ed, -ness,* and *-ly* are listed under the base word.

ab·stract (ab strakt′ *or* ab′ strakt) *adj.* thought of apart from any particular act or object.

Pronunciation Key

a	fat	**i**	hit	**oo**	look		**a** *in* ago	**ch**	chin
ā	ape	**ir**	here	**ōō**	tool		**e** *in* agent	**sh**	she
ä	car, lot	**ī**	bite, fire	**ou**	out	**ə**	**i** *in* unity	**th**	thin
							o *in* collect	***th***	then
e	ten	**ō**	go	**u**	up		**u** *in* focus	**zh**	leisure
er	care	**ô**	law, horn	**ur**	fur			**ng**	ring
ē	even	**oi**	oil			**'l**	able		

A

a·bate (ə bāt′) *v.* to become less; weaken.

ab·bey (ab′ē) *n.* a place where a group of monks or nuns live.

ab·bot (ab′ət) *n.* a man who is the head of a group of monks.

a·bol·ish (ə bäl′ish) *v.* to do away with completely.

ab·stract (ab strakt′ *or* ab′strakt) *adj.* thought of apart from any particular act or object.

a·buse (ə byo͞oz′) *v.* to use improperly or wrongly.

a·byss (ə bis′) *n.* a great, deep crack or opening in the earth.

ac·ro·bat (ak′rə bat) *n.* a performer who does tumbling tricks.

a·cute (ə kyo͞ot′) *adj.* very severe.

ad·a·mant (ad′ə mənt) *adj.* not giving in; unyielding.

a·dapt (ə dapt′) *v.* to change so as to be made usable for a specific purpose.

af·flic·tion (a flik′shən) *n.* pain; suffering.

a·ghast (ə gast′) *adj.* feeling great shock or horror.

al·a·bas·ter (al′ə bas′tər) *adj.* smooth and white like alabaster, a stone that is carved into statues or vases.

al·cove (al′kōv) *n.* a small part of a room, set off from the main part.

al·der (ôl′dər) *n.* a small tree.

al·lies (al′īz) *n.* countries joined together by agreement or united for a special purpose.

al·lure·ment (ə lo͞or′mənt) *n.* something that attracts or tempts.

a·loft (ə lôft′) *adv.* high above the ground.

am·ber (am′bər) *adj.* having a brownish-yellow color.

am·bi·tion (am bish′ən) *n.* **1.** strong desire to be successful or to gain fame. **2.** the thing that one strongly desires.

a·men·i·ties (ə men′ə tēz) *n. plural* the polite ways people are supposed to behave.

am·pu·tate (am′pyə tāt) *v.* to cut off, surgically.

an·nals (an′ ′lz) *n. plural* a history or record of events.

an·vil (an′vəl) *n.* a steel or iron block on which heated metal objects are shaped.

anx·i·e·ty (aŋ zī′ə tē) *n.* the condition of being worried about what may happen.

a·poth·e·car·y (ə päth′ə ker′ē) *n.* a person who makes and sells medicines.

ap·plaud (ə plôd′) *v.* to show enjoyment or approval, usually by clapping one's hands or cheering.—**applause** *n.*

ap·por·tion (ə pôr′shən) *v.* to separate and give out in shares.

ap·pro·pri·ate (ə prō′prē it) *adj.* just right, or suitable for the purpose.

as·cend (ə send′) *v.* to go up; rise.

as·sail (ə sāl′) *v.* to attack with questions or arguments.

as·sault (ə sôlt′) *n.* a sudden attack.

as·ton·ish·ment (ə stän′ish ment) *n.* the state of being filled with wonder; great surprise.

as·tound (ə stound′) *v.* to amaze or greatly surprise.

a·stride (ə strīd′) *adv.* having one leg on each side.

as·tro·nom·i·cal (as′trə näm′i k′l) *adj.* having to do with the science of the stars, planets, and comets.

at·trib·ute (a′trə byo͞ot′ *or* ə trib′yoot) *n.* a quality or characteristic of a person or thing.

aug·ment (ôg ment′) *v.* to become greater.

au·to·crat·ic (ôt′ə krat′ik) *adj.* having complete power over others; forcing others.

awe (ô) *n.* deep respect mixed with wonder and fear.

az·ure (azh′ər) *adj.* sky blue.

B

ban·ish (ban′ish) *v.* **1.** to force a person to leave his or her country as a punishment. **2.** get rid of.—banishment *n.*

bank·rupt (bangk′ rupt) *adj.* not able to pay all of one's debts.

bap·tism (bap′tiz′m) *n.* the religious ceremony of dipping people in water or sprinkling water on them.

barge (barj) *n.* a large boat.

bar·rack (bar′ək) *n.* a building where soldiers live.

bar·ri·er (bar′ē ər) *n.* thing that blocks the way or keeps one from going on.

bat·tal·ion (bə tal′yən) *n.* a large group of soldiers.

ba·zaar (bə zär′) *n.* a sale of many kinds of articles, usually to raise money for charity.

bed·cham·ber (bed′chām′bər) *n.* bedroom.

bel·fry (bel′frē) *n.* the part of a tower in which a bell is hung.

bel·low (bel′ō) *v.* to roar loudly.

be·nef·i·cence (bə nef′ə səns) *n.* a gift or kind act.

be·tray (bi trā′) *v.* to fail to keep a promise or secret.

be·wil·der (bi wil′dər) *v.* to make confused.

bi·ol·o·gy (bī äl′ə jē) *n.* the science of living things.

blub·ber (blub′ər) *n.* the fat of whales.

blun·der (blun′dər) *v.* to move clumsily.

bolt (bōlt) *n.* a large amount of cloth on a roll.

boul·der (bōl′dər) *n.* a large rock.

bow·er (bou′ər) *n.* a place shaded by trees or vines.

brooch (brōch *or* brōōch) *n.* an ornamental pin often worn on a woman's dress.

buck·skin (buk′skin) *n.* a soft leather made from the skins of deer or sheep.

buf·fa·lo (buf′ə lō) *n.* a wild ox, sometimes tamed as a work animal.

bun·gle (bung′g'l) *v.* to spoil by clumsy work.

bus·tle (bus′'l) *n.* a padding worn by women to puff out the back of a skirt.

C

ca·lam·i·ty (kə lam′ə tē) *n.* a terrible happening; deep trouble; misery.

can·ton (kan′tən *or* kan tän′) *n.* a state or section of a country.

ca·pri·cious (kə prish′əs) *adj.* likely to change suddenly; flighty.

cap·tive (kap′tiv) *n.* a person caught and kept against his or her will.

car·cass (kär′kəs) *n.* the dead body of an animal.

ca·reen (kə rēn′) *v.* to move from side to side while in motion.

ca·tas·tro·phe (kə tas′trə fē) *n.* a sudden happening that causes suffering or damage.

ca·the·dral (kə thē′dral) *n.* a church.

cen·taur (sen′tôr) *n.* a creature in myths that is part man and part horse.

cha·grin (shə grin′) *n.* a feeling of being disappointed because one has failed.

chaise (shāz) *n.* a light carriage.

cham·ber (chām′bər) *n.* a room, usually a bedroom.

cha·os (kā′äs) *n.* confusion; disorder.

chap·el (chap′'l) *n.* a place to worship in.

char (chär) *v.* to burn.

chime (chīm) *v.* to ring or sound.

chop·sticks (chäp′stiks) *n. plural* a pair of small sticks used to eat with.

chor·e·o·graph (kôr′ē ə graf′) *v.* to plan dance steps and movements.—**choreographer** *n.*

---

at, āte, fär; pen, ēqual; sit, mīne; sō, côrn, join, took, fōōl, our; us, turn; **ch**ill, **sh**op, **th**ick, ***th***ey, sing; **zh** *in* measure; 'l *in* idle;
ə *in* alive, cover, family, robot, circus.

cin·der (sin′dər) *n.* a tiny bit of partly burned matter, such as coal or lava.

clar·i·fy (klar′ə fī) *n.* to make something easier to understand.

clas·sic (klas′ik) *n.* literature of high excellence.

cliff (klif) *n.* large, steep side of rock.

clois·ter (kloi s′tər) *n.* a place where nuns or monks live.

com·i·cal (käm′i k'l) *adj.* funny; amusing.

com·men·ta·tor (käm′ən tāt′ər) *n.* a person who works at reporting and commenting on the news, as on radio or TV.

com·mut·er (kə myōō′tər) *adj.* a type of vehicle used to take people to work or school.

com·pel (kəm pel′) *v.* to force to do something.

com·pet·i·tor (kəm pet′ə tər) *n.* a person who challenges another for something.

com·rade (käm′rad) *n.* a close friend or companion.

con·dense (kən dens′) *v.* to become more closely packed together; shortened.

con·de·scend (kän də send′) *v.* to mildly agree to do something beneath one's dignity.

Con·fed·er·a·cy (kən fed′ər ə sē) *n.* the eleven Southern States that seceded from the U.S. in 1860 and 1861.

con·firm (kən furm′) *v.* to make firm by approving or agreeing.

con·gest·ed (kən jest′əd) *adj.* overcrowded.

con·ges·tion (kən jes′chən) *n.* the condition of being filled with blood or other fluids.

con·jec·ture (kən jek′chər) *n.* guess; opinion formed without facts.

con·sci·en·tious (kän′shē en′shəs) *adj.* trying to be careful and correct.

con·se·crate (kän′sə krāt) *v.* to set apart as holy.

con·sent (kən sent′) *v.* to give approval.

con·stant (kän′stənt) *adj.* not changing; fixed.

con·tempt (kən tempt′) *n.* the feeling one has toward someone or something one considers low or evil.

con·ti·nent (känt′'n ənt) *n.* any of the large land areas of the earth.

con·tour (kän′toor) *n.* the outline of the shape of something.

con·trast (kän′trast) *n.* a comparison of things, noting the differences.

con·vent (kän′vent) *n.* the place where nuns live.

con·verse (kən vurs′) *v.* to talk; to have a conversation.

cor·don (kôr′ d'n) *n.* a line or circle placed around an area to guard or protect it, sometimes made up of police.

corpse (kôrps) *n.* the dead body of a person.

cor·ri·dor (kôr′ə dər) *n.* a long hall or passageway.

cos·mo·pol·i·tan (käz′mə päl′ət'n) *adj.* feeling at home anywhere.

coun·cil (koun′s'l) *n.* a group of people who gives advice to or makes laws for a village, town, or city.

coun·ci·lor (koun′sə lər) *n.* a person who advises, usually a member of a council.

coun·te·nance (koun′tə nəns) *n.* the look on a person's face.

cowl·ish (koul′ish) *adj.* shaped like a hood.

crin·o·line (krin′'l in) *n.* an old-fashioned hoop skirt.

crouch (krouch) *n.* the position of stooping with the legs bent close to the ground.

croup (krōōp) *n.* a disease that causes hoarse coughing and hard breathing.

cyl·in·der (sil′ən dər) *n.* a rounded figure with two flat ends.

D

dank (daŋgk) *adj.* unpleasantly damp.

de·cath·lon (di kath′län) *n.* an athletic contest that includes ten different events.

de·cep·tion (di sep′shən) *n.* something that deceives, or fools.

ded·i·cate (ded′ə kāt) *v.* to set aside for a special purpose.

de·fect (dē′fekt *or* di fekt′) *n.* a fault or weakness.

de·fi·ance (di fī′əns) *n.* the act of opposing a person or thing.

dell (del) *n.* a valley or sheltered place.

de·scend·ant (di sen′dənt) *n.* one who is an offspring of, or has a trait of, certain family members or ancestors.

de·scent (di sent′) *n.* the act of moving down to a lower place.

des·per·ate (des′pər it) *adj.* having lost hope.

de·spair (di sper′) *n.* a giving up or loss of hope. *v.* to give up or lose hope.

de·spise (di spīz′) *v.* to dislike strongly.

des·tin·y (des′tə nē) *n.* one's fate.

de·tract (di trakt′) *v.* to remove something desirable.

de·vice (di vīs′) *n.* a thing made or invented for some special purpose or use.

de·vise (di vīz′) *v.* to think up or plan.

de·vo·tion (di vō′shən) *n.* loyalty or strong affection.

dice (dīs) *n. plural* small cubes marked on each side with a different number of dots, used in pairs for games of chance.

di·lem·ma (di lem′ə) *n.* a situation where one must choose between two equally difficult or unpleasant things.

dis·com·fit·ed (dis cum′fit id) *adv.* in a confused or embarrassed way.

dis·com·fort (dis kum′fərt) *n.* uneasiness or lack of comfort.

dis·may (dis mā′) *n.* fear; dread; uncertainty.

dis·pose (dis pōz′) *v.* to get rid of by giving or throwing away.

dis·po·si·tion (dis′pə zish′ən) *n.* one's general nature or mood.

dis·si·pate (dis′ə pāt) *v.* to break up or make disappear.

dis·tinct (dis tiŋgkt′) *adj.* different; clearly seen, heard, or felt.

dis·trac·tion (dis trak′shən) *n.* a drawing away of attention.

doc·u·ment (däk′yə mənt) *n.* a printed or written record used to prove something.

doff (däf) *v.* to take off, as one's hat.

dole·ful (dōl′fəl) *adj.* very sad.

do·min·ion (də min′yən) *n.* land or country ruled over.

duch·y (duch′ē) *n.* land that is ruled by a duke or duchess.

du·el (do͞o′əl *or* dyo͞o′əl) *n.* a pre-arranged fight with deadly weapons between two persons; the duel is governed by strict rules and must take place in front of witnesses.

doubt (dout) *n.* being unsure of something.

down·trod·den (doun′träd′′n) *n.* those forced to live in poverty and slavery.

draw·bridge (drô′brij) *n.* a bridge that can be raised or lowered to keep someone from crossing.

dumb·found (dum′found′) *v.* to astonish.

dun·geon (dun′jən) *n.* a dark underground room used as a prison.

dwel·ler (dwel′′r) *n.* one who lives in a particular place.

dy·na·mo (dī′nə mō) *n.* a machine for changing mechanical energy into electricity.

---

at, āte, fär; pen, ēqual; sit, mīne; sō, côrn, join, took, fo͞ol, our; us, turn; **ch**ill, **sh**op, **th**ick, ***th***ey, siŋ; **zh** *in* measure; ′l *in* idle;
ə *in* alive, cover, family, robot, circus.

E

e·clipse (i klips′) *n.* a hiding of the sun by the moon as it passes between the sun and the earth.

ec·stat·ic (ek stat′ik) *adj.* full of joy.

em·bed (im bed′) *v.* to set in earth.

e·ma·ci·ate (i mā′shē āt) *v.* to make very thin.

e·merge (i murj′) *v.* to come out so as to be seen.

em·i·nent (em′ə nənt) *adj.* very famous.

en·camp·ment (in kamp′mənt) *n.* a place set up for people to camp or rest.

en·dure (in door′ *or* in dyoor′) *v.* to put up with pain or weariness.

en·trails (en′trālz) *n. plural* the parts inside an animal's body.

e·rad·i·cate (i rad′ə kāt) *v.* to remove completely; get rid of.

e·rup·tion (i rup′shən) *n.* an explosion; a bursting or throwing forth.

es·cort (es kôrt′) *v.* to accompany someone.

es·sence (es′'ns) *n.* the most important or basic quality of something.

e·ter·nal (i tur′n'l) *adj.* seeming to have no end; continual.

e·the·re·al (i thir′ē əl) *adj.* like the upper regions of space.

e·vac·u·ate (i vak′yoo wāt) *v.* to leave.

ex·as·per·ate (ig zas′pə rāt) *n.* to annoy very much.

ex·cuse (ik skyōōs′) **1.** *n.* an explanation for an action. **2.** *v.* to forgive or pardon.

ex·e·cu·tion (ek′sə kyōō′shən) *n.* the act of putting someone to death.

ex·pose (ik spōz′) *v.* to let be seen; leave unprotected.

ex·ter·mi·nate (ik stur′mə nāt) *v.* to destroy completely.

ex·trav·a·gant (ik strav′ə gənt) *adj.* too ornate or showy. — **extravagantly** *adv.*

F

fa·ble (fā′b'l) *n.* a story that is not true.

fates (fāts) *n. plural* three goddesses who controlled human life in Greek mythology.

fath·om (fa*th*′əm) *n.* a length of six feet, used as a unit of measure for the depth of water.

fa·tigue (fə tēg′) *n.* a tired feeling as from hard work or not enough rest.

feat (fēt) *n.* something done that shows great skill or strength.

fis·tu·la (fis′choo lə) *n.* an open sore or ulcer.

flex (fleks) *v.* to bend.

floss (flôs) *n.* soft and silky fiber.

fluc·tu·ate (fluk′choo wāt) *v.* to rise and fall; keep changing.—**fluctuation** *n.*

fol·ly (fäl′ē′) *n.* a foolish action.

fore·man (fôr′mən) *n.* a person in charge of a group of workers.

for·feit (fôr′fit) *v.* to give up or lose something.

for·lorn (fər lôrn′) *adj.* sad because of being lonely or uncared for.

for·tress (fôr′trəs) *n.* a building with strong walls for defending against an enemy.

fra·grance (frā′grəns) *n.* a pleasant smell.

fran·tic (fran′tik) *adj.* very upset with anger or worry.—**frantically** *adv.*

fraud (frôd) *n.* a cheating or tricking; dishonesty.

fric·tion (frik′shən) *n.* the contact of one thing against another.

frus·trate (frus′trāt) *v.* to keep a person from doing what that person wants, or to keep a thing from being done.—**frustration** *n.*

G

gal·lant (gal′ənt) *adj.* brave and daring.

gal·li·vant (gal′ə vant′) *v.* to go out in search of amusement or excitement.

gan·grene (gaŋ′grēn) *n.* decay of a part of the body from which the blood is blocked by injury or disease.
gar·ment (gär′mənt) *n.* a piece of clothing.
gasp (gasp) *v.* to breathe in suddenly, as in surprise.
gaud·y (gôd′ē) *adj.* bright and showy.
gav·el (gav′'l) *n.* a small wooden hammer that a judge or chairperson taps on the table to call for attention.
gaunt (gônt) *adj.* looking worn and thin.
gen·darme (zhän′därm) *n.* a police officer in France.
gen·er·a·tion (jen′ə rā′shən) *n.* people born about the same time.
ges·tic·u·late (jes tik′yoo͞ lāt) *v.* to make motions with the hands and arms.
gore (gôr) *v.* to stab with a horn or tusk.
gran·deur (gran′jər) *n.* great dignity or style.
gran·ite (gran′it) *n.* rock used for buildings and monuments.
grap·ple (grap′'l) *v.* to fight or struggle.
grav·i·ty (grav′ə tē) *n.* the condition of being serious.
gren·a·dier (gren ə dir′) *n.* a soldier.
grieve (grēv) *v.* to feel deep sadness.
grim (grim) *adj.* frightful; cruel.
grope (grōp) *v.* to look for or find by feeling about.
grove (grōv) *n.* a group of trees.
guil·der (gil′dər) *n.* a unit of money in the Netherlands.
gul·ly (gul′ē) *v.* a narrow channel worn by water.
gust (gust) *n.* a strong, sudden rush of something carried by the air, such as rain.

H

hag·gard (hag′ərd) *adj.* having a wild-eyed, exhausted look.
halt (hôlt) *v.* to stop.
hap·haz·ard (hap haz′ərd) *adj.* not in any planned order.—**haphazardly** *adv.*
has·sle (has′'l) *v.* to argue about the price of something.
haugh·ty (hôt′ē) *adj.* showing too much pride in oneself.
her·mit (hʉr′mit) *n.* one who lives alone.
her·mit·age (hʉr′mit ij) *n.* a place where a person can live apart from other people.
hid·e·ous (hid′ē əs) *adj.* very ugly.
hom·age (häm′ij *or* äm′ij) *n.* the act of showing honor or respect.
ho·ri·zon (hə rī′z'n) *n.* the line where the sky seems to meet the earth.
hos·pi·tal·i·ty (häs′pə tal′ə tē) *n.* a friendly and kind way of treating guests.
hov·er (huv′ər *or* häv′ər) *v.* to stay or wait near one place.
hulk (hulk) *n.* the body of a ship.
hum·bug (hum′bug) *n.* a fraud, or hoax.
hum·drum (hum′drum) *adj.* dull or boring, monotonous.
hu·mil·i·ate (hyoo͞ mil′ē āt) *v.* to make one feel ashamed or embarrassed.
hys·te·ri·a (his ter′ē ə) *n.* an outbreak of emotional excitement or anxiety.

I

ig·loo (ig′lo͞o) *n.* a small house built by using blocks of packed snow.
im·meas·ur·a·ble (i mezh′ər ə b'l) *adj.* too large or too much to be measured.
im·mi·grant (im′ə grənt) *adj.* relating to those who come into a different land to make a new home.

---

at, āte, fär; pen, ēqual; sit, mīne; sō, côrn, join, to͝ok, fo͞ol, our; us, turn; chill, shop, thick, they, siŋ; zh *in* measure; 'l *in* idle;
ə *in* alive, cover, family, robot, circus.

im·pas·sioned (im pash′ ənd) *adj.* having or showing strong feelings or emotions.

im·pa·tient (im pā′shənt) *adj.* lack of patience.

im·pet·u·ous (im pech′o͞o wəs) *adj.* rushing into action.

im·pulse (im′puls) *n.* a sudden feeling that makes one want to do something.

in·can·des·cent (in′kən des′′nt) *adj.* glowing with great heat.

in·ca·pac·i·tate (in′kə pas′ə tāt) *v.* to disable.

in·cen·tive (in sen′tiv) *n.* the thing that makes one want to work or try something.

in·ci·dent (in′si dənt) *n.* something that happened; event.

in·de·cent (in dē′s′nt) *adj.* not proper, moral, or modest.

in·de·scrib·a·ble (in′di skrī′bə b′l) *adj.* too beautiful or too horrible to describe.

in·dig·nant (in dig′nənt) *adj.* angry about something.

in·flux (in′fluks) *n.* a coming in or pouring in.

in·scrip·tion (in skrip′shən) *n.* something printed or written on a large stone, a coin, or in a book.

in·spi·ra·tion (in′spə rā′shən) *n.* an idea or action that gives one cause or influence to do something.

in·ter·mit·tent (in′tər mit′′nt) *adj.* stopping and starting again.

in·ter·vene (in tər vēn′) *v.* to come in so as to help or settle.

in·tri·cate (in′tri kit) *adj.* full of difficult or complicated parts.

in·tu·i·tive (in to͞o′ i tive *or* in tyo͞o′ i tive) *adj.* knowing about something without actually thinking it out.—**intuitively** *adv.*

in·vi·o·late (in vī′ə lit *or* in vī′ə lāt) *adj.* not broken or violated; kept sacred.

in·vis·i·ble (in viz′ə b′l) *adj.* cannot be seen.

ir·rel·e·vant (i rel′ə vənt) *adj.* having nothing to do with the subject.—**irrelevantly** *adv.*

ir·ri·gate (ir′ə gāt) *v.* to water by means of canals, ditches, or pipes.—**irrigation** *n.*

i·so·late (ī′sə lāt) *v.* to set apart from others; place alone.—**isolation** *n.*

J

joust (joust *or* just) *n.* a fight between two knights on horseback using a sword-like pole.

K

ki·mo·no (kə mō′nə) *n.* a loose robe with wide sleeves and a sash.

knap·sack (nap′sak) *n.* a leather or canvas bag worn on the back to carry supplies.

knight (nīt) *n.* a man who is given a military rank of honor for service or deeds.

knight·hood (nīt′ho͝od) *n.* the rank or position of being a knight.

L

la·bour (lā′bər) *n.* British spelling of *labor,* meaning work.

la·dle (lā′d′l) *n.* a cuplike spoon with a long handle.

land·scape (land′skāp) *n.* a stretch of land that can be seen in one view.

lan·guor (laŋ′gər) *n.* a feeling of being weak or tired.

lar·i·at (lar′ē it) *n.* a rope used for tying a horse or other animal.

le·gion (lē′jən) *n.* a large group of soldiers.

list·less (list′lis) *adj.* having little energy or interest because one is tired, sick, or sad.—**listlessly** *adv.*

lodg·ings (läj′iŋz) *n. plural* a place to live, usually rented from somebody.

log·ger·heads (lôg′ər hedz) *n. plural* arguing; disagreeing.

lot (lät) *n.* **1.** a counter or slip of paper that people choose without looking, in deciding something by chance. **2.** one's condition; fate.

lu·na·tic (lo͞o'nə tik) *adj.* of or for insane or mentally ill persons.

M

mag·na·nim·i·ty (mag'nə nim'ə tē) *n.* the act of being generous.

mag·nif·i·cence (mag nif'ə s'ns) *n.* grand beauty; splendor.

mag·ni·fy (mag'nə fī) *v.* to make, look, or seem larger than is really so.

ma·jes·tic (mə jes'tik) *adj.* grand; stately; dignified.—**majestically** *adv.*

mare (mer) *n.* a female horse.

mast (mast) *n.* a tall pole set upright on a ship for supporting the sails.

mea·ger (mē'gər) *adj.* small amount.

mel·an·cho·ly (mel'ən käl'ē) *adj.* sad or depressed.

mem·bra·nous (mem'brə nəs) *adj.* of or like a thin layer of tissue that covers a part of an animal or plant.

mer·ci·ful (mur'si fəl) *adj.* kind; forgiving.

me·te·or (mēt'ē ər) *n.* a small solid body that moves with great speed from outer space into the air around the earth.

me·te·or·ite (mēt'ē ə rīt) *n.* a small chunk of metal or stone remaining from a meteor that has fallen upon the earth.

mill (mil) *v.* to move slowly.

min·i·a·ture (min'ē ə chər *or* min'i chər) *adj.* that is a small copy of something larger.

min·now (min'ō) *n.* a very small fish.

min·strel (min'strəl) *n.* an entertainer who travels about singing and reciting poems.

mi·ser (mī'zər) *n.* a greedy, stingy person who saves up money.

mod·er·a·tor (mäd'ə rāt'ər) *n.* a person in charge of a discussion or debate.

mole (mōl) *n.* a small, insect-eating, furry animal that burrows underground.

mon·arch (män'ərk) *n.* a ruler, as a king, queen, or emperor.

mon·grel (muŋ'grəl *or* mäŋ'grəl) *n.* an animal who has mixed breed or origin.

mo·not·o·ny (mə nät''nē) *n.* lack of variety.

moor·ings (mo͝or'iŋz) *n. plural* a place where a ship is anchored.

mor·sel (môr's'l) *n.* a small bit of food.

mor·tal (môr't'l) *adj.* of people as beings who must die.

moss (môs) *n.* tiny green plants.

moult (mōlt) *v.* British spelling of *molt,* meaning to shed skin, or feathers, before getting a new growth.

mount (mount) *n.* a horse for riding.

mul·ti·lat·er·al (mul'ti lat'ər əl) *adj.* having many sides.

mul·ti·tude (mul'tə to͞od *or* mul'tə tyo͞od) *n.* a large number of persons or things.

mul·ti·tu·di·nous (mul'tə'to͞od 'n əs *or* mul' tə tyo͞od''n əs) *adj.* very many; numerous

mus·ter (mus'tər) *n.* the gathering.

mu·tu·al (myo͞o'cho͞o wəl) *adj.* shared.

myth·i·cal (mith'i k'l) *adj.* of, in, or like a myth; imaginary.

N

new·fan·gled (no͞o faŋ'g'ld *or* nyo͞o'faŋ g'ld) *adj.* new and strange.

North Pole (nôrth' pōl') *n.* that point on the earth that is farthest north.

nudge (nuj) *v.* to push or poke gently.

numb·ness (num'nis) *n.* the condition of not being able to feel, or feel very little.

---

at, āte, fär; pen, ēqual; sit, mīne; sō, côrn, join, to͝ok, fo͞ol, our; us, turn; **ch**ill, **sh**op, **th**ick, ***th***ey, siŋ; **zh** *in* measure; 'l *in* idle;
ə *in* alive, cover, family, robot, circus.

O

o·be·di·ent (ō bē′dē ənt) *adj.* doing what one is told.

ob·serv·a·tory (əb zʉr′və tôr′ē) *n.* a building with telescopes and other equipment in it for studying things in space.

ob·sta·cle (äb′sti k'l) *n.* something that gets in the way or keeps one from going ahead.

oc·u·list (äk′yə list) *n.* a doctor who treats diseases of the eye.

om·in·ous (äm′ə nəs) *adj.* like a bad omen; threatening.—**ominously** *adv.*

om·nis·cient (äm nish′ənt) *adj.* knowing everything.

op·pres·sor (ə pres′ər) *n.* one who rules in a cruel way.

out·land·ish (ʊut lan′dish) *adj.* unusual or strange.

P

pact (pakt) *n.* an agreement between persons or groups.

pa·go·da (pə gō′də) *n.* a temple in the form of a tower, found in Japan or China.

pal·ate (pal′it) *n.* appreciation, or taste.

pal·lor (pal′ər) *n.* paleness of the face, that comes from being sick, worried, or tired.

pan·o·ra·ma (pan′ə ram′ə) *n.* a picture or model of a view or event.

par·a·bol·ic (par′ə bäl′ik) *adj.* curved, bowl-shaped.

par·a·sol (par′ə sôl) *n.* a light umbrella.

pas·sion (pash′ən) *n.* strong feeling or emotion.—**passionate** *adj.*

pass·port (pas′pôrt) *n.* an official paper given by a government to a citizen to prove that person's identity.

pas·tor·al (pas′tər əl) *adj.* peaceful, as life in the country.

pa·tience (pā′shəns) *n.* ability to bear discomfort while remaining calm.

pa·tri·ot (pā′trē ət) *n.* a person who shows great love for his or her country.

pa·tron (pā′trən) *n.* supporter or regular customer.

pea·cock (pē′käk) *n.* a large bird, having long tail feathers of bright colors.

peb·ble (peb′'l) *n.* a small stone.

pen·ance (pen′əns) *n.* suffering that one takes on to show apology for one's wrongdoing.

pen·e·trate (pen′ə trāt) *v.* to spread through.

per·cep·tion (pər sep′shən) *n.* the ability to understand.

per·di·tion (pər dish′ən) *n.* evil; ruin.

per·il (per′əl) *n.* a condition of possible danger and destruction.

per·ish (per′ish) *v.* to die; be destroyed.

per·pet·u·al (pər pech′ʊʊ wəl) *adj.* lasting for a long time or forever.

per·plex (pər pleks′) *v.* to make unsure of what to do; confuse or puzzle.

pe·so (pā′sō) *n.* a unit of money in Puerto Rico and other Hispanic countries.

phan·tom (fan′təm) *adj.* ghostly; shadowy.

phe·nom·e·non (fi näm′ə nän) *n.* something unusual or remarkable.

pi·ous (pī′əs) *adj.* dutiful; devoted.

pir·ou·ette (pir′ʊʊ wet′) *v.* to whirl on one's toes, as in dancing.

plague (plāg) *n.* a deadly disease.

plat·form (plat′fôrm) *n.* a stage higher than the ground or floor around it.

plum·met (plum′it) *n.* a metal weight hung at the end of a line, used to find how deep the water is.

plun·der (plun′dər) *v.* to rob or take something away.

poise (pɔiz) *v.* to balance or be held in balance.

pon·der (pän′dər) *v.* to think deeply; consider carefully.

pop·lar (päp′lər) *n.* a tall tree.
por·ti·co (pôr′tə kō) *n.* a porch or covered walk.
pounce (pouns) *v.* to spring on; attack.
pov·er·ty-strick·en (päv′ər tē strik′′n) *adj.* very poor.
prai·rie schoon·er (prar′ē sko͞o′nər) *n.* a large covered wagon used by pioneers.
pre·cede (pri sēd′) *v.* to go or come before.
prel·ude (prel′yo͞od *or* pre′lo͞od) *n.* the part that comes before or leads up to what follows.
prey (prā) *n.* a person or animal that is the victim of someone or something.
pri·mal (prī′m'l) *adj.* first in time; original.
prim·i·tive (prim′ə tiv) *adj.* like that of earliest times.
pro·ceeds (prō′sēdz) *n. plural* the money or profit from a business activity.
pro·ces·sion (prə sesh′ən) *n.* a group of persons or things moving forward in an orderly way.
pro·claim (prō klām′) *v.* to announce; make known publicly.
proc·la·ma·tion (prök′lə mā′shən) *n.* a public announcement.
pro·found (prə found′) *adj.* intense; very strong or deep.—**profoundly** *adv.*
pro·phet·ic (prə fet′ik) *adj.* telling what will happen in the future.
prop·o·si·tion (präp′ə zish′ən) *n.* a belief or idea, discussed and decided upon.
pros·per·i·ty (prä spar′ə tē) *n.* a condition of good fortune or success.
pros·trate (präs′trāt) *adj.* lying flat, as on one's back or one's face.
pul·sate (pul′sāt) *v.* to beat or throb in a regular rhythm.
pu·ri·fy (pyoor′ə fī) *v.* to make clean.
pur·sue (pər so͞o′ *or* per syo͞o′) *v.* to follow in order to catch.—**pursuer** *n.*

Q

quad·rant (kwäd′rənt) *n.* section or part, usually a fourth of a circle.
quar·ry (kwôr′ē) *v.* take from a place where stone is cut or blasted out of the earth.
quest (kwest) *n.* a journey or search, often for adventure.
quick·sil·ver (kwik′sil′vər) *adj.* like the liquid metal mercury; often used to mean fast or flowing.
quill (kwil) *n.* a large tail feather of a bird. **quillwork**—a number of quills tied or sewed in a design.

R

ra·di·ant (rā′dē ənt) *adj.* **1.** shining brightly; **2.** showing pleasure.
ra·di·us (rā′dē əs) *n.* a distance measured from a line that goes from the center to the outside of a circular area.
ram·ble (ram′b'l) *v.* to walk along without any special goal.
ran·som (ran′səm) *n.* the price asked or paid for freeing a captured person.
rap·ture (rap′chər) *n.* a deep feeling of joy.
ras·cal (ras′k'l) *n.* a dishonest person, usually full of tricks.
raw·hide (rô′hīd) *n.* cattle hide; a kind of leather.
realm (relm) *n.* a region or area, sometimes of the imagination.
re·buke (ri byo͞ok′) *v.* to scold sharply.
re·con·struc·tion (rē kən struk′shən) *n.* the process of rebuilding.
reed (rēd) *n.* the stem of tall grass, growing in wet land.

---

at, āte, fär; pen, ēqual; sit, mīne; sō, côrn, join, took, fo͞ol, our; us, turn; chill, shop, thick, *th*ey, sing; zh *in* measure; 'l *in* idle;
ə *in* alive, cover, family, robot, circus.

reign (rān) *n.* the rule of a king, queen, or emperor. *v.* to rule.

rein (rān) *v.* to pull or guide with reins, narrow straps used to control a horse.

re·pent (ri pent′) *v.* to feel sorry for having done something wrong.

rep·u·ta·tion (rep′yo͞o tā′shən) *n.* what people generally think about a person or thing.

res·er·va·tion (rez′ər vā′shən) *n.* land set aside for special use, as for Indians.

re·solve (ri zälv′) *n.* something decided upon; one's intention.

re·sound (ri zound′) *v.* to make a loud sound.

ret·i·nue (ret′'n o͞o *or* ret′'n yo͞o) *n.* the servants or followers of an important person.

rev·e·nue (rev′ə no͞o *or* rev′ə nyo͞o) *n.* money received, especially the money a government gets from taxes or duties.

re·vive (ri vīv′) *v.* to bring back, such as interest in something.

rheu·ma·tism (ro͞o′ mə tiz′m) *n.* a disease in which the joints and muscles become stiff, sore, and swollen.

rogue (rōg) *n.* a tricky person, sometimes dishonest, who often likes to have fun.

ru·di·ment (ro͞o′də mənt) *n.* something to be learned first; something basic.

S

sa·cred (sā′krid) *adj.* having to do with a religious or holy purpose.

sac·ris·ty (sak′ris tē) *n.* a room in a church where the vestments, linens and altar articles are kept.

sash (sash) *n.* a band or scarf worn over the shoulder or around the waist.

sat·in (sat′'n) *n.* a cloth or like a cloth, having a smooth, glossy finish.

schol·ar (skäl′ər) *n.* a person who has learned much through study.

scorn·ful (skôrn′fəl) *adj.* showing dislike or hatred towards something mean or evil.

scoun·drel (skoun′drəl) *n.* a dishonest person; rascal.

scroll (skrōl) *n.* a roll of paper or parchment, usually with writing or a design on it.

scru·ti·nize (skro͞ot′'n īz) *v.* to look at very carefully; examine closely.

scur·vy (skur′vē) *n.* a disease that is caused by a lack of vitamin C; involves weakness and bleeding gums.

sedge (sej) *n.* a plant like coarse grass.

seed·ling (sēd′liŋ) *n.* a young plant grown from a seed.

seis·mo·graph (sīz′mə graf) *n.* an instrument used to measure the strength of earthquakes or explosions.

se·lect·man (sə lekt′mən) *n.* an officer elected to serve on a board, or committee, of a town or city.

sem·i·cir·cu·lar (sem′i sur′kyə lər) *adj.* having a half-circle shape.

sen·si·tive (sen′sə tiv) *adj.* quick to feel, notice, or appreciate.

sen·ti·nel (sen′ti n'l) *n.* a person who keeps watch to guard a group.

se·ren·i·ty (sə ren′ə tē) *n.* a state of calmness.

serf·dom (surf′dum) *n.* the practice of keeping slaves, called serfs.

se·ver·i·ty (sə ver′ə tē) *n.* seriousness; harshness.

shaft (shaft) *n.* an arrow or spear.

sheath (shēth) *n.* a case for holding a sword.

sheer (shir) *adj.* straight up or down; very deep.

shep·herd (shep′ərd) *n.* a person who takes care of sheep.

shil·ling (shil′iŋ) *n.* a silver coin in Great Britain.

shorn (shôrn) *v.* cut.

shreds (shredz) *n.* pieces cut or torn off.

shrewd (shro͞od) *adj.* sharp; piercing, as in looks.

shroud (shrʊud) *n.* a sheet or gown which a dead person wears before burial.
shud·der (shud'ər) *v.* to tremble.
si·dle (sī'd'l) *v.* to move sideways.
sig·nif·i·cance (sig nif'ə kəns) *n.* importance.
si·lo (sī'lō) *n.* a storage tower, usually for grain.
sin·is·ter (sin'is tər) *adj.* that threatens something bad.
sledge (slej) *n.* a large sled for carrying loads over ice and snow.
smith·er·eens (smi*th* ə rēnz') *n. plural* small bits and pieces.
sol·emn (säl'əm) *adj.* serious.
sol·i·tar·y (säl'ə ter'ē) *adj.* living or being alone; single.
so·lo (sō'lō) *adj.* for or by one person, as a dancer or singer.
som·bre (säm'bər) *adj.* an old spelling of somber, meaning gloomy or serious.
spar (spär) *n.* a strong, heavy pole for holding up the sails on a ship.
spec·tral (spek'trəl) *adj.* ghostly; like a phantom.
spec·u·late (spek'yə lāt) *v.* to think about or make guesses; ponder.—**speculation** *n.*
sphere (sfir) *n.* the place or range of action or being.
sphe·roid (sfir'ʊid) *n.* a round object, shaped like a sphere, such as a planet.
sprat (sprat) *n.* a small fish.
stal·lion (stal'yən) *n.* a male horse.
stam·i·na (stam'ə nə) *n.* the strength to carry on or endure.
stealth·y (stel'thē) *adj.* quiet, so as not to be seen or heard.
steed (stēd) *n.* a horse, especially a lively riding horse.
stim·u·late (stim'yə lāt) *v.* to make more active; arouse.
stim·u·lus (stim'yə ləs) *n.* something that causes some action or activity.
sting·ray (stiŋ'rā) *n.* a large flat fish with a sharp spine on its tail, that can cause serious wounds.
stress (stres) *n.* pressure, mental or physical.
strew (stro͞o) *v.* to scatter or spread about.—**strewn.**
strid·u·late (strij'yə lāt') *v.* a chirping or grating sound made by rubbing body parts, as certain insects do.—**stridulation** *n.*
strife (strīf) *n.* struggle; conflict.
stu·pe·fac·tion (sto͞o'pə fak'shən) *n.* amazement; astonishment.
sty·mie (stī'mē) *v.* to hold back a person from doing something.
sub·sti·tute (sub'stə to͞ot *or* sub'stə tyo͞ot) *n.* a person or thing that takes the place of another.
sub·tle (sut''l) *adj.* not strong; delicate.
suc·ces·sion (sək sesh'ən) *n.* a number of things coming one after another.
sulk (sulk) *v.* to turn away and be aloof.
sul·try (sul'trē) *adj.* hot and damp, without a breeze.
su·per·in·tend (so͞o'pər in tend') *v.* to direct or supervise.
su·per·in·tend·ent (so͞o'per in ten'dənt) *n.* a person in charge of a large building or group of people.
sur·cin·gle (sʉr'siŋ'g'l) *n.* a strap put around a horse to hold a saddle or a pack.
sur·rey (sʉr'ē) *n.* a light covered carriage.
sur·vey (sər'vā) *n.* the act of measuring the size and shape of a piece of land by the use of special instruments.
swerve (swʉrv) *v.* to move or turn from a straight line or path.

---

at, āte, fär; pen, ēqual; sit, mīne; sō, côrn, jʊin, tʊok, fo͞ol, ʊur; us, tʉrn; **ch**ill, **sh**op, **th**ick, ***th***ey, siŋ; **zh** *in* measure; 'l *in* idle;
ə *in* alive, cover, family, robot, circus.

sym·met·ri·cal (si met′ri k'l) *adj.* balanced; alike in arrangement.

sym·pa·thize (sim′pə thīz) *v.* to share the feelings or ideas of another.

T

tan·gi·ble (tan′jə b'l) *adj.* that can be touched.

tan·ner (tan′ər) *n.* a person who makes leather from animal hides, by tanning (soaking in acid).—**tannery** *n.*

tat·tered (tat′ərd) *adj.* torn and ragged.

taunt (tônt *or* tänt) *v.* to make fun of; to tease with scorn.

taut (tôt) *adj.* tightly stretched, as a rope.

tax (taks) *v.* to accuse.

tech·nique (tek nēk′) *n.* style; a particular way of doing something.

tem·pest (tem′pist) *n.* a wild outburst of feeling or action.

ter·mite (tur′mīt) *n.* a small insect that eats wood and damages wooden buildings.

ter·race (ter′əs) *n.* a flat area of earth, as on a hillside.

ter·rain (tə rān′) *n.* ground or area of land.

thim·ble (thim′b'l) *n.* a cap of metal worn as a protection on the finger in sewing.

thong (thông) *n.* a narrow strip of leather, used as lace or strap.

thor·ough·fare (thur′ə fer) *n.* a main street or highway.

thresh·old (thresh′ōld *or* thresh′hōld) *n.* a piece of wood or stone beneath a door.

throb (thräb) *v.* to beat hard or fast, as the heart does when excited.

throne (thrōn) *n.* the position of power of a king or other monarch.

tour·na·ment (toor′nə mənt) *n.* a contest.

traipse (trāps) *v.* to walk or wander in an aimless way.

trai·tor (trāt′ər) *n.* a person who betrays his or her country, friends, or cause.

tran·quil (traŋ′kwəl) *adj.* calm; peaceful.

trans·con·ti·nen·tal (trans′kän tə nen′t'l) *adj.* that goes across a continent, or land area.

trans·fix (trans fiks′) *v.* to make unmovable; to hold fast.

trans·mis·sion (trans mish′ən) *n.* the moving of radio waves through space.

trans·verse (trans vurs′) *adj.* lying across; set crosswise.

trav·erse (tra vurs′ *or* trav′ərs) *v.* to pass over or through; cross.

treach·er·y (trech′ər ē) *n.* the act of disloyalty or betraying those who have trusted one.

tread (tred) *n.* a way or sound of walking.

trea·son (trē′z'n) *n.* the act of betraying one's country.

trem·u·lous (trem′yoo ləs) *adj.* trembling or quivering.

tri·col·ored (trī′kul ərd) *adj.* having three colors.

tri·pod (trī′päd) *n.* a stand or frame with three legs, often used to hold up cameras or telescopes.

troop (troop) *v.* to move in a crowd.

truce (troos) *n.* a stop in fighting or war, because both sides have agreed.

trun·dle (trun′d'l) *v.* to move or roll along.

tu·mult (too′mult *or* tyoo′mult) *n.* loud noise or uproar.

turn·key (turn′kē) *n.* a person in charge of the keys of a prison.

tur·moil (tur′moil) *n.* an excited or confused condition.

tusk (tusk) *n.* a long, pointed tooth, usually one of a pair, that sticks out of the mouth, as in elephants.

tus·sle (tus′'l) *n.* a short struggle.

tyr·an·ny (tir′ə nē) *n.* a cruel and unjust use of power.

ty·rant (tī′rənt) *n.* a cruel person, often a ruler.

U

un·con·scious (un kän′shəs) *adj.* not able to feel and think.
u·nite (yoo nīt′) *v.* to join together; combine.
un·prec·e·dent·ed (un pres′ə den′tid) *adj.* not done or known before.
ul·ti·mate (ul′tə mit) *adj.* greatest possible.

V

vag·a·bond (vag′ə bänd) *n.* a person who wanders from place to place.
vague (vāg) *adj.* not clear or definite as in form or meaning.
vain (vān) *adj.* **1.** having too high an opinion of oneself. **2.** with little or no result; not successful.—**vainly** *adv.*
val·iant (val′yənt) *adj.* brave; courageous.
van·guard (van′gärd) *n.* the front of an army.
van·i·ty (van′ə tē) *n.* the quality of being vain, having too high an opinion of oneself.
var·i·a·tion (ver′ē ā′shən) *n.* the act of changing, or differing.
venge·ance (ven′jəns) *n.* the act of getting even for a wrong or injury.
venge·ful (venj′fəl) *adj.* wanting to get even or punish someone for some wrongdoing.
ven·ture (ven′chər) *v.* to go in spite of danger or risk.
ver·ba·tim (vər bāt′əm) *adj.* in exactly the same words.
vex (veks) *v.* to trouble, disturb, or annoy.
vin·dic·tive (vin dik′tiv) *adj.* wanting to get revenge or do harm in return for harm.—**vindictiveness** *n.*
vis·age (viz′ij) *n.* the face, especially as showing one's feelings.
vi·sion (vizh′ən) *n.* something seen in the mind, in a dream, or in a supernatural way.
vo·cal (vō′k'l) *adj.* speaking or making sounds openly or strongly.
void (void) *n.* an empty space.
vol·ca·no (väl kā′nō) *n.* an opening in the earth's surface through which molten rock is thrown up.—**volcanic** *adj.*
vo·rac·i·ty (vô ras′ə tē) *n.* the act of eating food rapidly or greedily.
vow (vou) *n.* a solemn promise or pledge.
vul·ture (vul′chər) *n.* a large bird related to eagles and hawks that eats dead animals.

W

wasp (wäsp *or* wôsp) *n.* a flying insect.
wa·ver (wā′ver) *v.* to flutter; tremble.
wea·ry (wir′ē) *adj.* tired; worn out.
whin·ny (hwin′ē) *v.* to make a low neighing sound, as a horse.
whole·sale (hōl′sāl) *adj.* widespread; general.
wield (wēld) *v.* to use with skill.
wind·jam·mer (wind′jam′ər) *n.* a large sailing ship.
witch·craft (wich′kraft) *n.* the magic power of a witch.
wit·ty (wit′ē) *adj.* clever in an amusing way.
wrench (rench) *v.* to pull sharply.
writhe (rīth) *v.* to twist and turn; squirm.

Y

yawn (yôn) *v.* to open wide.

Z

zeal·ous (zel′əs) *adj.* very eager; enthusiastic.—**zealously** *adv.*
ze·nith (zē′nith) *n.* the highest point that one can see in the sky.
zone (zōn) *n.* an area set apart in some special way.

---

at, āte, fär; pen, ēqual; sit, mīne; sō, côrn, join, took, fool, our; us, turn; chill, shop, thick, they, sing; zh *in* measure; ′l *in* idle;
ə *in* alive, cover, family, robot, circus.

Biographies of Authors

Joan Aiken

Joan Aiken *(born 1924)* has been writing stories and poems since the age of five. She grew up in England, the daughter of an American poet. Aiken's writing career included working for a magazine and a radio station. She has a rich imagination and makes use of fantasy, mystery, and humor. *The Whispering Mountain* and *The Wolves of Willoughby Chase* are two of her popular books.

Ricardo Alegría *(born 1921)* lives in San Juan, Puerto Rico, the place of his birth. He writes mostly about history, but is also well known for a collection of Puerto Rican folk tales, *The Three Wishes.* Alegria has taught history at the University of Puerto Rico and is now the director of the Center of Advanced Studies of Puerto Rico and the Caribbean.

Sally Andresen *(born 1947)* was raised on a farm in Iowa. After graduating from Iowa State University, she became a junior high school teacher. Andresen wrote the poem "Fall" when she was in the ninth grade, for an English assignment.

Photograph © 1985 by Jill Krementz

Isaac Asimov

Isaac Asimov *(born 1920)* came with his family to the United States from Russia at the age of three. As a boy, he loved reading science fiction magazines. This reading stimulated Asimov's interest in science. He studied at Columbia University and then became a professor at Boston University School of Medicine. Asimov has written hundreds of books and articles on scientific and other subjects, but he is best known for his science fiction stories.

Herbert Asquith *(1881–1947)* was the son of a statesman who was a member of Parliament in England. He became a lawyer and served as a captain in the army. Asquith was known for his novels as well as his poetry.

Stephen Vincent Benét

Katharine Lee Bates *(1859–1929)* was born in Massachusetts and graduated from Wellesley College, where she later taught. Bates won fame for writing the words for the patriotic song, "America the Beautiful." The melody for the song was written by Samuel A. Ward. Bates is also known for her short stories and travel books.

Stephen Vincent Benét *(1898–1943)* was born in Bethlehem, Pennsylvania, to a family of famous writers. He studied literature at Yale University and then traveled to Paris to study and write. There he met his future wife, Rosemary, who was working as a newspaper reporter. Benét's works include novels, short stories, and poetry, as well as radio and film scripts. He won fame for the short story "The Devil and Daniel Webster" and a short novel in ballad form, *John Brown's Body.*

Hal Borland

Hal Borland *(born 1900)* grew up on the American frontier. He was greatly influenced by his childhood experiences. After completing high school, he worked his way through the University of Colorado by taking a job as a newspaper correspondent. Borland lived on a farm and had a deep interest in nature. His essays about outdoor life appeared in the *New York Times* for more than twenty years.

Pearl S. Buck

Pearl S. Buck *(1892–1973)* left her birthplace of West Virginia as a child to live in China, where her parents were missionaries. She came back to the United States to attend college, but returned to China many times. Buck's stories and novels depict the lives of common Chinese people, many of them farmers or fishermen. *The Good Earth* won a Pulitzer Prize in 1932.

Dorothy Canfield *(1879–1958)* was born in Kansas, the daughter of a teacher and an artist. She attended college in Ohio, New York, and France, but felt most at home in rural Vermont. Canfield wrote short stories and novels, also under her married name of Dorothy Canfield Fisher. Two other popular books are *The Bent Twig* and *Understood Betsy.*

Geoffrey Chaucer

Frances Carpenter *(1890–1972)* was the daughter of a well-known geographer. Her father traveled all over the world on research trips and often took his family along. Frances Carpenter used information gained on those trips as background for much of her writing. Two of her popular books are *Tales of a Chinese Grandmother* and *African Wonder Tales.*

Geoffrey Chaucer *(perhaps 1340–1400)* is considered one of the greatest poets of all time. He was born in London, and served a while as a page to King Edward III's son. Chaucer was influenced by French literature and Italian culture. He used these sources, as well as his knowledge of English life, to create *The Canterbury Tales*. These tales are in poetry form, filled with humor and memorable characterization.

Anton Chekhov

Anton Chekhov *(1860–1904)* was a noted Russian playwright and short story writer. He pursued a medical career while writing stories for magazines. Eventually Chekhov became a doctor, but still continued to write stories. After he married an actress, he turned to writing plays. Two of his well-known plays are *The Three Sisters* and *Uncle Vanya.* His plots are known for their humorous twists.

Francisco A. de Icaza *(1863–1925)* was born in Mexico City, but lived in Spain for many years. He served as secretary to the Minister of Mexico in Spain, who was his friend. That career came to an end because of the Revolution of 1914. Icaza then turned to writing poetry and essays.

Walter de la Mare

Walter de la Mare *(1873–1956)* was raised and educated in London, England. He began writing at the age of seventeen, when he founded a high school newspaper. While working as a bookkeeper; he devoted his spare time to writing. Eventually, he received a government grant, which allowed him to spend all his time writing. He is known for his poems, nursery rhymes, and stories. In 1953, he earned the Order of Merit from Queen Elizabeth II.

Emily Dickinson

Beatrice Schenk de Regniers grew up in Crawfordsville, Indiana. She was active in a theater-dance group in Chicago, and then began writing books for young people. *The Snow Party, The Shadow Book,* and *May I Bring a Friend?* have won book awards. Regniers has served as editor of a book club.

Emily Dickinson *(1830–1886)* lived in Massachusetts. She led a normal life until the age of twenty-six, when she suddenly began to spend most of her time alone. Dickinson stayed indoors and had few visitors. Secretly, she wrote more than a thousand poems—most reflected deep feelings about life, love, and nature. Only seven of Emily Dickinson's poems were published while she was alive. The rest were discovered after her death, written on scraps of paper and hidden away in her bedroom.

Ralph Waldo Emerson

Ralph Waldo Emerson *(1803–1882)* was born into a family of ministers. After working his way through Harvard University, he became the pastor of a Boston church. He gave up that vocation, however, because he felt better suited to the work of writing and lecturing. Two of Emerson's prose works are titled *The Conduct of Life* and *Essays. Poems* and *May-Day* are well known collections of his poetry.

Genevieve Foster *(1893–1979)* was inspired by her grandparents, who had a deep interest in history. Her favorite subjects to write about were historical figures, such as Columbus, the Pilgrims, and Abraham Lincoln. Born in New York City, Foster grew up and attended college in Wisconsin. She studied art and worked in advertising for a few years before writing became her career.

Robert Francis

Robert Francis *(born 1901)* has devoted his life to writing and teaching. In his home on the outskirts of Amherst, Massachusetts, Francis lives a quiet life, gardening, reading, and writing. His award-winning works include fiction, essays, autobiography, and poetry. Robert Francis has published many collections of poems, including *Come Out into the Sun, The Orb Weaver,* and *The Sound I Listened For.*

O. Henry

O. Henry *(1862–1910)* was the pen name of William Sydney Porter. Before he achieved fame as a writer, O. Henry worked as a store clerk, journalist, and bank teller. He served a prison term for bookkeeping irregularities at the bank, but always claimed innocence. O. Henry's stories usually have surprise endings. Two popular collections of his stories are *Of Cabbages and Kings* and *The Four Million.*

Oliver Herford *(1863–1935)* was born in England, but moved to the United States with his family at an early age. He attended Antioch College in Ohio, and he also spent time studying in London and Paris. Herford was a popular literary figure of the early 1900's. His poems and humorous stories were published in many magazines, including *Life* and *Harper's Weekly.* Herford was also an artist. Animals were his favorite subjects, and his drawings often accompanied his writings.

Langston Hughes

Edwin A. Hoey *(born 1930)* attended Swarthmore College, served in the army, and then worked for a publishing company. His poems and articles have appeared in magazines, journals, and textbooks.

Langston Hughes *(1902–1967)* was a playwright, poet, song writer, and lecturer as well as an author of short stories and novels. He worked at many jobs before he achieved recognition for his writing talent. Hughes wrote about many facets of life, basing much of the writing upon his varied experiences, including travel to Africa. Many of Hughes's works reflect the speech patterns and jazz rhythms he heard on the streets of Harlem.

Victor Hugo

Victor Hugo *(1802–1885)* was a French author who had a deep interest in politics. Because his father was a general in Napoleon's army, Hugo was aware from childhood of his country's problems. He wrote twenty-three poems by the time he was fourteen, winning an early reputation as a genius. He eventually wrote plays, novels, and essays. One of his famous novels, *Les Misèrables,* deals with a reformed criminal who tries to lead an honest life.

Helen Keller

Issa *(1763–1828)* was a Japanese poet, born in the Province of Shinano, Japan. He was a sad, lonely child who grew up to be rather unhappy. He had no fixed home until he reached the age of fifty, so Issa always considered himself an orphan. He loved living things and wrote many of his haiku about birds and insects. In his lifetime, Issa produced over fifteen thousand poems.

Helen Keller *(1880–1968)* overcame the loss of sight, hearing, and speech, caused by an illness at the age of two. For five years, she was cut off from contact with others until her teacher, Anne Sullivan, was hired. Sullivan taught her to communicate through touch, to write and read Braille, and eventually to speak. Keller graduated with honors from Radcliffe College. She mastered several languages and lectured throughout the world. Her speaking tours helped in raising money to improve conditions for blind people.

Abraham Lincoln

Richmond Lattimore *(born 1906)* is a graduate of Dartmouth College who became a Rhodes scholar. He has served on the faculty of Bryn Mawr College. Lattimore is known for his translations of Homer as well as his original poetry and critical writings.

Abraham Lincoln *(1809–1865)* was a self-educated man who grew up on the frontier of Kentucky and Indiana. He held jobs as postmaster and lawyer and served as a member of the Illinois legislature. Lincoln was elected to the Presidency of the United States in 1860. He remained in office until his assassination in 1865. As leader of the North during the Civil War, he was an inspiration to people all over the world. Lincoln's literary style, reflected in his speeches and letters, was straightforward and sincere. His sense of humor still delights readers today.

Vachel Lindsay

Vachel Lindsay *(1879–1931)* studied art when he was young and then later became a poet. He left his hometown of Springfield, Illinois, to travel around the country performing his poems. Lindsay tried to combine music, poetry, and stage directions into a form of poetry that sounds best when read aloud.

Jack London

Jack London *(1876–1916)* was born in California. He had to work as soon as he was able, and ran away at fifteen to travel the country as a hobo. At nineteen, he returned to high school. The following year, after graduating, he went to Alaska in search of gold. His experiences there were all used in his highly imaginative stories. London is best known for *The Call of the Wild,* a novel.

Henry Wadsworth Longfellow

Henry Wadsworth Longfellow *(1807–1882)* was one of the most popular and respected poets of his time. One of his narrative poems, "The Song of Hiawatha," sold more than one million copies in his lifetime. Longfellow was born in Portland, Maine, and graduated from Bowdoin College. He traveled and studied in Europe, and then returned to the United States to teach college. Much of his life was spent at Harvard University, inspiring students in their creative writing. Other well-known poems by Longfellow are "Paul Revere's Ride" and "The Village Blacksmith."

Edna St. Vincent Millay *(1892–1950)* won fame at the age of nineteen for her poem "Renascence." After graduating from Vassar College, she moved to New York City. There she lived in Greenwich Village among other noted writers of the 1920's and 1930's. Millay continued to write poetry, as well as stories and plays. She was awarded a Pulitzer Prize for *The Harp Weaver*.

Rosalie Moore *(born 1910)* has had a varied career. After graduating from the University of California, she worked at a radio station as a writer and announcer. She has lectured to college students at universities in the United States and in Mexico and has conducted poetry workshops. In 1977 she won an award for *Year of the Children,* a collection of her poems.

Edna St. Vincent Millay

Lillian Morrison *(born 1917)* writes about subjects that interest her—jazz, dance, and sports. She was born in New Jersey and eventually moved to New York City. There she worked in the public library, interested mainly in improving services to young people. Morrison is known for *The Ghosts of Jersey City,* a collection of her own poems, and *Sprints and Distances,* an anthology of sports poems which she edited.

Ogden Nash

Ogden Nash *(1901–1971)* worked as a salesman, in an advertising firm, and for a book publisher before devoting himself to the job of full-time writer. He always was amused by the way misspelled words made a story or an article funny by chance. This led him to write poems with unusual rhymes, often using incorrect spelling. Nash became one of America's best known writers of humorous poetry.

Amado Nervo *(1870–1919)* studied for the priesthood in his native Mexico. He gave up that vocation to become a journalist, novelist, and poet. Nervo served as a diplomat in Madrid, Spain, for more than eighteen years. He enjoyed the friendships of many writers, who encouraged him to pursue a literary career.

Carl Sandburg

Carl Sandburg *(1878–1967)* was the son of Swedish immigrants who settled in Illinois. Sandburg held a variety of jobs, served in the army, and traveled around the country. He sang and played his guitar, collected folk music, and listened to folk tales. Those experiences are reflected in his poetry, fiction, and nonfiction. Sandburg's language of writing—free verse, slang, dialect, and street talk—make his writing come alive with the sights and sounds of America of the past. Sandburg's biography of Abraham Lincoln, which won a Pulitzer Prize, is still popular reading.

William Saroyan *(1908–1981),* the son of Armenian immigrants, grew up in Fresno, California. He loved to read, and later claimed that he had read every book in the public library. He never finished his formal education because family financial problems caused him to leave school at the age of fifteen. Saroyan's wide reading led to his career in writing. *The Human Comedy* and *The Time of Your Life* are two of his well-known works.

William Saroyan

William Jay Smith *(born 1918)* is known for his humorous poetry as well as plays, critical reviews, and English translations of other people's writings. Smith was born in Winnfield, Louisiana, and claims one-sixteenth Cherokee heritage from his mother. He has been a college professor and educational consultant, and has served as a member of the Vermont House of Representatives.

Lincoln Steffens

Lincoln Steffens *(1866–1936)* wrote his autobiography in 1931, when he was sixty-five years old. By that time, Steffens had achieved fame as a writer, lecturer, and editor. He was born in San Francisco, attended the University of California, and further pursued his studies in Europe. His special interests were politics and the problems of business and labor.

Alfred, Lord Tennyson

Alfred, Lord Tennyson *(1809–1892)* was a shy, optimistic man who tried to deal positively with the unhappiness he encountered. His long poem *In Memorium* was written over a seventeen-year period and was about Tennyson's attempts to deal with the death of a close friend. Tennyson lived in England and was made its Poet Laureate by Queen Victoria. He became one of the best-known poets in the English-speaking world. His noted works include "The Lady of Shallot."

Ernest Lawrence Thayer *(1863–1940)* was born in Worcester, Massachusetts. He attended Harvard University, where he was the editor-in-chief of the student humor magazine, *Lampoon.* He joined his classmate William Randolph Hearst as a journalist on the *San Francisco Examiner.* Thayer wrote a number of poems for newspapers and is most noted for his famous poem, "Casey at the Bat."

Tobi Tobias *(born 1938)* has always been interested in people who have become famous in the arts. She enjoys researching and interviewing to get the information she needs for stories. Some people Tobias has written about include opera singer Marian Anderson; ballerina Maria Tallchief; and Isami Noguchi, a sculptor who grew up in Japan. Tobias also writes for television and magazines.

Mark Twain

Mark Twain *(1835–1910)* was the pen name of Samuel Clemens. Twain grew up in Hannibal, Missouri, where he had many adventures as a boy on the Mississippi River. He loved the river and enjoyed fishing and rafting. Twain wrote about these experiences in *The Adventures of Tom Sawyer* and *The Adventures of Huckleberry Finn,* two of his most popular books. As a young man, he worked as a printer, a riverboat pilot, and a journalist. His humorous newspaper articles and lectures were well received by the public.

Louis Untermeyer *(1895–1977)* gave up a career as a professional pianist to become a writer. He has edited collections of written works and served as poetry editor of a magazine. Untermeyer translated traditional tales into modern English.

Alice Walker

Alice Walker *(born 1944)* was raised on a small farm in Georgia. She worked her way through college to become an award-winning writer. Walker, who has taught at several colleges, won an award in 1973 for *In Love and Trouble,* a collection of stories. *Revolutionary Petunias,* a book of poems, was nominated for an award in the same year. Walker has also written *The Third Life of Grange Copeland,* a novel.

H.G. Wells

H. G. Wells *(1866–1946)* was a noted British writer who believed strongly in scientific progress. He attended London University and received a science degree with honors. He published hundreds of books in various fields, but is best-known for his science fiction writing. His famous works include *The War of the Worlds* and *The Time Machine.* Wells wrote of airplanes, submarines, and moon voyages long before people believed such things could become reality.

William Carlos Williams

William Carlos Williams *(1883–1963)* was born in Rutherford, New Jersey. He was a practicing physician who wrote forty-nine books. These included novels, short stories, plays, and poetry. Williams is praised for writing of everyday life in a style to which many can relate. Among his works are *Paterson,* a long poem set in Paterson, New Jersey, and *Pictures from Breughal,* for which he won the 1964 Pulitzer Prize.

Valerie Worth *(born 1933)* grew up in Philadelphia, Pennsylvania. She attended Swarthmore College, from which she earned a bachelor's degree. Worth has published *Small Poems,* a collection of poems about life, the earth, and the stars. In addition, Worth has written *Gypsy Gold,* a popular young adults' novel.

Index of Titles and Authors

Index of Fine Art

Index of Skills

Skills in Comprehending Literature

Vocabulary Skills

Writing Skills

Study and Research Skills

Speaking and Listening Skills

Skills in Critical Thinking

602

Art Credits

Cover

That, 1958–59, Kenneth Noland.
Collection, Mr. and Mrs. David Mirvish, Toronto, Canada.

Illustrations

Kinuko Y. Craft, 69, 72–73, 81, 83, 88, 92–93; William Cigliano, 30–31; Roberta Polfus, 51, 54, 474–475, 510, 515, 522; Jean Helmer, 107, 296, 447; Robert Masheris, 150, 154, 159; Sarah Woodward, 167, 168–169; Yoshi Miyake, 212, 217, 492, 499; Christa Kieffer, 225; John Sandford, 255; Glenn Wolff, 272–273; Judith Friedman, 360, 363; Dale Bēda, 376.

Photographs of Authors

The Bettmann Archive, Inc.: Stephen Vincent Benét, Pearl Buck, Geoffrey Chaucer, Anton Chekhov, Walter de la Mare, Emily Dickinson, Ralph Waldo Emerson, O. Henry, Langston Hughes, Victor Hugo, Helen Keller, Jack London, Carl Sandburg, William Saroyan, Alfred, Lord Tennyson, Mark Twain, H. G. Wells. Culver Pictures, Inc., Vachel Lindsay, Henry Wadsworth Longfellow, Ogden Nash, Lincoln Steffens, William Carlos Williams. Alex Gottfryd: Joan Aiken. Jill Krementz: Isaac Asimov. Library of Congress: Abraham Lincoln. Jerome Liebling: Robert Francis. New York Times: Hal Borland. Vassar College Library: Edna St. Vincent Millay. Newsweek; James Wilson: Alice Walker.

604

Acknowledgments

(continued from copyright page)

Lincoln," and "Benjamin Franklin" by Stephen Vincent Benét, from *A Book of Americans* by Rosemary & Stephen Vincent Benét, Holt, Rinehart and Winston, Inc.; copyright 1933 by Rosemary & Stephen Vincent Benét; copyright renewed © 1961 by Rosemary Carr Benét. For "The Rocking Donkey" by Joan Aiken, from *Smoke from Cromwell's Time and Other Stories;* copyright © 1959, 1966, 1969, 1970 by Joan Aiken. Delacorte Press/Seymour Lawrence: For "Seal," excerpted from *Laughing Time* by William Jay Smith; copyright © 1953, 1955, 1956, 1957, 1959, 1968, 1974, 1977, 1980 by William Jay Smith. Dodd, Mead & Company, Incorporated: For "Matthew A. Henson," from *Famous American Negroes* by Langston Hughes; copyright 1954 by Langston Hughes; copyright renewed 1982 by George Houston Bass. Doubleday & Company, Inc.: For an excerpt from *The Story of My Life* by Helen Keller; copyright 1902, 1903, 1905 by Helen Keller. For "The Six Horsemen," from *African Wonder Tales* by Frances Carpenter; copyright © 1963 by Frances Carpenter Huntington. For "Hearts and Hands," from *Waifs and Strays* by O. Henry; copyright 1917 by Doubleday & Company, Inc. Dover Publications, Inc.: For "The Dog (As Seen by the Cat)" by Oliver Herford, from *Rainbow in the Sky;* copyright 1935. E. P. Dutton, Inc.: For "The Flower-Fed Buffaloes" by Vachel Lindsay, from *Going to the Stars;* copyright 1926 by D. Appleton & Co., renewed by Elizabeth C. Lindsay. For "America the Beautiful" by Katharine Lee Bates, from *Poems.* Education Development Center, Inc.: For "Magic Words to Feel Better," from *Songs and Stories of the Netsilik Eskimos,* translated by Edward Field from text collected by Knud Rasmussen, courtesy Education Development Center, Inc., Newton, MA. M. Evans and Company, Inc.: Pages 41–43, 44–49, 56–57, 175–179, 191–194, 223–229, from *The World's Great Stories* by Louis Untermeyer; copyright © 1964 by Louis Untermeyer. Farrar, Straus & Giroux, Inc.: For "Sea Lions," from *More Small Poems* by Valerie Worth, with pictures by Natalie Babbitt; poems copyright © 1976 by Valerie Worth. Gail M. Griffin: For 'How the Three Young Men Found Death" by Gail M. Griffin, an adaptation of "The Pardoner's Tale" by Geoffrey Chaucer; copyright © 1969 by Gail M. Griffin. Harcourt Brace Jovanovich, Inc.: For "Summer of the Beautiful White Horse" by William Saroyan, from *My Name is Aram:* copyright 1938, 1966 by William Saroyan. For an abridged version of "I Get a Colt to Break In" by Lincoln Steffens, from *Boy on Horseback* by Lincoln Steffens; copyright 1931 by Harcourt Brace Jovanovich, Inc.; renewed 1959 by Peter Steffens. For "The Old Soldier," from *Four-Square* by Dorothy Canfield; copyright 1949 by Dorothy Canfield, renewed, 1977 by Sarah Fisher Scott. For excerpts from Chapter XVIII in *Abe Lincoln Grows Up* by Carl Sandburg; copyright 1926, 1928 by Harcourt Brace Jovanovich, Inc., renewed 1954, 1956 by Carl Sandburg. For "Women," from *Revolutionary Petunias & Other Poems* by Alice Walker; copyright © 1970 by Alice Walker. For "Chicago" from *Chicago Poems* by Carl Sandburg; copyright 1916 by Holt Rinehart and Winston, Inc.; renewed 1944 by Carl Sandburg. For an excerpt from "Fourth of July Night" in *Wind Song* by Carl Sandburg; copyright © 1956 by Carl Sandburg. Harper & Row, Publishers, Inc.: For "Snowy Benches," from *Out In the Dark and Daylight* by Aileen Fisher; text copyright © 1980 by Aileen Fisher. For an excerpt from page 24 (text only) of *Witcracks: Jokes and Jests* from American folklore collected by Alvin Schwartz (J. B. Lippincott Company). For "Cynthia in the Snow" (text only), from *Bronzeville Boys and Girls* by Gwendolyn Brooks; copyright © 1956 by Gwendolyn Brooks Blakely. For "Scene" (text only), from *River Winding: Poems* by Charlotte Zolotow (T. Y. Crowell Company); texty copyright © 1970 by Charlotte Zolotow. For "Strange Wind" (text only), from *A Light in the Attic* by Shel Silverstein; copyright © 1981 by Shel Silverstein. For an abridged and adapted text of *Maria Tallchief* by Tobi Tobias, A Crowell Biography (Thomas Y. Crowell); copyright © 1970 by Tobi Tobias. Harvard University Press: For "The Duel" and "Bee! I'm Expecting You!" by Emily Dickinson, from *The Poems of Emily Dickinson,* ed. by Thomas H. Johnson, Cambridge, Mass.: The Belknap Press of Harvard University Press, copyright © 1951, © 1955, 1979, 1983 by the President and Fellows of Harvard College, reprinted by permission of the publishers and the Trustees of Amherst College. The Hoksueido Press: For a haiku poem "Woodpecker" by Issa, from *A History of Haiku* by R. H. Blyth: Vol. I, *From the Beginning up to Issa;* copyright © 1964. Holt, Rinehart and Winston, Publishers: For "Steam Shovel," from *Upper Pasture* by Charles Malam; copyright 1930, © 1958 by Charles Malam. International Creative Management, Inc.: For "Invasion from Mars" by Howard Koch, from *The Panic Broadcast;* copyright 1940 Princeton University Press, 1968 by Howard Koch. Richmond Lattimore: For "Sky Diving" by Richmond Lattimore, from *Poems from Three Decades.* Little, Brown and Company: For "The Hippopotamus," "The Canary," "The Panther," and "The Termite," from *Verses from 1929 On* by Ogden Nash; copyright 1935, 1940, 1942 by The Curtis Publishing Company, first appeared in *The Saturday Evening Post.* Liveright Publishing Corp., Inc.: For "Who knows if the moon's," from *Tulips & Chimneys;* copyright 1923, 1925 and renewed 1951, 1953 by E. E. Cummings, copyright © 1973, 1976 by the Trustees for the E. E. Cummings Trust, copyright © 1973, 1976 by George James Firmage. Macmillan Publishing Co.: For "Skating," from *Pillicock Hill* by Herbert Asquith, New York: Macmillan, 1926. Norma Millay Ellis: For "The Courage That My Mother Had" by Edna St. Vincent Millay, from *Collected Poems,* Harper & Row; copyright 1954 by Norma Millay Ellis. William Morrow & Company, Inc.: For "The Women's 400 Meters," from *The Sidewalk Racer and Other Poems of Sports and Motion* by Lillian Morrison; copyright © 1968, 1977 by Lillian Morrison, by permission of Lothrop, Lee & Shepard Books (A Division of William Morrow & Company). New Directions Publishing Corporation: For "Poem" by William Carlos Williams, from *Collected Earlier Poems of William Carlos Williams;* copyright 1938 by New Directions Publishing Corporation. The New Yorker Magazine:

For "Catalogue" by Rosalie Moore, from *The New Yorker Magazine,* May 25, 1940; copyright © 1940, 1968 by The New Yorker Magazine, Inc. Harold Ober Associates: For "The Big Wave" by Pearl S. Buck, from *Jack & Jill,* October 1947; copyright 1947 by the Curtis Publishing Co., copyright 1948 by Pearl S. Buck, renewed 1975 by Pearl S. Buck. Open Court Publishing Company: For "Round Table Riddles," from *Cricket,* March 1983. Plays, Inc.; For *A Connecticut Yankee in King Arthur's Court,* adapted by Lewy Olfson, from *Radio Plays of Famous Stories,* by Lewy Olfson; Boston: Plays, Inc., Publishers, copyright © 1956 by Plays, Inc. This play is for reading purposes only; for permission to produce the play, write to Plays, Inc., 8 Arlington Street, Boston, MA 02116. Modern Poetry Association: For "Pole Vault" by Shiro Murano, translated from the Japanese by Satoru Sato with the assistance of Constance Urdang, from *Poetry,* May 1956. Random House, Inc.: For "Spotted Eagle and Black Crow," told by Jenny Leading Cloud (text only), from *The Sound of Flutes and Other Indian Legends* by Richard Erdoes; copyright © 1976 by Richard Erdoes; reprinted by permission of Pantheon Books, a division of Random House, Inc. For "The Dream Keeper," from *The Dream Keeper and Other Poems* by Langston Hughes; copyright 1932 and renewed 1960 by Langston Hughes, by permission of Alfred A. Knopf, Inc. Beatrice Schenk de Regniers: For anecdotes about Abraham Lincoln, from *The Abraham Lincoln Joke Book* by Beatrice Schenk de Regniers. Marie Rodell-Frances Collin Literary Agency: For "April and Robins," "The Prelude," and "Shortest Month," from *Sundial of the Seasons* by Hal Borland; copyright 1964 by Hal Borland, by permission of Barbara Dodge Borland. Charles Scribner's Sons: For "Day of Light and Shadow," from *Abraham Lincoln's World, 1809–1865;* copyright 1944 by Genevieve Foster; copyright renewed 1972. Simon & Schuster, Inc.: For two Lincoln letters from *A Treasury of the World's Great Letters* by M. Lincoln Schuster, editor; copyright 1940, 1968 by Simon & Schuster, Inc. For the pronunciation key on page 217 from *Webster's New World Dictionary,* Basic School Edition; copyright © 1979 by Simon & Schuster, Inc. The Society of Authors: For "All But Blind" by Walter de la Mare, permission granted by The Literary Trustees of Walter de la Mare and The Society of Authors. Sally Stolte: For "Fall" by Sally Andresen. The University of Massachusetts Press: For "Like Ghosts of Eagles" by Robert Francis; copyright © 1973 by Robert Francis, reprinted from *Robert Francis: Collected Poems, 1936–1976* (University of Massachusetts Press, 1976). Viking Penguin, Inc.: For "Gazelle" by Mary Ann Hoberman, from *The Raucous Ark* by Mary Ann Hoberman, illustrated by Joseph Low; copyright © 1973 by Mary Ann Hoberman. Robert Wallace: For "The Double Play" by Robert Wallace, copyright © 1961 by Robert Wallace. Wesleyan University Press: For "The Base Stealer" by Robert Francis, from *The Orb Weaver;* copyright © 1948 by Robert Francis. Xerox Education Publications: For "Foul Shot" by Edwin A. Hoey, from *Read* magazine; copyright © 1962, Xerox Corp., reprinted by permission of *Read* magazine. The authors and editors have made every effort to trace the ownership of all copyrighted selections found in this book and to make full acknowledgment for their use.

Staff Credits

Editor-in-Chief: Joseph F. Littell
Project Director: Patricia Opaskar

Administrative Editor: Kathleen Laya
Managing Editor: Geraldine Macsai

Associate Editors: Elizabeth M. Garber, Bernice Rappoport
Rights and Permissions: Irma Rosenberg
Associate Designer: Linda Schifano FitzGibbon

Special Contributors

Nora Brooks Blakely; Katherine Fischer; Charlene Griffin-Jordan; Catherine Hobbins; Donna Levine; Sister Margaret Murphy, O.P.; Jeffrey Taggart; Gerry Tremaine. Picture Research: Katherine Nolan.

Class Record Sheet

Chapter	Student Names															
1	Grade for Assignments															
	Mastery Test Score															
	Overall Grade															
2	Grade for Assignments															
	Mastery Test Score															
	Overall Grade															
3	Grade for Assignments															
	Mastery Test Score															
	Overall Grade															
4	Grade for Assignments															
	Mastery Test Score															
	Overall Grade															
5	Grade for Assignments															
	Mastery Test Score															
	Overall Grade															
6	Grade for Assignments															
	Mastery Test Score															
	Overall Grade															
7	Grade for Assignments															
	Mastery Test Score															
	Overall Grade															

End of Year

	Mastery Test Score															
	Overall Grade															

 Student's Name ____________________

Student Record Sheet Part 1

Chapter Evaluation

	Chapter 1	2	3	4	5	6	7	End of Year
Date								
Evaluation of Assignments								
Comprehension			How Writers Write					
Reading Literature								
Vocabulary			Sounds of Language					
Writing								
Study and Research			Figures of Speech					
Speaking and Listening								
Critical Thinking								
Score on Mastery Test	%	%	%	%	%	%	%	%
Overall Grade								

Note: Recording of separate strand grades is optional. Suggested Grades: A, B, C, D, F *or* Excellent, Satisfactory, Unsatisfactory

Diagnostic Tests

		Chapter 1	2	3	4	5	6	7
Date								
Reading Literature	Points			How Writers Write Points				
	Score			Score				
Comprehension	Points			Sounds of Language Points				
	Score			Score				
Vocabulary	Points			Figures of Speech Points				
	Score			Score				
Total	Score	%	%	%	%	%	%	%

Note: Recording of subtest scores is optional.

 Student's Name ______________________

Student Record Sheet Part 2

Mastery Tests

		Chapter 1	2	3	4	5	6	7	End of Year
Date									
Reading Literature	Points			How Writers Write					
	Score			Points					
Comprehension	Points			Score					
	Score								
Vocabulary	Points			Sounds of Language					
	Score			Points					
Writing	Points			Score					
	Score								
Study and Research	Points			Figures of Speech					
	Score			Point					
Critical Thinking	Points			Score					
	Score								
Total	Score	%	%	%	%	%	%	%	%

Bonus Writing	Points								

Note: Recording of subtest scores is optional.

Guidelines for Evaluating Composition

Most educators would agree that constant, helpful evaluation of student writing is the only way to help young writers develop their skills. For many teachers, however, this "helpful" feedback has come to mean endless amounts of time spent with a stack of papers and a red pencil, marking every incorrect spelling or misplaced comma. Such an evaluation is suffered through for the good of the students. Yet how much does this evaluation system aid the developing writer?

When a child is learning to talk, a parent will accept and respond to single words or incomplete phrases, recognizing that the child has a message to communicate even if the form of the message is undeveloped. Similarly, when a student is learning to write, he or she needs the encouragement of a response to a written message, no matter what the form of that message is. A teacher cannot afford to require correct sentence structure, grammar, capitalization, punctuation, and spelling before looking at the ideas in a piece of writing.

The practical classroom application of these ideas, advanced by recent research into the writing process, is that students should be given opportunities to write as frequently as possible and that they be given some evaluation of the sense and style of their writing as frequently as possible. This emphasis on quantity means that some teachers may need to rethink their evaluation procedures.

Types of Evaluation

In order to give student writers the constant practice and feedback they need, teachers must have a practical method of evaluation. Obviously, if the student will be writing constantly, a teacher cannot be expected to evaluate each piece in a line-by-line, word-by-word manner. Nor would such an evaluation necessarily be useful to the developing writer. It is therefore suggested that a teacher learn to use two different evaluation methods—the holistic method and the more detailed analytic method.

Holistic evaluation of writing is a quick, guided method of rating pieces of writing. It can best be used to evaluate daily writing samples or first drafts of more complex pieces. With holistic evaluation, an evaluator reads the written piece as a whole, considers certain features, and immediately assigns a grade. The grade may be a single rating for the entire piece of writing or a set of ratings for the different features being considered.

The evaluation form provided on page T27 of this Teacher's Edition is of this second type of holistic evaluation, but will also guide teachers who wish to use the single rating evaluation. It lists the major characteristics of content and form that can be identified in most types of writing. When the teacher desires to evaluate a certain type of writing, such as narrative composition, he or she might supplement the general questions about content with more specific guidelines.

Analytic evaluation should occur only when the student has turned in the clean, final copy of a piece of writing. In this detailed type of evaluation, the teacher analyzes each aspect of a piece of writing, including both content and mechanics. By this point, many of the student's errors will have been spotted and corrected during the revision process. Problems that remain in the final copy are likely to be indicative of where the student's real weaknesses lie, and both student and teacher can concentrate on identifying and correcting them.

Evaluators

The evaluation process can be utilized by three types of evaluators: the writer of the piece, other students, and the teacher. Each type of evaluation offers unique benefits to the developing writer.

1. Self-Evaluation. In this type of evaluation, a writer comments on his or her own work, noting which parts were successful and which unsuccessful. During self-evaluation, a student may be guided by a chart such as the one on page T27, as well as by what "feels" right.

It will not always be possible for a student to pinpoint exactly what is wrong in a piece of writing. When this occurs, the writer should be encouraged to underline any sentence or section that doesn't "feel" right, verbalize the problem as he or she perceives it, and then seek further clarification and help from the teacher. This estimation of errors will eventually become more precise as the student learns to recognize similar problems in later writing.

It is very helpful for students to be guided through the evaluation process before they attempt self-evaluation. The teacher might, for example, project a sample composition using an overhead projector, and then guide the class to an understanding of the types of questions they should ask during the revision process. Such guided evaluation helps the young writer develop a sense of when information is incomplete or ideas unclear. This knowledge can then be applied during self evaluation.

2. Peer Evaluation. Evaluating the writing of others is often a strong learning experience. In peer evaluation, students work together in small groups to improve a piece of writing. Student evaluators should always be given a list of specific criteria that the writing is expected to meet, and should then comment on how well each paper succeeds. Peer evaluation is most effective when the writer is given time to make revisions after the group suggests ways to improve the work.

3. Teacher Evaluation. The teacher's comments and suggestions may be incorporated at any point in the writing process. Studies indicate that evaluation by the teacher is most successful when it is done in combination with self- and peer evaluation. The evaluation form on page T27, therefore, provides for such a combination of evaluation procedures.

Teacher evaluation should also involve direct communication with every student. Such help can be provided in student-teacher conferences. These conferences provide an opportunity for students to ask the questions they develop during self-evaluation. They also give teachers a chance to comment on the strong points of the paper, offer additional suggestions, provide individualized instruction when it is needed.

Teacher evaluation of a final copy should be the last step in the evaluation process. When a student turns in a clean, final copy of a paper, the teacher should require that previous drafts be turned in with it. The teacher should then provide an in-depth analysis of the final copy, judging it not only on its final content, but also on how well the student incorporated earlier suggestions.

Keeping a Record of Improvement

Both the teacher and students benefit when writing folders are maintained throughout the school year. A piece of writing from early in the year, along with its evaluations, can be compared with later pieces. Progress from one piece to the next will be erratic, as the writer takes risks using new techniques and appears to move backwards until gaining mastery of each new technique. However, over the course of the year, progress should be evident.

Bibliography

Cooper, Charles R. and Lee Odell, eds. *Evaluating Writing: Describing, Measuring, Judging.* Urbana, Illinois: National Council of Teachers of English, 1977.

Everrts, Eldonna L., ed. *Explorations in Children's Writing.* Urbana, Illinois: National Council of Teachers of English, 1970.

Graves, Donald H. *Balance the Basics: Let Them Write.* New York: The Ford Foundation, 1978.

Murray, Donald M. *A Writer Teaches Writing: A Practical Method of Teaching Composition.* Boston: Houghton Mifflin, 1968.

Sager, Carol, "Improving the Quality of Written Composition in the Middle Grades," in *Language Arts* 54 (1977): 760–762.

Using the Composition Evaluation Form

The following form for composition evaluation may be used at any stage of the writing process, and may be re-used after each revision.

The form should be filled out by the student and turned in with the writing. There is also space on the form for peer evaluation, if desired. The teacher may ask students to turn in only final copies, or may ask to see work in progress. The student states whether the submitted writing is the final copy.

On the evaluation form, content may be rated at any point; mechanics should be graded only on a final copy.

Copies of the form should be kept by both the student and the teacher.

Self-Evaluation: Besides the questions on the form, the student can ask himself or herself the questions concerning revising listed in the relevant composition chapter. The student may use 1, 3, and 5 subjectively.

Peer Evaluation: Members of the peer group should rate each feature as objectively as possible. In order to focus on ideas and organizations, the group should evaluate content only.

Teacher Evaulation: The following standards for evaluating composition are provided to assist the teacher in rating papers with objectivity and consistency. In a conference, the teacher might discuss one or two of these areas in detail.

Standards for Holistic Evaluation

Content

	1—Low	3—Average	5—High
1	Unclear, unimaginative writing.	Understandable but unimaginative writing.	Imaginative, interesting writing.
2	Boring or poorly defined topic.	Topic adequately limited and defined.	Well-chosen, precisely developed topic.
3	Purpose unclear, or not achieved in the writing.	Purpose defined adequately. Not completely achieved.	Clear, well-defined purpose. Writing achieves purpose successfully.
4	Writing so lacking in detail that topic remains undeveloped.	Incomplete development. More information needed.	Topic thoroughly covered. Writing is rich in detail and supporting information.
5	Many irrelevant sentences or details.	Few irrelevant sentences or details.	Well-chosen, relevant sentences and details.
6	Disjointed ideas. No transitional words, phrases, or ideas.	Inconsistent flow. Some transitional devices.	Ideas flow well. Good use of transitional devices.
7	Lack of any logical organization of ideas.	Some organization of ideas evident.	Well-organized ideas. Type of organization suited to topic and purpose.
8	Dull, general words, poorly chosen. Inappropriate to audience.	Suitable but unimaginative language. Generally appropriate to audience.	Specific, vivid language. Appropriate to audience.

Mechanics

1	Many fragments and run-on sentences. Frequent mistakes in the use of nouns, verbs, pronouns, and subject-verb agreement.	Few fragments and run-ons. Some mistakes in the use of nouns, verbs, pronouns, and subject-verb agreement.	No fragments or run-ons. Few mistakes in the use of nouns, verbs, pronouns, and subject-verb agreement.
2	Frequent mistakes in capitalization.	Occasional mistakes in capitalization.	Infrequent mistakes in capitalization.
3	Punctuation marks frequently misused or missing.	Punctuation marks usually used correctly.	Infrequent mistakes in punctuation.
4	Frequent mistakes in spelling, without any indication of awareness of spelling patterns.	Occasional misspellings, usually indicating an approximation of the correct spelling and an awareness of spelling patterns.	Infrequent spelling mistakes.
5	Paragraphs not indented. Writing illegible. Incorrect headings or margins.	Some carelessness or inconsistency in form. Occasionally hard to read.	Correct form. Neat, legible handwriting.

Composition Evaluation Form

Writer ______________________ Date ____________

Title ______________________ **Circle one:** Unfinished Final Copy

Evaluation Symbols
1. Needs a great deal of work
3. Acceptable—could be improved
5. Very good. Needs no further revision.

Content	Writer's Opinion	Peer Group Opinion	Teacher's Evaluation	**Teacher's Comments**
1. **Interest.** Is the writing interesting and understandable? Does it hold the reader's attention?				
2. **Topic.** Is the topic a good one? Has it been narrowed sufficiently?				
3. **Purpose.** Is the purpose of the writing clear? Has the writer accomplished this purpose?				
4. **Development.** Has the topic been developed well? Is there sufficient information?				
5. **Unity.** Are all ideas and details related to the topic? Do they all help to develop or strengthen the main idea?				
6. **Continuity.** Do ideas flow smoothly? Has the writer avoided any breaks in thought?				
7. **Organization.** Were ideas arranged in a logical order? Does this order suit the purpose of the writing?				
8. **Language.** Is the language appropriate to the writing? Does it suit the audience? Are the words vivid?				
Additional Guidelines				

Mechanics (to be graded by teacher on final copy only)

1. **Grammar and Usage.** Are there any fragments or run-ons? Is the correct form of every pronoun or verb used? Are adjectives and adverbs used correctly?				
2. **Capitalization.** Are all first words, initials, proper nouns, proper adjectives, and titles capitalized?				
3. **Punctuation.** Does each sentence have the proper end mark? Are all punctuation marks used correctly?				
4. **Spelling.** Are all words spelled correctly? Are plurals and possessive forms spelled correctly?				
5. **Forms.** Is the writing legible? Is the heading correct? Are there sufficient margins?				

Evaluating Speaking and Listening

Recognizing What Can Be Evaluated

A student's speaking ability can be evaluated by any careful listener; a student's listening skills can only be estimated on the basis of observable behavior. Therefore, it is possible that students may be involved in evaluation of a peer's speaking skills. However, only the teacher should evaluate listening skills.

Using the Forms

The forms on this page and the following page may be used to evaluate either a single session or to summarize observations over a period of time. It is strongly recommended that each student be evaluated at least once per chapter on each of these skills.

Evaluation of Speaking Skills. Students may participate in peer evaluation of speaking skills. The evaluation form should first be presented and explained to the class as a whole. Then, one to four students may be asked to use the form at any one presentation.

Share peer evaluations with the speakers. Awareness of the audience as a group of individuals rather than a frighteningly large organism will help any student become more comfortable in the speaker's role and more concerned with the needs of the audience.

To evaluate discussion skills, direct each participant in a discussion to evaluate another member (perhaps without letting the group members know who is evaluating each of them). Afterwards, with your guidance, students may critique each other's behaviors.

In each case, to be aware of the standards to be considered, evaluators should have the forms before them during the activity but should mark nothing until the activity has ended.

Evaluation of Listening Skills. To attempt an objective evaluation of listening skills, the teacher should consciously compare a single student's behaviors with those listed on the form for a period of at least five minutes when the major classroom activity involves listening. Whenever possible, note specific behaviors that can be improved and, at a later conference with the student, make specific suggestions in a positive way.

Listening Evaluation Form

Student's Name ______________________ Date ______________________

For each item, circle the most accurate response. In the space below the choices, note any relevant behaviors.

1. The listener shows a conscious intention to hear by making an observable effort to eliminate or overcome difficulties, as by changing position, asking the speaker to speak more loudly or slowly, or avoiding distractions.	Never Sometimes Usually Often
2. The listener shows attention to what is being said by reacting appropriately, as by laughing at humorous statements and showing concern or concentration at more serious moments.	Never Sometimes Usually Often
3. The listener shows understanding of what has been said by asking appropriate questions of the speaker, answering questions on the content, or using information from the presentation in a succeeding discussion or in later oral or written work.	Never Sometimes Usually Often
4. The listener shows appreciation of what is said by a mannerly behavior during the presentation and by constructive comments concerning its delivery, content, or the like afterwards.	Never Sometimes Usually Often

Speaking Evaluation Form

Speaker ______________________ Date of Presentation ______________________

For each item, check the box with the most accurate description.

Presentation (Oral Interpretation of Original Material)	Poor	Satisfactory	Good
Volume. Was the speaker's voice loud enough?	Too loud or too soft	Usually loud enough	Easily heard, with voice loud or soft as required
Diction. Were the speaker's words easy to understand?	Mumbling or monotonous	Usually understandable	Clear, easily understood
Pacing. Was the speaker's speed appropriate?	Too fast or too slow	Speed usually good	Good speed, going fast or slow to fit material
Eye Contact. Did the speaker use eye contact effectively?	Little or no eye contact	Some eye contact	Frequent eye contact
Gestures. Did the speaker use appropriate body movements that contributed to understanding the meaning?	Few or no gestures used	Occasional gestures used	Gestures used frequently and appropriately
Expression. Did the speaker's voice express feeling?	Little or no expression	Some expression	Consistently expressed appropriate feeling
Understanding of Material. Did the speaker indicate an understanding of the material?	Uncertain or confused delivery	Usually in control	Strong, purposeful presentation
Effect on Audience. Did the speaker make it easy for you to understand and have an interest in what was said?	No enthusiasm, dull	Showed enthusiasm for subject	Created enthusiasm or other appropriate feeling in audience

Content and Organization (Original Material only)	Poor	Satisfactory	Good
Introduction. Did the speaker let you know immediately what the speech would be about?	Introduction dull, confusing	Made topic clear	Made topic clear and created interest in it quickly
Body of Speech. Did the speaker lead you steadily from one idea to the next, with examples where needed?	Disorganized, confused	Ideas seemed to be connected	Well organized, maintained high interest
Summary or Conclusion. Did the speaker pull together all the ideas of the speech and end it logically?	Trailed off at the end	Let you know the speech was over	Tied up all loose ends but left you wanting to hear more

Date ___________________________

Dear Parent,

In this year's study, your child will be using *Reading Literature, Green Level.* This text contains appealing selections, from both traditional and contemporary writers, in their original form. The study questions that accompany the selections are designed to lead students toward mastery of essential reading, comprehension, and writing skills. They also provide instruction and practice in word attack skills, to improve vocabulary development. In addition, the text develops skills in the areas of study and research, speaking and listening, and critical thinking. Topics are presented and developed fully, with extensive exercises for development provided.

Your assistance and reinforcement will add to the effectiveness of the text and your child's classroom experience. It would be helpful for you to become familiar with the subjects covered in the lessons and to encourage your child to share with you what he or she is studying.

No reading program is complete if it is limited to the classroom. Reading can inform and enrich a person only when that person exercises the ability to read. Here are some ways you can contribute to your child's reading development.

> Encourage your child to read by letting him or her see you read. Make sure that reading materials—books, newspapers, magazines—are present in your home.
>
> Guide your child's television viewing to include some of the better young people's specials and series. Encourage your child to evaluate each program's content as you discuss it together. Discover any books that may be relevant to the programs your child watches, and guide him or her to these materials.
>
> Provide a quiet place and time for reading, writing, and school assignments.

I am confident that, with your assistance, your child's understanding and appreciation of literature will increase throughout this year. If you have any questions or suggestions, please feel free to contact me.

Sincerely,

Fecha ______________________________

Estimados Padres,

Durante este año escolar, sus hijos van a estudiar *Reading Literature, Nivel Verde.* Este texto contiene selecciones atractivas, de escritores ambos tradicionally contemporáneo, en sus formas originales. Las preguntas de estudio que acompañan cada selección están diseñadas a dirigir cada estudiante hacia el dominio de habilidades esenciales en lectura, comprensión, y escritura. Al mismo tiempo, dan instrucción y practica en ampliar y desarrolar habilidades para mejorar vocabulario. Además, el texto desarrolla habilidades en areas de estudio e investigación, hablar y escuchar, y pensamiento crítico. Los temas del libro están presentados y extendidos completamente, con amplia oportunidad para práctica y desarrollo.

Les sugiero que se familaricen con el programa y con la clase de sus hijos. Asi Uds. comprenderán el sentido de la lección y podrán animar a sus hijos a compartirla con Uds.

Ningún programa de lectura es completo si nos limitamos a la clase. La lectura puede informar y enriquezer a la persona solamente cuando esa persona ejecuta la habilidad de la lectura. Es aquí donde Uds. pueden hacer una gran contribución. Pienso que las siguientes actividades tienen el mismo valor tanto en ingles como en español:

- Despierten en sus hijos el deseo y hábito de la lectura. Cuando Uds. lean aseguren que sus hijos los vean. Mantengan libros y revistas en casa.
- Guien a sus hijos para que vean los programas de televisión que son propios para niños de su edad. Discutan y juzgen con sus niños el valor del contenido de estos programas.
- Seleccionen un sitio apropriado para leer y escribir.

Sé que con su ayuda e interés en el transcurso del año escolar, sus hijos tendrán un gran exito en este programa. Les pido que se comuniquen conmigo, si tienen preguntas o sugerencias.

Atentamente,

Date ____________________

Dear Parent,

During the past few months, your child has been using the textbook, *Reading Literature, Green Level.* He or she has been participating in the following activities:

- reading legends and short stories for enjoyment and to gain an understanding and appreciation of literature and its elements
- strengthening comprehension of each selection by identifying such characteristics as setting, character, and plot
- improving vocabulary through developing word attack skills
- learning the process of writing and applying the techniques writers use to their own work
- developing study and research, speaking and listening, and critical thinking skills

In the coming months your child will be reading, poetry, nonfiction, and drama. Concepts and skills already introduced will be reviewed and new ones added, extended, and reinforced.

Your continued help and encouragement are most important as your child takes on these challenges.

Here are some ways you can reinforce and further expand your child's reading development.

> Discuss with your child his or her school experiences. Ask your child to explain what he or she is studying, and why it is important. Encourage your child to share his or her literary favorites with you and enjoy them together.
>
> Let your child see that reading is important by letting him or her see you read, and by providing quiet times and a quiet place in which the child can read. Encourage your child to bring home books from the library.

I am sure that, with your continued help, your child will make further progress in reading and appreciating literature throughout this school year. If you have any questions or suggestions, please feel free to contact me.

Sincerely,

Fecha ______________________________

Estimados Padres,

Durante los meses pasados, sus hijos han usando el texto *Reading Literature, Nivel Verde,* ellos han participado en las siguientes actividades:

- leyendo historietas e leyendas para su placer y para poder apreciar y entender la literatura y sus elementos
- reforzando la comprensión de cada selección identificando características como escenario, carácteres, y argumento
- mejorando su vocabulario con el empleo de nuevas estrategias para aprender palabras
- aprendiendo el proceso de escribir y aplicando las técnicas que usan autores a su proprio escrito
- desarrolando habilidades en estudio e investigacion, hablar y escuchar, y pensamiento crítico.

En los proximos meses, sus hijos van a leer poesiá, historias reales, y drama. Conceptos y habilidades ya presentados serán revisados, y las nuevas agregadas, extendidas, y reforzadas.

Les pido que continuen dando a sus hijos el apoyo y aliento que hasta hoy les han brindado. Asi podrán alcanzar estas metas con exito.

Les sugiero las siguientes activades para repasar y continuar el desarrollo de la lectura:

> Hable con sus hijos sobre las activades y estudios de la clase. Pídanles que expliquen lo que están estudiando en la escuela y por que es importante. Invite a sus hijos a compartir con Uds. sus cuentos favoritos y disfrútenlos juntos.
>
> Fomenten en sus hijos la importancia de la lectura. Cuando estén leyendo, asegúrense que ellos los vean. Animen a sus hijos que traigan a casa libros de la biblioteca.

Creo que con su ayuda y apoyo, sus hijos continuarán su progreso en el estudio de lectura y literatura durante el año. Les pido se comuniquen conmigo, si tienen preguntas o sugerencias.

Atentamente,

Date ______________________

Dear Parent,

Throughout this past school year, through the classroom use of *Reading Literature, Green Level*, your child has developed a variety of skills in reading, comprehension, vocabulary development, and writing. In addition, your child has improved skills in study and research, speaking and listening, and critical thinking. It is important to maintain these skills at a high level throughout the coming vacation.

Here are some ways you can assist your child in maintaining these skills:

Encourage reading for pleasure. Help your child to visit a library regularly. Accompany your child, if possible. Discuss with your child what he or she has learned or enjoyed in this independent reading. Through discussion your child will increase his or her reading comprehension.

If possible, have a dictionary for young people available at home, so that your child can continue to improve his or her vocabulary skills. Also, encourage your child to use such library resources as the encyclopedia and nonfiction books to learn more about his or her special interests.

Encourage your child in writing letters, keeping a diary, or writing original stories or poems for fun. Offer to read your child's writing, not to criticize, but to provide an audience. Your interest and support will give your child a stronger feeling for communication through writing, and will provide more incentive for clear and correct writing. Personal experiences with writing will reinforce your child's understanding and appreciation of literature.

Encouraging your child to participate in more purposeful activities such as these will provide an enriching alternative to watching television throughout the summer.

I hope these suggestions will help to make the coming vacation stimulating as well as enjoyable for both you and your child.

Sincerely,

Fecha ______________________________

Estimados Padres,

En el transcuro de este año escolar, con el uso en la clase del texto *Reading Literature, Nivel Verde,* sus hijos han aprendido una variedad de habilidades en lectura, comprensión, aumento de vocabulario, y escritura. Ademaś, sus hijos han mejorado habilidades en estudio e investigación, hablar y escuchar, y pensamiento crítico. Es sumamente importante que sus hijos conserven estos conocimientos ya adquiridos durante las vacaciones de verano que se aproximan.

Su ayuda, en inglés o español, tiene mucho valor. Les sugiero las siguientes activadades para ayudar a sus hijos mantener las habilidades que han aprendido.

Despierten en sus hijos el interés y hábito de la lectura, animándolos a visitar la biblioteca con frecuencia. Acompáñenlos cada vez que les sea posible. Discutan con sus hijos lo que han aprendido o disfrutado en su lectura. Atravez de esto, Uds. ayudarán a sus hijos a mejorar su comprensión de lo leido.

Si es posible, tengan un diccionario juvenil en casa para el desarrollo y comprensión del vocabulario. Ademas, animen a sus hijos a usar libros en la biblioteca como la enciclopedia, e historias reales, para que ellos aprendan más sobre sus intereses especiales.

Animen a sus ninos para que escribán sus propias cartas, un diario, o cuentos y poesias originales. Lean en voz alta lo que han escrito, no para criticar, sino para que tengan oyentes. Esta experiencia fomentará en sus hijos el deseo de expresarse por escrito clara y correctamente. La experiencia propia de sus hijos con la escritura contribuirá a asegurar el entendimiento y la apreciación de la literatura.

Estas actividades les darána sus hijos una alternativa enriquecida para no ver tantos programas de televisión.

Espero que estas sugerencias sean productivas y les ayuden a Uds. y a sus hijos a disfrutar un verano grato e interesante.

Atentamente,

Contents of Reading Literature

Reading Literature Red Level (7)

Chapter 1 Fables

Reading Literature: Fables
Comprehension Skills: Time Order
Vocabulary Skills: Word Parts

Ten Fables	Aesop
The Fox and the Grapes	Jean de La Fontaine
Two Ways To Count to Ten	Liberian Fable
The Thief and the Bell	Chinese Fable
The King and the Shirt	Leo Tolstoy
The Learned Son	Leo Tolstoy
Equal Inheritance	Leo Tolstoy
Three Rolls and a Pretzel	Leo Tolstoy
The Fox and the Crow	James Thurber

Review

Chapter 2 American Folklore

Reading Literature: American Folklore
Comprehension Skills: Cause and Effect
Vocabulary Skills: The Dictionary

Paul Bunyan and Babe, the Blue Ox	Traditional American Folk Tale
When Paul Bunyan Was Ill	Willie Reader
The Ballad of John Henry	Southern Folk Ballad
Pecos Bill: America's Greatest Cowboy	Traditional American Folk Tale
Davy Crockett	Michael Gorham
They Tell Yarns	Carl Sandburg
The Snakebit Hoe Handle	Appalachian Folk Tale
How To Tell Bad News	Colonial Folk Tale
Yankee Exaggerations	Folklore from the 1800's

Review

Chapter 3 How Writers Write

Using the Process of Writing

Pre-Writing, Writing, Revising

Using the Sounds of Language

Alliteration, Rhyme, Rhythm, Onomatopoeia

Using Figures of Speech

Simile, Metaphor, Personification, Hyperbole

Review

Chapter 4 Short Stories

Reading Literature: Short Stories
Comprehension Skills: Inferences and Outcomes
Vocabulary Skills: Context Clues

Great Classic Stories

The Necklace	Guy de Maupassant
Appointment in Baghdad	Traditional Story retold by Edith Wharton
How the Camel Got His Hump	Rudyard Kipling
The Emperor's New Clothes	Hans Christian Andersen
The Huckabuck Family and How They Raised Popcorn in Nebraska and Quit and Came Back	Carl Sandburg

Great Modern Stories

Reading Literature: More About Short Stories

The Dinner Party	Mona Gardner
Many Moons	James Thurber
Keplik, the Match Man	Myron Levoy
The Jar of Tassai	Grace P. Moon
The Fun They Had	Isaac Asimov
The Great Detective	Stephen Leacock

Review

Chapter 5 Poetry

Reading Literature: Poetry
Comprehension Skills: Figurative Language
Vocabulary Skills: Multiple Meanings

Poems About Individual Growth

Endless Search	Alonzo Lopez
One for Novella Nelson	Myra Cohn Livingston
Not in Vain	Emily Dickinson
Trifle	Georgia Douglas Johnson
Old English Prayer	Traditional
Your World	Georgia Douglas Johnson
Time	Traditional
Advice to Travelers	Walker Gibson
Little Dead	Myra Cohn Livingston
Faith	From a sign over an old inn at Bray, England
74th Street	Myra Cohn Livingston
To Satch	Samuel Allen
You Whose Day It Is	Nootka Indian Tribe

Poems About the Individual and Others

Reading Literature: More About Poetry

Faults	Sara Teasdale
A Choice of Weapons	Phyllis McGinley
The Quarrel	Eleanor Farjeon
A Love Song	Raymond Richard Patterson
While I Slept	Robert Francis
To Young People	Henry W. Longfellow

Poems About the World at Large

Orbiter 5 Shows How Earth Looks from the Moon	May Swenson
The First	Lilian Moore
Earth	Oliver Herford
The Computer's First Christmas Card	Edwin Morgan

Review

Chapter 6 Nonfiction

Reading Literature: Nonfiction
Comprehension Skills: Main Idea
Vocabulary Skills: Context Clues

Biographies

Florence Nightingale: Lady with a Lamp	May McNeer and Lynd Ward
George Washington Carver: Plant Wizard	May McNeer and Lynd Ward
Jane Addams: Good Neighbor	May McNeer and Lynd Ward
Jim Thorpe: Indian Athlete	Guernsey Van Riper, Jr.

True Adventure Stories

First to the South Pole!	Walker Chapman
from The Conquest of Everest	Sir Edmund Hillary
Neil Armstrong: First on the Moon	Paul Westman

Essays

Reading Nonfiction: More About Nonfiction

Morning—The Bird Perched for Flight	Anne Morrow Lindbergh
A Changing Landscape	Archibald MacLeish

Review

Chapter 7 Drama

Reading Literature: Drama
Comprehension Skills: Sentences and Punctuation
Vocabulary Skills: Levels of Language

The Tinker of Toledo	Nellie McCaslin
Miss Louisa and the Outlaws	Frances B. Watts

Review

Handbook for Reading and Writing

Literary Terms
Summary of Comprehension Skills
Summary of Vocabulary Skills
Guidelines for the Process of Writing
Guidelines for Study and Research
Summary of Skills in Critical Thinking
Glossary
Biographies of Authors
Index of Titles and Authors
Index of Fine Art
Index of Skills

Reading Literature Green Level (8)

Chapter 1 Legends

Reading Literature: Legends
Comprehension Skills: Main Idea
Vocabulary Skills: Context Clues

Richard the Lion-Hearted	Traditional Tale
King John and the Abbot	Traditional Tale
The Pied Piper of Hamelin	Traditional Tale
William Tell	Traditional Tale
Spotted Eagle and Black Crow	Traditional American Indian Legend
The Six Horsemen	Traditional West African Legend
Lazy Peter and His Three-Cornered Hat	Traditional Puerto Rican Legend

Review

Chapter 2 The Legend of King Arthur

Reading Literature: The Legend of King Arthur
Comprehension Skills: Inferences and Conclusions
Vocabulary Skills: Word Parts

The Legend of King Arthur — *Traditional Legend, A Retelling of* Le Morte d'Arthur *by Sir Thomas Malory*
Review

Chapter 3 How Writers Write

Using the Process of Writing
Pre-Writing, Writing, Revising

Using the Sounds of Language
Alliteration, Assonance, Rhyme, Rhythm, Onomatopoeia

Using Figures of Speech
Simile, Metaphor, Personification, Hyperbole

Review

Chapter 4 Short Stories

Reading Literature: Short Stories
Comprehension Skills: Relationships
Vocabulary Skills: Multiple Meanings

Great Classic Stories

How the Three Young Men Found Death — Geoffrey Chaucer
The Bishop's Candlesticks — Victor Hugo
Hearts and Hands — O. Henry
The Bet — Anton Chekhov
The Story of Keesh — Jack London

Great Modern Stories

Reading Literature: More About Short Stories

The Old Soldier — Dorothy Canfield
The Big Wave — Pearl S. Buck
The Summer of the Beautiful White Horse — William Saroyan
The Rocking Donkey — Joan Aiken
The Disappearing Man — Isaac Asimov

Review

Chapter 5 Poetry

Reading Literature: Poetry
Comprehension Skills: Inferences and Outcomes
Vocabulary Skills: Context Clues

Poems About Individual Growth

The Dream Keeper — Langston Hughes
The Duel — Emily Dickinson
The Courage That My Mother Had — Edna St. Vincent Millay
All But Blind — Walter de la Mare
Magic Words To Feel Better — Netsilik Eskimo
The Song by the Way — Francisco A. de Icaza
I Was Born Today — Amado Nervo

Poems About Animals

Reading Literature: More About Poetry

Poem — William Carlos Williams
Catalog — Rosalie Moore
Sea Lions — Valerie Worth
Seal — William Jay Smith
Woodpecker (haiku) — Issa
Fall (haiku) — Sally Andresen
Bee! I'm Expecting You! — Emily Dickinson
The Eagle — Alfred, Lord Tennyson
The Mountain and the Squirrel — Ralph Waldo Emerson
The Dog (As Seen by the Cat) — Oliver Herford
The Panther — Ogden Nash
The Termite — Ogden Nash
The Hippopotamus — Ogden Nash
The Canary — Ogden Nash
The Purist — Ogden Nash

Poems About Sports

The Base Stealer — Robert Francis
The Double-Play — Robert Wallace
Casey at the Bat — Ernest Lawrence Thayer
Foul Shot — Edwin A. Hoey
The Women's 400 Meters — Lillian Morrison
Skating — Herbert Asquith
Pole Vault — Shiro Murano
Sky Diving — Richmond Lattimore

Poems About American History

Like Ghosts of Eagles — Robert Francis
The Flower-Fed Buffaloes — Vachel Lindsay
Benjamin Franklin 1706–1790 — Stephen Vincent Benét and Rosemary Benét
Paul Revere's Ride — Henry W. Longfellow
Western Wagons — Stephen Vincent Benét and Rosemary Benét
Abraham Lincoln 1809–1865 — Stephen Vincent Benét and Rosemary Benét
Women — Alice Walker
America the Beautiful — Katharine Lee Bates

Review

Chapter 6 Nonfiction

Reading Literature: Nonfiction
Comprehension Skills: Connotations, Denotations
Vocabulary Skills: Reference Sources

Autobiographies

I Get a Colt To Break In — Lincoln Steffens
from The Story of My Life — Helen Keller

Biographies

Peculiarsome Abe — Carl Sandburg
Matthew A. Henson 1866–1955 — Langston Hughes
Maria Tallchief — Tobi Tobias

Humorous Sayings, Writings, and Anecdotes

Sayings and Writings — Abraham Lincoln
Anecdotes About Abraham Lincoln — Beatrice Schenk de Regniers

Essays

Reading Literature: Types of Nonfiction

April and Robins — Hal Borland
The Prelude — Hal Borland
Shortest Month — Hal Borland

Letters

Abraham Lincoln: Letter to His Step-Brother — Abraham Lincoln
Abraham Lincoln: Letter to Mrs. Bixby — Abraham Lincoln

Speeches

Farewell Address — Abraham Lincoln
The Gettysburg Address — Abraham Lincoln

Vignette

Day of Light and Shadow — Genevieve Foster

Review

Chapter 7 Drama

Reading Literature: Drama
Comprehension Skills: Author's Purpose
Vocabulary Skills: Context Clues

A Connecticut Yankee in King Arthur's Court — Mark Twain
Invasion from Mars — H.G. Wells

Review

Handbook for Reading and Writing

Literary Terms
Summary of Comprehension Skills
Summary of Vocabulary Skills
Guidelines for the Process of Writing
Guidelines for Study and Research
Summary of Skills in Critical Thinking
Glossary
Biographies of Authors
Index of Titles and Authors
Index of Fine Art
Index of Skills

Reading Literature Orange Level (9)

Chapter 1 Greek Myths and Legends

Reading Literature: Greek Myths and Legends
Comprehension Skills: Direct Statements
Vocabulary Skills: Four Ways To Find Meanings

Greek Myths

The Beginning of the World — Traditional Greek Myths
Pandora, the First Woman
The Flood
Perseus Slays the Gorgon
The Labors of Hercules
Theseus and the Minotaur — Traditional Greek Legends
The Flight of Icarus

Greek Legends

Reading Literature: Greek Legends

The Trojan War — Traditional Greek Legends
The Voyage of Odysseus
Circe, the Enchantress
The Perils of Odysseus
The End of Odysseus's Voyage
The Fate of the Suitors
The Kyklops — Homer, translated by Robert Fitzgerald

Review

Chapter 2 Norse Myths and Legends

Reading Literature: Norse Myths and Legends
Comprehension Skills: Comparisons and Contrasts
Vocabulary Skills: Word Parts

Norse Myths

The Beginning of a World — Traditional Norse Myths
How Odin Lost His Eye
Frigga's Necklace
Sif's Golden Hair
Thor's Voyage to the Land of the Giants

Norse Legend

The Song of Beowulf	Traditional Norse Legend

Review

Chapter 3 Myths from Many Lands

Reading Literature: Myths from Many Lands
Comprehension Skills; Paragraph Organization
Vocabulary Skills: Context Clues

Legend of Creation	Miwok Indian Myth
The Story of the Cuckoo	New Guinea Myth
The Fish	Australian Myth
The Tale of Superman	Hausa People, Nigeria
Superman	Jerome Siegel, Joe Shuster

Review

Chapter 4 How Writers Write

Using the Process of Writing

Pre-Writing, Writing, Revising

Using the Sounds of Language

Alliteration, Rhyme, Rhythm, Onomatopoeia, Assonance

Using Figures of Speech

Simile, Metaphor, Personification, Hyperbole
Review

Chapter 5 Short Stories

Reading Literature: Short Stories
Comprehension Skills: Inferences
Vocabulary Skills: Context Clues

Great Classic Stories

The Lady, or the Tiger?	Frank R. Stockton
A Spark Neglected	Leo Tolstoy
After Twenty Years	O. Henry
Charles	Shirley Jackson

Great Modern Stories

Reading Literature: More About Short Stories

A Man Who Had No Eyes	MacKinlay Kantor
Thank You, M'am	Langston Hughes
Raymond's Run	Toni Cade Bambara
Lather and Nothing Else	Hernando Téllez
The Third Wish	Joan Aiken

Science Fiction Stories

All Summer in a Day	Ray Bradbury
The Weapon	Fredric Brown
The Assassin	Robert Silverberg

Review

Chapter 6 Poetry

Reading Literature: Poetry
Comprehension Skills: Figurative Language
Vocabulary Skills: Origins of English Words

Observations

To Look at Any Thing	John Moffitt
I Hear America Singing	Walt Whitman
Song of the Truck	Doris Frankel
Unfolding Bud	Naoshi Koriyama
Fueled	Marcie Hans
Steam Shovel	Charles Malam
Macavity: The Mystery Cat	T. S. Eliot
Crossing	Philip Booth
Child on Top of a Greenhouse	Theodore Roethke
Central Park Tourney	Mildred Weston
Apartment House	Gerald Raftery
Southbound on the Freeway	May Swenson
For a Dead Kitten	Sara Henderson Hay
The High School Band	Reed Whittemore
Nine Triads	Lillian Morrison

Human Relationships

Reading Literature: More About Poetry

Ingratitude	William Shakespeare
Never Seek To Tell Thy Love	William Blake
When I Was One-And-Twenty	A.E. Housman
Faces	Sara Teasdale
The Storyteller	Mark Van Doren
Mother to Son	Langston Hughes
Lament	Edna St. Vincent Millay
Those Winter Sundays	Robert Hayden
Piñones	Leroy Quintana
Eviction	Lucille Clifton
Outwitted	Edwin Markham

Psalms of Life

A Psalm of Life	Henry W. Longfellow
Footprints	Henry W. Longfellow
Miracles	Walt Whitman
Lineage	Margaret Walker
Dreams	Langston Hughes
Thumbprint	Eve Merriam
"to be nobody-but-yourself"	e.e. cummings
The Road Not Taken	Robert Frost
Stopping by Woods on a Snowy Evening	Robert Frost
Requiem	Robert Louis Stevenson

Review

Chapter 7 Nonfiction

Reading Literature: Nonfiction
Comprehension Skills: Fact and Opinion
Vocabulary Skills: The Dictionary

Diaries

The Life of Davy Crockett by Himself	Davy Crockett
The Diary of a Young Girl	Anne Frank

Autobiographies

The Washwoman	Isaac Bashevis Singer
Langston Terrace	Eloise Greenfield and Lessie Jones Little

Biographies

We'll Always Sing His Songs	Carl Carmer
Banker Maggie Walker	Olive W. Burt

Personal Recollections

Mama and Her Bank Account	Kathryn Forbes
The First Day of the War	Maia Wojciechowska

Humorous Sketches

Reading Literature: Different Types of Nonfiction

Punch, Brothers, Punch	Mark Twain
Learning To Drive	Billy Rose

Articles

People	Isaac Asimov
How Smart Are Dolphins?	Russell Freedman

Sayings and Proverbs

Proverbs from Many Lands	Traditional
Chinese Proverbs	Traditional
African Proverbs	Traditional

Review

Chapter 8 Drama

Reading Literature: Drama
Comprehension Skills: Evaluations
Vocabulary Skills: Levels of Language

Sherlock Holmes and the Stock-broker's Clerk	Arthur Conan Doyle
Grandpa and the Statue	Arthur Miller

Review

Handbook for Reading and Writing

Literary Terms
Summary of Comprehension Skills
Summary of Vocabulary Skills
Guidelines for the Process of Writing
Guidelines for Study and Research
Summary of Skills in Critical Thinking
Glossary
Biographies of Authors
Index of Titles and Authors
Index of Fine Art
Index of Skills

Reading Literature Blue Level (10)

Chapter 1 How Writers Write

Understanding the Process of Writing

Pre-Writing, Writing, Revising
Review

Chapter 2 Short Stories

Reading Literature: Short Stories
Comprehension Skills: Relationships and Inferences
Vocabulary Skills: Context Clues

Setting

Feathered Friend	Arthur C. Clarke
Zlateh the Goat	Isaac Bashevis Singer
The Dog of Pompeii	Louis Untermeyer

Characterization

The Fan Club	Rona Maynard
A Mother in Mannville	Marjorie Kinnan Rawlings
The Storyteller	Saki

Plot

Reading Literature: More About Short Stories

The Test	Theodore L. Thomas
The Beau Catcher	Frederick Laing
The Most Dangerous Game	Richard Connell

Theme

Humans Are Different	Alan Bloch
Beauty Is Truth	Anna Guest
The Force of Luck	Latin American Folk Legend retold by Rudolfo A. Anaya
The Confession	Anton Chekov

Mood

The Ransom of Red Chief	O. Henry
The Old Man	Daphne du Maurier
The Richer, the Poorer	Dorothy West
The Foghorn	Ray Bradbury

Review

Chapter 3 Techniques Writers Use

Using the Sounds of Language

Alliteration, Assonance, Rhyme, Rhythm, Onomatopoeia

Using Figures of Speech

Simile, Metaphor, Personification, Hyperbole

Review

Chapter 4 Poetry

Reading Literature: Poetry
Comprehension Skills: Structure and Meaning
Vocabulary Skills: The Dictionary

Sound

The Optileast and the Pessimost	Eve Merriam
Rain	Richard Armour
The Sloth	Theodore Roethke
The Bat	Theodore Roethke
Life	Paul Laurence Dunbar

Shape

Reading Literature: More About Poetry

Football	Walt Mason
Arithmetic	Carl Sandburg
Medicine	Alice Walker
Voice in the Crowd	Ted Joans
Tears	Alonzo Lopez
who knows if the moon's	e.e. cummings
Absolutes	Gustave Keyser
The Universe	May Swenson

Speaker and Tone

The Way It Is	Gloria Oden
Youth to Age	Pauli Murray
Kidnap Poem	Nikki Giovanni
I'm Nobody! Who Are You?	Emily Dickinson
Two Friends	David Ignatow
Poem	Langston Hughes
Where the Rainbow Ends	Richard Rive
Friendship	Oglala Sioux

Imagery and Mood

Troubled Woman	Langston Hughes
Driving to Town Late To Mail a Letter	Robert Bly
Bicycles	Andrei Voznesensky
Concrete Trap	Elizabeth Coatsworth
time and space	Naoshi Koriyama

Figurative Language

Barter	Sara Teasdale
The Distant Drum	Calvin C. Hernton
Get Up, Blues	James A. Emanuel
A Penguin	Oliver Herford
Words	Pauli Murray

Theme

Lodged	Robert Frost
Seagulls	Robert Francis
Ride a Wild Horse	Hannah Kahn
Television-Movie	Kirby Congdon
Richard Cory	E.A. Robinson
Earth	John Hall Wheelock
Saying Yes	Diana Chang

Review

Chapter 5 Nonfiction

Reading Literature: Nonfiction
Comprehension Skills: Evaluating Nonfiction
Vocabulary Skills: Using Word Parts

True Adventure Stories

from Of Men and Mountains	William O. Douglas
Not To Go with the Others	John Hersey
Rattlesnake Hunt	Marjorie Kinnan Rawlings
from Never Cry Wolf	Farley Mowat

Biographies

Babe Didrikson Zaharias	Harry Gersh
Wilma Rudolph	Marc Dachter
Eleanor Roosevelt	Aylesa Forsee

Autobiographies

from Everything But Money	Sam Levenson
"Not Poor, Just Broke"	Dick Gregory
from Growing Up	Russell Baker
from My Life in and Out of Baseball	Willie Mays as told to Charles Einstein

Journals

from Travels with Charley	John Steinbeck
from Blue Highways	Willian Least Heat Moon
from North to the Orient	Anne Morrow Lindbergh

Humorous and Personal Essays

Fresh Air Will Kill You	Art Buchwald
At the Funeral	Mark Twain
The Fraudulent Ant	Mark Twain
A Loud Sneer for Our Feathered Friends	Ruth McKenney
Primal Screen	Ellen Goodman

Articles

Your Chances for the Presidency	Richard Armour
The First Basketball Game	Raymond P. Kaighn as told to Bob Brooks
Clever Hans	Evon Z. Vogt and Ray Hyman
Body Talk	Kathlyn Gay
Pompeii	Robert Silverberg

Review

Chapter 6 The Long Short Story

Reading Literature: The Long Short Story
Comprehension Skills: Grammar and Mechanics
Vocabulary Skills: How New Words Are Created

Flowers for Algernon	Daniel Keyes

Review

Chapter 7 Drama

Reading Literature: Drama
Comprehension Skills: Evaluation
Vocabulary Skills: Levels of Language

The Hitchhiker	Lucille Fletcher
The Monsters Are Due on Maple Street	Rod Sterling
The Monkey's Paw	W.W. Jacobs

Review

Handbook for Reading and Writing

Literary Terms
Summary of Comprehension Skills
Summary of Vocabulary Skills
Guidelines for the Process of Writing
Guidelines for Study and Research
Summary of Critical Thinking Terms
Glossary
Biographies of Authors
Index of Titles and Authors
Index of Fine Art
Index of Skills

Reading Literature Yellow Level (11)

Chapter 1 The Colonial Period (1600–1750)

Historical Background: The Colonial Period
Reading Literature: The Colonial Period
Comprehension Skills: Inferences and Conclusions
Vocabulary Skills: How Language Grows

This Newly Created World	Winnebago Indian
Song of the Sky Loom	Tewa Indian
I Went To Kill the Deer	Taos Pueblo Indian
I Have Killed the Deer	Taos Pueblo Indian
The Algonquian Confederacy Speech, 1609	Powhatan
Pocahontas	John Smith
from Of Plymouth Plantation	William Bradford
Psalm 23	King James Bible
Psalm 23	Bay Psalm Book
Desiderata	Anonymous
A Puritan Code	Jonathan Edwards
To My Dear and Loving Husband	Anne Bradstreet
Boast Not, Proud English	Roger Williams

Review

Chapter 2 How Writers Write

Understanding the Process of Writing

Pre-Writing, Writing, Revising

Review

Chapter 3 The Revolutionary Period (1750–1800)

Historical Background: The Revolutionary Period
Reading Literature: The Revolutionary Period
Comprehension Skills: Subjective Writing
Vocabulary Skills: Levels of Language

What Is an American?	Jean de Crévecoeur

Focus on Benjamin Franklin
from The Autobiography
Epigrams from *Poor Richard's Almanack*
Benjamin Franklin Hurls Defiance at an Old Comrade
On Being Learned
Benjamin Franklin Writes His Own Epitaph

The Crisis	Thomas Paine
The Declaration of Independence	Thomas Jefferson
The Education of a Lady	Thomas Jefferson
The Letters of Abigail and John Adams	Abigail and John Adams

Review

Chapter 4 Techniques Writers Use

Using the Sounds of Language

Alliteration, Assonance, Consonance, Rhyme, Rhythm, Onomatopoeia

Using Figures of Speech
Simile, Metaphor, Personification, Hyperbole

Review

Chapter 5 The Early National Period (1800–1855)

Historical Background: The Early National Period
Reading Literature: The American Romantics
Comprehension Skills: Relationships Between Ideas
Vocabulary Skills: Context Clues

Prayer at Sunrise	Zuñi Indian
Spring Song	Ojibwa Indian
Darkness Song	Iroquois Indian
Rip Van Winkle	Washington Irving
The Devil and Daniel Webster	Stephen Vincent Benét

Focus on Edgar Allen Poe
The Tell-Tale Heart
The Raven
Annabel Lee

Old Ironsides	Oliver Wendell Holmes
Killed at the Ford	Henry W. Longfellow
The Tide Rises, the Tide Falls	Henry W. Longfellow
from Self-Reliance	Ralph Waldo Emerson
Epigrams	Ralph Waldo Emerson
Concord Hymn	Ralph Waldo Emerson
from Walden	Henry David Thoreau
Declaration of Women's Rights	Elizabeth Cady Stanton

Review

Chapter 6 The Late Nineteenth Century (1855–1900)

Historical Background: The Late Nineteenth Century
Reading Literature: Realism and Naturalism
Comprehension Skills: Literal and Figurative Language
Vocabulary Skills: Word Parts

The Civil War

The Gettysburg Address	Abraham Lincoln
Letter to Mrs. Bixby	Abraham Lincoln
from The Emancipation Proclamation	Abraham Lincoln
Epigrams	Abraham Lincoln
from Robert E. Lee	Stephen Vincent Benét
from My Bondage and My Freedom	Frederick Douglass
An Occurence at Owl Creek Bridge	Ambrose Bierce
A Mystery of Heroism	Stephen Crane
Cavalry Crossing a Ford	Walt Whitman
Beat! Beat! Drums!	Walt Whitman
When I Heard the Learn'd Astronomer	Walt Whitman

Focus on Emily Dickinson
Fame Is a Bee
The Brain Is Wider Than the Sky
Faith Is a Fine Invention
Because I Could Not Stop for Death
The Bustle in a House

Native American

Rain-in-the-Face	Charles Eastman
I Kill Her Enemies	Norman H. Russell
The Sioux Woman	Mari Sandoz
The Last Song of Sitting Bull, the Teton Chief	Sioux Indian
Song of a Man About To Die in a Strange Land	Ojibwa Indian
There Is No Death	Chief Seattle

The Frontier
Focus on Mark Twain
from The Adventures of Huckleberry Finn
from Life on the Mississippi
An Encounter with an Interviewer
Epigrams

To Build a Fire	Jack London

Review

Chapter 7 Twentieth Century Fiction

Historical Background: The Twentieth Century
Reading Literature: Short Stories
Comprehension Skills: Tone, Mood, and Emphasis
Vocabulary Skills: Inference and Word Meaning

The Gift of the Magi	O. Henry
A Visit of Charity	Eudora Welty
The Far and the Near	Thomas Wolfe
Old Man at the Bridge	Ernest Hemingway
Migrant People	John Steinbeck
from To Kill a Mockingbird	Harper Lee
The Possibility of Evil	Shirley Jackson
Time in Thy Flight	Ray Bradbury

Review

Chapter 8 Twentieth Century Nonfiction

Reading Literature: Nonfiction
Comprehension Skills: Purpose and Audience
Vocabulary Skills: The Dictionary

Autobiographies and Biographies

from Black Boy	Richard Wright
from Stelmark	Harry Mark Petrakis
from I Know Why the Caged Bird Sings	Maya Angelou
The Legend of Amelia Earhart	Pete Hamill

Speeches

Inaugural Address	John F. Kennedy
from I Have a Dream	Martin Luther King, Jr.

Essays

It All Started with Columbus	Richard Armour
Seeing	Annie Dillard
Silent Spring	Rachel Carson

Review

Chapter 9 Twentieth Century Poetry

Reading Literature: Poetry
Comprehension Skills: Poetic Language
Vocabulary Skills: Application

Lucinda Matlock	Edgar Lee Masters
George Gray	Edgar Lee Masters
Sympathy	Paul Laurence Dunbar
The Debt	Paul Laurence Dunbar
Chicago	Carl Sandburg
Buffalo Dusk	Carl Sandburg
Jazz Fantasia	Carl Sandburg
Grass	Carl Sandburg
Mending Wall	Robert Frost
A Time To Talk	Robert Frost
The Road Not Taken	Robert Frost
Fire and Ice	Robert Frost

Reading Literature: More About Poetry

If You SHould Go	Countee Cullen
The Red Wheelbarrow	William Carlos Williams
in Just–	e.e. cummings

Focus on Langston Hughes
Aunt Sue's Stories
The Negro Speaks of Rivers
Harlem
Blues at Dawn
Subway Rush Hour

Ancient History	Arthur Guiterman
Money	Richard Armour
The Unknown Citizen	W.H. Auden
The Death of the Ball Turret Gunner	Randall Jarrell
Night Practice	May Swenson
Breaking and Entering	Joyce Carol Oates
In the Pocket	James Dickey
The Bean Eaters	Gwendolyn Brooks
Expect Nothing	Alice Walker
If There Be Sorrow	Mari Evans
Celebration	Alonzo Lopez
The New Direction	Emerson Blackhorse Mitchell
Choices	Nikki Giovanni
For Poets	Al Young

Review

Chapter 10 Twentieth Century Drama

Reading Literature: Drama
Comprehension Skills: Inferences and Outcomes
Vocabulary Skills: Multiple Meanings

The Miracle Worker	William Gibson

Review

Handbook for Reading and Writing
Literary Terms
Summary of Comprehension Skills
Summary of Vocabulary Skills
Guidelines for the Process of Writing
Guidelines for Study and Reseach
Summary of Critical Thinking Terms
Glossary
Biographies
Index of Titles and Authors
Index of Fine Art
Index of Skills

Reading Literature Purple Level (12)

Chapter 1 Our Classical Heritage

Historical Background: Our Classical Heritage
Reading Literature: Greek and Roman Literature
Comprehension Skills: Inferences and Conclusions
Vocabulary Skills: Context Clues

Ancient Greece

The Riddle of the Sphinx	Ancient Riddle
from The Iliad	Homer
Fables	Aesop
Aesop's Last Fable	William March
Four Fragments	Sappho
Epigrams	Sophocles
Epigrams	Euripides
Dialogue Between Two Young Men	Agathias

Ancient Rome

from The Metamorphoses	Ovid
A Total Abstainer	Martial

To Quintas	Martial
Galla's Hair	Martial

Review

Chapter 2 The Anglo-Saxon Period

Historical Background: The Anglo-Saxon Period
Reading Literature: Anglo-Saxon Literature
Comprehension Skills: Punctuation Clues
Vocabulary Skills: Inference

Five Anglo-Saxon Riddles
from Beowulf
The Seafarer

Review

Chapter 3 The Medieval Period

Historical Background: The Medieval Period
Reading Literature: Medieval Literature
Comprehension Skills: Identifying Relationships
Vocabulary Skills: The History of Language

Edward, Edward	Traditional English Ballad
Lord Randal	Traditional Scottish Ballad
Brian O Linn	Traditional Irish Ballad
from The Canterbury Tales	Geoffrey Chaucer
A Knight	
A Squire	
A Prioress	
The Intimations Kill Me	Giovanni Boccaccio
Federigo's Falcon	Giovanni Boccaccio
The One-Legged Crane	Giovanni Boccaccio
from The Divine Comedy	Dante Alighieri
Virgil	
The Gate of Hell	
Ulysses	

Review

Chapter 4 How Writers Write

Understanding the Process of Writing
Pre-Writing, Writing, Revising

Using the Sounds of Language
Alliteration, Assonance, Consonance, Rhyme, Rhythm, Onomatopoeia

Using Figures of Speech
Simile, Metaphor, Personification, Hyperbole

Review

Chapter 5 The Renaissance

Historical Background: The Renaissance
Reading Literature: Renaissance Literature
Comprehension Skills: Levels of Reading
Vocabulary Skills: Word Origins

William Shakespeare

The Story of Shakespeare's *Macbeth*	Marchette Chute
Famous Passages from Shakespeare	
Blow, Blow	William Shakespeare
Silvia	William Shakespeare
Sweet-and-Twenty	William Shakespeare
Sonnets	William Shakespeare
The Passionate Shepherd to His Love	Christopher Marlowe
The Nymph's Reply to the Shepherd	Sir Walter Raleigh
from Don Quixote	Miguel de Cervantes

Review

Chapter 6 The Seventeenth and Eighteenth Centuries

Historical Background: The Seventeenth and Eighteenth Centuries
Reading Literature: The Literature of the Period
Comprehension Skills: The Language of Poetry
Vocabulary Skills: Using the Dictionary

The Seventeenth Century

Logical English	Traditional
English Riddles	Traditional
Dare To Be True	George Herbert
To the Virgins, To Make Much of Time	Robert Herrick
Song to Celia	Ben Jonson
To Lucasta, On Going to the Wars	Richard Lovelace
Quotations	John Milton
from the King James Bible	

The Eighteenth Century

My Love Is Like a Red Red Rose	Robert Burns
To a Blockhead	Alexander Pope
Epigrams	Alexander Pope
To Hayley	William Blake
A Poison Tree	William Blake
Never Seek To Tell Thy Love	William Blake
To See a World	William Blake

Review

Chapter 7 The Nineteenth Century

Historical Background: The Nineteenth Century
Reading Literature: Romanticism and Realism
Comprehension Skills: Purpose and Audience
Vocabulary Skills: Word Parts

Fiction

from Great Expectations	Charles Dickens
The Piece of String	Guy de Maupassant
A Slander	Anton Chekhov
God Sees the Truth, But Waits	Leo Tolstoy

Poetry

Reading Literature: Poetry

My Heart Leaps Up	William Wordsworth
She Dwelt Among the Untrodden Ways	William Wordsworth
She Was A Phantom of Delight	William Wordsworth
She Walks in Beauty	George Gordon, Lord Byron
from Childe Harold's Pilgrimage	George Gordon, Lord Byron
An Epitaph	George Gordon, Lord Byron
Ozymandias	Percy Bysshe Shelley
Bards of Passion and of Mirth	John Keats
The Rime of the Ancient Mariner	Samuel Taylor Coleridge
Jabberwocky	Lewis Carroll
Jabber-Whacky	Isabelle di Caprio
Break, Break, Break	Alfred, Lord Tennyson
'Tis Better To Have Loved and Lost	Alfred, Lord Tennyson
A Prophecy	Alfred, Lord Tennyson
Ring Out, Wild Bells	Alfred, Lord Tennyson
from Pippa Passes	Robert Browning
If Thou Must Love Me	Elizabeth Barrett Browning
How Do I Love Thee	Elizabeth Barrett Browning
Remember	Christina Rossetti
Precious Stones	Christina Rossetti
Invictus	William Ernest Henley
The Secret of the Machines	Rudyard Kipling
The Convict and Boy with the Violin	Thomas Hardy
Epitaph on a Pessimist	Thomas Hardy
The Alderking	Johann Wolfgang von Goethe
Wings	Victor Hugo
The Lorelei	Heinrich Heine
Good Advice	Heinrich Heine

Nonfiction

Reading Literature: Nonfiction

The Gentleman	John Henry Newman
Nonsense Botany	Edward Lear
Three Recipes for Domestic Cookery	Edward Lear
Irish Folklore and Humor	
The Sparrow	Ivan Turgenev

Drama

Reading Literature: Drama

A Marriage Proposal	Anton Chekhov
from Cyrano de Bergerac	Edmond Rostand

Review

Chapter 8 The Twentieth Century

Historical Background: The Twentieth Century
Reading Literature: Other Elements of Fiction
Comprehension Skills: Evaluations
Vocabulary Skills: Levels of Language

Fiction

The Open Window	Saki
Beware of the Dog	Roald Dahl
A Cup of Tea	Katherine Mansfield
Difficulty with a Bouquet	William Sansom
The Laugher	Heinrich Böll
The Secret	Alberto Moravia

Poetry

Reading Literature: Other Elements of Poetry

Sea Fever	John Masefield
The Listeners	Walter de la Mare
Bones	Walter de la Mare
When I Was One-and-Twenty	A.E. Housman
To an Athlete Dying Young	A.E. Housman
An Irish Airman Foresees His Death	William Butler Yeats
The Soldier	Rupert Brooke
My Parents	Stephen Spender
Postscript	W.H. Auden
Traveler's Curse After Misdirection	Robert Graves
The Naming of Cats	T.S. Eliot
Lizard	D.H. Lawrence
Ever After Happily	Ian Serrailler
Rebecca	Hillaire Belloc
A Boy's Head	Miroslav Holub
To Paint the Portrait of a Bird	Jacques Prévert
Growing Blind	Rainer Maria Rilke
Alone	Hermann Hesse
Tonight I Can Write	Pablo Neruda
If You Hear That a Thousand People Love You	Guadalupe de Saavedra

Nonfiction

Reading Literature: More About Nonfiction

The Wit and Wisdom of George Bernard Shaw	George Bernard Shaw
Shooting an Elephant	George Orwell
On War and Peace	Winston Churchill
By Any Other Name	Santha Rama Rau
from Out of Africa	Isak Dinesen
Father and I	Par Lagerkvist
Silent Song	Pablo Neruda
Letter to an Unborn Child	A Yugoslav Patriot

Drama

Reading Literature: More About Drama

The Patient	Agatha Christie
The Jewels of the Shrine	James Ene Henshaw

Review

Handbook for Reading and Writing

Literary Terms
Summary of Comprehension Skills
Summary of Vocabulary Skills
Guidelines for the Process of Writing
Guidelines for Study and Reseach
Summary of Critical Thinking Terms
Glossary
Biographies
Index of Titles and Authors
Index of Fine Art
Index of Skills

Overview of Skills in Reading Literature

Reading Literature

		Level	Red	Green	Orange	Blue	Yellow	Purple
		Grade	**7**	**8**	**9**	**10**	**11**	**12**
Oral Tradition	Legends, Myths, Fables, Proverbs, Riddles, etc.		■	■	■	■	■	■
Short Stories			■	■	■	■	■	■
Poetry *See also* Forms of Poetry.			■	■	■	■	■	■
Nonfiction	Biography, Autobiography, Essays, Letters, Speeches, Articles, etc.		■	■	■	■	■	■
Drama			■	■	■	■	■	■
Character	Major and Minor Characters		■	■	■	■	■	■
	Static and Dynamic Characters		■	■	■	■	■	■
	Character Interpretation		■	■	■	■	■	■
	Dialogue		■	■	■	■	■	■
Setting			■	■	■	■	■	■
Plot			■	■	■	■	■	■
Conflict	External and Internal Conflict		■	■	■	■	■	■
	Types of External Conflict				■	■	■	■
Sequence or Organization	Chronological		■	■	■	■	■	■
	Logical		■	■	■	■	■	■
	Spatial				■	■	■	■
	Order of Importance				■	■	■	■
	Order of Familiarity					■	■	■
Narrator and Point of View	First-Person		■	■	■	■	■	■
	Third-Person		■	■	■	■	■	■
	Limited, Omniscient		■	■	■	■	■	■
Other Major Elements and Techniques	Speaker		■	■	■	■	■	■
	Mood		■	■	■	■	■	■
	Tone		■	■	■	■	■	■
	Theme		■	■	■	■	■	■

Shaded boxes indicate coverage.

Reading Literature (continued)

	Level	Red	Green	Orange	Blue	Yellow	Purple
	Grade	**7**	**8**	**9**	**10**	**11**	**12**
Other Major Elements and Techniques (continued)	Purpose	■	■	■	■	■	■
	Audience				■	■	■
	Irony	■	■	■	■	■	■
	Foreshadowing		■	■	■	■	■
	Parody	■		■	■	■	■
	Humor	■	■	■	■	■	■
	Allusions	■	■	■	■	■	■
	Flashback		■	■	■	■	■
	Style of Individual Writer	■	■	■	■	■	■
	Imagery, Sensory Images	■	■	■	■	■	■
	Satire, Paradox				■	■	■
Forms of Poetry	Lyric	■	■	■	■	■	■
	Narrative		■	■	■	■	■
	Concrete Poetry		■	■	■	■	■
	Free Verse		■	■	■	■	■
	Blank Verse					■	■
	Sonnet						■
	Ballad						■
Figurative Language	Simile	■	■	■	■	■	■
	Metaphor	■	■	■	■	■	■
	Personification	■	■	■	■	■	■
	Hyperbole	■	■	■	■	■	■
	Understatement	■	■	■	■	■	■
Sounds of Language	Alliteration	■	■	■	■	■	■
	Onomatopoeia	■	■	■	■	■	■
	Repetition	■	■	■	■	■	■
	Rhyme	■	■	■	■	■	■
	Rhyme Scheme	■	■	■	■	■	■
	Sonnet Form						■
	Rhythm	■	■	■	■	■	■
	Assonance		■	■	■	■	■
	Consonance					■	■

Shaded boxes indicate coverage.

Comprehension

		Level	Red	Green	Orange	Blue	Yellow	Purple
		Grade	7	8	9	10	11	12
Literal Reading	Chronological (or Time) Order		■	■	■	■	■	■
	Logical Order		■	■	■	■	■	■
	Spatial (or Natural) Order				■	■	■	■
	Order of Importance				■	■	■	■
	Order of Familiarity					■	■	■
	Stated Main Idea, Stated Details		■	■	■	■	■	■
	Stated Cause and Effect		■	■	■	■	■	■
Sentences and Fragments, Punctuation			■	■	■	■	■	■
Interpretive Meaning	Inferences about Characters, Events, Setting		■	■	■	■	■	■
	Predicting Outcomes		■	■	■	■	■	■
	Interpreting Figurative Language		■	■	■	■	■	■
	Inferring the Main Idea or Theme		■	■	■	■	■	■
	Application of Literature to Life		■	■	■	■	■	■
	Analysis of Literary Elements		■	■	■	■	■	■
	Making Inferences about a Culture from Its Literature				■		■	■
Recognition of Three Levels of Reading								■
Critical Reading *See also* Critical Thinking.	Fact and Opinion		■	■	■	■	■	■
	Objective and Subjective Statements			■	■	■	■	■
	Generalizations		■	■	■	■	■	■
	Stereotype			■	■	■	■	■
	Techniques of Argument or Persuasion				■	■	■	■
	Errors in Reasoning					■	■	■
	Evaluation of Elements of a Selection		■	■	■	■	■	■

Vocabulary

		7	8	9	10	11	12
Context Clues	Definition and Restatement	■	■	■	■	■	■
	Synonyms	■	■	■	■	■	■
	Antonyms	■	■	■	■	■	■
	Comparison and Contrast	■	■	■	■	■	■

Shaded boxes indicate coverage.

Vocabulary (continued)

	Level	Red	Green	Orange	Blue	Yellow	Purple
	Grade	7	8	9	10	11	12
Context Clues (continued)	Example	■	■	■	■	■	■
	Inference	■	■	■	■	■	■
	Others (Series, Grammar and Spelling, etc.)	■	■	■	■	■	■
Word Parts	Affixes and Base Words	■	■	■	■	■	■
	Word Parts from Greek and Latin			■	■	■	■
Word Origins	Other Languages, Proper Names, Sounds			■	■	■	■
	Clipped Words and Compounds			■	■	■	■
	Acronyms				■	■	■
Dictionary and Glossary	Respelling	■	■	■	■	■	■
	Pronunciation and Pronunciation Key	■	■	■	■	■	■
	Definition	■	■	■	■	■	■
	Part of Speech	■	■	■	■	■	■
	Etymologies			■	■	■	■
Thesaurus		■	■	■	■	■	■
Denotation, Connotation, Multiple Meanings	Choosing the Best Meaning	■	■	■	■	■	■
	Choosing the Best Word	■	■	■	■	■	■
	Recognizing Connotations	■	■	■	■	■	■
Levels of Language	Nonstandard English	■	■	■	■	■	■
	Slang, Colloquialisms, Dialect	■	■	■	■	■	■
	Standard English	■	■	■	■	■	■
	Formal, Informal	■	■	■	■	■	■
Active and Passive Vocabularies	Active, speaking and writing; Passive, listening and reading						■

Writing

		7	8	9	10	11	12
Process of Writing	Pre-Writing	■	■	■	■	■	■
	Writing	■	■	■	■	■	■
	Revising	■	■	■	■	■	■
Figures of Speech	Simile	■	■	■	■	■	■
	Metaphor	■	■	■	■	■	■

Shaded boxes indicate coverage.

Writing (continued)

		Level	Red	Green	Orange	Blue	Yellow	Purple
		Grade	**7**	**8**	**9**	**10**	**11**	**12**
Figures of Speech (continued)	Personification		■	■	■	■	■	■
	Hyperbole		■	■	■	■	■	■
Sound Techniques	Alliteration		■	■	■	■	■	■
	Onomatopoeia		■	■	■	■	■	■
	Rhyme		■	■	■	■	■	■
	Rhythm		■	■	■	■	■	■
	Assonance			■	■	■	■	■
	Consonance						■	■
Analytical Writing	Definition		■	■	■	■	■	■
	Explanation		■	■	■	■	■	■
	Comparison		■	■	■	■	■	■
	Opinion, Argument		■	■	■	■	■	■
	Analysis		■	■	■	■	■	■
	Report				■	■	■	■
Appreciating Types of Expository Writing			■	■	■	■	■	■
Creative Writing	Description of a Character or a Setting		■	■	■	■	■	■
	Narrative		■	■	■	■	■	■
	Autobiography, Biography		■	■	■	■	■	■
	Poetry		■	■	■	■	■	■
	Dialogue or Dramatic Scene		■	■	■	■	■	■
	Personal Essay		■	■	■	■	■	■
	Parody		■		■	■	■	■

Study and Research

		7	8	9	10	11	12
Reference Books	Dictionary, Encyclopedia, Atlas	■	■	■	■	■	■
	Specialized Reference Works				■	■	■
Library Resources	Card Catalog	■	■	■	■	■	■
	Picture File, Vertical File, Audio-Visual	■	■	■	■	■	■
	Readers' Guide to Periodical Literature	■	■	■	■	■	■
	Microfilm and Computerized Resources						■

Shaded boxes indicate coverage.

Study and Research (continued)

		Level	Red	Green	Orange	Blue	Yellow	Purple
		Grade	7	8	9	10	11	12
Nonfiction Books	Tables of Contents, Front Matter		■	■	■	■	■	■
	Indexes, Glossaries		■	■	■	■	■	■
Studying	Scanning, Skimming, and Study-Type Reading		■	■	■	■	■	■
	SQ3R		■	■	■	■	■	■
	Study Habits		■	■	■	■	■	■
	Graphs and Charts		■	■	■	■	■	■
Note-Taking			■	■	■	■	■	■
Organizing Information	Organizing Notes		■	■	■	■	■	■
	Informal, Formal Outlines		■	■	■	■	■	■
Interviewing	Preparing Questions		■	■	■	■	■	■
	Interviewing Techniques		■	■	■	■	■	■

Speaking and Listening

		Red 7	Green 8	Orange 9	Blue 10	Yellow 11	Purple 12
Individual Oral Interpretation	Interpreting a Character	■	■	■	■	■	■
	Reading a Narrative	■	■	■	■	■	■
	Reading a Poem	■	■	■	■	■	■
	Reciting	■	■	■	■	■	■
	Using Gestures		■	■	■	■	■
Choral Interpretation		■	■	■	■	■	■
Dialogue or Drama	Interpreting Dialogue	■	■	■	■	■	■
	Reading a Play	■	■	■	■	■	■
Telling a Narrative		■	■	■	■	■	■
Giving Directions		■	■	■	■	■	■
Presenting Speeches		■	■	■	■	■	■
Listening	Listening for Information	■	■	■	■	■	■
	Listening for Rhythm, Other Sound Techniques	■	■	■	■	■	■
	Listening To Evaluate a Speech	■	■	■	■	■	■
	Listening to a Play				■	■	■
	Listening to and Appreciating Music				■	■	■
Group Discussion					■	■	■

Shaded boxes indicate coverage.

Critical Thinking

	Level	Red	Green	Orange	Blue	Yellow	Purple
	Grade	**7**	**8**	**9**	**10**	**11**	**12**
Identification and Translation of Directly Stated Information		■	■	■	■	■	■
Classifying, Categorizing	Identifying Common Characteristics	■	■	■	■	■	■
	Determining Meaningful Categories	■	■	■	■	■	■
	Defining Terms			■	■	■	■
Interpretation and Analysis of Elements of a Work	Style	■	■	■	■	■	■
	Purpose	■	■	■	■	■	■
	Organization	■	■	■	■	■	■
	Literary Elements	■	■	■	■	■	■
Comparison and Contrast of Selections and Their Elements		■	■	■	■	■	■
Making Inferences and Predicting Outcomes *See also* Comprehension.		■	■	■	■	■	■
Fact, Opinion, and Slanted Writing	Separating Fact from Opinion	■	■	■	■	■	■
	Identifying Slanted Writing	■	■	■	■	■	■
	Loaded Language			■	■	■	■
Generalizations	Accurate and Inaccurate Generalizations	■	■	■	■	■	■
Reasoning	Analogies		■	■	■	■	■
	Inductive and Deductive Reasoning		■	■	■	■	■
	Errors in Reasoning; Circular Reasoning, False Analogies, Either-Or Thinking, etc.				■	■	■
Evaluation *See also* Comprehension.	Developing Standards	■	■	■	■	■	■
	Of Elements of a Work	■	■	■	■	■	■
	Of Reasoning and of Other Factors				■	■	■
	Of Soundness of Opinions		■	■	■	■	■
	Of Author's Credibility		■	■	■	■	■

Shaded boxes indicate coverage.